Commentary on Aristotle's Metaphysics

Aristotelian Commentary Series

Commentary on Aristotle's *Metaphysics*

St. Thomas Aquinas

Translation and Introduction by
John P. Rowan

Preface by
Ralph McInerny

DUMB OX BOOKS
Notre Dame, Indiana

Manufactured in the United States of America

ISBN: 978-1-883357-61-0

4 5 6 7 8 28 27 26 25

Contents

Introduction vii

Preface xxvi

St. Thomas's Prologue xxix

I. Introduction to First Philosophy: History of Metaphysical Inquiry 1

II. The Search for Truth and Causes 106

III. Metaphysical Problems 127

IV. Being and First Principles 196

V. Lexicon of Philosophical Terms 276

VI. The Scope of Metaphysics 396

VII. Substance, Essence and Definition 424

VIII. The Principles of Sensible Substances: Matter and Form 554

IX. Actuality and Potentiality 584

X. Unity 633

XI. Recapitulation on the Nature and Subject of Metaphysics. Motion. 695

XII. Mobile and Immobile Substance. The Prime Mover. 769

INTRODUCTION

I. The Translation

The following translation of St. Thomas's *Commentary on the Metaphysics of Aristotle* includes a translation of the version of Aristotle's text that is found in the printed editions of the Commentary now in use and commonly thought to be the one employed by St. Thomas. The inclusion of a translation of this version appeared necessary from the very beginning for two reasons. First, since the Commentary is a detailed analysis and exposition of the text of Aristotle, it becomes fully intelligible only in relation to the text, to which it makes constant reference as its point of departure. Second, since the version frequently departs in some measure from the original, it would not have proved feasible to employ one of the modern English translations[1] based on the Greek.

The translation both of the Commentary and of the version of Aristotle is based on the edition of Raymund M. Spiazzi, O.P. This edition is fundamentally that of M. R. Cathala, O.P., with emendations.[2] Some assistance in clearing up obscurities, such as typographical errors and the like, was obtained by consulting the edition of Parma[3] and that of Vivès.[4] However, the usefulness of these

---

1 *[Although much has been written since 1961 on the matters discussed in this Introduction, it retains its interest. RM]* For such translations see MacMahon, John H., *The Metaphysics of Aristotle* (London: H. G. Bohn, 1857; G. Bell and Sons, 1889; 1896; 1912); Ross, William D. (Oxford trans.), *Metaphysics*, in *The Works of Aristotle*, Vol. VIII (Oxford: Clarendon Press, 1908; 2nd ed., 1928), and in *The Student's Oxford Aristotle*, Vol. IV (London, New York: Oxford University Press, 1942); and in *The Basic Works of Aristotle*, ed. by Richard McKeon (New York: Random House, 1941), pp. 689–926; Taylor, Thomas, *The Metaphysics of Aristotle* (London: Davis, Wilks and Taylor, 1801); Tredennik, Hugh, *The Metaphysics* (Greek text with English translation), 2 vols. (In Loeb Classical Library) (London:W. Heinemann, and New York: G. P. Putnam, 1933–1935, 2nd ed. revised, 2. vols., Cambridge, Mass.: Harvard University Press, 1945); Hope, Richard, *Aristotle's Metaphysics* (New York: Columbia University Press, 1952).

2 *In Duodecim Libros Metaphysicorum Aristotelis Expositio*, editio iam a M. R. Cathala, O.P., exrata retraactatur cura et studio P. Fr. Raymundi M. Spiazzi, O.P.: Turin, 1950. This is referred to hereafter as the Cathala-Spiazzi edition. For a list of the emendations of Spiazzi (based on other editions and some manuscripts) see G. Ducoin, "St. Thomas commentateur d'Aristote," *Archives de Philosophie*, XX (1957), 84, n. 13.

3 *Sancti Thomae Aquinatis Opera Omnia*, 25 volumes (Parma: Fiaccadori, 1852–1873).

4 *Doctoris Angelici Divi Thomae Aquinatis Opera Omnia*, vols. XXIV and XXV, edited by

editions in this regard proved to be limited inasmuch as both the edition of Vivès and that of Cathala use Parma as their basic text.[5]

Since the Cathala-Spiazzi edition is not a critical one, it was necessary in certain instances to alter the reading of the text. Where such alterations are made and are not obvious, they are indicated in a footnote, and the reason for making them is stated when such justification appears necessary. The more important variations between the Greek text as given in Bekker and the Latin version of Aristotle's text are also indicated in footnotes. If the reader wishes to make comparisons between the version, the Greek text, and the English translations, he will find the Bekker reference numbers given at the beginning of each lesson useful in locating the passages in which he is interested.

The translation does not pretend to be a transliteration of the original. Since strict adherence to this method very often results in the use of *latinisms* and word structures that are foreign to the English reader, it seemed advisable, if the thought of the original was to be presented in as accurate and readily understandable a form as possible, to render the Latin as idiomatically and meaningfully as current English usage permits. Where the English words and phrases used to translate technical Latin terms are not those commonly employed in presenting the thought of St. Thomas and of Aristotle, the reader will find this indicated either by a footnote or by giving the Latin in parenthesis after the word or phrase in question. Throughout the whole translation the aim has been to produce as faithful and accurate a rendition of St. Thomas's work as circumstances permit. The extent to which this has been achieved will be left for the critics to decide.

The reader will find that the form of the introductory statements customarily used by St. Thomas to designate the passages of Aristotle's text which he is about to explain has been abbreviated. This has been done to avoid repetition and simplify the reading; for example, such statements as, "Then when Aristotle says, 'Animals by nature (2) . . . ,'" and, "Then when he says, 'Furthermore, it is necessary (126) . . . ,'" have been shortened to read, "Animals by nature (2)," and "Furthermore, it is necessary (126)."

The sections of the Commentary are indicated by numbers preceded by C and are the same as those originally established by Cathala. Numbers not preceded by C designate the sections of the version of Aristotle and are identical with those given by Spiazzi in his revision of the Cathala edition. The use of such numbers, singly or in combination, throughout the text, simplifies the matter of references and cross references where such are specified by the author, or where they would otherwise seem to be helpful. Thus in the case (267:C 489) the first number designates the section of the version of Aristotle and the second, the section of St. Thomas's Commentary on this passage.

S. E. Frette and P. Mare (Paris: Vives, 1889).

5 See A. Mansion, "Sure le texte de la version laitine medievale de le Metaphysique et de la Physique d'Aristote dans les editions de Saint Thomas d'Aquin," in *Revue Neo-Scolastique de Philosophie*, XXXIV (1932), 67.

II. The Nature of the Commentary

A commentary or exposition of the thought of some writer constituted one of the basic methods of teaching employed in medieval schools. Medieval writers inherited the commentary as a pedagogical instrument from two sources, the Fathers and Arabic writers, both of whom adopted it in turn from a common source—the literary and scientific writings of the last period of Greek thought. In the West the commentary took various forms. One type which appears as early as the sixth century is that employed by Boethius in certain of his writings, for example, his expositions of the *Categories* and the *De Interpretatione* of Aristotle. Here a portion of the original text in translation is given first, and then an explanation of its content in simpler form. Glosses upon a text constituted another form of commentary, and this became a popular form of exposition from the ninth to the twelfth century. During the twelfth and thirteenth centuries the West was introduced to the thought of antiquity by way of translations from the Greek and the Arabic. The latter were more numerous and presumably the first to appear,[6] and it was through them that Europe first came in contact with a large part of Aristotle's thought of which it had heretofore been ignorant. While there is ample evidence that these early translations extended to certain of Aristotle's works, and the *Metaphysics* was one of these,[7] the translations for the most part were of summaries or paraphrases of his writings, such as those composed by Alfarabi and Algazel, and especially the *Kitâb assifâ* of Avicenna, which is his principal work and a sort of philosophic encyclopedia covering the fields of logic, physics, metaphysics, and mathematics. The method of paraphrasing was imitated by Latin writers since it provided a simple means of presenting and popularizing Aristotle's views. St. Albert the Great, for example, made an extensive use of it in his "adapting Aristotle for the use of the Latin races."[8]

In addition to the paraphrase the West was also introduced to a more technical form of commentary, a more systematic method of analysis and explanation, which came to be known as the *lectio*, and was so named because it consisted fundamentally of a number of *readings* or *lessons (lectiones)* of the text of an

---

6 Whether translations were first made from the Greek or from the Arabic has been a matter of dispute among scholars. For a brief survey of the various opinions in this issue and the probable source of translation of certain of Aristotle's works, see Maurice de Wulf, *History of Medieval Philosophy*, trans. from the 5th French edition by E. C. Messenger (London and New York: Longmans, Green & Co.), vol. I, pp. 70–75, 237–46.

7 The decree of 1215 in the University of Paris prohibiting the use of certain works of Aristotle mentions specifically his books on natural philosophy and metaphysics, together with such commentaries or summaries of them as were used in explaining their content. See Denifle and Chatelain, *Chartularium Universitatis Parisiensis* (Paris, 1889–1891), vol. I, p. 78, n. 20. Alfred of Sareshel (Alfredus Anglicus) cites the *Metaphysics (litera Boethii)* in his *De motu cordis* (1217).

8 See Albert's *Physics*, lib. I, tr. 1, c. 1. In keeping with this guiding idea he made a complete paraphrase of Aristotle.

authority, accompanied by a literal explanation. This method of procedure, the literal commentary, eventually took precedence over the other forms of exposition and came to be widely used during the thirteenth and fourteenth centuries. Its originator is Averroes (The Commentator), who utilized it in what are called his "major commentaries."[9] In these the text of Aristotle is given paragraph by paragraph, and the views, intentions, and expressions of the author exposed in detail.

Considering the importance of Aristotle for the West, and the need for a true understanding of his thought, it is not surprising that St. Thomas should have adopted the method of literally commenting upon his writings in preference to the procedure of paraphrasing, which had previously been used. He adopted it as "a new way of treating the text," as Ptolemy of Lucca points out,[10] because it provided him with the best critical instrument for keeping in contact with the original and interpreting it accurately. The influence of Averroes upon St. Thomas in his commentaries generally, and in his exposition of the *Metaphysics* in particular, cannot be denied; and many interesting comparisons can be drawn between the expositions of the two men; for example, even in the matter of the divisions of the text into lessons, St. Thomas is evidently following The Commentator.

While it is clear that St. Thomas's primary aim is to explain literally what Aristotle said, it should also be noted that, in keeping with his respect for authority, he does not hesitate to "interpret" Aristotle, when the occasion demands. Attention must be drawn also to the fact that, since St. Thomas is principally concerned with the advancement of truth, he sometimes proceeds to draw out what he feels is implicit in Aristotle's doctrines. In so doing he introduces his own personal views into his explanations inasmuch as he sees a fundamental agreement between them and those of the Philosopher. In the same spirit he sometimes finds it necessary to disagree with the interpretations of other commentators, chiefly those of Avicenna and of Averroes,[11] when he feels that they fail to grasp the thought of the master on some specific point of doctrine. But he can also use the opinions of those whom he has criticized in other respects,[12] when it is evident that their interpretations add something to the understanding of Aristotle's teachings.

In his role as commentator St. Thomas makes a masterful use, both of the many dialectical instruments which Aristotle puts at the disposal of his readers in his methodological treatises, as well as of those developed by medieval logicians.[13]

---

9 For a brief description of the three methods of treating a text used by Averroes (the simple paraphrase, middle commentary, and major commentary), his role as originator of the literal commentary, and his connection with St. Thomas, see Leon Gauthier, *Ibn Rochd (Averroes)* (Paris: Presses Univ. de France, 1948), p. 16.

10 Quodam singulari et novo modo tradendi utebatur," in *Hist. Eccles.*, XXII, c. 24.

11 For example, in nn. 286, 1467–68, and 2418, he considers Averroes to be in error; and in nn. 556–58, 894, 1981, and 2559, he criticizes the views of Avicenna.

12 In nn. 345, 442, 1442, he notes what Averroes adds to an understanding of the text; and in nn. 46, 766–69, 1165, and 1469, he makes use of certain views of Avicenna.

In this respect alone the Commentary is an outstanding piece of work. Since Aristotle's text is fundamentally an inquiry or investigation into problems relevant to a specific subject matter, conducted along the lines recommended in the *Analytics* and *Topics*, it lends itself admirably to the kind of treatment to which St. Thomas subjects it. Aristotle's text might be described as an exercise in dialectic aimed at ascertaining truth in a certain sphere, and whose logical structure the reader is aware of only vaguely if at all. But in the treatment of the Commentary this structure is laid bare in order to better evaluate the conclusions to which it leads. For the medievals as for Aristotle a knowledge of method provided at once both the tools necessary for scientific research and the criteria, in large part at least, for judging the value of such research.

With this in mind St. Thomas proceeds from the very start to make evident with great precision both the content of Aristotle's thought and the process which he uses in formulating and presenting it. He divides and subdivides the text to reveal its essential structure, and within these divisions he follows step by step Aristotle's analyses of his predecessor's opinions and his evaluation of them; his examination of the various meanings of terms; the kind of arguments that are being used, and their demonstrative or probable character in the light of the premises from which they are derived.

The divisions of the text, which are given in the Commentary at the beginning of each lesson, serve to break up the passages to be commented upon into their constituent parts or members, thereby presenting the student with a schema that enables him to proceed in an orderly way to an understanding of the discussion contained therein. Sometimes the divisions given in one lesson will extend to subsequent lessons when the latter have an essential connection with it. There are also cases where the division extends to the work at large, indicating the issues dealt with in other books. Thus in Book III, after explaining the *aporiae* or difficulties which Aristotle raises, St. Thomas notes the respective books in which they will be solved; and again in Book XI, lesson 1, his division refers not only to certain issues that have yet to be treated, and where this will occur, but also designates topics that have already been discussed in previous books.

In his treatment of the text St. Thomas exhibits none of the critical and historical spirit that is so characteristic of our own era and began with the advances in philological studies and historical methodology made in the nineteenth century. This does not mean that he is lacking in historical sense or in critical ability (quite the reverse is true) but that he does not have at his disposal the variety of instruments in these fields that we now possess. His only method of ascertaining the true sense of Aristotle's text was to consult the various versions available to him. If he saw any development in Aristotle's thought, such as might be suggested by the text, and of the kind outlined in the works of

---

13 For a general picture of the knowledge and use of Aristotle's logical works during the thirteenth century, and of the developments in medieval logic, see Philotheus Boehner, O.F.M., *Medieval Logic* (Chicago: University of Chicago Press, 1952), and J. T. Clark, S.J., *Conventional Logic and Modern Logic* (Woodstock, Md.: Woodstock College Press, 1952).

modern scholars,[14] he gives no indication of it. Neither does he remark on the possibility of the various books which comprise the total work having been composed as distinct treatises at different times and combined into a whole by later hands. For him the work has the appearance of a single treatise whose parts have been skilfully knit together with the ultimate aim of exposing the nature of entity, its properties and causes.

III. Researches on the Commentary

The most important issues with which scholars have been concerned in the matter of the Commentary are (1) the period of its composition and date of completion; (2) the version or versions upon which St. Thomas based his exegesis, and the exact status of the printed version now in use; (3) the history of certain of the books commented upon, and the possibility of an earlier and later writing. These issues have been investigated at length, and much progress has been made despite the obstacles that have had to be faced. However, the tentative character of many of the solutions proposed for them indicates that considerable work yet remains to be done.

One of the main obstacles in the way of attaining definitive answers is the state of the printed editions and the manuscripts of this work with which investigators have had to deal. Both are admittedly imperfect, containing errors of various kinds. It is quite possible too that the manuscripts representing the versions of Aristotle's text which St. Thomas used in his exposition are not yet completely known. There is also the matter of the interpretation which should be given to the passages in various works[15] which refer in some way to the Commentary or to the versions of Aristotle and have been used as evidence by one or other investigator in support of his position regarding some phase of this work. These passages are often obscure, ambiguous, and perhaps even inaccurate, and so have led in many instances to different and even contradictory hypotheses.

Although little if anything has been published on the errors to be found in the manuscripts, sufficient information is at hand regarding the kind of inaccuracies one can expect to meet in the printed editions, and the reasons for their occurrence. In this matter one can cite the brief article of A. Mansion, dealing with the Commentaries on the *Physics* and *Metaphysics*,[16] and the article of L. W. Keeler, S.J., which, while it deals specifically with one of the *Opuscula* of St. Thomas,[17] is nevertheless of importance for the *Commentary on the Metaphysics.*

Mansion draws attention to the role that simple negligence has played in falsifying the text of the Commentary, and uses as an example a passage at the beginning of Book I, corresponding to Bekker 980a27–28, which, rendered into

---

14 E.g. Werner Jaeger.

15 Some of these passages are from other works of St. Thomas, and some are from the writings of his predecessors, contemporaries, and successors.

16 Sure le texte..." *Rev. Neo-Scol.*, XXXIV (1932), 66–67.

17 "Editions of the *De Unitate Intellectus*," *Gregorianum*, XVII (1936), 55–62.

Latin, reads, "Animalia quidem igitur natura sensum habentia fiunt." The phrase, as he points out, is given in the editions of Venice 1519, Rome 1570, Venice 1603, and Antwerp 1612, but is omitted in the edition of Parma 1866, and therefore also in the edition of Vivès 1889 and in that of Cathala 1915 (although corrected in the 1926 and following editions), since both of the latter employ Parma as their basic text without any apparent revision. Mansion's conclusion is that in all probability there are many other such errors in the printed editions (which has been borne out by more recent studies) and that an examination of the manuscripts upon which these editions have been based will reveal inaccuracies of a similar kind.

Father Keeler's work reveals another and different kind of error in his descriptions of the procedures followed by the editors of the sixteenth century, whose editions have been employed in printings down to our own time. The outstanding weakness of early editors, he notes, consisted in their "undue readiness" to take all sorts of liberties with the text. Thus Paulus Soncinas did not hesitate to substitute certain passages from humanist translations of Aristotle's text for those in medieval Latin when the latter appeared obscure or were too strange or archaic to suit his taste. Thus in the case of St. Thomas's exposition of the *De Generatione Animalium* of Aristotle, Soncinas substituted passages of the *nova translatio* of this work for certain parts of the *media translatio*, which seems to have been the one that St. Thomas employed. The same kind of procedure is also characteristic of the work of Anthony Pizamanus, who, in his edition of the *De Unitate Intellectus*, is responsible for what Keeler calls the "scandal" connected with St. Thomas's supposed assertion that he had seen certain books of Aristotle, fourteen in number, which treat of separate substances but had not yet been translated into Latin (presumably the fourteen books of the *Metaphysics*). Keeler's researches reveal that there are no manuscripts that contain the reading *numero XIV*, but that all having a numerical reference read *numero X*, while one (St. Genevieve 238) omits the words in question altogether. Apparently Pizamanus, who was following an earlier edition of Soncinas, which omits any mention of the number of books, considered this a lacuna and supplied the reading *numero XIV* on the basis of a reading found in another edition of this work prepared by a certain Didascalus, which edition he was also following. The issue is significant for the history of the Commentary inasmuch as one thesis of D. Salman, O.P., an investigator in this field, depends on the assumption that the reading *numero XIV* is correct.

Difficulties of this kind will disappear only when critical editions have been made of all of St. Thomas's writings. In the meantime they will continue to make the undertaking of translation and historical investigation extremely difficult.

1. *The Date of the Commentary*

The extensive researches that have been made into the history and chronology of St. Thomas's writings[18] would indicate that the commentaries on Aristotle

18 See for example, M. Grabmann, *Die Werke des hl. Thomas von Aquin*, 2nd ed. (Munster,

were composed between the years 1266 and 1272.[19] Some were at least begun while St. Thomas resided in Italy, and some were completed at Paris after his return there to teach for the second time. The *Commentary on the Metaphysics* is generally considered to belong to this second group. However, while there seems to be agreement as to the proximate date of its completion, both the time and place of its origin still remains a matter of dispute. One can appreciate the complexity of the problem and the tentative character of many of the solutions proposed for it only by surveying the studies that have been made.

One of the earliest dates given for the composition of the Commentary is that found in the account of St. Thomas's life and writings by Ptolemy of Lucca,[20] who ascribes it to the pontificate of Urban IV. According to Ptolemy, St. Thomas commented during this period upon the whole of philosophy, both moral and natural, and "especially upon the Ethics and Metaphysics." This would mean that the Commentary was written between 1261 and 1264. Ptolemy's authority in this matter has been questioned by M. Grabmann because of a discrepancy in the dates involved, inasmuch as St. Thomas resided at Rome from 1265 to 1267, whereas Urban IV reigned from 1261 to 1264.[21] However, P. Mandonnet has argued in favor of Ptolemy's statement on the grounds that, since one of these periods immediately succeeds the other, and since St. Thomas did teach at the court of Urban IV at Orvieto, which is adjacent to Rome, Ptolemy was very likely thinking of the whole period from 1261 to 1267.[22]

As early as 1921 Grabmann expressed the view that the Commentary could not have been completed before 1265, the date set earlier by Mandonnet,[23] but must have been in the process of composition during 1266. His opinion was based on a reference which St. Thomas makes in Book III, lesson 11 (C 468) to Simplicius' *Commentary on the Categories* of Aristotle, the translation of which was only completed by William of Moerbeke in March 1266 and was the one available to St. Thomas.

In 1925 A. Mansion published his findings to the effect that the work could not have been completed before 1271 but must have reached its final state toward the end of that year or at the beginning of 1272. His decision was based on the date of the translation of Simplicius' *Commentary on the De Coelo* of Aristotle, which was completed by Moerbeke in June 1271. St. Thomas makes three references to this work in Book XII of the Commentary when he sets out to explain the use that Aristotle made of Eudoxus and Calippus in the formation of his astronomical system. Two of these references are paraphrases (C 2573; C

1931), pp. 262 ff., and A. Walz, O.P., *San Tommaso d'Aquino* (Rome, 1945), p. 117.

19 *Hist. Eccles.*, XXII, c. 24.

20 Die Aristoteleskommentare des hl. Thomas von Aquin," in *Mittelalterliches Geistesleben*, vol. I (Munich, 1926), pp. 272—73.

21 Saint Thomas d'Aquin, Lecteur a la Curie Romaine," in *Xenia Thomistica*, vol. III (Rome, 1925), 9 ff.

22 "Des ecrits authentiques de Saint Thomas d'Aquin," 2nd ed. (Fribourg, 1910).

23 Die echten Schriften des hl Thomas von Aquin," in *Beitraege zur Geschichte der Philosophie des Mittelalters*, XXII, 1–2 (Munster, 1920).

2582), and one is an exact citation (C 2578), and this would have been possible only if he had possessed the translation at the time of writing.[24]

In 1942 T. Deman published his researches on St. Thomas's opinion of Aristotle as an interpreter of Plato and indicated in this article that the reference to Simplicius' *Commentary on the Categories,* given in Book III of St. Thomas's Commentary, appeared rather to be a reference to Simplicius' *Commentary on the De Coelo.*[25] This conclusion, contrary to that reached earlier by Grabmann, would necessitate putting the writing of Book III sometime after June 1271. But granted that this were the case, it would follow that St. Thomas must have composed the whole of his exposition in a much shorter period than the many demands on his time as teacher, scholar, and writer would reasonably allow. This has been the view expressed by D. Salman, and on the basis of this and what he considers to be internal evidence supplied by the Commentary and by other writings of St. Thomas, he argues in favor of an earlier writing composed in Italy between 1266 and 1268 and a revision of this made later at Paris between the end of 1270 and the beginning of 1272.[26] He also thinks that Ptolemy's account could simply refer to such a first writing and that this might have taken the form of a simple *reportatio.*[27] In his opinion the argument for an earlier writing is not invalidated by the evidence summoned in support of a later period of composition, for example, the reference made to Simplicius in Book III, and the mentioning of Books XIII and XIV of Aristotle's work as early as the exposition of Book I, since these could have been added later at the time of revision.[28] In this matter Salman is in agreement with the view expressed earlier by Mansion,[29] and also with that of A. Dondaine, O.P.,[30] although the latter's argument for an earlier date of composition was based on the assumption that the *translatio media* constituted the basic text upon which the Commentary was made, and that the *translatio nova* was employed later when the work was revised.

The researches of F. Pelster, S.J., which have been aimed primarily at establishing the version or versions of Aristotle's text that were used by St. Thomas, deserves special attention in regard to the present problem. Pelster's findings agree with those of other scholars as to the proximate time of completion of the Commentary; and while he admits that the hypothesis of an earlier writing is not impossible, he thinks that such a hypothesis is unnecessary, since what is used as evidence in support of it can be explained in another way,[31] as will be noted later.

---

24 "Pour l'histoire du Commentaire de Saint Thomas sur la Metaphysique," in *Revue Neo-Scolastique de Philosophie,* Louvain, XXVII (1925), 274 ff.

25 Remarques critiques de Saint Thomas sur Aristote interprete de Platon," in *Les Sciences Philosophiques et Theologiques* (Paris, 1941–42), pp. 133–48.

26 "Saint Thomas et les traductions latines des Metaphysiques d'Aristote," in *Archives d'Histoire Doctrinale et Litteraire du Moyen Age,* VII (1932), 111.

27 *Art. cit.,* pp. 110–11.

28 *Ibid.,* p. 118.

29 "Pour l'histoire," *art. cit.,* 284.

30 Saint Thomas et les traductions latines de la Metaphysique d'Aristote," *Bulletin thomiste* III (1933), 201–4.

From such investigations, then, it appears probable that the Commentary was completed at Paris toward the end of 1271 or at the beginning of 1272 but that the time and place of its origin are still not definitely known. It seems possible that it could have been written in its entirety during St. Thomas's last period at Paris; or that it was begun during his stay in Italy and completed at Paris as a single writing; or that a first writing was composed in Italy, and this subsequently revised at Paris.

2. *The Versions on Which the Commentary Is Based*

In order to give an accurate exposition of the true thought of Aristotle, St. Thomas required a faithful version of the original texts as a basis for his commentaries. The various paraphrases then in vogue could, therefore, hardly serve his purpose. Being merely summaries they neither contained the actual text of Aristotle nor pretended to follow the original order of exposition but employed instead a simpler and more systematic one established by the summarists themselves. Moreover, they frequently incorporated the views of their composers, views that sometimes made the Philosopher the exponent of doctrines that were often difficult if not impossible to reconcile with the principles of Christian wisdom. In view of the possibility that Aristotle himself might have something quite different to say, prudence dictated the exclusion of such paraphrases as the starting point for a satisfactory exposition.

The translation of certain of Aristotle's works made from the Arabic also proved to have serious defects and therefore were useful only in a limited way as a point of departure for the exegetical work St. Thomas had in mind. This at least was true of the translation of the *Metaphysics*, which he reputedly knew from the very beginning of his literary career. For one thing it was clearly inadequate inasmuch as it lacked Books XI, XIII and XIV, and contained only a garbled version of Books I ({A}) and II ({a})—Book I being comprised of Book {a} and part of Book {A} (chapters 5 and 8), and Book II of the remainder of Book A. The possibility too of such translations misrepresenting the thought of Aristotle had already been recognized and indicated in the pronouncements prohibiting their use on the part of the Masters and students at the University of Paris, as set forth in the earlier decrees of 1210 and 1215, mentioned above, and in the later decree of 1263.[32] That these versions should be held suspect is not to be wondered at considering the fact that the original works had undergone successive translations from the Greek to the Syriac, from this to the Arabic, and from this again to the Latin through some vernacular language[33]

Somewhat the same situation prevailed in the case of certain translations of the *Metaphysics* that were presumably based on the Greek and date from the end

31 . Pelster, S.J., "Die Uebersetzungen der aristotelischen Metaphysik in den Werken des hl. Thomas von Aquin," *Gregorianum*, XVII (1936), 378.

32 See F. van Steenberghen, *Siger de Brabant d'apres les oeuvres inedites*, II, 430–90.

33 See G. Lucquet, "Herman le Dalmate," in *Revue de l'histoire des Religions*, XLIV (1901), 415.

of the twelfth or the early years of the thirteenth century. The translation attributed to Boethius (the *littera Boethii*) and another entitled the *translatio vetus* belong to this group. Both of these are incomplete, containing only a small part of the whole.

If the commentaries were to do justice to the real thought of Aristotle, it became evident that they would have to be based on complete and faithful translations made from the original; and so it was, as William of Tocco tells us that, when St. Thomas wrote his expositions on natural philosophy, moral philosophy, and metaphysics, "he had these books newly translated so that the genuine thought of Aristotle should be more clearly expressed."[34] The translations of which William of Tocco speaks are those of William of Moerbeke, made at the request of St. Thomas himself. For the role that Moerbeke played as Greek translator and the invaluable assistance that he lent St. Thomas and others in their own work, one can profitably consult the work of M. Grabmann, *Guglielmo di Moerbeke, O.P., Il Traduttore delle Opere di Aristotele* (Rome, 1946). In the matter of the translations of Aristotle, Moerbeke made, in certain instances, a revision of already existing versions, completing them where necessary, and also rendered into Latin certain texts that had not yet been translated. With such works in his possession St. Thomas was able to attain a knowledge of Aristotle superior to that of his predecessors and contemporaries, and give the first faithful explication of his doctrines.

Granted that certain versions of the *Metaphysics* anteceded that of Moerbeke and were known to St. Thomas, the following questions have been raised by scholars in their investigations into the history of his Commentary on this work: Did St. Thomas base his exegesis solely upon the translation of Moerbeke, or did he also make use of these other versions? And if the latter, what versions were involved, and to what extent? Again, is the version of Aristotle now found in the printed editions of the Commentary to be identified with the translation of Moerbeke?

In regard to the version referred to in this last question, some clarification is necessary. As indicated earlier, the printed editions of the Commentary now in use are, for the most part, republications of editions dating from the sixteenth century. In some of these, for example the Parma, one finds at the beginning of each lesson two parallel versions. One is called the *versio antiqua*, and the other the *versio recens*. Since the latter is attributable to Cardinal Bessarion, a humanist of the Renaissance period, it has no bearing on St. Thomas's own work, and therefore is excluded from the present discussion. The *versio antiqua*, on the other hand, is presumably the version of William of Moerbeke, and therefore the one employed by St. Thomas.[35]

Although some of the studies devoted to finding solutions for these questions have not always been in agreement in terms of their results, it would nevertheless appear that we are now in a fair position to understand what actually occurred in the matter of the various versions.

---

34 *Vita S. Thomae Aquinatis*, c. 17.

35 This is the version contained in the Cathala-Spiazzi edition.

In an article published in 1932, D. Salman outlines for us, by way of an introduction to the results of his own investigations, the discoveries of four scholars who have been chiefly responsible up to his own time for the progress made in the matter of the Latin translations used in the composition of the Commentary.[36] First, there is the work of Monsignor Grabmann, whose researches revealed two manuscripts containing two distinct versions of the *Metaphysics*. One of these, which came to be called the *translatio nova*, was complete, while the other, which was entitled the *metaphysica vetus* or *translatio vetus*, was not, but contained only the first three books and a part of Book IV (up to 1007a30). The latter was considered to be the work of Boethius, and the former was identified as that of Moerbeke.[37]

In 1917 there appeared a work by B. Geyer which was devoted to a study of the citations from the *Metaphysics* as given in the works of St. Albert the Great and St. Thomas. By comparing the citations of St. Thomas drawn from a work which he referred to as the *littera Boethii* with the corresponding passages in the *vetus*, Geyer concluded that they were one and the same text. Moreover, since St. Thomas refers to the *littera Boethii* even for passages drawn from Books V and XII, Geyer also concluded that this translation, and therefore the *vetus*, which he identified with it, must go as far as Book XII rather than terminate with Book IV.[38] Additional researches, however, have not fulfilled his hope of discovering the whole text. In fact the studies of F. Pelster, published in 1923, revealed eight new manuscripts all terminating in Book IV, which would seem to indicate that the original version itself was incomplete and had undergone a number of revisions.[39] But since this conclusion fails to account for St. Thomas's references to later books of the *littera Boethii*, Geyer's identification of this version with the *vetus* was considered to be untenable.

The main contribution to this issue made by Pelster in this early study consisted in the discovery of two manuscripts containing a heretofore unknown version in thirteen books (XI being excluded), which he named the *translatio media*. By comparing the citations from the *Metaphysics* in the *Summa Contra Gentiles* with the corresponding passages in the *media*, Pelster concluded that it was this version that St. Thomas had used and that it must therefore have been known in 1260. This being so, it would have provided one source for the writing of the Commentary, and later investigations proved this to be true. Pelster also indicated that this text was the same as that known and used by St. Albert the Great in his paraphrase of the *Metaphysics*, which contains thirteen books, one corresponding to each of the books in question. Since comparisons also revealed

---

36 Saint Thomas et les traductions latines des Metaphysiques d'Aristote," *Archives d'histoire Doctrinale et Literaire du Moyen Age*, VII (1932), 85–87.

37 "Forschungen über die lateinishcen Aristotelesübersetzungen des XIII Jahrhunderts," in *Beitraege*, XVII (1916), 105 ff.

38 Die Übersetzungen der aristotelischen Metaphysik bei Albertus Magnus und Thomas von Aquin," *Philsophisches Jahrbuch*, XXX (1917), 392 ff.

39 *Die Griechish-Lateinishcen Metaphysikuebersetzungen der Mittelalters, Beitraege*, Supplementband, II (Munster, 1923), pp. 89–118.

that this version differed widely from the *vetus* but came very close to the *translatio nova*, identified as the work of Moerbeke, Pelster therefore decided that Moerbeke had employed the *media* in composing his own translation, retouching it where necessary in the light of the Greek text and completing it by translating Book XI into Latin for the first time.

In a subsequent study, published in 1928, M. Birkenmajer added to the complexity of the problem by introducing still another version, whose existence he supported by three new manuscripts that he had discovered. This version, whose date he placed around the middle of the twelfth century, would be older than any of the others and therefore was called by him the *vetustissima*. It resembled the *littera Boethii* and the *vetus* in being composed of the first three books and a part of the fourth. The *media* he dated earlier than Pelster, maintaining that it was in circulation as early as 1230 or even 1210, although he agreed with Pelster on the *nova* as the work of Moerbeke. The *vetus* he considered to be a reworking of the *vetustissima* in the light of the *media*.[40]

To the work of his predecessors Salman adds the results of his own researches to the effect that, if the facts were to be adequately accounted for, it would appear necessary to admit the existence of yet another translation, which would come between the *vetustissima* and the *media*, and would lack Books XI, XIII, and XIV. In his opinion it would be upon this text rather than the *media* that St. Thomas relied in composing his first writing of the Commentary, since the *media* could not have been known as early as 1230 as Birkenmajer had claimed, or even as early as 1260 as Pelster had maintained.

Salman's argument for a later dating of the *media* is based upon certain passages in some of St. Thomas's works. According to him these passages indicate that St. Thomas came to know the last books of the *Metaphysics* only in the very last years of his career; and this being so, the *media* could not have been known or used by him, since it contained the books in question. The passages referred to are those in which St. Thomas speaks of a treatise of Aristotle on separate substances, belonging to the realm of metaphysics, and which Salman identifies, on the strength of the reading in the *De Unitate*, with Books XIII and XIV of the *Metaphysics*. In his opinion these books could not have reached St. Thomas before the later part of 1270. Indeed, according to the passage in the *Commentary on the De Anima*, Book III, lesson 12 (n. 785), at the time of its composition (after 1266), St. Thomas was not even certain that such a treatise had ever been written; but he states categorically that it was still unknown in the West. The passages from the *Commentary on the De Sensu*, lesson 1 (n. 4) (dated after 1261), the *De Veritate*, q. 18, art. 5, obj. 8 and ans. (dated the beginning of 1258), and the *Quaestio Disputata de Anima*, art. 16 (dated the beginning of 1270), also bear witness to his ignorance of this treatise.[41] However, by the time of writing of the *De Unitate Intellectus* (dated 1270) St. Thomas knew that such a treatise actually existed, having seen the Greek text, and that it brought the total

---

40 etter to Geyer in Überweg-Geyer, *Die Patristische und Scholastische Philosophie* (Berlin, 1928), p. 346 ff.

41 For Salman's analyses of these texts and his conclusion, see *art. cit.*, pp. 87–89.

number of books up to fourteen but that it had not yet been translated into Latin. The passage from the *De Unitate* to which Salman refers in support of his interpretation runs thus: "Hujusmodi autem quaestiones certissime colligi potest Aristotelem solvisse in his libros quos patet eum scripsisse de substantiis separatis, ex his quae dicit in principio XII Metaphysicae, quos etiam libros vidimus numero XIV, licet nondum translatos in linguam nostram."[42] Assuming, then, that St. Thomas did not know Books XIII and XIV until 1270 and that these books were presented for the first time in the *media,* he could not have employed this version in the first writing of the Commentary, which was composed, in Salman's opinion, during the period of his career in Italy. But neither could he have depended solely upon the *vetus* or *littera Boethii,* since these versions go only as far as Book IV, whereas the first writing must have covered all books with the exception of XI, XIII, and XIV. Some other version therefore must have been available to him, and it would have to contain eleven books (I–X and XII).

According to Salman this version would be a combination of the *vetustissima* and an early translation based on the Arabic—one version making up for the deficiencies of the other. The existence of such a translation, he notes, is attested to by a document published by Lacombe, which describes three translations of the *Metaphysics* done at different times: a first or early version that was incomplete (which Salman identifies with the *vetustissima*); a second and later translation which is clearly identifiable with the Arabic by reason of its lacking Books XI, XIII, and XIV, and the confusion of the first two books; and a third and still later translation containing thirteen books (which Salman presumably identifies as the *media*). Since this new version which Salman proposes as the foundation for St. Thomas's work would depend predominantly on the *second translation,* he named it the *metaphysica secunda.*[43]

However, Salman's argument appears to have lost most if not all of its force in the light of the investigations of Keeler and the extensive studies of Pelster. If the reading *numero XIV* of the *De Unitate Intellectus* cannot be substantiated by any documentary evidence other than the faulty edition of Pizamanus, as Keeler has apparently shown (since most manuscripts contain the reading *numero X,* while others make no specific mention of the number of books at all), it would seem reasonable to maintain, as Pelster has done, that the work to which St. Thomas alludes in the passages singled out by Salman might be the *Theology of Aristotle* (an apocryphal work in ten parts) or some other work which Aristotle is supposed to have written on separate substances.[44] This interpretation, however, does not appear to be confirmed by any positive evidence, and Salman himself has rejected it on the ground that, since the *Theology of Aristotle* is generally admitted to have been in circulation in the West as early as the

---

42 For the analysis of this passage in relation to the others see *art. cit.*, pp. 91–98.

43 Salman, *art. cit.*, pp. 106–8. See also "Medieval Latin Versions of the *Parva Naturalia,*" *The New Scholasticism,* V (October, 1931), 296.

44 Pelster, *Die Griechisch*, p. 11; see also "Die Übersetzungen," *Gregorianum* XVI (1935), 330.

beginning of the thirteenth century and would thus be known to St. Thomas, it can hardly be the treatise to which he refers.[45]

The researches of Pelster, published in 1935 and 1936, are of special significance for the present problem.[46] His conclusions are based on an extensive study of the manuscripts of the various versions, and in this undertaking he has made great use of the collection of texts assembled earlier by Geyer. By comparing the citations from the *Metaphysics* that St. Thomas gives throughout his works at large, and the direct references that he makes to the text of Aristotle in his exposition of the *Metaphysics*, with the corresponding passages in the various versions, Pelster has been able to identify the translations that St. Thomas knew and used during his literary career. As a result of such studies he has concluded that St. Thomas knew the *metaphysica vetus* and the translation based on the Arabic from the very beginning of his career and that, while he unquestionably employed the *vetus* in various works, he does not appear to have made any use of the translation from the Arabic (at least not in the Commentary); the *littera Boethii*, which for St. Thomas went beyond Book IV, is taken, not from the *metaphysica vetustissim*, but from the *translatio vetus*, so that the latter version and that of the *littera Boethii* are different; St. Thomas knew the *metaphysica nova* when he wrote the *De Unitate Intellectus* in 1270 and also when he composed the first part of the *Summa Theologiae*, shortly after 1265, since both of these works contain citations from this version; St. Thomas both knew and used the *translatio media* in the *De Unitate Intellectus* and in the *Summa Contra Gentiles*, composed about 1260, and probably also in the *De Veritate*, as some passages would seem to indicate[47] There are of course some references which it is impossible or difficult to identify either with the *nova* or the *media*, since St. Thomas sometimes gives Aristotle's thought only in digested form.

It is in identifying the sources to which St. Thomas refers throughout the Commentary that the versions used in its composition become evident. According to Pelster's investigations these texts are evidently the *vetus*, *littera Boethii*, *media*, and *nova*, and presumably another translation based on the Greek that went beyond Book IV, unless the readings indicative of its existence are merely variants of the *media* and the *nova*, as could be the case. The undertaking has not been an easy one inasmuch as St. Thomas refers to the various versions which he is using simply as "this reading" (*haec littera*) when they constitute the basic text or first reading on which he is depending, and as "another reading" or "another translation" (*alia littera* or *alia translatio*) when they fill the role of a secondary text or alternative reading. It is only in the case of the text attributed to Boethius that his source is clearly designated.

Generally it can be said that it was by reason of the clarity of its presentation

---

45 Salman, *art. cit.*, p. 93.

46 "Die Übersetzungen der Aristotelischen Metaphysik in den Werken des hl. Thomas von Aquin," *Gregorianum* XVI (1935), 325–48, 531–61; XVII (1936), 377–406. See also "Neure Forschungen über die Aristotelesübersetzungen des XII und XIII Jahrhunderts," *Gregorianum* XXX (1949), 46–77.

47 *Art. cit.*, *Gregorianum* XVI (1935), 330–43.

(and this established by comparison) that one of these versions was given precedence over the others as the basic reading to be followed; and since this varied from version to version in relation to the particular book or chapter that was being considered, it became necessary to change the basic reading. In this way a version that constituted a primary reading in some parts became a secondary or alternative reading in others, its place being taken by one that had previously been secondary.

Pelster's conclusions given in summary form amount to the following: from Books I to IV St. Thomas constantly used the *vetus* and the *media*, and often gave first place to the former, as in Book II, lesson 2, and Book IV, lesson 5. In Book V the *media* appears to be the basic text, and beginning with lesson 20 of this book the *nova* appears for the first time as "another reading," although sometimes the *vetus* can be understood in this role. It would seem too that St. Thomas knew the *nova* as early as the writing of Book I; but since the *vetus* and the *nova* have the same reading, it is difficult to decide in favor of the *nova*. While the *nova* cannot be shown to be the fundamental reading for the first five books, there is every indication that by the time of writing of Book VI St. Thomas began to make greater use of it as his point of departure and often does this without taking the *media* into account at all. In the matter of the divisions that are given for the text of Aristotle, the *media* appears to have been used as an aid, and St. Thomas probably also derives from it the Greek words which are translated along with the *nova*. Sometimes, however, the *vetus* is preferred to the *media* in the establishing of these divisions. After Book IX St. Thomas appears to have relied solely upon the *nova*, since no alternative readings are given thereafter. The *versio antiqua* given in the printed editions is not simply the *nova* of Moerbeke, but a mixed form of the *nova* and *media*.[48]

Having established the foregoing, Pelster feels justified in dismissing Dondaine's opinion that the *media* constituted the basic text for St. Thomas's exposition, while the *nova* was used later only in a revisory capacity. Such a hypothesis is inadmissible in view of the position that the *nova* holds in the later books. Salman's assumption of a *metaphysica secunda* is similarly untenable inasmuch as St. Thomas was fully acquainted with the *media*, as numerous comparisons have shown.

3. *The Problem of the Last Books*

One of the central problems which scholars have had to face in their investigations into the history of the Commentary concerns the last books of the *Metaphysics*, specifically Books XI, XIII, and XIV. Were they available or not to St. Thomas when he began his exposition? Some have felt that they were, while others have adopted the opposite position, maintaining that he came to know and use them only at a later date.

The doxology that St. Thomas gives at the end of Book XII seems to clearly indicate that he considered his work to be completed at this point. In this respect

---

48 *Ibid.*, 532–61.

the *Commentary on the Metaphysics* is unique, as Mansion has pointed out, since other commentaries of Aquinas, as those on the *De Interpretatione*, the *De Coelo*,the *De Generatione et Corruptione*,, the *Meteorologica* and the *Politica* remain unfinished, terminating either at the end of some book or at the end of some lesson.[49]

The supposition that St. Thomas did not comment upon the last two books—XIII and XIV—because he lacked a Latin translation of them, cannot be maintained. Mansion noted the untenableness of such a hypothesis as early as 1925,[50] using in support of his claim the earlier work of Pelster, mentioned above, which contains a collection of the various references to these books in certain works of St. Thomas and St. Albert the Great, which are evidently drawn from the *media*.[51] But the most direct evidence of St. Thomas's knowledge of the last books is to be found in the many references made to them in the Commentary itself, especially in the early part of the work. The majority of such references are given in Book III, which contains the fifteen *aporiae* or difficulties that Aristotle intends to consider in the development of subsequent books. In lessons 4–15 of this book St. Thomas examines these difficulties, and in each lesson designates the respective books in which they will be treated. In so doing he refers to Books XIII and XIV and describes the problems with which they actually deal.[52] In mentioning Book XIII he even cites the opening lines of chapter 1.[53] The objection that such references have been added later in a second writing would have to be dismissed in the light of Pelster's later researches.

It therefore could not have been the lack of a translation that prevented St. Thomas from commenting upon the books in question; and inasmuch as he gives no explanation for bringing his work to a close at the point at which he did, we are forced to look elsewhere for an answer. Here the suggestion of Mansion appears to be the most reasonable one.[54] He bases his opinion on a statement in Sylvester Maurus, who, in his synopsis immediately preceding Book XIII, says of the last two books that their teaching is most obscure and of little value and that, in any event, since the subjects treated therein have already been dealt with in previous books, it would be pointless to dispute them any further.[55] Sylvester is referring to the fact that in these books Aristotle gives a systematic criticism of the theory of Ideas as interpreted by Plato's successors, Speusippus and Xenocrates, who identified the Ideas with numbers and extensions; and since this subject has nothing to do with the development of Aristotle's metaphysical

49 "Pour l'histoire," *Rev. Neo-scol.*, XXVII (1925), 278.
50 *Ibid.*, p. 279.
51 I.e., Die Griechish-lateinish," p. 105.
52 See nn. 422, 501, 514, 518.
53 See n. 2488: "De sensibili quidem igitur substantia . . ."
54 "Pour l'histoire," 279–80.
55 *Aristotelis opera omnia quae extant brevi paraphrasi et litterae perpetuo inhaerente expositione illustrata a Sylvestro Mauro*, S.J. (Rome, 1669; rev. ed., Paris, 1885–87), by F. Ehrle, S.J. and A. Bringman, S.J., vol. IV, p. 569.

views, properly speaking, and has already been exposed in great detail in earlier books, St. Thomas probably thought it unnecessary to deal with it again.

The problems regarding Book XI are not as easily solved. It is generally admitted that this book was the last one to have been introduced into the West, and its translation would without doubt be due to William of Moerbeke. However, the time at which St. Thomas first came to know of the existence of this book, and then received and used the translation of it in his exposition, is still an open question. Two different and opposite stands have been taken in this matter—one by Mansion and the other by Pelster—and both have something to be said in their favor.

Mansion's position, later accepted by Salman, is that St. Thomas was unaware of the existence of Book XI at the beginning of his exposition and even after his work was well under way. He grounds his argument on the fact that St. Thomas makes no mention of this book at the start of his Commentary, and even fails to take account of it as late as Book VII; for in the schematic division given at the beginning of this book, in which the issues to be dealt with in the remaining books are outlined, no reference at all is made to Book XI. One large division covers Books VII to IX, and another covers Book X. But at the beginning of Book XI a new division is found, which, while not in absolute opposition to the previous one, is still not in complete agreement with it. Mansion concluded from this that, when St. Thomas composed his exposition of Book VII, he was either unaware of Book XI altogether, or at least had not yet received the translation of it, and so made no mention of it in his division. However, when this book came into his possession later on, he incorporated it into his work and had therefore to make a new division which would account for it and also extend to the balance of his work. He would have received this new book just before he began his commentary of Book XII or after he had completed it; and assuming the later alternative to be true, it would then have been necessary for him to revise Book XII. Mansion feels that there is evidence to support such a second writing in a number of references given in early books, especially Book III, in which Book {L} is sometimes referred to as XI, following the numeration of the *media*.[56]

In Pelster's view the hypothesis of Mansion deserves attention, but it is not necessary to accept it.[57] That is to say, from the fact that St. Thomas in Book VII does not consider XI, it does not necessarily follow that he was unaware of it. He may have known it but simply found no occasion to use it. Since there is evidence that St. Thomas possessed the *nova* at the time he began his exposition, it is quite possible that he knew Book XI, which is found only in that version. He could have decided at first against using it and later changed his mind. This assumption is a reasonable one according to Pelster if certain facts are taken into consideration. St. Thomas in commenting upon Aristotle was interested primarily in explaining the development of his metaphysical views, and in this undertaking Book XI has no essential part to play, being neither a continuation of the thought of Book X nor an introduction in any necessary and proper sense to Book XII.

---

56 Mansion, *art. cit.*, 280–84.

57 For Pelster's argument, see *art. cit.*, *Gregorianum*, XVII (1936) 376–80.

This becomes evident when the contents of the book are examined, for they are merely a recapitulation of the main points developed in certain of the earlier books, to which extracts from the *Physics* have been added.[58] This book then could easily have been set aside without in any way affecting the development of Aristotle's main trend of thought. Pelster feels that when St. Thomas came to treat Book XI he decided to introduce it into his exposition as an introduction to Book XII inasmuch as it can be used as a kind of preparation for the doctrine presented in this book. St. Thomas's change of mind can be accounted for, he thinks, in the light of the circumstances under which the Commentary was written. St. Thomas composed his commentaries for the use of teachers and students in the schools, and since the *vetus*, the *media*, and the translation from the Arabic were all considered to be first class texts and the ones customarily employed, he would also have used them. But since these versions lacked Book XI, he would not have had to take this book into account. The *nova*, being new, would not be well enough known at first to use as a classroom text. However, when it did become better known and its superiority was recognized, St. Thomas would have begun to employ it as his basic text, and so would have to consider Book XI which it contained.

Granted that this simpler hypothesis is acceptable, Pelster also thinks that it is unnecessary to admit a second writing or revision, in whole or in part, as others have proposed on the basis of the occasional appearances of the numeration of the *media* along with that of the *nova*. The designation of Book ({L}) sometimes as XI and sometimes as XII, and of Books ({M}) and ({N}) sometimes as XII and XIII, and sometimes as XIII and XIV, admits of a simpler explanation: Since St. Thomas found himself in a transitional stage, he is sometimes thinking of the older numeration of the *media* and sometimes of the newer numeration of the *nova*. His readers and custom would force him to use the older numeration, while his new findings would incline him to use the newer. If the degree of simplicity with which a hypothesis takes care of known facts determines its acceptableness, Pelster's hypothesis cannot be lightly dismissed.

The completing of this translation has been possible only as a result of the unfailing assistance I have received from several persons who have my most sincere thanks. I am quite unable to express my gratitude to Fathers Robert W. Schmidt and James J. Doyle, S.J., for their untiring patience in reading the greater part of the manuscript, for their criticisms and the innumerable valuable suggestions they have made in the matter of emendations. I am particularly indebted to Father Schmidt for his excellent supervision throughout the whole undertaking and for locating a number of references, especially those to Avicenna. I also wish to acknowledge my indebtedness to Father Robert F. Harvanek, S.J., whose original interest in this work made its ultimate publication possible; and to

58 The first eight chapters of Book XI (K) present in condensed form the doctrines of chapters 2–6 of Book III, chapters 1–8 of Book IV, and chapters 1, 2–4 of Book VI, while the last four chapters are made up of extracts from the *Physics*: chapters 5 and 6 of Book II, chapters 1–7 of Book III and chapters 1–3 of Book V.

Fathers George A. Curran, S.J., and Michael Montague, S.J., for their help in reading some parts of the manuscript.

J. P. R.

PREFACE

The welcome accorded our project to put back in circulation English translations of St. Thomas's commentaries on works of Aristotle that have long been out of print, emboldens us to continue. In 1993, we published Thomas's *Commentary on Aristotle's Nicomachean Ethics*, and the following year his *Commentary on Aristotle's De Anima*. Our edition of the *Commentary on Aristotle's Metaphysics* is modeled on our earlier edition of the *Ethics* commentary. The Henry Regnery edition of these commentaries made of each of them a beautiful two-volume set. This had the disadvantage, however, of making the translation less usable than it might have been. Accordingly, we reset the *Ethics* commentary and published it as a single volume. The same has been done with the Commentary on the *Metaphysics*.

A commentary is to be consulted in close conjunction with the work on which it comments. The inclusion of the text of Aristotle in the commentary, with a passage from the *Metaphysics* followed by Thomas's explanation of it, makes it easy to use the commentary. And to have all twelve of the books of the *Metaphysics* commentary in a single volume facilitates consulting earlier and later books. This is important since, as a commentator, Thomas takes it to be his primary task to explain the order and interrelationships of the parts of the integral work. To have the whole of the *Metaphysics* and the whole of the commentary in one volume thus enables the student more easily to appraise the claims Thomas makes for the order of the text.

For much of this century, it has seemed quaint to read the *Metaphysics* as if it were a literary whole whose parts can be taken to comment on one another. The enormous influence exercised by the imaginative flights of Werner Jaeger in his two books on Aristotle[1] led to a frenzy of imitative efforts to fragment the work. Under this onslaught, scarcely two lines of text retained a fixed relation to one another. There was a reverse Heraclitization of the *Metaphysics, ut ita dicam*. Scholars sought to construct a unity out of the snippets of Heraclitus that have come down to us; but in the case of the *Metaphysics*, they took a marvelously unified work and sought to break it into unrelated pieces. One who looks back on those efforts, now that the frenzy has subsided, can only wonder at the leaps and gambols in the argumentation of otherwise sober, even Teutonic, folk.

With the appearance of Giuseppe Reale's book[2] on the *Metaphysics*, twentieth-

---

1 W. Jaeger, *Entstehungsgeschichte der Metaphysik des Aristoteles* (Berlin, 1912); *Aristoteles: Grundlegung einer Geschichte seiner Entwicklung* (Berlin, 1923).

2 Giuseppe Reale, *The Concept of First Philosophy and the Unity of the Metaphysics of*

century Aristotelian studies rejoined the efforts that had been made over the centuries to understand the Aristotelian treatises. Nowadays, an effort like that of Thomas Aquinas can count on getting a respectful reading from students of Aristotle. The Thomistic commentary gives us an interpretation of the *Metaphysics* which not only sees the overall sequence of books as manifesting an orderly procedure but also finds a marvelous order among the chapters of each book and indeed in the details of each chapter. No reader can fail to be struck by the way in which Thomas sees Book Five not only as occurring just where it ought to but also as having an internal order based upon the elements of Aristotelian scientific methodology—the subject of the science, its properties, its principles—which shows the book to be anything but random and/or self-standing introduction to Aristotelian terminology (one edition set it at the beginning of the work, another called it a Philosophical Lexicon). Not even Reale managed to see Book Five as an integral part of the whole.

The Leonine edition of the commentary, edited by James Reilly, has been eagerly awaited for many years. It is now complete, but publication may yet take a little while. One day, *deo volente*, all of the commentaries will be translated again from the text of the critical edition. In the meantime, in between time, our reprints can serve a transitional function.

Ralph McInerny
July 1995

Aristotle, translated by J. Catan (Albany, N.Y.: SUNY Press, 1980). For a recurrence of the evolutionary approach, though more apparent than real, see Bertrand Dumoulin, *Analyse Genetique de la Metaphysique d'Aristote* (Montreal, 1986).

ST. THOMAS'S PROLOGUE

When several things are ordained to a single thing, one of them must rule or govern and the rest be ruled or governed, as the Philosopher[1] teaches in the *Politics.*[2] This indeed is evident in the union of soul and body, for the soul naturally commands and the body obeys. The same thing is also true of the soul's powers, for the concupiscible and irascible appetites are ruled in a natural order by reason. Now all the sciences and arts are ordained to a single thing, namely, to man's perfection, which is happiness. Hence one of these sciences and arts must be the mistress of all the others, and this one rightly lays claim to the name *wisdom;* for it is the office of the wise man to direct others.

We can discover which science this is and the sort of things with which it is concerned by carefully examining the qualities of a good ruler; for just as men of superior intelligence are naturally the rulers and masters of others, whereas those of great physical strength and little intelligence are naturally slaves, as the Philosopher says in the aforementioned book,[3] in a similar way that science which is intellectual in the highest degree should be naturally the ruler of the others. This science is the one which treats of the most intelligible objects.

Now the phrase "most intelligible objects" can be understood in three ways. First, from the viewpoint of the order of knowing; for those things from which the intellect derives certitude seem to be more intelligible. Therefore, since the certitude of science is acquired by the intellect knowing causes, a knowledge of causes seems to be intellectual in the highest degree. Hence that science which considers first causes also seems to be the ruler of the others in the highest degree.

Second, this phrase can be understood by comparing the intellect with the senses; for while sensory perception is a knowledge of particulars, the intellect seems to differ from sense by reason of the fact that it comprehends universals. Hence that science is pre-eminently intellectual which deals with the most universal principles. These principles are *being* and those things which naturally accompany being, such as *unity* and *plurality, potency* and *act.* Now such principles should not remain entirely undetermined, since without them a complete knowledge of the principles which are proper to any genus or species cannot be had. Nor again should they be dealt with in any one particular science; for, since a knowledge of each class of beings stands in need of these principles, they would with equal reason be investigated in every particular science. It follows, then,

---

1 The title of "Philosopher" was the one which medieval writers reserved for Aristotle.

2 *Politica,* I, 5 (1254a20).

3 *Ibid.,* I, 1 (1254a31); 5 (1254b29).

that such principles are treated by one common science, which, since it is intellectual in the highest degree, is the mistress of the others.

Third, this phrase can be understood from the viewpoint of the intellect's own knowledge. For since each thing has intellective power by virtue of being free from matter, those things must be intelligible in the highest degree which are altogether separate from matter. For the intelligible object and the intellect must be proportionate to each other and must belong to one and the same genus, since the intellect and the intelligible object are one in actuality. Now those things are separate from matter in the highest degree which abstract not only from designated matter, "as the natural forms taken universally, of which the philosophy of nature (*scientia naturalis*)[4] treats," but from sensible matter altogether; and these are separate from matter not only in their intelligible constitution (*ratio*), as the objects of mathematics, but also in being, as God and the intelligences. Therefore the science which considers such things seems to be the most intellectual and the ruler or mistress of the others.

Now this threefold consideration should be assigned to one and the same science and not to different sciences. For the separate substances mentioned above are the universal and first causes of being. Moreover, it pertains to one and the same science to consider both the proper causes of some genus and the genus itself; for example, the philosophy of nature considers the principles of a natural body. Consequently it must be the office of one and the same science to consider separate substances and *being in general* (*ens commune*), which is the genus[5] of which the substances mentioned above are the common and universal causes.

From this it is evident that, although this science [i.e., metaphysics or first philosophy] studies the three classes of things mentioned above,[6] it does not investigate any one of them as its subject, but only being in general. For the subject of a science is the genus whose causes and properties we seek, and not the causes themselves of the particular genus studied, because a knowledge of the causes of some genus is the goal to which the investigation of a science attains. Now although the subject of this science is being in general, the whole of it is predicated of those things which are separate from matter both in their intelligible constitution and in being (*esse*). For it is not only those things which can never exist in matter which are said to be separate from matter in their intelligible constitution and in being, such as God and the intellectual substances, but also those things which can exist without matter, such as being in general. This could not be the case, however, if their being depended on matter.

---

4 In the works of Aristotle and St. Thomas the term *natural science* (*scientia naturalis*) is equivalent to the term *philosophy of nature* or *natural philosophy* (*philosophia naturalis*). The ancients drew no explicit distinction between a philosophic and what we call "scientific" study of nature.

5 According to St. Thomas the term *being* or *being in general* is not a *genus* or generic term in the strict logical sense, for being is predicated of things analogically or proportionally and not univocally. Cf. *Metaphysics*, Book III, Lesson 8, C 433.

6 I.e., God, the intellectual substances, and being in general.

Therefore in accordance with the three classes of objects mentioned above from which this science derives its perfection, three names arise. It is called *divine science* or *theology* inasmuch as it considers the aforementioned substances. It is called *metaphysics* inasmuch as it considers being and the attributes which naturally accompany being (for things which transcend the physical order are discovered by the process of analysis, as the more common are discovered after the less common). And it is called *first philosophy* inasmuch as it considers the first causes of things. Therefore it is evident what the subject of this science is, and how it is related to the other sciences, and by what names it is designated.

BOOK I
INTRODUCTION TO FIRST PHILOSOPHY

History of Metaphysical Inquiry

LESSON 1
The Dignity and Object of This Science

ARISTOTLE'S TEXT Chapter 1: 980a21–983a3

1. *All men naturally desire to know. A sign of this is the delight we take in the senses; for apart from their usefulness they are loved for themselves, and most of all the sense which operates through the eyes. For not only that we may act, but even when we intend to do nothing, we prefer sight, as we may say, to all the other senses. The reason is that of all the senses this most enables us to know and reveals many differences between things.* **980a21–27**

2. *Animals by nature, then, are born with sensory power.* **980a27–28**

3. *Now in some animals memory arises from the senses, but in others it does not; and for this reason the former are prudent and more capable of being taught than those which are unable to remember. Those which cannot hear sounds are prudent but unable to learn, as the bee and any other similar type of animal there may be. But any which have this sense together with memory are able to learn.* **980a28–980b25**

4. *Thus other animals live by imagination and memory and share little in experience, whereas the human race lives by art and reasoning.* **980b25–28**

5. *Now in men experience comes from memory, for many memories of the same thing produce the capacity of a single experience. And experience seems to be somewhat like science and art.* **980b28–981a2**

6. *But in men science and art come from experience; for "Experience causes art, and inexperience, luck," as Polus rightly states.[Plato, Gorgias, 448C] Art comes into being when from many conceptions acquired by experience a single universal judgment is formed about similar things. For to judge that this [medicine] has been beneficial to Callias and Socrates and many other individuals who suffer from this disease, is a matter of experience; but to judge that it has been beneficial to all individuals of a particular kind, as the phlegmatic, the bilious, or the feverish, taken as a class, who suffer from this disease, is a matter of art.* **981a2–12**

7. *In practical matters, then, experience seems to differ in no way from art. But we see that men of experience are more proficient than those who have theory without experience. The reason is that experience is a knowledge of singulars, whereas art is a knowledge of universals. But all actions and processes of generation are concerned with singulars. For the physician heals man only incidentally, but he heals Socrates or Callias, or some individual that can be named, to whom the nature man happens to belong. Therefore, if anyone has the theory without experience, and knows the universal but not the singulars contained in this, he will very often make mistakes; for it is rather the individual man who is able to be cured.* **981a12–24**

8. *Yet we think that scientific knowledge and the ability to refute objections belong to art rather than to experience, and we are of the opinion that those who are proficient in art are wiser than men of experience, implying that it is more according to wisdom to know as one pursuing all things.* **981a24–27**

9. *Now this is because the former know the cause whereas the latter do not. For those who have experience know that something is so but do not know why, whereas the others know the why and the cause. For this reason, too, we think that the master planners in each art are to be held in greater esteem, and that they know more and are wiser than the manual laborers, because they understand the reasons for the things which are done. Indeed, we think that the latter*

resemble certain inanimate things, which act but do not know what they do, as fire burns. Therefore inanimate things perform each of their actions as a result of a certain natural disposition, whereas manual laborers perform theirs through habit, implying that some men are wiser not insofar as they are practical but insofar as they themselves have the theories and know the causes. **981a28–981b6**

10. In general a sign of scientific knowledge is the ability to teach, and for this reason we think that art rather than experience is science. For those who have an art are able to teach, whereas the others are not. **981b7–10**

11. Furthermore, we do not hold that any one of the senses is wisdom, since the cognition of singular things belongs especially to the senses. However, these do not tell us why a thing is so; for example, they do not tell us why fire is hot but only that it is so. **981b10–13**

12. It is only fitting, then, that the one who discovered any art whatsoever that went beyond the common perceptions of men should be admired by men, not only because of some usefulness of his discoveries, but as one who is wise and as distinguishing [a thing] from others. And as more of the arts were discovered, some to supply the necessities of life, and others to introduce us [to the sciences], those who discovered the latter were always considered to be wiser than those who discovered the former, because their sciences were not for the sake of utility. Hence, after all such arts had already been developed, those sciences were discovered which are pursued neither for the sake of pleasure nor necessity. This happened first in those places where men had leisure. Hence the mathematical arts originated in Egypt, for there the priestly class was permitted leisure. The difference between art and science and similar mental states has been stated in our work on morals.[Ethics, 1139b14-1141b8] **981b13–27**

13. Now the reason for undertaking this investigation is that all men think that the science which is called wisdom deals with the primary causes and principles of things. Hence, as we have said before (8, 9), the man of experience is considered to be wiser than one who has any of the senses; the artist wiser than the man of experience; the master planner wiser than the manual laborer; and speculative knowledge wiser than practical knowledge. It is quite evident, then, that wisdom is a science of certain causes and principles. **981b27–982a3**

COMMENTARY

1. Aristotle first sets down an introduction to this science, in which he treats of two things. First [1], he points out with what this science is concerned. Second [Lesson 3], he explains what kind of science it is ("That this is not a practical science").

In regard to the first he does two things. First, he shows that the office of this science, which is called wisdom, is to consider the causes of things. Second [Lesson 2], he explains with what causes or kinds of causes it is concerned ("But since we are in search").

In regard to the first he prefaces certain preliminary considerations from which he argues in support of his thesis. Second [13], he draws a conclusion from these considerations ("Now the reason for undertaking").

In regard to the first he does two things. First, he makes clear the dignity of scientific knowledge in general. Second [2], he explains the hierarchy in knowing ("Animals by nature").

Now he establishes the dignity of scientific knowledge from the fact that it is naturally desired as an end by all men. Hence, in regard to this he does two things. First, he states what he intends [to prove]. Second [1], he proves it ("A sign of this").

Accordingly, he says, first, that the desire to know belongs by nature to all men.

2. Three reasons can be given for this. The first is that each thing naturally desires its own perfection. Hence matter is also said to desire form as any imperfect thing desires its perfection. Therefore, since the intellect, by which man is what he is, considered in itself is all things potentially, and becomes them actually only through knowledge, because the intellect is none of the things that exist before it understands them, as is stated in Book III of *The Soul* [429a23]; so each man naturally desires knowledge just as matter desires form.

3. The second reason is that each thing has a natural inclination to perform its proper operation, as something hot is naturally inclined to heat, and something heavy to be moved downwards. Now the proper operation of man as man is to understand, for by reason of this he differs from all other things. Hence the desire of man is naturally inclined to understand, and therefore to possess scientific knowledge.

4. The third reason is that it is desirable for each thing to be united to its source, since it is in this that the perfection of each thing consists. This is also the reason why circular motion is the most perfect motion, as is proved in Book VIII of the *Physics*[261a12], because its terminus is united to its starting-point. Now it is only by means of his intellect that man is united to the separate substances, which are the source of the human intellect and that to which the human intellect is related as something imperfect to something perfect. It is for this reason, too, that the ultimate happiness of man consists in this union. Therefore man naturally desires to know. The fact that some men do not devote any study to this science does not disprove this thesis; for those who desire some end are often prevented from pursuing it for some reason or other, either because of the difficulty of attaining it, or because of other occupations. And in this way, too, even though all men desire knowledge, still not all devote themselves to the pursuit of it because they are held back by other things, either by pleasures or the needs of the present life; or they may even avoid the effort that learning demands because they are lazy. Now Aristotle makes this statement in order to show that it is not pointless to search for a science that is not useful for anything else, as happens in the case of this science, since a natural desire cannot exist in vain.

5. Then he establishes his thesis by means of an example. Since our senses serve us in two respects: in knowing things and in meeting the needs of life, we love them for themselves inasmuch as they enable us to know and also assist us to live. This is evident from the fact that all men take the greatest delight in that sense which is most knowing, i.e., the sense of sight, which we value not merely in order to do something, but even when we are not required to act at all. The reason is that this sense—that of sight—is the most knowing of all our senses and makes us aware of many differences between things.

6. In this part it is clear that he gives two reasons why sight is superior to the other senses in knowing. The first is that it knows in a more perfect way; and this belongs to it because it is the most spiritual of all the senses. For the more immaterial a power is, the more

perfectly it knows. And evidently sight is a more immaterial sense, if we consider the modification produced in it by its object. For all other sensible objects change both the organ and medium of a sense by a material modification, for example, the object of touch by heating and cooling, the object of taste by affecting the organ of taste with some flavor through the medium of saliva, the object of hearing by means of motion in the body, and the object of smell by means of the evaporation of volatile elements. But the object of sight changes the organ and medium of sight only by a spiritual modification; because neither the pupil of the eye nor the air becomes colored, but these only receive the form of color in a spiritual mode of being. Therefore, because actual sensation consists in the actual modification of a sense by its object, it is evident that that sense which is changed in a more immaterial and spiritual way is more spiritual in its operation. Hence sight judges about sensible objects in a more certain and perfect way than the other senses do.

7. The other reason which he gives for the superiority of sight is that it gives us more information about things. This is attributable to the nature of its object, for touch and taste, and likewise smell and hearing, perceive those accidents by which lower bodies are distinguished from higher ones. But sight perceives those accidents which lower bodies have in common with higher ones. For a thing is actually visible by means of light, which is common both to lower and higher bodies, as is said in Book II of *The Soul [418b5]*. Hence the celestial bodies are perceptible only by means of sight.

8. There is also another reason. Sight informs us of many differences between things, for we seem to know sensible things best by means of sight and touch, but especially by means of sight. The reason for this can be drawn from the fact that the other three senses perceive those accidents which in a way flow from a sensible body and do not remain in it. Thus sound comes from a sensible body inasmuch as it flows away from it and does not remain in it. The same thing is true of the evaporation of volatile elements, with which and by which odor is diffused. But sight and hearing perceive those accidents which remain in sensible bodies, such as color, warmth and coldness. Hence the judgment of sight and touch is extended to things themselves, whereas the judgment of hearing and smell is extended to those accidents which flow from things and not to things themselves. It is for this reason that figure and size and the like, by which a sensible being itself is disposed, are perceived more by sight and touch than by the other senses. And they are perceived more by sight than by touch, both because sight knows more efficaciously, as has been pointed out (C 6), and also because quantity and those [accidents] which naturally follow from it, which are seen to be the common sensibles, are more closely related to the object of sight than to that of touch. This is clear from the fact that the object of sight belongs in some degree to every body having some quantity, whereas the object of touch does not.

9. **Animals by nature, then** [2].

Here he considers the hierarchy in knowledge. He does this, first [2], with respect to brute animals; and, then [4], with respect to men ("Thus other animals").

With respect to brute animals he mentions first what all animals have in common; and second [3], that by which they differ and surpass one another ("Now in some animals").

Now all animals are alike in the respect that they possess by nature the power of sensation. For an animal is an animal by reason of the fact that it has a sentient soul, which is the nature of an animal in the sense in which the distinctive form of each thing is its nature. But even though all animals are naturally endowed with sensory power, not all animals have all the senses, but only perfect animals. All have the sense of touch, for this sense in a way is the basis of all the other senses. However, not all have the sense of sight, because this sense knows in a more perfect way than all the other senses. But touch is more necessary; for it perceives the elements of which an animal is composed, namely, the hot, cold, moist and dry. Hence, just as sight knows in a more perfect way than the other senses, in a similar way touch is more necessary inasmuch as it is the first to exist in the process of generation. For those things which are more perfect according to this process come later in the development of the individual which is moved from a state of imperfection to one of perfection.

10. **Now in some animals** [3].

Here he indicates the different kinds and three levels of knowing found among brute animals. For there are certain animals which have sensation, although they do not have memory which comes from sensation. For memory accompanies imagination, which is a movement caused by the senses in their act of sensing, as we find in Book II of *The Soul [428b10]* But in some animals imagination does not accompany sensation, and therefore memory cannot exist in them. This is found verified in imperfect animals which are incapable of local motion, such as shellfish. For since sensory cognition enables animals to make provision for the necessities of life and to perform their characteristic operations, then those animals which move towards something at a distance by means of local motion must have memory. For if the anticipated goal by which they are induced to move did not remain in them through memory, they could not continue to move toward the intended goal which they pursue. But in the case of immobile animals the reception of a present sensible quality is sufficient for them to perform their characteristic operations, since they do not move toward anything at a distance. Hence these animals have an indefinite movement as a result of confused [or indeterminate] imagination alone, as he points out in Book III of *The Soul [434a1]*.

11. Again, from the fact that some animals have memory and some do not, it follows that some are prudent and some not. For, since prudence makes provision for the future from memory of the past (and this is the reason why Tully in his *Rhetoric*, Book II, makes memory, understanding and foresight parts of prudence), prudence cannot be had by those animals which lack memory. Now those animals which have memory can have some prudence, although prudence has one meaning in the case of brute animals and another in the case of man. Men are prudent inasmuch as they deliberate rationally about what they ought to do. Hence it is said in Book VI of the *Ethics [1140b5]*, that prudence is a rationally regulated plan of things to be done. But the judgment about things to be done which is not a result of any rational deliberation but of some natural instinct is called prudence in other

animals. Hence in other animals prudence is a natural estimate about the pursuit of what is fitting and the avoidance of what is harmful, as a lamb follows its mother and runs away from a wolf.

12. But among those animals which have memory some have hearing and some do not. And all those which cannot hear (as the bee or any other similar type of animal that may exist), even though they have prudence, are still incapable of being taught, i.e., in the sense that they can be habituated to the doing or avoiding of something through someone else's instruction, because such instruction is received chiefly by means of hearing. Hence in *The Senses and Their Objects [437a12]* it is stated that hearing is the sense by which we receive instruction. Furthermore, the statement that bees do not have hearing is not opposed in any way to the observation that they are frightened by certain sounds. For just as a very loud sound kills an animal and splits wood, as is evident in the case of thunder, not because of the sound but because of the violent motion of the air in which the sound is present, in a similar fashion those animals which lack hearing can be frightened by the sounding air even though they have no perception of sound. However, those animals which have both memory and hearing can be both prudent and teachable.

13. It is evident, then, that there are three levels of knowing in animals. The first level is that had by animals which have neither hearing nor memory, and which are therefore neither capable of being taught nor of being prudent. The second level is that of animals which have memory but are unable to hear, and which are therefore prudent but incapable of being taught. The third level is that of animals which have both of these faculties, and which are therefore prudent and capable of being taught. Moreover, there cannot be a fourth level, so that there would be an animal which had hearing but lacked memory. For those senses which perceive their sensible objects by means of an external medium—and hearing is one of these—are found only in animals which have locomotion and which cannot do without memory, as has been pointed out [n. 10].

14. **Thus other animals** [4].

Here he explains the levels of human knowing; and in regard to this he does two things. First [4], he explains how human knowing surpasses the knowing of the above-mentioned animals. Second [5], he shows how human knowing is divided into different levels ("Now in men").

Accordingly, in the first part [4] he says that the life of animals is ruled by imagination and memory: by imagination in the case of imperfect animals, and by memory in the case of perfect animals. For even though the latter also have imagination, still each thing is said to be ruled by that [power] which holds the highest place within it. Now in this discussion life does not mean the being of a living thing, as it is understood in Book II of *The Soul, [413a22]* when he says that "for living things to live is to be"; for the life of an animal in this sense is not a result of memory or imagination but is prior to both of these. But life is taken to mean vital activity, just as we are also accustomed to speak of association as the life of men. But by the fact that he establishes the truth about the cognition of animals with reference to the management of life, we are given to understand that knowing belongs to these animals, not for the sake of knowing, but because of the need for action.

15. Now, as is stated below [n. 18], in men the next thing above memory is experience, which some animals have only to a small degree. For an experience arises from the association of many singular [intentions] received in memory. And this kind of association is proper to man, and pertains to the cogitative power (also called particular reason), which associates particular intentions just as universal reason associates universal ones. Now since animals are accustomed to pursue or avoid certain things as a result of many sensations and memory, for this reason they seem to share something of experience, even though it be slight. But above experience, which belongs to particular reason, men have as their chief power a universal reason by means of which they live.

16. And just as experience is related to particular reason [in men], and customary activity to memory in animals, in a similar way art is related to universal reason. Therefore, just as the life of animals is ruled in a perfect way by memory together with activity that has become habitual through training, or in any other way whatsoever, in a similar way man is ruled perfectly by reason perfected by art. Some men, however, are ruled by reason without art; but this rule is imperfect.

17. **Now in men** [5].

Here he explains the different levels of human knowing; and in regard to this he does two things. First [5], he compares art with experience; and, second [12], he compares speculative art with practical art ("It is only fitting").

He treats the first point in two ways. First [5], he explains how art and experience originate. Second [7], he explains how one is superior to the other ("In practical matters").

In regard to the first he does two things. First [5], he explains how each of the above originates. Second [6], he makes this clear by means of an example ("For to judge").

In regard to the first he does two things. First [5], he describes how experience originates, and second [6], how art originates ("But in men, science").

He says first [5], then, that in men experience is caused by memory. The way in which it is caused is this: from several memories of a single thing a man acquires experience about some matter, and by means of this experience he is able to act easily and correctly. Therefore, because experience provides us with the ability to act easily and correctly, it seems to be almost the same as science and art. For they are alike inasmuch as in either case from many instances a single view of a thing is obtained. But they differ inasmuch as universals are grasped by art and singular things by experience, as is stated later.

18. **But in men science and art** [6].

Here he describes the way in which art arises. He says that in men science and art come from experience, and he proves this on the authority of Polus, who says that "Experience causes art and inexperience luck." For when an inexperienced person acts correctly, this happens by chance. Furthermore, the way in which art arises from experience is the same as the way spoken of above in which experience arises from memory. For just as one experiential cognition comes from many memories of a thing, so does one universal judgment about all similar things come from the apprehension of many experiences. Hence art has this [unified view] more than experience, because experience is concerned only with singulars, whereas art has to do with universals.

19. Thereupon he makes this clear by means of examples ("But in men [6]"). For when a man has learned that this medicine has been beneficial to Socrates and Plato, and to many other individuals who were suffering from some particular disease, whatever it may be, this is a matter of experience; but when a man learns that this particular treatment is beneficial to all men who have some particular kind of disease and some particular kind of physical constitution, as it has benefited the feverish, both the phlegmatic and the bilious, this is now a matter of art.

20. **In practical matters** [7].

He compares art to experience from the viewpoint of pre-eminence; and in regard to this he does two things. First [7], he compares them from the viewpoint of action; and, second [8], from the viewpoint of knowledge ("Yet we think").

He says then that in practical matters experience seems to differ in no way from art; for when it comes to acting, the difference between experience and art, which is a difference between the universal and the singular, disappears, because art operates with reference to singulars just as experience does. Therefore the aforesaid difference pertains only to the way in which they come to know. But even though art and experience do not differ in the way in which they act, because both act on singular things, nevertheless they differ in the effectiveness of their action. For men of experience act more effectively than those who have the universal knowledge of an art but lack experience.

21. The reason is that actions have to do with singular things, and all processes of generation belong to singular things. For universals are generated or moved only by reason of something else, inasmuch as this belongs to singular things. For man is generated when this man is generated. Hence a physician heals man only incidentally, but properly he heals Plato or Socrates, or some man that can be individually named, to whom the nature man belongs, or rather to whom it is accidental inasmuch as he is the one healed. For even though the nature man belongs essentially to Socrates, still it belongs only accidentally to the one healed or cured; for the proposition "Socrates is a man" is an essential one, because, if Socrates were defined, man would be given in his definition, as will be said below in Book IV. But the proposition "What is healed or cured is man" is an accidental one.

22. Hence, since art has to do with universals and experience with singulars, if anyone has the theoretical knowledge of an art but lacks experience, he will be perfect insofar as he knows the universal; but since he does not know the singular, because he lacks experience, he will very often make mistakes in healing. For healing belongs to the realm of the singular rather than to that of the universal, because it belongs to the former essentially and to the latter accidentally.

23. **Yet we think** [8].

Here he compares art with experience from the viewpoint of knowing; and in regard to this he does two things. First [8], he states how art is superior to experience; and second [9], he proves this ("Now this is because").

He claims that art and science are superior to experience in three respects. First, they are superior from the viewpoint of scientific knowledge, which we think is attained by art rather than by experience. Second, they are superior from the viewpoint of meeting objections, which occurs in disputes. For in a dispute the one who has an art is able to meet the objections raised against that art, but one who has experience [alone] cannot do this. Third, they are superior from this point of view, that those who have an art come nearer to the goal of wisdom than men of experience, "Implying that it is," i.e., happens to be, "more truly to know if wisdom pursues all things," i.e., insofar as it pursues universals. For one who has an art is judged wiser than one who has experience, by reason of the fact that he considers universals. Or in another version: "Implying that it is more according to wisdom to know as one pursuing all things," i.e., universals. Another reading has: "As more conformable to knowing, since wisdom pursues all things," as if to say: "As more dependent upon knowing" than upon doing, "since wisdom pursues all things," i.e., it seeks to reach each single thing; so that those are rather called wise who are more knowing, not those who are more men of action. Hence another reading expresses this meaning more clearly, saying: "Implying that all pursue wisdom more with respect to knowing."

24. **Now this is** [9].

Then he proves the superiority of art and science mentioned above, and he does this by means of three arguments. The first runs thus: those who know the cause and reason why a thing is so are more knowing and wiser than those who merely know that it is so but do not know why. Now men of experience know that something is so but do not know the reason, whereas men who have an art know not merely that something is so but also know its cause and reason. Hence those who have an art are wiser and more knowing than those who have experience.

25. **For this reason too**[9].

Here he proves the first aspect of superiority, and this runs as follows. Those who know the cause and reason why a thing is so are compared to those who merely know that it is so as the architectonic arts are to the arts of manual laborers. But the architectonic arts are nobler. In a similar way, then, those who know the causes and reasons of things are more knowing than those who merely know that things are so.

26. The first part of this proof becomes clear from the fact that architects, or master artists, know the causes of the things that are done. In order to understand this we must note that architect means chief artist, from {techne} meaning chief, and {archos} meaning art. Now that art is said to be a chief art which performs a more important operation. Indeed, the operations of artists are distinguished in this way; for some operations are directed to disposing the material of the artifact. Carpenters, for example, by cutting and planing the wood, dispose matter for the form of a ship. Another operation is directed to introducing this form into the matter, for example, when someone builds a ship out of wood which has been disposed and prepared. A third operation is directed to the use of the finished product, and this is the highest operation. But the first operation is the lowest because it is directed to the second and the second to the third. Hence the shipbuilder is a superior artist compared with the

one who prepares the wood; and the navigator, who uses the completed ship, is a superior artist compared with the shipbuilder.

27. Further, since matter exists for the sake of form, and ought to be such as to befit the form, the shipbuilder knows the reason why the wood should be shaped in some particular way; but those who prepare the wood do not know this. And in a similar way, since the completed ship exists in order to be used, the one who uses the ship knows why it should have some particular form; for the form should be one that befits its use. Thus it is evident that the reason for the operations which dispose the matter is taken from the design of the product in the artist's mind, and the reason for the operations which produce the form of the artifact is taken from the use [to which the artifact is put].

28. It is evident, then, that the master artists know the causes of the things which are done. In fact we judge and speak about the others, i.e., the manual laborers, as we do about certain inanimate things. This is not because they do not perform artful operations, but because the things which they do they do without knowing the cause; for they know that something is to be done but not why it is, just as fire burns without knowing why. Hence there is a likeness between inanimate things and manual laborers from this point of view, that, just as inanimate things act without knowing the causes, inasmuch as they are directed to their proper end by a superior intellect, so also do manual laborers. But they differ in this respect, that inanimate things perform each of their operations as a result of their nature, whereas manual laborers perform theirs through habit. And while habit is practically the same as nature inasmuch as it is inclined to one definite effect, still habit differs from nature inasmuch as it is open to opposites by reason of human knowledge. For we do not habituate natural bodies, as is stated in Book II of the *Ethics [1103a20]* nor, indeed, is it possible to cause habits in things that lack knowledge. Now the statements that have been made, as is evident from the statements themselves, must be interpreted as meaning that some men are wiser, not insofar as they are "practical," i.e., men of action, as befits men of experience, but insofar as they have a plan for things to be done and know their causes, which are the basis of such a plan; and this befits master artists.

29. **In general a sign of scientific knowledge** [10].

Here he gives the second argument, which is as follows: a sign of knowledge is the ability to teach, and this is so because each thing is perfect in its activity when it can produce another thing similar to itself, as is said in Book IV of *Meteors [390a10]*. Therefore, just as the possession of heat is indicated by the fact that a thing can heat something else, in a similar way the possession of knowledge is indicated by the fact that one can teach, that is, cause knowledge in another. But men who have an art can teach, for since they know causes they can demonstrate from these; and demonstration is a syllogism which produces knowledge, as is said in Book I of the *Posterior Analytics [71b18]*. But men who have experience [only] cannot teach; for since they do not know the causes, they cannot cause knowledge in someone else. And if they do teach others the things which they know by experience, these things are not learned after the manner of scientific knowledge but after that of opinion or belief. Hence, it is clear that men who have an art are wiser and more knowing than those who have experience.

30. **Furthermore, we do not hold** [11].

Here he gives the third argument, which is as follows: knowing singular things is proper to the senses rather than to any other type of knowing [power], since our entire knowledge of singular things originates with the senses. Yet we do not hold that "any one of these," i.e., any one of the senses, is wisdom, because even though each sense knows that a thing is so, it does not know why it is so; for touch judges that fire is hot but does not know why it is hot. Therefore men of experience, who have a knowledge of singular things but do not know their causes, cannot be called wise men.

31. **It is only fitting** [12].

Here he compares practical art with speculative art; and in regard to this he does three things. First [12], he shows that a speculative art is wisdom to a greater degree than a practical art. Second *(ibid.)*, he answers an objection ("The difference").

He proves his first statement by this argument: in any of the sciences or arts we find that men with scientific knowledge are more admired and are held in higher esteem than all other men, because their knowledge is held to be nobler and more worthy of the name of wisdom. Now the discoverer of any art at all is admired because he perceives, judges and discerns a cause beyond the perceptions of other men, and not because of the usefulness of his discoveries. We admire him rather "as being wise, and as distinguishing [a thing] from others." As being wise, indeed, in the subtle way in which he investigates the causes of his discoveries, and as distinguishing [a thing] from others insofar as he investigates the ways in which one thing differs from another. Or, according to another interpretation, "as being distinct from the others" is to be read passively, as being distinguished in this respect from others. Hence another text has "one who is different." Some sciences, then, are more admirable and worthy of the name of wisdom because their observations are more outstanding, not because they are useful.

32. Therefore, since many useful arts have been discovered (some to provide the necessities of life, as the mechanical arts, and others to introduce us to the sciences, as the logical disciplines), those artists must be said to be wiser whose sciences were discovered not for the sake of utility but merely for the sake of knowing, that is to say, the speculative sciences.

33. That the speculative sciences were not discovered for the sake of utility is made clear by this fact, that after all sciences of this kind "had already been developed," i.e., acquired or discovered, which can serve as introductions to the other sciences, or provide the necessities of life, or give pleasure (as those arts whose object is to delight man), the speculative sciences were discovered, not for this kind of end, but for their own sake. The fact that they were not discovered for the sake of utility becomes evident from the place in which they were discovered. For they originated in those places where men first applied themselves to such things. Another version reads, "And first in those places where men had leisure," i.e., they had time for study because they were released from other occupations as a result of the abundance of things necessary [for life]. Hence the mathematical arts,

which are speculative in the highest degree, were first discovered in Egypt by the priests, who were given time for study, and whose expenses were defrayed by the community, as we also read in *Genesis* (47:22).

34. But because the names "wisdom," "science" and "art" have been used indifferently, lest someone should think that these terms are synonymous, he excludes this opinion and refers to his work on morals, i.e., to Book VI of the *Ethics [1139b15-1141b23]*, where he has explained the difference between art, wisdom, science, prudence, and understanding. And to give the distinction briefly—wisdom, science and understanding pertain to the speculative part of the soul, which he speaks of in that work as the scientific part of the soul. But they differ in that understanding is the habit of the first principles of demonstration, whereas science has to do with conclusions drawn from subordinate causes, and wisdom with first causes. This is the reason it is spoken of there as the chief science. But prudence and art belong to the practical part of the soul, which reasons about our contingent courses of action. And these also differ; for prudence directs us in actions which do not pass over into some external matter but are perfections of the one acting (which is the reason why prudence is defined in that work as the reasoned plan of things to be done), but art directs us in those productive actions, such as building and cutting, which pass over into external matter (which is the reason why art is defined as the reasoned plan of things to be made).

35. **Now the reason for undertaking** [13].

From what has been said he proves his major thesis, that is to say, that wisdom deals with the causes of things. He says that the reason "for undertaking this investigation," i.e., the above piece of reasoning, is that the science which is called wisdom seems to be about first causes and principles. This is evident from the foregoing; for the more a man attains to a knowledge of the cause, the wiser he is. This is also evident from the foregoing; because the man of experience is wiser than one who has sensation alone without experience; and the artist is wiser than any man of experience; and among artists the architect is wiser than the manual laborer. And similarly among the arts and sciences the speculative are more scientific than the practical. All these things are clear from the foregoing remarks. It follows, then, that that science which is wisdom in an absolute sense is concerned with the causes of things. The method of arguing would be similar if we were to say that that which is hotter is more afire, and therefore that that which is afire in an absolute sense is hot in an absolute sense.

LESSON 2
Wisdom Considers Universal First Causes and First Principles

ARISTOTLE'S TEXT Chapter 2: 982a4–982b10

1. But since we are in search of this science, it will therefore be necessary to consider with what kind of causes and principles wisdom or science deals. This will perhaps become evident if we take the opinions which we have about the wise man. First of all, then, we think that the wise man is one who knows all things in the highest degree, as becomes him, without having a knowledge of them individually. **982a4–10**

2. Next, we say that that man is wise who is capable of knowing things that are difficult and not easy for man to understand. For sensory perception is common to all, and is therefore easy and not a matter of wisdom. **982a10–12**

3. Again, [we consider him wise who is] more certain. **982a12–13**

4. And in every branch of science we say that he is wiser who is more capable of teaching us about the causes of things. **982a13–14**

5. Again, among the sciences we think that that science which exists for itself and is desirable for the sake of knowledge is wisdom to a greater degree than one which is desirable for the sake of contingent effects. **982a14–16**

6. And we think that a superior science which is rather the more basic comes nearer to wisdom than a subordinate science. For a wise man must not be directed but must direct, and he must not obey another but must be obeyed by one who is less wise. Such then and so many are the opinions which we have about the wise and about wisdom. **982a16–21**

7. Now of these attributes, that of knowing all things necessarily belongs to him who has universal knowledge in the highest degree, because he knows in some respect all things which are subordinate. **982a21–23**

8. But the things which are just about the most difficult for man to understand are also those which are most universal; for they are farthest removed from the senses. **982a23–25**

9. Again, the most certain of the sciences are those which are most concerned with primary things. For sciences based on fewer principles are more certain than those which have additional principles, as arithmetic is more certain than geometry. **982a25–28**

10. Moreover, that science which speculates about the causes of things is more instructive. For those who teach us are those who assign the causes of every single thing. **982128–30**

11. Again, understanding and scientific knowledge for their own sake are found in the highest degree in the science which has as its object what is most knowable. For one who desires scientific knowledge for itself will desire in the highest degree the science which is most truly science, and such a science has for its object what is most knowable. Now first principles and causes are most knowable; for it is by reason of these and from these that other things are known, and not these from things which are subordinate to them. **982130–982b4**

12. But that science is highest and superior to subordinate sciences which knows the reason why each single thing must be done. This is the good of every single thing, and viewed universally it is the greatest good in the whole of nature. **982b4–7**

13. In view of everything that has been said, then, the term which we are investigating evidently falls to the same science. For this science must speculate about first principles and causes, because the good, or that for the sake of which something is done, is also one of the causes. **982b7–10**

COMMENTARY

36. Having shown that wisdom is a knowledge of causes, the Philoso-

pher's aim here is to establish with what kinds of causes and what kinds of principles it is concerned. He shows that it is concerned with the most universal and primary causes, and he argues this from the definition of wisdom.

In regard to this he does three things. First [1], he formulates a definition of wisdom from the different opinions which men have about the wise man and about wisdom. Second [7], he shows that all of these are proper to that universal science which considers first and universal causes ("Now of these"). Third [13], he draws the conclusion at which he aims ("In view of everything").

In regard to the first he gives six common opinions which men have entertained about wisdom. He states the first [14] where he says "But since we are in search"; and this opinion is this: in general we all consider those especially to be wise who know all things, as the case demands, without having a knowledge of every singular thing. For this is impossible, since singular things are infinite in number, and an infinite number of things cannot be comprehended by the intellect.

37. **Next, we say that** [15].

Here he gives the second opinion, which is this: we hold that man to be wise who is capable, by reason of his intellect, of knowing difficult things, and those which are not easy for ordinary men to understand. For sensory perception, i.e., the knowing of sensible things, is common to all men, and is therefore easy and so not a matter of wisdom. That is to say, it is neither a mark nor the office of a wise man. Thus it is clear that whatever pertains properly to wisdom is not easily known by all.

38. **Again, [we consider]** [16].

Here he gives the third opinion, namely, that we say that he is wise who, regarding what he knows, is more certain than other men generally are.

39. **And in every branch** [17].

Here he gives the fourth opinion, namely, that that man is said to be wiser in every science who can give the causes of anything that is brought into question, and can teach by means of this.

40. **Again, among the sciences** [18].

Here he gives the fifth opinion, which is this: among the many sciences that science which is more desirable and willed for its own sake, i.e., chosen for the sake of knowledge and for knowledge itself alone, is more of the nature of wisdom than one which is for the sake of any of the other contingent effects which can be caused by knowledge, such as the necessities of life, pleasure, and so forth.

41. **And we think** [19].

Here he gives the sixth opinion, namely, that this wisdom, of which mention has been made, must be or is said to be "rather the more basic," i.e., nobler, than "a subordinate science." This can be understood from the foregoing. For in the field of the mechanical arts, subordinate artists are those who execute by manual operations the commands of superior artists, whom he referred to above as master artists and wise men.

42. That the notion of wisdom belongs to sciences which give orders rather than to those which take them, he proves by two arguments. The first is that subordinate sciences are directed to superior sciences. For subordinate arts are directed to the end of a superior art, as the art of horsemanship to the end of the military art. But in the opinion of all it is not fitting that a wise

man should be directed by someone else, but that he should direct others. The second is that inferior artists are induced to act by superior artists inasmuch as they rely upon superior artists for the things which they must do or make. Thus the shipbuilder relies upon the instructions of the navigator for the kind of form which a ship ought to have. However, it does not befit a wise man that he should be induced to act by someone else, but that he should use his knowledge to induce others to act.

43. These, then, are the kind of opinions which men have of wisdom and the wise; and from all of these a description of wisdom can be formulated, so that the wise man is described as one who knows all, even difficult matters, with certitude and through their cause; who seeks this knowledge for its own sake; and who directs others and induces them to act. And in this way the major premise of the syllogism becomes evident. For every wise man must be such, and conversely whoever is such is wise.

44. **Now of these** [20].

Here he shows that all of the above attributes come together in the man who knows the first and universal causes of things; and he follows the same order as he did above. Thus he held first that knowledge of all things in the highest degree belongs to him who has universal knowledge. This was the first opinion, and it is made clear in this way: Whoever knows universals knows in some respect the things which are subordinate to universals, because he knows the universal in them. But all things are subordinate to those which are most universal. Therefore the one who knows the most universal things, knows in a sense all things.

45. **But the things** [21].

Here he proves that the second attribute belongs to the same person, by the following argument. Those things which are farthest removed from the senses are difficult for men to know; for sensory perception is common to all men since all human knowledge originates with this. But those things which are most universal are farthest removed from sensible things, because the senses have to do with singular things. Hence universals are the most difficult for men to know. Thus it is clear that that science is the most difficult which is most concerned with universals.

46. But the statement which appears in Book I of the *Physics [184a24]* seems to contradict this. For it is said there that more universal things are known first by us; and those things which are known first are those which are easier. Yet it must be said that those things which are more universal according to simple apprehension are known first; for being is the first thing that comes into the intellect, as Avicenna says, and animal comes into the intellect before man does. For just as in the order of nature, which proceeds from potentiality to actuality, animal is prior to man, so too in the genesis of knowledge the intellect conceives animal before it conceives man. But with respect to the investigations of natural properties and causes, less universal things are known first, because we discover universal causes by means of the particular causes which belong to one genus or species. Now those things which are universal in causing are known subsequently by us (notwithstanding the fact that they are things which are primarily knowable according to their nature), although things which are universal by predication are

known to us in some way before the less universal (notwithstanding the fact that they are not known prior to singular things). For in us sensory knowledge, which is cognitive of singular things, precedes intellective knowledge, which is about universals. And some importance must also be attached to the fact that he does not say that the most universal things are the most difficult absolutely, but "just about." For those things which are entirely separate from matter in being, as immaterial substances, are more difficult for us to know than universals. Therefore, even though this science which is called wisdom is the first in dignity, it is still the last to be learned.

47. **Again, the most certain** [22].

Here he shows that the third attribute belongs to the same science, by this argument: the more any sciences are prior by nature, the more certain they are. This is clear from the fact that those sciences which are said to originate as a result of adding something to the other sciences are less certain than those which take fewer things into consideration; for example, arithmetic is more certain than geometry because the objects considered in geometry are a result of adding to those considered in arithmetic. This becomes evident if we consider what these two sciences take as their first principle, namely, the point and the unit. For the point adds to the unit the notion of position, because undivided being constitutes the intelligible structure of the unit; and insofar as this has the function of a measure it becomes the principle of number. And the point adds to this the notion of position. However, particular sciences are subsequent in nature to universal sciences, because their subjects add something to the subjects of universal sciences. For example, it is evident that *mobile being*, with which the philosophy of nature deals, adds to *being* pure and simple, with which metaphysics is concerned, and to *quantified being*, with which mathematics is concerned. Hence that science which treats of being and the most universal things is the most certain. Moreover, the statement here that this science deals with fewer principles is not opposed to the one made above, that it knows all things; for the universal takes in fewer inferiors actually, but many potentially. And the more certain a science is, the fewer actual things it has to consider in investigating its subject-matter. Hence the practical sciences are the least certain, because they must consider the many circumstances attending individual effects.

48. **Moreover, that science** [23].

Here he proves that the fourth attribute belongs to the same science, by this argument: that science is more instructive, or better able to teach, which is concerned to a greater degree with causes. For only those teach who assign the causes of every single thing, because scientific knowledge comes about through some cause, and to teach is to cause knowledge in another. But that science which considers universals considers the first of all the causes. Hence it is evidently the best fitted to teach.

49. **Again, understanding** [24].

Here he proves that the fifth attribute belongs to the same science, by this argument: it is the office of those sciences which deal with things that are most knowable most properly to know and understand for their own sake, i.e., for the sake of those sciences themselves and not for something else. But it is the sciences that deal with first causes which consider the most knowable things. Therefore those sciences are desired most for their own sake. He proves the first premise thus: One who most desires knowledge for the sake of knowledge most desires scientific knowledge. But the highest kind of knowledge is concerned with things that are most knowable. Therefore those sciences are desired most for their own sake which have to do with things that are most knowable. He proves the second premise thus: Those things from which and by reason of which other things are known are more knowable than the things which are known by means of them. But these other things are known through causes and principles, and not vice versa, etc.

50. **But that science** [25].

Here he proves that the sixth attribute belongs to the same science, by the following argument: that science which considers the final cause, or that for the sake of which particular things are done, is related to the other sciences as a chief or master science is to a subordinate or ancillary one, as is evident from the foregoing remarks. For the navigator, to whom the use, or end, of the ship belongs, is a kind of master artist in relation to the shipbuilder who serves him. But the aforesaid science is concerned most with the final cause of all things. This is clear from the fact that that for the sake of which all particular things are done is the good of each, i.e., a particular good. But the end in any class of things is a good; and that which is the end of all things, i.e., of the universe itself, is the greatest good in the whole of nature. Now this belongs to the consideration of the science in question, and therefore it is the chief or architectonic science with reference to all the others.

51. **In view of everything** [26].

Here he draws from the foregoing arguments his intended conclusion, saying that it is clear from everything that has been said that the name wisdom which we are investigating belongs to the same science which considers or speculates about first principles and causes. This is evident from the six primary conditions which clearly pertain to the science that considers universal causes. But because the sixth condition touched on the consideration of the end, which was not clearly held to be a cause among the ancient philosophers, as will be said below [cf. n. 177], he therefore shows in a special way that this condition belongs to the same science, namely, the one which considers first causes. For the end, which is a good and that for the sake of which other things are done, is one of the many causes. Hence the science which considers first and universal causes must also be the one which considers the universal end of all things, which is the greatest good in the whole of nature.

LESSON 3
The Nature and Goal of Metaphysics

ARISTOTLE'S TEXT Chapter 2: 982b11–983a23

1. That this is not a practical science is evident from those who first philosophized. For it is because of wonder that men both now and formerly began to philosophize, wondering at first about less important matters, and then progressing little by little, they raised questions about more important ones, such as the phases of the moon and the courses of the sun and the stars and the generation of the universe. But one who raises questions and wonders seems to be ignorant. Hence the philosopher is also to some extent a lover of myth, for myths are composed of wonders. If they philosophized, then, in order to escape from ignorance, they evidently pursued their studies for the sake of knowledge and not for any utility. **982b11–21**

2. And what has happened bears witness to this; for when nearly all the things necessary for life, leisure and learning were acquired, this kind of prudence began to be sought. It is evident, then, that we do not seek this knowledge for the sake of any other necessity. **982b22–25**

3. But just as we say that a man is free who exists for himself and not for another, in a similar fashion this is the only free science, because it alone exists for itself. **982b25–28**

4. For this reason, too, it might rightly be thought that this science is not a human possession, since in many respects human nature is servile. **982b28–30**

5. Hence, according to Simonides, "Only God has this honor," and it is unfitting that a man should not seek a knowledge which befits him. Some poets accordingly say that the deity is naturally envious; and it is most likely that it should happen in this case, and that all those who are imperfect are unfortunate. But it is not fitting that the deity should be envious, for as the proverb says: "The poets tell many lies." **982b30–983a3**

6. Nor must we think that any other science is more honorable than this. For what is most divine is most honorable. But then it alone will be such, and in two ways. For of all knowledge that which God most properly has is divine; and if there is any such knowledge, it is concerned with divine matters. But this science alone has both of these characteristics; for God seems to be a cause and in some sense a principle according to all men; and such [knowledge as this] God either alone has, or has in the highest degree. Therefore, all the other sciences are more necessary, but none is more excellent. **983a4–11**

7. But it is necessary in a sense to bring to a halt the progression of this science at the contrary of our original questions. Indeed, as we have said, all men begin by wondering whether things are as strange as chance occurrences appear to those who do not yet know the cause; or by wondering about the changes in the course of the sun, or about the incommensurability of the diagonal [of a square]. For it would seem an object of wonder to all if something having the nature of number were immeasurable. But it is necessary to advance to the contrary view and, as the proverb says, the worthier one, as also happens in a sense in these matters when men have learned them. For nothing would surprise a geometrician more than if the diagonal [of a square] should become commensurable [with a side]. It has been stated, then, what the nature is of the science which we are seeking, and what its goal is for which our search and whole method must be undertaken. **983a11–23**

COMMENTARY

52. Having indicated the things with which this science deals, Aristotle now shows what kind of science it is. In regard to this he does two things. First [1], he reveals the dignity of this science; and second [7], the goal which it

attempts to reach ("But it is necessary").

In regard to the first he does four things. First, he shows that this is not a practical science but a speculative one; second [3], that it is free in the highest degree ("But just as we say"); third [4], that it is not a human [possession] ("For this reason"); and fourth [6], that it is the most honorable science ("Nor must we think that").

He proves the first in two ways. First, by an argument, and second [2], by an example ("And what has happened").

53. First [1], he gives this argument. No science in which knowledge itself is sought for its own sake is a practical science, but a speculative one. But that science which is wisdom, or philosophy as it is called, exists for the sake of knowledge itself. Hence it is speculative and not practical. He proves the minor premise in this way. Whoever seeks as an end to escape from ignorance tends toward knowledge for itself. But those who philosophize seek as an end to escape from ignorance. Therefore they tend towards knowledge for itself.

54. That they seek to escape from ignorance is made clear from the fact that those who first philosophized and who now philosophize did so from wonder about some cause, although they did this at first differently than now. For at first they wondered about less important problems, which were more obvious, in order that they might know their cause; but later on, progressing little by little from the knowledge of more evident matters to the investigation of obscure ones, they began to raise questions about more important and hidden matters, such as the changes undergone by the moon, namely, its eclipse, and its change of shape, which seems to vary inasmuch as it stands in different relations to the sun. And similarly they raised questions about the phenomena of the sun, such as its eclipse, its movement and size; and about the phenomena of the stars, such as their size, arrangement, and so forth; and about the origin of the whole universe, which some said was produced by chance, others by an intelligence, and others by love.

55. Further, he points out that perplexity and wonder arise from ignorance. For when we see certain obvious effects whose cause we do not know, we wonder about their cause. And since wonder was the motive which led men to philosophy, it is evident that the philosopher is, in a sense, a philomyth, i.e., a lover of myth, as is characteristic of the poets. Hence the first men to deal with the principles of things in a mythical way, such as Perseus and certain others who were the seven sages, were called the theologizing poets. Now the reason why the philosopher is compared to the poet is that both are concerned with wonders. For the myths with which the poets deal are composed of wonders, and the philosophers themselves were moved to philosophize as a result of wonder. And since wonder stems from ignorance, they were obviously moved to philosophize in order to escape from ignorance. It is accordingly evident from this that "they pursued" knowledge, or diligently sought it, only for itself and not for any utility or usefulness.

56. Now we must note that, while this science was first designated by the name wisdom, this was later changed to the name philosophy, since they mean the same thing. For while the ancients who pursued the study of wisdom were called sophists, i.e., wise

men, Pythagoras, when asked what he professed himself to be, refused to call himself a wise man as his predecessors had done, because he thought this was presumptuous, but called himself a philosopher, i.e., a lover of wisdom. And from that time the name "wise man" was changed to "philosopher," and "wisdom" to "philosophy." This name also contributes something to the point under discussion, for that man seems to be a lover of wisdom who seeks wisdom, not for some other reason, but for itself alone. For he who seeks one thing on account of something else, has greater love for that on whose account he seeks than for that which he seeks.

57. **And what has happened** [2].

Here he proves the same point by means of an example. The statement (he says) that wisdom or philosophy is not sought for any utility but for knowledge itself is proved by "what has happened," i.e., by what has occurred in the case of those who have pursued philosophy. For when nearly all those [arts] were discovered which are necessary for life, "leisure" (i.e., for the sort of pleasure which consists in a life of ease), and learning, such as the logical sciences, which are not sought for themselves but as introductions to the other arts, then man began for the first time to seek this kind of prudence, namely, wisdom. And from this it is clear that wisdom is not sought because of any necessity other than itself but for itself alone; for no one seeks something which he already possesses. Hence, because wisdom was sought after all other knowledge had been discovered, it is evident that it was not sought for some reason other than itself but for itself.

58. **But just as** [3].

Here he proves the second attribute, namely, that wisdom is free; and he uses the following argument: that man is properly said to be free who does not exist for someone else but for himself. For slaves exist for their masters, work for them, and acquire for them whatever they acquire. But free men exist for themselves inasmuch as they acquire things for themselves and work for themselves. But only this science exists for itself; and therefore among all the sciences only this science is free.

59. Now we must note that this can be understood in two ways. In one way, the expression "only this" may indicate every speculative science as a class. And then it is true that only this class of science is sought for itself. Hence, only those arts which are directed to knowing are called free [or liberal] arts, whereas those which are directed to some useful end attained by action are called mechanical or servile arts. Understood in another way, the expression may specifically indicate this philosophy or wisdom which deals with the highest causes; for the final cause is also one of the highest causes, as was stated above [n. 51]. Therefore this science must consider the highest and universal end of all things. And in this way all the other sciences are subordinated to it as an end. Hence only this science exists in the highest degree for itself.

60. **For this reason** [4].

Here he proves the third attribute, namely, that this science is not a human [possession]. In regard to this he does two things. First [4], he proves his thesis. Second [5], he criticizes an erroneous view held by certain men ("Hence, according to Simonides").

He proves his thesis by the following argument. A science which is free in the highest degree cannot be a possession of that nature which is servile and subordinate in many respects. But human nature is servile "in many respects," i.e., in many ways. Therefore this science is not a human possession. Now human nature is said to be servile insofar as it stands in need of many things. And on this account it happens that man sometimes neglects what should be sought for its own sake because of the things necessary for life. Thus it is said in Book III of the *Topics [118a10]* that it is better to philosophize than to become wealthy, although sometimes becoming wealthy is more desirable, that is, to one lacking life's necessities. From this it is clear that that wisdom is sought for itself alone which does not belong to man as his proper possession. For man has as his possession what he can have at his command and use freely. But that science which is sought for itself alone, man cannot use freely, since he is often kept from it because of the necessities of life. Nor again is it subject to man's command, because man cannot acquire it perfectly. Yet that very small part of it which he does have outweighs all the things known through the other sciences.

61. **Hence, according to Simonides** [5].

Here he rejects the error of a certain poet, Simonides, who said that it is proper to God alone to have the honor of desiring that knowledge which ought to be sought for its own sake and not for the sake of something else. But it is not fitting that man should not seek that knowledge which is in keeping with his own condition, namely, that which is directed to the necessities of life required by man.

62. Now Simonides' error came from that of certain poets who said that the Deity is envious, and that since He is envious He does not desire that the things which pertain to His honor should be shared by all. And if God is envious of men in other things, He is rightly more so in this case, i.e., in the case of the science which is sought for its own sake, which is the most honorable of all the sciences. And according to the opinion of these men it follows that all who are imperfect are unfortunate, for they said that men are fortunate as a result of the providence of the gods, who communicate their goods to men. Hence as a result of the envy of the gods, who are unwilling to communicate their goods, it follows that men, who remain outside the perfection of this science, are unfortunate.

63. But the basis of this opinion is most false, because it is not fitting that any divine being should be envious. This is evident from the fact that envy is sadness at someone else's prosperity. But this can occur only because the one who is envious thinks that someone else's good diminishes his own. Now it is impossible that God should be sad, because He is not subject to evil of any kind. Nor can His goodness be diminished by someone else's goodness, since every good flows from His goodness as from an unfailing spring. Hence Plato also said that there is no envy of any kind in God. [*Phaedrus*, 247A; *Timaeus*, 29E] But the poets have lied not only in this matter but in many others, as is stated in the common proverb.

64. **Nor must we think** [6].

Here he proves the fourth attribute, namely, that this is the most honorable science, by the following argument. That science which is most divine is most honorable, just as God Himself is also the most honorable of all things. But this science is the most divine, and is therefore the most honorable. The minor premise is proved in this way: a science is said to be divine in two ways, and only this science is said to be divine in both ways. First, the science which God has is said to be divine; and second, the science which is about divine matters is said to be divine. But it is evident that only this science meets both of these requirements, because, since this science is about first causes and principles, it must be about God; for God is understood in this way by all inasmuch as He is one of the causes and a principle of things. Again, such a science which is about God and first causes, either God alone has or, if not He alone, at least He has it in the highest degree. Indeed, He alone has it in a perfectly comprehensive way. And He has it in the highest degree inasmuch as it is also had by men in their own way, although it is not had by them as a human possession, but as something borrowed from Him.

65. From these considerations he draws the further conclusion that all other sciences are more necessary than this science for use in practical life, for these sciences are sought least of all for themselves. But none of the other sciences can be more excellent than this one.

66. **But it is necessary** [7].

He now gives the goal toward which this science moves. He says that its progression comes to rest, or is terminated, in the contrary of what was previously found in those who first sought this science, as also happens in the case of natural generations and motions. For each motion is terminated in the contrary of that from which the motion begins. Hence, since investigation is a kind of movement towards knowledge, it must be terminated in the contrary of that from which it begins. But, as was stated above (27:C 53), the investigation of this science began with man's wonder about all things, because the first philosophers wondered about less important matters and subsequent philosophers about more hidden ones. And the object of their wonder was whether the case was like that of strange chance occurrences, i.e., things which seem to happen mysteriously by chance. For things which happen as if by themselves are called chance occurrences. For men wonder most of all when things happen by chance in this way, supposing that they were foreseen or determined by some cause. For chance occurrences are not determined by a cause, and wonder results from ignorance of a cause. Therefore when men were not yet able to recognize the causes of things, they wondered about all things as if they were chance occurrences; just as they wondered about changes in the course of the sun, which are two in number, namely, the solstices, that of winter and that of summer. For at the summer solstice the sun begins to decline toward the south, after previously declining toward the north. But at the winter solstice the opposite occurs. And they wondered also that the diagonal of a square is not commensurable with a side. For since to be immeasurable seems to belong to the indivisible alone (just as unity alone is what is not measured by number but itself measures all numbers), it seems to be a matter of wonder that something which is not indivisible is immeasurable, and consequently that what is not a smallest part is immeasurable. Now it is evident that the diagonal of a square and its side are neither indivisible nor smallest parts. Hence it seems a matter of wonder if they are not commensurable.

67. Therefore, since philosophical

investigation began with wonder, it must end in or arrive at the contrary of this, and this is to advance to the worthier view, as the common proverb agrees, which states that one must always advance to the better. For what that opposite and worthier view is, is evident in the case of the above wonders, because when men have already learned the causes of these things they do not wonder. Thus the geometrician does not wonder if the diagonal is incommensurable with a side. For he knows the reason for this, namely, that the proportion of the square of the diagonal to the square of a side is not as the proportion of the square of a number to the square of a number, but as the proportion of two to one. Hence it follows that the proportion of a side to the diagonal is not as the proportion of number to number. And from this it is evident that they cannot be made commensurable. For only those lines are commensurable which are proportioned to each other as number to number. Hence the goal of this science to which we should advance will be that in knowing the causes of things we do not wonder about their effects.

68. From what has been said, then, it is evident what the nature of this science is, namely, that it is speculative and free, and that it is not a human possession but a divine one; and also what its aim is, for which the whole inquiry, method, and art must be conducted. For its goal is the first and universal causes of things, about which it also makes investigations and establishes the truth. And by reason of the knowledge of these it reaches this goal, namely, that there should be no wonder because the causes of things are known.

LESSON 4
Opinions about the Material Cause

ARISTOTLE'S TEXT Chapter 3: 983a24–984a18

1. *It is evident, then, that one must acquire scientific knowledge of those causes which stand at the beginning, for we say that we have scientific knowledge of each thing when we think we comprehend its first cause. Now causes are spoken of in four ways. Of these we say that one is the substance or quiddity of a thing, for the first "why" of a thing is reduced to its ultimate intelligible structure, and the first why of a thing is a cause or principle; another is the matter or subject; a third is the source of motion; and a fourth is the cause which is opposite to this, namely, that for the sake of which, or the good; for this is the goal of every generation and motion. There has been sufficient consideration of these in our works on nature. [Physics 194b15]* **983a24–983b1**

2. *However, let us examine those who have undertaken an investigation of existing things and have philosophized about the truth before us. For evidently they too speak of certain principles and causes. Therefore, to us who come later [their views] will serve as an introduction to the study which we are now making; for we shall either discover some other class of cause, or be more convinced of those which have just been expounded.* **983b1–6**

3. *Most of those who first philosophized thought that only the things which belong to the class of matter are the principles of all things. For that of which all things are composed, from which they first come to be, and into which they are finally dissolved, while their substance remains although it is changed in its attributes—this they call the element and principle of existing things.* **983b6–11**

4. *And for this reason they thought that nothing is either generated or corrupted, as if such a reality always remained in existence. And just as we do not say that Socrates comes to be in an unqualified sense when he becomes good or musical, or is corrupted when he loses these states, because the subject Socrates himself remains, in the same way they say that nothing else is generated or corrupted. For there must be some matter, either one or more than one, from which other things come to be, and which itself remains in existence. However, they do not all speak in the same way about the number and nature of such a principle.* **983b11–20**

5. *Thales, the originator of this kind of philosophy, says that this principle is water; and this is why he also claimed that the earth rests upon water.* **983b20–22**

6. *For presumably he took this position because he saw that the nutriment of all things is moist, that heat itself is generated from this, and that animal life comes from this. But that from which each thing comes to be is a principle of all things. He bases his opinion on this, then, and on the fact that the seeds of all things have a moist nature, whereas water is by nature the principle of moist things.* **983b22–27**

7. *Moreover, there are some who think that the ancients who lived long before the present generation and were the first to speculate about the gods also held this view about the nature of things. For they made Oceanus and Tethys the parents of generation, and held the oath of the gods to be by a body of water, to which the poets gave the name Styx. For what is oldest is most honorable, and what is most honorable is that by which one swears. Whether this view of nature is in fact the ancient and primary one is perhaps uncertain. Thales is said to have expressed himself in this way about the first cause, but no one could say that Hippo is to be included in this group, because of the weakness of his understanding.* **983b27–984a5**

8. *Anaximenes and Diogenes hold that air is prior to water and is the most fundamental of the simple bodies.* **984a5–7**

9. Hippasus of Metopontium and Heraclitus of Ephesus hold that fire [is the primary principle]. **984a7–8**

10. Empedocles holds that there are four [simple bodies], since he adds a fourth—earth—to those already mentioned. For he says that these always remain and only become many or few in number by being combined into a unity and separated out of a unity. **984a8–11**

11. Anaxagoras of Clazomenae, who was prior to Empedocles in years but later in his speculations, says that the principles of things are infinite in number. For he says that nearly all bodies which are made up of parts like themselves, such as fire or water, are generated or corrupted in this way, merely by combining and separating; but that otherwise they are neither generated nor corrupted but always remain in existence. From these views, then, one might think that the only cause is the one which is said to belong to the class of matter. **984a11–18**

COMMENTARY

69. Having set forth a preface in which he indicates the aim of this science, its dignity and goal, Aristotle begins to deal with this science; and this is divided into two parts. In the first [1], he explains what the first philosophers had to say about the causes of things. In the second (cf. n. 274), he begins to pursue the truth of this science. He does this in Book II ("Theoretical, i.e., speculative, knowledge").

The first part is divided into two members. First, he gives the opinions of the philosophers about the causes of things. Second [cf. n. 181], he criticizes them insofar as their statements are unsatisfactory ("Therefore all those").

In regard to the first he does two things. First, he takes up again the enumeration of causes which was treated in greater detail in Book II of the *Physics [194b15]*. Second [2], he presents the opinions of the philosophers ("However, let us examine").

70. Accordingly, he says, first (1), that since it is evident that wisdom speculates about causes, we ought to begin by acquiring knowledge from the causes of things. This also seems to be in keeping with the intelligible structure of science, because we say that we know each thing scientifically when we think we are not ignorant of its cause. Now causes are spoken of in four ways. One of these is the formal cause, which is the very substance of a thing by which we know what each thing is. For it is well known, as is stated in Book II of the *Physics [193b7]*, that we do not say that anything has a nature before it has received a form. Now it is clear that a form is a cause, because the question "Why is something so?" we reduce to its formal cause as its ultimate explanation, beginning with proximate forms and proceeding to the ultimate form. But evidently the "why?" asks about a cause and principle. Hence it is evident that a form is a cause. A second cause is the material cause. A third is the efficient cause, which is the source of motion. A fourth is the final cause, which is opposite to the efficient cause as a goal is to a starting-point; for motion begins with the efficient cause and terminates with the final cause. This [latter] cause is also that for the sake of which a thing comes to be, and the good of each nature.

71. He makes the final cause known by three considerations. It is the goal of motion, and thus is opposite to the source of motion, which is the efficient cause. It is first in intention, and for this reason is said to be that for the sake of

which [something is done]. It is desirable of itself, and for this reason is called a good; for the good is what all desire. Hence, in explaining how the final cause is opposite to the efficient cause, he says that it is the goal [or end] of every process of generation and motion, whose starting-point is the efficient cause. By these two types of change he seems to imply that there is a twofold goal. For the goal of a process of generation is the form itself, which is a part of a thing. But the goal of motion is something sought for outside the thing moved. He says that he has treated these causes at sufficient length in the *Physics, [194b15]* lest he should be asked to make a more extensive treatment of them.

72. **However, let us examine** [2].

Here he states what the philosophers had to say about the causes; and in regard to this he does two things. First, he gives the reasons why this must be done; and, second [3], he begins to carry out his plan ("Most of those").

Accordingly, he says that even though there is a treatise on the causes in the *Physics,[ibid.]* it is still necessary to consider the opinions of the philosophers who first undertook an investigation of the natures of existing things, and have philosophized about the truth before him; because they too set down causes and principles. Therefore, for us who have come later, a consideration of their opinions will be "a first [step]," or preamble, "to the investigation," i.e., to the art which we are now seeking. Hence the text of Boethius also says: "Therefore as we enter upon the task of this science, their opinions will constitute a preamble to the road that is now to be travelled." Another text has: "Therefore to us who are beginning this inquiry it will be a certain vital work in the investigation that now confronts us," and it must be read in this way: "Therefore, as we enter upon our present course," i.e., upon the present study and art, it will be necessary to consider the opinion of these men "as a work of life," that is to say, as necessary, like works which are done for the preservation of life, so that this reading is interpreted as a metaphorical way of speaking, meaning by "work of life" anything necessary. Now this is useful, because from the opinions of these men we will either discover another class of causes over and above those already enumerated, or be more convinced of the things that have just been stated about the causes, namely, that there are four classes of them.

73. **Most of those** [3].

Here he begins to deal with the opinions of the ancient philosophers; and in regard to this he does two things. First [3], he states their opinions; and, second [cf n. 181] he finds fault with them ("Therefore all those").

In regard to the first he does two things. First, he states the opinions which each one of the philosophers held about the causes. Second [cf. n. 171], he summarizes the discussion ("We have examined").

The first part is divided into two members. In the first [3], he gives the opinions of those who omitted the formal cause. In the second [cf. n. 151], he gives the opinion of Plato, who was the first to posit a formal cause ("After the philosophies").

In regard to the first he does two things. First, he gives the opinion of those who claimed that certain evident things are principles. Second [cf. n. 112], he gives the opinions of those who devised extrinsic principles ("Leucippus").

In regard to the first he does two things. First, he touches on the opinions which the ancient philosophers held about the material cause; and, second [see Lesson 5], on their opinions about the efficient cause ("But as men").

In regard to the first he does two things. First [3], he states in a general way the views of those who posited a material cause. Second [5], he examines their views in detail ("Thales, the originator").

In regard to the first he does two things. First [3], he states their opinions about the material cause. Second [4], he states their opinions about the generation of things, which follow from the first ("And for this reason").

74. Accordingly he says, first [3], that most of those who first philosophized about the natural world held that the principles of all things are merely those which are referred to the class of material cause. In regard to this it must be said that they took the four conditions of matter which seem to belong to the notion of a principle. For, [first], that of which a thing is composed seems to be a principle of that thing. But matter is such a thing; for we say that a thing that has matter is of its matter, as a knife is of iron. [Second], that from which a thing comes to be, being also a principle of the process of generation of that thing, seems to be one of its causes, because a thing comes into being by way of generation. But a thing first comes to be from matter, because the matter of things precedes their production. And a thing does not come from matter in an accidental way; for a thing is generated in an accidental way from its contrary or privation, as when we say that white comes from black. Third, that into which all things are ultimately dissolved by corruption seems to be a principle of things. For just as principles are first in the process of generation, in a similar way they are last in the process of dissolution; and obviously this too pertains to matter. Fourth, since a principle must remain in existence, then that which remains throughout the process of generation and corruption seems to be a principle. Now the matter which they said is the substance of a thing remains throughout every transmutation, although its attributes, such as its form and everything that accrues to it over and above its material substance, are changed. From all these considerations they concluded that matter is the element and principle of all beings.

75. **And for this reason** [4].

Then he gives, as a secondary point, what they held as following from the above, namely, that in the world nothing is generated or corrupted in an absolute sense. For when some change occurs with regard to a thing's attributes, and its substance remains unchanged, we do not say that it is generated or corrupted in an absolute sense, but only in a qualified one; for example, when Socrates becomes good or musical, we do not say that he simply comes to be, but comes to be this. And similarly when he loses a state of this kind, we do not say that he is corrupted in an absolute sense, but only in a qualified one. But matter, which is the substance of things according to them, always remains; and every change affects some of a thing's accidents, such as its attributes. From this they concluded that nothing is generated or corrupted in an absolute sense, but only in a qualified one.

76. Yet even though they all agreed on this point, in positing a material cause, nevertheless they differed in

their position in two respects: first, with respect to the number of material causes, because some held that there is one, and others many; and second, with respect to its nature, because some held that it is fire, others water, and so on. Similarly, among those who posited many material causes, some assigned certain ones as the material principles of things, and some the others.

77. **Thales, the originator** [5].

Here he begins to give the opinions of each of the philosophers about the material cause. First [5], he gives the opinions of those who posited one material cause; and second [10], the opinions of those who posited many ("Empedocles").

In regard to the first he does three things. First, he gives the opinions of those who claimed that water is the principle of all things; second [8], he gives the opinion of those who made air the principle of things ("Anaximenes"); and third [9], the opinion of those who claimed that fire is the principle of things ("Hippasus").

In regard to the first he does two things. First [5], he gives the opinion of Thales, who said that water is the principle of things; and second [6], the reason for this opinion ("For presumably").

He says then [5] that Thales, the originator of this kind of philosophy, i.e., speculative philosophy, said that water is the first principle of all things. Thales is said to have been the originator of speculative philosophy because he was the only one of the seven wise men, who came after the theological poets, to make an investigation into the causes of things, the other sages being concerned with moral matters. The names of the seven wise men are as follows. The first was Thales of Miletus, who lived during the time of Romulus and when Achaz, King of Israel, was reigning over the Hebrews. The second was Pittacus of Mitylene, who lived when Sedecias was reigning over the Hebrews and when Tarquinius Priscus was reigning over the Romans. The other five sages were Solon of Athens, Chilo of Lacedaemon, Periander of Corinth, Cleobulus of Lydia, and Bias of Prienne, all of whom lived during the period of the Babylonian captivity. Hence, since Thales alone among these men investigated the natures of things and distinguished himself by committing his arguments to writing, he is described here as the originator of this science.

78. Nor should it be thought unfitting if he touches here on the opinions of those who have treated only the philosophy of nature; because according to the ancients, who knew no other substance except the corporeal and mobile, it was necessary that first philosophy be the philosophy of nature, as is stated in Book IV. And from this position Thales next adopted this one, that the earth rests upon water, as anything having a principle is based on its principle.

79. **For presumably he took** [6].

Here he gives the reasons by which Thales could be led to the above position. First, he shows how he was led to this position by his own reasoning; and second [7], by the authority of his predecessors ("Moreover, there are some").

Now he was led by two lines of reasoning; one is taken from the cause itself of a thing, and the other from a consideration of the generation of things ("And on the fact"). Therefore these premises are related. For the second follows from the first, because that which is a principle of being of other things is also the first principle from which things are generated. The third follows from the second, because by corruption each thing is dissolved into that from which it was generated. The fourth follows from the second and the third; for that which precedes the generation of things and remains after they have been corrupted must always remain in being.

80. In the first line of reasoning he uses three indications to show that water is the principle of being of things. The first of these is that the nutriment of living things must be moist. But living things derive nourishment and being from the same principle; and thus moisture appears to be the principle of being of things. The second indication is that the being of any physical thing, and especially of a living one, is conserved by its proper and natural heat. But heat seems to be generated from moisture, since moisture itself is in a sense the matter of heat. Hence from this it appears that moisture is a principle of being of things. The third indication is that animal life depends on moisture. Hence an animal dies as a result of its natural moisture being dried up and is kept in existence as a result of its moisture being preserved. But in living things to live is to be. Hence it is also evident from this that moisture is a principle of being of things. These three indications also have a natural connection with one another. For an animal is nourished by moisture, because its natural heat is sustained by moisture. And from these two it follows that animal life is always due to moisture. But that from which a thing comes to be, i.e., from which a thing gets its being, is a principle of everything that derives being from it. And for this reason he adopted this opinion that moisture is the principle of all things.

81. In a similar way he also draws an indication of this from the generation of things, because the processes of generation of living things, which are the noblest of [natural] beings, come from seed. But the seed or spermata of all living things have a moist nature. Hence from this it also appears that moisture is a principle of generation of things. Again, if we add to all of the above points the fact that water is the principle of moisture, it follows that water is the first principle of things.

82. **Moreover, there are** [7].

Here he shows how Thales was led to the above position by the authority of the ancients. He says that prior to Thales and many years before the men of Aristotle's time there were some men, the first to speculate about the gods, who seem to have held this opinion about nature, namely, that water is the principle of all things.

83. With a view to making this clear, we must bear in mind that among the Greeks the first who were famous for their learning were certain theological poets, so called because of the songs which they wrote about the gods. These poets, who were three in number, Orpheus, Museus and Linus, of whom Orpheus was the more famous, lived during the time when the judges ruled over the Jewish people. Hence it is clear that they lived long before Thales and much longer before Aristotle, who lived during the time of Alexander. These poets dealt to some extent with the nature of things by means of certain figurative representations in myths. For they said that Oceanus [i.e., the ocean], where the greatest aggregation of waters is found, and Tethys, which is the name they gave to the goddess of the waters, are the parents of generation, implying

by this, under the form of a myth, that water is the principle of generation.

84. They cloaked this view in another fabulous story, saying that the oath or vow of the gods was by a certain body of water, which the poets call Styx and describe as an underground swamp. And when they said that the gods swore by water, they implied that water was nobler than the gods themselves, because an oath or vow is taken on what is most honorable. Now that which is prior is more honorable; for the perfect is prior absolutely to the imperfect, both in nature and in time, although in a particular being imperfection is prior temporally to perfection. Hence, from this it is evident that they thought that water is prior to the gods themselves, whom they thought to be celestial bodies. And since these earliest thinkers said that water is the principle of things, if there was any opinion about natural bodies prior to theirs, we do not know what it was. Thus what Thales is said to have thought about the first cause of things is now clear.

85. A certain philosopher named Hippo was not credited with adding anything to those mentioned because of the imperfection of his knowledge or understanding. Hence, in *The Soul [405b1]*, Hippo is placed among the ruder [thinkers]; for in that work it is stated that Hippo, basing his argument on the seeds of things, as was said here of Thales, held water to be the soul and principle of things. Hence it is clear that he adds nothing to Thales' view. Or the statement can mean that, since he spoke imperfectly, he did not make himself worthy to have his doctrine included here with the others.

86. **Anaximenes and Diogenes** [8].

Here he gives the opinions of those who held that air is the principle of things, namely, Diogenes and Anaximenes, who held that air is naturally prior to water and is the principle of all simple bodies, i.e., of the four elements, and thus of all other things. Anaximenes is the third philosopher after Thales and the disciple of Anaximander, who was the disciple of Thales; and Diogenes is said to have been the disciple of Anaximenes. Yet there is this difference between the opinion of Diogenes and that of Anaximenes: Anaximenes held that air is the principle of things in an absolute sense, whereas Diogenes said that air could be the principle of things only if it possessed a divine nature. From this comes the opinion which is touched on in *The Soul*, Book I [405a21]. Now the reason why he held that air is the principle of things could be taken from the process of respiration, by which the life of animals is conserved, and because the processes whereby things are generated and corrupted seem to be modified as a result of changes in the air.

87. **Hippasus of Metopontium** [9].

Here he states that the two philosophers, Hippasus and Heraclitus, held that fire is the material principle of things. And they could have been influenced by its subtileness, as is said below.

88. **Empedocles** [10].

Here he gives the opinions of those who posited many material principles. First, he gives the opinion of Empedocles, who held that there are a limited number of such principles; and second [11], that of Anaxagoras, who held that there are an infinite number ("Anaxagoras").

First [10], he gives Empedocles' opinion regarding the three elements mentioned above, water, air, and fire, which he says are the principles of things, adding to them a fourth, earth.

89. Second, he gives Empedocles' opinion about the permanence of these elements; for, like those who hold that there is one material cause, he holds that these elements always remain and are neither generated nor corrupted. However, he said that other things are generated from and dissolved into these elements according as a greater or smaller number of them are combined or separated out, i.e., inasmuch as these four are united by the process of combination and lose their unity by the process of separation.

90. **Anaxagoras** [11].

Here he gives the opinion of Anaxagoras, who was the other disciple of Anaximenes and the classmate of Diogenes. A native of Clazomenae, he was prior to Empedocles in years but later in his activity or work, either because he began to philosophize later, or because his explanation of the number of principles is less satisfactory than that of Empedocles. For he said that there are an infinite number of material principles, whereas it is better to take a limited and smaller number, as Empedocles did, as is stated in Book I of the *Physics.[188a16]* For Anaxagoras not only said that fire, water, and the other elements are the principles of things, as Empedocles did, but also claimed that all things having like parts, such as flesh, bones, marrow and so forth, whose smallest parts are infinite in number, are the principles of things. For he claimed that in each being there are an infinite number of parts of each type of thing, because he found that in the case of inferior things one of these can be generated from another. He said, in fact, that things could be generated only by being separated out from a mixture, as Aristotle has explained more fully in the *Physics*, Book I.[187a20]

91. Second, Anaxagoras also agrees with Empedocles on this point, namely, that things are generated and corrupted only insofar as the parts of these infinite principles are combined or separated out, and that if this were not the case nothing would be generated or corrupted. But he said that the infinite number of principles of this kind, from which the substances of things are produced, always remain in being.

92. From the opinions of these philosophers, then, Aristotle concludes that the only cause which these men recognized was the one which belongs to the class of material cause.

LESSON 5
Opinions about the Efficient Cause

ARISTOTLE'S TEXT Chapters 3 & 4: 984a18–984b33

1. But as men proceeded in this way, reality itself again opened up a path and forced them to make investigations. For if every process of generation and corruption is from some one thing or more than one, why does this occur, and what is the cause? For certainly the subject itself does not cause itself to change. I mean, for example, that neither wood nor bronze is the cause of the change undergone by either one of them; for wood does not produce a bed, or bronze a statue, but something else is the cause of the change. But to seek this is to seek another principle, as if one were to say that from which the beginning of motion comes. **984a18–25**

2. Now in general those who have taken such a course from the very beginning, and who said that the subject is one, created no difficulty for themselves when they said that everything is one. [But some of those who say that it is one], being baffled, so to speak, by this question, say that this [one subject] and the whole of nature is immobile not only with respect to generation and corruption (for this is an ancient opinion and one which all men confess to be true), but also with respect to every other change. This opinion is peculiar to them. Hence, of those who said that the [universe] itself is one, it occurred to none of them to conceive of such a cause, except perhaps Parmenides, and to him only insofar as he claims that there is not one cause but also in a sense two causes. But for those who make the elements of things many, such as the hot and cold, or fire and earth, a better explanation is possible, because they use fire as if it were a material principle which is active in nature, but water and earth and the like they use in the opposite way. **984a25–984b8**

3. After these men and such principles, as if they were insufficient to generate the natures of existing things, men were again compelled (as we said [45]) by the truth itself to seek for the next principle. For perhaps it is unlikely that either fire or earth or anything else of this kind should be the cause of the good dispositions of things which are or come to be; nor was it consistent that they should think this to be the case. Nor again would it be right to attribute so important a matter to chance occurrence and fortune. **984b8–15**

4. And when someone [Anaxagoras] said that there is one intellect present in nature as in animals, and that this is the cause of the world and the arrangement of the whole, he seemed to atone for the untenable statements made by his predecessors. We know that Anaxagoras expressed these views, although Hermotimus of Clazomenae was the first to speak of such a cause. Those, therefore, who held these opinions likewise posited a principle in existing things which is the cause of their goodness, and that sort of cause which is the source of motion in the world. **984b15–22**

Chapter 4

5. Now someone might have suspected that Hesiod was the first to have investigated this sort of cause, or anyone else who held that love or desire is a principle in existing things, as Parmenides did. For in the place where he attempts to explain the generation of the universe, he says that "Love, the first of all the gods, was made." And Hesiod says that "The first of all things to be made was chaos, then broad earth, and love, who is pre-eminent among the immortals"—as though there must be in the world some cause which moves things and brings them together. How one must arrange these thinkers in sequence will be decided later on. **984b23–32**

COMMENTARY

93. Having given the philosophers' opinions about the material cause,

Aristotle now gives their opinions about the efficient cause, which is the source of motion. This is divided into two parts. First [1], he gives the opinion of those who assigned without qualification a cause of motion and generation. Second [3], he examines the opinion of those who posited an efficient cause, which is also the principle of good and evil in the world ("After these men").

In regard to the first he does two things. First, he gives the reasoning which compelled them to posit an efficient cause. Second [2], he shows the different positions which different men have held regarding this ("Now in general").

He says [1], then, that some philosophers have proceeded in this way in positing a material cause, but that the very nature of reality clearly provided them with a course for understanding or discovering the truth, and compelled them to investigate a problem which led them to the efficient cause. This problem is as follows: no thing or subject changes itself; for example, wood does not change itself so that a bed comes from it, nor does bronze cause itself to be changed in such a way that a statue comes from it; but there must be some other principle which causes the change they undergo, and this is the artist. But those who posited a material cause, whether one or more than one, said that the generation and corruption of things come from this cause as a subject. Therefore there must be some other cause of change, and to seek this is to seek another class of principle and cause, which is called the source of motion.

94. **Now in general** [2].

He shows here that the philosophers have adopted three positions with respect to the foregoing issue. For those who adopted this course from the very beginning, and said that there is one material cause, were not greatly concerned with the solution of this problem. For they were content with their view of matter and neglected the cause of motion altogether.

95. But others, who said that all things are one, being defeated as it were by this issue, as they were unable to go so far as to assign a cause of motion, denied motion altogether. Hence they said that the whole universe is one immobile being. In this respect they differed from the first philosophers of nature, who said that one cause is the substance of all things although it is moved by rarefaction and condensation, so that in this way many things come to be in some measure from one principle. However, they did not say that this principle is subject to generation and corruption in an absolute sense. For the view that nothing was generated or corrupted without qualification is an ancient one admitted by all of them, as is clear from what was said above (cf. n. 75). But it was peculiar to these later thinkers to say that the whole of reality is one immobile being, devoid of every kind of motion. These men were Parmenides and Melissus, as will be explained below (cf. n. 138). Hence it is evident that it was impossible for those who said that the whole is one immobile being to conceive of "such a cause," i.e., a cause of motion. For, by the very fact that they did away with motion, they sought in vain for a cause of motion. An exception was Parmenides; for even though he held that there is only one thing according to reason, he held that there are many things according to the senses, as will be stated below [5]. Hence, inasmuch as Parmenides held that there are many things, it was in

keeping with his position to hold that there are many causes, one of which would be a mover and the others something moved. For just as he held that there are many things according to the senses, in a similar way it was necessary for him to hold that there is motion according to the senses, because a plurality of things can be understood to be produced from one subject only by some kind of motion.

96. Third, there were those who, in making the substances of things many, assented to the aforesaid reasoning by positing a cause of motion. For they maintained that the hot or the cold, i.e., fire or earth, are causes; and of these they used fire as having a mobile, i.e., an active, nature, but water, earth and air they used in the opposite way, i.e., as having a passive nature. Thus fire was a sort of efficient cause, but the others a sort of material cause.

97. **After these men** [3].

Here he gives the opinion of those who posited an efficient cause, not only as a principle of motion, but also as a principle of good and evil in things. In regard to this he does two things. First [3], he expounds their views. Second (see next lesson), he shows in what respect they failed in assigning the causes of things ("These thinkers").

In regard to the first he does two things. First, he gives the reasons for their position by which they were induced to posit another cause besides the foregoing one. Second [4], he shows how they posited this kind of cause in different ways ("And when someone").

He says first [3], then, that after the foregoing philosophers who held that there is only one material cause, or many bodies, one of which was active and the others passive, and after the other first principles given by them, men were again compelled by the truth itself, "as we have said," i.e., as was stated above [1], to seek the "next" principle, i.e., the one which naturally follows the foregoing one, namely, the cause of good, which is really the final cause, although it was held by them only incidentally, as will be seen below (Lesson 11). For they held that there is a cause of goodness in things only after the manner of an efficient cause. They were compelled to do this because the foregoing principles were not sufficient to account for the generation of the natural world, in which some things are found to be well disposed. The fact that bodies are conserved in their proper places and are corrupted outside of them proves this; and so do the benefits resulting from the parts of animals, which are found to be disposed in this manner according as this is in keeping with an animal's good state of being.

98. But neither fire nor earth nor any such bodies were held to be adequate causes of this kind of good disposition or state of being which some things already have but others acquire by some kind of production. For these bodies act in one definite way according to the necessity of their proper forms, as fire heats things and tends upward, and water cools things and tends downward. But the aforesaid benefits and good states of being of things must have a cause which is not limited to one effect only, since the parts of different animals are found to be disposed in different ways, and in each one insofar as it is in keeping with its nature.

99. Hence, it is not reasonable that fire or earth or the like should be the cause of the aforesaid good state of being which things have, nor was it

reasonable that these men should have thought this to be the case. Nor again would it be reasonable to say that these things are chance occurrences, i.e., that they are accidental or come about by chance, and that their causality is changed only fortuitously; although some of these thinkers had said this, as Empedocles and all those who posited a material cause, as is evident in Book II of the *Physics.[196a21]* However, this is also seen to be false by reason of the fact that good dispositions of this kind are found either always or for the most part, whereas things that come about by chance or fortune do not occur always or for the most part but seldom. For this reason, then, it was necessary to discover besides the four elements some other principle which would account for the good dispositions of things. Another text has "Nor would it be right that these should be attributed to chance occurrence and fortune," but this means the same as the above.

100. **And when someone said** [4].

Here he gives in detail the opinions about the aforesaid principle. First [4], he gives the opinions of those who held that there is one [efficient] cause; and second (next lesson), the opinions of those who held that there are two such causes ("But since there would seem").

In regard to the first he does two things. First, he gives the views of those who held that the first efficient cause is an intellect; and second [5], the opinions of those who held that it is love ("Now someone might").

He says [4], then, that after the foregoing doctrine someone appeared who said that there is an intellect present in nature at large, just as there is in animals, and that this is the cause of the world and the order of the whole, i.e., of the universe, in which order the good of the entire universe and that of every single part consists. And this man atoned for the first philosophers by reducing to pure truth those who said unreasonable things and did not mention this kind of cause. Now Anaxagoras clearly stated this doctrine, although another philosopher—Hermotimus of Clazomenae—first gave him the idea of proposing this opinion. Hence it is evident that those who held this opinion claimed at the same time that the principle by which things are well disposed and the one which is the source of motion in things, are one and the same.

101. **Now someone might** [49].

Here he gives the opinion of those who claimed that love is the first principle, although they did not hold this very explicitly or clearly. Accordingly, he says that some suspected that Hesiod had sought for such a principle to account for the good disposition of things, or anyone else who posited love or desire in nature. For when Parmenides attempted to explain the generation of the universe, he said that in the establishing of the universe "Love, the first of all the gods, was made." Nor is this opposed to his doctrine that there is one immobile being, of which Aristotle speaks here; because this man held that there are many things according to the senses, although there is only one thing according to reason, as was stated above and will be stated below. Moreover, he called the celestial bodies, or perhaps certain separate substances, gods.

102. But Hesiod said that first of all there was chaos, and then broad earth was made, to be the receptacle of everything else; for it is evident that the receptacle [or void] and place are principles, as is stated in Book IV of the *Physics.[208b25]* And he also held that

love, which instructs all the immortals, is a principle of things. He did this because the communication of goodness seems to spring from love, for a good deed is a sign and effect of love. Hence, since corruptible things derive their being and every good disposition from immortal beings of this kind, this must be attributed to the love of the immortals. Furthermore, he held that the immortals are either the celestial bodies themselves, or material principles themselves. Thus he posited chaos and love as though there had to be in existing things not only a material cause of their motions, but also an efficient cause which moves and unites them, which seems to be the office of love. For love moves us to act, because it is the source of all the emotions, since fear, sadness and hope proceed only from love. That love unites things is clear from this, that love itself is a certain union between the lover and the thing loved, seeing that the lover regards the beloved as himself. This man Hesiod is to be numbered among the poets who lived before the time of the philosophers.

103. Now, as to which one of these thinkers is prior, i.e., more competent in knowledge, whether the one who said that love is the first principle, or the one who said that intellect is, can be decided later on, that is, where God is discussed. He calls this decision an arrangement, because the degree of excellence belonging to each man is allotted to him in this way. Another translation states this more clearly: "Therefore, in what order it is fitting to go over these thinkers, and who in this order is prior, can be decided later on."

LESSON 6
Love and Hate as Efficient Causes of Good and Evil

ARISTOTLE'S TEXT Chapter 4: 984b32–985b4

1. But since there would seem to be in nature things which are contrary to those that are good, and not only order and good but also disorder and what is base, and evil things more numerous than good ones, and base things more numerous than noble ones, for this reason another thinker introduced love and strife as causes, each of its own type of effects. For if anyone grasps what Empedocles said, taking it according to its meaning rather than according to its faltering expression, he will find that love is the cause of things which come to be by aggregation, and strife the cause of evil things. Hence, if anyone were to say that Empedocles, in a sense, both said and was the first to say that good and evil are principles, he would perhaps speak correctly, i.e., if the cause of all good things is good and that of all evil things is evil. **984b32–985a10**

2. These thinkers, then, as we have said, to this extent have touched on two of the causes which we established in the Physics, [194b15]—matter and the source of motion—though only obscurely and with no clarity, much as untrained men conduct themselves in battle. For the latter, though encircled, often deal telling blows, but without science. In the same way these thinkers do not seem to be aware of what they are saying. For it seems that they almost never make use of the causes except to a small degree. **985a10–18**

3. Anaxagoras uses "intellect" in an artificial way in generating the world. For when he is in difficulty as to what is necessarily the cause of something, he drags in this intellect; but in other cases he makes everything but intellect the cause of what comes to be. **985a18–21**

4. Empedocles, it is true, makes greater use of causes than Anaxagoras, though not sufficiently; nor does one find in his use of them what he professed. In many places he argues that love separates things, and that strife brings them together. For when being itself is separated out into its elements by strife, then fire and each of the other elements are brought together into a unity. But when they are united by love, the particles must again be separated out from each element. **985a21–29**

5. In contrast to the first philosophers, then, Empedocles was the first to introduce this cause, dividing it in such a way as to make the source of motion not a single principle but different and contrary ones. Moreover, he was the first to claim that the elements, which are said to belong to the class of matter, are four in number, although he does not use them as four but as two, taking fire by itself alone, and its opposites—earth, air, and water—as a single nature (46). But anyone may see this by studying his basic sayings. This philosopher, then, as we have said, has spoken in this way about the principles of things and their number. **985a29–985b4**

COMMENTARY

104. Here Aristotle gives the opinion of those who posited contrariety in beings of this kind, and the reason which moved them, which is as follows. There would seem to be in nature things which are contrary to those that are good, because in nature one finds not only things which are ordered and good, but sometimes things which are disordered and base. Now it cannot be said that evil things have no cause but happen by chance, because evil things are more numerous than good ones, and base things more numerous than those which are unqualifiedly noble. But those things which come to be by chance without a definite cause do not occur for the most part but in the smaller number of cases. Hence, since contrary effects have contrary causes,

it was necessary to hold as a cause of things not only love, from which the order and good in things originate, but also hate, which is the source of disorder and baseness or evil in things, so that in this way particular instances of evil and good have their own type of causes.

105. That this was the reason which moved Empedocles is evident if anyone grasps what he says, taking his statement according to its meaning rather than according to the words which he used imperfectly and, as it were, in a faltering way. For he said that it is the office of love to bring the elements together, and of hate to separate them. But since the generation of things is a result of the coming together [of the elements], by reason of which there is being and good in things, and their corruption a result of the separation [of the elements], which is the way to non-being and evil, it is now evident that he wanted love to be the cause of things which come to be by aggregation, i.e., of good things, and hate the cause of evil things. Thus if one were to say that Empedocles was the first to maintain that good and evil are principles, he would perhaps speak correctly.

106. That is to say, this would follow if Empedocles did hold that good is the cause of all good things, and evil the cause of all evil things. For it is evident that he posited evil as the cause of some evil things, namely, of corruption, and good as the cause of some good things, namely, of generation. But because it would not follow that all good things would be caused by friendship or all evil things by hate, since the parts of the world would be differentiated by hate and fused together by friendship, therefore he did not always hold that good is the cause of good things, and evil the cause of evil things.

107. **These thinkers** [2].

Here he shows that in giving these causes the philosophers treated them inadequately. First [2], he mentions them in a general way. Second [3]), he treats each one individually ("Anaxagoras").

He says first [2], then, that these philosophers—Anaxagoras and Empedocles—arrived at a doctrine of two of the causes which have been established in the *Physics,[194b15]* namely, matter and the cause of motion, although they treated these obscurely and with no clarity, because they did not explain that those principles which they held to be the causes of things could be reduced to these classes of causes. But insofar as they posited two of these causes, they may be likened to untrained warriors who, though encircled by the enemy, sometimes strike good blows, not by art but by chance. This is evident from the fact that, even though they happen to do this sometimes, this does not occur always or for the most part. In like manner, too, these philosophers were not accustomed to express themselves accurately, nor was it their custom to speak with awareness, i.e., as men who know. Hence another translation has, "But these men neither have science, nor are they to be compared with men who realize what they are saying." This is shown by the fact that, although they had proposed these causes, they hardly ever used them, because they employed them in few instances. Hence it seems that they introduced them not as a result of art but by accident, because they were moved to do so by necessity.

108. **Anaxagoras** [3].

Here he shows in what particular respect the view of each is unsatisfactory. First, he speaks of Anaxagoras; and second [4], of Empedocles ("Empedocles").

He says first, then, that Anaxagoras uses "intellect" to generate the world, and in so doing he seems to speak of it in an artificial way. For when he inquires about the causes of the world's generation, he drags it in of necessity, i.e., he invents this intelligence only because he is unable to attribute the generation of the world to any other cause which would differentiate things except to one which is essentially distinct and unmixed, and intellect is a thing of this kind. But in all other cases he draws his causes from any other source rather than intellect, for example, in the case of the particular natures of things.

109. **Empedocles** [4].

Here he shows in what respect Empedocles' doctrine is inadequate; and in regard to this he does two things. First, he shows in what respect Empedocles' doctrine is inadequate. Second [5], he explains what Empedocles himself held in contrast to the other philosophers ("In contrast").

He says, first [4], that Empedocles, in dealing with the particular natures of things, "makes greater use of the causes" posited by him (the four elements, and love and hate) than Anaxagoras did, because he reduced the generation and corruption of particular things to these causes, and not to intelligence as Anaxagoras did. But Empedocles failed in two ways.

First, he failed because he does not treat causes of this kind adequately enough; for he uses things which are not self-evident as though they were self-evident axioms, as is stated in the *Physics*, Book I,[189a4] that is, insofar as he assumed that they are self-evident, because at one definite time strife has dominion over the elements and at another, love.

110. Second, he failed because in the matters which he investigates, one does not find what he has professed, i.e., what he held as a principle, namely, that love combines things and that strife separates them, because in many places love must on the contrary "separate" or divide things, and strife "bring them together," i.e., unite them. For when the universe itself "is separated out," i.e., divided into its parts, by hate, as occurs when the world is generated, all particles of fire are then combined into one whole, and so also are the individual particles of the other elements "brought together," i.e., joined to each other. Hence, strife not only separates the particles of fire from those of air, but also brings together the particles of fire. But, on the other hand, when the elements come together through love, which occurs when the universe is destroyed, the particles of fire must then be separated from each other, and so also must the particles of the other elements. For fire can be mixed with air only if the particles of fire are separated from each other; and the same is true of the particles of air only if these elements penetrate one another, so that love not only unites unlike things but also separates like things, according to what follows from his position.

111. **In contrast** [5].

Here he shows in what respect Empedocles' own doctrine differs from that of the other philosophers. He says that Empedocles maintained two things in contrast to the others. First, he divided the cause which is the source of motion into two contrary parts. Second, he held the material cause to be constituted of four elements—not that he uses the four elements as four, but rather as two, because he contrasts fire with the other three, saying that fire is active in nature and the others passive in nature. Anyone can gather this from the elements of things treated by him, or from his "basic sayings" in the sense of the rudiments of the doctrine which he propounded. Another version reads "from his verses," because he is said to have written his philosophy in meters. And still another version which says "from his statements," agrees with this. As has been stated, then, this philosopher was the first to stipulate in this way that the principles of things are so many in number, namely, four, and to speak of those which have been mentioned.

LESSON 7
The Views of the Atomists and the Pythagoreans

ARISTOTLE'S TEXT Chapters 4 & 5: 985b4–986a13

1. Leucippus and his colleague Democritus say that the elements of things are the full and the void, calling the one being and the other non-being. Of these they say that the full or solid is being, and the void, non-being. For this reason too they say that being no more is than non-being, because the void no more is than body; and they hold that these are the material causes of things. **985b4–10**

2. And just as those who make the underlying substance one generate other things from this by means of its attributes, holding that rarity and density are the principles of these attributes, in the same way these men say that the differences [of the atoms] are the causes of other things. These differences, they say, are three: shape, arrangement, and position. For they claim that what exists differs only by rhythm, inter-contact, and turning; and of these rhythm means shape, inter-contact arrangement, and turning position. For A differs from N in shape, AN from NA in arrangement, and Z from N in position. But with regard to motion, from whence it comes or how it is present in things, these men carelessly dismissed this question as the other thinkers did. As we have said before, then, these two types of causes seem to have been investigated to this extent by the first thinkers. **985b10–22**

Chapter 5

3. But during the time of these and prior to them, lived the group called the Pythagoreans, who dealt with mathematics and were the first to develop it; and having been brought up in these sciences, they thought that their principles were the principles of all things. But since among these principles numbers are naturally first, they thought they saw in numbers, more than in fire and earth, many resemblances to things which are and come to be, because [according to them] this particular attribute of numbers is justice, another is soul and mind, and still another is opportunity. The case is the same, so to speak, with every other thing. **985b23–31**

4. Moreover, since they considered the attributes and ratios of harmonies in terms of numbers, and since other things in their whole nature seemed to be likened to numbers, and since numbers are the first things in the whole of nature, they thought that the elements of numbers are the elements of all things, and that the whole heaven is a harmony and number. And whatever they had revealed in the case of numbers and harmonies [which they could] show [to be in agreement] with the motions and parts of the heavens, and its whole arrangement, they collected and adapted to these. And if anything was lacking anywhere, they called it in in order that their undertaking might be complete. I mean that since the number ten seems to be the perfect number and to comprise the whole nature of numbers, they said that the bodies which move in the heavens are ten in number; but as only nine are observable they therefore invented a tenth, the counter-earth. These things have been dealt with more exactly in another work. [On the Heavens, 293a24] **985b31–986a13**

COMMENTARY

112. Here he begins to give the positions of those who held strange and obscure views about the principles of things. First [1], he gives the position of those who held that there are many principles of things; and second (Lesson 9), the position of those who held that there is only one being ("But there are some").

In regard to the first he does two things. First, he gives the opinion of Leucippus and Democritus, who held that the principles of things are corporeal. Second [3], he gives the opinion of the Pythagoreans, who held that the principles of things are incorporeal entities ("But during the time").

In regard to the first he does two things. First, he gives the opinion of Democritus and Leucippus about the material cause of things; and second [2], their opinion about the cause of diversity, that is, how matter is differentiated into many things. In this discussion the cause of the generation and corruption of things also becomes evident; and this is a point on which these men agreed with the ancient philosophers ("And just as those who").

He says [1], then, that two philosophers, Democritus and Leucippus, who are called friends because they followed each other in all things, held that the principles of things are the full and the void or empty, of which the full is being, and the void or empty, non-being.

113. Now in order to clarify this opinion we must recall what the Philosopher says in Book I of *Generation, [325a1-326b129]* where he treats it more fully. For certain philosophers had held that everything is one continuous immobile being, because it seems that there cannot be motion without a void, or any distinction between things, as they said. And though they could not comprehend the privation of continuity, by reason of which bodies must be understood to be differentiated, except by means of a void, they claimed that the void existed in no way. Democritus, who came after them, and who agreed with their reasoning but was unable to exclude diversity and motion from things, held that the void existed, and that all bodies are composed of certain indivisible bodies [i.e., the atoms]. He did this because it seemed to him that no reason could be given why the whole of being should be divided in one part rather than another. And lest he should hold that the whole of being is continuous, he therefore chose to maintain that this whole is divided everywhere and in its entirety; and this could not be the case if anything divisible remained undivided. And according to him indivisible bodies of this kind can neither exist nor be joined together except by means of the void. For if the void did not come between any two of them, one continuous whole would result from the two; which he did not hold for the above reason. Hence he said that the continuous quantity of each body is constituted both of those indivisible bodies filling indivisible spaces and of certain empty spaces, which he called pores, coming between these indivisible bodies.

114. And since the void is non-being and the full is being, it is evident from this that he did not hold that a thing was constituted by being rather than non-being, because the [indivisible] bodies did not constitute things more than the void, or the void more than bodies; but he said that a body is composed at once of these two things, as is clear in the text. Hence he held that these two things are the causes of beings as their matter.

115. **And just as those** [2].

Here he shows in what respect these philosophers agreed with the ancients who claimed that there is only one matter. He indicates agreement in two respects.

First, just as the ancient philosophers held that there is one matter, and from that one matter generated something else according to the different attributes of matter (i.e., the rare and dense, which they accepted as the principles of all other attributes), in a similar way these philosophers—Democritus and Leucippus—said that there were different causes of different things (namely, of the bodies composed of these indivisible bodies), i.e., that different beings were produced as a result of certain differences of these indivisible bodies and their pores.

116. Now they said that these differences are, first, differences in shape, which is noted from this that things are angular, circular or square; second, differences in arrangement, i.e., insofar as the indivisible bodies are prior or subsequent; and, third, differences in position, i.e., insofar as these bodies are in front or behind, right or left, or above and below. Hence they said that one being differs from another "either by rhythm," which is shape, "or by intercontact," which is arrangement, "or by turning," which is position.

117. He illustrates this by using the letters of the Greek alphabet, which differ from each other in shape just as in our alphabet one letter also differs from another; for A differs from N in shape. Again, AN differs from NA in arrangement, because one letter is placed before the other. And one letter also differs from another in position, as Z from N, just as in our language we also see that semivowels cannot stand after liquids preceded by mutes in the same syllable. Therefore, just as tragedy and comedy come from the same letters as a result of the letters being disposed in different ways because of this threefold difference, in a similar fashion different species of things are produced from the same indivisible bodies as a result of the latter being disposed in different ways.

118. The second respect in which these philosophers agreed with the ancients is this: just as the ancient philosophers neglected to posit a cause which accounts for motion in things, so also did these men, although they would say that these indivisible bodies are capable of self-motion. Thus it is evident that these philosophers mentioned only two of the causes, i.e., all of them spoke of the material cause, and some of the efficient cause.

119. **But during the time of these** [3].

Here he gives the opinions of the Pythagoreans, who held that numbers are the substances of things. In regard to this he does two things. First [3], he gives their opinions about the substance of things; and second (next lesson), their opinions about the principles of things ("But the reason").

In regard to the first he gives two reasons by which they were led to assert that numbers are the substances of things. He gives the second reason [4] where he says "Moreover, since they considered."

He says [3] that the Pythagoreans were philosophers who lived "during the time of these," i.e., they were contemporaries of some of the foregoing philosophers; "and prior to them," because they preceded some of them. Now it must be understood that there were two groups of philosophers. One group was called the Ionians, who inhabited the land which is now called Greece. This group originated with Thales, as was pointed out above (see n. 77). The other group of philosophers were the Italians, who lived in that part of Italy which was once called Greater Greece and is now called Apulia and Calabria. The leader of these philosophers was Pythagoras, a native of Samos, so called from a certain city of Calabria. These two groups of philosophers lived at the same time, and this is why he says that they lived "During the time of these and prior to them."

120. These Italian philosophers, also called Pythagoreans, were the first to develop certain mathematical entities, so that they said that these are the substances and principles of sensible things. He says that they were "the first" because the Platonists were their successors. They were moved to bring in mathematics because they were brought up in the study of these sciences, and therefore they thought that the principles of mathematics are the principles of all existing things. For men are wont to judge about things in terms of what they already know. And since among mathematical entities numbers are first, these men therefore tried to see resemblances of natural things, both as regards their being and generation, in numbers rather than in the sensible elements—earth, water and the like. For just as the foregoing philosophers adapted the attributes of sensible things to those of natural things because of a certain resemblance which they bear to the properties of fire, water, and bodies of this kind, in a similar fashion these mathematicians adapted the properties of natural things to the attributes of numbers when they said that some one attribute of number is the cause of justice, another the cause of soul and intellect, and still another the cause of opportunity, and so on for other things. And in this way the attributes of numbers are understood to be the intelligible structures and principles of all things appearing in the sensible world, both in the realm of voluntary matters, signified by justice, and in that of the substantial forms of natural things, signified by soul and intellect, and in that of accidents, signified by opportunity.

121. **Moreover, since they** [4].

Here he gives the second reason which motivated them. For they thought of the attributes of harmonies, musical consonants and their ratios, i.e., proportions, in terms of the nature of numbers. Hence, since harmonious sounds are certain sensible things, they attempted by the same reasoning to liken all other sensible things, both in their intelligible structure and in their whole nature, to numbers, so that numbers are the first things in the whole of nature.

122. For this reason too they thought that the principles of numbers are the principles of all existing things, and they said that the whole heaven is merely a kind of nature and harmony of numbers, i.e., a kind of numerical proportion similar to the proportion found in harmonies. Hence, whatever they had "revealed," i.e., had shown, which they could adapt to numbers and harmonies, they also adapted both to the changes undergone by the heavens, as its motion, eclipses and the like; and to its parts, as the different orbs; and to the whole arrangement of the heavens, as the different stars and different figures in the constellations.

123. And if anything was lacking in the observable order of things which did not seem to be adapted to numbers, "they called it in," i.e., they invented something new "in order that their whole undertaking might be complete," i.e., in order that their whole undertaking, which was to adapt sensible things to numbers, might be made complete, until they had adapted all sensible things to numbers, as is evident in one example. For the number ten seems to be the perfect number, because it constitutes the first limit and contains within itself the nature of all numbers; for all other numbers are merely a kind of repetition of the number ten. This is why

Plato counted up to ten, as Aristotle says in the *Physics,* Book IV.[206b33] Hence Pythagoras also said that the spheres which move in the heavens are ten in number, although only nine of these are observable; because we observe seven in the motions of the planets, an eighth in the motion of the fixed stars, and a ninth in the daily motion, which is the first motion. But Pythagoras adds a tenth sphere, which was that of the "counter-earth," i.e., which is moved in the opposite direction to the motion in the lower spheres and therefore produces a contrary sound. For he said that a kind of harmony results from the motion of the celestial bodies, so that just as a harmony is produced from a proportion of contrary sounds, i.e., of low and high notes, in a similar way he claimed that in the heavens there was a single motion in the opposite direction to that of the other motions in order that a harmony might result. According to this position the daily motion belonged to the tenth sphere, which moves from east to west, the other spheres being revolved in the opposite direction from west to east. In fact, according to him, it could have been the ninth sphere which first revolved all the lower spheres in the opposite direction to the first motion. The things that pertain to this opinion of Pythagoras are considered more extensively and more definitely in the last books of this science.

LESSON 8
The Pythagorean Doctrine about Contraries

ARISTOTLE'S TEXT Chapter 5: 986a13–986b10

1. *But the reason we have come [to examine these philosophers] is that we may also learn from them what they hold the principles of things to be, and how these principles fall under the causes already described. Now these men also seem to think that number is the principle of existing things both as their matter and as their attributes and states. According to them the elements of number are the even and odd, and of these the latter is limited and the former, unlimited. The unit is composed of both of these, since it is both even and odd, and number is derived from the unit. And number, as has been stated (58), constitutes the whole heaven.*

986a13–21

2. *But other members of the same school say that the principles of things are ten in number, which they give as co-elements: the limited and unlimited, even and odd, one and many, right and left, masculine and feminine, rest and motion, straight and curved, light and darkness, good and evil, square and oblong.* **986a22–26**

3. *Alcmaeon of Croton seems to have formed his opinion in the same way, and either he derived the theory from them or they from him; for Alcmaeon (who had reached maturity when Pythagoras was an old man) expressed views similar to those of the Pythagoreans. For he says that many things in the realm of human affairs are in twos [i.e., pairs], calling them contrarieties, not distinguished as these men had distinguished them, but such as are taken at random, for example, white and black, sweet and bitter, good and evil, small and great. It is true that this philosopher threw out vague remarks about the other contrarieties, but the Pythagoreans have declared both what the contrarieties are and how many there are.*

986a27–986b2

4. *From both of these, then, we can gather this much, that contraries are the principles of existing things; but how many they are and that they are these [determinate ones must be learned] from other thinkers. The way in which many principles can be brought together under the causes described is not clearly expressed by them, although they seem to allot their elements to the class of matter; for they say that substance is composed and moulded out of these as something inherent. From these remarks, then, it is possible to get an adequate understanding of the meaning of the ancient philosophers who said that the elements of things are many.*

986b2–10

COMMENTARY

124. Here he states what the Pythagoreans had to say about the principles of things. In regard to this he does two things. First [1], he expounds their opinions about the principles of things; and second [4], he indicates to what class of cause the principles laid down by them are reduced ("From both of these").

In regard to the first he gives three opinions. The second [2] begins at the words "But other members"; and the third [3], where he says "Alcmaeon of Croton."

He says first [1], then, that the reason he came to examine the opinions of the Pythagoreans is that he might show from their opinions what the principles of things are and how the principles laid down by them fall under the causes given above. For the Pythagoreans seem to hold that number is the principle of existing things as matter, and that the attributes of number are the attributes and states of existing things. By "attributes" we mean transient accidents, and by "states," permanent accidents. They also held that the attribute of any number according to which any number is said to be even is justice, because of the equality of division, since such a number is evenly divided into two parts right down to the unit. For example, the number eight is divided into two fours, the number four into two twos, and the number two into two units. And in a similar way they likened the other accidents of things to the accidents of numbers.

125. In fact, they said that the even and odd, which are the first differences of numbers, are the principles of numbers. And they said that even number is the principle of unlimitedness and odd number the principle of limitation, as is shown in the *Physics*, Book III, [203a10] because in reality the unlimited seems to result chiefly from the division of the continuous. But an even number is capable of division; for an odd number includes within itself an even number plus a unit, and this makes it indivisible. He also proves this as follows: when odd numbers are added to each other successively, they always retain the figure of a square, whereas even numbers change their figure. For when the number three is added to the unit, which is the principle of numbers, the number four results, which is the first square [number], because 2 X 2 = 4. Again, when the number five, which is an odd number, is added to the number four, the number nine results, which is also a square number; and so on with the others. But if the number two, which is the first even number, is added to the number one, a triangular number results, i.e., the number three. And if the number four, which is the second even number, is added to the number three, there results a septangular number, i.e., the number seven. And when even numbers are added to each other successively in this way, they do not retain the same figure. This is why they attributed the unlimited to the even and the limited to the odd. And since limitedness pertains to form, to which active power belongs, they therefore said that even numbers are feminine, and odd numbers, masculine.

126. From these two, namely, the even and odd, the limited and unlimited, they produced not only number but also the unit itself, i.e., unity. For unity is virtually both even and odd; because all differences of number are virtually contained in the unit; for all differences of number are reduced to the unit. Hence, in the list of odd numbers the unit is found to be the first. And the same is true in the list of even numbers, square numbers, and perfect numbers. This is also the case with the other differences of number, because even though the unit is not actually a number, it is still virtually all numbers. And just as the unit is said to be composed of the even and odd, in a similar way number is composed of units. In fact, [according to them], the heavens and all sensible things are composed of numbers. This was the sequence of principles which they gave.

127. **But other members** [2].

Here he gives another opinion which the Pythagoreans held about the principles of things. He says that among these same Pythagoreans there were some who claimed that there is not just one contrariety in principles, as the foregoing did, but ten principles, which are presented as co-elements, that is, by taking each of these principles with its co-principle, or contrary.

The reason for this position was that they took not only the first principles but also the proximate principles attributed to each class of things. Hence, they posited first the limited and the unlimited, as did those who have just been mentioned; and subsequently the even and the odd, to which the limited and unlimited are attributed. And because the even and odd are the first principles of things, and numbers are first produced from them, they posited, third, a difference of numbers, namely, the one and the many, both of which are produced from the even and the odd. Again, because continuous quantities are composed of numbers, inasmuch as they understood numbers to have position (for according to them the point was merely the unit having position, and the line the number two having position), they therefore claimed next that the principles of positions are the right and left; for the right is found to be perfect and the left imperfect. Therefore the right is determined from the aspect of oddness, and the left from the aspect of evenness. But because natural bodies have both active and passive powers in addition to mathematical extensions, they therefore next maintained that masculine and feminine are principles. For masculine pertains to active power, and feminine to passive power; and of these masculine pertains to odd number and feminine to even number, as has been stated (n. 125).

128. Now it is from active and passive power that motion and rest originate in the world; and of these motion is placed in the class of the unlimited and even, because it partakes of irregularity and otherness, and rest in the class of the unlimited and odd. Furthermore, the first differences of motions are the circular and straight, so that as a consequence of this the straight pertains to even number. Hence they said that the straight line is the number two; but that the curved or circular line, by reason of its uniformity, pertains to odd number, which retains its undividedness because of the form of unity.

129. And they not only posited principles to account for the natural operations and motions of things, but also to account for the operations of living things. In fact, they held that light and darkness are principles of knowing, but that good and evil are principles of appetite. For light is a principle of knowing, whereas darkness is ascribed to ignorance; and good is that to which appetite tends, whereas evil is that from which it turns away.

130. Again, [according to them] the difference of perfection and imperfection is found not only in natural things and in voluntary powers and motions, but also in continuous quantities and figures. These figures are understood to be something over and above the substances of continuous quantities, just as the powers responsible for motions and operations are something over and above the substances of natural bodies. Therefore with reference to this they held that what is quadrangular, i.e., the square and oblong, is a principle. Now a square is said to be a figure of four equal sides, whose four angles are right angles; and such a figure is produced by multiplying a line by itself. Therefore, since it is produced from the unit itself, it belongs to the class of odd number. But an oblong is defined as a figure whose angles are all right angles and whose opposite sides alone, not all sides, are equal to each other. Hence it is clear that, just as a square is produced by multiplying one line by itself, in a similar way an oblong

is produced by multiplying one line by another. Hence it pertains to the class of even number, of which the first is the number two.

131. **Alcmaeon of Croton** [3].

Here he gives the third opinion of the Pythagoreans, saying that Alcmaeon of Croton, so named from the city in which he was raised, seems to maintain somewhat the same view as that expressed by these Pythagoreans, namely, that many contraries are the principles of things. For either he derives the theory from the Pythagoreans, or they from him. That either of these might be true is clear from the fact that he was a contemporary of the Pythagoreans, granted that he began to philosophize when Pythagoras was an old man. But whichever happens to be true, he expressed views similar to those of the Pythagoreans. For he said that many of the things "in the realm of human affairs," i.e., many of the attributes of sensible things are arranged in pairs, understanding by pairs opposites which are contrary. Yet in this matter he differs from the foregoing philosophers, because the Pythagoreans said that determinate contraries are the principles of things. But he throws them in, as it were, without any order, holding that any of the contraries which he happened to think of are the principles of things, such as white and black, sweet and bitter, and so on.

132. **From both of these** [4].

Here he gathers together from the above remarks what the Pythagoreans thought about the principles of things, and how the principles which they posited are reduced to some class of cause.

He says, then, that from both of those mentioned above, namely, Alcmaeon and the Pythagoreans, it is possible to draw one common opinion, namely, that the principles of existing things are contraries; which was not expressed by the other thinkers. This must be understood with reference to the material cause. For Empedocles posited contrariety in the case of the efficient cause; and the ancient philosophers of nature posited contrary principles, such as rarity and density, although they attributed contrariety to form. But even though Empedocles held that the four elements are material principles, he still did not claim that they are the first material principles by reason of contrariety but because of their natures and substance. These men, however, attributed contrariety to matter.

133. The nature of the contraries posited by these men is evident from the foregoing discussion. But how the aforesaid contrary principles posited by them can be "brought together under," i.e., reduced to, the types of causes described, is not clearly "expressed," i.e., distinctly stated, by them. Yet it seems that such principles are allotted to the class of material cause; for they say that the substance of things is composed and moulded out of these principles as something inherent, and this is the notion of a material cause. For matter is that from which a thing comes to be as something inherent. This is added to distinguish it from privation, from which something also comes to be but which is not inherent, as the musical is said to come from the non-musical.

LESSON 9
The Opinions of the Eleatics and Pythagoreans about the Causes of Things

ARISTOTLE'S TEXT Chapter 5: 986b10–987a28

1. But there are some [the Eleatics] who spoke of the whole as if it were a single nature, although the statements which they made are not all alike either with regard to their acceptableness or their conformity with nature. **986b10–12**

2. Therefore a consideration of these men pertains in no way to the present investigation of causes. For they do not, like certain of the philosophers [the early physicists] who supposed being to be one, still generate it from the one as matter; but they speak of this in another way. For the others assume motion when they generate this whole, whereas these thinkers say it is immobile. **986b12–17**

3. Yet their opinion is relevant to the present investigation to some extent; for Parmenides seems to touch on unity according to intelligible structure and Melissus on unity according to matter. This is why the former says that it is limited, and the latter that it is unlimited. Xenophanes, the first of those to speak of the one (for Parmenides is said to have been his disciple), made nothing clear, nor does he seem to have touched on either of these. But with regard to the whole heaven he says that the one is God. **986b17–25**

4. As we have stated, then, these men must be dismissed for the purposes of the present inquiry. In fact, two of them—Xenophanes and Melissus—are to be disregarded altogether as being a little too rustic. Parmenides, however, seems to speak with more insight; for he thought that besides being there is only non-being, and this is nothing. This is why he thinks that being is necessarily one and nothing else. We have discussed this point more clearly in the Physics.[186b5] But being compelled to follow the observed facts, and having assumed that what is one from the viewpoint of reason is many from the viewpoint of the senses, he postulates in turn two principles, i.e., two causes, the hot and cold, calling the one fire and the other earth; and of these he ranks the hot with being and the cold with nonbeing. **986b25–987a2**

5. From what has been said, then, and from the wise men who have already agreed with this reasoning, we have acquired these things. From the first philosophers we have learned that the principle of things is corporeal, because water and fire and the like are bodies; and from some we have learned that there is one corporeal principle, and from others, many; although both suppose that these belong to the class of matter. And from others we have learned that in addition to this cause there is the source from which motion begins, which some claim to be one and others two. Down to the Italian philosophers, then, and independent of them, others have spoken of these things in a more trivial way, except that, as we have said, they have used two kinds of causes, and one of these—the source of motion—some thinkers consider as one and others as two. **987a2–13**

6. Now the Pythagoreans have spoken of these two principles in the same way, but added this much, which is peculiar to them, that they did not think that the limited, unlimited and one are different natures, like fire or earth or anything else of this kind, but that the unlimited itself and the one itself are the substance of the things of which they are predicated. And this is why they considered number as the substance of all things. These thinkers, then, have expressed themselves thus with regard to these things, and they began to discuss and define the "what" itself of things, although they treated it far too simply. For they defined things superficially and thought that the substance of a thing is that to which a given definition first applies; just as if one supposed that double and two are the same because that to which the double first belongs is the number two. But perhaps "to be double" is not the same as "to be two"; and if they are not, then the one itself will be many. This, indeed, is the conclusion which they reached. From the first philosophers and others, then, this much can be learned. **987a13–28**

COMMENTARY

134. Here he gives the opinions of those philosophers who spoke of the whole universe as one being; and in regard to this he does two things. First [1], he gives the opinion which they held in common; and second [2], he shows how a consideration of this opinion is relevant to the present treatise, and how it is not ("Therefore a consideration").

He says [1], then, that there were certain philosophers, other than those just mentioned, who spoke "of the whole," i.e., of the universe, as if it were of one nature, i.e., as if the whole universe were a single being or a single nature. However, not all maintained this position in the same way, as he will make clear below (see nn. 138–49). Yet in the way in which they differ their statements are neither acceptable nor in conformity with nature. None of their statements are in conformity with nature, because they did away with motion in things. And none of them are acceptable, because they held an impossible position and used sophistical arguments, as is clear in Book I of the Physics.[191a26-191b25]

135. **Therefore a consideration** [2].

Here he shows how a consideration of this position pertains to the present investigation and how it does not. He shows, first, that it has no bearing on this investigation if we consider their position itself; and, second [3], that it does have a bearing on this investigation if the reasoning or method behind their position is considered ("Yet their opinion").

He says [2], then, that since these philosophers held that there is only one being, and a single thing cannot be its own cause, it is clear that they could not discover the causes. For the position that there is a plurality of things demands a diversity of causes in the world. Hence, a consideration of their statements is of no value for the purposes of the present study, which deals with causes. But the situation is different in the case of the ancient philosophers of nature, who held that there is only one being, and whose statements must be considered here. For they generated many things from that one principle as matter, and thus posited both cause and effect. But these men with whom we are now dealing speak of this in a different way. For they do not say that all things are one materially, so that all things are generated from one matter, but that all things are one in an absolute sense.

136. The reason for this difference is that the ancient philosophers of nature added motion to the view of those who posited one being and one principle, and said that this one being is mobile; and therefore different things could be generated from that one principle by a certain kind of motion, i.e., by rarefaction and condensation. And they said that the whole universe with respect to the diversity found in its parts is generated in this way. Yet since they held that the only change affecting substance is accidental, as was stated above (see n. 75), the conclusion then followed that the whole universe is one thing substantially but many things accidentally. But these thinkers [i.e., the Eleatics], said that the one being which they posited is immobile in

an absolute sense; and therefore a diversity of things could not be produced from that one being. For since this being is immobile they could not posit any plurality in the world, either substantial or accidental.

137. **Yet their opinion** [3].

Here he shows how their opinion is relevant to the present inquiry. First [3]), he deals with all of these thinkers in general; and second [4], with Parmenides in particular ("As we have stated").

He says, first [3], that although they did away with diversity in the world, and consequently with causality,

nevertheless their opinion is relevant to the present study to this extent, let us say: as regards the method by which they establish their position and the reason for their position.

138. Parmenides, who was a member of this group, seems to touch on unity according to intelligible structure, i.e., according to form; for he argued as follows: besides being there is only non-being, and non-being is nothing. Therefore besides being there is nothing. But being is one. Therefore, besides the one there is nothing. In this argument he clearly considered the intelligible structure itself of being, which seems to be one, because nothing can be understood to be added to the concept of being by which it might be diversified. For whatever is added to being must be other than being. But anything such as this is nothing. Hence it does not seem that this can diversify being; just as we also see that differences added to a genus diversify it, even though these differences are outside the substance of that genus. For differences do not participate in a genus, as is stated in the *Topics*, Book IV, [121a10] otherwise a genus would have the substance of a difference. And definitions would be nonsense if when a genus is given the difference were added, granted that the genus were the substance of the difference, just as it would be nonsense if the species were added. Moreover a difference would not differ in any way from a species. But those things which are outside the substance of being must be non-being, and thus cannot diversify being.

139. But they were mistaken in this matter, because they used being as if it were one in intelligible structure and in nature, like the nature of any genus. But this is impossible. For being is not a genus but is predicated of different things in many ways. Therefore in Book I of the *Physics [185a20]* it is said that the statement "Being is one" is false. For being does not have one nature like one genus or one species.

140. But Melissus considered being in terms of matter. For he argued that being is one by reason of the fact that being is not generated from something prior, and this characteristic pertains properly to matter, which is ungenerated. For he argued in this way: whatever is generated has a starting-point. But being is not generated and therefore does not have a starting-point. But whatever lacks a starting-point lacks an end and therefore is unlimited. And if it is unlimited, it is immobile, because what is unlimited has nothing outside itself by which it is moved. That being is not generated he proves thus. If being were generated, it would be generated either from being or from non-being. But it is not generated from non-being, because non-being is nothing and from nothing nothing comes. Nor is it generated from being, because then a thing would be before it came to be. Therefore it is not generated in any way. In this argument he obviously treats being as matter, because it is of

the very nature of matter not to be generated from something prior. And since limitation pertains to form, and unlimitedness to matter, Melissus, who considered being under the aspect of matter, said that there is one unlimited being. But Parmenides, who considered being under the aspect of form, said that being is limited. Hence, insofar as being is considered under the aspect of form and matter, a study of these men is relevant to the present investigation; because matter and form are included among the causes.

141. But Xenophanes, who was the first of those to say that everything is one (and therefore Parmenides was his disciple), did not explain by what reasoning he maintained that all things are one, either by arguing from the viewpoint of matter, or from that of form. Hence, with respect to neither nature, i.e., neither matter nor form, does he seem "to come up to these men," that is, to reach and equal them in their irrational manner of arguing. But concerning the whole heaven he says that the one is God. For the ancients said that the world itself is God. Hence, seeing that all parts of the universe are alike insofar as they are bodies, he came to think of them as if they were all one. And just as the foregoing philosophers held that beings are one by considering those things which pertain either to matter or to form, in a similar way these philosophers maintained this position regarding the composite itself.

142. **As we have stated** [4].

His aim here is to explain in a special way how the opinion of Parmenides pertains to the present investigation. He concludes from the foregoing that, since these men did away with diversity in the world and therefore with causality, all of them must be disregarded so far as the present study is concerned. Two of them—Xenophanes and Melissus—must be disregarded altogether, because they are a little too "rustic," i.e., they proceeded with less accuracy. But Parmenides seems to have expressed his views "with more insight," i.e., with greater understanding. For he employs the following argument: besides being there is only non-being, and whatever is non-being "is thought to be nothing"; i.e., he considers it worthy to be nothing. Hence he thought that it necessarily followed that being is one, and that whatever is other than being is nothing. This argument has been treated more clearly in the *Physics*, Book I. [186b5]

143. But even though Parmenides was compelled by this argument to hold that all things are one, yet, because there appeared to the senses to be many things in reality, and because he was compelled to accept what appeared to the senses, it was his aim to make his position conform to both of these, i.e., to what is apprehended both by the senses and by reason. Hence he said that all things are one according to reason but many according to the senses. And inasmuch as he held that there is a plurality of things according to the senses, he was able to hold that there is in the world both cause and effect. Hence he posited two causes, namely, the hot and the cold, one of which he ascribed to fire, and the other to earth. And one of these—the hot or fire—seemed to pertain to the efficient cause, and the other—cold or earth—to the material cause. And lest his position should seem to contradict the conclusion of his own argument that whatever is besides being is nothing, he said that one of these causes—the hot—is being, and that the other

cause—the one besides being, or the cold—is nonbeing, according to both reason and the truth of the thing itself, and is a being only according to sensory perception.

144. Now in this matter he comes very close to the truth; for the material principle, which he held to be earth, is not an actual being. And in a similar way, too, one of two contraries is a privation, as is said in Book I of the *Physics. [192a3]* But privation does not belong to the intelligible constitution of being. Hence in a sense cold is the privation of heat, and thus is non-being.

145. **From what has been said** [5].

Here he summarizes the remarks which have been made about the doctrines of the ancient philosophers; and in regard to this he does two things. First [5], he summarizes the remarks made about the doctrines of the ancient philosophers of nature; and second [6], those made about the doctrines of the Pythagoreans, who introduced mathematics ("Now the Pythagoreans").

Therefore from the above remarks he concludes, first [5], that from the foregoing philosophers, who adopted the same opinion, namely, that the material cause is the substance of things, and who were already beginning by the use of reason to know the causes of things by investigating them, we learn the causes which have been mentioned. For from the first philosophers it was learned that the principle of all things is corporeal. This is evident from the fact that water and the like, which are given as the principles of things, are bodies. However, they differed in this respect, that some, such as Thales, Diogenes and similar thinkers, claimed that there is only one corporeal principle, whereas others, such as Anaxagoras, Democritus and Leucippus, held that there are several corporeal principles. Yet both groups, i.e., both those who posited one principle and those who posited many, placed such corporeal principles in the class of material cause. And some of them not only posited a material cause but added to this the cause from which motion begins: some holding it to be one, as Anaxagoras did in positing intellect, and Parmenides, love, and others to be two, as Empedocles did in positing love and hate.

146. Hence, it is clear that these philosophers who lived down to the time of the Italians, or Pythagoreans, "and [were] independent of them," i.e., who had their own opinions about reality and were unaware of those of the Pythagoreans, spoke obscurely about the principles of things; for they did not designate to what class of cause such principles might be reduced. Yet they made use of two causes, i.e., the source from which motion begins and matter: some saying that the former—the source from which motion begins—is one, and others two; as has been pointed out (see n. 145).

147. **Now the Pythagoreans** [6].

Here he summarizes the opinions expressed by the Pythagoreans, both what they held in common with the foregoing philosophers, and what was peculiar to themselves. Now the opinion common to some of the foregoing philosophers and to the Pythagoreans was this that they posited, in a sense, two principles in the same way as the foregoing philosophers did. For Empedocles held that there are two contrary principles, one being the principle of good things, and the other the principle of evil things, and the Pythagoreans did the same thing, as is clear from the co-ordination of contrary principles which they posited.

148. However, they did not do this in the same way; because Empedocles placed these contrary principles in the class of material cause, as was stated above (see n. 111), whereas the Pythagoreans added their own opinion to that of the other thinkers. The first thing that they added is this: they said that what I call the one, the limited and the unlimited are not accidents of any other natures, such as fire or earth or the like, but claimed that what I call the one, the limited and the unlimited constitute the substance of the same things of which they are predicated. From this they concluded that number, which is constituted of units, is the substance of all things. But while the other philosophers of nature posited the one, the limited and the unlimited, they nevertheless attributed these to another nature, as accidents are attributed to a subject, for example, to fire or water or something of this kind.

149. The second addition which they made to the views of the other philosophers is this: they began to discuss and to define "the whatness itself," i.e., the substance and quiddity of things, although they treated this far too simply by defining things superficially. For in giving definitions they paid attention only to one thing; because they said that, if any given definition were to apply primarily to some thing, this would be the substance of that thing; just as if one were to suppose that the ratio "double" is the substance of the number two, because such a ratio is found first in the number two. And since being was found first in the one rather than in the many (for the many is composed of ones), they therefore said that being is the substance itself of the one. But this conclusion of theirs is not acceptable; for although the number two is double, the essence of twoness is not the same as that of the double in such a way that they are the same conceptually, as the definition and the thing defined. But even if their statements were true, it would follow that the many would be one. For some plurality can belong primarily to something one; for example, evenness and the ratio double belong first to the number two. Hence [according to them] it would follow that the even and the double are the same. And it would likewise follow that that to which the double belongs is the same as the number two, so long as the double is the substance of the number two. This, indeed, is also the conclusion which the Pythagoreans drew; for they attributed plurality and diversity to things as if they were one, just as they said that the properties of numbers are the same as the properties of natural beings.

150. Hence, Aristotle concludes that it is possible to learn this much from the early philosophers, who posited only one material principle, and from the later philosophers, who posited many principles.

LESSON 10
The Platonic Theory of Ideas

ARISTOTLE'S TEXT Chapter 6: 987a29–988a17

1. *After the philosophies described came the system of Plato, which followed them in many respects, but also had other [theses] of its own in addition to the philosophy of the Italians. For Plato agreeing at the very beginning with the opinions of Cratylus (362) and Heraclitus that all sensible things are always in a state of flux, and that there is no scientific knowledge of them, also accepted this doctrine in later years. However, when Socrates, concerning himself with moral matters and neglecting nature as a whole, sought for the universal in these matters and fixed his thought on definition, Plato accepted him because of this kind of investigation, and assumed that this consideration refers to other entities and not to sensible ones. For [according to him] it is impossible that there should be a common definition of any one of these sensible things which are always changing. Such entities, then, he called Ideas or Forms (species); and he said that all sensible things exist because of them and in conformity with them; for there are many individuals of the same name because of participation in these Forms. With regard to participation, he [merely] changed the name; for while the Pythagoreans say that things exist by imitation of numbers, Plato says that they exist by participation, changing the name. Yet what this participation or imitation of Forms is they commonly neglected to investigate.* **987a29–987b14**

2. *Further, he says that besides sensible things and Ideas there are the objects of mathematics, which constitute an intermediate class. These differ from sensible things in being eternal and immobile; and from the Ideas in that there are many alike, whereas each Idea is itself only one.* **987b14–18**

3. *And since the Forms [or Ideas] are the causes of other things, he thought that the elements of these are the elements of all existing things. Hence, according to him, the great and small are principles as matter, and the one as substance [or form]; for it is from these by participation in the one that the Ideas are numbers.* **987b18–22**

4. *Yet Plato said that the one is substance and that no other being is to be called one, just as the Pythagoreans did; and like them too he said that numbers are the causes of real substance.* **987b22–25**

5. *But to posit a dyad in place of the indeterminate one, and to produce the unlimited out of the great and small, is peculiar to him. Moreover, he says that numbers exist apart from sensible things, whereas they say that things themselves are numbers. Further, they do not maintain that the objects of mathematics are an intermediate class.* **987b25–29**

6. *Therefore, his making the one and numbers to exist apart from things and not in things, as the Pythagoreans did, and his introducing the separate Forms, were due to his investigation into the intelligible structures of things; for the earlier philosophers were ignorant of dialectic.* **987b29–33**

7. *But his making the dyad [or duality] to be a different nature was due to the fact that all numbers, with the exception of prime numbers, are naturally generated from the number two as a matrix* **987b33–988a1**

8. *Yet what happens is the contrary of this. For this view is not a reasonable one; because the Platonists produce many things from matter but their form generates only once.* **988a1–3**

9. *And from one matter one measure [table] seems to be produced, whereas he who induces the form, even though he is one, produces many measures [tables]. The male is also related to the female in a similar way; for the latter is impregnated by one act, but the male impregnates many*

females. And such are the changes in these principles. Concerning the causes under investigation, then, Plato defines them thus. **988a3–8**

10. From the foregoing account it is evident that Plato used only two causes: one being the whatness of a thing, and the other, matter; for the Forms are the cause of the quiddity in other things, and the one is the cause of the quiddity in the Forms. What the underlying matter is of which the Forms are predicated in the case of sensible things, and the one in the case of the Forms, is also evident, namely, that it is this duality, the great and small. Moreover, he assigned the cause of good and evil to these two elements, one to each of them; which is rather a problem, as we say (48:C 100), that some of the first philosophers, such as Empedocles and Anaxagoras, [have attempted] to investigate. **988a8–17**

COMMENTARY

151. Having given the opinion of the ancient phiolsophers about the material and efficient cause, he gives a third opinion, that of Plato, who was the first to clearly introduce the formal cause. This is divided into two parts. First [1], he gives Plato's opinion. Second (Lesson 11), from all of the foregoing remarks he makes a summary of the opinions which the other philosophers expressed about the four classes of causes ("We have examined").

In regard to the first he does two things. First, he gives Plato's opinion about the substances of things; and second [3], his opinion about the principles of things ("And since the Forms").

In regard to the first he does two things. First, he gives Plato's opinion insofar as he posited Ideas; and second [2], insofar as he posited intermediate substances, namely, the separate mathematical entities ("Further, he says").

He says, first [1], that after all the foregoing philosophers came the system of Plato, who immediately preceded Aristotle; for Aristotle is considered to have been his disciple. And even if Plato followed in many respects the natural philosophers who preceded him, such as Empedocles, Anaxagoras and the like, he nevertheless had certain other doctrines of his own in addition to those of the preceding philosophers, because of the philosophy of the Italians, or Pythagoreans. For insofar as he was devoted to the study of truth he sought out the philosophers of all lands in order to learn their teachings. Hence he came to Tarentum in Italy, and was instructed in the teachings of the Pythagoreans by Archytas of Tarentum, a disciple of Pythagoras.

152. Now Plato would seem to follow the natural philosophers who lived in Greece; and of this group some of the later members held that all sensible things are always in a state of flux, and that there can be no scientific knowledge of them (which was the position of Heraclitus and Cratylus). And since Plato became accustomed to positions of this kind from the very beginning, and agreed with these men in this position, which he acknowledged to be true in later years, he therefore said that scientific knowledge of particular sensible things must be abandoned. And Socrates (who was Plato's master and the disciple of Archelaus, a pupil of Anaxagoras), because of this position, which arose in his time, that there can be no science of sensible things, was unwilling to make any investigation into the nature of physical things, but only busied himself with moral

matters. And in this field he first began to investigate what the universal is, and to insist upon the need for definition.

153. Hence, Plato, being Socrates' pupil, "accepted Socrates," i.e., followed him, and adopted this method for the purpose of investigating natural beings. He did so believing that in their case the universal in them could successfully be grasped and a definition be assigned to it, with no definition being given for any sensible thing; because, since sensible things are always "changing," i.e., being changed, no common intelligible structure can be assigned to any of them. For every definition must conform to each thing defined and must always do so, and thus requires some kind of immutability. Hence universal entities of this kind, which are separate from sensible things and that to which definitions are assigned, he called the Ideas or Forms of sensible things. He called them Ideas, or exemplars, inasmuch as sensible things are made in likeness to them; and he called them Forms inasmuch as [sensible things] have substantial being by participating in them. Or he called them Ideas inasmuch as they are principles of being, and Forms inasmuch as they are principles of knowledge. Hence all sensible things have being because of them and in conformity with them. They have being because of the Ideas insofar as the Ideas are the causes of the being of sensible things, and "in conformity with them" insofar as they are the exemplars of sensible things.

154. The truth of this is clear from the fact that "many individuals of the same name" are attributed to one Form alone, i.e., there are many individuals which have the same Form predicated of them, and predicated by participation. For the Form or Idea [of man] is the specific nature itself by which there exists *man* essentially. But an individual is man by participation inasmuch as the specific nature [man] is participated in by this designated matter. For that which is something in its entirety does not participate in it but is essentially identical with it, whereas that which is not something in its entirety but has this other thing joined to it, is said properly to participate in that thing. Thus, if heat were a self-subsistent heat, it would not be said to participate in heat, because it would contain nothing but heat. But since fire is something other than heat, it is said to participate in heat.

155. In a similar way, since the separate Idea of man contains nothing but the specific nature itself, it is man essentially; and for this reason it was called by him man-in-itself. But since Socrates and Plato have in addition to their specific nature an individuating principle, which is designated matter, they are therefore said to participate in a Form, according to Plato.

156. Now Plato took this term *participation* from Pythagoras, although [in doing so] he made a change in the term. For the Pythagoreans said that numbers are the causes of things, just as the Platonists said that the Ideas are, and claimed that sensible things of this kind exist as certain imitations of numbers. For inasmuch as numbers, which have no position of themselves, received positions, they caused bodies. But because Plato held that the Ideas are unchangeable in order that there might be scientific knowledge of them, he did not agree that the term *imitation* could be used of the Ideas, but in place of it he used the term participation. However, it must be noted that, even though the Pythagoreans posited par-

ticipation or imitation, they still did not investigate the way in which a common Form is participated in by individual sensible things or imitated by them. But the Platonists have treated this.

157. **Further, he says** [2].

Here he gives Plato's opinion about the mathematical substances. He says that Plato posited other substances—the objects of mathematics—in addition to the Forms and sensible things. Moreover, he said that beings of this kind were an intermediate class among the three kinds of substances; or that they were above sensible substances and below the Forms, and differed from both. The mathematical substances differed from sensible substances, because sensible substances are corruptible and changeable, whereas the mathematical substances are eternal and immobile. The Platonists got this idea from the way in which mathematical science conceives its objects; for mathematical science abstracts from motion. The mathematical substances also differed from the Forms, because the objects of mathematics are found to be numerically different and specifically the same, otherwise the demonstrations of mathematics would prove nothing. For unless two triangles belonged to the same class, geometry would attempt in vain to demonstrate that some triangles are alike; and the same thing is true of other figures. But this does not happen in the case of the Forms. For, since a Form is just the specific nature itself of a thing, each Form can only be unique. For even though the Form of man is one thing, and the Form of ass another thing, nevertheless the Form of man is unique, and so is the Form of ass; and the same thing is true of other things.

158. Now to one who carefully examines Plato's arguments it is evident that Plato's opinion was false, because he believed that the mode of being which the thing known has in reality is the same as the one which it has in the act of being known. Therefore, since he found that our intellect understands abstractions in two ways: in one way as we understand universals abstracted from singulars, and in another way as we understand the objects of mathematics abstracted from sensible things, he claimed that for each abstraction of the intellect there is a corresponding abstraction in the essences of things. Hence he held that both the objects of mathematics and the Forms are separate. But this is not necessary. For even though the intellect understands things insofar as it becomes assimilated to them through the intelligible form by which it is put into act, it still is not necessary that a form should have the same mode of being in the intellect that it has in the thing known; for everything that exists in something else exists there according to the mode of the recipient. Therefore, considering the nature of the intellect, which is other than the nature of the thing known, the mode of understanding, by which the intellect understands, must be one kind of mode, and the mode of being, by which things exist, must be another. For although the object which the intellect understands must exist in reality, it does not exist there according to the same mode [which it has in the intellect]. Hence, even though the intellect understands mathematical entities without simultaneously understanding sensible substances, and understands universals without understanding particulars, it is not therefore necessary that the objects of mathematics should exist apart

from sensible things, or that universals should exist apart from particulars. For we also see that sight perceives color apart from flavor, even though flavor and color are found together in sensible substances.

159. **And since the Forms** [3].

Here he gives Plato's opinion concerning the principles of things; and in regard to this he does two things. First [3], he states the principles which Plato assigned to things; and second [10], the class of cause to which they are reduced ("From the foregoing").

In regard to the first he does two things. First, he tells us what kind of principles Plato had assigned to things. Second [4], he shows in what respect Plato agreed with the Pythagoreans, and in what respect he differed from them ("Yet Plato").

He says, first [3], that, since the Forms are the causes of all other beings according to Plato, the Platonists therefore thought that the elements of the Forms are the elements of all beings. Hence, they assigned as the material principle of things the great and small, and said that "the substance of things," i.e., their form, is the one. They did this because they held these to be the principles of the Forms. For they said that just as the Forms are the formal principles of sensible things, in a similar way the one is the formal principle of the Forms. Therefore, just as sensible things are constituted of universal principles by participation in the Forms, in a similar way the Forms, which he said are numbers, are constituted "of these," i.e., of the great and small. For the unit constitutes different species of numbers by addition and subtraction, in which the notion of the great and small consists. Hence, since the one was thought to be the substance of being (because he did not distinguish between the one which is the principle of number, and the one which is convertible with being), it seemed to him that a plurality of different Forms might be produced from the one, which is their common substance, in the same way that a plurality of different species of numbers is produced from the unit.

160. **Yet Plato** [4].

Here he compares the position of Plato with that of Pythagoras. First [4], he shows in what respect they agreed; and second [5], in what respect they differed ("But to posit").

Now they agreed in two positions; and the first is that the one is the substance of things. For the Platonists, like the Pythagoreans, said that what I call the one is not predicated of some other being as an accident is of a subject, but signifies a thing's substance. They said this, as we have pointed out (see n. 159), because they did not distinguish between the one which is convertible with being and the one which is the principle of number.

161. The second position follows from the first; for the Platonists, like the Pythagoreans, said that numbers are the causes of the substance of all beings; and they held this because [in their opinion] number is just a collection of units. Hence if the one is substance, number must also be such.

162. **But to posit** [5].

Here he shows in what respect they differed; and in regard to this he does two things. First, he states how they differed. Second [6], he gives the reason for this difference ("Therefore, his making").

Now this difference involves two things. First, the Pythagoreans, as has already been stated, posited two principles of which things are constituted, namely, the limited and the unlimited, of which one, i.e., the unlimited, has the character of matter. But in place of this one principle—the unlimited—which the Pythagoreans posited, Plato created a dyad, holding that the great and small have the character of matter. Hence the unlimited, which Pythagoras claimed to be one principle, Plato claimed to consist of the great and small. This is his own opinion in contrast with that of Pythagoras.

163. The second difference is that Plato held that numbers are separate from sensible things, and this in two ways. For he said that the Forms themselves are numbers, as was pointed out above (see n. 159); and he also held, as was stated above (see n. 157), that the objects of mathematics are an intermediate class between the Forms and sensible things, and that they are numbers by their very essence. But the Pythagoreans said that sensible things themselves are numbers, and did not make the objects of mathematics an intermediate class between the Forms and sensible things; nor again did they hold that the Forms are separate from things.

164. **Therefore, his making** [6].

Here he gives the reason for the difference. First [6], he gives the reason for the second difference; and then [7], the reason for the first difference ("But his making").

He says, then, that the Platonists adopted the position that both the one and numbers exist apart from sensible things and not in sensible things, as the Pythagoreans claimed; and they also introduced separate Forms because of the investigation "which was made into the intelligible structures of things," i.e., because of their investigation of the definitions of things, which they thought could not be attributed to sensible substances, as has been stated (see n. 151). This is the reason they were compelled to hold that there are certain things to which definitions are assigned. But the Pythagoreans, who came before Plato, were ignorant of dialectic, whose office it is to investigate definitions and universals of this kind, the study of which led to the introduction of the Ideas.

165. **But his making** [7].

Here he gives the reason for the other difference, that is, the one concerning matter. First [7], he gives the reason for such a difference. Second [8], he shows that Plato was not reasonably motivated ("Yet what happens").

He accordingly says [7] that the Platonists made the dyad [or duality] to be a number of a different nature than the Forms, because all numbers with the exception of prime numbers are produced from it. They called prime numbers those which are not measured by any other number, such as three, five, seven, eleven, and so on; for these are produced immediately from unity alone. But numbers which are measured by some other number are not called prime numbers but composite ones, for example, the number four, which is measured by the number two; and in general every even number is measured by the number two. Hence even numbers are attributed to matter, since unlimitedness, which belongs to matter, is attributed to them, as has been stated above (see n. 125). This is why he posited the dyad, from which as "a matrix," or exemplar, all other even numbers are produced.

166. **Yet what happens** [8].

Here he proves that Plato made unreasonable assumptions; and in regard to this he does two things. For, first [8], he proves this by an argument from nature. Second [9], he gives the argument based on the nature of things, which led Plato to adopt this position ("And from one matter").

He says [8] that, although Plato posited a dyad on the part of matter, still what happens is the contrary of this, as the opinions of all the other natural philosophers testify; for they claimed that contrariety pertains to form and unity to matter, as is clear in Book I of the *Physics. [187a16]* For they held that the material principle of things is air or water or something of this kind, from which the diversity of things is produced by rarefaction and condensation, which they regarded as formal principles; for Plato's position is not a reasonable one. Now the natural philosophers adopted this position because they saw that many things are generated from matter as a result of a succession of forms in matter. For that matter which now supports one form may afterwards support many forms as a result of one form being corrupted and another being generated. But one specifying principle or form "generates only once," i.e., constitutes the thing which is generated. For when something is generated it receives a form, and the same form numerically cannot become the form of another thing that is generated but ceases to be when that which was generated undergoes corruption. In this argument it is clearly apparent that one matter is related to many forms, and not the reverse, i.e., one form to many matters. Thus it seems more reasonable to hold that unity pertains to matter but duality or contrariety to form, as the philosophers of nature claimed. This is the opposite of what Plato held.

167. **And from one matter** [9].

Here he gives an opposite argument taken from sensible things according to the opinion of Plato. For Plato saw that each thing is received in something else according to the measure of the recipient. Hence receptions seem to differ according as the capacities of recipients differ. But one matter is one capacity for reception. And Plato also saw that the agent who induces the form, although he is one, causes many things to have this form; and this comes about because of diversity on the part of matter. An example of this is evident in the case of male and female; for a male is related to a female as an agent and one who impresses a form on matter. But a female is impregnated by one act of a male, whereas one male can impregnate many females. This is why he held that unity pertains to form and duality to matter.

168. Now we must note that this difference between Plato and the philosophers of nature is a result of the fact that they considered things from different points of view. For the philosophers of nature considered sensible things only insofar as they are subject to change, in which one subject successively acquires contrary qualities. Hence they attributed unity to matter and contrariety to form. But Plato, because of his investigation of universals, went on to give the principles of sensible things. Therefore, since the cause of the diversity of the many singular things which come under one universal is the division of matter, he held that diversity pertains to matter and unity to form. "And such are the changes of those principles" which Plato posited, i.e., participations, or, as I may say, influences in the things generated. For Pythagoras understands the word change in this way. Or Aristotle says "changes" inasmuch as Plato changed the opinion which the first philosophers of nature had about principles, as is evident from the foregoing. Hence it is evident from the foregoing

that Plato dealt thus with the causes which we are investigating.

169. **From the foregoing** [10].

Here he shows to what class of cause the principles given by Plato are referred. He says that it is evident from the foregoing that Plato used only two kinds of causes. For he used as "one" cause of a thing the cause of its "whatness," i.e., its quiddity, or its formal cause, which determines its quiddity; and he also used matter itself. This is also evident from the fact that the Forms which he posited "are the causes of other things," i.e., the causes of the whatness of sensible things, namely, their formal causes, whereas the formal cause of the Forms themselves is what I call the one, which seems to be the substance of which the Forms are composed. And just as he holds that the one is the formal cause of the Forms, in a similar fashion he holds that the great and small are their material cause, as was stated above (71:C 159). And these causes—the formal and the material cause—are referred not only to the Forms but also to sensible substances, because [there is some subject of which] the one is predicated in the case of the Forms. That is to say, that which is related to sensible substances in the same way as the one is to the Forms is itself a Form, because that duality which relates to sensible things as their matter is the great and small.

170. Furthermore, Plato indicated the cause of good and evil in the world, and he did this with reference to each of the elements which he posited. For he made Form the cause of good and matter the cause of evil. However, some of the first philosophers attempted to investigate the cause of good and evil, namely, Anaxagoras and Empedocles, who established certain causes in the world with this special end in view that by means of these causes they might be able to give the principles of good and evil. And in touching upon these causes of good and evil they came very close to positing the final cause, although they did not posit this cause directly but only indirectly, as is stated below (84:C 177).

LESSON 11

A Summary of the Early Opinions about the Causes

ARISTOTLE'S TEXT Chapter 7: 988a18–988b21

1. We have examined, then, in a brief and summary way those philosophers who have spoken about the principles of things and about the truth, and the way in which they did this. Yet we have learned from them this much: that none of those who have discussed principle and cause have said anything beyond the points established by us in the Physics.[194b15-195b30] **988a18–22**

2. Yet all have approached these causes obscurely. **988a22–23**

3. For some speak of the [first] principle as matter, whether they suppose it to be one or many, and whether they assume it to be a body or something incorporeal, as Plato speaks of the great and small; the Italians of the unlimited; Empedocles of fire, earth, water and air; and Anaxagoras of an infinite number of like parts. All these have touched on this kind of cause, and so also have those who make the first principle air or fire or water or something denser than fire or rarer than air. For they have said that some such body is the primary element. These thinkers, then, have touched only on this cause. **988a23–32**

4. But others [have introduced] the source of motion, for example, those who make friendship and strife, or intellect, or love, or something besides these a principle of things. **988a32–34**

5. But the quiddity or substance no one has presented clearly. Those who express it best are those who posit the Ideas and the intelligible natures inherent in the Ideas. For they do not think of the Ideas and the things inherent in them as the matter of sensible things; nor do they think of them as the source from which motion originates, for they say that these things are the causes rather of immobility and of that which is at rest. But [according to them] the Forms are responsible for the quiddity of all other things, and the one for the quiddity of the Forms. **988a34–988b6**

6. That for the sake of which there are actions and changes and motions they affirm in some way to be a cause, but not in the way we are determining causes, or in the way in which it is truly a cause. For while those who speak of intellect or love posit these causes as good, they do not say that anything exists or comes to be because of them, but claim that the motion of things stems from them. In like manner those who say that the one or being is such a reality, say that it is the cause of substance, but not that things either are or come to be for the sake of this. Hence, it happens to them that in a way they both say and do not say that the good is a cause; for they do not speak of it in its principal aspect but in a secondary one. **988b616**

7. Therefore all these philosophers, being unable to touch on any other cause, seem to bear witness to the fact that we have dealt correctly with the causes, both as to their number and their kinds. Moreover, it is evident that all principles must be sought in this way or in some similar one. As to the way in which each of these philosophers has spoken, and how they have raised possible problems about the principles of things, let us discuss these points next. **988b16–21**

COMMENTARY

171. Here he makes a summary of everything that the early philosophers have said about causes; and in regard to this he does three things. First [1], he shows that the early philosophers were unable to add another kind of cause to the four classes of causes given above (see n. 70). Second [2], he indicates the way in which they touched upon these causes ("Yet all").

Third [7] he draws the conclusion at which he chiefly aims ("Therefore, all these").

He says, first [1], that in giving this brief and summary account he has stated who the philosophers are, and how they have spoken of the principles of things and of what is true of the substance itself of things. And from their statements this much can be learned: that none of those who have spoken about causes and principles were able to mention any causes other than those distinguished in Book II of the *Physics.[194b15-195b30]*

172. **Yet all** [2].

Here he gives the way in which they dealt with each of the causes. He does this, first [2], in a general way: and, second [3], in a special way ("For some speak").

Accordingly he says, first, that they not only have not added anything, but in the way in which they approached these causes they proceeded obscurely and not clearly. For they have not stated to what class of cause the principles posited by them would belong; but they gave as principles things that can be adapted to some class of cause.

173. **For some speak** [3].

Here he shows in a special way how they touched on each of these causes. He shows, first [3], how they touched on the material cause; second [4], on the efficient cause ("But others"); third [5], on the formal cause ("But the quiddity"); and fourth [6], on the final cause ("That for the sake of which").

He says, first [3], then, that those philosophers, i.e., the early ones, all agree insofar as they assign some material cause to things. Yet they differ in two respects. First, they differ in that some, such as Thales, Diogenes and the like, held that the material principle is one, whereas others, such as Empedocles, claimed that it is many; and second, they differ in that some, such as the first group above, held that the material principle of things is a body, whereas others, such as Plato, who posited a dyad, claimed that it is something incorporeal. For Plato posited the great and small, which the Platonists do not speak of as a body. The Italians, or Pythagoreans, posited the unlimited; but neither is this a body. Empedocles, on the other hand, posited the four elements, which are bodies; and Anaxagoras also posited "an infinite number of like parts," i.e., [he claimed] that the principles of things are an infinite number of like parts. All of these thinkers have touched on "this kind of cause," i.e., the material cause, and so also have those who said that the principle of things is air or water or fire or something midway between these elements, i.e., what is denser than fire and rarer than air. For all philosophers such as those just mentioned have claimed that some kind of body is the first element of things. Thus Aristotle's statement is evident, namely, that in the light of the foregoing remarks these philosophers have posited only the material cause.

174. **But others** [4].

Here he gives their opinions about the efficient cause. He says that some of the foregoing philosophers have posited, in addition to the material cause, a cause from which motion begins, for example, those who made love or hate or intellect a cause of things, or those who introduced some other active principle distinct from these, as Parmenides, who made fire an efficient cause.

175. **But the quiddity** [5].

Here he gives their opinions about the formal cause. He says that the cause through which a thing's substance is known, i.e., the formal cause, no one attributed to things with any clarity. And if the ancient philosophers touched on something that might pertain to the formal cause, as Empedocles did when he claimed that bone and flesh contain some proportion [of the elements], by which they are things of this kind, nevertheless they did not treat what belongs to the formal cause after the manner of a cause.

176. But among the other philosophers, those who posited the Forms and those intelligible aspects which belong to the Forms, such as unity, number and the like, came closest to positing the formal cause. For the Forms and everything that belongs to the Forms in the aforesaid way, such as unity and number, are not acknowledged or assumed by them to be the matter of sensible things, since they place matter rather on the side of sensible things; nor do they claim that the Forms are the causes from which motion originates in the world, but rather that they are the cause of immobility in things. For they said that whatever is found to be necessary in sensible things is caused by the Forms, and that these, i.e., the Forms, are immobile. For they claimed that the Forms, because immobile, are uniform in being, as has been said (see n. 156), so that definitions can be given of them and demonstrations made about them. But according to the opinion of these men the Forms are responsible for the quiddity of particular things after the manner of a formal cause, and the one is responsible for the quiddity of the Forms.

177. **That for the sake of which** [6].

Here he gives the opinions of certain thinkers about the final cause. He says that in one sense the philosophers say that the goal for the sake of which motions, changes and activities occur is a cause, and in another sense they do not. And they neither speak of it in the same way, nor in the way in which it is a true cause. For those who affirm that intellect or love is a cause, posit these causes as good. For they said that things of this kind are the causes of things being well disposed, since the cause of good can only be good. Hence it follows that they could make intellect and love to be causes, just as the good is a cause. But good can be understood in two ways: in one way as a final cause, in the sense that something comes to be for the sake of some good; and in another way as an efficient cause, as we say that the good man does good. Now these philosophers did not say that the foregoing causes are good in the sense that they are the reason for the existence or coming to be of some beings, which pertains to the intelligibility of the final cause, but in the sense that there proceeds from these causes—intellect and will—a kind of motion toward the being and coming-to-be of things; and this pertains to the intelligibility of the efficient cause.

178. In a similar way the Pythagoreans and Platonists, who said that the substance of things is the one itself or being, also attributed goodness to the one or being. Thus they said that such a reality, i.e., the good, is the cause of the substance of sensible things, either in the manner of a formal cause, as the Platonists maintained, or in the manner of a material cause, as the Pythagoreans claimed. However, they did not say that the being and coming-to-be of things exists for the sake of this, i.e., the one or being; and this is something that pertains to the intelligibility of the final cause. Hence, just as the philosophers of nature claimed

that the good is a cause in the manner of an efficient cause and not in that of a formal cause, in a similar way the Platonists claimed that the good is a cause in the manner of a formal cause, and not in that of a final cause. The Pythagoreans, on the other hand, considered it to be a cause in the manner of a material cause.

179. It is evident, then, that in one sense they happened to speak of the good as a cause and in another not. For they did not speak of it as a cause in its principal aspect but in a secondary one; because according to its proper intelligible structure the good is a cause in the manner of a final cause. This is clear from the fact that the good is what all desire. Now that to which an appetite tends is a goal. Therefore according to its proper intelligible structure the good is a cause in the manner of a goal. Hence those who make the good a cause in its principal aspect claim that it is a final cause. But those who attribute a different mode of causality to the good claim that the good is a cause but only in a secondary way; because they do not hold that it is such by reason of being good, but by reason of that to which good happens to belong—by reason of its being active or perfective. Hence it is clear that those philosophers posited a final cause only incidentally, because they posited as a cause something that is fitting to be an end, namely, the good. However, they did not claim that it is a cause in the manner of a final cause, as has been stated.

180. **Therefore all these** [7].

Here he draws the conclusion at which he chiefly aims: that the things established about the causes, both as to their number and their kinds, are correct. For the foregoing philosophers seem to bear witness to this in being unable to add another class of cause to those discussed above. This is one of the useful pieces of information resulting from the account of the foregoing views. Another is that evidently the principles of things must be investigated in this science, either all those which the ancient philosophers posited, and which have been established above, or some of them. For this science considers chiefly the formal and final cause, and also in a sense the efficient cause. Now it is not only necessary that the above views be discussed, but after this examination it is also necessary to describe the way in which each of these men has spoken (both in what sense their statements are acceptable and in what sense not), and how the statements which have been made about the principles of things contain a problem.

LESSON 12

Criticism of the Views about the Number of Material Principles

ARISTOTLE'S TEXT Chapter 8: 988b22–989b24

1. *Therefore all those who hold that the whole is one and say that there is a certain single nature as matter, and that this is corporeal and has measure, are clearly at fault in many ways. For they give only the elements of bodies and not those of incorporeal things, as if incorporeal things did not exist.* **988b22–26**

2. *And in attempting to state the cause of generation and corruption, and in treating all things according to the method of natural philosophy, they do away with the cause of motion.* **988b26–28**

3. *Furthermore, they did not claim that the substance or whatness of a thing is a cause of anything.* **988b28–29**

4. *And they were wrong in holding that any of the simple bodies except earth is a principle, without considering how they are generated from each other.* **988b29–31**

5. *I mean fire, earth, water and air; for some of these are generated from each other by combination and others by separation. Now it makes the greatest difference as to which of these is prior and which subsequent.* **988b31–34**

6. *For in one way it would seem that the most basic element of all is that from which a thing first comes to be by combination. But such an element will be one which has the smallest parts and is the subtlest of bodies. Hence all those who posit fire as the first principle make statements that conform most closely to this theory. But each of the other thinkers admits that the primary element of bodies is something of this kind.* **988b34–989a5**

7. *For none of the later thinkers, and none of those who spoke about the one, wanted earth to be an element, evidently because of the size of its particles. But each of the other three elements finds some supporter, for some say that this primary element is fire, others water, and others air. But why do they not say that it is earth, as in a sense most men do? For they say that everything is earth. And Hesiod says that earth is the first of bodies to be generated; for this happens to be the ancient and common view. Therefore, according to this theory, if anyone says that any of these bodies with the exception of fire is the primary element of things, or if anyone holds that it is something denser than air but rarer than water, he will not speak the truth.* **989a5–15**

8. *However, if that which is later in generation is prior in nature, and if that which is condensed and compounded is later in generation, then the reverse will be true—water will be prior to air, and earth to water. Let these points suffice, then, regarding those who posit one cause such as we have described.* **989a15–19**

9. *The same consequence will also be true if anyone posits many elements, as Empedocles says that the four [elemental] bodies are the matter of things. For these same consequences must befall this man, as well as some which are peculiar to himself. For we see things being generated from each other in such a way that the same body does not always remain fire or earth. But we have spoken of these matters in our physical treatises.* **989a19–24**

10. *And concerning the cause of things in motion, whether one or more than one must be posited, it must not be thought that what has been said is either entirely correct or reasonable.* **989a25–26**

11. *And in general those who speak thus must do away with alteration, because the cold will not come from the hot, nor the hot from the cold. For what is it that undergoes these contraries, and what is the one nature which becomes fire and water? Such a thing Empedocles does not admit.* **989a26–30**

12. But if anyone were to maintain that Anaxagoras speaks of two elements, they would acknowledge something fully in accord with a theory which he himself has not stated articulately, although he would have been forced to follow those who express this view. For to say, as he did, that in the beginning all things are mixed together is absurd, both because it would be necessary to understand that things previously existed in an unmixed state, and because it is not fitting that anything should be mixed with just anything; and also because properties and accidents could be separated from substances (for there is both mixture and separation of the same things). Yet, if anyone were to follow him up and articulate what he means, his statement would perhaps appear more astonishing. For when nothing was distinct from anything else, evidently nothing would be truly predicated of that substance. I mean that it would neither be white nor black nor tawny, nor have any color, but would necessarily be colorless; for otherwise it would have one of these colors. And, similarly, it would be without humors. And for the same reason it would have no other similar attribute. For it could not have any quality or quantity or whatness, because, if it had, some of the attributes described as formal principles would inhere in it. But this is obviously impossible, since all things are mixed together; for they would already be distinct from each other. But he said that all things are mixed together except intellect, and that this alone is unmixed and pure. Now from these statements it follows for him that there are two principles, one being the intellect itself (for this is unmixed in an absolute sense), and the other being the kind of thing we suppose the indeterminate to be before it is limited and participates in a form. Hence, what he says is neither correct nor clear, although he intends something similar to what later thinkers said and what is now more apparent. But these thinkers are concerned only with theories proper to generation, corruption and motion; for usually it is only of this kind of substance that these men seek the principles and causes. **989a30–989b24**

COMMENTARY

181. Having stated the opinions which the philosophers held about the principles of things, Aristotle begins here to criticize them; and this is divided into two parts. First [1], he criticizes each opinion. Second (see n. 272), he summarizes his discussion and links it up with what follows ("From the foregoing").

The first is divided into two parts. First, he criticizes the opinions of those who have treated things according to the method of natural philosophy. Second (Lesson 13), he criticizes the opinions of those who have not treated things according to the method of natural philosophy, i.e., Pythagoras and Plato, because they posited higher principles than the natural philosophers did ("But all those").

In regard to the first part he does two things. First, he criticizes the opinions of those who posited one material cause; and second [9], the opinions of those who posited many ("The same consequence").

In regard to the first he does two things. First, he criticizes the foregoing opinions in a general way; and second [4], in a special way ("And they were wrong").

He criticizes these opinions in a general way by means of three arguments. The first [1] is this: in the world there are not only bodies but also certain incorporeal things, as is clear from *The Soul. [411a23]* But these men posited only corporeal principles, which is clear from the fact that they maintained that "the whole is one," i.e., that the universe is one thing substantially, and that there is a single nature as matter, and that this is corporeal and has "measure," i.e., dimension. But a body cannot be the cause of an incorporeal thing. Therefore it is evident that they were at fault in this respect that they treated the principles of things inadequately. And they were at fault not only in this respect but in many others, as is clear from the following arguments.

182. **And in attempting** [2].

Here he gives the second argument, which runs thus: whoever feels obliged to establish the truth about motion must posit a cause of motion. But these philosophers felt obliged to treat motion, which is clear for two reasons: first, because they tried to state the causes of generation and corruption in the world, which do not occur without motion; and second, because they wanted to treat things according to the method of natural philosophy. But since a treatment of things according to this method involves motion (because nature is a principle of motion and rest, as is clear in Book II of the *Physics [192b22]*), they should therefore have dealt with that cause which is the source of motion. And since they did away with the cause of motion by saying nothing about it, obviously they were also at fault in this respect.

183. **Furthermore, they did not** [3].

Here he gives the third argument: every natural being has "a substance," i.e., a *form of the part,* "and whatness," i.e., quiddity, which is the *form of the whole.* He says *form* inasmuch as it is a principle of subsistence, and *whatness* inasmuch as it is a principle of knowing, because *what a thing is* is known by means of this. But the foregoing philosophers did not claim that form is a cause of anything. They treated things inadequately, then, and were also at fault in neglecting the formal cause.

184. **For none of the later** [7].

Here he criticizes their opinions in a special way; and he does this with respect to two things. First [7], he criticizes them for maintaining that all the elements with the exception of fire are the principles of things. Second [8], he criticizes them for omitting earth ("However, if").

First [7], he takes up once more the position of those who claimed that each of the simple bodies except earth is the [primary] element of things. The reason which he gives for this position is that these men saw that the simple bodies are generated from each other in such a way that some come from others by combination or compacting, as grosser things come from more refined ones.

185. He also explains how to proceed against their opinions from their own arguments. For they claimed that one of these elements is the principle of things by arguing that other things are generated from it either by combination or by separation. Now it makes the greatest difference as to which of these two ways is prior and which subsequent, for on this depends the priority or posteriority of that from which something is generated. For, on the one hand, that seems to be prior from which something is produced by combination; and he gives this argument first. Yet, on the other hand, that seems to be prior from which something is produced by rarefaction; and he bases his second argument on this.

186. For the fact that the primary element is that from which something is produced by combination supports the opinion which is now held that the most basic element is that from which

other things are produced by combination. This in fact is evident both from reason and from the things that they held. It is evident from reason, because that from which other things are produced by combination is the most refined type of body, and the one having the smallest parts; and this seems to be the simpler body. Hence, if the simple is prior to the composite, this body seems to be first. It is also evident from the things that they held, because all those who posited fire as the principle of things asserted that it is the first principle. Similarly, others have been seen to follow this argument, for they thought that the primary element of bodies is the one having the finest parts. This is evident from the fact that none of the later philosophers followed the theological poets, who said that earth is the primary element of things. Evidently they refused to do this "because of the size of its parts," i.e., because of the coarseness of its parts. However, it is a fact that each of the other three elements finds some philosopher who judges it to be the principle of things. But their refusal to make earth a principle is not to be explained by a refusal to reject a common opinion; for many men thought that earth is the substance of things. Hesiod, who was one of the theological poets, also said that earth is the first of all bodies to come into being. Thus the opinion that earth is the principle of things is evidently an ancient one, because it was maintained by the theological poets, who preceded the philosophers of nature. It was also the common opinion, because many men accepted it. It follows, then, that the later philosophers avoided the position that earth is a principle only because of the coarseness of its parts. But it is certain that earth has coarser parts than water, and water than air, and air than fire; and if there is any intermediate element, it is evident that it is grosser than fire. Hence by following this argument it is clear that none of them spoke correctly, except him who held that fire is the first principle. For as soon as some element is held to be a principle by reason of its minuteness, the most minute element must be held to be the first principle of things.

187. **However, if that which** [8].

Here he gives another argument, and according to it the opposite seems to be true, namely, that earth is the most basic element of things. For it is evident that whatever is subsequent in generation is prior in nature, because nature tends to the goal of generation as the first thing in its intention. But the denser and more composite something is, the later it appears in the process of generation; for the process of generation proceeds from simple things to composite ones, just as mixed bodies come from the elements, and the humors and members [of a living body] from mixed bodies. Hence, whatever is more composite and condensed is prior in nature. In this way a conclusion is reached which is the opposite of that following from the first argument; i.e., water is now prior to air and earth to water as the first principle of things.

188. It should be noted, however, that it is a different thing to look for what is prior in one and the same entity and for what is prior without qualification. For if one seeks what is prior without qualification, the perfect must be prior to the imperfect, just as actuality is prior to potentiality; because a thing is brought from a state of imperfection to one of perfection, or from potentiality to actuality, only by some-

thing completely actual. Therefore, if we speak of what is first in the whole universe, it must be the most perfect thing. But in the case of one particular thing which goes from potentiality to complete actuality, potentiality is prior to actuality in time, although it is subsequent in nature. It is also clear that the first of all things must be one that is simplest; for the composite depends on the simple, and not the reverse. It was necessary, then, that the ancient philosophers should attribute both of these properties (the greatest perfection along with the greatest simplicity) to the first principle of the whole universe. However, these two properties cannot be attributed simultaneously to any corporeal principle, for in bodies subject to generation and corruption the simplest entities are imperfect. They were compelled, then, as by contrary arguments, to posit different principles. Yet they preferred the argument of simplicity, because they considered things only insofar as something passes from potentiality to actuality, and in this order it is not necessary that anything which is a principle should be more perfect. But this kind of opposition can be resolved only by maintaining that the first principle of things is incorporeal, because this principle will be the simplest one, as Aristotle will prove below (see n. 2548).

189. Last of all he concludes that for the purpose of the present discussion enough has been said about the positions of those who affirm one material cause.

190. **The same consequence** [9].

Here he gives the arguments against those who posited many material causes. First [9], he argues against Empedocles; and second [12], against Anaxagoras ("But if anyone").

First [9], he says that the same consequence faces Empedocles, who held that the four [elemental] bodies are the matter of things, because he experienced the same difficulty with regard to the above contrariety. For according to the argument of simplicity fire would seem to be the most basic principle of bodies; and according to the other argument earth would seem to be such, as has been stated [8]. And while Empedocles faced some of the same absurd conclusions as the preceding philosophers (i.e., he did not posit either a formal cause or the aforesaid contrariety of simplicity and perfection in corporeal things), there is no argument against him for doing away with the cause of motion. But he did face certain other absurd conclusions besides those that confronted the philosophers who posited one material cause.

191. This is shown by three arguments, of which the first is as follows. First principles are not generated from each other, because a principle must always remain in existence, as is pointed out in Book I of the *Physics.[188a26]* But we perceive that the four elements are generated from each other, and for this reason their generation is dealt with in natural philosophy. Hence his position that the four elements are the first principles of things is untenable.

192. **And concerning the cause** [10].

Here he gives the second absurdity, which has to do with the cause of motion. For to posit many and contrary causes of motion is not at all correct or reasonable; because if the causes of motion are understood to be proximate ones, they must be contraries, since their effects seem to be contraries. But if the first cause is understood, then it must be unique, as is apparent in Book XII (see n. 2492) of this work, and in Book VIII of the *Physics.[259a14]* Therefore, since he intends to posit the first causes of motion, his position that they are contraries is untenable.

193. **And in general** [11].

Here he gives the third argument which leads to an absurdity: in every process of alteration it must be the same subject which undergoes contraries. This is true because one contrary does not come from another in such a way that one is converted into the other; for example, the cold does not come from the hot in such a way that heat itself becomes cold or the reverse, although the cold does come from the hot when the underlying subject is one only inasmuch as the single subject which is now the subject of heat is afterwards the subject of cold. But Empedocles did not hold that contraries have one subject. In fact he held that they are found in different subjects, as heat in fire and cold in water. Nor again did he hold that there is one nature underlying these two. Therefore he could not posit alteration in any way. Yet it is absurd that alteration should be done away with altogether.

194. **But if anyone** [12].

Here he deals with Anaxagoras' opinion; and in regard to this he does two things. First, he shows in general in what respect Anaxagoras' opinion should be accepted as true, and in what respect not. Second [12], he explains each of these in particular ("For to say").

He says, first, that if anyone wishes to maintain that Anaxagoras' opinion is true insofar as he posited two principles, i.e., matter and efficient cause, let him understand this according to the reasoning which Anaxagoras himself seems to have followed, as if compelled by some need for truth, inasmuch as he would have followed those who expressed this theory. But "he himself has not stated it articulately"; i.e., he has not expressed it distinctly. Therefore, with reference to what he has not expressly stated his opinion is true; but with reference to what he has expressly stated his opinion is false.

195. This is made clear in particular as follows. If his opinion is taken in its entirety according to a superficial understanding of his statements, a greater absurdity will appear for four reasons. First, his opinion that all things were mixed together at the beginning of the world is absurd; for in Aristotle's opinion the distinction between the parts of the world is thought to be eternal. The second reason is this: what is unmixed is related to what is mixed as the simple to the composite. But simple bodies are prior to composite ones, and not the reverse. Therefore what is unmixed must be prior to what is mixed. This is the opposite of what Anaxagoras said. The third reason is this: in the case of bodies not anything at all is naturally disposed to be mixed with anything else, but only those things are naturally disposed to be mixed which are naturally inclined to pass over into each other by some kind of alteration; for a mixture is a union of the altered things which are capable of being mixed. But Anaxagoras held that anything is mixed with just anything. The fourth reason is this: there is both mixture and separation of the same things; for only those things are said to be mixed which are naturally disposed to exist apart. But properties and accidents are mixed with substances, as Anaxagoras said. Therefore it follows that properties and accidents can exist apart from substances. This is evidently false. These absurdities appear

then, if Anaxagoras' opinion is considered in a superficial way.

196. Yet if anyone were to follow him up "and articulate," i.e., investigate clearly and distinctly, the things which Anaxagoras "means," i.e., what he intended, although he did not know how to express this, his statement would appear to be more astonishing and subtler than those of the preceding philosophers. This will be so for two reasons. First, he came closer to a true understanding of matter. This is clear from the fact that in that mixture of things, when nothing was distinguished from anything else but all things were mixed together, nothing could be truly predicated of that substance which is so mixed, which he held to be the matter of things. This is clear in the case of colors; for no special color could be predicated of it so that it might be said to be white or black or have some other color; because, according to this, that color would necessarily be unmixed with other things. Nor, similarly, could color in general be predicated of it so that it might be said to be colored; because everything of which a generic term is predicated must also have a specific term predicated of it, whether the predication be univocal or denominative. Hence, if that substance were colored, it would necessarily have some special color. But this is opposed to the foregoing statement. And the argument is similar with respect to "humors," i.e., savors, and to all other things of this kind. Hence the primary genera themselves could not be predicated of it in such a way that it would have quality or quantity or some attribute of this kind. For if these genera were predicated of it, some particular species would necessarily belong to it. But this is impossible, if all things are held to be mixed together. For this species which would be predicated of that substance would already be distinguished from the others. And this is the true nature of matter, namely, that it does not have any form actually but is in potentiality to all forms. For the mixed body itself does not have actually any of the things which combine in its mixture, but has them only potentially. And it is because of this likeness between prime matter and what is mixed that he seems to have posited the above mixture; although there is some difference between the potentiality of matter and that of a mixture. For even though the elements which constitute a mixture are present in the mixture potentially, they are still not present in a state of pure passive potency; for they remain virtually in the mixture. This can be shown from the fact that a mixture has motion and operations as a result of the bodies of which the mixture is composed. But this cannot be said of the things which are present potentially in prime matter. And there is also another difference, namely, that even though a mixture is not actually any of the mixed bodies which it contains, yet it is something actual. This cannot be said of prime matter. But Anaxagoras seems to do away with this difference, because he has not posited any particular mixture but the universal mixture of all things.

197. The second reason is this: he spoke more subtly than the others, because he came closer to a true understanding of the first active principle. For he said that all things are mixed together except intellect, and that this alone is unmixed and pure.

198. From these things it is clear that he posited two principles: one of these he claimed to be the intellect itself, insofar as it is simple and unmixed with

other things; and the other is prime matter, which we claim is like the indeterminate before it is limited and participates in a form. For since [prime] matter is [the subject] of an infinite number of forms, it is limited by a form and acquires some species by means of it.

199. It is clear, then, that, in regard to the things which he stated expressly, Anaxagoras neither spoke correctly nor clearly. Yet he would seem to say something directly which comes closer to the opinions of the later philosophers, which are truer (namely, to those of Plato and Aristotle, whose judgments about prime matter were correct) and which were then more apparent.

200. In concluding Aristotle excuses himself from a more diligent investigation of these opinions, because the statements of these philosophers belong to the realm of physical discussions, which treat of generation and corruption. For these men usually posited principles and causes of this kind of substance, i.e., of material and corruptible substance. He says "usually," because, while they did not treat other substances, certain of the principles laid down by them can also be extended to other substances. This is most evident in the case of intellect. Therefore, since they have not posited principles common to all substances, which pertains to this science, but only principles of corruptible substances, which pertains to the philosophy of nature, a diligent study of the foregoing opinions belongs rather to the philosophy of nature than to this science.

LESSON 13
Criticism of the Pythagoreans' Opinions

ARISTOTLE'S TEXT Chapters 8 & 9: 989b24–990a34

1. *But all those who make a study of all existing things, and who claim that some are sensible and others not, evidently make a study of both classes. And for this reason one should dwell at greater length on the statements they have made, whether they be acceptable or not, for the purposes of the present study which we now propose to make.* **989b24–29**

2. *Therefore, those who are called Pythagoreans used principles and elements which are foreign to the physicists; and the reason is that they did not take them from sensible things. For the objects of mathematics, with the exception of those that pertain to astronomy, are devoid of motion. Nevertheless they discuss and treat everything that has to do with the physical world; for they generate the heavens and observe what happens in regard to its parts, affections and operations. And in doing this they use up their principles and causes, as though they agreed with the others, i.e., the physicists, that whatever exists is sensible and is contained by the so-called heavens. But, as we have stated, the causes and principles [of which they speak] are sufficient to extend even to a higher class of beings, and are better suited to these than to their theories about the physical world.* **989b29–990a8**

3. *Yet how there will be motion if only the limited and unlimited and even and odd are posited as principles, they do not say. But how can there be generation or corruption, or the activities of those bodies which traverse the heavens, if there is no motion or change?* **990a8–12**

4. *And further, whether one grants them that continuous quantities come from these things, or whether this is demonstrated, how is it that some bodies are light and others heavy? For from what they suppose and state, they say nothing more about mathematical bodies than they do about sensible ones. Hence they have said nothing about fire, earth and other bodies of this kind, since they have nothing to say that is proper to sensible things.* **990a12–18**

5. *Further, how are we to understand that the attributes of number and number itself are [the causes] of what exists and comes to pass in the heavens, both from the beginning and now? And how are we to understand that there is no other number except that of which the world is composed? For when they [place] opportunity and opinion in one part of the heavens, and a little above or below them injustice and separation or mixture, and when they state as proof of this that each of these is a number, and claim that there already happens to be in this place a plurality of quantities constituted [of numbers], because these attributes of number correspond to each of these places, [we may ask] whether this number which is in the heavens is the same as that which we understand each [sensible] thing to be, or whether there is another kind of number in addition to this? For Plato says there is another. In fact, he also thinks that both these things and their causes are numbers, but that some are intellectual causes and others sensible ones.*

Chapter 9

Regarding the Pythagoreans, then, let us dismiss them for the present; for it is enough to have touched upon them to the extent that we have. **990a18–34**

COMMENTARY

201. Here he argues dialectically against the opinions of Pythagoras and Plato, who posited different principles than those which pertain to the philosophy of nature. In regard to this he does two things. First [1]), he shows that a study of these opinions rather than those mentioned above belongs

to the present science. Second [2], he begins to argue dialectically against these opinions ("Therefore those who").

He says, first [1], then, that those who "make a study," i.e., an investigation, of all existing things, and hold that some are sensible and others non-sensible, make a study of both classes of beings. Hence an investigation of the opinions of those who spoke either correctly or incorrectly, belongs rather to the study which we now propose to make in this science. For this science deals with all beings and not with some particular class of being. Hence, the things which pertain to every class of being are to be considered here rather than those which pertain to some particular class of being.

202. **Therefore those who** [2].

Here he argues against the opinions of the foregoing philosophers. First (99), he argues against Pythagoras; and second (103:C 208), against Plato ("But those who posited Ideas").

In regard to the first he does two things. First, he shows in what way Pythagoras agreed with the philosophers of nature, and in what way he differed from them. Second [3], he argues against Pythagoras' position ("Yet how").

We must understand [2], then, that in one respect the Pythagoreans agreed with the philosophers of nature, and in another respect they differed from them. They differed from them in their position regarding principles, because they employed principles of things in a way foreign to the philosophers of nature. The reason is that they did not take the principles of things from sensible beings, as the natural philosophers did, but from the objects of mathematics, which are devoid of motion, and are therefore not physical. And the statement that the objects of mathematics are devoid of motion must be referred to those sciences which are purely mathematical, such as arithmetic and geometry. Astronomy considers motion, because astronomy is a science midway between mathematics and natural philosophy. For astronomy and the other intermediate sciences apply their principles to natural things, as is clear in Book II of the *Physics.[194a8]*

203. Now Pythagoras agreed with the philosophers of nature concerning the things whose principles he sought; for he discussed and treated all natural beings. He dealt with the generation of the heavens, and observed everything that happens to the parts of the heavens, by which are meant the different spheres, or also the different stars. He also considered what happens to its affections, or to the eclipses of the luminous bodies; and what happens to the operations and motions of the heavenly bodies, and their effects on lower bodies. And he used up causes on particular things of this kind by applying to each one its proper cause. He also seemed to agree with the other philosophers of nature in thinking that that alone has being which is sensible and is contained by the heavens which we see. For he did not posit an infinite sensible body as the other philosophers of nature did. Nor again did he hold that there are many worlds, as Democritus did. He therefore seemed to think that there are no beings except sensible ones, because he assigned principles and causes only for such substances. However, the causes and principles which he laid down are not proper or limited to sensible things, but are sufficient for ascending to higher beings, i.e., intellectual ones. And they were better fitted to these

than the theories of the natural philosophers which could not be extended beyond sensible things, because these philosophers claimed that principles are corporeal. But since Pythagoras posited incorporeal principles, i.e., numbers, although he only posited principles of sensible bodies, he came very close to positing principles of intelligible beings, which are not bodies, as Plato did later on.

204. **Yet how** [3].

Here he gives three arguments against the opinion of Pythagoras. The first is this: Pythagoras could not explain how motion originates in the world, because he posited as principles only the limited and unlimited and the even and odd, which he held to be principles as substance, or material principles. But he had to admit that there is motion in the world. For how could there be generation and corruption in bodies, and how could there be any activities of the heavenly bodies, which occur as a result of certain kinds of motion, unless motion and change existed? Evidently they could not exist in any way. Hence, since Pythagoras considered generation and corruption and the operations of the heavenly bodies without assigning any principle of motion, his position is clearly unsatisfactory.

205. **And further** [4].

Here he gives the second argument. For Pythagoras claimed that continuous quantities are composed of numbers. But whether he proves this or takes it for granted, he could not give any reason on the part of numbers as to why some things are heavy and others light. This is clear from the fact that his theories about numbers are no more adapted to sensible bodies than they are to the objects of mathematics, which are neither heavy nor light. Hence they obviously said nothing more about sensible bodies than they did about the objects of mathematics. Therefore, since sensible bodies, such as earth and fire and the like, considered in themselves, add something over and above the objects of mathematics, it is evident that they said nothing proper in any true sense about these sensible bodies. Thus it is also evident that the principles which they laid down are not sufficient, since they neglected to give the causes of those [attributes] which are proper to sensible bodies.

206. **Further, how are we** [5].

Here he gives the third argument, which is based on the fact that Pythagoras seemed to hold two contrary [positions]. For, on the one hand, he held that number and the attributes of number are the cause both of those events which occur in the heavens and of all generable and corruptible things from the beginning of the world. Yet, on the other hand, he held that there is no other number besides that of which the substance of things is composed; for he held that number is the substance of things. But how is this to be understood, since one and the same thing is not the cause of itself? For Pythagoras says that the former position may be demonstrated from the fact that each one of these sensible things is numerical in substance; because in this part of the universe there are contingent beings, about which there is opinion, and which are subject to time inasmuch as they sometimes are and sometimes are not. But if generable and corruptible things were partly above or partly below, there would be disorder in the order of the universe: either after the manner of injustice, i.e., insofar as some being would receive a nobler or less noble place than it ought to have; or after the manner of separation, i.e., in the sense that, if a body were located outside its own place, it would be separated from bodies of a like nature; or after the manner of mixture and mingling, provided that a body located outside its proper place must be mixed with some other body, for example, if some part of water occupied a place belonging to air or to earth. In this discussion he seems to touch on two ways in which a natural body conforms to its proper place: one pertains to the order of position, according to which nobler bodies receive a higher place, in which there seems to be a kind of justice; and the other pertains to the similarity or dissimilarity between bodies in place, to which separation and mingling may be opposed. Therefore, insofar as things have a definite position, they are fittingly situated in the universe. For if their position were changed ever so little, something unfitting would result, inasmuch as it has been stated and shown that all parts of the universe are arranged in a definite proportion; for every definite proportion is numerical. And it was from this that Pythagoras showed that all things would be numbers. But, on the other hand, we see that the continuous quantities established in different places are many and different, because the particular places in the universe correspond to the proper attributes by which bodies are differentiated. For the attributes of bodies which are above differ from those which are below. Hence, since Pythagoras by means of the above argument affirms that all sensible things are numbers, and we see that the difference in sensible bodies is attributable to difference in place, the question arises whether the number which exists "in the heavens," i.e., in the whole visible body which comprises the heavens, is merely the same as that which must be understood to be the substance of each sensible thing, or whether besides this number which constitutes the substance of sensible things there is another number which is their cause. Now Plato said that there is one kind of number which is the substance of sensible things, and another which is their cause. And while both Plato himself and Pythagoras thought that numbers are both sensible bodies themselves and their causes, Plato alone considered intellectual numbers to be the causes of things that are not sensible, and sensible numbers to be the causes and forms of sensible things. And since Pythagoras did not do this, his position is unsatisfactory.

207. In concluding Aristotle says that these remarks about the Pythagoreans' opinions will suffice; for it is enough to have touched upon them to this extent.

LESSON 14
Arguments against the Platonic Ideas

ARISTOTLE'S TEXT Chapter 9: 990a34–991a8

1. *But those who posited Ideas, and were the first to seek an understanding of the causes of sensible things, introduced other principles equal in number to these—as though one who wishes to count things thinks that this cannot be done when they are few, but believes that he can count them after he has increased their number. For the separate Forms are almost equal to, or not fewer than, these sensible things in the search for whose causes these thinkers have proceeded from sensible things to the Forms. For to each thing there corresponds some homogeneous entity bearing the same name; and with regard to the substances of other things there is a one-in-many, both in the case of these sensible things and in those which are eternal.* **99034–990b8**

2. *Furthermore, with regard to the ways in which we prove that there are Forms, according to none of these do they become evident. For from some no syllogism necessarily follows, whereas from others there does; and [according to these] there are Forms of things of which we do not think there are Forms.* **990b8–11**

3. *For according to those arguments from [the existence of] the sciences there will be Forms of all things of which there are sciences; and according to the argument of the one-in-many there will also be Forms of negations.* **990b11–13**

4. *Again, according to the argument that there is some understanding of corruption, there will be Forms of corruptible things; for of these there is some sensible image.* **990b13–15**

5. *Again, according to the most certain arguments [for the Forms] some establish Forms of relations, of which they deny there is any essential class; whereas others lead to "the third man."* **990b15–17**

6. *And in general the arguments for the Forms do away with the existence of the things which those who speak of the Forms are more anxious to retain than the Forms themselves. For it happens that the dyad [or duality] is not first, but that number is; and that the relative is prior to that which exists of itself. And all the other [conclusions] which some [reach] by following up the opinions about the Ideas are opposed to the principles [of the theory].* **990a17–22**

7. *Again, according to the opinion whereby we claim that there are Ideas [or Forms], there will be Forms not only of substances but also of many other things. For there is one concept not only in the case of substances but also in that of other things; and there are sciences not only of substance itself but also of other things. And a thousand other such [difficulties] face them.* **990a22–27**

8. *But according to logical necessity and the opinions about the Ideas, if the Forms are participated in, there must be Ideas only of substances. For they are not participated in according to what is accidental. But things must participate in each Form in this respect: insofar as each Form is not predicated of a subject. I mean that if anything participates in doubleness itself, it also participates in the eternal, but only accidentally; for it is an accident of doubleness to be eternal. Hence the Forms will be substances.* **990a27–34**

9. *But these things signify substance both here and in the ideal world; [otherwise] why is it necessary that a one-in-many appear in addition to these sensible things? Indeed, if the form of the Ideas and that of the things which participate in them are the same, there will be something in common. For why should duality be one and the same in the case of corruptible twos and in those which are many but eternal, rather than in the case of this [Idea of duality] and a particular two? But if the form is not the same, there will be pure equivocation; just as if one*

were to call both Callias and a piece of wood man, without observing any common attribute which they might have. **990b34–991a8**

COMMENTARY

208. Here he argues disputatively against Plato's opinion. This is divided into two parts. First (103:C 208), he argues against Plato's opinion with reference to his position about the substances of things; and second [1], with reference to his position about the principles of things ("And in general").

The first is divided into two parts. First, he argues against Plato's position that the Forms are substances; and second (see n. 239), against the things that he posited about the objects of mathematics ("Further, if the Forms").

In regard to the first he does two things. First, he argues against this position of Plato; and second [2], against the reasoning behind it ("Furthermore, with regard to").

He says, first [1], that the Platonists, in holding that the Ideas are certain separate substances, seemed to be at fault in that, when they sought for the causes of these sensible beings, they neglected sensible beings and invented certain other new entities equal in number to sensible beings. This seems to be absurd, because one who seeks the causes of certain things ought to make these evident and not add other things, the premising of which only adds to the number of points which have to be investigated. For it would be similar if a man who wished to count certain things which he did not think he was able to count because they are few, believed that he could count them by increasing their number through the addition of certain other things. But it is evident that such a man has a foolish motive, because the path is clearer when there are fewer things; for it is better and easier to make certain of fewer things than of many. And the smaller a number is, the more certain it is to us, inasmuch as it is nearer to the unit, which is the most accurate measure. And just as the process of counting things is the measure we use to make certain of their number, in a similar fashion an investigation of the causes of things is the accurate measure for making certain of their natures. Therefore, just as the number of fewer numerable things is made certain of more easily, in a similar way the nature of fewer things is made certain of more easily. Hence, when Plato increased the classes of beings to the extent that he did with a view to explaining sensible things, he added to the number of difficulties by taking what is more difficult in order to explain what is less difficult. This is absurd.

209. That the Ideas are equal in number to, or not fewer than, sensible things, whose causes the Platonists seek (and Aristotle includes himself among their number because he was Plato's disciple), and which they established by going from sensible things to the aforesaid Forms, becomes evident if one considers by what reasoning the Platonists introduced the Ideas. Now they reasoned thus: they saw that there is a one-in-many for all things having the same name. Hence they claimed that this one-in-many is a Form. Yet with respect to all substances of things other than the Ideas we see that there is found to be a one-in-many which is predicated of them univocally inasmuch as there are found to be many things which are specifically one. This

occurs not only in the case of sensible things but also in that of the objects of mathematics, which are eternal; because among these there are also many things which are specifically one, as was stated above (see n. 157). Hence it follows that some Idea corresponds to each species of sensible things; and therefore each Idea is something having the same name as these sensible things, because the Ideas agree with them in name. For just as Socrates is called man, so also is the Idea of man. Yet they differ conceptually; for the intelligible structure of Socrates contains matter, whereas that of the ideal man is devoid of matter. Or, according to another reading, each Form is said to be something having the same name [as these sensible things] inasmuch as it is a one-in-many and agrees with the things of which it is predicated so far as the intelligible structure of the species is concerned. Hence he says that they are equal to, or not fewer than, these things. For either there are held to be Ideas only of species, and then they would be equal in number to these sensible things (granted that things are counted here insofar as they differ specifically and not individually, for the latter difference is infinite); or there are held to be Ideas not only of species but also of genera, and then there would be more Ideas than there are species of sensible things, because all species would be Ideas and in addition to these each and every genus [would be an Idea]. This is why he says that they are either not fewer than or more. Or, in another way, they are said to be equal inasmuch as he claimed that they are the Forms of sensible things. And he says not fewer than but more inasmuch as he held that they are the Forms not only of sensible things but also of the objects of mathematics.

210. **Furthermore, with regard to** [2].

Here he argues dialectically against the reasoning behind Plato's position; and in regard to this he does two things. First (104), he gives a general account of the ways in which Plato's arguments fail. Second [3], he explains them in detail ("For according to those").

He says, first [2], that with regard to the ways in which we Platonists prove the existence of the Forms, according to none of these are the Forms seen to exist. The reason is that "no syllogism follows" necessarily from some of these ways, i.e., from certain arguments of Plato, because they cannot demonstrate with necessity the existence of the Ideas. However, from other arguments a syllogism does follow, although it does not support Plato's thesis; for by certain of his arguments there are proved to be Forms of certain things of which the Platonists did not think there are Forms, just as there are proved to be Forms of those things of which they think there are Forms.

211. **For according to** [3].

Here he examines in detail the arguments by which the Platonists establish Ideas. First, he examines the second argument; and he does this by showing that from Plato's argument it follows that there are Forms of some things for which the Platonists did not posit Forms. Second (Lesson 15), he examines the first argument; and he does this by showing that Plato's arguments are not sufficient to prove that Ideas exist ("But the most").

In regard to the first member of this division he gives seven arguments. The first is this: one of the arguments that induced Plato to posit Ideas is taken from scientific knowledge; for since science is concerned with necessary things, it cannot be concerned with sensible things, which are corruptible, but must be concerned with separate entities which are incorruptible. According to the argument taken from the sciences, then, it follows that there are Forms of every sort of thing of which there are sciences. Now there are sciences not only of that which is one-in-many, which is affirmative, but also of negations; for just as there are some demonstrations which conclude with an affirmative proposition, in a similar way there are demonstrations which conclude with a negative proposition. Hence it is also necessary to posit Ideas of negations.

212. **Again, according to the argument** [4].

Here he gives the second argument. For in the sciences it is not only understood that some things always exist in the same way, but also that some things are destroyed; otherwise the philosophy of nature, which deals with motion, would be destroyed. Therefore, if there must be Ideas of all the things which are comprehended in the sciences, there must be Ideas of corruptible things as such, i.e., insofar as these are singular sensible things; for thus are things corruptible. But according to Plato's theory it cannot be said that those sciences by which we understand the processes of corruption in the world attain any understanding of the processes of corruption in sensible things; for there is no comprehension of these sensible things, but only imagination or phantasy, which is a motion produced by the senses in their act of sensing, as is pointed out in *The Soul,* Book II.[428b10]

213. **Again, according to the most** [5].

Here he gives the third argument, which contains two conclusions that he says are drawn from the most certain arguments of Plato. One conclusion is this: if there are Ideas of all things of which there are sciences, and there are sciences not only of absolutes but also of things predicated relatively, then in giving this argument it follows that there are also Ideas of relations. This is opposed to Plato's view. For, since the separate Ideas are things which exist of themselves, which is opposed to the intelligibility of a relation, Plato did not hold that there is a class of Ideas of relations, because the Ideas are said to exist of themselves.

214. The second conclusion is one which follows from other most certain arguments, namely, that there is "a third man." This phrase can be understood in three ways. First, it can mean that the ideal man is a third man distinct from two men perceived by the senses, who have the common name man predicated of both of them. But this does not seem to be what he has in mind, even though it is not mentioned in the *Sophistical Refutations,* Book II; for this is the position against which he argues. Hence according to this it would not lead to an absurdity.

215. The second way in which this expression can be understood is this: the third man means one that is common to the ideal man and to one perceived by the senses. For since both a man perceived by the senses and the ideal man have a common intelligible structure, like two men perceived by the senses, then just as the ideal man is held to be a third man in addition to two men perceived by the senses, in a similar way there should be held to be another third man in addition to the ideal man and one perceived by the senses. But neither does this seem to be what he has in mind here, because he

leads us immediately to this absurdity by means of another argument. Hence it would be pointless to lead us to the same absurdity here.

216. The third way in which this expression can be understood is this: Plato posited three kinds of entities in certain classes of things, namely, sensible substances, the objects of mathematics and the Forms. He does this, for example, in the case of numbers, lines and the like. But there is no reason why intermediate things should be held to exist in certain classes rather than in others. Hence in the class of man it was also necessary to posit an intermediate man, who will be a third man midway between the man perceived by the senses and the ideal man. Aristotle also gives this argument in the later books of this work (cf.n. 2160).

217. **And in general** [6].

Here he gives the fourth argument, which runs as follows. Whoever by his own reasoning does away with certain [principles] which are better known to him than the ones which he posits, adopts an absurd position. But these theories about the Forms which Plato held do away with certain principles whose reality the Platonists (when they said that there are Ideas) were more convinced of than the existence of the Ideas. Therefore Plato's position is absurd. The minor premise is proved in this way. According to Plato the Ideas are prior both to sensible things and to the objects of mathematics. But according to him the Ideas themselves are numbers; and they are odd numbers rather than even ones, because he attributed odd number to form and even number to matter. Hence he also said that the dyad [or duality] is matter. Therefore it follows that other numbers are prior to the dyad, which he held to be the matter of sensible things, and identified with the great and small. Yet the Platonists asserted the very opposite of this, that is to say, that the dyad is first in the class of number.

218. Again, if, as has been proved by the above argument [5], there must be Ideas of relations, which are self-subsistent relations, and if the Idea itself is prior to whatever participates in the Idea, it follows that the relative is prior to the absolute, which is said to exist of itself. For sensible substances of this kind, which participate in Ideas, are said to be in an unqualified sense. And in like manner whatever those who follow the opinion about the Ideas say of all things is opposed to self-evident principles which even they themselves are most ready to acknowledge.

219. **Again, according to the opinion** [7].

Here he gives the fifth argument, which is as follows: Ideas were posited by Plato in order that the intelligible structures and definitions of things given in the sciences might correspond to them, and in order that there could be sciences of them. But there is "one concept," i.e., a simple and indivisible concept, by which the quiddity of each thing is known, i.e., not only the quiddity of substances "but also of other things," namely, of accidents. And in a similar way there are sciences not only of substance and about substance, but there are also found to be sciences "of other things," i.e., of accidents. Hence according to the opinion by which you Platonists acknowledge the existence of Ideas, it evidently follows that there will be Forms not only of substances but also of other things, i.e., of accidents. This same conclusion follows not only because of definitions and the sciences, but there also happen to be many "other such" [reasons], i.e., very many reasons why it is necessary to posit Ideas of accidents according to Plato's arguments. For example, he held that the Ideas are the principles of being and of becoming in the world, and of many such aspects which apply to accidents.

220. But, on the other hand, according to Plato's opinion about the Ideas and according to logical necessity, insofar as the Ideas are indispensable to sensible things, i.e., "insofar" as they are capable of being participated in by sensible things, it is necessary to posit Ideas only of substances. This is proved thus: things which are accidental are not participated in. But an Idea must be participated in by each thing insofar as it is not predicated of a subject. This becomes clear as follows: if any sensible thing participates in "doubleness itself," i.e., in a separate doubleness (for Plato spoke of all separated things in this way, namely, as self-subsisting things), it must participate in the eternal. But it does not do this essentially (because then it would follow that any double perceived by the senses would be eternal), but accidentally, i.e., insofar as doubleness itself, which is participated in, is eternal. And from this it is evident that there is no participation in things which are accidental, but only in substances. Hence according to Plato's position a separate Form was not an accident but only a substance. Yet according to the argument taken from the sciences there must also be Forms of accidents, as was stated above [7].

221. **But these things** [9].

Then he gives the sixth argument, which runs thus: these sensible things signify substance both in the case of things perceived by the senses and in that of those in the ideal world, i.e., in the case of intelligible things, which signify substance; because they held that both intelligible things and sensible ones are substance. Therefore it is necessary to posit in addition to both of these substances—intelligible and sensible ones—some common entity which is a one-in-many. For the Platonists maintained that the Ideas exist on the grounds that they found a one-in-many which they believed to be separate from the many.

222. The need for positing a one apart from both sensible substances and the Forms he proves thus: the Ideas and the sensible things which participate in them either belong to one class or not. If they belong to one class, and it is necessary to posit, according to Plato's position, one common separate Form for all things having a common nature, then it will be necessary to posit some entity common to both sensible things and the Ideas themselves, which exists apart from both. Now one cannot answer this argument by saying that the Ideas, which are incorporeal and immaterial, do not stand in need of any higher Forms; because the objects of mathematics, which Plato places midway between sensible substances and the Forms, are similarly incorporeal and immaterial. Yet since many of them are found to belong to one species, Plato held that there is a common Form for these things, in which not only the objects of mathematics participate but also sensible substances. Therefore, if the twoness [or duality] which is the Form or Idea of twoness is identical with that found in sensible twos, which are corruptible (just as a pattern is found in the things fashioned after it), and with that found in mathematical twos, which are many in one class (but are nevertheless eternal), then for the same reason in the case of the same

twoness, i.e., the Idea two, and in that of the other twoness, which is either mathematical or sensible, there will be another separate twoness. For no reason can be given why the former should exist and the latter should not.

223. But if the other alternative is admitted—that sensible things, which participate in the Ideas, do not have the same form as the Ideas—it follows that the name which is predicated of both the Ideas and sensible substances is predicated in a purely equivocal way. For those things are said to be equivocal which have only a common name and differ in their intelligible structure. And it follows that they are not only equivocal in every way but equivocal in an absolute sense, like those things on which one name is imposed without regard for any common attribute, which are said to be equivocal by chance; for example, if one were to call both Callias and a piece of wood man.

224. Now Aristotle added this because someone might say that a name is not predicated of an Idea and of a sensible substance in a purely equivocal way, since a name is predicated of an Idea essentially and of a sensible substance by participation. For, according to Plato, the Idea of man is called "man in himself," whereas this man whom we apprehend by the senses is said to be a man by participation. However, such an equivocation is not pure equivocation. But a name which is predicated by participation is predicated with reference to something that is predicated essentially; and this is not pure equivocation but the multiplicity of analogy. However, if an Idea and a sensible substance were altogether equivocal by chance, it would follow that one could not be known through the other, as one equivocal thing cannot be known through another.

LESSON 15
The Destruction of the Platonists' Arguments for Ideas

ARISTOTLE'S TEXT Chapter 9: 991a8–991b9

1. But the most important problem of all that one might raise is what the Forms contribute to sensible things, either to those which are eternal or to those which are generated and corrupted. **991a8–10**

2. For they are not the cause of motion or of any change whatever in these things. **991a11**

3. Nor are they of any assistance in knowing other things; for they are not the substance of other things, because if they were they would exist in them. Nor do they contribute anything to the being of other things; for they are not present in the things which participate in them. For if they were they would perhaps seem to be causes, as whiteness mixed with some white thing. But this theory, which was first stated by Anaxagoras and later by Hesiod and certain other thinkers, is easily disposed of. For it is easy to bring many absurd conclusions against such a view. In fact other things are not derived from the Forms in any of the customary senses. **991a12–20**

4. Again, to say that they are exemplars, and that other things participate in them, is to speak with empty talk and to utter poetic metaphors. **991a20–22**

5. For what is the work which looks towards the Ideas [as an examplar]? [Timaeus, 28C] For one thing may both be and become similar to another thing and not be made in likeness to it. So whether Socrates exists or not, a man such as Socrates might come to be. **991a22–26**

6. Similarly, it is evident that this will be the case even if Socrates is eternal. And there will be many exemplars of the same thing, and for this reason many Forms, as animal and two-footed and man-in-himself will be the Form of man. **991a26–29**

7. Further, the Forms will be the exemplars not only of sensible things but also of the Forms themselves, as the genus of the species. Hence the same thing will be both an exemplar and a copy. **991a29–991b1**

8. Again, it is thought to be impossible that the substance of a thing and that of which it is the substance should exist apart. Hence, if the Forms are the substances of things, how will they exist apart from them? **9981b1–991b3**

9. But in the Phaedo [100D] it is stated that the Forms are the causes both of being and of coming to be. Yet even if the Forms do exist, still the things which participate in them will not come to be unless there is something which produces motion. **991b3–5**

10. And many other things come to be, such as a house and a ring, of which we do not say that there are any Forms. It is evident, then, that other things can exist and come to be because of such causes as those [responsible for the things] just mentioned. **991b6–9**

COMMENTARY

225. Here Aristotle attacks the opinion of Plato insofar as he did not draw the conclusion which he intended to draw. For Plato intended to conclude that there are Ideas by this argument that they are necessary in some way for sensible things. Hence, Aristotle, by showing that the Ideas cannot contribute anything to sensible things, destroys the arguments by which Plato posits Ideas. Thus he says [1] that of all the objections which may be raised against Plato the foremost is that the Forms which Plato posited do not seem to contribute anything to sensible things, either to those which are eternal, as the celestial bodies, or to those which are generated and corrupted, as

the elemental bodies. He shows [2] that this criticism applies to each of the arguments by which Plato posited Ideas ("For they are not").

226. At this point in the text [2] he begins to present his five objections [against the Platonic arguments for Ideas].

He argues, first [2], that they are useless in explaining motion; second [3], that they are useless in explaining our knowledge of sensible things ("Nor are they"); third [4], that they are of no value as exemplars ("Again, to say"); fourth [8], that they are of no value as the substances of things ("Again, it is thought"); and fifth [9], that they are of no value as causes of generation ("But in the *Phaedo*").

Accordingly, he says, first [2], that the Forms cannot contribute anything to sensible things in such a way as to be the cause of motion or of any kind of change in them. He does not give the reason for this here but mentioned it above [9], because it is clear that the Ideas were not introduced to explain motion but rather to explain immutability. For since it seemed to Plato that all sensible things are always in motion, he wanted to posit something separate from sensible things that is fixed and immobile, of which there can be certain knowledge. Hence, according to him, the Forms could not be held to be sensible principles of motion, but rather to be immutable things and principles of immutability; so that, undoubtedly, whatever is found to be fixed and constant in sensible things will be due to participation in the Ideas, which are immutable in themselves.

227. **Nor are they of any assistance** [3].

Second, he shows that the Forms do not contribute anything to the knowledge of sensible things, by the following argument: knowledge of each thing is acquired by knowing its own substance, and not by knowing certain substances which are separate from it. But these separate substances, which they call Forms, are altogether other than sensible substances. Therefore a knowledge of them is of no assistance in knowing other sensible things.

228. Nor can it be said that the Forms are the substances of these sensible things; for the substance of each thing is present in the thing whose substance it is. Therefore, if these Forms were the substances of sensible things, they would be present in sensible things. This is opposed to Plato's opinion.

229. Nor again can it be said that the Forms are present in these sensible substances as in things which participate in them; for Plato thought that some Forms are the causes of sensible things in this way. For just as we might understand whiteness itself existing of itself as a certain separate whiteness to be mingled with the whiteness in a subject, and to participate in whiteness, in a similar way we might say that man [in himself], who is separate, is mingled with this man who is composed of matter and the specific nature in which he participates. But this argument is easily "disposed of," i.e., destroyed; for Anaxagoras, who also held that forms and accidents are mingled with things, was the first to state it. Hesiod [Eudoxus] and certain other thinkers were the second to mention it. Therefore I say that it is easily disposed of, because it is easy to bring many absurd conclusions against such an opinion. For it would follow, as he pointed out above (see n. 194) against Anaxagoras, that accidents and forms could exist without substances. For

only those things can exist separately which are naturally disposed to be mixed with other things.

230. It cannot be said, then, that the Forms contribute in any way to our knowledge of sensible things as their substances. Nor can it be said that they are the principles of being in these substances by way of participation. Nor again can it be said that from these Forms as principles other things—sensible ones—come to be in any of the ways in which we are accustomed to speak. Therefore, if principles of being and principles of knowledge are the same, the Forms cannot possibly make any contribution to scientific knowledge, since they cannot be principles of being. Hence he says "in any of the customary ways" of speaking, because Plato invented many new ways of deriving knowledge of one thing from something else.

231. **Again, to say** [4].

Here he gives the third objection against the arguments for separate Forms. He says that the Forms are of no value to sensible things as their exemplars. First [4], he states his thesis; and second [5], he proves it ("For what is the work").

Accordingly he says, first [4], that to say that the Forms are the exemplars both of sensible things and the objects of mathematics (because the latter participate in causes of this kind), is untenable for two reasons. First, because it is vain and useless to posit exemplars of this kind, as he will show; and second, because this manner of speaking is similar to the metaphors which the poets introduce, which do not pertain to the philosopher. For the philosopher ought to teach by using proper causes. Hence he says that this manner of speaking is metaphorical, because Plato likened the generation of natural substances to the making of works of art, in which the artisan, by looking at some exemplar, produces something similar to his artistic idea.

232. **For what is the work** [5].

Here he proves his thesis by three arguments. For the work, i.e., the use, of an exemplar, seems to be this, that the artisan by looking at an exemplar induces a likeness of the form in his own artifact. But in the operations of natural beings we see that like things are generated by like, as man is generated by man. Therefore this likeness arises in things which are generated, either because some agent looks toward an exemplar or not. If not, then what is "the work," or utility, of the agent's so looking toward the Ideas as exemplars?—as if to say, none. But if the likeness results from looking at a separate exemplar, then it cannot be said that the cause of this likeness in the thing generated is the form of an inferior agent. For something similar would come into being with reference to this separate exemplar and not with reference to this sensible agent. And this is what he means when he says "and not be like it," i.e., like the sensible agent. From this the following absurdity results: someone similar to Socrates will be generated whether Socrates is held to exist or not. This we see is false; for unless Socrates plays an active part in the process of generation, no one similar to Socrates will ever be generated. Therefore, if it is false that the likeness of things which are generated does not depend on proximate agents, it is pointless and superfluous to posit separate exemplars of any kind.

233. However, it should be noted that, even though this argument does away with the separate exemplars postulated by Plato, it still does not do

away with the fact that God's knowledge is the exemplar of all things. For since things in the physical world are naturally inclined to induce their likeness in things which are generated, this inclination must be traced back to some directing principle which ordains each thing to its end. This can only be the intellect of that being who knows the end and the relationship of things to the end. Therefore this likeness of effects to their natural causes is traced back to an intellect as their first principle. But it is not necessary that this likeness should be traced back to any other separate forms; because in order to have the above-mentioned likeness this direction of things to their end, according to which natural powers are directed by the first intellect, is sufficient.

234. **Similarly, it is evident** [6].

Here he gives the second argument, which runs as follows: just as Socrates because he is Socrates adds something to man, in a similar way man adds something to animal. And just as Socrates participates in man, so does man participate in animal. But if besides this Socrates whom we perceive there is held to be another Socrates who is eternal, as his exemplar, it will follow that there are several exemplars of this Socrates whom we perceive, i.e., the eternal Socrates and the Form man. And by the same reasoning the Form man will have several exemplars; for its exemplar will be both animal and two-footed and also "man-in-himself," i.e., the Idea of man. But that there should be several exemplars of a single thing made in likeness to an exemplar is untenable. Therefore it is absurd to hold that things of this kind are the exemplars of sensible things.

235. **Further** [7].

Here he gives the third argument, which runs thus: just as a Form is related to an individual, so also is a genus related to a species. Therefore, if the Forms are the exemplars of individual sensible things, as Plato held, there will be also certain exemplars of these Forms, that is to say, their genus. But this is absurd, because then it would follow that one and the same thing, i.e., Form, would be an exemplar of one thing, namely, of the individual whom we perceive by the senses, and a copy made in likeness to something else, namely, a genus. This seems to be absurd.

236. **Again, it is thought** [8].

Here he proves his fourth objection, namely, that the Forms contribute nothing to sensible things as their substances or formal causes; because "It is thought by him," that is to say, it is a matter of opinion (to put this impersonally), that it is impossible for a thing's substance to exist apart from the thing whose substance it is. But the Forms exist apart from the things of which they are the Forms, i.e., apart from sensible things. Therefore they are not the substances of sensible things.

237. **But in the "Phaedo"** [9].

Here he shows that the Forms are of no value in accounting for the coming to be of sensible things, although Plato said "in the *Phaedo*,"^2 i.e., in one of his works, that the Forms are the causes both of the being and of the coming to be of sensible things.

But Aristotle disproves this by two arguments. The first is as follows: to posit the cause is to posit the effect. However, even if the Forms exist, the particular or individual things which participate in the Forms will come into being only if there is some agent which moves them to acquire form. This is evident from Plato's opinion that the

Forms are always in the same state. Therefore, assuming that these Forms exist, if individuals were to exist or come into being by participating in them, it would follow that individual substances of this kind would always be. This is clearly false. Therefore it cannot be said that the Forms are the causes of both the coming to be and the being of sensible things. The chief reason is that Plato did not hold that the Forms are efficient causes, as was stated above (see n. 226). For Aristotle holds that the being and coming to be of lower substances proceeds from immobile separate substances, inasmuch as these substances are the movers of the celestial bodies, by means of which generation and corruption are produced in these lower substances.

238. **And many other** [10].

Here he gives the second argument, which runs thus: just as artifacts are related to artificial causes, so are natural bodies to natural causes. But we see that many other things besides natural bodies come into being in the realm of these lower bodies, as a house and a ring, for which the Platonists did not posit any Forms. Therefore "other things," namely, natural things, can both be and come to be because of such proximate causes as those just mentioned, i.e., artificial ones; so that, just as artificial things come to be as a result of proximate agents, so also do natural things.

LESSON 16
Arguments against the View that Ideas Are Numbers

ARISTOTLE'S TEXT Chapter 9: 991b9–992a24

1. Further, if the Forms are numbers, in what way will they be causes? Will it be because existing things are other numbers, so that this number is man, another Socrates, and still another Callias? In what respect, then, are the former the cause of the latter? For it will make no difference if the former are eternal and the latter are not. But if it is because the things here are ratios of numbers, like a harmony, then clearly there will be one kind of thing of which they are the ratios. And if this is matter, evidently the numbers themselves will be certain ratios of one thing to something else. I mean that, if Callias is a numerical ratio of fire, water, earth and air, [his Idea will also be a ratio of certain things], and man-in-himself, whether it be a number or not, will still be a numerical ratio of certain things and not just a number; nor will it be any number because of these. **991b9–21**

2. Again, one number will come from many numbers, but how or in what way can one Form come from [many] Forms? **991b22–23**

3. But if one number is not produced from them but from the units which they contain, as the units in the number ten thousand, how are the units related? For if they are specifically the same, many absurdities will follow; and if they are not, neither will they be the same as one another nor all the others the same as all. **991b23–26**

4. For in what way will they differ, if they have no attributes? For these statements are neither reasonable nor in accord with our understanding. **991b26–27**

5. Further, [if the Forms are numbers], it is necessary to set up some other class of number: that with which arithmetic deals. And all the things which are said to be intermediate, from what things or what principles in an absolute sense will they come, or why will they be [an intermediate class] between the things at hand and those [in the ideal world]? **991b27–31**

6. Again, each of the units which are contained in the number two will come from a prior two. But this is impossible. **991b31–992a1**

7. Further, why is a number something composed of these? **992a1–2**

8. And, again, in addition to what has been said, if the units are different, it will be necessary to speak of them in the same way as do those who say that the elements are four or two. For none of them designate as an element what is common, namely, body, but fire and earth, whether body is something in common or not. But now we are speaking of the one as if it were one thing made up of like parts, as fire or water. But if this is the case, numbers will not be substances. Yet it is evident that, if the one itself is something common and a principle, then the one is used in different senses; otherwise this will be impossible. **992a2–10**

9. Now when we wish to reduce substances to their principles, we claim that lengths come from the long and short, i.e., from a kind of great and small; and the plane from the wide and narrow; and body from the deep and shallow. **992a10–13**

10. Yet how will a surface contain a line, or a solid a line or surface? For the wide and narrow is a different class from the deep and shallow. Hence, just as number is not present in these, because the many and few differ from these, it is evident that no one of the other higher classes will be present in the lower. And the broad is not in the class of the deep, for then the solid would be a kind of surface. **992a13–19**

11. Further, from what will points derive being? Plato was opposed to this class of objects as a geometrical fiction, but he called them the principle of a line. And he often holds that there are indivisible lines. Yet these must have some [limit]. Therefore any argument that proves the existence of the line also proves the existence of the point. **992a19–24**

COMMENTARY

239. Here he destroys Plato's opinion about the Forms inasmuch as Plato claimed that they are numbers. In regard to this he does two things. First [1], he argues dialectically against Plato's opinion about numbers; and second ([9], against his opinion about the other objects of mathematics ("Now when we wish").

In regard to the first part he gives six arguments. The first [1] is this: in the case of things which are substantially the same, one thing is not the cause of another. But sensible things are substantially numbers according to the Platonists and Pythagoreans. Therefore, if the Forms themselves are numbers, they cannot be the cause of sensible things.

240. But if it is said that some numbers are Forms and others are sensible things, as Plato literally held (as though we were to say that this number is man and another is Socrates and still another is Callias), even this would not seem to be sufficient; for according to this view the intelligible structure of number will be common both to sensible things and the Forms. But in the case of things which have the same intelligible structure, one does not seem to be the cause of another. Therefore the Forms will not be the causes of sensible things.

241. Nor again can it be said that they are causes for the reason that, if those numbers are Forms, they are eternal. For this difference, namely, that some things differ from others in virtue of being eternal and non-eternal in their own being considered absolutely, is not sufficient to explain why some things are held to be the causes of others. Indeed, things differ from each other as cause and effect rather because of the relationship which one has to the other. Therefore things that differ numerically do not differ from each other as cause and effect because some are eternal and some are not.

242. Again, it is said that sensible things are certain "ratios" or proportions of numbers, and that numbers are the causes of these sensible things, as we also observe to be the case "in harmonies," i.e., in the combinations of musical notes. For numbers are said to be the causes of harmonies insofar as the numerical proportions applied to sounds yield harmonies. Now if the above is true, then just as in harmonies there are found to be sounds in addition to numerical proportions, in a similar way it was obviously necessary to posit in addition to the numbers in sensible things something generically one to which the numerical proportions are applied, so that the proportions of those things which belong to that one genus would constitute sensible things. However, if that to which the numerical proportion in sensible things is applied is matter, evidently those separate numbers, which are Forms, had to be termed proportions of some one thing to something else. For this particular man, called Callias or Socrates, must be said to be similar to the ideal man, called "man-in-himself," or humanity. Hence, if Callias is not merely a number, but is rather a kind of ratio or numerical proportion of the elements, i.e., of fire, earth, water and air, and if the ideal man-in-himself is a kind of ratio or numerical proportion of certain things, the ideal man will not be a number by reason of its own substance. From this it follows that there will be no number "apart from these," i.e., apart from the things numbered. For if the number which constitutes the Forms is separate in the

highest degree, and if it is not separate from things but is a kind of proportion of numbered things, no other number will now be separate. This is opposed to Plato's view.

243. It also follows that the ideal man is a proportion of certain numbered things, whether it is held to be a number or not. For according to those who held that substances are numbers, and according to the philosophers of nature, who denied that numbers are substances, some numerical proportions must be found in the substances of things. This is most evident in the case of the opinion of Empedocles, who held that each one of these sensible things is composed of a certain harmony or proportion [of the elements].

244. **Again, one number** [2].

Here he gives the second argument which runs thus: one number is produced from many numbers. Therefore, if the Forms are numbers, one Form is produced from many Forms. But this is impossible. For if from many things which differ specifically something specifically one is produced, this comes about by mixture, in which the natures of the things mixed are not preserved; just as a stone is produced from the four elements. Again, from things of this kind which differ specifically one thing is not produced by reason of the Forms, because the Forms themselves are combined in such a way as to constitute a single thing only in accordance with the intelligible structure of individual things, which are altered in such a way that they can be mixed together. And when the Forms themselves of the numbers two and three are combined, they give rise to the number five, so that each number remains and is retained in the number five.

245. But since someone could answer this argument, in support of Plato, by saying that one number does not come from many numbers, but each number is immediately constituted of units, Aristotle is therefore logical in rejecting this answer [3] ("But if one number").

For if it is said that some greater number, such as ten thousand, is not produced "from them," namely, from twos or many smaller numbers, but from "units," i.e., ones, this question will follow: How are the units of which numbers are composed related to each other? For all units must either conform with each other or not.

246. But many absurd conclusions follow from the first alternative, especially for those who claim that the Forms are numbers. For it will follow that different Forms do not differ substantially but only insofar as one Form surpasses another. It also seems absurd that units should differ in no way and yet be many, since difference is a result of multiplicity.

247. But if they do not conform, this can happen in two ways. First, they can lack conformity because the units of one number differ from those of another number, as the units of the number two differ from those of the number three, although the units of one and the same number will conform with each other. Second, they can lack conformity insofar as the units of one and the same number do not conform with each other or with the units of another number. He indicates this distinction when he says, "For neither will they be the same as one another [4]," i.e., the units which comprise the same number, "nor all the others the same as all," i.e., those which belong to different numbers. Indeed, in whatever way there is held to be lack of conformity between units an absurdity is appar-

ent. For every instance of non-conformity involves some form or attribute, just as we see that bodies which lack conformity differ insofar as they are hot and cold, white and black, or in terms of similar attributes. Now units lack qualities of this kind, because they have no qualities, according to Plato. Hence it will be impossible to hold that there is any non-conformity or difference between them of the kind caused by a quality. Thus it is evident that Plato's opinions about the Forms and numbers are neither "reasonable" (for example, those proved by an apodictic argument), nor "in accord with our understanding" (for example, those things which are self-evident and verified by [the habit of] intellect alone, as the first principles of demonstration).

248. **Further, [if the Forms]** [5].

Here he gives the third argument against Plato, which runs thus: all objects of mathematics, which Plato affirmed to be midway between the Forms and sensible substances, are derived unqualifiedly from numbers, either as proper principles, or as first principles. He says this because in one sense numbers seem to be the immediate principles of the other objects of mathematics; for the Platonists said that the number one constitutes the point, the number two the line, the number three surface, and the number four the solid. But in another sense the objects of mathematics seem to be reduced to numbers as first principles and not as proximate ones. For the Platonists said that solids are composed of surfaces, surfaces of lines, lines of points, and points of units, which constitute numbers. But in either way it followed that numbers are the principles of the other objects of mathematics.

249. Therefore, just as the other objects of mathematics constituted an intermediate class between sensible substances and the Forms, in a similar way it was necessary to devise some class of number which is other than the numbers that constitute the Forms and other than those that constitute the substance of sensible things. And arithmetic, which is one of the mathematical sciences, evidently deals with this kind of number as its proper subject, just as geometry deals with mathematical extensions. However, this position seems to be superfluous; for no reason can be given why number should be midway "between the things at hand," or sensible things, and "those in the ideal world," or the Forms, since both sensible things and the Forms are numbers.

250. **Again, each of the units** [6].

Here he gives the fourth argument, which runs thus: those things which exist in the sensible world and those which exist in the realm of mathematical entities are caused by the Forms. Therefore, if some number two is found both in the sensible world and in the realm of the objects of mathematics, each unit of this subsequent two must be caused by a prior two, which is the Form of twoness. But it is "impossible" that unity should be caused by duality. For it would be most necessary to say this if the units of one number were of a different species than those of another number, because then these units would acquire their species from a Form which is prior to the units of that number. And thus the units of a subsequent two would have to be produced from a prior two.

251. **Further, why is** [7].

Here he gives the fifth argument, which runs thus: many things combine so as to constitute one thing only by reason of some cause, which can be considered to be either extrinsic, as some agent which unites them, or intrinsic, as some unifying bond. Or if some things are united of themselves, one of them must be potential and another actual. However, in the case of units none of these reasons can be said to be the one "why a number," i.e., the cause by which a number, will be a certain "combination," i.e., collection of many units; as if to say, it will be impossible to give any reason for this.

252. **And, again, in addition** [8].

Here he gives the sixth argument, which runs thus: if numbers are the Forms and substances of things, it will be necessary to say, as has been stated before [3], either that units are different, or that they conform. But if they are different, it follows that unity as unity will not be a principle. This is clarified by a similar case drawn from the position of the natural philosophers. For some of these thinkers held that the four [elemental] bodies are principles. But even though being a body is common to these elements, these philosophers did not maintain that a common body is a principle, but rather fire, earth, water and air, which are different bodies. Therefore, if units are different, even though all have in common the intelligible constitution of unity, it will not be said that unity itself as such is a principle. This is contrary to the Platonists' position; for they now say that the unit is the principle of things, just as the natural philosophers say that fire or water or some body with like parts is the principle of things. But if our conclusion against the Platonists' theory is true—that unity as such is not the principle and substance of things—it will follow that numbers are not the substances of things. For number is held to be the substance of things only insofar as it is constituted of units, which are said to be the substances of things. This is also contrary to the Platonists' position which is now being examined, i.e., that numbers are Forms.

253. But if you say that all units are undifferentiated, it follows that "the whole," i.e., the entire universe, is a single entity, since the substance of each thing is the one itself, and this is something common and undifferentiated. Further, it follows that the same entity is the principle of all things. But this is impossible by reason of the notion involved, which is inconceivable in itself, namely, that all things should be one according to the aspect of substance. For this view contains a contradiction, since it claims that the one is the substance of all things, yet maintains that the one is a principle. For one and the same thing is not its own principle, unless, perhaps, it is said that "the one" is used in different senses, so that when the senses of the one are differentiated all things are said to be generically one and not numerically or specifically one.

254. **Now when we wish** [9].

Here he argues against Plato's position with reference to his views about mathematical extensions. First [9], he gives Plato's position; and second [10], he advances an argument against it ("Yet how will").

He says, first, that the Platonists, wishing to reduce the substances of things to their first principles, when they say that continuous quantities themselves are the substances of sensible things, thought they had discovered the principles of things when they assigned line, surface and solid as the principles of sensible things. But in giving the principles of continuous quantities they said that "lengths," i.e., lines, are composed of the long and short, because they held that contraries are the principles of all things. And since the line is the first of continuous quantities, they first attributed to it the great and small; for inasmuch as these two are the principles of the line, they are also the principles of other continuous quantities. He says "from the great and small" because the great and small are also placed among the Forms, as has been stated (see n. 217). But insofar as they are limited by position, and are thus particularized in the class of continuous quantities, they constitute first the line and then other continuous quantities. And for the same reason they said that surface is composed of the wide and narrow, and body of the deep and shallow.

255. **Yet how will a surface** [10].

Here he argues against the foregoing position, by means of two arguments. The first is as follows. Things whose principles are different are themselves different. But the principles of continuous quantities mentioned above are different, according to the foregoing position, for the wide and narrow, which are posited as the principles of surface, belong to a different class than the deep and shallow, which are held to be the principles of body. The same thing can be said of the long and short, which differ from each of the above. Therefore, line, surface and body all differ from each other. How then will one be able to say that a surface contains a line, and a body a line and a surface? In confirmation of this argument he introduces a similar case involving number. For the many and few, which are held to be principles of things for a similar reason, belong to a different class than the long and short, the wide and narrow, and the deep and shallow. Therefore number is not contained in these continuous quantities but is essentially separate. Hence, for the same reason, the higher of the above mentioned things will not be contained in the lower; for example, a line will not be contained in a surface or a surface in a body.

256. But because it could be said that certain of the foregoing contraries are the genera of the others, for example, that the long is the genus of the broad, and the broad the genus of the deep, he destroys this [objection] by the following argument: things composed of principles are related to each other in the same way as their principles are. Therefore, if the broad is the genus of the deep, surface will also be the genus of body. Hence a solid will be a kind of plane, i.e., a species of surface. This is clearly false.

257. **Further, from what will** [11].

Here he gives the second argument, which involves points; and in regard to this Plato seems to have made two errors. First, Plato claimed that a point is the limit of a line, just as a line is the limit of a surface and a surface the limit of a body. Therefore, just as he posited certain principles of which the latter are composed, so too he should have posited some principle from which points derive their being. But he seems to have omitted this.

258. The second error is this: Plato seems to have held different opinions about points. For sometimes he maintained that the whole science of geometry treats this class of things, namely, points, inasmuch as he held that points are the principles and substance of all continuous quantities. And he not only implied this but even explicitly stated that a point is the principle of a line, defining it in this way. But many times he said that indivisible lines are the principles of lines and

other continuous quantities, and that this is the class of things with which geometry deals, namely, indivisible lines. Yet by reason of the fact that he held that all continuous quantities are composed of indivisible lines, he did not avoid the consequence that continuous quantities are composed of points, and that points are the principles of continuous quantities. For indivisible lines must have some limits, and these can only be points. Hence, by whatever argument indivisible lines are held to be the principles of continuous quantities, by the same argument too the point is held to be the principle of continuous quantity.

LESSON 17

Arguments against the View that the Ideas Are Principles of Being and Knowledge

ARISTOTLE'S TEXT Chapters 9 & 10: 992a24–993a27

1. *And, in general, even though wisdom investigates the causes of apparent things, we have neglected this study. For we say nothing about the cause from which motion originates. And while we think that we are stating the substance of these sensible things, we introduce other substances. But the way in which we explain how the latter are the substances of the former is empty talk; for to participate, as we have said before (115), signifies nothing. Moreover, that which we see to be the cause in the sciences, that by reason of which all intellect and all nature operates, on that cause which we say is one of the principles the Forms do not touch in any way. But mathematics has been turned into philosophy by present-day thinkers (566), although they say that mathematics must be treated for the sake of other things.* **992a24–992a1**

2. *Further, one might suppose that the underlying substance [which they consider] as matter is too mathematical, and that it is rather a predicate and difference of substance and matter, like the great and small; just as the philosophers of nature speak of the rare and dense (56), which they say are the primary differences of the underlying subject; for these are a kind of excess and defect.* **992b1–7**

3. *And with regard to motion, if these entities [the great and small] are motion, evidently the Forms are moved; but if they are not, from what does motion come? For [if it has no cause], the whole study of nature is destroyed.* **992b7–9**

4. *And what seems easy to show is that all things are not one; for from their position all things do not become one. But if someone should assert that all things are some one thing, not even this is true unless one grants that the universal is a class; and in certain other cases this is impossible.* **992b9–13**

5. *For they do not have any theory about the lengths, widths, and solids which come after the numbers: either as to how they now exist or will exist, or what importance they have. For it is impossible that they should be Forms (since they are not numbers), or intermediate things (for those are the objects of mathematics), or corruptible things; but, on the contrary, it seems that they form a fourth class.* **992b13–18**

6. *And, in general, to look for the elements of existing things without distinguishing the different senses in which things are said to be, makes it impossible to discover them. And [their view is unsatisfactory] in another way, i.e., in the way in which they seek for the elements of which things are composed. For it is impossible to understand of what things action or passion or straightness is composed. But if this is possible only in the case of substances, then to look for the elements of all existing things, or to think that we have found them, is a mistake.* **992b18–24**

7. *But how will one acquire knowledge of the elements of all things? For it is clearly impossible to have prior knowledge of anything. For just as one acquiring knowledge of geometry must have a prior knowledge of other things, but not of the things which this science [investigates], and which he is to learn, so it is in the case of the other sciences. Hence, if there is a science of all things (and there must be a science of these), as some say, the one learning this science does not have any prior knowledge of it. But all learning proceeds from things previously known, either all or some of them, whether the learning be by demonstration or by definitions. For [the parts] of which definitions are composed must already be known beforehand and be evident. The same thing is true in the case of things discovered by induction.* **992b24–33**

8. *But if this science were connatural, it is a wonder how we could be unconscious of having the most important of the sciences.* **992b33–993a2**

9. Again, how is anyone to know the elements of which things are composed, and how is this to be made evident? For this also presents a difficulty; because one might argue in the same way as one does about certain syllables. For some say that sma is made up of s, m and a, whereas others say that it is a totally different sound and not any of those which are known to us. **993a2–7**

10. Again, how could one know the things of which a sense is cognizant without having that sense? Yet this will be necessary if they [i.e., sensible things] are the elements of which all things are composed, just as spoken words are composed of their proper elements. **993a7–10**

Chapter 10

11. From the foregoing, then, it is evident that all [the early philosophers] seem to seek the causes mentioned in the Physics, [194b16] and that we cannot state any other in addition to these. But they understood these obscurely; and while in one sense all causes have been mentioned before, in another sense they have not been mentioned at all. Indeed, the earliest philosophy seems to speak in a faltering way about all subjects inasmuch as it was new as regards principles and the first of its kind. For even Empedocles says that ratios are present in bone, and that this is the quiddity or substance of a thing. But [if this is true], there must likewise be a ratio of flesh and of every other thing or of nothing. For it is because of this that flesh and bone and every other thing exists, and not because of their matter, which he says is fire, earth, air and water. But if someone else had said this, he would have been forced to agree to the same thing. But he has not said this. Such things as these, then, have been explained before. So let us return again to whatever problems one might raise about the same subject; for perhaps in the light of these we shall be able to make some investigation into subsequent problems.
993a11–27

COMMENTARY

259. Here Aristotle destroys Plato's opinion about the principles of things. First [1], he destroys Plato's opinion about principles of being; and second [7], his opinion about principles of knowledge ("But how will one").

In regard to the first part he gives six arguments. The first is based on the fact that Plato neglected to deal with the classes of causes. Thus he says that, "in general, wisdom," or philosophy, has as its aim to investigate the causes "of apparent things," i.e., things apparent to the senses. For men began to philosophize because they sought for the causes of things, as was stated in the prologue (see n. 53). But the Platonists, among whom he includes himself, neglected the principles of things, because they said nothing about the efficient cause, which is the source of change. And by positing the Ideas they thought they had given the formal cause of things. But while they thought that they were speaking of the substance of these things, i.e., sensible ones, they posited the existence of certain other separate substances which differ from these. However, the way in which they assigned these separate substances as the substances of sensible things "is empty talk," i.e., it proves nothing and is not true. For they said that the Forms are the substances of sensible things inasmuch as they are participated in by sensible things. But what they said about participation is meaningless, as is clear from what was said above (see n. 225). Furthermore, the Forms which they posited have no connection with the final cause, although we see that this is a cause in certain sciences which demonstrate by means of the final cause, and that it is by reason of this cause that every intellectual agent and every natural one operates, as has been shown in the *Physics*, Book II. [199a10] And just as they do not touch on that cause which is called an end [or goal], when they postulate the existence of the Forms (n. 169), neither do they treat of that cause which is called the source of motion, namely, the efficient cause, which is the opposite, so to speak, of the final cause. But the Platonists by omitting causes of this kind (since they did omit a starting-point and end of motion), have dealt with natural things as if they were objects of mathematics, which lack motion. Hence they said that the objects of mathematics should be studied not only for themselves but for the sake of other things, i.e., natural bodies; inasmuch as they attributed the properties of the objects of mathematics to sensible bodies.

260. **Further, one might** [2].

Here he gives the second argument, which runs thus: that which is posited as the matter of a thing is the substance of a thing, and is predicable of a thing to a greater degree than something which exists apart from it. But a Form exists apart from sensible things. Therefore, according to the opinion of the Platonists, one might suppose that the underlying substance as matter is the substance of the objects of mathematics rather than a separate Form. Furthermore, he admits that it is predicated of a sensible thing rather than the above Form. For the Platonists held that the great and small is a difference of substance or matter; for they referred these two principles to matter, just as the philosophers of nature (n. 115) held that rarity and density are the primary differences of the "underlying subject," or matter, by which matter is changed, and spoke of them in a sense as the great and small. This is clear from the fact that rarity and density are a kind of excess and defect. For the dense is what contains a great deal of matter under the same dimensions, and the rare is what contains very little matter. Yet the Platonists said that the Forms are the substance of sensible things rather than the objects of mathematics, and that they are predicable of them to a greater degree.

261. **And with regard** [3].

Here he gives the third argument, which runs thus: if those attributes which exist in sensible things are caused by separate Forms, it is necessary to say either that there is an Idea of "motion" among the Forms or there is not. If there is a Form or Idea of motion among the Forms, and there cannot be motion without something that is moved, it also follows that the Forms must be moved. But this is opposed to the Platonists' opinion, for they claimed that the Forms are immobile. On the other hand, if there is no Idea of motion, and these attributes which exist in sensible things are caused by the Ideas, it will be impossible to assign a cause for the motion which occurs in sensible things; and thus the entire investigation of natural philosophy, which studies mobile things, will be destroyed.

262. **And what seems easy** [4].

Then he gives the fourth argument, which runs thus: if unity were the substance of all things, as the Platonists assumed, it would be necessary to say that all things are one, just as the philosophers of nature also did in claiming that the substance of all things is water, and so on for the other elements. But it is easy to show that all things are not one. Hence the position that unity is the substance of all things is not held in high repute.

263. But let us assume that someone might say that it does not follow, from

Plato's position, that all things are one in an unqualified sense but in a qualified sense, just as we say that some things are one generically or specifically. And if someone wished to say that all things are one in this way, even this could be held only if what I call the one were a genus or universal predicate of all things. For then we could say that all things are one specifically, just as we say that both a man and an ass are animal substantially. But in certain cases it seems impossible that there should be one class of all things, because the difference dividing this class would necessarily not be one, as will be said in Book III (n. 432). Therefore, in no way can it be held that the substance of all things is one.

264. **For they do not have** [5].

Here he gives the fifth argument, which runs thus: Plato placed lengths, widths and solids after numbers as the substances of sensible things, i.e., that of which they are composed. But according to Plato's position there seems to be no reason why they should be held to exist either now or in the future. Nor does this notion seem to have any efficacy to establish them as the causes of sensible things. For things which exist "now" must mean immobile things (because these always exist in the same way), whereas things which "will exist" must mean those which are capable of generation and corruption, which acquire being after non-being. This becomes clear thus: Plato posited three classes of things—sensible things, the Forms and the objects of mathematics, which are an intermediate class. But such lines and surfaces as those of which sensible bodies are composed cannot be Forms; for the Forms are essentially numbers, whereas such things [i.e., the lines and surfaces composing bodies] come after numbers. Nor can such lines and surfaces be said to be an intermediate class between the Forms and sensible things; for the things in this intermediate class are the objects of mathematics, and exist apart from sensible things; but this cannot be said of the lines and surfaces of which sensible bodies are composed. Nor again can such lines and surfaces be sensible things; for the latter are corruptible, whereas these lines and surfaces are incorruptible, as will be proved below in Book III (n. 466). Therefore these things are either nothing at all or they constitute a fourth class of things, which Plato omitted.

265. **And, in general** [6].

Here he gives the sixth argument, which runs thus: it is impossible to discover the principles of anything that is spoken of in many senses, unless these many senses are distinguished. Now those things which agree in name only and differ in their intelligible structure cannot have common principles; otherwise they would have the same intelligible structure, since the intelligible structure of a thing is derived from its own principles. But it is impossible to assign distinct principles for those things which have only the name in common, unless it be those whose principles must be indicated to differ from each other. Therefore, since being is predicated both of substance and the other genera in different senses and not in the same sense, Plato assigned inadequate principles for things by failing to distinguish beings from each other.

266. But since someone could assign principles to things which differ in their intelligible structure and have a common name, by adjusting proper principles to each without distinguishing the many senses of the common

name, and since the Platonists have not done this, then "in another way," i.e., by another argument, they assigned inadequate principles to things when they looked for the elements of which things are made, i.e., in the way in which they sought for them, inasmuch as they did not assign principles which are sufficient for all things. For from their statements it is impossible to understand the principles of which either action and passion, curvature and straightness, or other such accidents, are composed. For they only indicated the principles of substances and neglected accidents.

267. But if in defense of Plato someone wished to say that it is possible for the elements of all things to have been acquired or discovered at the moment when the principles of substances alone happen to have been acquired or discovered, this opinion would not be true. For even if the principles of substances are also in a sense the principles of accidents, nevertheless accidents have their own principles. Nor are the principles of all genera the same in all respects, as will be shown below in Book XI (n. 2173) and Book XII (n. 2455) of this work.

268. **But how will one** [7].

Here he argues dialectically against Plato's position that the Ideas are the principles of our scientific knowledge.

He gives four arguments, of which the first is this: if our scientific knowledge is caused by the Ideas themselves, it is impossible for us to acquire knowledge of the principles of things. But it is evident that we do acquire knowledge. Therefore our knowledge is not caused by the Ideas themselves. That it would be impossible to acquire knowledge of anything, he proves thus: no one has any prior knowledge of that object of which he ought to acquire knowledge; for example, even though in the case of geometry one has prior knowledge of other things which are necessary for demonstration, nevertheless the objects of which he ought to acquire knowledge he must not know beforehand. The same thing is also true in the case of the other sciences. But if the Ideas are the cause of our knowledge, men must have knowledge of all things, because the Ideas are the intelligible structures of all knowable things. Therefore we cannot acquire knowledge of anything, unless one might be said to acquire knowledge of something which he already knew. If it is held, then, that someone acquires knowledge, he must not have any prior knowledge of the thing which he comes to know, but only of certain other things through which he becomes instructed; i.e., one acquires knowledge through things previously known, [either] "all," i.e., universals, "or some of them," i.e., singular things. One learns through universals in the case of those things which are discovered by demonstration and definition, for in the case of demonstrations and definitions the things of which definitions or universals are composed must be known first. And in the case of things which are discovered by induction singular things must be known first.

269. **But if this science** [8].

Here he gives the second argument, which runs thus: if the Ideas are the cause of our knowledge, it must be connatural to us; for men grasp sensible things through this proper nature, because sensible things participate in Ideas according to the Platonists. But the most important knowledge or science is one that is connatural to us and which we cannot forget, as is evident of our knowledge of the first principles of demonstration, of which no one is ignorant. Hence there is no way in which we can forget the knowledge of all things caused in us by the Ideas. But this is contrary to the Platonists' opinion, who said that the soul as a result of its union with the body forgets the knowledge which it has of all things by nature, and that by teaching a man acquires knowledge of something that he previously knew, as though the process of acquiring knowledge were merely one of remembering.

270. **Again, how is anyone** [9].

Here he gives the third argument, which runs thus: in order to know things a man must acquire knowledge not only of the forms of things but also of the material principles of which they are composed. This is evident from the fact that occasionally questions arise regarding these; for example, with regard to this syllable *sma,* some raise the question whether it is composed of the three letters *s, m* and *a,* or whether it is one letter which is distinct from these and has its own sound. But only the formal principles of things can be known through the Ideas, because the Ideas are the forms of things. Hence the Ideas are not a sufficient cause of our knowledge of things when material principles remain unknown.

271. **Again, how could** [10].

Here he gives the fourth argument, which runs thus: in order to know reality we must know sensible things, because sensible things are the apparent material element of which all things are composed, just as complex sounds (such as syllables and words) are composed of their proper elements. If, then, knowledge is caused in us by the Ideas, our knowledge of sensible things must be caused by the Ideas. But the knowledge which is caused in us by the Ideas is grasped without the senses, because we have no connection with the Ideas through the senses. Therefore in the act of perception it follows that anyone who does not have a sense can apprehend the object of that sense. This is clearly false; for a man born blind cannot have any knowledge of colors.

272. **From the foregoing** [11].

Here he summarizes the statements made by the ancient philosophers. He says that from what has been said above it is evident that the ancient philosophers attempted to investigate the cause which he [Aristotle] dealt with in the *Physics, [194b16]* and that in their statements we find no cause in addition to those established in that work. However, these men discussed these causes obscurely; and while in a sense they have mentioned all of these causes, in another sense they have not mentioned any of them. For just as young children at first speak imperfectly and in a stammering way, in a similar fashion this philosophy, since it was new, seems to speak imperfectly and in a stammering way about the principles of all things. This is borne out by the fact that Empedocles was the first to say that bones have a certain ratio, or proportional mixture [of the elements], and that this is a thing's quiddity or substance. But the same thing must also be true of flesh and of every other single thing or of none of them, for all of these things are mixtures of the elements. And for this reason it is evident that flesh and bone and all things of this kind are not what they are because of their matter, which he identified with the four elements, but because of this principle—their form. However, Empedocles, compelled as it were by the need for truth, would have maintained this view if it had been expressed more clearly by someone else, but he did not express it clearly. And just as the ancient philosophers have not clearly expressed the nature of form, neither have they clearly expressed the nature of matter, as was said above about Anaxagoras (n. 90). Nor have they clearly expressed the nature of any other principles. Therefore, concerning such things as have been stated imperfectly, we have spoken of this before (n. 190). And with regard to these matters we will restate again in Book III (n. 423) whatever difficulties can be raised on both sides of the question. For perhaps from such difficulties we will discover some useful information for dealing with the problems which must be examined and solved later on throughout this whole science.

BOOK II
THE SEARCH FOR TRUTH AND CAUSES

LESSON 1
The Acquisition of Truth: Its Ease and Its Difficulty

ARISTOTLE'S TEXT Chapter 1: 993a30–993b19

1. *Theoretical, i.e., speculative, knowledge of truth is in one sense difficult and in another, easy.* **993a30–31**

2. *An indication of this is found in the fact that, while no one can attain an adequate knowledge of it, all men together do not fail, because each one is able to say something true about nature.* **993a31–993b2**

3. *And while each one individually contributes nothing or very little to the truth, still as a result of the combined efforts of all a great amount of truth becomes known.* **993b2–4**

4. *Therefore, if the situation in the case of truth seems to be like the one which we speak of in the proverb "Who will miss a door?" then in this respect it will be easy to know the truth.* **993b4–5**

5. *But the fact that we cannot simultaneously grasp a whole and its parts shows the difficulty involved.* **993b6–7**

6. *However, since the difficulty is twofold, perhaps its cause is not in things but in us; for just as the eyes of owls are to the light of day, so is our soul's intellective power to those things which are by nature the most evident of all.* **993b7–11**

7. *Now it is only right that we should be grateful not merely to those with whose views we agree but also to those who until now have spoken in a superficial way; for they too have made some contribution because they have made use of the habit which we now exercise. Thus if there had been no Timotheus, we would not have a great part of our music; and if there had been no Phrynis, there would have been no Timotheus. The same is true of those who have made statements about the truth; for we have accepted certain opinions from some of them, and others have been the cause of them attaining their knowledge as they have been the cause of us attaining ours.* **993b11–19**

COMMENTARY

273. Having criticized the ancient philosophers' opinions about the first principles of things, with which first philosophy is chiefly concerned, the Philosopher now begins to establish what is true.

First philosophy considers truth in a different way than the particular sciences do. Each of the particular sciences considers a particular truth about a definite class of beings; e.g., geometry deals with the continuous quantities of bodies, and arithmetic with numbers; whereas first philosophy considers what is universally true of beings. Therefore, it pertains to this science to consider in what respects man is capable of knowing the truth.

274. This part is divided into two sections. In the first [1] he deals with the things that belong to a universal consideration of truth. In the second he begins to investigate what is true of first principles and of everything else with which this philosophy deals. He does this in Book III, which begins with the words "With a view to."

The first part is again divided into three parts. In the first of these he explains in what respects man is capable of knowing the truth. In the second (Lesson 2) he indicates to what science the knowledge of truth principally belongs ("It is only right to call"). In the third (Lesson 5) he explains the method by which truth is investigated ("The way in which people are affected").

In regard to the first he does three things. First, he shows in what respect it is easy to know the truth. Second [6], he gives the reason for the difficulty involved ("However, since the difficulty is twofold"). Third [7], he shows how men assist each other to know the truth ("Now it is only right").

In regard to the first he does two things. First, he states what he intends to prove. He says that "theoretical knowledge," i.e., the contemplative or speculative understanding of truth, is in one sense easy and in another, difficult.

275. **An indication of this** [2].

Second, he explains what he intends to prove: first, in what sense it is easy to know the truth; and second [5], in what sense it is difficult ("But the fact").

He shows in what sense it is easy to know the truth, by giving three indications. The first is this: while no man can attain a complete knowledge of the truth, still no man is so completely devoid of truth that he knows nothing about it. This is shown by the fact that anyone can make a statement about the truth and the nature of things, which is a sign of intellectual reflection.

276. **And while each one individually** [3].

Here he gives the second indication. He says that, while the amount of truth that one man can discover or contribute to the knowledge of truth by his own study and talents is small compared with a complete knowledge of truth, nevertheless what is known as a result of "the combined efforts" of all, i.e., what is discovered and collected into one whole, becomes quite extensive. This can be seen in the case of the particular arts, which have developed in a marvelous manner as a result of the studies and talents of different men.

277. **Therefore, if the situation** [4].

Third, he shows that the same thing is true by citing a common proverb. He concludes from the foregoing that since anyone can attain some knowledge of the truth, even though it be little, the situation in the case of knowledge is like the one that we speak of in the proverb "Who will miss a door?" i.e., the outer door of a house. For it is difficult to know what the interior of a house is like, and a man is easily deceived in such matters; but just as no one is mistaken about the entrance of a house, which is evident to all and is the first thing that we perceive, so too this is the case with regard to the knowledge of truth; for those truths through which we enter into a knowledge of others are known to all, and no man is mistaken about them. Those first principles which are naturally apprehended are truths of this sort, e.g., "It is impossible both to affirm and deny something at the same time," and "Every whole is greater than each of its parts," and so on. On the other hand, there are many ways in which error may arise with respect to the conclusions into which we enter through such principles as through an outer door. Therefore, it is easy to know the truth if we consider that small amount of it which is comprised of self-evident principles, through which we enter into other truths, because this much is evident to all.

278. **But the fact that we cannot** [5].

Here he explains in what sense it is

difficult to know the truth. He says that our inability to grasp the whole truth and a part of it shows the difficulty involved in the search for truth. In support of this we must consider his statement that the truth through which we gain admission to other truths is known to all. Now there are two ways in which we attain knowledge of the truth. The first is the method of analysis, by which we go from what is complex to what is simple or from a whole to a part, as it is said in Book I of the *Physics [184a21]* that the first objects of our knowledge are confused wholes. Now our knowledge of the truth is perfected by this method when we attain a distinct knowledge of the particular parts of a whole. The other method is that of synthesis, by which we go from what is simple to what is complex; and we attain knowledge of truth by this method when we succeed in knowing a whole. Thus the fact that man is unable to know perfectly in things a whole and a part shows the difficulty involved in knowing the truth by both of these methods.

279. **However, since the difficulty is twofold** [6].

He gives the reason for this difficulty. Here too it must be noted that, in all cases in which there is a certain relationship between two things, an effect can fail to occur in two ways, i.e., because of either one of the things involved. For example, if wood does not burn, this may happen either because the fire is not strong enough or because the wood is not combustible enough. And in a similar way the eye may be prevented from seeing a visible object either because the eye is weak or because the visible object is in the dark. Therefore, in like manner, it may be difficult to know the truth about things either because things themselves are imperfect in some way or because of some weakness on the part of our intellect.

280. Now it is evident that we experience difficulty in knowing the truth about some things because of the things themselves; for since each thing is knowable insofar as it is an actual being, as will be stated below in Book IX (see n. 1894) of this work, then those things which are deficient and imperfect in being are less knowable by their very nature; e.g., matter, motion, and time are less knowable because of the imperfect being which they have, as Boethius says in his book *The Two Natures*.

281. Now there were some philosophers who claimed that the difficulty experienced in knowing the truth is wholly attributable to things themselves, because they maintained that nothing is fixed and stable in nature but that everything is in a state of continual change, as will be stated in Book IV (n. 683) of this work. But the Philosopher denies this, saying that even though the difficulty experienced in knowing the truth can perhaps be twofold because of different things, i.e., our intellect and things themselves, still the principal source of the difficulty is not things but our intellect.

282. He proves this in the following way. If this difficulty were attributable principally to things, it would follow that we would know best those things which are most knowable by nature. But those things which are most knowable by nature are those which are most actual, i.e., immaterial and unchangeable things, yet we know these least of all. Obviously, then, the difficulty experienced in knowing the truth is due principally to some weakness on the part of our intellect. From this it follows that our soul's intellectual

power is related to those immaterial beings, which are by nature the most knowable of all, as the eyes of owls are to the light of day, which they cannot see because their power of vision is weak, although they do see dimly lighted things.

283. But it is evident that this simile is not adequate; for since a sense is a power of a bodily organ, it is made inoperative as a result of its sensible object being too intense. But the intellect is not a power of a bodily organ and is not made inoperative as a result of its intelligible object being too intelligible. Therefore, after understanding objects that are highly intelligible our ability to understand less intelligible objects is not decreased but increased, as is stated in Book III of *The Soul.* *[429b1]*

284. Therefore it must be said that a sense is prevented from perceiving some sensible object for two reasons: first, because a sensory organ is rendered inoperative as a result of its sensible object being too intense (this does not occur in the case of the intellect); second, because of some deficiency in the ability of a sensory power to perceive its object; for the powers of the soul in all animals do not have the same efficacy. Thus, just as it is proper to man by nature to have the weakest sense of smell, in a similar way it is proper to an owl to have the weakest power of vision, because it is incapable of perceiving the light of day.

285. Therefore, since the human soul occupies the lowest place in the order of intellective substances, it has the least intellective power. As a matter of fact, just as it is by nature the actuality of a body, although its intellective power is not the act of a bodily organ, in a similar way it has a natural capacity to know the truth about corporeal and sensible things. These are less knowable by nature because of their materiality, although they can be known by abstracting sensible forms from phantasms. And since this process of knowing truth befits the nature of the human soul insofar as it is the form of this kind of body (and whatever is natural always remains so), it is possible for the human soul, which is united to this kind of body, to know the truth about things only insofar as it can be elevated to the level of the things which it understands by abstracting from phantasms. However, by this process it cannot be elevated to the level of knowing the quiddities of immaterial substances because these are not on the same level as sensible substances. Therefore it is impossible for the human soul, which is united to this kind of body, to apprehend separate substances by knowing their quiddities.

286. For this reason the statement which Averroes makes at this point in his *Commentary* is evidently false, i.e., that the Philosopher does not prove here that it is just as impossible for us to understand abstract substances as it is for a bat to see the sun. The argument that he gives is wholly ridiculous; for he adds that, if this were the case, nature would have acted in vain because it would have made something that is naturally knowable in itself to be incapable of being known by anything else. It would be the same as if it had made the sun incapable of being seen.

This argument is not satisfactory for two reasons. First, the end of separate substances does not consist in being understood by our intellect, but rather the converse. Therefore, if separate substances are not known by us, it does not follow that they exist in vain; for only that exists in vain which fails to attain the end for which it exists. Second, even though the quiddities of separate substances are not understood by us, they are understood by other intellects. The same is true of the sun; for even though it is not seen by the eye of the owl, it is seen by the eye of the eagle.

287. **Now it is only right** [7].

He shows how men assist each other to know the truth; for one man assists another to consider the truth in two ways—directly and indirectly.

One is assisted directly by those who have discovered the truth; because, as has been pointed out, when each of our predecessors has discovered something about the truth, which is gathered together into one whole, he also introduces his followers to a more extensive knowledge of truth.

One is assisted indirectly insofar as those who have preceded us and who were wrong about the truth have bequeathed to their successors the occasion for exercising their mental powers, so that by diligent discussion the truth might be seen more clearly.

288. Now it is only fitting that we should be grateful to those who have helped us attain so great a good as knowledge of the truth. Therefore he says that "It is only right that we should be grateful," not merely to those whom we think have found the truth and with whose views we agree by following them, but also to those who, in the search for truth, have made only superficial statements, even though we do not follow their views; for these men too have given us something because they have shown us instances of actual attempts to discover the truth. By way of an example he mentions the founders of music; for if there "had been no Timotheus," who discovered a great part of the art of music, we would not have many of the facts that we know about melodies. But if Timotheus had not been preceded by a wise man named "Phrynis," he would not have been as well off in the subject of music. The same thing must be said of those philosophers who made statements of universal scope about the truth of things; for we accept from certain of our predecessors whatever views about the truth of things we think are true and disregard the rest. Again, those from whom we accept certain views had predecessors from whom they in turn accepted certain views and who were the source of their information.

LESSON 2
The Supreme Science of Truth, and Knowledge of Ultimate Causes

ARISTOTLE'S TEXT Chapters 1 & 2: 993b19–994b11

1. It is only right to call philosophy the science of truth. For the end of theoretical knowledge is truth, whereas that of practical knowledge is action; for even when practical men investigate the way in which something exists, they do not consider it in itself but in relation to some particular thing and to the present moment. But we know a truth only by knowing its cause. Now anything which is the basis of a univocal predication about other things has that attribute in the highest degree. Thus fire is hottest and is actually the cause of heat in other things. Therefore that is also true in the highest degree which is the cause of all subsequent things being true. For this reason the principles of things that always exist must be true in the highest degree, because they are not sometimes true and sometimes not true. Nor is there any cause of their being, but they are the cause of the being of other things. Therefore insofar as each thing has being, to that extent it is true. **993b19–31**

Chapter 2

2. Further, it is evident that there is a [first] principle, and that the causes of existing things are not infinite either in series or in species. For it is impossible that one thing should come from something else as from matter in an infinite regress, for example, flesh from earth, earth from air, air from fire, and so on to infinity. Nor can the causes from which motion originates proceed to infinity, as though man were moved by the air, the air by the sun, the sun by strife, and so on to infinity. Again, neither can there be an infinite regress in the case of the reason for which something is done, as though walking were for the sake of health, health for the sake of happiness, and happiness for the sake of something else, so that one thing is always being done for the sake of something else. The same is true in the case of the quiddity. **994a1–11**

COMMENTARY

289. Having shown how man is disposed for the study of truth, the Philosopher now shows that the knowledge of truth belongs pre-eminently to first philosophy. Regarding this he does two things. First [1], he shows that a knowledge of truth belongs pre-eminently to first philosophy. Second [2], he rejects a false doctrine that would render his proof untenable ("Further it is evident").

In regard to the first he does two things. First, he shows that knowledge of the truth belongs to first philosophy. Second that it belongs in the highest degree to this science ("But we know a truth").

He proves these two propositions from two things established above in the prologue of this book, i.e., that wisdom is not a practical but a speculative science (n. 53), and that it knows first causes (n. 48).

290. He argues from the first of these to the first conclusion in this way. Theoretical, i.e., speculative, knowledge differs from practical knowledge by its end; for the end of speculative knowledge is truth, because it has knowledge of the truth as its objective. But the end of practical knowledge is action, because, even though "practical men," i.e., men of action, attempt to understand the truth as it belongs to certain things, they do not seek this as an ultimate end; for they do not consider the cause of truth in and for itself as an end but in relation to action, either by applying it to some definite individual, or to some definite time.

Therefore, if we add to the above the fact that wisdom or first philosophy is not practical but speculative, it follows that first philosophy is most fittingly called the science of truth.

291. But since there are many speculative sciences, which consider the truth, such as geometry and arithmetic, therefore it was necessary to show that first philosophy considers truth in the highest degree inasmuch as it has been shown above that it considers first causes (n. 48). Hence he argues as follows. We have knowledge of truth only when we know a cause. This is apparent from the fact that the true things about which we have some knowledge have causes which are also true, because we cannot know what is true by knowing what is false, but only by knowing what is true. This is also the reason why demonstration, which causes science, begins with what is true, as is stated in Book I of the *Posterior Analytics. [74b5]*

292. Then he adds the following universal proposition. When a univocal predicate is applied to several things, in each case that which constitutes the reason for the predication about other things has that attribute in the fullest sense. Thus fire is the cause of heat in compounds. Therefore, since heat is predicated univocally both of fire and of compound bodies, it follows that fire is hottest.

293. Now he says "univocal" because sometimes it happens that an effect does not become like its cause, so as to have the same specific nature, because of the excellence of that cause; for example, the sun is the cause of heat in these lower bodies, but the form which these lower bodies receive cannot be of the same specific nature as that possessed by the sun or any of the celestial bodies, since they do not have a common matter. This is why we do not say that the sun is hottest, as we say fire is, but that it is something superior to the hottest.

294. Now the term *truth* is not proper to one class of beings only, but is applied universally to all beings. Therefore, since the cause of truth is one having the same name and intelligible structure as its effect, it follows that whatever causes subsequent things to be true is itself most true.

295. From this he again concludes that the principles of things which always exist, i.e., the celestial bodies, must be most true. He does this for two reasons. First, they are not "sometimes true and sometimes not true," and therefore surpass the truth of things subject to generation and corruption, which sometimes exist and sometimes do not. Second, these principles have no cause but are the cause of the being of other things. And for this reason they surpass the celestial bodies in truth and in being; and even though the latter are incorruptible, they have a cause not only of their motion, as some men thought, but also of their being, as the Philosopher clearly states in this place.

296. Now this is necessary, because everything that is composite in nature and participates in being must ultimately have as its causes those things which have existence by their very essence. But all corporeal things are actual beings insofar as they participate in certain forms. Therefore a separate substance which is a form by its very essence must be the principle of corporeal substance.

297. If we add to this conclusion the fact that first philosophy considers first causes, it then follows, as was said above [1], that first philosophy considers those things which are most true.

Consequently this science is pre-eminently the science of truth.

298. From these conclusions he draws a corollary: since those things which cause the being of other things are true in the highest degree, it follows that each thing is true insofar as it is a being; for things which do not always have being in the same way do not always have truth in the same way, and those which have a cause of their being also have a cause of their truth. The reason for this is that a thing's being is the cause of any true judgment which the mind makes about a thing; for truth and falsity are not in things but in the mind, as will be said in Book VI (558:C 1230) of this work.

299. **Further, it is evident** [2].

He rejects a position that would render the above proof untenable; for this proof proceeded on the supposition that first philosophy considers first causes. But if there were an infinite regress in causes, this proof would be destroyed, for then there would be no first cause. So his aim here is to refute this position. Concerning this he does two things. First [2]), he points out what he intends to prove. Second (Lesson 3), he proceeds to do so ("For intermediate things").

He says, first, that from what has been said it can clearly be shown that there is some [first] principle of the being and truth of things. He states that the causes of existing things are not infinite in number because we cannot proceed to infinity in a series of causes belonging to one and the same class, e.g., the class of efficient causes. Nor again are causes infinite in species, as though the classes of causes were infinite in number.

300. Then he explains his statement about an infinite number of causes in a series. He does this, first, in regard to the class of material causes. For it is impossible to have an infinite series in the sense that one thing always comes from something else as its matter, e.g., that flesh comes from earth, earth from air, and air from fire, and that this does not terminate in some first entity but goes on to infinity. Second, he gives an example of this in the class of efficient cause. He says that it is impossible to have an infinite series in the class of cause which we define as the source of motion; e.g., when we say that a man is moved to put aside his clothing because the air becomes warm, the air having been heated in turn by the sun, the sun having been moved by something else, and so on to infinity. Third, he gives an example of this in the class of final causes. He says that it is also impossible to proceed to infinity in the case of "the reason for which" something is done, i.e., the final cause; for example, if we were to say that a journey or a walk is undertaken for the sake of health, health for the sake of happiness, happiness for the sake of something else, and so on to infinity. Finally, he mentions the formal cause. He says that it is also impossible to proceed to infinity in the case of the "quiddity," i.e., the formal cause, which the definition signifies. However, he omits examples because these are evident, and because it was shown in Book I of the *Posterior Analytics [81b10]* that it is impossible to proceed to infinity in the matter of predication, as though animal were predicated quidditatively of man, living of animal, and so on to infinity.

LESSON 3

The Existence of a First Efficient Cause and of a First Material Cause

ARISTOTLE'S TEXT Chapter 2: 994a11–994b9

1. *For intermediate things in a series limited by some first and last thing must have as their cause the first member of the series, which they follow; because if we had to say which one of these three is the cause of the others, we would say that it is the first. What is last is not the cause, since what is last is not a cause of anything. Neither is the intermediate the cause, because it is the cause of only one; for it makes no difference whether one or several intermediates exist, or an infinite or finite number. Indeed, in series that are infinite in this way or in the infinite in general, all parts are intermediates to the same degree right down to the present one. Therefore, if there is nothing first in the whole series, nothing in the series is a cause.* **994a11–19**

2. *Neither is it possible to proceed to infinity in a downward direction, where there is a starting-point in an upward direction, so that water comes from fire, earth from water, and some other class of things always being generated in this way.* **994a19–22**

3. *Now there are two ways in which one thing comes from (ex) another. I do not mean from in the sense of after, as the Olympian games are said to come from the Isthmian, but either in the way in which a man comes from a boy as a result of a boy changing, or in the way in which air comes from water.* **994a22–24**

4. *We say, then, that a man comes from a boy in the sense that what has come into being comes from what is coming into being, or in the sense that what has been completed comes from what is being completed. For generation is always midway between being and non-being, and thus whatever is coming into being is midway between what is and what is not. Now a learner is one who is becoming learned, and this is the meaning of the statement that the man of science comes from the learner. But water comes from air in the sense that it comes into being when the latter ceases to be.* **994a25–31**

5. *This is why changes of the former kind are not reversible, and thus a boy does not come from a man. The reason is that the thing which comes into being does not come from generation but exists after generation. This is the way in which the day comes from the dawn, i.e., in the sense that it exists after the dawn; and this is why the dawn cannot come from the day. On the other hand, changes of the latter sort are reversible.* **994a31–994b3**

6. *Now in neither way is it possible to proceed to infinity; for existing intermediaries must have some end, and one thing may be changed into the other because the corruption of one is the generation of the other.* **994b3–6**

7. *At the same time it is impossible that an eternal first cause should be corrupted; for since generation is not infinite in an upward direction, then a first principle by whose corruption something else is produced could not be eternal.* **994b6–9**

COMMENTARY

301. Having assumed above that the causes of beings are not infinite in number, the Philosopher now proves this. First [1], he proves that there are not an infinite number of causes in a series; and second (n. 330), that the classes of causes are not infinite in number ("Again, if the classes of causes").

In regard to the first he does four things. First, he proves his assumption in the case of efficient or moving causes; second [2], in the case of material causes ("Neither is it possible");

third (Lesson 4), in the case of final causes ("Again, that for the sake of which"); and fourth (see n. 320), in the case of formal causes ("Nor can the quiddity").

In regard to the first he proceeds as follows. First, he lays down this premise: in the case of all those things which lie between two extremes, one of which is last and the other first, the first is necessarily the cause of those which come after it, namely, what is intermediate and what is last.

302. Then he proves this premise by a process of elimination. For if we had to say which of the three, i.e., the first, the intermediate, or the last, is the cause of the others, we would have to say that the first is the cause. We could not say that what is last is the cause of all the others, because it is not a cause of anything; for in other respects what is last is not a cause, since an effect follows a cause. Nor could we say that the intermediate is the cause of all the others, because it is the cause of only one of them, namely, what is last.

303. And lest someone should think that an intermediate is followed by only one thing, i.e., what is last (for this occurs only when there is a single thing between two extremes), in order to exclude this interpretation he adds that it makes no difference to the premise given above whether there is only one intermediate or several, because all intermediates are taken together as one insofar as they have in common the character of an intermediate. Nor again does it make any difference whether there are a finite or infinite number of intermediates, because so long as they have the nature of an intermediate they cannot be the first cause of motion. Further, since there must be a first cause of motion prior to every secondary cause of motion, then there must be a first cause prior to every intermediate cause, which is not an intermediate in any sense, as though it had a cause prior to itself. But if we were to hold that there is an infinite series of moving causes in the above way, then all causes would be intermediate ones. Thus we would have to say without qualification that all parts of any infinite thing, whether of a series of causes or of continuous quantities, are intermediate ones; for if there were a part that was not an intermediate one, it would have to be either a first or a last; and both of these are opposed to the nature of the infinite, which excludes every limit, whether it be a starting-point or a terminus.

304. Now there is another point that must be noted, i.e., that if there are several intermediate parts in any finite thing, not all parts are intermediate to the same degree; for some are closer to what is first, and some to what is last. But in the case of some infinite thing in which there is neither a first nor last part, no part can be closer to or farther away from either what is first or what is last. Therefore all parts are intermediates to the same degree right down to the one you designate now. Consequently, if the causes of motion proceed to infinity in this way, there will be no first cause. But a first cause is the cause of all things. Therefore it will follow that all causes are eliminated; for when a cause is removed the things of which it is the cause are also removed.

305. **Neither is it possible** [2].

He shows that it is impossible to proceed to infinity in the case of material causes. First [2], he states what he intends to prove. Second [3], he proceeds with his proof ("Now there are two ways").

In regard to the first it must be noted

that a patient is subjected to the action of an agent. Therefore to pass from agent to agent is to proceed in an upward direction, whereas to pass from patient to patient is to proceed in a downward direction. Now just as *action* is attributed to the cause of motion, so is *undergoing action* attributed to matter. Therefore among the causes of motion the process is in an upward direction, whereas among material causes the process is in a downward direction. Consequently, since he showed among moving causes that it is impossible to proceed to infinity, as it were, in an upward direction, he adds that it is impossible to proceed to infinity in a downward direction, i.e., in the process of material causes, granted that there is a starting-point in an upward direction among the causes of motion.

306. He illustrates this by way of the process of natural bodies, which proceeds in a downward direction, as if we were to say that water comes from fire, earth from water, and so on to infinity. He uses this example in accordance with the opinion of the ancient philosophers of nature, who held that one of these elements is the source of the others in a certain order.

307. However, this can also be explained in another way, inasmuch as we understand that in the case of moving causes there are evident to the senses certain ultimate effects which do not move anything else. Therefore we do not ask if there is an infinite regress in the lower members of that class, but if there is an infinite regress in the higher ones. But in regard to the class of material causes, he assumes that there is one first cause which is the foundation and basis of the others; and he inquires whether there is an infinite regress in a downward direction in the process of those things which are generated from matter. The example which he gives illustrates this, because he does not say that fire comes from water and this in turn from something else, but the converse, i.e., that water comes from fire, and something else again from this. For this reason first matter is held to exist; and he asks whether the things that are generated from matter proceed to infinity.

308. **Now there are two ways in which** [3].

He proves his original thesis. Concerning this he does four things. First [3], he distinguishes between the two ways in which one thing *comes from* something else. Second [4], he shows that these two ways differ in two respects ("We say, then, that a man"). Third [6], he shows that it is impossible to proceed to infinity in either of these ways ("Now in neither way"). Fourth [7], he shows in which of these ways other things come from the first material principle ("At the same time").

He says, first, that one thing "comes from" another properly and essentially in two ways. He speaks thus in order to exclude that way in which something is said in an improper sense to *come from* something else only by reason of the fact that it *comes after* it, as when it is said that certain feasts of the Greeks called the Olympian come from those called the Isthmian, or as if we were to say that the feast of the Epiphany comes from the feast of the Nativity. But this is an improper use of the word, because the process of coming to be is a change, and in a change it is not only necessary that an order exist between the two limits of the change but also that both limits have the same subject. Now this is not the case in the above example, but we speak in this way insofar as we think of time as the subject of different feasts.

309. Now properly speaking it is necessary to say that one thing *comes from* something else when some subject is changed from *this* into *that*. This occurs in two ways: first, as when we say that a man comes from a boy in the sense that a boy is changed from boyhood to manhood; second, as when we say that air comes from water as a result of substantial change.

310. **We say, then, that a man** [4].

He explains the twofold sense in which these two ways differ. First, we say that a man comes from a boy in the sense that what has already come into being comes from what is coming into being, or in the sense that what has already been completed comes from what is being completed. For anything in a state of becoming and of being completed is midway between being and non-being, just as generation is midway between existence and nonexistence. Therefore, since we reach an extreme through an intermediate, we say that what has been generated comes from what is being generated, and that what has been completed comes from what is being completed. Now this is the sense in which we say that a man comes from a boy, or a man of science from a learner, because a learner is one who is becoming a man of science. But in the other sense, i.e., the one in which we say that water comes from fire, one of the limits of the change is not related to the other as a passage or intermediate, as generation is to being, but rather as the limit from which a thing starts in order to reach another limit. Therefore one comes from the other when the other is corrupted.

311. **This is why changes** [5].

He infers another difference from the foregoing one. For since, in the first way, one thing is related to the other as generation is to being, and as an intermediate to a limit, it is evident that one is naturally ordained to the other. Therefore they are not reversible so that one comes from the other indifferently. Consequently we do not say that a boy comes from a man, but the reverse. The reason for this is that those two things, of which one is said to come from the other in this way, are not related to each other in the same way as the two limits of a change, but as two things one of which comes after the other in sequence. And this is what he means when he says that "what has come into being" (i.e., the terminus of generation or being) does not come from generation as though generation itself were changed into being, but is that which exists after generation, because it follows generation in a natural sequence; just as one's destination comes after a journey, and as what is last comes after what is intermediate. Therefore, if we consider these two things, i.e., generation and being, the way in which they are related does not differ from the one we have excluded, in which sequence alone is considered, as when we say that the day comes from the dawn because it comes after the dawn. Moreover, this natural sequence prevents us from saying in an opposite way that the dawn comes "from the day," i.e., after the day; and for the same reason a boy cannot come from a man. But in the other sense in which one thing comes from another, the process is reversible; for just as water is generated by reason of air being corrupted, in a similar way air is generated by reason of water being corrupted. The reason is that these two are not related to each other in a natural sequence, i.e., as an intermediate to a limit, but as two limits, either one of which can be first or last.

312. **Now in neither way** [6].

He shows that it is impossible to proceed to infinity in either of these ways. First, in the way in which we say that a man comes from a boy; for the thing from which we say something else comes as a man comes from a boy has the position of an intermediary between two limits, i.e., between being and non-being. But an infinite number of intermediates cannot exist when certain limits are held to exist, since limits are opposed to infinity. Therefore, it is impossible to have an infinite series in this way.

313. In like manner it is impossible to have an infinite series in the other way; for in that way one limit is converted into the other, because the corruption of one is the generation of the other, as has been explained. Now wherever a reversible process exists there is a return to some first thing in the sense that what was at first a starting-point is afterwards a terminus. This cannot occur in the case of things that are infinite, in which there is neither a starting-point nor a terminus. Consequently, there is no way in which one thing can come from another in an infinite regress.

314. **At the same time it is impossible** [7].

He shows in which of these ways something comes from first matter. Now it must be noted that in this place Aristotle uses two common suppositions accepted by all of the ancient philosophers: first, that there is a primary material principle, and therefore that in the process of generation there is no infinite regress on the part of the higher, i.e., of that from which a thing is generated; second, that matter is eternal. Therefore, from this second supposition he immediately concludes that nothing comes from first matter in the second way, i.e., in the way in which water comes from air as a result of the latter's corruption, because what is eternal cannot be corrupted.

315. But since someone could say that the philosophers did not hold that the first material principle is eternal because it remains numerically one eternally but because it is eternal by succession (as if the human race were held to be eternal), he therefore excludes this from the first supposition. He says that since generation is not infinite in an upward direction but stops at a first material principle, then if there is a first material principle by reason of whose corruption other things come into being, it must not be the eternal principle of which the philosophers speak. The reason is that the first material principle cannot be eternal if other things are generated by reason of its corruption, and it in turn is generated by the corruption of something else. It is evident, then, that a thing comes from this first material principle as something imperfect and potential which is midway between pure nonbeing and actual being, but not as water comes from air by reason of the latter's corruption.

LESSON 4
The Existence of a First in Final and Formal Causes

ARISTOTLE'S TEXT Chapter 2: 994b9–994b31

1. Again, that for the sake of which something comes to be is an end. Now such a thing is not for the sake of something else, but other things are for its sake. Therefore, if there is such a thing as an ultimate end, there will not be an infinite regress; but if there is no ultimate end, there will be no reason for which things come to be. **994b9–12**

2. Now those who posit infinity do away with the nature of the good without realizing it. **994b12–13**

3. But no one will attempt to do anything unless he thinks he can carry it through to its term. **994b13–14**

4. Nor will there be any intelligence in such matters, because one who has intelligence always acts for the sake of something since this limit is the end of a thing. **994b14–16**

5. Nor can the quiddity be reduced to a definition which adds to the defining notes. **994b16–18**

6. For a prior definition is always more of a definition, whereas a subsequent one is not; and where the first note does not apply, neither does a later one. **994b18–20**

7. Again, those who speak in this way do away with science, because it is impossible to have science until we reach what is undivided. **994b20–21**

8. Nor will knowledge itself exist; for how can one understand things which are infinite in this way? **994b21–23**

9. This case is not like that of a line, whose divisibility has no limit, for it would be impossible to understand a line if it had no limits. This is why no one will count the sections, which proceed to infinity. **994b23–25**

10. But it is necessary to understand that there is matter in everything that is moved, and that the infinite involves nothingness, but essence does not. But if there is no infinite, what essence [i.e., definition] does the infinite have? **994b25–27**

11. Again, if the classes of causes were infinite in number, it would also be impossible to know anything; for we think that we have scientific knowledge when we know the causes themselves of things; but what is infinite by addition cannot be traversed in a finite period of time. **994b27–31**

COMMENTARY

316. Having shown that there is no infinite regress either among the causes of motion or among material causes, the Philosopher now shows that the same thing is true of the final cause, which is called "that for the sake of which" something comes to be [1].

He proves this by four arguments. The first is as follows. That for the sake of which something comes to be has the character of an end. But an end does not exist for the sake of other things, but others exist for its sake. Now such a thing either exists or not. If there is something of such a kind that all things exist for its sake and not it for the sake of something else, it will be the last thing in this order; and thus there will not be an infinite regress. However, if no such thing exists, no end will exist; and thus the class of cause called "that for the sake of which" will be eliminated.

317. **Now those who posit infinity** [2].

He gives the second argument,

which is derived from the foregoing one; for from the first argument he concluded that those who posit an infinite regress in final causes do away with the final cause. Now when the final cause is removed, so also is the nature and notion of the good; because *good* and *end* have the same meaning, since the good is that which all desire, as is said in Book I of the *Ethics.[1094a2]* Therefore those who hold that there is an infinite regress in final causes do away completely with the nature of the good, although they do not realize this.

318. **But no one will attempt** [3].

He gives the third argument, which is as follows. If there were an infinite number of final causes, no one could reach a last terminus, because there is no last terminus in an infinite series. But no one will attempt to do anything unless he thinks he is able to accomplish something as a final goal. Therefore, those who hold that final causes proceed to infinity do away with every attempt to operate and even with the activities of natural bodies; for a thing's natural movement is only toward something which it is naturally disposed to attain.

319. **Nor will there be** [4].

He states the fourth argument, which is as follows. One who posits an infinite number of final causes does away with a limit, and therefore with the end for the sake of which a cause acts. But every intelligent agent acts for the sake of some end. Therefore it would follow that there is no intellect among causes which are productive; and thus the practical intellect is eliminated. But since these things are absurd, we must reject the first position, from which they follow, i.e., that there is an infinite number of final causes.

320. **Nor can the quiddity** [5].

He shows that there is not an infinite number of formal causes. In regard to this he does two things. First [5], he states what he intends to prove. Second [6], he proves it ("For a prior definition").

Regarding the first we must understand that each thing derives its particular species from its proper form, and this is why the definition of a species signifies chiefly a thing's form. Therefore we must understand that a procession of forms is consequent upon a procession of definitions; for one part of a definition is prior to another just as genus is prior to difference and one difference is prior to another. Therefore an infinite regress in forms and in the parts of a definition is one and the same thing. Now since Aristotle wishes to show that it is impossible to proceed to infinity in the case of formal causes, he holds that it is impossible to proceed to infinity in the parts of a definition. Hence he says that it is impossible for a thing's quiddity to be reduced to another definition, and so on to infinity, so that the defining notes are always increased in number. For example, one who defines man gives animal in his definition, and therefore the definition of man is reduced to that of animal, and this in turn to the definition of something else, thereby increasing the defining notes. But to proceed to infinity in this way is absurd.

321. Now we do not mean by this that there are the same number of forms in each individual as there are genera and differences, so that in man there is one form by which he is man, another by which he is animal, and so on; but we mean that there must be as many grades of forms in reality as there are orders of genera and differences [in knowledge]. For we find in reality one form which is not the form

of a body, another which is the form of a body but not of an animated body, and so on.

322. **For a prior definition** [6].

He proves his premise by four arguments. The first is this. Wherever there are a number of forms or defining notes, a prior definition is always "more of a definition." This does not mean that a prior form is more complete (for specific forms are complete), but that a prior form belongs to more things than a subsequent form, which is not found wherever a prior form is found; e.g., the definition of man is not found wherever that of animal is found. From this he argues that if the first note [of a series] does not fit the thing defined, "neither does a later one." But if there were an infinite regress in definitions and forms, there would be no first definition or definitive form. Hence all subsequent definitions and forms would be eliminated.

323. **Again, those who speak** [7].

He gives the second argument, which is as follows. It is impossible to have scientific knowledge of anything until we come to what is undivided. Now in this place "undivided" cannot mean the singular, because there is no science of the singular. However, it can be understood in two other ways. First, it can mean the definition itself of the last species, which is not further divided by essential differences. In this sense his statement can mean that we do not have complete knowledge of a thing until we reach its last species; for one who knows the genus to which a thing belongs does not yet have a complete knowledge of that thing. According to this interpretation we must say that, just as the first argument concluded that it is impossible to have an infinite regress in an upward direction among formal causes, in a similar fashion this second argument concludes that it is impossible to have an infinite regress in a downward direction, otherwise it would be impossible to reach a last species. Therefore this position destroys any complete knowledge.

324. Now a formal division exists not only when a genus is divided by differences (and when such division is no longer possible the last species can be said to be undivided), but also when the thing defined is divided into its definitive parts, as is evident in Book I of the Physics.[184a11] Therefore in this place "undivided" can also mean a thing whose definition cannot be resolved into any definitive parts. Now according to this the supreme genus is undivided; and from this point of view his statement can mean that we cannot have scientific knowledge of a thing by definition unless we reach its supreme genera; because when these remain unknown it is impossible to know its subsequent genera. And according to this the second argument concludes, as the former one did, that it is impossible to proceed to infinity in an upward direction among formal causes.

325. Or, in order to reach the same conclusion, "undivided" can be explained in another way, i.e., in the sense that an immediate proposition is undivided. For if it were possible to proceed to infinity in an upward direction in the case of definitions, there would be no immediate proposition, and thus science as such, which is about conclusions derived from immediate principles, would be destroyed.

326. **Nor will knowledge** [8].

He gives the third argument, which proceeds to [show that such an infinite regress would] destroy not only science but any kind of human knowing whatsoever. In regard to this argument he does two things. First [8], he gives his argument. Second [9], he refutes an objection raised against it ("This case is not like").

The argument is as follows. We know each thing by understanding its form. But if there were an infinite regress in forms, these forms could not be understood, because the intellect is incapable of understanding the infinite as infinite. Therefore this position destroys knowing in its entirety.

327. **This case is not like** [9].

He disposes of an objection; for someone could say that a thing having an infinite number of forms can be understood in the same way as a line which is divided to infinity. But he denies this. He says that this case is not the same as that of a line, whose divisions do not stop but go on to infinity. For it is impossible to understand anything unless some limit is set to it. Therefore a line can be understood inasmuch as some actual limit is given to it by reason of its extremes. However, it cannot be understood insofar as its division does not terminate. Hence no one can count the divisions of a line insofar as they are infinite. But as applied to forms "infinite" means actually infinite, and not potentially infinite as it does when applied to the division of a line. Therefore, if there were an infinite number of forms, there would be no way in which a thing could be known either scientifically or in any way at all.

328. **But it is necessary** [10].

He gives the fourth argument, which runs thus. Matter must be understood to exist in everything that is moved; for whatever is moved is in potentiality, and what is in potentiality is matter. But matter itself has the character of the infinite, and nothingness belongs to the infinite in the sense of matter, because matter taken in itself is understood without any of kind of form. And since nothingness belongs to the infinite, it follows contrariwise that the principle by which the infinite is a being is itself not infinite, and that it does not belong "to the infinite," i.e., to matter, to be infinite in being. But things are by virtue of their form. Hence there is no infinite regress among forms.

329. However, it must be noted that in this place Aristotle holds that the infinite involves the notion of nothingness, not because matter involves the notion of privation (as Plato claimed when he failed to distinguish between privation and matter), but because the infinite involves the notion of privation. For a potential being contains the notion of the infinite only insofar as it comes under the nature of privation, as is evident in Book III of the *Physics*. *[207b35]*

330. **Again, if the classes** [11].

He shows that the classes of causes are not infinite in number, and he uses the following argument. We think that we have scientific knowledge of each thing when we know all its causes. But if there were an infinite number of causes in the sense that one class of cause may be added to another continuously, it would be impossible to traverse this infinity in such a way that all causes could be known. Hence in this way too the knowing of things would be destroyed.

LESSON 5
The Method to Be Followed in the Search for Truth

ARISTOTLE'S TEXT Chapter 3: 994b32–995a20

1. The way in which people are affected by what they hear depends upon the things to which they are accustomed; for it is in terms of such things that we judge statements to be true, and anything over and above these does not seem similar but less intelligible and more remote. For it is the things to which we are accustomed that are better known. **994b32–995a3**

2. The great force which custom has is shown by the laws, in which legendary and childish elements prevail over our knowledge of them, because of custom. **995a3–6**

3. Now some men will not accept what a speaker says unless he speaks in mathematical terms; and others, unless he gives examples; while others expect him to quote a poet as an authority. Again, some want everything stated with certitude, while others find certitude annoying, either because they are incapable of comprehending anything, or because they consider exact inquiry to be quibbling; for there is some similarity. Hence it seems to some men that, just as liberality is lacking in the matter of a fee for a banquet, so also is it lacking in arguments. **995a6–12**

4. For this reason one must be trained how to meet every kind of argument; and it is absurd to search simultaneously for knowledge and for the method of acquiring it; for neither of these is easily attained. **995a12–14**

5. But the exactness of mathematics is not to be expected in all cases, but only in those which have no matter. This is why its method is not that of natural philosophy; for perhaps the whole of nature contains matter. Hence we must first investigate what nature is; for in this way it will become evident what the things are with which natural philosophy deals, and whether it belongs to one science or to several to consider the causes and principles of things. **995a14–20**

COMMENTARY

331. Having shown that the study of truth is in one sense difficult and in another easy, and that it belongs preeminently to first philosophy, the Philosopher now exposes the proper method of investigating the truth. In regard to this he does two things. First [1], he gives the different methods which men follow in the study of truth. Second [4], he shows which method is the proper one ("For this reason one must").

In regard to the first he does two things. First, he shows how powerful custom is in the study of truth. Second [3], he concludes that the different methods which men employ in the study of truth depend on the different things to which they are accustomed ("Now some men").

In regard to the first he does two things. First, he shows how powerful custom is in the study of truth. Second [3], he makes this clear by an example ("The great force").

He says, first, that the way in which people are affected by what they hear depends upon the things to which they are accustomed, because such things are more willingly heard and more easily understood. For things spoken of in a manner to which we are accustomed seem to us to be acceptable; and if any things are said to us over and above what we have been accustomed to hear, these do not seem to have the same degree of truth. As a matter of fact they seem less intelligible to us and further removed from reason just because we are not accustomed to them; for it is the things which we are accustomed to hear that we know best of all.

332. Now the reason for this is that things which are customary become natural. Hence a habit, which disposes us in a way similar to nature, is also acquired by customary activity. And from the fact that someone has some special sort of nature or special kind of habit, he has a definite relationship to one thing or another. But in every kind of cognition there must be a definite relationship between the knower and the object of cognition. Therefore, to the extent that natures and habits differ, there are diverse kinds of cognition. For we see that there are innate first principles in men because of their human nature, and that what is proper to some special virtue appears good to one who has this habit of virtue; and, again, that something appears palatable to the sense of taste because of its disposition. Therefore, since custom produces a habit which is similar to nature, it follows that what is customary is better known.

333. **The great force** [2].

Here he makes his previous statement clear by giving a concrete case. He says that the laws which men pass are positive evidence of the force of custom; for the legendary and childish elements in these laws are more effective in winning assent than is knowledge of the truth. Now the Philosopher is speaking here of the laws devised by men, which have as their ultimate end the preservation of the political community. Therefore the men who have established these laws have handed down in them, in keeping with the diversity of peoples and nations involved, certain directives by which human souls might be drawn away from evil and persuaded to do good, although many of them, which men had heard from childhood and of which they approved more readily than of what they knew to be true, were empty and foolish. But the law given by God directs men to that true happiness to which everything false is opposed. Therefore there is nothing false in the divine law.

334. **Now some men** [3].

Here he shows how men as a result of custom use different methods in the study of truth. He says that some men listen to what is said to them only if it is mathematical in character; and this is acceptable to those who have been educated in mathematics because of the habits which they have. Now since custom is like nature, the same thing can also happen to certain men because they are poorly disposed in some respect, e.g., those who have a strong imagination but little intelligence. Then there are others who do not wish to accept anything unless they are given a concrete example, either because they are accustomed to this or because their sensory powers dominate and their intellect is weak. Again, there are some who think that nothing is convincing enough unless a poet or some authority is cited. This is also a result either of custom or of poor judgment, because they cannot decide for themselves whether the conclusion of an argument is certain; and therefore, having no faith in their own judgment, as it were, they require the judgment of some recognized authority. Again there are others who want everything said to them with certitude, i.e., by way of careful rational investigation. This occurs because of the superior intelligence of the one making the judgment and the arguments of the one conducting the investigation, provided that one does not look for certitude where it cannot be had. On the other hand there are some who are annoyed if some matter is investigated in an exact way by means of a careful discussion. This can occur for two reasons. First, they lack the ability to comprehend anything; for since their reasoning power is poor they are unable to understand the order in which premises are related to conclusions. Second, it occurs because of quibbling, i.e., reasoning about the smallest matters, which bears some resemblance to the search for certitude since it leaves nothing undiscussed down to the smallest detail. Then there are some who think that, just as liberality is lacking when the smallest details are taken into account in estimating the fee for a banquet, in a similar way there is a lack of civility and liberality when a man also wishes to discuss the smallest details in the search for truth.

335. **For this reason one must be trained** [4].

He exposes the proper method of investigating the truth. Concerning this he does two things. First (174:C 335), he shows how a man can discover the proper method of investigating the truth. Second (175:C 336), he explains that the method which is absolutely the best should not be demanded in all matters ("But the exactness of mathematics").

He says, first, that since different men use different methods in the search for truth, one must be trained in the method which the particular sciences must use to investigate their subject. And since it is not easy for a man to undertake two things at once (indeed, so long as he tries to do both he can succeed in neither), it is absurd for a man to try to acquire a science and at the same time to acquire the method proper to that science. This is why a man should learn logic before any of the other sciences, because logic considers the general method of procedure in all the other sciences. Moreover, the method appropriate to the particular sciences should be considered at the beginning of these sciences.

336. **But the exactness of mathematics** [5].

He shows that the method which is absolutely the best should not be demanded in all the sciences. He says that the "exactness," i.e., the careful and certain demonstrations, found in mathematics should not be demanded in the case of all things of which we have science, but only in the case of those things which have no matter; for things that have matter are subject to motion and change, and therefore in their case complete certitude cannot be had. For in the case of these things we do not look for what exists always and of necessity, but only for what exists in the majority of cases. Now immaterial things are most certain by their very nature because they are unchangeable, although they are not certain to us because our intellectual power is weak, as was stated above (149:C 279). The separate substances are things of this kind. But while the things with which mathematics deals are abstracted from matter, they do not surpass our understanding; and therefore in their case most certain reasoning is demanded. Again, because the whole of nature involves matter, this method of most certain reasoning does not belong to natural philosophy. However, he says "perhaps" because of the celestial bodies, since they do not have matter in the same sense that lower bodies do.

337. Now since this method of most certain reasoning is not the method proper to natural science, therefore in order to know which method is proper to that science we must investigate first what nature is; for in this way we will discover the things which natural phi-

losophy studies. Further, we must investigate "whether it belongs to one science," i.e., to natural philosophy, or to several sciences, to consider all causes and principles; for in this way we will be able to learn which method of demonstration is proper to natural philosophy. He deals with this method in Book II of the *Physics*,^1 as is obvious to anyone who examines it carefully.

BOOK III
METAPHYSICAL PROBLEMS

LESSON 1

The Need of Questioning Everything in the Search for Universal Truth

ARISTOTLE'S TEXT Chapter 1: 995a24–995b4

1. *With a view to the science under investigation we must attack first those subjects which must first be investigated. These are all the subjects about which some men have entertained different opinions, and any other besides these which has been omitted.* **995a24–27**

2. *Now for those who wish to investigate the truth it is worth the while to ponder these difficulties well. For the subsequent study of truth is nothing else than the solution of earlier problems. For it is impossible to untie a knot without knowing it. But a perplexity on the part of the mind makes this evident in regard to the matter at hand; for insofar as the mind is perplexed, to that extent it experiences something similar to men who are bound; for in both cases it is impossible to move forward. For this reason, then, it is first necessary to consider all the difficulties and the reasons for them.* **995a27–34**

3. *[This is also necessary] for another reason, namely, that those who make investigations without first recognizing the problem are like those who do not know where they ought to go.* **99ba34–36**

4. *Again, one would not even know when he finds the thing which he is seeking [and when not]; for the goal is not evident to such a man, but it is evident to one who previously discussed the difficulties.* **995a34–95b2**

5. *Furthermore, one who has heard all the arguments of the litigants, as it were, and of those who argue the question, is necessarily in a better position to pass judgment.* **995b2–4**

COMMENTARY

338. Having indicated in Book II the method of considering the truth, the Philosopher now proceeds with his study of the truth. First [1], he proceeds disputatively, indicating those points which are open to question so far as the truth of things is concerned. Second, he begins to establish what is true, and he does this in Book IV, which begins: "There is a certain science."

The first part is divided into two sections. In the first, he states what he intends to do. In the second (Lesson 2), he proceeds to do it ("The first problem").

In regard to the first he does two things. First [1], he states what he intends to do. Second [2], he gives the reasons for this ("Now for those").

He says first [1], then, that with a view to this science which we are seeking about first principles and what is universally true of things, we must attack, first of all, those subjects about which it is necessary to raise questions before the truth is established. Now there are disputed points of this kind for two reasons, either because the ancient philosophers entertained a different opinion about these things than is really true, or because they completely neglected to consider them.

339. **Now for those** [2].

Here he gives four arguments in support of this thesis. First, he says that for those who wish to investigate the truth it is "worth the while," i.e., worth the effort, "to ponder these difficulties well," i.e., to examine carefully those matters which are open to question. This is necessary because the subsequent study of truth is nothing else than the solution of earlier difficulties. Now in loosening a physical knot it is evident that one who is unacquainted with this knot cannot loosen it. But a difficulty about some subject is related to the mind as a physical knot is to the body, and manifests the same effect. For insofar as the mind is puzzled about some subject, it experiences something similar to those who are tightly bound. For just as one whose feet are tied cannot move forward on an earthly road, in a similar way one who is puzzled, and whose mind is bound, as it were, cannot move forward on the road of speculative knowledge. Therefore, just as one who wishes to loosen a physical knot must first of all inspect the knot and the way in which it is tied, in a similar way one who wants to solve a problem must first survey all the difficulties and the reasons for them.

340. **[This is also necessary]** [3].

Here he gives the second argument. He says that those who wish to investigate the truth without first considering the problem are like those who do not know where they are going. This is true for this reason, that, just as the terminus of a journey is the goal intended by one who travels on foot, in a similar way the solution of a problem is the goal intended by one who is seeking the truth. But it is evident that one who does not know where he is going cannot go there directly, except perhaps by chance. Therefore, neither can one seek the truth directly unless he first sees the problem.

341. **Again, one would** [4].

Here he gives the third argument. He says that, just as one who is ignorant of where he is going does not know whether he should stop or go further when he reaches his appointed goal, in a similar way one who does not know beforehand the problem whose solution marks the terminus of his search cannot know when he finds the truth which he is seeking and when not. For he does not know what the goal of his investigations is, but this is evident to one who knew the problem beforehand.

342. **Furthermore** [5].

He gives the fourth argument, which is taken from the viewpoint of a judge. For a judge must pass judgment on the things which he hears. But just as one can pass judgment in a lawsuit only if he hears the arguments on both sides, in a similar way one who has to pass judgment on a philosophy is necessarily in a better position to do so if he will hear all the arguments, as it were, of the disputants.

343. Now it must be noted that it was for these reasons that Aristotle was accustomed, in nearly all his works, to set forth the problems which emerge before investigating and establishing what is true. But while in other works Aristotle sets down the problems one at a time in order to establish the truth about each one, in this work he sets forth all the problems at once, and afterwards in the proper order establishes the things that are true. The reason for this is that other sciences consider the truth in a particular way, and therefore it belongs to them to raise problems of a particular kind about individual truths. But just as it belongs to this science to make a universal study of truth, so also does it belong to it to discuss all the problems which pertain to the truth. Therefore it does not discuss its problems one at a time but all at once.

344. There can also be another reason [why Aristotle proceeds in this way], namely, that those problems on which he touches are chiefly those

about which the philosophers have held different opinions. However, he does not proceed to investigate the truth in the same order as the other philosophers did. For he begins with things which are sensible and evident and proceeds to those which are separate from matter, as is evident below in Book VII (650:C 1566), whereas the other philosophers wanted to apply intelligible and abstract principles to sensible things. Hence, because he did not intend to establish the truth in the same order as that followed by the other philosophers, and from whose views these problems arise, he therefore decided to give first all the problems in a separate section, and afterwards to solve these problems in their proper order.

345. Averroes gives another reason [for Aristotle's procedure]. He says that Aristotle proceeds in this way because of the relationship of this science to logic, which will be touched on below in Book IV; and therefore he made dialectical discussion a principal part of this science.

LESSON 2
Questions Concerning the Method of This Science

ARISTOTLE'S TEXT Chapter 1: 995b4–995b27

1. *The first problem concerns the things about which we raised questions in our introductory statements, i.e., whether it belongs to one science or to many to speculate about the causes.* **995b4–6**

2. *And there is also the problem whether it belongs to this science to know only the principles of substance, or also the principles on which all sciences base their demonstrations, e.g., whether it is possible to affirm and deny one and the same thing at the same time or not; and other such principles. And if this science deals with substance, there is the question whether one science deals with all substances, or many sciences. And if many, whether all are cognate, or whether some should be called wisdom and others something else.* **995b6–13**

3. *It is also necessary to inquire whether sensible substances alone must be said to exist, or whether there are other substances in addition to these; and whether they are unique, or whether there are many classes of substances, as was claimed by those who created the Forms and made the objects of mathematics an intermediate class between these Forms and sensible substances. As we have said, then, it is necessary to examine these questions.* **995b13–18**

4. *There is also the problem whether this speculation has to do with substances alone or also with the proper accidents of substances. And we must inquire about sameness and difference, likeness and unlikeness, contrariety, priority and posteriority, and all other such things which the dialecticians attempt to treat (basing their investigations only on probabilities); for to them too it belongs to theorize about all these things. Furthermore, we must investigate all those essential accidents of these same things; and not only what each one of them is, but also whether there is one contrary for each one.* **995b18–27**

COMMENTARY

346. Following out his announced plan, the Philosopher begins to set down the problems which are encountered in establishing the truth; and he divides this into two parts. In the first [1], he gives these problems; and in the second (Lesson 4), he gives the reasons for these problems, by indicating the arguments on either side of the question ("Therefore let us discuss").

Now it was stated in Book II that it is necessary to seek the method of a science before seeking the science itself. Therefore he gives, first [1], the problems which pertain to this science's method of investigation. Second (Lesson 2), he gives the problems which pertain to the first principles with which this science deals, as has been stated in Book I (see n. 36) ("And we must inquire").

Now a science is concerned with two things, as was said in Book II, namely, a study of the causes by which it demonstrates and the things with which it deals. Hence in regard to the first point he does two things. First [1], he presents a problem concerning the investigation of causes. Second [2], he presents several problems concerning the things with which this science deals ("And there is also the problem").

He says [1], then, that the first problem is one which we proposed in the issues raised at the end of Book II (see n. 336), which is, so to speak, the prologue to the whole of science, i.e., whether a study of the four causes in their four classes belongs to one science or to many different sciences. And this is to ask whether it belongs to one science, and especially to this science, to demonstrate by means of all the causes, or rather whether some sciences demonstrate by one cause and some by another.

347. **And there is also the problem** [2].

Here he raises problems about the things which this science considers. First [2], he inquires about the things which this science considers about substances; and second [3], about substances themselves ("It is also necessary").

In regard to the first [2] he raises three questions. For if it is supposed, from what was said in Book I, that this science considers first principles, the first question here will be whether it belongs to this science to know only the first principles of substances, or also to consider the first principles of demonstration, by means of which all sciences demonstrate. For example, should this science consider whether it is possible to affirm and deny one and the same thing at the same time or not? And the same thing applies to the other first and self-evident principles of demonstration.

348. And if this science considers substance as the primary kind of being, the second question is whether there is one science which considers all substances, or whether there are many sciences which consider different substances. For it seems that there should be many sciences which consider many substances.

349. And if there are many sciences which consider many substances, the third question is whether all are "cognate," i.e., whether all belong to one class, as geometry and arithmetic belong to the class of mathematical science, or whether they do not, but some to the class of wisdom and some to another class, for example, to the class of natural philosophy or to that of mathematical science. For according to the first point of view it seems that they do not belong to one class, since material and immaterial substances are not known by the same method.

350. **It is also necessary** [3].

Here he adds to the number of questions about substance; and he does this by raising two questions. The first question is whether sensible substances alone must be held to exist, as the philosophers of nature claimed, or whether there are in addition to sensible substances other immaterial and intelligible substances, as Plato claimed.

351. And if there are some substances separate from sensible things, the second question is whether "they are unique," i.e., whether they belong only to one class, or whether there are many classes of such substances. For certain men, understanding that there is a twofold abstraction, namely, of the universal from the particular, and of the mathematical form from sensible matter, held that each class is self-subsistent. Thus they held that there are separate substances which are subsisting abstract universals, and between these and particular sensible substances they placed the objects of mathematics—numbers, continuous quantities, and figures—which they regarded as separate subsisting things. Concerning the questions which have now been raised, then, it is necessary to investigate them below. He does this, first, by arguing both sides of the question, and, second, by determining its truth.

352. **There is also the problem** [4].

Here he asks whether this science's investigations extend to accidents; and he raises three questions. The first is whether this science, seeing that it is called the philosophy of substance, speculates about substance alone, or whether it also speculates about the proper accidents of substance; for it seems to be the office of the same science to consider a subject and the proper accidents of that subject.

353. The second question is whether this science considers certain things which seem to be proper accidents of being and which belong to all beings, namely, sameness and difference, likeness and unlikeness, contrariety, priority, and posteriority, and all others of this kind which are treated by the dialecticians, who deal with all things. However, they do not examine such things according to necessary premises but according to probable ones. For from one point of view it seems that, since these accidents are common ones, they pertain to first-philosophy; but from another point of view it seems that, since they are considered by the dialecticians, whose office it is to argue from probabilities, an examination of them does not belong to the consideration of the philosopher, whose office it is to demonstrate.

354. And since certain proper attributes naturally flow from these common accidents of being, the third question is whether it is the function of the philosopher to consider in regard to the common accidents only their quiddity or also their properties; for example, whether there is one opposite for each one.

LESSON 3
Questions Concerning the Things with Which This Science Deals

ARISTOTLE'S TEXT Chapter 1: 995b27–996a17

1. And we must inquire whether it is genera that constitute the principles and elements of things, or the parts into which each existing thing is divided. And if it is genera, whether it is those that are predicated of individuals first or last. And we must also inquire whether animal or man is a principle, and exists more truly than the singular. **995b27–31**

2. But most of all it is necessary to investigate and treat the question whether besides matter there is any cause in the proper sense or not; and whether it is separable or not; and whether it is numerically one or many. And we must ask whether there is anything besides the synolon (and by synolon I mean matter when something is predicated of it), or nothing; or whether this is true of some things but not of others, [and what these things are]. **995b31–36**

3. Further, we must inquire whether the principles of things are limited in number or in kind, both those in the intelligible structures of things and those in the underlying subject; and whether the principles of corruptible and of incorruptible things are the same or different; and whether they are all incorruptible, or whether those of corruptible things are corruptible. And the most difficult question of all, and the most disputed one, is whether unity and being are not something different from the substances of existing things, as the Pythagoreans and Plato say, or whether this is not the case, but the underlying subject is something different, as Empedocles holds of love, another thinker of fire, another of water, and another of air. And we must inquire whether the principles of things are universals or singular things. **996a1–10**

4. Again, we must inquire whether they exist potentially or actually. And also whether they are principles of things in some other way or in reference to motion; for these questions present great difficulty. **996a10–12**

5. And in addition to these questions we must inquire whether numbers or lengths and points are somehow substances or not. And if they are substances, whether they are separate from sensible things or are found in them. Concerning all of these matters it is not only difficult to discover what is true, but it is not even easy to state the problems well. **996a12–17**

COMMENTARY

355. Having raised questions pertaining to the method of investigation which this science uses, the Philosopher now raises questions pertaining to the things which this science considers. And since this science considers first principles, as has been stated in Book I, he therefore raises here questions pertaining to the principles of things.

Now both the Forms and the objects of mathematics were held to be the first principles of things. Therefore, first [1], he raises questions concerning the Forms; and second [5], concerning the objects of mathematics ("And in addition to these").

In regard to the first he does two things. First, he asks what things are principles; and second [3], what sort of beings they are ("Further, we must inquire").

And since separate universals were held to be the principles of things, he asks, first, whether universals are the principles of things; and second [2], whether separate entities are the principles of things ("But most of all").

Concerning the first [1], he asks two questions. The first is whether genera constitute the principles and elements of things, or the ultimate parts into which each individual thing is dissolved. This question arises because an element is that of which a thing is first composed and into which it is ultimately dissolved. Now we find a twofold mode of composition and dissolution. One has to do with the intelligible constitution, in which species are resolved into genera, and according to this mode genera seem to be the principles and elements of things, as Plato claimed. The other mode of composition and dissolution has to do with the real order; for example, natural bodies are composed of fire, air, water and earth, and are dissolved into these. It was for this reason that the natural philosophers claimed that the elements constitute the first principles of things.

356. And assuming that genera are the principles of things, the second question is whether the principles of things are to be identified with the universals which are predicated of individual things, i.e., the lowest species, which he calls genera after the usage of the Platonists, because the lowest species contain under themselves many individuals just as genera contain many species; or whether it is rather the first and most common genera that constitute principles, for example, which of the two is more of a principle, animal or man; for man is a principle according to the Platonists, and is more real than any singular man. Now this problem arises because of two divisions which reason makes. One of these is that whereby we divide genera into species, and the other is that whereby we resolve species into genera. For it seems that whatever is the last term in a process of division is always the first principle and element in a process of composition.

357. **But most of all** [2].

Here he inquires whether separate entities are the principles of things; and he raises four questions. For since the first philosophers of nature posited only a material cause, the first question is whether besides matter there is anything else that is a cause in the proper sense or not.

358. And granted that there is some other cause besides matter, the second question is whether it is separable from matter, as Plato held, or as Pythagoras held.

359. And if there is something separable from matter, the third question is whether it is a single thing, as Anaxagoras claimed, or many, as Plato and Aristotle himself claimed.

360. The fourth question is whether there is anything "besides the *synolon,*" i.e., the concrete whole, or nothing; or whether there is something in certain cases and not in others; and what kind of things they are in those cases in which there is something else, and what kind of things they are in those in which there is not. And he explains what a *synolon* or concrete whole is; i.e., it is matter when something is predicated of it. Now in order to understand this we must note that Plato claimed that man and horse, and universals which are predicated in this way, are certain separate Forms; and that man is predicated of Socrates or Plato by reason of the fact that sensible matter participates in a separate Form. Hence Socrates or Plato is called a *synolon* or concrete whole, because each is constituted as a result of matter participating in a separate form. And each is, as it were, a kind of predicate of matter. Hence the Philosopher asks here whether the whatness of the individual thing is something else in addition to the individual thing itself, or not; or also whether it is something else in the

case of some things and not in that of others. The Philosopher will answer this question in Book VII (see n. 1356).

361. **Further, we must inquire** [3].

Here he raises questions about the way in which principles exist. And since being is divided by the one and many, and by act and potency, he asks, first, whether these principles are one or many; and second [4], whether they are actual or potential ("Again, we must inquire").

In regard to the first he asks four questions. The first is whether the principles of things are limited in number or in kind; as we say, for example, that there are three principles of nature. Now the statement that they are limited in number can mean that the principle of nature is numerically a single form and a single matter and privation. And the statement that they are limited in kind can mean that there are many material principles which have in common the specific nature of material principle, and so on for the rest. And since some of the philosophers, such as the Platonists, attributed formal causes to things, while others, such as the ancient natural philosophers, attributed only material causes to things, he adds that this question is applicable both "in the intelligible structures," i.e., in formal causes, "and in the underlying subject," i.e., in material causes.

362. The second question is whether the principles of corruptible and of incorruptible things are the same or different. And if they are different, whether all are incorruptible, or whether the principles of corruptible things are corruptible and those of incorruptible things are incorruptible.

363. The third question is whether unity and being signify the very substance of things and not something added to the substance of things, as the Pythagoreans and Platonists claimed; or whether they do not signify the substance of things, but something else is the subject of unity and being, for example, fire or air or something else of this kind, as the ancient philosophers of nature held. Now he says that this question is the most difficult and most puzzling one, because on this question depends the entire thought of Plato and Pythagoras, who held that numbers are the substance of things.

364. The fourth question is whether the principles of things are "somehow universals or are in some sense singular things," i.e., whether those things which are held to be principles have the character of a principle in the sense of a universal intelligible nature, or according as each is a particular and singular thing.

365. **Again, we must inquire** [4].

Here he asks whether these principles exist potentially or actually. This question seems to refer especially to material principles; for it can be a matter of dispute whether the first material principle is some actual body, such as fire or air, as the ancient philosophers of nature held, or something which is only potential, as Plato held. And since motion is the actualization of something in potency, and is, in a sense, midway between potentiality and actuality, he therefore adds another question: whether the principles of things are causes only in reference to motion, as the philosophers of nature posited only principles of motion, either material or efficient, or also whether they are principles which act in some other way than by motion, as Plato claimed that sensible things are caused by immaterial entities by a certain participation in these. Furthermore, he says that these questions have been raised because they present the greatest difficulty, as is clear from the manner in which the philosophers have disagreed about them.

366. **And in addition to these** [5].

Here he raises questions concerning the objects of mathematics, which are posited as the principles of things. He raises two questions. The first is whether numbers, lengths, figures and points are somehow substances, as the Pythagoreans or Platonists held, or whether they are not, as the philosophers of nature held.

367. And if they are substances, the second question is whether they are separate from sensible things, as the Platonists held, or exist in sensible things, as the Pythagoreans held.

368. Now these questions are raised as problems which must be debated and settled below, because in these matters it is not only difficult to discover the truth, but it is not even easy to debate the matter adequately by finding probable arguments for either side of the question.

LESSON 4
Are All the Classes of Causes Studied by One Science or by Many?

ARISTOTLE'S TEXT Chapter 2: 996a18–996b26

1. Therefore let us discuss first the problem about which we first spoke: whether it is the office of one science or of many to study all the classes of causes. **996a18–20**

2. For how will it be the office of one science to come to principles since they are not contrary? **99a20–21**

3. Furthermore, in the case of many existing things not all the principles are present. For how can a principle of motion be present in all immobile things, or how can the nature of the good be found there? For everything which is a good in itself and by reason of its own nature is an end and thus a cause, because it is for its sake that other things come to be and exist. Further, the end and that for the sake of which something comes to be is the terminus of some action. But all actions involve motion. Therefore it would be impossible for this principle to be present in immobile things, nor could there be an autoagathon, i.e., a good in itself. Hence in mathematics too nothing is proved by means of this cause, nor is there any demonstration on the grounds that a thing is better or worse. Nor does anyone make any mention at all of anything of this kind. And for this reason some of the Sophists, for example, Aristippus, disregarded these. For in the other arts, even in the servile ones, such as building and cobbling, all things are to be explained on the grounds that they are better or worse; but the mathematical sciences give no account of things which are good or evil. **996a21–996b1**

4. But on the other hand, if there are many sciences of the causes, and different sciences for different principles, which of these must be said to be the one that is being sought, or which one of those who have them is best informed about the subject under investigation? **996b1–5**

5. For it is possible for the same thing to have all the classes of causes; for example, in the case of a house the source of motion is the art and the builder, the reason for which is its function, the matter is earth and stones, and the form is the plan. **996b5–8**

6. Therefore, from the things which were established a little while ago as to which of the sciences one should call wisdom, there is reason for calling every one of them such. For inasmuch as wisdom takes precedence and is a more authoritative science, and one which the others, like slaves, have no right to contradict, then the science which deals with the end and the good is such a science, because other things are for the sake of this. **996b8–13**

7. But insofar as wisdom has been defined as the science of first causes and of what is most knowable, such a science will be about substance. For while a subject may be known in many ways, we say that he who knows what a thing is in its being knows it better than he who knows it in its non-being. And in the former case one knows better than another, especially he who knows what a thing is, and not how great it is or of what sort it is or anything that it is naturally disposed to do or to undergo. Further, in the case of other things too we think that we know every single thing, and those of which there are demonstrations, when we know what each is, for example, what squaring is, because it is finding the middle term. The same thing is true in other cases. **996b13–22**

8. But with regard to processes of generation and actions and every change, we think that we know these perfectly when we know the principle of motion. But this differs from and is opposite to the end of motion. And for this reason it seems to be the province of a different science to speculate about each one of these causes. **996b22–26**

COMMENTARY

369. Having raised the questions which cause difficulty in this science,

Aristotle begins here to treat them dialectically. This is divided into three parts. In the first part [1], he treats the questions which pertain to the method of investigation of this science. In the second (Lesson 7), he treats the questions which pertain to substances ("Furthermore, there is"). In the third (Lesson 8), he treats the questions which pertain to the principles of substances ("Concerning the principles").

In regard to the first he does three things. First, he argues dialectically about this science's method of investigation, with reference to the causes by means of which it demonstrates; second [7], with reference to the first principles of demonstration ("But insofar"); and third (Lesson 6), with reference to substances themselves ("And there is the problem").

In regard to the first he does two things. First [1], he takes up again the question about which he plans to argue dialectically, concluding from the order in which the questions have been listed that it is necessary first to debate those issues which were stated first in the list of questions, namely, whether it is the function of one science or of many to investigate all the classes of causes; so that in this way the order of argument corresponds to the order in which the questions have been raised.

370. **For how will it be** [2].

Second, he gives the arguments relating to this question; and in regard to this he does three things. First [2], he gives an argument for the purpose of showing that it is not the office of a single science to consider all the classes of causes. Second [4], assuming that it belongs to different sciences to consider the different classes of causes, he asks which class of cause it is that is investigated by first philosophy. He argues on both sides of this question ("But on the other hand"). Third [8], he draws from this second dispute the conclusion of the first arguments ("But with regard to").

In regard to the first [2] he gives two arguments. He says that since it belongs to one science to consider contraries, how will it belong to one science to consider principles since they are not contrary? This view, if it is considered superficially, seems to be of no importance; for it appears to follow from the destruction of the antecedent, as if one were to argue thus: if principles are contraries, they belong to one science; therefore, if they are not contraries, they do not belong to one science.

371. Therefore it can be said that in these disputes the Philosopher not only uses probable arguments but sometimes also uses sophistical ones when he gives arguments introduced by others. But it does not seem reasonable that in such an important matter so great a philosopher would have introduced an argument which is both trifling and insignificant. Hence a different explanation must be given, namely, that if one rightly considers the nature of the various things which belong to the same science, some belong to a single science insofar as they are different, but others insofar as they are reduced to some one thing. Hence many other different things are found to belong to one science insofar as they are reduced to one thing, for example, to one whole, one cause, or one subject. But contraries and all opposites belong essentially to one science by reason of the fact that one is the means of knowing the other. And from this comes this probable proposition that all different things which are contraries belong to one science. Therefore, if principles were different and were not contraries,

it would follow that they would not belong to one science.

372. **Furthermore, in the case of** [3].

Here he gives the second argument, which runs thus. In the case of different things which belong to one science, whatever science considers one also considers another. This is evident in the case of contraries, which are different and belong essentially to one science without being reduced to some other unity. But not every science which considers one cause considers all causes. Therefore the study of all the causes does not belong to a single science.

373. He proves the minor premise thus: Different sciences deal with different beings, and there are many beings to which all the causes cannot be assigned. He makes this clear, first, with regard to that cause which is called the source of motion; for it does not seem that there can be a principle of motion in immobile things. Now certain immobile things are posited, especially by the Platonists, who claim that numbers and substances are separate entities. Hence, if any science considers these, it cannot consider the cause which is the source of motion.

374. Second, he shows that the same thing is true of the final cause, which has the character of good. For it does not seem that the character of goodness can be found in immobile things, if it is conceded that everything which is good in itself and by reason of its own nature is an end. And it is a cause in the sense that all things come to be and exist because of it and for its sake. However, he says "everything which is good in itself and by reason of its own nature" in order to exclude the useful good, which is not predicated of the end but of the means to the end. Hence those things which are said to be good only in the sense that they are useful for something else are not good in themselves and by reason of their own nature. For example, a bitter potion is not good in itself but only insofar as it is directed to the end, health, which is a good in itself. But an end, or that for the sake of which something comes to be, seems to be the terminus of an action. But all actions seem to involve motion. Therefore it seems to follow that this principle, i.e., the final cause, which has the character of goodness, cannot exist in immobile things. Further, since those things which exist of themselves apart from matter must be immobile, it therefore does not seem possible that "an *autoagathon*," i.e., a good-in-itself, exists, as Plato held. For he called all immaterial and unparticipated things entities which exist of themselves, just as he called the Idea of man, man-in-himself, as though not something participated in matter. Hence he also called the good-in-itself that which is its own goodness unparticipated, namely, the first principle of all things.

375. Moreover, with a view to strengthening this argument he introduces an example. For, from the fact that there cannot be an end in the case of immobile things, it seems to follow that in the mathematical sciences, which abstract from matter and motion, nothing is proved by means of this cause, as in the science of nature, which deals with mobile things, something is proved by means of the notion of good. For example, we may give as the reason why man has hands that by them he is more capable of executing the things which reason conceives. But in the mathematical sciences no demonstration is made in this way, that something is so because it is better for it to be so, or worse if it were not so; as

if one were to say, for example, that the angle in a semi-circle is a right angle because it is better that it should be so than be acute or obtuse. And because there can be, perhaps, another way of demonstrating by means of the final cause (for example, if one were to say that, if an end is to be, then what exists for the sake of an end must first be), he therefore adds that in the mathematical sciences no one makes any mention at all of any of those things which pertain to the good or to the final cause. And for this reason certain sophists, as Aristippus, who belonged to the Epicurean school, completely disregarded any demonstrations which employ final causes, considering them to be worthless in view of the fact that in the servile or mechanical arts, for example, in the "art of building," i.e., in carpentry, and in that of "cobbling," all things are explained on the grounds that something is better or worse; whereas in the mathematical sciences, which are the noblest and most certain of the sciences, no mention is made of things good and evil.

376. **But on the other hand** [4].

Here he interjects another question. First, he states this question, which has two parts. The first part of the question is this. If different causes are considered by many sciences, so that a different science considers a different cause, then which of these sciences should be called the one "that is being sought," i.e., first philosophy? Is it the one which considers the formal cause, or the one which considers the final cause, or the one which considers one of the other causes? The second part of the question is this: If there are some things which have many causes, which one of those who consider those causes knows that subject best?

377. **For it is possible** [5].

He clarifies the second part of the question by the fact that one and the same thing is found to have every type of cause. For example, in the case of a house the source of motion is the art and the builder; the reason for which, or the final cause of the house, "is its function," i.e., its use, which is habitation; its material cause is the earth, from which the walls and floor are made; and its specifying or formal cause is the plan of the house, which the architect, after first conceiving it in his mind, gives to matter.

378. **Therefore from the things** [6].

Here he takes up again the question as to which of the aforesaid sciences we can call wisdom on the basis of the points previously established about wisdom at the beginning of this work (see n. 36), namely, whether it is the science which considers the formal cause, or the one which considers the final cause, or the one which considers one of the other causes. And he gives in order arguments relating to each of the three causes, saying that there seems to be some reason why "every one of the sciences," i.e., any one which proceeds by means of any cause at all, should be called by the name of wisdom. First, he speaks of that science which proceeds by means of the final cause. For it was stated at the beginning of this work that this science, which is called wisdom, is the most authoritative one, and the one which directs others as subordinates. Therefore, inasmuch as wisdom "takes precedence," i.e., is prior in the order of dignity and more influential in its authoritative direction of the other sciences (because it is not right that the others should contradict it but they should take their principles from it as its servants), it seems that that science "which deals with the end and the good," i.e., the one which proceeds by means of the final cause, is worthy of the name of wisdom. And this is true because everything else exists for the sake of the end, so that in a sense the end is the cause of all the other causes. Thus the science which proceeds by means of the final cause is the most important one. This is indicated by the fact that those arts which are concerned with ends are more important than and prior to the other arts; for example, the art of navigation is more important than and prior to the art of ship-building. Hence, if wisdom is preeminent and regulative of the other sciences, it seems that it proceeds especially by means of the final cause.

379. **But insofar as wisdom** [7].

Here he introduces the arguments relating to the formal cause. For it was said in the prologue of this work that wisdom is concerned with first causes and with whatever is most knowable and most certain. And according to this it seems to be concerned with "substance," i.e., it proceeds by means of the formal cause. For among the different ways of knowing things, we say that he who knows that something exists, knows more perfectly than he who knows that it does not exist. Hence in the *Posterior Analytics*[86b35] the Philosopher proves that an affirmative demonstration is preferable to a negative demonstration. And among those who know something affirmatively, we say that one knows more perfectly than another. But we say that he knows more perfectly than any of the others who knows what a thing is, and not he who knows how great it is, or what it is like, or what it can do or undergo. Therefore, to know a thing itself in the most perfect way absolutely is to know what it is, and this is to know its substance. But even in knowing other things, for example, a thing's properties, we say that we know best every single thing about which there are demonstrations when we also know the whatness of their accidents and properties; because whatness is found not only in substance but also in accidents.

380. He gives the example of squaring, i.e., squaring a surface of equally distant sides which is not square but which we say we square when we find a square equal to it. But since every rectangular surface of equally distant sides is contained by the two lines which contain the right angle, so that the total surface is simply the product of the multiplication of one of these lines by the other, then we find a square equal to this surface when we find a line which is the proportional mean between these two lines. For example, if line A is to line B as line B is to line C, the square of line B is equal to the surface contained by C and A, as is proved in Book VI of Euclid's *Elements.*

381. This becomes quite evident in the case of numbers. For 6 is the proportional mean between 9 and 4; for 9 is related to 6 in the ratio of 1 1/2 to 1, and so also is 6 to 4. Now the square of 6 is 36, which is also produced by multiplying 4 by 9; for 4 X 9 = 36. And it is similar in all other cases.

382. **But with regard to processes** [8].

Here he gives an argument pertaining to the cause of motion. For in processes of generation and actions and in every change we see that we may say that we know a thing when we know its principle of motion, and that motion is nothing else than the actuality of something mobile produced by a mover, as is stated in the *Physics,* Book III.[202a5] He omits the material cause, however, because that cause is a principle of knowing in the most imperfect way; for the act of knowing is not caused by what is potential but by what is actual, as is stated below in Book IX.

383. Then after having given those arguments which pertain to the second question, he introduces an argument which is based on the same reasons as were given above (see nn. 370 ff.) in reference to the first question, namely, that it is the office of a different science to consider all these causes by reason of the fact that in different subject-matters different causes seem to have the principal role, for example, the source of motion in mobile things, the quiddity in demonstrable things, and the end in things which are directed to an end.

384. However, we do not find that Aristotle explicitly solves this question later on, though his solution can be ascertained from the things which he establishes below in different places. For in Book IV (see n. 533) he establishes that this science considers being as being, and therefore that it also belongs to it, and not to the philosophy of nature, to consider first substances; for there are other substances besides mobile ones. But every substance is either a being of itself, granted that it is only a form; or it is a being by its form, granted that it is composed of matter and form. Hence inasmuch as this science considers being, it considers the formal cause before all the rest. But the first substances are not known by us in such a way that we know what they are, as can be understood in some way from the things established in Book IX (see n. 1904); and thus in our knowledge of them the formal cause has no place. But even though they are immobile in themselves, they are nevertheless the cause of motion in other things after the manner of an end. Hence inasmuch as this science considers first substances, it belongs to it especially to consider the final cause and also in a way the efficient cause. But to consider the material cause in itself does not belong to it in any way, because matter is not properly a cause of being but of some definite kind of being, namely, mobile substance. However, such causes belong to the consideration of the particular sciences, unless perhaps they are considered by this science inasmuch as they are contained under being; for it extends its analysis to all things in this way.

385. Now when these things are seen it is easy to answer the arguments which have been raised. For, first, nothing prevents the different causes in this science from belonging to a single existing thing, even though they are not contraries, because they are reducible to one thing—being in general—as has been stated (n. 384). And in a similar way, even though not every science considers all of the causes, still nothing prevents one science from being able to consider all of the causes or several of them insofar as they are reducible to some one thing. But to be more specific, it must be said that in the case of immobile things nothing prevents the source of motion and the end or good from being investigated. By immobile things I mean here those which are still causes of motion, as the first substances. However, in the case of those things which are neither moved nor cause motion there is no investigation of the source of motion, or of the end in the sense of the end of motion, although an end can be considered as the goal of some operation which does not involve motion. For if there are held to be intellectual

substances which do not cause motion, as the Platonists claimed, still insofar as they have an intellect and will it is necessary to hold that they have an end and a good which is the object of their will. However, the objects of mathematics neither are moved nor cause motion nor have a will. Hence in their case the good is not considered under the name of good and end, although in them we do consider what is good, namely, their being and what they are. Hence the statement that the good is not found in the objects of mathematics is false, as he proves below in Book IX (see n 1888).

386. The reply to the second question is already clear; for a study of the three causes, about which he argued dialectically, belongs to this science.

LESSON 5

Are the Principles of Demonstration and Substance Considered by One Science or by Many?

ARISTOTLE'S TEXT Chapter 2: 996b26–997a15

1. But with respect to the principles of demonstration there is also the problem whether they are studied by one science or by many. By principles of demonstration I mean the common axioms from which [all] demonstrations proceed, e.g., "everything must either be affirmed or denied," and "it is impossible both to be and not to be at the same time," and all other such propositions. Is there one science which deals with these principles and with substance or are there different sciences? And, if not one, which of the two must be called the one that is now being sought?

996b26–33

2. Now it would be unreasonable that these things should be studied by one science; for why should the study of these be proper to geometry rather than to any other science? In a similar way, then, if this study pertains to any science but cannot pertain to all, an understanding of these principles is no more proper to the science which studies substance than it is to any other science. **996b33–997a2**

3. But at the same time how will there be a science of these principles? For we already know what each one of them is; and therefore the other arts use them as something known. However, if there is demonstration of them, there will have to be some subject-genus, and some of the principles will have to be properties and others axioms. For there cannot be demonstration of all things, since demonstration must proceed from something, and be about something, and [be demonstration] of certain things. It follows, then, that there is a single genus of demonstrable things; for all demonstrative sciences use axioms. **997a2–11**

4. But on the other hand, if the science which considers substance differs from the one which considers axioms, which of these sciences is the more important and prior one? For axioms are most universal and are the principles of all things. And if it does not belong to the philosopher to establish the truth and falsity [of these principles], to what other person will it belong?

997a11–15

COMMENTARY

387. Having debated the first question, which had to do with the study of causes, Aristotle's intention here is to argue dialectically about the science which is concerned with the study of the first principles of demonstration; and in regard to this he does three things. First [1], he raises the question. Second [2], he argues one side of the question ("Now it would be"). Third [4], he argues on the other side of the question ("But on the other hand").

Accordingly, he states, first [1], the problem relating to the first principles of demonstration, namely, whether the study of these principles belongs to one science or to many. Further, he explains what the principles of demonstration are, saying that they are the common conceptions of all men on which all demonstrations are based, i.e., inasmuch as the particular principles of the proper demonstrated conclusions derive their stability from these common principles. And he gives an example of first principles, especially this one, that everything must either be affirmed or denied [of some subject]. Another principle which he mentions is that it is impossible for the same thing both to be and not to be at the same time. Hence the question arises whether these principles and similar ones pertain to one science or to many. And if they pertain to one science, whether they pertain to the science which investigates substance or to another science. And if to another science, then which of these must be called wisdom, or first philosophy, which we now seek.

388. **Now it would be** [2].

Here he argues one side of the question with a view to showing that it is not the office of one science to consider all first principles, i.e., the first principles of demonstration and substance. He gives two arguments, of which the first runs thus: since all sciences employ these principles of demonstration, there seems to be no reason why the study of them should pertain to one science rather than to another; nor again does it seem reasonable that they should be studied by all sciences, because then it would follow that the same thing would be treated in different sciences; but that would be superfluous. Hence it seems to follow that no science considers these principles. Therefore, for the very same reason that it does not belong to any of the other sciences to give us a knowledge of such principles, for this reason too it follows that it does not belong to the science whose function it is to consider substance.

389. **But at the same time** [3].

Here he gives the second argument, which runs thus. In the sciences there are two methods by which knowledge is acquired. One is that by which the whatness of each thing is known, and the other is that by which knowledge is acquired through demonstration. But it does not belong to any science to give us a knowledge of the principles of demonstration by means of the first method, because such knowledge of principles is assumed to be prior to all the sciences. For "we already know" what each one of them is, i.e., we know from the very beginning what these principles signify, and by knowing this the principles themselves are immediately known. And since such knowledge of principles belongs to us immediately, he concludes that all the arts and sciences which are concerned with other kinds of cognitions make use of these principles as things naturally known by us.

390. But it is proved in the same way that a knowledge of these principles is not presented to us in any science by means of demonstration, because if there were demonstration of them, then three principles would have to be considered, namely, some subject-genus, its properties and the axioms. In order to clarify this he adds that there cannot be demonstration of all things; for subjects are not demonstrated but properties are demonstrated of subjects. Concerning subjects, however, it is necessary to know beforehand whether they exist and what they are, as is stated in Book I of the *Posterior Analytics*.[71a10] The reason is that demonstration must proceed from certain things as principles, which are the axioms, and be about something, which is the subject, and [be demonstration] of certain things, which are properties. Now according to this it is immediately evident of one of these three, i.e., the axioms, that they are not demonstrated, otherwise there would have to be certain axioms prior to the axioms; but this is impossible. Therefore, having dismissed this method of procedure as obvious, he proceeds to consider the subject-genus. For since one science has one subject-genus, then that science which would demonstrate axioms would have one subject-

genus. Thus there would have to be one subject-genus for all demonstrative sciences, because all demonstrative sciences use axioms of this kind.

391. **But on the other hand** [4].

Here he argues the other side of the question. For if it is said that there is one science which deals with such principles, and another which deals with substance, the problem will remain as to which of these sciences is the more important and prior one. For, on the one hand, since the axioms are most universal and are the principles of everything that is treated in any of the sciences, it seems that the science which deals with such principles is the most important one. Yet, on the other hand, since substance is the first and principal kind of being, it is evident that first-philosophy is the science of substance. And if it is not the same science which deals with substance and with the axioms, it will not be easy to state to which of the other sciences it belongs to consider the truth and falsity of these axioms, i.e., if it does not belong to first philosophy, which considers substance.

392. The Philosopher answers this question in Book IV (see n. 590) of this work. He says that the study of the axioms belongs chiefly to the [first] philosopher inasmuch as it pertains to him to consider being in general, to which first principles of this kind essentially belong, as is most evident in the case of the very first principle: it is impossible for the same thing both to be and not to be [at the same time]. Hence all the particular sciences use principles of this kind just as they use being itself, although it is the first philosopher who is chiefly concerned with this. And the first argument is solved in this way. But the second argument is solved thus: the [first] philosopher does not consider principles of this kind in such a way as to make them known by defining them or by demonstrating them in an absolute sense, but by refutation, i.e., by arguing disputatively against those who deny them, as is stated in Book IV (see n. 608).

LESSON 6

Are All Substances Considered by One Science or by Many? Does the Science of Substance Consider the Essential Accidents of Substance?

ARISTOTLE'S TEXT Chapter 2: 997a15–997a34

1. *And there is the problem whether there is one science which deals with all substances, or many sciences.* **997a15–16**

2. *If there is not one science, then with what substances must this science deal?* **997a16–17**

3. *But it is unreasonable that there should be one science of all substances; for then one science would demonstrate all essential accidents, i.e., if it is true that every demonstrative science speculates about the essential accidents of some subject by proceeding from common opinions. Hence it is the office of the same science to study the essential accidents of the same subject-genus by proceeding from the same opinions. For it belongs to one science to consider that something is so, and it belongs to one science to consider the principles from which demonstrations proceed, whether to the same science or to a different one. Hence it belongs to one science to consider accidents, whether they are studied by these sciences or by one derived from them.* **997a17–25**

4. *Further, there is the problem whether this science is concerned only with substances or also with accidents. I mean, for example, that if a solid is a kind of substance, and also lines and surfaces, the question arises whether it is the function of the same science to know these and also the accidents of each class of things about which the mathematical sciences make demonstrations, or whether it is the concern of a different science.* **997a25–30**

5. *For if it is the concern of the same science, a particular one will undertake these demonstrations and this will be the one which deals with substance. However, there does not seem to be any demonstration of the quiddity.* **997a30–32**

6. *But if it is the concern of a different science, which science will it be that studies the accidents of substances? For to solve this is very difficult.* **997a32–34**

COMMENTARY

393. Having debated the questions which pertain to the scope of investigation of this science, he now treats the third question, which pertains to the study of substances and accidents. This is divided into two parts inasmuch as he discusses two questions on this point. The second (Lesson 7) begins where he says, "Furthermore, there is."

In regard to the first he does three things. First [1], he raises the question whether there is one science that considers all substances, or whether there are many sciences that consider different substances.

394. **If there is not** [2].

Second, he argues the first side of the question with a view to showing that there is one science of all substances. For if there were not one science of all substances, then apparently it would be impossible to designate the substance which this science considers, because substance as substance is the primary kind of being. Hence it does not seem that one substance rather than another belongs to the consideration of the basic science.

395. **But it is unreasonable** [3].

Third, he argues the other side of the question, saying that it is unreasonable to hold that there is one science of all substances. For it would follow that there would be one demonstrative science of all essential accidents. And this is true because every science which demonstrates certain accidents speculates about the essential accidents of some particular subject, and it does this from certain common conceptions. Therefore, since a demonstrative science considers the accidents only of some particular subject, it follows that the study of some subject-genus belongs to the same science that is concerned with the study of the essential accidents of that genus and vice versa, so long as demonstrations proceed from the same principles.

396. But sometimes it happens to be the function of some science to demonstrate from certain principles that a thing is so, and sometimes it happens to be the function of some science to demonstrate the principles from which it was demonstrated that a thing is so, sometimes to the same science and sometimes to a different one. An example of its being the function of the same science is seen in the case of geometry, which demonstrates that a triangle has three angles equal to two right angles in virtue of the principle that the exterior angle of a triangle is equal to the two interior angles opposite to it; for to demonstrate this belongs to geometry alone. And an example of its being the function of a different science is seen in the case of music, which proves that a tone is not divided into two equal semitones by reason of the fact that a ratio of 9 to 8, which is superparticular, cannot be divided into two equal parts. But to prove this does not pertain to the musician but to the arithmetician. It is evident, then, that sometimes sciences differ because their principles differ, so long as one science demonstrates the principles of another science by means of certain higher principles.

397. But if it is assumed that the principles are identical, sciences could not differ so long as the accidents are the same and the subject-genus is the same, as if one science considered the subject and another its accidents. Hence it follows that that science which considers a substance will also consider its accidents, so that if there are many sciences which consider substances, there will be many sciences which consider accidents. But if there is only one science which considers substances, there will be only one science which considers accidents. But this is impossible, because it would then follow that there would be only one science, since there is no science which does not demonstrate the accidents of some subject. Therefore it is the function of one science to consider all substances.

398. This is treated in Book IV (see n. 546) of this work, where it is shown that the examination of substance as substance belongs to the first science, whose province it is to consider being as being; and thus it considers all substances according to the common aspect of substance. Therefore it belongs to this science to consider the common accidents of substance. But it belongs to the particular sciences, which deal with particular substances, to consider the particular accidents of substances, just as it belongs to the science of nature to consider the accidents of mobile substance. However, among substances there is also a hierarchy, for the first substances are immaterial ones. Hence the study of them belongs properly to first-philosophy, just as the philosophy of nature would be first philosophy if there were no other substances prior to mobile corporeal substances, as is stated below in Book VI (see n. 1170).

399. **Further, there is the problem** [4].

Here he raises another question regarding the study of substance and accidents. Concerning this he does three things. First, he raises the question whether the investigation of this science is concerned with substance alone or also with the attributes that are accidents of substances. For example, if we say that lines, surfaces and solids are substances of some sort, as some held, the question arises whether it belongs to the same science to consider such things and also their proper accidents, which are demonstrated in the mathematical sciences, or whether it belongs to another science.

400. **For if it is the concern** [5].

Second, he argues one side of the question. For if it belongs to the same science to consider accidents and substances, then, since a science which considers accidents demonstrates accidents, it follows that a science which considers substance demonstrates substances. But this is impossible; for the definition of a substance, which expresses the quiddity, is indemonstrable. Hence it will belong to the same science to consider substances and accidents.

401. **But if it is the concern** [6].

Third, he argues the other side of the question: if different sciences consider substance and accident, it will not be possible to state which science it is that speculates about the accidents of substance; because the science which would do this would consider both, although this would seem to pertain to all sciences; for every science considers the essential accidents of its subject, as has been explained.

402. The Philosopher answers this question in Book IV (see n. 570) of this work, saying that it is also the office of that science which is concerned with the study of substance and being to consider the proper accidents of substance and being. Yet it does not follow that it would consider each in the same way, i.e., by demonstrating substance as it demonstrates accidents, but by defining substance and by demonstrating that accidents either belong to or do not belong to it, as is explained more fully at the end of Book IX of this work.

LESSON 7

Are There Certain Other Substances Separate from Sensible Things? Criticism of the Different Opinions Regarding the Objects of Mathematics

ARISTOTLE'S TEXT Chapters 2 & 3: 997a34–998a21

1. *Furthermore, there is the problem whether sensible substances alone must be said to exist, or others besides these. And whether there is one genus or many genera of substances, as is held by those who speak of the Forms and the intermediate entities with which they say the mathematical sciences deal.* **997a34–997b3**

2. *Now the way in which we say that the Forms are both causes and substances in themselves has been treated in our first discussions concerning all of these things.* **997b3–5**

3. *But while they involve difficulty in many respects, it is no less absurd to say that there are certain other natures besides those which exist in the heavens, and that these are the same as sensible things, except that the former are eternal whereas the latter are corruptible. For they [i.e., the Platonists] say nothing more or less than that there is a man-in-himself and horse-in-itself and health-in-itself, which differ in no respect [from their sensible counterparts]; in which they act like those who say that there are gods and that they are of human form. For just as the latter made nothing else than eternal men, in a similar way the former make the Forms nothing else than eternal sensible things.* **997b5–12**

4. *Furthermore, if anyone holds that there are intermediate entities in addition to the Forms and sensible substances, he will face many problems. For evidently there will be, in like manner, lines in addition to ordinary sensible lines, and the same will be true of other classes of things. Therefore, since astronomy is one of these [mathematical sciences], there will be a heaven in addition to the one we perceive, and a sun and moon, and the same will be true of the other celestial bodies. And how are we to accept these things? For it is unreasonable that a heaven should be immobile, but that it should be mobile is altogether impossible. The same thing is true of the things with which the science of perspective is concerned, and of harmonics in mathematics, because for the same reasons it is also impossible that these should exist apart from sensible things. For if there are intermediate sensible objects and senses, evidently there will be intermediate animals between animals-in-themselves and those which are corruptible.* **997b12–24**

5. *Again, one might also raise the question as to what things these sciences must investigate. For if geometry, which is the art of measuring the earth, differs from geodesy, which is the art of dividing the earth, only in this respect that the latter deals with things which are perceptible by the senses, whereas the former deals with those which are imperceptible, evidently there will be, in addition to the science of medicine, another science midway between the science of medicine itself and this particular science of medicine; and this will be true of the other sciences. But how is this possible? For then there will be certain healthy things besides those which are sensible and besides health-in-itself.* **997b25–32**

6. *Similarly, neither does it seem that geodesy is concerned with continuous quantities which are sensible and corruptible. For in this case it would be destroyed when they are destroyed.* **997b32–34**

7. *Nor again will astronomy deal with sensible continuous quantities, or with this heaven. For the lines we perceive by the senses are not such as those of which geometry speaks, since none of the things perceived by the senses are straight or round in this way. For the circle does not touch the rule at a point, but in the way in which Protagoras spoke in arguing against the geometricians. Neither are the motions or revolutions of the heavens similar to the things of which geometry speaks, nor do points have the same nature as the stars.* **997b34–998a6**

8. However, there are also some who say that these intermediate entities, which are below the Forms and above sensible things, do not exist outside of sensible things but in them. But to enumerate all the impossible consequences which follow from this theory would require too long a discussion. It will be sufficient to propose the following consideration. **998a7–11**

9. It is unreasonable that this should be so only in the case of such things, but evidently it is also possible for the Forms to exist in sensible things, because both of these views depend on the same argument. **998a11–13**

10. Furthermore, it would be necessary for two solids to occupy the same place. **998a13–14**

11. And [the objects of mathematics] would not be immobile since they exist in sensible things, which are moved. **998a14–15**

12. Moreover, on the whole, to what end would anyone hold that they exist but exist in sensible things? For the same absurdities as those described will apply to these suppositions. For there will be a heaven in addition to the one which we perceive, although it will not be separate but in the same place; but this is quite impossible.

Chapter 3

In these matters, then, it is difficult to see how it is possible to have any positive truth. **998a15–21**

COMMENTARY

403. Having debated the questions which pertain to the scope of this science, the Philosopher now treats dialectically the questions which pertain to the substances themselves with which this science is chiefly concerned. In regard to this he does three things. First [1], he raises the questions. Second [2], he indicates the source from which arguments can be drawn in support of one side of the question ("Now the way"). Third [3], he argues on the other side of the question ("But while they involve").

In regard to the first part of this division he raises two questions. The first question is whether sensible substances alone are found in the universe, as certain of the ancient philosophers of nature claimed, or whether besides sensible substances there are certain others, as the Platonists claimed.

404. And assuming that besides sensible substances there are certain others, the second question is whether these substances belong to one genus, or whether there are many genera of substances. For he considers both opinions. For some thinkers held that in addition to sensible substances there are only separate Forms, i.e., an immaterial man-in-himself and horse-in-itself and so on for the other classes of things, whereas others held that there are certain other substances midway between the Forms and sensible things, namely, the objects of mathematics, with which they said the mathematical sciences deal.

405. The reason for this view is that they posited on the part of the intellect a twofold process of abstracting things: one whereby the intellect is said to abstract the universal from the particular, and according to this mode of abstraction they posited separate Forms, which subsist of themselves; and another [whereby the intellect is said to abstract] from sensible matter certain forms in whose definition sensible matter is not given, for example, the abstraction of circle from brass. And according to this mode of abstraction they posited separate objects of mathematics, which they said are midway

between the Forms and sensible substances, because they have something in common with both: with the Forms inasmuch as they are separate from sensible matter, and with sensible substances inasmuch as many of them are found in one class, as many circles and many lines.

406. **Now the way in which** [2].

Then he shows how it is possible to argue one side of the question, saying that it has been stated "in our first discussions," i.e., in Book I (see n. 151), how the Forms are held to be both the causes of sensible things and substances which subsist of themselves. Hence, from the things which have been said there in presenting the views of Plato, arguments can be drawn in support of the affirmative side of the question.

407. **But while they involve** [3].

Here he advances reasons for the negative side. He does this, first [3], for the purpose of showing that the Forms are not separate from sensible things; and, second [4], for the purpose of showing that the objects of mathematics are not separate ("Furthermore, if anyone").

Now above in Book I (see n. 208) he gave many arguments against those who posited separate Forms; and, therefore, passing over those arguments, he gives the line of reasoning which seems most effective. He says [3] that while the position of those who posit separate Forms contains many difficulties, the position of those which is now given is no less absurd than any of the others, i.e., that someone should say that there are certain natures in addition to the sensible ones which are contained beneath the heavens. For the heavens constitute the limit of sensible bodies, as is proved in Book I of *The Heavens and the World*.[278b23] But those who posited the Forms did not place them below the heavens or outside of it, as is stated in Book III of the *Physics*.[203a5] Hence, in accordance with this he says that they posited certain other natures in addition to those which exist in the heavens. And they said that these opposite natures are the same as these sensible things both in kind and in their intelligible constitution, and that they exist in these sensible things; or rather they said that those natures are the Forms of these sensible things. For example, they said that a separate man constitutes the humanity of this particular man who is perceived by the senses, and that a man who is perceived by the senses is a man by participating in that separate man. Yet they held that these differ in this respect, that those immaterial natures are eternal, whereas these sensible natures are corruptible.

408. That they hold those natures to be the same as these sensible things is clear from the fact that, just as man, horse, and health are found among sensible things, in a similar way they posited among these natures "a man-in-himself," i.e., one lacking sensible matter; and they did the same with regard to horse and health. Moreover, they claimed that nothing else existed in the class of separate substances except [the counterpart of] what existed materially in the sensible world. This position seems to be similar to that of those who held that the gods are of human form, which was the position of the Epicureans, as Tully states in *The Nature of the Gods*. For just as those who held that the gods are of human form did nothing else than make men eternal in nature, in a similar way those who claimed that there are Forms do nothing else than hold that there are

eternal sensible things, such as horse, ox, and the like.

409. But it is altogether absurd that what is naturally corruptible should be specifically the same as what is naturally incorruptible; for it is rather the opposite that is true, namely, that corruptible and incorruptible things differ in kind to the greatest degree, as is said below in Book X (see n. 2137) of this work. Yet it can happen that what is naturally corruptible is kept in being perpetually by Divine power.

410. **Furthermore, if anyone** [4].

Then he argues against those who claimed that the objects of mathematics are midway between the Forms and sensible things. First [4], he argues against those who held that the objects of mathematics are intermediate entities and are separate from sensible things; and, second [8], against those who held that the objects of mathematics exist but exist in sensible things ("However, there are").

In regard to the first he does two things. First, he introduces arguments against the first position. Second [7], he argues in support of this position ("Nor again").

He brings up three arguments against the first position. The first argument is this: just as there is a mathematical science about the line, in a similar way there are certain mathematical sciences about other subjects. If, then, there are certain lines in addition to the sensible ones with which geometry deals, by the same token there will be, in all other classes of things with which the other mathematical sciences deal, certain things in addition to those perceived by the senses. But he shows that it is impossible to hold this with regard to two of the mathematical sciences.

411. He does this, first, in the case of astronomy, which is one of the mathematical sciences and which has as its subject the heavens and the celestial bodies. Hence, according to what has been said, it follows that there is another heaven besides the one perceived by the senses, and similarly another sun and another moon, and so on for the other celestial bodies. But this is incredible, because that other heaven would be either mobile or immobile. If it were immobile, this would seem to be unreasonable, since we see that it is natural for the heavens to be always in motion. Hence the astronomer also makes some study of the motions of the heavens. But to say that a heaven should be both separate and mobile is impossible, because nothing separate from matter can be mobile.

412. Then he shows that the same view is unacceptable in the case of other mathematical sciences, for example, in that of perspective, which considers visible lines, and "in the case of harmonics," i.e., in that of music, which studies the ratios of audible sounds. Now it is impossible that there should be intermediate entities between the Forms and sensible things; because, if these sensible things—sounds and visible lines—were intermediate entities, it would also follow that there are intermediate senses. And since senses exist only in an animal, it would follow that there are also intermediate animals between the Form animal, and corruptible animals; but this is altogether absurd.

413. **Again, one might** [5].

The second argument [which he uses against the possibility of the objects of mathematics being an intermediate class of entities separate from sensible things] is as follows. If in those classes of things with which the mathematical sciences deal there are three classes of things—sensible substances, Forms and intermediate entities, then since the intelligible structure of all sensible things and of all Forms seems to be the same, it appears to follow that there are intermediate entities between any sensible things at all and their Forms. Hence there remains the problem as to what classes of things are included in the scope of the mathematical sciences. For if a mathematical science such as geometry differs from geodesy, which is the science of sensible measurements, only in this respect that geodesy deals with sensible measurements, whereas geometry deals with intermediate things which are not sensible, there will be in addition to all the sciences which consider sensible things certain [other] mathematical sciences which deal with these intermediate entities. For example, if the science of medicine deals with certain sensible bodies, there will be in addition to the science of medicine, and any like science, some other science which will be intermediate between the science of medicine which deals with sensible bodies and the science of medicine which deals with the Forms. But this is impossible; for since medicine is about "healthy things," i.e., things which are conducive to health, then it will also follow, if there is an intermediate science of medicine, that there will be intermediate health-giving things in addition to the health-giving things perceived by the senses and absolute health, i.e., health-in-itself, which is the Form of health separate from matter. But this is clearly false. Hence it follows that these mathematical sciences do not deal with certain things which are intermediate between sensible things and the separate Forms.

414. **Similarly, neither** [6].

Then he gives the third argument [against the possibility of the objects of mathematics being an intermediate class]; and in this argument one of the points in the foregoing position is destroyed, namely, that there would be a science of continuous quantities which are perceptible; and thus, if there were another science of continuous quantities, it would follow from this that there would be intermediate continuous quantities. Hence he says that it is not true that geodesy is a science of perceptible continuous quantities, because such continuous quantities are corruptible. It would follow, then, that geodesy is concerned with corruptible continuous quantities. But it seems that a science is destroyed when the things with which it deals are destroyed; for when Socrates is not sitting, our present knowledge that he is sitting will not be true. Therefore it would follow that geodesy, or geosophics as other readings say, is destroyed when sensible continuous quantities are destroyed; but this is contrary to the character of science, which is necessary and incorruptible.

415. Yet this argument can be brought in on the opposite side of the question inasmuch as one may say that he intends to prove by this argument that there are no sciences of sensible things, so that all sciences must be concerned with either the intermediate entities or the Forms.

416. **Nor again will** [7].

Here he argues in support of this position, as follows: it belongs to the very notion of science that it should be concerned with what is true. But this would not be the case unless it were about things as they are. Therefore the things about which there are sciences must be the same in themselves as they are shown to be in the sciences. But perceptible lines are not such as geometry says they are. He proves this on the grounds that geometry demonstrates that a circle touches "the rule," i.e., a straight line, only at a point, as is shown in Book III of Euclid's *Elements. [III,16]* But this is found to be true of a circle and a line in the case of sensible things. Protagoras used this argument when he destroyed the certainties of the sciences against the geometricians. Similarly, the movements and revolutions of the heavens are not such as the astronomers describe them; for it seems to be contrary to nature to explain the movements of the celestial bodies by means of eccentrics and epicycles and other different movements which the astronomers describe in the heavens. Similarly, neither are the quantities of the celestial bodies such as the astronomers describe them to be, for they use stars as points even though they are still bodies having extension. It seems, then, that geometry does not deal with perceptible continuous quantities, and that astronomy does not deal with the heaven which we perceive. Hence it remains that these sciences are concerned with certain other things, which are intermediate.

417. **However, there are** [8].

Here he argues against another position. First, he states the point at issue. Second [9], he brings in arguments germane to his purpose ("It is unreasonable").

Accordingly, he says, first [8], that some thinkers posit natures midway between the Forms and sensible things, yet they do not say that these natures are separate from sensible things but exist in sensible things themselves. This is clear regarding the opinion of those who held that there are certain self-subsistent dimensions which penetrate all sensible bodies, which some thinkers identify with the place of sensible bodies, as is stated in Book IV of the *Physics [209b32]* and is disproved there. Hence he says here that to pursue all the absurd consequences of this position is a major undertaking, but that it is now sufficient to touch on some points briefly.

418. **It is unreasonable** [9].

Then he brings four arguments against this position. The first runs as follows. It seems to be for the same reason that in addition to sensible things the Forms and objects of mathematics are posited, because both are held by reason of abstraction on the part of the intellect. If, then, the objects of mathematics are held to exist in sensible things, it is fitting that not only they but also the Forms themselves should exist there. But this is contrary to the opinion of those who posit [the existence of] the Forms. For they hold that these are separate, and not that they exist anywhere in particular.

419. **Furthermore, it would be** [10].

Here he gives the second argument, which runs thus: if the objects of mathematics differ from sensible things yet exist in them, since a body is an object of mathematics, it follows that a mathematical body exists simultaneously with a sensible body in the same subject. Therefore "two solids," i.e., two bodies, will exist in the same place. This is impossible not only for two sensible bodies but also for a sensible body and a mathematical one, because each has dimensions, by reason of which two bodies are prevented from being in the same place.

420. **And [the objects of mathematics]** [11].

Here he gives the third argument. For when something is moved, anything that exists within it is moved. But sensible things are moved. Therefore, if the objects of mathematics exist in sensible things, it follows that the objects of mathematics are moved. But this is contrary to the intelligible constitution of mathematical objects, which abstract not only from matter but also from motion.

421. **Moreover, on the whole** [12].

Then he gives the fourth argument, which runs thus: no position is thought to be reasonable unless it is based on one of the causes, and especially if a more untenable conclusion follows from such a position. But this position is held without a cause. For the same absurdities face those who hold the objects of mathematics to be intermediate entities and to exist in sensible things, as face those who hold that they do not exist in sensible things, as well as certain other peculiar and greater difficulties, as is clear from what has been said above. Hence, this position is an unreasonable one. In concluding he states that the questions mentioned above involve much difficulty as to what is true in these matters.

422. Now the Philosopher treats these questions below in Books XII, XIII and XIV of this work, where he shows that there are neither separate mathematical substances nor Forms. The reasoning which moved those who posited the objects of mathematics and the Forms, which are derived from an abstraction of the intellect, is given at the beginning of Book XIII. For nothing prevents a thing which has some particular attribute from being considered by the intellect without its being viewed under this aspect and yet be considered truly, just as a white man can be considered without white being considered. Thus the intellect can consider sensible things not inasmuch as they are mobile and material but inasmuch as they are substances or continuous quantities; and this is to abstract the thing known from matter and motion. However, so far as the thing known is concerned, the intellect does not abstract in such a way that it understands continuous quantities and forms to exist without matter and motion. For then it would follow either that the intellect of the one abstracting is false, or that the things which the intellect abstracts are separate in reality.

LESSON 8

Are Genera Principles of Things? And If So, Does This Apply to The Most Universal Genera or to Those Nearest to Individuals?

ARISTOTLE'S TEXT Chapter 3: 998a21–999a23

1. *Concerning the principles of things there is the problem whether genera must be regarded as the elements and principles of things, or rather the first things of which each thing is composed inasmuch as they are intrinsic.* **998a21–23**

2. *Just as the elements and principles of a word seem to be those things of which all words are first composed, but not word in common. And just as we say that the elements of diagrams are those things whose demonstrations are found in the demonstrations of others, either of all or of most of them.* **998a23–27**

3. *Furthermore, those who say that the elements of bodies are many, and those who say that they are one, call the things of which bodies are composed and constituted their principles, as Empedocles says that fire and water and those things which are included with these are the elements from which existing things derive their being; but he does not speak of them as the genera of existing things* **998a28–32**

4. *And again if anyone wished to speculate about the nature of other things, in finding out in regard to each (a bed, for example) of what parts it is made and how it is put together, he will come to know its nature. And according to these arguments genera are not the principles of existing things.* **998a32–998b4**

5. *But if we know each thing through definitions, and genera are the principles of definitions, genera must be the principles of the things defined.* **998b4–6**

6. *And if in order to acquire scientific knowledge of existing things it is necessary to acquire scientific knowledge of their species, according to which they are said to be beings, then genera are the principles of species.* **998b6–8**

7. *Moreover, some of those who say that the elements of existing things are the one or being or the great and small, seem to use these as genera.* **998b9–11**

8. *But it is not possible to speak of principles in both ways; for the meaning of substance is one. Therefore a definition by means of genera will differ from one which gives the intrinsic constituents.* **998b11–14**

9. *Again, if genera are the principles of things in the fullest sense, there is the question whether the first genera must be thought to be principles, or those which are lowest and are predicated of individual things. For this also raises a problem.* **998b14–17**

10. *For if universals are the principles of things to a greater degree, evidently these must be the highest genera, because it is most properly these which are predicated of all existing things. Therefore there will be as many principles of existing things as there are first genera. Hence being and unity will be principles and substances, for it is these especially which are predicated of all existing things. It is impossible, however, that unity or being should be a single genus of existing things; for it is necessary both that the differences of each genus exist and that each be one. But it is impossible either that species be predicated of the differences of their own genera, or that a genus be so predicated independently of its species. If, then, unity or being is a genus, no difference will be one and a being. But if unity and being are not genera, neither will they be principles, supposing that genera are principles.* **998b17–28**

11. *Further, those things which are intermediate and are taken along with differences will be genera down to individuals. But some seem to be such, whereas others do not. Again, differences are principles to a greater degree than genera; and if they are principles, principles will be*

infinite in number, so to speak. And [this will appear] in another way also if one holds that the first genus is a principle. **998b28–999a1**

12. But, on the other hand, if unity is a specific principle to a greater degree, and unity is indivisible, and everything indivisible is such either in quantity or in species, and what is indivisible in species is prior, and genera are divisible into species, then it will be rather the lowest predicate which is one. For man is not the genus of particular men. **999a1–6**

13. Further, in the case of those things to which prior and subsequent apply, it is not possible in their case that there should be something which exists apart from them. For example, if the number two is the first of numbers, there will not be any number apart from the species of numbers; nor, likewise, any figure apart from the species of figures. But if the genera of these things do not [exist apart from the species], then in the case of other things the teaching will be that there are genera apart from the species; for of these things there seem especially to be genera. But among individual things one is not prior and another subsequent. **999a6–13**

14. Further, where one thing is better and another worse, that which is better is always prior; so that there will be no genus of these things. From these considerations, then, it seems that it is the terms predicated of individuals, rather than genera, which are principles. **999a13–16**

15. But again it is not easy to state how one must conceive these to be the principles of things. For a principle or cause must be distinct from the things of which it is the principle or cause, and must be able to exist apart from them. But why should one think that anything such as this exists apart from singular things, except that it is predicated universally and of all things? But if this is the reason, then the more universal things are, the more they must be held to be principles. Hence the first genera will be principles of things. **999a16–23**

COMMENTARY

423. Having debated the questions which were raised about substances, the Philosopher now treats dialectically the questions which were raised about principles. This is divided into two parts. In the first [1] he discusses the questions which asked what the principles of things are; and in the second (Lesson 10), the questions which asked what kind of things the principles are ("Again, there is the problem").

In the first part of this division he discusses two questions: first, whether universals are the principles of things; and second (Lesson 9), whether any principles are separate from matter ("But there is a problem").

In regard to the first he discusses two questions, of which the first is whether genera are the principles of things. The second [9] asks which genera these are, whether the first genera or the others ("Again, if genera").

In regard to the first he does two things: first, he raises the question; and second [2], he treats it dialectically ("Just as the elements").

The first question [1] has to do with the principles of things: whether it is necessary to accept or believe that those genera which are predicated of many things are the elements and principles of things, or rather that those parts of which every single thing is composed must be called the elements and principles of things. But he adds two conditions, one of which is "inasmuch as they are intrinsic," which is given in order to distinguish these parts from a contrary and a privation. For white is said to come from black, or the non-white, although these are not intrinsic to white. Hence they are not its elements. The other condition is what he calls "the first things," which is given in order to distinguish them from secondary components. For the bodies of animals are composed of flesh and nerves, which exist within the animal; yet these are not called the elements of animals, because they are not the first things of which an animal is composed, but rather fire, air, water and earth, from which flesh and nerves derive their being.

424. **Just as the elements** [2].

Here he treats this question dialectically; and in regard to this he does three things. First, he shows that the first things of which anything is composed are its principles and elements. Second [5], he argues the opposite side of the question ("But if we know"). Third [8], he rejects one answer by which it could be said that both of these [i.e., genera and constituent parts] are the principles and elements of things ("But it is not").

In regard to the first he gives three arguments. The first of these proceeds from natural phenomena, in which he makes his thesis evident by two examples. The first example which he gives if that of a word, whose principle and element is not said to be the common term word but rather the first constituents of which all words are composed, which are called letters. He gives as a second example, diagrams, i.e., the demonstrative descriptions of geometrical figures. For the elements of these diagrams are not said to be the common term diagram but rather those theorems whose demonstrations are found in the demonstrations of other geometrical theorems, either of all or of most of them, because the other demonstrations proceed from the supposition of the first demonstrations. Hence the book of Euclid is called *The Book of Elements*, because the first theorems of geometry, from which the other demonstrations proceed, are demonstrated therein.

425. **Furthermore, those who** [3].

Here he gives the second argument, which also employs certain examples drawn from nature. He says that those who hold that the elements of bodies are either one or many, say that the principles and elements of bodies are those things of which bodies are composed and made up as intrinsic constituents. Thus Empedocles says that the elements of natural bodies are fire and water and other things of this kind, which along with these he calls the elements of things; and natural bodies are constituted of these first things inasmuch as they are intrinsic. Moreover, they [i.e., the philosophers of nature] held that in addition to these two principles there are four others—air, earth, strife and friendship—as was stated in Book I (see n. 104). But neither Empedocles nor the other philosophers of nature said that the genera of things are the principles and elements of these natural bodies.

426. **And again if anyone** [4].

Here he gives the third argument, which involves things made by art. He says that if someone wished to "speculate about their nature," i.e., about the definition which indicates the essence of other bodies than natural ones, namely, of bodies made by human art, for example, if one wished to know a bed, it would be necessary to consider of what parts it is made and how they are put together; and in this way he would know the nature of a bed. And after this he concludes that genera are not the principles of existing things.

427. **But if we know** [5].

Here he argues the other side of the question. He gives three arguments, the first of which is as follows. Each thing is known through its definition. Therefore, if a principle of being is the same as a principle of knowing, it seems that anything which is a principle of definition is also a principle of the thing defined. But genera are principles of definitions, because definitions are first composed of them. Hence genera are the principles of the things defined.

428. **And if in order to** [6].

Here he gives the second argument, which runs thus. Scientific knowledge of each thing is acquired by knowing the species from which it gets its being, for Socrates can be known only by understanding that he is man. But genera are principles of species, because the species of things are composed of genera and differences. Therefore genera are the principles of existing things.

429. **Moreover, some of those** [7].

Here he gives a third argument, which is based on the authority of the Platonists, who held that the one and being are the principles of things, and also the great and small, which are used as genera. Therefore genera are the principles of things.

430. **But it is not possible** [8].

Here he excludes one answer which would say that both of these are principles. He says that it is impossible to say that both of these are "principles," i.e., both the elements, or the parts of which something is composed, and genera. He proves this by the following argument. Of each thing there is one definite concept which exposes its substance, just as there is also one substance of each thing. But the definitive concept which involves genera is not the same as the one which involves the parts of which a thing is composed. Hence it cannot be true that each definition indicates a thing's substance. But the definitive concept which indicates a thing's substance cannot be taken from its principles. Therefore it is impossible that both genera and the parts of which things are composed should be simultaneously the principles of things.

431. **Again, if genera** [9].

Then he treats the second question dialectically. First, he raises the question; and second [10], he brings up arguments relative to this question ("For if universals").

Accordingly, he says that if we hold that genera are the principles of things in the fullest sense, which of these genera should be considered to be the principles of things to a greater degree? Must we consider those "genera" which are first in number, namely, the most common, or also the lowest genera, which are proximately predicated of the individual, i.e., the lowest species. For this is open to question, as is clear from what follows.

432. **For if universals** [10].

Here he argues about the question which was proposed; and in regard to this he does three things. First, he introduces arguments to show that the first genera cannot be principles. Second [12], he introduces arguments to show that the last species should rather be called the principles of things ("But, on the other hand"). Third [15], he debates the proposed question ("But again it is").

In regard to the first [10] he gives three arguments, of which the first runs thus: if genera are principles to the extent that they are more universal, then those which are most universal, i.e., those which are predicated of all things, must be the first genera and the principles of things in the highest degree. Hence there will be as many principles of things as there are most common genera of this kind. But the most common of all genera are unity and being, which are predicated of all things. Therefore unity and being will be the principles and substances of all things. But this is impossible, because unity and being cannot be genera of all things. For, since unity and being are most universal, if they were principles of genera, it would follow that genera would not be the principles of things. Hence the position which maintains that the most common genera are principles is an impossible one, because from it there follows the opposite of what was held, namely, that genera are not principles.

433. That being and unity cannot be genera he proves by this argument: since a difference added to a genus constitutes a species, a species cannot be predicated of a difference without a genus, or a genus without a species. That it is impossible to predicate a species of a difference is clear for two reasons. First, because a difference applies to more things than a species, as Porphyry says; and second, because, since a difference is given in the definition of a species, a species can be predicated essentially of a difference only if a difference is understood to be the subject of a species, as number is the subject of evenness in whose definition it is given. This, however, is not the case; but a difference is rather a formal principle of a species. Therefore a species cannot be predicated of a difference except, perhaps, in an incidental way. Similarly too neither can a genus, taken in itself, be predicated of a difference by essential predication. For a genus is not given in the definition of a difference, because a difference does not share in a genus, as is stated in Book IV of *The Topics;[122b20]* nor again is a difference given in the definition of a genus. Therefore a genus is not predicated essentially of a difference in any way. Yet it is predicated of that which "has a difference," i.e., of a species, which actually contains a difference. Hence he says that a species is not predicated of the proper differences of a genus, nor is a genus independently of its species, because a genus is predicated of its differences inasmuch as they inhere in a species. But no difference can be conceived of which unity and being are not predicated, because any difference of any genus is a one and a being, otherwise it could not constitute any one species of being. It is impossible, then, that unity and being should be genera.

434. **Further, those things** [11].

Then he gives the second argument, which runs thus: if genera are called principles because they are common and predicated of many things, then for a like reason all those things which are principles because they are common and predicated of many will have to be genera. But all things which are intermediate between the first genera and individuals, namely, those which are considered together with some differences, are common predicates of many things. Hence they are both principles and genera. But this is evidently false. For some of them are genera, as subaltern species, whereas others are not, as the lowest species. It is not true, then, that the first or common genera are the principles of things.

435. Further, if the first genera are principles, because they are the principles by which we know species, then differences will be principles to a greater degree, because differences are the formal principles of species; and form or actuality is chiefly the princi-

ple of knowing. But it is unfitting that differences should be the principles of things, because in that case there would be an infinite number of principles, so to speak; for the differences of things are infinite, so to speak; not infinite in reality but to us. That they are infinite in number is revealed in two ways: in one way if we consider the multitude of differences in themselves; in another way if we consider the first genus as a first principle, for evidently innumerable differences are contained under it. The first genera, then, are not the principles of things.

436. **But on the other hand** [12].

Then he shows that the lowest species are principles to a greater degree than genera. He gives three arguments, of which the first runs thus: according to the Platonists it is the one which seems to have "the nature," or character, of a principle to the greatest degree. Indeed, unity has the character of indivisibility, because a one is merely an undivided being. But a thing is indivisible in two ways, namely, in quantity and in species: in quantity, as the point and unit, and this is a sort of indivisibility opposed to the division of quantity; and in species, as what is not divided into many species. But of these two types of indivisibility the first and more important one is indivisibility in species, just as the species of a thing is prior to its quantity. Therefore that which is indivisible in species is more of a principle because it is indivisible in quantity. And in the division of quantity the genus seems to be more indivisible, because there is one genus of many species; but in the division of species one species is more indivisible. Hence the last term which is predicated of many, which is not a genus of many species, namely, the lowest species, is one to a greater degree in species than a genus; for example, man or any other lowest species is not the genus of particular men. Therefore a species is a principle to a greater degree than a genus.

437. **Further, in the case of** [13].

Then he gives the second argument, which is based on a certain position of Plato; for at one time Plato held that there is some one thing which is predicated of many things without priority and posteriority, and that this is a separate unity, as man is separate from all men; and at another time he held that there is some one thing which is predicated of many things according to priority and posteriority, and that this is not a separate unity. This is what Aristotle means when he says "in the case of those things to which prior and subsequent apply," i.e., that when one of the things of which a common term is predicated is prior to another, it is impossible in such cases that there should be anything separate from the many things of which this common term is predicated. For example, if numbers stand in such a sequence that two is the first species of number, no separate Idea of number will be found to exist apart from all species of numbers. And on the same grounds no separate figure will be found to exist apart from all species of figures.

438. The reason for this can be that a common attribute is held to be separate so as to be some first entity in which all other things participate. If, then, this first entity is a one applicable to many in which all other things participate, it is not necessary to hold that there is some separate entity in which all things participate. But all genera seem to be things of this kind, because all types of genera are found to differ insofar as they are more or less perfect, and thus insofar as they are prior and

subsequent in nature. Hence, if in those cases in which one thing is prior to another it is impossible to regard anything common as a separate entity, on the supposition that there is a genus apart from species, then "in the case of other things the teaching" will [differ], i.e., there will be another doctrine and rule concerning them, and the foregoing rule will not apply to them. But considering the individuals of one species, it is evident that one of these is not prior and another subsequent in nature but only in time. And thus according to Plato's teaching a species is separate. Since, then, these common things are principles inasmuch as they are separate, it follows that a species is a principle to a greater degree than a genus.

439. **Further, where one thing** [14].

Here he gives the third argument, which makes use of the notions "better or worse." For in all those cases where one thing is better than another, that which is better is always prior in nature. But there cannot be held to be one common genus of those things which exist in this way. Hence there cannot be held to be one separate genus in the case of those things in which one is better and another worse; and thus the conclusion is the same as the above. For this argument is introduced to strengthen the preceding one, so to speak, i.e., with a view to showing that there is priority and posteriority among the species of any genus.

440. And from these three arguments he draws the conclusion in which he is chiefly interested, namely, that the lowest species, which are predicated immediately of individuals, seem to be the principles of things to a greater degree than genera.

441. **But again it is not** [15].

Here he argues the opposite side of the question, as follows: a principle and a cause are distinct from the things of which they are the principle and cause, and are capable of existing apart from them. And this is true, because nothing is its own cause. He is speaking here of extrinsic principles and causes, which are causes of a thing in its entirety. But the only thing that is held to exist apart from singular things is what is commonly and universally predicated of all things. Therefore the more universal a thing is, the more separate it is, and the more it should be held to be a principle. But the first genera are most universal. Therefore the first genera are the principles of things in the highest degree.

442. Now the solution to these questions is implied in this last argument. For according to this argument genera or species are held to be universal principles inasmuch as they are held to be separate. But the fact that they are not separate and self-subsistent is shown in Book VII (see n. 1592) of this work. Hence the Commentator also shows, in Book VIII, that the principles of things are matter and form, to which genus and species bear some likeness. For a genus is derived from matter and difference from form, as will be shown in the same book (n. 1721). Hence, since form is more of a principle than matter, species will consequently be principles more than genera. But the objection which is raised against this, on the grounds that genera are the principles of knowing a species and its definitions, is answered in the same way as the objection raised about their separateness. For, since a genus is understood separately by the mind without understanding its species, it is a principle of knowing. And in the same way it would be a principle of being, supposing that it had a separate being.

LESSON 9

Do Any Universals Exist Apart from the Singular Things Perceived by the Senses and from Those Which Are Composed of Matter and Form?

ARISTOTLE'S TEXT Chapter 4: 999a24–999b20

1. *But there is a problem connected with these things, which is the most difficult of all and the most necessary to consider, with which our analysis is now concerned.* **999a24–26**

2. *For if there is nothing apart from singular things, and singular things are infinite in number, how is it possible to acquire scientific knowledge of them? For insofar as there is something that is one and the same, and insofar as there is something universal [which relates to singular things], to that extent we acquire knowledge of them.* **999a26–29**

3. *But if this is necessary, and there must be something apart from singular things, it will be necessary that genera exist apart from singular things, and they will be either the last or the first. But the impossibility of this has already appeared from our discussion.* **999a29–32**

4. *Further, if there is something apart from the concrete whole (which is most disputable), as when something is predicated of matter, if there is such a thing, the problem arises whether it must exist apart from all concrete wholes, or apart from some and not from others, or apart from none.* **999a32–999b1**

5. *If, then, there is nothing apart from singular things, nothing will be intelligible, but all things will be sensible, and there will be no science of anything, unless one might say that sensory perception is science.* **999b1–3**

6. *Further, neither will anything be eternal or immobile; for all sensible things perish and are subject to motion.* **999b3–5**

7. *But if there is nothing eternal, neither can there be generation; for there must be something which has come to be and something from which it comes to be; and the last of these must be ungenerated, since the process of generation must have a limit, and since it is impossible for anything to come to be from non-being.* **999b5–8**

8. *Further, since generation and motion exist, there must be a terminus; for no motion is infinite but every motion has a terminus. And that which is incapable of coming to be cannot be generated. But that which has come to be must exist as soon as it has come to be.* **999b8–12**

9. *Further, if matter exists because it is ungenerated, it is much more reasonable that substance should exist, since that is what it (matter) eventually comes to be. For if neither the one nor the other exists, nothing at all will exist. But if this is impossible, there must be something besides the synolon, and this is the form or specifying principle.* **999b12–16**

10. *But again if anyone holds this to be true, the problem arises in what cases one may hold this and in what not. For evidently this is not thought to be so in all cases. For we do not hold that there is a house apart from particular houses.* **999b16–20**

COMMENTARY

443. Having debated the question whether universals are the principles of things, the Philosopher now raises a question about their separability, namely, whether there is anything separate from sensible things as their principle. In regard to this he considers two questions. The first [1] of these is whether universals are separate from singular things. The second [4] is whether there is any formal [principle] separate from things which are composed of matter and form ("Further, if there is something").

In regard to the first he does three things. First, he describes the problem.

Second [2], he argues one side of the question ("For if there is nothing"). Third [3], he argues the other side of the question ("But if this is").

Accordingly, this problem arises with regard to a point mentioned in the last argument of the preceding question, namely, whether a universal is separate from singular things, as the aforesaid argument supposed. He describes this problem as "the one with which our analysis is now concerned [1]," i.e., the one which immediately preceded the foregoing argument. And he speaks of it in this way: first, that "it is connected with," i.e., is a consequence of, the foregoing one, because, as has already been stated, the consideration of the preceding question depends on this. For if universals are not separate, they are not principles; but if they are separate, they are principles. Second, he speaks of this problem as the most difficult of all the problems in this science. This is shown by the fact that the most eminent philosophers have held different opinions about it. For the Platonists held that universals are separate, whereas the other philosophers held the contrary. Third, he says that this problem is one which it is most necessary to consider, because the entire knowledge of substances, both sensible and immaterial, depends on it.

444. **For if there is nothing** [2].

Here he advances an argument to show that universals are separate from singular things. For singular things are infinite in number, and what is infinite cannot be known. Hence all singular things can be known only insofar as they are reduced to some kind of unity which is universal. Therefore there is science of singular things only inasmuch as universals are known. But science is only about things which are true and which exist. Therefore universals are things which exist of themselves apart from singular things.

445. **But if this is** [3].

Then he argues the other side of the question in this way: if it is necessary that universals be something apart from singular things, it is necessary that genera exist apart from singular things, either the first genera or also the last, which are immediately prior to singular things. But this is impossible, as is clear from the preceding discussion. Therefore universals are not separate from singular things.

446. The Philosopher solves this problem in Book VII (see n. 1592) of this work, where he shows in many ways that universals are not substances which subsist of themselves. Nor is it necessary, as has often been said, that a thing should have the same mode of being in reality that it has when understood by the intellect of a knower. For the intellect knows material things immaterially, and in a similar way it knows universally the natures of things which exist as singulars in reality, i.e., without considering the principles and accidents of individuals.

447. **Further, if there is something** [4].

Here he raises another question, namely, whether anything is separate from things composed of matter and form; and in regard to this he does two things. First, he raises the question. Second [5], he proceeds to deal with it ("If, then, there is").

In regard to the first it should be observed that he first raises the question whether a universal is separate from singular things. Now it happens to be the case that some singular things are composed of matter and form. But not all singular things are so composed, either according to the real state of affairs, since separate substances are particular because existing and operating of themselves, or even according to the opinion of the Platonists, who held that even among separate mathematical entities there are particulars inasmuch as they held that there are many of them in a single species. And while it is open to dispute whether there is anything separate in the case of those things which are not composed of matter and form, as the universal is separate from the particular, the problem is chiefly whether there is anything separate in the case of things which are composed of matter and form. Hence he says that the point which causes most difficulty is whether there is something "apart from the concrete whole," i.e., apart from the thing composed of matter and form. The reason why a composite thing is called a concrete whole he explains by adding "when something is predicated of matter." For Plato held that sensible matter participates in separate universals, and that for this reason universals are predicated of singular things. These participations in universal forms by material sensible things constitute a concrete whole inasmuch as a universal form is predicated of matter through some kind of participation. Now in regard to these things he raises a question which has three parts, namely, whether there is anything that exists apart from all things of this kind, or apart from some and not from others, or apart from none.

448. **If, then, there is** [5].

Here he proceeds to deal with this problem; and concerning it he does two things. First, he argues against the position that nothing can be held to be separate from things composed of matter and form. Second [10], he argues the other side of the question ("But again if anyone holds this").

In regard to the first [5] he advances two arguments. First, he argues from the principle that those things which are composed of matter and form are sensible things; and therefore he proposes that those things which are composed of matter and form are singulars. However, singular things are not intelligible but sensible. Therefore, if there is nothing apart from singular things which are composed of matter and form, nothing will be intelligible but all beings will be sensible. But there is science only of things which are intelligible. Therefore it follows that there will be no science of anything, unless one were to say that sensory perception and science are the same, as the ancient philosophers of nature held, as is stated in Book I of *The Soul. [404b8]* But both of these conclusions are untenable, namely, that there is no science and that science is sensory perception. Therefore the first position is also untenable, namely, that nothing exists except singular things which are composed of matter and form.

449. **Further, neither will anything** [6].

Second, he argues on the grounds that things composed of matter and form are mobile. He gives the following argument. All sensible things composed of matter and form perish and are subject to motion. Therefore, if there is nothing apart from beings of this kind, it will follow that nothing is eternal or immobile.

450. **But if there is** [7].

Here he shows that this conclusion is untenable, namely, that nothing is eternal and immobile. He does this, first, with respect to matter; and second [8], with respect to form ("Further, since generation").

Accordingly, he says first [7] that if nothing is eternal, it is impossible for anything to be generated. He proves this as follows. In every process of generation there must be something which comes to be and something from which it comes to be. Therefore, if that from which a thing comes to be is itself generated, it must be generated from something. Hence there must either be an infinite regress in material principles, or the process must stop with some first thing which is a first material principle that is ungenerated, unless it might be said, perhaps, that it is generated from non-being; but this is impossible. Now if the process were to go on to infinity, generation could never be completed, because what is infinite cannot be traversed. Therefore it is necessary to hold either that there is some material principle which is ungenerated, or that it is impossible for any generation to take place.

451. **Further, since generation** [8].

Here he proves the same thing with respect to the formal cause; and he gives two arguments, the first of which is as follows. Every process of generation and motion must have some terminus. He proves this on the grounds that no motion is infinite, but that each motion has some terminus. This is clear in the case of other motions which are completed in their termini. But it seems that a contrary instance is had in the case of circular motion, which can be perpetual and infinite, as is proved in Book VIII of the *Physics*. *[251b20]* And even though motion is assumed to be eternal, so that the entire continuity of circular motion is infinite insofar as one circular motion follows another, still each circular motion is both complete in its species and finite. That one circular motion should follow another is accidental so far as the specific nature of circular motion is concerned.

452. The things which he said about motion in general he proves specially in regard to generation; for no process of generation can be infinite, because that thing cannot be generated whose process of generation cannot come to an end, since the end of generation is to have been made. That its being made is the terminus of generation is clear from the fact that what has been generated must exist "as soon as it has come to be," i.e., as soon as its generation is first terminated. Therefore, since the form whereby something is, is the terminus of generation, it must be impossible to have an infinite regress in the case of forms, and there must be some last form of which there is no generation. For the end of every generation is a form, as we have said. Thus it seems that just as the matter from which a thing is generated must itself be ungenerated because it is impossible to have an infinite regress, in a similar way there must be some form which is ungenerated because it is impossible to have an infinite regress in the case of forms.

453. **Further, if matter exists** [9].

He gives the second argument, which runs thus. If there is some first matter which is ungenerated, it is much more reasonable that there should be some substance, i.e., some form, which is ungenerated, since a thing has being through its form, whereas matter is rather the subject of generation and transmutation. But if neither of these is ungenerated, then absolutely nothing will be ungenerated, since everything which exists has the character of matter or form or is composed of both. But it is impossible that nothing should be ungenerated, as has been proved [8]. Therefore it follows that there must be something else "besides the *synolon*," or concrete whole, i.e., besides the singular thing which is composed of matter and form. And by something else I mean the form or specifying principle. For matter in itself cannot be separated from singular things, because it has being only by reason of something else. But this seems to be true rather of form, by which things have being.

454. **But again if anyone** [10].

Here he argues the other side of the question. For if one holds that there is some form separate from singular things which are composed of matter and form, the problem arises in which cases this must be admitted and in which not. For obviously this must not be held to be true in the case of all things, especially in that of those made by art. For it is impossible that there should be a house apart from this sensible house, which is composed of matter and form.

455. Now Aristotle solves this problem partly in Book XII (n. 2488) of this work, where he shows that there are certain substances separate from sensible things and intelligible in themselves; and partly in Book VII (n. 1503), where he shows that the forms or specifying principles of sensible things are not separate from matter. However, it does not follow that no science of sensible things can be had or that science is sensory perception. For it is not necessary that things have in themselves the same mode of being which they have in the intellect of one who knows them. For those things which are material in themselves are known in an immaterial way by the intellect, as has also been stated above (see n. 446). And even though a form is not separate from matter, it is not therefore necessary that it should be generated; for it is not forms that are generated but composites, as will be shown in Book VII of this work. It is clear, then, in what cases it is necessary to posit separate forms and in what not. For the forms of all things which are sensible by nature are not separate from matter, whereas the forms of things which are intelligible by nature are separate from matter. For the separate substances do not have the nature of sensible things, but are of a higher nature and belong to another order of existing things.

LESSON 10

Do All Things Have a Single Substance? Do All Things Have the Same or Different Principles?

ARISTOTLE'S TEXT Chapter 4: 999b20–1000a4

1. *Again, there is the problem whether all things, for example, all men, have a single substance.* **999b20–21**

2. *But this is absurd; for not all things whose substance is one are themselves one, but are many and different. But this too is untenable.* **999b21–23**

3. *And at the same time there is the problem how matter becomes each of the many things and a concrete whole.* **999b23–24**

4. *And again one might also raise this problem about principles. For if they are specifically one, there will be nothing that is numerically one. Nor again will unity itself and being be one. And how will there be science unless there is some unity in all things?* **999b24–27**

5. *But, on the other hand, if they are numerically one, each of the principles will also be one, and not as in the case of sensible things, different for different things; for example, if the syllable ba is taken as a species, its principles in every case are specifically the same, for they are numerically different. However, if this is not so, but the things which are the principles of beings are numerically one, there will be nothing else besides the elements. For it makes no difference whether we say "numerically one" or "singular," because it is in this way that we say each thing is numerically one. But the universal is what exists in these. For example, if the elements of a word were limited in number, there would have to be as many letters as there are elements. Indeed, no two of them would be the same, nor would more than two.* **999b27–1000a4**

COMMENTARY

456. Having asked what the principles are, and whether some are separate from matter, the Philosopher now asks what the principles are like. First [1], he asks whether the principles are one or many; second (Lesson 15), whether they exist potentially or actually ("And connected with these problems"); and third (see below n. 523), whether they are universals or singular things ("And there is also the problem").

In regard to the first he does two things. First [1], he inquires how the principles stand with respect to unity; and second (Lesson 12), what relationship unity has to the notion of principle ("But the most difficult").

In regard to the first he does three things. First [1], he inquires specially about the formal principle: whether all things that are specifically the same have a single form. Second [4], he asks the same question of all principles in general ("And again one might"). Third (Lesson 11), he asks whether corruptible and incorruptible things have the same principles or different ones ("Again there is the problem").

In regard to the first he does two things. First [1], he introduces the problem. Second [2], he debates it ("But this is absurd").

The problem [1], then, is whether all things that belong to the same species, for example, all men, have a single substance or form.

457. **But this is absurd** [2].

Then he advances arguments on one side of the question, to show that all things belonging to one species do not have a single form. He does this by means of two arguments, the first of which runs thus. Things that belong to one species are many and different. Therefore, if all things that belong to one species have a single substance, it follows that those which have a single substance are many and different. But this is unreasonable.

458. **And at the same time** [3].

Then he gives the second argument, which runs thus. That which is one and undivided in itself is not combined with something divided in order to constitute many things. But it is evident that matter is divided into different singular things. Hence, if substance in the sense of form is one and the same for all things, it will be impossible to explain how each of these singular things is a matter having a substance of the kind that is one and undivided, so that as a singular thing it is a concrete whole having two parts: a matter and a substantial form which is one and undivided.

459. Now he does not argue the other side of the question, because the very same arguments which were advanced above regarding the separateness of universals are applicable in the inquiry which follows it against the arguments just given. For if a separate universal exists, it must be held that things having the same species have a single substance numerically, because a universal is the substance of singular things. Now the truth of this question will be established in Book VII (see n. 1356) of this work, where it is shown that the whatness or essence of a thing is not other than the thing itself, except in an accidental way, as will be explained in that place.

460. **And again one might** [4].

Here he raises a difficulty concerning the unity of principles in general: whether the principles of things are numerically the same, or only specifically the same and numerically distinct. And in regard to this he does two things. First, he advances arguments to show that they are numerically the same. Second [5], he argues on the other side of the question ("But, on the other hand").

In regard to the first [4] he gives three arguments; and he introduces the problem, saying that the same question which was raised about substance can be raised about principles in general, i.e., whether the principles of things are numerically the same.

461. He introduces the first argument to show that they are numerically the same. For things composed of principles merely contain what they receive from these principles. Therefore, if principles are not found to be one numerically but only specifically, the things composed of these principles will not be one numerically but only specifically.

462. The second argument runs thus: unity itself or being itself must be numerically one. And by unity itself or being itself he means unity or being in the abstract. Hence, if the principles of things are not one numerically but only specifically, it will follow that neither unity itself or being itself will subsist of themselves.

463. The third argument is this: science is had of things because there is found to be a one-in-many, as man in common is found in all men; for there is no science of singular things but of the unity [i.e., common attribute] found in them. Moreover, all science or cognition of things which are composed of principles depends on a knowledge of these principles. If, then, principles are not one numerically but only specifically, it will follow that there is no science of beings.

464. **But, on the other hand** [5].

Here he argues the opposite side of

the question in the following fashion. If principles are numerically one so that each of the principles considered in itself is one, it will be impossible to say that the principles of beings exist in the same way as the principles of sensible things. For we see that the principles of different sensible things are numerically different but specifically the same, just as the things of which they are the principles are numerically different but specifically the same. We see, for example, that syllables which are numerically distinct but agree in species have as their principles letters which are the same specifically though not numerically. And if anyone were to say that this is not true of the principles of beings, but that the principles of all beings are the same numerically, it would follow that nothing exists in the world except the elements, because what is numerically one is a singular thing. For what is numerically one we call singular, just as we call universal what is in many. But what is singular is incapable of being multiplied, and is encountered only as a singular. Therefore, if it is held that numerically the same letters are the principles of all syllables, it will follow that those letters could never be multiplied so that there could be two of them or more than two. Thus a could not be found in these two different syllables *ba* or *da*. And the argument is the same in the case of other letters. Therefore, by the same reasoning, if the principles of all beings are numerically the same, it will follow that there is nothing besides these principles. But this seems to be untenable; because when a principle of anything exists it will not be a principle unless there is something else besides itself.

465. Now this question will be solved in Book XII (see n. 2464); for it will be shown there that the principles which things have, namely, matter and form or privation, are not numerically the same for all things but analogically or proportionally the same. But those principles which are separate, i.e., the intellectual substances, of which the highest is God, are each numerically one in themselves. Now that which is one in itself and being is God; and from Him is derived the numerical unity found in all things. And there is science of these, not because they are numerically one in all, but because in our conception there is a one in many. Moreover, the argument which is proposed in support of the opposite side of the question is true in the case of essential principles but not in that of separate ones, which is the class to which the agent and final cause belong. For many things can be produced by one agent or efficient cause, and can be directed to one end.

LESSON 11

Do Corruptible and Incorruptible Things Have the Same or Different Principles?

ARISTOTLE'S TEXT Chapter 4: 1000a5–1001a3

1. *Again, there is a problem which has been neglected no less by the moderns than by their predecessors: whether the principles of corruptible and incorruptible things are the same or different.* **1000a5–7**

2. *For if they are the same, how is it that some things are incorruptible and others corruptible? And what is the cause?* **1000a7–8**

3. *The followers of Hesiod and all those who were called theologians paid attention only to what was plausible to themselves and have neglected us. For, making the principles of things to be gods or generated from the gods, they say that whatever has not tasted nectar and ambrosia became mortal.* **1000a9–13**

4. *And it is clear that they are using these terms in a way known to themselves, but what they have said about the application of these causes is beyond our understanding. For if it is for the sake of pleasure that the gods partake of these things, nectar and ambrosia are not the cause of their being. But if they partake of them to preserve their being, how will the gods be eternal in requiring food?* **1000a13–18**

5. *But with regard to those who have philosophized by using fables, it is not worth our while to pay any serious attention to them.* **1000a18–19**

6. *However, from those who make assertions by means of demonstration it is necessary to find out, by questioning them, why some of the things which are derived from the same principles are eternal in nature and others are corrupted. But since these philosophers mention no cause, and it is unreasonable that things should be as they say, it is clear that the principles and causes of these things will not be the same.* **1000a19–24**

7. *For the explanation which one will consider to say something most to the point is that of Empedocles, who has been subject to the same error. For he posits a certain principle, hate, which is the cause of corruption.* **1000a24–28**

8. *Yet even hate would seem to generate everything except the one. For all things except God are derived from this. Hence he says: "From which have blossomed forth all that was and is [and will be]: trees, and men and women, and beasts and flying things, and water-nourished fish, and the long-lived gods." And apart from these things it is evident that, if hate did not exist in the world, all things would be one, as he says: "For when they have come together, then hate will stand last of all."* **1000a28–1000b2**

9. *For this reason too it turns out that God, who is most happy, is less wise than other beings. For he does not know all the elements, because hate he does not have, and knowledge is of like by like. "For one knows earth by earth, water by water, affection by affection, and hate by mournful hate."* **1000b3–8**

10. *But it is also clear (and this is where our discussion began) that hate no more turns out to be the cause of corruption than of being.* **1000b8–11**

11. *Nor, similarly, is love the cause of existence; for in blending things together into a unity it corrupts other things.* **1000b11–12**

12. *Moreover, he does not speak of the cause of change itself, except to say that it was naturally disposed to be so.* **1000b12–13**

13. *[He says]: "But thus mighty hate was nourished among the members and rose to a position of honor when the time was fulfilled, which being changeable dissolved the bond." Hence change is a necessity, but he gives no reason for its necessity.* **1000b14–17**

14. Yet he alone speaks expressly to this extent. For he does not make some beings corruptible and others incorruptible, but makes all things corruptible except the elements. But the problem that has been stated is why some things are corruptible and others are not, supposing that they come from the same principles. To this extent, then, it has been said that the principles of things will not be the same. **1000b17–22**

15. But if the principles are different, one problem is whether they will be incorruptible or corruptible. For supposing that they are corruptible, it is evident that they must also come from certain things, because all things that are corrupted are dissolved into those elements from which they come. Hence it follows that there are other principles prior to these principles. But this is also unreasonable, whether the process stops or goes on to infinity. Further, how will corruptible things exist if their principles are destroyed? But if they are incorruptible, why will corruptible things come from incorruptible principles, and incorruptible things from others? For this is unreasonable, and is either impossible or requires a great deal of reasoning. **1000b23–32**

16. Further, no one has attempted to say that these things have different principles, but [all thinkers] say that all things have the same principles. But they admit the first problem, considering it a trifling matter. **1000b32–1001a2**

COMMENTARY

466. Having investigated in a general way whether all principles belonging to one species are numerically the same, the Philosopher inquires here whether the principles of corruptible and incorruptible things are numerically the same. In regard to this he does three things. First [1], he raises the question. Second [2], he introduces an argument to show that the principles of corruptible and those of incorruptible things are not the same ("For if they are the same"). Third [15], he introduces arguments to show that they are not different ("But if the principles").

He says first [1], then, that there is a problem which has been neglected no less by the modern philosophers, who followed Plato, than by the ancient philosophers of nature, who also were puzzled whether the principles of corruptible and incorruptible things are the same or different.

467. **For, if they are the same** [1].

Here he advances an argument to show that the principles of corruptible and of incorruptible things are not the same. In regard to this he does three things. First [2], he gives the argument. Second [3], he criticizes the solution of the proposed argument which the theological poets gave ("The followers of Hesiod"). Third [6], he criticizes the solution which some philosophers of nature gave ("However, from those who").

He says first [2], then, that if the principles of corruptible and of incorruptible things are held to be the same, since from the same principles there follow the same effects, it seems that either all things are corruptible or all are incorruptible. Therefore the question arises how some things are corruptible and others incorruptible, and what the reason is.

468. The **followers of Hesiod** [3].

He criticizes the solution given by the theological poets. First [3], he gives their solution. Second [4], he argues against it ("And it is clear that"). Third [5], he gives the reason why he does not criticize this position with more care ("But with regard to those").

Concerning the first [3] it must be

noted that there were among the Greeks, or philosophers of nature, certain students of wisdom, such as Orpheus, Hesiod and certain others, who were concerned with the gods and hid the truth about the gods under a cloak of fables, just as Plato hid philosophical truth under mathematics, as Simplicius says in his *Commentary on the Categories.* Therefore he says that the followers of Hesiod, and all those who were called theologians, paid attention to what was convincing to themselves and have neglected us, because the truth which they understood was treated by them in such a way that it could be known only to themselves. For if the truth is obscured by fables, then the truth which underlies these fables can be known only to the one who devised them. Therefore the followers of Hesiod called the first principles of things gods, and said that those among the gods who have not tasted a certain delectable food called nectar or manna became mortal, whereas those who had tasted it became immortal.

469. But some part of the truth could lie hidden under this fable, provided that by nectar or manna is understood the supreme goodness itself of the first principle. For all the sweetness of love and affection is referred to goodness. But every good is derived from a first good. Therefore the meaning of these words could be that some things are incorruptible by reason of an intimate participation in the highest good, as those which participate perfectly in the divine being. But certain things because of their remoteness from the first principle, which is the meaning of not to taste manna and nectar, cannot remain perpetually the same in number but only in species, as the Philosopher says in Book II of *Generation. [338b12]* But whether they intended to treat this obscurely or something else, cannot be perceived any more fully from this statement.

470. **And it is clear** [4].

He argues against the aforesaid position. He says that the meaning which these followers of Hesiod wished to convey by the terms nectar or manna was known to them but not to us. Therefore their explanation of the way in which these causes are meant to solve this question and preserve things from corruption is beyond our understanding. For if these terms are understood in their literal sense, they appear to be inadequate, because the gods who tasted nectar or manna did so either for the sake of pleasure or because these things were necessary for their existence, since these are the reasons why men partake of food. Now if they partook of them for the sake of pleasure, nectar and manna could not be the cause of their existence so as to make them incorruptible, because pleasure is something that follows on being. But if they partook of the aforesaid nourishment because they needed it to exist, they would not be eternal, having repeated need of food. Therefore it seems that gods who are first corruptible, as it were, standing as they do in need of food, are made incorruptible by means of food. This also seems to be unreasonable, because food does not nourish a thing according to its species unless it is corrupted and passes over into the species of the one nourished. But nothing that is corruptible can be responsible for the incorruptibility of something else.

471. **But with regard to those** [5].

Here he gives his reason for not investigating this opinion with more care. He says that it is not worth our while to pay any attention to those who have philosophized "by using fables," i.e., by hiding philosophical truth under fables. For if anyone argues against their statements insofar as they are taken in a literal sense, these statements are ridiculous. But if one wishes to inquire into the truth hidden by these fables, it is not evident. Hence it is understood that Aristotle, in arguing against Plato and other thinkers of this kind who have treated their own doctrines by hiding them under something else, does not argue about the truth which is hidden but about those things which are outwardly expressed.

472. **However, from those who make assertions** [6].

Then he argues against the answer given by some of the philosophers of nature; and in regard to this he does three things. First [6], he gives the argument. Second [7], he gives the answer ("For the explanation"). Third [8], he criticizes it ("Yet even hate").

Accordingly, he says, first [6], that, having dismissed those who treated the truth by using fables, it is necessary to seek information about the aforesaid question from those who have treated the truth in a demonstrative way, by asking them why it is that, if all beings are derived from the same principles, some beings are eternal by nature and others are corrupted. And since these men give no reason why this is so, and since it is unreasonable that things should be as they say (that in the case of beings having the same principles some should be corruptible and others eternal), it seems clearly to follow that corruptible and eternal things do not have the same principles or the same causes.

473. **For the explanation** [7].

Then he gives one solution. He says that the explanation given to the aforesaid question which seems to fit it best is the one which Empedocles gave, although he was subject to the same error as the others, because the explanation which he gave is no more adequate than theirs, as is about to be shown. For he maintained that corruptible and incorruptible things have certain common principles, but that a special principle, hate, causes the corruption of the elements in such a way that the coming together of this cause and another principle produces corruption in the world.

474. **Yet even hate** [8].

Here he criticizes Empedocles' argument, and he does this in three ways. First [8], he does this by showing that the argument which Empedocles gave is not in keeping with his position; second [12], by showing that it is not adequate ("Moreover, he does not"); third [14], by showing that it is not to the point ("Yet he alone speaks").

In regard to the first he does three things. First, he shows that Empedocles' argument does not agree with his other views about hate; second [9], that it does not agree with his view about God himself ("For this reason"); and third [11], that it does not agree with his view about love ("Nor, similarly").

Accordingly, he says, first [8], that Empedocles' position that hate is the cause of corruption is untenable, because according to his position hate also seems to be the cause of the generation of all things except one. For he held that everything else is composed essentially of hate along with the other principles, with the exception of God alone, whom he claimed to be composed of the other principles without hate. Moreover, he called the heavens God, as was stated above in Book I (see n. 101), because Xenophanes, after reflecting upon the whole heaven, said that the one itself is God. And Empedocles, considering the indestructibleness of the heavens, held that the heavens are composed of the four elements and love, but not of strife or hatred. But in the case of other things he said that all those which are or were or will be, come from hate, such as sprouting trees, and men and women, and beasts (which are terrestrial animals), and vultures (which are flying and long-lived animals), and fish (which are nourished in the water), and the long-lived gods. And by the gods he seems to mean either the stars, which he held are sometimes corrupted, although after a long period of time, or the demons, which the Platonists held to be ethereal animals. Or by the gods he also means those beings whom the Epicureans held to be of human form, as was stated above (n. 408). Therefore, from the fact that all living things except one are generated from hate, it can be said that hate is the cause of generation.

475. And in addition to this there is another reason [why hate can be said to be the cause of generation]; for according to Empedocles' position it is evident that, if hate did not exist in the world, all things would be one, since hate is the reason why things are distinct, according to Empedocles. Hence he quotes Empedocles' words to the effect that, when all things come together into a unity, for example, when chaos comes into being, hate will stand last of all, separating and dissolving things. Hence the text of Boethius says: "When it comes together, then chaos knows the ultimate discord." Thus it is clear that, since the being of the world consists in the distinction of things, hate is the cause of the world's generation.

476. **For this reason** [9].

Here he gives a second argument, which pertains to the deity. He says that, since Empedocles would hold that hate is not a constituent of the divine composition, it follows, according to his arguments, that God, who is said by all men to be most happy, and consequently most knowing, is less prudent than all other beings who have knowledge. For according to Empedocles' position it follows that God does not know the elements because He does not contain hate. Hence He does not know himself. And like knows like according to the opinion of Empedocles, who said that by earth we know earth, by water water, "and by affection," i.e., love or concord, we know affection, or love or concord. And in a similar way we know "hate by hate," which is sadness, whether unpleasant or evil, according to the text of Boethius, who says that "by evil discord we know discord." It is evident, then, that Aristotle thought this untenable and contrary to the position that God is most happy because He himself would not know some of the things that we know. And since this argument seemed to be beside the point, therefore, returning to his principal theme, he says [10] that, in returning to the point from which the first argument began, it is evident, so far as Empedocles is concerned, that hate is no more a cause of corruption than of being.

477. **Nor, similarly, is love** [11].

Here he gives the third argument, which pertains to love. He says that in like manner love is not the cause of generation or being, as Empedocles claimed, if another position of his is considered. For he said that, when all the elements are combined into a unity, the corruption of the world will then take place; and thus love corrupts all things. Therefore, with respect to the world in general, love is the cause of corruption, whereas hate is the cause of generation. But with respect to singular things, hate is the cause of corruption and love of generation.

478. **Moreover, he does** [12].

Here he shows that Empedocles' argument is not adequate. For Empedocles said that there exists in the world a certain alternation of hate and friendship, in such a way that at one time love unites all things and afterwards hate separates them. But as to the reason why this alternation takes place, so that at one time hate predominates and at another time love, he said nothing more than that it was naturally disposed to be so.

479. And next he gives Empedocles' words, which, because they are written in Greek verse, are difficult and differ from the common way of speaking. These words are [13]: "But thus mighty hate was nourished among the members and rose to a position of honor when the time was fulfilled, which being changeable dissolved the bond." But the text of Boethius runs thus: "But when mighty discord in the members was promoted to a place of honor, because it marched forward in a completed year, which, when these things have been changed, returns to a full bond." Now in order to understand this it must be noted that he speaks poetically of the whole world as though it were a single living thing in whose members and parts there is found at first the greatest harmony, which he calls love or concord, and afterwards there begins to exist little by little a certain dissonance, which he calls discord. And, similarly, in the parts of the universe at first there was maximum concord, and afterwards hate was nourished little by little until it acquired "the place of honor," i.e., it acquired dominion over the elements. This comes about when a completed time is reached or a year is completed, as Empedocles held, "which" (hate or discord, or the year), being changeable, dissolves "the bond," i.e., the former union of the elements; or the year or hate returns to a full bond, because by a certain ability and hidden power it returns to predominate over things.

480. After these words of Empedocles, Aristotle, in giving the meaning of the word "changeable" which he used, adds the explanation as though change were necessary; for he says that Empedocles made the foregoing statements as though it were necessary that there should be an alternation of hate and love, but he gives no reason for this necessity. For in the case of this one living thing it is evident that what causes the alternation of hate and love is the motion of the heavens which causes generation and corruption in the world. But no such cause can be assigned why the whole should be changed in this way by love and hate. Hence it is clear that his argument was inadequate.

481. **Yet he alone** [14].

Here he shows that this argument of Empedocles is not to the point. He says that Empedocles seems to say "expressly," i.e., clearly, only that he does not hold that some of the things derived from these principles are corruptible and others incorruptible, but he holds that all things are corruptible with the exception of the elements alone. Thus he seems to avoid the foregoing problem inasmuch as the question remains why some things are corruptible and some not, if they come from the same principles. Hence it is also clear that his argument is not to the point, because he neglects the very point that requires explanation.

482. But it can be asked how he can say here that Empedocles held all things to be corruptible except the elements, since Empedocles has said above that the one is God, i.e., what is composed of the other principles except hate. It must be noted, however, that Empedocles posited two processes of corruption in the world, as is clear from what was said above. He posited one with respect to the blending of the whole universe, which was brought about by love; and from this process he did not make even God immune, because in God he placed love, which caused other things to be mixed with God. And he posited another process of corruption for singular things, and the principle of this process is hate. But he excluded this kind of corruption from God, seeing that he did not posit hate in God. In summing up, then, Aristotle concludes that this much has been said for the purpose of showing that corruptible and incorruptible things do not have the same principles.

483. **But if the principles** [15].

Here he argues the other side of the question, with two arguments. The first is this: if the principles of corruptible and incorruptible things are not the same, the question arises whether the principles of corruptible things are corruptible or incorruptible. If one says that they are corruptible, he proves that this is false by two arguments. The first runs thus: every corruptible thing is dissolved into the principles of which it is composed. If, then, the principles of corruptible things are corruptible, it will be necessary to hold also that there are other principles from which they are derived. But this is untenable, unless an infinite regress is posited. Now it was shown in Book II (n. 299) that it is impossible to have an infinite regress in principles in any class of cause. And it would be just as untenable for someone to say that this condition applies in the case of corruptible principles, since corruption seems to come about as a result of something being dissolved into prior principles.

484. The second argument runs thus. If the principles of corruptible things are corruptible, they must be corrupted, because every corruptible thing will be corrupted. But after they have been corrupted they cannot be principles, for what is corrupted or has been corrupted cannot cause anything. Therefore, since corruptible things are always caused in succession, the principles of corruptible things cannot be said to be corruptible.

485. Again, if it is said that the principles of corruptible things are incorruptible, evidently the principles of incorruptible things are incorruptible. Therefore the question remains why it is that from certain incorruptible principles corruptible effects are produced, and from certain others incorruptible effects are produced; for this seems to be unreasonable and is either impossible or requires considerable explanation.

486. **Further, no one** [16].

Then relative to his main thesis he gives his second argument, which is drawn from the common opinions of all men. For no one has attempted to say that corruptible and incorruptible things have different principles, but all say that all things have the same principles. Yet the first argument, given in favor of the first part of the question, all pass over lightly, as though it were of little importance; but this is to acknowledge its truth. Hence the text of Boethius says: "But they swallow the first argument as though they considered it a minor matter."

487. Now the solution to this problem is given in Book XII (see n. 2553), where the Philosopher shows that the first active or motive principles of all things are the same but in a certain sequence. For the first principles of things are unqualifiedly incorruptible and immobile, whereas the second are incorruptible and mobile, i.e., the celestial bodies, which cause generation and corruption in the world as a result of their motion. Now the intrinsic principles of corruptible and of incorruptible things are the same, not numerically but analogically. Still the intrinsic principles of corruptible things, which are matter and form, are not corruptible in themselves but only in reference to something else. For it is in this way that the matter and form of corruptible things are corrupted, as is stated in Book I of the *Physics*.[190a33]

LESSON 12
Are Unity and Being the Substance and Principle of All Things?

ARISTOTLE'S TEXT Chapter 4: 1001a4–1001b 25

1. But the most difficult problem which has to be considered, and the one which is most necessary for a knowledge of the truth, is whether unity and being are the substance of existing things, and whether each of them is nothing else than unity and being. Or whether it is necessary to investigate what being and unity themselves are, as though there were some other nature which underlies them. **1001a4–8**

2. For some think that reality is of the former sort, and some of the latter. For Plato and the Pythagoreans thought that being and unity were nothing else [than themselves], and that this is their nature, their substance being simply unity and being. But among the other philosophers [there are different opinions] about the nature of unity. Empedocles, for example, as though reducing it to something better known, says that unity is being; for he would seem to say that this is love, since this is the cause why unity belongs to all things. Others say that this unity and being of which existing things consist and have been made is fire, and others say it is air. And those who hold that there are many elements say the same thing; for they must also speak of unity and being in as many ways as they say there are principles. **1001a8–19**

3. But if anyone holds that unity and being are not substances, it will follow that no other universals are such; for these are the most universal of all. But if there is no one-in-itself or being-in-itself, there will hardly be any other things that exist apart from what are called singular things. Further, if unity is not a substance, evidently number will not exist as another reality separate from existing things; for number is units, and a unit is truly something one. But if there is a one-in-itself and being-in-itself, the substance of these must be unity itself and being itself. For nothing else is predicated universally of all things but these two. **1001a19–29**

4. But, on the other hand, if there is to be a one-in-itself and being-in-itself, there is great difficulty in seeing how there will be anything else besides these. I mean, how will there be more beings than one? For that which differs from being does not exist. Hence according to Parmenides' argument it must follow that all beings are one, and that this is being. **1001a29–1001b1**

5. But there is a difficulty in either case; for whether unity itself is not a substance, or whether there is a unity itself, it is impossible for number to be a substance. Now it has already been stated why this follows if unity is not a substance; but if it is, the same difficulty will arise with regard to being. For from something outside of being something else will be one; for it must be not one. But all beings are either one or many, each of which is a one. **1001b1–6**

6. Further, if unity itself is indivisible, according to Zeno's axiom it will be nothing. For that which when added does not make a thing greater or when subtracted does not make it smaller, this, he says, does not belong to the realm of existing things, as though it were evident that whatever has being is a continuous quantity. And if it is a continuous quantity, it is corporeal; for this in every respect is a being. But other quantities, for example, a surface and a line, when added in one way will make a thing greater, but in another way they will not; and a point and a unit will do so in no way. **1001b7–13**

7. But this philosopher speculates clumsily, and it is possible for a thing to be indivisible in such a way that some answer may be made against him; for when something of this kind is added it will not make a thing greater but more. **1001b13–16**

8. Yet how will continuous quantity come from such a unity or from many of them? For this would be like saying that a line is made up of points. **1001b17–19**

9. But even if someone were to think that the situation is such that number has come, as some say, from unity itself and from something else that is not one, none the less it would be necessary to inquire why and how the thing which has come to be would sometimes be a number and sometimes a continuous quantity, if that not-one were inequality and the same nature in either case. For it is not clear how continuous quantities would be produced from unity and this principle, or from some number and this principle. **1001b19–25**

COMMENTARY

488. Having asked whether the principles of things are the same or different, the Philosopher now asks how unity itself could have the nature of a principle; and in regard to this he does three things. First [1], he asks whether unity itself is a principle; second (Lesson 13), he asks whether numbers, which arise or follow from unity, are the principles of things ("And connected with"); and third (Lesson 14), whether the Forms, which are certain separate unities, are the principles of things ("But in general").

In regard to the first he does three things. First, he raises the question. Second [2], he gives the opinions on both sides ("For some think"). Third [3], he advances arguments on both sides ("But if anyone").

He says, first [1], that of all the different questions which have been raised, one is more difficult to consider because of the weight of the arguments on both sides, and that this question is also one about which it is necessary to know the truth, because our decision about the substances of things depends on it. Now this question is whether unity and being are the substances of things, not so that either of them must be attributed to some other nature which would be informed, as it were, by unity and being, but rather so that the unity and being of a thing are its substance; or, in an opposite way, whether it is necessary to ask what that thing is to which unity and being properly belong, as though there were some other nature which is their subject.

489. **For some think** [2].

Here he gives the opinions on each side of the question. He says that some philosophers thought that reality was of one kind, and some of another. For Plato and the Pythagoreans did not hold that unity and being are the attributes of some nature, but that they constitute the nature of things, as though being itself and unity itself were the substance of things. But some philosophers, in speaking about the natural world, attributed unity and being to certain other natures, as Empedocles reduced the one to something better known, which he said is unity and being; and this seems to be love, which is the cause of unity in the world. But other philosophers of nature attributed these to certain elementary causes, whether they posited one first principle, as fire or air, or more than one. For since they would hold that the material principles of things are the substances of things, it was necessary that each of these should constitute the unity and being of things; so that whichever one of these anyone might hold to be a principle, he would logically think that through it being and unity would be attributed to all things, whether he one.

490. **But if anyone** [3].

Here he gives arguments on both sides of the question. First, he gives arguments in support of the view of

Plato and Pythagoras. Second [4], he gives arguments on the other side of the question, in support of the view of the philosophers of nature ("But, on the other hand").

In regard to the first [3], he makes use of elimination as follows. It is necessary to hold either that unity and being, separate and existing apart, are a substance, or not. Now if it is said that unity and being are not a substance, two untenable consequences will follow. The first of these is this: unity and being are said to be the most universal of all, and therefore, if unity and being are not separate in such a way that unity itself or being itself is a certain substance, it will then follow that no universal is separate. Thus it will follow that there is nothing in the world except singular things, which seems to be inappropriate, as has been stated in earlier questions (n. 443).

491. The other untenable consequence is this. Number is nothing else than units, because number is composed of units; for a unit is nothing else than unity itself. Therefore, if unity itself is not separate as a substance existing of itself, it will follow that number will not be a reality separate from those things which are found in matter. This can be shown to be inappropriate in view of what has already been stated above. Hence it cannot be said that unity and being are not a substance which exists by itself.

492. Therefore, if the other part of the division is conceded, that there is something which is unity itself and being itself, and that this exists separately, it must be the substance of all those things of which unity and being are predicated. For everything that is separate and is predicated of many things is the substance of those things of which it is predicated. But nothing else is predicated of all things in as universal a way as unity and being. Therefore unity and being will be the substance of all things.

493. **But, on the other hand** [4].

Then he argues the other side of the question; and he gives two arguments. The second [6] of these begins where he says, "Further, if unity itself."

In regard to the first he does two things. First, he gives the argument. Second [5], he shows how the question is made difficult as a result of the argument given ("But there is a difficulty in either case").

The first [4] argument, then, is as follows: if there is something which is itself being and unity as something existing separately, it will be necessary to say that unity is the very same thing as being. But that which differs from being is non-being. Therefore it follows, according to the argument of Parmenides, that besides the one there is only non-being. Thus all things will have to be one, because it could not be held that that which differs from the one, which is essentially separate, is a being.

494. **But there is a difficulty** [5].

Here he shows how this argument creates a difficulty in the case of the position of Plato, who held that number is the substance of things. He says that Plato faces a difficulty in either case, whether it is said that this separate one is a substance or not. For whichever view is held, it seems impossible that number should be the substance of things. For if it is held that unity is not a substance, it has already been stated [4] why number cannot be held to be a substance.

495. But if unity itself is a substance, the same problem will arise with respect to both unity and being. For either there is some other unity besides

this unity which exists separately of itself, or there is not. And if there is no other, a multitude of things will not exist now, as Parmenides said. But if there is another unity, then that other unity, since it is not unity itself, must have as a material element something that is other than unity itself, and, consequently, other than being. And that material element from which this second unity comes to be, will have not to be a being. Thus a multitude of beings cannot be constituted from this unity which exists apart from unity itself, because all beings are either one or many, each of which is a one. But this one has as its material element something that is neither unity nor being.

496. **Further, if unity** [6].

Here he gives the second argument; and in regard to this he does three things. First [6], he gives the argument. Second [7], he criticizes it ("But this"). Third [8], he shows that the difficulty remains ("Yet how will continuous quantity").

He says first [6], then, that if this separate unity is indivisible, there follows from this the other position, which Zeno assumed, that nothing exists. For Zeno supposed that that which when added does not make a thing greater and when taken away does not make it smaller, is nothing in the real order. But he makes this assumption on the grounds that continuous quantity is the same as being. For it is evident that this is not a continuous quantity—I mean that which when added does not make a thing greater and when subtracted does not make it smaller. Therefore, if every being were a continuous quantity, it would follow that that which when added does not make a thing greater and when subtracted does not make it smaller, is non-being.

497. And better still, if any particular thing were to bear this out, every being would have to be a corporeal continuous quantity. For anything added to or subtracted from a body in any one of its dimensions, makes the body greater or less. But other continuous quantities, such as lines and surfaces, become greater insofar as one dimension is added, whereas others do not. For line added to line in length causes increase in length but not in width; and surface added to surface causes increase in width and in length but not in depth. But a point and a unit do not become greater or less in any way. Hence according to Zeno's axiom it would follow that a point and a unit are non-beings in an absolute sense, whereas a body is a being in every respect, and surfaces and lines are beings in one respect and non-beings in another respect.

498. **But this** [7].

Here he criticizes the argument which has been given. He says that Zeno, by proposing such an axiom, speculated "clumsily," i.e., in an unskilled and rude manner, so that according to him there cannot by anything indivisible. And for this reason some answer must be given to the foregoing argument; and if not to the point at issue, at least to the man. Now we say that even though a unity when added to something else does not make it larger, it does cause it to be more. And it is sufficient for the notion of being that in the case of what is continuous it should make a thing larger, and that in the case of what is discrete it should make it more.

499. **Yet how will** [8].

Then he states the difficulty which still faces the Platonists after the above solution. And he advances two difficulties. The first of these is that the

Platonists held that the one which is indivisible is the cause not only of number, which is a plurality, but also of continuous quantity. Therefore, if it is granted that when a one is added it makes a thing more, as would seem to suffice for the one which is the cause of number, how will it be possible for continuous quantity to come from an indivisible one of this kind, or from many such ones, as the Platonists held? For this would seem to be the same thing as to hold that a line is composed of points. For unity is indivisible just as a point is.

500. **But even if someone** [9].

Here he gives the second difficulty. He says that if anyone were to think that the situation is such that number is the result of the indivisible one and of something else which is not one, but participates in the one as a kind of material nature, as some say, the question would still remain why and how that which comes from the one as form and from another material nature, which is called the not-one, is sometimes a number and sometimes a continuous quantity. The difficulty would be most acute if that material not-one were inequality, as is implied in the continuously extended, and were to be the same reality. For it is not clear how numbers come from this inequality as matter and from the one as form; nor again is it clear how continuous quantities come from some number as form and from this inequality as matter. For the Platonists held that number comes from a primary one and a primary two, and that from this number and material inequality continuous quantity is produced.

501. The solution of this problem is treated by Aristotle in the following books. For the fact that there is something separate, which is itself one and being, he will prove below in Book XII (see n. 2553), when he establishes the oneness of the first principle which is separate in an absolute sense, although it is not the substance of all things which are one, as the Platonists thought, but is the cause and principle of the unity of all things. And insofar as unity is predicated of other things it is used in two ways. In one way it is interchangeable with being, and in this way each thing is one by its very essence, as is proved below in Book IV (n. 548); and unity in this sense adds nothing to being except merely the notion of undividedness. Unity is used in another way insofar as it has the character of a first measure, either in an absolute sense or with respect to some genus. And this unity if it is both a minimum in the absolute sense and indivisible, is the one which is the principle and measure of number. But if it is not both a minimum in an absolute sense and indivisible, it will not be a unit and measure in an absolute sense, as a pound in the case of weights and a half-tone in the case of melodies, and a foot in the case of lengths. And nothing prevents continuous quantities from being composed of this kind of unity. He will establish this in Book X (see n. 1940) of this work. But because the Platonists thought that the one which is the principle of number and the one which is interchangeable with being are the same, they therefore held that the one which is the principle of number is the substance of each thing, and consequently that number, inasmuch as it is composed of many substantial principles, makes up or comprises the substance of composite things. But he will treat this question at greater length in Books XIII and XIV of this work.

LESSON 13

Are Numbers and Continuous Quantities the Substances and Principles of Sensible Things?

ARISTOTLE'S TEXT Chapter 5: 1001b26–1002b11

1. *And connected with these is the question whether numbers and bodies and surfaces and points are substances, or not.* **1001b26–28**

2. *For if they are not, we are in a quandary as to what being is, and what the substances of things are. For affections and motions and relations and dispositions and their complex conceptions do not seem to signify substance; because all are predicated of some subject, and no one of them is a particular thing. And those things which seem to signify substance most of all, as fire, water, earth [and air], of which composite bodies are constituted, their heat and cold and similar affections, are not substances. And it is only the body which undergoes these that remains as a being and is a substance.* **1001b28–1002a4**

3. *Yet a body is a substance to a lesser degree than a surface, and this than a line, and this in turn than a unit and a point; for a body is defined by means of these, and these seem to be capable of existing without a body, but that a body should exist without these is impossible.* **1002a4–8**

4. *For this reason many of the natural philosophers, including the first, thought that substance and being are bodies, and that other things are attributes of this kind of thing; and hence too that the principles of bodies are the principles of beings. But the later philosophers, who were wiser than these, thought that the principles of things are numbers. Therefore, as we have said, if these are not substance, there is no substance or being at all; for the accidents of these things are not worthy to be called beings.* **1002a8–14**

5. *But if it is admitted that lengths and points are substances to a greater degree than bodies, and we do not see to what sort of bodies these belong (because it is impossible for them to exist in sensible bodies), there will then be no substance at all.* **1002a15–18**

6. *Further, all of these seem to be dimensions of bodies, one according to width, another according to depth, and another according to length.* **1002a18–20**

7. *And, similarly, any figure whatever already exists in a solid. Hence if neither Mercury is in the stone, nor one half of a cube in a cube as something segregated, neither will surface exist in a solid; for if this were true of anything whatever, it would also be true of that which divides a thing in half. And the same argument would apply in the case of a line, a point and a unit. If, then, a body is substance in the highest degree, and these things are such to a greater degree than it is, and these do not exist and are not substances, it escapes our understanding as to what being itself is and what the substance of beings is.* **1002a20–28**

8. *For along with what has been said there happen to be certain unreasonable views about generation and corruption. For if substance, not existing before, exists now, or existing before, does not exist afterwards, it seems to suffer these changes through generation and corruption. But it is impossible for points and lines and surfaces either to come to be or to be destroyed, even though they sometimes exist and sometimes do not. For when bodies are joined or divided, at one time, when they are joined, they [i.e., the two surfaces] simultaneously become one, and at another time, when they are divided, two surfaces are produced; because it [i.e., one of the two surfaces in question] is not in the bodies which have been joined but has perished. And when bodies are divided surfaces exist which did not exist before. For the indivisible point is not divided into two, and if things are generated and corrupted, they are generated from something.* **1002a28–1002a8**

9. *And it is similar with regard to the now in time, for this cannot be generated and corrupted.*

Yet it seems always to exist, although it is not a substance. It is also clear that this is true of points, lines and surfaces, because the argument is the same; for they are all similarly either limits or divisions. **1002b8–11**

COMMENTARY

502. Having inquired whether unity and being are the substances of sensible things, the Philosopher now asks whether numbers and continuous quantities are the substances of sensible things; and in regard to this he does three things. First [1], he presents the question. Second [2], he argues in support of one side of the question ("For if they are not"). Third [5], he argues on the other side ("But if it is admitted").

Accordingly he says, first [1], that "connected with these," i.e., following from the foregoing problem, there is the question whether numbers and continuous quantities, i.e., bodies, surfaces, and their extremities, such as points, are either substances that are separate from sensible things, or are the substances of sensible things themselves, or not. He says that this problem is a result of the foregoing one, because in the foregoing problem it was asked whether unity is the substance of things. Now unity is the principle of number. But number seems to be the substance of continuous quantity inasmuch as a point, which is a principle of continuous quantity, seems to be merely the number one having position, and a line to be the number two having position, and the primary kind of surface to be the number three having position, and a body the number four having position.

503. **For if they are not** [2].

Then he advances an argument to show that these are the substances of sensible things; and in regard to this he does two things. First [2], he introduces an argument to show that these are the substances of sensible things. Second [4], he shows how the early philosophers followed out the first arguments ("For this reason").

In regard to the first he does two things. For, first, he advances an argument to show that body is the substance of things; and second [3], to show that many other things are substances to an even greater degree ("Yet a body").

He says, first [2], that if these things are not substances, we are in a quandary as to what being is essentially, and what the substances of beings are. For it is evident that affections and motions and relations and dispositions or arrangements, and their complex conceptions according as they are put into words, do not seem to signify the substance of anything; because all things of this kind seem to be predicated of a subject as something belonging to the genus of quantity, and no one of them seems to signify "this particular thing," i.e., something that is complete and subsists of itself. This is especially evident in regard to the foregoing things, which are not said to be complete things but things whose nature consists in a kind of relation. But of all things those which especially seem to signify substance are fire, earth, and water, of which many bodies are composed. But he omits air, because it is less perceptible; and this is the reason why some thought air to be nothing. But in these bodies there are found certain dispositions, namely, hot and cold and other affections and passible qualities of this kind, which are not substances according to what has been said. It follows, then, that body alone is substance.

504. **Yet a body** [3].

Here he proceeds to examine those things which appear to be substance to an even greater degree than a body. He says that a body seems to be a substance to a lesser degree than a surface, and a surface than a line, and a line than a point or a unit. He proves this in two ways, of which the first is as follows. That by which a thing is defined seems to be its substance, for a definition signifies substance. But a body is defined by a surface, a surface by a line, a line by a point, and a point by a unit, because they say that a point is a unit having position. Therefore surface is the substance of body, and so on for the others.

505. The second argument runs as follows. Since substance is the primary kind of being, whatever is prior seems to be substance to a greater degree. But a surface is naturally prior to a body, because a surface can exist without a body but not a body without a surface. Therefore a surface is substance to a greater degree than a body. The same reasoning can be applied to all the others in turn.

506. **For this reason** [4].

Then he shows how the earlier philosophers followed out the foregoing arguments. He says that it was because of the foregoing arguments that many of the ancient philosophers, especially the first, thought that body alone was being and substance, and that all other things were accidents of bodies. Hence when they wanted to study the principles of beings, they studied the principles of bodies, as was stated above in Book I (see n. 74) with regard to the positions of the ancient natural philosophers. But the other philosophers who came later, and were reputed to be wiser than the aforesaid philosophers inasmuch as they dealt more profoundly with the principles of things, i.e., the Pythagoreans and Platonists, were of the opinion that numbers are the substances of sensible things inasmuch as numbers are composed of units. And the unit seems to be one substance of things. Hence, according to the foregoing arguments and opinions of the philosophers, it seems that if these things—numbers, lines, surfaces, and bodies—are not the substances of things, there will be no being at all. For if these are not beings, it is unfitting that their accidents should be called beings.

507. **But if it is** [5].

Then he argues in support of the other side of the question; and he gives four arguments, the first of which is as follows. If anyone were to admit that lengths and points are substances to a greater degree than bodies, then supposing that things of this sort are not substances, it also follows that bodies are not substances. Consequently, no substance will exist, because the accidents of bodies are not substances, as has been stated above (n. 503). But points, lines and surfaces are not substances. For these must be the limits of some bodies, because a point is the limit of a line, a line the limit of a surface, and a surface the limit of a body. But it is not evident to what sort of bodies these surfaces, lines and points, which are substances, belong. For it is evident that the lines and surfaces of sensible bodies are not substances, because they are altered in the same way as the other accidents in reference to the same subject. Therefore it follows that there will be no substance whatever.

508. **Further, all of these** [6].

Here he gives the second argument,

which is as follows. All of the above-mentioned things seem to be certain dimensions of bodies, either according to width, as a surface, or according to depth, as a solid, or according to length, as a line. But the dimensions of a body are not substances. Therefore things of this kind are not substances.

509. **And, similarly** [7].

Here he gives a third argument, which is as follows. Any figure which can be educed from a solid body according to some dimension is present in that body in the same way, i.e., potentially. But in the case of a large piece of stone which has not yet been cut, it is evident that "Mercury," i.e., the figure of Mercury, is not present in it actually but only potentially. Therefore, in like manner, "in a cube," i.e., in a body having six square surfaces, one half of the cube, which is another figure, is not present actually; but it becomes actual in this way when a cube has already been divided into two halves. And since every eduction of a new figure in a solid which has been cut is made according to some surface which limits a figure, it is also evident that such a surface will not be present in a body actually but only potentially. For if each surface besides the external one were actually present in a solid body, then for the same reason the surface which limits one half of the figure would also be actually present in it. But what has been said of a surface must also be understood of a line, a point, and a unit; for these are actually present in the continuum only insofar as they limit the continuum, and it is evident that these are not the substance of a body. But the other surfaces and lines cannot be the substance of a body, because they are not actually present in it; for substance is actually present in the thing whose substance it is. Hence he concludes that of all of these body especially seems to be substance, and that surfaces and lines seem to be substance to a great degree than bodies. Now if these are not actual beings or substances, it seems to escape our comprehension as to what being is and what the substances of things are.

510. **For along with** [8].

Here he gives the fourth argument. First, he states it, and second [9], he clarifies it by using a similar case ("And it is similar").

Accordingly, he says, first [8], that along with the other untenable consequences mentioned there also happen to be certain unreasonable views about generation and corruption on the part of those who hold that lines and surfaces are the substances of sensible things. For every substance which at first did not exist and later does exist, or which first was and afterwards is not, seems to suffer this change by way of generation and corruption. This is most evident in the case of all those things which are caused by way of motion. But points and lines and surfaces sometimes are and sometimes are not. Yet they are not generated or corrupted. Neither, then, are they substances.

511. He then proves each assumption. The first of these, is that they sometimes are and sometimes are not. For it happens that bodies which were at first distinct are afterwards united, and that those which were at first united are afterwards divided. For when bodies which were initially separated are united, one surface is produced for the two of them, because the parts of a continuous body are united in having one common boundary, which is one surface. But when one body is divided into two, two surfaces are produced, because it cannot be said

that when two bodies are brought together their surfaces remain intact, but that both "perish," i.e., cease to be. In like manner, when bodies are divided there begin to exist for the first time two surfaces which previously did not exist. For it cannot be said that a surface, which is indivisible according to depth, is divided into two surfaces according to depth; or that a line, which is indivisible according to width, is divided according to width; or that a point, which is indivisible in every respect, is divided in any respect whatsoever. Thus it is clear that two things cannot be produced from one thing by way of division, and that one thing cannot be produced from two of these things by way of combination. Hence it follows that points, lines and surfaces sometimes begin to be and sometimes cease to be.

512. After having proved this, he proves the second assumption, namely, that these things are neither generated nor corrupted. For everything that is generated is generated from something, and everything that is corrupted is dissolved into something as its matter. But it is impossible to assign any matter whatever from which these things are generated and into which they are dissolved, because they are simple. Therefore they are neither generated nor corrupted.

513. **And it is similar** [9].

Then he makes the foregoing argument clear by using a similar case. For the now in time stands to time as a point to a line. But the now in time does not seem to be generated and corrupted, because if it were its generation and corruption would have to be measured by some particular time or instant. Thus the measure of this now either would be another now and so on to infinity, or would be time itself. But this is impossible. And even though the now is not generated or corrupted, still each now always seems to differ, not substantially but existentially, because the substance of the now corresponds to the mobile subject. But the difference of the now in terms of existence corresponds to the variation in motion, as is shown in Book IV of the *Physics. [219b12]* Therefore the same thing seems to be true of a point in relation to a line, and of a line in relation to a surface, and of a surface in relation to a body, namely, that they are neither corrupted nor generated, although some variation is observable in things of this kind. For the same holds true of all of these, because all things of this kind are, in like manner, limits if regarded as at the extremities, or divisions if they are found in between. Hence, just as the now varies existentially as motion flows by, although it remains substantially the same because the mobile subject remains the same, so also does the point vary. And it does not become different because of the division of a line, even though it is not corrupted or generated in an absolute sense. The same holds true of the others.

514. But the Philosopher will treat this question in Books XIII and XIV. And the truth of the matter is that mathematical entities of this kind are not the substances of things, but are accidents which accrue to substances. But this mistake about continuous quantities is due to the fact that no distinction is made between the sort of body which belongs to the genus of substance and the sort which belongs to the genus of quantity. For body belongs to the genus of substance according as it is composed of matter and form; and dimensions are a natural consequence of these in corporeal mat-

ter. But dimensions themselves belong to the genus of quantity, and are not substances but accidents whose subject is a body composed of matter and form. The same thing too was said above (n. 501) about those who held that numbers are the substances of things; for their mistake came from not distinguishing between the one which is the principle of number and that which is interchangeable with being.

LESSON 14

Are There Separate Forms in Addition to the Objects of Mathematics and Sensible Things?

ARISTOTLE'S TEXT Chapter 6: 1002b12–1002b32

1. *But in general one will wonder why, in addition to sensible things and those which are intermediate, it is necessary to look for certain other things which we posit as the specific essences (or Forms) of sensible things.* **1002b12–14**

2. *For if it is because the objects of mathematics differ in one respect from the things which are at hand, they do not differ in being many things that are specifically the same. Hence the principles of sensible things will not be limited in number but only in species; unless one were to consider the principles of this particular syllable or word, for these are limited in number. And this is likewise true of the intermediate entities; for in their case too there are an infinite number of things that are specifically the same. Hence, if in addition to sensible substances and the objects of mathematics there are not certain other things, such as some call the Forms, there will be no substance which is one both numerically and specifically. Nor will the principles of beings be limited in number, but only in species. Therefore, if this is necessary, it will also be necessary on this account that there should be Forms. And even if those who speak of the Forms do not express themselves clearly, although this is what they wanted to say, they must affirm that each of the Forms is a substance, and that nothing accidental pertains to them.* **1002b14–30**

3. *But if we hold that the Forms exist, and that principles are one numerically but not specifically, we have stated the untenable conclusions that follow from this view.* **1002b30–32**

COMMENTARY

515. Having inquired whether the objects of mathematics are the principles of sensible substances, the Philosopher now inquires whether in addition to the objects of mathematics there are certain other principles, such as those which we call Forms, which are the substances and principles of sensible things. In regard to this he does three things. First [1], he presents the question. Second [2], he argues one side of the question ("For if it is because"). Third [3], he argues the other side ("But if we hold").

Accordingly, he says, first [1], that if one assumes that the objects of mathematics are not the principles of sensible things and their substances, one will next have the problem why, in addition to both sensible things and the objects of mathematics (which are an intermediate class between sensible things and the Forms), it is necessary to posit a third class of entities, namely, the specific essences, i.e., the Ideas or separate Forms.

516. **For if it is because** [2].

Here he argues one side of the question. The reason why it is necessary to posit separate Forms over and above sensible substances and the objects of mathematics seems to be that the objects of mathematics differ in one respect "from the things at hand," i.e., from sensible things, which exist in the universe; for the objects of mathematics abstract from sensible matter. Yet they do not differ but rather agree in another respect. For just as we find many sensible things which are specifically the same but numerically different, as many men or many horses, in a similar way we find many objects of mathematics which are specifically the same but numerically different, such as many equilateral triangles and many equal lines. And if this is true, it follows that, just as the principles of sensible things are not limited in number but in species, the same thing is true "of the intermediate entities"—the objects of mathematics. For since in the case of sensible things there are many individuals of one sensible species, it is evident that the principles of sensible things are not limited in number but in species, unless of course we can consider the proper principles of a particular individual thing, which are also limited in number and are individual. He gives as an example words; for in the case of a word expressed in letters it is clear that the letters are its principles, yet there are not a limited number of individual letters taken numerically, but only a limited number taken specifically, some of which are vowels and some consonants. But this limitation is according to species and not according to number. For a is not only one but many, and the same applies to other letters. But if we take those letters which are the principles of a particular syllable, whether written or spoken, then they are limited in number. And for the same reason, since there are many objects of mathematics which are numerically different in one species, the mathematical principles of mathematical science could not be limited in number but only in species. We might say, for example, that the principles of triangles are three sides and three angles; but this limitation is according to species, for any of them can be multiplied to infinity. Therefore, if there were nothing besides sensible things and the objects of mathematics, it would follow that the substance of a Form would be numerically one, and that the principles of beings would not be limited in number but only in species. Therefore, if it is necessary that they be limited in number (otherwise it would happen that the principles of things are infinite in number), it follows that there must be Forms in addition to the objects of mathematics and sensible things.

517. This is what the Platonists wanted to say, because it necessarily follows from the things which they held that in the case of the substance of sensible things there is a single Form to which nothing accidental belongs. For something accidental, such as whiteness or blackness, pertains to an individual man, but to this separate man, who is a Form, according to the Platonists, there pertains nothing accidental but only what belongs to the definition of the species. And although they wanted to say this, they did not "express themselves" clearly; i.e., they did not clearly distinguish things.

518. **But if we hold that** [3].

Then he counters with an argument for the other side of the question. He says that, if we hold that there are separate Forms and that the principles of things are limited not only in species but also in number, certain impossible consequences will follow, which are touched on above in one of the questions (see n. 464). But the Philosopher will deal with this problem in Book XII (see n. 2450) and Book XIV of this work. And the truth of the matter is that, just as the objects of mathematics do not exist apart from sensible things, neither do Forms exist apart from the objects of mathematics and from sensible substances. And while the efficient and moving principles of things are limited in number, the formal principles of things, of which there are many individuals in one species, are not limited in number but only in species.

LESSON 15
Do First Principles Exist Actually or Potentially, and Are They Universal or Singular?

ARISTOTLE'S TEXT Chapter 6: 1002b32–1003b17

1. *And connected with these problems there is the question whether the elements of things exist potentially or in some other way.* **1002b32–34**

2. *If they exist in some other way, then there will be something else prior to [first] principles. For potentiality is prior to that cause, but the potential need not exist in that way.* **1002b34–1003a2**

3. *But if the elements exist potentially, it is possible for nothing to exist; for even that which does not yet exist is capable of existing, because that which does not exist may come to be. But nothing that is incapable of existing may come to be. It is necessary, then, to investigate these problems.* **1003a2–6**

4. *And there is also the problem whether [first] principles are universals or singular things, as we maintain.* **1003a6–7**

5. *For if they are universals, they will not be substances, because a common term signifies not a particular thing but what sort of thing; and a substance is a particular thing.* **1003a7–9**

6. *But if it is a particular thing, and is held to be the common whatness which is predicated of things, Socrates himself will be many animals: [himself] and man and animal; i.e., if each of these signifies a particular thing and a one. If, then, the first principles of things are universals, these consequences will follow.* **1003a9–13**

7. *However, if they are not universals but have the nature of singular things, they will not be knowable; for all scientific knowledge is universal. Hence, if there is to be any scientific knowledge of [first] principles, there will have to be different principles which are predicated universally and are prior to [first] principles.* **1003a13–17**

COMMENTARY

519. Having inquired what the principles are, the Philosopher now asks how they exist. First [1], he asks whether they exist potentially or actually; and second [4], whether they are universals or singulars ("And there is also the problem").

In regard to the first he does three things. First, he raises the question. Second [2], he argues one side ("If they exist"). Third [3], he argues the opposite side ("But if the elements").

His first question [1], then, is whether first principles exist potentially or "in some other way," i.e., actually. This problem is introduced because of the ancient philosophers of nature, who held that there are only material principles, which are in potency. But the Platonists, who posited separate Forms as formal principles, claimed that they exist actually.

520. **If they exist** [2].

He proves that principles exist potentially. For if they were to exist "in some other way," i.e., actually, it would follow that there would be something prior to principles; for potentiality is prior to actuality. This is clear from the fact that one thing is prior to another when the sequence of their being cannot be reversed; for if a thing exists, it follows that it can be, but it does not necessarily follow that, if a thing is possible, it will exist actually. But it is impossible for anything to be prior to a first principle. Therefore it is impossible for a first principle to exist in any other way than potentially.

521. **But if the elements** [3].

Here he argues the other side of the question. If the principles of things exist potentially, it follows that no beings exist actually; for that which exists potentially does not yet exist actually. He proves this on the grounds that that which is coming to be is not a being. For that which exists is not coming to be; but only that comes to be which exists potentially. Therefore everything that exists potentially is nonbeing. Hence if principles exist only potentially, beings will not exist. But if principles do not exist, neither will their effects. It follows, then, that it is possible for nothing to exist in the order of being. And in summing this up he concludes that according to what has been said it is necessary to inquire about the principles of things for the reasons given.

522. This question will be answered in Book IX (see n. 1844) of this work, where it is shown that actuality is prior to potentiality in an unqualified sense, but that in anything moved from potentiality to actuality, potentiality is prior to actuality in time. Hence it is necessary that the first principle exist actually and not potentially, as is shown in Book XII (see n. 2500) of this work.

523. **And there is also the problem** [4].

Here he asks whether the principles of things exist as universals or as singular things; and in regard to this he does three things. First [4], he presents the question. Second [5], he argues one side ("For if they are universals"). Third [7], he argues the other side ("However, if they are not universals").

The problem [4], then, is whether principles are universals or exist in the manner of singular things.

524. **For if they are** [5].

Then he proves that principles are not universals, by the following argument. No predicate common to many things signifies a particular thing, but signifies such and such a thing or of what sort a thing is; and it does this not according to accidental quality but according to substantial quality, as is stated below in Book V (see n. 987) of this work. The reason for this is that a particular thing is said to be such insofar as it subsists of itself. But that which subsists of itself cannot be something that exists in many, as belongs to the notion of common. For that which exists in many will not subsist of itself unless it is itself many. But this is contrary to the notion of common, because what is common is what is one-in-many. Hence it is clear that a particular thing does not signify anything common, but signifies a form existing in many things.

525. Further, he adds the minor premise, namely, that substance signifies a particular thing. And this is true of first substances, which are said to be substances in the full and proper sense, as is stated in the *Categories; [2b15]* for substances of this kind are things which subsist of themselves. Thus it follows that, if principles are universals, they are not substances. Hence either there will be no principles of substances, or it will be necessary to say that the principles of substances are not substances.

526. But since it is possible for someone to affirm that some common predicate might signify this particular thing, he therefore criticizes this when he says "But if it is [6]."

He explains the untenable consequence resulting from this. For if a common predicate were a particular thing, it would follow that everything to which that common predicate is applied would be this particular thing which is common. But it is clear that both animal and man are predicated of Socrates, and that each of these—animal and man—is a common predicate. Hence, if every common predicate were a particular thing, it would follow that Socrates would be three particular things; for Socrates is Socrates, which is a particular thing; and he is also a man, which is a particular thing according to the above; and he is also an animal, which is similarly a particular thing. Hence he would be three particular things. Further, it would follow that there would be three animals; for animal is predicated of itself, of man, and of Socrates. Therefore, since this is impossible, it is also impossible for a common predicate to be a particular thing. These, then, will be the impossible consequences which follow if principles are universals.

527. **However, if they are not** [7].

He argues the other side of the question. Since all sciences are universal, they are not concerned with singulars but with universals. Therefore, if some principles were not universals but were singular things, they would not be knowable in themselves. Hence, if any science were to be had of them, there would have to be certain prior principles, which would be universals. It is necessary, then, that first principles be universals in order that science may be had of things; because if principles remain unknown, other things must remain unknown.

528. This question will be answered in Book VII (see n. 1584) of this work, where it is shown that universals are neither substances nor the principles of things. However, it does not follow for this reason that, if the principles and substances of things were singulars, there could be no science of them, both because immaterial things, even though they subsist as singulars, are nevertheless also intelligible, and also because there is science of singulars according to their universal concepts which are apprehended by the intellect.

BOOK IV
BEING AND FIRST PRINCIPLES

LESSON 1

The Proper Subject Matter of This Science: Being as Being, and Substance and Accidents

ARISTOTLE'S TEXT Chapters 1 & 2: 1003a21–1003b22

1. There is a certain science which studies being as being and the attributes which necessarily belong to being. **1003a21–23**

2. This science is not the same as any of the so-called particular sciences; for none of the other sciences attempt to study being as being in general, but cutting off some part of it they study the accidents of this part. This, for example, is what the mathematical sciences do. **1003a23–26**

3. Now since we are seeking the principles and ultimate causes of things, it is evident that these must be of themselves the causes of some nature. Hence, if those who sought the elements of beings sought these principles, they must be the elements of beings not in any accidental way but inasmuch as they are beings. Therefore the first causes of being as being must also be understood by us. **1003a26–32**

Chapter 2

4. The term being is used in many senses, but with reference to one thing and to some one nature and not equivocally. Thus everything healthy is related to health, one thing because it preserves health, another because it causes it, another because it is a sign of it (as urine) and still another because it is receptive of it. The term medical is related in a similar way to the art of medicine; for one thing is called medical because it possesses the art of medicine, another because it is receptive of it, and still another because it is the act of those who have the art of medicine. We can take other words which are used in a way similar to these. And similarly there are many senses in which the term being is used, but each is referred to a first principle. For some things are called beings because they are substances; others because they are affections of substances; others because they are a process toward substance, or corruptions or privations or qualities of substance, or because they are productive or generative principles of substance, or of things which are related to substance, or the negation of some of these or of substance. For this reason too we say that non-being is non-being. **1003a33–1003b10**

5. Therefore, just as there is one science of all healthy things, so too the same thing is true in other cases. For it is the office of one and the same science to study not only those things which are referred to one thing but also those which are referred to one nature. For those too in a sense are referred to one thing. **1003b11–15**

6. It is evident, then, that it is the function of one science to study beings as beings. **1003b15–16**

7. But in every respect a science is concerned with what is primary, and that on which other things depend, and from which they derive their name. Hence, if this is substance, it must be of substances that the philosopher possesses the principles and causes. **1003b16–19**

8. Now of every single class of things there is one sense and one science; for example, grammar, which is one science, studies all words. And for this reason too it belongs to a general science to study all species of being as being and the species of these species. **10003b19–22**

COMMENTARY

529. In the preceding book the Philosopher proceeded to treat dialectically the things which ought to be considered in this science. Here he begins

to proceed demonstratively by establishing the true answer to those questions which have been raised and argued dialectically.

In the preceding book he treated dialectically both the things which pertain to the method of this science, namely, those to which the consideration of this science extends, as well as those which fall under the consideration of this science. And because it is first necessary to know the method of a science before proceeding to consider the things with which it deals, as was explained in Book II (see n. 335), this part is therefore divided into two members. First [1], he speaks of the things which this science considers; and second, of those which fall under its consideration. He does this in Book V ("In one sense the term *principle*").

The first part is divided into two members. First, he establishes what the subject matter of this science is. Second [4], he proceeds to answer the questions raised in the preceding book about the things which this science considers ("The term *being*").

In regard to the first he does three things. First, he submits that there is a science whose subject is being. Second [2], he shows that it is not one of the particular sciences ("But this science"); and third [3], he shows that it is the science with which we are now dealing ("Now since").

Now because a science should investigate not only its subject but also the proper accidents of its subject, he therefore says, first [1], that there is a science which studies being as being, as its subject, and studies also "the attributes which necessarily belong to being," i.e., its proper accidents.

530. He says "as being" because the other sciences, which deal with particular beings, do indeed consider being (for all the subjects of the sciences are beings), yet they do not consider being as being, but as some particular kind of being, for example, number or line or fire or the like.

531. He also says "and the attributes which necessarily belong to being," and not just those which belong to being, in order to show that it is not the business of this science to consider those attributes which belong accidentally to its subject, but only those which belong necessarily to it. For geometry does not consider whether a triangle is of bronze or of wood, but only considers it in an absolute sense according as it has three angles equal to two right angles. Hence a science of this kind, whose subject is being, must not consider all the attributes which belong accidentally to being, because then it would consider the accidents investigated by all sciences; for all accidents belong to some being, but not inasmuch as it is being. For those accidents which are the proper accidents of an inferior thing are related in an accidental way to a superior thing; for example, the proper accidents of man are not the proper accidents of animal. Now the necessity of this science, which considers being and its proper accidents, is evident from this, that such things should not remain unknown since the knowledge of other things depends on them, just as the knowledge of proper objects depends on that of common objects.

532. **This science** [2].

Then he shows that this science is not one of the particular sciences, and he uses the following argument. No particular science considers universal being as such, but only some part of it separated from the others; and about this part it studies the proper accidents. For example, the mathematical sciences study one kind of being, quantitative being. But the common science considers universal being as being, and therefore it is not the same as any of the particular sciences.

533. **Now since** [3].

Here he shows that the science with which we are dealing has being as its subject, and he uses the following argument. Every principle is of itself the principle and cause of some nature. But we are seeking the first principles and ultimate causes of things, as was explained in Book I (see n. 57), and therefore these are of themselves the causes of some nature. But this nature can only be the nature of being. This is clear from the fact that all philosophers, in seeking the elements of things inasmuch as they are beings, sought principles of this kind, namely, the first and ultimate ones. Therefore in this science we are seeking the principles of being as being. Hence being is the subject of this science, for any science seeks the proper causes of its subject.

534. **The term "being"** [4].

Then he proceeds to answer the questions raised in the preceding book about the things which this science considers, and this is divided into three parts. First [4], he answers the question whether this science considers substances and accidents together, and whether it considers all substances. Second (Lesson 2), he answers the question whether it belongs to this science to consider all of the following: one and many, same and different, opposites, contraries, and so forth ("Now although"). Third (Lesson 5), he answers the question whether it belongs to this science to consider the principles of demonstration ("Moreover, it is necessary").

In regard to the first he does three things. First, he shows that it is the office of this science to consider both substances and accidents. Second [6], he shows that this science is chiefly concerned with substances ("But in every respect"). Third [8], he shows that it pertains to this science to consider all substances ("Now of every").

In regard to the first part he uses this kind of argument: those things which have one term predicated of them in common, not univocally but analogously, belong to the consideration of one science. But the term being is thus predicated of all beings. Therefore all beings, i.e., both substances and accidents, belong to the consideration of one science which considers being as being.

535. Now in this argument he gives, first [4], the minor premise; second [5], the major premise ("Therefore, just as"); and third [7], the conclusion ("It is evident, then").

He accordingly says, first [4], that the term being, or what is, has several meanings. But it must be noted that a term is predicated of different things in various senses. Sometimes it is predicated of them according to a meaning which is entirely the same, and then it is said to be predicated of them univocally, as animal is predicated of a horse and of an ox. Sometimes it is predicated of them according to meanings which are entirely different, and then it is said to be predicated of them equivocally, as *dog* is predicated of a star and of an animal. And sometimes it is predicated of them according to meanings which are partly different and partly not (different inasmuch as they imply different relationships, and the same inasmuch as these different relationships are referred to one and the same thing), and then it is said "to be predicated analogously," i.e., proportionally, according as each one by its own relationship is referred to that one same thing.

536. It must also be noted that the one thing to which the different relationships are referred in the case of analogical things is numerically one and not just one in meaning, which is the kind of oneness designated by a univocal term. Hence he says that, although the term being has several senses, still it is not predicated equivocally but in reference to one thing; not to one thing which is one merely in meaning, but to one which is one as a single definite nature. This is evident in the examples given in the text.

537. First, he gives the example of many things being related to one thing as an end. This is clear in the case of the term *healthy* or *healthful*. For the term healthy is not predicated univocally of food, medicine, urine and an animal; because the concept healthy as applied to food means something that preserves health; and as applied to medicine it means something that causes health; and as applied to urine it means something that is a sign of health; and as applied to an animal it means something that is the recipient or subject of health. Hence every use of the term healthy refers to one and the same health; for it is the same health which the animal receives, which urine is a sign of, which medicine causes, and which food preserves.

538. Second, he gives the example of many things being related to one thing as an efficient principle. For one thing is called medical because it possesses the art of medicine, as the skilled physician. Another is called medical because it is naturally disposed to have the art of medicine, as men who are so disposed that they may acquire the art of medicine easily (and according to this some men can engage in medical activities as a result of a peculiar natural constitution). And another is called medical or medicinal because it is necessary for healing, as the instruments which physicians use can be called medical. The same thing is also true of the things called medicines, which physicians use in restoring health. Other terms which resemble these in having many senses can be taken in a similar way.

539. And just as the above-mentioned terms have many senses, so also does the term being. Yet every being is called such in relation to one first thing, and this first thing is not an end or an efficient cause, as is the case in the foregoing examples, but a subject. For some things are called beings, or are said to be, because they have being of themselves, as substances, which are called beings in the primary and proper sense. Others are called beings because they are affections or properties of substances, as the proper accidents of any substance. Others are called beings because they are processes toward substance, as generation and motion. And others are called beings because they are corruptions of substances; for corruption is the process toward non-being just as generation is the process toward substance. And since corruption terminates in privation just as generation terminates in form, the very privations of substantial forms are fittingly called beings. Again, certain qualities or certain accidents are called beings because they are productive or generative principles of substances or of those things which are related to substance according to one of the foregoing relationships or any other relationship. And similarly the negations of those things which are related to substances, or

even substance itself, are also called beings. Hence we say that non-being is non-being. But this would not be possible unless a negation possessed being in some way.

540. But it must be noted that the above-mentioned modes of being can be reduced to four. For one of them, which is the most imperfect, i.e., negation and privation, exists only in the mind. We say that these exist in the mind because the mind busies itself with them as kinds of being while it affirms or denies something about them. In what respect negation and privation differ will be treated below (n. 564).

541. There is another mode of being inasmuch as generation and corruption are called beings, and this mode by reason of its imperfection comes close to the one given above. For generation and corruption have some admixture of privation and negation, because motion is an imperfect kind of actuality, as is stated in the *Physics*, Book III. [201b31]

542. The third mode of being admits of no admixture of non-being, yet it is still an imperfect kind of being, because it does not exist of itself but in something else, for example, qualities and quantities and the properties of substances.

543. The fourth mode of being is the one which is most perfect, namely, what has being in reality without any admixture of privation, and has firm and solid being inasmuch as it exists of itself. This is the mode of being which substances have. Now all the others are reduced to this as the primary and principal mode of being; for qualities and quantities are said to be inasmuch as they exist in substances; and motions and generations are said to be inasmuch as they are processes tending toward substance or toward some of the foregoing; and negations and privations are said to be inasmuch as they remove some part of the preceding three.

544. **Therefore, just as** [5].

Here he gives the major premise of the first argument. He says that it is the office of one science to study not only those things which are referred "to one thing," i.e., to one common notion, but also those which are referred to one nature according to different relationships. And the reason for this is that the thing to which they are referred is one; just as it is clear that one science, medicine, considers all health-giving things. The same thing holds true of other things which are spoken of in the same way.

545. **It is evident** [7].

Then he draws his intended conclusion. This is evident of itself.

546. **But in every** [6].

Then he shows that this science, even though it considers all beings, is chiefly concerned with substances. He uses the following argument. Every science which deals with many things that are referred to one primary thing is properly and principally concerned with that primary thing on which other things depend for their being and from which they derive their name; and this is true in every case. But substance is the primary kind of being. Hence the philosopher who considers all beings ought to consider primarily and chiefly the principles and causes of substances. Therefore his consideration extends primarily and chiefly to substances.

547. **Now of every** [8].

Then he shows by the following argument that it is the business of the first philosopher to consider all substances. There is one sense and one science of all things belonging to one class; for example, sight is concerned with all colors, and grammar with all words. Therefore, if all beings somehow belong to one class, all species of being must belong to the consideration of one science which is a general science, and different species of being must belong to the different species of that science. He says this because it is not necessary for one science to consider all the species of one genus according to the special notes of every single species, but only inasmuch as they agree generically. But according to their specific notes the different species of one genus belong to the special sciences, as happens in the present case. For inasmuch as all substances are beings or substances, they belong to the consideration of this science; but inasmuch as they are a particular kind of substance, as a lion or an ox, they belong to the special sciences.

LESSON 2
This Science Considers Being and Unity. The Parts of Philosophy Based on the Divisions of Being and Unity

ARISTOTLE'S TEXT Chapter 2: 1003b22–1004a9

1. *Now although being and unity are the same and are a single nature in the sense that they are associated like principle and cause, they are not the same in the sense that they are expressed by a single concept. Yet it makes no difference even if we consider them to be the same; in fact this will rather support our undertaking.* **1003b22–26**

2. *For one man and human being and man are the same thing; and nothing different is expressed by repeating the terms when we say, "This is a human being, a man, and one man." And it is evident that they are not separated either in generation or in corruption. The same holds true of what is one. Hence it is evident that any addition to these expresses the same thing, and that unity is nothing else than being.* **1003b26–32**

3. *Further, the substance of each thing is one in no accidental way; and similarly it is something that is.* **1003b32–33**

4. *Hence there are as many species of being as there are of unity, of which it is the office of the same general science to treat. I mean, for example, sameness and likeness and other such attributes. And almost all contraries may be referred to this starting point. But these have been studied by us in our selection, i.e., in our explanation or treatment, of contraries.* **1003b33–1004a2**

5. *And there are just as many parts of philosophy as there are substances, so that there must be a first philosophy and one which is next in order to it. For being and unity are things which straightway have genera; and for this reason the sciences will correspond to these. For the term philosopher is used like the term mathematician; for mathematics too has parts, and there is a first and a second science and then others following these among the mathematical sciences.* **1004a2–9**

COMMENTARY

548. Here he proceeds to show that the study of common attributes such as one and many and same and different belongs to the consideration of one and the same science; and in regard to this he does two things. First [1], he shows that this is true of each attribute taken separately by arguing from proper or specific principles. Second (Lesson 4), he shows that this is true of all attributes taken together by arguing from common principles ("And it is also evident").

In regard to the first he does two things. First, he shows that the philosopher ought to investigate all these attributes. Second (Lesson 3, see n. 568), he tells us how to investigate them ("Hence, since the term").

In regard to the first he does two things. First, he shows that it is the office of this science to consider unity and its species. Second (Lesson 3), he shows that it is the office of one and the same science to consider all opposites ("Now since").

In regard to the first he does two things. First [1], he shows that it is the office of this science to consider unity. Second [4], he shows that it also belongs to it to examine the species of unity ("Hence there are").

He therefore says, first [1], that being and unity are the same and are a single nature. He says this because some things are numerically the same which are not a single nature but different natures, for example, Socrates, this white thing, and this musician. Now the terms *one* and *being* do not signify different natures but a single nature. But things can be one in two ways; for some things are one which are associated as interchangeable things, like principle and cause; and some are interchangeable not only in the sense that they are one and the same numerically [or in subject] but also in the sense that they are one and the same conceptually, like garment and clothing.

549. Now the terms one and being signify one nature according to different concepts, and therefore they are like the terms principle and cause, and not like the terms tunic and garment, which are wholly synonymous.—Yet it makes no difference to his thesis if we consider them to be used in the same sense, as those things which are one both numerically and conceptually. In fact this will "rather support our undertaking," i.e., it will serve his purpose better; for he intends to prove that unity and being belong to the same study, and that the species of the one correspond to those of the other. The proof of this would be clearer if unity and being were the same both numerically and conceptually rather than just numerically and not conceptually.

550. He proves that they are the same numerically by using two arguments. He gives the first where he says, "For one man," and it runs as follows. Any two things which when added to some third thing cause no difference are wholly the same. But when one and being are added to man or to anything at all, they cause no difference. Therefore they are wholly the same. The truth of the minor premise is evident; for it is the same thing to say "man" and "one man." And similarly it is the same thing to say "human being" and "the thing that is man;" and nothing different is expressed when in speaking we repeat the terms, saying, "This is a human being, a man, and one man." He proves this as follows.

551. It is the same thing for man and the thing that is man to be generated and corrupted. This is evident from the fact that generation is a process toward being, and corruption a change from being to non-being. Hence a man is never generated without a human being being generated, nor is a man ever corrupted without a human being being corrupted; and those things which are generated and corrupted together are themselves one and the same.

552. And just as it has been said that being and man are not separated either in generation or in corruption, so too this is evident of what is one; for when a man is generated, one man is generated, and when a man is corrupted, one man is also corrupted. It is clear, then, that the apposition of these [i.e., of one or being to man] expresses the same thing, and that just because the term one or being is added to man it is not to be understood that some nature is added to man. And from this it is clearly apparent that unity does not differ from being, because any two things which are identical with some third thing are identical with each other.

553. It is also evident from the foregoing argument that unity and being are the same numerically but differ conceptually; for if this were not the case they would be wholly synonymous, and then it would be nonsense to say, "a human being," and "one man." For it must be borne in mind that the term *man* is derived from the quiddity or the nature of man, and the term *thing* from the quiddity only; but

the term *being* is derived from the act of being, and the term *one* from order or lack of division; for what is one is an undivided being. Now what has an essence, and a quiddity by reason of that essence, and what is undivided in itself, are the same. Hence these three—thing, being, and one—signify absolutely the same thing but according to different concepts.

554. **Further, the substance** [3].

Then he gives the second argument, which has to do with sameness or identity of subject. This argument is as follows. Any two attributes which are predicated essentially and not accidentally of the substance of each thing are the same in subject, or numerically. But unity and being are such that they are predicated essentially and not accidentally of the substance of each thing; for the substance of a thing is one in itself and not accidentally. Therefore the terms being and one signify the same thing in subject.

555. That the terms being and one are predicated essentially and not accidentally of the substance of each thing can be proved as follows. If being and one were predicated of the substance of each thing by reason of something added to it [i.e., accidentally], being would have to be predicated also of the thing added, because anything at all is one and a being. But then there would be the question whether being is predicated of this thing (the one added) either essentially or by reason of some other thing that is added to it in turn. And if the latter were the case, then the same question would arise once again regarding the last thing added, and so on to infinity. But this is impossible. Hence the first position must be held, namely, that a thing's substance is one and a being of itself and not by reason of something added to it.

556. But it must be noted that Avicenna felt differently about this; for he said that the terms being and one do not signify a thing's substance but something added to it. He said this of being because, in the case of anything that derives its existence from something else, the existence of such a thing must differ from its substance or essence. But the term being signifies existence itself. Hence it seems that being, or existence, is something added to a thing's essence.

557. He spoke in the same way of one, because he thought that the one which is interchangeable with being and the one which is the principle of number are the same. And the one which is the principle of number must signify a reality added to the substance, otherwise number, since it is composed of ones, would not be a species of quantity, which is an accident added to substance. He said that this kind of one is interchangeable with being, not in the sense that it signifies the very substance of a thing or being, but in the sense that it signifies an accident belonging to every being, just as the ability to laugh belongs to every man.

558. But in regard to the first point he does not seem to be right; for even though a thing's existence is other than its essence, it should not be understood to be something added to its essence after the manner of an accident, but something established, as it were, by the principles of the essence. Hence the term being, which is applied to a thing by reason of its very existence, designates the same thing as the term which is applied to it by reason of its essence.

559. Nor does it seem to be true that the one or unity which is interchangeable with being and that which is the principle of number are the same; for nothing that pertains to some special

class of being seems to be characteristic of all beings. Hence the unity which is limited to a special class of being—discrete quantity—does not seem to be interchangeable with universal being. For, if unity is a proper and essential accident of being, it must be caused by the principles of being as being, just as any proper accident is caused by the principles of its subject. But it is not reasonable that something having a particular mode of being should be adequately accounted for by the common principles of being as being. It cannot be true, then, that something which belongs to a definite genus and species is an accident of every being.

560. Therefore the kind of unity which is the principle of number differs from that which is interchangeable with being; for the unity which is interchangeable with being signifies being itself, adding to it the notion of undividedness, which, since it is a negation or a privation, does not posit any reality added to being. Thus unity differs from being in no way numerically but only conceptually; for a negation or a privation is not a real being but a being of reason, as has been stated (n. 540). However, the kind of unity which is the principle of number adds to substance the note of a measure, which is a special property of quantity and is found first in the unit. And it is described as the privation or negation of division which pertains to continuous quantity; for number is produced by dividing the continuous. Hence number belongs to mathematical science, whose subject cannot exist apart from sensible matter but can be considered apart from sensible matter. But this would not be so if the kind of unity which is the principle of number were separate from matter in being and existed among the immaterial substances, as is true of the kind of unity which is interchangeable with being.

561. **Hence there are** [4].

Then he concludes that it is the business of the philosopher to consider the parts of unity, just as it is to consider the parts of being. First, he proves this; and second [5], he shows that there are different parts of philosophy corresponding to the different parts of being and unity ("And there are").

He says, first [4], that since being and unity signify the same thing, and the species of things that are the same are themselves the same, there must be as many species of being as there are of unity, and they must correspond to each other. For just as the parts of being are substance, quantity, quality, and so on, in a similar way the parts of unity are sameness, equality and likeness. For things are the same when they are one in substance, equal when they are one in quantity, and like when they are one in quality. And the other parts of unity could be taken from the other parts of being, if they were given names. And just as it is the office of one science, philosophy, to consider all parts of being, in a similar way it is the office of this same science to consider all parts of unity, i.e., sameness, likeness and so forth. And to this "starting point," i.e., unity, "almost" all contraries may be referred.

562. He adds this qualification because in some cases this point is not so evident. Yet it must be true; for since one member of every pair of contraries involves privation, they must be referred back to certain primary privatives, among which unity is the most basic. And plurality, which stems from unity, is the cause of otherness, difference and contrariety, as will be stated below. He says that this has been

treated "in our selection," or extract, "of contraries," i.e., a treatise which is the part selected to deal with contraries, namely, Book X (see nn. 2000–21) of this work.

563. **And there are** [5].

Here he shows that the parts of philosophy are distinguished in reference to the parts of being and unity. He says that there are as many parts of philosophy as there are parts of substance, of which being and unity chiefly are predicated, and of which it is the principal intention or aim of this science to treat. And because the parts of substance are related to each other in a certain order, for immaterial substance is naturally prior to sensible substance, then among the parts of philosophy there must be a first part. Now that part which is concerned with sensible substance is first in the order of instruction, because any branch of learning must start with things which are better known to us. He treats of this part in Books VII (see n. 1300) and VIII of this work. But that part which has to do with immaterial substance is prior both in dignity and in the aim of this science. This part is treated in Book XII (see n. 2488) of this work. Yet whatever parts are first must be continuous with the others, because all parts have unity and being as their genus. Hence all parts of this science are united in the study of being and unity, although they are about different parts of substance. Thus it is one science inasmuch as the foregoing parts are things which correspond to "these," i.e., to unity and being, as common attributes of substance. In this respect the philosopher resembles the mathematician; for mathematical science has different parts, one of which is primary, as arithmetic, another secondary, as geometry, and others following these in order, as optics, astronomy and music.

LESSON 3
The Same Science Considers Unity and Plurality and All Opposites. The Method of Treating These

ARISTOTLE'S TEXT Chapter 2: 1004a9–1004a34

1. Now since it is the office of a single science to study opposites, and plurality is the opposite of unity, it is also the office of a single science to study negation and privation, because in both cases we are studying the unity of which there is negation or privation. And this (negation or privation) is what is stated either absolutely because an attribute is not present in a thing or (not absolutely) because it is not present in some determinate class. Therefore this difference is present in unity over and above what is implied in negation; for negation is the absence of the thing in question. But in the case of privation there is an underlying subject of which the privation is predicated. **1004a9–16**

2. But plurality is the opposite of unity. Hence the opposites of the above-mentioned concepts, otherness, unlikeness, and inequality, and any others which are referred to plurality or unity, must come within the scope of the science mentioned above. And contrariety is one of these; for contrariety is a kind of difference, and difference is a kind of otherness. **1004a16–22**

3. Hence, since the term one is used in many senses, the terms designating the foregoing opposites will also be used in many senses. Yet it is the business of one science to know them all. For even if some term is used in many senses, it does not therefore follow that it belongs to another science. Hence if terms are not used with one meaning, and their concepts are not referred to one thing, then it is the office of a different science to study them. But since all things are referred to some primary thing, as all things which are one are referred to a primary one, the same thing must hold true of sameness, otherness, and the contraries. It is necessary, then to distinguish all the senses in which each term is used and then refer them back to the primary thing signified in each of the predicates in question to see how each is related to it. For one thing is given a particular predicate because it possesses it, another because it produces it, and others in other ways. **1004a22–31**

4. Hence it is evident, as has been stated in our problems, that it is the office of a single science to give an account of these predicates as well as of substance; and this was one of the problems. **1004a31–34**

COMMENTARY

564. Here he shows that it is the office of this science to consider opposites; and in regard to this he does two things. First [1], he shows that it is the office of this science to consider privation and negation; and second [2], to consider contraries ("But plurality").

He accordingly says [1] that, since it pertains to one science to consider opposites (for example, it belongs to medicine to consider health and sickness, and to grammar to consider agreement and disagreement), and since plurality is the opposite of unity, the study of privation and negation must belong to that science which deals with unity and plurality. For the consideration "of both" involves unity; that is, the study of unity, whose concept entails negation and privation, depends on both of these. For, as has been said above (n. 553), what is one is an undivided being, and division relates to plurality, which is the opposite of unity. Hence the study of negation and privation belongs to that science whose business it is to consider unity.

565. Now there are two kinds of

negation: simple negation, by which one thing is said absolutely not to be present in something else, and negation in a genus, by which something is denied of something else, not absolutely, but within the limits of some determinate genus. For example, not everything that does not have sight is said absolutely to be blind, but something within the genus of an animal which is naturally fitted to have sight. And this difference is present in unity over and above "what is implied in negation"; i.e., it is something by which it differs from negation, because negation expresses only the absence of something, namely, what it removes, without stating a determinate subject. Hence simple negation can be verified both of a non-being, which is not naturally fitted to have something affirmed of it, and of a being which is naturally fitted to have something affirmed of it and does not. For *unseeing* can be predicated both of a chimera and of a stone and of a man. But in the case of privation there is a determinate nature or substance of which the privation is predicated; for not everything that does not have sight can be said to be blind, but only that which is naturally fitted to have sight. Thus since the negation which is included in the concept of unity is a negation in a subject (otherwise a non-being could be called one), it is evident that unity differs from simple negation and rather resembles the nature of privation, as is stated below in Book X (see n. 2069) of this work.

566. But it must be noted that, although unity includes an implied privation, it must not be said to include the privation of plurality; for, since a privation is subsequent in nature to the thing of which it is the privation, it would follow that unity would be subsequent in nature to plurality. And it would also follow that plurality would be given in the definition of unity; for a privation can be defined only by its opposite. For example, if someone were to ask what blindness is, we would answer that it is the privation of sight. Hence, since unity is given in the definition of plurality (for plurality is an aggregate of units), it would follow that there would be circularity in definitions. Hence it must be said that unity includes the privation of division, although not the kind of division that belongs to quantity; for this kind of division is limited to one particular class of being and cannot be included in the definition of unity. But the unity which is interchangeable with being implies the privation of formal division, which comes about through opposites, and whose primary root is the opposition between affirmation and negation. For those things are divided from each other which are of such a kind that one is not the other. Therefore being itself is understood first, and then non-being, and then division, and then the kind of unity which is the privation of division, and then plurality, whose concept includes the notion of division just as the concept of unity includes the notion of undividedness. However, some of the things that have been distinguished in the foregoing way can be said to include the notion of plurality only if the notion of unity is first attributed to each of the things distinguished.

567. **But plurality** [2].

Here he shows that it is the business of the philosopher to consider contraries, or opposites; for plurality is the opposite of unity, as has been said [1], and it is the office of one science to consider opposites. Hence, since this science considers unity, sameness, likeness and equality, it must also consider their opposites, plurality, otherness or diversity, unlikeness and inequality, and all other attributes which are reduced to these or even to unity and plurality. And contrariety is one of these; for contrariety is a kind of difference, namely, of things differing in the same genus. But difference is a kind of otherness or diversity, as is said in Book X see n. 2017). Therefore contrariety belongs to the consideration of this science.

568. **Hence, since** [3].

Then he deals with the method by which the philosopher ought to establish these things. He says that, since all of the above-mentioned opposites are derived from unity, and the term one is used in many senses, all of the terms designating these must also be used in many senses, i.e., *same, other,* and so on. Yet even though all of these are used in many senses, it is still the work of one science, philosophy, to know the things signified by each of these terms. For if some term is used in many senses, it does not therefore follow that it belongs to another or different science. For if the different things signified are not referred to "with one meaning," or according to one concept, i.e., univocally, or are not referred to one thing in different ways, as in the case of analogous things, then it follows that it is the office of another, i.e., of a different, science, to consider them; or at least it is the office of one science accidentally, just as astronomy considers a star in the heavens, i.e., the dog star, and natural science considers a dog-fish and a dog.—But all of these are referred to one starting point. For things signified by the term one, even though diverse, are referred back to a primary thing signified as one; and we must also speak in the same way of the terms same, other, contrary, and others of this kind. Regarding each of these terms, then, the philosopher should do two things. First, he should distinguish the many senses in which each may be used; and second, he should determine regarding "each of the predicates," i.e., each of the names predicated of many things, to what primary thing it is referred. For example, he should state what the first thing signified by the term same or other is, and how all the rest are referred to it; one inasmuch as it possesses it, another inasmuch as it produces it, or in other ways of this kind.

569. **Hence it is evident** [4].

He draws his conclusion from what has been said, namely, that it belongs to this science to reason about these common predicates and about substance; and this was one of the problems investigated in the questions treated dialectically in Book III (see nn. 346 and 393).

LESSON 4
First Philosophy Considers All Contraries. Its Distinction from Logic

ARISTOTLE'S TEXT Chapter 2: 1004a34–1005a18

1. *And it is also evident that it is the function of the philosopher to be able to study all things. For if it is not the function of the philosopher, who is it that will investigate whether Socrates and Socrates sitting are the same person, or whether one thing has one contrary, or what a contrary is, or how many meanings it has? And the same applies to other questions of this kind. Therefore, since these same things are the essential properties of unity as unity and of being as being, but not as numbers or lines or fire, evidently it is the office of this science to know both the quiddities of these and their accidents. Therefore those who have been studying these things do not err by being unphilosophical, but because substance, to which they pay no attention, is first. Now there are properties of number as number, for example, oddness and evenness, commensurability and equality, excess and defect, and these belong to numbers either in themselves or in relation to one another. And similarly there are properties of the solid, and of what is changeable and what is unchangeable, and of what is heavy and what is light. And in a similar fashion there are properties of being as being; and these are the ones about which the philosopher has to investigate the truth.* **1004a34–1004b17**

2. *An indication of this is the following. Dialecticians and sophists assume the same guise as the philosopher, for sophistry is apparent wisdom, and dialecticians dispute about all things, and being is common to all things. But evidently they dispute about these matters because they are common to philosophy. For sophistry and dialectics are concerned with the same class of things as philosophy.* **1004b17–23**

3. *But philosophy differs from the latter in the manner of its power, and from the former in the choice, i.e., selection, of a way of life. For dialectics is in search of knowledge of what the philosopher actually knows, and sophistry has the semblance of wisdom but is not really such.* **1004b23–26**

4. *Further, one corresponding member of each pair of contraries is privative, and all contraries are referred to being and to non-being and to unity and to plurality; for example, rest pertains to unity and motion to plurality.* **1004b27–29**

5. *And almost all men admit that substance and beings are composed of contraries; for all say that principles are contraries. For some speak of the odd and even, others of the hot and cold, others of the limited and unlimited, and others of love and hate.* **1004b29–33**

6. *And all the other contraries seem to be reducible to unity and plurality. Therefore let us take that reduction for granted. And all the principles which have to do with other things fall under unity and being as their genera.* **1004b33–1005a2**

7. *It is clear from these discussions, then, that it is the office of one science to study being as being. For all beings are either contraries or composed of contraries, and the principles of contraries are unity and plurality. And these belong to one science, whether they are used in one sense or not. And perhaps the truth is that they are not. Yet even if the term one is used in many senses, all will be referred to one primary sense; and the same is true of contraries. Hence, even if unity or being is not a universal and the same in all things or is something separate (as presumably it is not), still in some cases the thing will be referred to unity and in others it will be referred to what follows on unity.* **1005a2–11**

8. *And for this reason it is not the province of geometry to examine what a contrary is, or what the perfect is, or what unity is, or what sameness or otherness is, but to assume them.* **1005a11–13**

9. *It is evident, then, that it is the office of one science to study both being as being and the*

attributes which belong to being as being. And it is evident too that the same science studies not only substances but also their accidents, both those mentioned above, and prior and subsequent, genus and species, whole and part, and others such as these. **1005a13–18**

COMMENTARY

570. Here he uses arguments based on common principles to prove what the philosopher ought to consider regarding all of the foregoing attributes. First [1], he proves his thesis; and second [9], he introduces his intended conclusion ("It is evident").

In regard to the first part he does two things. First, he proves his thesis; and second [8], he draws a corollary from what has been said ("And for this reason").

He gives three arguments to prove his thesis. The second [2] begins where he says, "An indication of this"; and the third [4], at "Further, one corresponding."

The first argument [1] is as follows. All questions that can be raised must be answered by some science. But questions are raised about the common attributes mentioned above, for example, that raised about sameness and otherness: whether Socrates and Socrates sitting are the same; and that raised about contraries: whether one thing has one contrary, and how many meanings the term contrary has. Hence these questions must be answered by some science which considers sameness and contrariety and the other attributes mentioned above.

571. That this is the job of the philosopher and of no one else he proves thus: that science whose office is to consider being as being is the one which must consider the first properties of being. But all of the above-mentioned attributes are proper accidents of unity and being as such. For number as number has properties, such as excess, equality, commensurability, and so on, some of which belong to a number taken absolutely, as even and odd, and some to one number in relation to another, as equality. And even substance has proper attributes, "as the resistant," or body, and others of this kind. And in a similar way being as being has certain properties, which are the common attributes mentioned above; and therefore the study of them belongs to the philosopher. Hence those dealing with philosophy have not erred in their treatment of these things "by being unphilosophical," i.e., by considering them in a way that does not pertain to the investigations of philosophy, but because in treating them they pay no attention to substance, as though they were completely unmindful of it despite the fact that it is the first thing which the philosopher ought to consider.

572. **An indication** [2].

Then he gives a second argument to prove the same point. This argument employs an example and runs thus: dialecticians and sophists assume the same guise as the philosopher inasmuch as they resemble him in some respect. But the dialectician and sophist dispute about the above-mentioned attributes. Therefore the philosopher should also consider them. In support of his first premise he shows how dialectics and sophistry resemble philosophy and how they differ from it.

573. Dialectics resembles philosophy in that it is also the office of the dialectician to consider all things. But this could not be the case unless he considered all things insofar as they agree in some one respect; because

each science has one subject, and each art has one matter on which it operates. Therefore, since all things agree only in being, evidently the subject matter of dialectics is being and those attributes which belong to being; and this is what the philosopher also investigates. And sophistry likewise resembles philosophy; for sophistry has "the semblance of wisdom," or is apparent wisdom, without being wisdom. Now anything that takes on the appearance of something else must resemble it in some way. Therefore the philosopher, the dialectician and the sophist must consider the same thing.

574. Yet they differ from each other. The philosopher differs from the dialectician in power, because the consideration of the philosopher is more efficacious than that of the dialectician. For the philosopher proceeds demonstratively in dealing with the common attributes mentioned above, and thus it is proper to him to have scientific knowledge of these attributes. And he actually knows them with certitude, for certain or scientific knowledge is the effect of demonstration. The dialectician, however, proceeds to treat all of the above-mentioned common attributes from probable premises, and thus he does not acquire scientific knowledge of them but a kind of opinion. The reason for this difference is that there are two kinds of beings: beings of reason and real beings. The expression *being of reason* is applied properly to those notions which reason derives from the objects it considers, for example, the notions of genus, species and the like, which are not found in reality but are a natural result of the consideration of reason. And this kind of being, i.e., being of reason, constitutes the proper subject of logic. But intellectual conceptions of this kind are equal in extension to real beings, because all real beings fall under the consideration of reason. Hence the subject of logic extends to all things to which the expression *real being* is applied. His conclusion is, then, that the subject of logic is equal in extension to the subject of philosophy, which is real being. Now the philosopher proceeds from the principles of this kind of being to prove the things that have to be considered about the common accidents of this kind of being. But the dialectician proceeds to consider them from the conceptions of reason, which are extrinsic to reality. Hence it is said that dialectics is in search of knowledge, because in searching it is proper to proceed from extrinsic principles.

575. But the philosopher differs from the sophist "in the choice," i.e., in the selection or willing, or in the desire, of a way of life. For the philosopher and sophist direct their life and actions to different things. The philosopher directs his to knowing the truth, whereas the sophist directs his so as to appear to know what he does not.

576. Now although it is said that philosophy is scientific knowledge, and that dialectics and sophistry are not, this still does not do away with the possibility of dialectics and sophistry being sciences. For dialectics can be considered both from the viewpoint of theory and from that of practice. From the viewpoint of theory it studies these conceptions and establishes the method by which one proceeds from them to demonstrate with probability the conclusions of the particular sciences; and it does this demonstratively, and to this extent it is a science. But from the viewpoint of practice it makes use of the above method so as to reach certain probable conclusions in the particular sciences; and in this

respect it falls short of the scientific method. The same must be said of sophistry, because from the viewpoint of theory it treats by means of necessary and demonstrative arguments the method of arguing to apparent truth. From the viewpoint of practice, however, it falls short of the process of true argumentation.

577. But that part of logic which is said to be demonstrative is concerned only with theory, and the practical application of it belongs to philosophy and to the other particular sciences, which are concerned with real beings. This is because the practical aspect of the demonstrative part of logic consists in using the principles of things, from which proceeds demonstration (which properly belongs to the sciences that deal with real beings), and not in using the conceptions of logic. Thus it appears that some parts of logic are at the same time scientific, theoretical, and practical, as exploratory dialectics and sophistry; and one is concerned with theory and not practice, namely, demonstrative logic.

578. **Further, one corresponding** [4].

Then he gives the third argument in support of his thesis. It runs as follows: everything that is reducible to unity and being should be considered by the philosopher, whose function is to study unity and being. But all contraries are reducible to unity and being. Therefore all contraries belong to the consideration of the philosopher, whose function is to study unity and being.

579. Then he proves that all contraries are reducible to unity and being. He does this, first, with regard to being; and he proceeds thus: of any two contraries which the philosophers posited as the principles of things, as is said in Book I (n. 132), one contrary is always the correlative of the other and is related to it as its privation. This is clear from the fact that one of two contraries is always something imperfect when compared with the other, and thus implies some privation of the perfection of the other. But a privation is a kind of negation, as was stated above (n. 564), and thus is a non-being. Hence it is clear that all contraries are reducible to being and non-being.

580. He also shows by an example that all contraries are reducible to unity and plurality. For rest or repose is reducible to unity, since that is said to be at rest which is in the same condition now as it was before, as is stated in Book VI of the *Physics. [234b5]* And motion is reducible to plurality, because whatever is in motion is in a different condition now than it was before, and this implies plurality.

581. **And almost all** [5].

Then he uses another argument to show that contraries are reducible to being. Both the principles of things and the things composed of them belong to the same study. But the philosophers admit that contraries are the principles of being as being; for all say that beings and the substances of beings are composed of contraries, as was stated in Book I of the *Physics [188a19]* and in the first book of this work (see n. 132). Yet while they agree on this point, that the principles of beings are contraries, still they differ as to the contraries which they give. For some give the even and odd, as the Pythagoreans; others the hot and cold, as Parmenides; others "the end" or terminus "and the unlimited," i.e., the finite and infinite, as did the same Pythagoreans (for they attributed limitedness and unlimitedness to the even and the odd, as is stated in Book I (see n. 124); and still others gave friendship and strife, as Empedocles. Hence it is clear that contraries are reducible to the study of being.

582. **And all the other** [6].

He says that the above-mentioned contraries are reducible not only to being but also to unity and plurality. This is evident. For oddness by reason of its indivisibility is affiliated with unity, and evenness by reason of its divisibility has a natural connection with plurality. Thus end or limit pertains to unity, which is the terminus of every process of resolution, and lack of limit pertains to plurality, which may be increased to infinity. Again, friendship also clearly pertains to unity, and strife to plurality. And heat pertains to unity inasmuch as it can unite homogeneous things, whereas cold pertains to plurality inasmuch as it can separate them. Further, not only these contraries are reducible in this way to unity and plurality, but so also are the others. Yet this "reduction," or introduction, to unity and plurality let us now accept or "take for granted," i.e., let us now assume it, because to examine each set of contraries would be a lengthy undertaking.

583. Next he shows that all contraries are reducible to unity and being. For it is certain that all principles, inasmuch as they have to do "with other things," i.e., the things composed of them, fall under unity and being as their genera, not in the sense that they truly are genera, but in the sense that they bear some likeness to genera by reason of what they have in common. Hence, if all contraries are principles or things composed of principles, they must be reducible to unity and being.—Thus it is clear that he shows that contraries are reducible to being for two reasons: first, because of the nature of privation, and second, by reason of the fact that contraries are principles. He shows that they are reducible to unity by giving an example and by using a process of reduction. Last, he shows that they are reducible to unity and being inasmuch as they have the character of genera.

584. **It is clear** [7].

Here he proves in a converse way that this science considers being because it considers the things mentioned above. His argument is this: all beings are reducible to contraries because they are either contraries or composed of contraries. And contraries are reducible to unity and plurality because unity and plurality are the principles of contraries. But unity and plurality belong to one science, philosophy. Therefore it is the office of this science to consider being as being. Yet it must be noted that all the contraries mentioned above fall under the consideration of one science whether they are used "in one sense," i.e., univocally, or not, as perhaps is the case. However, even if the term one is used in many senses, all the others, i.e., all the other senses, are reducible to one primary sense. Hence, even if unity or being is not one universal, like a genus, as was stated above (whether a universal is said to be a one-in-all, as we maintain, or something separate from things, as Plato thought, and as is presumably not the case), still each is used in a primary and a secondary sense. And the same holds true in the case of other terms, for some senses are referred to one primary sense, and others are secondary with respect to that primary sense. An adverb designating uncertainty is used inasmuch as we are now assuming things that will be proved below.

585. But nevertheless it must be borne in mind that the statement

which he made, that all beings are either contraries or composed of contraries, he did not give as his own opinion but as one which he took from the ancient philosophers; for unchangeable beings are not contraries or composed of contraries. And this is why Plato did not posit any contrariety in the unchangeable sensible substances; for he attributed unity to form and contrariety to matter. But the ancient philosophers claimed that only sensible substances exist and that these must contain contrariety inasmuch as they are changeable.

586. **And for this reason** [8].

Then he draws a corollary from what has been said. He says that it is not the province of geometry to investigate the foregoing things, which are accidents of being as being, i.e., to investigate what a contrary is, or what the perfect is, and so on. But if a geometer were to consider them, he would "assume them," i.e., presuppose their truth, inasmuch as he would take them over from some prior philosopher from whom he accepts them insofar as they are necessary for his own subject matter. What is said about geometry must be understood to apply also in the case of any other particular science.

587. **It is evident** [9].

He now summarizes the points established above. He says that obviously the consideration of being as being and the attributes which belong to it of itself pertain to one science. Thus it is clear that that science considers not only substances but also accidents since being is predicated of both. And it considers the things which have been discussed, namely, sameness and otherness, likeness and unlikeness, equality and inequality, privation and negation, and contraries—which we said above are the proper accidents of being. And it considers not only those things which fall under the consideration of this science, about which demonstration was made individually by means of arguments based on proper principles, but it in like manner also considers prior and subsequent, genus and species, whole and part, and other things of this kind, because these too are accidents of being as being.

LESSON 5

Answers to Questions Raised in Book III about Principles of Demonstration

ARISTOTLE'S TEXT Chapter 3: 1005a19–1005b8

1. *Moreover, it is necessary to state whether it is the office of one science or of different sciences to inquire about those principles which are called axioms in mathematics, and about substance.* **1005a19–21**

2. *Now it is evident that it is the office of one science—that of the philosopher—to investigate these.* **1005a21–22**

3. *For these principles apply to all beings and not to some class distinct from the others. And all men employ them, because they pertain to being as being; for each class is being. But they employ them just so far as to satisfy their needs, i.e., so far as the class contains the things about which they form demonstrations. Hence, since it is evident that these principles pertain to all things inasmuch as they are beings (for this is what they have in common), the investigation of them belongs to him who considers being as being.* **1005a22–29**

4. *Hence no one who is making a special inquiry attempts to say anything about their truth or falsity, neither the geometer nor the arithmetician.* **1005a29–31**

5. *However, some of the philosophers of nature have done this, and with reason; for they thought that they alone were inquiring about the whole of nature and about being. But since there is one kind of thinker who is superior to the philosopher of nature (for nature is only one class of being), the investigation of these principles will belong to him who studies the universal and deals with first substance. The philosophy of nature is a kind of wisdom, but it is not the first.* **1005a31–1005b2**

6. *And whatever certain ones of those who speak about the truth attempt to say concerning the way in which it must be accepted, they do this through ignorance of analytics. For they must know these principles in order to attain scientific knowledge and not be seeking them when they are learning a science.* **1005b2–5**

7. *It is evident, then, that it is also the business of the philosopher, i.e., of him who investigates all substance insofar as its nature permits, to investigate all syllogistic principles.* **1005b5–8**

COMMENTARY

588. Here he answers another question raised in Book III (n. 387): whether it belongs to this science to consider the first principles of demonstration. This is divided into two parts. In the first [1] he shows that it belongs to this science to make a general study of all these principles; and in the second (Lesson 6) he shows that it also belongs to it to make a special study of the first of these principles ("And it is fitting").

In regard to the first he does three things. First, he raises the question whether it belongs to one or to different sciences to consider substance and the principles which are called axioms in the mathematical sciences. He assigns these principles more to the mathematical sciences because such sciences have more certain demonstrations and use these self-evident principles in a more manifest way inasmuch as they refer all of their demonstrations to them.

589. **Now it is evident** [2].

Second, he answers this question by saying that a single science investigates both of the foregoing things, and that this is the philosophy with which we are now concerned.

590. **For these principles** [3]).

Third, he proves his proposed answer, and in regard to this he does two things. First [3], he proves it. Second [7], he introduces his main conclusion ("It is evident").

Now he proves his proposed answer in two ways. He does this, first, by an argument; and second [4], by an example ("Hence no one").

The argument is as follows: whatever principles pertain to all beings, and not just to one class of beings distinct from the others, belong to the consideration of the philosopher. But the above-mentioned principles are of this kind. Therefore they belong to the consideration of the philosopher. He proves the minor premise as follows. Those principles which all sciences use pertain to being as being. But first principles are principles of this kind. Therefore they pertain to being as being.

591. The reason which he gives for saying that all sciences use these principles is that the subject genus of each science has being predicated of it. Now the particular sciences do not use the foregoing principles insofar as they are common principles, i.e., as extending to all beings, but insofar as they have need of them; that is, insofar as they extend to the things contained in the class of beings which constitutes the subject of a particular science, about which it makes demonstrations. For example, the philosophy of nature uses them insofar as they extend to changeable beings and no further.

592. **Hence no one** [4].

Then he proves what he had said by using an example. First, he introduces the proof; and second [5], he rejects a false notion held by some men ("However, some").

He accordingly says, first [4], that no one whose chief intention is to hand down scientific knowledge of some particular being has attempted to say anything about the truth or falsity of first principles. Neither the geometer nor the arithmetician does this even though they make the greatest use of these principles, as was said above (n. 588). Hence it is evident that the investigation of these principles belongs to this science.

593. **However, some** [5].

Here he rejects the false notion held by some men, and in regard to this he does two things. First, he rejects the false notion of those who occupied themselves with these principles even though they did not concern them. Second, [6], he rejects the false notion of those who wanted to deal with these principles in a different way than they should be dealt with ("And whatever").

He accordingly says, first [5], that even though none of the particular sciences ought to deal with the above-mentioned principles, nevertheless some of the natural philosophers have dealt with them; and they did so not without reason. For the ancients did not think that there was any substance besides the changeable corporeal substance with which the philosophy of nature is concerned. Hence they believed that they alone established the truth about the whole of nature and therefore about being, and thus about first principles, which must be considered along with being. But this is false, because there is still a science which is superior to the science of nature. For nature itself, i.e., natural being, which has its own principle of motion, constitutes in itself one class of universal being. But not every being is of this kind, because it has been proved in the *Physics*, Book VIII, [256a3 ff.] that an unchangeable being exists. Now this unchangeable being is superior to and nobler than changeable being, with which the philosophy of nature is concerned. And since the consideration of common being belongs to that science which studies the primary kind of being, then the consideration of common being belongs to a different science than the philosophy of nature. And the consideration of common principles of this kind will also belong to this science. For the philosophy of nature is a part of philosophy but not the first part, which considers common being and those attributes which belong to being as being.

594. **And whatever** [6].

Then he rejects the other false notion, which concerns the way in which such principles should be treated. For some men investigated these principles with the aim of demonstrating them. And whatever they said about the truth of these principles, i.e., how they must be accepted as true by force of demonstration, or how the truth found in all these principles must be reached, they did through ignorance of, or lack of skill in, "analytics," which is that part of logic in which the art of demonstration is treated.^2 For "they must know these principles in order to attain scientific knowledge"; i.e., every science acquired by demonstration depends on these principles. But "those who are learning," i.e., the pupils who are being instructed in some science, must not seek these principles as something to be demonstrated. Or, according to another text, "those who have scientific knowledge must attain science from these principles"; i.e., those who attain knowledge by demonstration must come to know common principles of this kind and not ask that they be demonstrated to them.

595. **It is evident** [7].

He draws the conclusion primarily intended, namely, that it will be the function of the philosopher to consider every substance as such and also the first syllogistic principles. In order to make this clear it must be noted that self-evident propositions are those which are known as soon as their terms are known, as is stated in Book I of the *Posterior Analytics. [72b18]* This occurs in the case of those propositions in which the predicate is given in the definition of the subject, or is the same as the subject. But it happens that one kind of proposition, even though it is self-evident in itself, is still not self-evident to all, i.e., to those who are ignorant of the definition of both the subject and the predicate. Hence Boethius says in the *Hebdomads* that there are some propositions which are self-evident to the learned but not to all. Now those are self-evident to all whose terms are comprehended by all. And common principles are of this kind, because our knowledge proceeds from common principles to proper ones, as is said in Book I of the *Physics.[184a21]* Hence those propositions which are composed of such common terms as whole and part (for example, every whole is greater than one of its parts) and of such terms as equal and unequal (for example, things equal to one and the same thing are equal to each other), constitute the first principles of demonstration. And the same is true of similar terms. Now since common terms of this kind belong to the consideration of the philosopher, then it follows that these principles also fall within his scope. But the philosopher does not establish the truth of these principles by way of demonstration, but by considering the meaning of their terms. For example, he considers what a whole is and what a part is; and the same applies to the rest. And when the meaning of these terms becomes known, it follows that the truth of the above-mentioned principles becomes evident.

LESSON 6

First Philosophy Must Examine the First Principle of Demonstration. The Nature of This Principle. The Errors about It

ARISTOTLE'S TEXT Chapters 3 & 4: 1005b8–1006a18

1. *And it is fitting that the person who is best informed about each class of things should be able to state the firmest principles of his subject. Hence he who understands beings as beings should be able to state the firmest principles of all things. This person is the philosopher.* **1005b8–11**

2. *And the firmest of all principles is that about which it is impossible to make a mistake; for such a principle must be both the best known (for all men make mistakes about things which they do not know) and not hypothetical. For the principle which everyone must have who understands anything about beings is not hypothetical; and that which everyone must know who knows anything must be had by him when he comes to his subject. It is evident, then, that such a principle is the firmest of all.* **1005b11–18**

3. *And let us next state what this principle is. It is that the same attribute cannot both belong and not belong to the same subject at the same time and in the same respect; and let us stipulate any other qualifications that have to be laid down to meet dialectical difficulties. Now this is the firmest of all principles, since it answers to the definition given; for it is impossible for anyone to think that the same thing both is and is not, although some are of the opinion that Heraclitus speaks in this way; for what a man says he does not necessarily accept. But if it is impossible for contraries to belong simultaneously to the same subject (and let us then suppose that the same things are established here as in the usual proposition), and if one opinion which expresses the contradictory of another is contrary to it, evidently the same man at the same time cannot think that the same thing can both be and not be; for one who is mistaken on this point will have contrary opinions at the same time. And it is for this reason that all who make demonstrations reduce their argument to this ultimate position. For this is by nature the starting point of all the other axioms.* **1005b18–34**

Chapter 4

4. *Now as we have said, there are some who claimed that the same thing can both be and not be, and that this can be believed. And many of those who treat of nature adopt this theory. But now we take it to be impossible for a thing both to be and not be at the same time, and by means of this we shall show that this is the firmest of all principles.* **1005b35–1006a5**

5. *But some deem it fitting that even this principle should be demonstrated, and they do this through want of education. For not to know of what things one should seek demonstration and of what things one should not shows want of education. For it is altogether impossible that there should be demonstration of all things, because there would then be an infinite regress so that there would still be no demonstration. But if there are some things of which it is not necessary to seek demonstration, these people cannot say what principle they think to be more indemonstrable.* **1006a6–11**

6. *But even in this case it is possible to show by refutation that this view is impossible, if only our opponent will say something. But if he says nothing, it is ridiculous to look for a reason against one who has no reason, on the very point on which he is without reason; for such a man is really like a plant. Now I say that demonstration by refutation is different from demonstration [in the strict sense], because he who would demonstrate this principle in the strict sense would seem to beg the question. But when someone argues for the sake of convincing another there will be refutation, not demonstration.* **1006a11–18**

COMMENTARY

596. He shows here that it is the first philosopher who is chiefly concerned with the first principle of demonstration; and in regard to this he does two things. First [1], he shows that it is the business of the first philosopher to consider this principle; and second (Lesson 7), he begins to examine this principle ("The starting point").

In regard to the first he does three things. First, he shows that it is the office of this science to consider the first principle of demonstration. Second [2], he indicates what this principle is ("And the firmest"). Third [4], he rejects certain errors regarding this same principle ("Now as we have said").

In regard to the first point he uses the following argument. In every class of things that man is best informed who knows the most certain principles, because the certitude of knowing depends on the certitude of principles. But the first philosopher is best informed and most certain in his knowledge; for this was one of the conditions of wisdom, as was made clear in the prologue of this work (see n. 35), namely, that he who knows the causes of things has the most certain knowledge. Hence the philosopher ought to consider the most certain and firmest principles of beings, which he considers as the subject-genus proper to himself.

597. **And the firmest** [2].

Then he shows what the firmest or most certain principle is; and in regard to this he does two things. First [2], he states the conditions for the most certain principle; and then [3] he shows how they fit a single principle ("And let us").

He accordingly gives, first [2], the three conditions for the firmest principle. The first is that no one can make a mistake or be in error regarding it. And this is evident because, since men make mistakes only about those things which they do not know, then that principle about which no one can be mistaken must be the one which is best known.

598. The second condition is that it must "not be hypothetical," i.e., it must not be held as a supposition, as those things which are maintained through some kind of common agreement. Hence another translation reads "And they should not hold a subordinate place," i.e., those principles which are most certain should not be made dependent on anything else. And this is true, because whatever is necessary for understanding anything at all about being "is not hypothetical," i.e., it is not a supposition but must be self-evident. And this is true because whatever is necessary for understanding anything at all must be known by anyone who knows other things.

599. The third condition is that it is not acquired by demonstration or by any similar method, but it comes in a sense by nature to the one having it inasmuch as it is naturally known and not acquired. For first principles become known through the natural light of the agent intellect, and they are not acquired by any process of reasoning but by having their terms become known. This comes about by reason of the fact that memory is derived from sensible things, experience from memory, and knowledge of those terms from experience. And when they are known, common propositions of this kind, which are the principles of the arts and sciences, become known.

Hence it is evident that the most certain or firmest principle should be such that there can be no error regarding it; that it is not hypothetical; and that it comes naturally to the one having it.

600. **And let us next** [3].

Then he indicates the principle to which the above definition applies. He says that it applies to this principle, as the one which is firmest: it is impossible for the same attribute both to belong and not belong to the same subject at the same time. And it is necessary to add "in the same respect"; and any other qualifications that have to be given regarding this principle "to meet dialectical difficulties" must be laid down, since without these qualifications there would seem to be a contradiction when there is none.

601. That this principle must meet the conditions given above he shows as follows: it is impossible for anyone to think, or hold as an opinion, that the same thing both is and is not at the same time, although some believe that Heraclitus was of this opinion. But while it is true that Heraclitus spoke in this way, he could not think that this is true; for it is not necessary that everything that a person says he should mentally accept or hold as an opinion.

602. But if one were to say that it is possible for someone to think that the same thing both is and is not at the same time, this absurd consequence follows: contraries could belong to the same subject at the same time. And "let us suppose that the same things are established," or shown, here as in the usual proposition established in our logical treatises. For it was shown at the end of the *Perihermineas [23b23]* that contrary opinions are not those which have to do with contraries but those which have to do with contradictories, properly speaking. For when one person thinks that Socrates is white and another thinks that he is black, these are not contrary opinions in the primary and proper sense; but contrary opinions are had when one person thinks that Socrates is white and another thinks that he is not white.

603. Therefore, if someone were to think that two contradictories are true at the same time by thinking that the same thing both is and is not at the same time, he will have contrary opinions at the same time; and thus contraries will belong to the same thing at the same time. But this is impossible. It is impossible, then, for anyone to be mistaken in his own mind about these things and to think that the same thing both is and is not at the same time. And it is for this reason that all demonstrations reduce their propositions to this proposition as the ultimate opinion common to all; for this proposition is by nature the starting point and axiom of all axioms.

604. The other two conditions are therefore evident, because, insofar as those making demonstrations reduce all their arguments to this principle as the ultimate one by referring them to it, evidently this principle is not based on an assumption. Indeed, insofar as it is by nature a starting point, it clearly comes unsought to the one having it and is not acquired by his own efforts.

605. Now for the purpose of making this evident it must be noted that, since the intellect has two operations, one by which it knows quiddities, which is called the understanding of indivisibles, and another by which it combines and separates, there is something first in both operations. In the first operation the first thing that the intellect conceives is *being*, and in this operation nothing else can be conceived unless being is understood. And because this

principle—it is impossible for a thing both to be and not be at the same time—depends on the understanding of being (just as the principle, every whole is greater than one of its parts, depends on the understanding of whole and part), then this principle is by nature also the first in the second operation of the intellect, i.e., in the act of combining and separating. And no one can understand anything by this intellectual operation unless this principle is understood. For just as a whole and its parts are understood only by understanding being, in a similar way the principle that every whole is greater than one of its parts is understood only if the firmest principle is understood.

606. **Now as we have said** [4].

Then he shows how some men erred regarding this principle; and in regard to this he does two things. First, he touches on the error of those who rejected the foregoing principle; and second [5] he deals with those who wished to demonstrate it ("But some").

He accordingly says that some men, as was stated above about Heraclitus [3], said that the same thing can both be and not be at the same time, and that it is possible to hold this opinion; and many of the philosophers of nature adopt this position, as will be made clear below (see n. 665). For our part, however, we now take as evident that the principle in question is true, i.e., the principle that the same thing cannot both be and not be; but from its truth we show that it is most certain. For from the fact that a thing cannot both be and not be it follows that contraries cannot belong to the same subject, as will be said below (see n. 663). And from the fact that contraries cannot belong to a subject at the same time it follows that a man cannot have contrary opinions and, consequently, that he cannot think that contradictories are true, as has been shown (n. 603).

607. **But some** [5].

Then he mentions the error of certain men who wished to demonstrate the above-mentioned principle; and in regard to this he does two things. First, he shows that it cannot be demonstrated in the strict sense; and second [6], that it can be demonstrated in a way ("But even").

Thus he says, first [5], that certain men deem it fitting, i.e., they wish, to demonstrate this principle; and they do this "through want of education," i.e., through lack of learning or instruction. For there is want of education when a man does not know what to seek demonstration for and what not to; for not all things can be demonstrated. For if all things were demonstrable, then, since a thing is not demonstrated through itself but through something else, demonstrations would either be circular (although this cannot be true, because then the same thing would be both better known and less well known, as is clear in Book I of the *Posterior Analytics[72a30. 72b5 ff.]*, or they would have to proceed to infinity. But if there were an infinite regress in demonstrations, demonstration would be impossible, because the conclusion of any demonstration is made certain by reducing it to the first principle of demonstration. But this would not be the case if demonstration proceeded to infinity in an upward direction. It is clear, then, that not all things are demonstrable. And if some things are not demonstrable, these men cannot say that any principle is more indemonstrable than the above-mentioned one.

608. **But even in this case** [6].

Here he shows that the above-mentioned principle can be demonstrated in a certain respect. He says that it may be demonstrated by disproof. In Greek the word is {elegktikos} which is better translated as *by refutation*, for an {elegchos} is a syllogism that establishes the contradictory of a proposition, and so is introduced to refute some false position. And on these grounds it can be shown that it is impossible for the same thing both to be and not be. But this kind of argument can be employed only if the one who denies that principle because of difficulties "says something," i.e., if he signifies something by a word. But if he says nothing, it is ridiculous to look for a reason against one who does not make use of reason in speaking; for in this dispute anyone who signifies nothing will be like a plant, for even brute animals signify something by such signs.

609. For it is one thing to give a strict demonstration of this principle, and another to demonstrate it argumentatively or by refutation. For if anyone wished to give a strict demonstration of this principle, he would seem to be begging the question, because any principle that he could take for the purpose of demonstrating this one would be one of those that depend on the truth of this principle, as is clear from what has been said above (n. 607). But when the demonstration is not of this kind, i.e., demonstration in the strict sense, there will then be disproof or refutation at most.

610. Another text states this better by saying, "But when one argues for the sake of convincing another, there will then be refutation but not demonstration"; i.e., when a process of this kind from a less well known to a better known principle is employed for the sake of convincing another man who denies this, there will then be disproof or refutation but not demonstration; i.e., it will be possible to have a syllogism which contradicts his view, since what is less known absolutely is admitted by the opponent, and thus it will be possible to proceed to demonstrate the above-mentioned principle so far as the man is concerned but not in the strict sense.

LESSON 7
Contradictories Cannot Be True at the Same Time

ARISTOTLE'S TEXT Chapter 4: 1006a18–1007b18

1. *The starting point of all such discussions is not the desire that someone shall state that something either is or is not, for this might perhaps be thought to be begging the question, but that he shall state something significant both for himself and for someone else; for this he must do if he is to say anything. For if he does not, no discussion will be possible for such a person either with himself or with another. But if anyone will grant this, demonstration will be possible; for there will already be something definite. But this will not have the effect of demonstrating but of upholding, for he who destroys reason upholds reason.* **1006a18–26**

2. *First of all, then, it is evident that this at least is true, that the term to be or not to be signifies something, so that not everything will be so and not so.* **1006a26–31**

3. *Again, if the term man signifies one thing, let this be a two-footed animal.* **1006a31–32**

4. *Now by signifying one thing I mean this: granted that man is a two-footed animal, then if something is a man, this will be what being a man is. And it makes no difference even if someone were to say that this term signifies many things, provided that there are a definite number; for a different term might be assigned to each concept. I mean, for example, that if one were to say that the term man signifies not one thing but many, one of which would have a single concept, namely, two-footed animal, there might still be many others, if only there are a limited number; for a particular term might be assigned to each concept. However, if this were not the case, but one were to say that a term signifies an infinite number of things, evidently reasoning would be impossible; for not to signify one thing is to signify nothing. And if words signify nothing, there will be no discourse with another or even with ourselves. For it is impossible to understand anything unless one understands one thing; but if this does happen, a term may be assigned to this thing. Let it be assumed, then, as we said at the beginning, that a term signifies something, and that it signifies one thing.* **1006a32–1006b13**

5. *It is impossible, then, that being a man should mean not being a man, if the term man not only signifies something about one subject but also signifies one thing. For we do not think it fitting to identify signifying one thing with signifying something about one subject, since the terms musical, white and man would then signify one thing. And therefore all things would be one, because all would be synonymous. And it will be impossible to be and not to be the same thing, except in an equivocal sense, as occurs if one whom we call man others call not-man. But the problem is not whether the same thing can at the same time be and not be a man in name, but whether it can in fact.* **1006b13–22**

6. *Now if man and not-man do not signify something different, it is evident that not being a man will not differ from being a man. Thus being a man will be identical with not being a man, for they will be one thing. For being one means this: being related as clothing and garment are, if they are taken in the same sense. And if being a man and not being a man are to be one, they must signify one thing. But it has been shown that they signify different things.* **1006b22–28**

7. *Therefore, if it is true to say that something is a man, it must be a two-footed animal, for this is what the term man signifies. But if this is necessary, it is impossible for this very thing not to be a two-footed animal; for this is what to-be-necessary means, namely, unable not to be. Hence it cannot be true to say that the same thing is and is not a man at the same time. The same argument also applies to not being a man.* **1006b28–1007a1**

8. *For being a man and not being a man signify different things, since being white and being a man are different; for there is much greater opposition in the former case, so that they signify different things. And if one were to say also that white signifies the same thing as man and is*

one in concept, we shall say the same thing as was said before, namely, that all things are one, and not merely opposites. But if this is impossible, then what has been said will follow. **1007a1–8**

9. That is to say, it will follow if our opponent answers the question. And if in giving a simple answer to the question he also adds the negations, he is not answering the question. For there is nothing to prevent the same thing from being man and white and a thousand other things numerically. Still if one asks whether it is or is not true to say that this is a man, his opponent should reply by stating something that means one thing and not add that it is also white or black or large. Indeed, it is impossible to enumerate the accidents of being, which are infinite in number; so therefore let him enumerate either all or none. Similarly, even if the same thing is a thousand times a man and a not-man, he must not, in answering the question whether this is a man, add that it is also at the same time a not-man, unless he also gives all the other corresponding accidents, whatever are so or are not so. And if he does not do this, there will be no debate with him. **1007a8–20**

10. And those who say this do away completely with substance or essence, for they must say that all attributes are accidents, and that there is no such thing as being a man or being an animal. For if there is to be such a thing as being a man, this will not be being a not-man or not being a man; in fact these are the negations of it. For there was one thing which the term signified, and this was the substance of something. And to signify the substance of a thing is to signify that its being is not something else. And if being essentially a man is being essentially a not-man, then the being of man will be something else. Hence they are compelled to say that nothing will have such a concept as this, but that all attributes are accidental. For this distinguishes substance from accident; for white is an accident of man, because while some man is white he is not the essence of whiteness. **1007a20–33**

11. Moreover, if all attributes are accidental predicates, there will be no first universal. And if the accidental always implies a predication about some subject, the process must go on to infinity. But this is impossible; for not more than two terms are combined in accidental predication. For an accident is an accident of an accident only because both are accidents of the same subject. I mean, for example, that white is an accident of musical and musical of white only because both are accidental to man; but Socrates is not musical in the sense that both are accidental to something else. Therefore, since some accidents are predicated in the latter and some in the former sense, all those that are predicated as white is predicated of Socrates cannot form an infinite series in an upward direction so that there should be another accident of white Socrates; for no one thing results from all of these. Nor again will white have another accident, such as musical; for this is no more an accident of that than that of this. And at the same time it has been established that some things are accidents in this sense and some in the sense that musical is an accident of Socrates. And whatever attributes are predicated accidentally in the latter sense are not accidents of accidents but only those predicated in the former sense. Not all attributes, then, are said to be accidents; and thus there must be some term which also signifies substance. And if this is so, then we have proved that contradictories cannot be predicated at the same time of the same subject. **1007a33–1007b18**

COMMENTARY

611. Here he begins to argue dialectically against those who deny the foregoing principle, and this is divided into two parts. In the first [1] he argues against those who say that contradictories are true at the same time; and in the second (Lesson 16), against those who say that they are false at the same time ("Neither can there be").

In regard to the first he does two

things. First, he argues in a general way against those who make the aforesaid errors. Second (Lesson 10), he shows how we must argue specifically against different positions ("But the same method").

In regard to the first he does two things. First, he argues dialectically against the reasoning of those who deny the foregoing principle. Second (Lesson 9, text 5), he shows that Protagoras' opinion is fundamentally the same as the one just mentioned ("The doctrine of Protagoras").

In regard to the first point he gives seven arguments. He gives the second [10] at the words "And those who"; the third (Lesson 8) at "Furthermore, if all"; the fourth (Lesson 8, text 5) at "Again, either this"; the fifth (Lesson 9) at "Again, how"; the sixth (Lesson 9, text 2) at "It is most evident"; and the seventh (Lesson 9, text 4) at "Further, even if all."

In regard to the first he does two things. First, he indicates the starting point from which one must proceed to argue against those who deny the first principle. Second [2], he proceeds to argue from that starting point ("First of all, then").

He therefore says, first [1], that with respect to all such unreasonable positions there is no need for us to take as a starting point that someone wishes to suppose that this thing definitely is "or is not"; i.e., it is not necessary to take as a starting point some proposition in which some attribute is either affirmed or denied of a subject (for this would be a begging of the question, as was said above [n. 609]), but it is necessary to take as a starting point that a term signifies something both to the one who utters it, inasmuch as he himself understands what he is saying, and to someone else who hears him. But if such a person does not admit this, he will not say anything meaningful either for himself or for someone else, and it will then be idle to dispute with him. But when he has admitted this, a demonstration will at once be possible against him; for there is straightway found to be something definite and determinate which is signified by the term distinct from its contradictory, as will become clear below. Yet this will not strictly be a demonstration of the foregoing principle but only an argument upholding this principle against those who deny it. For he who "destroys reason," i.e., his own intelligible expression, by saying that a term signifies nothing, must uphold its significance, because he can only express what he denies by speaking and by signifying something.

612. **First of all, then** [2].

He proceeds from the assumption he had made to prove what he intends. First, he deals with one particular case; and second [3], he treats all cases in a general way ("Again, if the term").

He accordingly says, first [2], that if a term signifies something, it will be evident first of all that this proposition will be true, and that its contradictory, which he denies, will be false; and thus this at least will be true, that not every affirmation is true together with its negation.

613. **Now by signifying** [4].

Then he shows that this applies universally to all cases, namely, that contradictories are not true at the same time. In regard to this he does four things. First, he makes certain assumptions which are necessary for drawing his intended conclusion. Second [7], he draws his conclusion ("Therefore, if it is true"). Third [8], he proves one assumption which he had made ("For *being a man").* Fourth [9], he rejects a quibble ("That is to say").

In regard to the first he does three things. First, he shows that a term signifies one thing; and second [5], he shows from this that the term man signifies what being a man is, but not what it is not ("It is impossible, then"). Third [6], he shows that the term *man* signifies one thing ("Now if man").

He accordingly says, first [4], that if the term man signifies one thing, let this be two-footed animal. For a term is said to signify this one thing which is the definition of the thing signified by the term, so that if "two-footed animal" is the being of man, i.e., if this is what the essence of man is, this will be what is signified by the term man.

614. But if one were to say that a term signifies many things, it will signify either a finite or an infinite number of them. But if it signifies a finite number, it will differ in no way, according to another translation, from the term which is assumed to signify one thing; for it signifies many finite concepts of different things, and different terms can be fitted to each single concept. For example, if the term man were to signify many concepts, and the concept two-footed animal is one of them, one term is assigned to the concept man. And if there are many other concepts, many other terms may be assigned so long as those concepts are finite in number. Thus he will be forced back to the first position, that a term signifies one thing.

615. But if a term does not signify a finite but an infinite number of concepts, evidently neither reasoning nor debate will be possible. This becomes clear as follows: any term that does not signify one thing signifies nothing. This is proved thus: terms signify something understood, and therefore if nothing is understood, nothing is signified. But if one thing is not understood, nothing is understood, because anyone who understands anything must distinguish it from other things. If a term does not signify one thing, then, it signifies nothing at all; and if terms signify nothing, discourse will be impossible, both the kind which establishes truth and the kind which refutes an assertion. Hence it is clear that, if terms signify an infinite number of things, neither reasoning nor dispute will be possible. But if it is possible to understand one thing, a term may be given to it. So let it be held then that a term signifies something.

616. **It is impossible** [5].

He proves the second point, namely, that the term *man* does not signify *not being a man;* for a term that signifies one thing signifies not only what is one in subject (and is therefore said to be one because it is predicated of one subject) but what is one absolutely, i.e., in concept. For if we wanted to say that a term signifies one thing because it signifies the attributes which are verified of one thing, it would then follow that the terms musical, white and man all signify one thing, since all are verified of one thing. And from this it would follow that all things are one; for if white is predicated of man and is therefore identical with him, then when it is also predicated of a stone it will be identical with a stone; and since those things which are identical with one and the same thing are identical with each other, it would follow that a man and a stone are one thing and have one concept. Thus the result would be that all terms are univocal, i.e., one in concept, or synonymous, as another text says, i.e., meaning absolutely the same thing in subject and in concept.

617. Now although being and non-being are verified of the same subject according to those who deny the first principle, still being a man and not being a man must differ in concept, just as white and musical differ in concept even though they are verified of the same subject. Hence it is evident that being and non-being cannot be the same in concept and in subject in the sense that they are signified by one univocal term.

618. Now it must be noted that the expression *being a man* or *to be a man* or *having the being of a man* is taken here for the quiddity of man, and therefore it is concluded from this that the term man does not signify not being a man as its proper concept. But because he had said above (n. 614) that the same term can signify many things according to different concepts, he therefore adds "except in an equivocal sense" in order to make clear that the term man does not signify in a univocal sense both being a man and not being a man, but it can signify both in an equivocal sense; i.e., in the sense that what we call man in one language others might call not-man in another language. For we are not debating whether the same thing can both be and not be man in name, but whether it can in fact.

619. **Now if man** [6].

Then he proves the third point: that the terms *man* and *not-man* do not signify the same thing, and he uses the following argument. The term man signifies being a man or what man is, and the term not-man signifies not being a man or what man is not. If, then, man and not man do not signify something different, being a man will not differ from not being a man, or being a not-man, and therefore one of these will be predicated of the other. And they will also have one concept; for when we say that some terms signify one thing, we mean that they signify one concept, as the terms clothing and garment do. Hence, if being a man and not being a man are one in this way, i.e., in concept, there will then be one concept which will signify both being a man and not being a man. But it has been granted or demonstrated that the term which signifies each is different; for it has been shown that the term man signifies man and does not signify not-man. Thus it is clear that being a man and not being a man do not have a single concept, and therefore the thesis that man and not-man signify different things becomes evident.

620. **Therefore, if it is true** [7].

Here he proves his main thesis from the assumptions made earlier, and he uses the following argument. A man must be a two-footed animal, as is true from the foregoing, for this is the concept which the term man signifies. But what is necessary cannot not be; for this is what the term necessary means, namely, unable not to be, or incapable of not being, or impossible not to be. Hence it is not possible, or incapable, or impossible for man not to be a two-footed animal, and therefore it is evident that the affirmation and the negation cannot both be true; i.e., it cannot be true that man is both a two-footed animal and not a two-footed animal. The same reasoning based on the meanings of terms can be understood to apply to what is not-man, because what is not-man must be not a two-footed animal, since this is what the term signifies. Therefore it is impossible that a not-man should be a two-footed animal.

621. Now the things demonstrated above are useful to his thesis, because if someone were to think that the terms man and not-man might signify the

same thing, or that the term man might signify both being a man and not being a man, his opponent could deny the proposition that man must be a two-footed animal. For he could say that it is no more necessary to say that man must be a two-footed animal than to say that he is not a two-footed animal, granted that the terms man and not-man signify the same thing, or granted that the term man signifies both of these—being a man and not being a man.

622. **For being a man** [8].

Then he proves one of the assumptions which he had made; for in order to prove that the term man does not signify not being a man, he assumed that being a man and not being a man are different, even though they might be verified of the same subject. His aim here is to prove this by the following argument. There is greater opposition between being a man and not being a man than between man and white; but man and white have different concepts, although they may be the same in subject. Therefore being a man and not being a man also have different concepts. He proves the minor thus: if all attributes which are predicated of the same subject have the same concept and are signified by one term, it follows that all are one, as has been stated and explained (n. 616). Now if this is impossible, the position we have maintained follows, namely, that being a man and not being a man are different. And for this reason the final conclusion given above will follow, namely, that man is a two-footed animal, and that it is impossible for him to be what is not a two-footed animal.

623. **That is to say** [9].

He rejects one quibble by which the foregoing process of reasoning could be obstructed. For when an opponent has been asked whether man must be a two-footed animal, he need not reply either affirmatively or negatively but could say that man must be both a two-footed animal and not a two-footed animal. But the philosopher rejects this here, saying that the foregoing conclusion follows so long as an opponent wishes to give a simple answer to the question. But if in giving a simple answer to the question on the side of the affirmative he also wishes to include in his answer the negative aspect, he will not be answering the question. He proves this as follows. One and the same thing can be both a man and white and a thousand other things of this kind. Yet if it is asked here whether a man is white, we must give in our answer only what is signified by one word, and not add all the other attributes. For example, if one asks whether this is a man, we must answer that it is a man, and not add that it is both a man and white and large and the like; for we must give either all of the accidents of a thing at once or not. But not all accidents can be given at once since they are infinite in number; for there are an infinite number of accidents belonging to one and the same thing by reason of its relationship to an infinite number of antecedents and consequents, and what is infinite in number cannot be traversed. In answering the question, then, we must not give any of the attributes which are accidental to the thing about which the question is raised but only the attribute which is asked for. Hence, even if it is supposed a thousand times that man and not-man are the same, still, when the question is asked about man, the answer must not include anything about not-man, unless all those things which are accidental to man are given. And if this were done, no dispute would be possible, because it would never reach completion, since an infinite number of things cannot be traversed.

624. **And those who** [10].

Then he gives the second argument, and it is based on the notion of substantial and accidental predicates. This is his argument: if an affirmation and a negation are verified of the same subject, it follows that no term will be predicated quidditatively, or substantially, but only accidentally; and therefore there will have to be an infinite regress in accidental predicates. But the consequent is impossible, and thus the antecedent must be impossible.

625. In this argument he does two things. First, he gives a conditional proposition. Second [11]), he gives a proof that destroys the consequent ("Moreover, if all").

Regarding the first part he proceeds as follows. He says that those who state that an affirmation and a negation may be true at the same time completely do away with "substance," i.e., with a substantial predicate, "or essence," i.e., with an essential predicate; for they must say "that all attributes are accidents," or accidental predicates, and that there is no such thing as being a man or being an animal, and that what the quiddity of man or the quiddity of animal signifies does not exist.

626. He proves this as follows: if there is something which is being a man, i.e., which is the substantial essence of man, which is predicated of man, it will not be not being a man or being a not-man; for these two, i.e., not being a man and being a not-man, are the negations of being a man. It is clear, then, that an affirmation and a negation are not verified of the same subject, for not being a man or being a not-man is not verified of being a man.

627. And the assumption made, namely, that if there is such a thing as being a man, this will not be not being a man or being a not-man, he proves in the following way. It was posited and proved above that the thing which a term signifies is one. And it was also posited that the thing which a term signifies is the substance of something, namely, a thing's quiddity. Hence it is clear that some term signifies a thing's substance, and that the thing which was signified is not something else. Therefore, if the essence or quiddity of man should be either not being a man or being a not-man, it is quite clear that it would differ from itself. It would be necessary to say, then, that there is no definition signifying a thing's essence. But from this it would follow that all predicates are accidental ones.

628. For substance is distinguished from accident, i.e., a substantial predicate is distinguished from an accidental one, in that each thing is truly what is predicated substantially of it. Thus it cannot be said that a substantial predicate is not one thing, for each thing exists only if it is one. But man is said to be white because whiteness or white is one of his accidents, although not in such a way that he is the very essence of white or whiteness. It is not necessary, then, that an accidental predicate should be one only, but there can be many accidental predicates. A substantial predicate, however, is one only; and thus it is clear that what being a man is is not what not being a man is. But if a substantial predicate is both, it will no longer be one only, and thus will not be substantial but accidental.

629. **Moreover, if all** [11].

He destroys the consequent. He shows that it is impossible that all predicates should be accidental and none substantial because, if all were accidental, there would be no universal predicate. (And universal predicate here means the same thing as it does in the *Posterior Analytics, [73b27]* i.e., an attribute which is predicated of something in virtue of itself and in reference to what it itself is). But this is impossible; for if one attribute is always predicated of another accidentally, there will be an infinite regress in accidental predication; but this is impossible for this reason.

630. For there are only two ways in which accidental predication occurs. One way is had when one accident is predicated accidentally of another; and this happens because both are accidents of the same subject, for example, when white is predicated of musical because both are accidents of man. The other way is had when an accident is predicated of a subject (as when Socrates is said to be musical), not because both are accidents of some other subject, but because one of them is an accident of the other. Hence, even though there are two ways in which accidents may be predicated, in neither way can there be an infinite regress in predication.

631. For it is clear that there cannot be an infinite regress in that way in which one accident is predicated of another, because one must reach some subject. For it has been stated already that the essential note of this kind of predication is that both accidents are predicated of one subject. And thus by descending from a predicate to a subject, the subject itself can be found to be the terminus.

632. And there cannot be an infinite regress in an upward direction in the way of predicating in which an accident is predicated of a subject, as when Socrates is said to be white, by ascending from a subject to a predicate so as to say that white is an accident of Socrates and that some other attribute is an accident of white Socrates. For this could occur only in two ways. One way would be that one thing would come from white and Socrates; and thus just as Socrates is one subject of whiteness, in a similar way white Socrates would be one subject of another accident. But this cannot be so, because one thing does not come from all of these predicates. For what is one in an absolute sense does not come from a substance and an accident in the way that one thing comes from a genus and a difference. Hence it cannot be said that white Socrates is one subject.

633. The other way would be that, just as Socrates is the subject of whiteness, in a similar way some other accident, such as musical, would have whiteness as its subject. But neither can this be so, and for two reasons. First, there can be no special reason why musical should be said to be an accident of white rather than the reverse; neither white nor musical will be prior to the other, but they will rather be of equal rank. Second, in conjunction with this it has been established or determined at the same time that this way of predicating in which an accident is predicated of an accident differs from that in which an accident is predicated of a subject, as when musical is predicated of Socrates. But in the way of which he is now speaking accidental predication does not mean that an accident is predicated of an accident; but it is to be so taken in the way we first described.

634. It is evident, then, that an infinite regress in accidental predication is impossible, and therefore that not all

predications are accidental. And it is also evident that there will be some term which signifies substance; and again, that contradictories are not true of the same subject.

635. Now with regard to the argument given it must be noted that, even though one accident is not the subject of another, and thus one accident is not related to the other as its subject, still one is related to the other as cause and thing caused. For one accident is the cause of another. Heat and moistness, for example, are the cause of sweetness, and surface is the cause of color. For by reason of the fact that a subject is receptive of one accident it is receptive of another.

LESSON 8
Other Arguments Against the Foregoing Position

ARISTOTLE'S TEXT Chapter 4: 1007b18–1008b2

1. *Furthermore, if all contradictories are true of the same subject at the same time, it is evident that all things will be one. For the same thing will be a trireme, a wall and a man, if it is possible either to affirm or to deny anything of everything.* **1007b18–22**

2. *And this is what must follow for those who agree with Protagoras' view. For if it appears to anyone that a man is not a trireme, it is evident that he is not a trireme; so that he also is a trireme if contradictories are true. And thus there arises the view of Anaxagoras that all things exist together at the same time, so that nothing is truly one. Hence they seem to be speaking about the indeterminate; and while they think they are speaking about being, they are speaking about non-being; for the indeterminate is what exists potentially and is not complete.* **1007b22–29**

3. *But the affirmation and the negation of every predicate of every subject must be admitted by them; for it would be absurd if each subject should have its own negation predicated of it while the negation of something else which cannot be predicated of it should not be predicated of it. I mean that, if it is true to say that a man is not a man, evidently it is also true to say that he is not a trireme. Therefore, if the affirmation is predicable of him, so also must the negation be. But if the affirmation is not predicable of him, the negation of the other term will be predicable of him to a greater degree than his own negation. If, then, the latter negation is predicable of him, the negation of trireme will also be predicable of him; and if this is predicable of him, the affirmation will be too. This is what follows, then, for those who hold this view.* **1007b29–1008a3**

4. *And it also follows for them that it is not necessary either to affirm or to deny. For if it is true that the same thing is both a man and a not-man, evidently it will be neither a man nor a not-man; for of the two affirmations there are two negations. And if the former is taken as a single proposition composed of the two, the latter also will be a single proposition opposed to the former.* **1008a3–7**

5. *Again, either this is true of all things, and a thing is both white and not-white, and both being and not-being, and the same applies to other affirmations and negations; or it is not true of all but is true of some and not of others. And if not of all, the exceptions will be admitted. But if it is true of all, then either the negation will be true of everything of which the affirmation is, and the affirmation will be true of everything of which the negation is, or the negation will be true of everything of which the affirmation is, but the affirmation will not always be true of everything of which the negation is. And if the latter is true, there will be something that certainly is not, and this will be an unshakeable opinion. And if that it is not is something certain and knowable, more known indeed will be the opposite affirmation than the negation. But if in denying something it is equally possible to affirm what is denied, it is necessary to state what is true about these things, either separately (for example, to say that a thing is white and that it is not-white), or not. And if it is not true to affirm them separately, then an opponent will not be saying what he professes to say, and nothing will exist. But how could non-existent things speak or walk, as he does? Again, [according to this view] all things will be one, as has been said before, and man and God and a trireme and their contradictories will be the same. Similarly, if this is true of each thing, one thing will differ in no respect from another; for if it differs, this difference will be something true and proper to it. And similarly if it is possible for each to be true separately, the results described will follow. And to this we may add that all will speak the truth and all speak falsely; and that each man will admit of himself that he is in error. And at the same time it is evident that up to this point the discussion is about*

nothing at all, because our opponent says nothing. For he does not say that a thing is so or is not so, but that it is both so and not so; and again he denies both of these and says that it is neither so nor not so. For if this were not the case there would already be some definite statement. Further, if when the affirmation is true the negation is false, and if when the negation is true the affirmation is false, it will be impossible both to affirm and to deny the same thing truly at the same time. But perhaps someone will say that this was the contention from the very beginning. **1008a8–1008b2**

COMMENTARY

636. Then he gives a third argument, which involves oneness and difference. The argument runs thus: if an affirmation and a negation are true of the same subject at the same time, all things will be one. But the consequent is false. Hence the antecedent must be false. In regard to this argument he does three things.

First [1], he lays down a conditional proposition and gives an example, namely, that if contradictories are true of the same subject at the same time, it will follow that the same thing will be a trireme (i.e., a ship with three banks of oars), a wall and a man.

637. **And this is what** [2].

Then he shows that the same impossible conclusion follows with regard to two other positions. He does this, first, with regard to the opinion of Protagoras, who said that whatever seems so to anyone is wholly true for him; for if it seems to someone that a man is not a trireme, then he will not be a trireme; and if it seems to someone else that a man is a trireme, he will be a trireme; and thus contradictories will be true.

638. Second, he does this with regard to the opinion of Anaxagoras, who said that all things exist together, so that nothing which is truly one is distinguished from other things, but all are one in a kind of mixture. For he said that everything is found in everything else, as has been shown in Book I of the *Physics.[187a30]* This is the position which Anaxagoras adopted because he seems to be speaking about indeterminate being, i.e., what has not been made actually determinate. And while he thought he was speaking about complete being, he was speaking about potential being, as will become clear below (see n. 667). But the indeterminate is what exists potentially and is not "complete," i.e., actual; for potency is made determinate only by actuality.

639. **But the affirmation** [3].

Third, he proves that the first conditional proposition is true. He does this, first, on the grounds that all things would have to be affirmed to be one; and second [4], on the grounds that affirmations would not be distinguished from their negations from the viewpoint of truth and falsity ("And it also follows").

He accordingly says, first [3], that the first conditional proposition must be admitted by them inasmuch as they hold than an affirmation and a negation are true of the same subject at the same time because an affirmation and a negation are true of anything at all. For it is clear that the negation of some other thing seems to be predicable of each thing to a greater degree than its own negation. For it would be absurd if some subject should have its own negation predicated of it and not the negation of something else by which it is signified that this other thing is not predicable of it. For example, if it is true to say that a man is not a man, it is much truer to say that a man is not a trireme. Hence it is clear that anything of which a negation must be predicated must also have an affirmation predicated of it. Therefore a negation will be predicated of it since an affirmation and a negation are true at the same time; or if an affirmation is not predicated of it, the negation of the other term will be predicated of it to a greater degree than its own negation. For example, if the term trireme is not predicable of man, non-trireme will be predicated of him inasmuch as it may be said that a man is not a trireme. But if the affirmation is predicable, so also must the negation be, since they are verified of the same thing. A man, then, must be a trireme, and he must also be anything else on the same grounds. Hence all things must be one. Therefore this is what follows for those who maintain the position that contradictories are true of the same subject.

640. **And it also follows** [4].

He now draws the other impossible conclusion which follows from this view, namely, that a negation will not be distinguished from an affirmation as regards falsity, but each will be false. Thus he says that not only the foregoing impossible conclusions follow from the above-mentioned position, but also the conclusion that it is not necessary "either to affirm or to deny," i.e., it is not necessary that either the affirmation or the negation of a thing should be true, but each may be false; and so there will be no difference between being true and being false. He proves this as follows.

641. If it is true that something is both a man and a not-man, it is also true that it is neither a man nor a not-man. This is evident. For of these two terms, *man* and *not-man*, there are two negations, *not man* and *not not-man*. And if one proposition were formed from the first two, for example, if one were to say that Socrates is neither a man nor a not-man, it would follow that neither the affirmation nor the negation is true but that both are false.

642. **Again, either this** [5].

Then he gives a fourth argument, and this is based on certitude in knowing. It runs thus. If an affirmation and a negation are true at the same time, either this is true of all things, or it is true of some and not of others. But if it is not true of all, then those of which it is true will be "admitted"; i.e., they will be conceded simply and absolutely, or according to another translation "they will be certain," i.e., true with certainty; that is, in their case the negation will be true because the affirmation is false, or the reverse.

643. But if it is true in all cases that contradictories are verified of the same subject, this might happen in two ways. In one way anything of which affirmations are true, negations are true, and the reverse. In another way anything of which affirmations are true, negations are true, but not the reverse.

644. And if the second is true, this impossible conclusion will follow: there will be something that firmly or certainly is not; and so there will be an unshakeable opinion regarding a negative proposition. And this will be the case because a negation is always true since whenever an affirmation is true its negation is also true. But an affirmation will not always be true, because it was posited that an affirmation is not true of anything at all of which a negation is true; and thus a negation will be more certain and knowable

than an affirmation. But this seems to be false because, even though non-being is certain and knowable, an affirmation will always be more certain than its opposite negation; for the truth of a negation always depends on that of some affirmation. Hence a negative conclusion can be drawn only if there is some kind of affirmation in the premises. But an affirmative conclusion can never be drawn from negative premises.

645. Now if one were to speak in the first way and say that of anything of which an affirmation is true the negation is also true, and similarly that of anything of which the negation is true the affirmation is also true, inasmuch as affirmation and negation are interchangeable, this might happen in two ways. For if an affirmation and a negation are both true at the same time, either it will be possible to state what is true of each separately, for example, to say that each of these propositions is true separately—"Man is white" and "Man is not white"; or it will not be possible to state that each is true separately but only both together. For example, if we were to say that this copulative proposition is true—"Man is white and man is not white."

646. And if we were to speak in the second way and say that neither one is true separately but only both together, two impossible conclusions would then follow. The first is that "an opponent will not be saying what he professes to say," i.e., he will assert neither the affirmation nor the negation of something, and "neither will exist," i.e., both will be false; or according to another text, "nothing will exist," i.e., it will follow that nothing is true, neither the affirmation nor the negation. And if nothing is true it will be impossible to understand or to express anything. For how can anyone understand or express non-being? Implied is the reply: in no way.

647. The second impossible conclusion would be that all things are one, as has been stated in a previous argument (n. 639). For it would follow that a man and God and a trireme, and also their contradictories, a not-man, not-God and not-trireme, are the same. Thus it is clear that, if an affirmation and a negation are true of any subject at the same time, one thing will not differ from another. For if one were to differ from another, something would have to be predicated of the one which is not predicated of the other; and so it would follow that something is definitely and properly true of this thing which does not fit the other. Therefore an affirmation and a negation will not be true of anything whatever. But it is clear that things which differ in no way are one. Thus it would follow that all things are one.

648. But if one were to speak in the first way and say that it is possible for an affirmation and a negation to be true, not only together but also separately, four impossible conclusions will follow. The first is that this position "indicates that this statement is true"; i.e., it proves that the statement just made is true. Hence another text reads, "the results described will follow," i.e., all things will be one, because it will then be possible both to affirm and to deny each thing, and one will not differ from the other.

649. A second impossible conclusion is that all will speak the truth, because anyone at all must make either an affirmation or a negation, and each will be true. And each man will also admit of himself that he is wrong when

he says that the affirmation is true; for, since he says that the negation is true, he admits that he was in error when he made the affirmation.

650. A third impossible conclusion is that up to this point there obviously could not be any investigation or dispute. For it is impossible to carry on a dispute with someone who admits nothing, because such a person really says nothing since he does not say absolutely that something is so or is not so; but he says that it is both so and not so. And again he denies both of these, for he says that it is neither so nor not so, as is evident from the preceding argument. For if he does not deny all of these he will know that something is definitely true, and this is contrary to his original position. Or according to another translation which expresses this more clearly, "there would already be some definite statement."

651. A fourth impossible conclusion will follow because of the definition of the true and the false. For truth exists when one says that what is, is, or that what is not, is not. But falsity exists when one says that what is, is not, or that what is not, is. Hence from the definition of the true and the false it is clear that, when an affirmation is true, its negation is false; for one then says that what is, is not. And when a negation is true, its affirmation is false; for what is not is then said to be. Therefore it is impossible both to affirm and to deny the same thing truly. But perhaps an opponent could say that this last argument is begging the question; for he who claims that contradictories are true at the same time does not accept this definition of the false: the false is to say that what is not, is, or that what is, is not.

LESSON 9
Three Further Arguments Against Those Who Deny the First Principle

ARISTOTLE'S TEXT Chapters 4 & 5: 1008b2–1009a 16

1. *Again, how is that man wrong who judges that a thing is so or is not so, and is he right who judges both? For if the second is right, what will his statement mean except that such is the nature of beings? And if he is not right, he is more right than the one who holds the first view, and beings will already be of a certain nature, and this will be true and not at the same time not true. But if all men are equally right and wrong, anyone who holds this view can neither mean nor state anything; for he will both affirm and not affirm these things at the same time. And if he makes no judgment but equally thinks and does not think, in what respect will he differ from plants?* **1008b2–12**

2. *It is most evident, then, that no one, either among those who profess this theory or any others, is really of this mind. For why does a man walk home and not remain where he is when he thinks he is going there? He does not at dawn walk directly into a well or into a brook if he happens on such; but he seems to be afraid of doing so because he does not think that to fall in is equally good and not good. Therefore he judges that the one is better and the other not. And if this is so in the case of what is good and what is not good, it must also be so in the case of other things. Thus he must judge that one thing is a man and another not a man, and that one thing is sweet and another not sweet. For when he thinks that it is better to drink water and to see a man and then seeks these things, he does not make the same judgment about all of them, though this would be necessary if the same thing were equally a man and not a man. But according to what has been said there is no one who does not seem to fear some things and not others. Hence, as it appears, all men make an unqualified judgment, and if not about all things, still about what is better or worse.* **1008b12–27**

3. *And if they do not have science but opinion, they ought to care all the more about the truth, just as one who is ill ought to care more about health than one who is well. For one who has opinion in contrast to one who has science is not healthily disposed towards the truth.* **1008b27–31**

4. *Further, even if all things are so and not so as much as you like, still difference of degree belongs to the nature of beings. For we should not say that two and three are equally even; and he who thinks that four is five is not equally as wrong as he who thinks that it is a thousand. Therefore, if they are not equally wrong, obviously one is less wrong and so more right. Hence, if what is truer is nearer to what is true, there must be some truth to which the truer is nearer. And even if there is not, still there is already something truer and more certain, and we shall be freed from that intemperate theory which prevents us from determining anything in our mind.* **1008b31–1009a5**

Chapter 5

5. *The doctrine of Protagoras proceeds from the same opinion, and both of these views must be alike either true or not true. For if all things which seem or appear are true, everything must be at once true and false. For many men have opinions which are contrary to one another, and they think that those who do not have the same opinions as themselves are wrong. Consequently the same thing must both be and not be. And if this is so, it is necessary to think that all opinions are true; for those who are wrong and those who are right entertain opposite opinions. If, then beings are such, all men will speak the truth. Hence it is evident that both contraries proceed from the same way of thinking.* **1009a6–16**

COMMENTARY

652. Here [1] he gives a fifth argument, which is based on the notion of truth, and it runs as follows. It has been stated that both the affirmation and the negation of something are held to be true at the same time. Therefore he who judges or thinks that "a thing is so," i.e., that the affirmation alone is true, "or is not so," i.e., that the negation alone is true, is wrong; and he who judges that both are true at the same time is right. Hence, since truth exists when something is such in reality as it is in thought, or as it is expressed in words, it follows that what a man expresses will be something definite in reality; i.e., the nature of beings will be such as it is described to be; so that it will not be at once the subject both of an affirmation and of a negation. Or according to another text, "beings will already be of a certain nature," as if to say that since the statement is definitely true, it follows that a thing has such a nature. However, if one were to say that it is not he who judges that an affirmation and a negation are true at the same time that has a true opinion, but rather he who thinks that either the affirmation alone is true or the negation alone is true, it is evident that beings will already exist in some determinate way. Hence another translation says more clearly, "and in a sense this will be definitely true and not at the same time not true," because either the affirmation alone is true or the negation alone is true.

653. But if all of those just mentioned, i.e., both those who affirm both parts of a contradiction and those who affirm one of the two, "are wrong," and all are also right, it will be impossible to carry on a dispute with anyone who maintains this, or even to say anything that might provoke a dispute with him. Or according to another text, "such a man will not affirm or assert anything." For, as another translation says, "he cannot assert or affirm anything of this kind," because he equally affirms and denies anything at all. And if this man takes nothing to be definitely true, and similarly thinks and does not think, just as he similarly affirms and denies something in speech, he seems to differ in no way from plants; because even brute animals have certain definite conceptions. Another text reads, "from those disposed by nature," and this means that such a one who admits nothing does not differ in what he is actually thinking from those who are naturally disposed to think but are not yet actually thinking. For those who are naturally disposed to think about any question do not affirm either part of it, and similarly neither do the others.

654. **It is most evident** [2].

Then he gives a sixth argument, which is based on desire and aversion. In regard to this he does two things. First, he gives the argument. Second [3], he rejects an answer which is a quibble ("And if they").

He accordingly says, first [2], that it is evident that no man is of such a mind as to think that both an affirmation and a negation can be verified of the same subject at the same time. Neither those who maintain this position nor any of the others can think in this way. For if to go home were the same as not to go home, why would someone go home rather than remain where he is, if he were of the opinion that to remain where he is is the same as to go home?

Therefore, from the fact that someone goes home and does not remain where he is it is clear that he thinks that to go and not to go are different.

655. Similarly, if someone walks along a path which happens to lead directly to a well or a brook, he does not proceed straight along that path but seems to fear that he will fall into the well or brook. This happens because he judges that to fall into a well or a brook is not equally good and not good, but he judges absolutely that it is not good. However, if he were to judge that it is both good and not good, he would not avoid the above act any more than he would desire it. Therefore, since he avoids doing this and does not desire it, obviously he judges or thinks that the one course is better, namely, not to fall into the well, because he knows that it is better.

656. And if this is true of what is good and what is not good, the same thing must apply in other cases, so that clearly one judges that one thing is a man and another not a man, and that one thing is sweet and another not sweet. This is evident from the fact that he does not seek all things to the same degree or make the same judgment about them, since he judges that it is better to drink water which is sweet than to drink that which is not sweet; and that it is better to see a man than to see something which is not a man. And from this difference in opinion it follows that he definitely desires the one and not the other; for he would have to desire both equally, i.e., both the sweet and the not-sweet, and both man and not-man, if he thought that contradictories were the same. But, as has been said before (n. 655), there is no one who does not seem to avoid the one and not the other. So by the very fact that a man is differently disposed to various things inasmuch as he avoids some and desires others, he must not think that the same thing both is and is not.

657. It is evident, then, that all men think that truth consists in affirmation alone or in negation alone and not in both at the same time. And if they do not think that this applies in all cases, they at least are of the opinion that it applies in the case of things which are good or evil or of those which are better or worse; for this difference accounts for the fact that some things are desired and others are avoided.

658. **And if they** [3].

Then he rejects a quibble. For someone could say that men desire some things inasmuch as they are good and avoid others inasmuch as they are not good, not because they know the truth but because they are of the opinion that the same thing is not both good and not good, although this amounts to the same thing in reality. But if it is true that men do not have science but opinion, they ought to care all the more about learning the truth. This is made clear as follows: one who is ill cares more about health than one who is well. But one who has an untrue opinion, in comparison with one who has scientific knowledge, is not healthily disposed towards the truth, because he is in the same state with regard to scientific knowledge as a sick man is with regard to health; for a false opinion is a lack of scientific knowledge just as illness is a lack of health. Thus it is evident that men ought to care about discovering the truth. However, this would not be the case if nothing were definitely true, but only if something were both true and not true at the same time.

659. **Further, even if all** [4].

Then he gives a seventh argument, which is based on the different degrees of falsity. He says that even if it should be most true that everything is so and not so, i.e., that an affirmation and its negation are true at the same time, still it is necessary that different degrees of truth should exist in reality. For obviously it is not equally true to say that two is even and that three is even; nor is it equally false to say that four is five, and that it is a thousand. For if both are equally false, it is evident that one is less false, i.e., it is less false to say that four is five than to say that it is a thousand. But what is less false is truer, or nearer to the truth, just as that is also less black which is nearer to white. Therefore it is clear that one of them speaks more truly, i.e., he comes nearer to the truth; and this is the one who says that four is five. But nothing would be closer or nearer to the truth unless there were something which is absolutely true in relation to which the nearer or closer would be truer and less false. It follows, then, that it is necessary to posit something which is unqualifiedly true, and that not all things are both true and false, because otherwise it would follow from this that contradictories are true at the same time. And even if it does not follow from the foregoing argument that there is something which is unqualifiedly true, still it has been stated already that one thing is truer and firmer or more certain than another; and thus affirmation and negation are not related in the same way to truth and certitude. Hence as a result of this argument and the others given above we shall be freed or liberated from this theory, i.e., from this non-mixed opinion, or one that is not tempered (and for this reason another text has "intemperate"); for an opinion is well tempered when the predicate is not repugnant to the subject. But when an opinion involves opposite notions, it is not well tempered; and the position mentioned above, which says that contradictories can be true, is an opinion of this kind.

660. Further, this position prevents us from being able to define or settle anything in our mind. For the first notion of difference is considered in affirmation and negation. Hence he who says that an affirmation and a negation are one does away with all definiteness or difference.

661. **The doctrine of Protagoras** [5].

Here he shows that the opinion of Protagoras is reduced to the same position as the one mentioned above. For Protagoras said that everything which seems to be true to anyone is true. And if this position is true, the first one must also be true, namely, that an affirmation and its negation are true at the same time. Hence all things must be true and false at the same time inasmuch as this follows from this position, as has been shown above (n. 659). He proves this as follows. Many men have opinions which are contrary to one another, and they think that those who do not have the same opinions as themselves are wrong, and vice versa. If, then, whatever seems so to anyone is true, it follows that both are wrong and both are right, because the same thing is and is not. Hence according to the opinion of Protagoras it follows that both parts of a contradiction are true at the same time.

662. Similarly, if it is true that both parts of a contradiction are true at the same time, the opinion of Protagoras must be true, namely, that all things which seem true to anybody are true.

For it is clear that people have different opinions, and some of these are false and others are true because they have opinions which are opposed to each other. If, then, all opposites are true at the same time (and this follows if contradictories are true at the same time), the result must be that all are right, and that what seems so to anyone is true. Thus it is clear that each position contains the same opinion, theory, or way of thinking, because one necessarily follows from the other.

LESSON 10
The Procedure Against Those Who Say that Contradictories Are True at the Same Time

ARISTOTLE'S TEXT Chapter 5: 1009a16–1009a38

1. *But the same method of discussion is not applicable in all of these cases, because some men need persuasion and others force. For the ignorance of those who have formed their opinions as a result of difficulties is easily cured, because refutation is directed not against their words but against their thought. But the cure for all of those who argue for the sake of argument consists in refuting what they express in speech and in words.* **1009a16–22**

2. *Those who have experienced difficulties have formed this opinion because of things observed in the sensible world, i.e., the opinion that contradictories and contraries can both be true at the same time, inasmuch as they see that contraries are generated from the same thing. Therefore, if it is impossible for non-being to come into being, the thing must have existed before as both contraries equally. This is Anaxagoras' view, for he says that everything is mixed in everything else. And Democritus is of the same opinion, for he holds that the void and the full are equally present in any part, and yet one of these is non-being and the other being.* **1009a22–30**

3. *Concerning those who base their opinions on these grounds, then, we say that in one sense they speak the truth, and that in another they do not know what they are saying. For being has two meanings, so that in one sense a thing can come to be from non-being and in another sense it cannot. Hence the same thing can both be and not be at the same time, but not in the same respect; for while the same thing can be potentially two contraries at the same time, it cannot in complete actuality.* **1009a30–36**

4. *Further, we shall expect them to believe that among beings there is also another kind of substance to which neither motion nor generation nor corruption belongs in any way.* **1009a36–38**

COMMENTARY

663. Having raised arguments against those who deny the first principle, and having settled the issue, here the Philosopher indicates how one must proceed differently against various men who adopted different versions of the above-mentioned error. This is divided into two parts.

In the first [1] he shows that one must proceed differently against different men. In the second [2] he begins to proceed in a different way than he did above ("Those who").

He accordingly says, first [1], that the same method "of discussion," i.e., of popular address (or "of good grammatical construction," according to another translation, or of well ordered argument "or intercession," as is said in the Greek, i.e., of persuasion) is not applicable to all of the foregoing positions; that is, to the position that contradictories can be true, and to the position that truth consists in appearances. For some thinkers adopt the foregoing positions for two reasons. Some do so because of some difficulty; for since certain sophistical arguments occur to them, from which the foregoing positions seem to follow, and they do not know how to solve them, they accept the conclusion. Hence their ignorance is easily cured. For one must not oppose them or attack the arguments which they give, but must appeal to their thought, clearing up the mental difficulties which have led them to form such opinions; and then they will give up these positions.

664. Others adopt the foregoing positions, not because of any difficulty which leads them to such positions, but only because they want to argue "for the sake of argument," i.e., because of a certain insolence, inasmuch as they want to maintain impossible theories of this kind for their own sake since the contrary of these cannot be demonstrated. The cure for these men is the refutation or rejection "of what they express in speech and in words," i.e., on the grounds that the word in a statement has some meaning. Now the meaning of a statement depends on the meaning of the words, so that it is necessary to return to the principle that words signify something. This is the principle which the Philosopher used above (see n. 611).

665. **Those who** [2].

Since the Philosopher met the difficulties above on this point by considering the meaning of words, he begins here to meet those who are in difficulties by solving their problems.

First [2], he deals with those who held that contradictories are true at the same time; and second (Lesson 11), he deals with those who held that everything which appears so is true ("And similarly").

In regard to the first he does two things. First, he sets forth the difficulty which led some men to admit that contradictories are true at the same time. Second ([3], he clears up this difficulty ("Concerning those").

He says, then, that the opinion on this point, that the parts of a contradiction may be true at the same time, was formed by some men as a result of a difficulty which arose with regard to sensible things, in which generation and corruption and motion are apparent. For it seemed that contraries were generated from the same thing; for example, air, which is warm, and earth, which is cold, both come from water. But everything which is generated comes from something that existed before; for non-being cannot come into being, since nothing comes from nothing. A thing therefore had to have in itself contradictories simultaneously, because if both the hot and the cold are generated from one and the same thing, then it turns out to be hot and not-hot itself.

666. It was because of such reasoning that Anaxagoras claimed that everything is mixed in everything else. For from the fact that anything at all seemed to come from anything else he thought that one thing could come from another only if it already existed in it. Democritus also seems to have agreed with this theory, for he claimed that the void and the full are combined in any part of a body. And these are like being and non-being, because the full has the character of being and the void the character of non-being.

667. **Concerning those** [3].

Here he solves the foregoing difficulty in two ways. First, he says that the opinion of those who have adopted the foregoing absurd views because of some difficulty must be met by appealing to their thought, as has been stated (n. 663). Therefore "concerning those who base their opinions," i.e., those who think that contradictories are true at the same time, "on these grounds," i.e., on the reasoning mentioned above, we say that in one sense they speak the truth and in another they do not know what they are saying since their statements are absurd. For being has two meanings: actual being and potential being; and therefore when they say that being does not come from non-being, in one sense they are right and in another they are not. For being does not come from actual being but from potential being. Hence in one sense the same thing can be at the same time both being and non-being, and in another sense it cannot; for the same thing can be contraries potentially, but it cannot be both "in complete actuality," i.e., actually. For if something warm is potentially both hot and cold, it still cannot be actually both.

668. **Further, we shall** [4].

Then he gives the second solution. He says that we deem it fitting that they should accept or think that there is some kind of substance to which neither motion nor generation nor corruption belongs, as is proved in Book VIII of the *Physics.[258b5]* Now one could not conclude to the existence of this kind of substance by reason of what has been said above, namely, that contraries belong to it, because nothing is generated from them. This solution seems to be like the one reached by the Platonists, who, because of the changeable character of sensible things, were compelled to posit unchangeable separate Forms (i.e., those of which definitions are given, and demonstrations made, and certain knowledge is had) on the grounds that there could be no certain knowledge of sensible things because of their changeableness and the mixture of contrariety which they contain. But the first solution is a better one.

LESSON 11

The Reason Why Some Considered Appearances to Be True

ARISTOTLE'S TEXT Chapter 5: 1009a38–1009b12

1. And similarly the theory that truth consists in appearances comes to some thinkers from sensible things. For they think that the truth should not be judged by the large or small number who uphold some view; and they point out that the same thing appears to be sweet to some when they taste it and bitter to others. Hence, if all men were ill or all were mad, and only two or three were healthy or in possession of their wits, the latter would appear ill or mad and not the former. Further, they say that the impressions made upon many of the other animals are contrary to those made upon us, and that to the senses of each person things do not always appear to be the same. Therefore it is not always evident which of these views is true or which is false, but both appear equally so. And it is for this reason that Democritus says that either nothing is true or it is not evident to us. **1009a38–1009b12**

COMMENTARY

669. Having solved the difficulty which led the ancient philosophers to maintain that contradictories are true at the same time, the Philosopher now dispels the difficulty which led some thinkers to maintain that every appearance is true.

This part is divided into two. First [1], he gives the difficulties which led some thinkers to hold the position mentioned above. Second (Lesson 13), he dispels these difficulties ("But in reply").

In regard to the first he does two things. First, he gives the reason which led these men to maintain that every appearance is true. Second (Lesson 12), he explains why they reasoned in this way ("In general").

He therefore says, first [1], that, just as the opinion which maintained that contradictories are true at the same time came from certain sensible things in which it happens that contradictories come from the same thing, so too "the theory that truth consists in appearances," or the opinion about the truth of appearances, is derived from certain sensible things; that is, by those who are not perverse but are drawn into this position because of difficulties. This occurs because they find that different men hold contrary opinions about the same sensible things; and they give three reasons in support of their position. First, they point out that the same thing appears to taste sweet to some and bitter to others, so that men have contrary opinions about all sensible things. Second, they note that many animals make judgments about sensible things which are contrary to ours; for what seems tasty to the ox or to the ass is judged by man to be unpalatable. Third, they say that the same man at different times makes different judgments about sensible things; for what now appears to be sweet and palatable to him at another time seems bitter or tasteless.

670. And no certain reason can be given that clearly indicates which of these opinions is true or which is false, because one of these seems no truer to one person than the other does to another person. Therefore they must be equally true or equally false. Hence Democritus said that either nothing is definitely true or, if anything is true, it is not evident to us; for even though we acquire our knowledge of things through the senses, their judgment is

not certain since they do not always judge in the same way. Hence we do not seem to have any certainty regarding the truth so that we can say that this opinion is definitely true and its contrary definitely false.

671. But someone could say, in opposing this position, that some rule can be adopted whereby a person can discern among contrary opinions the one that is true. That is, we might say that the judgment which healthy people make about sensible things is right, and the one which sick people make is not; and that the judgment which wise and intelligent people make in matters of truth is right, and the one which foolish or ignorant people make is not. He rejects this reply at the very start on the grounds that no certain judgment about the truth of any theory can be fittingly based on the number, large or small, of persons who hold it, according to which that would be said to be true which seems so to many, and that to be false which seems so to a few; for sometimes what many believe is not simply true. Now health and sickness or wisdom and foolishness do not seem to differ only by reason of the greater or smaller number of people involved. For if all or most persons were like those who are now thought to be ignorant or foolish, they would be considered wise, and those who are now thought to be wise would be considered foolish. The same applies in the case of health and sickness. Hence the judgment regarding truth and falsity of one who is healthy and wise is no more credible than the judgment of one who is ill and foolish.

LESSON 12
Two Reasons Why Some Identify Truth with Appearances

ARISTOTLE'S TEXT Chapter 5: 1009b12–1010a15

1. *And in general it is because these philosophers think that discretion is sensory perception, and that this in turn is alteration, that they say that what appears to the senses is necessarily true.* **1009b12–15**

2. *For it is for these reasons that both Empedocles and Democritus and, we may probably say, every one of the other philosophers became involved in such opinions. For Empedocles also says that when men change their condition they change their knowledge, "for understanding varies in men in relation to what is seen," according to him. And elsewhere he says, "Insofar as they are changed into a different nature, to that extent it is proper for them always to think other thoughts." And Parmenides also speaks in the same way: "For just as each has his mixture of many-jointed limbs, so intellect is present in men; for it is the same thing, the nature of the limbs, which exercises discretion in men—in all and in each; for that which is more is intellect." Anaxagoras is also recorded as saying to some of his companions that things were such to them as they thought them to be. And men also say that Homer maintained this view, because he made Hector, after he was stunned by the blow, think other thoughts; implying that people of sound and unsound mind both think but not the same thoughts. It is evident, then, that if both of these states of mind are forms of knowledge, beings must also be so and not so at the same time.* **1009b15–33**

3. *Hence their conclusion happens to be the most serious one. For if those who have seen most clearly the truth which it is possible for us to have (and these are those who seek and love it most), maintain such opinions and express such views about the truth, how is it unfitting that those who are trying to philosophize should abandon the attempt? For to seek the truth will be like chasing birds.* **1009b33–1010a1**

4. *Now the reason these men held this opinion is that, while they investigated the truth about beings, they thought that sensible things alone exist; and in these much of the nature of the indeterminate, i.e., the kind of being which we have described, is present. Hence, while they speak in a plausible way, they do not say what is true; for it is more plausible to speak as they do than as Epicharmus did to Xenophanes.* **1010a1–7**

5. *Again, since they saw that the whole of the natural world is in motion, and that we can say nothing true about what is undergoing change, they came to the conclusion that it is impossible to say anything true about what is always changing altogether. For it was from this view that the most extreme of the opinions mentioned above blossomed forth; that is, the opinion held by those who are said to Heraclitize, and such as Cratylus expressed, who finally thought that he should say nothing but only moved his finger, and criticized Heraclitus for saying that it is impossible to step into the same river twice; for he himself thought that this could not be done even once.* **1010a7–15**

COMMENTARY

672. He gives the reason why these philosophers adopted the foregoing position. First [1], he shows how sensory perception provided one reason for adopting this position; and second [4], how sensible objects provided another ("Now the reason").

In regard to the first part he does three things. First, he explains how sensory perception provided one reason for adopting this position. Second [2], he recounts the opinions of different men which have this reason as their common basis ("For it is"). Third [3], he attacks these opinions ("Hence their conclusion").

He accordingly says, first [1], that the ancients were of the opinion that discretion, i.e., wisdom or science, is merely sensory perception; for they did not make any distinction between sense and intellect. Now sensory perception comes about through a certain alteration of a sense with reference to sensible objects. And so the fact that a sense perceives something results from the impression which a sensible thing makes on the sense. Thus a sensory perception always corresponds to the nature of the sensible object as it appears. Hence, according to these thinkers, whatever appears to the senses is necessarily true; and since we must add that all knowing is sensory, it follows that whatever appears in any way at all to anyone is true.

673. But this argument fails, not only because it holds that sense and intellect are the same, but also because it maintains that the judgment which a sense makes about sensible objects is never false. For while a sense may make a mistake about common and accidental sensible objects, it does not do this with regard to its proper sensible object, except perhaps when the sensory organ is indisposed. And even though a sense is altered by its sensible object, the judgment of a sense does not have to conform to the conditions of the sensible object; for it is not necessary that the action of an agent be received in the patient according to the mode of being of the agent but only according to that of the patient or subject. This is why a sense sometimes is not disposed to receive the form of a sensible object according to the mode of being which the form has in the sensible object, and it therefore sometimes judges a thing to be otherwise than it really is.

674. **For it is** [2].

He presents the opinions which different men held for the reasons stated above. Now all of the statements of these men which he adduces imply two things: first, that intellect is the same as sense, and, second, that every appearance is true. Thus he says that it is for the reasons mentioned above that Empedocles and Democritus and each of the other philosophers became involved in such opinions about reality "we may probably say," i.e., we can conjecture on the basis of their statements.

675. For Empedocles said that those who change "their condition," i.e., some bodily disposition, also change their understanding; implying that the intellect, to which knowledge belongs, depends on a condition of the body, just as a sense does. For understanding increases in men "in relation to what is seen"; that is, an increase in knowledge takes place in a man by reason of the fact that something new begins to appear to him, and this comes about as a result of some change in a bodily disposition. Another translation states this more clearly, saying, "For purpose or decision develops in man in relation to what is at hand"; as if to say, according to the different dispositions which are actually present in men, new decisions or new purposes or new judgments develop in them. And the implication is that decision or purpose does not depend on any intellective power in man over and above the senses but only on a disposition of the body, which is changed with the presence of different things. But in other

works of his Empedocles says that, to the extent that alteration occurs, that is, to the extent that men are changed to another bodily disposition, to that extent, he says, there is always thoughtfulness in them; that is, thought, concern, or planning arises in them proportionately. This translation is a difficult one to understand, but another states this notion more clearly, saying, "to the extent that men have been changed, to that extent they are always determined to think other thoughts or even foolish ones." Or according to another text, "It is proper for them [always to think other thoughts]," as if to say that, insofar as a man is changed in some bodily disposition, to that extent his basic outlook is different—implying that he has a different understanding and a different outlook.

676. Then he gives Parmenides' opinion in this matter. He says that Parmenides speaks about the truth of things in the same way that Empedocles does, for Parmenides says that, just as each man has an arrangement of jointed members, or "of many-jointed limbs," according to another text, so intellect is present in men; implying that there is a great deal of variety and circumvolution in the members of man in order that such an arrangement of members may be adjusted for the operation of the intellect, which depends on the way in which the members are combined, according to him. For he says that it is the same thing "which cares for," i.e., which has the care or supervision of the members because of the nature of the members, and which is "in each," i.e., in the individual parts of the universe, and "in all," i.e., in the whole universe. Yet insofar as it is present in the whole universe and in its individual parts and in men, it is designated by different names. In the whole universe it is called God, in the individual parts it is called nature, and in men it is called thought. Thus it is present to a greater degree in man than it is in the other parts of the universe; for in man this power thinks as a result of the determinate way in which his members are combined, but this does not apply in the case of other things. In this statement he also wants it understood that thought is a result of the way in which the body is composed, and thus does not differ from sensory perception. Another translation states this more clearly, saying, "For it is the same thing, the nature of the limbs, which exercises discretion in men—in all and in each; for that which is more is intellect."

677. Then he gives the opinion of Anaxagoras, who expressed it to some of his companions and friends and had them commit it to memory, namely, that things are such to them as they take or believe them to be. This is the second point which is touched on in these statements of the philosophers, namely, that truth depends on opinion.

678. Then he gives the view of Homer, who seemed to be of the same opinion according to what people said of him. For in his story he made Hector lie, as it were, in a trance from the blow which he had been dealt, "lingering in another place," i.e., to think other thoughts than he had thought before, or, according to another text, to be of a different opinion from the one which he had before; as if in lingering and not lingering, i.e., in the state in which he lay after being struck down, he would both think and not think, although not about the same thing. For he knew those things which then appeared to him, but not those which he had

known before and had then ceased to know. Another translation expresses the idea thus: "Implying that people of sound and unsound mind both think but not the same thoughts"; as if to say that, just as this is true of Hector, who had strange opinions after the blow, so too it is possible for others to have sound and foolish opinions at the same, although not about the same things but about different ones.

679. Now from all of the foregoing views of the philosophers he draws his intended conclusion that, if both of these states of mind constitute knowledge, i.e., those states in which a man thinks contrary things when he is changed from one state to another, it follows that whatever anyone thinks is true; for knowing would not consist in thinking what is false. Hence it follows that beings are equally so and not so.

680. **Hence, their conclusion** [3].

Here he attacks the above-mentioned philosophers. He says that the conclusion which they drew is the most serious one. For if those who have seen the truth most clearly, insofar as it is possible for man to see it (namely, the foregoing philosophers, who are also the ones that love and seek it most of all) offer such opinions and views about the truth, how is it unfitting that these philosophers should grieve about the ineffectualness of their study if truth cannot be found? Another text reads, "How is it unfitting that those who are trying to philosophize should give up or abandon the attempt?" i.e., that a man should not cling to those who want to philosophize but despise them. For, if a man can know nothing about the truth, to seek the truth is to seek something which he cannot attain. In fact he resembles someone who chases or hunts birds; for the more he pursues them the farther they get away from him.

681. **Now the reason** [4].

He indicates how sensible things influenced this opinion, i.e., how they provided a basis for the above-mentioned position. For, since sensible things are naturally prior to the senses, the dispositions of the senses must depend on those of sensible things. He gives two ways in which sensible things provided a basis for this position. The second [5] is treated at the words, "Again, since they."

He accordingly says, first, that the reason why the foregoing philosophers adopted this position is this: since they aimed to know the truth about beings, and it seemed to them that sensible things alone exist, they therefore based their doctrine about truth in general on the nature of sensible things. Now in sensible things much of the nature of the infinite or indeterminate is present, because they contain matter, which is not in itself limited to one form but is in potency to many; and in these the nature of being is also found just as we have pointed out: the being of sensible things is not determinate but is open to various determinations. It is not to be wondered at, then, if he does not assign a definite knowledge to the senses, but one kind of knowledge to one sense, and another kind to another sense.

682. And for this reason the above-mentioned philosophers use the foregoing argument plausibly or fittingly, though they are not right in claiming that there is nothing definite in sensible things; for even though matter in itself is indeterminately disposed for many forms, nevertheless by a form it is determined to one mode of being. Hence, since things are known by their

form rather than by their matter, it is wrong to say that we can have no definite knowledge of them. Yet, since the opinion of these philosophers has some plausibility, it is more fitting to speak as they do than as Epicharmus did to Xenophanes, who seems to have said that all things are immovable, necessary and known with certainty.

683. **Again, since they** [5].

He gives the second way in which sensible things provided a basis for this opinion. He says that the philosophers saw that the whole of the natural world, i.e., the sensible world, is in motion, and they also saw that no attribute can be predicated of anything that is being changed insofar as it is being changed; for whatever is being changed insofar as it is being changed is neither white nor black. Hence, if the nature of sensible things is being changed always and "altogether," i.e., in all respects, so that there is nothing fixed in reality, it is impossible to make any statement about them that is definitely true. Thus it follows that the truth of an opinion or proposition does not depend on some determinate mode of being in reality but rather on what appears to the knower; so that it is what appears to each individual that is true for him.

684. That such was their argument becomes clear as follows. For from this assumption or opinion there sprouted "the most serious or extreme" opinion of the philosophers of whom we have spoken, i.e., the opinion which is found to be the most serious or extreme in this class. And this is the one which he called "Heraclitizing," i.e., following the opinion of Heraclitus, or the opinion of those who were disciples of Heraclitus, according to another text, or of those who professed to follow the opinion of Heraclitus, who claimed that all things are in motion and consequently that nothing is definitely true. This opinion also was maintained by Cratylus, who finally arrived at such a pitch of madness that he thought that he should not express anything in words, but in order to express what he wanted he would only move his finger. He did this because he believed that the truth of the thing which he wanted to express would pass away before he had finished speaking. But he could move his finger in a shorter space of time. This same Cratylus also reprimanded or rebuked Heraclitus. For Heraclitus said that a man cannot step into the same river twice, because before he steps in a second time the water of the river already has flowed by. But Cratylus thought that a man cannot step into the same river even once, because even before he steps in once the water then in the river flows by and other water replaces it. Thus a man is incapable not only of speaking twice about anything before his disposition is changed but even of speaking once.

LESSON 13
Change in Sensible Things Not Opposed to Their Truth

ARISTOTLE'S TEXT Chapter 5: 1010a15–1010b1

1. *But in reply to this theory we shall also say that there is some reason why these men should think that what is changing, when it is changing, does not exist.* **1010a15–17**

2. *Yet there is a problem here; for what is casting off some quality retains something of what is being cast off, and something of what is coming to be must already exist. And in general if a thing is ceasing to be, there must be something which is; and if a thing is coming to be, there must be something from which it comes to be and something by which it comes to be; and this process cannot proceed to infinity.* **1010a17–22**

3. *But setting aside these considerations, let us say that change in quantity and change in quality are not the same. Let it be granted, then, that a thing does not remain the same in quantity; but it is by reason of its form that we know each thing.* **1010a22–25**

4. *Again, those who hold this view deserve to be criticized, because what they saw in the case of a very small number of sensible things they asserted to be true also of the whole universe. For it is only that region of the sensible world about us which is always in process of generation and corruption. But this is, so to speak, not even a part of the whole, so that it would have been juster for them to have esteemed the changing because of the whole than to misjudge as they did the whole because of its changing part.* **1010a25–32**

5. *Further, it is evident that in answering these men we shall say the same things as we said before; for we must show them and make them understand that there is a kind of nature which is immobile.* **1010a32–35**

6. *And those who say that the same thing both is and is not at the same time can also say that all things are at rest rather than in motion. For according to this view there is nothing into which anything may be changed, since everything is already present in everything.* **1010a35–1010b1**

COMMENTARY

685. He argues against the foregoing opinions. First [1], he argues against the views that were held about the changeable character of sensible things; and second (Lesson 14),

against the statements that were made regarding sensory appearances ("Now concerning the truth").

In regard to the first part [1] he gives six arguments. The first of these is as follows: he who thinks that what is not does not exist, has a true opinion and makes a true statement if he expresses this. But what is being changed, while it is being changed, is neither that to which it is being changed nor that from which it is being changed; and thus some true statement can be made about a thing that is undergoing change. Hence, in opposing the foregoing theory or "account" (i.e., the opinion that no true statement can be made about anything which is changing), we can say that there is some ground or valid reason "in their case," i.e., according to the opinion of the foregoing philosophers, for thinking "that what is changing," or what is being changed, "when it is changing," i.e., while it is undergoing change, does not exist; that is, there is some reason for thinking that it has no being.

686. **Yet there is** [2].

Then he gives the second argument, and it runs thus: everything which is being changed already has some part of the terminus to which it is being changed, because what is being changed, while it is being changed, is partly in the terminus to which it is being changed, and partly in the terminus from which it is being changed, as is proved in Book VI of the *Physics [235b6]* (or, according to another text, "that which is casting off some quality retains something of what is being cast off"). And by this statement we are given to understand that anything which is being moved retains some part of the terminus from which it is being moved, because so long as a thing is being moved it is casting off the terminus from which it is being moved; and it is possible only to cast off some quality which belongs to a mobile subject. And something of what is coming to be must already exist, because everything which is coming to be was coming to be, as is proved in Book VI of the *Physics.[237b10]* And it is also evident that, if something is ceasing to be, there must be something which is; for if it did not exist in any way at all, it already would have ceased to be and would not be ceasing to be. Similarly, if something is coming to be, there must be a matter from which it is coming to be and an agent by which it is coming to be. But this cannot go on to infinity, because, as is proved in Book II (see n. 301), there cannot be an infinite regress either in the case of material causes or in that of efficient causes. Hence a major problem faces those who say that no true statement can be made about anything which is being moved or generated, both because each thing which is being moved or generated has some part of the terminus to which it is being moved, and because in every process of generation or motion there must be held to be something unproduced and unchangeable both on the part of the matter and on that of the agent.

687. **But setting aside** [3].

Then he gives the third argument, and this rejects the very ground on which these thinkers base their opinion that all sensible things are always in motion. For they were led to make this statement because of things which increase as a result of growth. For they saw that a thing increases in quantity to a very small degree during one year, and they thought that the motion of growth was continuous, so that quantity, in which increase is observed, might be divided in proportion to the parts of time. Thus an increase in some part of quantity would take place in some part of time, and this part of quantity would be related to a whole quantity as some part of a period of time to the whole of that period. And since this kind of motion is imperceptible, they also thought that things which appear to be at rest are being moved, although by an imperceptible motion.

688. In opposing these thinkers, then, he says that, even apart from the considerations which have been made, it is clear that change in quantity and in quality or form are not the same. And although they admit that change in quantity is continuous in reality, and that all things are always being moved imperceptibly by this motion, it is not therefore necessary for this reason that all things should be being moved in quality or form. Hence it will be possible to have a definite knowledge of things, because things are known by their form rather than by their quantity.

689. **Again, those who** [4].

Then he gives the fourth argument. He says that "those who think in this way," i.e., those who entertain the opinion that all sensible things are always being moved because they find a small number of sensible things of which this is true, deserve to be criticized; for there are many sensible things which are capable of being moved only from the viewpoint of local motion. For it is obvious that it is only the sensible things around us here in the sphere of active and passive things which are in process of generation and corruption. But this sphere or place amounts to nothing, so to speak, in comparison with the whole universe; for the entire earth has no sensible quantity in comparison with the outermost sphere. Hence this place is related to the universe as its central point, as the astronomers prove on the grounds that the six signs of the zodiac always appear above the earth. But this would not be the case if the earth were to hide from us some part of the heavens which are perceived by the senses. For it would be foolish to make a judgment about the whole sensible world in the light of these few things. Indeed, it would have been more acceptable if the whole sensible world had been judged according to the motion of the celestial bodies, which far surpass the others in quantity.

690. **Further, it is evident** [5].

He gives the fifth argument. He says that we must also use the same arguments against these men as were used above in this same book; that is, we must show them that there is a kind of nature which is immobile, namely, that of the primary mover, as is proved in Book VIII of the *Physics.[258b5]* And this argument must be used against them, and they ought to accept it, as has been proved elsewhere (see n. 668). It is not true, then, that all things are always in motion, and that it is impossible to make any true statement about anything.

691. **And those who say** [6].

He gives the sixth argument. He says that their position that all things are being moved is opposed to their first position, that contradictories are true of the same subject at the same time, because if something is and is not at the same time, it follows that all things are at rest rather than in motion. For nothing is being changed in terms of any attribute which already belongs to it; for example, what is already white is not being changed as regards whiteness. But if it is possible for the same thing both to be and not be at the same time, all attributes will be present in all things, as has been proved above (n. 639), because all will be one. Hence there will not be anything to which a thing can be changed.

LESSON 14
Seven Arguments against the View that Truth Consists in Appearances

ARISTOTLE'S TEXT Chapter 5: 1010b1–1011a2

1. *Now concerning the truth that not everything which appears is true, the following points must be taken into consideration: first, that a sense is not false with regard to its proper object, but imagination is not the same as a sense.* **1010b1–3**

2. *Second, that it is surprising if some should raise the question whether continuous quantities are as great and colors really such as they appear to those who are at a distance or as they appear to those who are close at hand, and whether things are such as they appear to those who are healthy or to those who are ailing, and whether heavy things are such as they appear to those who are weak or to those who are strong, and whether those things are true which appear to those who are asleep or to those who are awake. For it is clear that they do not think so. Therefore no one who is in Lybia, having dreamed that he was in Athens, would go to the Odeon.* **1010b3–11**

3. *Again, concerning future things, as Plato says, the opinion of a physician and that of a person who is ignorant of the art of medicine are not of equal value as to whether someone will get well or not.* **1010b11–14**

4. *Again, in the case of the senses the perception of a foreign object and that of a proper object, or that of a kindred object and that of the object of the sense concerned, are not of equal value. In the case of colors it is sight and not taste which passes judgment; and in the case of flavors it is taste and not sight which does this.* **1010b14–17**

5. *And no one of these senses ever affirms at the same time about the same subject that it is simultaneously both so and not so. Nor at another time does it experience any difficulty about a modification, but only about the object of which the modification is an accident. I mean, for example, that the same wine, either as a result of a change in itself or in the body, might seem at one time sweet and at another not. But sweetness, such as it is when it exists, has never changed; but one is always right about it, and sweetness itself is necessarily such as it is.* **1010b18–26**

6. *Yet all these theories destroy this, for just as things will have no substance, neither will they have any necessity; for that is necessary which cannot be in one way and in another. Hence, if anything is necessary, it will not be both so and not so.* **1010b26–30**

7. *And in general if only the sensible actually exists, there would be nothing if living things did not exist; for there would be no senses. Therefore the position that neither sensible objects nor sensory perceptions would exist is perhaps true, for these are modifications of the one sensing. But that the underlying subjects which cause perception should not exist apart from perception is impossible; for a perception is not the perception of itself, but there is some other thing besides the perception which must be prior to the perception. For that which causes motion is naturally prior to that which is moved, and this is no less true if they are correlative terms.* **1010b30–1011a2**

COMMENTARY

692. Here he begins to argue dialectically against the opinion that truth if equivalent to appearances; and in regard to this he does two things. First [1], he rejects this opinion. Second (Lesson 15, text 6), he draws his intended conclusion ("Let this suffice").

In regard to the first he does two things. First, he argues dialectically against those who held this opinion because of some theory or difficulty. Second (*ibid.*, text 1), he argues against those who held this opinion because of insolence ("Now there are some").

In regard to the first part [1] he gives seven arguments. The first of these is as follows: it has been shown (n. 690) that not all things are changeable, and "concerning the truth that not everything which appears is true," these points must be considered. First, the proper cause of falsity is not the senses but the imagination, which is not the same as the senses. That is to say, the diversity of judgments made about sensible objects is not attributable to the senses but to the imagination, in which errors are made about sensory perceptions because of some natural obstacle. Now imagination is not the same as perception, as is proved in Book III of *The Soul, [428b10]* but is a motion produced as a result of actual sensing. Therefore in attributing to the senses this diversity of judgments by which one person is considered to have a false perception of a particular object about which another has a true perception, they do not proceed as they should.

Another translation states this better, saying, "And, first, it must be understood that a sense is not false with regard to its proper object," implying that no sense makes a mistake about its own proper object; for example, sight is not mistaken about colors. From this it is evident that the judgment which a sense makes about its proper sensible object is a definite one, so that there must be some definite truth in the world.

693. And if someone raises the objection that error sometimes arises even with regard to proper sensibles, his answer is that this is attributable not to the senses but to the imagination; for when the imagination is subject to some sort of abnormality, it sometimes happens that the object apprehended by a sense enters the imagination in a different way than it was apprehended by the sense. This is evident, for example, in the case of madmen, in whom the organ of imagination has been injured.

694. **Second, that it is** [2].

Then he gives his second argument, and it runs thus: it is surprising if some "should raise the question," or "be puzzled," as another text says, whether continuous quantities are such as they appear to those who are at a distance or to those who are close at hand. For it is just about self-evidently true that a sense judges quantities which are close at hand to be such as they are, and those which are far away to be smaller than they are, because what seems farther away appears small, as is proved in the science of optics.

695. The same thing applies if someone raises the question whether colors are such as they appear to those who are close at hand; for it is evident that the farther an agent's power is extended when it acts, the more imperfect is its effect; for fire heats those things which are far away to a lesser degree than those which are close at hand. And for the same reason the color of a perfect sensible body does not change that part of the transparent medium which is far away from it as completely as it changes that part which is close to it. Hence the judgment of a sense is truer about sensible colors in things close at hand than it is about those in things far away.

696. The same thing is also true if someone asks whether things are such as they appear to those who are healthy or "to those who are ailing,"

i.e., those who are ill. For healthy people have sensory organs which are well disposed, and therefore the forms of sensible things are received in them just as they are; and for this reason the judgment which healthy people make about sensible objects is a true one. But the organs of sick people are not properly disposed, and therefore they are not changed as they should be by sensible objects. Hence their judgment about such objects is not a true one. This is clear with regard to the sense of taste; for when the organ of taste in sick people has been rendered inoperative as a result of the humors being destroyed, things which have a good taste seem tasteless to them.

697. The same thing also applies regarding the question whether things having weight are as heavy as they seem to those who are weak or to those who are strong; for it is clear that the strong judge about heavy things as they really are. But this is not the case with the weak, who find it difficult to lift a weight not only because of the heaviness of it (and this sometimes happens even with the strong) but also because of the weakness of their power, so that even less heavy things appear heavy to them.

698. The same thing again applies if the question is raised whether the truth is such as it appears to those who are asleep or to those who are awake. For the senses of those who are asleep are fettered, and thus their judgment about sensible things cannot be free like the judgment of those who are awake and whose senses are unfettered. For it has been pointed out above that it would be surprising if they should be perplexed, because it appears from their actions that they are not perplexed, and that they do not think that all of the above-mentioned judgments are equally true. For if someone in Lybia seems in his dreams to be in Athens, or if someone in Paris seems in his dreams to be in Hungary, he does not when he awakens act in the same way that he would if he were to perceive this when he is awake. For if he were awake in Athens, he would go to the Odeon, i.e., a building in Athens; but he would not do this if he had merely dreamed it. It is clear, then, that he does not think that what appears to him when he is asleep and what appears when he is awake are equally true.

699. We can argue in the same way with regard to the other issues mentioned above; for even though men often raise questions about these issues, they are not in their own mind perplexed about them. Hence it is clear that their reason for holding to be true everything which appears, is invalid; for they held this position because of the impossibility of deciding which of several opinions is the truer, as has been stated above (n. 663).

700. **Again, concerning future** [3].

Here he gives his third argument. He says that in the case of future events, as Plato points out, the opinion of a physician and that of a person who is ignorant of the art of medicine are not "of equal value," i.e., equally important, certain, true or acceptable, as to the future possibility of some sick person being cured or not. For, while a physician knows the cause of health, this is unknown to someone who is ignorant of the art of medicine. It is clear, then, that the opinion which some held that all opinions are equally true is a foolish one.

701. **Again, in the case** [4].

He gives his fourth argument, which runs thus: in the case of sensible objects the judgment which a sense makes about some sensible object foreign to it and that which it makes about its proper sensible object are not of equal "value," i.e., equally true and acceptable; for example, sight and taste do not make the same sort of judgment about colors and flavors, but in the case of colors the judgment of sight must be accepted, "and in the case of flavors," or savors, the judgment of taste must be accepted. Hence, if sight judges a thing to be sweet and taste judges it to be bitter, taste must be accepted rather than sight.

702. And in the same way too the judgment which a sense makes about its proper sensible object and the one which it makes about something akin to its proper object are not of equal value. Now those things which are said here to be akin to proper sensible objects are called common sensibles, for example, size, number and the like, about which a sense is deceived to a greater degree than it is about its proper sensible object, although it is deceived about them to a lesser degree than it is about the sensible objects of another sense or about things which are called accidental sensible objects. Hence it is clearly foolish to say that all judgments are equally true.

703. **And no one** [5].

He now gives his fifth argument. He says that no sense affirms at one instant of time that a thing is simultaneously both so and not so. For sight does not at the same moment affirm that something is white and not white or that it is two cubits and not two cubits or that it is sweet and not sweet. But while a sense's power of judging may seem at different times to form opposite judgments about the same thing, still from this judgment no difficulty ever arises about the sensible modification itself, but only about the subject of this modification. For example, if we take the same subject, wine, sometimes it appears to the sense to taste sweet and sometimes not. This happens either because of some change in the sentient body, i.e., in the organ, which is infected by bitter humors, so that whatever it tastes does not seem sweet to it, or else because of some change in the wine itself. But the sense of taste never changes its judgment without judging sweetness itself to be such as it considered it to be in the sweet thing when it judged it to be sweet; but about sweetness itself it always makes a true affirmation, and always does this in the same way. Hence, if the judgment of a sense is true, as these men claimed, it also follows that the nature of sweetness is necessarily such as it is; and thus something will be definitely true in reality. And it also follows that both an affirmation and a negation can never be true at the same time, because a sense never affirms that something is both sweet and not sweet at the same time, as has been stated.

704. **Yet all these** [6].

He gives the sixth argument. He says that, just as all of the above-mentioned theories or opinions destroy substantial predicates, as has been shown above (n. 625), in a similar way they destroy all necessary predicates. For it follows that nothing could ever be predicated of anything else either substantially or necessarily. That nothing could be predicated of anything else substantially is clear from what has been stated above. That nothing could be predicated of anything else necessarily is proved as follows. That is necessary which cannot be otherwise than it is; therefore, if everything which is can exist in one way or in another way, as is held by those who say that contradictories and opposite opinions are true at the same time, it follows that nothing is necessary in the world.

705. **And in general** [7].

Then he gives the seventh argument. He says that, if everything which appears is true, and a thing is true only insofar as it appears to the senses, it follows that a thing exists only insofar as it is actually being sensed. But if something exists only in this way, i.e., insofar as it is being sensed, then it follows that nothing would exist if the senses did not exist; and this would follow if there were no animals or living things. But this is impossible.

706. For this can be true, that sensibles under the aspect of their sensibility do not exist; i.e., if they are considered under the aspect of sensibles actualized, they do not exist apart from the senses, for they are sensibles actualized insofar as they are present in a sense. And according to this every actualized sensible is a certain modification of the subject sensing, although this would be impossible if there were no sensory beings. But that the sensible objects which cause this modification in a sense should not exist is impossible. This becomes clear as follows: when some subsequent thing is removed it does not follow that a prior thing is removed. But the thing producing the modification in a sense is not the perception itself, because a perception is not the perception of itself but of something else, and this must be naturally prior to the perception just as a mover is prior to the thing which is moved. For sight does not see itself but sees color.

707. And even if someone were to raise the objection that a sensible object and a sense are correlative and thus naturally simultaneous, so that when one is destroyed the other is destroyed, Aristotle's thesis is still true; for what is potentially sensible is not said to be relative to a sense because it is referred to a sense, but because the sense is referred to it, as is stated in Book V of this work (see n. 1027). It is clearly impossible, then, to say that some things are true because they appear to the senses; yet this is what those men maintain who claim that all appearances are true, as is evident from the foregoing statements.

LESSON 15

Refutation of the View that Contradictories Can Be Shown to Be True at the Same Time. Contraries Cannot Belong to the Same Subject at the Same Time

ARISTOTLE'S TEXT Chapter 6: 1011a3–1011b22

1. *Now there are some, both of those who have been convinced by theories of this kind and of those who merely state them, who raise a difficulty; for they ask who it is that judges a man to be healthy, and in general who it is that judges rightly in each particular case. But such difficulties are like wondering whether we are now asleep or awake; and all such difficulties amount to the same thing. For these people think it fitting that there should be a reason for everything; for they are seeking a starting point, and they think they can get this by demonstration. Yet that sometimes they are not convinced they make evident in their actions. But according to what we have said this is characteristic of them; for they are seeking a reason for things for which no reason can be given, because the starting point of demonstration is not demonstration. These men, then, might easily believe this truth, for it is not difficult to grasp.* **1011a3–14**

2. *But those who seek compulsion only in words are seeking the impossible. For they deem it right to speak as they do, and immediately say contrary things.* **1011a15–16**

3. *Yet if not all things are relative but some things are absolute, not everything which appears will be true; for that which appears appears to someone. Thus he who says that all things which appear are true, makes all things which are, relative. Hence, those who look for compulsion in words, and think it fitting to maintain this view at the same time, must be careful to add that it is not what appears that is true, but what appears for him to whom it appears, and at the time when it appears, and in the manner in which it appears, and so on. And if they maintain their view but not in this way, it will soon happen that they are saying contrary things. For it is possible that the same thing may appear to be honey to the sense of sight but not to the sense of taste, and that, since we have two eyes, things will not appear the same to each if their sight is unequal. Now, as we have stated, there are some who say, for the reasons already given, that what appears is true, and that all things are therefore equally true and false, because they do not always appear the same to all men or to the same man (for they do not always happen to be the same) but often have contrary appearances at the same time. For touch says there are two objects when the fingers are crossed, but sight says there is one. And in answering these men we must say that what appears is true, but not for the same man and in the same way and at the same time, so that when these qualifications are added what appears will be true. But perhaps it is for this reason that those who argue thus, not because of some difficulty but for the sake of argument, must say that this is not true but true for this person.* **1011a18–1011b3**

4. *And, as has been said before, they must make everything relative both to opinion and to perception, so that nothing has come to be or will come to be unless someone has first formed an opinion about it. But if something has come to be or will come to be, it is evident that not all things depend on opinion.* **1011b4–7**

5. *Further, if a thing is one, it is relative to one thing or to a determinate number; and if the same thing is both half and equal, still the equal is not relative to the double or the half to the equal. If, then, in relation to the thinking subject, man and the object of thought are the same, man will not be the thinking subject but the object of thought. And if each thing is relative to the thinking subject, the thinking subject will be relative to things infinite in species.* **1011b7–12**

6. *Let this suffice, then, regarding the points under discussion: that the firmest opinion of all is the one which asserts that opposite statements are not true at the same time; the conclusions that follow for those who say that they are true; and why they speak as they do.* **1011b13–15**

7. But since it is impossible for contradictories to be true of the same subject at the same time, it is evident that contraries cannot belong to the same subject at the same time; for one of two contraries is a privation. But a privation is nothing less than the negation of substance from some determinate genus. Therefore, if it is impossible to affirm and deny something truly at the same time, it is also impossible for contraries to belong to the same subject at the same time; but either both belong in a certain respect, or the one in a certain respect and the other absolutely.

1011b15–22

COMMENTARY

708. He argues against those who adopted the above-mentioned theory not because of any reason but merely because they are obstinate; and in regard to this he does two things. First [1], he shows how these men were moved to adopt this opinion; and second [2], how this opinion must be dealt with ("But those who").

He accordingly says, first [2], that, besides the foregoing thinkers who adopted the above-mentioned opinion because of certain difficulties, there are some "among those who have been persuaded to accept these views," or opinions (i.e., those who continue to deceive themselves and have only these arguments to support their view), who raise a question. Another translation reads: "Now there are some, both of those who have been convinced by theories of this kind and of those who merely state them, who are puzzled or raise a question." And this statement means that some of those who are puzzled, i.e., some of those who hold the above-mentioned opinion, consider only these difficulties and use the arguments which are given below. For if someone says to them that in the case of contrary opinions we should believe those persons who are healthy rather than those who are ill, and those who are wise rather than those who are ignorant, and those who are awake rather than those who are asleep, they will immediately ask how it is possible to distinguish with certainty between a healthy person and a sick one, and one who is awake and one who is asleep, and one who is wise and one who is foolish. In short, regarding all differences of opinion they will ask how it is possible to decide which one of these judges rightly in each particular case; for a man may seem to be wise to some and foolish to others, and the same applies in other cases.

709. But these questions are foolish, for they are similar to the question whether we are now asleep or awake; for the distinction between all of these is not essential. Yet all of the foregoing difficulties amount to the same thing since they have a common root. For these sophists desire that demonstrative arguments should be given for all things; for it is obvious that they wanted to take some starting point which would be for them a kind of rule whereby they could distinguish between those who are healthy and those who are ill, and between those who are awake and those who are asleep. And they were not content to know this rule in just any way at all but wanted to acquire it by demonstration. That these men were in error, then, becomes evident from their actions, according to what has been said. And from these considerations it appears that their position is false; for if the judgments of one who is asleep and of one who is awake were equally good, then the same thing would result from each

judgment when men act. But this is clearly false. Another text says, "But that sometimes they are not convinced they make evident in their actions"; and this statement is the clearer one in the light of the things laid down above. For although these men maintain this view and raise such questions, still they are not deceived in their own mind so that they believe the judgment of one who is asleep and the judgment of one who is awake to be equally true. And this is clear from their actions, as has been pointed out.

710. But even though they are not deceived so as to be perplexed in this matter, this "nevertheless is characteristic of them," i.e., this weakness of mind that they should seek a demonstrative argument for things for which no demonstration can be given. For "the starting point of demonstration is not demonstration"; i.e., there can be no demonstration of it. And this is easy for them to believe, because this too is not difficult to grasp by demonstration; for a demonstrative argument proves that not all things can be demonstrated, otherwise there would be an infinite regress.

711. **But those who** [2].

He now argues against the other philosophers, i.e., against those who were not moved to maintain that all appearances are true on the grounds that no rule can be established demonstratively whereby it is possible to distinguish with certainty between those who judge rightly and those who do not, but who hold the above-mentioned theory or view only because they are insolent.

In regard to this he does three things. First (377:C 711), he shows that such insolence tends to lead to an impossible conclusion. Second [3], he indicates the way in which it seems necessary to oppose them ("Yet if not all things"). Third [4], he explains how we must meet their argument from the viewpoint of truth ("And, as has been").

He accordingly says, first [2], that those who seek "compulsion merely in words," i.e., those who are not moved by any reason or because of the difficulty involved in some problem or because of some failure in demonstration but depend solely on words and believe that they can say anything which cannot be disproved—such people as these want to argue to an impossible conclusion. For they want to adopt the principle that contraries are true at the same time on the grounds that all appearances are true.

712. **Yet if not all** [3].

Then he shows how we may oppose these men by using their own position and avoid the foregoing impossible conclusion. He says that, unless everything which is, is claimed to be relative, it cannot be said that every appearance is true. For if there are some things in the world which have absolute being and are not relative to perception or to opinion, being and appearing will not be the same; for appearing implies a relation to perception or to opinion, because that which appears appears to someone; and thus whatever is not an appearance must be true. It is clear, then, that whoever says that all appearances are true, makes all beings relative, i.e., to perception or to opinion. Hence, in opposing the foregoing sophists who seek compulsion in words, we may say that, if anyone thinks it fitting "to grant this view," i.e., to concede this opinion which they maintain, he must be careful, or observant, lest he be led to admit that contradictories are true at the same time; for it should not be said unqualifiedly that everything which appears is true, but that what appears is true for the one to whom it appears, and inasmuch as it appears, and when it appears, and in the manner in which it appears. We would be allowed to add these qualifications on the grounds that a thing does not have being in an absolute sense but only relatively.

713. Now this should be noted by those who want to adopt this position, because if someone were to grant them that every appearance is true, and thus not admit the above-mentioned qualifications, as has been stated, it would follow immediately that he is saying that contraries are true at the same time. For it is possible that the same thing may appear to be honey to the sense of sight because its color resembles that of honey, and not appear to be honey to the sense of taste because it does not taste like honey. And similarly when two eyes are unlike, the vision which is had through each is not the same, or the visual impressions which we get through each eye do not seem the same. For example, if the pupil of one eye were infected by some gross or dark vapor, and the other were free of this, all things would seem dark or obscure through the infected eye but not through the good one. I say, then, that one must be careful, or observant, because this is necessary in confronting the foregoing sophists, who say, for the reasons given above (n. 708), that every appearance is true.

714. And from this position it would also follow that all things are equally true and false, because they do not appear the same to all men or even the same to one man, since the same man very often makes contrary judgments about the same thing at the same time on the basis of different senses; for example, sight judges that thing to be one which touch judges to be two, because when the fingers are crossed it happens that the same tangible object is sensed by different organs of touch; that is, the contact through different fingers affects the tactual power as though there were two tangible objects. But it does not seem to the same man through the same sense and in the same way and at the same time that this is true, namely, that contraries are true at the same time.

715. Therefore, it is perhaps necessary to use this answer against the above-mentioned sophists who argue thus not because of some difficulty but for the sake of argument (as though upholding this statement for its own sake because they are perverse), namely, that this is not true absolutely but true for this person. For it does not follow from this that contradictories are true at the same time, because it is not contradictory that something should be true for one person and not true for another.

716. **And, as has been said** [4].

He tells us that we should oppose the foregoing sophists from the standpoint of the truth and not just offer an argument *ad hominem,* namely, not by granting the false opinion which they maintain. And he does this by means of two arguments. The first is this: as has been stated before, if everything which appears is true, they must "make all things relative," i.e., to perception or to opinion. Now from this the untenable position follows that nothing may exist or come to be if it is not thought of in some way. But if this is false (because many things are and come to be of which there is neither opinion nor knowledge, for example, things which exist in the depths of the sea or in the bowels of the earth), it is evident that not all things are relative, i.e., to perception or to opinion. Hence not every appearance is true.

717. **Further, if a thing** [5].

He gives the second argument. He says that what is one is relative only to one thing, and not to any one thing at all but to a determinate one. For example, it is clear that the half and the equal may be the same in their subject, yet the double is not said to be relative to the equal but rather to the half; but equal is said to be relative to equal. Similarly, if man himself as a thinking subject is also the object of thought, man is not relative to the thinking subject as a thinking subject, but as the object of thought. If, then, all beings are relative to a thinking subject as such, it follows that what I call the thinking subject is not one, since one is relative only to one, but it is an infinite number of things in species, since an infinite number of things are related to it. But this is impossible. Hence it cannot be said that all things are said to be relative to a thinking subject, or that everything which appears so, or is thought to be so, is therefore true.

718. **Let this suffice** [6].

He now draws his intended conclusion, and in regard to this he does two things. First, he draws his main conclusion; and second [7], he derives a corollary from it ("But since it is impossible").

He accordingly says, first [6], that it is clear from the above statement that the most certain of all opinions or views is the one which states that opposite statements or propositions, i.e., contradictory ones, are not true at the same time. And the impossible conclusions which face those who say that they are true at the same time, and the reason which moved them to say this, have also been explained.

719. **But since it is impossible** [7].

He draws the corollary. He says that, since it is impossible, from what has been said, for two contradictories to be true of the same subject at the same time, it is also evident that contraries cannot belong to the same subject; for the privative character of one of two contraries is no less evident in the case of contraries than it is in the case of other opposites, although each of two contraries is a positive reality; for it does not consist in affirmation and negation or in privation and possession. For one of them is imperfect when compared with the other, as black when compared with white, and bitter with sweet; and thus it has a kind of privation added to it. But privation is negation of substance, i.e., in some determinate subject. And it is also the deprivation of some determinate genus; for it is a negation within a genus. For not everything which does not see is said to be blind, but only that which is found in the genus of seeing things. It is clear, then, that a contrary includes privation, and that privation is a kind of negation. Hence, if it is impossible both to affirm and to deny something at the same time, it is also impossible for contraries to belong absolutely to the same subject at the same time; but either "both belong to it," i.e., relatively, as when both are present potentially or partially, or one is present in a certain respect and the other absolutely; or one is present in many and the more important parts, and the other only in some part; for example, an Ethiopian is black absolutely and white as regards his teeth.

LESSON 16
No Intermediate between Contradictories. How Heraclitus and Anaxagoras Influenced This Position

ARISTOTLE'S TEXT Chapter 7: 1011b23–1012a28

1. *Neither can there be an intermediate between contradictories, but of each subject it is necessary either to affirm or to deny one thing. This first becomes evident when people define what truth and falsity are; for to say that what is, is not, or that what is not, is, is false; and to say that what is, is, or that what is not, is not, is true. Hence he who affirms that something is or is not will say either what is true or what is false. But neither what is nor what is not is said to be or not to be.* **1011b23–29**

2. *Further, an intermediate between contradictories will be such either in the way that green is an intermediate between white and black, or as what is neither a man nor a horse is an intermediate between a man and a horse. If it is of the latter sort, there will then be no change; for change is from what is good to what is not-good, or from the latter to the former. But that this now occurs is always apparent; for change takes place only between opposites and intermediates. But if it is a true intermediate, then in this case there will be a kind of change to something white, but not from what is not-white. However, this is not now apparent.* **1011b29–1012a1**

3. *Further, the mind either affirms or denies every sensible and intelligible object. This is clear from the definition, because it expresses what is true or what is false. Indeed, when the mind composes in this way by affirming or denying, it says what is true; and when it does it otherwise, it says what is false.* **1012a2–5**

4. *Again, there must be an intermediate in addition to all contradictories, unless one is arguing for the sake of argument. In that case one will say what is neither true nor false. And then there will be something else besides being and non-being; and therefore there will also be some kind of change besides generation and corruption.* **1012a5–9**

5. *Again, there will also be an intermediate in all those classes of things in which the negation of a term implies its contrary; for example, in the class of numbers there will be a number which is neither even nor odd. But this is impossible, as is evident from the definition.* **1012a9–12**

6. *Further, there will be an infinite regress, and there will be things which are related not only as half again as much but even more. For it will also be possible to deny the intermediate both with reference to its affirmation and to its negation; and this again will be something, for its substance is something different.* **1012a12–15**

7. *Again, when one answers "no" to the question whether a thing is white, he has denied nothing except that it is; and its not-being is a negation.* **1012a15–17**

8. *Now some men have formed this opinion in the same way that other unreasonable opinions have been formed; for when they cannot refute eristic arguments, they assent to the argument and claim that the conclusion is true. Some men hold this view, then, for this reason, and others because they seek an explanation for everything.* **1012a17–21**

9. *The starting point to be used against all of these people is the definition, and the definition results from the necessity of their meaning something; for the concept, of which the word is a sign, is a definition.* **1012a21–24**

10. *Now the statement of Heraclitus, which says that all things are and are not, seems to make all things true; and the statement of Anaxagoras that there is an intermediate between contradictories seems to make everything false; for when all things are mixed together, the mixture is neither good nor not good, so that it is impossible to say anything true.* **1012a24–28**

COMMENTARY

720. Having argued dialectically against those who maintain that contradictories are true at the same time, Aristotle now argues against those who maintain that there is an intermediate between contradictories; for these thinkers do not always say that the one or the other part of a contradiction is true. In regard to this he does two things. First [1], he argues against this position. Second (Lesson 17), he argues against certain other unreasonable questions which follow from this position and from the one above ("With these points").

In regard to the first he does two things. First, he raises arguments against the position mentioned. Second [8], he gives the reason why some thinkers have been moved to hold this position ("Now some men").

In regard to the first part he gives seven arguments. He says, first [1], that, just as contradictories cannot be true at the same time, neither can there be an intermediate between contradictories, but it is necessary either to affirm or deny one or the other.

721. This first becomes evident from the definition of truth and falsity; for to say what is false is simply to say that what is, is not, or that what is not, is. And to say what is true is simply to say that what is, is, or that what is not, is not. It is clear, then, that whoever says that something is, says either what is true or what is false; and if he says what is true, it must be so, because to say what is true is to say that what is, is. And if he says what is false, it must not be so, because to say what is false is simply to say that what is, is not. The same thing applies if he says that something is not; for if he says what is false, it must be; and if he says what is true, it must not be. Therefore, either the affirmation or the negation is necessarily true. But he who holds that there is an intermediate between contradictories does not claim that it is necessary to say that what is either is or is not; nor does he claim that it is necessary to speak in this way about what is not. Thus neither he who affirms nor he who denies need say what is true or what is false.

722. **Further, an intermediate** [2].

He gives the second argument, which runs thus: an intermediate between any two contradictories can be understood in one way as something that participates in each of the extremes, and this is an intermediate in the same genus, as green or yellow is an intermediate between white and black; or in another way as something that is the negation of each extreme, and such an intermediate is different in genus; for example, a stone, which is neither a man nor a horse, is an intermediate between a man and a horse. Therefore, if there is an intermediate between contradictories, it will be such either in the first way or in the second.

723. If it is an intermediate in the second way, there will be no change. This becomes clear as follows: every change is from what is not-good to what is good, or from what is good to what is not-good. Hence, since change is between contraries, for example, white and black, change must take place between things which are opposed as contradictories; for black is not white, as is clear from the above statements. But according to the foregoing position there cannot be change from what is not-good to what is good, or the reverse. Hence there will be no change. Yet it always appears or seems

that change proceeds from what is not-good to what is good, or the reverse. That every change of this sort would be destroyed if the foregoing position is true becomes clear as follows. Change can take place only between contraries and intermediates which belong to the same genus. But there can be a change from one extreme to another only through an intermediate. Therefore, if there is an intermediate between contradictories as the negation of both, i.e., as something belonging to a different genus, it will be impossible for change to take place between an extreme and an intermediate, and therefore between one extreme and another.

724. And if it is an intermediate in the first way, so that the intermediate between contradictories belongs to the same genus by participating in both, as yellow is an intermediate between white and black, this impossible conclusion follows: there will be some process of generation which terminates in white and does not come from the not-white, because change proceeds not only from one extreme to another but also from an intermediate. But it does not seem to be true that there is any process of change terminating in the white which does not proceed from the not-white. Thus it is clear that there is no way at all in which there can be an intermediate between contradictories.

725. **Further, the mind** [3].

He gives the third argument, which runs thus: in every one of the conceptions by which the intellect knows or understands, it either affirms or denies something. Now from the definition of truth and falsity it seems that whether one affirms or denies he must say what is true or what is false; because when the intellect composes in this way, either by affirming or denying as the matter stands in reality, it expresses what is true; but when it does it otherwise, it expresses what is false. Thus it is clear that a true statement must always be either an affirmation or a negation, because some opinion must be true, and every opinion is either an affirmation or a negation. Hence it must always be either an affirmation or a negation that is true; and thus there is no intermediate between contradictories.

726. **Again, there must** [4].

Then he gives the fourth argument, which runs thus: if one maintains that there must be an intermediate between contradictories, then it is necessary to say that in the case of all contradictories there must be besides the contradictories themselves something true which is an intermediate between them, unless this person is arguing "for the sake of argument," i.e., without any real reason but only because it pleases him to speak in this way. But this cannot be true in all cases, because the true and the not-true are contradictories. Thus it would follow that there is someone who says what is neither true nor false. But the opposite of this was made clear from the definition of truth and falsity.

727. Similarly, since being and non-being are contradictories, it will follow that there is something besides being and non-being, and thus there will be some kind of change besides generation and corruption; for generation is a change to being, and corruption a change to non-being. Therefore there can be no intermediate between contradictories.

728. **Again, there will** [5].

He gives the fifth argument. He says that in some genera a negation takes the place of a contrary difference; or, according to another text, "negation supplies the contrary," because one of two contraries, which must be in the same genus, derives its definition from negation, as is clear in the case of the even and the odd, and the just and unjust. Therefore, if there is an intermediate between affirmation and negation, there will be some intermediate between all these contraries, since they obviously depend on affirmation and negation; for example, in the case of number, there will be some number which is neither even nor odd. But this is clearly impossible in the light of the definition of the even and the odd; for the even is what can be divided into equal numbers, and the odd is what cannot. Therefore it follows that there cannot be an intermediate between affirmation and negation.

729. **Further, there will** [6].

He now gives the sixth argument: those who claim that there is an intermediate between an affirmation and a negation hold some third thing besides these two, which all posit in common, saying that there is nothing intermediate between them. But three is related to two "as half again as much," i.e., in a proportion of one and a half to one. Therefore, according to the opinion of those who hold an intermediate between an affirmation and a negation it appears at first sight that all things "will be related as half again as much," i.e., in a proportion of one and a half to one to the things which are given, because there will be not only affirmations and negations but also intermediates. And this is not the only conclusion that follows, but it also follows that there will be many more things in infinite regression. For it is evident that everything which can be affirmed can also be denied. But if it is possible to affirm that the following three things exist: an affirmation, a negation and an intermediate, it is then also possible to deny these three. And just as a negation differs from an affirmation, in a similar way there will also be some fourth thing which differs from the three mentioned; for it will have a different substance and intelligible structure than those just mentioned, in the same way that a negation has a different substance and intelligible structure from an affirmation. And it is possible to deny these four, and the negations of these will be true; and so on to infinity. Hence there will be infinitely more things than have just been posited. This seems absurd.

730. **Again, when one** [7].

He gives the seventh argument, and it runs as follows: if someone were to ask whether a man or some other thing is white, the one answering him must say either "yes" or "no." If he says "yes," it is plain that he says that the affirmation is true; but if he does not affirm this but says "no," it is clear that he denies this. Now the only thing which he denies is what he was asked, and the negation of this is non-being because it is negative. Therefore it follows that, when he answers this question, he must of necessity either admit the affirmative or assert the negative. Hence there is no intermediate between these two.

731. **Now some men** [8].

He gives the reason why some men adopt this opinion, and in regard to this he does three things. First, he shows why some men have held this opinion. Second [9], he explains how one can argue dialectically against them ("The starting point"). Third [10], he notes the philosophical views on which the foregoing opinions depend ("Now the statement").

He accordingly says, first [8], that

the foregoing opinion, like other unreasonable opinions, is adopted by certain thinkers for one of two reasons. The first is this: when some men cannot refute "eristic arguments," i.e., disputatious or sophistical arguments, which are presented to them either by others or by themselves, they agree with the one giving the argument and assent to the conclusion, saying that what has been shown is true. And then they try to confirm this by devising other arguments.

732. The second reason why men adopt this position is that some men want to discover an argument to prove everything, and therefore whatever cannot be proved they do not want to affirm but deny. But first principles, which are the common conceptions of all men, cannot be proved. Hence these men deny them and thereby adopt unreasonable views.

733. **The starting point** [9].

He indicates the starting point from which one must proceed to argue against such opinions. He says that the starting point is derived from the definitions of truth and falsity, or from the definitions of other terms, as is clear from the arguments given above. For men must admit the definitions of things if they hold that words signify something; for the intelligible expression of a thing which a word signifies is a thing's definition. But if they do not admit that all words signify something, they do not differ from plants, as has been said above (n. 652).

734. **Now the statement** [10].

Here he gives the opinion on which the foregoing opinions depend. He says that these opinions stem from the position of Heraclitus, who said that all things are in motion, and therefore that they both are and are not at the same time. And since what is being moved has non-being mixed with being, it follows that everything is true.

735. And from the position of Anaxagoras it follows that there is an intermediate between contradictories; for he held that everything is mixed with everything, because everything comes from everything. But neither of the extremes can be predicated of the mixture; for example, intermediate colors are neither whiteness or blackness. Hence the mixture is neither good nor not-good, neither white nor not-white; and thus there is an intermediate between contradictories. It follows, then, that everything is false; for according to the common opinion we posit nothing but affirmation and negation. Hence, if both an affirmation and its negation are false, it follows that everything is false.

LESSON 17

Rejection of the Opinions that Everything Is True and False, and that Everything Is at Rest and in Motion

ARISTOTLE'S TEXT Chapter 8: 1012a29–1012b31

1. *With these points settled it is evident that the theories which have been expressed univocally and about all things cannot be true as some affirm them to be. Now some say that nothing is true (for they say that there is nothing to prevent all statements from being like the statement that the diagonal of a square is commensurable with one of its sides), and others say that everything is true. These views are almost the same as that of Heraclitus; for he who says that all things are true and all false admits both views apart from his own words. Hence, if those are impossible, these also must be impossible.* **1012a29–1012b2**

2. *Further, it is evident that there are contradictories which cannot be true at the same time. Nor can they all be false, though this would seem more possible from what has been said.* **1012b2–4**

3. *But in opposing all such views it is necessary to postulate, as has been stated in the above discussion, not that something is or is not, but that a word signifies something. Hence it is necessary to argue from a definition, once we have accepted what truth and falsity mean. But if to say what is true is merely to deny what is false, not everything can be false. For one part of a contradiction must be true.* **1012b5–11**

4. *Again, if everything must be either affirmed or denied, both cannot be false; for one part of a contradiction is false.* **1012b11–13**

5. *And the view commonly expressed applies to all such theories—they destroy themselves; for he who says that everything is true makes the contrary of his own statement true, and thus makes his own not true; for the contrary denies that it is true. And he who says that everything is false makes his own statement false. But if the former makes an exception of the contrary statement, saying that it alone is not true, and the latter makes an exception of his own statement, saying that it is not false, still they will have to consider the truth and falsity of an infinite number of statements. For he who says that a true statement is true is right; and this process will go on to infinity.* **1012b13–22**

6. *Now it is evident that those who say that all things are at rest do not speak the truth, and neither do those who say that all things are in motion.* **1012b22–24**

7. *For if all things are at rest, the same thing will always be true and false; but this seems to be something that changes, for he who makes a statement at one time was not and again will not be.* **1012b24–26**

8. *And if all things are in motion, nothing will be true, and so everything will be false. But it has been shown that this is impossible.* **1012b26–28**

9. *Further, it must be some being which is changed; for change is from something to something.* **1012b28–29**

10. *But it is not true that all things are at rest or in motion sometimes, and nothing always; for there is something which always moves the things that are being moved, and the first mover is itself immovable.* **1012b28–31**

COMMENTARY

736. He argues dialectically against certain positions which stem from those mentioned above. First [1], he argues against certain men who destroy the principles of logic; and second [6], against certain men who

destroy the principles of natural philosophy ("Now it is evident").

For first philosophy should argue dialectically against those who deny the principles of the particular sciences, because all principles are based on the principle that an affirmation and a negation are not true at the same time, and that there is no intermediate between them. Now these principles are the most specific principles of this science, since they depend on the concept of being, which is the primary subject of this branch of philosophy. But the true and the false belong specifically to the study of logic; for they depend on the kind of being which is found in the mind, with which logic deals; for truth and falsity exist in the mind, as is stated in Book VI of this work (see n. 1231). Motion and rest, on the other hand, belong properly to the study of natural philosophy, because nature is defined as a principle of motion and of rest. Now the error made about truth and falsity is a result of the error made about being and nonbeing, for truth and falsity are defined by means of being and non-being, as has been said above. For there is truth when one says that what is, is, or that what is not, is not; and falsity is defined in the opposite way. And similarly the error made about rest and motion is a result of the error made about being and non-being; for what is in motion as such does not yet exist, whereas what is at rest already is. Hence, when the errors made about being and non-being have been removed, the errors made about truth and falsity and rest and motion will then also be removed.

737. Regarding the first part of this division he does two things. First [1], he gives the erroneous opinions about truth and falsity. Second [2], he criticizes these opinions ("Further, it is evident").

Thus he says [1] that, "with these points settled," i.e., with the foregoing points established which have to be used against the paradoxical positions mentioned above, it is obviously impossible that the views of some men should be true, namely, that we must form an opinion "univocally," i.e., think in the same way, about all things, so that we should say that all things are equally true or equally false. For some thinkers said that nothing is true but everything false, and that there is nothing to prevent us from saying that all statements are just as false as the statement (which is false) that the diameter of a square is commensurate with one of its sides. But others have said that all things are true. Statements of the latter kind are a result of the opinion of Heraclitus, as has been pointed out (n. 684); for he said that a thing is and is not at the same time, and from this it follows that everything is true.

738. And lest perhaps someone might say that besides these opinions there is also a third one, which states that everything is both true and false at the same time, he replies, as though meeting a tacit objection, that anyone who maintains this opinion also maintains both of the foregoing ones. Hence, if the first two opinions are impossible, the third must also be impossible.

739. **Further, it is evident** [2].

Then he presents arguments against the foregoing opinions, and the first of these is as follows: it is evident that there are certain contradictories which cannot be true at the same time or false at the same time, for example, the true and not-true, being and non-being. This can be better understood from what has been said. Therefore, if one of these two contradictories must be false and the other true, not all things can be true or all false.

740. **But in opposing** [3].

He gives the second argument. He says that in opposing "these views," or positions, "it is necessary to postulate," or request, not that someone should admit that something either is or is not in reality, as has been stated above (n. 611), because this seems to be begging the question, but that he should admit that a word signifies something. Now if this is not granted, the dispute comes to an end; but if it is granted, it is then necessary to give definitions, as has already been stated above (*ibid.*). Hence we must argue against these thinkers by proceeding from definitions, and in the case of the present thesis we must do this especially by considering the definition of falsity. Now if truth consists merely in affirming what it is false to deny, and vice versa, it follows that not all statements can be false, because either the affirmation or the negation of something must be true. For obviously truth consists simply in saying that what is, is, or in saying that what is not, is not; and falsity consists in saying that what is, is not, or in saying that what is not, is. Hence it is clear that it is true to say that that is of which it is false that it is not, or to say that that is not of which it is false that it is; and it is false to say that that is of which it is true that it is not, or to say that that is not of which it is true that it is. Thus from the definition of truth and falsity it is clear that not all things are false. And for the same reason it is clear that not all things are true.

741. **Again, if everything** [4].

Here he gives the third argument, which runs thus: it is clear from what has been said above that we must either affirm or deny something of each thing since there is no intermediate between contradictories. It is impossible, then, for everything to be false. And by the same reasoning it is proved that it is impossible for everything to be true, i.e., by reason of the fact that it is impossible both to affirm and to deny something at the same time.

742. **And the view** [5].

He gives the fourth argument: all of the foregoing statements, or opinions, face this unreasonable result—they destroy themselves. This is "the view commonly expressed," i.e., a frequently heard statement made by all; and thus another text says, "It happens that it is commonly held." He proves this view as follows: anyone who says that everything is true makes the contrary of his own opinion true. But the contrary of his own opinion is that his own opinion is not true. Therefore he who says that everything is true says that his own opinion is not true; and thus he destroys his own opinion. Similarly it is evident that he who says that everything is false also says that his own opinion is false.

743. And because someone could say that he who claims that everything is true makes an exception of the one contrary to his own statement, or bars it from what holds universally (and the same thing applies to one who says that everything is false), he therefore rejects this answer. He says that, if the one who says that everything is true makes his own contrary opinion an exception, saying that it alone is not true, and if the one who says that everything is false makes his own opinion an exception, saying that it alone is not false, none the less it follows that they will be able "to consider," or bring forward, an infinite

number of true statements against those who hold that all are false, and an infinite number of false statements against those who hold that all are true. For granted that one opinion is true, it follows that an infinite number are true. And granted that one opinion is false, it follows that an infinite number are false. For if the position, or opinion, that Socrates is sitting is true, then the opinion that it is true that Socrates is sitting will also be true, and so on to infinity. For he who says that a true statement is true is always right; and he who says that a false statement is true is always wrong; and this can proceed to infinity.

744. **Now it is** [6].

He argues against those who destroy the principles of nature, i.e., motion and rest, and in regard to this he does three things.

First, he mentions the falsity of these opinions, saying that it is evident, from what has been said above, that neither the opinion which states that everything is in motion, nor the one which states that everything is at rest, is true.

745. **For if all things** [7].

Second, he shows that these opinions are false. First of all he shows that the opinion which holds that everything is at rest is false; for if everything were at rest, nothing would then be changed from the state in which it sometimes is. Hence, whatever is true would always be true, and whatever is false would always be false. But this seems to be absurd; for the truth and falsity of a proposition is changeable. Nor is this to be wondered at, because the man who has an opinion or makes a statement at one time was not and now is and again will not be.

746. Second, he uses two arguments to show that the opinion which holds that all things are in motion is false. He gives the first [8] where he says, "And if all things." It is as follows. If all things are in motion and nothing is at rest, nothing will be true in the world; for what is true already exists, but what is in motion does not yet exist. Hence everything must be false. But this is impossible, as has been shown (n. 740).

747. **Further, it must be** [9].

He gives the second argument, and it runs thus: everything that is undergoing change is necessarily a being, because everything that is being changed is being changed from something to something else, and everything that is being changed in something else belongs to the subject that is undergoing change. Hence it is not necessary to say that everything in the subject undergoing change is being changed, but that there is something which remains. Hence not everything is in motion.

748. **But it is not** [10].

He gives the third argument, and it disposes of a false opinion which could arise from what has been said above. For, since not all things are in motion nor all at rest, someone could therefore think that all things are sometimes in motion and sometimes at rest. In disposing of this opinion he says that, it is not true that all things are sometimes in motion and sometimes at rest, for there are certain movable things which are always being moved, namely, the celestial bodies above us, and there is a mover, namely, the first, which is always immovable and ever in the same state, as has been proved in Book VIII of the *Physics*.*[258b5]*

BOOK V
LEXICON OF PHILOSOPHICAL TERMS

LESSON 1
Five Senses of the Term "Principle." The Common Definition of Principle

ARISTOTLE'S TEXT Chapter 1: 1012b34–1013a23

1. *In one sense the term principle [beginning or starting point] means that from which someone first moves something; for example, in the case of a line or a journey, if the motion is from here, this is the principle, but if the motion is in the opposite direction, this is something different. In another sense principle means that from which a thing best comes into being, as the starting point of instruction; for sometimes it is not from what is first or from the starting point of the thing that one must begin, but from that from which one learns most readily. Again, principle means that first inherent thing from which something is brought into being, as the keel of a ship and the foundation of a house, and as some suppose the heart to be the principle in animals, and others the brain, and others anything else of the sort. In another sense it means that non-inherent first thing from which something comes into being; and that from which motion and change naturally first begins, as a child comes from its father and mother, and a fight from abusive language. In another sense principle means that according to whose will movable things are moved and changeable things are changed; in states, for example, princely, magistral, imperial, or tyrannical power are all principles. And so also are the arts, especially the architectonic arts, called principles. And that from which a thing can first be known is also called a principle of that thing, as the postulates of demonstrations. And causes are also spoken of in the same number of senses, for all causes are principles.* **1012b34–1013a17**

2. *Therefore, it is common to all principles to be the first thing from which a thing either is, comes to be, or is known. And of these some are intrinsic and others extrinsic. And for this reason nature is a principle, and so also is an element, and mind, purpose, substance, and the final cause; for good and evil are the principles both of the knowledge and motion of many things.* **1013a17–23**

COMMENTARY

749. Having established in the preceding book the things which pertain to the consideration of this science, here the Philosopher begins to deal with the things which this science considers.

And since the attributes considered in this science are common to all things, they are not predicated of various things univocally but in a prior and subsequent way, as has been stated in Book IV (see n. 535). Therefore, first [1], he distinguishes the meanings of the terms which come under the consideration of this science. Second [2], he begins to deal with the things which come under the consideration of this science. He does this in the sixth book, which begins with the words, "The principles."

Now since it is the office of each science to consider both its subject and the properties and causes of its subject, this fifth book is accordingly divided into three parts. First, he establishes the various senses of the terms which signify causes; second (Lesson 7), the various senses of the terms which signify the subject or parts of the subject of this science ("The term *one*"); and third (Lesson 18), the various senses of the terms which signify the properties of being as being ("That thing").

The first part is divided into two

members. First, he distinguishes the various senses in which the term *cause* is used. Second (Lesson 6), he explains the meaning of a term which signifies something associated with a cause—the term *necessary;* for a cause is that on which something else follows of necessity ("*Necessary* means").

The first part is divided into two members. First, he distinguishes the various senses of the terms which signify cause in a general way. Second (Lesson 5), he gives the meaning of a term which signifies a special kind of cause, i.e., the term *nature* ("*Nature* means").

750. The first part is divided into three members. First, he gives the various meanings of the term *principle;* second (Lesson 2), of the term *cause* ("In one sense the term *cause*"); and third (Lesson 4), of the term *element* ("The inherent principle").

He follows this order because the term principle is more common than the term cause, for something may be a principle and not be a cause; for example, the principle of motion is said to be the point from which motion begins. Again, a cause is found in more things than an element is, for only an intrinsic cause can be called an element.

In regard to the first he does two things. First [1], he gives the meanings of the term principle. Second [2], he reduces all of these to one common notion ("Therefore, it is common").

751. Now it should be noted that, although a principle and a cause are the same in subject, they nevertheless differ in meaning; for the term principle implies an order or sequence, whereas the term cause implies some influence on the being of the thing caused. Now an order of priority and posteriority is found in different things; but according to what is first known by us order is found in local motion, because that kind of motion is more evident to the senses. Further, order is found in three classes of things, one of which is naturally associated with the other, i.e., continuous quantity, motion and time. For insofar as there is priority and posteriority in continuous quantity, there is priority and posteriority in motion; and insofar as there is priority and posteriority in motion, there is priority and posteriority in time, as is stated in Book IV of the *Physics. [219a14]* Therefore, because a principle is said to be what is first in any order, and the order which is considered according to priority and posteriority in continuous quantity is first known by us (and things are named by us insofar as they are known to us), for this reason the term principle, properly considered, designates what is first in a continuous quantity over which motion passes. Hence he says that a principle is said to be "that from which someone first moves something," i.e., any part of a continuous quantity from which local motion begins. Or, according to another reading, "Some part of a thing from which motion will first begin"; i.e., some part of a thing from which it first begins to be moved; for example in the case of a line and in that of any kind of journey the principle is the point from which motion begins. But the opposite or contrary point is "something different or other," i.e., the end or terminus. It should also be noted that a principle of motion and a principle of time belong to this class for the reason just given.

752. But because motion does not always begin from the starting point of a continuous quantity but from that part from which the motion of each

thing begins most readily, he therefore gives a second meaning of principle, saying that we speak of a principle of motion in another way "as that from which a thing best comes into being," i.e., the point from which each thing begins to be moved most easily. He makes this clear by an example; for in the disciplines one does not always begin to learn from something that is a beginning in an absolute sense and by nature, but from that from which one "is able to learn" most readily, i.e., from those things which are better known to us, even though they are sometimes more remote by their nature.

753. Now this sense of principle differs from the first. For in the first sense a principle of motion gets its name from the starting point of a continuous quantity, whereas here the principle of continuous quantity gets its name from the starting point of motion. Hence in the case of those motions which are over circular continuous quantities and have no starting point, the principle is also considered to be the point from which the movable body is best or most fittingly moved according to its nature. For example, in the case of the first thing moved [the first sphere] the starting point is in the east. The same thing is true in the case of our own movements; for a man does not always start to move from the beginning of a road but sometimes from the middle or from any terminus at all from which it is convenient for him to start moving.

754. Now from the order considered in local motion we come to know the order in other motions. And for this reason we have the senses of principle based upon the principle of generation or coming to be of things. But this is taken in two ways; for it is either "inherent," i.e., intrinsic, or "non-inherent," i.e., extrinsic.

755. In the first way, then, a principle means that part of a thing which is first generated and from which the generation of the thing begins; for example, in the case of a ship the first thing to come into being is the base or keel, which is in a certain sense the foundation on which the whole superstructure of the ship is raised. And, similarly, in the case of a house the first thing that comes into being is the foundation. And in the case of an animal the first thing that comes into being, according to some, is the heart, and according to others, the brain or some such member of the body. For an animal is distinguished from a non-animal by reason of sensation and motion. Now the principle of motion appears to be in the heart, and sensory operations are most evident in the brain. Hence those who considered an animal from the viewpoint of motion held that the heart is the principle in the generation of an animal. But those who considered an animal only from the viewpoint of the senses held that the brain is this principle; yet the first principle of sensation is also in the heart even though the operations of the senses are completed in the brain. And those who considered an animal from the viewpoint of operation, or according to some of its activities, held that the organ which is naturally disposed for that operation, as the liver or some other such part is the first part which is generated in an animal. But according to the view of the Philosopher the first part is the heart because all of the soul's powers are diffused throughout the body by means of the heart.

756. In the second way, a principle means that from which a thing's process of generation begins but which is

outside the thing. This is made clear in the case of three classes of things. The first is that of natural beings, in which the principle of generation is said to be the first thing from which motion naturally begins in those things which come about through motion (as those which come about through alteration or through some similar kind of motion; for example, a man is said to become large or white); or that from which a complete change begins (as in the case of those things which are not a result of motion but come into being through mutation alone). This is evident in the case of substantial generation; for example, a child comes from its father and mother, who are its principles, and a fight from abusive language, which stirs the souls of men to quarrel.

757. The second class in which this is made clear is that of human acts, whether ethical or political, in which that by whose will or intention others are moved or changed is called a principle. Thus those who hold civil, imperial, or even tyrannical power in states are said to have the principal places; for it is by their will that all things come to pass or are put into motion in states. Those men are said to have civil power who are put in command of particular offices in states, as judges and persons of this kind. Those are said to have imperial power who govern everyone without exception, as kings. And those hold tyrannical power who through violence and disregard for law keep royal power within their grip for their own benefit.

758. He gives as the third class things made by art; for the arts too in a similar way are called principles of artificial things, because the motion necessary for producing an artifact begins from an art. And of these arts the architectonic, which "derive their name" from the word principle, i.e., those called principal arts, are said to be principles in the highest degree. For by architectonic arts we mean those which govern subordinate arts, as the art of the navigator governs the art of ship-building, and the military art governs the art of horsemanship.

759. Again, in likeness to the order considered in external motions a certain order may also be observed in our apprehensions of things, and especially insofar as our act of understanding, by proceeding from principles to conclusions, bears a certain resemblance to motion. Therefore in another way that is said to be a principle from which a thing first becomes known; for example, we say that "postulates," i.e., axioms and assumptions, are principles of demonstrations.

760. Causes are also said to be principles in these ways, "for all causes are principles." For the motion that terminates in a thing's being begins from some cause, although it is not designated a cause and a principle from the same point of view, as was pointed out above (n. 751).

761. **Therefore, it is** [2].

Then he reduces all of the above-mentioned senses of principle to one that is common. He says that all of the foregoing senses have something in common inasmuch as that is said to be a principle which comes first either with reference to a thing's being (as the first part of a thing is said to be a principle) or with reference to its coming to be (as the first mover is said to be a principle) or with reference to the knowing of it.

762. But while all principles agree in the respect just mentioned, they nevertheless differ, because some are intrin-

sic and others extrinsic, as is clear from the above. Hence nature and element, which are intrinsic, can be principles—nature as that from which motion begins, and element as the first part in a thing's generation. "And mind," i.e., intellect, and "purpose," i.e., a man's intention, are said to be principles as extrinsic ones. Again, "a thing's substance," i.e., its form, which is its principle of being, is called an intrinsic principle, since a thing has being by its form. Again, according to what has been said, that for the sake of which something comes to be is said to be one of its principles. For the good, which has the character of an end in the case of pursuing, and evil in that of shunning, are principles of the knowledge and motion of many things; that is, all those which are done for the sake of some end. For in the realm of nature, in that of moral acts, and in that of artifacts, demonstrations make special use of the final cause.

LESSON 2

The Four Classes of Causes. Several Causes of the Same Effect. Causes May Be Causes of Each Other. Contraries Have the Same Cause

ARISTOTLE'S TEXT Chapter 2: 1013a24–1013b16

1. In one sense the term cause means that from which, as something intrinsic, a thing comes to be, as the bronze of a statue and the silver of a goblet, and the genera of these. In another sense it means the form and pattern of a thing, i.e., the intelligible expression of the quiddity and its genera (for example, the ratio of 2:1 and number in general are the cause of an octave chord) and the parts which are included in the intelligible expression. Again, that from which the first beginning of change or of rest comes is a cause; for example, an adviser is a cause, and a father is the cause of a child, and in general a maker is a cause of the thing made, and a changer a cause of the thing changed. Further, a thing is a cause inasmuch as it is an end, i.e., that for the sake of which something is done; for example, health is the cause of walking. For if we are asked why someone took a walk, we answer, "in order to be healthy"; and in saying this we think we have given the cause. And whatever occurs on the way to the end under the motion of something else is also a cause. For example, reducing, purging, drugs and instruments are causes of health; for all of these exist for the sake of the end, although they differ from each other inasmuch as some are instruments and others are processes. These, then, are nearly all the ways in which causes are spoken of. **1013a24–1013b4**

2. And since there are several senses in which causes are spoken of, it turns out that there are many causes of the same thing, and not in an accidental way. For example, both the maker of a statue and the bronze are causes of a statue not in any other respect but insofar as it is a statue. However, they are not causes in the same way, but the one as matter and the other as the source of motion. **1013b4–9**

3. And there are things which are causes of each other. Pain, for example, is a cause of health, and health is a cause of pain, although not in the same way, but one as an end and the other as a source of motion. **1013b9–11**

4. Further, the same thing is sometimes the cause of contraries; for that which when present is the cause of some particular thing, this when absent we sometimes blame for the contrary. Thus the cause of the loss of a ship is the absence of the pilot whose presence is the cause of the ship's safety. And both of these—the absence and the presence—are moving causes. **1013b9–16**

COMMENTARY

763. Here the Philosopher distinguishes the various senses in which the term *cause* is used; and in regard to this he does two things. First [1], he enumerates the classes of causes. Second (Lesson 3, n 783), he gives the modes of causes ("Now the modes").

In regard to the first part he does two things. First, he enumerates the various classes of causes. Second (Lesson 3), he reduces them to four ("All the causes").

In regard to the first part he does two things. First, he enumerates the different classes of causes. Second [2], he clarifies certain things about the classes of causes ("And since").

He accordingly says, first [1], that in one sense the term cause means that from which a thing comes to be and is "something intrinsic," i.e., something which exists within the thing. This is said to distinguish it from a privation and also from a contrary; for a thing is said to come from a privation or from a contrary as from something which is not intrinsic; for example, white is said to come from black or from not-white. But a statue comes from bronze and a goblet from silver as from something which is intrinsic; for the nature bronze is not destroyed when a statue comes into being, nor is the nature silver destroyed when a goblet comes into being. Therefore the bronze of a statue and the silver of a goblet are causes in the sense of matter. He adds "and the genera of these," because if matter is the species of anything it is also its genus. For example, if the matter of a statue is bronze, its matter will also be metal, compound and body. The same holds true of other things.

764. In another sense cause means the form and pattern of a thing, i.e., its exemplar. This is the formal cause, which is related to a thing in two ways. In one way it stands as the intrinsic form of a thing, and in this respect it is called the formal principle of a thing. In another way it stands as something which is extrinsic to a thing but is that in likeness to which it is made, and in this respect an exemplar is also called a thing's form. It is in this sense that Plato held the Ideas to be forms. Moreover, because it is from its form that each thing derives its nature, whether of its genus or of its species, and the nature of its genus or of its species is what is signified by the definition, which expresses its quiddity, the form of a thing is therefore the intelligible expression of its quiddity, i.e., the formula by which its quiddity is known. For even though certain material parts are given in the definition, still it is from a thing's form that the principal part of the definition comes. The reason why the form is a cause, then, is that it completes the intelligible expression of a thing's quiddity. And just as the genus of a particular matter is also matter, in a similar way the genera of forms are the forms of things; for example, the form of the octave chord is the ratio of 2:1. For when two notes stand to each other in the ratio of 2:1, the interval between them is one octave. Hence twoness is its form; for the ratio of 2:1 derives its meaning from twoness. And because number is the genus of twoness, we may therefore say in a general way that number is also the form of the octave, inasmuch as we may say that the octave chord involves the ratio of one number to another. And not only is the whole definition related to the thing defined as its form, but so also are the parts of the definition, i.e., those which are given directly in the definition. For just as two-footed animal capable of walking is the form of man, so also are animal, capable of walking and two-footed. But sometimes matter is given indirectly in the definition, as when the soul is said to be the actuality of a physical organic body having life potentially.

765. In a third sense cause means that from which the first beginning of change or of rest comes, i.e., a moving or efficient cause. He says "of change or of rest," because motion and rest which are natural are traced back to the same cause, and the same is true of motion and of rest which are a result of force. For that cause by which something is moved to a place is the same as that by which it is made to rest there. "An adviser" is an example of this kind of cause, for it is as a result of an adviser that motion begins in the one who acts upon his advice for the sake of safeguarding something. And in a similar way "a father is the cause of a child." In these two examples Aristotle touches upon the two principles of motion from which all things come to be,

namely, purpose in the case of an adviser, and nature in the case of a father. And in general every maker is a cause of the thing made and every changer a cause of the thing changed.

766. Moreover, it should be noted that according to Avicenna [*Sufficientia*, I, 10] there are four modes of efficient cause, namely, perfective, dispositive, auxiliary and advisory.

An efficient cause is said to be perfective inasmuch as it causes the final perfection of a thing, as the one who induces a substantial form in natural things or artificial forms in things made by art, as a builder induces the form of a house.

767. An efficient cause is said to be dispositive if it does not induce the final form that perfects a thing but only prepares the matter for that form, as one who hews timbers and stones is said to build a house. This cause is not properly said to be the efficient cause of a house, because what he produces is only potentially a house. But he will be more properly an efficient cause if he induces the ultimate disposition on which the form necessarily follows; for example, man generates man without causing his intellect, which comes from an extrinsic cause.

768. And an efficient cause is said to be auxiliary insofar as it contributes to the principal effect. Yet it differs from the principal efficient cause in that the principal efficient cause acts for its own end, whereas an auxiliary cause acts for an end which is not its own. For example, one who assists a king in war acts for the king's end. And this is the way in which a secondary cause is disposed for a primary cause. For in the case of all efficient causes which are directly subordinated to each other, a secondary cause acts because of the end of a primary cause; for example, the military art acts because of the end of the political art.

769. And an advisory cause differs from a principal efficient cause inasmuch as it specifies the end and form of the activity. This is the way in which the first agent acting by intellect is related to every secondary agent, whether it be natural or intellectual. For in every case a first intellectual agent gives to a secondary agent its end and its form of activity; for example, the naval architect gives these to the shipwright, and the first intelligence does the same thing for everything in the natural world.

770. Further, to this genus of cause is reduced everything that makes anything to be in any manner whatsoever, not only as regards substantial being, but also as regards accidental being, which occurs in every kind of motion. Hence he says not only that the maker is the cause of the thing made, but also that the changer is the cause of the thing changed.

771. In a fourth sense cause means a thing's end, i.e., that for the sake of which something is done, as health is the cause of walking. And since it is less evident that the end is a cause in view of the fact that it comes into being last of all (which is also the reason why this cause was overlooked by the earlier philosophers, as was pointed out in Book I [see n. 177], he therefore gives a special proof that an end is a cause. For to ask why or for what reason is to ask about a cause, because when we are asked why or for what reason someone walks, we reply properly by answering that he does so in order to be healthy. And when we answer in this way we think that we are stating the cause. Hence it is evident that the end is a cause. Moreover, not only the ultimate reason for which an agent acts

is said to be an end with respect to those things which precede it, but everything that is intermediate between the first agent and the ultimate end is also said to be an end with respect to the preceding agents. And similarly those things are said to be causes from which motion arises in subsequent things. For example, between the art of medicine, which is the first efficient cause in this order, and health, which is the ultimate end, there are these intermediates: reducing, which is the most proximate cause of health in those who have a superfluity of humors; purging, by means of which reducing is brought about; "drugs," i.e., laxative medicine, by means of which purging is accomplished; and "instruments," i.e., the instruments by which medicine or drugs are prepared and administered. And all such things exist for the sake of the end, although one of them is the end of another. For reducing is the end of purging, and purging is the end of purgatives. However, these intermediates differ from each other in that some are instruments, i.e., the instruments by means of which medicine is prepared and administered (and the administered medicine itself is something which nature employs as an instrument); and some—purging and reducing—are processes, i.e., operations or activities.

772. He concludes, then, that "these are the ways in which causes are spoken of [1]," i.e., the four ways; and he adds "nearly all" because of the modes of causes which he gives below. Or he also adds this because the same classes of causes are not found for the same reason in all things.

773. **And since** [2].

Then he indicates certain points which follow from the things said above about the causes, and there are four of these. The first is that, since the term cause is used in many senses, there may be several causes of one thing not accidentally but properly. For the fact that there are many causes of one thing accidentally presents no difficulty, because many things may be accidents of something that is the proper cause of some effect, and all of these can be said to be accidental causes of that effect. But that there are several proper causes of one thing becomes evident from the fact that causes are spoken of in various ways. For the maker of a statue is a proper cause and not an accidental cause of a statue, and so also is the bronze, but not in the same way. For it is impossible that there should be many proper causes of the same thing within the same genus and in the same order, although there can be many causes providing that one is proximate and another remote; or that neither of them is of itself a sufficient cause, but both together. An example would be many men rowing a boat. Now in the case in point these two things are causes of a statue in different ways: the bronze as matter, and the artist as efficient cause.

774. **And there are** [3].

Then he sets down the second fact that may be drawn from the foregoing discussion. He says that it may also happen that any two things may be the cause of each other, although this is impossible in the same class of cause. But it is evident that this may happen when causes are spoken of in different senses. For example, the pain resulting from a wound is a cause of health as an efficient cause or source of motion, whereas health is the cause of pain as an end. For it is impossible that a thing should be both a cause and something caused. Another text states this better, saying that "exercise is the cause of physical fitness," i.e., of the good disposition caused by moderate exercise, which promotes digestion and uses up superfluous humors.

775. Now it must be borne in mind that, although four causes are given above, two of these are related to one another, and so also are the other two. The efficient cause is related to the final cause, and the material cause is related to the formal cause. The efficient cause is related to the final cause because the efficient cause is the starting point of motion and the final cause is its terminus. There is a similar relationship between matter and form. For form gives being, and matter receives it. Hence the efficient cause is the cause of the final cause, and the final cause is the cause of the efficient cause. The efficient cause is the cause of the final cause inasmuch as it makes the final cause be, because by causing motion the efficient cause brings about the final cause. But the final cause is the cause of the efficient cause, not in the sense that it makes it be, but inasmuch as it is the reason for the causality of the efficient cause. For an efficient cause is a cause inasmuch as it acts, and it acts only because of the final cause. Hence the efficient cause derives its causality from the final cause. And form and matter are mutual causes of being: form is a cause of matter inasmuch as it gives actual being to matter, and matter is a cause of form inasmuch as it supports form in being. And I say that both of these together are causes of being either in an unqualified sense or with some qualification. For substantial form gives being absolutely to matter, whereas accidental form, inasmuch as it is a form, gives being in a qualified sense. And matter sometimes does not support a form in being in an unqualified sense but according as it is the form of this particular thing and has being in this particular thing. This is what happens in the case of the human body in relation to the rational soul.

776. **Further, the same thing** [4].

Then he gives the third conclusion that may be drawn from the foregoing discussion. He says that the same thing can be the cause of contraries. This would also seem to be difficult or impossible if it were related to both in the same way. But it is the cause of each in a different way. For that which when present is the cause of some particular thing, this when absent "we blame," i.e., we hold it responsible, "for the contrary." For example, it is evident that by his presence the pilot is the cause of a ship's safety, and we say that his absence is the cause of the ship's loss. And lest someone might think that this is to be attributed to different classes of causes, just as the preceding two were, he therefore adds that both of these may be reduced to the same class of cause—the moving cause. For the opposite of a cause is the cause of an opposite effect in the same line of causality as that in which the original cause was the cause of its effect.

LESSON 3
All Causes Reduced to Four Classes

ARISTOTLE'S TEXT Chapter 2: 1013b16–1014a25

1. All the causes mentioned fall under one of the four classes which are most evident. For the elements of syllables, the matter of things made by art, fire and earth and all such elements of bodies, the parts of a whole, and the premises of a conclusion, are all causes in the sense of that from which things are made. But of these some are causes as a subject, for example, parts, and others as the essence, for example, the whole, the composition and the species, whereas the seed, the physician, the adviser, and in general every agent, are all sources of change or of rest. But the others are causes as the end and the good of other things. For that for the sake of which other things come to be is the greatest good and the end of other things. And it makes no difference whether we say that it is a good or an apparent good. These, then, are the causes, and this the number of their classes. **1013b16–29**

2. Now the modes of causes are many in number, but these become fewer when summarized. For causes are spoken of in many senses; and of those which belong to the same class, some are prior and some subsequent. For example, both the physician and one possessing an art are causes of health, and both the ratio of 2:1 and number are causes of the octave chord; and always those classes which contain singulars. Further, a thing may be a cause in the sense of an accident, and the classes which contain these; for example, in one sense the cause of a statue is Polyclitus and in another a sculptor, because it is accidental that a sculptor should be Polyclitus. And the universals which contain accidents are causes; for example, man is the cause of a statue, and even generally animal, because Polyclitus is a man and an animal. And of accidental causes some are more remote and some more proximate than others. Thus what is white and what is musical might be said to be the causes of a statue, and not just Polyclitus or man. Again, in addition to all of these, i.e., both proper causes and accidental causes, some are said to be causes potentially and some actually, as a builder and one who is building. And the distinctions which have been made will apply in like manner to the effects of these causes, for example, to this statue, or to a statue, or to an image generally, or to this bronze, or to bronze, or to matter in general. And the same applies to accidental effects. Again, both proper and accidental causes may be spoken of together, so that the cause of a statue may be referred to as neither Polyclitus nor a sculptor but the sculptor Polyclitus. But while all these varieties of causes are six in number, each is spoken of in two ways; for causes are either singular or generic; either proper or accidental, or generically accidental; or they are spoken of in combination or singly; and again they are either active or potential causes. But they differ in this respect, that active causes, i.e., singular causes, exist or cease to exist simultaneously with their effects, as this particular one who is healing with this particular person who is being healed, and as this particular builder with this particular thing which is being built. But this is not always true of potential causes; for the builder and the thing built do not cease to exist at the same time. **1013b29–1014a25**

COMMENTARY

777. Here the philosopher reduces all causes to the classes of causes mentioned above [1], saying that all those things which are called causes fall into one of the four classes mentioned above. For "elements," i.e., letters, are said to be the causes of syllables; and the matter of artificial things is said to be their cause; and fire and earth and all simple bodies of this kind are said to be the causes of compounds. And parts are said to be the causes of a

whole, and "premises," i.e., propositions previously set down from which conclusions are drawn, are said to be the causes of the conclusion. And in all of these cases cause has a single formal aspect according as cause means that from which a thing is produced, and this is the formal aspect of material cause.

778. Now it must be noted that propositions are said to constitute the matter of a conclusion, not inasmuch as they exist under such a form, or according to their force (for in this way they would rather have the formal aspect of an efficient cause), but with reference to the terms of which they are composed. For a conclusion is constituted of the terms contained in the premises, i.e., of the major and minor terms.

779. And of those things of which something is composed, some are like a subject, for example, parts and the other things mentioned above, whereas some are like the essence, for example, the whole, the composition and the species, which have the character of a form whereby a thing's essence is made complete. For it must be borne in mind that sometimes one thing is the matter of something else in an unqualified sense (for example, silver of a goblet), and then the form corresponding to such a matter can be called the species. But sometimes many things taken together constitute the matter of a thing; and this may occur in three ways. For sometimes things are united merely by their arrangement, as the men in an army or the houses in a city; and then the whole has the role of a form which is designated by the term army or city. And sometimes things are united not just by arrangement alone but by contact and a bond, as is evident in the parts of a house; and then their composition has the role of a form. And sometimes the alteration of the component parts is added to the above, as occurs in the case of a compound; and then the compound state itself is the form, and this is still a kind of composition. And a thing's essence is derived from any one of these three—the composition, species, or whole—as becomes clear when an army, a house, or a goblet is defined. Thus we have two classes of cause.

780. But the seed, the physician and the adviser, and in general every agent, are called causes for a different reason, namely, because they are the sources of motion and rest. Hence this is now a different class of cause because of a different formal aspect of causality. He puts seed in this class of cause because he is of the opinion that the seed has active power, whereas a woman's menstrual fluid has the role of the matter of the offspring.

781. There is a fourth formal aspect of causality inasmuch as some things are said to be causes in the sense of the end and good of other things. For that for the sake of which something else comes to be is the greatest good "and the end" of other things, i.e., it is naturally disposed to be their end. But because someone could raise the objection that an end is not always a good since certain agents sometimes inordinately set up an evil as their end, he therefore replies that it makes no difference to his thesis whether we speak of what is good without qualification or of an apparent good. For one who acts does so, properly speaking, because of a good, for this is what he has in mind. And one acts for the sake of an evil accidentally inasmuch as he happens to think that it is good. For no one acts for the sake of something with evil in view.

782. Moreover, it must be noted that, even though the end is the last thing to come into being in some cases, it is always prior in causality. Hence it is called the cause of causes, because it is the cause of the causality of all causes. For it is the cause of efficient causality, as has already been pointed out (see n. 775); and the efficient cause is the cause of the causality of both the matter and the form, because by its motion it causes matter to be receptive of form and makes form exist in matter. Therefore the final cause is also the cause of the causality of both the matter and the form. Hence in those cases in which something is done for an end (as occurs in the realm of natural things, in that of moral matters, and in that of art), the most forceful demonstrations are derived from the final cause. Therefore he concludes that the foregoing are causes, and that causes are distinguished into this number of classes.

783. **Now the modes** [2].

Then he distinguishes between the modes of causes. And causes are distinguished into classes and into modes. For the division of causes into classes is based on different formal aspects of causality, and is therefore equivalently a division based on essential differences, which constitute species. But the division of causes into modes is based on the different relationships between causes and things caused, and therefore pertains to those causes which have the same formal aspect of causality. An example of this is the division of causes into proper and accidental causes, and into remote and proximate causes. Therefore this division is equivalently a division based on accidental differences, which do not constitute different species.

784. He accordingly says that there are many modes of causes, but that these are found to be fewer in number when "summarized," i.e., when brought together under one head. For even though proper causes and accidental causes are two modes, they are still reduced to one head insofar as both may be considered from the same point of view. The same thing is true of the other different modes. For many different modes of causes are spoken of, not only with reference to the different species of causes, but also with reference to causes of the same species, namely, those which are reduced to one class of cause.

785. For one cause is said to be prior and another subsequent; and causes are prior or subsequent in two ways: In one way, when there are many distinct causes which are related to each other, one of which is primary and remote, and another secondary and proximate (as in the case of efficient causes man generates man as a proximate and subsequent cause, but the sun as a prior and remote cause); and the same thing can be considered in the case of the other classes of causes. In another way, when the cause is numerically one and the same, but is considered according to the sequence which reason sets up between the universal and the particular; for the universal is naturally prior and the particular subsequent.

786. But he omits the first way and considers the second. For in the second way the effect is the immediate result of both causes, i.e., of both the prior and subsequent cause; but this cannot happen in the first way. Hence he says that the cause of health is both the physician and one possessing an art, who belong to the class of efficient cause: one possessing an art as a universal

and prior cause, and the physician as a particular, or special, and subsequent cause. The same thing is true of the formal cause, since this cause may also be considered in two ways; for example, for an octave chord "double," or the ratio of 2:1, or the number two, is a formal cause as one that is special and subsequent, whereas number, or the ratio of one number to another or to the unit, is like a universal and prior cause. And in this way too "always those classes which contain singulars," i.e., universals, are said to be prior causes.

787. Causes are distinguished in another way inasmuch as one thing is said to be a proper cause and another an accidental cause. For just as proper causes are divided into universal and particular, or into prior and subsequent, so also are accidental causes. Therefore, not only accidental causes themselves are called such, but so also are the classes which contain these. For example, a sculptor is the proper cause of a statue, and Polyclitus is an accidental cause inasmuch as he happens to be a sculptor. And just as Polyclitus is an accidental cause of a statue, in a similar way all universals "which contain accidents," i.e., accidental causes, are said to be accidental causes, for example, man and animal, which contain under themselves Polyclitus, who is a man and an animal.

788. And just as some proper causes are proximate and some remote, as was pointed out above, so also is this the case with accidental causes. For Polyclitus is a more proximate cause of a statue than what is white or what is musical. For an accidental mode of predication is more remote when an accident is predicated of an accident than when an accident is predicated of a subject. For one accident is predicated of another only because both are predicated of a subject. Hence when something pertaining to one accident is predicated of another, as when something pertaining to a builder is predicated of a musician, this mode of predication is more remote than one in which something is predicated of the subject of an accident, as when something pertaining to a builder is predicated of Polyclitus.

789. Now it must be borne in mind that one thing can be said to be the accidental cause of something else in two ways: in one way, from the viewpoint of the cause; because whatever is accidental to a cause is itself called an accidental cause, for example, when we say that something white is the cause of a house. In another way, from the viewpoint of the effect, i.e., inasmuch as one thing is said to be an accidental cause of something else because it is accidental to the proper effect. This can happen in three ways. The first is that the thing has a necessary connection with the effect. Thus that which removes an obstacle is said to be a mover accidentally. This is the case whether that accident is a contrary, as when bile prevents coolness (and thus scammony is said to produce coolness accidentally, not because it causes coolness, but because it removes the obstacle preventing coolness, i.e., bile, which is its contrary); or even if it is not a contrary, as when a pillar hinders the movement of a stone which rests upon it, so that one who removes the pillar is said to move the stone accidentally. In a second way, something is accidental to the proper effect when the accident is connected with the effect neither necessarily nor in the majority of cases but seldom, as the discovery of a treasure is connected

with digging in the soil. It is in this way that fortune and chance are said to be accidental causes. In a third way things are accidental to the effect when they have no connection except perhaps in the mind, as when someone says that he is the cause of an earthquake because an earthquake took place when he entered the house.

790. And besides the distinction of all things into causes in themselves or proper causes and accidental causes, there is a third division of causes inasmuch as some things are causes potentially and some actually, i.e., actively. For example, the cause of building is a builder in a state of potency (for this designates his habit or office), or one who is actually building.

791. And the same distinctions which apply to causes can apply to the effects of which these causes are the causes. For effects, whether particular or universal, can be divided into prior and subsequent, as a sculptor may be called the cause of this statue, which is subsequent; or of a statue, which is more universal and prior; or of an image, which is still more universal. And similarly something is the formal cause of this particular bronze; or of bronze, which is more universal; or of matter, which is still more universal. The same things can be said of accidental effects, i.e., of things produced by accident. For a sculptor who is the cause of a statue is also the cause of the heaviness, whiteness or redness which are in it as accidents from the matter and are not caused by this agent.

792. Again, he gives a fourth division of causes, namely, the division into simple causes and composite causes. A cause is said to be simple when, for example, in the case of a statue, the proper cause alone is considered, as a sculptor, or when an accidental cause alone is considered, as Polyclitus. But a cause is said to be composite when both are taken together, for example, when we say that the cause of a statue is the sculptor Polyclitus.

793. There is moreover another way in which causes are said to be composite, i.e., when several causes act together to produce one effect, for example, when many men act together in order to row a boat, or when many stones combine in order to constitute the matter of a house. But he omits the latter way because no one of these things taken in itself is the cause, but a part of the cause.

794. And having given these different modes of causes, he brings out their number, saying that these modes of causes are six in number, and that each of these have two alternatives so that twelve result. For these six modes are either singular or generic (or, as he called them above, prior and subsequent); either proper or accidental (to which the genus of the accident is also reduced, for the genus to which an accident belongs is an accidental cause); and again, either composite or simple. Now these six modes are further divided by potency and actuality and thus are twelve in number. Now the reason why all these modes must be divided by potency and actuality is that potency and actuality distinguish the connection between cause and effect. For active causes are at one and the same time particulars and cease to exist along with their effects; for example, this act of healing ceases with this act of recovering health, and this act of building with this thing being built; for a thing cannot be actually being built unless something is actually building.

But potential causes do not always cease to exist when their effects cease; for example, a house and a builder do not cease to exist at one and the same time. In some cases, however, it does happen that when the activity of the efficient cause ceases the substance of the effect ceases. This occurs in the case of those things whose being consists in coming to be, or whose cause is not only the cause of their coming to be but also of their being. For example, when the sun's illumination is removed from the atmosphere, light ceases to be. He says "singular causes" because acts belong to singular things, as was stated in Book I of this work (see n. 21).

LESSON 4

The Proper Meaning of Element; Elements in Words, Natural Bodies, and Demonstrations. Transferred Usages of "Element" and Their Common Basis

ARISTOTLE'S TEXT Chapter 3: 1014a26–1014b15

1. *The inherent principle of which a thing is first composed and which is not divisible into another species is called an element. For example, the elements of a word are the parts of which a word is composed and into which it is ultimately divided and which are not further divided into other words specifically different from them. But if they are divided, their parts are alike, as the parts of water are water; but this is not true of the syllable. Similarly, people who speak of the elements of bodies mean the component parts into which bodies are ultimately divided and which are not divided into other bodies specifically different. And whether such parts are one or many, they call them elements. And similarly the parts of diagrams are called elements, and in general the parts of demonstrations; for the primary demonstrations which are contained in many other demonstrations are called the elements of demonstrations; and such are the primary syllogisms which are composed of three terms and proceed through one middle term.*

1014a26–1014b3

2. *People also use the term element in a transferred sense of anything which is one and small and useful for many purposes; and for this reason anything which is small and simple and indivisible is called an element. Hence it follows that the most universal things are elements, because each of them, being one and simple, is found in many things, either in all or in most of them. And to some the unit and the point seem to be principles. Therefore, since what are called genera are universal and indivisible (for their formal character is one), some men call the genera elements, and these more than a difference, since a genus is more universal. For where the difference is present the genus also follows, but the difference is not always present where the genus is. And in all these cases it is common for the element of each thing to be the primary component of each thing.* **1014b3–15**

COMMENTARY

795. Here he distinguishes the different senses of the term *element*, and in regard to this he does two things. First [1], he gives the different senses in which the term element is used. Second [2], he indicates what all of them have in common ("And in all these").

In regard to the first he does two things. First, he explains how the term element is used in its proper sense; and second [2], how it is used in transferred senses ("People also use").

First [1], he gives a sort of description of an element, and from this one can gather the four notes contained in its definition. The first is that an element is a cause in the sense of that from which a thing comes to be; and from this it is clear that an element is placed in the class of material cause.

796. The second is that an element is the principle from which something first comes to be. For copper is that from which a statue comes to be, but it is still not an element because it has some matter from which it comes to be.

797. The third is that an element is inherent or, intrinsic; and for this reason it differs from everything of a transitory nature from which a thing comes to be, whether it be a privation or a contrary or the matter subject to contrariety and privation, which is transitory; for example, when we say that a musical man comes from a non-musical man, or that the musical comes

from the non-musical. For elements must remain in the things of which they are the elements.

798. The fourth is that an element has a species which is not divisible into different species; and thus an element differs from first matter, which has no species, and also from every sort of matter which is capable of being divided into different species, as blood and things of this kind.

Hence he says, as the first note, that an element is that of which a thing is composed; as the second, that it is that of which a thing is "first" composed; as the third, that it is "an inherent principle"; and as the fourth, that it is "not divisible into another species."

799. He illustrates this definition of element in four cases in which we use the term element. For we say that letters are the elements of a word because every word is composed of them, and of them primarily. This is evident from the fact that all words are divided into letters as ultimate things; for what is last in the process of dissolution must be first in the process of composition. But letters are not further divided into other words which are specifically different. Yet if they should be divided in any way, the parts in which the division results would be "alike," i.e., specifically the same, just as all parts of water are water. Now letters are divided according to the amount of time required to pronounce them, inasmuch as a long letter is said to require two periods of time, and a short letter one. But while the parts into which letters are so divided do not differ as the species of words do, this is not the case with a syllable; for its parts are specifically different, since the sounds which a vowel and a consonant make, of which a syllable is composed, are specifically different.

800. He gives as a second example natural bodies, certain of which we also call the elements of certain others. For those things into which all compounds are ultimately dissolved are called their elements; and therefore they are the things of which bodies of this kind are composed. But those bodies which are called elements are not divisible into other bodies which are specifically different, but into like parts, as any part of water is water. And all those who held for one such body into which every body is dissolved and which is itself incapable of being further divided, said that there is one element. Some said that it is water, some air, and some fire. But those who posited many such bodies also said there are many elements. Now it should be borne in mind that when it is set down in the definition of an element that an element is not divisible into different species, this should not be understood of the parts into which a thing is divided in a quantitative division (for wood would then be an element, since any part of wood is wood), but in a division made by alteration, as compounds are dissolved into simple bodies.

801. As a third example he gives the order of demonstrations, in which we also employ the word element; for example, we speak of Euclid's *Book of Elements*. And he says that, in a way similar and close to those mentioned, those things which "are parts of diagrams," i.e., the constituents of geometrical figures, are called elements. This can be said not only of the demonstrations in geometry but universally of all demonstrations. For those demonstrations which have only three terms are called the elements of other demonstrations, because the others are composed of them and resolved into

them. This is shown as follows: a second demonstration takes as its starting point the conclusion of a first demonstration, whose terms are understood to contain the middle term which was the starting point of the first demonstration. Thus the second demonstration will proceed from four terms, the first from three only, the third from five, and the fourth from six; so that each demonstration adds one term. Thus it is clear that first demonstrations are included in subsequent ones, as when this first demonstration—every B is A, every C is B, therefore every C is A—is included in this demonstration—every C is A, every D is C, therefore every D is A; and this again is included in the demonstration whose conclusion is that every E is A, so that for this final conclusion there seems to be one syllogism composed of several syllogisms having several middle terms. This may be expressed thus: every B is A, every C is B, every D is C, every E is D, therefore every E is A. Hence a first demonstration, which has one middle term and only three terms, is simple and not reducible to another demonstration, whereas all other demonstrations are reducible to it. Hence first syllogisms, which come from three terms by way of one middle term, are called elements.

802. **People also use** [2].

Here he shows how the term element is used in a transferred sense. He says that some men, on the basis of the foregoing notion or meaning of element, have used the term in a transferred sense to signify anything that is one and small and useful for many purposes. For from the fact that an element is indivisible they understood that it is one; and from the fact that it is first they understood that it is simple; and from the fact that other things are composed of elements they understood that an element is useful for many purposes. Hence they set up this definition of an element in order that they might say that everything which is smallest in quantity and simple (inasmuch as it is not composed of other things) and incapable of division into different species, is an element.

803. But when they had set up this definition of element, it turned out that by using it in a transferred sense they had invented two senses of element. First, they called the most universal things elements; for a universal is one in definition and is simple (because its definition is not composed of different parts) and is found in many things, and thus is useful for many purposes, whether it be found in all things, as unity and being are, or in most things, as the other genera. And by the same reasoning it came about, second, that they called points and units principles or elements because each of them is one simple thing and useful for many purposes.

804. But in this respect they fell short of the true notion of a principle, because universals are not the matter of which particular things are composed but predicate their very substance. And similarly points are not the matter of a line, for a line is not composed of points.

805. Now with this transferred notion of element established, the solution to a question disputed in Book III (see nn. 431–36) becomes clear, i.e., whether a genus or a species is more an element, and whether a genus or a difference is more an element; for it clearly follows that genera are elements to a greater degree because genera are more universal and indivisible. For there is no concept or definition of them which must be composed of gen-

era and differences, but it is species which are properly defined. And if a genus is defined, it is not defined insofar as it is a genus but insofar as it is a species. Hence a species is divided into different parts and thus does not have the character of an element. But a genus is not divisible into different parts, and therefore they said that genera are elements more than species. Another translation reads, "For their formal character is one," that is, indivisible, because even though genera do not have a definition, still what is signified by the term genus is a simple conception of the intellect which can be called a definition.

806. And just as a genus is more an element than a species is because it is simpler, in a similar way it is more an element than a difference is, even though a difference is simple, because a genus is more universal. This is clear from the fact that anything which has a difference has a genus, since essential differences do not transcend a genus; but not everything which has a genus necessarily has a difference.

807. Last of all he says that all of the foregoing senses of element have this note in common, that an element is the primary component of each being, as has been stated.

LESSON 5
Five Senses of the Term Nature

ARISTOTLE'S TEXT Chapter 4: 1014b15–1015a20

1. *Nature means, in one sense, the generation of things that are born, as if one were to pronounce the letter {y} [in {physis}] long. And in another sense it means the immanent principle from which anything generated is first produced. Again, it means the source of the primary motion in any beings which are by nature, and it is in each inasmuch as it is such. Now all those things are said to be born which increase through something else by touching and by existing together, or by being naturally joined, as in the case of embryos. But being born together differs from touching, for in the latter case there need be nothing but contact. But in things which are naturally joined together there is some one same thing in both, instead of contact, which causes them to be one, and which makes them to be one in quantity and continuity but not in quality. Again, nature means the primary thing of which a natural being is composed or from which it comes to be, when it is unformed and immutable by its own power; for example, the bronze of a statue or of bronze articles is said to be their nature, and the wood of wooden things, and the same applies in the case of other things. For each thing comes from these though its primary matter is preserved. For it is also in this sense that men speak of the elements of natural beings as their nature; some calling it fire, others earth, others water, others air, and others something similar to these, whereas others call all of them nature. In still another sense nature means the substance of things which are by nature, as those who say that nature is the primary composition of a thing, as Empedocles says, "Of nothing that exists is there nature, but only the mixing and separating-out of what has been mixed. Nature is but the name men give to these." For this reason we do not say that things which are or come to be by nature have a nature, even when that from which they can be or come to be is already present, so long as they do not have their form or species. Hence that which is composed of both of these exists by nature, as animals and their parts.* **1014b16–1015a7**

2. *Again, nature is the primary matter of a thing, and this in two senses: either what is primary with respect to this particular thing, or primary in general; for example, the primary matter of bronze articles is bronze, but in general it is perhaps water, if everything capable of being liquefied is water. And nature is also a thing's form or substance, i.e., the terminus of the process of generation. But metaphorically speaking every substance in general is called nature because of form or species, for the nature of a thing is also a kind of substance.* **1015a7–13**

3. *Hence, from what has been said, in its primary and proper sense nature is the substance of those things which have within themselves as such the source of their motion. For matter is called nature because it is receptive of this. And processes of generation and growth are called nature because they are motions proceeding from it. And nature is the source of motion in those things which are by nature, and it is something present in them either potentially or in complete actuality.* **1015a13–19]**

COMMENTARY

808. Here he gives the different meanings of the term *nature*. And even though an investigation of the term nature appears not to belong to first philosophy but rather to the philosophy of nature, he nevertheless gives the different meanings of this term here, because according to one of its common meanings nature is predicated of every substance, as he will make clear. Hence it falls under the consideration of first philosophy just as universal substance does.

In regard to the first he does two

things. First [1], he distinguishes the different senses in which the term nature is used. Second [3], he reduces all of these to one primary notion ("Hence, from what").

In regard to the first he does two things. First, he gives five principal senses in which the term nature is used. Second [2], he gives two additional senses connected with the last two of these ("Again, nature").

He accordingly says, first [1], that in one sense nature means the process of generation of things that are generated, or, according to another text which states this in a better way, "of things that are born." For not everything that is generated can be said to be born but only living things, for example, plants and animals and their parts. The generation of non-living things cannot be called nature, properly speaking, according to the common use of the term, but only the generation of living things inasmuch as nature may mean the nativity or birth of a thing—as the word seems to mean, "as if one were to pronounce nature long." This text has been corrupted, as is evident from another translation which says, "as if one were to pronounce the {y} [in {physis}] long." For, if {physis}, which means nature in the Greek, is taken to mean the generation of living things, the first {y} is pronounced long; but if it is taken to mean a principle, and this is the way in which it is commonly used, the first {y} is pronounced short. Yet even from this text it can be understood that the term nature means the generation of living things by a certain lengthening or extension of usage.

809. Again, from the fact that nature was first used to designate the birth of a thing there followed a second use of the term, so that nature came to mean the principle of generation from which a thing comes to be, or that from which as from an intrinsic principle something born is first generated.

810. And as a result of the likeness between birth and other kinds of motion the meaning of the term nature has been extended farther, so that in a third sense it means the source from which motion begins in any being according to its nature, provided that it is present in it insofar as it is such a being and not accidentally. For example, the principle of health, which is the medical art, is not present in a physician who is ill insofar as he is ill but insofar as he is a physician. And he is not healed insofar as he is a physician but insofar as he is ill; and thus the source of motion is not in him insofar as he is moved. This is the definition of nature given in Book II of the *Physics*. *[192b22]*

811. And because he mentioned things that are born, he also shows what it means in the proper sense "to be born," as another text says, and in place of which this text incorrectly says "to be generated." For the generation of living things differs from that of non-living things, because a non-living thing is not generated by being joined or united to its generator, as fire is generated by fire and water by water. But the generation of a living thing comes about through some kind of union with the principle of generation. And because the addition of quantity to quantity causes increase, therefore in the generation of living things there seems to be a certain increase, as when a tree puts forth foliage and fruit. Hence he says that those things are said to be born which "increase," i.e., have some increase together with the principle of generation.

812. But this kind of increase differs from that class of motion which is

called increase [or augmentation], by which things that are already born are moved or changed. For a thing that increases within itself does so because the part added passes over into the substance of that thing, as food passes over into the substance of the one nourished. But anything that is born is added to the thing from which it is born as something other and different, and not as something that passes over into its substance. Hence he says that it increases "through something distinct" or something else, as if to say that this increase comes about through the addition of something that is other or different.

813. But addition that brings about increase can be understood to take place in two ways: in one way, "by touching," i.e., by contact alone; in another way, "by existing together," i.e., by the fact that two things are produced together and naturally connected with each other, as the arms and sinews; "and by being joined," i.e., by the fact that something is naturally adapted to something else already existing, as hair to the head and teeth to the gums. In place of this another text reads, more appropriately, "by being born together with," and "by being connected with at birth." Now in the generation of living things addition comes about not only by contact but also by a kind of joining together or natural connection, as is evident in the case of embryos, which are not only in contact in the womb, but are also bound to it at the beginning of their generation.

814. Further, he indicates the difference between these two, saying that "being fused," i.e., being bound together, or "being connected at birth," as another text says, differs from contact, because in the case of contact there need be nothing besides the things in contact which makes them one. But in the case of things which are bound together, whether naturally connected or born together and joined at birth, there must be some one thing "instead of contact," i.e., in the place of contact, which causes them "to be naturally joined," i.e., joined or bound together or born together. Moreover, it must be understood that the thing which causes them to be one makes them one in quantity and continuity but not in quality; because a bond does not alter the things bound from their own dispositions.

815. And from this it is evident that anything that is born is always connected with the thing from which it is born. Hence nature never means an extrinsic principle, but in every sense in which it is used it is taken to mean an intrinsic principle.

816. And from this third meaning of nature there follows a fourth. For if the source of motion in natural bodies is called their nature, and it seemed to some that the principle of motion in natural bodies is matter, it was for this reason that matter came to be called nature, which is taken as a principle of a thing both as to its being and as to its becoming. And it is also considered to be without any form, and is not moved by itself but by something else. He accordingly says that nature is spoken of as that primary thing of which any being is composed or from which it comes to be.

817. He says this because matter is a principle both of being and of becoming. Hence he says that "it is without order," i.e., form; and for this reason another text says "when it is unformed"; for in the case of some things

their order (or arrangement) is regarded as their form, as in the case of an army or of a city. And for this reason he says that it is "immutable by its own power," i.e., it cannot be moved by its own power but by that of a higher agent. For matter does not move itself to acquire a form but is moved by a higher and extrinsic agent. For instance, we might say that "bronze is the nature of a statue or of bronze vessels" or "wood of wooden," as if such vessels were natural bodies. The same is true of everything else that is composed of or comes to be from matter; for each comes to be from its matter though this is preserved. But in the process of generation the dispositions of a form are not preserved; for when one form is introduced another is cast out. And for this reason it seemed to some thinkers that forms are accidents and that matter alone is substance and nature, as he points out in the *Physics*, Book II. [193a9]

818. They held this view because they considered the matter and form of natural bodies in the same way as they did the matter and form of things made by art, in which forms are merely accidents and matter alone is substance. It was in this sense that the philosophers of nature said that the elements are the matter of things which come to be by nature, i.e., water, air, or fire—or earth, which no philosopher has held to be the element of natural beings all by itself, although some of those who were not philosophers of nature did hold this, as was stated in Book I (see n. 134). And some philosophers, such as Parmenides, held that some of these are the elements and natures of things; others, such as Empedocles, held that all four are the elements of things; and still others, such as Heraclitus, held that something different is the element of things, for he claimed that vapor plays this role.

819. Now because motion is caused in natural bodies by the form rather than by the matter, he therefore adds a fifth sense in which the term nature is used: that in which nature means the form of a thing. Hence in another sense nature means "the substance of things," i.e., the form of things, which are by nature. It was in this sense that some said that the nature of things is the composition of mixed bodies, as Empedocles said that there is nothing absolute in the world, but that only the alteration or loosening (or mixing, according to another text) of what has been mixed is called nature by men. For they said that things composed of different mixtures have different natures.

820. Now they were led to hold that form is nature by this process of reasoning: whatever things exist or come to be by nature are not said to have a nature, even though the matter from which they are naturally disposed to be or to come to be is already present, unless they have a proper species and a form through which they acquire their species. Now the term species seems to be given in place of substantial form and the term form in place of figure, which is a natural result of the species and a sign of it. Hence, if form is nature, a thing cannot be said to have a nature unless it has a form. Therefore, that which is composed of matter and form "is said to be by nature," i.e., according to nature, as animals and the parts of animals, such as flesh and bones and the like.

821. **Again, nature** [2].

Then he gives two meanings of nature which are connected with the last two preceding ones, and the first of these is added to the fourth sense of nature, in which it means the matter of a thing. And he says that not every kind of matter is said to be the nature of a thing but only first matter. This can be understood in two senses: either with reference to something generic, or with reference to something that is first absolutely or without qualification. For example, the first matter generically of artificial things produced from bronze is bronze; but their first matter without qualification is water; for all things which are liquefied by heat and solidified by cold have the character of water, as he says in Book IV of the *Meteors.[389a24-389b22]*

822. He links up the second of these additional meanings with the fifth sense of nature mentioned above, according to which nature means form. And in this sense not only the form of a part *(forma partis)* is called nature but the species is the form of the whole *(forma totius)*. For example, we might say that the nature of man is not only a soul but humanity and the substance signified by the definition. For it is from this point of view that Boethius says *[De duabus naturis, 1]* that the nature of a thing is the specific difference which informs each thing, because the specific difference is the principle that completes a thing's substance and gives it its species. And just as form or matter is called nature because it is a principle of generation, which is the meaning of nature according to the original use of the term, in a similar way the species or substance of a thing is called its nature because it is the end of the process of generation. For the process of generation terminates in the species of the thing generated, which is a result of the union of matter and form.

823. And because of this every substance is called nature according to a kind of metaphorical and extended use of the term; for the nature which we spoke of as the terminus of generation is a substance. Thus every substance is similar to what we call nature. Boethius also gives this meaning of the term. Moreover, it is because of this meaning that the term nature is distinguished from other common terms. For it is common in this way just as substance also is.

824. **Hence, from what** [3].

Then he reduces all of the foregoing senses of the term nature to one common notion. But it must be noted that the reduction of the other senses to one primary sense can happen in two ways: in one way, with reference to the order which things have; and in another way, with reference to the order which is observed in giving names to things. For names are given to things according as we understand them, because names are signs of what we understand; and sometimes we understand prior things from subsequent ones. Hence something that is prior for us receives a name which subsequently fits the object of that name. And this is what happens in the present case; for since the forms and powers of things are known from their activities, the process of generation or birth of a thing is the first to receive the name of nature and the last is the form.

825. But with reference to the order which things have in reality the concept of nature primarily fits the form, because, as has been said [1], nothing is said to have a nature unless it has a form.

826. Hence from what has been said it is evident that "in its primary and proper sense nature is the substance," i.e., the form, of those things which

have within themselves as such the source of their motion. For matter is called nature because it is receptive of form; and processes of generation get the name of nature because they are motions proceeding from a form and terminating in further forms. And this, namely, the form, is the principle of motion in those things which are by nature, either potentially or actually. For a form is not always the cause of actual motion but sometimes only of potential motion, as when a natural motion is prevented by an external obstacle, or even when a natural action is prevented by a defect in the matter.

LESSON 6

Four Senses of the Term Necessary. Its First and Proper Sense Immobile Things, though Necessary, Are Exempted from Force

ARISTOTLE'S TEXT Chapter 5: 1015a20–1015b15

1. Necessary means that without which, as a contributing cause, a thing cannot be or live; for example, breathing and food are necessary to an animal because it cannot exist without them. **1015a20–22**

2. And it also means that without which the good for man cannot be or come to be, and that without which one cannot get rid of or remain free of some evil; for example, the drinking of some drug is necessary in order that one may not be in distress, and sailing to Aegina is necessary in order that one may collect money. **1015a22–26**

3. Again, it means what applies force and force itself, and this is something which hinders and prevents, in opposition to desire and choice. For that which applies force is said to be necessary, and for this reason anything necessary is also said to be lamentable, as Evenus says, "For every necessary thing is mournful." And force is a kind of necessity, as Sophocles [Electra, 256] says, "But force compels me to do this." And necessity seems to be something blameless, and rightly so, for it is contrary to motion which stems from choice and from knowledge. **1015a26–33**

4. Again, we say that anything which cannot be otherwise is necessarily so. **1015a33–35**

5. And from this sense of the term necessary all the other senses are derived. For whatever is forced is said either to do or to undergo something necessary when it cannot do something according to its inclination as a result of force, as if there were some necessity by reason of which the thing could not be otherwise. The same thing applies to the contributing causes of life and of good. For when in the one case good, and in the other life or being, is impossible without certain contributing causes, these are necessary; and this cause is a kind of necessity. **1015a35–1015b6**

6. Further, demonstration belongs to the class of necessary things, because whatever has been demonstrated in the strict sense cannot be otherwise. The reason for this is the principles, for the principles from which a syllogism proceeds cannot be otherwise. **1015b6–9**

7. Now of necessary things some have something else as the cause of their necessity and others do not, but it is because of them that other things are necessary. Hence what is necessary in the primary and proper sense is what is simple, for this cannot be in more ways than one. Therefore it cannot be in one state and in another; otherwise there would be more ways than one. If, then, there are any beings which are eternal and immobile, in them nothing forced or contrary to nature is found. **1015b9–15**

COMMENTARY

827. Having distinguished the different senses of the terms which signify causes, the Philosopher now gives the different senses of a term which designates something pertaining to the notion of cause, i.e., the term *necessary;* for a cause is that from which something else follows of necessity. In regard to this he does two things. First [1], he distinguishes the different senses of the term necessary. Second [5], he reduces all of these to one primary sense ("And from this sense").

In the first part [1] he gives four senses in which the term *necessary* is used. First, it means that without which a thing cannot be or live; and even when this is not the principal cause of a thing, it is still a contributing cause. Breathing, for example, is necessary to an animal which breathes, because it cannot live without this. And while breathing is not the [principal] cause of life, none the less it is still a contributing cause inasmuch as it helps to restore what is lost and prevents the total consumption of moisture, which is a cause of life. Hence things of this kind are said to be necessary because it is impossible for things to exist without them.

828. **And it also means** [2].

Then he gives a second sense in which things are said to be necessary. He says that in a second way those things are said to be necessary without which some good cannot be or come about, or some evil be avoided or expelled. For example, we say that "the drinking of some drug," i.e., a laxative medicine, is necessary, not because an animal cannot live without it, but because it is required to expel something, namely, an evil, illness, or even to avoid it. For this is necessary "in order that one may not be in distress," i.e., to avoid being ill. And similarly "sailing to Aegina," i.e., to a definite place, is necessary, not because a man cannot exist without this, but because he cannot acquire some good, i.e., money, without doing this. Hence, such a voyage is said to be necessary in order to collect a sum of money.

829. **Again, it means** [3].

Here he gives a third sense in which things are said to be necessary. He says that anything which exerts force, and even force itself, is termed necessary. For force is said to be necessary, and one who is forced is said to do of necessity whatever he is compelled to do. He shows what is meant by something that exerts force both in the case of natural beings and in that of beings endowed with will. In natural beings there is a desire for or an inclination toward some end or goal, to which the will of a rational nature corresponds; and for this reason a natural inclination is itself called an appetite. For both of these, i.e., both the desire of a natural inclination and the intention of the will, can be hindered and prevented—hindered in carrying out a motion already begun, and prevented from initiating motion. Therefore, that is said to be forced "which is done in opposition to desire," i.e., against the inclination of a natural being; and it is "something that hinders choice," i.e., the end intended in executing a voluntary motion already begun, and also something that prevents it from beginning. Another text says, "and this is according to impetuousness," i.e., according to impulse. For force is found when something is done through the impulse of an external agent and is opposed to the will and power of the subject. And that is forced which is done as a result of an impulse applying force.

830. Now from this definition of the forced he draws two conclusions. The first is that everything forced is sad or mournful. He proves this by using the statement of a certain poet or teacher, saying that everything which is necessary or forced is sad or lamentable; for force is a kind of necessity, as the poet Sophocles says: "Force," i.e., necessity, "compelled me to do this." For it has been said [3] that force is something which hinders the will; and things which are opposed to the will cause sorrow, because sorrow has to do with things which happen to us against our will.

831. The second conclusion is that anything which is necessary is rightly said to be without blame or reproach. For it is said that necessity deserves forgiveness rather than blame; and this is true because we deserve to be

blamed only for the things which we do voluntarily and for which we may also be reasonably rebuked. But the kind of necessity which pertains to force is opposed to the will and to reason, as has been stated [3]; and thus it is more reasonable to say that things done by force are not subject to blame.

832. **Again, we say** [4].

He gives a fourth sense in which things are said to be necessary. He says that being in such a state that it cannot be otherwise we also call necessary, and this is what is necessary in an absolute sense. Things necessary in the first senses, however, are necessary in a relative sense.

833. Now whatever is absolutely necessary differs from the other types of necessity, because absolute necessity belongs to a thing by reason of something that is intimately and closely connected with it, whether it be the form or the matter or the very essence of a thing. For example, we say that an animal is necessarily corruptible because this is a natural result of its matter inasmuch as it is composed of contraries; and we say that an animal is necessarily capable of sensing because this is a result of its form; and we also say that an animal is necessarily a living sensible substance because this is its essence.

834. However, the necessity of something which is necessary in a relative sense and not absolutely depends on an extrinsic cause. And there are two kinds of extrinsic causes—the end and the agent. The end is either existence taken absolutely, and the necessity taken from this end pertains to the first kind; or it is well disposed existence or the possession of some good and necessity of the second kind is taken from this end.

835. Again, the necessity which comes from an external agent pertains to the third kind of necessity. For force exists when a thing is moved by an external agent to something which it has no aptitude for by its own nature. For if something is disposed by its own nature to receive motion from an external agent, such motion will not be forced but natural. This is evident in the motion of the celestial bodies by separate substances, and in that of lower bodies by higher ones.

836. **And from this** [5].

Here he reduces all of the senses in which things are necessary to one; and in regard to this he does three things. First [5], he shows that all the types of necessity found in reality pertain to this last type. Second [6], he shows that necessity in matters of demonstration is taken in this last sense ("Further, demonstration"). Third [7], he draws a corollary from what has been set down above ("Now of necessary things").

He accordingly says, first [5], that all the other senses of the term necessary are somehow referred to this last sense. He makes this clear, first, with reference to the third way in which things are said to be necessary. For whatever is forced is said to do or to undergo something of necessity on the grounds that it cannot act through its own power because of the force exerted on it by an agent; and this is a kind of necessity by which it cannot be otherwise than it is.

837. Then he shows that the same thing is true of the first and second ways in which things are said to be necessary: in the first way with reference to the causes of living and being absolutely, and in the second with reference to the causes of good. For the term necessary was so used in these other ways: in one way to designate that without which a thing cannot be

well off, and in the other to designate that without which a thing cannot live or exist. Hence that cause without which a thing cannot live or exist or possess a good or avoid an evil is said to be necessary; the supposition being that the primary notion of the necessary derives from the fact that something cannot be otherwise.

838. **Further, demonstration** [6].

Then he shows that the necessary in matters of demonstration is taken from this last sense, and this applied both to principles and to conclusions. For demonstration is said to be about necessary things, and to proceed from necessary things. It is said to be about necessary things because what is demonstrated in the strict sense cannot be otherwise. He says "demonstrated in the strict sense" in order to distinguish this from what is demonstrated by the kind of demonstration which refutes an opponent, and does not strictly demonstrate. In the fourth book (see n. 609) he called this an *ad hominem* argument. In demonstrations of this kind which refute an opponent we conclude to the impossible from certain impossible premises. But since in demonstrations the premises are the causes of the conclusion, for demonstrations in the strict sense are productive of science and this is had only by way of a cause, the principles from which a syllogism proceeds must also be necessary and thus cannot be otherwise than they are. For a necessary effect cannot come from a non-necessary cause.

839. **Now of necessary things** [7].

Here he draws three conclusions from the points set down above, one of which follows from the other. The first is that, since in demonstrations the premises are the causes of the conclusion and both of these are necessary, it follows that some things are necessary in one of two ways. For there are some things whose necessity is caused by something else, and there are others whose necessity has no cause; and such things are necessary of themselves. This is said against Democritus, who claimed that we must not look for the causes of necessary things, as is stated in Book VIII of the *Physics.[265b23]*

840. The second conclusion is that, since there must be one first necessary being from which other beings derive their necessity (for there cannot be an infinite regress in causes, as was shown in the second book [see n. 301]), this first necessary being, which is also necessary in the most proper sense because it is necessary in all ways, must be simple. For composite things are changeable and thus can be in more ways than one. But things which can be in more ways than one can be now in one way and now in another, and this is opposed to the notion of necessity; for that is necessary which cannot be otherwise. Hence the first necessary being must not be now in one way and now in another, and consequently cannot be in more ways than one. Thus he must be simple.

841. The third conclusion is that, since the forced is something which is moved by an external agent in opposition to its own nature, and necessary principles are simple and unchangeable, as has been shown ([7], therefore if there are certain eternal and unchangeable beings, as the separate substances are, in them there must be nothing forced or contrary to their nature. He says this lest a mistake should be made in the case of the term necessity, since it is predicated of immaterial substances without implying on this account that anything forced is found in them.

LESSON 7
The Kinds of Accidental Unity and of Essential Unity

ARISTOTLE'S TEXT Chapter 6: 1015b16–1016b3

1. *The term one is used both of what is accidentally one and of what is essentially one. A thing is said to be accidentally one, for example, when we say "Coriscus" and "musical" and "musical Coriscus." For to say "Coriscus" and "musical" and "musical Coriscus" amounts to the same thing; and this is also true when we say "just" and "musical" and "just musical Coriscus." For all of these are said to be accidentally one; just and musical because they are accidents of one substance, and musical and Coriscus because the one is an accident of the other. And similarly in a sense musical Coriscus is one with Coriscus, because one of the parts of this expression is an accident of the other. Thus musical is an accident of Coriscus and musical Coriscus is an accident of just Coriscus, because one part of each expression is an accident of one and the same subject. For it makes no difference whether musical is an accident of Coriscus [or whether just Coriscus is an accident of musical Coriscus]. The same thing also holds true if an accident is predicated of a genus or of any universal term, for example, when one says that man and musical man are the same; for this occurs either because musical is an accident of man, which is one substance, or because both are accidents of some singular thing, for example, Coriscus. Yet both do not belong to it in the same way, but one perhaps as the genus and substance, and the other as a habit or modification of the substance. Therefore whatever things are said to be accidentally one are said to be such in this way.* **1015b16–36**

2. *But in the case of things which are said to be essentially one, some are said to be such by nature of their continuity; for example, a bundle becomes one by means of a binding, and pieces of wood become one by means of glue. And a continuous line, even if it is bent, is said to be one, just as each part [of the human body] is, for example, a leg or an arm. And of these things themselves those which are continuous by nature are one to a greater degree than those which are continuous by art. And that is said to be continuous whose motion is essentially one and cannot be otherwise. And motion is one when it is indivisible, i.e., indivisible in time.* **1015b36–1016a6**

3. *Again, all those things are essentially continuous which are one not merely by contact; for if you place pieces of wood so that they touch each other, you will not say that they are one, either one board or one body or any other continuous thing. Hence those things which are continuous throughout are said to be one even though they are bent. And those which are not bent are one to an even greater degree; for example, the lower leg or the thigh is one to a greater degree than the leg, because the motion of the leg may not be one. And a straight line is one to a greater degree than a bent line. But what is bent and angular we refer to as either one or not one, because its motion may be either simultaneous or not. But the motion of a straight line is always simultaneous, and no part of it which has extension is at rest when another moves, as in a bent line.* **1016a7–17**

4. *Again, a thing is said to be one in another sense because its underlying subject is uniform in species; and it is uniform in species as those things whose form is indivisible from the viewpoint of sensory perception. And the underlying subject is either one that is primary or one that is last in relation to the end. For wine is said to be one and water is said to be one inasmuch as they are indivisible in species. And all liquids are said to be one, as oil, wine and fluids, because the ultimate subject of all is the same; for all of these are made up of water or of air.* **1016a17–24**

5. *And those things are said to be one whose genus is one and differs by opposite differences. And all these things are said to be one because the genus, which is the subject of the differences, is one; for example, man, dog and horse are one because all are animals; and it is such in a way*

closest to that in which matter is one. And sometimes these things are said to be one in this way, and sometimes in their higher genus, which is said to be the same if those which are higher than these are the last species of the genus; for example, the isosceles and the equilateral triangle are one and the same figure because both are triangles; but they are not the same triangles.

1016a24–32

6. Further, any two things are said to be one when the definition expressing the essence of one is indistinguishable from that signifying the essence of the other. For in itself every definition is divisible. And what has increased and what has decreased are one in this way, because their definition is one. An example of this is found in plane figures, which are one in species.

1016a32–1016b1

7. And those things are altogether one and in the highest degree whose concept, which grasps their essence, is indivisible and cannot be separated either in time or in place or in its intelligible structure; and of these, all those which are substances are especially such. **1016b1–3**

COMMENTARY

842. Having given the various senses of the terms which signify causes, the Philosopher now proceeds to do the same thing with those terms which signify in some way the subject of this science. This is divided into two parts. In the first [1] he gives or distinguishes the different senses of the terms which signify the subject of this science; and in the second (Lesson 11) he distinguishes the different senses of the terms which signify the parts of this subject ("Things are said to be the *same*").

Now the subject of this science can be taken either as that which has to be considered generally in the whole science, and as such it is unity and being, or as that with which this science is chiefly concerned, and this is substance. Therefore, first [1], he gives the different senses of the term *one;* second (Lesson 9) of the term *being* ("The term *being*"); and third (Lesson 10), of the term *substance* ("The term *substance*").

In regard to the first part of this division he does two things. First, he makes a distinction between what is essentially one and what is accidentally one, and he also indicates the various senses in which things are said to be accidentally one. Second [2], he notes the various senses in which things are said to be essentially one ("But in the case").

843. He says [1], then, that the term *one* signifies both what is essentially one and what is accidentally one. And he tells us that what is accidentally one we should consider first in the case of singular terms. Now singular terms can be accidentally one in two ways: in one way according as an accident is related to a subject; and in another way according as one accident is related to another. And in both cases three things have to be considered—one composite thing and two simple ones. For if what is accidentally one is considered to be such according as an accident is related to a subject, then there are, for example, these three things: first, Coriscus; second, musical; and third, musical Coriscus. And these three are accidentally one; for Coriscus and what is musical are the same in subject. Similarly when an accident is related to an accident, three terms must be considered: first, musical; second, just; and third, just musical Coriscus. And all these are said to be accidentally one, but for different reasons.

844. For just and musical, which are two simple terms in the second way,

are said to be accidentally one because both are accidents of one and the same subject. But musical and Coriscus, which are two simple terms in the first way, are said to be accidentally one because "the one," namely, musical, "is an accident of the other," namely, of Coriscus. And similarly in regard to the relationship of musical Coriscus to Coriscus (which is the relationship of a composite term to one of two simple terms), these are said to be accidentally one in the first way, because in this expression, i.e., in the complex term, musical Coriscus, one of the parts, namely, musical, is an accident of the other, which is designated as a substance, namely, Coriscus. And for the same reason it can be said that musical Coriscus is one with just Coriscus, which are two composites in the second way, because two of the parts of each composite are accidents of one subject, Coriscus. For if musical and musical Coriscus, and just and just Coriscus, are the same, then whatever is an accident of musical is also an accident of musical Coriscus; and whatever is an accident of Coriscus is also an accident of just Coriscus. Hence, if musical is an accident of Coriscus, it follows that musical Coriscus is an accident of just Coriscus. Therefore it makes no difference whether we say that musical Coriscus is an accident of just Coriscus, or that musical is an accident of Coriscus.

845. But because accidental predicates of this kind are first applied to singular things and then to universals (although the reverse is true of essential predicates), he therefore makes clear that what he showed in the case of singular terms also applies in that of universal terms. He says that, if an accident is used along with the name of a genus or of any universal term, accidental unity is taken in the same way as it is in the above cases when an accident is joined to a singular term; for example, when it is said that man and musical man are accidentally one, although they differ in some respect.

846. For singular substances are neither present in a subject nor predicated of a subject, so that while they are the subject of other things, they themselves do not have a subject. Now universal substances are predicated of a subject but are not present in a subject, so that while they are not the subjects of accidents, they have something as their subject. Hence, when an accident is joined to a singular substance, the expression stating this can only mean that an accident belongs to a singular substance, as musical belongs to Coriscus when Coriscus is said to be musical.

847. But when we say musical man, the expression can mean one of two things: either that musical is an accident of man, by which substance is designated, and from this it derives its ability to be the subject of an accident; or it means that both of these, man and musical, belong to some singular thing, for example, Coriscus, in the way that musical was predicated of just, because these two belong to the same singular thing and in the same way, i.e., accidentally. But perhaps the one term does not belong to the other in the same way, but in the way that universal substance belongs to the singular as a genus, as the term *animal;* or if it is not a genus, it at least belongs to the substance of the subject, i.e., as an essential predicate, as the term *man.* But the other term, namely, musical, does not have the character of a genus or essential predicate, but that of a habit or modification of the subject, or whatever sort of accident it may be. He

gives these two, habit and modification, because there are some accidents which remain in their subject, such as habits, which are moved with difficulty, and others which are not permanent but transient, such as modifications. It is clear, then, that these are the ways in which things are said to be accidentally one.

848. **But in the case** [2].

Then he gives the ways in which things are essentially one, and in regard to this he does two things. First [2], he indicates the different senses in which the term *one* is used; and second (Lesson 8, text 5), the different senses in which the term *many* is used ("Moreover, it is evident").

In regard to the first he does two things. First, he gives the different senses in which things are one from the viewpoint of nature, i.e., according to the conditions found in reality; and second (Lesson 8, text 4), from the viewpoint of logic, i.e., according to the considerations of logic ("Further, some things").

In regard to the first he does two things. First, he distinguishes the different senses in which things are said to be one. Second (Lesson 8, text 3), he indicates a property which accompanies unity ("But the essence of oneness").

In regard to the first he does two things. First, he sets down the different senses in which things are said to be one. Second (Lesson 8, text 1), he reduces all of them to a single sense ("For in general").

In the first part [2] he gives five senses in which the term one is used.

849. The first is this: some of the things which are said to be essentially one are such "by nature of their continuity," i.e., by being continuous, or "because they are continuous," as another translation says. But things are said to be continuous in two ways; for, as another text says, some things are continuous by reason of something other than themselves, and some in themselves.

850. First, he proceeds to deal with those things which are continuous by reason of something other than themselves. He says that there are things which are continuous as a result of something else; for example, a bundle of sticks is continuous by means of a cord or binding; and in this way too pieces of wood which have been glued together are said to be one by means of the glue. Now there are also two ways in which this occurs, because the continuity of things which are fastened together sometimes takes the form of a straight line, and sometimes that of a line which is not straight. This is the case, for example, with a bent line having an angle, which results from the contact of two lines in one surface in such a way that they are not joined in a straight line. And it is in this way that the parts of an animal are said to be one and continuous; for example, the leg, which is bent, and contains an angle at the knee, is said to be one and continuous; and it is the same with the arm.

851. But since this kind of continuity which comes about by reason of something else can exist or come to be both by nature and by art, those things which are continuous by nature are one to a greater degree than those which are continuous by art; for the unity that accounts for the continuity of things which are continuous by nature is not extrinsic to the nature of the thing which is made continuous by it, as happens in the case of things which are one by art, in which the binding or glue or something of the sort is entirely extrinsic to the nature of the things

which are joined together. Hence those things which are joined by nature hold the first place among those which are essentially continuous, which are one in the highest degree.

852. In order to make this clear he defines the continuous. He says that that is said to be continuous which has only one motion essentially and cannot be otherwise. For the different parts of any continuous thing cannot be moved by different motions, but the whole continuous thing is moved by one motion. He says "essentially" because a continuous thing can be moved in one way essentially and in another or others accidentally. For example, if a man in a ship moves against the motion of the ship essentially, he is still moved accidentally by the motion of the ship.

853. Now in order for motion to be one it must be indivisible; and by this I mean from the viewpoint of time, in the sense that at the same time that one part of a continuous thing is moved another is also moved. For it is impossible that one part of a continuous thing should be in motion and another at rest, or that one part should be at rest and another in motion, so that the motion of the different parts should take place in different parts of time.

854. Therefore the Philosopher defines the continuous here by means of motion, and not by means of the oneness of the boundary at which the parts of the continuous things are joined, as is stated in the *Categories,[5a1]* and in the *Physics [227a10]* because from this definition he can consider different grades of unity in different continuous things (as will be made clear later on [see n. 856]), but he cannot do this from the definition given there.

855. Moreover, it should be noted that what is said here about the motion of a continuous thing being indivisible from the viewpoint of time is not opposed to the point proved in Book VI of the *Physics, [235a10-24]* that the time of a motion is divided according to the parts of the thing moved. For here the Philosopher is speaking of motion in an unqualified sense, because one part of a continuous thing does not begin to be moved before another part does; but there he is speaking of some designation which is made in the continuous quantity over which motion passes. For that designation, which is the first part of a continuous quantity, is traversed in a prior time, although in that prior time other parts of the continuous thing that is in motion are also moved.

856. **Again, all those** [3].

Then he proceeds to deal with things which are essentially continuous. He says that those things are essentially continuous which are said to be one not by contact. He proves this as follows: things which touch each other, as two pieces of wood, are not said to be one piece of wood or one body or any other kind of one which belongs to the class of the continuous. Hence it is evident that the oneness of things which are continuous differs from that of things which touch each other. For those things which touch each other do not have any unity of continuity of themselves but by reason of some bond which unites them; but those things which are continuous are said to be essentially one even though they are bent. For two bent lines are continuous in relation to one common boundary, which is the point at which the angle is formed.

857. Yet those things are one to a greater degree which are essentially continuous and without a bend. The reason is that a straight line can have only one motion in all of its parts,

whereas a bent line can have one or two motions. For the whole of a bent line can be understood to be moved in one part; and it can also be understood that when one part is at rest, the other part, which makes an angle with the part at rest, can come closer by its motion to the unmoved part; for example, when the lower leg or shin is bent in the direction of the upper leg, which here is called the thigh. Hence each of these—the shin and thigh—is one to a greater degree "than the scelos," as the Greek text says, i.e., the whole composed of the shin and thigh.

858. Further, it must be noted that the text which reads "curved" instead of "bent" is false. For, since the parts of a curved line do not contain an angle, it is evident that they must be in motion together or at rest together, just as the parts of a straight line are; but this does not happen in the case of a bent line, as has been stated [3].

859. **Again, a thing** [4].

Here he gives the second way in which things are one. He says that a thing is said to be one in a second way not merely by reason of continuous quantity but because of the fact that the whole subject is uniform in species. For some things can be continuous even though they differ in species; for example, when gold is continuous with silver or something of this kind. And then two such things will be one if quantity alone is considered but not if the nature of the subject is considered. But if the whole continuous subject is uniform in species, it will be one both from the viewpoint of quantity and from that of nature.

860. Now a subject is said to be uniform in species when the same sensible form is not divided in such a way that there are different sensible forms in different parts of the subject, as it sometimes happens, for example, that one part of a sensible body is white and another black. And this subject, which does not differ in species, can be taken in two ways: in one way as the first subject, and in another as the last or ultimate subject which is reached at the end of a division. It is evident, for example, that a whole amount of wine is said to be one because its parts are parts of one common subject which is undifferentiated specifically. The same is true of water. For all liquids or moist things are said to be one insofar as they have a single ultimate subject. For oil and wine and the like are ultimately dissolved into water or air, which is the root of moistness in all things.

861. **And those things** [5].

Then he indicates the third way in which things are said to be one. He says that those things are said to be one whose genus is one, even though it is divided by opposite differences. And this way resembles the preceding one; for some things were said to be one in the preceding way because their subject-genus is one, and now some things are said to be one because their genus, which is the subject of differences, is one; for example, a man and a horse and a dog are said to be one because they have animality in common as one genus, which is the subject of differences. Yet this way differs from the preceding, because in the preceding way the subject was one thing which was not differentiated by forms; but here the subject-genus is one thing which is differentiated by various differences, as though by various forms.

862. Thus it is evident that some things are said to be one in genus in a most proximate sense, and in a way similar to that in which some things are said to be one in matter. For those things which are said to be one in mat-

ter are also differentiated by forms. For even though a genus is not matter, because it would then not be predicated of a species since matter is part of a thing, still the notion of a genus is taken from what is material in a thing, just as the notion of a difference is taken from what is formal. For the rational soul is not the difference of man (since it is not predicated of man), but something having a rational soul (for this is what the term rational signifies). Similarly, sensory nature is not the genus of man but a part. But something having a sensory nature, which the term animal signifies, is the genus of man. In a similar fashion, then, the way in which things are one in matter is closely related to that in which they are one in genus.

863. But it must be borne in mind that to be one in generic character has two meanings. For sometimes some things are said to be one in genus, as has been stated, because they belong to one genus, whatever it may be. But sometimes some things are said to be one in genus only in reference to a higher genus, which, along with the designation "one" or "the same," is predicated of the last species of a lower genus when there are other higher species in one of which the lower species agree. For example, figure is one supreme genus which has many species under it, namely, circle, triangle, square, and the like. And triangle also has different species, namely, the equilateral, which is called isopleural, and the triangle with two equal sides, which is called equi-legged or isosceles. Hence these two triangles are said to be one figure, which is their remote genus, but not one triangle, which is their proximate genus. The reason for this is that these two triangles do not differ by any differences which divide figure, but by differences which divide triangle. And the term *same* means that from which something does not differ by a difference.

864. **Further, any two** [6].

He now describes the fourth way in which things are said to be one. He says that things such that the definition of one (which is the concept signifying its quiddity) is not distinguished from the definition of the other (which also signifies its quiddity) are also said to be one. For while every definition must be divisible or distinguishable in itself, or essentially, since it is composed of genus and difference, it is possible for the definition of one thing to be indistinguishable from that of another when the two have one definition. And this applies whether those definitions signify the total [intelligible structure] of the thing defined, as tunic and clothing (and then things whose definition is one are one in an absolute sense), or whether that common definition does not totally comprehend the intelligible structure of the two things which have it in common, as an ox and a horse have in common the one definition of animal. Hence they are never one in an absolute sense, but only in a relative sense inasmuch as each is an animal. The same applies in the case of increase and decrease; for there is one common definition of the genus, because each is a motion relating to quantity. And the same thing is true of plane figures, for there is one definition of the species, plane figure.

865. **And those things** [7].

He gives the fifth way in which things are one. He says that those things are "altogether" one, i.e., perfectly, and in the highest degree, whose concept, which grasps their quiddity, is altogether indivisible, like simple things, which are not composed of material and formal principles. Hence the concept which embraces their quiddity does not comprehend them in such a way as to form a definition of them from different principles, but rather grasps them negatively, as happens in the case of a point, which has no parts; or it even comprehends them by relating them to composite things, as happens, for example, when someone defines the unit as the principle of number. And because such things have in themselves an indivisible concept, and things which are divided in any way at all can be understood separately, it therefore follows that such things are indivisible both in time and in place and in their intelligible structure. Hence these things are one in the highest degree, and especially those which are indivisible in the genus of substance. For even though what is indivisible in the genus of accident is not composite in itself, none the less it does form a composite with something else, namely, the subject in which it inheres. But an indivisible substance is neither composite in itself nor does it form a composite with something else. Or the term substance can be taken in the ablative case, and then the sense is that, even though some things are said to be one because they are indivisible in time and in place and in definition, still those things in this class which are indivisible in substance are said to be one in the highest degree. This sense is reduced to the preceding one.

LESSON 8

The Primary Sense of One. One in the Sense of Complete. One as the Principle of Number. The Ways in Which Things Are One. The Ways in Which Things Are Many

ARISTOTLE'S TEXT Chapter 6: 1016b3–1017a6

1. For in general those things which do not admit of division are said to be one insofar as they do not admit of division. Thus, if two things do not admit of division insofar as they are man, they are one man; and if they do not admit of division insofar as they are animal, they are one animal; and if they do not admit of division insofar as they have continuous quantity, they are one continuous quantity. Hence many things are said to be one because they do or undergo or have or are related to some other thing which is one. But those things are said to be one in a primary sense whose substance is one; and they are one either by continuity or in species or in intelligible structure. For we count as many those things which are not continuous, or those whose form is not one, or those whose intelligible structure is not one. **1016b3–11**

2. Again, in one sense we say that anything at all is one by continuity if it is quantitative and continuous; and in another sense we say that a thing is not one unless it is a whole, i.e., unless it has one form. Thus in looking at the parts of a shoe which are put together in any way at all, we would not say that they are one, except by reason of their continuity; but if they are put together in such a way as to be a shoe and to have a certain form, there would then be one thing. And for this reason among lines the circular line is one in the highest degree because it is whole and complete. **1016b11–17**

3. But the essence of oneness is to be a principle of some number; for the first measure is a principle, because that by which we first come to know each class of things is its first measure. Unity, then, is the first principle of what is knowable about each class. But this unity or unit is not the same in all classes; for in one it is the lesser half tone, and in another it is the vowel or consonant; and in the case of weight the unit is different; and in that of motion different still. But in all cases what is one is indivisible either in quantity or in species. Thus a unit is indivisible in quantity as quantity in every way and has no position; and a point is indivisible in every way and has position. A line is divisible in one dimension; a surface, in two; and a body, in three. And conversely, that which is divisible in two dimensions is a surface; in one, a line; and quantitatively indivisible in every way, a point and a unit. If it has no position, it is a unit; and if it has position, it is a point. **1016b17–31**

4. Further, some things are one in number, some in species, some in genus, and some analogically or proportionally. Those things are one in number which have one matter; in species, which have one intelligible structure; in genus, which have the same figure of predication; and proportionally, which are related to each other as some third thing is to a fourth. And the latter types of unity always follow the former. Thus things which are one in number are one in species, but not all which are one in species are one in number; and all which are one in species are one in genus, but not all which are one in genus are one in species, although they are all one proportionally. And not all which are one proportionally are one in genus. **1016b31–1017a3**

5. Moreover, it is evident that things are said to be many in a way opposite to that in which they are one. For some things are many because they are not continuous; others, because their matter, either the first or ultimate, is divisible in species; and others because they have many conceptions expressing their essence. **1017a3–6**

COMMENTARY

866. Here the Philosopher reduces all senses in which things are said to be one to one primary sense, and in regard to this he does two things. First [1], he makes this reduction; and second [2], to those senses in which things are said to be one, which have already been given, he adds another ("Again, in one sense").

He accordingly says, first [1], that it is evident from what precedes that things which are indivisible in every way are said to be one in the highest degree. For all the other senses in which things are said to be one are reducible to this sense, because it is universally true that those things which do not admit of division are said to be one insofar as they do not admit of division. For example, those things which are undivided insofar as they are man are said to be one in humanity, as Socrates and Plato; those which are undivided in the notion of animality are said to be one in animality; and those which are undivided from the viewpoint of extension or measure are said to be one in quantity, as continuous things.

867. And from this we can also derive number and the types of unity given above, because what is one is indivisible either in an absolute sense or in a qualified one. If it is indivisible in an absolute sense, it is the last type of unity, which is a principle; but if it is indivisible in a qualified sense, it is so either in quantity alone or in nature. If it is indivisible in quantity, then it is the first type. If it is indivisible in nature, it is so either in reference to its subject or to the division which depends upon the form. If it is divisible in reference to its subject, it is so either in reference to a real subject, and then it is the second type, or to a logical subject, and then it is the third type. And indivisibility of form, which is indivisibility of intelligible structure, or definition, constitutes the fourth type.

868. Now from these senses of the term one certain others are again derived. Thus there are many things which are said to be one because they are doing one thing. For example, many men are said to be one insofar as they are rowing a boat. And some things are said to be one because they are subject to one thing; for example, many men constitute one people because they are ruled by one king. And some are said to be one because they possess one thing; for example, many owners of a field are said to be one in their ownership of it. And some things are also said to be one because they are something which is one; for example, many men are said to be one because each of them is white.

869. But considering all of these secondary senses in which things are said to be one, which have already been stated in the five ways given above, we can say that those things are one in the primary sense which are one in their substance. For a thing is one in substance either by reason of its continuity, as in the first way; or because of the species of the subject, as in the second way; and again in the third way because the unity of the genus is somewhat similar to the unity of the species; or also because of the intelligible structure, as in the fourth and fifth ways. That some things are said to be one in these ways is clear from the opposite of one. For things are many in number, i.e., they are counted as many, either because they are continuous, or because they do not have one species, or

because they do not have one common intelligible structure.

870. **Again, in one sense** [2].

Then he gives an additional sense in which the term one is used, which differs from the preceding ones. This sense is not derived from the notion of indivision, as the foregoing are, but rather from the notion of division. He says that sometimes some things are said to be one because of continuity alone, and sometimes they are said to be one only if they constitute a whole and something complete. Now this happens when the thing has one form, not in the sense that a homogeneous subject is said to have one form, which pertains to the second type given above, but in the sense that the form consists in a kind of totality requiring a definite order of parts. Thus it is clear that we do not say that a thing is one, for example, some artifact such as a shoe, when we see the parts put together in any way at all (unless perhaps it is taken to be one insofar as it is continuous); but we say that all parts of a shoe are one when they are united in such a way that the thing is a shoe and has one form—that of a shoe.

871. And from this it is clear that a circular line is one in the highest degree. For a circular line is not only continuous like a straight line, but also has a totality and completeness which a straight line does not have; for that is complete and whole which lacks nothing. Now this characteristic belongs to a circular line; for nothing can be added to a circular line, but something can be added to a straight one.

872. **But the essence** [3].

Then he indicates a property which flows from oneness or unity. He says that the essence of one consists in being the principle of some number. This is clear from the fact that the unit is the primary numerical measure by which every number is measured. Now a measure has the character of a principle, because measured things are known by their measure, and things are known by their proper principles. And it is clear from this that unity is the first principle of what is known or knowable about each thing, and that it is the principle of knowing in all classes.

873. But this unity which is the principle of knowing is not the same in all classes of things. For in the class of musical sounds it is the lesser half tone, which is the smallest thing in this class; for a lesser half tone is less than a half tone since a tone is divided into two unequal half tones one of which is called a lesser half tone. And in the class of words the first and smallest unity is the vowel or consonant; and the vowel to a greater degree than the consonant, as will be stated in Book X (see n. 1971). And in the class of heavy things or weights there is some smallest thing which is their measure, i.e., the ounce or something of this kind. And in the class of motions there is one first measure which measures the other motions, namely, the simplest and swiftest motion, which is the diurnal motion.

874. Yet all of these have this feature in common that the first measure is indivisible in quantity or in species. Hence, in order that something be one and first in the genus of quantity it must be indivisible, and indivisible in quantity. It is called a unit if it is indivisible in every way and has no position, and a point if it is altogether indivisible in quantity but has position. A line is something divisible in one dimension only; a surface, in two; and a body, in all, i.e., in three dimensions. And these descriptions are re-

versible; for everything that is divisible in two dimensions is a surface, and so on with the others.

875. Again, it must be noted that being a measure is the distinctive characteristic of unity insofar as it is the principle of number. But this unity or one is not the same as that which is interchangeable with being, as has been stated in Book IV (see n. 557). For the concept of the latter kind of unity involves only being undivided, but that of the former kind involves being a measure. But even though this character of a measure belongs to the unity which is the principle of number, still by a kind of likeness it is transferred to the unity found in other classes of things, as the Philosopher will show in Book X of this work (see n. 1921). And according to this the character of a measure is found in any class of things. But this character of a measure is a natural consequence of the note of undividedness, as has been explained [3]. Hence the term one is not predicated in a totally equivocal sense of the unity which is interchangeable with being and of that which is the principle of number, but it is predicated of one primarily and of the other secondarily.

876. **Further, some things** [4].

Then he gives another way of dividing unity, and this division is rather from the viewpoint of logic. He says that some things are one in number, some in species, some in genus, and some analogically. Those things are one in number whose matter is one; for insofar as matter has certain designated dimensions it is the principle by which a form is individuated. And for this reason a singular thing is numerically one and divided from other things as a result of matter.

877. Those things are said to be one in species which have one "intelligible structure," or definition; for the only thing that is defined in a proper sense is the species, since every definition is composed of a genus and a difference. And if any genus is defined, this happens insofar as it is a species.

878. Those things are one in genus which have in common one of the "figures of predication," i.e., which have one way of being predicated. For the way in which substance is predicated and that in which quality or action is predicated are different; but all substances have one way of being predicated inasmuch as they are not predicated as something which is present in a subject.

879. And those things are proportionally or analogically one which agree in this respect that one is related to another as some third thing is to a fourth. Now this can be taken in two ways: either in the sense that any two things are related in different ways to one third thing (for example, the term healthy is predicated of urine because it signifies the relationship of a sign of health [to health itself]; and of medicine because it signifies the relationship of a cause to the same health); or it may be taken in the sense that the proportion of two things to two other things is the same (for example, tranquillity to the sea and serenity to the air; for tranquillity is a state of rest in the sea, and serenity is a state of rest in the air).

880. Now with regard to the ways in which things are one, the latter types of unity always follow the former, and not the reverse; for those things which are one in number are one in species, but not the other way about. The same thing is clear in the other cases.

881. **Moreover, it is evident** [5].

From the ways in which things are said to be one he now derives the ways in which things are said to be many. He says that things are said to be many in just as many ways as they are said to be one, because in the case of opposite terms one is used in as many ways as the other. Hence some things are said to be many because they are not continuous, which is the opposite of the first way in which things are one.

882. Other things are said to be many because their matter is divisible in species, whether we understand by matter "the first," i.e., their proximate matter, or the final or ultimate matter into which they are ultimately dissolved. Indeed, it is by the division of their proximate matter that wine and oil are said to be many, and by the division of their remote matter that wine and a stone are said to be many. And if matter be taken both for real matter and for conceptual matter, i.e., for a genus, which resembles matter, many in this sense is taken as the opposite of the second and third ways in which things are said to be one.

883. And still other things are said to be many when the conceptions which express their essence are many. And many in this sense is taken as the opposite of the fourth way in which things are said to be one.

884. But the opposite of the fifth way in which things are one does not have the notion of many except in a qualified sense and potentially; for the fact that a thing is divisible does not make it many except potentially.

LESSON 9
Division of Being into Accidental and Essential. The Types of Accidental and of Essential Being

ARISTOTLE'S TEXT Chapter 7: 1017a7–1017b9

1. *The term being (ens) signifies both accidental being (ens per accidens) and essential being (ens per se).* **1017a7–8**

2. *Accidental being is designated when we say, for example, that the just person is musical, and that the man is musical, and that the musician is a man. And the same thing applies when we say that the musician builds, because it is accidental to a builder to be a musician, or to a musician to be a builder. For to say that "this is that" means that this is an accident of that. And so it is in the cases given; for when we say that the man is musical, and that the musician is a man, or that what is musical is white, in the latter case we mean that both are accidents of the same thing, and in the former that the attribute is accidental to the being. But when we say that what is musical is a man, we mean that musical is an accident of this person. And in this sense too white is said to be, because the thing of which it is an accident is. Therefore those things which are said to be in an accidental sense are said to be such either because both belong to the same being, or because the attribute belongs to the being, or because the thing to which it belongs and of which it is predicated is.* **1017a8–22**

3. *On the other hand those things are said to be essentially which signify the figures of predication; for being is signified in just as many ways as predications are made. Therefore, since some of these predications signify what a thing is, others what it is like, others how much, others how related, others what it does, others what it undergoes, others where, and others when, to each of these there corresponds a mode of being which signifies the same thing. For there is no difference between "the man is recovering" and "the man recovers," or between "the man is walking" or "cutting" and "the man walks" or "cuts." And the same is true in other cases.* **1017a22–30**

4. *Again, being signifies that something is true, and non-being signifies that something is not true but false. This also holds true of affirmation and negation. For example, to say that Socrates is musical means that this is true. Or to say that Socrates is not white means that this is true. But to say that the diagonal of a square is not incommensurable with a side means that this is false.* **1017a31–35**

5. *Again, to be, or being, signifies that some of the things mentioned are potentially and others actually. For in the case of the terms mentioned we predicate being both of what is said to be potentially and of what is said to be actually. And similarly we say both of one who is capable of using scientific knowledge and of one who is actually using it, that he knows. And we say that that is at rest which is already so or capable of being so. And this also applies in the case of substances; for we say that Mercury is in the stone, and half of the line in the line, and we call that grain which is not yet ripe. But when a thing is potential and when not must be settled elsewhere (773:C 1832).* **1017a35–1017b9**

COMMENTARY

885. Here the Philosopher gives the various senses in which the term *being* is used, and in regard to this he does three things. First [1], he divides being into essential being and accidental being. Second [2], he distinguishes between the types of accidental being ("Accidental being"). Third [3], he distinguishes between the types of essential being ("On the other hand").

He says [1], then, that while things are said to be both essentially and accidentally, it should be noted that this division of being is not the same as that whereby being is divided into substance and accident. This is clear from the fact that he later divides essential being into the ten predicaments, nine of which belong to the class of accident [3]. Hence being is divided into substance and accident insofar as it is considered in an absolute sense; for example, whiteness considered in itself is called an accident, and man a substance. But accidental being, in the sense in which it is taken here, must be understood by comparing an accident with a substance; and this comparison is signified by the term is when, for example, it is said that the man is white. Hence this whole "the man is white" is an accidental being. It is clear, then, that the division of being into essential being and accidental being is based on the fact that one thing is predicated of another either essentially or accidentally. But the division of being into substance and accident is based on the fact that a thing is in its own nature either a substance or an accident.

886. **Accidental being** [2].

Then he indicates the various senses in which a thing is said to be accidentally. He says that this occurs in three ways: first, when an accident is predicated of an accident, as when it is said that someone just is musical: second, when an accident is predicated of a subject, as when it is said that the man is musical; and third, when a subject is predicated of an accident, as when it is said that the musician is a man. And since he has shown above (see n. 787) how an accidental cause differs from an essential cause, he therefore now shows that an accidental being is a result of an accidental cause.

887. He says that in giving an accidental cause we say that the musician builds, because it is accidental to a builder to be a musician, or vice versa; for it is evident that the statement "this is that," i.e., the musician is a builder, simply means that "this is an accident of that." The same is true of the foregoing senses of accidental being when we say that the man is musical by predicating an accident of a subject, or when we say that what is white is musical, or conversely that what is musical is white by predicating an accident of an accident. For in all of these cases is signifies merely accidental being: "in the latter case," i.e., when an accident is predicated of an accident, is signifies that both accidents are accidental to the same subject; "and in the former," i.e., when an accident is predicated of a subject, is signifies "that the attribute is accidental to the being," i.e., to the subject. But when we say that what is musical is a man, we mean "that musical is an accident of this person," i.e., that musical, which holds the position of a subject, is an accident of the predicate. And the reason for making the predication is similar in a sense when a subject is predicated of an accident and when an accident is predicated of an accident. For a subject is predicated of an accident by reason of the fact that the subject is predicated of that to which the accident, which is expressed in the subject, is accidental; and in a similar fashion an accident is predicated of an accident because it is predicated of the subject of an accident. And for this reason the attribute musical is predicated not only of man but also of white, because that of which the attribute musical is an accident, i.e., the subject, is white.

888. It is evident, then, that those things which are said to be in an accidental sense are said to be such for three reasons: either "because both," namely, the subject and predicate, belong to the same thing (as when an accident is predicated of an accident); or "because the attribute," namely, the predicate, such as musical, "belongs to the being," i.e., to the subject which is said to be musical (and this occurs when an accident is predicated of a subject); or "because the thing," i.e., the subject which is expressed in the predicate, to which belongs the accident of which it (the subject) is itself predicated, itself is (and this occurs when a subject is predicated of an accident, as when we say that what is musical is a man).

889. **On the other hand** [3].

Here he distinguishes between the types of essential being; and in regard to this he does three things. First [3], he divides the kind of being which lies outside the mind, which is complete being, by the ten predicaments. Second [4], he gives another type of being, inasmuch as being exists only in the mind ("Again, being signifies"). Third [5], he divides being by potentiality and actuality—and being divided in this way is more common than complete being, for potential being is being only imperfectly and in a qualified sense ("Again, to be").

He says, first [3], that all those things which signify the figures of predication are said to be essentially. For it must be noted that being cannot be narrowed down to some definite thing in the way in which a genus is narrowed down to a species by means of differences. For since a difference does not participate in a genus, it lies outside the essence of a genus. But there could be nothing outside the essence of being which could constitute a particular species of being by adding to being; for what is outside of being is nothing, and this cannot be a difference. Hence in Book III of this work (see n. 433) the Philosopher proved that being cannot be a genus.

890. Being must then be narrowed down to diverse genera on the basis of a different mode of predication, which flows from a different mode of being; for "being is signified," i.e., something is signified to be, "in just as many ways" (or in as many senses) as we can make predications. And for this reason the classes into which being is first divided are called predicaments, because they are distinguished on the basis of different ways of predicating. Therefore, since some predicates signify what (i.e., substance); some, of what kind; some, how much; and so on; there must be a mode of being corresponding to each type of predication. For example, when it is said that a man is an animal, is signifies substance; and when it is said that a man is white, is signifies quality; and so on.

891. For it should be noted that a predicate can be referred to a subject in three ways. This occurs in one way when the predicate states what the subject is, as when I say that Socrates is an animal; for Socrates is the thing which is an animal. And this predicate is said to signify first substance, i.e., a particular substance, of which all attributes are predicated.

892. A predicate is referred to a subject in a second way when the predicate is taken as being in the subject, and this predicate is in the subject either essentially and absolutely and as something flowing from its matter, and then it is quantity; or as something flowing from its form, and then it is quality; or it is not present in the sub-

ject absolutely but with reference to something else, and then it is relation. A predicate is referred to a subject in a third way when the predicate is taken from something extrinsic to the subject, and this occurs in two ways. In one way, that from which the predicate is taken is totally extrinsic to the subject; and if this is not a measure of the subject, it is predicated after the manner of attire, as when it is said that Socrates is shod or clothed. But if it is a measure of the subject, then, since an extrinsic measure is either time or place, the predicament is taken either in reference to time, and so it will be *when;* or if it is taken in reference to place and the order of parts in place is not considered, it will be *where;* but if this order is considered, it will be position. In another way, that from which the predicate is taken, though outside the subject, is nevertheless from a certain point of view in the subject of which it is predicated. And if it is from the viewpoint of the principle, then it is predicated as an action; for the principle of action is in the subject. But if it is from the viewpoint of its terminus, then it will be predicated as a passion; for a passion is terminated in the subject which is being acted upon.

893. But since there are some predications in which the verb is is clearly not used (for example, when it is said that a man walks), lest someone think that these predications do not involve the predication of being, for this reason Aristotle subsequently rejects this, saying that in all predications of this kind something is signified to be. For every verb is reduced to the verb is plus a participle. For there is no difference between the statements "the man is recovering" and "the man recovers"; and it is the same in other cases. It is clear, then, that "being" is used in as many ways as we make predications.

894. And there is no truth in Avicenna's statement [*Metaphysica,* III,7] that predicates which belong to the class of accidents primarily signify substance and secondarily accidents, as the terms *white* and *musical.* For the term white, as it is used in the categories, signifies quality alone. Now the term white implies a subject inasmuch as it signifies whiteness after the manner of an accident, so that it must by implication include the subject in its notion, because the being of an accident consists in being in something. For even though whiteness signifies an accident, it still does not signify this after the manner of an accident but after that of a substance. Hence it implies a subject in no way. For if it were to signify a subject primarily, then the Philosopher would not put accidental predicates under essential being but under accidental being. For the whole statement "the man is white" is a being in an accidental sense, as has been stated [2].

895. **Again, being signifies** [4].

Then he gives another sense in which the term being is used, inasmuch as the terms being and is signify the composition of a proposition, which the intellect makes when it combines and separates. He says that being signifies the truth of a thing, or as another translation better expresses it, being signifies that some statement is true. Thus the truth of a thing can be said to determine the truth of a proposition after the manner of a cause; for by reason of the fact that a thing is or is not, a discourse is true or false. For when we say that something is, we signify that a proposition is true; and when we say that something is not, we signify that it is not true. And this applies both to affirmation and to negation. It applies to affirmation, as when we say that Socrates is white because this is true; and to negation, as when we say that Socrates is not white, because this is true, namely, that he is not white. And in a similar way we say that the diagonal of a square is not incommensurable with a side, because this is false, i.e., its not being incommensurable.

896. Now it must be noted that this second way in which being is used is related to the first as an effect is to a cause. For from the fact that something is in reality it follows that there is truth and falsity in a proposition, and the intellect signifies this by the term is taken as a verb copula. But since the intellect considers as a kind of being something which is in itself a nonbeing, such as a negation and the like, therefore sometimes being is predicated of something in this second way and not in the first. For blindness is said to be in the second way on the grounds that the proposition in which something is said to be blind is true. However, it is not said to be true in the first way; for blindness does not have any being in reality but is rather a privation of some being. Now it is accidental to a thing that an attribute should be affirmed of it truly in thought or in word, for reality is not referred to knowledge but the reverse. But the act of being which each thing has in its own nature is substantial; and therefore when it is said that Socrates is, if the *is* is taken in the first way, it belongs to the class of substantial predicates; for being is a higher predicate with reference to any particular being, as animal with reference to man. But if it is taken in the second way, it belongs to the class of accidental predicates.

897. **Again, to be, or being** [5].

Here he gives the division of being into the actual and the potential. He says that to be and being signify something which is expressible or utterable potentially or actually. For in the case of all of the foregoing terms which signify the ten predicaments, something is said to be so actually and something else potentially; and from this it follows that each predicament is divided by actuality and potentiality. And just as in the case of things which are outside the mind some are said to be actually and some potentially, so also is this true in the case of the mind's activities, and in that of privations, which are only conceptual beings. For one is said to know both because he is capable of using scientific knowledge and because he is using it; and similarly a thing is said to be at rest both because rest belongs to it already and because it is capable of being at rest. And this is true not only of accidents but also of substances. For "Mercury," we say, i.e., the image of Mercury, is present potentially in the stone; and half of a line is present potentially in a line, for every part of a continuum is potentially in the whole. And the line is included in the class of substances according to the opinion of those who hold that the objects of mathematics are substances—an opinion which he has not yet disproved. And when grain is not yet ripe, for example, when it is still in blade, it is said to be potentially. Just when, however, something is potential and when it is no longer such must be established elsewhere, namely, in Book IX of this work (see n. 1832).

LESSON 10
Meanings of Substance

ARISTOTLE'S TEXT Chapter 8: 1017b10–1017b26

1. *The term substance (substantia) means the simple bodies, such as earth, fire, water and the like; and in general bodies and the things composed of them, both animals and demons and their parts. All of these are called substances because they are not predicated of a subject, but other things are predicated of them.* **1017b10–14**

2. *In another sense substance means that which, being present in such things as are not predicated of a subject, is the cause of their being, as the soul in an animal.* **1017b14–16**

3. *Again, substance means those parts which, being present in such things, limit them and designate them as individuals and as a result of whose destruction the whole is destroyed; for example, body is destroyed when surface is, as some say, and surface when line is. And in general it seems to some that number is of this nature; for [according to them] if it is destroyed, nothing will exist, and it limits all things.* **1017b18–21**

4. *Again, the quiddity of a thing, whose intelligible expression is the definition, also seems to be the substance of each thing.* **1017b21–23**

5. *It follows, then, that the term substance is used in two senses. It means the ultimate subject, which is not further predicated of something else; and it means anything which is a particular being and capable of existing apart. The form and species of each thing is said to be of this nature.* **1017b23–26**

COMMENTARY

898. Aristotle now explains the various senses in which the term *substance* is used; and in regard to this he does two things. First [1], he gives the various senses in which the term substance is used. Second [4], he reduces all of these to two ("It follows").

In treating the first part he gives four senses of the term substance. First, it means particular substances, such as the simple bodies: earth, fire, water and the like. And in general it means all bodies, even though they are not simple, i.e., compound bodies of like parts, such as stones, blood, flesh and the like. Again, it means animals, which are composed of such sensible bodies, and also their parts, such as hands and feet and so on; "and demons," i.e., the idols set up in temples and worshipped as gods. Or by demons he means certain animals which the Platonists claimed are capable of reasoning, and which Apuleius defines thus: demons are animals composed of an ethereal body, rational in mind, passive in soul, and eternal in time. Now all of the foregoing things are called substances because they are not predicated of another subject but other things are predicated of them. This is the description of first substance given in the *Categories*.[2a10]

899. **In another sense** [2].

He says that in another sense substance means the cause of the being of the foregoing substances which are not predicated of a subject; and it is not extrinsic to them like an efficient cause but is intrinsic like a form. It is in this sense that the soul is called the substance of an animal.

900. **Again, substance** [3].

He gives a third meaning of substance, which is the one used by the Platonists and Pythagoreans. He says that all those parts of the foregoing substances which constitute their limits and designate them as individuals, according to the opinion of these thinkers, and by whose destruction the whole is destroyed, are also termed substances. For example, body is destroyed when surface is, as some say, and surface when line is. It is also clear that surface is the limit of body and line the limit of surface. And according to the opinion of the philosophers just mentioned the line is a part of surface and surface a part of body. For they held that bodies are composed of surfaces, surfaces of lines, and lines of points; and thus it would follow that the point is the substance of the line, the line the substance of surface, and so on for the rest. And according to this position number seems to constitute the entire substance of all things, because when number is destroyed nothing remains in the world; for what is not one is nothing. And similarly things which are not many are non-existent. And number is also found to limit all things, because all things are measured by number.

901. But this sense of substance is not a true one. For that which is found to be common to all things and is something without which they cannot exist does not necessarily constitute their substance, but it can be some property flowing from the substance or from a principle of the substance. These philosophers also fell into error especially regarding unity and number because they failed to distinguish between the unity which is interchangeable with being and that which is the principle of number.

902. **Again, the quiddity** [4].

He says that the quiddity of each thing, which the definition signifies, is also called its substance. Now the quiddity or essence of a thing, whose intelligible expression is the definition, differs from a form, which he identified with the second meaning of substance, just as humanity differs from a soul, for a form is part of a thing's essence or quiddity, but the essence or quiddity itself of a thing includes all its essential principles. It is in this last sense, then, that genus and species are said to be the substance of the things of which they are predicated; for genus and species do not signify the form alone but the whole essence of a thing.

903. **It follows** [5].

Then he reduces the foregoing senses of substance to two. He says that from the above-mentioned ways in which the term substance is used we can understand that it has two meanings. It means the ultimate subject in propositions, and thus is not predicated of something else. This is first substance, which means a particular thing which exists of itself and is capable of existing apart because it is distinct from everything else and cannot be common to many. And a particular substance differs from universal substance in these three respects: first, a particular substance is not predicated of inferiors, whereas a universal substance is; second, universal substance subsists only by reason of a particular substance, which subsists of itself; and third, universal substance is present in many things, whereas a particular substance is not but is distinct from everything else and capable of existing apart.

904. And the form and species of a thing also "is said to be of this nature," i.e., substance. In this he includes the second and fourth senses of substance; for essence and form have this note in common that both are said to be that by which something is. However, form, which causes a thing to be actual, is related to matter, whereas quiddity

or essence is related to the supposit, which is signified as having such and such an essence. Hence "the form and species" are comprehended under one thing—a being's essence.

905. He omits the third sense of substance because it is a false one, or because it is reducible to form, which has the character of a limit. And he omits matter, which is called substance, because it is not substance actually. However, it is included in the first sense of substance, because a particular substance is a substance and is individuated in the world of material things only by means of matter.

LESSON 11
The Ways in Which Things Are the Same Essentially and Accidentally

ARISTOTLE'S TEXT Chapter 9: 1017b27–1018a9

1. Things are said to be the same accidentally; for example, "white" and "musical" are the same because they are accidents of the same subject. And "man" and "musical" are the same because the one is an accident of the other. And "musical" is the same as "man" because it is an accident of a man. And the composite is the same as each of these simple terms, and each the same as it. For both "man" and "musical" are said to be the same as "musical man," and this the same as they. And for this reason none of these predications are universal. For it is not true to say that every man is the same as the musical; for universal predicates are essential, whereas accidental predicates are not, but are said of singulars in an unqualified sense. For "Socrates" and "musical Socrates" seem to be the same because Socrates is not found in many. And for this reason we do not say "every Socrates" as we say "every man." Some things, then, are said to be the same in this way. **1017b27–1018a5**

2. And others are said to be the same essentially, and in the same number of ways in which they are said to be one. For those things whose matter is one in species or in number, and those whose substance is one, are said to be the same. Hence it is evident that sameness (identitas) is a kind of unity of the being of many things or of one thing taken as many; for example, when a person says that something is the same as itself, he uses the same thing as though it were two. **1018a5–9**

COMMENTARY

906. Having given the various senses of the terms which signify the subject of this science, here the Philosopher gives those which signify the parts of such things as constitute the subject of this science. This is divided into two parts. In the first [1] he gives the various senses of the terms which signify the parts of unity; and in the second (Lesson 14), those which signify the parts of being ("In one sense"). For substance, which is also posited as the subject of this science, is a single category which is not divided into many categories.

The first part is divided into two sections. In the first he gives the various senses of the terms which signify the parts of unity; and in the second (Lesson 13), those which signify something that flows from the notion of unity, namely, *prior* and *subsequent* ("Things are said to be"). For to be one is to be a principle or starting point, as has been explained above (see n. 872).

907. The first part is divided into two sections. In the first he gives the various senses of the terms which signify the primary parts of unity and of its opposite, plurality; and in the second (Lesson 12, text 5), he gives those which signify certain secondary parts of unity ("By opposites").

Now the parts of unity are *sameness*, which is oneness in substance; *likeness*, which is oneness in quality; and *equality*, which is oneness in quantity. And, opposed to these, the parts of plurality are *otherness*, *unlikeness* and *inequality*.

In regard to the first he does two things. First, he gives the various senses in which the term *same* is used, and the senses of its opposite. Second (Lesson 12, text 3), he gives the various senses of the term *like*, and of its opposite, *unlike* ("Things are said to be *like*"). He makes no mention here, however, of the term *equal* and its opposite, because in the case of these terms plurality is not so evident.

In regard to the first part he does three things. First, he gives the various senses of the term *same;* second (Lesson 12, text 1), of the term *other*, or *diverse* ("Those things are said to be *other*"); and third (*ibid.*, text 2), of the term *different* ("Things are said to be *different*").

In regard to the first he does two things. First, he gives the ways in which things are said to be accidentally the same; and second [2], he gives those in which things are said to be essentially the same ("And others").

908. He says [1] that things are said to be accidentally the same *(idem per accidens)* in three ways. In one way they are the same in the sense that two accidents are; thus "white" and "musical" are said to be the same because they are accidents of the same subject. Things are accidentally the same in a second way when a predicate is said to be the same as a subject inasmuch as it is predicated of it; thus when it is said that the man is musical, these (man and musical) are said to be the same because musical is an accident of a man, i.e., the predicate is an accident of the subject. And things are accidentally the same in a third way when the subject is said to be the same as an accident inasmuch as it is predicated of it. For example, when it is said that the musical thing is a man, it is understood that the man is the same as the musical thing; for what is predicated of some subject is identified with that subject. And sameness in this sense means that the subject is an accident of the predicate.

909. Now besides these ways in which things are accidentally the same, in which an accident and a subject are taken in themselves, there are also others, i.e., those in which an accident is taken in conjunction with a subject. And when this occurs two senses of the term same have to be distinguished. One of these is signified when an accident taken singly is predicated of the composite of subject and accident; and then the meaning is that the accident is the same as both of the simple terms taken together; for example, "musical" is the same as "musical man." The other is signified when the composite of accident and subject is predicated of the subject taken singly, as when we say that the man is a musical man; and then both of these (the composite "musical man") are signified as being the same as this, i.e., as the subject taken singly. The same notion applies if an accident is taken singly and a subject is taken in combination with the accident. This would be the case, for example, if we were to say that what is musical is a musical man, or the reverse; for both "man" and "musical" are said to be accidentally the same as "musical man," which is the composite, when these two are predicated of that one thing, and vice versa.

910. From this he draws the further conclusion that, in all of the foregoing modes of predication in which things are said to be accidentally the same, no term is predicated universally. For it is not true to say that every man is the same as what is musical. This becomes clear as follows: Only those attributes which belong essentially to the same subject are predicated universally of universals; for a predicate is predicated essentially of a subject because the mode of predication, which is a universal one, agrees with the condition of the subject, which is universal. However, accidents are not predicated essentially of universals, but only by reason of singular things; and thus

they are not predicated universally of universals. But while accidents are predicated in an unqualified sense of singular things (for Socrates and musical Socrates seem to be the same in subject), they are not predicated universally of singular things; for nothing can be predicated universally of something that is not universal. But Socrates is not universal, because he is not present in many. Hence nothing can be predicated of Socrates so that we should say "every Socrates" as we say "every man." The things of which we have spoken, then, are said to be one in this way, i.e., accidentally, as has been stated.

911. **And others** [2].

Then he gives the ways in which things are said to be essentially the same *(idem per se)*. He says that things are said to be essentially the same in the same number of ways in which they are said to be essentially one. Now all of the ways in which things are said to be essentially one are reduced to two. Thus, in one sense, things are said to be essentially one because their matter is one, whether we take the matter to be the same in species or in number. The second and third ways in which things are one are reduced to this. And, in another sense, things are said to be one because their substance is one, whether by reason of continuity, which pertains to the first way in which things are one, or by reason of the unity and indivisibility of their intelligible structure, which pertains to the fourth and fifth ways. Therefore some things are said to be the same in these ways too.

912. From this he further concludes that sameness *(identitas)* is a unity or union. For things which are said to be the same are either many in being, but are said to be the same inasmuch as they agree in some respect, or they are one in being, but the intellect uses this as many in order to understand a relationship; for a relationship can be understood only between two extremes. This is what happens, for example, when we say that something is the same as itself; for the intellect then uses something which is one in reality as though it were two, otherwise it could not designate the relationship of a thing to itself. Hence it is clear that, if a relationship always requires two extremes, and in relations of this kind there are not two extremes in reality but only in the mind, then the relationship of sameness according to which something is said to be absolutely the same, will not be a real relation but only a conceptual relation. This is not the case, however, when any two things are said to be the same either in genus or in species. For if the relationship of sameness were something in addition to what we designate by the term *same,* then since this reality, which is a relation, is the same as itself, it would have to have for a like reason something that is also the same as itself; and so on to infinity. Now while it is impossible to proceed to infinity in the case of real beings, nothing prevents this from taking place in the case of things which have being in the mind. For since the mind may reflect on its own act it can understand that it understands; and it can also understand this act in turn, and so on to infinity.

LESSON 12

Various Senses of Diverse, Different, Like, Contrary, and Diverse in Species

ARISTOTLE'S TEXT Chapters 9 & 10: 1018a9–1018b8

1. Things are said to be other or diverse (diversa) of which either the forms or the matter or the intelligible structure of the essence is many; and in general the term other has senses opposite to those of the same. **1018a9–11**

2. Things are said to be different (differentia) which, while being diverse, are the same in some respect, and not merely in number, but in species or in genus or proportionally. And so also are those things whose genus is not the same, and contraries, and all those things which have diversity or otherness in their essence. **1018b12–15**

3. Things are said to be like (similia) which undergo the same modifications; or undergo more of the same than of different modifications; or whose quality is one. **1018b15–17**

4. And whatever has a greater number or the more important of those contraries in reference to which alteration is possible is said to be like something else. And things are said to be unlike (dissimilia) in ways opposite to those in which they are like. **1018b17–19**

Chapter 10

5. By opposites (opposita) we mean contraries, contradictories, relatives, and privation and possession. **1018b20–21**

6. And opposites also mean the ultimate parts of which things are composed and into which they are dissolved, as in processes of generation and corruption. And those things which cannot be present at the same time in a subject which is receptive of them are called opposites: either they themselves or the things of which they are composed. Gray and white, for example, are not present at the same time in the same subject, and therefore the things of which they are composed are opposites. **1018b21–25**

7. By contraries (contraria) we mean those attributes which, differing in genus, cannot be present at the same time in the same subject; and also those which differ most in the same genus; and those which differ most in the same subject; and those which differ most among those which come under the same power; and things which differ most either absolutely or in genus or in species. **1018b25–31**

8. Other things are called contraries either because they have contrary attributes or because they are receptive of them; and others because they are capable of causing them or undergoing them, or because they are actually causing them or undergoing them, or because they are rejections or acquisitions or possessions or privations of such attributes. **1018b31–35**

9. But since the term being and the term one are used in many ways, all other terms which are used in relation to them must follow upon them; so that the terms same, diverse and contrary vary according to each category. **1018b35–38**

10. Those things are said to be diverse (or other) in species which belong to the same genus but are not subalternate. And so are those which belong to the same genus and have a difference; and also those which have contrariety in their substance. For contraries differ from each other in species, either all of them, or those which are called such in a primary sense; and so are those things whose intelligible structures differ in the lowest species of the genus (for example, man and horse do not differ in genus but their intelligible structures are different); and those attributes which belong to the same substance and have a difference. Things which are the same in species are said to be such in ways opposite to those just given. **1018b38–1018b8**

COMMENTARY

913. Here he explains the various ways in which the term *diverse* (or

other) is used, and he gives three senses. Thus some things are said to be diverse in species because their species are many, as an ass and an ox; others are said to be diverse in number because their matters differ, as two individuals of one species; and others are said to be diverse because "the intelligible structure of the essence," i.e., the definition designating their substance, is different. For some things may be the same in number, i.e., from the viewpoint of matter, but diverse in their intelligible structure, as Socrates and this white man.

914. And since many modes of diversity can be considered (for example, diversity in genus, and the diversity resulting from the division of the continuous), he therefore adds that the term *diverse* means the very opposite of *the same;* for to every way in which things are the same there corresponds an opposite way in which they are diverse. Hence things are said to be diverse in the same number of senses in which they are said to be the same.

915. Yet the other ways in which things are said to be one, i.e., the same, can be reduced to those stated here. For diversity of genus is included in diversity of species, and diversity of quantity is included in diversity of matter, because the parts of a quantity have the character of matter in relation to the whole.

916. **Things are said to be "different"** [2].

Then he gives the various senses in which the term *different* is used, and there are two of them. First, any two things are said properly to be different which, while being diverse, are "the same in some respect," i.e., they have some one thing in common. And this is so whether they have some one thing in common numerically, as Socrates sitting and Socrates not sitting; or whether they have some one thing in common specifically, as Socrates and Plato have man in common; or whether they have a common genus, as man and ass share in the genus animal; or whether they share in some one thing proportionally, as quantity and quality both share in being. And from this it is evident that everything different is diverse, but not the reverse. For diverse things which agree in no respect cannot properly be called different, because they do not differ in some other respect but only in themselves; but that is said to be different which differs in some particular respect. The term different is used in a second way when it is taken commonly in place of the term diverse; and then those things are also said to be different which belong to diverse genera and have nothing in common.

917. Next he indicates the kind of things which admit of difference in the first way, which is the proper one. Now those things which are said properly to differ must agree in some respect. Those which agree in species differ only by accidental differences; for example, Socrates insofar as he is white or just differs from Plato insofar as he is black or musical. And those things which agree in genus and are diverse in species differ by substantial differences. And since this is so, then those things are said to differ most properly which are the same in genus and diverse in species. For every genus is divided into contrary differences, but not every genus is divided into contrary species. Thus the species of color, white and black, are contraries, and so are their differences, expanding and contracting. And the differences of animal, rational and irrational, are contraries; but the species of animal, such

as man, horse, and the like, are not. Therefore things which are said to differ most properly are either those which are contrary species, as white and black, or those species of one genus which are not contrary but have contrariety in their essence because of the contrariety of differences which belong to the essence of the species.

918. **Things are said to be "like"** [3].

Here he points out the various ways in which the term *like* is used, and in regard to this he does two things. First [3], he indicates the various ways in which this term is used; and second [5], he gives those senses in which the term *unlike* is used ("By opposites").

In regard to the first he does two things. First, he gives the ways in which the term like is used; and second [4], he explains how one thing is said to be most like another ("And whatever").

He gives three ways in which things are like. Now it is evident that oneness in quality causes likeness. Further, undergoing or affection *(passio)* is associated with quality, because undergoing is most noticeable in the case of qualitative change or alteration; and thus one species of quality is called affection or possible quality. Hence things are observed to be like not only insofar as they have a common quality but also insofar as they undergo or suffer something in common. And this can be taken from two points of view: either from that of the affection or undergoing, or from that of the subject in which the affection is terminated.

919. Some things are like, then, for three reasons. First, they undergo or suffer the same thing; for example, two pieces of wood which are consumed by fire can be said to be like. Second, several things are like merely because they are affected or undergo something, whether this be the same or different; for example, two men, one of whom is beaten and the other imprisoned, are said to be like in that they both undergo something or suffer. Third, those things are said to be like which have one quality; for example, two white things are alike in whiteness, and two stars in the heaven are alike in brightness or in power.

920. **And whatever** [4].

Then he shows how one thing is said to be most like some other thing. For when there are several contraries of the sort which are observed to be alterable, whatever resembles some other thing in having the more important of these contraries is said to be more properly like that thing. For example, garlic, which is hot and dry, is said to be more properly like fire than sugar, which is hot and moist. The same holds true of any two things which are like some third thing in terms of only one quality; for whatever resembles some other thing in terms of some quality which is more proper to itself, is said to be more properly like that thing. For example, air is more properly like fire than earth; for air is like fire in reference to warmth, which is a quality proper to fire itself to a greater degree than dryness, in reference to which earth is like air.

921. Then he states that things are said to be *unlike* in ways opposite to those in which they are *like.*

922. **By "opposites"** [5].

Here he distinguishes between the secondary parts of plurality, i.e., those contained under difference and diversity, which are its primary parts; and in regard to this he does three things. First, he gives the various ways in which the term *opposite* is used; second [7], those in which the term *contrary* is used ("By contraries"); and third [10], those in which things are said to be *diverse or other in species* ("Those things are said to be").

In regard to the first he does two things. First [5], he gives the various ways in which we speak of *opposites;* and there are four of these: contradictories, contraries, privation and possession, and relatives. For one thing is contraposed or opposed to another either by reason of dependence, i.e., insofar as one depends on another, and then they are opposed as relatives, or by reason of removal, i.e., because one removes another. This occurs in three ways: either one thing removes another entirely and leaves nothing, and then there is negation; or the subject alone remains, and then there is privation; or the subject and genus remain, and then there is contrariety. For there are contraries not only in the same subject but also in the same genus.

923. **And opposites** [6].

Second, he gives two ways in which things can be recognized as opposites. The first of these pertains to motion, for in any motion or change the *terminus from which* is the opposite of the *terminus to which.* Hence those things from which motion begins and those in which it ends are opposites. This is evident in processes of generation; for the white is generated from the not-white, and fire is generated from what is not-fire.

924. The second pertains to the subject. For those attributes which cannot belong at the same time to the same subject must be the opposite of each other, either they themselves or the things in which they are present. For the same body cannot be at the same time both white and black, which are contraries; nor can the terms *man* and *ass* be predicated of the same thing, because their intelligible structures contain opposite differences, i.e., rational and irrational. The same holds true of gray and white, because gray is composed of black, which is the opposite of white. And we should note that he expressly says, "in the same subject"; for certain things cannot exist at the same time in the same subject, not because they are opposed to each other, but because the subject is not receptive of the one or the other; for example, whiteness and music cannot exist at the same time in an ass, but they can exist at the same time in a man.

925. **By "contraries"** [7].

Then he states the various ways in which the term *contrary* is used, and in regard to this he does three things. First, he gives the principal ways in which things are said to be contrary. Among these he includes, first, one improper usage of the term, i.e., that whereby some attributes are called contraries which, while differing in genus, cannot belong at the same time to the same subject; for properly speaking contraries are attributes which belong to one genus. An example of this would be found if we were to say that heaviness and circular motion cannot belong to the same subject.

926. Then he gives a second usage of the term, which is a proper one, according to which contraries are said to be things that agree in some respect; for contraries agree in three respects, namely, in reference to the same genus, or to the same subject, or to the same power. Then he uses these three to expose the things which are real contraries. He says that those attributes which differ most in the same genus are called contraries, as white and black in the genus of color; and those which differ most in the same subject, as health and disease in an animal; and

those which differ most in reference to the same power, as what is correct and what is incorrect in reference to grammar; for rational powers extend to opposites. He says "most" in order to differentiate contraries from the intermediate attributes which lie between them, which also agree in the same genus, subject and power, yet do not differ to the greatest degree.

927. Hence he adds the universal notion involved in things which are designated as contraries, namely, that contraries are things which differ most either absolutely or in the same genus or in the same species. They differ "absolutely," for example, in the case of local motion, where the extremes are separated most widely, as the most easterly and westerly points of the whole universe, which are the limits of its diameter. And they differ "in the same genus," as the specific differences which divide a genus; and "in the same species," as contrary differences of an accidental kind by which individuals of the same species differ from each other.

928. **Other things** [8].

Here he shows in what respect some things are said to be contraries in a secondary way because they are related to those things which are contraries in the primary way. For some things are contraries either because they actually possess contraries, as fire and water are called contraries because one is hot and the other cold; or because they are the potential recipients of contraries, as what is receptive of health and of disease; or because they are potentially causing contraries or undergoing them, as what is capable of heating and of cooling, and what is able to be heated and to be cooled; or because they are actually causing contraries or undergoing them, as what is heating and cooling or being heated and being cooled; or because they are expulsions or rejections or acquisitions of contraries, or even possessions or privations of them. For the privation of white is the opposite of the privation of black, just as the possession of the former is the opposite of that of the latter.

929. It is evident, then, that he touches on a threefold relationship of contraries to things: one is to a subject which is either in act or in potency; another is to something that is active or passive in act or in potency; and a third is to processes of generation and corruption, either to the processes themselves or to their termini, which are possession and privation.

930. **But since the term** [9].

He gives a third way in which the term contrary is used, and he also shows why the foregoing terms are used in many ways. For since the terms *one* and *being* have several meanings, the terms which are based upon them must also have several meanings; for example, *same* and *diverse*, which flow from *one* and *many;* and *contrary,* which is contained under *diverse.* Hence diverse must be divided according to the ten categories just as being and one are.

931. **Those things** [10].

He now explains the various ways in which things are said to be *diverse* (or *other*) *in species*, and he gives five of these. First, they belong to the same genus and are not subalternate; for example, science and whiteness both come under quality, yet they are not distinguished from each other by opposite differences.

932. Second, they belong to the same genus and are distinguished from each other by some difference, whether

such differences are contrary or not, as two-footed and four-footed.

933. Third, their subjects contain contrariety; i.e., those things which are distinguished by contrary differences, whether the subjects are contrary themselves (as white and black, which are distinguished by the differences "expanding" and "contracting") or not (as man and ass, which are distinguished by the differences "rational" and "irrational"). For contraries must differ in species, either all of them, or those which are called contraries in the primary sense.

934. Fourth, the lowest species are diverse and are the last in some genus, as man and horse. For those things which differ only in species are said more properly to differ in species than those which differ both in species and in genus.

935. Fifth, they are accidents in the same subject, yet differ from each other; for many accidents of one and the same kind cannot exist in the same subject. And things are said to be *the same in species* in ways opposite to those given above.

LESSON 13
The Ways in Which Things Are Prior and Subsequent

ARISTOTLE'S TEXT Chapter 11: 1018b9–1019a14

1. *Things are said to be prior and subsequent insofar as there is some primary thing or principle in each class; for prior means what is nearer to some principle determined either in an absolute sense and by nature, or relatively, or in reference to place, or in certain other ways.* **1018b9–12**

2. *For example, a thing is prior in place because it is nearer either to some naturally determined place, as the middle or last, or to one that depends on chance. And what is farther away is subsequent.* **1018b12–14**

3. *Other things are prior in time. For some are prior because they are farther away from the present, as in the case of things which have taken place. Thus the Trojan war is prior to that of the Medes because it is farther away from the present. And others are prior in time because they are nearer to the present, as in the case of future events; for the Nemean [games] are prior to the Pythian because they are nearer to the present, provided that the present is taken as the principle or primary point.* **1018b14–19**

4. *Other things are prior in motion; for what is nearer to a first mover is prior; for example, the boy is prior to the man. And this too is a kind of principle in an absolute sense. Other things are prior in power; for whatever surpasses another in power, or is more powerful, is prior. And such is that according to whose will another, i.e., a subsequent, thing necessarily follows, because if the one does not move, the other is not moved, and if it does move, the other is moved; and will is a principle.* **1018b19–26**

5. *Other things are prior in arrangement, and these are the things which have a different place in relation to some one determinate thing according to some plan; for example, one who stands second is prior to one who stands third; and among the strings of the lyre the paranete is prior to the nete. For in the one case it is [the leader] who is taken as the principle or starting point; and in the other it is the middle string. These things, then, are said to be prior in this way.* **1018b26–30**

6. *In another way, whatever is prior in knowledge is considered to be prior in an absolute sense. And of such things some are prior in a different way, for some are prior in reference to reason, and others in reference to the senses. For universals are prior in reference to reason, but singulars in reference to the senses.* **1018b30–34**

7. *And in the intelligible structure the attribute is prior to the whole, as "musical" is prior to "musical man." For the intelligible structure is not complete without one of its parts, and "musical man" cannot exist unless there is someone who is musical.* **1018b34–37**

8. *Again, the attributes of prior things are said to be prior, as straightness is prior to smoothness; for the former is a property of a line considered in itself, and the latter a property of surface. Some things, then, are said to be prior and subsequent in this way.* **1018b37–1019a2**

9. *But others are said to be prior in nature and in substance, namely, all those things which can exist without others, although others cannot exist without them; and this is the division which Plato used. And since the term being is used in many ways, the first subject is prior, and therefore substance is prior. And things which exist potentially and those which exist actually are prior in various ways. For some things are prior in being potential, and others in being actual; for example, potentially half a line is prior to the entire line, and a part is prior to the whole, and matter is prior to substance. But in reference to actuality they are subsequent; for when the whole has been dissolved into such parts they will exist actually.* **1019a2–11**

10. *In a sense, then, all things which are prior and subsequent are said to be such in this [last] way. For some things can exist without others so far as the process of generation is concerned*

(as the whole without the parts), and some again without others so far as the process of corruption is concerned (as the parts without the whole). The same thing applies in other cases.

1019a11–14

COMMENTARY

936. Having given the various senses of the terms which signify the parts of unity, here Aristotle gives those which signify order, namely, *prior* and *subsequent*. For unity implies a certain order, because the essence of unity consists in being a principle, as was stated above (see n. 872). In regard to the first he does two things. First [1], he indicates the common meaning of the terms prior and subsequent; and second [2], he gives the various senses in which these terms are commonly taken ("For example, a thing").

He accordingly says, first [1], that the meaning of the term *prior* depends on that of the term *principle* (or starting point); for the principle in each class of things is what is first in that class, and the term prior means what is nearest to some determinate principle. Now the relationship between a principle of this kind and something which is near it can be considered from several points of view. For something is a principle or primary thing either in an absolute sense and by nature (as a father is a principle of a child), or "relatively," i.e., in relation to some extrinsic thing (for example, something that is subsequent by nature is said to be prior in relation to something else). Things which are prior in this last sense are such either in reference to knowledge or to perfection or to dignity, or in some such way. Or a thing is also said to be a principle and to be prior in reference to place; or even in certain other ways.

937. **For example, a thing** [2].

Then he gives the various ways in which things are said to be prior and subsequent. And since the terms prior and subsequent are used in reference to some principle, and a principle is what is first either in being or in becoming or in knowledge (as has been stated above [see n. 761]), this part is therefore divided into three sections.

In the first he explains how a thing is said to be prior in motion and in quantity, because the order found in motion flows from that found in quantity. For the prior and subsequent in motion depends on the prior and subsequent in continuous quantity, as is stated in Book IV of the *Physics.[219a15]* Second [6], he shows how one thing is said to be prior to another in knowledge ("In another way"). Third [9], he explains how one thing is said to be prior to another in being, i.e., in nature ("But others").

In regard to the first he does two things. First, he shows how one thing is said to be prior and another subsequent in quantity in the case of continuous things; and second [5], how one thing is prior and another subsequent in the case of discrete things ("Other things are prior in arrangement").

938. In treating the first member of this division [2] he gives three ways in which things are prior. The first has to do with place; for example, a thing is said to be prior in place inasmuch as it is nearer to some determinate place, whether that place be the middle point in some continuous quantity or an extreme. For the center of the world, to which heavy bodies gravitate, can be taken as the principle (or starting point) of the order involving place, and

then we put the elements in the following order, saying that earth is first, water second, and so on. Or the outermost sphere can be taken as the principle, and then we say that fire is first, air second, and so on.

939. Now nearness to a principle of place, whatever it may be, can be taken in two ways: in one way with reference to an order naturally determined, as water is naturally nearer to the middle of the universe than air, and air nearer to the extreme, i.e., the outermost sphere; and in another way with reference to an order that depends "on chance," i.e., insofar as some things have a certain order purely as a result of chance, or on some other cause than nature. For example, in the case of stones which lie on top of one another in a heap, the highest is prior according to one order, and the lowest according to another. And just as what is nearest to a principle is prior, in a similar way what is farther away from a principle is subsequent.

940. **Other things are prior in time** [3].

Things are understood to be prior and subsequent in a second way with reference to the order in time. And he now describes this order, saying that other things are said to be prior in time, and this in various ways. For some things are prior because they are farther away from the present, as occurs "in the case of things which have taken place," i.e., past events. For the Trojan wars are said to be prior to those of the Medes and the Persians (in which Xerxes, the king of the Persians and Medes, fought against the Greeks), because they are farther away from the present. And some things are said to be prior because they are closer or nearer to the present; for example, Meneleus is said to be prior to Pyrrho because he is nearer to some present moment in reference to which each was future. But this text seems to be false, because both of them lived before the time of Aristotle, when these words were written. And it is said in the Greek that the Nemean are prior to the Pythian, these being two holidays or feasts one of which was nearer to the moment at which these words were written although both were future.

941. Now it is clear that in this case we are using the present as a principle or starting point in time, because we say that something is prior or subsequent on the grounds that it is nearer to or farther away from the present. And those who hold that time is eternal must say this; for, when this is supposed, the only principle or starting point of time which can be taken is one that relates to some present moment, which is the middle point between the past and the future, inasmuch as time might proceed to infinity in both directions.

942. **Other things are prior in motion** [4].

The term prior is used in a third way with reference to the order in motion; and he first shows how this applies to natural things. He says that some things are said to be prior in the order found in motion; for what is nearer to a first cause of motion is prior. A boy, for example, is prior to a man because he is nearer to his primary mover, i.e., the one begetting him. And the latter is also said to be prior because of his nearness to some principle. For that—the one moving and begetting—is in a sense a principle, though not in just any way at all (as happened in the case of place), but in an absolute sense and by nature. Second, he also mentions this order of motion in the realm of the voluntary, saying that some things are said to be prior in power, as men who are placed in positions of authority. For one who surpasses another in power, or is more powerful, is said to be prior. This is the order of dignity.

943. Now it is evident that this order also involves motion; for one who is more powerful, or surpasses another in power, is one "according to whose will," i.e., intention, something necessarily follows, because it is through him that some subsequent thing is put in motion. Hence, when the more powerful or prior does not move, no subsequent thing moves; but when the former moves, the latter is also moved. This is the position of a prince in a state; for it is by his authority that others are moved to carry out the things which he commands, and if he does not command them they do not move. And it is clear that the term prior is used here too because of the nearness of a thing to some principle. For "the will," i.e., the intention, of the ruler is taken here as a principle, and those who are nearer to the ruler, and therefore prior, are the ones through whom his commands are made known to his subjects.

944. **Other things are prior in arrangement** [5].

He now explains how a thing is prior in the order found among discrete things. He says that some things are said to be prior in order only because they (the associated things) have some kind of arrangement, and not because of continuity, as happened in the previous cases. And things of this kind have a different place in relation to some one determinate thing from a given point of view, as one who stands second and one who stands third—the one who stands second being prior to the one who stands third. By one who stands second is meant one who stands next to someone, such as a king; and by one who stands third is meant one who stands third from the king. Hence another text reads, "The leader is prior to the one who stands third." It is evident, then, that things are understood to have different places inasmuch as one is second and another third. And in a similar way the *paranete* is prior to the *nete;* for among the strings of the lyre the low-pitched string is called the *hypate;* the high-pitched, the *nete;* and the middle, the *mese.* And the *paranete* refers to that which is next to the *nete* and nearer to the *mese.*

945. It is also evident that something is said to be prior here because of its nearness to some principle, although this happens differently in both of the examples given above. For in the former case—that of one who stands second and one who stands third—the thing which is taken as a principle is a real starting point and extreme, namely, the one who is highest among them, or the chief of the others, as a king or some other person of this kind. But in the case of the strings of the lyre it is the middle one, i.e., the middle string, termed the *mese,* that is taken as the principle; and since those which are nearer to this are called the paranete, the paranete are therefore said to be prior to the nete. These things are said to be prior in this way, then, i.e., by the order in quantity, whether continuous or discrete.

946. **In another way** [6].

Here he shows how one thing is said to be prior to another in knowledge. Now what is prior in knowledge is also prior in an absolute sense and not in a qualified one, as was the case with place; for a thing is known through its principles. But since knowledge is twofold: intellectual or rational, and sensory, we say that things are prior in one way in reference to reason, and in another in reference to the senses.

947. He gives three ways in which something is prior in reference to reason or intellectual knowledge. First, there is the way in which universals are prior to singulars, although the opposite occurs in the case of sensory knowledge because there singulars are prior. For reason has to do with universals and the senses with singulars; and thus the senses know universals only accidentally inasmuch as they know the singular of which the universals are predicated. For a sense knows man inasmuch as it knows Socrates, who is a man; and in the opposite way the intellect knows Socrates inasmuch as it knows man. But what is essential is always prior to what is accidental.

948. **And in the intelligible structure** [7].

Here he gives the second way in which a thing is prior in reference to reason. He says that in the intelligible structure "the attribute is prior to the whole," i.e., to the composite of subject and attribute; thus "musical man" cannot be known without grasping the meaning of the part "musical." And in the same way all other simple things are prior in intelligibility to the composite, although the opposite is true from the viewpoint of the senses; for it is composite things which are first offered to the senses.

949. **Again, the attributes** [6].

Then he gives the third way. He says that the attributes of prior things are also said to be prior from the viewpoint of reason, as straightness is said to be prior to smoothness. For straightness is an essential property of a line, and smoothness a property of surface, and a line is naturally prior to surface. But from the viewpoint of the senses surface is prior to a line, and the attributes of composite things are prior to those of simple ones. These things, then, are said to be prior in this way, namely, according to the order in knowing.

950. **But others** [9].

He then gives the ways in which a thing is said to be prior according to the order in being, and in regard to this he does two things. First, he gives three ways in which a thing is said to be prior in being; and second [10], he reduces them to one ("In a sense, then").

He says, first [9], that some things are said to be prior in being, i.e., "in nature and substance," or according to the natural order in being. And this is so for three reasons. First, priority is attributed because of community or dependence; and according to this those things are said to be prior which can exist without others, although others cannot exist without them. And one thing is prior to another when the sequence of their being cannot be reversed, as is stated in the *Categories.[14a30]* "This is the division," i.e., the mode of division of prior and subsequent, which Plato used against others; for it was because of community or dependence that he wanted universals to be prior in being to singular things, surfaces prior to bodies, lines to surfaces, and numbers to all other things.

951. Second, things are said to be prior in being because of the relationship of substance to accident. For since the term being is used in many senses and not univocally, all senses of being must be reduced to one primary sense, according to which being is said to be the subject of other things and to subsist of itself. Hence the first subject is

said to be prior; and thus substance is prior to accident.

952. Third, things are said to be prior in being inasmuch as being is divided into the actual and the potential. For a thing is said to be prior in one way potentially and in another actually. A thing is said to be prior potentially in the sense that half a line is prior to an entire line, and any part to its whole, and matter "to substance," i.e., to form. For all of the first things mentioned in these instances are related to the others, to which they are said to be prior, as something potential to something actual. However, from the viewpoint of actuality the first things mentioned are said to be subsequent, since they become actual only by the dissolution of some whole. For when a whole is dissolved into its parts, the parts then begin to exist actually.

953. **In a sense, then** [10].

Here he concludes that all of the ways in which the terms prior and subsequent are used can be reduced to the last one given; and especially to the first of these inasmuch as the term prior means something which can exist without other things, but not the reverse. For from the viewpoint of generation some things can exist without others, and it is in this way that a whole is prior to its parts; for when a whole has been generated its parts do not exist actually but only potentially. And from the viewpoint of corruption some things can exist without others; for example, the parts can exist without the whole after the whole has been corrupted and dissolved into its parts. And in the same way too the other senses of prior and subsequent can be reduced to this sense. For it is certain that prior things do not depend upon subsequent ones, but the reverse. Hence all prior things can exist without subsequent ones, but not the reverse.

LESSON 14

Various Senses of the Terms Potency, Capable, Incapable, Possible and Impossible

ARISTOTLE'S TEXT Chapter 12: 1019a15–1020a6

1. *In one sense the term potency or power (potestas) means the principle of motion or change in some other thing as other; for example, the art of building is a potency which is not present in the thing built; but the art of medicine is a potency and is present in the one healed, but not inasmuch as he is healed. In general, then, potency means the principle of change or motion in some other thing as other.* **1019a15–20**

2. *Or it means the principle of a thing's being moved or changed by some other thing as other. For by reason of that principle by which a patient undergoes some change we sometimes say that it has the potency of undergoing if it is possible for it to undergo any change at all. But sometimes we do not say this by reason of every change which a thing can undergo but only if the change is for the better.* **1019a20–23**

3. *And in another sense potency means the ability or power to do this particular thing well or according to intention. For sometimes we say of those who can merely walk or talk but not well or as they planned, that they cannot walk or talk. And the same applies to things which are undergoing change.* **1019a23–26**

4. *Further, all states in virtue of which things are altogether unsusceptible to change or immutable, or are not easily changed for the worse, are called potencies or powers. For things are broken and crushed and bent and in general destroyed, not because they have a potency, but because they do not have one and are deficient in some way. And things are not susceptible to such processes when they are hardly or slightly affected by them because they have the potency and the ability to be in some definite state.* **1019a26–32**

5. *And since the term potency is used in these senses, the term capable or potent (possibilis) will be used in the same number of senses. Thus in one sense whatever has [within itself] the source of the motion or change which takes place in some other thing as other (for even something that brings another to rest is potent in a sense) is said to be capable. And in another sense that which receives such a potency or power from it is said to be capable.* **1019a32–1019b1**

6. *And in still another sense a thing is said to be capable if it has the potency of being changed in some way, whether for the worse or for the better. For anything which is corrupted seems to be capable of being corrupted, since it would not have been corrupted if it had been incapable of it. But as matters stand it already has a certain disposition and cause and principle to undergo such change. Hence sometimes a thing seems to be such (i.e., capable) because it has something, and sometimes because it is deprived of something.* **1019b1–6**

7. *But if privation is in a sense a having, all things will be capable or potent by having something. But being is used in two different senses. Hence a thing is capable both by having some privation and principle, and by having the privation of this, if it can have a privation.* **1019b6–10**

8. *And in another sense a thing is capable because there is no potency or power in some other thing as other which can corrupt it.* **1019b10–11**

9. *Again, all these things are capable either because they merely might happen to come into being or not, or because they might do so well. For this sort of potency or power is found in inanimate things such as instruments. For men say that one lyre can produce a sound, and that another cannot, if it does not have a good tone.* **1019b11–15**

10. *Incapacity (impotentia), on the other hand, is a privation of capacity, i.e., a kind of removal of such a principle as has been described, either altogether, or in the case of something which is*

naturally disposed to have it, or when it is already naturally disposed to have it and does not. For it is not in the same way that a boy, a man and an eunuch are said to be incapable of begetting. **1019b15–19**

11. Again, there is an incapacity corresponding to each kind of capacity, both to that which can merely produce motion, and to that which can produce it well. **1019b19–21**

12. And some things are said to be incapable according to this sense of incapacity, but others in a different sense, namely, as possible and impossible. Impossible means that of which the contrary is necessarily true; thus it is impossible that the diagonal of a square should be commensurable with a side, because such a statement is false of which the contrary is not only true but also necessarily so, i.e., that the diagonal is not commensurable. Therefore, that the diagonal is commensurable is not only false but necessarily false. **1019b21–27**

13. And the contrary of this, i.e., the possible, is when the contrary is not necessarily false. For example, it is possible that a man should be seated, because it is not necessarily false that he should not be seated. Hence the term possible means in one sense (as has been stated), whatever is not necessarily false; and in another sense, whatever is true; and in still another, whatever may be true. **1019b27–33**

14. And what is called "a power" in geometry is called such metaphorically. These senses of capable, then, do not refer to potency. **1019b33–35**

15. But those senses which do refer to potency are all used in reference to the one primary sense of potency, namely, a principle of change in some other thing inasmuch as it is other. And other things are said to be capable [in a passive sense], some because some other thing has such power over them, some because it does not, and some because it has it in a special way. The same applies to the term incapable. Hence the proper definition of the primary kind of potency will be: a principle of change in some other thing as other. **1019b35–1020a6**

COMMENTARY

954. Having treated the various senses of the terms which signify the parts of unity, here Aristotle begins to treat those which signify the parts of being. He does this, first [1], according as being is divided by act and potency; and second (Lesson 15), according as it is divided by the ten categories ("*Quantity* means").

In regard to the first, he gives the various senses in which the term *potency* or *power (potestas)* is used. But he omits the term *act*, because he could explain its meaning adequately only if the nature of forms had been made clear first, and he will do this in Books VIII (see n. 1703) and IX (see n. 1823). Hence in Book IX he immediately settles the question about potency and act together.

This part, then, is divided into two members. In the first he explains the various senses in which the term potency is used; and in the second [15], he reduces all of them to one primary sense ("But those senses").

In regard to the first he does two things. First, he gives the various senses in which the term potency is used; and second [10], the various senses in which the term *incapacity* is used *("Incapacity")*.

In treating the first he does two things. First, he gives the senses in which the term potency is used; and second [5], those in which the term *capable* or *potent* is used ("And since the term").

955. In dealing with the first part, then, he gives four senses in which the term *potency* or *power* is used. First, potency means a principle of motion or

change in some other thing as other. For there is some principle of motion or change in the thing changed, namely, the matter, or some formal principle on which the motion depends, as upward or downward motion is a result of the forms of lightness or heaviness. But a principle of this kind cannot be designated as the active power on which this motion depends. For everything which is moved is moved by another; and a thing moves itself only by means of its parts inasmuch as one part moves another, as is proved in Book VIII of the *Physics.[257b29]* Hence insofar as a potency is a principle of motion in that in which motion is found, it is not included under active power but under passive potency. For heaviness in earth is not a principle causing motion but rather one which causes it to be moved. Hence active power must be present in some other thing than the one moved; for example, the power of building is not in the thing being built but rather in the builder. And while the art of medicine is an active power, because the physician heals by means of it, it may also be found in the one who is healed, not inasmuch as he is healed, but accidentally, i.e., inasmuch as the physician and the one who is healed happen to be the same. So therefore generally speaking potency or power means in one sense a principle of motion or change in some other thing as other.

956. **Or it means** [2].

Here he gives a second sense in which the term potency is used. He says that in another sense the term potency means the principle whereby something is moved or changed by another thing as other. Now this is passive potency, and it is by reason of it that a patient undergoes some change. For just as every agent or mover moves something other than itself and acts in something other than itself, so too every patient is acted upon by something other than itself, i.e., everything moved is moved by another. For that principle whereby one thing is properly moved or acted upon by another is called passive potency.

957. Now there are two ways in which we can say that a thing has the potency to be acted upon by another. Sometimes we attribute such a potency to something, whatever it may be, because it is able to undergo some change, whether it be good or bad. And sometimes we say that a thing has such a potency, not because it can undergo something evil, but because it can be changed for the better. For example, we do not say that one who can be overpowered has a potency [in this last sense], but we do attribute such a potency to one who can be taught or helped. And we speak thus because sometimes an ability to be changed for the worse is attributed to incapacity, and the ability not to be changed in the same way is attributed to potency, as will be said below [8].

958. Another text reads, "And sometimes this is not said of every change which a thing undergoes but of change to a contrary"; and this should be understood thus: whatever receives a perfection from something else is said in an improper sense to undergo a change; and it is in this sense that to understand is said to be a kind of undergoing. But that which receives along with a change in itself something other than what is natural to it is said in a proper sense to undergo a change. Hence such undergoing is also said to be a removing of something from a substance. But this can come about only by way of some contrary. There-

fore, when a thing is acted upon in a way contrary to its own nature or condition, it is said in a proper sense to undergo a change or to be passive. And in this sense even illnesses are called undergoings. But when a thing receives something which is fitting to it by reason of its nature, it is said to be perfected rather than passive.

959. **And in another sense** [3].

He now gives a third sense in which the term potency is used. He says that in another sense potency means the principle of performing some act, not in any way at all, but well or according to "intention," i.e., according to what a man plans. For when men walk or talk but not well or as they planned to do, we say that they do not have the ability to walk or to talk. And "the same thing applies when things are being acted upon," for a thing is said to be able to undergo something if it can undergo it well; for example, some pieces of wood are said to be combustible because they can be burned easily, and others are said to be incombustible because they cannot be burned easily.

960. **Further, all states** [4].

He gives a fourth sense in which the term potency is used. He says that we designate as potencies all habits or forms or dispositions by which some things are said or made to be altogether incapable of being acted upon or changed, or to be not easily changed for the worse. For when bodies are changed for the worse, as those which are broken or bent or crushed or destroyed in any way at all, this does not happen to them because of some ability or potency but rather because of some inability and the weakness of some principle which does not have the power of resisting the thing which destroys them. For a thing is destroyed only because of the victory which the destroyer wins over it, and this is a result of the weakness of its proper active power. For those things which cannot be affected by defects of this kind, or can "hardly or only gradually" be affected by them (i.e., they are affected slowly or to a small degree) are such "because they have the potency and the ability to be in some definite state"; i.e., they have a certain perfection which prevents them from being overcome by contraries. And, as is said in the *Categories, [9a22]* it is in this way that *hard* or *healthy* signifies a natural power which a thing has of resisting change by destructive agents. But *soft* and *sickly* signify incapacity or lack of power.

961. **And since the term** [5].

Here he gives the senses of the term *capable* or *potent*, which correspond to the above senses of potency. And there are two senses of capable which correspond to the first sense of potency. For according to its active power a thing is said to be capable of acting in two ways: in one way, because it acts immediately of itself; and in another way, because it acts through something else to which it communicates its power, as a king acts through a bailiff.

Hence he says that, since the term potency is used in this number of senses, the term capable or potent must also be used in the same number of senses. Thus in one sense it means something which has an active principle of change within itself, "as what brings another to rest or to a stop"; i.e., what causes some other thing to stand still is said to be capable of bringing something different from itself to a state of rest. And it is used in another sense when a thing does not act directly but another thing receives such power from it that it can act directly.

962. **And in still another** [6].

Next, he gives a second sense in which the term capable is used, and this corresponds to the second sense of the term potency, i.e., passive potency. He says that, in a different way from the foregoing, a thing is said to be capable or potent when it can be changed in some respect, whatever it may be, i.e., whether it can be changed for the better or for the worse. And in this sense a thing is said to be corruptible because "it is capable of being corrupted," which is to undergo change for the worse, or it is not corruptible because it is capable of not being corrupted, assuming that it is impossible for it to be corrupted.

963. And what is capable of being acted upon in some way must have within itself a certain disposition which is the cause and principle of its passivity, and this principle is called passive potency. But such a principle can be present in the thing acted upon for two reasons. First, this is because it possesses something; for example, a man is capable of suffering from some disease because he has an excessive amount of some inordinate humor. Second, a thing is capable of being acted upon because it lacks something which could resist the change. This is the case, for example, when a man is said to be capable of suffering from some disease because his strength and natural power have been weakened. Now both of these must be present in anything which is capable of being acted upon; for a thing would never be acted upon unless it both contained a subject which could receive the disposition or form induced in it as a result of the change and also lacked the power of resisting the action of an agent.

964. Now these two ways in which the principle of passivity is spoken of can be reduced to one, because privation can be designated as "a having." Thus it follows that to lack something is to have a privation, and so each way will involve the having of something. Now the designation of privation as a having and as something had follows from the fact that being is used in two different ways; and both privation and negation are called being in one of these ways, as has been pointed out at the beginning of Book IV (see n. 564). Hence it follows that negation and privation can also be designated as "havings." We can say, then, that in general something is capable of undergoing because it contains a kind of "having" and a certain principle that enables it to be acted upon; for even to lack something is to have something, if a thing can *have* a privation.

965. **And in another sense** [8].

Here he gives a third sense in which the term capable is used; and this sense corresponds to the fourth sense of potency inasmuch as a potency was said to be present in something which cannot be corrupted or changed for the worse. Thus he says that in another sense a thing is said to be capable because it does not have some potency or principle which enables it to be corrupted. And I mean by some other thing as other. For a thing is said to be potent or powerful in the sense that it cannot be overcome by something external so as to be corrupted.

966. **Again, all these** [9].

He gives a fourth sense in which the term capable is used, and this corresponds to the third sense of potency inasmuch as potency designated the ability to act or be acted upon well. He says that according to the foregoing senses of potency which pertain both to acting and to being acted upon, a thing can be said to be capable either because it merely happens to come into being or not or because it happens to come into being well. For a thing is said to be capable of acting either because it can simply act or because it can act well and easily. And in a similar way a thing is said to be capable of being acted upon and corrupted because it can be acted upon easily. And this sense of potency is also found in inanimate things "such as instruments," i.e., in the case of the lyre and other musical instruments. For one lyre is said to be able to produce a tone because it has a good tone, and another is said not to because its tone is not good.

967. **Incapacity** [10].

Then he gives the different senses of the term *incapacity*, and in regard to this he does two things. First [10], he gives the various senses in which we speak of incapacity; and second [12], he treats the different senses in which the term *impossible* is used ("And some things").

In treating the first part he does two things. First, he gives the common meaning of the term incapacity. Second [11], he notes the various ways in which it is used ("Again, there is").

He accordingly says, first [10], that incapacity is the privation of potency. Now two things are required in the notion of privation, and the first of these is the removal of an opposite state. But the opposite of incapacity is potency. Therefore, since potency is a kind of principle, incapacity will be the removal of that kind of principle which potency has been described to be. The second thing required is that privation properly speaking must belong to a definite subject and at a definite time; and it is taken in an improper sense when taken without a definite subject and without a definite time. For properly speaking only that is said to be blind which is naturally fitted to have sight and at the time when it is naturally fitted to have it.

968. And he says that incapacity, such as it has been described, is the removal of a potency, "either altogether," i.e., universally, in the sense that every removal of a potency is called incapacity, whether the thing is naturally disposed to have the potency or not; or it is the removal of a potency from something which is naturally fitted to have it at some time or other or only at the time when it is naturally fitted to have it. For incapacity is not taken in the same way when we say that a boy is incapable of begetting, and when we say this of a man and of an eunuch. For to say that a boy is incapable of begetting means that, while the subject is naturally fitted to beget, it cannot beget before the proper time. But to say that an eunuch is incapable of begetting means that, while he was naturally fitted to beget at the proper time, he cannot beget now; for he lacks the active principles of begetting. Hence incapacity here retains rather the notion of privation. But a mule or a stone is said to be incapable of begetting because neither can do so, and also because neither has any real aptitude for doing so.

969. **Again, there is** [11].

Then he explains the various senses of *incapacity* by contrasting them with the senses of potency. For just as potency is twofold, namely, active and passive, and both refer either to acting and being acted upon simply, or to acting and being acted upon well, in a similar fashion there is an opposite sense of incapacity corresponding to each type of potency. That is to say, there is a sense of incapacity corresponding "both to that which can merely produce motion and to that which can produce it well," namely, to active potency, which is the potency to simply move a thing or to move it well, and to passive potency, which is the potency to simply be moved or to be moved well.

970. **And some things** [12].

Then he explains the various senses in which the term *impossible* is used; and in regard to this he does two things. First, he gives the various senses in which the term impossible is used; and then [15] he reduces them to one ("But those senses").

In regard to the first he does three things. First [12], he says that in one sense some things are said to be impossible because they have the foregoing incapacity which is opposed to potency. And impossible in this sense is used in four ways corresponding to those of incapacity.

971. Accordingly, when he says "in a different sense [12]," he gives an other way in which some things are said to be impossible. And they are said to be such not because of the privation of some potency but because of the opposition existing between the terms in propositions. For since potency is referred to being, then just as being is predicated not only of things that exist in reality but also of the composition of a proposition inasmuch as it contains truth and falsity, in a similar fashion the terms possible and impossible are predicated not only of real potency and incapacity but also of the truth and falsity found in the combining or separating of terms in propositions. Hence the term impossible means that of which the contrary is necessarily true. For example, it is impossible that the diagonal of a square should be commensurable with a side, because such a statement is false whose contrary is not only true but necessarily so, namely, that it is not commensurable. Hence the statement that it is commensurable is necessarily false, and this is impossible.

972. **And the contrary** [13].

Here he shows that the possible is the opposite of the impossible in the second way mentioned; for the impossible is opposed to the possible in the second way mentioned. He says, then, that the possible, as the contrary of this second sense of the impossible, means that whose contrary is not necessarily false; for example, it is possible that a man should be seated, because the opposite of this—that he should not be seated—is not necessarily false.

973. From this it is clear that this sense of possible has three usages. For in one way it designates what is false but is not necessarily so; for example, it is possible that a man should be seated while he is not seated, because the opposite of this is not necessarily true. In another way possible designates what is true but is not necessarily so because its opposite is not necessarily false, for example, that Socrates should be seated while he is seated. And in a third way it means that, although a thing is not true now, it may be true later on.

974. **And what is called "a power"** [14].

He shows how the term *power* is used metaphorically. He says that in geometry the term power is used metaphorically. For in geometry the square of a line is called its power by reason of the following likeness, namely, that just as from something in potency something actual comes to be, in a similar way from multiplying a line by itself its square results. It would be the same if we were to say that the number three is capable of becoming the number nine, because from multiplying the number three by itself the number nine results; for three times three makes nine. And just as the term impossible taken in the second sense does not correspond to any incapacity, in a similar way the senses of the term possible which were given last do not correspond to any potency, but they are used figuratively or in the sense of the true and the false.

975. **But those senses** [15].

He now reduces all senses of capable and incapable to one primary sense. He says that those senses of the term capable or potent which correspond to potency all refer to one primary kind of potency—the first active potency—which was described above (see n. 955) as the principle of change in some other thing as other; because all the other senses of capable or potent are referred to this kind of potency. For a thing is said to be capable by reason of the fact that some other thing has active power over it, and in this sense it is said to be capable according to passive potency. And some things are said to be capable because some other thing does not have power over them, as those which said to be capable because they cannot be corrupted by external agents. And others are said to be capable because they have it "in some special way," i.e., because they have the power or potency to act or be acted upon well or easily.

976. And just as all things which are said to be capable because of some potency are reduced to one primary potency, in a similar way all things which are said to be incapable because of some impotency are reduced to one primary incapacity, which is the opposite of the primary potency. It is clear, then, that the proper notion of potency in the primary sense is this: a principle of change in some other thing as other; and this is the notion of active potency or power.

LESSON 15

The Meaning of Quantity. Its Kinds. The Essentially and Accidentally Quantitative

ARISTOTLE'S TEXT Chapter 13: 1020a7–1020a32

1. *Quantity [or the quantitative] means what is divisible into constituent parts, both or one of which is by nature a one and a particular thing.* **1020a7–8**

2. *Therefore plurality [or multitude] is a kind of quantity if it is numerable; and so also is magnitude [or continuous quantity] if it is measurable. Plurality means what is potentially divisible into non-continuous parts; and magnitude means what is divisible into continuous parts. Again, of the kinds of magnitude, what is continuous in one dimension is length; in two, breadth; and in three, depth. And of these, limited plurality is number; limited length, a line; limited breadth, a surface; and limited depth, a body [or solid].* **1020a8–14**

3. *Again, some things are said to be quantitative essentially and others accidentally; for example, a line is quantitative essentially, but the musical accidentally.* **1020a14–17**

4. *And of those things which are quantitative essentially, some are such by reason of their substance, as a line is quantitative quidditatively. For in the definition expressing its quiddity some kind of quantity is found. Others are properties and states of this kind of substance, as much and little, long and short, broad and narrow, deep and shallow, heavy and light, and the like. And large and small, and larger and smaller, whether they are spoken of essentially or in relation to each other, are properties of quantity. And these terms are also transferred to other things.* **1020a17–26**

5. *But of things which are quantitative accidentally, some are said to be such in the sense in which the musical and the white are quantitative, i.e., because the subject to which they belong is quantitative. Others are said to be quantitative in the sense in which motion and time are, for these too are said to be in a sense quantitative and continuous because the things of which they are the properties are divisible. And I mean not the thing which is moved, but the space through which it is moved. For since space is quantitative, motion is also quantitative; and through it, i.e., motion, time is also quantitative.* **1020a26–32**

COMMENTARY

977. Since being is divided not only into potency and actuality but also into the ten categories, having given the different senses of the term potency (see nn. 954–60), the Philosopher begins here to give the different senses of the terms which designate the categories. First [1], he considers the term *quantity;* and second (Lesson 16), the term *quality* ("*Quality* means"). Third (Lesson 17), he gives the different meanings of the term *relative* ("Some things"). He omits the other categories because they are limited to one class of natural beings, as is especially evident of action and passion, and of place and time.

In regard to the first he does three things. First, he gives the meaning of quantity. He says that quantity means what is divisible into constituent parts. Now this is said to distinguish this kind of division from that of compounds. For a compound is dissolved into the elements, and these are not present in it actually but only virtually. Hence, in the latter case there is not just division of quantity, but there must also be some alteration by means of which a compound is dissolved into its elements. He adds that both or one of these constituents is by nature "a one," that is, something which is pointed out. He says this in order to exclude the division of a thing into its essential parts, which are matter and form; for neither one of these is fitted by nature to be a particular thing of itself.

978. **Therefore plurality** [2].

Second, he gives the kinds of quantity; and of these there are two primary kinds: plurality or multitude, and magnitude or measure. And each of these has the character of something quantitative inasmuch as plurality is numerable and magnitude is measurable. For mensuration pertains properly to quantity. However, plurality is defined as what is divisible potentially into parts which are not continuous; and magnitude as what is divisible into parts which are continuous. Now this occurs in three ways, and therefore there are three kinds of magnitude. For if magnitude is divisible into continuous parts in one dimension only, it will be length; if into two, width; and if into three, depth. Again, when plurality or multitude is limited, it is called number. And a limited length is called a line; a limited width, surface; and a limited depth, body. For if multitude were unlimited, number would not exist, because what is unlimited cannot be numbered. Similarly, if length were unlimited, a line would not exist, because a line is a measurable length (and this is why it is stated in the definition of a line that its extremities are two points). The same things holds true of surface and of body.

979. **Again, some things** [3].

Third, he gives the different ways in which things are quantitative; and in regard to this he does three things. First, he draws a distinction between what is essentially quantitative, as a line, and what is accidentally quantitative, as the musical.

980. **And of those** [4].

Second, he gives the different senses in which things are essentially quantitative, and there are two of these. For some things are said to be such after the manner of a substance or subject, as line, surface or number; for each of these is essentially quantitative because quantity is given in the definition of each. For a line is a limited quantity divisible in length. The same is true of the other dimensions.

981. And other things belong essentially to the genus of quantity and are signified after the manner of a state or property of such substance, i.e., of a line, which is essentially quantitative, or of other similar kinds of quantity. For example, much and little are signified as properties of number; long and short, as properties of a line; broad and narrow, as properties of surface; and high and low or deep, as properties of body. And the same is true of heavy and light according to the opinion of those who said that having many surfaces, or atoms, causes bodies to be heavy, and having few causes them to be light. But the truth of the matter is that heavy and light do not pertain to quantity but to quality, as he states below (see n. 993). The same thing is true of other such attributes as these.

982. There are also certain attributes which are common properties of any continuous quantity, as large and small, and larger and smaller, whether these are taken "essentially," i.e., absolutely, or "in relation to each other," as something is said to be large and small relatively, as is stated in the *Categories*.[5b20] But these terms which signify the properties of quantity pure

and simple are also transferred to other things besides quantities. For whiteness is said to be large and small, and so also are other accidents of this kind.

983. But it must be borne in mind that of all the accidents quantity is closest to substance. Hence some men think that quantities, such as line, number, surface and body are substances. For next to substance only quantity can be divided into distinctive parts. For whiteness cannot be divided, and therefore it cannot be understood to be individuated except by its subject. And it is for this reason that only in the genus of quantity are some things designated as subjects and others as properties.

984. **But of things** [5].

Then he gives the different senses in which things are said to be accidentally quantitative. These senses are two. In one sense, things are said to be accidentally quantitative only because they are accidents of some quantity; for example, white and musical are said to be quantitative because they are accidents of a subject which is quantitative.

985. In another sense, some things are said to be accidentally quantitative, not because of the subject in which they exist, but because they are divided quantitatively as a result of the division of some quantity; for example, motion and time (which are said to be quantitative and continuous because of the subjects to which they belong) are divisible and are themselves divided as a result of the division of the subjects to which they belong. For time is divisible and continuous because of motion, and motion is divisible because of magnitude—not because of the magnitude of the thing which is moved, but because of the magnitude of the space through which it is moved. For since that magnitude is quantitative, motion is also quantitative; and since motion is quantitative, it follows that time is quantitative. Hence these can be said to be quantitative not merely accidentally but rather subsequently, inasmuch as they receive quantitative division from something prior.

986. However, it must be noted that in the *Categories*[5a5] the Philosopher held that time is essentially quantitative, while here he holds that it is accidentally quantitative. There he distinguished between the species of quantity from the viewpoint of the different kinds of measure. For time, which is an external measure, has the character of one kind of measure, and continuous quantity, which is an internal measure, has a different one. Hence in the *Categories* time is given as another species of quantity, whereas here he considers the species of quantity from the viewpoint of the being of quantity. Therefore those things which only receive their quantitative being from something else he does not give here as species of quantity, but as things which are accidentally quantitative, as motion and time. But motion has no other manner of measure than time and magnitude. Hence neither in this work nor in the *Categories* does he give it as a species of quantity. Place, however, is given there as a species of quantity. But it is not given as such here because it has a different manner of measure, although not a different quantitative being.

LESSON 16
The Senses of Quality

ARISTOTLE'S TEXT Chapter 14: 1020a33–1020b25

1. *Quality (the qualified or of what sort [quale]) means in one sense substantial difference; for example, How is man's quiddity qualified? as a two-footed animal. How is a horse's? as a four-footed animal. A circle's? as a figure which is non-angular; as if substantial difference were quality. In this one sense, then, quality (qualitas) means substantial difference.* **1020a33–1020b1**

2. *In another sense the term applies to immobile things and to the objects of mathematics, as numbers are of a certain type (quales), for example, those which are compound, and not only those of one dimension but also those of which surface and solid are the counterpart (for there are numbers which are so many times so much and so many times so many times so much). And in general it means what is present in substance besides quantity. For the substance of each number is what it is once; for example, the substance of six is not two times three but six taken once, for six times one is six.* **1020b1–8**

3. *Again, all the modifications of substances which are moved, such as heat and cold, whiteness and blackness, heaviness and lightness, and any other attributes of this sort according to which the bodies of changing things are said to be altered, are called qualities.* **1020b8–12**

4. *Further, the term quality is used of virtue and vice, and in general of good and evil.* **1020b12–13**

5. *The senses of quality, then, come down to two; and one of these is more basic than the other. For the primary kind of quality is substantial difference. And the quality found in number is a part of this, for this is a substantial difference, but either of things which are not moved, or not of them insofar as they are moved. The others, however, are the modifications of things which are moved inasmuch as they are moved, and are the differences of motions. And virtue and vice are parts of these modifications, for they indicate clearly the differences of the motion or activity according to which things in motion act or are acted upon well or badly. For what is capable of being moved or of acting in this way is good, and what cannot do so but acts in a contrary way is bad. And good and bad signify quality especially in the case of living things, and especially in those which have the power of choice.* **1020b13–25**

COMMENTARY

987. Here he gives the various senses in which the term *quality* is used, and in regard to this he does two things. First [1], he gives four senses of the term quality; and second [5], he reduces them to two ("The senses of quality").

He accordingly says, first (487), that the term quality is used in one sense as "substantial difference," i.e., the difference by which one thing is distinguished substantially from another and which is included in the definition of the substance. And for this reason it is said that a difference is predicated as a substantial qualification. For example, if one were to ask what sort of *(quale)* animal man is, we would answer that he is two-footed; and if one were to ask what sort of animal a horse is, we would answer that it is four-footed; and if one were to ask what sort of figure a circle is, we would answer that it is "non-angular," i.e., without angles; as if a substantial difference were quality. In one sense, then, quality means substantial difference.

988. Now Aristotle omits this sense of quality in the *Categories* [8b25] because it is not contained under the cate-

gory of quality, which he deals with there. But here he is dealing with the meaning of the term quality.

989. **In another sense** [2].

Here he gives a second sense in which the term quality is used. He says that the term quality or "qualified" is used in another sense insofar as immobile things and the objects of mathematics are said to be qualified in a certain way. For the objects of mathematics are abstracted from motion, as is stated in Book VI of this work (see n. 1161). Such objects are numbers and continuous quantities, and of both we use the term quality. Thus we say that surfaces are qualified as being square or triangular. And similarly numbers are said to be qualified as being compound. Those numbers are said to be compound which have some common number that measures them; for example, the number six and the number nine are measured by the number three, and are not merely referred to one as a common measure. But those which are measured by no common number other than one are called uncompounded or first in their proportion.

990. Numbers are also spoken of as having quality in a metaphor taken from surface and from "solid," i.e., body. They are considered like a surface inasmuch as one number is multiplied by another, either by the same number or by a different one, as in the phrase "twice three" or "three times three." And this is what he means by "so many times so much"; for something like one dimension is designated by saying "three," and a sort of second dimension by saying "twice three" or "three times three."

991. Numbers are considered like a solid when there is a twofold multiplication, either of the same number by itself, or of different numbers by one; as in the expression "three times three times three" or "two times three times two" or "two times three times four." And this is what he means by "so many times so many times so much." For we treat of three dimensions in a number in somewhat the same way as in a solid; and in this arrangement of numbers there is something which is treated as a substance, as three, or any other number that is multiplied by another. And there is something else which is treated as quantity, as the multiplication of one number by another or by itself. Thus when I say "twice three," the number two is signified after the manner of a measuring quantity, and the number three after the manner of a substance. Therefore what belongs to the substance of number besides quantity itself, which is the substance of number, is called a quality of it, as what is meant in saying twice or three times.

992. Another text reads "according to quantity," and then the substance of number is said to be the number itself expressed in an unqualified sense, as "three." And insofar as we consider the quality of a quantity, this is designated by multiplying one number by another. The rest of the text agrees with this, saying that the substance of any number is what it is said to be once; for example, the substance of six is six taken once, and not three taken twice or two taken three times; and this pertains to its quality. For to speak of a number in terms of surface or solid, whether square or cube, is to speak of its quality. And this type of quality is the fourth kind given in the *Categories*. [10a10]

993. **Again, all the modifications** [3].

Then he gives the third sense in

which quality is used. He says that qualities also mean the modifications of mobile substances according to which bodies are changed through alteration, as heat and cold and accidents of this kind. And this sense of quality belongs to the third kind of quality given in the *Categories. [9a28]*

994. **Further, the term quality** [4].

Next he gives the fourth sense in which quality is used. He says that quality or "qualified" is used in a fourth sense insofar as something is disposed by virtue or vice, or in whatever way it is well or badly disposed, as by knowledge or ignorance, health or sickness, and the like. This is the first kind of quality given in the *Categories.*[8b26]

995. Now he omits the second of these senses of quality because it is contained rather under power, since it is signified only as a principle which resists modification. But it is given in the *Categories* [9a13] among the kinds of quality because of the way in which it is named. However, according to its mode of being it is contained rather under power, as he also held above (see n. 960).

996. **The senses of quality** [5].

Then he reduces to two the four senses of quality so far given, saying that a thing is said to be qualified in a certain way in two senses, inasmuch as two of these four senses are reduced to the other two. The most basic of these senses is the first one, according to which quality means substantial difference, because by means of it a thing is designated as being informed and qualified.

997. The quality found in numbers and in other objects of mathematics is reduced to this as a part. For qualities of this kind are in a sense the substantial differences of mathematical objects, because they are signified after the manner of substance to a greater degree than the other accidents, as was stated in the chapter on quantity (see n. 980). Further, qualities of this kind constitute substantial differences, "either of things which are not moved, or not of them insofar as they are moved"; and he says this in order to show that it makes no difference to his thesis whether the objects of mathematics are self-subsistent substances, as Plato claimed, and are separate from motion; or whether they exist in substances which are mobile in reality but separate in thought. For in the first sense they would not be qualities of things which are moved; but in the second sense they would be, but not inasmuch as they are moved.

998. The second basic sense in which quality is used is that in which the modifications of things which are moved as such, and also the differences of things which are moved, are called qualities. They are called the differences of motions because alterations differ in terms of such qualities, as becoming hot and becoming cold differ in terms of heat and cold.

999. The sense in which virtue and vice are called qualities is reduced to this last sense, for it is in a way a part of this sense. For virtue and vice indicate certain differences of motion and activity based on good or bad performance. For virtue is that by which a thing is well disposed to act or be acted upon, and vice is that by which a thing is badly disposed. The same is true of other habits, whether they are intellectual, as science, or corporal, as health.

1000. But the terms *well* and *badly* relate chiefly to quality in living things, and especially in those having "election," i.e., choice. And this is true because good has the role of an end or goal. So those things which act by choice act for an end. Now to act for an end belongs particularly to living things. For non-living things act or are moved for an end, not inasmuch as they know the end, or inasmuch as they themselves act for an end, but rather inasmuch as they are directed by something else which gives them their natural inclination, just as an arrow, for example, is directed toward its goal by an archer. And non-rational living things apprehend an end or goal and desire it by an appetite of the soul, and they move locally toward some end or goal inasmuch as they have discernment of it; but their appetite for an end, and for those things which exist for the sake of the end, is determined for them by a natural inclination. Hence they are acted upon rather than act; and thus their judgment is not free. But rational beings, in whom alone choice exists, know both the end and the proportion of the means to the end. Therefore, just as they move themselves toward the end, so also do they move themselves to desire the end and the means; and for this reason they have free choice.

LESSON 17
The Senses of Relative

ARISTOTLE'S TEXT Chapter 15: 1020b26–1021b11

1. *Some things are said to be relative (ad aliquid) directly, as double to half and triple to a third part; and in general what is multiplied to a part of what is multiplied, and what includes to what is included in it. And in another sense as what heats to what can be heated, and what cuts to what can be cut; and in general everything active to everything passive. And in another sense as what is measurable to a measure, and what is knowable to knowledge, and what is sensible to sense.* **1020b26–32**

2. *The first things which are said to be relative numerically are such, either without qualification, or in some definite relation to them, or to unity; as double is related to half as a definite number. And the multiple is related numerically to the unit, but not in a definite numerical relation such as this or that. But what is one and a half times as great as something else is related to it in a definite numerical relation to a number. And the superparticular is related to the subparticular in an indefinite relation, as what is multiple is related to a number. And what includes is related to what is included in it as something altogether indefinite in number, for number is commensurable. For what includes is related to what is included in it according to so much and something more; but this something more is indefinite. For whatever the case may be, it is either equal or not equal to it. Therefore all these relations are said to be numerical and are properties of number.* **1026b32–1021a9**

3. *Further, equal, like and same are said to be relative, but in a different way, because all these terms are referred to unity. For those things are the same whose substance is one; and those are alike whose quality is one; and those are equal whose quantity is one. And unity is the principle and measure of number. Hence all these are said to be relative numerically, yet not in the same way.* **1021a9–14**

4. *Active and passive things are relative in virtue of active and passive potencies and the operations of potencies; for example, what can heat is relative to what can be heated, because it can heat it; and what is heating is relative to what is being heated; and what is cutting to what is being cut, inasmuch as they are doing these things. But of those things which are relative numerically there are no operations, except in the sense stated elsewhere; [Physics, II, 2] and operations which imply motion are not found in them. Moreover, of things which are relative potentially, some are said to be relative temporally also, as what makes to what is made, and what will make to what will be made. For in this way a father is said to be the father of his son, because the former has acted, whereas the latter has been acted upon. Again, some things are said to be relative according to the privation of potency; for example, the incapable and other terms used in this way, as the invisible.* **1021a14–26**

5. *Therefore things which are said to be relative numerically and potentially are all relative because the subject of the reference is itself referred to something else, not because something else is referred to it. But what is measurable and knowable and thinkable are said to be relative because in each case something else is referred to them, not because they are referred to something else. For by what is thinkable is meant that of which there may be a thought. However, a thought is not relative to the one whose thought it is, for then the same thing would be expressed twice. And similarly sight is relative to that of which it is the sight and not to the one whose sight it is (although it is true to say this); but it is relative to color or to something of this sort. But then the same thing would be said twice, that sight is of the one whose sight it is. Things which are said to be relative directly, then, are spoken of in this way.* **1021a26–1021b4**

6. *And other things are said to be relative because their genera are such; for example, medicine*

is relative because its genus, science, seems to be relative. Furthermore, of this type are all things which are said to be relative by reason of their subject; for example, equality is said to be relative because equal is relative; and likeness, because like is relative. **1021b4–8**

7. But other things are said to be relative indirectly, as man is relative because he happens to be double, and this is relative; or the white is said to be relative because the same thing happens to be white and double. **1021b8–11**

COMMENTARY

1001. Here the Philosopher establishes the meaning of the *relative* or *relation;* and in regard to this he does two things. First [1], he gives the senses in which things are said to be relative directly; and second [6], those in which things are said to be relative indirectly ("And other things").

In regard to the first he does two things. First, he enumerates the senses in which things are said to be relative directly. Second [2], he proceeds to deal with these ("The first things").

He accordingly gives, first [1], three senses in which things are said to be relative directly. The first of these has to do with number and quantity, as double to half and triple to a third, and "what is multiplied," i.e., the multiple, to a part "of what is multiplied," i.e., the submultiple, "and what includes to what is included in it." But what includes is here taken for what is greater in quantity. For everything which is greater in quantity includes within itself that which it exceeds. For it is this and something more; for example, five includes within itself four, and three cubits include two.

1002. The second sense is that in which some things are said to be relative according to acting and undergoing, or to active and passive potency; for example, in the realm of natural actions, as what can heat to what can be heated; and in the realm of artificial actions, as what can cut to what can be cut; and in general as everything active to everything passive.

1003. The third sense of relation is that in which something measurable is said to be relative to a measure. Here measure and measurable are not taken quantitatively (for this pertains to the first sense, in which either one is said to be relative to the other, since double is said to be relative to half and half to double), but according to the measurement of being and truth. For the truth of knowledge is measured by the knowable object. For it is because a thing is so or is not so that a statement is known to be true or false, and not the reverse. The same thing applies in the case of a sensible object and sensation. And for this reason a measure and what is measurable are not said to be related to each other reciprocally, as in the other senses, but only what is measurable is related to its measure. And in a similar fashion too an image is related to that of which it is the image as what is measurable is related to its measure. For the truth of an image is measured by the thing whose image it is.

1004. These senses are explained as follows: since a real relation consists in the bearing of one thing upon another, there must be as many relations of this kind as there are ways in which one thing can bear upon another. Now one thing bears upon another either in being, inasmuch as the being of one thing depends on another, and then we have the third sense; or according to active or passive power, inasmuch as one thing receives something from another or confers it upon the other, and then we have the second sense; or according as the quantity of one thing can be measured by another, and then we have the first sense.

1005. But the quality as such of a thing pertains only to the subject in which it exists, and therefore from the viewpoint of quality one thing bears upon another only inasmuch as quality has the character of an active or passive power, which is a principle of action or of being acted upon. Or it is related by reason of quantity or of something pertaining to quantity; as one thing is said to be whiter than another, or as that which has the same quality as another is said to be like it. But the other classes of things are a result of relation rather than a cause of it. For the category *when* consists in a relation to time; and the category *where* in a relation to place. And *posture* implies an arrangement of parts; and *having* (attire), the relation of the thing having to the things had.

1006. **The first things** [2].

Then he proceeds to deal with the three senses of relation which have been enumerated. First [3], he considers the first sense. Second [4], he treats the second sense ("Active and passive"). Third [5], he attends to the third sense ("Therefore, things").

In regard to the first he does two things. First [2], he describes the relations which are based simply on number; and second [3], he treats those which are based simply on unity ("Further, *equal*").

He says, first [2], that the first way in which things are relative, which is numerical, is divided inasmuch as the relation is based on the ratio of one number to another or on that of a number to unity. And in either case it may be taken in two ways, for the number which is referred to another number or to unity in the ratio on which the relation is based is either definite or indefinite. This is his meaning in saying that the first things which are said to be relative numerically are said to be such "without qualification," i.e., in general or indefinitely, "or else definitely." And in both ways "to them," namely, to numbers, "or to unity," i.e., to the unit.

1007. Now it should be borne in mind that every measure which is found in continuous quantities is derived in some way from number. Hence relations which are based on continuous quantity are also attributed to number.

1008. It should also be borne in mind that numerical ratios are divided first into two classes, that of equality and that of inequality. And there are two kinds of inequality: the larger and smaller, and more and less. And the larger is divided into five kinds.

1009. For a number is larger whenever it is multiple with respect to a smaller number, i.e., when it includes it many times, as six includes two three times. And if it includes it twice, it is called double; as two in relation to one, or four to two. And if it includes it three times, it is called triple; and if four times, quadruple; and so on.

1010. But sometimes a larger number includes a whole smaller number once and some part of it besides; and then it is said to be superparticular. If it includes a whole smaller number and a half of it besides, it is called sesquialteral, as three to two; and if a third part besides, it is called sesquitertian, as four to three; and if a fourth part besides, it is called sesquiquartan, as five to four; and so on.

1011. Sometimes a larger number includes a whole smaller number once and not merely one part but many parts besides, and then it is called superpartient. And if it includes two parts, it is called superbipartient, as five to three. Again, if it includes three parts, then it is called supertripartient, as seven to four; and if it includes four parts, it is superquadripartient, and then it is related as nine to five; and so on.

1012. Sometimes a larger number includes a whole smaller number many times and some part of it besides, and then it is called multiple superparticular. If it includes it two and a half times, it is called double sesquialteral, as five to two. If it includes it three and a half times, it is called triple sesquialteral, as seven to two. And if it includes it four and a half times, it is called quadruple sesquialteral, as nine to two. And the species of this kind of ratio can also be considered in the case of the superparticular, inasmuch as we speak of the double sesquitertian ratio when a greater number includes a smaller number two and a third times, as seven to three; or of the double sesquiquartan, as nine to four; and so on.

1013. Sometimes too a larger number includes a whole smaller number many times and many parts of it besides, and then it is called multiple superpartient. And similarly a ratio can be divided from the viewpoint of the species of multiplicity, and from that of the species of the superpartient, provided that we may speak of a double superbipartient, when a greater number includes a whole smaller number twice and two parts of it, as eight to three; or even of triple superbipartient, as eleven to three; or even of double supertripartient, as eleven to four. For it includes a whole number twice and three parts of it besides.

1014. And there are just as many species of inequality in the case of a smaller number. For a smaller number is called submultiple, subpartient, submultiple superparticular, submultiple superpartient, and so on.

1015. But it must be noted that the first species of ratio, namely, multiplicity, consists in the relation of one number to the unit. For any species of it is found first in the relation of some number to the unit. Double, for example, is found first in the relation of two to the unit. And similarly a triple ratio is found in the relation of three to the unit; and so on in other cases. But the first terms in which any ratio is found give species to the ratio itself. Hence in whatever other terms it is subsequently found, it is found in them according to the ratio of the first terms. For example, the double ratio is found first between two and the unit. It is from this, then, that the ratio receives its meaning and name; for a double ratio means the ratio of two to the unit. And it is for this reason [too that we use the term in other cases; for] even though one number is said to be double another, this happens only inasmuch as a smaller number takes on the role of the unit and a larger number the role of two; for six is related to three in a double ratio, inasmuch as six is to three as two is to one. And it is similar in the case of a triple ratio, and in all other species of multiplicity. Hence he says that the relation of double is a result of the fact that a definite number, i.e., two, "is referred to unity," i.e., to the unit.

1016. But the term *multiple* implies the relation of a number to the unit, not of any definite number but of number in general. For if a definite number were taken, as two or three, there would be one species of multiplicity, as double or triple. And just as the double is related to two and the triple to three, which are definite numbers, so too the multiple is related to multiplicity, because it signifies an indefinite number.

1017. Other ratios, however, cannot be reduced to the relation of a number to the unit: either a superparticular ratio, or a superpartient, or a multiple superparticular, or a multiple superpartient. For all of these species of ratios are based on the fact that a larger number includes a smaller number once, or some part of it, and one or several parts of it besides. But the unit cannot have a part, and therefore none of these ratios can be based on the relation of a number to the unit but on the relation of one number to another. Thus the double ratio is either that of a definite number, or that of an indefinite number.

1018. And if it is that of a definite number, then "it is what is one and a half times as great," i.e., sesquialteral, or "that which it exceeds," i.e., supersesquialteral. For a sesquialteral ratio consists first in these terms: three and two; and in the ratio of these it is found in all other cases. Hence what is called one and a half times as great, or sesquialteral, implies the relation of one definite number to another, namely, of three to two.

1019. But the relation which is called superparticular is relative to the subparticular, not according to any definite number, as the multiple is relative also to the unit, but according to an indefinite number. For the first species of inequality given above (see n. 1008) are taken according to indefinite numbers, for example, the multiple, superparticular, superpartient, and so on. But the species of these are taken according to definite numbers, as double, triple, sesquialteral, sesquiquartan, and so on.

1020. Now it happens that some continuous quantities have a ratio to each other which does not involve any number, either definite or indefinite. For there is some ratio between all continuous quantities, although it is not a numerical ratio. For there is one common measure of any two numbers, namely, the unit, which, when taken many times, yields a number. But no common measure of all continuous quantities can be found, since there are certain incommensurable continuous quantities, as the diameter of a square is incommensurable with one of its sides. The reason is that there is no ratio between it and one of its sides like the ratio of one number to another or of a number to the unit.

1021. Therefore, when it is said in the case of quantities that this quantity is greater than that one, or is related to that one as what includes is related to what is included in it, not only is this ratio not considered according to any definite species of number, but it is not even considered according to number at all, because every number is commensurable with another. For all numbers have one common measure, which is the unit. But what includes and what is included in it are not spoken of according to any numerical measure; for it is what is so much and something more that is said to have the relation of what includes to what is included in it. And this is indefinite, whether it be commensurable or incommensurable; for whatever quantity may be taken, it is either equal or unequal. If it is not equal, then it follows that it is unequal and includes something else, even though it is not commensurable. Hence it is clear that all of the above-mentioned things are said to be relative according to number and to the properties of numbers, which are commensuration, ratio, and the like.

1022. **Further, equal** [3].

He now treats those relative terms which have a reference to unity or oneness and are not based on the relation of one number to another or to the unit. He says that *equal, like* and *same* are said to be relative in a different way than the foregoing. For these are called such in reference to unity. For those things are the same whose substance is one; and those are alike whose quality is one; and those are equal whose quantity is one. Now since unity is the principle and measure of number, it is also clear that the former terms are said to be relative "numerically," i.e., in reference to something belonging to the class of number. But these last terms are not said to be relative in the same way as the first. For the first relations seen are those of number to number, or of a number to the unit; but this relation has to do with unity in an absolute sense.

1023. **Active and passive** [4].

Here he proceeds to treat the second type of relations, which pertains to active and passive things. He says that relative beings of this kind are relative in two ways: in one way according to active and passive potency; and in a second way according to the actualizations of these potencies, which are action and passivity; for example, what can heat is said to be relative to what can be heated in virtue of active and passive potency. For it is what is capable of heating that can heat, and it is what is capable of being heated that can become hot. Again, what is heating in relation to what is heated, and what is cutting in relation to what is being cut, are said to be relative according to the operations of the aforesaid potencies.

1024. Now this type of relation differs from those previously given; for those which are numerical are operations only figuratively, for example, to multiply, to divide, and so forth, as has also been stated elsewhere, namely, in Book II of the *Physics,* [193b30] where he shows that the objects of mathematics abstract from motion, and therefore they cannot have operations of the kind that have to do with motion.

1025. It should also be noted that among relative terms based on active and passive potency we find diversity from the viewpoint of time; for some of these terms are predicated relatively with regard to past time, as what has made something to what has been made; for instance, a father in relation to his son, because the former has begot and the latter has been begotten; and these differ as what has acted and what has been acted upon. And some are used with respect to future time, as when what will make is related to what will be made. And those relations which are based on privation of potency, as the impossible and the invisible, are reduced to this class of relations. For something is said to be impossible for this person or for that one; and the invisible is spoken of in the same way.

1026. **Therefore, things** [5].

Next he proceeds to deal with the third type of relations. He says that this third type differs from the foregoing in this way, that each of the foregoing things is said to be relative because each is referred to something else, not because something else is referred to it.

For double is related to half, and vice versa; and in a similar way a father is related to his son, and vice versa. But something is said to be relative in this third way because something is referred to it. It is clear, for example, that the sensible and the knowable or intelligible are said to be relative because other things are related to them; for a thing is said to be knowable because knowledge is had of it. And similarly something is said to be sensible because it can be sensed.

1027. Hence they are not said to be relative because of something which pertains to them, such as quality, quantity, action, or undergoing, as was the case in the foregoing relations, but only because of the action of other things, although these are not terminated in them. For if seeing were the action of the one seeing as extending to the thing seen, as heating extends to the thing which can be heated, then just as what can be heated is related to the one heating, so would what is visible be related to the one seeing. But to see and to understand and actions of this kind, as is stated in Book IX (see n. 1788) of this work, remain in the things acting and do not pass over into those which are acted upon. Hence what is visible or what is knowable is not acted upon by being known or seen. And on this account these are not referred to other things but others to them. The same is true in all other cases in which something is said to be relative because something else is related to it, as right and left in the case of a pillar. For since right and left designate starting points of motion in living things, they cannot be attributed to a pillar or to any nonliving thing except insofar as living things are related to a pillar in some way. It is in this sense that one speaks of a right-hand pillar because a man stands to the left of it. The same holds true of an image in relation to the original; and of a denarius, by means of which one fixes the price of a sale. And in all these cases the whole basis of relation between two extremes depends on something else. Hence all things of this kind are related in somewhat the same way as what is measurable and its measure. For everything is measured by the thing on which it depends.

1028. Now it must be borne in mind that, even though verbally knowledge would seem to be relative to the knower and to the object of knowledge (for we speak both of the knowledge of the knower and of the knowledge of the thing known), and thought to the thinker and to what is thought, nevertheless a thought as predicated relatively is not relative to the one whose thought it is as its subject, for it would follow that the same relative term would then be expressed twice. For it is evident that a thought is relative to what is thought about as to its object. Again, if it were relative to the thinker, it would then be called relative twice; and since the very existence of what is relative is to be relative in some way to something else, it would follow that the same thing would have two acts of existence. Similarly in the case of sight it is clear that sight is not relative to the seer but to its object, which is color, "or something of this sort." He says this because of the things which are seen at night but not by means of their proper color, as is stated in *The Soul*, Book II. [419a1]

1029. And although it is correct to say that sight is of him who sees, sight is not related to the seer formally as sight but as an accident or power of the seer. For a relation has to do with something external, but a subject does not, except insofar as it is an accident. It is clear, then, that these are the ways in which some things are said to be relative directly.

1030. **And other things** [6].

He now gives three ways in which some things are said to be relative not directly but indirectly. The first of these is that in which things are said to be relative because their genera are relative, as medicine is said to be relative because science is relative. For medicine is called the science of health and sickness. And science is relative in this way because it is an accident.

1031. The second way is that in which certain abstract terms are said to be relative because the concrete things to which these abstract terms apply are relative to something else. For example, equality and likeness are said to be relative because the like and the equal are relative. But equality and likeness are not considered relative as words.

1032. The third way is that in which a subject is said to be relative because of an accident. For example, a man or some white thing is said to be relative because each happens to be double; and in this way a head is said to be relative because it is a part.

LESSON 18
The Senses of Perfect

ARISTOTLE'S TEXT Chapter 16: 1021b12–1022a3

1. *That thing is said to be perfect (or complete) outside of which it is impossible to find even a single part; for example, the perfect time of each thing is that outside of which it is impossible to find any time which is a part of it. And those things are perfect whose ability (virtus) and goodness admit of no further degree in their class; for example, we speak of a perfect physician and a perfect flute player when they lack nothing pertaining to the form of their particular ability. And thus in transferring this term to bad things, we speak of a perfect slanderer and a perfect thief, since we also call them good, as a good slanderer and a good thief. For any ability is a perfection, since each thing is perfect and every substance is perfect when, in the line of its particular ability, it lacks no part of its natural measure.* **1021b12–23**

2. *Further, those things are said to be perfect which have a goal or end worth seeking. For things are perfect which have attained their goal. Hence, since a goal is something final, we also say, in transferring the term perfect to bad things, that a thing has been perfectly spoiled and perfectly corrupted when nothing pertaining to its corruption and evil is missing but it is at its last point. And for this reason death is described metaphorically as an end; for both of these are final things. But an end is a final purpose.* **1021b23–30**

3. *Things which are said to be perfect in themselves, then, are said to be such in all of these senses: some because they lack no part of their goodness and admit of no further degree and have no part outside; others in general inasmuch as they admit of no further degree in any class and have no part outside.* **1021b30–1022a1**

4. *And other things are now termed perfect in reference to these, either because they make something such, or have something such, or know something such, or because they are somehow referred to things which are said to be perfect in the primary senses.* **1022a1–3**

COMMENTARY

1033. Having treated the various senses of the terms which signify the causes, the subject and the parts of the subject of this science, here the Philosopher begins to treat the various senses of the terms which designate attributes having the character of properties. This is divided into two parts. In the first [1] he gives the various senses of the terms which refer to the perfection or completeness of being. In the second (Lesson 22, text 3) he treats those which refer to a lack of being ("*False* means").

In regard to the first he does two things. First, he gives the different senses of the terms which designate attributes pertaining to the perfection of being; and second (Lesson 21), he treats those which designate the wholeness of being. For the terms *perfect* and *whole* have the same or nearly the same meaning, as is said in the *Physics*, Book III. [207a12] He considers the second part of this division where he says, *"To come from something."*

In regard to the first part he does two things. First, he treats the various senses of the term perfect. Second (Lesson 19), he treats the various senses of the terms which signify certain conditions of that which is perfect ("The term *limit*").

In regard to the first he does two things. First, he considers the senses in which things are said to be *perfect in themselves;* and second [4], he treats those in which things are said to be *perfect* by *reason of something else* ("And other things").

In regard to the first he does two things. First, he gives three senses in which a thing is said to be perfect in itself. Second [3], he shows how, according to these senses, a thing is said to be perfect in different ways ("Things which are said").

1034. He accordingly says, first [1], that in one sense that thing is said to be perfect outside of which it is impossible to find any of its parts. For example, a man is said to be perfect when no part of him is missing; and a period of time is said to be perfect when none of its parts can be found outside of it. For example, a day is said to be perfect or complete when no part of it is missing.

1035. A thing is said to be perfect in another sense with reference to some ability. Thus a thing is said to be perfect which admits of "no further degree," i.e., excess or superabundance, from the viewpoint of good performance in some particular line, and is not deficient in any respect. For we say that that thing is in a good state which has neither more nor less than it ought to have, as is said in Book II of the *Ethics. [1106b10]* Thus a man is said to be a perfect physician or a perfect flute player when he lacks nothing pertaining to the particular ability by reason of which he is said to be a good physician or a good flute player. For the ability which each thing has is what makes its possessor good and renders his work good.

1036. And it is in this sense that we also transfer the term perfect to bad things. For we speak of a perfect "slanderer," or scandal monger, and a perfect thief, when they lack none of the qualities proper to them as such. Nor is it surprising if we use the term perfect of those things which rather designate a defect, because even when things are bad we predicate the term good of them in an analogous sense. For we speak of a good thief and a good scandal monger because in their operations, even though they are evil, they are disposed as good men are with regard to good operations.

1037. The reason why a thing is said to be perfect in the line of its particular ability is that an ability is a perfection of a thing. For each thing is perfect when no part of the natural magnitude which belongs to it according to the form of its proper ability is missing. Moreover, just as each natural being has a definite measure of natural magnitude in continuous quantity, as is stated in Book II of *The Soul, [416a15]* so too each thing has a definite amount of its own natural ability. For example, a horse has by nature a definite dimensive quantity, within certain limits; for there is both a maximum quantity and minimum quantity beyond which no horse can go in size. And in a similar way the quantity of active power in a horse has certain limits in both directions. For there is some maximum power of a horse which is not in fact surpassed in any horse; and similarly there is some minimum which never fails to be attained.

1038. Therefore, just as the first sense of the term perfect was based on the fact that a thing lacks no part of the dimensive quantity which it is naturally determined to have, in a similar way this second sense of the term is based on the fact that a thing lacks no part of the quantity of power which it is naturally determined to have. And each of these senses of the term has to do with internal perfection.

1039. **Further, those things** [2].

Here he gives the third sense in which the term perfect is used, and it pertains to external perfection. He says that in a third way those things are said to be perfect "which have a goal," i.e., which have already attained their end, but only if that end is "worth seeking," or good. A man, for instance, is called perfect when he has already attained happiness. But one who has attained some goal that is evil is said to be deficient rather than perfect, because evil is a privation of the perfection which a thing ought to have. Thus it is evident that, when evil men accomplish their will, they are not happier but sadder. And since every goal or end is something final, for this reason we transfer the term perfect somewhat figuratively to those things which have reached some final state, even though it be evil. For example, a thing is said to be perfectly spoiled or corrupted when nothing pertaining to its ruin or corruption is missing. And by this metaphor death is called an end, because it is something final. However, an end is not only something final but is also that for the sake of which a thing comes to be. This does not apply to death or corruption.

1040. **Things which are said** [3].

Here he shows how things are perfect in different ways according to the foregoing senses of perfection. He says that some things are said to be perfect in themselves; and this occurs in two ways. For some things are altogether perfect because they lack absolutely nothing at all; they neither have any "further degree," i.e., excess, because there is nothing which surpasses them in goodness; nor do they receive any good from outside, because they have no need of any external goodness. This is the condition of the first principle, God, in whom the most perfect goodness is found, and to whom none of all the perfections found in each class of things are lacking.

1041. Some things are said to be perfect in some particular line because "they do not admit of any further degree," or excess, "in their class," as though they lacked anything proper to that class. Nor is anything that belongs to the perfection of that class external to them, as though they lacked it; just as a man is said to be perfect when he has already attained happiness.

1042. And not only is this distinction made with reference to the second sense of perfection given above, but it can also be made with reference to the first sense of the term, as is mentioned at the beginning of *The Heavens*. *[268a20]* For any individual body is a perfect quantity in its class, because it has three dimensions, which are all there are. But the world is said to be universally perfect because there is absolutely nothing outside of it.

1043. **And other things** [4].

He now gives the sense in which some things are said to be perfect by reason of their relation to something else. He says that other things are said to be perfect "in reference to these," i.e., in reference to things which are perfect in themselves, either because they make something perfect in one of the preceding ways, as medicine is perfect because it causes perfect health; or because they have some perfection, as a man is said to be perfect who has perfect knowledge; or because they represent such a perfect thing, as things which bear a likeness to those that are perfect (as, for example, an image which represents a man perfectly is said to be perfect); or in any other way in which they are referred to things that are said to be perfect in themselves in the primary senses.

LESSON 19

The Senses of Limit, of "According to Which," of "In Itself," and of Disposition

ARISTOTLE'S TEXT Chapters 17 & 18: 1022a4–1022a36

1. The term limit (boundary or terminus) means the extremity of anything, i.e., that beyond which nothing of that being can be found, and that within which everything belonging to it is contained. **1022a4–5**

2. And limit means the form, whatever it may be, of a continuous quantity or of something having continuous quantity; and it also means the goal or end of each thing. And such too is that toward which motion and action proceed, and not that from which they proceed. And sometimes it is both, not only that from which, but also that to which. And it means the reason for which something is done; and also the substance or essence of each. For this is the limit or terminus of knowledge; and if of knowledge, also of the thing. **1022a5–10**

3. Hence it is clear that the term limit has as many meanings as the term principle has, and even more. For a principle is a limit, but not every limit is a principle. **1022a10–13**

Chapter 18

4. The phrase according to which (secundum quod) has several meanings. In one sense it means the species or substance of each thing; for example, that according to which a thing is good is goodness itself. And in another sense it means the first subject in which an attribute is naturally disposed to come into being, as color in surface. Therefore, in its primary sense, "that according to which" is the form; and in its secondary sense it is the matter of each thing and the first subject of each. And in general that according to which is used in the same way as a reason. For we speak of that according to which he comes, or the reason of his coming; and that according to which he has reasoned incorrectly or simply reasoned, or the reason why he has reasoned or reasoned incorrectly. Further, that according to which is used in reference to place, as according [i.e., next] to which he stands, or according to [i.e., along] which he walks; for in general these signify position and place. **1022a14–24**

5. Hence the phrase in itself (secundum se) must be used in many senses. For in one sense it means the quiddity of each thing, as Callias and the quiddity of Callias. And in another sense it means everything that is found in the quiddity of a thing. For example, Callias is an animal in himself, because animal belongs to his definition; for Callias is an animal. Again, it is used of a thing when something has been manifested in it as its first subject or in some part of it; for example, a surface is white in itself, and a man is alive in himself. For the soul is a part of man in which life is first present. Again, it means a thing which has no other cause. For there are many causes of man, namely, animal and two-footed, yet man is man in himself. Further, it means any attributes that belong to a thing alone and inasmuch as they belong to it alone, because whatever is separate is in itself. **1022a24–36**

COMMENTARY

1044. Here Aristotle proceeds to examine the terms which signify the conditions necessary for perfection. Now what is perfect or complete, as is clear from the above, is what is determinate and absolute, independent of anything else, and not deprived of anything but having whatever befits it in its own line. Therefore, first [1], he deals with the term *limit (boundary* or *terminus);* second [4], with the phrase *in itself* ("The phrase *according to which*"); and third (Lesson 20, text 2), with the term *having* ("*Having* means").

In regard to the first he does three things. First [1], he gives the meaning of *limit*. He says that limit means the last part of anything, such that no part of what is first limited lies outside this limit; and all things which belong to it are contained within it. He says "first" because the last part of a first thing may be the starting point of a second thing; for example, the now of time, which is the last point of the past, is the beginning of the future.

1045. **And limit means the form** [2].

Second, he gives four senses in which the term limit is used. The first of these applies to any kind of continuous quantity insofar as the terminus of a continuous quantity, or of a thing having continuous quantity, is called a limit; for example, a point is called the limit of a line, and a surface the limit of a body, or also of a stone, which has quantity.

1046. The second sense of limit is similar to the first inasmuch as one extreme of a motion or activity is called a limit, i.e., that toward which there is motion, and not that from which there is motion, as the limit of generation is being and not non-being. Sometimes, however, both extremes of motion are called limits in a broad sense, i.e., both that from which as well as that to which, inasmuch as we say that every motion is between two limits or extremes.

1047. In a third sense limit means that for the sake of which something comes to be, for this is the terminus of an intention, just as limit in the second sense meant the terminus of a motion or an operation.

1048. In a fourth sense limit means the substance of a thing, i.e., the essence of a thing or the definition signifying what a thing is. For this is the limit or terminus of knowledge, because knowledge of a thing begins with certain external signs from which we come to know a thing's definition, and when we have arrived at it we have complete knowledge of the thing. Or the definition is called the limit or terminus of knowledge because under it are contained the notes by which the thing is known. And if one difference is changed, added, or subtracted, the definition will not remain the same. Now if it [i.e., the definition] is the limit of knowledge, it must also be the limit of the thing, because knowledge is had through the assimilation of the knower to the thing known.

1049. **Hence it is clear** [4].

Here he concludes by comparing a limit with a principle, saying that limit has as many meanings as principle has, and even more, because every principle is a limit but not every limit is a principle. For that toward which there is motion is a limit, but it is not in any way a principle, whereas that from which there is motion is both a principle and a limit, as is clear from what was said above (504:C 1046).

1050. **The phrase "according to which"** [4].

Here he deals with the phrase *in itself*; and in regard to this he does three things. First [4], he lays down the meaning of the phrase *according to which*, which is more common than the phrase *in itself*. Second [5], he draws his conclusion as to the ways in which the phrase *in itself* is used ("Hence the phrase"). Third (Lesson 20), he establishes the meaning of the term *disposition* ("*Disposition* means"), because each of the senses in which we use the phrases mentioned above somehow signifies disposition.

In regard to the first [4], he gives four senses in which the phrase *according to which* is used. The first has to do with the "species," i.e., the form, or "the substance of each thing," or its essence, inasmuch as this is that according to which something is said to be; for example, according to the Platonists "the good itself," i.e., the Idea of the Good, is that according to which something is said to be good.

1051. This phrase has a second meaning insofar as the subject in which some attribute is naturally disposed to first come into being is termed "that according to which," as color first comes into being in surface; and therefore it is said that a body is colored according to its surface. Now this sense differs from the preceding one, because the preceding sense pertains to form, but this last sense pertains to matter.

1052. There is a third sense in which this phrase is used, inasmuch as any cause or reason in general is said to be "that according to which." Hence the phrase "according to which" is used in the same number of senses as the term reason. For it is the same thing to ask, "According to what does he come?" and "For what reason does he come?" And in like manner it is the same to ask, "According to what has he reasoned incorrectly or simply reasoned, and, for what reason has he reasoned?"

1053. This phrase *according to which* is used in a fourth sense inasmuch as it signifies position and place; as in the statement, "according to which he stands," i.e., next to which, and, "according to which he walks," i.e., along which he walks; and both of these signify place and position. This appears more clearly in the Greek idiom.

1054. **Hence the phrase** [5].

From what has been said above he draws four senses in which the phrase *in itself* or *of itself* is used. The first of these is found when the definition, which signifies the quiddity of each thing, is said to belong to each in itself, as Callias "and the quiddity of Callias," i.e., the essence of the thing, are such that one belongs to the other "in itself." And not only the whole definition is predicated of the thing defined in itself, but so too in a way everything which belongs to the definition, which expresses the quiddity, is predicated of the thing defined in itself. For example, Callias is an animal in himself. For animal belongs in the definition of Callias, because Callias is an individual animal, and this would be given in his definition if individual things could have a definition. And these two senses are included under one, because both the definition and a part of the definition are predicated of each thing in itself for the same reason. For this is the first type of essential predication given in the *Posterior Analytics [73a34]* and it corresponds to the first sense given above (see n. 1050) in which we use the phrase *according to which.*

1055. This phrase is used in a second sense when something is shown to be in something else as in a first subject, when it belongs to it of itself. This can happen in two ways: for either the first subject of an accident is the whole subject itself of which the accident is predicated (as a surface is said to be colored or white in itself; for the first subject of color is surface, and therefore a body is said to be colored by reason of its surface); or also the subject of the accident is some part of the subject, just as a man is said to be alive in himself, because part of him, namely, the soul, is the first subject of life. This is the second type of essential predication given in the *Posterior Analytics,* [73a38] namely, that in which the subject is given in the definition of the predicate. For the first and proper subject is given in the definition of a proper accident.

1056. This phrase is used in a third sense when something having no cause is spoken of as *in itself;* as all immediate propositions, i.e., those which are not proved by a middle term. For in *a priori* demonstrations the middle term is the cause of the predicate's belonging to the subject. Hence, although man has many causes, for example, animal and two-footed, which are his formal cause, still nothing is the cause of the proposition "Man is man," since it is an immediate one; and for this reason man is man in himself. And to this sense is reduced the fourth type of essential predication given in the *Posterior Analytics,* [73b10] the case in which an effect is predicated of a cause; as when it is said that the slain man perished by slaying, or that the thing cooled was made cold or chilled by cooling.

1057. This phrase is used in a fourth sense inasmuch as those things are said to belong to something in themselves which belong to it alone and precisely as belonging to it alone. He says this in order to differentiate this sense of *in itself* from the preceding senses, in which it was not said that a thing belongs to something in itself because it belongs to it alone; although in that sense too something would belong to it alone, as the definition to the thing defined. But here something is said to be in itself by reason of its exclusiveness. For *in itself* signifies something separate, as a man is said to be by himself when he is alone. And to this sense is reduced the third sense given in the *Posterior Analytics,* [73b5] and the fourth sense of the phrase *according to which,* which implies position.

LESSON 20

The Meanings of Disposition, of Having, of Affection, of Privation, and of "To Have"

ARISTOTLE'S TEXT Chapters 19–23: 1022b1–1023a25

1. *Disposition means the order of what has parts, either as to place or as to potentiality or as to species. For there must be a certain position, as the term disposition itself makes clear.* **1022b1–3**

Chapter 20

2. *Having (possession or habit) means in one sense a certain activity of the haver and of the thing had, as a sort of action or motion. For when one thing makes and another is made, the making is intermediate. And likewise between one having clothing and the clothing had, the having is intermediate. It is accordingly clear that it is not reasonable to have a having; for if it were possible to have the having of what is had, this would go on to infinity. In another sense having means a certain disposition whereby the thing disposed is well or badly disposed, either in relation to itself or to something else; for example, health is a sort of having and is such a disposition. Again, the term having is used if there is a part of such a disposition. And for this reason any virtue pertaining to the powers of the soul is a sort of having.* **1022b4–14**

Chapter 21

3. *Affection (passio) means in one sense (modification), the quality according to which alteration occurs, as white and black, sweet and bitter, heavy and light, and all other such attributes. And in another sense (undergoing), it means the actualizations and alterations of these; and of these, particularly harmful operations and motions; and most especially those which are painful and injurious (suffering). Again, great rejoicing and grieving are called affections (passiones).* **1022b15–21**

Chapter 22

4. *The term privation is used in one sense when a thing does not have one of those attributes which it is suitable for some things to have, even though that particular thing would not naturally have it. In this sense a plant is said to be deprived of eyes. And it is used in another sense when a thing is naturally disposed to have something, either in itself or according to its class, and does not have it. A man and a mole, for example, are deprived of sight but in different ways: the latter according to its class and the former in itself. Again, we speak of privation when a thing is by nature such as to have a certain perfection and does not have it even when it is naturally disposed to have it. For blindness is a privation, although a man is not blind at every age but only if he does not have sight at the age when he is naturally disposed to have it. And similarly we use the term privation when a thing does not have some attribute which it is naturally disposed to have, in reference to where, and to what, and to the object in relation to which, and in the manner in which it may have it by nature if it does not have it. Again, the removal of anything by force is called a privation.* **1022b22–33**

5. *And in all instances in which negations are expressed by the privative particle {a}- [i.e., un- or in-], privations are expressed. For a thing is said to be unequal because it does not have the equality which it is naturally fitted to have. And a thing is said to be invisible either because it has no color at all or because its color is deficient; and a thing is said to be footless either because it lacks feet altogether or because its feet are imperfect. Again, we use the term privation of a thing when it has something to a very small degree, for example, "unignited," and this means to have it in a deficient way. And privation also designates what is not had easily or well; for example, a thing is uncuttable not only because it cannot be cut but because it cannot be cut easily or well. And we use the term privation of what is not had in any way. For it is not only a*

one-eyed man that is said to be blind, but one who lacks sight in both eyes. And for this reason not every man is good or bad, just or unjust, but there is an intermediate state. **1022b33–1023b7**

Chapter 23

6. To have (to possess or to hold) has many meanings. In one sense it means to treat something according to one's own nature or to one's own impulse; and for this reason a fever is said to possess a man, and tyrants are said to possess cities, and people who are clothed are said to possess clothing. And in another sense a thing is said to have something when this is present in the subject which receives it; thus bronze has the form of a statue, and a body, disease. And whatever contains something else is said to have or to hold it; for that which is contained is said to be held by the container; for example, we say that a bottle holds a liquid and a city men and a ship sailors. It is in this way too that a whole has parts. Again, whatever prevents a thing from moving or from acting according to its own impulse is said to hold it, as pillars hold the weight imposed on them. It is in this sense that the poets make Atlas hold the heavens, as if otherwise it would fall on the earth, as certain of the physicists also say. And it is in this sense that that which holds something together is said to hold what it holds together, because otherwise it would be separated, each according to its own impulse. And to be in something is expressed in a similar way and corresponds to the meanings of to have. **1023a8–25**

COMMENTARY

1058. Because the phrase *according to which* signifies in one sense position, the Philosopher therefore proceeds to examine next [1] the term *disposition.* He gives the common meaning of this term, saying that a disposition is nothing else than the order of parts in a thing which has parts. He also gives the senses in which the term disposition is used; and there are three of these. The first designates the order of parts in place, and in this sense disposition or posture is a special category.

1059. Disposition is used in a second sense inasmuch as the order of parts is considered in reference to potency or active power, and then disposition is placed in the first species of quality. For a thing is said to be disposed in this sense, for example, according to health or sickness, by reason of the fact that its parts have an order in its active or passive power.

1060. Disposition is used in a third sense according as the order of parts is considered in reference to the form and figure of the whole; and then disposition or position is held to be a difference in the genus of quantity. For it is said that one kind of quantity has position, as line, surface, body and place, but that another has not, as number and time.

1061. He also points out that the term disposition signifies order; for it signifies position, as the derivation itself of the term makes clear, and order is involved in the notion of position.

1062. **"Having" means** [2].

He now proceeds to examine the term *having.* First [2], he gives the different senses of the term having. Second [3], he gives the different senses of certain other terms which are closely connected with this one ("*Affection* means").

He accordingly gives, first [2], the two senses in which the term having is used. First, it designates something intermediate between the haver and the thing had. Now even though having is not an action, none the less it signifies something after the manner of an action. Therefore having is understood to be something intermediate between the haver and the thing had and to be a sort of action; just as heating is understood to be something intermediate between the thing being heated and the heater, whether what is intermediate be taken as an action, as when heating is taken in an active sense, or as a motion, as when heating is taken in a passive sense. For when one thing makes and another is made, the making stands between them. In Greek the term {*poiesis*} is used, and this signifies making. Moreover, if one goes from the agent to the patient, the intermediate is making in an active sense, and this is the action of the maker. But if one goes from the thing made to the maker, then the intermediate is making in a passive sense, and this is the motion of the thing being made. And between a man having clothing and the clothing had, the having is also an intermediate; because, if we consider it by going from the man to his clothing, it will be like an action, as is expressed under the form "to have." But if we consider it in the opposite way, it will be like the undergoing of a motion, as is expressed under the form "to be had."

1063. Now although having is understood to be intermediate between a man and his clothing inasmuch as he has it, none the less it is evident that there cannot be another intermediate between the having and the thing had, as though there were another having midway between the haver and the intermediate having. For if one were to say that it is possible to have the having "of what is had," i.e., of the thing had, an infinite regress would then result. For the man has "the thing had," i.e., his clothing, but he does not have the having of the thing had by way of another intermediate having. It is like the case of a maker, who makes the thing made by an intermediate making, but does not make the intermediate making itself by way of some other intermediate making. It is for this reason too that the relations by which a subject is related to something else are not related to the subject by some other intermediate relation and also not to the opposite term; paternity, for example, is not related to a father or to a son by some other intermediate relation. And if some relations are said to be intermediate, they are merely conceptual relations and not real ones. Having in this sense is taken as one of the categories.

1064. In a second sense the term having means the disposition whereby something is well or badly disposed; for example, a thing is well disposed by health and badly disposed by sickness. Now by each of these, health and sickness, a thing is well or badly disposed in two ways: in itself or in relation to something else. Thus a healthy thing is one that is well disposed in itself, and a robust thing is one that is well disposed for doing something. Health is a kind of having, then, because it is a disposition such as has been described. And having (habit) designates not only the disposition of a whole but also that of a part, which is a part of the disposition of the whole. For example, the good dispositions of an animal's parts are themselves parts of the good disposition of the whole animal. The virtues pertaining to the parts of the soul are also habits; for example, temperance is a habit of the concupiscible part, fortitude a habit of the irascible part, and prudence a habit of the rational part.

1065. **"Affection"** [3].

Here he proceeds to treat the terms which are associated with having. First [3], he deals with those which are associated as an opposite; and second [6], he considers something which is related to it as an effect, namely, *to have,* which derives its name from having ("To have").

Now there is something which is opposed to having as the imperfect is opposed to the perfect, and this is affection (being affected). And privation is opposed by direct opposition. Hence, first [3], he deals with affection; and second [4], with privation ("The term privation").

He accordingly gives, first [3], four senses of the term affection. In one sense (modification) it means the quality according to which alteration takes place, such as white and black and the like. And this is the third species of quality; for it has been proved in Book VII of the *Physics* [245b1] that there can be alteration only in the third species of quality.

1066. Affection is used in another sense (undergoing) according as the actualizations of this kind of quality and alteration, which comes about through them, are called affections. And in this sense affection is one of the categories, for example, being heated and cooled and other motions of this kind.

1067. In a third sense (suffering) affection means, not any kind of alteration at all, but those which are harmful and terminate in some evil, and which are lamentable or sorrowful; for a thing is not said to suffer insofar as it is healed but insofar as it is made ill. Or it also designates anything harmful that befalls anything at all—and with good reason. For a patient by the action of some agent which is contrary to it is drawn from its own natural disposition to one similar to that of the agent. Hence, a patient is said more properly to suffer when some part of something fitting to it is being removed and so long as its disposition is being changed into a contrary one, than when the reverse occurs. For then it is said rather to be perfected.

1068. And because things which are not very great are considered as nothing, therefore in a fourth sense (passion) affection means not any kind of harmful alteration whatsoever, but those which are extremely injurious, as great calamities and great sorrows. And because excessive pleasure becomes harmful (for sometimes people have died or become ill as a result of it), and because too great prosperity is turned into something harmful to those who do not know how to make good use of it, therefore another text reads "great rejoicing and grieving are called affections." And still another text agrees with this, saying, "very great sorrows and prosperities."

1069. Now it should be noted that because these three—disposition, habit or having, and affection—signify one of the categories only in one of the senses in which they are used, as is evident from what was said above, he therefore did not place them with the other parts of being, i.e., with quantity, quality and relation. For either all or most of the senses in which they were used pertained to the category signified by these terms.

1070. **The term "privation"** [4].

Here he gives the different senses in which the term *privation* is used. And since privation includes in its intelligible structure both negation and the fitness of some subject to possess some attribute, he therefore gives, first [4], the different senses of privation which refer to this fitness or aptitude for some attribute. Second [5], he treats the various senses of negation ("And in all instances").

In regard to the first [4] he gives four senses of privation. The first has to do with this natural fitness taken in reference to the attribute of which the subject is deprived and not in reference to the subject itself. For we speak of a privation in this sense when some attribute which is naturally fitted to be had is not had, even though the subject which lacks it is not designed by nature to have it. For example, a plant is said to be deprived of eyes because eyes are naturally designed to be had by something, although not by a plant. But in the case of those attributes which a subject is not naturally fitted to have, the subject cannot be said to be deprived of them, for example, that the eye by its power of vision should penetrate an opaque body.

1071. A second sense of the term privation is noted in reference to a subject's fitness to have some attribute. For in this sense privation refers only to some attribute which a thing is naturally fitted to have either in itself or according to its class; in itself, for example, as when a blind person is said to be deprived of sight, which he is naturally fitted to have in himself. And a mole is said to be deprived of sight, not because it is naturally fitted to have it, but because the class, animal, to which the mole belongs, is so fitted. For there are many attributes which a thing is not prevented from having by reason of its genus but by reason of its differences; for example, a man is not prevented from having wings by reason of his genus but by reason of his difference.

1072. A third sense of the term privation is noted in reference to circumstances. And in this sense a thing is said to be deprived of something if it does not have it when it is naturally fitted to have it. This is the case, for example, with the privation *blindness;* for an animal is not said to be blind at every age but only if it does not have sight at an age when it is naturally fitted to have it. Hence a dog is not said to be blind before the ninth day. And what is true of the circumstance *when* also applies to other circumstances, as "to *where,*" or place. Thus *night* means the privation of light in a place where light may naturally exist, but not in caverns, which the sun's rays cannot penetrate. And it applies "to what part," as a man is not said to be toothless if he does not have teeth in his hand but only if he does not have them in that part in which they are naturally disposed to exist; and "to the object in relation to which," as a man is not said to be small or imperfect in stature if he is not large in comparison with a mountain or with any other thing with which he is not naturally comparable in size. Hence a man is not said to be slow in moving if he does not run as fast as a hare or move as fast as the wind; nor is he said to be ignorant if he does not understand as God does.

1073. Privation is used in a fourth sense inasmuch as the removal of anything by violence or force is called a privation. For what is forced is contrary to natural impulse, as has been said above (see n. 829); and thus the removal of anything by force has reference to something that a person is naturally fitted to have.

1074. **And in all** [5].

Then he gives the different senses of privation which involve negation. For the Greeks use the prefix {a}, when compounding words, to designate negations and privations, just as we use the prefix *in-* or *un-*; and therefore he says that in every case in which one expresses negations designated by the prefix a, used in composition at the beginning of a word, privations are designated. For *unequal* means in one sense what lacks equality, provided that it is naturally such as to have it; and *invisible* means what lacks color; and footless, what lacks feet.

1075. Negations of this kind are used in a second sense to indicate not what is not had at all but what is had badly or in an ugly way; for example, a thing is said to be colorless because it has a bad or unfitting color; and a thing is said to be footless because it has defective or deformed feet.

1076. In a third sense an attribute is signified privatively or negatively because it is had to a small degree; for example, the term {apyrenon} i.e., unignited, is used in the Greek text, and it signifies a situation where the smallest amount of fire exists. And in a way this sense is contained under the second, because to have something to a small degree is in a way to have it defectively or unfittingly.

1077. Something is designated as a privation or negation in a fourth sense because it is not done easily or well; for example, something is said to be uncuttable not only because it is not cut but because it is not cut easily or well.

1078. And something is designated as a privation or negation in a fifth sense because it is not had in any way at all. Hence it is not a one-eyed person who is said to be blind but one who lacks sight in both eyes.

1079. From this he draws a corollary, namely, that there is some intermediate between good and evil, just and unjust. For a person does not become evil when he lacks goodness to any degree at all, as the Stoics said (for they held all sins to be equal), but when he deviates widely from virtue and is brought to a contrary habit. Hence it is said in Book II of the *Ethics, [1109b18]* that a man is not to be blamed for deviating a little from virtue.

1080. **"To have"** [6].

Then he gives four ways in which the term *to have* (to possess or hold) is used. First, to have a thing is to treat it according to one's own nature in the case of natural things, or according to one's own impulse in the case of voluntary matters. Thus a fever is said to possess a man because he is brought from a normal state to one of fever. And in the same sense tyrants are said to possess cities, because civic business is carried out according to the will and impulse of tyrants. And in this sense too those who are clothed are said to possess or have clothing, because clothing is fitted to the one who wears it so that it takes on his figure. And to have possession of a thing is also reduced to this sense of to have, because anything that a man possesses he uses as he wills.

1081. To have is used in a second way inasmuch as that in which some attribute exists as its proper subject is said to have it. It is in this sense that bronze has the form of a statue, and a body has disease. And to have a science or quantity or any accident or form is included under this sense.

1082. To have is used in a third way (to hold) when a container is said to have or to hold the thing contained, and the thing contained is said to be held by the container. For example, we say that a bottle has or "holds a liquid," i.e., some fluid, such as water or wine; and a city, men; and a ship, sailors. It is in this sense too that a whole is said to have parts; for a whole contains a part just as a place contains the thing in place. But a place differs from a whole in this respect that a place may be separated from the thing which occupies it, whereas a whole may not be separated from its parts. Hence, anything that occupies a place is like a separate part, as is said in Book IV of the *Physics*. [209b22-32]

1083. To have is used in a fourth way (to hold up) inasmuch as one thing is said to hold another because it prevents it from operating or being moved according to its own impulse. It is in this sense that pillars are said to hold up the heavy bodies placed upon them, because they prevent these bodies from falling down in accordance with their own inclination. And in this sense too the poets said that Atlas holds up the heavens; for the poets supposed Atlas to be a giant who prevents the heavens from falling on the earth. And certain natural philosophers also say this, holding that the heavens will at some time be corrupted and fall in dissolution upon the earth. This is most evident in the opinions expressed by Empedocles, for he held that the world is destroyed an infinite number of times and comes into being an infinite number of times. And the fables of the poets have some basis in reality; for Atlas, who was a great astronomer, made an accurate study of the motion of the celestial bodies, and from this arose the story that he holds up the heavens. But this sense of the term to have differs from the first. For according to the first, as was seen, the thing having compels the thing had to follow by reason of its own impulse, and thus is the cause of forced motion. But here the thing having prevents the thing had from being moved by its own natural motion, and thus is the cause of forced rest. The third sense of having, according to which a container is said to have or hold the thing contained, is reduced to this sense, because the individual parts of the thing contained would be separated from each other by their own peculiar impulse if the container did not prevent this. This is clear, for example, in the case of a bottle containing water, inasmuch as the bottle prevents the parts of the water from being separated.

1084. In closing he says that the phrase *to be in a thing* is used in the same way as *to have*, and the ways of *being in a thing* correspond to those of *having a thing*. Now the eight ways of being in a thing have been treated in Book IV of the *Physics*. [210a14] Two of these are as follows: that in which an integral whole is in its parts, and the reverse of this. Two others are: the way in which a universal whole is in its parts, and vice versa. And another is that in which a thing in place is in a place, and this corresponds to the third sense of having, according to which a whole has parts, and a place has the thing which occupies it. But the way in which a thing is said to be in something as in an efficient cause or mover (as the things belonging to a kingdom are in the king) corresponds to the first sense of having given here [6]. And the way in which a thing is in an end or goal is reduced to the fourth sense of having given here [6], or also to the first, because those things which are related to an end are moved or at rest because of it.

LESSON 21
The Meanings of "To Come from Something," Part, Whole, and Mutilated

ARISTOTLE'S TEXT Chapters 24–27: 1023a26–1024a28

1. To come from something (esse or fieri ex aliquo) means in one sense to come from something as matter, and this in two ways: either in reference to the first genus or to the ultimate species; for example, all liquefiable things come from water, and a statue comes from bronze. And in another sense it means to come from a thing as a first moving principle; for example, From what did the fight come? From a taunt; because this was the cause of the fight. In another sense it means to come from the composite of matter and form, as parts come from a whole, and a verse from the Iliad, and stones from a house. For the form is an end or goal, and what is in possession of its end is complete. And one thing comes from another in the sense that a species comes from a part of a species, and man from two-footed, and a syllable from an element. For this is different from the way in which a statue comes from bronze, because a composite substance comes from sensible matter, but a species also comes from the matter of a species. These are the senses, then, in which some things are said to come from something. But other things are said to come from something if they come from a part of that thing in any of the aforesaid senses. For example, a child comes from its father and mother, and plants come from the earth, because they come from some part of them. And some things come from others only because they come one after the other in time, as night comes from day, and a storm from a calm. And some of these are so described only because they admit of change into each other, as in the cases just mentioned. And some only because they follow one another in time, as a voyage is made from the equinox because it takes place after the equinox. And feasts come one from another in this way, as the Thargelian from the Dionysian, because it comes after the Dionysian. **1023a26–1023b11**

Chapter 25

2. Part means in one sense that into which a quantity is divided in any way; for what is subtracted from a quantity is always called a part of it. For example, the number two is said in a sense to be a part of the number three. And in another sense part means only such things as measure a whole. And for this reason the number two is said in a sense to be a part of the number three, and in another, not. Again, those things into which a species is divided irrespective of quantity are also called parts of this species; and it is for this reason that species are said to be parts of a genus. Again, parts mean those things into which a whole is divided or of which a whole is composed, whether the whole is a species or the thing having the species, as bronze is a part of a bronze sphere or of a bronze cube (for this is the matter in which the form inheres). An angle also is a part. And those elements contained in the intelligible expression, which manifests what each thing is, are also parts of a whole. And for this reason the genus is also called a part of the species, although in another respect the species is called a part of the genus. **1023b12–25**

Chapter 26

3. Whole means that from which none of the things of which it is said to consist by nature are missing; and that which contains the things contained in such a way that they form one thing. **1023b26–28**

4. But this occurs in two ways: either inasmuch as each is the one in question, or inasmuch as one thing is constituted of them. **1023b28–29**

5. For a whole is a universal or what is predicated in general as being some one thing as a universal is one, in the sense that it contains many things, because it is predicated of each, and all of them taken singly are that one thing, as man, horse and god, because all are living things. **1023b29–32**

6. A whole is something continuous and limited when one thing is constituted of many parts which are present in it, particularly when they are present potentially; but if not, even when they are present in activity. **1023b32–34**

7. And of these same things, those which are wholes by nature are such to a greater degree than those which are wholes by art, as we also say of a thing that is one (424:C 848), inasmuch as wholeness is a kind of unity. **1023b34–36**

8. Again, since a quantity has a beginning, a middle point and an end, those quantities to which position makes no difference we designate by the term all; but those to which position makes a difference we designate by the term whole; and those to which both descriptions apply we designate by both terms—all and whole. Now these are the things whose nature remains the same in being rearranged but whose shape does not, as wax and a garment; for both all and whole are predicated of them since they verify both. But water and all moist things and number have all applied to them, although water and number are called wholes only in a metaphorical sense. But those things of which the term every is predicated with reference to one, have the term all predicated of them with reference to several, for example, all this number, all these units. **1024b1–10**

Chapter 27

9. It is not any quantity at all that is said to be mutilated, but it must be a whole and also divisible. For two things are not mutilated when one is taken away from the other, because the mutilated part is never equal to the remainder. And in general no number is mutilated, for its substance must remain. If a goblet is mutilated it must still be a goblet; but a number is not the same when a part is taken away. Again, all things composed of unlike parts are not said to be mutilated. For a number is like something having unlike parts, as two and three. And in general those things to which position makes no difference, such as water and fire, are not mutilated; but they must have position in their substance. And they must be continuous; for a harmony is made up of unlike parts and has position but is not mutilated. **1024a11–22**

10. Further, neither is every whole mutilated by the privation of every part. For the parts which are removed must not be things which are proper to the substance or things which exist anywhere at all; for example, a goblet is not mutilated if a hole is made in it, but only if an ear or some extremity is removed; and a man is not mutilated if his flesh or spleen is removed, but only if an extremity is removed. And this means not any extremity whatever, but those which, when removed from the whole, cannot regenerate. Hence to have one's head shaven is not a mutilation. **1024a22–28**

COMMENTARY

1085. Here he begins to treat the things which pertain to the notion of whole and part. First [1], he deals with those which pertain to the notion of *part;* and second [3], with those which pertain to the notion of *whole* ("*Whole* means").

And because a whole is constituted of parts, he therefore does two things in dealing with the first member of this division. First, he explains the various ways in which a thing is said *to come from something;* and second [2], he considers the different senses in which the term *part* is used ("*Part* means").

In regard to the first he does three things. First, he considers the ways in which a thing is said *to come from something* in the primary and proper sense. Second [1], he indicates the ways in which one thing comes from another but not in the primary sense ("But other things"). Third [1], he considers the ways in which one thing comes from another but not in the proper sense ("And some things").

In dealing with the first part [1] he gives four ways in which a thing is said to come from something. First, a thing is said to come from something as from matter, and this can happen in two ways: In one way, inasmuch as matter is taken to be "the matter of the first genus," i.e., common matter; as water is the matter of all liquids and liquables, all of which are said to come from water. In another way, "in reference to the ultimate species," i.e., the lowest species; as the species statue is said to come from bronze.

1086. In a second way a thing is said to come from something as "from a first moving principle," as a fight comes from a taunt, which is the principle moving the soul of the taunted person to fight. And it is in this way too that a house is said to come from a builder, and health from the medical art.

1087. In a third way one thing is said to come from another as something simple "comes from the composite of matter and form." This pertains to the process of dissolution; and it is in this way that we say parts come from a whole, "and a verse from the *Iliad*" (i.e., from the whole treatise of Homer about Troy); for the *Iliad* is divided into verses as a whole is divided into parts. And it is in the same way that stones are said to come from a house. The reason for this is that the form is the goal or end in the process of generation; for it is what has attained its end that is said to be perfect or complete, as was explained above (see n. 1039). Hence it is evident that that is perfect which has a form. Therefore, when a perfect whole is broken down into its parts, there is motion in a sense from form to matter; and in a similar way when parts are combined, there is an opposite motion from matter to form. Hence the preposition *from*, which designates a beginning, applies to both processes: both to the process of composition, because it signifies a material principle, and to that of dissolution, because it signifies a formal principle.

1088. In a fourth way a thing is said to come from something as "a species comes from a part of a species." And part of a species can be taken in two ways: either in reference to the conceptual order or to the real order. It is taken in reference to the conceptual order when we say, for example, that *two-footed* is a part of *man;* because while it is part of his definition, it is not a real part, otherwise it would not be predicated of the whole. For it is proper to the whole man to have two feet. And it is taken in reference to the real order when we say, for example, that "a syllable comes from an element," or letter, as from a part of the species. But here the fourth way in which the term is used differs from the first; for in the first way a thing was said to come from a part of matter, as a statue comes from bronze. For this substance, a statue, is composed of sensible matter as a part of its substance. But this species is composed of part of the species.

1089. For some parts are parts of a species and some are parts of matter. Those which are called parts of a species are those on which the perfection of the species depends and without which it cannot be a species. And it is for this reason that such parts are placed in the definition of the whole, as body and soul are placed in the definition of an animal, and an angle in the definition of a triangle, and a letter in the definition of a syllable. And those parts which are called parts of matter are those on which the species does not depend but are in a sense accidental to the species; for example, it is accidental to a statue that it should come from bronze or from any particular matter at all. And it is also accidental that a circle should be divided into two semi-circles; and that a right angle should have an acute angle as part of it. Parts of this sort, then, are not placed in the definition of the whole species but rather the other way around, as will be shown in Book VII of this work (see n. 1542). Hence it is clear that in this way some things are said to come from others in the primary and proper sense.

1090. But some things are said to come from something not in the primary sense but according to a part of that thing in "any of the aforesaid senses." For example, a child is said to come from its father as an efficient principle, and from its mother as matter; because a certain part of the father causes motion, i.e., the sperm, and a certain part of the mother has the character of matter, i.e., the menstrual fluid. And plants come from the earth, although not from the whole of it but from some part.

1091. And in another way a thing is said to come from something in an improper sense, namely, from the fact that this implies order or succession alone; and in this way one thing is said to come from another in the sense that it comes after it, as "night comes from day," i.e., after the day, "and a storm from a calm," i.e., after a calm. And this is said in reference to two things. For in those cases in which one thing is said to come from another, order is sometimes noted in reference to motion and not merely to time; because either they are the two extremes of the same motion, as when it is said that white comes from black, or they are a result of different extremes of the motion, as night and day are a result of different locations of the sun. And the same thing applies to winter and summer. Hence in some cases one thing is said to come from another because one is changed into the other, as is clear in the above examples.

1092. But sometimes order or succession is considered in reference to time alone; for example, it is said that "a voyage is made from the equinox," i.e., after the equinox. For these two extremes are not extremes of a single motion but pertain to different motions. And similarly it is said that the Thargelian festival [of Apollo and Artemis] comes from the Dionysian because it comes after the Dionysian, these being two feasts which were celebrated among the gentiles, one of which preceded the other in time.

1093. **"Part" means** [2].

He now gives four senses in which something is said to be a part. In one sense part means that into which a thing is divided from the viewpoint of quantity; and this can be taken in two ways. For, in one way, no matter how much smaller that quantity may be into which a larger quantity is divided, it is called a part of this quantity. For anything that is taken away from a quantity is always called a part of it; for example, the number two is in a sense a part of the number three. And, in another way, only a smaller quantity which measures a larger one is called a part. In this sense the number two is not a part of the number three but a part of the number four, because two times two equals four.

1094. In a second sense parts mean those things into which something is divided irrespective of quantity; and it is in this sense that species are said to be parts of a genus. For a genus is divided into species, but not as a quantity is divided into quantitative parts. For a whole quantity is not in each one of its parts, but a genus is in each one of its species.

1095. In a third sense parts mean those things into which some whole is divided or of which it is composed, whether the whole is a species or the thing having a species, i.e., the individual. For, as has been pointed out already [1], there are parts of the species and parts of matter, and these (species and matter) are parts of the individual. Hence bronze is a part of a bronze sphere or of a bronze cube as the matter in which the form is received, and thus bronze is not a part of the form but of the thing having the form. And a cube is a body composed of square surfaces. And an angle is part of a triangle as part of its form, as has been stated above [1].

1096. In a fourth sense parts mean those things which are placed in the definition of anything, and these are parts of its intelligible structure; for example, animal and two-footed are parts of man.

1097. From this it is clear that a genus is part of a species in this fourth sense, but that a species is part of a genus in a different sense, i.e., in the second sense. For in the second sense a part was taken as a subjective part of a universal whole, whereas in the other three senses it was taken as an integral part. And in the first sense it was taken as a part of quantity; and in the other two senses as a part of substance; yet in such a way that a part in the third sense means a part of a thing, whether it be a part of the species or of the individual. But in the fourth sense it is a part of the intelligible structure.

1098. **"Whole" means** [3].

He proceeds to treat the things which pertain to a *whole.* First [3], he considers a whole in a general way; and second (Lesson 22), he deals with a particular kind of whole, namely a genus ("The term *genus*").

In regard to the first part he does two things. First, he proceeds to deal with the term whole; and second ([9], with its opposite, *mutilated* ("It is not any quantity").

In regard to the first he does three things. First [3], he states the common meaning of whole, which involves two things. The first is that the perfection of a whole is derived from its parts. He indicates this when he says "a whole means that from which none of the things," i.e., the parts, "of which it is said to consist by nature," i.e., of which the whole is composed according to its own nature, "are missing." The second is that the parts become one in the whole. Thus he says that a whole is "that which contains the things contained," namely, the parts, in such a way that the things contained in the whole are some one thing.

1099. **But this occurs.** [4].

Second, he notes two ways in which a thing is a whole. He says that a thing is said to be a whole in two ways: either in the sense that each of the things contained by the containing whole is "the one in question," i.e., the containing whole, which is in the universal whole that is predicated of any one of its own parts; or in the sense that it is one thing composed of parts in such a way that none of the parts are that one thing. This is the notion of an integral whole, which is not predicated of any of its own integral parts.

1100. **For a whole** [5].

Third, he explains the foregoing senses of whole. First, he explains the first sense. He says that a whole is a universal "or what is predicated in general," i.e., a common predicate, as being some one thing as a universal is one, in the sense that it is predicated of each individual just as the universal, which contains many parts, is predicated of each of its parts. And all of these are one in a universal whole in such a way that each of them is that one whole; for example, *living thing* contains man and horse and god, because "all are living things," i.e., because living thing is predicated of each. By a god he means here a celestial body, such as the sun or the moon, which the ancients said were living bodies and considered to be gods; or he means certain ethereal living beings, which the Platonists called demons, and which were worshipped by the pagans as gods.

1101. **A whole is something** [6].

Second, he explains the meaning of whole in the sense of an integral whole; and in regard to this he does two things. First, he gives the common meaning of this kind of whole, and particularly of that which is divided into quantitative parts, which is more evident to us. He says that a whole is something "continuous and limited," i.e., perfect or complete (for what is unlimited does not have the character of a whole but of a part, as is said in Book III of the *Physics* [207a26]) when one thing is composed of many parts which are present in it. He says this in order to exclude the sense in which one thing comes from another as from a contrary.

1102. Now the parts of which a whole is composed can be present in it in two ways: in one way potentially, and in another actually. Parts are potentially present in a whole which is continuous, and actually present in a whole which is not continuous, as stones are actually present in a heap. But that which is continuous is one to a greater degree, and therefore is a whole to a greater degree, than that which is not continuous. Hence he says that parts must be present in a whole, especially potential parts, as they are in a continuous whole; and if not potentially, then at least "in activity," or actually. For "activity" means interior action.

1103. Now although a thing is a whole to a greater degree when its parts are present potentially than when they are present actually, none the less if we look to the parts, they are parts to a greater degree when they exist actually than when they exist potentially. Hence another text reads, "especially when they are present perfectly and actually; but otherwise, even when they are present potentially." And it also adds the words given above: "particularly when they are present potentially; but if not, even when they are present in activity." Hence it seems that the translator found two texts, which he translated, and then made the mistake of combining both so as to make one text. This is clear from another translation, which contains only one of these statements; for it reads as follows: "And a whole is continuous and limited when some one thing is composed of many intrinsic parts, especially when they are present potentially; but if not, when they are present actually."

1104. **And of these same things** [7].

Second, he indicates two differences within this second sense of whole. The first is that some continuous things are such by art and some by nature. Those which are continuous by nature are "such," i.e., wholes, to a greater degree than those which are such by art. And since we spoke in the same way above (see n. 848) about things which are one, saying that things which are continuous by nature are one to a greater degree, as though wholeness were oneness, it is clear from this that anything which is one to a greater degree is a whole to a greater degree.

1105. **Again, since a quantity** [8].

He gives the second difference. For since it is true that there is an order of parts in quantity, because a quantity has a beginning, a middle point and an end, and the notion of position involves these, the positions of the parts in all these quantities must be continuous. But if we consider the position of the parts, a whole is found to be continuous in three ways. For there are some wholes which are unaffected by a difference of position in their parts. This is evident in the case of water, for it makes no difference how the parts of water are interchanged. The same thing is true of other liquids, as oil and wine and the like. And in these things a whole is signified by the term *all* and not by the term *whole*. For we say all the water or all the wine or all the numbers, but not the whole, except metaphorically. This perhaps applies to the Greek idiom, but for us it is a proper way of speaking.

1106. And there are some things to which the position of the parts does make a difference, for example, a man and any animal and a house and the like. For a thing is not a house if its parts are arranged in just any way at all, but only if they have a definite arrangement; and of these we use the term whole and not the term all. And similarly a thing is not a man or an animal if its parts are arranged in just any way at all. For when we speak of only one animal, we say the whole animal and not all the animal.

1107. And there are some things to which both of these apply, because in a sense the position of their parts accounts for their differences; and of these we use both terms—all and whole. And these are the things in which, when the parts are interchanged, the matter remains the same but not the form or shape. This is clear, for example, in the case of wax; for no matter how its parts are interchanged the wax still remains, but it does not have the same shape. The same is true of a garment and of all things which have like parts and take on a different shape. For even though liquids have like parts, they cannot have a shape of their own, because they are not limited by their own boundaries but by those of other things. Hence when their parts are interchanged no change occurs in anything that is proper to them.

1108. The reason for this difference is that the term all is distributive and therefore requires an actual multitude or one in proximate potency to act; and because those things have like parts, they are divided into parts entirely similar to the whole, and in that manner multiplication of the whole takes place. For if every part of water is water, then in each part of water there are many waters, although they are present potentially, just as in one number there are many units actually. But a whole signifies a collection of parts into some one thing; and therefore in those cases in which the term whole is properly used, one complete thing is made from all the parts taken together, and the perfection of the whole belongs to none of the parts. A house and an animal are examples of this. Hence, "every animal" is not said of one animal but of many. Therefore at the end of this part of his discussion he says that those wholes of which the term every is used, as is done of one thing when reference is made to a whole, can have the term all (in the plural) used of them, as is done of several things when reference is made to them as parts. For example, one says "all this number," and "all these units," and "all this water," when the whole has been indicated, and "all these waters" when the parts have been indicated.

1109. **It is not any quantity** [9].

Here he clarifies the issue about the opposite of "whole," which is *mutilated,* in place of which another translation reads "diminished (or reduced) by a member"; but this does not always fit. For the term mutilated is used only of animals, which alone have members. Now mutilated seems to mean "cut off," and thus Boethius translated it "maimed," i.e., "defective." Hence the Philosopher's aim here is to show what is required in order that a thing may be said to be mutilated: and first, what is required on the side of the whole; and second [10], what is required on the side of the part which is missing ("Further, neither").

1110. Now in order that a whole can be said to be mutilated, seven things are required. First, the whole must be a quantified being having parts into which it may be divided quantitatively. For a universal whole cannot be said to be mutilated if one of its species is removed.

1111. Second, not every kind of quantified being can be said to be mutilated, but it must be one that is "divisible into parts," i.e., capable of being separated, and be "a whole," i.e., something composed of different parts. Hence the ultimate parts into which any whole is divided, such as flesh and sinew, even though they have quantity, cannot be said to be mutilated.

1112. Third, two things are not mutilated, i.e., anything having two parts, if one of them is taken away from the other. And this is true because a "mutilated part," i.e., whatever is taken away from the mutilated thing, is never equal to the remainder, but the remainder must always be larger.

1113. Fourth, no number can be mutilated no matter how many parts it may have, because the substance of the mutilated thing remains after the part is taken away. For example, when a goblet is mutilated it still remains a goblet; but a number does not remain the same no matter what part of it is taken away. For when a unit is added to or subtracted from a number, it changes the species of the number.

1114. Fifth, the thing mutilated must have unlike parts. For those things which have like parts cannot be said to be mutilated, because the nature of the whole remains verified in each part. Hence, if any of the parts are taken away, the others are not said to be mutilated. Not all things having unlike parts, however, can be said to be mutilated; for a number cannot, as has been stated, even though in a sense it has unlike parts; for example, the number twelve has the number two and the number three as parts of it. Yet in a sense every number has like parts because every number is constituted of units.

1115. Sixth, none of those things in which the position of the parts makes no difference can be said to be mutilated, for example, water or fire. For mutilated things must be such that the intelligible structure of their substance contains the notion of a determinate arrangement of parts, as in the case of a man or of a house.

1116. Seventh, mutilated things must be continuous. For a musical harmony cannot be said to be mutilated when a note or a chord is taken away, even though it is made up of low and high pitched sounds, and even though its parts have a determinate position; for it is not any low and high pitched sounds arranged in any way at all that constitute such a harmony.

1117. **Further, neither is** [10].

Then he indicates the conditions which must prevail with regard to the part cut off in order that a thing may be mutilated; and there are three of these. He says that, just as not every kind of whole can be said to be mutilated, so neither can there be mutilation by the removal of every part. For, first, the part which is removed must not be a principal part of the substance, that is, one which constitutes the substance of the thing and without which the substance cannot be, because the thing that is mutilated must remain when a part is removed, as has been stated above (see n. 1113). Hence a man cannot be said to be mutilated when his head has been cut off.

1118. Second, the part removed should not be everywhere, but in some extremity. Thus, if a goblet is perforated about the middle by removing some part of it, it cannot be said to be mutilated; but this is said if someone removes "the ear of a goblet," i.e., a part which is similar to an ear, or any other extremity. Similarly a man is not said to be mutilated if he loses some of his flesh from his leg or from his arm or from his waist, or if he loses his spleen or some part of it, but if he loses one of his extremities, such as a hand or a foot.

1118a. Third, a thing is not said to be mutilated if just any part that is an extremity is removed, but if it is such a part which does not regenerate if the whole of it is removed, as a hand or a foot. But if a whole head of hair is cut off, it grows again. So if such parts are removed, the man is not said to be mutilated, even though they are extremities. And for this reason people with shaven heads are not said to be mutilated.

LESSON 22
The Meanings of Genus, of Falsity, and of Accident

ARISTOTLE'S TEXT Chapters 28–30: 1024a29–1025a34

1. *The term genus (or race) is used if there is a continuous generation of things having the same species; for example, "as long as the genus of man lasts" means "while there is continuous generation of men." And the term also designates that from which things are first brought into being. For it is in this way that some men are called Hellenes by race and others Ionians, because the former come from Hellen and the latter from Ion as the ones who begot them. Again the term is applied to the members of the genus more from the begetter than from the material principle. For some people are also said to derive their race from the female, as those who come from Pleia. Further, the term is used in the sense that the plane is called the genus of plane figures, and the solid the genus of solid figures. For each of the figures is either a plane of such and such a kind or a solid of such and such a kind; and this is the subject underlying the differences. Again, genus means the primary element present in definitions, which is predicated quidditatively of the thing whose differences are called qualities. The term genus, then, is used in all these senses: in one as the continuous generation of a species; in another as the primary mover of the same species; and in another as matter. For that to which the difference or quality belongs is the subject which we call matter.* **1024a29–1024b9**

2. *Things are said to be diverse (or other) in species whose first subject is diverse and cannot be resolved one into the other or both into the same thing. For example, form and matter are diverse in genus. And all things which are predicated according to a different categorical figure of being are diverse in genus. For some signify the quiddity of beings, others quality, and others something else, in the sense of our previous distinctions. For they are not analyzed into each other or into some one thing.* **1024b9–16**

Chapter 29

3. *False means in one sense what is false as a thing, and that either because it is not combined or is incapable of being combined. For example, the statement that the diagonal is commensurable or that you are sitting belong to this class; for the former is always false and the latter is sometimes so; for it is in these senses that these things are non-beings. But there are things which exist and are fitted by nature to appear either other than they are or as things that do not exist, as a shadowgraph and dreams. For these in fact are something, but not that of which they cause an image in us. Therefore things are said to be false either because they do not exist or because the image derived from them is not of something real.* **1024b17–26**

4. *A false notion inasmuch as it is false is the notion of something non-existent. Hence every notion is false when applied to something other than that of which it is true; for example, the notion of a circle is false when applied to a triangle. Now of each thing there is in a sense one notion, which is its essence; but there are also in a sense many, since the thing itself and the thing with a modification are in a sense the same, as Socrates and musical Socrates. But a false notion is absolutely speaking not the notion of anything. And it is for this reason that Antisthenes entertained a silly opinion when he thought that nothing could be expressed except by its proper notion—one term always for one thing. From this it would follow that there can be no contradiction and almost no error. It is possible, however, to express each thing not only by its own notion but also by that which belongs to something else not only falsely but also truly, as eight may be said to be double through the notion of two. These are the ways, then, in which things are said to be false.* **1024b26–1025a2**

5. *A false man is one who chooses such thoughts not for any other reason but for themselves;*

and one who is the cause of such thoughts in others; just as we say that those things are false which produce a false image or impression. **1025a2–6**

6. Hence, the speech in the Hippias, which says that the same man is true and false, is refuted; for it assumes that that man is false who is able to deceive, even though he is knowing and prudent. **1025a6–8**

7. And further it assumes that one who is capable of willing evil things is better. And this false opinion is arrived at by way of induction. For one who limps voluntarily is better than one who does so involuntarily; and by limping we mean imitating a limp. For if a man were to limp voluntarily, he would be worse in this way, just as he would be in the case of moral character. **1025a8–13**

Chapter 30

8. An accident is what attaches to anything and which it is true to affirm is so, although not necessarily or for the most part; for example, if someone discovers a treasure while digging a hole for a plant, the discovery of the treasure is an accident to the digger. For the one does not necessarily come from the other or come after it, nor does it happen for the most part that someone will find a treasure when he digs a hole to set out a plant. And a musician may be white; but since this does not happen necessarily or for the most part, we say that it is accidental. But since something belongs to something, and some belong somewhere and at some time, then whatever attaches to a subject, but not because it is now or here, will be an accident. Nor does an accident have any determinate cause, but only a contingent or chance cause, i.e., an indeterminate one. For it was by accident that someone came to Aegina; and if he did not come there in order to get there, but because he was driven there by a storm or was captured by pirates, the event has occurred and is an accident; yet not of itself but by reason of something else. For the storm is the cause of his coming to the place to which he was not sailing, and this was Aegina. And in another sense accident means whatever belongs to each thing of itself but not in its substance; for example, it is an accident of a triangle to have its angles equal to two right angles. And these same accidents may be eternal, but none of the others can be. But an account of this has been given elsewhere. **1025a14–24**

COMMENTARY

1119. Here he gives his views about a particular kind of whole, namely, a genus. First [1], he gives the different senses in which the term *genus* is used; and second [2], he treats the different senses in which things are said to be *diverse* (or *other*) in *genus* ("Things are said").

He accordingly says, first [1], that the term genus is used in four senses. First, it means the continuous generation of things that have the same species; for example, it is said, "as long as 'the genus of man' will exist," i.e., "while the continuous generation of men will last." This is the first sense of genus given in Porphyry, i.e., a multitude of things having a relation to each other and to one principle.

1120. In a second sense genus (race) means that from which "things are first brought into being," i.e., some things proceed from a begetter. For example, some men are called Hellenes by race because they are descendants of a man called Hellen; and some are called Ionians by race because they are descendants of a certain Ion as their first begetter. Now people are more commonly named from their father, who is their begetter, than from their mother, who produces the matter of generation, although some derive the name of their race from the mother; for example, some are named from a certain woman called Pleia. This is the second sense of genus given in Porphyry.

1121. The term genus is used in a third sense when surface or the plane is called the genus of plane figures, "and the solid," or body, is called the genus of solid figures, or bodies. This sense of genus is not the one that signifies the essence of a species, as animal is the genus of man, but the one that is the proper subject in the species of different accidents. For surface is the subject of all plane figures. And it bears some likeness to a genus, because the proper subject is given in the definition of an accident just as a genus is given in the definition of a species. Hence the proper subject of an accident is predicated like a genus. "For each of the figures," i.e., plane figures, is such and such a surface. "And this," i.e., a solid figure, is such and such a solid, as though the figure were a difference qualifying surface or solid. For surface is related to plane (surface) figures, and solid to solid figures, as a genus, which is the subject of contraries; and difference is predicated in the sense of quality. And for this reason, just as when we say rational animal, such and such an animal is signified, so too when we say square surface, such and such a surface is signified.

1122. In a fourth sense genus means the primary element given in a definition, which is predicated quidditatively, and differences are its qualities. For example, in the definition of man, animal is given first and then two-footed or rational, which is a certain substantial quality of man.

1123. It is evident, then, that the term genus is used in so many different senses: in one sense as the continuous generation of the same species, and this pertains to the first sense; in another as the first moving principle, and this pertains to the second sense; and in another as matter, and this pertains to the third and fourth senses. For a genus is related to a difference in the same way as a subject is to a quality. Hence it is evident that genus as a predicable and genus as a subject are included in a way under one meaning, and that each has the character of matter. For even though genus as a predicable is not matter, still it is taken from matter as difference is taken from form. For a thing is called an animal because it has a sentient nature; and it is called rational because it has a rational nature, which is related to sentient nature as form is to matter.

1124. **Things are said** [2].

Here he explains the different senses in which things are said to be *diverse* (or *other*) *in genus;* and he gives two senses of this corresponding to the last two senses of genus. For the first two senses are of little importance for the study of philosophy.

In the first sense, then, some things are said to be diverse in genus because their first subject is diverse; for example, the first subject of color is surface, and the first subject of flavors is something moist. Hence, with regard to their subject-genus, flavor and color are diverse in genus.

1125. Further, the two different subjects must be such that one of them is not reducible to the other. Now a solid is in a sense reducible to surfaces, and therefore solid figures and plane figures do not belong to diverse genera. Again, they must not be reducible to the same thing. For example, form and matter are diverse in genus if they are considered according to their own essence, because there is nothing common to both. And in a similar way the celestial bodies and lower bodies are diverse in genus inasmuch as they do not have a common matter.

1126. In another sense those things are said to be diverse in genus which are predicated "according to a different figure of the category of being," i.e., of the predication of being. For some things signify quiddity, some quality, and some signify in other ways, which are given in the division made above where he dealt with being (see nn. 889–94). For these categories are not reducible one to the other, because one is not included under the other. Nor are they reducible to some one thing, because there is not some one common genus for all the categories.

1127. Now it is clear, from what has been said, that some things are contained under one category and are in one genus in this second sense, although they are diverse in genus in the first sense. Examples of this are the celestial bodies and elemental bodies, and colors and flavors. The first way in which things are diverse in genus is considered rather by the natural scientist and also by the philosopher, because it is more real. But the second way in which things are diverse in genus is considered by the logician, because it is conceptual.

1128. **"False" means** [3].

Here he gives the various senses of the terms which signify a lack of being or incomplete being. First [3], he gives the senses in which the term *false* is used. Second [8], he deals with the various senses of *accident*.

In regard to the first he does three things. First, he shows how the term false is used of real things; and second [4], how it is used of definitions ("A *false notion*"); and third [5], how men are said to be false ("A *false man*").

He accordingly says, first [3], that the term false is applied in one sense to real things inasmuch as a statement signifying a reality is not properly composed. And there are two ways in which this can come about: In one way by forming a proposition which should not be formed; and this is what happens, for instance, in the case of false contingent propositions. In another way by forming a proposition about something impossible; and this is what happens in the case of false impossible propositions. For if we say that the diagonal of a square is commensurable with one of its sides, it is a false impossible proposition; for it is impossible to combine "commensurable" and "diagonal." And if someone says that you are sitting while you are standing, it is a false contingent proposition; for the predicate does not attach to the subject, although it is not impossible for it to do so. Hence one of these—the impossible—is always false; but the other—the contingent—is not always so. Therefore those things are said to be false which are non-beings in their entirety; for a statement is said to be false when what is signified by the statement is nonexistent.

1129. The term false is applied to real things in a second way inasmuch as some things, though beings in themselves, are fitted by nature to appear either to be other than they are or as things that do not exist, as "a shadowgraph," i.e., a delineation in shadow. For sometimes shadows appear to be the things of which they are the shadows, as the shadow of a man appears to be a man. The same applies to dreams, which seem to be real things yet are only the likenesses of things. And one speaks in the same way of false gold, because it bears a resemblance to real gold. Now this sense differs from the first, because in the first sense things were said to be false because they did not exist, but here things are said to be false because, while being something in themselves, they are not the things "of which they cause an image," i.e., which they resemble. It is clear, then, that things are said to be false either because they do not exist or because there arises from them the appearance of what does not exist.

1130. **A "false notion"** [4].

He indicates how the term false applies to definitions. He says that "a notion," i.e., a definition, inasmuch as it is false, is the notion of something non-existent. Now he says "inasmuch as it is false" because a definition is said to be false in two ways. It is either a false definition in itself, and then it is not the definition of anything but has to do entirely with the nonexistent; or it is a true definition in itself but false inasmuch as it is attributed to something other than the one properly defined; and then it is said to be false inasmuch as it does not apply to the thing defined.

1131. It is clear, then, that every definition which is a true definition of one thing is a false definition of something else; for example, the definition which is true of a circle is false when applied to a triangle. Now for one thing there is, in one sense, only one definition signifying its quiddity; and in another sense there are many definitions for one thing. For in one sense the subject taken in itself and "the thing with a modification," i.e., taken in conjunction with a modification, are the same, as Socrates and musical Socrates. But in another sense they are not, for it is the same thing accidentally but not in itself. And it is clear that they have different definitions. For the definition of Socrates and that of musical Socrates are different, although in a sense both are definitions of the same thing.

1132. But a definition which is false in itself cannot be a definition of anything. And a definition is said to be false in itself, or unqualifiedly false, by reason of the fact that one part of it cannot stand with the other; and such a definition would be had, for example, if one were to say "inanimate living thing."

1133. Again, it is clear from this that Antisthenes' opinion was foolish. For, since words are the signs of things, he maintained that, just as a thing does not have any essence other than its own, so too in a proposition nothing can be predicated of a subject but its own definition, so that only one predicate absolutely or always may be used of one subject. And from this position it follows that there is no such thing as a contradiction; because if animal, which is included in his notion, is predicated of man, non-animal cannot be predicated of him, and thus a negative proposition cannot be formed. And from this position it also follows that one cannot speak falsely, because the proper definition of a thing is truly predicated of it. Hence, if only a thing's own definition can be predicated of it, no proposition can be false.

1134. But his opinion is false, because of each thing we can predicate not only its own definition but also the definition of something else. And when this occurs in a universal or general way, the predication is false. Yet in a way there can be a true predication; for example, eight is said to be double inasmuch as it has the character of duality, because the character of duality is to be related as two is to one. But inasmuch as it is double, eight is in a sense two, because it is divided into two equal quantities. These things, then, are said to be false in the foregoing way.

1135. **A "false man"** [5].

Then he shows how the term false may be predicated of a man; and in regard to this he does two things. First, he gives two ways in which a man is said to be false. In one way a man is said to be false if he is ready to think, or takes pleasure in thinking, thoughts of this kind, i.e., false ones, and chooses such thoughts not for any other reason but for themselves. For anyone who has a habit finds the operation relating to that habit to be pleasurable and readily performed; and thus one who has a habit acts in accordance with that habit and not for the sake of anything extrinsic. For example, a debauched person commits fornication because of the pleasure resulting from coition; but if he commits fornication for some other end, for instance, that he may steal, he is more of a thief than a lecher. And similarly one who chooses to speak falsely for the sake of money is more avaricious than false.

1136. In a second way a man is said to be false if he causes false notions in others, in much the same way as we said above that things are false which cause a false image or impression. For it is clear from what has been said that the false has to do with the non-existent. Hence a man is said to be false inasmuch as he makes false statements, and a notion is said to be false inasmuch as it is about something non-existent.

1137. **Hence, the speech** [6].

Second, he excludes two false opinions from what has been laid down above. He draws the first of these from the points made above. He says that, since a false man is one who chooses and creates false opinions, one may logically refute or reject a statement made in the *Hippias*, i.e., one of Plato's works, which said that the same notion is both true and false. For this opinion considered that man to be false who is able to deceive, so that, being able both to deceive and to speak the truth, the same man is both true and false. And similarly the same statement will be both true and false, because the same statement is able to be both true and false; for example, the statement "Socrates sits" is true when he is seated, but is false when he is not seated. Now it is evident that this is taken unwarrantedly, because even a man who is prudent and knowing is able to deceive; yet he is not false, because he does not cause or choose false notions or opinions, and this is the reason why a man is said to be false, as has been stated [5].

1138. **And further** [7].

Then he rejects the second false opinion. This opinion maintained that a man who does base things and wills evil is better than one who does not. But this is false. For anyone is defined as being evil on the grounds that he is ready to do or to choose evil things. Yet this opinion wishes to accept this sense of false on the basis of a sort of induction from a similar case. For one who voluntarily limps is better and nobler than one who limps involuntarily. Hence he says that to do evil is like limping inasmuch as the same notion applies to both. And in a sense this is true; for one who limps voluntarily is worse as regards his moral character, although he is more perfect as regards his power of walking. And similarly one who voluntarily does evil is worse as regards his moral character, although perhaps he is not worse as regards some other power. For example, even though that man is more evil, morally speaking, who voluntarily says what is false, still he is more intelligent than one who believes that he speaks the truth when he in fact speaks falsely, though not wilfully.

1139. **An "accident"** [8].

Here, finally, he gives the different senses in which the term *accident* is used; and there are two of these. First, an accident means anything that attaches to a thing and is truly affirmed of it, although not necessarily or "for the most part," i.e., in the majority of cases, but in a minority; for example, if one were to find a treasure while digging a hole to set out a plant. Hence, finding a treasure while digging a hole is an accident. For the one is not necessarily the cause of the other so that the one necessarily comes from the other. Neither do they necessarily accompany each other so that the latter comes after the former as day follows night, even though the one is not the cause of the other. Neither does it happen for the most part, or in the majority of cases, that this should occur, i.e., that one who sets out a plant finds a treasure. And similarly a musician is said to be white, although this is not necessarily so nor does it happen for the most part. Hence our statement is accidental. But this example differs from the first; for in the first example the term accident is taken in reference to becoming, and in the second example it is taken in reference to being.

1140. Now just as something belongs to some definite subject, so too it is considered "to belong somewhere," i.e., in some definite place, "and at some time," i.e., at some definite time. And therefore it happens to belong to all of these accidentally if it does not belong to them by reason of their own nature; for example, when white is predicated of a musician, this is accidental, because white does not belong to a musician as such. And similarly if there is an abundance of rain in summer, this is accidental, because it does not happen in summer inasmuch as it is summer. And again if what is heavy is high up, this is accidental, for it is not in such a place inasmuch as the place is such, but because of some external cause.

1141. And it should be borne in mind that there is no determinate cause of the kind of accident here mentioned, "but only a contingent cause," i.e., whatever one there happens to be, or "a chance cause," i.e., a fortuitous one, which is an indeterminate cause. For example, it was an accident that someone "came to Aegina," i.e., to that city, if he did not come there "in order to get there," i.e., if he began to head for that city not in order that he might reach it but because he was forced there by some external cause; for example, because he was driven there by the winter wind which caused a tempest at sea, or even because he was captured by pirates and was brought there against his will. It is clear, then, that this is accidental, and that it can be brought about by different causes. Yet the fact that in sailing he reaches this place occurs "not of itself," i.e., inasmuch as he was sailing (since he intended to sail to another place), but "by reason of something else," i.e., another external cause. For a storm is the cause of his coming to the place "to which he was not sailing," i.e., Aegina; or pirates; or something else of this kind.

1142. In a second sense accident means whatever belongs to each thing of itself but is not in its substance. This is the second mode of essential predication, as was noted above (C 1055); for the first mode exists when something is predicated essentially of something which is given in its definition, as animal is predicated of man, which is not an accident in any way. Now it belongs essentially to a triangle to have two right angles, but this does not belong to its substance. Hence it is an accident.

1143. This sense of accident differs from the first, because accidents in this second sense can be eternal. For a triangle always has three angles equal to two right angles. But none of those things which are accidents in the first sense can be eternal, because they are always such as occur in the minority of cases. The discussion of this kind of accident is undertaken in another place, for example in Book VI of this work (see n. 1172), and in Book II of the *Physics. [196b10]* Accident in the first sense, then, is opposed to what exists in itself; but accident in the second sense is opposed to what is substantial. This completes Book V.

BOOK VI
THE SCOPE OF METAPHYSICS

LESSON 1
The Method of Investigating Being as Being. How This Science Differs from the Other Sciences

ARISTOTLE'S TEXT Chapter 1: 1025b3–1026a32

1. *The principles and causes of beings are the object of our search, and it is evident that [we must investigate the principles and causes of beings] as beings. For there is a cause of health and of its recovery; and there are also principles and elements and causes of the objects of mathematics; and in general every intellectual science, to whatever degree it participates in intellect, deals with principles and causes: either with those which are more certain or with those which are simpler.* **1025b3–7**

2. *But all these sciences single out some one thing, or some particular class, and confine their investigations to this, but they do not deal with being in an unqualified sense, or as being. Nor do they make any mention of the whatness itself of things. But proceeding from this, some making it evident by means of the senses, and others taking it by assuming it [from some other science], they demonstrate with greater necessity or more weakly the essential attributes of the class of things with which they deal. For this reason it is evident that there is no demonstration of a thing's substance or whatness from such an inductive method, but there is another method of making it known. And similarly they say nothing about the existence or non-existence of the class of things with which they deal, because it belongs to the same science to show what a thing is and whether it exists.* **1025b7–18**

3. *And since the philosophy of nature is concerned with some class of being (for it deals with that kind of substance in which there is a principle of motion and rest), it is evident that it is neither a practical nor a productive science. For the principle of productive sciences is in the maker, whether it be intellect or art or some kind of power; but the principle of practical sciences is prohaeresis in the agent, for the object of action and that of choice are the same. Thus if every science is either practical, productive or theoretical, the philosophy of nature will be a theoretical science. But it will be theoretical of that kind of being which is subject to motion, and of that kind of substance which is inseparable from matter in its intelligible structure for the most part only.* **1025b18–28**

4. *Now the essence and the conceptual expression of the way in which a thing exists must not remain unknown, because without this our investigation will be unfruitful. And regarding things defined, or their whatness, some are like snub and others like concave. And these differ, because snub is conceived with sensible matter (for snub is a concave nose), whereas concave is conceived without sensible matter. But all physical things are spoken of in a way similar to snub, for example, nose, eye, face, flesh, bone and animal in general; leaf, root, bark and plant in general (for the definition of none of these is without motion but always includes matter). Thus it is clear how we must investigate and define the essence in the case of physical things, and why it also belongs to the natural philosopher to speculate about one kind of soul—that which does not exist without matter. From these facts, then, it is evident that the philosophy of nature is a theoretical science.* **1025b28–1026a7**

5. *But mathematics is also a theoretical science, although it is not yet evident whether it deals with things which are immobile and separable from matter. However, it is evident that mathematics speculates about things insofar as they are immobile and insofar as they are separable from matter.* **1026a7–10**

6. Now if there is something which is immobile, eternal and separable from matter, evidently a knowledge of it belongs to a theoretical science. However, it does not belong to the philosophy of nature (for this science deals with certain mobile things), or to mathematics, but to a science prior to both. For the philosophy of nature deals with things which are inseparable from matter but not immobile. And some mathematical sciences deal with things which are immobile, but presumably do not exist separately, but are present as it were in matter. First philosophy, however, deals with things which are both separable from matter and immobile. Now common causes must be eternal, and especially these; since they are the causes of the sensible things visible to us. **1026a10–17**

7. Hence there will be three theoretical philosophies: mathematics, the philosophy of nature, and theology. **1026a17–19**

8. For it is obvious that, if the divine exists anywhere, it exists in this kind of nature. **1026a19–22**

9. And the most honorable of the sciences must deal with the most honorable class of things. Therefore the theoretical sciences are more desirable than the other sciences. **1026a22–23**

10. But someone will raise the question whether first philosophy is universal or deals with some particular class, i.e., one kind of reality; for not even in the mathematical sciences is the method the same, because both geometry and astronomy deal with a particular kind of nature, whereas the first science is universally common to all. **1026a23–27**

11. Therefore, if there is no substance other than those which exist in the way that natural substances do, the philosophy of nature will be the first science; but if there is an immobile substance, this substance will be prior, and [the science which investigates it will be] first philosophy, and will be universal in this way. And because it will be first and about being, it will be the function of this science to investigate both what being is and what the attributes are which belong to it as being. **1026a27–32**

COMMENTARY

1144. Having shown in Book IV (see n. 535) of this work that this science considers being and unity and those attributes which belong to being as such, and that all of these are used in several senses; and having distinguished the number of these in Book V (n. 843;n. 885) of this work, here the Philosopher begins to establish the truth about being and those attributes which belong to being.

This part is divided into two sections. In the first [1] he explains the method by which this science should establish what is true about being. In the second (Lesson 5) he begins to settle the issue about being. He does this at the beginning of Book VII ("The term *being* is used in many senses").

The first part is divided into two sections. In the first he explains the method of treating beings, which is proper to this science, by showing how it differs from the other sciences. In the second (Lesson 2) he excludes certain senses of being from the investigation of this science, namely, those senses which are not the chief concern of this science ("Being in an unqualified sense").

The first part is again divided into two sections. In the first he shows how this science differs from the others because it considers the principles of being as being. In the second [3] he shows how this science differs from the others in its method of treating principles of this kind ("And since the philosophy of nature"). In regard to the first he does two things.

1145. First [1], he shows how this science agrees with the other sciences in its study of principles. He says that since being is the subject of this kind of science, as has been shown in Book IV (nn. 529–31), and every science must investigate the principles and causes which belong to its subject inasmuch as it is this kind of thing, we must investigate in this science the principles and causes of beings as beings. And this is also what occurs in the other sciences. For there is a cause of health and of its recovery, which the physician seeks. And similarly there are also principles, elements and causes of the objects of mathematics, as figure and number and other things of this kind which the mathematician investigates. And in general every intellectual science, to whatever degree it participates in intellect, must always deal with causes and principles. This is the case whether it deals with purely intelligible things, as divine science does, or with those which are in some way imaginable or sensible in particular but intelligible in general; or even if it deals with sensible things inasmuch as there is science of them, as occurs in the case of mathematics and in that of the philosophy of nature. Or again whether they proceed from universal principles to particular cases in which there is activity, as occurs in the practical sciences, it is always necessary that such sciences deal with principles and causes.

1146. Now these principles are either more certain to us, as occurs in the natural sciences, because they are closer to sensible things, or they are simpler and prior in nature, as occurs in the mathematical sciences. But cognitions which are only sensory are not the result of principles and causes but of the sensible object itself acting upon the senses. For to proceed from causes to effects or the reverse is not an activity of the senses but only of the intellect. Or "more certain principles" means those which are better known and more deeply probed, and "simple" means those which are studied in a more superficial way, as occurs in the moral sciences, whose principles are derived from those things which occur in the majority of cases.

1147. **But all these** [2].

Second, he shows how the other sciences differ from this science in their study of principles and causes. He says that all these particular sciences which have now been mentioned are about one particular class of being, for example, number, continuous quantity or something of this kind; and each confines its investigations to "its subject genus," i.e., dealing with this class and not with another; for example, the science which deals with number does not deal with continuous quantity. For no one of the other sciences deals "with being in an unqualified sense," i.e., with being in general, or even with any particular being as being; for example, arithmetic does not deal with number as being but as number. For to consider each being as being is proper to metaphysics.

1148. And since it belongs to the same science to consider both being and the whatness or quiddity, because each thing has being by reason of its quiddity, therefore the other particular sciences make "no mention of," i.e., they do not investigate, the whatness or quiddity of a thing and the definition signifying it. But they proceed "from this," i.e., from the whatness itself of a thing, to other things, using this as an already established principle for the purpose of proving other things.

1149. Now some sciences make the

whatness of their subject evident by means of the senses, as the science which treats of animals understands what an animal is by means of what "is apparent to the senses," i.e., by means of sensation and local motion, by which animal is distinguished from non-animal. And other sciences understand the whatness of their subject by assuming it from some other science, as geometry learns what continuous quantity is from first philosophy. Thus, beginning from the whatness itself of a thing, which has been made known either by the senses or by assuming it from some other science, these sciences demonstrate the proper attributes which belong essentially to the subject-genus with which they deal; for a definition is the middle term in a causal demonstration. But the method of demonstration differs; because some sciences demonstrate with greater necessity, as the mathematical sciences, and others "more weakly," i.e., without necessity, as the sciences of nature, whose demonstrations are based on things that do not pertain to something always but for the most part.

1150. Another translation has "condition" in place of "assumption," but the meaning is the same; for what is assumed is taken, as it were, by stipulation. And since the starting point of demonstration is definition, it is evident that from this kind of inductive method "there is no demonstration of a thing's substance," i.e., of its essence, or of the definition signifying its whatness; but there is some other method by which definitions are made known, namely, the method of elimination and the other methods which are given in the *Posterior Analytics*, Book II. [96a20]

1151. And just as no particular science settles the issue about the whatness of things, neither does any one of them discuss the existence or nonexistence of the subject-genus with which it deals. This is understandable, because it belongs to the same science to settle the question of a thing's existence and to make known its whatness. For in order to prove that a thing exists its whatness must be taken as the middle term of the demonstration. Now both of these questions belong to the investigation of the philosopher who considers being as being. Therefore every particular science assumes the existence and whatness of its subject, as is stated in Book I of the *Posterior Analytics*.76b5] This is indicated by the fact that no particular science establishes the truth about being in an unqualified sense, or about any being as being.

1152. **And since the philosophy of nature** [3].

Here he shows how this science differs from the other sciences in its method of considering the principles of being as being. And since the philosophy of nature was considered by the ancients to be the first science and the one which would consider being as being, therefore, beginning with it as with what is more evident, he shows, first [3], how the philosophy of nature differs from the practical sciences; and second [4], how it differs from the speculative sciences, showing also the method of study proper to this science ("Now the essence").

He says, first [3], that the philosophy of nature does not deal with being in an unqualified sense but with some particular class of being, i.e., with natural substance, which has within itself a principle of motion and rest; and from this it is evident that it is neither a practical nor a productive science. For action and production differ, because action is an operation that remains in the agent itself, as choosing, understanding and the like (and for this reason the practical sciences are called moral sciences), whereas production is an operation that passes over into some matter in order to change it, as cutting, burning and the like (and for this reason the productive sciences are called mechanical arts).

1153. Now it is evident that the philosophy of nature is not a productive science, because the principle of productive sciences is in the maker and not in the thing made, which is the artifact. But the principle of motion in natural bodies is within these natural bodies. Further, the principle of things made by art, which is in the maker, is, first, the intellect which discovers the art; and second, the art which is an intellectual habit; and third, some executive power, such as the motive power by which the artisan executes the work conceived by his art. Hence it is evident that the philosophy of nature is not a productive science.

1154. And for this reason it is evident that it is not a practical science; for the principle of practical sciences is in the agent, not in the actions or customary operations themselves. This principle is "prohaeresis," i.e., choice; for the object of action and that of choice are the same. Hence it is evident that the philosophy of nature is neither a practical nor a productive science.

1155. If, then, every science is either practical, productive or theoretical, it follows that the philosophy of nature is a theoretical science. Yet "it is theoretical," or speculative, of a special class of being, namely, that which is subject to motion; for mobile being is the subject matter of the philosophy of nature. And it deals only with "that kind of substance," i.e., the quiddity or essence of a thing, which is for the most part inseparable from matter in its intelligible structure. He adds this because of the intellect, which comes in a sense within the scope of the philosophy of nature, although its substance is separable from matter. Thus it is clear that the philosophy of nature deals with some special subject, which is mobile being, and that it has a special way of defining things, namely, with matter.

1156. **Now the essence** [4].

Here he shows how the philosophy of nature differs from the other speculative sciences in its method of defining things; and in regard to this he does two things. First [4], he explains this difference. Second [7], he draws a conclusion about the number of theoretical sciences ("Hence there will be").

In regard to the first he does three things. First, he exposes the method of defining things which is proper to the philosophy of nature. He says that, in order to understand how the speculative sciences differ from each other, the quiddity of a thing and the way in which "the conceptual expression," i.e., the definition signifying it, should be expressed in each science, must not remain unknown. For in seeking the aforesaid difference "without this," i.e., without knowing how to define things, our search would be unfruitful. For since a definition is the middle term in a demonstration, and is therefore the starting-point of knowing, the difference between the speculative sciences must depend on the different ways of defining things.

1157. Now concerning things which are defined it must be noted that some are defined like snub and others like concave. And these two differ because the definition of snub includes sensible matter (since snub is merely a curved or concave nose), whereas concavity is defined without sensible matter. For some sensible body, such as fire or water or the like, is not included in the definition of concave or curved. For that is said to be concave whose middle curves away from the ends.

1158. Now all natural things are defined in a way similar to snub, as is evident both of those parts of an animal which are unlike, for example, nose, eye and face; and of those which are alike, for example, flesh and bone; and also of the whole animal. And the same is true of the parts of plants, for example, leaf, root and bark; and also of the whole plant. For no one of these can be defined without motion; but each includes sensible matter in its definition, and therefore motion, because every kind of sensible matter has its own kind of motion. Thus in the definition of flesh and bone it is necessary that the hot and cold be held to be suitably mixed in some way; and the same is true of other things. From this it is evident what the method is which the philosophy of nature uses in investigating and defining the quiddity of natural things; i.e., it involves sensible matter.

1159. And for this reason the philosophy of nature also investigates one kind of soul—the kind that is not defined without sensible matter. For in Book II of *The Soul* [412a20] he says that a soul is the first actuality of a natural organic body having life potentially. But if any soul can exist separately from a body, then insofar as it is not the actuality of such a body, it does not fall within the scope of the philosophy of nature. Therefore it is evident from the above that the philosophy of nature is a theoretical science, and that it has a special method of defining things.

1160. **But mathematics** [5].

Second, he exposes the method proper to mathematics. He says that mathematics is also a speculative science; for evidently it is neither a practical nor a productive science, since it considers things which are devoid of motion, without which action and production cannot exist. But whether those things which mathematical science considers are immobile and separable from matter in their being is not yet clear. For some men, the Platonists, held that numbers, continuous quantities and other mathematical objects are separate from matter and midway between the Forms and sensible things, as is stated in Book I (see n. 157) and in Book III (see n. 350). But the answer to this question has not yet been fully established by him, but will be established later on. [XIII,2]

1161. However, it is evident that mathematical science studies some things insofar as they are immobile and separate from matter, although they are neither immobile nor separable from matter in being. For their intelligible structure, for example, that of concave or curved, does not contain sensible matter. Hence mathematical science differs from the philosophy of nature in this respect, that while the philosophy of nature considers things whose definitions contain sensible matter (and thus it considers what is not separate insofar as it is not separate), mathematical science considers things whose definitions do not contain sensible matter. And thus even though the things which it considers are not separate from matter, it nevertheless considers them insofar as they are separate.

1162. **Now if there is something** [6].

Third, he exposes the method proper to this science. He says that, if there is something whose being is immobile, and therefore eternal and separable from matter in being, it is evident that the investigation of it belongs to a theoretical science and not to a practical or productive one, whose investigations have to do with certain kinds of motion. However, the study of such being does not belong to the philosophy of nature, for the philosophy of nature deals with certain kinds of beings, namely, mobile ones. Nor likewise does the study of this being belong to mathematics, because mathematics does not consider things which are separable from matter in being but only in their intelligible structure, as has been stated (n. 1161). But the study of this being must belong to another science which is prior to both of these, i.e., prior to the philosophy of nature and to mathematics.

1163. For the philosophy of nature deals with things which are inseparable from matter and mobile, and mathematics deals with certain immobile things, although these are not separate from matter in being but only in their intelligible structure, since in reality they are found in sensible matter. And he says "presumably" because this truth has not yet been established. Further, he says that some mathematical sciences deal with immobile things, as geometry and arithmetic, because some mathematical sciences are applied to motion, as astronomy. But the first science deals with things which are separable from matter in being and are altogether immobile.

1164. Now common causes must be eternal, because the first causes of beings which are generated must not themselves be generated, otherwise the process of generation would proceed to infinity; and this is true especially of those causes which are altogether immobile and immaterial. For those immaterial and immobile causes are the causes of the sensible things evident to us, because they are beings in the highest degree, and therefore are the cause of other things, as was shown in Book II (151:C 290). From this it is evident that the science which considers beings of this kind is the first of all the sciences and the one which considers the common causes of all beings. Hence there are causes of beings as beings, which are investigated in first philosophy, as he proposed in Book I (14:C 36). And from this it is quite evident that the opinion of those who claimed that Aristotle thought that God is not the cause of the substance of the heavens, but only of their motion, is false.

1165. However, we must remember that even though things which are separate from matter and motion in being and in their intelligible structure belong to the study of first philosophy, still the philosopher not only investigates these but also sensible things inasmuch as they are beings. Unless perhaps we may say, as Avicenna does, that common things of the kind which this science considers are said to be separate from matter in being, not because they are always without matter, but because they do not necessarily have being in matter, as the objects of mathematics do.

1166. **Hence there will be** [7].

He draws a conclusion as to the number of theoretical sciences. And in regard to this he does three things. First [7], he concludes from what has been laid down above that there are three parts of theoretical philosophy: mathematics, the philosophy of nature, and theology, which is first philosophy.

1167. **For it is obvious** [8].

Second, he gives two reasons why this science is called theology. The first of these is that "it is obvious that if the divine exists anywhere," i.e., if something divine exists in any class of things, it exists in such a nature, namely, in the class of being which is immobile and separate from matter, which this science studies.

1168. **And the most honorable** [9].

He gives the second reason why this science is called theology; and the reason is this: the most honorable science deals with the most honorable class of beings, and this is the one in which divine beings are contained. Therefore, since this science is the most honorable of the sciences because it is the most honorable of the theoretical sciences, as was shown before (see n. 64)—and these are more honorable than the practical sciences, as was stated in Book I (see n. 35)—it is evident that this science deals with divine beings; and therefore it is called theology inasmuch as it is a discourse about divine beings.

1169. **But someone will** [10].

Third, he raises a question about a point already established. First, he states the question, saying that someone can inquire whether first philosophy is universal inasmuch as it considers being in general, or whether it investigates some particular class or a single nature. Now this does not seem to be the case. For this science and the mathematical sciences do not have one and the same method; because geometry and astronomy, which are mathematical sciences, deal with a special nature, whereas first philosophy is universally common to all. Yet the reverse seems to be true, namely, that it deals with a special nature, because it is concerned with things which are separable from matter and immobile, as has been stated (see n. 1163).

1170. **Therefore, if** [11].

Second, he answers this question, saying that if there is no substance other than those which exist in the way that natural substances do, with which the philosophy of nature deals, the philosophy of nature will be the first science. But if there is some immobile substance, this will be prior to natural substance; and therefore the philosophy of nature, which considers this kind of substance, will be first philosophy. And since it is first, it will be universal; and it will be its function to study being as being, both what being is and what the attributes are which belong to being as being. For the science of the primary kind of being and that of being in general are the same, as has been stated at the beginning of Book IV (see n. 533).

LESSON 2
The Being Which This Science Investigates

ARISTOTLE'S TEXT Chapter 2: 1026a33–1027a28

1. *Being in an unqualified sense has various meanings, of which one is the accidental, and another the true (and non-being may signify the false); and besides these there are the categorical figures, for example, the what, of what sort, how much, where, when, and anything else which signifies in this way; and besides all of these there is the potential and the actual.* **1026a33–1026b2**

2. *Since being is used in many senses, then, we must speak first of the accidental, because there is no speculation about it. And this is indicated by the fact that there is no science, either practical or speculative, that investigates it. For one who builds a house does not simultaneously cause all traits that are accidental to the completed house, since these are infinite in number. For nothing prevents the completed house from being pleasant to some, harmful to others, useful to others, and different, as I may say, from all other things, none of which the art of building produces. And similarly neither does the geometrician speculate about things which are accidents of figures in this way, nor whether a triangle differs from a triangle having two right angles.* **1026b2–12**

3. *And this is understandable, because the accidental is in a sense being only in name.* **1026b12–14**

4. *Hence in a way Plato was not wrong when he said that sophistry deals with non-being. For the arguments of the sophists, as I may say, are concerned chiefly with the accidental; [for example, they ask] whether the musical and the grammatical are the same or different; and whether musical Coriscus and Coriscus are the same; and whether everything which is but has not always been has come to be, so that if one who is musical has become grammatical, then one who is grammatical has become musical; and all other such arguments. For the accidental seems to be close to non-being.* **1026b14–21**

5. *Now this is also clear from these arguments: there is generation and corruption of those things which are in another way, but not of those things which are by accident.* **1026b22–24**

6. *Yet concerning the accidental it is necessary to state further, so far as it is possible, what its nature is and by what cause it exists; and perhaps at the same time it will also become evident why there is no science of it.* **1026b24–27**

7. *Therefore, since there are some beings which always are in the same way and of necessity (not necessity in the sense of compulsion, but in the sense of that which cannot be otherwise), and others which are neither of necessity nor always, but for the most part, this is the principle and this the cause of the accidental.* **1026b27–31**

8. *For that which is neither always nor for the most part, we call the accidental. For example, if there should be cold and wintry weather during the dog days, we say that this is accidental; but not if the weather is sultry and hot, because the latter occurs either always or for the most part, whereas the former does not. And it is accidental for a man to be white, for this is so neither always nor for the most part; but it is not accidental for him to be an animal. And it is accidental if a builder produces health, because it is not a builder but a physician who is naturally fitted to do this; but it is accidental for a builder to be a physician. Again, a confectioner, aiming to prepare something palatable, may produce something health-giving; but not according to the confectioner's art. Hence we say that it was accidental. And while there is a sense in which he produces it, he does not produce it in a primary and proper sense. For there are other powers which sometimes are productive of other things, but there is no art or*

determinate power which is productive of the accidental; for the cause of things which are or come to be by accident is also accidental. **1026b31–1027a8**

9. Hence, since not all things are or come to be of necessity and always, but most things occur for the most part, the accidental must exist; for example, a white man is neither always nor for the most part musical. But since this occurs only occasionally, it must be accidental; otherwise everything would be of necessity. Hence matter is the contingent cause of the accidental, which happens otherwise than usually occurs. And we must take as our starting point this question: Is there nothing that is neither always nor for the most part, or is this impossible? There is, then, besides these something which is contingent and accidental. But then there is the question: Does that which occurs for the most part and that which occurs always, have no existence, or are there some beings which are eternal? These questions must be investigated later (1055). **1027a8–19**

10. However, it is evident that there is no science of the accidental, for all scientific knowledge is of that which is always or for the most part; otherwise how could one be taught or teach anyone else? For a thing must be defined either as being so always or for the most part; for example, honey-water is beneficial in most cases to those with a fever. But with regard to what happens in the other cases, it will be impossible to state when they occur, for example, at the new moon; for whatever happens at the new moon also happens either always or for the most part; but the accidental is contrary to this. We have explained, then, what the accidental is, and by what cause it exists, and that there is no science of it. **1027a19–28**

COMMENTARY

1171. Here Aristotle indicates with what beings this science chiefly intends to deal; and in regard to this he does three things. First [1], he recalls the ways in which things are said to be; second [2], he establishes the nature of the two kinds of being with which he is not chiefly concerned ("Since being"); and third (Lesson 4. text 4), he shows that it is not his chief aim to consider these two kinds of being ("But since combination").

Accordingly he says, first [1], that being in an unqualified sense, i.e., in a universal sense, is predicated of many things, as has been stated in Book V (see n. 885). In one sense being means what is accidental; and in another sense it means the same thing as the truth of a proposition (and non-being the same as the falseness of a proposition); and in a third sense being is predicated of the things contained under the categorical figures; for example, the what, of what sort, how much, and so on; and in a fourth sense, in addition to all of the above, being applies to what is divided by potentiality and actuality.

1172. **Since being** [2].

Here he deals with the senses of being which he intends to exclude from this science. First [2], he deals with accidental being; and second (Lesson 4), with being which is identical with the true ("Again, being in the sense of the true").

In regard to the first he does two things. First, he shows that there can be no science of the accidental. Second [6], he establishes the things that must be considered about accidental being ("Yet concerning the accidental").

He says, first [2], that since being is used in many senses, as has been stated [1], it is necessary first of all to speak of accidental being, so that anything which has the character of being in a lesser degree may first be excluded from the study of this science. And with regard to this kind of being it must be said that no speculation of any science can be concerned with it; and he proves this in two ways.

1173. He does this first by giving a concrete indication. He says that the impossibility of there being any speculation about accidental being is indicated by the fact that no science, howsoever "investigative" it may be, or "thoughtful" as another translation says, i.e., no matter how carefully it investigates the objects which come within its scope, is found to deal with accidental being. No practical science (and this is divided into the science of action and productive science, as was said above [see n. 1152]) is concerned with it, nor even any speculative science.

1174. He makes this evident, first, in the case of the practical sciences; for one who builds a house, granted that he builds it, is only an accidental cause of those things which are accidental to the completed house, since these are infinite in number and thus cannot come within the scope of art. For nothing prevents the completed house from being "pleasant," or delightful, to those who dwell there happily; "harmful" to those who suffer some misfortune occasioned by it; "useful" to those who acquire some profit from it; and also "different" from and unlike all other things. But the art of building does not produce any of the things which are accidental to a house, but only produces a house and the things which are essential to it.

1175. Then he shows that the same thing is true in the case of the speculative sciences, because similarly neither does geometry speculate about those things which are accidents "of figures in this way," i.e., accidentally, but only about those attributes which belong essentially to figures. For it speculates about a triangle being a figure having "two right angles," i.e., having its three angles equal to two right angles; but it does not speculate whether a triangle is anything else, such as wood or something of the sort, because these things pertain to a triangle accidentally.

1176. **And this is understandable** [3].

Second, he proves the same thing by means of an argument. He says it is reasonable that no science should speculate about accidental being, because a science studies those things which are beings in a real sense, but accidental being is in a sense being only in name, inasmuch as one thing is predicated of another. For each thing is a being insofar as it is one. But from any two things which are accidentally related to each other there comes to be something that is one only in name, i.e., inasmuch as one is predicated of the other, for example, when the musical is said to be white, or the converse. But this does not happen in such a way that some one thing is constituted from whiteness and the musical.

1177. **Hence in a way** [4].

He proves in two ways that accidental being is in a sense being only in name. He does this, first, on the authority of Plato; and second [5], by an argument ("Now this is").

He says that since accidental being is in a sense being only in name, Plato in a way was not wrong when, in allotting different sciences to different kinds of substance, he assigned sophistical science to the realm of non-being. For the arguments of the sophists are concerned chiefly with the accidental, since hidden paralogisms have the fallacy of accident as their principal basis.

1178. Therefore in the first book of the *Sophistical Refutations* [166b29] it is said that in arguing against wise men the sophists construct syllogisms that are based on the accidental. This is evident, for example, in these paralogisms in which the question is raised whether the musical and the grammatical are the same or different. Let us construct such a paralogism. The musical differs from the grammatical; but the musical is the grammatical; hence the musical differs from itself. For the musical differs from the grammatical essentially speaking, but the musical is the grammatical by accident. Little wonder then that an absurd conclusion follows, for what is accidental is not distinguished from what is essential. And it would be similar if we were to speak thus: Coriscus differs from musical Coriscus; but Coriscus is musical Coriscus; therefore Coriscus differs from himself. Here too no distinction is drawn between what is accidental and what is essential. And it would be the same if we were to say: everything which is and has not always been, has come to be; but the musical is grammatical and has not always been so; therefore it follows that the musical has become grammatical and that the grammatical has become musical. But this is false, because no process of generation terminates in the grammatical being musical, but one process of generation terminates in a man being grammatical and another in a man being musical. It is also evident that in this argument the first statement is true of something that has being essentially, whereas in the second something is assumed that has being only by accident. And it is similar in all such argument based on the fallacy of accident. For accidental being seems to be close to non-being; and therefore sophistics, which is concerned with the apparent and nonexistent, deals chiefly with the accidental.

1179. **Now this is also clear** [5].

Second, he proves the same thing by an argument. He says that it is also evident, from these arguments which the sophists use, that the accidental is close to non-being; for there is generation and corruption of those things which are beings in a different way than the accidental is, but there is neither generation nor corruption of the accidental. For the musical comes to be by one process of generation and the grammatical by another, but there is not one process of generation of the grammatical musical as there is of two-footed animal or of risible man. Hence it is evident that accidental being is not called being in any true sense.

1180. **Yet concerning the accidental** [6].

He now establishes the truth about accidental being insofar as it is possible to do so. For even though those things which are properly accidental do not come within the scope of any science, still the nature of the accidental can be considered by some science. This is also what happens in the case of the infinite; for even though the infinite as infinite remains unknown, still some science treats of the infinite as infinite.

In regard to this he does two things. First [6], he settles the issue regarding those points which should be investigated about accidental being. Second (Lesson 3), he rejects an opinion that would abolish accidental being ("Now it is evident").

1181. In regard to the first he does two things. First [6], he says that there are three points which must be discussed about accidental being, insofar as it is possible to treat of it, namely, what its nature is, and what causes it;

and from this the third will become evident, why there can be no science of it.

1182. **Therefore, since there are** [7].

He discusses these three points. First, he shows what the cause of the accidental is. He says that there are some beings which always are in the same way and of necessity (not in the sense in which necessity is taken to mean compulsion, but in the sense of that which cannot be otherwise than it is, as "Man is an animal"); and there are other beings which are neither always nor of necessity, but for the most part, i.e., in the majority of cases, and "this," i.e., what occurs in the majority of cases, is the principle and the cause of the accidental. For in the case of those things which always are there can be nothing accidental, because only that which exists of itself can be necessary and eternal, as is also stated in Book V (see n. 839). Hence it follows that accidental being can be found only in the realm of contingent things.

1183. But that which is contingent, or open to opposites, cannot as such be the cause of anything. For insofar as it is open to opposites it has the character of matter, which is in potency to two opposites; for nothing acts insofar as it is in potency. Hence a cause which is open to opposites in the way that the will is, in order that it may act, must be inclined more to one side than to the other by being moved by the appetible object, and thus be a cause in the majority of cases. But that which takes place in only a few instances is the accidental, and it is this whose cause we seek. Hence it follows that the cause of the accidental is what occurs in the majority of cases, because this fails to occur in only a few instances. And this is what is accidental.

1184. **For that which** [8].

Second, he exposes the nature of accidental being; and he speaks thus: that which exists for the most part is the cause of the accidental, because we call that accidental which is neither always nor for the most part. And this is the absence of what occurs for the most part; so that "if there should be wintry weather," i.e., a period of rain and cold, "during the dog days," i.e., in the days of the dog star, we say that this is accidental. But we do not say this "if the weather is sultry" during that time, i.e., if there is a period of drought and heat; for the latter occurs always or almost always, but the former does not. Similarly we say that it is accidental for a man to be white, because this is so neither always nor for the most part. But we say that man is an animal essentially, not accidentally, because this is so always. And similarly a builder causes health accidentally, because a builder inasmuch as he is a builder is not naturally fitted to cause health, but only a physician can do this. However, a builder may cause health inasmuch as he happens to be a physician. Similarly a confectioner, or cook, "aiming," i.e., intending, to prepare "something palatable," or delightful in the line of food, may make something health-giving when he prepares a tasty dish. For food which is good and delightful sometimes promotes health. But it is not according to the "confectioner's art," i.e., the culinary art, that he produces something health-giving, but something delightful. And for this reason we say that this is accidental.

1185. And it should be noted that in the first example the accidental came about insofar as two things happen to occur at the same time; in the second, insofar as two things happen to be present in the same subject, as white and man; in the third, insofar as the same efficient cause happens to be a twofold agent, as a builder and a physician; and in the fourth, insofar as the effect happens to be twofold, as health and pleasure in the case of food; for while a cook prepares a pleasing dish, nevertheless this happens to be health-giving by accident. In fact a cook prepares something health-giving only in a secondary sense but not in a primary and proper sense, because an art operates through knowledge. Hence whatever lies outside the knowledge of an art is not produced primarily and properly by that art. Therefore the accidental, which lies outside the knowledge of an art, is not produced by art. For there are certain determinate powers which sometimes are productive of other beings which have being in the proper sense of the term, but there is no art or determinate power which is productive of beings in an accidental sense. Now the cause of those things which are or come to be by accident must be an accidental cause and not a proper cause. For effect and cause are proportionate to each other; and therefore whatever is an accidental effect has only an accidental cause, just as an effect in the proper sense has a cause in the proper sense.

1186. And since he had said above [7] that the cause of the accidental is what occurs for the most part, therefore when he says "Hence, since not all [9]," he shows how the accidental exists as a result of what occurs for the most part. He says that, since not all things are or come to be always and of necessity, "but most things happen for the most part," i.e., in the majority of cases, therefore the accidental must exist; and this is what does not occur always or for the most part, as when I say "The white man is musical." Yet because this sometimes happens, although not always or in the majority of cases, it follows that this comes about by accident. For if that which occurs only occasionally were never to occur, then that which occurs in the majority of cases would never fail to occur but would be always and of necessity. Thus all things would be eternal and necessary. But this is false. And since that which occurs in the majority of cases fails to occur because of matter (which is not completely subject to the active power of the agent, as happens in the majority of cases), then matter is the cause of that which happens to be otherwise "than usually occurs," i.e., of what happens only occasionally. This cause, I say, is not a necessary cause but a contingent one.

1187. Granted that not all things are necessary but that there is something which is neither always nor for the most part, then we must take as our starting-point the question whether there is nothing that is neither always nor for the most part. But obviously this is impossible; for since that which occurs for the most part is the cause of the accidental, then both that which always is and that which is for the most part must exist. Hence anything besides the things just mentioned is an accidental being.

1188. However, the question whether that which occurs for the most part is found in some being, and whether that which occurs always is not found in any being, or whether there are some things which are eternal, must be dealt with later in Book XII (see n. 2488), where he will show that there are some substances which are eternal. Hence in the first question he asks whether all things are accidental; and in the second, whether all things are contingent and nothing is eternal.

1189. **However, it is evident** [10].

Here he establishes the third point, namely, that there is no science of the accidental. He says that this is evident from the fact that every science is concerned with what is either always or for the most part. Therefore, since the accidental occurs neither always nor for the most part, there will be no science of it. He proves the first thus: one cannot be taught by another or teach another about something which does not occur either always or for the most part; for anything that may be taught must be defined on the grounds that it is so either always or for the most part; for example, that "honey-water" (a mixture of honey and water) is beneficial to those with a fever, is defined as something that occurs for the most part.

1190. But with regard to "what happens in the other cases [10]," i.e., in the case of things which are neither always nor for the most part, it cannot be said when they will occur, for example, at the time of the new moon; for whatever is destined to happen at that time also happens either always or for the most part. Or his statement about the new moon can be another example of something that is defined as occurring always; and he adds the phrase "or for the most part" because of the way in which the accidental differs, because it does not occur in either of these ways. Hence he adds that "the accidental is contrary to this," i.e., contrary to what occurs always or for the most part. And this is the minor premise of the principal argument used above. In bringing his discussion to a close he mentions the points which have been explained, namely, what the accidental is, and what its cause is, and that there can be no science of it.

LESSON 3
Refutation of Those Who Wished to Abolish the Accidental

ARISTOTLE'S TEXT Chapter 3: 1027a29–1027b16

1. *Now it is evident that there are principles and causes which are generable and corruptible without generation and corruption; for if this were not the case, everything would be of necessity, i.e., if there must be some cause, and not an accidental one, of that which is generated and corrupted. For if we ask: "Will this thing exist or not?" It will if some second thing happens; but if the latter does not, neither will the former. And this second thing will happen if some third thing does. And thus it is evident that when time is continually taken away from a limited period of time, one will finally come to the present moment. Hence this man will die either from illness or violence if he goes out; and he will do this if he gets thirsty; and this will happen if something else does. And in this way one will come to what exists now, or to something that has already happened; for example, he will go out if he gets thirsty, and this will happen if he eats highly seasoned food, and this is either the case or not. Therefore it will be from necessity that he dies or does not die. And similarly if one jumps back to something that has already happened, the same argument applies; for this—I mean what has already happened—is already present in something. Therefore everything that will be, will be of necessity; for example, one who lives shall die; because some part of the process has already been completed, as the presence of contraries in the same body. But whether he will die from illness or violence has not yet been determined, unless something else will have happened.* **1027a29–1027b11**

2. *It is evident, then, that this process goes back to some principle, but that this does not go back to anything else. Therefore this will be the principle of everything that happens by chance, and there will be no cause of its generation.* **1027b11–14**

3. *But to what kind of principle and what kind of cause such a process of reduction leads, whether to matter or to a final cause or to a cause of motion, must be given careful consideration. Let us dismiss accidental being, then, for it has been dealt with at sufficient length.* **1027b14–16**

COMMENTARY

1191. Having drawn his conclusions concerning accidental being, the Philosopher now rejects an opinion that would completely abolish this kind of being. For some men held that whatever comes to pass in the world has some proper cause, and again that given any cause its effect necessarily follows. Hence, as a result of the connection between causes it would follow that everything in the world happens of necessity and nothing by chance. Therefore the Philosopher's aim is to destroy this position; and in regard to this he does three things.

First [1], he destroys this position. Second [2], he draws a conclusion from his discussion ("It is evident"). Third [3], he poses a question that arises out of this discussion ("But to what kind of principle").

He says, first [1], that it will be evident from the following remarks that the principles and causes of the generation and corruption of some things "are generable and corruptible," i.e., they are capable of being generated and corrupted, "without generation and corruption," i.e., without generation and corruption taking place. For if the generation or corruption of one thing is the cause of the generation or corruption of another, it is not necessary that the generation or corruption of the effect necessarily follows when the generation or corruption of the cause takes place, because some causes are active only for the most part. Therefore, granted that these causes exist, their effect can be hindered accidentally, either because the matter is not disposed, or because an opposing agent interferes, or because of some such reason.

1192. Yet it must be noted that Avicenna proves in his *Metaphysics* that no effect is possible in relation to its own cause but only necessary. For if when the cause is posited it is possible for its effect not to follow, and it does follow (and the potential as such is made actual by some actual being), then something else besides this cause will have to cause the actual effect to follow. Therefore this cause was not sufficient. This appears to be contrary to what the Philosopher says here.

1193. But it must be noted that Avicenna's statement should be understood to apply only if we assume that no obstacle interferes with the cause. For given the cause its effect must follow unless there is some obstacle, and sometimes this occurs accidentally. Hence the Philosopher says that generation and corruption need not follow when the causes of generation and corruption are posited.

1194. For if this statement were not true, it would follow that all things would be of necessity, granted that along with this statement: given the cause the effect must follow, another position is also maintained, namely, that there must be some proper cause, and not merely an accidental one, of each thing which is generated and corrupted. For from these two propositions it follows that all things are of necessity. He proves this as follows.

1195. If it is asked whether a thing will be or not, it follows from the above remarks that one or the other is true of necessity; because if everything that is generated has a proper cause which produces it, and if given the cause its effect must ensue, then it follows that that thing about which it was asked whether it will exist or not, will come to be if its cause is held to exist; and if that cause will not exist, neither will its effect. And similarly it will be necessary to say that this cause will exist if some other thing which is its cause will exist.

1196. Further, it is evident that regardless of the amount of future time that may be taken, whether after a hundred or a thousand years, the amount of time beginning from the present moment up to that point is limited. However, since the generation of a cause is prior in time to the generation of its effect, then by proceeding from effect to cause we must subtract some part of future time and come closer to the present. But every limited thing is used up by having some part of it constantly taken away. Thus by proceeding from an effect to its cause and again from that cause to its cause and so on in this way, it follows that the whole period of future time is used up, since it is limited, and in this way the present moment is reached.

1197. This is clear in the following example. If every effect has some proper cause from which it follows of necessity, then this man must die of necessity, either from illness or violence, if he leaves the house. For his leaving the house is found to be the cause of his death by either violence (for example, if on leaving the house he is discovered by robbers and is killed), or illness (for example, if on leaving the house because he is hot he contracts a fever and dies). And in the same way it will also happen of necessity that he leaves the house in order to draw water from a well if he is thirsty; for thirst is the cause of his leaving the house in order to draw water. And similarly by the same argument it will also happen of necessity that he is thirsty if there is something else which causes his thirst; and thus by proceeding from effect to cause in this way one comes to "something which exists now," i.e., to some present thing or to "something that has already happened," i.e., to some past event. For example, if we were to say that a man will be thirsty if he eats highly seasoned or salty food which makes him thirsty, his eating or not eating salty food is in the present. Thus it follows that "the aforesaid future event," namely, that this man will die or not die, will happen of necessity.

1198. For since every conditional proposition is a necessary one, then granted the antecedent the consequent must follow; for example, this conditional proposition is true: "If Socrates runs, he moves." Therefore, granted that he runs, he must be moving so long as he runs. But if any effect has a proper cause from which it follows of necessity, then that conditional proposition must be true of which the antecedent is the cause and the consequent is the effect. And although there are sometimes several intermediates between a cause which exists at the present moment and an effect which will exist in the future (each of which is an effect in relation to those preceding it and a cause in relation to those following it), nevertheless it follows from first to last that any conditional proposition is true whose antecedent is present and whose consequent exists at some future time, for example, the proposition: "If a man eats salty food, he will be killed." Now the antecedent refers to what is present, and therefore it will be by necessity that he is killed. And in this way all other future events whose proximate or remote causes exist in the present will be necessary.

1199. The same argument applies if one in proceeding from effects to causes "jumps back to something that has already happened," or to past events, that is to say, if one traces future effects back to some past cause that is not present; for that which is past nevertheless still is in some sense. I say this insofar as it has occurred, or is past. For even though Caesar's life is not now, in the present, nevertheless it is in the past, because it is true that Caesar has lived. Thus it is possible to hold as true now the antecedent of a conditional proposition in whose antecedent clause there is a past cause and in whose consequent clause there is a future effect. And thus since all future effects must be traced back to such present or past causes, it follows that all future events happen of necessity. For example, we say that it is absolutely necessary that one now living is going to die, because this follows of necessity in reference to something that has already come to pass, namely, that there are two contraries in the same body by reason of its composition; for this conditional proposition is true, "If a body is composed of contraries, it will be corrupted."

1200. But it is impossible that all future events should happen of necessity. Therefore the two premises from which this conclusion would follow are impossible, namely, that any effect has a proper cause, and that given the cause its effect must follow. For from this would follow the position already mentioned, namely, that there are some causes already posited for any future effect; for example, some causes have already been posited for the corruption of an animal. But no cause has yet been posited from which it will follow of necessity that this man will die either from illness or violence.

1201. **It is evident** [2].

He draws a conclusion from the foregoing discussion. He says that, since not everything which comes to be has a proper cause, it is therefore evident that in the case of future contingent events the reduction of a future effect to some proper cause goes back to some principle, and that this principle is not reduced to some other proper principle but will be the cause of "everything that happens by chance," i.e., an accidental cause, and that there will be no other cause of that accidental cause; just as we have already said (550:C 1184) that accidental being has no cause and is not generated. For example, the cause of this man being killed by robbers is a proper cause, because he is wounded by robbers; and this also has a proper cause, because he is found by the robbers; but this has only an accidental cause. For if on his way to work this man is wounded by robbers, this is accidental, as is evident from the foregoing; and therefore it is not necessary to posit a cause for this. For that which is accidental is not generated, and thus it is not necessary to look for some proper cause which produces it, as was said above.

1202. **But to what kind of principle** [3].

Here he poses a question arising out of the foregoing discussion; for he has just said above that the causes of those beings which are accidental are ultimately reduced to some principle for which it is impossible to give another cause. Hence he inquires here about this process of reduction or {anagoge}, which means the same as "to what kind of principle and what kind of cause it should be reduced," i.e., to what class of cause or principle, whether to some first cause which is a material cause, or to one which is a final cause (or that for the sake of which a thing comes to be), or to one which is a mover. He omits the formal cause because the question here involves the cause responsible for the generation of things that come to be by accident. But in the process of generation a form has no causal role except that of an end, because in the process of generation the end and the form are identical. Now he does not answer the question which is raised here, but assumes its solution from what has been established in Book II of the *Physics; [198b3]* for it was shown there that fortune and chance, which are the causes of things that come to be by accident, are reduced to the class of efficient cause. Hence he concludes from the above that we must omit any discussion of accidental being, because the truth concerning it has been established as completely as it is possible to do so.

1203. It must be noted, however, that the doctrine of the Philosopher set forth here seems to do away with certain things which some thinkers hold in philosophy, namely, fate and providence. For here the force of the Philosopher's argument is that not all that occurs may be traced back to some proper cause from which it follows of necessity, otherwise it would follow that everything in the world would be of necessity and nothing by accident. But those who posit fate say that the contingent events occurring here, which appear to be accidental, can be traced back to some power of a celestial body, whose activity produces in a certain order those things which, viewed in themselves, seem accidental. And similarly those who posit providence say that whatever occurs here is ordained by the order of providence.

1204. From both of these positions, then, there seem to follow two conclusions which are opposed to what the philosopher establishes here. The first is that nothing in the world happens accidentally either by fortune or by chance; for those things which occur in a certain order are not accidental, since they occur either always or for the most part. The second is that all things happen of necessity. For if all those things whose cause is placed in the present or has been placed in the past occur of necessity, as the Philosopher's argument maintains, and if the cause of those things which come under providence or fate is placed in the present or has already been placed in the past (because providence is unchangeable and eternal, and the motion of the heavens is also invariable), it seems to follow that those things which come under providence or fate happen of necessity. Thus if everything that occurs here is subject to fate and providence, it follows that everything happens of necessity. Therefore according to the mind of the Philosopher it seems impossible to posit either fate or providence.

1205. In clearing up this difficulty it must be noted that the higher a cause the more extensive is its causality, for a higher cause produces its own proper higher effect, which is more general and extends to many things. For example, in the case of the arts it is evident that the political art, which is higher than the military art, has jurisdiction over the entire political community, whereas the military art has jurisdiction only over those things which fall within the military sphere. But the order found in the effects of a cause extends only so far as the causality of that cause extends, for every cause in the proper sense has definite effects which it produces in a certain order. It is evident, then, that when effects are referred to lower causes they seem to be unrelated and to coincide with each other accidentally, but that when they are referred to some higher common cause they are found to be related and not accidentally connected but to be produced simultaneously by one proper cause.

1206. For example, if the blossoming of one plant is referred to a particular power in this plant and the blossoming of a second plant is referred to a particular power in that plant, there seems to be no reason (indeed it seems to be accidental) why the first plant should blossom when the second does. And this is true, because the cause of the power of the first plant extends to the blossoming of this plant and not to that of the second, so that while it causes the first plant to blossom, it does not cause it to blossom at the same time as the second. But if this is attributed to the power of a celestial body, which is a universal cause, then we find that the first plant blossoms when the second does, not by accident, but by the direction of some first cause, which ordains this and moves each plant to blossom at the same time.

1207. Now we find three grades of causes in the world. First, there is a cause which is incorruptible and immutable, namely, the divine cause; second, beneath this there are causes which are incorruptible but mutable, namely, the celestial bodies; and third, beneath this there are those causes which are corruptible and mutable. Therefore causes in this third grade are particular causes and are determined to proper effects of the same kind; for example, fire generates fire, man generates man, and plants generate plants.

1208. Now a cause belonging to the second grade is in one sense universal and in another particular. It is particular because it extends to some special class of beings, namely, to those which are generated by motion; for it is both a cause of motion and something that is moved. And it is universal because its causality extends not only to one class of changeable things but to everything that is altered, generated and corrupted; for that which is first moved must be the cause of everything that is subsequently moved.

1209. But the cause belonging to the first grade is universal without qualification, because its proper effect is existence. Hence whatever exists, and in whatever way it exists, comes properly under the causality and direction of that cause.

1210. If, then, we attribute all contingent events here to particular causes only, many things will be found to occur accidentally. This will be so for a number of reasons. First, because of the conjunction of two causes one of which does not come under the causality of the other, as when robbers attack me without my intending this; for this meeting is caused by a twofold motive power, namely, mine and that of the robbers. Second, because of some defect in the agent, who is so weak that he cannot attain the goal at which he aims, for example, when someone falls on the road because of fatigue. Third, because of the indisposition of the matter, which does not receive the form intended by the agent but another kind of form. This is what occurs, for example, in the case of the deformed parts of animals.

1211. But if these contingent events are traced back further to a celestial body, we find that many of them are not accidental; because even though particular causes are not contained under each other, they are nevertheless contained under one common celestial cause. Hence their concurrence can be attributed to one definite celestial cause. Again, since the power of a celestial body is incorruptible and impassible, no effect can escape from the sphere of its causality because of any defect or weakness of its power. But since it acts by moving, and since every agent of this kind requires a matter which is properly determined or disposed, then in the case of natural beings it can happen that the power of a celestial body fails to produce its effect because the matter is not disposed; and this will be accidental.

1212. Therefore, even though many things which seem to be accidental when traced back to these particular causes are found not to be accidental when traced back to a common universal cause, namely, to a celestial body, yet even when this reduction has been made some things are found to be accidental, as the Philosopher stated above (554:C 1201). For when an agent produces its effect for the most part but not always, it follows that it fails in a few instances; and this is accidental. If, then, the celestial bodies cause their effects in these lower bodies for the most part but not always, because the matter is not properly disposed, then it follows that, when the power of a celestial body fails to produce its effect, this happens accidentally.

1213. There is also another reason why things happen accidentally even if causality is traced back to a celestial body. It is that in the sphere of lower bodies there are some efficient causes which can act of themselves without the influence of a celestial body. These causes are rational souls, to which the power of a celestial body does not extend (since they are not forms subjected to bodies), except in an accidental way, i.e., inasmuch as the influence of a celestial body produces some change in the [human] body, and accidentally in the powers of the soul which are actualities of certain parts of the body, by which the rational soul is disposed to act. However, no necessity is involved, since the soul's dominion over the passions is free inasmuch as it may not assent to them. Therefore in the sphere of lower bodies whatever things are found to happen accidentally when reduced to these causes, i.e., rational souls, insofar as they do not follow the inclination produced by the influence of a celestial body, will not be found to be generated in any essential way by being traced back to the power of a celestial body.

1214. Thus it is evident that to posit fate, which is a certain disposition present in lower bodies as a result of the activity of a celestial body, is not to do away with everything that happens by chance.

1215. But if these contingent events are traced back further to the highest, divine cause, it will be impossible to find anything that lies outside its sphere of influence, since its causality extends to all things insofar as they are beings. Hence its causal activity cannot be thwarted as a result of the matter being indisposed, because matter itself and its dispositions do not lie outside the domain of this agent, since He is the agent who gives things their being and not merely moves and changes them.

For it cannot be said that matter is presupposed as the subject of being as it is presupposed as the subject of motion; it is rather part of the essence of a thing. Therefore, just as the power of changing and moving is not hindered by the essence of motion or its terminus but by the subject which is presupposed, in a similar fashion the power of the one giving being is not hindered by matter or anything which accrues in any way to the being of a thing. From this it is also evident that in the sphere of lower bodies no efficient cause can be found which is not subject to the control of this first cause.

1216. It follows, then, that everything which occurs here insofar as it is related to the first divine cause, is found to be ordained by it and not to be accidental, although it may be found to be accidental in relation to other causes. This is why the Catholic faith says that nothing in the world happens by chance or fortuitously, and that everything is subject to divine providence. But in this place Aristotle is speaking of those contingent events which occur here as a result of particular causes, as is evident from his example.

1217. It now remains to see how the affirming of fate and providence does not eliminate contingency from the world, as though all things were to happen of necessity. From the things that have been said above it is evident that fate does not do away with contingency. For it has been shown already that, even though the celestial bodies and their motions and activities are necessary, nevertheless their effects in these lower bodies can fail either because the matter is not disposed or because the rational soul may freely choose to follow or not follow the inclinations produced in it by the influence of a celestial body. Thus it follows that effects of this sort do not happen of necessity but contingently; for to posit a celestial cause is not to posit a cause of such a kind that its effect follows of necessity, as the death of an animal is a result of its being composed of contraries, as he mentions in the text [1].

1218. But there is greater difficulty with regard to providence, because divine providence cannot fail; for these two statements are incompatible, namely, that something is foreknown by God, and that it does not come to pass. Hence it seems that, once providence is posited, its effect follows of necessity.

1219. But it must be noted that an effect and all of its proper accidents depend on one and the same cause; for just as a man is from nature, so also are his proper accidents, such as risibility and susceptibility to mental instruction. However, if some cause does not produce man in an absolute sense but such and such a man, it will not be within the power of this cause to produce the proper attributes of man but only to make use of them. For while the statesman makes man a citizen, he does not make him susceptible to mental instruction. Rather he makes use of this property in order to make a citizen of him.

1220. Now, as has been pointed out (n. 1215), being as being has God himself as its cause. Hence just as being itself is subject to divine providence, so also are all the accidents of being as being, among which are found necessity and contingency. Therefore it belongs to divine providence not only to produce a particular being but also to give it contingency or necessity; for insofar as God wills to give contingency or necessity to anything, He has prepared for it certain intermediate causes from which it follows either of necessity or contingently. Hence the effect of every cause is found to be necessary insofar as it comes under the control of providence. And from this it follows that this conditional proposition is true: "If anything is foreknown by God, it will be."

1221. However, insofar as any effect is considered to come under its proximate cause, not every effect is necessary; but some are necessary and some contingent in proportion to their cause. For effects are likened in their nature to their proximate causes, but not to their remote causes, whose state they cannot attain.

1222. It is evident, then, that when we speak of divine providence we must say that this thing is foreseen by God not only insofar as it is but also insofar as it is either contingent or necessary. Therefore, just because divine providence is held to exist, it does not follow, according to the argument which Aristotle gives here, that every effect happens of necessity, but only that it must be either contingent or necessary. In fact this applies solely in the case of this cause, i.e., divine providence, because the remaining causes do not establish the law of necessity or contingency, but make use of this law established by a higher cause. Hence the only thing that is subject to the causality of any other cause is that its effect be. But that it be either necessary or contingent depends on a higher cause, which is the cause of being as being, and the one from which the order of necessity and of contingency originates in the world.

LESSON 4

The True and the False as Being and Non-Being. Accidental Being and Being in the Sense of the True Are Excluded from This Science

ARISTOTLE'S TEXT Chapter 4: 1027b17–1028a6

1. Again, being in the sense of the true and non-being in the sense of the false [are not to be considered] since such being depends on combination and separation, and these taken together form both parts of a contradiction. For truth resides in the affirmation of one side of a contradiction when there is combination, and in the negation when there is separation. But falsity consists in the reverse of this division. **1027b17–23**

2. But how [the intellect] happens to understand [things which are combined and separated, whether] together or separately, pertains to another discussion; and by understanding things together or separately I mean understanding them not successively but insofar as they form a unity. **1027b23–25**

3. For what is true and what is false are not in things themselves, so that what is good is true and what is evil is false, but only in the mind. And with regard to simple concepts and the whatness of things there is neither truth nor falsity in the mind. Hence the things which must be investigated about being and non-being in this sense must be considered later on. **1027b25–29**

4. But since combination and separation exist in thought and not in things, and being in this sense is different from being in the proper senses (for these are either what a thing is, or of what sort, or how much, or anything else that the mind combines or separates), then being in the sense of what is accidental and being in the sense of what is true must be omitted from this science. For the cause of the former is the indeterminate, and of the latter some positive state of mind; and both of these pertain to the remaining class of being and do not indicate the existence of any definite kind of being outside of the mind. For this reason, then, let us exclude them from our study, and let us look for the causes and principles of being as being. Now from our discussions of the different meanings of words it is evident that being is used in several senses. **1027b29–1028a6**

COMMENTARY

1223. Having drawn his conclusions about accidental being, the Philosopher now settles the issue about the being which signifies the truth of a proposition; and in regard to this he does two things. First [1], he determines the meaning of this kind of being. Second [4], he excludes it from the principal study of this science ("But since combination").

In regard to the first he does three things. First, he determines the meaning of this kind of being. Second [2], he answers a question ("But how [the intellect]"). Third [3] he clarifies a statement which he had made ("For what is true").

He says [1], then, that "in one sense being means what is true," i.e., it signifies nothing else than truth; for when we ask if man is an animal, the answer is that he is, by which it is meant that this proposition is true. And in the same way non-being signifies in a sense what is false; for when one answers that he is not, it is meant that the statement made is false. Now this being which means what is true, and non-being which means what is false, depend on combination and separation; for simple terms signify neither truth nor falsity, whereas complex terms have truth and falsity through affirmation or negation. And here affirmation is called combination because it signifies that a predicate belongs to a subject, whereas negation is called separation because it signifies that a predicate does not belong to a subject.

1224. Further, since words are the signs of concepts, we must speak in the same way about the concepts of the intellect; for those which are simple do not have truth and falsity, but only those which are complex through affirmation or negation.

1225. And since the being and non-being just mentioned—the true and the false—depend on combination and separation, they therefore also depend on the division of a contradiction; for each part of a contradiction separates the true and the false from each other, so that one part is true and the other is false. For since a contradiction is constituted of an affirmation and a negation, and each of these is constituted of a predicate and a subject, then a predicate and a subject can be related to each other in two ways; because they are either connected in reality, as man and animal, or are unconnected, as man and ass.

1226. Hence, if two contradictions are formed, one from connected terms, as "Man is an animal" and "Man is not an animal," and another from unconnected terms, as "Man is an ass" and "Man is not an ass," then truth and falsity divide each contradiction between themselves, so that the true on its side "resides in affirmation when there is combination," i.e., in connected terms, and "in negation when there is separation," i.e., in unconnected terms. For these two propositions "Man is an animal" and "Man is not an ass" are true. But the false on its side resides in the reverse of this division, i.e., in the contradictory of those statements which fall on the side of the true, because it consists in the negating of connected terms and in the affirming of unconnected terms; for these two propositions "Man is not an animal" and "Man is an ass" are false.

1227. **But how [the intellect]** [2].

Here he dismisses a problem that could arise from the foregoing remarks. For he said that the true and the false consist secondarily in the combination and separation of words, but primarily and properly in the combination and separation which the intellect makes. Now every combination and separation involves a plurality, and therefore the problem can arise how the intellect understands things which are combined and separated, whether together or separately. But he says that this pertains to another discussion namely, to *The Soul.* [430a26-431b4]

1228. Now *together* is used in two senses. For sometimes it signifies a unity, as when we say that those things which exist at one and the same instant are together in time; and sometimes it signifies the connection and proximity of things which succeed each other, as when we say that two men are together in place when their places are joined and next to each other, and in time when their times succeed each other. And since this is so, he therefore answers the proposed question which asks whether the intellect understands things which are combined or separated, together or separately, by saying that it does not understand them together according as some things are said to be together insofar as they succeed each other, but according as they are said to be together insofar as they form one thing.

1229. And in this way he indicates the solution of this question. For if the intellect understands a man and an animal as they are in themselves, as two distinct things, it understands them successively by two simple concepts without forming an affirmation or a negation from them. But when it combines or separates them, it understands them both as one thing, i.e., according as one thing is constituted from them; just as the intellect also understands the parts of a whole as one thing by understanding the whole itself. For the intellect does not understand a house by understanding first the foundation and then the walls and then the roof, but it understands all of these together insofar as one thing is constituted from them. And in a similar way it understands a predicate and a subject together insofar as one judgment is constituted from them, namely, an affirmation or a negation.

1230. **For what is true** [3].

He explains a statement which he had made to the effect that truth and falsity consist in combination and separation; and he proves this by means of the process of elimination. For some of the things signified by a word are found in things outside of the mind, but others are found only in the mind. For white and black are found outside of the mind, but their concepts are found only in the mind. Now someone might think that the true and the false are also found in things, just as good and evil are, so that the true is a kind of good and the false a kind of evil; for this would be necessary if truth and falsity were found in things, since truth signifies a certain perfection of nature, and falsity a defect. Moreover, every perfection existing in things pertains to the perfection and goodness of their nature, whereas every defect and privation pertains to evil.

1231. But he denies this, saying that the true and the false are not found in things in such a way that what is true on the part of reason is a kind of natural good, and what is false a kind of evil, but "they are found only in the mind," or intellect.

1232. The intellect, however, has two operations. One of these is called the understanding of indivisibles, and this is the operation by which the intellect forms simple concepts of things by understanding the whatness of each one of them. The other operation is that by which the intellect combines and separates.

1233. Now while truth and falsity are in the mind, they do not pertain to that operation by which the mind forms simple concepts and the whatness of things. This is what he means when he says "with regard to simple concepts and the whatness of things there is neither truth nor falsity in the mind." Hence as a result of this process of elimination it follows that since truth and falsity are neither in things nor in the mind when it apprehends simple concepts and the whatness of things, they must pertain primarily and principally to the combination and separation which the mind makes, and secondarily to that of words, which signify the mind's conceptions. Further, he concludes that everything which must be considered about being and nonbeing in this sense, namely, insofar as being signifies the true, and non-being the false, "must be considered later on," i.e., at the end of Book IX (see n. 1895), and also in *The Soul,* [430a26-431b4] and in his works on logic. [*On Interpretation*, 17b12 ff.] For the whole of logic seems to be devoted to the being and non-being spoken of in this way.

1234. Now it must be noted that any

kind of knowing attains its completion as a result of the likeness of the thing known existing in the knowing subject. Therefore, just as the completion of the thing known depends upon this thing having the kind of form which makes it to be such and such a thing, in a similar fashion the completion of the act of knowing depends upon the knowing subject having the likeness of this form. Moreover, just as the thing known is said to be good because it has the form which it ought to have, and evil because it is defective in some way, in a similar fashion the knowledge of the knowing subject is said to be true because this subject possesses a likeness of the thing known, and false because its knowledge falls short of such a likeness. Therefore, just as good and evil designate perfections of things, in a similar way truth and falsity designate perfections of knowledge.

1235. But even though in sensory perception there can be a likeness of the thing known, nevertheless it does not belong to the senses to know the formality of this likeness but only to the intellect. Hence, even though the senses can be true in relation to sensible objects, they still cannot know the truth, but only the intellect can do this. And this is why it is said that truth and falsity are in the mind.

1236. And although the intellect has within itself a likeness of the things known according as it forms concepts of incomplex things, it does not for that reason make a judgment about this likeness. This occurs only when it combines or separates. For when the intellect forms a concept of mortal rational animal, it has within itself a likeness of man; but it does not for that reason know that it has this likeness, since it does not judge that "Man is a mortal rational animal." There is truth and falsity, then, only in this second operation of the intellect, according to which it not only possesses a likeness of the thing known but also reflects on this likeness by knowing it and by making a judgment about it. Hence it is evident from this that truth is not found in things but only in the mind, and that it depends upon combination and separation.

1237. And if a thing is sometimes said to be false, and the same applies to a definition, this will be so in reference to affirmation and negation. For a false thing, as is said at the end of Book V (see n. 1128), means one that does not exist in any way (for example, the commensurability of a diagonal) or one that exists but is naturally disposed to appear otherwise than it is. Similarly a definition is said to be false either because it is not the definition of any existing thing or because it is assigned to something other than that of which it is the definition. For it is evident that falsity is said to be in things or in definitions in all of these ways by reason of a false statement made about them.

1238. The same thing is evident in the case of truth. For a thing is said to be true when it has the proper form which is shown to be present in it; and a definition is said to be true when it really fits the thing to which it is assigned.

1239. It is also evident that nothing prevents truth from being a kind of good insofar as the knowing intellect is taken as a thing. For just as every other thing is said to be good because of its perfection, in a similar fashion the intellect which knows is said to be good because of its truth.

1240. It is also evident from the statements made here that the true and the false, which are objects of knowing, are found in the mind, but that good and evil, which are the objects of appetite, are found in things. And it is also evident that, just as the act of knowing attains its completion as a result of the things known existing in the knowing subject, in a similar fashion every appetite attains its completion as a result of the ordering of the appetitive subject to its appetible objects.

1241. **But since combination** [4].

Here he excludes being in the sense of the true and being in the sense of the accidental from the principal consideration of this science. He says that combination and separation, on which truth and falsity depend, are found in the mind and not in things; and that if any combination is also found in things, such combination produces a unity which the intellect understands as one by a simple concept. But that combination or separation by which the intellect combines or separates its concepts is found only in the intellect and not in things. For it consists in a certain comparison of two concepts, whether these two are identical or distinct in reality. For sometimes the intellect uses one concept as two when it forms a combination, as when we say "Man is man"; and it is clear from this that such a combination is found only in the intellect and not in things. Therefore whatever is a being in the sense of the true, and consists in such a combination, differs from those things which are beings in the proper sense and are realities outside of the mind, each of which is "either what a thing is," i.e., substance, or of what sort, or how much, or any of the simple concepts which the mind combines or separates.

1242. Therefore both being in the sense of the accidental and being in the sense of the true must be excluded from this science. For the cause of the former—being in the sense of the accidental—is the indeterminate, and therefore it does not come within the scope of art, as has been shown (see n. 1174); and the cause of the latter—being in the sense of the true—is "some positive state of mind," i.e., the operation of the intellect combining and separating, and therefore it belongs to that science which studies the intellect.

1243. Another reason for excluding them is that, while "both of these," namely, being in the sense of the true and accidental being, belong to some class of being, they do not belong to being in the proper sense, which is found in reality. Nor do they designate another kind of being distinct from beings in the proper sense. For it is evident that accidental being is a result of the coincidental connection of beings which exist outside the mind, each of which is a being of itself. For even though the grammatical musical has being only accidentally, nevertheless both grammatical and musical are beings in the proper sense, because each of these taken by itself has a definite cause. Similarly the intellect combines and separates those things which are contained in the categories.

1244. If, then, the class of being contained in the categories is sufficiently dealt with, the nature of accidental being and being in the sense of the true will be evident. And for this reason we must exclude these types of being and investigate the causes and principles of beings as beings in the proper sense. This is also evident from what has been established in Book V (n. 885), where, in discussing the different senses of such terms, it was stated that being is used in many senses, as follows below at the beginning of Book VII (n. 1245).

BOOK VII
SUBSTANCE, ESSENCE, AND DEFINITION

LESSON 1
The Primacy of Substance. Its Priority to Accidents

ARISTOTLE'S TEXT Chapters 1 & 2: 1028a10–1028b32

1. *The term being is used in many senses, as we have explained in our discussions on the different meanings of words (435). For in one sense it signifies the whatness of a thing and this particular thing; and in another sense it signifies of what sort a thing is or how much or any one of the other things which are predicated in this way. But of all the senses in which being is used, it is evident that the first of these is the whatness of a thing, which indicates substance.* **1028a10–15**

2. *For when we state of what sort a thing is, we say that it is good or evil, and not that it is three cubits long or a man; but when we state what a thing is, we do not say that it is white or black or three cubits long, but that it is a man or a god. And other things are called beings because they belong to such a being; for some are qualities of it, others quantities, others affections, and so on.* **1028a15–20**

3. *Hence one may even be puzzled whether each of the following terms, namely, to walk, to be healthy and to sit, is a being or a non-being. And it is similar in the case of other things such as these; for no one of them is fitted by nature to exist of itself or is capable of existing apart from substance. But if anything is a being, it is rather the thing that walks and sits and is healthy. Now these appear to be beings to a greater degree because there is some subject which underlies them; and this is substance and the individual, which appears in a definite category; for the term good or sitting is not used without this. Evidently then it is by reason of this that each of the other categories is a being. Hence the first kind of being, and not being of a special sort but being in an unqualified sense, will be substance.* **1028a20–31**

4. *Now there are several senses in which a thing is said to be first; but substance is first in every respect: in definition, in the order of knowing, and in time; for none of the other categories can exist separately, but only substance. And it is first in definition, because in the definition of each thing it is necessary to include the definition of substance. And we think that we know each thing best when we know what it is (for example, what a man is or what fire is) rather than when we know of what sort it is or how much it is or where it is; for we know each of these things only when we know what the quality or quantity is.* **1028a31–1028b2**

5. *And the question which was raised formerly and is raised now and always, and which always causes difficulty, is what being is; and this is the question what substance is. For some say that it is one, and others more than one; and some say that it is limited, and others, unlimited. And for this reason we must investigate chiefly and primarily and solely, as we might say, what this kind of being is.* **1028b2–7**

Chapter 2

6. *Now it seems that substance is found most evidently in bodies. Hence we say that animals and plants and their parts are substances, and also natural bodies, such as fire, water, earth and particular things of this kind, and all things which are either parts of these or composed of these, either of parts or of all, for example, the heaven and its parts, such as the stars, the moon and the sun. But whether these alone are substances, or other things also are, or none of these but certain other things, must be investigated.* **1028b8–15**

7. *Again, it seems to some that the limits of a body, such as surface, line, point and unit, are substances to a greater degree than a body or solid. And some are of the opinion that there is*

nothing of this sort apart from sensible substances, while others think that there are eternal substances which are more numerous and possess being to a greater degree. Thus Plato claimed that there are two kinds of substances: the separate Forms and the objects of mathematics, and a third kind: the substances of sensible bodies. And Speusippus admitted still more kinds of substances, beginning with the unit; and he posited principles for each kind of substance: one for numbers, another for continuous quantities, and still another for the soul; and by proceeding in this way he increases the kinds of substance. And some say that the separate Forms and numbers have the same nature, and that other things, such as lines and surfaces, depend on these; and so on until one comes to the substance of the heavens and sensible bodies. **1028b16–27**

8. Regarding these matters, then, it is necessary to investigate which statements are true and which are not; and what things are substances; and whether there are or are not any substances in addition to sensible ones; and how these exist; and whether there is any separable substance (and if so, why and how), or whether there is no such substance apart from sensible ones. This must be done after we have first described what substance is. **1028b27–32**

COMMENTARY

1245. Having dismissed both accidental being and being which signifies the true from the principal study of this science, here the Philosopher begins to establish the truth about essential being *(ens per se)*, which exists outside the mind and constitutes the principal object of study in this science. This is divided into two parts; for this science discusses both being as being and the first principles of being, as has been stated in Book VI (see n. 1145). Thus in the first part [1] he establishes the truth about being; and in the second, about the first principles of being. He does this in Book XII ("The study").

But since being and unity accompany each other and come within the scope of the same study, as has been stated at the beginning of Book IV (n. 548), the first part is therefore divided into two sections. In the first he establishes the truth about being as being; and in the second, about unity and those attributes which naturally accompany it. He does this in Book X ("It was pointed out").

Now essential being, which exists outside the mind, is divided in two ways, as has been stated in Book V (n. 889); for it is divided, first, into the ten categories, and second, into the potential and the actual. Accordingly, the first part is divided into two sections. In the first he establishes the truth about being as divided into the ten categories; and in the second, about being as divided into the potential and the actual. He does this in Book IX ("We have dealt").

1246. The first part is divided again into two sections. In the first he shows that in order to establish the truth about being as divided into the ten categories, it is necessary to establish the truth about substance; and in the second (Lesson 2), he begins to do this ("The term *substance*").

In regard to the first he does two things. First [1], he shows that it is necessary to settle the issue about substance. Second [6], he indicates the things that have to be discussed about substance ("Now it seems").

In regard to the first he does two things. He shows that one who intends to treat being should investigate substances separately; and he does this, first, by giving an argument; and second [5], by considering what others have been accustomed to do ("And the question").

Hence in the first part his aim is to give the following argument. That which is the first among the kinds of being, since it is being in an unqualified sense and not being with some qualification, clearly indicates the nature of being. But substance is being of this kind. Therefore to know the nature of being it suffices to establish the truth about substance.

In regard to the first he does two things. First, he shows that substance is the first kind of being; and second [4], he shows in what way it is said to be first ("Now there are several"). In regard to the first he does two things.

1247. First [1], he explains his thesis. He says that the term *being* is used in many senses (as has been stated in Book V [n. 885] where he distinguished the different senses in which terms of this kind are used); for in one sense being signifies the whatness of a thing and this particular thing, i.e., substance, inasmuch as by "the whatness of a thing" is meant the essence of a substance, and by "this particular thing," an individual substance; and the different senses of substance are reduced to these two, as has been stated in Book V (n. 898). And in another sense it signifies quality or quantity or any one of the other categories. And since being is used in many senses, it is evident that being in the primary sense is the whatness of a thing, i.e., the being which signifies substance.

1248. **For when we state** [2].

Second, he proves his thesis by using the following argument: in every class of things that which exists of itself and is a being in an unqualified sense is prior to that which exists by reason of something else and is a being in a qualified sense. But substance is a being in an unqualified sense and exists of itself, whereas all classes of beings other than substance are beings in a qualified sense and exist by reason of substance. Therefore substance is the primary kind of being.

1249. He makes the minor premise clear in two ways. He does this, first, by considering the way in which we speak or make predications. He says that it is evident from this that substance is the primary kind of being, because when we state of what sort a thing is we say that it is either good or evil; for this signifies quality, which differs from substance and quantity. Now three cubits long signifies quantity and man signifies substance. Therefore when we state of what sort a thing is, we do not say that it is three cubits long or a man. And when we state what a thing is, we do not say that it is white or hot, which signify quality, or three cubits long, which signifies quantity, but we say that it is a man or a god, which signifies substance.

1250. From this it is clear that terms signifying substance express what a thing is in an unqualified sense, whereas those signifying quality do not express what a thing is in an unqualified sense, but what sort of thing it is. The same is true of quantity and the other genera.

1251. From this it is clear that substance itself is said to be a being of itself, because terms which simply signify substance designate what this thing is. But other classes of things are said to be beings, not because they have a quiddity of themselves (as though they were beings of themselves, since they do not express what a thing is in an unqualified sense), but because "they belong to such a being," i.e., because they have some connection with substance, which is a being of itself. For they do not signify quiddity, since some of them are clearly qualities of such a being, i.e., of substance, other quantities, other affections, or something of the sort signified by the other genera.

1252. **Hence one may** [3].

Second he proves the same point by means of an example. The other kinds of beings are beings only inasmuch as they are related to substance. Therefore, since other beings when signified in the abstract do not designate any connection with substance, the question can arise whether they are beings or non-beings, for example, whether to walk, to be healthy, and to sit, and any one of these things which are signified in the abstract, is a being or a non-being. And it is similar in the case of other things such as these, which are signified in the abstract, whether they designate some activity, as the foregoing do, or whether they do not, as is the case with whiteness and blackness.

1253. Now accidents signified in the abstract seem to be non-beings, because no one of them is fitted by nature to exist of itself. In fact the being of each of them consists in their existing in something else, and no one of them is capable of existing apart from substance. Therefore when they are signified in the abstract as though they were beings of themselves and separate from substance, they seem to be non-beings. The reason is that words do not signify things directly according to the mode of being which they have in reality, but indirectly according to the mode in which we understand them; for concepts are the likenesses of things, and words the likenesses of concepts, as is stated in Book I of the *Perihermenias.* [16a4]

1254. Moreover, even though the mode of being which accidents have is not one whereby they may exist of themselves but only in something else, still the intellect can understand them as though they existed of themselves; for it is capable by nature of separating things which are united in reality. Hence abstract names of accidents signify beings which inhere in something else, although they do not signify them as inhering. And non-beings would be signified by names of this kind, granted that they would not inhere in something else.

1255. Further, since these accidents signified in the abstract appear to be non-beings, it seems rather to be the concrete names of accidents that signify beings. And "if anything is a being," it seems rather to be "the thing that walks and sits and is healthy," because some subject is determined by them by reason of the very meaning of the term, inasmuch as they designate something connected with a subject. Now this subject is substance. Therefore every term of this kind which signifies an accident in the concrete "appears in a definite category," i.e., it seems to involve the category of substance, not in such a way that the category of substance is a part of the meaning of such terms (for white in the categorical sense indicates quality alone), but so that terms of this sort signify accidents as inhering in a substance. And we do not use the terms "good or sitting without this," i.e., without substance; for an accident signifies something connected with substance.

1256. Again, since accidents do not seem to be beings insofar as they are signified in themselves, but only insofar as they are signified in connection with substance, evidently it is by reason of this that each of the other beings is a being. And from this it also appears that substance is "the first kind of being and being in an unqualified sense and not being of a special sort," i.e., with some qualification, as is the case with accidents; for to be white is not to be in an unqualified sense but with some qualification. This is clear from the fact that when a thing begins to be white we do not say that it begins to be in an unqualified sense, but that it begins to be *white*. For when Socrates begins to be a man, he is said to begin to be in an unqualified sense. Hence it is obvious that being a man signifies being in an unqualified sense, but that being white signifies being with some qualification.

1257. **Now there are several** [4].

Here he shows in what respect substance is said to be first. He says that, since the term *first* is used in several senses, as has been explained in Book V (n. 936), then substance is the first of all beings in three respects: in the order of knowing, in definition, and in time. He proves that it is first in time by this argument: none of the other categories is capable of existing apart from substance, but substance alone is capable of existing apart from the others; for no accident is found without a substance, but some substance is found without an accident. Thus it is clear that an accident does not exist whenever a substance does, but the reverse is true; and for this reason substance is prior in time.

1258. It is also evident that it is first in definition, because in the definition of any accident it is necessary to include the definition of substance; for just as nose is given in the definition of snub, so too the proper subject of any accident is given in the definition of that accident. Hence just as animal is prior to man in definition, because the definition of animal is given in that of man, in a similar fashion substance is prior to accidents in definition.

1259. It is evident too that substance is first in the order of knowing, for that is first in the order of knowing which is better known and explains a thing better. Now each thing is better known when its substance is known rather than when its quality or quantity is known; for we think we know each thing best when we know what man is or what fire is, rather than when we know of what sort it is or how much it is or where it is or when we know it according to any of the other categories. For this reason too we think that we know each of the things contained in the categories of accidents when we know what each is; for example, when we know what being this sort of thing is, we know quality; and when we know what being how much is, we know quantity. For just as the other categories have being only insofar as they inhere in a substance, in a similar way they can be known only insofar as they share to some extent in the mode according to which substance is known, and this is to know the whatness of a thing.

1260. **And the question** [5].

Here he proves the same point, namely, that it is necessary to treat substance separately, by considering what other philosophers have been accustomed to do. He says that when one raises the question what being is (and this is a question which has always caused difficulty for philosophers both "formerly," i.e., in the past, and "now," i.e., in the present), this is nothing else than the question or problem what the substance of things is.

1261. For some men, such as Parmenides (see n. 138) and Melissus (n. 140), said that "this being," i.e., substance, is one and immobile, whereas others, such as the ancient philosophers of nature, who maintained (n. 145) that there is only one material principle of things, said that it is mobile. And they thought that matter alone is being and substance. Hence when they claimed that there is one being because there is one material principle, they obviously understood by one being, one substance. Other men maintained that there are more beings than one, namely, those who posited (n. 145) many material principles, and, consequently, many substances of things. And some of this group held that these principles are limited in number, for example, Empedocles, who posited (n. 148) four elements; and others held that they are unlimited in number, for example, Anaxagoras, who posited (n. 90) an unlimited number of like parts, and Democritus, who posited (n. 113) an unlimited number of indivisible bodies.

1262. If, then, the other philosophers in treating of beings paid attention to substances alone, we too should investigate "what this kind of being is," i.e., what substance itself is. And this we must do, I say, chiefly, because this is our principal aim; and primarily, because by means of it the other kinds of being are known; and solely, as we might say, because by establishing what is true about substance by itself, one acquires a knowledge of all the other kinds of being. Thus in one sense he deals with substance separately, and in another sense not. He indicates this when he says "as we might say" or inasmuch as we might speak in this way, as we are accustomed to say of things which are not true in every respect.

1263. **Now it seems** [6].

Here he indicates the things that have to be discussed about substance; and in regard to this he does two things. First [6], he gives the opinions that other men have held about substance. Second [8], he states that it is necessary to determine which of their opinions are true ("Regarding these matters").

In regard to the first he does two things. First [6], he indicates the things that are evident about substance. He says that substantial being is found most obviously in bodies. Thus we say that animals and plants and their parts are substances, and also natural bodies such as fire, earth, water, "and particular things of this kind," i.e., such elemental bodies as earth and fire, according to the opinion of Heraclitus (n. 87), and other intermediate entities, according to the opinions of others. We also say that all parts of the elements are substances, as well as the bodies composed of the elements, whether of some of the elements, as particular compounds, or "of all the elements," i.e., the whole of the various elements, as this whole sphere of active and passive beings; and as we also say that "a heaven," which is a natural body distinct from the elements, is a substance, and also its parts, such as the stars, the moon and the sun.

1264. But whether these sensible substances are the only substances, as the ancient philosophers of nature claimed, or whether there are also some substances which differ from these, as the Platonists claimed, or whether these too are not substances but only certain things which differ from these, must be investigated.

1265. **Again, it seems** [7].

Second, he describes the philosophers' opinions about those substances which are not evident. He says that it seems to some philosophers that the limits of bodies are the substances of things, i.e., that surface, line, point and unit are substances to a greater degree than a body or solid. And those who held this opinion differed in their views; because some, the Pythagoreans, thought that no limits of this kind are separate from sensible bodies, while others thought that there are certain eternal beings which are separate from and more numerous than sensible things and have being to a greater degree. I say "have being to a greater degree," because they are incorruptible and immobile, whereas sensible bodies are corruptible and mobile; and "more numerous," because while sensible bodies belong only to one order, these separate beings belong to two, inasmuch as "Plato claimed that there are two kinds of separate substances," or two orders of separate substances, namely, the separate Forms or Ideas and the objects of mathematics; and he also posited a third order—the substances of sensible bodies.

1266. But Speusippus, who was Plato's nephew and his successor, posited many orders of substances, and in each order he also began with the unit, which he posited as the principle in each order of substance. But he posited one kind of unit as the principle of numbers, which he claimed to be the first substances after the Forms, and another as the principle of continuous quantities, which he claimed to be second substances; and finally he posited the substance of the soul. Hence by proceeding in this way he extended the order of substances right down to corruptible bodies.

1267. But some thinkers differed from Plato and Speusippus, because they did not distinguish between the Forms and the first order of mathematical objects, which is that of numbers. For they said that the Forms and numbers have the same nature, and that "all other things depend on these," i.e., are related successively to numbers, namely, lines and surfaces, right down to the first substance of the heavens and the other sensible bodies which belong to this last order.

1268. **Regarding these matters** [8].

Here he explains what should be said about the foregoing opinions. He says that it is necessary to determine which of the above opinions are true and which are not; and what things are substances; and whether the objects of mathematics and the separate Forms are substances in addition to sensible ones, or not; and if they are substances, what mode of being they have; and if they are not substances in addition to sensible ones, whether there is any other separate substance, and [if so], why and how; or whether there is no substance in addition to sensible substances.

1269. For he will settle this issue below and in Book XII (1055:C 2488) of this work. Yet before this is done it is first necessary to posit and explain what it is that constitutes the substance of these sensible bodies in which substance is clearly found. He does this in the present book (see n. 1270) and in Book VIII (see n. 1687), which follows.

LESSON 2

Substance as Form, as Matter, and as Body. The Priority of Form. The Procedure in the Investigation of Substance

ARISTOTLE'S TEXT Chapters 3 & 4: 1028b33–1029b12

1. The term substance is used chiefly of four things, if not of more; for the essence (or quiddity) and the universal and the genus seem to be the substance of each thing, and fourthly the subject. Now the subject is that of which the others are predicated, while it itself is not predicated of anything else. And for this reason it is first necessary to establish the truth about this, because this first subject seems in the truest sense to be substance. **1028b33–1029a2**

2. Now in one sense matter is said to be the subject, and in another, the form, and in still another, the thing composed of these. By matter I mean the bronze, and by form the specifying figure, and by the thing composed of these the whole statue. **1029a2–5**

3. If, then, the specifying principle is prior to the matter and is being to a greater degree, for the same reason it will also be prior to the thing composed of these. We have now sketched what substance is, namely, that it is not what is predicated of a subject, but that of which all other things are predicated. However, it must not be considered merely in this way; for this is not enough, since this is evident. **1029a5–10**

4. And from this point of view matter is substance; for if it is not, it eludes us to say what else is. For when everything else is taken away, nothing but matter appears to remain, because the other things are affections, activities and potencies of bodies. And length, width and depth are quantities and not substances; for quantity is not substance, but substance is rather the first thing to which these belong. But when length, width and depth are taken away, we see that nothing remains unless there is something which is limited by them. Hence to those who consider the situation in this way, matter alone must seem to be substance. **1029a10–19**

5. And by matter I mean that which in itself is neither a quiddity nor a quantity nor anything expressed by any of the other categories by which being is made determinate. For there is something of which each of these is predicated, whose being is different from that of each of the other categories, because the others are predicated of substance, but this is predicated of matter. Therefore the ultimate subject is in itself neither a quiddity nor a quantity nor anything else. Nor again is it the negations of these, for they too will be accidental to it. Therefore for those who ponder the question it follows from these arguments that matter is substance. **1029a20–27**

6. But this is impossible; for to exist separately and to be a particular thing seem to belong chiefly to substance; and for this reason it would seem that the specifying principle and the thing composed of both the specifying principle and matter are substance to a greater degree than matter. **1029a27–30**

7. Yet that substance which is now composed of both (I mean of form and matter) must be dismissed; for it is subsequent and open to view. And matter too is in a sense evident. But it is necessary to investigate the third kind of substance, for this is the most perplexing. **1029a30–33**

8. Now some admit that among sensible things there are substances, and therefore these must be investigated first. **1029a33–34**

Chapter 4

9. Since we have established at the very beginning (568) the different senses into which we have divided the term substance, and that one of these seems to be the essence of a thing, this must be investigated. **1029b11–13**

10. For this is a preparatory task in order that one may pass to what is more knowable, because learning is acquired by all in this way, by proceeding from things which are less knowable by nature to those which are more knowable. And just as in practical matters one's task is to proceed from things which are good for each individual to those which are totally good and good for each, in a similar fashion our task now is to proceed from things which are more knowable to us to those which are more knowable by nature. But what is knowable and first to individual men is often only slightly knowable and has little or nothing of being. Yet starting from what is only slightly knowable but knowable to oneself, we must try to acquire knowledge of things which are wholly knowable, by proceeding, as has been said, by way of the very things which are knowable to us. **1029b1–12**

COMMENTARY

1270. Having shown that the chief aim of this science is to study substance, he now begins to establish the truth about substance. This part is divided into two members. In the first [1] he explains the method and order to be followed in treating of substance. In the second (Lesson 3), he goes ahead with his treatment of substance ("And first let us make").

He explains the method and order to be followed in treating of substance by distinguishing its different senses; and by explaining which of these senses must be dealt with primarily and principally, which of them must be omitted, and which must be considered to be prior or subsequent. Hence the first part is divided into three members, according to the divisions and subdivisions of substance which he gives. This second part [2] begins where he says, "Now in one sense." The third [8] begins where he says, "Now some."

Accordingly he says, first [1], that the term *substance* is used at least of four things, if not "of more," i.e., in more senses. For there are several senses in which some speak of substance, as is clear in the case of those who said that the limits of bodies are substances, which sense he dismisses here. Now the first of these senses is that in which a thing's essence, i.e., its quiddity, essential structure, or nature, is called its substance.

1271. The second sense is that in which "the universal" is called the substance of a thing, according to the opinion of those who maintain that the Ideas are separate Forms, which are the universals predicated of particular things and the substances of these particular things.

1272. The third sense is that in which "the first genus seems to be the substance of each thing"; and in this sense they claim that unity and being are the substances of all things and their first genera.

1273. The fourth sense is that in which "the subject," i.e., a particular substance, is called a substance. Now a subject means that of which other things are predicated, either as superiors are predicated of inferiors, for example, genera, species and differences; or as common and proper accidents are predicated of a subject, for example, as man, animal, rational, capable of laughter and white are predicated of Socrates. However, a subject is not itself predicated of anything else, and this must be understood essentially. For nothing prevents Socrates from being predicated accidentally of this white thing or of animal or of man, because Socrates is the thing of which white or animal or man is an accident. For it is evident that the subject which is spoken of here is what is called first substance in the *Categories,* [2a10] for the definition of subject given here and that of first substance given there are the same.

1274. Hence he concludes that it is necessary to establish the truth "about this," i.e., about this subject or first substance, because such a subject seems in the truest sense to be substance. Therefore in the *Categories* [*ibid.*] it is said that such substance is said to be substance properly, principally and chiefly. For substances of this kind are by their very nature the subjects of all other things, namely, of species, genera and accidents; whereas second substance, i.e., genera and species, are the subjects of accidents alone. And they also have this nature only by reason of these first substances; for man is white inasmuch as *this* man is white.

1275. Hence it is evident that the division of substance given here is almost the same as that given in the *Categories,* for by subject here is understood first substance. And what he called the genus and the universal, which seem to pertain to genus and species, are contained under second substances. However, the essence, which is given here, is omitted in that work, because it belongs in the predicamental order only as a principle; for it is neither a genus nor a species nor an individual thing, but is the formal principle of all these things.

1276. **Now in one sense** [2].

Here he subdivides the fourth sense of substance given in his original division, i.e., substance in the sense of a subject; and in regard to this he does three things. First, he gives this subdivision. Second [3] he compares the parts of this subdivision with each other ("If, then"). Third [7], he shows how the parts of this division must be treated ("Yet that substance").

Accordingly he says, first [2], that a subject in the sense of a first or particular substance is divided into three parts, i.e., into matter, form, and the thing composed of these. This division is not one of genus into species, but of an analogous predicate, which is predicated in a primary and in a derivative sense of those things which are contained under it. For both the composite and the matter and the form are called particular substances, but not in the same order; and therefore later on [6] he inquires which of these has priority as substance.

1277. To clarify this part of his division he draws an example from the field of artifacts, saying that bronze is as matter, the figure as "the specifying form," i.e., the principle which gives a thing its species, and the statue as the thing composed of these. This example must not be understood to express the situation as it really is but only according to a proportional likeness; for figure and other forms produced by art are not substances but accidents. But since figure is related to bronze in the realm of artifacts as substantial form is to matter in the realm of natural bodies, he uses this example insofar as it explains what is unknown by means of what is evident.

1278. **If, then** [3].

Here he compares the parts of the foregoing division with each other; and in regard to this he does three things. First [3], he explains that the form is substance to a greater degree than the composite. Second [4], he explains that some men were of the opinion that matter constitutes substance in the truest sense ("And from this"). Third [6], he shows that the form and the composite are substance to a greater degree than matter ("But this is impossible").

He accordingly says, first [3], "that the specifying principle," i.e., the form, is prior to matter. For matter is a potential being, and the specifying principle is its actuality; and actuality is prior to potentiality in nature. And absolutely speaking it is prior in time, because the potential is brought to actuality only by means of something actual; although in one and the same subject which is at one time potential and at another actual, potentiality is prior to actuality in time. Hence it is clear that form is prior to matter, and that it is also a being to a greater degree than matter; because that by reason of which anything is such, is more so. But matter becomes an actual being only by means of form. Hence form must be being to a greater degree than matter.

1279. And from this it again follows for the same reason that form is prior to the thing composed of both, inasmuch as there is something having the nature of matter in the composite. Thus the composite shares in something which is secondary in nature, i.e., in matter. And it is also clear that matter and form are principles of the composite. Now the principles of a thing are prior to that thing. Therefore, if form is prior to matter, it will be prior to the composite.

1280. And since it might seem to someone, from the fact that the Philosopher gives all the senses in which the term *substance* is used, that this suffices for a knowledge of what substance is, he therefore adds that "we have now merely sketched" what substance is; i.e., stated only in a universal way that substance is not what is predicated of a subject, but that of which other things are predicated. But one must not merely understand substance and other things in this way, namely, by means of a universal and logical definition; for this is not a sufficient basis for knowing the nature of a thing, because the very formula which is given for such a definition is evident. For the principles of a thing, on which the knowledge of a thing depends, are not mentioned in a definition of this kind, but only some common condition of a thing by means of which such acquaintance is imparted.

1281. **And from this point** [4].

He examines the view that matter is in the truest sense substance; and in regard to this he does two things. First [4], he gives the argument by which the ancient philosophers maintained that matter most truly and solely is substance. Second [5], he explains what matter is ("And by matter").

Hence he says, first, that not only the form and the composite are substance but so also is matter, according to the argument mentioned above; for if matter itself is not substance, it eludes us to say what other thing besides matter is substance. For if the other attributes, which clearly are not substance, are taken away from sensible bodies, in which substance is clearly apparent, it seems that the only thing which remains is matter.

1282. For in these sensible bodies, which all men admit to be substances, there are certain attributes such as the affections of bodies, for example, hot and cold and the like, which are evidently not substances. And in these bodies there are also "certain activities," i.e., processes of generation and corruption and motions, which are clearly not substances. And in them there are also potencies, which are the principles of these activities and motions, i.e., potencies of acting and being acted upon, which are present in things; and it is also clear that these are not substances, but that they rather belong to the genus of quality.

1283. And, after all of these, we find

dimensions in sensible bodies, namely, length, width and depth, which are quantities and not substances. For it is evident that quantity is not substance, but that substance is that to which the foregoing dimensions belong as their first subject. But when these dimensions are taken away, nothing seems to remain except their subject, which is limited and differentiated by dimensions of this kind. And this subject is matter; for dimensive quantity seems to belong immediately to matter, since matter is divided in such a way as to receive different forms in its different parts only by means of this kind of quantity. Therefore, from a consideration of this kind it seems to follow not only that matter is substance, but that it alone is substance.

1284. Now it was their ignorance of substantial form that misled the ancient philosophers into giving this argument; for as yet they had not progressed in knowledge to the point where their mind might be elevated to something over and above sensible bodies. Hence they considered only those forms which are proper or common sensibles; and it is clear that such attributes as white and black, great and small, and the like, are accidents of this kind. But a substantial form is perceptible only indirectly, and therefore they did not acquire a knowledge of it so that they might know how to distinguish it from matter. In fact they said that the whole subject, which we maintain is composed of matter and form, is first matter, for example, air or water or something of the kind. And they called those things forms which we call accidents, for example, quantities and qualities, whose proper subject is not first matter but the composite substance, which is an actual substance; for it is by reason of this that every accident is something inhering in a substance, as has been explained (nn. 1254–56).

1285. **And by matter I mean** [5].

Now since the foregoing argument which shows that matter alone is substance seems to have come from their ignorance of matter, as has been pointed out, he therefore next states what matter really is, as is made clear in Book I of the *Physics*. [192a30] For matter can be adequately known by itself only by means of motion, and the study of it seems to belong chiefly to the philosophy of nature. Hence the Philosopher also accepts here the characteristics of matter investigated in his physical treatises, saying that "by matter I mean that which in itself," i.e., considered essentially, "is neither a quiddity," i.e., a substance, "nor a quantity nor any of the other categories into which being is divided or by which it is made determinate."

1286. This is especially evident in the case of motion; for, properly speaking, the subject of change and motion must differ from each of the limits of motion, as is proved in Book I of the *Physics*. [190b34] Now matter is the first subject which underlies not only those motions which are qualitative and quantitative, and those which pertain to the other accidents, but also those which are substantial. Hence it must differ essentially from all substantial forms and their privations, which are the limits of generation and corruption, and not just quantitatively or qualitatively or according to the other accidents.

1287. Yet the Philosopher does not use motion to prove that matter differs from all forms (for this proof belongs to the philosophy of nature); but he uses the method of predication, which is proper to dialectics and is closely allied with this science, as he says in Book IV (n. 574). Hence he says that there must be some subject of which all terms are predicated, yet in such a way that the being of that subject of which they are predicated differs from the being of each of the things which "are predicated of it"; i.e., they have a different quiddity or essence.

1288. Now it must be noted that what has been said here cannot be understood to apply to univocal predication, according to which genera are predicated of the species in whose definitions they are given, because man and animal do not differ essentially; but this must be understood to apply to denominative predication, as when white is predicated of man, for the quiddity of white differs from that of man. Hence he adds that the other genera are predicated of substance in this way, i.e., denominatively, and that substance is predicated of matter denominatively.

1289. It must not be understood, then, that actual substance (of which we are speaking here) is predicated of matter univocally or essentially; for he had already said above that matter is neither a quiddity nor any of the other categories. But it must be understood to be predicated denominatively, in the way in which accidents are predicated of substance. For just as the proposition "Man is white" is true, and the proposition "Man is whiteness" or "Humanity is whiteness" is not, in a similar way the proposition "This material thing is a man" is true, and the proposition "Matter is man" or "Matter is humanity" is not. Concretive or denominative predication, then, shows that, just as substance differs essentially from accidents, in a similar fashion matter differs essentially from substantial forms. Hence it follows that the ultimate subject, properly speaking, "is neither a quiddity," i.e., a substance, nor a quantity nor any of the other things contained in any genus of beings.

1290. Neither can negations themselves be predicated essentially of matter. For just as forms are something distinct from the essence of matter, and thus in a certain measure are related to it accidentally, in a similar way the different negations of forms, which are themselves privations, also belong to matter accidentally. For if they should belong essentially to matter, forms could never be received in matter without destroying it. The Philosopher says this in order to reject the opinion of Plato, who did not distinguish between privation and matter, as is said in Book I of the *Physics*. [192a3] Last, he concludes that for those who ponder the question according to the foregoing arguments it follows that matter alone is substance, as the preceding argument also concluded.

1291. **But this is impossible** [6].

He now proves the contrary of this conclusion, saying that matter alone cannot be substance or substance in the highest degree. For there are two characteristics which seem to belong most properly to substance. The first is that it is capable of separate existence, for an accident is not separated from a substance, but a substance can be separated from an accident. The second is that substance is a determinate particular thing, for the other genera do not signify a particular thing.

1292. Now these two characteristics—being separable and being a particular thing—do not fit matter; for matter cannot exist by itself without a form by means of which it is an actual being, since of itself it is only potential. And it is a particular thing only by means of a form through which it becomes actual. Hence being a particular thing belongs chiefly to the composite.

1293. It is clear, then, "that the specifying principle," i.e., the form, and "the thing composed of both," namely, of matter and form, seem to be substance to a greater degree than matter, because the composite is both separable and a particular thing. But even though form is not separable and a particular thing, it nevertheless becomes an actual being by means of the composite itself; and therefore in this way it can be both separable and a particular thing.

1294. **Yet that substance** [7].

He shows how one must proceed to deal with the parts of this division of substance which has been followed, i.e., the division of substance into matter, form and composite. He says that even though both the form and the composite are substance to a greater degree than matter, still it is now necessary to dismiss the kind of substance which "is composed of both," i.e., of matter and form; and there are two reasons for doing this.

1295. One reason is that it is subsequent to both in nature, namely, to matter and form, just as the composite is subsequent to the simple elements of which it is composed. Hence a knowledge of matter and form precedes a knowledge of the composite substance.

1296. The other reason is that this kind of substance "is open to view," i.e., evident, since it is the object of sensory perception; and therefore it is not necessary to dwell on the knowledge of it. And even though matter is not subsequent but is in a sense prior, still in a sense it is evident. Hence he says "in a sense," because it does not of itself have any traits by which it may be known, since the principle of knowing is form. But it is known by means of an analogy; for just as sensible substances of this kind are related to artificial forms, as wood is related to the form of a bench, so also is first matter related to sensible forms. Hence it is said in the *Physics*, Book I, [191a9] that first matter is known by an analogy. It follows, then, that we must investigate the third kind of substance, namely, form, because this is the most perplexing.

1297. **Now some admit** [8].

Here he explains the method and order and way in which the parts of the third division of substance must be dealt with, in which substance is distinguished into those which are sensible and those which are not. In regard to this he does three things.

1298. First, he shows what has to be done at the very beginning with regard to sensible substances, because sensible substances of this kind are admitted by all; for all admit that some sensible things are substances. But not all admit that there are substances which are not sensible. Hence it is first necessary to consider sensible substances as better known.

1299. **Since we have established** [9].

Second, he shows what has to be established about sensible substances. He says that since substance has been divided above according to the different senses in which the term is used, of which one is the essence of a thing, i.e., its quiddity or essential structure, it is therefore first necessary to investigate this by showing what it is that constitutes the quiddities of sensible substances.

1300. **For this is** [10].

Third, he gives the reason for the

order of treatment mentioned above. He says that we must speak first of the essences of sensible substances, because this is "a preparatory task," i.e., a work preparatory to and necessary for our undertaking, inasmuch as we pass from sensible substances, which are more evident to us, to what "is more knowable in an unqualified sense and by nature," i.e., to intelligible substances, in which we are chiefly interested. For knowledge is acquired in all matters, or by all men, by proceeding from those things which are less knowable by nature to those which are more knowable by nature.

1301. For since all learning proceeds from those things which are more knowable to the learner, who must have some prior knowledge in order to learn, we must proceed to learn by passing from those things which are more knowable to us, which are often less knowable by nature, to those which are more knowable by nature but less knowable to us.

1302. For with regard to the knowledge of those things which begins from the senses, it is those things which are closer to the senses that are more knowable. But those things are more knowable by nature which by reason of their own nature are capable of being known. Now these are the things which are more actual and are beings to a greater degree. And these lie outside the scope of sensation. But sensible forms are forms in matter.

1303. In matters of learning, then, it is necessary to proceed from things which are less knowable by nature to those which are more knowable. "And one's task is" the same here, i.e., it is necessary to act in the same way here, "as in practical matters," i.e., in the arts and active potencies, in which we go "from things which are good for each individual," i.e., from things which are good for this person and for that person, so as to reach those things which "are" totally good, or universally good, and therefore good for each individual. For the military art attains the victory of the whole army, which is a certain common good, from the victories of this and of that particular man. And similarly the art of building by combining particular stones succeeds in constructing a whole house. And so too in speculative matters we must proceed from those things which are more knowable to oneself, namely, to the one learning, in order to reach those which are knowable by nature, which also finally become known to the one learning.

1304. Now this does not occur because the things which are more knowable to this person or to that person are more knowable in an unqualified sense; for those things which are "knowable to individual men," i.e., to this or to that particular man, and are first in the process of knowing, are often only slightly knowable by nature. This happens because they have little or nothing of being; for a thing is knowable to the extent that it has being. For example, it is evident that accidents, motions and privations have little or nothing of being, yet they are more knowable to us than the substances of things; for they are closer to the senses, since of themselves they fall under sensory perception as proper or common sensibles. But substantial forms do so only accidentally.

1305. And he says "often" because sometimes the same things are more knowable both to us and by nature, for example, the objects of mathematics, which abstract from sensible matter.

Hence in such cases one always proceeds from things which are more knowable by nature, because the same things are more knowable to us. And while those things which are more knowable to us are only slightly knowable by nature, still from things of the kind which are only slightly knowable by nature (although they are more knowable to the one learning), one must attempt to know the things which are "wholly," i.e., universally and perfectly, knowable, by advancing to a knowledge of such things by way of those which are only slightly knowable by nature, as has already been explained.

LESSON 3
What Essence is. The Things to Which It Belongs

ARISTOTLE'S TEXT Chapter 4: 1029b13–1030a17

1. *And first let us make some dialectical comments about the essence of a thing, because the essence of each thing is what each is said to be essentially (per se). For being you is not being musical, because you are not musical essentially. Therefore your essence is what you are said to be essentially.* **1029b13–16**

2. *But not even all of this is the essence of a thing; for the essence of a thing is not what is predicated of it essentially in the way that white is predicated of surface, because being a surface is not being white. Nor is the essence of a thing the composite of the two, namely, being a white surface. Why? Because white inheres in surface. Therefore the concept (or formula) which expresses what each thing is but does not contain the thing itself is the concept of its essence. Hence, if being a white surface is always being a smooth surface, then being white and being smooth will be one and the same thing.* **1029b16–22**

3. *Now since there are also composites in the case of the other categories, for there is some subject of each, for example, of quantity, quality, when, where and motion, it is therefore necessary to inquire whether there is a concept of the essence of each one of them, and whether this essence is found in them, for example, whether the essence of white man is found in white man. Now let the name of this composite be garment. What is the essence of garment?* **1029b22–28**

4. *But neither is this one of those terms which are predicated essentially. Now there are two ways in which a term can be predicated in a non-essential way of a subject: one of these is by addition, and the other is not. For in one case the term is predicated of the thing defined because the term is added to something else. For example, if in defining white one might give the concept of white man. And in the other case it is so predicated because some other term is added to the subject; for example, if the word garment were to signify white man, and someone were to define a garment as white, then a white man would be something white, yet his essence does not consist in being white, but in being a garment. Therefore the essence is what a thing of a definite sort is, whether it expresses that thing wholly or not. Now a thing's essence is what a thing is. But when something is predicated of another this is not some definite thing; for example, white man is not really a definite thing, i.e., if being a definite thing belongs to substances alone. Hence essence belongs to those things whose concept is a definition. Now there is not a definition if the name signifies the same thing as the concept; for then all concepts would be limiting terms, because the name of any concept would be the same. Hence even the Iliad will be a definition. But there is a definition if the concept is of some primary thing. And such things are those which are predicated without predicating something else of the subject. Thus essence will not be found in any of those things which are not species of a genus, but in these alone; for it seems that these things are not predicated according to participation and affection, or as an accident. But of each of the other things, if it has a name, there will be a concept of what it means, namely, that this accident inheres in this subject; or in place of a simple term one will be able to give a more definite one; but there will be no definition or essence.* **1029b28–1030a17**

COMMENTARY

1306. Having settled the issue about the order to be followed in treating of substances, the Philosopher now begins to settle the issue about sensible substances, as he had said he would; and this is divided into two parts. In the first part [1] he settles the issue about the essence of sensible substances, by using dialectical and common arguments; and in the second, by considering the principles of sensible substances. He does this in Book VIII ("It is necessary, then").

The first part is divided into two members. In the first he indicates the kind of essence which sensible substances have. In the second (Lesson 17) he shows that this kind of essence has the role of a principle and cause ("But let us state").

The first part is divided into two. In the first he settles the issue about the essences of sensible substances. In the second (Lesson 13) he shows that universals are not the substances of sensible things, as some said ("But since our investigation").

1307. The first part is divided into two. In the first he shows what kind of substances sensible things have. In the second (Lesson 9) he shows what parts constitute their substance ("But since the definition").

The first part is divided into two. In the first he investigates the kind of essence which sensible substances have. In the second (Lesson 6) he inquires into the causes of their generation ("Now of those things").

The first part is divided into two. In the first he shows what constitutes the essence of sensible substances; and in the second (Lesson 5) he shows how essence is related to sensible substances, i.e., whether it is the same as these substances or different ("Moreover, it is necessary").

The first part is divided into two. In the first he shows what essence is. In the second [3] he indicates to what things it belongs ("Now since there are").

In regard to the first he does two things. First [1], he dismisses from the essence of a thing any term that is predicated accidentally; and second [2], any term that is predicated essentially *(per se)* in the way that properties are predicated of a subject ("But not even all").

1308. He says, first [1], then, that it is first necessary to speak of sensible substances and to show what their essence is. Therefore, let us first make some dialectical comments about the essence of a thing; for this science has a connection with dialectics, as was stated above (n. 574), because both are universal. Hence the dialectical method is proper to this science, and it is fitting that it should begin with the dialectical method. But he says that he is going to treat of essence in a way that is chiefly dialectical inasmuch as [in so doing] he investigates what essence is from the manner of predicating terms of a subject; for this belongs properly to dialectics.

1309. Regarding essence it should first of all be borne in mind that it must be predicated of a thing essentially; for those things which are predicated of a thing accidentally do not belong to its essence. For by the essence of a thing we mean the proper answer which can be given to the question asking what it is. And when we ask what a thing is we cannot give a proper answer by mentioning attributes which belong to it accidentally; for when someone asks what man is, one cannot answer that he is white or sitting or musical. Hence none of those attributes which are predicated of a thing accidentally belong to its essence; for being you is not being musical.

1310. Now throughout the whole of the following discussion it must be noted that by the phrase *to be this* or *being this* he understands the essence of a thing; for example, by *to be man* or *being man* he understands what pertains to the essence of man. Now the whatness of "being musical," i.e., the very essence of musical, has nothing to do with your whatness. For if one were to ask what you are, one could not answer that you are musical. Hence it follows that being you is not being musical, because those things which pertain to the quiddity of music are extrinsic to your quiddity, although musical may be predicated of you. And this is so because "you are not musical essentially," since musical is not predicated of you essentially but accidentally. Therefore what you are "essentially" pertains to your whatness, because it is predicated of you essentially and not accidentally; for example, man, animal, substance, rational, sensible, and other attributes of this kind, all of which belong to your whatness, are predicated of you essentially.

1311. **But not even** [2].

He excludes from the quiddity of a thing any attribute that is predicated essentially as properties are predicated of subjects. He says that not even everything that is predicated essentially of a thing belongs to its essence. For a property is predicated essentially of its proper subject as color is predicated of surface. Yet the essence of a thing is not something that is found in a thing essentially in the way that white is found in surface; because "being a surface" is not "being white"; i.e., the quiddity of surface is not that of whiteness; for the quiddity of surface differs from that of whiteness.

1312. And not only is being white not the quiddity of surface, but neither is the combination of the two, namely of surface and whiteness, i.e., to be a white surface, or being a white surface. For the quiddity or essence of white surface is not the quiddity or essence of surface. And if we were asked why, we could answer, "Because white inheres in surface," i.e., because when I say "white surface" I mean something which adheres to surface as extrinsic to its essence and not as intrinsic to its essence. Hence this whole which is white surface is not identical with the essence of surface.

1313. Now properties are predicated of their proper subjects in this way because their proper subjects are given in their definitions, as nose is given in the definition of snub and number in the definition of equal. And certain attributes are predicated essentially in such a way that subjects are not included in their definitions, as animal is predicated essentially of man, but man is not included in the definition of animal. Therefore since those attributes which are predicated accidentally do not belong to a thing's quiddity, and neither do those which are predicated essentially in whose definitions subjects are given, it follows that those attributes belong to a thing's quiddity in whose definitions subjects are not given. Hence he draws his conclusion, saying that the concept "which expresses what each thing is," i.e., which describes the predicate, "but does not contain the thing itself," i.e., the subject, will be the concept of the essence in each particular thing. Hence animal belongs to the essence of man.

1314. By a reduction to absurdity he proves that those things which are predicated essentially of a thing as a property is predicated of a subject, do not pertain to the whatness of a thing. For many different properties may be predicated essentially of the same subject, as the properties colored, rough and smooth, which are proper attributes of surface, are predicated essentially of a subject. And it is for the same reason that all predicates of this kind pertain to the quiddity of their subject. Therefore if whiteness pertains to the quiddity of surface, so also for a like reason will smoothness; for things identical with some third thing are identical with each other. "Hence, if being a white surface is always being a smooth surface," i.e., if it is true always and universally that the quiddity of a property is the same as that of its proper subject, it follows that being white and being smooth will be "one and the same thing," i.e., the quiddity of whiteness and that of smoothness will be one and the same. But this is obviously false. Therefore it follows that the essence of a property and that of its subject are not one and the same thing.

1315. **Now since there are** [3].

He inquires to what things essence belongs. First, he raises the question; and second [4] he answers it ("But neither").

He accordingly says, first [3], that there are certain composites in the case of the other categories and not merely in that of substance. He says this because he is investigating the quiddity of sensible substances, which are composite. For just as composite sensible substances have matter, which is the subject of substantial forms, so also do the other categories have their own subject. For there is some subject of each of them, namely, of quality, quantity, when, where, and also of motion, in which are included both action and being acted upon. Hence just as fire is a composite of matter and substantial form, in a similar way there is a kind of composition of substance and accidents.

1316. Therefore, since there is a definition of substances which are composed of matters and forms, we must also inquire whether there is "a concept of the essence" of all those things which are composites of accidents and subjects, i.e., whether they have a definition which is a concept signifying their essence; and also whether "this essence," which the definition signifies, is intrinsic to them, i.e., whether they have a quiddity or something that can answer the question "What?" For example, white man is a composite of subject and accident. The question, then, is whether there is an essence of white man as such.

1317. And since someone might perhaps say that white man is two things and not one, he therefore adds that white man might have one name, say, *garment.* The question about this one thing, then, i.e., garment, will be whether it has any whatness, so that we can ask, "What is the essence of a garment?" For then just as this word *man* signifies some composite, namely, rational animal, in like manner the word *garment* signifies some composite, namely, white man. And thus just as man has a definition, in a similar way it seems that garment can have a definition.

1318. **But neither is this** [4].

Here he answers the preceding question; and this part is divided twofoldly inasmuch as he gives two solutions. The second part (Lesson 4) begins where he says, "Or another solution."

He says, first [4], then, that *white man,* or *garment,* which is supposed to stand for "white man," is not one of those terms which are predicated essentially, but is rather one of those which are predicated accidentally; for the quiddity "white man" is one thing accidentally and not essentially, as was stated above (nn. 1313–14).

1319. Now there are two ways in which a thing is said to be one accidentally or non-essentially: first, in the sense that we say "Man is white," and second, in the sense that we say "This white thing is man"; because one of these is defined by addition, whereas the other is not. For in the definition of man it is not necessary to include the definition of white or the word white, but in the definition of white it is necessary to include man, or the word man, or his definition, provided that man is the proper subject of white, or whatever its proper subject happens to be.

1320. Now in order to explain this he adds that when one thing is predicated of another in a non-essential way, it is added to the other, because an accident is added to the subject given in the definition of that accident when it is defined; for example, if someone were to define white thing, he would have to express the concept white man, because in the definition of an accident it is necessary to include its subject. And then the definition includes white man; and thus it will be, as it were, the concept of white man and not the concept of white alone. This must be understood to be the case, as has already been said, if man is the proper and essential subject of white. But the one is added to the other accidentally, not because it is added to the definition of the other, but because the other is added to it in its own definition, as white is added to man accidentally, not because it is placed in the definition of man, but because man is placed in the definition of white. Hence, if by supposition the word *garment* signifies *white man*, then anyone who defines garment must define it in the same way that white is defined; for just as man and white must be given in the definition of garment, so also must each be given in the definition of white.

1321. It is clear, then, from what has been said, that white is predicated of man; for this proposition "A white man is white" is true, and vice versa. Yet the essence of white man is not that of white; and neither is the essence of garment, which signifies the composite white man, as has been stated. Thus it is evident that the essence of white and that of white man, or "garment," cannot be the same, by reason of the fact that, if white is also predicated of white man, it is still not its whatness.

1322. It is also evident that, if white has an essence and definition, it does not have a different one from that which belongs to white man; for since a subject is included in the definition of an accident, white must be defined in the same way that white man is, as has been stated. This is made clear as follows: white does not have a quiddity but only the thing of which it is predicated, man or white man. And this is what he means when he says: "Therefore the essence is what a thing of a definite sort is, whether it expresses that thing wholly or not"; i.e., from what has already been said it follows that essence belongs only to some definite thing, whether it expresses "that thing wholly," i.e., the composite, as white man, or not, as man. But white does not signify that it is some definite thing, but that it is of some sort.

1323. The fact that essence belongs only to some definite thing is shown as follows: the essence of a thing is what that thing is; for to have an essence means to be some definite thing. Hence those things which do not signify some definite thing do not have an essence. But when something is predicated of another as an accident is predicated of a subject, this is not some definite thing. For example, when I say "Man is white" I do not signify that it is some definite thing, but that it is of some special sort. For to be some definite thing belongs to substances alone. Hence it is clear that whiteness and the like cannot have an essence.

1324. But because someone might say that there are concepts of words signifying accidents as well as concepts of words signifying substance, he therefore concludes that essence does not belong to all things which have any kind of concept at all that explains their name, but only to those whose concept is a definition.

1325. Now the concept of a thing is not definitive if it is merely a concept of the sort which signifies the same thing as a name, as *one bearing arms* signifies the same thing as *arms-bearer*, because it would then follow that all concepts are "limiting terms," i.e., definitions. For a name can be given to any concept (for example, a name can be given to the concept *walking man* or *writing man*), yet it does not follow for this reason that these are definitions, because according to this it would follow that "even the *Iliad*," i.e., the poem written about the Trojan war, would be one definition; for that whole poem is a single account depicting the Trojan war. It is clear, then, that not every concept signifying the same thing as a name is a definition of it, but only if the concept "is of some primary thing," i.e., if it signifies something that is predicated essentially For that which is predicated essentially is first in the order of predication.

1326. But such things, i.e., primary ones, are all those which are predicated essentially, and such things do not involve predicating one thing of another; for example, white is not predicated essentially of man as though what white is and what man is are the same; but they are predicated of each other accidentally. For animal is predicated of man essentially, and in a similar way rational is predicated of animal. Hence the expression *rational animal* is the definition of man.

1327. Thus it is clear that essence will not be found in any of those things which are not classed among the species of some genus, but "in these alone," i.e., in the species alone. For species alone may be defined, since every definition is composed of genus and difference. But that which is contained under a genus and is constituted of differences is a species, and therefore definition pertains only to species. For species alone seem not to be predicated according to participation and affection or as an accident.

1328. In this statement he rejects three things which seem to make it impossible for anything to be defined by a genus. For, in the first place, those things of which a genus is predicated by participation cannot be defined by means of that genus, unless it belongs to the essence of the thing defined; for example, a fiery iron, of which fire is predicated by participation, is not defined by fire as its genus, because iron by its very essence is not fire but only participates to some degree in fire. However, a genus is not predicated of its species by participation but essentially; for man is an animal essentially and not merely something participating in animal, because man is truly an animal. Moreover, subjects are predicated of their properties, as nose is predicated of snub, yet the essence of nose is not the essence of snub; for species are not related to a genus as a property of that genus, but as something essentially the same as that genus. And white can be predicated of man accidentally, but the essence of man is not the essence of white, as the essence of a genus is the essence of its species. Hence it seems that only the concept of the species, which is constituted of genus and difference, is a definition.

1329. But if a name is given to other things, there can be a concept expressing what that name signifies, and this may occur in two ways. First, this occurs when a name that is less meaningful is explained by one that is more meaningful and is predicated of it, for example, when the name *philosophy* is explained by the name *wisdom.* And this is the meaning of his statement that "this accident inheres in this subject," namely, that sometimes the concept explaining the name is taken from a more meaningful term which is predicated of it.

1330. And, second, this occurs when a more meaningful phrase is used to explain a simple term; for example, when the phrase *lover of wisdom* is taken to explain the term *philosopher.* And this is what he means when he says "or in place of a simple term," as if in order to explain a simple term one might take "a more definite one." Yet such a concept will not be a definition, nor will the thing signified by it be an essence.

LESSON 4
The Analogous Character of Definition. Its Applicability to Accidents

ARISTOTLE'S TEXT Chapters 4 & 5: 1030a17–1031a14

1. *Or another solution is that definition, like the whatness of a thing, is used in many senses. For in one sense whatness signifies the substance and this particular thing, and in another sense it signifies any of the categories, such as quantity, quality, and others such as these. For just as being is found in all things, although not in the same way, but in one thing primarily and in the others secondarily, so too whatness is found in an unqualified sense in substance, but in another sense in the other categories. For we might even speak of the whatness of quality, so that quality is also one of those things which have whatness; not in an unqualified sense, however, but just as some say, in a logical sense, that non-being is, not in an unqualified sense, but insofar as it is nonbeing; and this is also the case with quality.* **1030a17–27**

2. *Therefore it is also necessary to consider how we must predicate it of each particular thing, yet not more than the condition of each warrants. Hence, too, since what is said is evident, essence (or whatness) will also be found in like manner primarily and unqualifiedly in substance, and then in the other categories, not as essence in an unqualified sense, but as the essence of quality and quantity. For these things must be said to be beings either equivocally or by adding or removing something, just as it is said that the unknowable is known. For the truth of the matter is that this word is used neither equivocally nor according to the same meaning, but just as the word medical is used in reference to one and the same thing, although not according to one and the same meaning or equivocally; for a body and an operation and an instrument are called medical neither equivocally nor according to one meaning, but in reference to one thing. It makes no difference, then, as to the way in which one wishes to express this.* **1030a27–1030b4**

3. *Now it is evident that definition and essence in the primary and unqualified sense belong to substances. And they belong not only to these but also to other things as well, although not in the primary sense. For if we maintain this, it is not necessary that there be a definition of any word which means the same thing as any concept, but it must mean the same thing as any determinate concept. And this will be the case if it is the concept of some one thing, not because it is continuous, like the Iliad, or one of the things which are one by being linked together, but if it is one according to one of the many meanings of that term. But the word one is used in the same number of senses as being is; and in one sense being signifies a particular thing, and in another, quantity, and in another, quality. And for this reason there will be a definition and concept of white man but in a different sense from that of whiteness and of substance.* **1030b4–13**

Chapter 5

4. *Now if one denies that a concept which involves the addition of something else is a definition, the problem arises how there can be a definition of things which are not simple but compound; for this must come about by way of addition. I mean, for example, that there is nose and concavity and snubness, which is a word compounded of the two, because the one is found in the other; and neither concavity nor snubness is an accidental attribute of nose, but an essential one. Nor do they belong to nose as white belongs to Callias or to man (because Callias, who happens to be a man, is white), but as male belongs to animal and equal to quantity, and as all those attributes which are said to belong to something else essentially. Now these attributes are those in which is found either the concept or name of the subject to which each one belongs, and which cannot be explained apart from it; for example, it is impossible to explain white apart from man, but not female apart from animal. Hence there is either no essence and definition of any of these things, or if there is, it is in the way we have described [texts 1–3].* **1030b14–28**

5. And there is also a second difficulty about them. For if snub nose and concave nose are the same, snub and concave will be the same; but if they are not, then, since it is impossible to use the word snub without the thing of which it is a proper attribute (because snub is concavity in a nose), either it is impossible to speak of a snub nose, or the same term is used twice—a concave nose nose. For a snub nose will be a concave nose nose. Hence it is absurd that such things should have an essence. And if they have, there will be an infinite regression; because some other nose will be found in the nose of snub-nose. It is clear, then, that there is definition of substance alone; for if the other categories also had a definition, this would have to be a result of adding something, just as there is no definition of equal and odd without number or of female without animal. And by "adding something" I mean those expressions in which the same thing happens to be said twice. And if this is true, there will not be any definition of those things which are compounded, for example, odd number. **1030b28–1031a6**

6. But this is hidden from us, because the concepts of these things are not expressed exactly. But if these things also have formulae, either they have such in a different way or, as we have said (582–84), definition and essence must be used in many senses. Hence in one sense there will be no definition of anything, and definition and essence will be found only in substance; and in another sense the other things will have a definition and essence. It is evident, then, that a definition is a concept of the essence of a thing, and that essence belongs to substances either alone, or chiefly, primarily, and without qualification. **1031a7–14**

COMMENTARY

1331. Here he gives the second solution to the question which was raised; and in regard to this he does three things. First [1], he gives the solution. Second [3], he proves it ("Now it is evident"). Third [4], he dispels certain difficulties which could arise from the previous discussion ("Now if one denies").

He accordingly says, first [1], that it is necessary to say, as was stated in the foregoing solution (n. 1325), that there is no definition and whatness of accidents but only of substances; or according to another solution it is necessary to say that the terms *definition* and *whatness* are used in many senses. For in one sense whatness signifies substance and this particular thing, and in another sense it signifies each of the other categories, such as quantity, quality and the like. Moreover, just as being is said to belong to all the other categories, although not in the same way, but primarily to substance and secondarily to the others, in a similar fashion whatness belongs in an unqualified sense to substance, "but in another sense to the other categories," i.e., in a qualified sense.

1332. For the fact that it belongs to the others "in another sense," i.e., in a qualified sense, is clear from the fact that in each of the other categories some reply may be made to the question "What is it?" For we ask of what sort a thing is, or what its quality is, as "What is whiteness?" And we answer, "Color." Hence it is evident that quality is one of the many things in which whatness is found.

1333. However, quality does not have whatness in an unqualified sense but the whatness of quality. For when I ask what man is, and one answers, "Animal," the term *animal*, since it belongs in the genus of substance, not only designates what man is, but also designates a *what*, i.e., a substance, in an unqualified sense. But when one asks what whiteness is, and someone answers, "Color," this word, even though it signifies what whiteness is, does not signify what something is in an unqualified sense, but of what sort it is. Hence quality does not have whatness in an unqualified sense, but with some qualification. For this kind of whatness is found in quality, as when we say that color is the whatness of whiteness; and this kind of whatness is substantial rather than substance.

1334. For by reason of the fact that all the other categories get the notion of being from substance, the mode of being of substance, i.e., being a *what,* is therefore participated in by all the other categories according to a certain proportional likeness; for example, we say that, just as animal is the whatness of man, in a similar fashion color is the whatness of whiteness, and number the whatness of double; and in this way we say that quality has whatness, not whatness in an unqualified sense, but a whatness of this particular kind; just as some say, for example, in speaking of non-being from a logical point of view, that non-being *is,* not because non-being is in an unqualified sense, but because non-being *is* non-being. And in a similar way quality does not have whatness in an unqualified sense, but the whatness of quality.

1335. **Therefore it is also** [2].

He now shows that whatness and definition are predicated of the nature found in substance and in accidents. He says that, since definition and whatness are found in some way both in substance and in accidents, therefore one must try to consider how we should "predicate it," i.e., predicate the definition, of each thing, yet no more than its condition warrants; so that, namely, we do not say that those predicates are applied univocally which do not have one essential character in reality.

1336. And for this reason the things which have been said about definition and whatness in regard to substance and accidents is clear, namely, that whatness will belong primarily and unqualifiedly to substance, and secondarily to the other categories, not, of course, so as to be whatness in an unqualified sense, but the whatness of this or that particular category, namely, of quantity or quality. For it is evident that definition and whatness must be predicated of substance and accidents either equivocally or by adding or removing something to a greater or lesser degree; or in a primary or secondary way, as being is predicated of substance and accident, and as we say that "the unknowable is known" in a qualified sense, i.e., secondarily, because so far as the unknowable is concerned we can know that it is not an object of knowledge; and thus we can also say of non-being that it is not.

1337. For the truth is that whatness and definition are not predicated of substance and accidents either equivocally or unqualifiedly and according to the same meaning, i.e., univocally, but as the term *medical* is predicated of different particulars in reference to one and the same thing, although it does not signify one and the same thing in the case of all the things of which it is predicated; nor is it also predicated equivocally. For a body is said to be medical because it is the subject of the art of medicine, and an activity is said to be medical because it is performed by the art of medicine, as purging; and an instrument, such as a syringe, is said to be medical because it is used by the art of medicine. Thus it is clear that the term *medical* is not used in a purely equivocal sense of these three things, since equivocal things have no relationship to some one thing. Nor again it is used univocally according to the same meaning, for the term *medical* is not predicated in the same sense of one who uses the art of medicine and of something that assists the art of medicine to produce its effect, but it is predicated analogically in reference to one thing, namely, to the art of medicine. And similarly whatness and definition are not predicated of substance and accident either equivocally or univocally, but in reference to one thing. For they are predicated of an accident in relation to substance, as has been explained.

1338. And since he had given two solutions, he adds that it makes no difference as to the way in which one wishes to answer the above question, i.e., whether one says that accidents do not have a definition, or that they have one in a secondary and qualified sense. However, the statement made in the first solution, to the effect that accidents do not have a definition, is to be understood in a primary and unqualified sense.

1339. **Now it is evident** [3].

Second he proves the solution which was given. He says that it is evident that definition and essence belong primarily and unqualifiedly to substances, yet not to substances alone since in a sense accidents also have a definition and essence, though not in the first way. This is made clear as follows: not every concept by which a word is explained is the same as a definition, nor is the word explained by each concept always something defined; but it is proper that there should be a definition of any determinate concept, namely, of one that signifies one thing. For if I say that Socrates is white and musical and curly-headed, this concept does not signify one thing, except perhaps accidentally, but signifies many; and therefore such a concept is not a definition.

1340. However, it is not enough that the thing signified by a concept should be one thing from the viewpoint of continuity in order that there may be a definition of it; for then the *"Iliad,"* i.e., the poem about the Trojan war, would be a definition, because that war was waged over a continuous period of time. Nor again is it enough that the thing should be one by connection; for example, if I were to say that a house is stones and mortar and wood, this concept would not be a definition of a house. But a concept that signifies one thing will be a definition if it signifies in some one of those senses in which the term *one* is predicated essentially; for the term one is used in as many senses as being is. And in one sense being signifies this particular thing, and in another, quantity, and in another, quality, and so on for the other categories. Yet it is predicated primarily of substance and secondarily of the other categories. Therefore the term one in an unqualified sense will apply primarily to substance and secondarily to the other categories.

1341. If, then, it is characteristic of the notion of definition that it should signify one thing, it follows that there will be a definition of white man, because white man is in a sense one thing. But the concept of white will be a definition in a different sense than the concept of substance, because the concept of substance will be a definition in a primary sense, and the concept of white will be a definition in a secondary sense, just as the term one is predicated of each in a primary and in a secondary sense.

1342. **Now if one denies** [4].

He clears up some of the difficulties pertaining to the point established above; and this is divided into two parts corresponding to the two difficulties which he removes. The second [5] begins where he says "And there is also."

Now there are two things which have to be noted first of all in order to make the first part of this division evident. The first is that some said that no definition comes about "by way of addition," i.e., no definition contains anything extrinsic to the essence of the thing defined. And they seemed to have in mind the fact that the definition signifies the essence of a thing. Hence it would seem that whatever is extrinsic to the essence of a thing should not be given in its definition.

1343. The second thing which has to be noted is that some accidents are simple and some compound. Those are said to be simple which have no determinate subject included in their definition, for example, curved and concave and other mathematical entities; and those are said to be compound which have a determinate subject without which they cannot be defined.

1344. Hence a problem arises if someone wants to say that a concept which is formed by addition is not a definition of those accidents which are simple, but of those which are compound; for it seems that none of these can have a definition. It is clear, then, that if compound accidents are defined, their definition must be formed by addition, since they cannot be defined without their proper subject. For example, if we take the following three things: nose, concavity, and snubness, then concavity is an accident in an unqualified sense, especially in relation to nose, since nose is not contained in the concept of concavity. And snubness is a compound accident, since nose is a part of its concept. Thus snubness will be an expression of both inasmuch as it signifies that "the one is found in the other," i.e., a definite accident in a definite subject, and neither concavity nor snubness is an attribute of nose in an accidental way, as white belongs accidentally to Callias and to man, inasmuch as Callias, who happens to be a man, is white. But snubness is an essential quality of nose, for it is proper to nose as such to be snub. Another translation has aquiline in place of concave, and its meaning is more evident, because nose is given in the definition of aquiline just as it is in the definition of snub. Concavity or snubness, then, belongs to nose essentially, just as male belongs to animal essentially, and equality to quantity, and all other things which are said to be present essentially in something else, because the concept of all is the same; and "these attributes are those in which," i.e., in the concepts of which, there is found either the name of the thing "to which this attribute belongs," namely, substance, or its concept. For in definitions the concept can always be given in place of the name; for example, when we say that man is a mortal rational animal, the definition can be given in place of the term animal, just as it may be said that man is a mortal rational sensory animated substance. And similarly if I say that a male is an animal capable of generating in another, I can also say that a male is a sensory animated substance capable of generating in another.

1345. Thus it is clearly impossible "to explain" this, i.e., to convey knowledge of, one of the accidents mentioned above which we called compound, apart from its subject, as it is possible to convey knowledge of whiteness without giving man in its definition or concept. But it is not possible to convey knowledge of female without mentioning animal, because animal must be given in the definition of female just as it must be given in the definition of male. Hence it is evident that none of the compound accidents mentioned above have a whatness and real definition if there is no definition by way of addition, as happens in the definitions of substances.

1346. Or if they have some kind of definition, since they can be defined only by way of addition, they will have a definition in a different way than substances do, as we said in the second solution. Hence in this conclusion he states the solution to the foregoing difficulty; for the statement which he made there, namely, that there is no definition by way of addition, is true of definition insofar as it applies to substances. Hence the accidents mentioned above do not have a definition in this way but differently, i.e., in a secondary sense.

1347. **And there is** [5].

Here he states the second difficulty; and in regard to this he does two things. First, he raises the difficulty; and second [6], he gives its solution ("But this is hidden").

He accordingly says, first [5], that there is another problem concerning the points discussed above. For to say "snub nose" and "concave nose" is either to say the same thing or not. If it is the same, it follows that snub and concave are the same, but this is clearly false since the definition of each is different.

1348. But if to say snub nose and concave nose is not to say the same thing, because snub cannot be understood "without the thing of which it is a proper attribute," i.e., without nose, since snubness is concavity in a nose (although concave can be spoken of without nose being involved), and if what I call snub involves more than concave, then it follows that this thing which I call nose either cannot be called a snub nose, or if it is called such, the word will be used twice, namely, inasmuch as we might say that a snub nose is "a concave nose nose"; for the definition of a word can always be given in place of that word. Hence when the word snub nose is used, the word snub can be removed and the definition of snub, which is a concave nose, can be added to the definition of nose. Thus it would seem that to speak of a snub nose is merely to speak of a concave nose nose, which is absurd. And for this reason it would seem absurd to say that such accidents have an essence.

1349. For if it is not true that they do not have an essence, the same word may be repeated an infinite number of times when the definition of the word is put in place of that word. For it is obvious that, when I say "concave nose," the word snub can be understood in place of concave, because snubness is merely concavity in a nose; and the term concave nose can also be understood in place of snub; and so on to infinity.

1350. Hence it would seem to be evident that only substance has a definition; for if the other categories also had a definition, this would have to be a result of adding something to their subject, as the definition of equal and that of odd must be derived from the definition of their subjects. For there is no definition of odd without number, or of female, which signifies a certain quality of animal, without animal. Therefore if some things are defined by way of addition, it follows that the same words may be used twice, as was shown in the example given above.

Hence if it is true that this absurd conclusion would result, it follows that compound accidents do not have a definition.

1351. **But this is hidden** [6].

He solves the problem raised above. He says that anyone who raises the above question is ignorant of the fact that these concepts are not expressed exactly, i.e., with exactness, as those which are used univocally, but are employed in a primary and secondary way, as was stated above [1]. But if the compound accidents mentioned above have a formula, or conceptual expression, they must have such in a different way than definitions do, or definition and essence, which is signified by definition, must be used in different senses.

1352. Hence "in one sense," i.e., primarily and without qualification, only substance will have a definition, and only substance will have an essence. "And in another sense," i.e., secondarily and with some qualification, the other categories will also have a definition. For substance, which has a quiddity in the absolute sense, does not depend on something else so far as its quiddity is concerned. An accident depends on its subject, however, although a subject does not belong to the essence of its accident (in much the same way as a creature depends on the creator, yet the creator does not belong to the essence of the creature), so that an extrinsic essence must be placed in its definition. In fact, accidents have being only by reason of the fact that they inhere in a subject, and therefore their quiddity depends on their subject. Hence a subject must be given in the definition of an accident at one time directly and at another, indirectly.

1353. Now a subject is given directly in the definition of an accident when an accident is signified concretely as an accident fused with a subject, as when I say that snubness is a concave nose; for nose is given in the definition of snub as a genus in order to signify that accidents subsist only in a subject. But when an accident is signified in the abstract, after the manner of a substance, then the subject is given in its definition indirectly, as a difference, as it is said that snubness is the concavity of a nose.

1354. Hence it is clear that when I say snub nose, it is not necessary to understand concave nose in place of nose; because nose is not included in the definition of snub as though it were part of its essence, but as something added to its essence. Hence snub and concave are essentially the same. But snub adds over and above concave a relation to a determinate subject; and thus in this determinate subject, nose, snub differs in no way from concave, nor is it necessary that any word should be put in place of snub except the word concave. Thus it will not be necessary to use concave nose in place of snub, but only concave.

1355. In bringing his discussion to a close he draws the conclusion which follows as obvious, namely, that a definition, which is the concept of a thing's essence and the essence itself, belongs to substances alone, just as the first solution maintained. Or substances are defined in a primary and unqualified sense, and accidents in a secondary and qualified sense, as has been stated in the second solution.

LESSON 5

The Relation of Essence to Thing in Essential and in Accidental Predication

ARISTOTLE'S TEXT Chapter 6: 1031a15–1032a11

1. *Moreover, it is necessary to inquire whether each thing and its essence are the same or different; for this is a kind of preamble to the inquiry about substance.* **1031a15–17**

2. *For each thing seems not to be different from its own substance, and the essence is said to be the substance of each thing.* **1031a17–18**

3. *Now in the case of accidental predications each thing would seem to be different from its essence, as a white man would seem to be different from the being of a white man. For if it were the same, then the being of a man and that of a white man would be the same; for a man and a white man are the same, as they say, and therefore the being of a white man is the same as that of a man. Or [perhaps] it is not necessary that all those things which are predicated accidentally should be the same. For the extreme terms of a syllogism do not become the same in an absolute sense. But perhaps it might seem to follow that extreme terms which are accidental become the same, as the being of white and the being of musical. However, this does not seem to be the case.* **1031a19–28**

4. *But in the case of essential predications a thing and its essence must always be the same. And this must be the case if there are substances which have no other substances or natures prior to them, such as some affirm the Ideas to be. For if the being of the good differs from the good-itself, and the being of animal from animal-itself, and the being of being from being-itself, there will be certain substances and natures and Ideas in addition to those mentioned, and these will be prior to substance, if essence belongs to substance.* **1031a28–1031b3**

5. *And if they are separated from each other, there will be no understanding of them, and they will not be beings. Now by separated is meant, if the being of the good is not present in the good-itself, and being good does not belong to this. For there is understanding of each thing by reason of the fact that its being is known; and the same thing applies to the good and to other things. Hence if the being of the good is not good, neither is the being of being being, nor the being of the one one. Now all essences are alike or none of them are. Hence if the essence of being is not being, neither will this be so in the case of other things. Furthermore, anything in which the being of the good is not found is not good.* **1031b3–11**

6. *It is necessary, then, that the good be one with the being of the good, and that the amicable be one with the being of the amicable, and the same is true of all those things which are not predicated of something else, but are predicated primarily and essentially. For it is enough if this is so, even if they are not separate Forms; and perhaps even more if they are. It is also evident at the same time that, if the Ideas are such as some claim, their subject will not be substance; for the Ideas must be substances but not be predicable of a subject; for if they were, they would exist only by participation in it. It is clear from these arguments, then, that each thing is one and the same as its essence, but not in an accidental way; and that to know each of these things is to know its essence. Hence according to this exposition both must be one thing.* **1031b11–22**

7. *But it is not true to say that a term which is predicated accidentally, as musical or white, is the same as its essence, in view of its twofold meaning; for both the subject to which the accident belongs and the accident itself are white. Hence in a sense an accident and its essence are the same, and in a sense they are not; for the essence of white is not the same as the essence of white man, but it is the same as the attribute white.* **1031b22–28**

8. *Now the absurdity will become apparent if a name is given to the essence of each one of these; for there will also be another essence besides the original essence; for example, besides the*

essence of horse there will be another essence of horse. And what will prevent some things from already being the same as their essence, if the essence of a thing is its substance? Indeed, they are not only one, but their intelligible structure is also the same, as is clear from what has been said; for the unity of the essence of the one and the one is not accidental.
1031b22–1032a2

9. Again, if they are different, there will be an infinite regress; for the one will be the essence of the being of the one, but the other will be the one itself. Hence the same reasoning will apply in the case of other things. It is clear, then, that in the case of those predications which are primary and essential, each thing and its being are identical. **1032a2–6**

10. Moreover, it is evident that the sophistical arguments raised against this position, and the question whether Socrates and the being of Socrates are the same, are answered in the same way; for there is no difference either in the things from which one asks the question, or in those from which one solves it. Hence it has now been stated how the essence of each thing is the same as that thing, and how it is not. **1032a6–11**

COMMENTARY

1356. Having established what essence is, and to what things it belongs, the Philosopher next inquires how essence is related to the thing of which it is the essence, i.e., whether it is the same as that thing or different; and in regard to this he does three things. First ([1], he presents the problem. Second [2], he gives its solution ("For each thing"). Third [10], he shows that the sophistical arguments which arise with regard to these matters can be met by using the above solution ("Moreover, it is evident").

He accordingly says, first [1], that it is necessary to inquire whether the essence of each thing and the thing of which it is the essence are the same or different, for example, whether the essence of a man and a man are the same or different; and it is the same in the case of other things. For to investigate this and make it evident is a "preamble to," i.e., a basic requirement for, "the inquiry about substance," which we intend to make in the following discussions. For it is his aim to investigate below whether universals are the substances of things, and whether the parts of things defined enter into their definition; and this inquiry which he now proposes to make is useful in solving that problem.

1357. **For each thing** [2].

Then he gives the solution to the problem which has been raised; and in regard to this he does three things. First [2], he gives the solution to this problem. Second [4], he proves it ("But in the case"). Third [8], he shows that the opposite of the solution given above is absurd and impossible ("Now the absurdity").

In regard to the first he does two things. First [8], he indicates what seems to be true at first glance with regard to the proposed problem. Second [3], he shows what follows from the contrary of this problem ("Now in the case").

He accordingly says, first [2], that it seems necessary at first glance, i.e., at once, to say that there is no case in which a particular thing differs from its own substance; and the reason is that the essence of a thing is the substance of the very thing of which it is the essence. Hence according to this argument it seems at first glance that the essence of a thing is the same as the thing itself and that one does not differ from the other.

1358. **Now in the case** [3].

Then he indicates the things to which the above premise does not apply. He says that insofar as the essence of a thing does not seem to differ from the thing of which it is the essence, since it is its substance, then in the case of accidental predications, which do not express the substance of their subject, the essence of the predicate seems to differ from the subject. For "the being of a white man," i.e., the essence of a white man, differs from a white man.

1359. This seems to be the case because, when someone says "white man," man is presupposed, for a man and a white man are the same, as they say. For if white had a different being than its subject, something might be predicated of the composite by means of the concept white, or it could be predicated of the composite because it was not opposed to the concept white. For whatever is predicated of a white man is so predicated only because it is predicated of a man; for an accident is a subject only by reason of a substance. Hence, insofar as man is understood in what is white, man and white are the same; and insofar as they are the same, then whatever constitutes the being of a white man will also constitute the being of a man. Hence if the essence of a white man is the same as a white man, it will also be the same as a man. But it is not the same as a man; and thus the essence of a white man is not the same as a white man. Therefore in the case of those things which are accidental, the essence of a thing and the thing itself are not the same.

1360. Now it is evident that the essence of a white man is not the same as a man, because not everything that is predicated accidentally of a subject is necessarily the same as that subject. For a subject is in a sense a mean between two accidents which are predicated of it, inasmuch as these two accidents are one only because their subject is one; for example, white and musical are one because the man of whom they are predicated is one. Therefore man is a mean, and white and musical are extremes. Now if white were essentially the same as man, then by the same argument musical would also be the same as man. Thus the two extremes, white and musical, would be essentially the same, because two things that are identical with some other thing are themselves identical. But it is false that these two extreme terms are essentially the same, although perhaps it might seem to be true that they are accidentally the same. Now it is certain that white and musical are accidentally the same.

1361. But according to this someone might think that, just as the white and the musical are accidentally the same, in a similar fashion "the being of white" and "the being of musical," i.e., the essences of both, are accidentally the same. However, this does not seem to be true; for the white and the musical are accidentally the same because each is accidentally the same as a man. Now the being of white and the being of musical are not the same as the being of man. Hence the being of white and the being of musical are not accidentally the same, but only the white and the musical.

1362. **But in the case** [4].

Then he explains the proposed solution; and in regard to this he does two things. First [4], he explains the solution with reference to essential predications; and second [8], with reference to accidental predications ("But it is not true").

In regard to the first he does two things. First, he explains the proposed solution with reference to essential predications; and second [6], he draws the conclusion at which he aims ("It is necessary").

In regard to the first he does two things. First, he shows that in the case of essential predications the essence of a thing does not differ from the thing of which it is the essence; and second [5], that it is not separated from it ("And if").

He accordingly says, first [4], that in the case of essential predications the essence of a thing and the thing itself must always be the same. This becomes clear if one holds that there are substances which are separate from these sensible substances and have no other separated substances or natures prior to them; for the Platonists say that abstract ideas are substances of this kind. For if the essence of a thing differs from the thing itself, this will have to be true of all things which have an essence. Now every substance has an essence. Therefore the essence of every substance will differ from that substance. Hence the essence of an ideal substance will also differ from that substance. Thus "if the good itself," i.e., the Idea of good, differs from "the being of the good," i.e., from the essence of this Idea, and if animal-itself also differs from the being of an animal and if being-itself differs from the being of being, and so on in the case of the other Ideas, it follows that, just as there are held to be Ideas apart from sensible substances, in a similar fashion there will also be other substances and natures and Ideas apart from those mentioned by the Platonists. And these other substances will constitute the essence of these Ideas and will be prior to them. Now I say that this follows "if essence belongs to substance," i.e., if each substance has an essence, as has been stated; or [in other words] if this essence belongs to the substance of the thing; for that on which a substance depends is prior to it.

1363. **And if** [5].

He shows that the essence of a thing is not separated from the thing of which it is the essence. He says, "And if they are separated from each other," i.e., if the essence of a thing and the thing itself are not only different but also separated from each other, two absurdities follow. The first is that there will be no understanding of those things whose essence is separated from them; and the second is that these same things will not be beings.

1364. He also explains what he means by "separated," namely, that "the being of the good," i.e., the essence of the good, which the Platonists posit, "is not present in the good-itself," i.e., in the Idea of good; and again that "being good," i.e., the quiddity of good, is not present in this good; as if to say that the foregoing separation must be understood to mean the separation of the quiddity of the good both from the Idea of good and from a particular good, which is called such through participation in the Idea of good. Or according to another text, "And being good does not belong to this," i.e., this essence is not proper to the being of the good in such a way that the essence of the good may be separated from the good, and vice versa.

1365. It is evident that the untenable conclusions mentioned above follow from the position described, because the understanding of each thing consists in a knowledge of its essence; and this applies in like manner both to the good and to all other things. Hence it follows that, if good is not present in "the being of the good," i.e., its essence, neither is being present in "the being of being," i.e., the essence of being, nor similarly is unity present in the being of the one, because either all of them alike or none of them are the same as their quiddities. If, however, by reason of the above-mentioned separation good is not present in the being of the good, then in an opposite way neither is the being of the good present in the good. Hence, too, neither will the essence of being be the same as being, nor will any other things have within themselves a single whatness. Thus if each thing is understood by means of its whatness, it follows that nothing can be known. This was the first absurdity mentioned.

1366. It is also evident that "the second absurdity follows"—that nothing will be a being or a good or an animal or anything of this kind; because that cannot be good in which "the being of the good," i.e., the whatness of the good, is not present. Hence if the whatness of the good is separated from the good, and the whatness of being is separated from being, it follows that the things which are said to be good and to be beings are neither good nor beings. This was the second absurdity mentioned.

1367. **It is necessary** [6].

The Philosopher now draws the conclusion in which he is chiefly interested. He says that, since it follows, as a result of the difference and separation of essence from things, that things are not understood and are not beings, and this is absurd, "it is necessary that the amicable be one with the being of the amicable," or the whatness of the amicable, "and that the good be one with the being of the good," i.e., the quiddity of the good. He gives these two examples: the amicable, pertaining to particular goods, which the Platonists said were good by participation; and the good, pertaining to the Idea of good. And it is similar in the case of all other predications which are essential and primary and which do not involve one thing being predicated of something else, i.e., accidental predications; for the latter type of predication is of a different nature, as has been stated (n. 1313). For in order that things may both be understood and be beings, it is enough "if this is so," i.e., if this is true, namely, that the quiddity of a thing is the same as the thing itself, even though the Ideal Forms which the Platonists posited do not exist.

1368. Now the Platonists claimed that there are separate Forms only for this reason, that certain knowledge of sensible things might be had by means of these Forms, inasmuch as sensible things would exist by participating in them. But perhaps it is sufficient for the foregoing position that the whatness of a thing should be the same as the thing itself rather than the Form, even if it is true that there are Forms, because the Forms exist apart from things. Moreover, a thing is understood and has being by means of something which is connected with it and is the same as itself, rather than by means of something which is separated from it.

1369. And from this consideration the Philosopher wants us to understand that separate Forms are destroyed. For if the Forms are held merely to account for our understanding of things and their being, and another position sufficiently accounts for this when it is held and the Platonic position is not, it follows that it is pointless to posit separate Forms.

1370. Similarly, the same point of the non-existence of separate Forms is evident from another consideration. If there are Ideas, it follows that the thing which is their subject, namely, this particular sensible thing, is not a substance. For the Platonists adopted the position that Ideas must be substances and so not belong to any subject; for it is proper for a substance not to inhere in a subject. But if the subjects hereabout, i.e., the sensible things about us, are substances, they must be such by participating in these separate Forms. Hence these Forms will inhere in a subject.

1371. From these arguments, then, it is evident that each thing and its whatness are one and the same in no accidental way; and similarly that in the act of understanding to know a particular thing is the same as to know its essence. "Hence according to this exposition" inasmuch as those things are said to be one which are one both from the viewpoint of being and that of being understood, it is necessary that both of these, i.e., a thing and its essence, should be one.

1372. **But it is not true** [7].

He explains the foregoing solution with reference to accidental predications. He says that in the case of accidental predications it is not true to say that the essence of a thing and the thing of which it is the essence are the same. This is so because of the twofold meaning of the term; for when a man is said to be white, something can be attributed to the subject either by reason of the subject or by reason of the accident. Hence if we were to say that the whatness of a white man is the same as a white man, two things could be meant: that it is either the same as a man or the same as white; for it can designate both the subject "to which the accident white belongs and the accident itself." Hence it is clear that in one sense the whatness of a white man is the same as a white man, and in another it is not. For it is not the same as a man or even the same as white man as regards the subject, but it is the same as "the attribute," i.e., white; for the essence of white and white itself are the same. However, it cannot be said that it is the same as a white man, lest it should be understood to be the same as the subject.

1373. **Now the absurdity** [8].

He shows that the opposite of the solution mentioned is absurd; and it was necessary to do this because he had proved that the solution given above is true when separate Forms are posited; which is a position that he afterwards destroyed. Hence he had to repeat his proof, showing that what he had proved about the Forms also applies to a thing's essence. In regard to this he gives two arguments.

1374. In the first of these arguments he says that to affirm that the essence of a thing and the thing itself are different will appear absurd if anyone gives a name to the essence of each of these; for by the same argument both the thing and its essence will then be different from its essence; for example, a horse is something having the essence of a horse. Now if this differs from a horse, this will have a different name, and let us call it A. Therefore, since A is a thing, it will have an essence different from itself, just as horse does. Thus this thing which constitutes the being of a horse will have a different essence. But this is clearly false. Now this argument proceeds in the same way with regard to the quiddity as the first argument did with regard to the Ideas. And if someone were to say that the essence of a horse is the substance itself, which is the quiddity of a horse, what will prevent us from saying right now at the very start that some things are their own essence? By this he implies the answer, "Nothing."

1375. But it must be understood that a thing and its essence are one in every respect, even in their intelligible structure, as can be made clear from what has been said. For the one and the essence of the one are one not in an accidental way but essentially; and thus they are one in their intelligible structure.

1376. **Again, if they are** [9].

Then he gives the second argument, which runs as follows: if the essence of a thing and the thing itself are different, there will be an infinite regress; for we must say that there are two things, one of which is the one, and the other the essence of the one; and by the same argument there will be a third thing, which would be the essence of the essence of the one, and so on to infinity. Now since an infinite regress is impossible, it is evident that, in the case of predications which are primary and essential and not accidental, each thing and its being are one and the same.

1377. **Moreover, it is evident** [10].

He says that the sophistical arguments which are raised against this position in order to show that the essence of a thing and the thing itself are not the same, are clearly met by means of the same solution which was given to the first problem. For example, the Sophists ask if Socrates and the being of Socrates are the same, and they show that they are not by saying that, if Socrates and the being of Socrates are the same, and Socrates is white, it follows that white and the being of Socrates, and so on, are the same. Now the solution is clear from what has been said above, "For there is no difference either in the things from which one asks the question, or in those from which one solves it," i.e., it makes no difference from what things one proceeds to argue, or to what questions one adapts the answer, inasmuch as the solution is basically the same. Hence from what has been said it is evident when the essence of each thing is the same as each thing and when it is not; for it is the same in the case of essential predications, but not in that of accidental ones.

1378. In support of the statements which he has made it must also be noted that the whatness of a thing is what its definition signifies. Hence when a definition is predicated of the thing defined, the whatness of that thing must also be predicated of it. Therefore, humanity, which is not predicated of man, is not the whatness of man, but mortal rational animal is; for the word *humanity* does not answer the question, "What is man?" But mortal rational animal does. Yet humanity is taken as the formal principle of the essence, just as animality is taken as the principle of the genus and not as the genus, and as rationality is taken as the principle of the difference and not as the difference.

1379. Now to this extent humanity is not absolutely the same as man, because it implies only the essential principles of man and excludes all accidents. For humanity is that by which man is man. But none of the accidents of a man is that whereby he is a man. Hence all accidents of man are excluded from the meaning of humanity. Now it is the particular thing itself, namely, a man, which contains the essential principles and is that in which accidents can inhere. Hence although a man's accidents are not contained in his intelligible expression, still man does not signify something apart from his accidents. Therefore man signifies as a whole and humanity as a part.

1380. Moreover, if there is some thing in which no accident is present, then is this thing the abstract must differ in no way from the concrete. This is most evident in the case of God.

LESSON 6

Becoming—by Nature, by Art, and by Chance. The Source and Subject of Becoming

ARISTOTLE'S TEXT Chapter 7: 1032a12–1033a23

1. *Now of those things which come to be, some come to be by nature, some by art, and some spontaneously.* **1032a12–13**

2. *And everything which comes to be comes to be by something and from something and becomes something. And this something which I say it comes to be may be in any category; for it may come to be either a this or so much or of such a sort or at some time.* **1032a13–15**

3. *Now natural generations are those which come about by nature.* **1032a15–17**

4. *And that from which a thing comes to be is what we call matter; and that by which it comes to be is one of those things which exist by nature. And this something which it comes to be is a man or a plant or some other one of those things which we chiefly claim to be substances.* **1032a17–19**

5. *Now all things which come to be either by nature or by art have matter; for it is possible for each one of them to be and not to be, and this possibility is the matter of each.* **1032a20–22**

6. *And in general both that from which they come to be and that according to which they come to be is nature; for the thing generated, such as a plant or an animal, has a nature. And that by which they are generated, i.e., the so-called specific nature, which is specifically the same, is also nature (although this is found in something else); for man begets man. The things which come to be by nature, then, are produced in this way.* **1032a22–26**

7. *But the other kinds of generation are called "productions"; and all productions are a result either of art, of power, or of mind. And some of these are a result of chance and fortune in the same way as things which come to be by nature; for some of these same things are generated both from seed and without seed. Therefore we shall have to investigate these later on (Lesson 8, text 5).* **1032a26–32**

8. *Now those things are produced by art whose form exists in the mind; and by form I mean the essence of each thing and its first substance. For even contraries have in a sense the same form; for the substance of a privation is the same as the substance of its opposite, as health is the substance of sickness, for sickness is made apparent by the absence of health; and the health which exists in the mind is the concept in scientific knowledge.* **1032a32–1032b6**

9. *Health comes about, then, as a result of thinking in this manner: since health is such and such, if health is to exist, such and such a condition must exist, for example, regularity; and if this is to exist there must be heat; and the physician continues to think in this way until he eventually comes to some final thing which he is capable of doing. Hence, the motion which begins from this, which is ordained to the acquisition of health, is called a production. Hence it turns out that in a sense health comes from health, and a house from a house, and what has matter from what is without matter; for the medical art and the building art are the form of health and the form of a house. And by substance without matter I mean the essence.* **1032b6–14**

10. *Now of generations and motions one part is called thinking and the other producing; for that which proceeds from the principle and the form is thinking, and that which proceeds from the terminus of thinking is producing. And each of the other, intermediate, things is produced in the same way. I mean that if health is to be restored a balance must be achieved. What, then, does a balance involve? Some particular thing. And this will occur if the body is heated. And what does this involve? Something else. And this exists potentially; and it is present already in the physician himself. The thing which produces the effect, then, and that from which the restoration of health begins if it comes to be by art, is the form in the mind.* **1032b15–23**

11. But if it comes to be by chance, the thing which produces it is the starting point of production for the one who acts by art. For instance, in the restoration of health the starting point may perhaps be the production of heat, which the physician causes by rubbing. The heat in the body, then, is either a part of health, or it is followed by some such thing as is a part of health, or it comes about through several intermediaries. Now this last thing is the one producing health, and what is such is a part of health, as stones are parts of a house and other materials are parts of other things. **1032b23–30**

12. Hence, as is said, it is impossible for anything to be produced if nothing pre-exists. Therefore that some part will necessarily pre-exist is evident; for the matter is a part, since it exists in the product and becomes something. Hence it is also one of those things which are contained in the intelligible expression of a thing. And we describe what brazen circles are in both ways, saying about the matter that it is bronze, and about the specifying principle that it is such and such a figure. And this is the genus in which circle is first placed. Hence a brazen circle has matter in its intelligible expression. **1032b30–1033a5**

13. Now as for that from which as matter a thing is produced, some things when they are produced are not said to be that but of that kind; for instance, a statue is not stone but of stone. And a man who is recovering his health is not said to be that from which he has come. The reason is that, although a thing comes both from its privation and from its subject, which we call matter (for example, what becomes healthy is both a man and one who is sick), we say that it comes rather from its privation (for example, a healthy person comes from a sick one rather than from a man). And for this reason a healthy person is not said to be a sick one, but to be a man, and the man is said to be healthy. However, as regards those things of which the privation is not evident and is nameless (for example, the privation of some particular figure in bronze or in the bricks and timbers of a house), the thing produced seems to come from these just as a healthy person comes from a sick one. Hence, just as in the former case a thing is not said to be that from which it comes to be, so too in this case the statue is not said to be wood but wooden, not bronze but brazen, not stone but of stone; and a house is not said to be bricks but of bricks. For if someone were to examine the question carefully, he would not say without qualification either that the statue comes from wood or the house from bricks, because there must be change in that from which something comes to be without remaining. It is for this reason, then, that we speak in this way. **1033a5–23**

COMMENTARY

1381. Having shown what essence is, and to what things it belongs, and that it does not differ from the thing to which it belongs, the Philosopher now aims to show that the essences and forms present in these sensible things are not generated by any forms existing apart from matter, but by forms present in matter. And this will be one of the ways in which the position of Plato is destroyed; for Plato claimed that there are separate Forms, and that these are necessary both in order that an understanding of sensible things may be had, and that sensible things may exist by participating in them, and that these Forms may be responsible for the generation of sensible things. Now he has already shown, in the preceding chapter (n. 1368), that separate Forms are not necessary either to account for our understanding of sensible things or their being, since these can be adequately explained on the grounds that the whatness of a sensible thing is both present in that thing and identical with it. Hence it remains to show that separate Forms are not required for the generation of sensible things; and he proves this in this chapter.

This undertaking is accordingly divided into two parts. In the first [1] he prefaces his discussion with certain points required for the proof of his thesis. In the second (Lesson 7), he proves his thesis ("Now since").

In regard to the first he does two things. First, he proposes certain divisions regarding the processes of generation which take place in the natural world. Second [3], he explains these ("Now natural generations").

He gives two divisions. The first has to do with things that are generated and with their mode of generation; and the second [2], with the conditions necessary for generation ("And everything").

He accordingly says, first [1], that of things which come to be, some come to be by nature, some by art, and some by chance, or "spontaneously," i.e., by itself without purpose. The reason for this division is that the cause of generation is either a proper cause or an accidental one. For if it is a proper cause, it is either the principle of motion intrinsic to a thing, and then it is nature, or it is extrinsic to the thing, and then it is art, for nature is a principle of motion in that in which it exists, but art does not exist in the thing produced by art but in something else.

1382. But if it is an accidental cause, then it is chance or fortune. It is fortune in reference to those things which act by mind, but chance occurs in other things also; and both of these come under "the spontaneous," i.e., what is of itself without purpose; for that is without purpose which is directed to a goal and does not reach it. And both chance and fortune are found among those things which are done for the sake of some goal, when some effect results besides the one intended by some definite proper cause. Hence an effect is said to be proper inasmuch as it has a definite cause, and to be without purpose inasmuch as it occurs apart from the intention of the agent.

1383. **And everything** [2].

Then he gives the second division, which involves the conditions of generation; for everything which comes to be is brought about by some agent, and is produced from something as its matter, and also becomes something, which is the terminus of generation. And since he had said above that this something belongs in the class of substances, he therefore now informs us that this must be understood in a more general way, inasmuch as by *something* is meant any category in which generation can occur, in an unqualified or qualified sense, essentially or accidentally. For the something of which he spoke is either "a this," i.e., a substance, or a quantity or quality or time or some other category.

1384. And the reason for this division is that in every generation something which was formerly potential becomes actual. Now a thing can be said to go from potency to actuality only by reason of some actual being, which is the agent by which the process of generation is brought about. Now potency pertains to the matter, from which something is generated, and actuality pertains to the thing generated.

1385. **Now natural generations** [3].

Then he explains that these three conditions required for generation are found in the three types mentioned; and in regard to this he does two things. First [3], he explains his thesis.

Second [12], he introduces the conclusion which he chiefly intends to draw ("Hence, as is said").

In regard to the first he does three things. First, he makes this clear in the case of natural generations; and second [7], in the case of generations resulting from art ("But the other"); and third [11], in the case of those generations which come about by chance ("But if it comes").

In regard to the first he does four things. First [3], he indicates what generations are natural. He says that those generations are natural whose principle is nature and not art or any mind, for example, when fire or a plant or an animal is generated as a result of the natural power inherent in things.

1386. **And that from which** [4].

Having posited these three conditions he now gives examples of natural generations. He says that in natural generation there is something from which any natural thing is generated, and this is called matter; and something by which it is generated, and this is called the agent; and there is this particular thing, namely, the thing generated, such as a man or a plant or something of this sort, which "we chiefly claim to be substances," i.e., particular composite substances, which are more evidently substances, as was stated above. But matter and the form, which is the principle of action in the agent, are substances only insofar as they are principles of composite substances.

1387. Now of these three conditions, two have the nature of principles of generation, namely, matter and the agent, and the third has the nature of a terminus of generation, i.e., the composite which is generated. And since nature is a principle of generation, both the matter as well as the form, which is the principle of generation in the agent, are called nature, as is evident in Book II of the *Physics*. [193a32] And the composite which is generated is said to be by nature or according to nature.

1388. **Now all things** [5].

Here he proves that one of these three conditions—the principle from which a thing comes to be—is found in every kind of generation, not only in natural generations but also in artificial ones (for the nature of the other two conditions is evident). He says that all the things which come to be by nature or by art have a matter from which they come to be; for everything that is generated by nature or by art is capable both of being and of not being. For since generation is a change from non-being to being, the thing generated must at one time be and at another not be, and this would be true only if it were possible for it both to be and not to be. Now the potential element which each thing has both for being and not being is matter; for it is in potentiality to the forms by which things have being, and to the privations by which they have non-being, as is clear from what was said above. Therefore it follows that there must be matter in every kind of generation.

1389. **And in general** [6].

Here he shows how the three conditions mentioned above are related to nature. He says that in general each of the three conditions mentioned above is in a sense nature. For the principle from which natural generation proceeds, namely, matter, is called nature; and for this reason the generations of simple bodies are said to be natural ones, even though the active principle of their generation is extrinsic to them.

This seems to be contrary to the very notion of nature, because nature is an intrinsic principle having a natural aptitude for such a form; and processes of generation which proceed from this principle are said to be natural.

1390. Again, the principle according to which generation comes about, namely, the form of the thing generated, is said to be its nature, as a plant or an animal; for a natural generation is one which is directed towards nature just as the act of whitening is one which is directed towards whiteness.

1391. Again, the principle by which generation comes about, as by an agent, is the specific nature, which is specifically the same as the nature of the thing generated, although it exists in something else; for man begets man. However, the thing generated and the one generating it are not numerically the same but only specifically the same.

1392. And for this reason it is said in Book II of the *Physics* [198a25] that the form and the goal of the process of generation coincide in one and the same individual. Now the agent coincides with these insofar as it is specifically the same but not insofar as it is numerically the same. But the matter is neither specifically the same nor numerically the same.

1393. Another text states that the principle by which a thing comes to be is the so-called specific nature or one conforming to it; for the thing generated and the one generating it are not always specifically the same, although they do have some conformity, as when a horse begets a mule. Finally, he concludes that the things generated by nature are generated in the manner described.

1394. **But the other kinds** [7].

He now settles the issue about the things generated by art; and in regard to this he does two things. First [7], he distinguishes processes of generation arising from art from other processes of generation, namely, natural ones. Second [8], he shows how generation comes about by art ("Now those things").

He accordingly says, first, that those processes of generation which differ from natural ones are called productions. For even though in the case of natural things we can use the word *production,* which is equivalent to *praxis* in Greek (as when we say that what is actually hot produces something which is actually hot), still we use the word properly in reference to those things which come about as a result of mind, in which the mind of the agent has dominion over the thing which he makes inasmuch as he can make it in this way or in that. But this does not occur in the case of natural things, for they rather act with a view to some effect in the definite manner provided for them by a superior agent. Moreover, productions of this kind are a result of art, of power, or of mind.

1395. Now the term *power* used here seems to be taken in the sense of *violence;* for certain of those things which do not come about by nature are produced by virtue of the agent's power alone, in which a minimum of art is required and a minimum of activity directed by mind. This occurs especially in pulling or throwing or casting out bodies.

1396. Moreover, when the direction of mind is required, at one time this comes about by art, and at another by mind alone, as when one does not yet have an artistic habit perfectly. For just as one person may argue by art, and another without art, as an unlearned person, so too in reference to those things which are made by art one can produce an artistic work by art, and someone else without art.

1397. Furthermore, of those processes of generation which are a result either of art, of power, or of mind, some are a result of chance and fortune, for example, when an agent by use of intelligence aims at some goal to be attained by his own activity, and a goal is reached which the agent did not intend. For example, someone intends to rub himself vigorously and health comes of it, as is said later (see n. 1403).

1398. And the same thing occurs in the case of things produced by art as in those produced by nature; for the power contained in the seed, as is said below (n. 1451), is similar to art, because just as art through certain definite intermediates attains the form at which it aims, so also does the formative power in the seed. And just as an effect produced by art may also occur apart from the intention of art or of mind, and then it is said to happen by chance, so too in the case of these things, i.e., natural ones, some things are generated both from seed and without seed. And when they are generated from seed, they are generated by nature; but when they are generated without seed, they are generated by chance. These things must also be investigated in this same chapter.

1399. Now the words used here give rise to two problems. The first is that, since every natural thing has a definite mode of generation, those things which are generated from seed and those which are generated from decay do not seem to be the same. This is what Averroes seems to feel in his commentary on Book VIII of the *Physics*, for he says that an animal which is generated from seed and one which is generated from decay cannot be specifically the same. Avicenna, however, feels that all things which are generated from seed can be generated in the same species without seed from decay, or by some method of blending terrestrial matters.

1400. Aristotle's view seems to be a mean between these two opinions, namely, that some things can be generated both from seed and without seed, but not all things, as he says below (see n. 1454); just as in the case of things produced by art not all things can be produced by art and without art, but some are produced by art alone, as a house. For perfect animals seem to be capable of being generated from seed, whereas imperfect animals, which are akin to plants, seem to be capable of being generated both from seed and without seed. For instance, plants are sometimes produced without seed by the action of the sun on the earth when it is rightly disposed for this effect; yet plants generated in this way produce seed from which plants of a similar kind are generated.

1401. And this is reasonable, because the more perfect a thing is the more numerous are the things required for its completeness. And, for this reason, in the generation of plants and imperfect animals it is sufficient that the power of the heavens alone should act. But in the case of perfect animals the power of the seed is also needed along with the power of the heavens. Hence it is said in Book II of the *Physics* [194b14] that man and the sun beget man.

1402. The second problem is that animals which are generated without seed from decay do not seem to be produced by chance but by some definite agent, namely, by the power of the heavens, which supplies in the generation of such animals the energy of the generative power found in the seed. The Commentator is also of this opinion in his commentary on Book IX of this work.

1403. But it must be noted that nothing prevents a process of generation from being a proper process when referred to one cause, and yet be an accidental or chance affair when referred to another cause, as is evident in the Philosopher's example. For when health results from a vigorous rubbing quite apart from the aim of the one doing the rubbing, the process of restoring health, if it is referred to nature, which governs the body, is not accidentally but properly aimed at. However, if it is referred to the aim of the one doing the rubbing, it will be accidental and a matter of chance. Similarly, if the process of generation of an animal generated from decay is referred to the particular causes acting here below, it will also be found to be accidental and a matter of chance; for heat, which causes decay, is not inclined by nature to have as its goal the generation of this or that particular animal which results from decay, as the power in the seed has as its goal the generation of something of a particular type. But if it is referred to the power of the heavens, which is the universal power regulating generation and corruption in these lower bodies, it is not accidental but is directly aimed at, because its goal is that all forms existing potentially in matter should be brought to actuality. Thus Aristotle has correctly compared here the things which come to be by art with those which come to be by nature.

1404. **Now those things** [8].

He now explains the way in which things are generated by art; and he does this chiefly with reference to the efficient principle, for the material principle has already been discussed where he spoke about natural generation. In regard to this he does two things. First, he shows what the active principle is in a process of generation resulting from art. Second [9], he shows how the process of generation proceeds from this principle ("Health comes about").

He accordingly says, first [8], that those things which come to be by art are those of which the productive form exists in the mind. And by *form* he means the essence of anything made by art, for example, the essence of a house, when it is a house that is made. He also calls this the "first substance," i.e., the first form; and he does this because the form present in the matter of things made by art proceeds from the form present in the mind. In the case of natural things, however, the opposite is true.

1405. Now the form present in the mind differs from the one present in matter; for in matter the forms of contraries are different and opposed, but in the mind contraries have in a sense the same form. And this is true because forms present in matter exist for the sake of the being of the things informed, but forms present in the mind exist according to the mode of what is knowable or intelligible. Now while the being of one contrary is destroyed by that of another, the knowledge of one contrary is not destroyed by that of another but is rather supported by it. Hence the forms of contraries in the mind are not opposed, but rather "the substance," i.e., the whatness, "of a privation," is the same as the substance of its contrary, as the concepts of health and of sickness in the mind are the same; for sickness is known by the absence of health. Further, the health which exists in the mind is the concept by which health and sickness are known; and it is found "in the scientific knowledge" of both, i.e., in knowing both.

1406. **Health comes about** [9].

He now shows how health is produced by this principle; and in regard to this he does two things. First, he shows how the health which exists in the mind is the principle (or starting point) for the restoring of health; and second [10], how the term *principle* is taken in different ways in regard to the activity of art ("Now of generations").

He accordingly says [9] that, since the health present in the mind is the principle of the health produced by art, health is brought about in a subject as a result of someone thinking in this manner: since health is such and such, i.e., either regularity or the balance of heat, cold, moisture and dryness, if health is to exist, it is necessary that this exist, i.e., regularity or the balance of humors; and if regularity or balance must exist, there must be heat, by which the humors are balanced; and thus by always going from what is subsequent to what is prior he thinks of the thing which is productive of heat, and then of the thing which is productive of this, until he reaches some final thing which he himself is immediately capable of doing, for example, the dispensing of some particular medicine; and finally the motion beginning from the thing which he can do immediately is said to be the activity directed to the production of health.

1407. Hence it is evident that, just as in the case of natural things man is generated from man, so too in the case of artificial things it turns out that health comes to be in a sense from health, and a house from a house; i.e., from what exists in the mind without matter there is produced something which has matter. For the medical art, which is the principle of health, is nothing else than the form of health existing in the mind; and this form or substance which exists without matter is the one which he speaks of above as the essence of the thing produced by art.

1408. **Now of generations** [10].

He shows how the word *principle* is taken in different ways in regard to the activities of art. He says that in artificial generations and motions there is one activity which is called *thinking* and another which is called *producing*. For the artist's planning, which begins from the principle which is the form of the thing to be made by his art, is itself called thinking; and this activity extends, as was said above, right down to what is last in the order of intention and first in the order of execution. Therefore the activity which begins from this last thing in which the activity of thinking terminates, is called producing, and this is then a motion affecting matter.

1409. And what we have said about the activity of art in reference to the form, which is the ultimate goal of artificial generation, also applies in the case of all other intermediate things; for example, in order that one may be healed the humors of the body must be balanced. Hence this process of balancing is one of the intermediate things which is nearest to health. And just as the physician when he aims to cause health must begin by considering what health is, so too when he intends to produce a balance he must know what a balance is, namely, that it is "some particular thing," i.e., the proportion of humors appropriate to human nature. "And this will occur if the body is heated"—supposing that someone is sick because of a lack of heat. And again he must know what this is, i.e., what being heated is, as if one might say that being heated consists in being changed by a hot medicine. And "this," namely, the administering of a hot medicine, is immediately within the physician's power; and "this is already present in the physician himself," i.e., it is within his power to administer such a medicine.

1410. Hence it is evident that the principle causing health, from which the process of restoring health begins, is the form existing in the mind, either of health itself, or of other intermediate things by means of which health is produced. And I say that this is the case if the process of restoring health comes about by art. But if it comes about in some other way, the principle of health will not be a form existing in the mind; for this is proper to artificial operations.

1411. **But if it** [11].

He shows how chance generations take place. He says that, when the restoring of health comes about by chance, the principle of health is the same as the one from which health comes about for him who causes health by art. But this must be understood of the principle of production, which is last in the order of intention and first in the order of execution, just as in the process of restoring health the principle of health may at times begin with the patient's being heated. And the process of restoring health also begins here when someone is healed by chance, because someone may produce heat by rubbing but not intend this as the goal of the rubbing. Thus the heat produced in the body by rubbing or by a medication either is a part of health, inasmuch as it is something entering into the substance of health, as when by itself the alteration of being heated is sufficient to promote health; or something which is a part of health may result from heat, as when health is produced as a result of the heat dissolving certain congested humors, the dissolution of which thereupon constitutes health. Or it can also be produced by several intermediates, as when heat consumes certain superfluous humors blocking some passage in the body, so that when these have been removed the proper movement of spirits to some parts of the body then begins; and this final step is the one then causing health. "And what is such," namely, the proximate cause of health, "is a part of health," i.e., something entering into the make-up of health. And it is the same with other things produced by art; for the parts of a house are the stones whose bonding in the course of construction goes to constitute a house.

1412. **Hence, as is said** [12].

Then he draws the conclusion at which he chiefly aims; and in regard to this he does two things. First, he introduces this conclusion; and second [13], he dispels a difficulty ("Now as for that").

He says, first [12], that, since everything which comes to be is generated from matter and is also generated by something like itself, it is impossible for anything to be generated unless something pre-exists, as is commonly said; for the common opinion of the philosophers of nature was that nothing comes to be from nothing. Further, it is evident that the thing which preexists must be part of the thing generated, and this can be shown from the fact that matter is present in the thing generated and becomes the thing generated when it is brought to actuality. And not only the material part of a thing pre-exists, as is clear from the explanation given, but so also does the part which exists in the mind, namely, the form; for these two principles, matter and form, are parts of the thing generated.

1413. For we can describe what brazen circles are in both ways, or, according to another text, what many circles are, i.e., particular and distinct circles, by stating the matter, which is bronze, and "by stating the specifying principle," i.e., the form, which is such and such a figure. And he is right in saying many particular circles; for a circle is one thing specifically and formally, but it becomes many and is individuated by matter. And this, the figure, is the genus in which brazen circle is first placed. Hence it is evident, from what has been said, that brazen circle has matter in its definition. And the fact that the form of the thing generated pre-exists has been made clear above both in reference to natural generations and to artificial productions.

1414. **Now as for that** [13].

Here he dispels a certain difficulty; for that from which a thing comes to be as its matter is sometimes predicated of it not abstractly but denominatively; for some things are not said to be "that," i.e., the matter, "but of that kind"; for instance, a statue is not said to be stone but of stone. And a man who is recovering his health "is not said to be that from which," i.e., one does not predicate of him the thing from which, he is said to come to be; for a person who is recovering his health comes from a sick person. But we do not say that a person who is recovering his health is a sick one.

1415. Now the reason for this kind of difficulty is that one thing is said to come from something else in two ways, namely, from a privation and from a subject, which is matter, for example, when it is said that a man recovers his health, and that a sick person recovers his health. But a thing is said to come from a privation rather than from a subject; for example, a healthy person is said to come from a sick one rather than from a man. But when one thing becomes another we say this in reference to the subject rather than to the privation; for properly speaking we say that a man rather than a sick person becomes healthy. Therefore a healthy person is not said to be a sick one, but rather a man; and in the opposite way it is a man that is said to be healthy. Hence the thing that comes to be is predicated of the subject, not of the privation.

1416. But in some cases the privation is not evident and is nameless; for example, the privation of any particular figure in bronze does not have a name, and neither does the privation of house in the stones and timbers. Therefore we use the term *matter* simultaneously to designate both the matter and the privation. Hence just as we say in the one case that a healthy person comes from a sick one, so too we say in the other case that a statue comes from bronze, and a house from stones and timbers. And for this reason, too, just as in the one case the thing that comes to be from something taken as a privation is not predicated of the subject, because we do not say that a healthy person is a sick one, neither do we say in the other case that a statue is wood; but the abstract term is predicated concretely by saying that it is not wood but wooden, not bronze but brazen, not stone but of stone. And similarly a house is not bricks but of bricks. For if someone were to examine the question carefully, he would not say in an unqualified sense either that the statue comes from wood or the house from bricks, but that it comes to be as a result of some change. For the former comes from the latter taken as something which is changed and not as something which remains, because bronze does not stay formless while it is being made into a statue, nor do bricks stay unbonded while a house is being built. And for this reason "we speak in this way," i.e., predication is made in this way, in the cases mentioned above.

LESSON 7

The Composite and Not the Form is Generated. The Ideas Are neither Principles of Generation nor Exemplars

ARISTOTLE'S TEXT Chapter 8: 1033a24–1034a8

1. Now since that which comes to be comes to be by something (and by this I mean the principle of generation), and from something (and by this let us understand not the privation but the matter; for this has already been defined [601] in our discussion about these things), and becomes something (i.e., a sphere or a circle or whatever else it may be), just as the agent does not produce the underlying subject, i.e., the bronze, neither does he produce a sphere, except accidentally, because a brazen sphere is a sphere and he produces the former. For to make this particular thing is to make it out of the subject totally. I mean that to make the bronze round is not to make round or sphere but something else, i.e., to cause this form in something else. For if he makes a form he makes it out of something else (this was assumed above); for example, he makes a brazen sphere. And he makes this in the sense that he makes this thing which is a sphere out of this thing which is bronze. Hence if he also produces the underlying subject itself, evidently he will produce it in the same way, and processes of generation will then proceed to infinity. Hence it is evident that neither the form nor anything else which we term the form in a sensible thing comes to be; i.e., the form or essence is not generated, for this is what comes to be in something else either by art, by nature or by power. **1033a24–1033b8**

2. But he does make a brazen sphere to be. For he makes it from bronze and a sphere, because he causes this form in this matter, and this constitutes a brazen sphere; and this is the being of a sphere. But if the being of sphere in general is to be produced, something will be produced from nothing; for that which comes to be must be divisible, and this is this and that is that. And by this I mean the matter, and by that the form. Therefore, if a sphere is a figure everywhere equidistant from a center, one part of this will be that in which the thing produced exists, and the other will be what exists in this. But this is all that has been produced, as in the case of a brazen sphere. It is evident from what has been said, then, that it is not the thing which is called the form or substance that is generated, but the concrete whole which gets its name from this; and there is matter in everything which is generated; and that this is this and that is that. **1033b8–19**

3. The problem, then, is as follows: is there a sphere apart from these particular spheres, or a house apart from bricks, or one that has never been produced? Now if this were true, no particular thing would exist. But since house means what is such and such, it is not a definite thing, yet the agent makes and generates something that is such and such from this. And when this has been generated it is such and such a particular thing; and this whole particular thing, such as Callias or Socrates, is like a brazen sphere, but man and animal are like brazen sphere in general. It is evident, then, that the cause which consists of the Forms, in the sense in which some are accustomed to speak of them, i.e., supposing that they do exist apart from singular things, is useless so far as processes of generation and substances are concerned. Nor will the Forms be, for this reason, substances existing by themselves. **1033b19–29**

4. And in some cases it is evident that the thing which generates is of the same kind as the thing which is generated, although they are not the same numerically but specifically, for example, in the case of natural generations (for man begets man), unless something contrary to nature is generated, as when a horse begets a mule. And even these cases are alike; for what is common both to horse and ass as their proximate genus has no name, but perhaps both might be something like mule. Hence there is evidently no need to furnish a Form as an examplar; for men would have searched for Forms especially in sensible things, since these are substances in the highest degree. But the thing which generates is adequate for producing the thing and for causing the form in the matter. And when the whole is such and such a form in this flesh and these bones, this is Callias or Socrates; and they differ in their matter (for the matter of each is different) but are the same in form, because form is indivisible. **1033b29–1034a8**

COMMENTARY

1417. The Philosopher posited above certain points about processes of generation in the world as prerequisites for proving his thesis, namely, to show that the causes of the generation of things must not be held to be separate Forms. And since two of these have already been made clear in the foregoing discussion, i.e., that every process of generation is from matter, and that everything which is generated is generated by something similar to itself, he now aims to prove his thesis from the questions which were investigated above.

This is divided into two parts. In the first [1] he shows what things are generated. In the second [3] he shows that the cause of generation is not a separate Form ("The problem, then"). In the third (Lesson 8) he clears up certain things which could be considered as problems pertaining to the points already established ("However, someone").

In regard to the first he does two things. First [1], he shows that a form is generated only accidentally; and second [2], that it is a composite thing which is generated ("But he does make").

He accordingly says, first [1], that the points explained above are true. The first of these is that everything which comes to be, comes to be by something, and this is the agent or generator, which is the principle of generation; and the second is that everything which comes to be, comes to be from something, and by this something from which generation takes place we mean the matter and not the privation. For it was said above that something comes to be from matter in a different way than it does from a privation. The third point is that in every process of generation there must be something which comes to be; and this is either a sphere or a circle or something else.

1418. From the things which have been posited it ought to be evident that, just as an agent does not produce the matter or subject of generation, for example, the bronze, when he generates something, so too "neither does he produce the form," namely, the thing itself which is a sphere, except perhaps accidentally; for he makes a brazen sphere, which is a composite. And since a brazen sphere is also a sphere, he therefore accidentally produces a sphere.

1419. Now the fact that the agent does not produce the matter is evident of itself, because matter is prior to the act of making. Hence it was not necessary for Aristotle to prove that matter is not generated. However, regarding forms there could be a difficulty, because a form is found only at the termination of an activity; and therefore it was necessary for him to prove that a form is produced only accidentally. And the reason is that forms do not have being, properly speaking, but are rather the principles by which things have being. Hence if the process of coming to be is the way to being, only those things properly come to be which have being by their forms; and forms begin to be in the sense that they exist in the things generated, which have being by these forms.

1420. The proof that forms are not generated is as follows. To make this particular thing is to make it from a subject, and this is "totally," i.e., universally, true of every generation. For to make what is bronze round is not to make "round" itself, i.e., roundness, or "sphere" itself, namely, the form of a sphere, but to make "something else," namely, a form, not in any way whatever, "but in something else," namely, in matter; and this is to make the composite. This is made evident as follows. If an agent makes something, he must make it from something else as its matter. And "this was assumed above," namely, that every process of generation is from matter, because of the proof adduced above; as an agent, for example, is said to make a brazen sphere. And this is true because he makes the thing which is a brazen sphere from bronze. Hence, if he also makes the form itself, it is clear that he will make it in the same way, namely, from some matter. And thus just as a brazen sphere will be composed of matter and form, so also will the form of brazen sphere be composed of matter and form; and the same question will be raised in turn about the form of this form, and so on to infinity; and in this way processes of generation will proceed to infinity, because everything generated has matter and form. It is evident, then, that the form of the thing generated does not come to be; and neither does any other thing, whatever it may be, which must be called a form in sensible things, for example, order, combination and shape, which has the character of a form in some things, especially in those made by art.

1421. And since generation pertains to the thing generated, it is evident that it is not the form that is generated but the composite. And so too the essence of the thing generated is not itself generated, except accidentally; for the form or essence "is what comes to be in something else," i.e., in matter, but not of itself. And I say that it comes to be either by art, by nature "or by power," i.e., by anything that acts by violence (See n. 841).

1422. Now he says that the essence of a thing is not generated, even though it is the same as the thing generated; for it was shown above (n. 1362) that each thing is the same as its own essence. But the essence of a thing refers properly to its form. Hence individual conditions, which pertain to a form accidentally, are excluded from it. And species and other universals are generated only accidentally when singular things are generated.

1423. Yet it must be noted that even though it is said in the text that form comes to be in matter, this is not a proper way of speaking; for it is not a form that comes to be, but a composite. For a form is said to exist in matter, although a form does not [properly] exist, but a composite exists by its form. Thus the proper way of speaking is to say that a composite is generated from matter according to such and such a form. For forms are not generated, properly speaking, but are brought from the potency of matter, inasmuch as matter, which is in potentiality to form, becomes actual under some form; and this is to produce a composite.

1424. **But he does make** [2].

Here he shows that it is composite things which are generated. He says that an agent does make a sphere to be;

for he makes it from bronze, which is the matter, as the principle of generation, and from sphere, which is the form and terminus of generation. For he causes "this form," i.e., the figure of a sphere, "in this," i.e., in the matter, in the sense that he changes this bronze into a sphere, and this is a brazen sphere, or the form of a sphere in bronze.

1425. "But this," namely, the figure of a sphere, "is the being of a sphere," i.e., the whatness of a sphere. "But of the being of sphere in general," i.e., of the whatness of the form, there is no generation whatever, because if it were generated it would have to be generated from something as its matter. For everything which comes to be must be divisible, so that "this is this," i.e., one part of it is this, "and that is that," i.e., another part is that. He explains this by saying that one part of it is matter and the other, form. Hence, if the whatness of a sphere in reference to the form itself is "that it is a figure everywhere equidistant from a center," i.e., that it is a certain solid figure of which all lines drawn from the center to the circumference are equal, then "one part," i.e., the matter "of this," namely, of a brazen sphere, must be that in which "the thing produced will exist," namely, the matter, and the other will be what exists in this, namely, the form, which is the figure everywhere equidistant from a center, and "this is all," i.e., the whole, "that has been produced," namely, a brazen sphere.

1426. Hence it is evident from our remarks that, if everything which comes to be must be divisible, the part which is called the form or "substance," i.e., the essence, does not come to be; but it is "the concrete whole," or the composite, which is spoken of and gets its name from such a form or quiddity or whatness which comes to be. Again, it is evident that matter is found in everything which is generated, and that of everything which is generated "this is this and that is that," i.e., one part is matter and the other is form.

1427. **The problem, then** [3].

Since it is not forms which are generated but composite things, he shows that it is not necessary to posit separate Forms as the causes of generation in these lower bodies. And it must be understood that the Platonists claimed that separate Forms cause generation in two ways: first, after the manner of a generator, and, second, after the manner of an exemplar.

Hence he shows, first [3], that separate Forms are not causes of generation after the manner of a generator; and second [4], that they are not causes after the manner of an exemplar ("And in some cases").

He accordingly says, first [3], that it is necessary to consider whether there is a form "which is universal and exists apart from singular forms of this kind," i.e., whether there is a sphere without matter apart from these spheres found in matter; or again whether there is a universal house without matter apart from the bricks of which these particular houses are made. Now he raises the question with reference to artificial things in order to throw light on natural ones, whose forms the Platonists claimed to be separate from matter; so that the question is understood to be whether there is a universal man apart from the flesh and bones of which individual men are composed.

1428. And for the purpose of answering this question he posits here that, if any substance is produced in this way, it will not be a particular thing in any sense, but will only signify such and such a thing, which is not a definite individual. For *Socrates* signifies this particular thing and a definite individual, but *man* signifies such and such a thing, because it signifies a common and indefinite form, since it signifies without the definiteness of a *this* or a *that*. Hence, if there should be a man separate from Socrates and Plato and other individuals of this kind, it will still be a particular or definite thing. But in processes of generation we see that the thing which makes and generates something "from this," i.e., from some particular matter, is "such and such a particular thing," i.e., this definite thing having a definite form; for just as the thing generated must be a particular thing, so also must the thing which generates it be a particular thing, since the thing generated is similar to the thing which generates it, as was proved above (n. 1391). Now that the thing generated is a particular thing is clear from the fact that it is a composite. "And this being," i.e., the composite, when it is "such and such a thing," i.e., a definite thing, is like Callias or Socrates, just as when we speak of this brazen sphere. But man and animal do not signify this matter from which generation proceeds, and neither does brazen sphere, taken universally. Therefore, if the composite is generated, and it is generated only from this matter whereby it is this particular thing, then what is generated must be a particular thing. And since the thing generated is similar to the one generating it, the latter must also be a particular thing. Hence there is no universal form without matter.

1429. It is therefore evident from what has been said that, if there are any forms separate from singular things, they are of no use for the generations and substances of things, just as some are accustomed to speak of "the cause which consists of the Forms," intending thus to posit such forms. For one reason why the Platonists posited separate Forms was that they might be the cause of processes of generation in the world. Hence, if separate Forms cannot be the cause of generation, it is evident that forms will not be certain substances existing by themselves.

1430. And it must be noted that all those who have failed to consider what the Philosopher proved above—that forms do not come to be—face the same difficulty with regard to the production of forms, because it was for this reason that some men were compelled to say that all forms are created; for while they held that forms come to be, they could not hold that they come from matter since matter is not a part of form; and therefore they concluded that forms come from nothing, and, consequently, that they are created. But because of this difficulty, on the other hand, some men claimed that forms actually pre-exist in matter, and this is to suppose that forms are hidden, as Anaxagoras maintained.

1431. Now the view of Aristotle, who claimed that forms are not generated but only composite things, excludes both of these other opinions. For it is not necessary to say that forms are caused by some external agent, or that they will always be present in matter actually, but only potentially, and that in the generation of the composite they are brought from potentiality to actuality.

1432. **And in some cases** [4].

He shows that separate Forms cannot be the cause of the generation of things after the manner of an exemplar. He says that even though in some cases one may encounter the problem whether the generator is similar to the thing generated, still in the case of some things it is evident that the generator is of the same kind as the thing generated: not numerically the same but specifically, as is clear in the case of natural beings; for man begets man, and similarly a horse begets a horse, and each natural thing produces something similar to itself in species, unless something beyond nature happens to result, as when a horse begets a mule. And this generation is beyond nature, because it is outside of the aim of a particular nature.

1433. For the formative power, which is in the sperm of the male, is designed by nature to produce something completely the same as that from which the sperm has been separated; but its secondary aim, when it cannot induce a perfect likeness, is to induce any kind of likeness that it can. And since in the generation of a mule the sperm of a horse cannot induce the form of a horse in the matter, because it is not adapted to receive the form of a horse, it therefore induces a related form. Hence in the generation of a mule the generator is similar in a way to the thing generated; for there is a proximate genus, which lacks a name, common to horse and to ass; and mule is also contained under that genus. Hence in reference to that genus it can be said that like generates like; for example, if we might say that that proximate genus is *beast of burden*, we could say that, even though a horse does not generate a horse but a mule, still a beast of burden generates a beast of burden.

1434. Hence it is evident that everything which is generated receives the likeness of its form from the power of the thing generating it. And for this reason it is obviously not necessary to posit some separate Form, as the exemplar of the things which are generated, from whose image the things generated receive a similar form, as the Platonists claimed. For exemplars of this kind are especially necessary in the case of the natural substances mentioned above, which are substances to a greater degree when compared with artificial things. Now in the case of the foregoing substances the generator is sufficient to cause a likeness of form; and it is enough to maintain that the generator causes the form in the matter, i.e., that the thing which causes the thing generated to receive such a form is not some form outside of matter, but a form in matter.

1435. "And every form" which is in the matter, namely, "in this flesh and these bones," is some singular thing, such as Callias or Socrates. And this form which causes a likeness in species in the process of generation, also differs numerically from the form of the thing generated because of difference in matter; for material diversity is the principle of diversity among individuals in the same species; for the matter containing the form of the man who begets and that of the man who is begotten are different. But both forms are the same in species; for the form itself is "indivisible," i.e., it does not differ in the one who generates and in the one who is generated. Hence it follows that it is not necessary to posit a form apart from singular things, which causes the form in the things generated, as the Platonists claimed.

LESSON 8

Generation by Art and by Nature or by Art Alone. Generation of Composites, Not Substantial or Accidental Forms

ARISTOTLE'S TEXT Chapter 9: 1034a9–1034b19

1. *However, someone might raise the question why some things come to be both by art and by chance, as health, while others do not, as a house.* **1034a9–10**

2. *And the reason is that in some of these the matter, which is the principle of generation in the making and producing of everything which comes to be by art, and in which some part of the thing made is present, the matter of these, I say, is such that it can set itself in motion, whereas the matters of others cannot. And of the former kind some can set itself is motion in a special way, and some cannot; for many things can move themselves but not in some special way, as in dancing. Those things, then, whose matter is of such a kind, for instance, stones, can only be moved by something else. Yet in another way they can move themselves, as in the case of fire. And for this reason some things will not exist apart from one who possesses an art, while others will; for they will be moved either by those things which do not have art or by those which have it in part.* **1034a10–21**

3. *And it is evident from what has been said that in a sense all things come from something which is univocal (as natural things), or from something which is univocal in part (as a house comes from a house, or by means of mind; for art is a form), or from a part or from something having a part, unless it comes to be accidentally.* **1034a21–25**

4. *For the first and proper cause of the production of anything is a part of the thing produced; for the hêat in the motion produces heat in the body; and this is either health or a part of health, or some part of health or health itself follows from it. Hence it is said to cause health, because it causes that from which health follows, and of which health is an accident. Hence, just as in syllogisms the basis of everything is substance (for a syllogism proceeds from the whatness of a thing), so too in this case processes of generation proceed from it.* **1034a25–32**

5. *And those things which are constituted by nature are similar to these; for the seed produces something in the same way as things which operate by art; for it contains the form potentially, and that from which the seed comes [and the thing which it generates] are in a sense univocal, for it is not necessary to inquire about all things in the same way as we do when we say that a man comes from a man; for a woman also comes from a man. Hence a mule does not come from a mule, unless there should be some defect. And whatever things arise by chance, as some artificial things do, are those whose matter can be moved by itself by the very motion by which the seed moves. But those things whose matter does not possess this capacity cannot be generated in any other way than by the agents themselves.* **1034a33–1034b7**

6. *Now it is not only with reference to substance that our argument proves that the specifying principle does not come to be, but the common reasoning also applies in a similar way to all the primary genera, such as quantity, quality and the other categories. For a brazen sphere as such comes to be, but not the sphere or the bronze, but if it does come to be, it comes to be in the bronze (because it is always necessary that the form and the matter pre-exist). This must also be the case with the quiddity, with quality, with quantity, and also with the other categories; for quality does not come to be, but wood of such a quality; and quantity does not come to be, but so much wood or so large an animal.* **1034b7–16**

7. *But from these remarks it is possible to learn a property of substance, namely, that there must always pre-exist another actual substance which produces it; for example, an animal must pre-exist if an animal is generated. But quantity and quality must pre-exist only potentially.* **1034b16–19**

COMMENTARY

1436. Having shown that separate forms are not the cause of generation in these lower bodies, the Philosopher now clears up certain things which could be regarded as problems relating to the points already established. This is divided into three parts insofar as there are three problems which he intends to clear up. The second part [3] begins where he says "And it is evident"; and the third [6], at the words, "Now it is not only." In regard to the first he does two things. First [1], he states the problem. Second [2], he solves it ("And the reason").

Now the first problem stems from a statement which he had made above (n. 1412) to the effect that, when the principle of health is the form in the mind, health is then a result of art; but when health is not a result of this principle but only of the act of heating, health then comes about by chance, for example, when health happens to result from a vigorous rubbing. But this cannot be true of everything that comes to be by art; for a house is never produced by any principle except the form of a house in the mind, and thus it will always come to be by art and never by chance. Hence the problem is why some things, for instance, health, sometimes come to be by art and sometimes by chance, while others, for instance, a house, come to be only by art and never by chance.

1437. **And the reason** [2].

He then solves the problem. He says that the reason for the above-mentioned difference in the case of artificial things lies in the fact that the matter from which generation begins, inasmuch as it is the basis of the making and producing any of the things which come about by art, is such as to contain some part of the thing generated. For the matter must have some aptitude for form, because not any artifact can be produced from any matter, but each from some definite matter; for example, a saw is not produced from wool but from iron. Hence the aptitude itself of the artifact for a form, which is in the matter, is already some part of the artifact which is in the matter; because without this aptitude the artifact cannot exist; for instance, there cannot be a saw without hardness, by which the iron is disposed for the form of a saw.

1438. But this part is found in matter in two ways: sometimes in such a way that the matter can move itself by this part, i.e., by the part of the form existing within it, and sometimes not. For example, in the case of the human body, which is the matter of health, there is an active power by which the body can heal itself, but in the case of stones and timbers there is no active power by which the matter can be moved to receive the form of a house.

1439. And if the matter can be so moved to receive a form by a part of the form which exists in it, this can occur in two ways. For sometimes it can be moved by an intrinsic principle, which is the part mentioned above, in the same way in which it is moved by art, as occurs in the restoration of health; for the nature of the human body acts in the same way with regard to health as art does. But sometimes the matter cannot be moved by an intrinsic principle in the same way in which it is moved by art, although it can be moved by itself in some way. For there are many things which can be moved by themselves, but not in the same way in which they are moved by art, as is clear in the case of dancing. For men who do not have the art of dancing can move about but not in the way in which those men do who have this art.

1440. Therefore those artificial things which have this kind of nature, such as a house made of bricks, cannot set themselves in motion; for they cannot be moved unless they are moved by something else. This is true not only of artificial things but also of natural ones; for in this way too the matter of fire cannot be moved to receive the form of fire unless it is moved by something else. And it is for this reason that the form of fire is generated only by something else. Hence it follows that some artificial things cannot come to be unless there is something which possesses art, i.e., those which do not have in their matter any principle which can move their matter to receive a form, or which cannot cause motion in the way in which art does.

1441. And those things which can be moved by some extrinsic principle which is not possessed of art, can both be and come to be without the intervention of art; for the matters of these are moved by things which do not possess art. He makes this clear in two ways: first, by pointing out that this can happen insofar as they can be moved by certain other extrinsic principles which do not possess art; and second, when "the matter is moved by a part" [i.e., of the composite] namely, by some intrinsic principle, which is some part of the form, for example, when health is restored to the human body by some intrinsic principle which is a part of the form.

1442a. Now it must be noted that some persons, because of the words which are used here, claim that in every natural generation the matter contains some active principle, which is the form pre-existing potentially in the matter and a kind of beginning of form, and thus it is called a part of the form. And they try to establish this, first, from the statements made here; for Aristotle seems to say here that those things whose matter contains no active principle are produced by art alone; and therefore they think that some active principle must be present in the matter of things which are generated by nature.

1442b. Second, they try to establish this from the fact that every motion whose principle is not intrinsic to the thing moved but extrinsic to it is a violent motion and not a natural one. For if there were no active principle in the matter of those things which are generated by nature, the process of generation of these things would not be natural but violent; or, in other words, there would be no difference between artificial generations and natural ones.

1442c. And when one argues against them that, if the generation of those things which come about by nature is from an intrinsic principle, such things do not therefore stand in need of any extrinsic generator, their answer is: just as an intrinsic principle is not a perfect form but a kind of beginning of form, neither is it a perfect active principle in the sense that it can act of itself so as to bring about generation; but it bears some likeness to an active power inasmuch as it cooperates with an extrinsic agent. For if the mobile object contributes nothing to the motion produced by an external agent, the motion is violent; because violence exists when the thing undergoing the change is moved by an extrinsic principle and does not itself contribute anything to the change, as is stated in Book III of the *Ethics*. [1110a1]

1442d. Now this opinion seems to

resemble the one expressed by those who claim that forms lie hidden; for since a thing acts only insofar as it is actual, if the parts or beginnings of the forms which exist in matter have some active power, it follows that they are actual to some degree; and this is to maintain that forms lie hidden. Furthermore, since being is prior to action, a form cannot be understood to act before it actually exists.

1442e. Therefore it must be said that, just as living things alone are found to move themselves locally, whereas other things are moved by an extrinsic principle, i.e., either by one which generates or which removes some obstacle, as is stated in Book VIII of the *Physics*, [255b24] so too only living things are found to move themselves with the other motions. This is because they are found to have different parts, one of which can be a mover and the other something moved; and this must be true of everything that moves itself, as is proved in Book VIII of the **Physics**. [258a17] Hence in the generation of living things we find an intrinsic efficient principle, which is the formative power in the seed. And just as living things have a power of growth, which is responsible for the motion of increase and decrease, in a similar fashion they have an intrinsic motive principle responsible for the qualitative change of being healed. For since the heart is not subject to disease, the natural power which is present in it, as in something healthy, changes the whole body to a state of health.

1442f. Hence the Philosopher is speaking here of such matter as has an efficient principle within itself, and not of inanimate things. This is clear from the fact that he compares the matter of fire with the matter of a house in this respect, that both are moved to receive their form by an extrinsic principle. It does not follow, however, that the process whereby inanimate bodies are generated is not natural; for in order to have natural motion it is not necessary that the principle of motion present in the thing moved should always be an active and formal principle; but sometimes it is passive and material. Hence in Book II of the *Physics* [193a9-b7] nature is distinguished into matter and form. And the natural generation of simple bodies is said to proceed from this principle, as the Commentator says in his commentary on Book II of the *Physics*. Yet there is a difference between the matter of natural things and that of things made by art, because in the matter of natural things there is a natural aptitude for form, and this can be brought to actuality by a natural agent; but this does not occur in the matter of things made by art.

1443. **And it is evident** [3].

Then he clears up the second problem which could arise from the foregoing discussion; for he had said above (n. 1432) that everything which is generated is generated by something having a similar form. Now this does not apply in the same way to all things, and therefore he intends here to clarify how this applies in a different way to different things.

In regard to this he does two things. First, he distinguishes the different ways in which the thing generated is like the thing which generates it. Second [4], he explains these ways ("For the first").

With regard to the first [3] it must be noted that everything which is generated by something is generated by it either properly or accidentally. Now whatever is generated by something accidentally is not generated by it according as it is a thing of some special kind. Hence in the generator there does not have to be any likeness of the thing generated; for example, the discovery of a treasure has no likeness in him who, when he digs in order to plant something, discovers the treasure accidentally. But a generator in the proper sense generates something of the same kind as itself. Hence in a proper generator the likeness of the thing generated must exist in some way.

1444. But this comes about in three ways: First, when the form of the thing generated pre-exists in the generator according to the same mode of being, and in a similar matter, as when fire generates fire or man begets man. This type of generation is wholly univocal.

1445. Second, when the form of the thing generated pre-exists in the generator, neither according to the same mode of being, nor in a substance of the same kind; for example, the form of a house pre-exists in the builder, not with the material being which it has in the stones and timbers, but with the immaterial being which it has in the mind of the builder. This type of generation is partly univocal, from the standpoint of form, and partly equivocal, from the standpoint of the being of the form in the subject.

1446. Third, when the whole form of the thing generated does not preexist in the generator, but only some part of it or a part of a part; as in the medicine which has been heated there pre-exists the heat which is a part of health, or something leading to a part of health. This type of generation is not univocal in any way.

1447. Hence he says, "It is evident from what has been said that in a sense all things come from something which is totally univocal, as natural things," for example, fire comes from fire, and a man from a man; or it comes from something which is univocal "in part," in reference to the form, and equivocal in part, in reference to the being which the form has in the subject; for example, a house comes from the house which is the art in the builder, "or by means of mind," or by a habit of art; for the building art is the form of the house. Or in a third way some things come from the form pre-existing in the generator, or from the generator himself who possesses a part of the above-mentioned form. For the process of generation can be said to be a result either of the form or of a part of the form, or of something having the form or a part of the form; but it comes from something having the form as from a generator, and from the form or a part of the form as from something by which the generator generates; for it is not the form that generates or acts, but the thing having the form generates and acts by means of it. By this I mean that a thing is generated by something like itself in the ways mentioned above, unless it comes about in an accidental way; for then it is not necessary that any likeness of this kind should be observed, as has been explained (n. 1443).

1448. **For the first** [4].

Here he explains the ways mentioned above in which one thing comes from something else. He does this first in the case of artificial things; and second [5], in the case of natural ones ("And those things which").

He accordingly says, first [4], that the thing produced must come from some part, because the first and proper cause of the production of anything produced is the part of it which preexists in the one producing it, and which is either the form itself of the producer or a part of the form. For when heat is caused by motion, heat is present in a sense in the motion itself as in an active power; for the power of causing heat which is in the motion is itself something belonging to the genus of heat; and the heat which is present virtually in the motion causes the heat in the body, not by a univocal generation but by an equivocal one; for the heat in the motion and that in the heated body are not of exactly the same nature. But heat is either health itself or some part of health, or it is accompanied by some part of health or health itself.

1449. Now by these four alternatives which he gives he wants us to understand the four modes in which the form of the thing causing generation can be referred to the form of the thing generated. The first of these is found when the form of the thing generated is totally in the thing which causes generation; as the form of a house is in the mind of the master builder, and the form of the fire which is generated is in the fire which generates it. The second mode is found when a part of the form of the thing generated is in the thing causing generation, as when a hot medicine restores health by heating; for the heat produced in the one who is being healed is a part of health. The third mode is found when part of the form is in the thing causing generation, not actually but virtually, as when motion restores health by heating; for heat is present in the motion virtually but not actually. The fourth mode is found when the whole form itself is present virtually but not actually in the thing which causes generation; for example, the form of numbness is in the eel which makes the hand numb. And it is similar in the case of other things which act by means of the whole form. Therefore he refers to the first mode by the words "Either health"; to the second mode, by the words "or a part"; to the third, by the words "or some part of health follows from it"; and to the fourth, by the words "or health itself." And since motion causes the heat from which health follows, for this reason too motion is said to cause health, because that causes health from which health follows or ensues. Or better "that which follows from and happens as a result of motion," namely, heat, causes health.

1450. Hence it is evident that, just as in syllogisms the basis of all demonstrations "is substance," i.e., the whatness (for demonstrative syllogisms proceed from the whatness of a thing, since the middle term in demonstrations is a definition), "so too in this case," namely, in matters of operation, processes of generation proceed from the quiddity. In this statement the likeness of the speculative intellect to the practical intellect is shown; for just as the speculative intellect proceeds to demonstrate the properties of subjects from a study of their quiddity, in a similar fashion the intellect proceeds from the form of the work, which is its quiddity, as was stated above.

1451. **And those things** [5].

Here he explains his statement about artificial things in their application to natural things. He says that those things which are constituted by nature are similar to those which come to be by art; for the seed acts for the purpose of generating, and this is what happens in the case of things which come to be by art; for just as a master builder is not a house actually and does not possess the form which constitutes a house actually but only potentially, so too the seed is not an animal actually, nor does it possess a soul actually, which is the form of an animal, but only potentially. For in the seed there is a formative power which is related to the matter of the thing conceived in the same way in which the form of the house in the mind of the builder is related to the stones and timbers; but there is this difference: the form of an art is wholly extrinsic to the stones and timbers, whereas the power of the seed is present in the seed itself.

1452. Now although the generation of an animal from seed does not proceed from the seed as from something univocal, since the seed is not an animal, still that from which the seed comes is in some measure univocal with the thing which comes from it; for the seed comes from an animal. And in this respect natural generation bears no likeness to artificial generation; because it is not necessary for the form of the house in the mind of the master builder to come from a house, although this sometimes happens, as when someone makes a plan of one house from that of another. But it is always necessary for seed to come from an animal.

1453. Moreover, he explains what he meant by the phrase "in a sense univocal," because in natural generations it is not necessary that there should always be univocity in every respect, as there is when a man is said to come from a man, "for a woman comes from a man" as an agent; and a mule does not come from a mule, but from a horse or an ass, and in this case there is some likeness, as he said above (n. 1433). Further, since he had said that there must be univocity to some degree because of that from which the seed comes, he adds that this must be understood "unless there should be some defect," i.e., unless there is some shortcoming of natural power in the seed; for then the generator produces something which is not similar to itself, as is evident in the birth of monsters.

1454. And "just as in those," i.e., in artificial things, some come to be not only by art but also by chance, when the matter can be moved by itself by the same motion according to which it is moved by art (but when it cannot be moved in this way, then that which comes to be by art cannot be produced by anything else than art), so too in this case some things can come to be by chance and without seed, whose matter can be moved by itself in this way "by the motion by which the seed moves," i.e., with the aim of generating an animal. This is evident in the case of those things which are generated from decay, and which are said in one sense to be a result of chance, and in another not, as was explained above (n. 1403). But those things whose matter cannot be moved by itself by that very motion by which the seed is moved, are incapable of being generated in another way than from their own seed; and this is evident in the case of man and horse and other perfect animals. Now it is clear from what is said here that not all animals can be generated both from seed and without seed, as Avicenna claims, and that none can be generated in both ways, as Averroes claims.

1455. Now it must be observed that from what has been said here it is possible to solve the problems facing those who claim that the forms generated in these lower bodies do not derive their being from natural generators but from forms which exist apart from matter. For they seem to maintain this position chiefly because of those living things which are generated from decay, whose forms do not seem to come from anything that is similar to them in form. And again since even in animals which are generated from seed the active power of generation, which is in the seed, is not a soul, they said that the soul of the animal which is generated cannot come from the seed. And they proceed to argue thus because they think that no active principle of generation is found in these lower bodies except heat and cold, which are accidental forms, and it does not seem that substantial forms can be generated by means of these. Nor does it seem that the argument which the Philosopher used against those who posited separate exemplars, holds in all cases, so that the forms in things causing generation are sufficient to account for the likeness of form in the things which are generated.

1456. But all these difficulties are solved by the text of Aristotle if it is examined carefully. For it is said in the text that the active power in the seed, even though it is not an animal actually, is nevertheless an animal virtually. Hence just as the form of a house in matter can come from the form of house in the mind, so too a complete soul can come from the power in the seed, exclusive of the intellect, which is from an extrinsic principle, as is said in Book XVI of ***Animals***. *[736b28; 737a9-10]* And this is true inasmuch as the power in the seed comes from a complete soul by whose power it acts; for intermediate principles act by virtue of primary principles.

1457. Now in the matter of those things which are generated from decay there also exists a principle which is similar to the active power in the seed, by which the soul of such animals is caused. And just as the power in the seed comes from the complete soul of the animal and from the power of a celestial body, in a similar fashion the power of generating an animal which exists in decayed matter is from a celestial body alone, in which all forms of things which are generated are present virtually as in their active principle. And even though active qualities are operative, they do not act by their own power but by virtue of their substantial forms to which they are related as instruments; as it is said in Book II of ***The Soul*** [416a14] that the heat of fire is like an instrument of the nutritive soul.

1458. **Now it is not only** [6].

Then he clears up the third problem that could arise from his remarks, for he had proved above that it is not forms which are generated but composite things, and someone could be puzzled whether this is true only of substantial forms or also of accidental forms. So his aim here is to meet this problem, and therefore he does two things. First, he shows that this is true of both types of forms. He says that the argument given above "with reference to substance," i.e., the category of substance, not only shows that the "specifying principle," or form, does not come to be, but is common in a similar way "to all genera," i.e., to the categories, such as quantity and quality and so on. "For a brazen sphere as such comes to be," i.e., a composite such as a brazen sphere, "but not the sphere," i.e., what has the character of a form, "or the bronze," i.e., what has the character of matter. And if a sphere does come to be in some manner of speaking, it does not come to be in itself, but comes to be in bronze; because, in order for generation to take place the matter and the form must pre-exist, as was shown above (nn. 1383–88). Thus it is "a brazen sphere as such," namely, the composite, which comes to be, "and this must also be the case with the quiddity," i.e., the category of substance, and with quality and quantity, and also with the other categories. For "quality" does not come to be, i.e., quality itself, but this whole which is "wood of such a quality"; nor does "quantity" come to be, i.e., quantity itself, but so much wood or so large an animal.

1459. **But from these remarks** [7].

He shows what the difference is between substance and accidents. He says that we must take this characteristic to be a property of substance as compared with accidents, namely, that when a substance is generated there must always exist another substance which causes its generation; for example, in the case of animals generated from seed, if an animal is generated, another animal which generates it must pre-exist. But in the case of quantity and quality and the other accidents it is not necessary that these pre-exist actually but only potentially, and this is the material principle and subject of motion. For the active principle of a substance can only be a substance; but the active principle of accidents can be something which is not an accident, namely, a substance.

LESSON 9

Parts of the Quiddity and Definition. Priority of Parts to Whole

ARISTOTLE'S TEXT Chapter 10: 1034b20–1035b3

1. *But since the definition is the intelligible expression of a thing, and every intelligible expression has parts, and just as the intelligible expression is related to the thing, so is a part of the intelligible expression to a part of the thing, the problem now arises whether the intelligible expression of the parts must be present in the intelligible expression of the whole or not; for in some cases they seem to be and in others they do not, for the intelligible expression of a circle does not include that of its segments [but the intelligible expression of a syllable includes that of its letters], yet a circle is divided into segments as a syllable is into elements.* **1034b20–28**

2. *Further, if parts are prior to a whole, and an acute angle is a part of a right angle, and a finger a part of a man, an acute angle will be prior to a right angle, and a finger prior to a man. However, the latter seem to be prior, for in the intelligible expression the parts are explained from them; and wholes are prior because they can exist without a part.* **1034b28–32**

3. *Or perhaps it happens that the term part is used in many senses, one of which is what measures a thing quantitatively. But let us dismiss this sense of the term and inquire about those things which constitute the parts of which substance is composed. Now if matter is one of these, and form another, and the thing composed of these a third, then there is one sense in which even matter is called a part of a thing, and there is another in which it is not, but only those things of which the intelligible expression or specifying principle consists. For example, flesh is not a part of concavity, because flesh is the matter in which concavity is produced; but it is a part of snubness. And bronze is a part of the whole statue, but it is not a part of the statue in the sense of form; for predications must be made according to a thing's form and insofar as each thing has a form, but the material principle should never be predicated of a thing essentially. And this is why the intelligible expression of a circle does not contain that of its segments, whereas the intelligible expression of a syllable does contain that of its letters; for the letters are parts of the intelligible expression of the form, and are not matter. But segments of this kind are parts of the matter in which the form is produced, yet they are more akin to the form than bronze is when roundness is produced in bronze. However, not all the elements of a syllable will be contained in its intelligible expression; for example, the letters inscribed in wax or produced in the air; for these are already parts of the syllable as its sensible matter. For even if a line when divided is dissolved into halves, or a man into bones and sinews and flesh, it does not follow for this reason that they are composed of these as parts of their substance, but as their matter; and these are parts of the concrete whole, but not of the specifying principle, or of that to which the intelligible expression belongs. Hence they are not included in the intelligible expression of these things. Therefore in some cases the intelligible expression of a thing will include that of such parts as those mentioned, but in other cases it need not include them unless taken together they constitute the intelligible expression of the thing. For it is by reason of this that some things are composed of these as the principles into which they are dissolved, while others are not. Hence all things which are matter and form taken together, as snub and brazen circle, are dissolved into these parts, and matter is one of them. But all things which are not conceived with matter but without it, as the intelligible expression of form alone, are not corrupted either in an unqualified sense or in such a way as this. Hence these material parts are the principles and parts which come under these, but they are neither parts nor principles of the form. Therefore a statue made of clay is dissolved into clay, and a sphere into bronze, and Callias into flesh and bones; and again a circle is dissolved into its segments, because it is something conceived with matter. For the term circle is used equivocally both of that which is*

called such without qualification and of an individual circle, because there is no proper name for individual circles. **1034b32–1035b3**

COMMENTARY

1460. Having shown what the quiddity (or essence) of a thing is, and to what things it belongs, and how it is related to the things to which it belongs, and that it is not necessary to posit separate quiddities in order to account for the generation of things, here the Philosopher's aim is to expose the principles of which a thing's quiddity is composed. This is divided into two parts. In the first [1] he describes the principles of which a thing's quiddity is composed; and in the second (Lesson 12) he explains how the thing which comes into being from these principles is one ("And now").

The first part is divided into two. In the first he raises a difficulty. In the second [3] he solves it ("Or perhaps").

The first part is divided into two insofar as he raises two difficulties about the same point. The second [2] is treated where he says, "Further, if parts."

He accordingly says, first [1], that every "definition is the intelligible expression of a thing," i.e., a certain combination of words arranged by reason. For one word cannot constitute a definition, because a definition must convey a distinct knowledge of the real principles which come together to constitute a thing's essence; otherwise a definition would not adequately expose a thing's essence. And for this reason it is said in Book I of the *Physics* [184b11] that a definition divides "the thing defined into its separate elements," i.e., it expresses distinctly each of the principles of the thing defined, and this can be done only by means of several words. Hence one word cannot be a definition, but it can give us information about something in the same way that a word which is better known can give us information about a word which is less well known. Now every intelligible expression has parts, because it is a composite utterance and not a simple word. Therefore it seems that, just as the intelligible expression of a thing is related to the thing, so also are the parts of the intelligible expression related to the parts of the thing. And for this reason the problem arises whether the intelligible expression of the parts must be given in that of the whole or not.

1461. This difficulty is confirmed by the fact that in some intelligible expressions of wholes the intelligible expressions of the parts seem to be present, and in some not; for in the definition of a circle the definition "of the segments of a circle" is not present, i.e., the definition of the parts which are separated from the circle, as the semicircle and quarter circle; but in the definition of a syllable the definition "of its elements," i.e., its letters, is present. For if a syllable is defined it is necessary to say that it is a sound composed of letters; and so we give in the definition of a syllable the letter and, consequently, its definition, because we can always substitute the definition for the word. Yet a circle is divided into segments as its parts, just as a syllable is divided "into its elements," or letters.

1462. Now his statement here that a part of the definition of a thing is related to a part of the thing as the definition is related to the thing, seems to involve a difficulty; for the definition is the same as the thing. Hence it seems to follow that the parts of the definition are the same as the parts of the thing; and this seems to be false. For the parts of the definition are predicated of the thing defined, as animal and rational are predicated of man, but no integral part is predicated of a whole.

1463. But it must be remarked that the parts of a definition signify the parts of a thing inasmuch as the parts of a definition are derived from the parts of a thing, yet not so that the parts of a definition are the parts of a thing. For neither animal nor rational are parts of man, but animal is taken from one part and rational from another; for an animal is a thing having a sentient nature, and a rational being is one having reason. Now sentient nature has the character of matter in relation to reason. And this is why genus is taken from matter and difference from form, and species from both matter and form together; for man is a thing having reason in a sentient nature.

1464. **Further, if parts** [2].

Then he gives the second difficulty; and this has to do with the priority of parts. For all parts seem to be prior to a whole as simple things are prior to what is composite, because an acute angle is prior to a right angle, since a right angle is divided into two or more acute angles, and in the same way a finger is prior to a man. Hence it seems that an acute angle is naturally prior to a right angle, and a finger prior to a man.

1465. But, on the other hand, the latter seem to be prior; namely, a right angle seems to be prior to an acute angle, and a man to a finger, and this seems to be so for two reasons. First, they are prior in meaning; for in this way those things which are given in the intelligible expression of other things are said to be prior to them, and not the other way around; "For in their intelligible expression an acute angle and a finger are explained from these," i.e., they are defined in reference to these, namely, to man and to right angle, as we have stated. Hence it seems that a man and a right angle are prior to a finger and to an acute angle.

1466. Second, some things are said to be prior because they can exist without others, for those things which can exist without others, and not the reverse, are said to be prior, as is stated in Book V (n. 950); for example, the number one can exist without the number two. Now a man can exist without a finger, but not a finger without a man, because a finger which has been severed from the body is not a finger, as is stated below (n. 1488). Hence it seems that a man is prior to a finger; and the same reasoning applies to a right angle and to an acute angle.

1467. **Or perhaps** [3].

Then he solves the difficulties which were raised; and this is divided into two parts. In the first he gives the solution. In the second (Lesson 10) he explains it ("The truth, then"). In the third (Lesson 11), he settles a problem that could arise from the foregoing solution ("Now the problem").

In support of what has been said in this chapter it should be noted that there are two opinions about the definitions of things and their essences. Some say that the whole essence of a species is the form; for example, the whole essence of man is his soul. And for this reason they say that in reality the form of the whole, which is signified by the word *humanity*, is the same as the form of the part, which is signified by the word *soul*, but that they differ only in definition; for the form of the part is so designated inasmuch as it perfects the matter and makes it to be actual, but the form of the whole is so designated inasmuch as the whole which is constituted by it is placed in its species. And for this reason they think that no material parts are given in the definition which designates the species, but only the formal principles of the species. This appears to be the opinion of Averroes and of certain of his followers.

1468. But this seems to be opposed to the opinion of Aristotle; for he says above, in Book VI (n. 1158), that natural things have sensible matter in their definition, and in this respect they differ from the objects of mathematics. Now it cannot be said that natural substances are defined by something that does not pertain to their being; for substances are not defined by addition but only accidents, as was stated above (n. 1352). Hence it follows that sensible matter is a part of the essence of natural substances, and not only of individuals but also of species themselves; for it is not individuals that are defined but species.

1469. And from this arises the other opinion, which Avicenna entertains. According to this opinion the form of the whole, which is the quiddity of the species, differs from the form of the part as a whole differs from a part; for the quiddity of a species is composed of matter and form, although not of this individual matter and this individual form; for it is an individual, such as Socrates or Callias, that is composed of these. This is the view which Aristotle introduces in this chapter in order to reject Plato's opinion about the Ideas, for Plato said that the forms of natural things have being of themselves without sensible matter, as though sensible matter were in no way a part of their species. Therefore, having shown that sensible matter is a part of the species of natural things, he now shows that there cannot be species of natural things without sensible matter; for example, the species *man* cannot exist without flesh and bones; and the same is true in other cases.

1470. Now this will constitute the third method by which the Ideas are rejected; for Aristotle rejected them, first, on the grounds that the essence of a thing does not exist apart from the thing to which it belongs; second, on the grounds that forms existing apart from matter are not causes of generation either in the manner of a generator or in that of an exemplar. And now in this third way he rejects Plato's thesis on the grounds that the intelligible expression of a species includes common sensible matter.

1471. Hence in solving this difficulty [3] he says that the word *part* is used in several senses, as was explained in Book V (n. 1093); for example, in one sense it means a quantitative part, i.e., one which measures a whole quantitatively, as half a cubit is part of a cubit, and the number two is part of the number six. But this type of part is at present omitted, because it is not his aim here to investigate the parts of quantity, but those of a definition, which signifies a thing's substance. Hence it is necessary to investigate the parts of which a thing's substance is composed.

1472. Now the parts of substance are matter and form and the composite of these; and any one of these three—matter, form and the composite—is substance, as was stated above (n. 1276). Therefore in one sense matter is part of a thing, and in another sense it is not, but this is true "of those things of which the intelligible expression or specifying principle consists," i.e., the form; for we understand concavity as form and nose as matter, and snub as the composite. And according to this, flesh, which is the matter or a part of the matter, is not a part of concavity, which is the form or specifying principle; for flesh is the matter in which the form is produced. Yet flesh is some part of snub, provided that snub is understood to be a composite and not merely a form. Similarly, bronze is a part of the whole statue, which is composed of matter and form; but it is not a part of the statue insofar as statue is taken here in the sense of the specifying principle, or form.

1473. And to insure an understanding of what the specifying principle is and what the matter is, it is necessary to point out that anything which belongs to a thing inasmuch as it has a specific form belongs to its specific form; for example, inasmuch as a thing has the form of a statue, it is proper for it to have a shape or some such quality. But what is related to a form as its matter must never be predicated essentially of a form. Yet it must be noted that no kind of matter, be it common or individual, is related essentially to a species insofar as species is taken in the sense of a form, but insofar as it is taken in the sense of a universal; for example, when we say that man is a species, common matter then pertains essentially to the species, but not individual matter, in which the nature of the form is included.

1474. Hence it must be said that the definition of a circle is not included in "the definition of its segments," i.e., the parts divided from a circle, whether they be semicircles or quarter circles. But the definition of a syllable includes that "of its elements," or letters; and the reason is that "the elements," or letters, are parts of a syllable with reference to its form, but not to its matter; for the form of a syllable consists in being composed of letters. The divisions of a circle, however, are not parts of a circle taken formally, but of this part of a circle, or of these circles, as the matter in which the form of a circle is produced.

1475. This can be understood from the rule laid down above; for he had said that what belongs essentially to each thing having a form pertains to the form, and that what belongs to the matter is accidental to the specific form; but it belongs essentially to a syllable, which is composed of letters. Now the fact that a circle may be actually divided into semicircles is accidental to a circle, not as a circle, but as *this* circle, of which this line, which is a material part of it, is a division. Hence it is clear that a semicircle is part of a circle in reference to individual matter. Therefore this matter, i.e., this line, is more akin to the form than bronze is, which is sensible matter, when roundness, which is the form of a circle, is produced in bronze; because the form of a circle never exists apart from a line, but it does exist apart from bronze. And just as the parts of a circle, which are accidents in reference to individual matter, are not given in its definition, in a similar fashion not all letters are given in the definition of a syllable, i.e., those which are parts along with matter, for example, those inscribed in wax or produced in the air, since these are already parts of a syllable as sensible matter.

1476. For not all the parts into which a thing is corrupted, when it is dissolved, must be parts of its substance; because even if a line when divided is dissolved into two parts, or a man into bones, sinews, and flesh, it does not therefore follow, if a line is thus composed of halves, or a man of flesh and bones, that these are parts of their substance; but these things are constituted of these parts as their matter. Hence these are parts of "the concrete whole," or composite, "but not of the specifying principle," i.e., the form, or "of that to which the intelligible expression belongs," i.e., of the thing defined. Therefore no such parts are properly given in the intelligible expressions of these things.

1477. Still it must be noted that in the definitions of some things the intelligible expressions of such parts are included, i.e., in the definitions of composite things, of which they are the parts. But in the definitions of other things this is not necessary, i.e., in the definitions of forms, unless such forms are taken along with matter. For even though matter is not part of a form, it must be given in the definition of a form, since the mind cannot conceive of a form without conceiving matter; for example, organic body is included in the definition of soul. For just as accidents have complete being only insofar as they belong to a subject, in a similar fashion forms have complete being only insofar as they belong to their proper matters. And for this reason, just as accidents are defined by adding their subjects, so too a form is defined by adding its proper matter. Hence when matter is included in the definition of a form, there is definition by addition, but not when it is included in the definition of a composite.

1478. Or his statement "unless taken together they constitute the intelligible expression of the thing" exemplifies his remark that "in other cases it need not include them." For in such cases it is not necessary that the material parts should be included in the definition, i.e., in the case of those things which are not taken together with matter, or which do not signify something composed of matter and form. This is evident; for since matter is not included in the intelligible expression of some things but is included in that of others, there can be some things which "are composed of these as the principles into which they are dissolved," i.e., the parts into which things are dissolved by corruption. And these are the things whose definitions include matter. But there are some things which are not composed of the foregoing material parts as principles, as those in whose definitions matter is not included.

1479. And since matter is included in the definitions of those things which are taken together with matter but not in those of others, "hence all things which are matter and form taken together," i.e., all things which signify something composed of matter and form, such as snub or brazen circle, such things are corrupted into material parts, and one of these is matter. But those things which are not conceived by the mind with matter but lack matter altogether, as those which belong to the notion of the species or form alone, these are not corrupted "in such a way as this," i.e., by being dissolved into certain material parts. For some forms are corrupted in no way, as the intellectual substances, which exist of themselves, whereas others which do not exist of themselves are corrupted accidentally when their subject is corrupted.

1480. Hence it is evident that material parts of this kind are the principles and parts of those things "which come under these," i.e., which depend on these, as a whole depends on its component parts; yet they are neither parts nor principles of the form. And for this reason when a composite, such as a statue made of clay, is corrupted, "it is dissolved into its matter," i.e., into clay, as a brazen sphere is dissolved into bronze, and as Callias, who is a particular man, is dissolved into flesh and bones. Similarly a particular circle depending on these divided lines is corrupted into its segments; for just as Callias is a man conceived with individual matter, so too a circle whose parts are these particular segments is a particular circle conceived with individual matter. Yet there is this difference, that singular men have a proper name, and therefore the name of the species is not applied equivocally to the individual, but the term *circle* is applied equivocally to the circle "which is called such in an unqualified sense," i.e., in a universal sense, and to singular particular circles. And the reason is that names are not given to several particular circles but they are given to particular men.

1481. Moreover it must be noted that the name of the species is not predicated of the individual in the sense that it refers the common nature of the species to it, but it is predicated of it equivocally, if it is predicated in such a way that it signifies this individual as such; for if I say "Socrates is a man," the word *man* is not used equivocally. But if this word man is imposed as a proper name on some individual man, it will signify both the species and this individual equivocally. It is similar in the case of the word circle, which signifies the species and this particular circle equivocally.

LESSON 10
Priority of Parts to Whole and Their Role in Definition

ARISTOTLE'S TEXT Chapter 10: 1035b3–1036a25

1. The truth, then, has now been stated; but let us state it even more clearly by repeating the same discussion. For all things which are parts of a thing's intelligible expression and that into which its intelligible expression is divided, are prior to it, either all or some of them. But the intelligible expression of a right angle is not divided into that of an acute angle, but the intelligible expression of an acute angle is divided into that of a right angle; and one who defines an acute angle uses a right angle, for an acute angle is less than a right angle. And the same thing is true of a circle and a semicircle; for a semicircle is defined by means of a circle, and a finger is defined by means of the whole man, because a finger is such and such a part of man. Hence all parts which have the nature of matter and are that into which the whole is divided as matter are subsequent [to the whole]. But all things which are parts of the intelligible expression and of the substance according to its intelligible expression are prior, either all or some of them. **1035b3–14**

2. And since the soul of animals (for this is the substance of living things) is their form according to the intelligible expression, and is the substance, species, or essence of such a body (for if a part of each animal is properly defined, it will not be defined without its function, and this will not be possible without sensation), therefore parts of this kind, either all or some of them, are prior to the concrete whole, the animal; and this is likewise true of every individual thing. But the body and parts of this kind are subsequent to this substance; and it is not substance but the concrete whole which is divided into these as its matter. Therefore in a sense these are prior to the concrete whole and in a sense they are not; for they cannot exist apart, because a finger is not a part of an animal when it is disposed in just any way at all; for a dead finger is called a finger equivocally. But some parts are simultaneous with the whole, and these are the principal parts in which the intelligible expression and substance are present, for example, the heart or the brain, because it makes no difference which of them is such. But man and horse and those terms which are applied in this way to singular things, but are taken universally, are not substance, but a certain concrete whole composed of this matter and this intelligible expression taken universally. Socrates, however, is already a singular thing by reason of ultimate matter; and it is similar in other cases. Hence a part is a part of the species (which means the essence of a thing) and of the concrete whole which is composed of species and matter itself. **1035b14–33**

3. But only the parts of the species are parts of the intelligible expression, and the intelligible expression is of the universal; for the being of a circle is the same as a circle, and the being of a soul the same as a soul. But in the case of a concrete whole, for example, this circle, or any singular thing, either sensible or intelligible (by sensible circles I mean those made of bronze and wood, and by intelligible, such as are the objects of mathematics), of these there is no definition; but they are known by intellect or by sense, i.e., when they are actually seen. And when they are removed from a state of actuality, it is not clear whether they exist or not; but they are always known and expressed by a universal formula. Now matter is unknowable in itself. And in one respect matter is sensible, and in another it is intelligible; sensible matter being such as brass and wood and anything mobile, and intelligible matter being what is present in sensible things but not as sensible, such as the objects of mathematics. How this applies to whole and part and to the prior and subsequent has therefore been stated. **1035b33–1036a13**

4. But when anyone asks whether a right angle and a circle and an animal are prior to the parts into which they are divided and of which they are composed, the answer must be that these are not parts without qualification. For if the soul is the same as an animal or a living thing, or the soul of each individual is the same as each individual, and if a circle is the same as the being of a circle, and a right angle is the same as the being of a right angle, the thing must be said to be subsequent to that by which it is, for example, to those parts which are included in its intelligible expression and to those in the universal right angle. For both the right angle which is found in matter, which is a bronze right angle, and that found in these particular lines, are subsequent to their parts; but the right angle which is immaterial is subsequent to the parts found in the intelligible expression, but is prior to those found in a particular thing. But to this question an unqualified answer must not be given. However, if the soul is something different and is not the same as an animal, even if this is so, in one sense it must be said that the parts are prior, and in another sense it must not, as has been stated. **1036a13–25**

COMMENTARY

1482. Since the foregoing solution was not always clear, for he had not yet shown how parts are prior and subsequent or even distinguished the universal composite from the particular or the species from the form, he therefore now explains the foregoing solution. This is divided into two parts. In the first [1] he explains the foregoing solution. In the second [4] he tells us how the solution should be applied to this question ("But when anyone").

The first part is divided into two sections. First, he answers the question about the priority of parts; and second [3], the question whether the parts of the thing defined enter into its definition ("But only").

The first part is again divided into two sections. First, he shows how parts are prior to wholes. Second [2], he clarifies this by an example ("And since the soul").

He accordingly says, first [1], that while the explanation given above in the solution advanced is true in itself, it is still necessary to go over it again so that it may become more evident in reference to the present discussion. For all parts of a thing's intelligible expression, i.e., those into which the intelligible expression is divided, must be prior to the thing defined, either all or some of them. This is said because sometimes the parts of the form are not necessarily parts of the species, but relate to the perfection of a thing; for example, sight and hearing, which are parts of the sentient soul, are not integral or necessary parts of an animal, inasmuch as there can exist an animal which does not have these senses. They nevertheless belong to the perfection of animal, because perfect animals do have these senses. Thus it is universally true that those parts which are given in the definition of anything are universally prior to it.

1483. But even though an acute angle is part of a right angle, it is still not given in its definition; but the opposite is true, for the intelligible expression of a right angle is not dissolved into the definition of an acute angle, but the reverse. For he who defines an acute angle uses right angle in its definition, because an acute angle is less than a right angle. The same is true of a circle and a semicircle, which is defined by means of a circle, because it is a half of a circle. And the same thing holds true of a finger and a man, who is given in the definition of a finger; for a finger is defined as such and such a part of man. For it was stated above that the parts of the form are parts of the intelligible expression but not those of the matter. Therefore, if only the parts of the intelligible expression are prior and not those of the matter, it follows that all things which are material parts of the thing defined, into which it is dissolved in the same way that a composite is dissolved into its material principles, are subsequent. "But all things which are parts of the intelligible expression and of the substance according to its intelligible expression," i.e., the parts of the form according to which the intelligible expression of the thing is understood, are prior to the whole, either all or some of them, according to the argument given above.

1484. **And since** [2].

Here he explains what he has said, by using an example. He says that since the soul of living things is their substance according to its intelligible expression, i.e., the form from which they derive their intelligible expression, then the soul of an animal "is the substance," i.e., the form or specifying principle or essence "of such a body," namely, of an organic body; for an organic body can be defined only by means of a soul. And from this point of view a soul is said to be the essence of such a body.

1485. The truth of this is shown by the fact that, if anyone properly defines a part of any animal at all, he can define it properly only by means of its proper operation, as, for example, if someone were to say that an eye is that part of an animal by which it sees. But the operation itself of the parts does not exist without sensation or motion or the other operations of the soul's parts; and thus one who defines some part of the body must use the soul.

1486. And since this is so, its parts, i.e., those of the soul, must be prior (either all of them, as happens in the case of perfect animals, or some of them, as happens in the case of imperfect animals) "to the concrete whole," i.e., to the composite of body and soul. The same thing is true of every other individual thing, because the formal parts must always be prior to any composite.

1487. But the body and its parts are subsequent "to this substance," i.e., to the form, which is the soul, since the soul must be given in the definition of the body, as has already been stated (C 1485); and what is divided into the parts of the body as its matter is not "the substance itself," but "the concrete whole," i.e., the composite. It is clear, then, that in a sense the parts of the body are prior to "the concrete whole," i.e., to the composite, and in a sense they are not.

1488. In fact they are prior in the way in which the simple is prior to the complex, inasmuch as the composite animal is constituted of them. However, they are not prior in the sense in which prior means something that can exist without something else; for the parts of the body cannot exist apart from the animal. Thus a finger is not a finger under all conditions, because one that is severed or dead is called such only equivocally, for example, the finger of a statue or that in a painting. But from this point of view parts of this kind are subsequent to the composite animal, because an animal can exist without a finger.

1489. But there are certain parts which, even though they are not prior to the whole animal with this sort of priority, are nevertheless simultaneous with the whole, from this point of view; because, just as the parts themselves cannot exist without the entire body, neither can the entire animal exist without them. And parts of this kind are the principal parts of the body in which "the form," i.e., the soul, first exists, namely, the heart or the brain. Nor does it make any difference to his thesis what things may be such.

1490. Yet it must be borne in mind that this composite, animal or man, can be taken in two ways: either as a universal or as a singular. An example of a universal composite would be animal and man, and of a singular composite, Socrates and Callias. Hence he says that man and horse and those predicates which are used in this way in reference to singular things but are taken universally, as man and horse, "are not substance," i.e., they are not just form alone, but are concrete wholes composed of a determinate matter and a determinate form (i.e., insofar as these are taken not individually but universally). For *man* means something composed of body and soul, but not of this body and this soul, whereas *a singular man* means something composed of "ultimate matter," i.e., individual matter; for Socrates is something composed of this body and this soul, and the same is true of other singular things.

1491. Hence it is clear that matter is a part of the species. But by *species* here we mean not just the form but the essence of the thing. And it is also clear that matter is a part of this whole which "is composed of species and matter," i.e., the singular, which signifies the nature of the species in this determinate matter. For matter is part of a composite, and a composite is both universal and singular.

1492. **But only the parts** [3].

Here he explains what parts should be given in a definition. For since it was shown (n. 1463) which parts are parts of the species as well as which are parts of the individual (because matter taken commonly is part of the species, whereas this definite matter is part of the individual), it is evident that only those parts which are parts of the species are parts of the intelligible expression, and not those which are parts of the individual; for flesh and bones, and not this flesh and these bones, are given in the definition of man; and the reason is that the definitive expression is applied only universally.

1493. For since the essence of a thing is the same as the thing of which it is the essence, as was shown above (n. 1362), there will be a definition which is the intelligible expression or essence only of that which is the same as its own essence. Now things of this kind are universal and not singular; for a circle and the being of a circle are the same, and it is similar in the case of a soul and the being of a soul. But there is no definition of those things which are composed of a form and individual matter, as of this circle or of any other singular thing.

1494. Nor does it make any difference whether the singulars are sensible or intelligible; sensible singulars being such things as brazen and wooden circles, and intelligible singulars being such as mathematical circles. Now that some singulars are considered among the objects of mathematics is clear from the fact that in this order many things of the same species are observed, as many equal lines and many similar figures. And such singulars are said to be intelligible insofar as they are grasped without the senses by means of imagination alone, which is sometimes referred to as an intellect, according to the statement in Book III of *The Soul:* [430a25] "The passive intellect is corruptible."

1495. Therefore there is no definition of singular circles, because those things of which there is definition are known by their own definition. But singulars are known only as long as they come under the senses or imagination, which is called an intellect here because it considers things without the senses just as the intellect does. But "when" singular circles of this kind "are removed from a state of actuality," i.e., when they are no longer considered by the senses (in reference to sensible circles) and by imagination (in reference to mathematical circles), it is not evident whether they exist as singulars; yet they are always referred to and known by their universal formula. For even when they are not actually being perceived, these sensible circles are known inasmuch as they are circles, but not inasmuch as they are these circles.

1496. The reason for this is that matter, which is the principle of individuation, is unknowable in itself and is known only by means of the form, from which the universal formula is derived. Therefore when singular things are absent, they are known only by their universals. Now matter is the principle of individuation not only in singular things but also in the objects of mathematics; for there are two kinds of matter, one sensible and the other intelligible. And by *sensible matter* is meant such things as bronze and wood, or any changeable matter, such as fire and water and all things of this sort; and singular sensible things are individuated by such matter. But by *intelligible matter* is meant what exists in things which are sensible but are not viewed as sensible, as the objects of mathematics. For just as the form of man exists in such and such matter, which is an organic body, in a similar way the form of a circle or of a triangle exists in this matter, which is a continuum, whether surface or solid.

1497. He therefore concludes that he has explained the relationship of whole and part, and the sense in which there is priority and posteriority, i.e., how a part is a part of the whole, and how it is prior and how subsequent. For the parts of individual matter are parts of the singular composite but not of the species or form, whereas the parts of universal matter are parts of the species but not of the form. And since universals and not singulars are defined, the parts of individual matter are therefore not given in a thing's definition, but only the parts of common matter together with the form or parts of the form.

1498. **But when anyone** [4].

He now adapts the proposed solution to the question previously noted. He says that when someone asks whether a right angle and a circle and an animal are prior to their parts, or the reverse: whether the parts into which these things are divided and of which they are composed are prior, we must meet this question by using the foregoing solution. Now in reply to this an unqualified answer cannot be given; for there are two opinions on this point. Some say that the whole species is the same as the form so that man is the same as his soul, and others say that they are not, but that man is a composite of body and soul. And it is necessary to answer each opinion in a different way.

1499. For if a soul is the same as an animal or a living thing, or in a similar way, if each thing is the same as its form (for example, a circle is the same as the form of a circle, and a right angle the same as the form of a right angle), we must answer by establishing which is subsequent and in what way it is subsequent; because from this point of view the parts of the matter are subsequent to those in the intelligible expression, and to those "in some right angle," i.e., in the universal right angle, but they are prior to those in a particular right angle. For this right angle which is bronze has sensible matter, and this right angle which is contained in singular lines has intelligible matter; but that right angle which is "immaterial," i.e., common, will be subsequent to the parts of the form present in the intelligible expression, and it will be prior to the parts of the matter which are the parts of singular things. And according to this opinion it will not be possible to distinguish between common matter and individual matter. Yet an unqualified answer must not be given to this question, because it will be necessary to distinguish between the parts of the matter and those of the form.

1500. If, however, the other opinion is true, namely, that the soul is different from the animal, it will be necessary both to say and not to say that the parts are prior to the whole, as was previously established; because with regard to this opinion he instructed us above to distinguish not only between matter and form, but also between common matter, which is part of the species, and individual matter, which is part of the individual.

LESSON 11

What Forms Are Parts of the Species and of the Intelligible Expression

ARISTOTLE'S TEXT Chapter II: 1036a26–1037b 7

1. *Now the problem rightly arises as to what parts are parts of the species, and which are not parts of the species but of the concrete whole. For if this is not clear it is impossible to define anything, because definition refers to the universal and the species. Hence, if it is not evident as to what parts are material and what are not, the intelligible expression of the thing will not be clearly known.* **1036a26–31**

2. *Therefore in the case of all those things which seem to be produced in specifically different matters, as a circle in bronze and in stone and in wood, it seems to be evident that none of these, either bronze or stone or wood, belong to the substance of a circle, because it can be separated from them. And with regard to those things which do not seem to be separable, nothing prevents them from being similar to these, as, for instance, if all sensible circles were of bronze; for none the less the bronze would be no part of the species. But it is difficult to separate it in the mind; for example, the species of man always appears in flesh and bones and such parts. Hence the question arises whether these are parts of the species and intelligible expression of man, or are not but have the character of matter. But since such species do not occur in other matters, we cannot separate them.* **1036a31–1036b7**

3. *Now since this seems to be possible, but it is not clear when, some thinkers are puzzled even in the case of a circle and a triangle, as if it were not right to define these by lines and by what is continuous, but that all these should be predicated in a way similar to the flesh and bones of a man and the bronze and stone of a circle. And they refer all things to numbers and say that the intelligible expression of a line is that of the number two. And of those who speak of Ideas, some claim that the number two is the line itself, and others claim that it is the Form of a line; for some say that a Form and the thing of which it is the Form are the same, for example, the number two and the Form of twoness; but this is not so in the case of a line.* **1036b7–17**

4. *It follows, then, that there is one Form of many things whose Form appears to be different; and this is a conclusion that also faced the Pythagoreans.* **1036b17–19**

5. *And it is possible [according to this view] to make one Form proper to all things, and to maintain that nothing else is a Form at all.* **1036b19–20**

6. *However, in this way all things will be one. Therefore that the questions about definitions constitute a problem, and why, has been stated.* **1036b20–22**

7. *Hence to reduce all things in this way and to do away with matter is superfluous; for perhaps some things are a this in this, or are things having these two principles. And the analogy of the animal, which the younger Socrates was accustomed to state, is not a good one; for it leads us away from the truth and makes us suppose that it is possible for man to exist without parts, as a circle exists without bronze. But this case is not similar; for an animal is something sensible and cannot be defined without motion, and therefore it cannot be defined without its parts being disposed in some way. For it is not a hand in any condition which is part of a man, but when it is capable of performing the function of a hand. Hence it is a part when it is animated, but it is not a part when it is not animated.* **1036b22–32**

8. *And with regard to the objects of mathematics the question arises why the intelligible structures of the parts are not parts of the intelligible structure of the whole (for example, why semicircles are not parts of the intelligible structure of a circle), for they are not sensible. But perhaps this makes no difference; for there will be matter of certain things and of those which are not sensible. And this will be true of everything which is not an essence or species considered in itself, but a particular thing. Therefore the semicircle will not be part of the circle which is*

universal, but semicircles will be parts of singular circles, as was said before (627); for some matter is sensible and some intelligible. **1036b32–1037a5**

9. And it is also evident that the soul is a primary substance, and that the body is matter, and that man or animal is the composite of both taken universally. And Socrates and Coriscus are composed of soul and body taken individually, i.e., if the term soul is taken in two senses; for some take soul as soul and others as the whole. But if soul and body without qualification mean this individual soul and this individual body, each term is used both as a universal and as a singular. **1037a5–10**

10. But whether there are besides the matter of such substances other substances as well, and whether it is necessary to look for some different substance in these, such as numbers or something of this kind, must be examined later (Books XIII & XIV); for it is for the sake of these too that we are trying to define sensible substances, since in a sense the study of sensible substances constitutes the work of the philosophy of nature, or second philosophy. For the philosopher of nature must have scientific knowledge not only of matter but of the part which is intelligible, and the latter is the more important. And with regard to definitions the philosopher must know how the parts in the intelligible expression are disposed, and why the definition is one intelligible expression; for it is evident that a thing is one. But how a thing having parts is one must be examined later. **1037a10–20**

11. We have stated, then, what the essence of a thing is and how it is predicated essentially of all things (582), as well as why the intelligible expression of the essence of some things contains the parts of the thing defined, and why that of others does not. And we have also stated that those parts which have the nature of matter are not found in the intelligible expression of substance; for they are not parts of that substance, but of the whole. And in one sense there is an intelligible expression of this and in another sense there is not; for there is no intelligible expression that involves matter, because this is indeterminate. But there is an intelligible expression of the whole with reference to primary substance; for example, in the case of man there is an intelligible expression of the soul; for the substance of a thing is the specifying principle intrinsic to it, and the whole substance is composed of this along with matter. Concavity, for example, is such a principle, for from this and from nose snubnose and snubness are derived. For nose is also contained twice in these expressions; but in the whole substance or in snubnose or in Callias matter is also present. And we have also stated that in some cases the essence of the thing is the same as the thing itself, as in the case of primary substances; for curvature and the essence of curvature are the same, if curvature is primary. And by primary I mean what does not refer to something as existing in something else as its subject or matter. But all things which have the nature of matter or are conceived with matter, are not the same—not even if they are one accidentally, as Socrates and musician, for they are accidentally the same. **1037a21–1037b7**

COMMENTARY

1501. In this part he solves a problem which could arise from the answer to the foregoing question; for in answering that question he had distinguished the parts of the species from those of the individual thing, which is composed of species and matter. Hence he now inquires as to what parts are parts of the species and what are not.

This part is therefore divided into three sections. In the first [1] he solves the problem. In the second [10] he shows what remains to be discussed

("But whether"). In the third [11] he summarizes the points discussed ("We have stated").

He accordingly says, first [1], that since it has been stated that the parts of the species are given in definitions, but not the parts of the thing composed of matter and species, there is a real problem as to what parts are parts of the species, and what are not parts of the species "but of the concrete whole," i.e., the individual thing, in which the nature of the species is taken along with individuating matter.

1502. For if this is not evident, we will be unable to define anything correctly, because definition never pertains to the singular but only to the universal, as was stated above (nn. 1493–97). And among universals the species is properly included, and this is constituted of genus and difference, of which every definition is composed; for a genus is defined only if there is also a species. Hence it is clear that unless we know what part has the nature of matter, and what part does not but pertains to the species itself, it will not be evident as to what definition should be assigned to a thing, since it is assigned only to the species. And in the definition of the species it is necessary to give the parts of the species and not those which are subsequent to it.

1503. **Therefore in the case** [2].

He solves the proposed problem; and in regard to this he does three things. First [2], he gives the solution according to the opinion of the Platonists. Second [4], he rejects it ("It follows"). Third [7], he solves it by giving his own opinion ("Hence to reduce").

In regard to the first he does two things. First, he solves the proposed difficulty in reference to sensible things; and second [3], in reference to the objects of mathematics ("Now since this seems").

He says, first [2], then, that in the case of some things it is evident that matter is not part of the species, for example, all those which appear to be produced in specifically different matters, as a circle is found to be produced in bronze, in stone and in wood. Hence it is evident that neither bronze nor stone nor wood is part of the substance of circle, as though it were a part of the form, circle. And this is evident by reason of the fact that circle may be separated from each of these matters, and nothing can be separated from something which is a part of its form.

1504. But there are some things whose species do not occur as produced in specifically different matters, but always in the same matters; for example, the species of man insofar as it is apparent to the sense of sight is found only in flesh and bones. However, nothing prevents those things which do not seem to be separate from their proper matter from also being related in the same way to their own matters as those things which can exist in different matters and be separated from each of them.

1505. For if we were to maintain that some circles would not be apparent to the senses unless they were composed of bronze, none the less bronze would not be in this way a part of the form of circle. And even though circle would not then be actually separate from bronze, it would still be separable in thought, since the species of circle can be understood without bronze, since bronze is not part of the form of circle, although it is difficult to mentally separate and isolate from each other those things which are not actually separate; for this belongs only to those things which can be raised above the sensible order by the intellect.

1506. And similarly, if the species of man always appears in flesh and bones and such parts, it is necessary to ask whether these are parts of man's species "and of the intelligible expression," or definition, of man; or whether they are not the species' parts, but only the matter of the species, as bronze is the matter of a circle. But because such a species does not arise in other material parts than these, therefore we cannot by means of our intellect easily separate man from flesh and bones; for the reasoning seems to be the same in this case as in that of a circle, if all circles were of bronze.

1507. **Now since this** [3].

Then he continues his discussion by examining the opinion just touched on insofar as it relates to the objects of mathematics. He says that in some cases it seems possible for matter not to be a part of the species, although the species occurs only in matter, but it is not evident when and in what instances this is possible or not possible. Therefore some thinkers are puzzled about this, not only in reference to natural things but also in reference to the objects of mathematics, such as circles and triangles.

1508. For it seems to them that, just as sensible matter is not a part of the species of natural beings, in a similar fashion intelligible matter is not a part of the species of mathematical entities. Now the intelligible matter of mathematical figures is continuous quantity, such as lines and surfaces. Hence it was thought that a line is not part of the species of a circle or triangle (as if it were not right that a triangle and a circle should be defined by lines and by continuous quantity, since they are not parts of the species), but that all those things are related to a circle and a triangle in the same way that flesh and bones are related to man, and bronze and stones to circles.

1509. But when the continuous quantity, line, is removed from triangles and circles, the only thing that remains is the unit and number, because a triangle is a figure having three lines, and a circle is a figure having one. Therefore, not holding that lines are parts of the species, they refer all species to numbers, saying that numbers are the species of all mathematical entities; for they say that the intelligible structure of the number two is that of a straight line, because a straight line is terminated by two points.

1510. But among the Platonists, who posit Ideas, there is a difference of opinion on this matter; for some of them, i.e., those who did not make the objects of mathematics an intermediate class between the Forms and sensible things but claimed that the Forms are numbers, said that the line is the number two, because they did not hold that there is an intermediate line differing from the Form of a line.

1511. But others said that the number two is not a line but the Form of a line; for according to them the line is a mathematical intermediate between the Forms and sensible things; and they said that the number two is the Form itself of the number two. And according to them there are some things in which the Form and the thing of which it is the Form do not differ, for example, numbers. Hence they said that the number two and the Form of twoness are the same. But this is not the case with a line, in their opinion, because a line already expresses something participating in a Form, since there are found to be many lines in one species; and this would not be so if the line itself were a separate Form.

1512. **It follows, then** [4].

He now rejects the solution given above; and he gives three arguments, of which the first is this: if numbers alone are separate Forms, all things which participate in one number will participate in one Form. But there are many specifically different things which participate in one number; for one and the same number is present in a triangle because of its three lines, and in a syllogism because of its three terms, and in a solid because of its three dimensions. Hence it follows that there is one Form of many things which are specifically different. This was the conclusion which faced not only the Platonists but also the Pythagoreans, who also claimed that the nature of everything consists in numbers.

1513. **And it is possible** [5].

Then he gives the second argument, which is as follows: if flesh and bones are not parts of the Form of man, and lines not parts of the Form of triangle, then for a like reason no matter is part of a Form. But in the case of numbers, according to the Platonists, the number two is attributed to matter and unity to Form. Therefore only unity constitutes Form. But the number two, and therefore all other numbers, inasmuch as they imply matter, will not be Forms. Hence there will only be one Form of all things.

1514. **However, in this way** [6].

Here he gives the third argument, which is as follows: those things are one whose Form is one. Hence if there is only one Form of all things, it follows that all things are one formally, and not just those which seem to be different [but in reality are not]. Yet it can be said that this third argument does not differ from the second one, but that it is an absurdity which follows as a conclusion of the second argument.

1515. Therefore having given the arguments on which the foregoing solution is based, and having given two arguments against this solution, he concludes that the questions about definitions constitute a problem, and that the reason for this has been stated. Thus it is evident that he wishes to use everything which has been set down to expose the difficulty connected with the foregoing problem.

1516. **Hence to reduce** [7].

He now gives the real solution of the foregoing problem based on his own doctrine. He does this first with regard to natural things; and second [8], with regard to the objects of mathematics ("And with regard").

He accordingly says, first [7], that since the absurdities mentioned above plague those removing from the species of a thing all material parts, whether they are sensible or not, it is evident from what has been said that it is futile to reduce all species of things to numbers or to the unit and to do away completely with sensible and intelligible matter as the Platonists did.

1517. For some forms of things are not forms without matter, but are "a this in this," i.e., a form in matter, in such a way that what results from the form existing in matter is the species. Or if they are not like a form in matter, they are like things which have a form in matter; for properly speaking natural things have form in matter, and the objects of mathematics also resemble these in a way inasmuch as the figure of a circle or a triangle is related to lines as the form of man is related to flesh and bones. Therefore just as man's species is not a form without flesh and bones, neither is the form of a triangle or of a circle a form without lines. Hence the analogy of animal, which the younger Socrates was accustomed to use, is not a good one.

1518. Now it seems that Plato himself is called the younger Socrates, because in all his works he introduces Socrates as the speaker, since Socrates was his master. And Plato's opinion about the materiality of natural species he calls an analogy, because it is similar to fables, which are devised for the purpose of conveying some opinion by means of a metaphor; and this is why he said above in Book III (see nn. 471, 474), that this opinion resembles the opinion of those who assume that there are gods and that their forms are like human ones. Hence the view expressed above is not a good one, because it leads us away from the truth insofar as it makes us think that it is possible for man to exist without flesh and bones, just as it is possible for a circle to exist without bronze, which clearly does not belong to the species of a circle.

1519. But this case is not similar; for a man is not related to flesh and bones in the same way that a circle is related to bronze, because a circle is not something sensible in its own intelligible expression; for it can be understood without sensible matter. Hence, bronze, which is sensible matter, is not part of the species of a circle. But an animal seems to be a sensible thing since it cannot be defined without motion; for an animal is distinguished from something that is not an animal by means of sensation and motion, as is clear in Book I of *The Soul.* [413b1] Therefore an animal cannot be defined without including bodily parts, which are disposed in a proper way for motion; for the hand is not a part of man when it exists in every state, but when it is disposed in such a way that it can perform the proper work of a hand; and this it cannot do without the soul, which is the principle of motion. Hence it is necessary that the hand be a part of man insofar as it is animated, but it is not a part of man insofar as it is not animated, like the hand of a corpse or that in a painting. Therefore such parts as are required for the carrying out of the proper operation of the species must be parts of the species; both those which pertain to the form and those which pertain to matter.

1520. **And with regard to** [8].

Next he answers the question with regard to the objects of mathematics; for though the solution has been given above with regard to natural things, it seems that the difficulty still remains with regard to the objects of mathematics; for he had said above that since an animal is sensible it cannot be defined without sensible parts, as a circle can be defined without bronze, which is sensible matter. Therefore "with regard to the objects of mathematics the question arises why the intelligible expressions of the parts," i.e., the definitions of the parts, "are not parts of the intelligible expression of the whole," e.g., why semicircles, or half-circles, are not given in the definition of a circle; for it cannot be said that these, namely, semicircles, are sensible things, as bronze is sensible matter.

1521. But he answers that it makes no difference to his thesis whether the material parts are sensible or not; because there is intelligible matter even in things which are not sensible. And such matter—the kind which is not a part of the species—belongs to everything whose essence or species is not the same as itself "but is a particular thing," i.e., a determinate particular, as if to say that in everything which is not its own species but is a definite individual determined in species there must be certain material parts which are not parts of the species. For since Socrates is not identical with his own humanity but has humanity, for this reason he has in himself certain material parts which are not parts of his species but of this individual matter, which is the principle of individuation, for example, this flesh and these bones.

1522. And, similarly, in this particular circle there are these particular lines which are not parts of the species. Hence it is clear that parts of this kind are not parts of the universal circle but of singular circles, as was stated above (n. 1492). And for this reason semicircles are not included in the definition of the universal circle, because they are parts of singular circles and not of the universal circle. This is true both of sensible and intelligible matter; for matter is found in both modes, as is evident from what has been said. But if there were some individual which was the same as its own species, for example, if Socrates were his own humanity, there would be no parts in Socrates which would not be parts of humanity.

1523. **And it is also** [9].

He now sums up the solution given above by using animal as an example. He says that it is evident that the soul "is a primary substance," i.e., the form of animal, and that the body is matter, and that "man is the composite of both," i.e., insofar as they are taken universally; but that Socrates or Coriscus is the composite of both taken particularly, because "soul is taken in two senses," i.e., universally and particularly, as soul and as this soul. Hence what is signified as a whole must be taken both universally and singularly, in the way in which soul is taken in two senses, because this is in keeping with both views which men take of the soul. For, as was said above (n. 1467), some claim that a man or an animal is its soul, whereas others say that a man or an animal is not its soul "but the whole," i.e., the composite of soul and body.

1524. It is evident, then, according to the opinion which affirms that man is his soul, that the term *soul* is taken both universally and singularly, as soul and this soul; and the term *man* is also taken both universally and particularly, i.e., singularly, as man and as this man. And similarly, too, according to the opinion which affirms that man is a composite of body and soul, it follows that, if simple things may be taken both universally and singularly, composites may also be taken both universally and singularly; for example, if the soul is this thing and the body is this thing, which are referred to in an unqualified sense as parts of the composite, it follows that the terms *universal* and *particular*, or *singular*, may be applied not only to the parts but also to the composite.

1525. **But whether** [10].

He explains what still remains to be established about substances; and he gives the two issues which have to be dealt with. The first is this: when it has been established that the substance and whatness of sensible and material things are parts of the species, the next thing that has to be established is whether there is some substance besides the matter "of such substances," i.e., of material and sensible substances, so that it is necessary to look for some other substance of these sensible things besides the one which has been dealt with; as some affirm that there are numbers existing apart from matter, "or something of the kind," i.e., that separate Forms or Ideas are the substances of these sensible things. This must be investigated later on (Books XIII and XIV).

1526. For this investigation is the one proper to this science, because in this science we attempt to establish something about sensible substances "for the sake of these," i.e., for the sake of immaterial substances, because the study of sensible and material substances belongs in a sense to the philosophy of nature, which is not first philosophy, but second philosophy, as was stated in Book IV (n. 593). For first philosophy is concerned with the first substances, which are immaterial ones, which it studies not only inasmuch as they are substances but inasmuch as they are such substances, namely, inasmuch as they are immaterial. But it does not study sensible substances inasmuch as they are such substances but inasmuch as they are substances, or also beings, or inasmuch as we are led by such substances to a knowledge of immaterial substances. But the philosopher of nature, on the other hand, deals with material substances, not inasmuch as they are substances, but inasmuch as they are material and have a principle of motion within themselves.

1527. And because someone might think that the philosophy of nature should not treat of material and sensible substances in their entirety, but only of their matters, he therefore rejects this, saying that the philosophy of nature must consider not only matter but also the part "which is intelligible," namely, the form. And it must also consider form more than matter, because form is nature to a greater degree than matter, as was proved in Book II of the *Physics*. [193b7]

1528. Second, it remains to be established how "the parts in the intelligible expression," i.e., in the definition, are disposed: whether they are parts of the substance actually. And it also remains to be established why the definition, when it is composed of many parts, is one intelligible expression; for it is evident that the definition of a thing must be only one intelligible expression, because a thing is one, and a definition signifies what a thing is. But how a thing having parts is one must be investigated later.

1529. **We have stated** [11].

Next he sums up the points which have been established. He says that it has been stated what the essence of a thing is, and how it is predicated of all things, and that it is predicated essentially. And it has also been stated why the intelligible expression signifying the essence of some things contains in itself the parts of the thing defined, just as the definition of a syllable contains its letters, and "why that of others does not," as the definition of a circle does not contain semicircles. And again it has also been stated that those parts which are material parts of substance are not given "in the intelligible expression of substance," i.e., of form, because such parts are not "parts of that substance," i.e., of the form, but are parts of the whole composite.

1530. Now in one sense there is a definition of this kind of composite, and in another sense there is not; for if it is taken "with matter," namely, the individual, there is no definition of it, since singulars are not defined, as was stated above (627:C 1493). The reason is that such individual matter is something unlimited and indeterminate; for matter is limited only by form. But if composite is taken "with reference to the primary substance," i.e., to form, it has a definition; for the composite is defined when taken specifically, but not when taken individually.

1531. And just as the individual is individuated by matter, in a similar fashion each thing is placed in its proper species by its form; for man is man, not because he has flesh and bones, but because he has a rational soul in this flesh and these bones. It is necessary, then, that the definition of the species should be taken from the form, and that only those material parts should be given in the definition of the species, in which the form has the primary and chief role, as the intelligible expression of man is one which contains soul; for man is man because he has such a soul. And for this reason, if man is defined, he must be defined by his soul, yet in his definition one must include the parts of the body in which the soul is first present, such as the heart or the brain, as was said above (n. 1489).

1532. For the substance, of which matter is not a part, "is the specifying principle," i.e., the form, which is present in matter; and from this form and matter "the whole substance" is derived, i.e., made determinate and defined; for example, concavity is a form of this kind, for from this and from nose snubnose and snubness are derived. And in the same way man and humanity are derived from soul and body. For if nose, which plays the part of matter, were part of curvature, then when curved nose is referred to, the term *nose* would be expressed twice; for it is expressed once by its own name, and it is included again in the definition of the curved. However, this would be the case if nose were placed in the definition of the curved as part of the essence of curvature, and not by addition, as was stated above (n. 1472). And even though matter is not present in the essence of form, it is nevertheless present in the whole composite substance; for example, curvature is present in snub nose, and individual matter is also present in Callias.

1533. It was also said above (n. 1362) that the essence of each thing is the same as the thing of which it is the essence. This is true without qualification in some cases, "as in the case of primary substances," i.e., in that of immaterial substances, just as curvature itself is the same as the essence of curvature, provided that curvature belongs to primary substances. He says this because curvature seems to be a form in matter, though not in sensible matter but in an intelligible matter—continuous quantity. Or, according to another text, "which is first"; for there is a primary curvature, like the curvature which exists among the separate Forms, according to the Platonists, and of these Forms it is universally true that each is the same as its own essence. But the other curvature which is present in sensible things or in the objects of mathematics is not a primary one. Hence it is not the same as its essence.

1534. And in explaining this he says that he does not use the term *primary substance* here to mean a particular substance, as he does in the ***Categories***, *[2b11]* but to mean something which does not exist in something else "as in a subject or matter," i.e., those things which are not forms in matter, such as the separate substances. But all those which have the nature of matter or are conceived with matter, such as composites, which have matter in their intelligible expression, are not the same as their essence. Nor do those predications which are accidental form a unity, as Socrates and musician are the same accidentally.

1535. Now it must be noted that from the opinion which he expressed here that each thing and its essence are the same, he now excludes two kinds of things: (1) things which are accidental, and (2) substances which are material, although above he excluded only those things which are said to be accidental. And it is necessary not only to exclude the former but also to exclude material substances; for, as was said above (n. 1460), what the definition signifies is the essence, and definitions are not assigned to individuals but to species; and therefore individual matter, which is the principle of individuation, is distinct from the essence. But in reality it is impossible for a form to exist except in a particular substance. Hence if any natural thing has matter which is part of its species, and this pertains to its essence, it must also have individual matter, which does not pertain to its essence. Therefore, if any natural thing has matter, it is not its own essence but is something having an essence; for example, Socrates is not humanity but something having humanity. And if it were possible for a man to be composed of body and soul and not be this particular man composed of this body and this soul, he would still be his own essence, even though he contained matter.

1536. Now even though man does not exist apart from singular men in reality, nevertheless man is separable in his intelligible expression, which pertains to the domain of logic. Therefore, above (n. 1308), where he considered essence from the viewpoint of logic, he did not exclude material substances from being their own essence; for man as a universal is the same as his essence, logically speaking. And now having come to natural principles, which are matter and form, and having shown how they are related to the universal in different ways, and to the particular thing which subsists in nature, he now excludes material substances, which exist in reality, from the statement which he had made above to the effect that the essence of a thing is the same as the thing of which it is the essence. Moreover it follows that those substances which are subsistent forms alone do not have any principle individuating them which is extrinsic to the intelligible expression (of the thing or of the species) which signifies their whatness. Concerning these things, then, it is true that each is unqualifiedly the same as its own essence.

LESSON 12
The Unity of the Thing Defined and of the Definition

ARISTOTLE'S TEXT Chapter 12: 1037b8–1038a35

1. And now let us speak first of definition insofar as it has not been discussed in the ***Analytics;***^1 *for the problem mentioned there*^2 *constitutes a preamble to the arguments about substance. And by this problem I mean: for what reason is that thing one whose intelligible expression we call a definition? For example, two-footed animal is the definition of man; for let this be his intelligible expression. Why, then, is this one thing and not many, namely, animal and two-footed?* **1037b8–14**

2. For man and white are many since the latter is not present in the former; but they are one when the latter is present in the former, and the subject, man, is the recipient of some attribute; for then one thing is produced, and this is white man. But in this case one does not participate in the other; a genus does not participate in its differences, for then the same thing would participate in contraries; for the differences by which a genus is distinguished are contraries. **1037b14–21**

3. And even if it does not participate in them, the same argument applies if the differences are many, for example, capable of walking, two-footed and wingless. For why are all these one and not many? It is not because they are found in one thing, because then one thing will be composed of all differences. **1037b21–24**

4. But all the elements of a definition must be one, because a definition is one intelligible expression and one substance. Hence it must be the intelligible expression of some one particular thing; for substance signifies one thing and a particular thing, as we have said (See Lesson 4). **1037b24–27**

5. Now it is necessary first to examine those definitions which are attained by the process of division. For there is nothing in a definition except the primary genus and the differences; and the other genera consist of the so-called primary genus and the differences included in this; for example, the primary genus is animal, and the next is two-footed, and the next is two-footed animal without wings. And the same thing also applies if a definition is expressed by many terms. And on the whole it makes no difference whether it is expressed by many or by few, or whether it is expressed by few or by two. Of the two, then, the one is the difference and the other the genus; for example, in the expression "two-footed animal," animal is the genus and the other term is the difference. Hence, if a genus in an unqualified sense does not exist apart from those things which are its species, or if it has the nature of matter (for the spoken word is both a genus and matter, and the differences make the species, i.e., the letters, out of this), it is clear that the definition is the intelligible expression composed of the differences. **1037b27–1038a9**

6. Again, it is necessary too that a difference should be divided by a difference, as "having feet" is a difference of animal; and it is necessary also to know the difference of animal having feet, inasmuch as it has feet. Therefore, if someone is to speak correctly of something having feet, he must not say that one kind is winged and another wingless; and if he does say this it will be because of incompetence. But he will speak correctly only if he says that one kind has cloven feet and the other not; because these are the differences of the difference having feet, since a cloven foot is a certain kind of foot. And one always wants to proceed in this way until he comes to the species which have no differences; and then there will be as many species of foot as there are differences, and the species of animals having feet will be equal in number to the differences. **1038a9–18**

7. If these things are so, then, it is evident that the ultimate difference will be the substance and definition of the thing, if the same thing is not to be expressed many times over in definitive

expressions, because this is superfluous.^3 However, this sometimes happens, for when one says "two-footed animal having feet," he has said nothing more than animal having feet and having two feet. And if he divides this by its proper difference, he will express the same thing many times, and equal in number to the differences. If, then, a difference of a difference may be produced, the one which is the ultimate difference will be the specific form and substance.
1038a18–26

8. But if the division is made according to what is accidental, as if one were to divide what has feet into what is white and what is black, there will be as many differences as there are divisions.
1038a26–28

9. Hence it is evident that the definition is an intelligible expression composed of differences, and that it is composed of the last of these if the definition is formed correctly. **1038a28–30**

10. Moreover, this will be evident if we change the order of the words in such definitions, for example, in the definition of man by saying "two-footed animal having feet"; for having feet is superfluous when two-footed has been stated. But there is no sequence of parts in substance, for how are we to understand that one part is subsequent and the other prior? Therefore with regard to those definitions which are formed by the process of division, let this much be a preliminary statement of the kind of things they are. **1038a30–35**

COMMENTARY

1537. After having shown what parts are given in definitions, here the Philosopher inquires how a definition, being composed of parts, can be one thing; and in regard to this he does three things. First [1], he raises a question. Second [2], he argues on one side ("For man"). Third [5], he answers the question ("Now it is necessary").

He accordingly says that with regard to definition we should speak now for the first time of the things which have not been stated about it "in the *Analytics*," i.e., in the ***Posterior Analytics***.^1 For in that work a certain difficulty was raised^2 about definition and left unsolved, and this must be answered here "because it constitutes a preamble to the arguments about substance," i.e., because the answer to this question is a prerequisite for establishing certain things about substance, which is the chief concern of this science. This difficulty is why the thing of which the intelligible expression, namely, the quiddity, is a definition, "is one thing." For a definition is an intelligible expression signifying a quiddity; for example, the definition of man is "two-footed animal," for let us assume that this is his definition. Therefore the question is: why is this thing which is called two-footed animal one thing and not many?

1538. **For man** [2].

Then he raises arguments on both sides of the question; and he does this, first [2], in order to show that one thing is not produced from them; and second [4], to show that the contrary is true ("But all the elements").

In regard to the first he does two things. First, he shows that one thing is not produced from a genus and a difference. Second [3], he shows that one thing is not produced from many differences ("And even if").

He accordingly says, first [2], that these two things, man and white, are many when one of them is not present in the other; for if white does not belong to man, then man and white are one in no way. But they are one when one of them is present in the other, and when the subject, man, "is the recipient of the other," i.e., when it receives the modification, white; and then something accidentally one is produced from these two things, namely, a white man. Now from these remarks it is understood that one thing is not produced from two things when one does not exist in the other. But "in this case," namely, when one speaks of two-footed animal, "one," i.e., animal, does not participate "in the other," namely, in two-footed, as white man participates in white. And this is so because animal is a genus and two-footed is a difference. But a genus does not seem to participate in differences, for it would follow that the same thing would participate in contraries at the same time; for differences are the contraries "by which a genus is distinguished," i.e., by which a genus is divided; and for the same reason that it participates in one it will participate in the other. But if it is impossible for the same thing to participate in contraries, it will be impossible for one thing to be produced from a genus and a difference.

1539. **And even if** [3].

Then he shows that one thing cannot be produced from many differences. He says that, even if it is admitted that a genus participates in some way in a difference (as, for example, animal is not taken under its common aspect but insofar as it is restricted to a species by a difference, and then one thing is produced from a genus and a difference), the same argument can still be used to show that a definition does not signify one thing, if many differences are given in the definition; for example, if in the definition of man these three differences are given: first, capable of walking or having feet, second, two-footed, and third, wingless; for it cannot be said why these things are one and not many.

1540. For to explain this it is not enough to give as a reason that they exist in one thing (as in the animal, man), because in this way it would follow that all accidents which inhere in any subject would be essentially one thing; for we do speak of one accident in relation to another accident as well as to the subject. And since those things which are accidents of one subject may also be accidents of another subject, it would follow that those two subjects would be one, for example, snow and a swan, in both of which whiteness is found. And thus by inference it would follow that all things would be one. Hence it cannot be said that one thing is produced from many differences, even though one thing is produced from a genus and a difference. Hence it seems that a definition does not signify one thing composed of two parts.

1541. **But all the elements** [4].

Here he argues one side of the question, showing that a definition does signify one thing. He says that all the attributes which are given in a definition must be one. And this is so because a definition is one intelligible expression, and what it signifies is the substance of a thing. Hence a definition must be an intelligible expression signifying one thing, because the substance of a thing, which the definition signifies, is one quiddity. And it was also stated above (n. 1331), where definition was shown to belong properly to substances, that a definition signifies a particular thing.

1542. **Now it is necessary** [5].

He answers the foregoing question by showing that a definition signifies one thing; and in regard to this he does two things. First [5], he shows how one thing is produced from a genus and a difference; and second [6], how one thing is produced from many differences ("Again, it is").

He accordingly says, first [5], that in order to investigate the unity of definitions it is necessary, first, to examine definitions which are based on the division of genus into differences. For those are true definitions which contain nothing but the primary genus and differences, because some definitions are based on certain accidents, or on certain properties, or also on certain extrinsic causes, which do not signify the substance of a thing. Hence such definitions are not to the point, since here he is treating of definitions with a view to investigating the substances of things.

1543. Therefore I say that in a definition there is a primary genus with differences, because, even if one sometimes gives in definitions certain intermediate genera between the primary genus, which is the most general, and the last species which are defined, nevertheless those intermediate genera are nothing but the primary genus and the differences included in the understanding of the intermediate genus "along with this," i.e., along with the primary genus; as when animal, which is an intermediate genus, is given in the definition of man, it is evident that animal is nothing but substance, which is the primary genus, along with certain differences; for an animal is a living sensible substance. And the case is the same when we understand the primary genus to be animal "having feet"; and again when we understand the third genus to be "two-footed animal without wings." And the same thing is true when any genus is limited by many differences; for a subsequent genus always includes a prior genus along with some difference. Hence it is evident that every definition is dissolved into a primary genus and certain differences.

1544. And in general it makes no difference whether the thing defined is defined by many terms or by few. Hence it makes no difference whether it is defined by few or by two, so long as one of these is a genus and the other a difference; for animal is the genus of two-footed animal, and the other term, namely, two-footed, is the difference. Therefore it must shown, first, how one thing is produced from these. This becomes clear as follows.

1545. A genus does not exist apart from the things which are its species, for no animal is found which is not a man or an ox or some other animal of this kind. Or if there is something which is a genus apart from its species, taken in the sense that it exists apart from its species, it is not a genus but matter, because it is possible for something to be both the genus and matter of certain things, as the vocal sound is both the genus of letters and their matter. That it is a genus is evident from the fact that differences added to the vocal sound make the species of articulate sounds; and that it is matter is evident because the differences "make the elements," i.e., the letters, "out of this," namely, out of the vocal sound, as something is made out of matter.

1546. Moreover, it must be understood that while genus and matter can be the same in name, they nevertheless do not mean the same thing; for matter is an integral part of a thing, and thus cannot be predicated of a thing, for it cannot be said that man is flesh and bones. But a genus is predicated of its species, and therefore it must in some way signify the whole thing, just as matter along with its privation is sometimes designated by the simple name of the matter in view of the namelessness of privations, as it was said above (n. 1416) that bronze is taken for formless bronze when we say that a statue is made of bronze; and in a similar fashion when the form is nameless, the composite of matter and form is designated by the simple name of the matter—not common matter, but some determinate matter. And in this way it is taken as a genus; for just as a species is a composite of matter and a determinate form, so too a genus is a composite of matter and a common form.

1547. This becomes evident in many ways. For body can be taken both as the matter and as the genus of animal, because, if we understand in the notion of body a substance completed by its ultimate form, having in itself three dimensions, then body is a genus and its species are the complete substances determined by these ultimate forms, as that of gold, of silver, of olive, or of man. But if one considers in the notion of body only that it is a thing having three dimensions with an aptitude for an ultimate form, then body is matter.

1548. And the same thing applies in the case of a vocal sound; for if in the intelligible expression of vocal sound one includes the formation of sound in common according to the form which is subdivided into the different forms of the letters and syllables, then vocal sound is a genus. But if in the intelligible expression of vocal sound one understands only the substance of sound, to which the foregoing formation can accrue, then vocal sound will be the matter of the letters. From this it is also evident that vocal sound, which is a genus, cannot exist without species; for a sound can be formed only if it has the definite form of this or that letter. But if it lacked altogether the form of a letter insofar as it is matter, then it would be found without letters, just as bronze is found without the things which are produced from it.

1549. If the foregoing statements are true, then, it is evident that a definition is an intelligible expression having unity from its differences in such a way that the whole essence of the definition is included in a certain way in the difference. For animal, which is a genus, cannot exist without species, because the forms of the species, the differences, are not different forms from the form of the genus but are the forms of the genus lacking determination; for example, it is evident that an animal is a thing having a sentient soul, that man is one having "such and such" a sentient soul, viz., with reason, and that a lion is one having "such and such" a soul, namely, with an abundance of daring. And it is the same in other cases. Hence, when a difference is added to a genus it is not added as though it were an essence distinct from the genus, but as though it were contained implicitly in the genus, as the determinate is contained in the indeterminate, for example, white in the thing colored.

1550. And in the light of this the problem raised above (n. 1537) is solved, since nothing prevents one and the same genus from containing within itself various differences, as the indeterminate contains within itself various determinate things. And in addition it is solved by reason of the fact that a difference does not accrue to a genus as constituting an essence distinct from it, as white accrues to man.

1551. **Again, it is** [6].

He next shows that a multitude of differences does not prevent a definition from being one; and in regard to this he does two things. First, he shows in what way a multitude of differences should be taken in a definition. Second [7], he shows that, if differences are taken in the right way, a multitude of differences does not prevent a definition from being one ("If these things").

He accordingly says, first [6], that in the case of those definitions which include many differences not only should the genus be divided by a difference but the first difference should also be divided by the second difference; for example, footed is the difference of animal according to which animal is said to have feet or to be capable of walking; but since this difference is also found to have many forms, it is again necessary to know the difference of such an animal, i.e., what its difference is, "inasmuch as it has feet," i.e., inasmuch as it is considered essentially and not accidentally.

1552. Therefore, since it is accidental to a thing having feet to have wings, it must not be said, in dividing the difference, that among those things which have feet, one kind is winged and another wingless, if a man wants to express correctly the division of the differences. Yet when someone in dividing differences "does this," in such a way that he divides it by means of those attributes which are accidental, this is why he cannot find proper and essential differences. For sometimes necessity compels us to use accidental differences in place of essential differences inasmuch as accidental differences are the signs of certain essential differences unknown to us.

1553. But this difference "having feet" must be divided in this way, namely, so that among animals of this kind one kind has cloven feet and another has not; for these, namely, cloven and uncloven, "are the differences of foot." Therefore having cloven feet divides essentially the difference having feet; for a cloven foot "is a certain kind of foot," i.e., the difference having cloven feet is something contained under the difference having feet; and they are related to each other as the determinate to the indeterminate, as we said of genus and difference.

1554. And it is always necessary to proceed in this way in the division of differences until the one making the division "comes to the species which have no difference," i.e., to ultimate differences, which are not divided further into other differences; and then there will be as many species of foot as there are differences, and the species of animals having feet will be equal in number to the differences; for any individual difference constitutes one ultimate species.

1555. **If these things** [7].

He shows here, from the things which have been set down, that a multitude of differences does not prevent a definition from being one. And in regard to this he does two things. First [7], he proves his thesis. Second [9], he draws the conclusion at which he aims ("Hence it is evident").

In regard to the first he does two things. First, he proves how one thing is produced from many differences, if differences are understood essentially. Second [8], he shows that this cannot be the case if the differences are understood accidentally ("But if the division").

He accordingly says, first [7], that if the differences taken in a definition are such "as has been indicated," i.e., so that differences are always taken essentially and not accidentally, it is obvious that the ultimate difference will constitute the whole substance of the thing and its entire definition; for it includes in itself all preceding parts.

1556. For on the grounds that a genus does not exist without differences it has been shown that a genus is included in its differences. But that the ultimate difference includes all preceding differences is evident from the fact that unless this were affirmed to be so, it would follow that "in the definitive expressions of things," i.e., in their definitions, the same thing would have to be expressed many times. This would be superfluous and meaningless.

1557. And this absurd conclusion follows because, if someone were to define an animal by saying "two-footed having feet" (as he must do if two-footed is a difference distinct from having feet and does not include it), when he defines it in this way he has said nothing but animal having feet having two feet; for two-footed is nothing but having two feet, in which the difference having feet is obviously included. Hence it is evident that, if both are used, we get nonsense.

1558. Moreover, if someone divides two-footed "by its proper difference," i.e., by those things which are essential and not accidental, it follows further that the same thing is expressed many times, and as many times as the number of differences used, so that, if I say that one kind of two-footed animal is one which has a foot divided into five toes, and another kind is one which has a foot divided into four toes, anyone wishing to give all intermediate differences in defining man would express the same thing many times, and as often as he added differences; for he would say that man is an animal having feet, having two feet, having feet divided into five toes.

1559. Now since these things are unacceptable, it is evident that, if differences are taken in a definition there will be one ultimate difference, namely, the one "which will be the specific form and substance," i.e., which comprises the substance and specific form of the thing defined; and as a result of the unity of this difference the definition will be one.

1560. **But if the division** [8].

Here he shows that the definition cannot be said to be one if the differences which are taken are accidental. He says that, if someone in dividing and defining were to take an accidental difference (for example, if things having feet were divided, one into black and another into white), there would be as many ultimate differences as the divisions which have been made, because one of them would not include another. And concerning differences taken in this way the argument introduced above was directed against the unity of the definition; for differences of this kind taken accidentally in this way would be one only in their subject, and this is not enough to account for the unity of the definition.

1561. **Hence it is evident** [9].

He now concludes to his thesis; and in regard to this he does two things. First he gives his conclusion. He says that it is evident from the above discussions that, even though a genus and a difference are given in a definition, still a definition is an intelligible expression composed only of differences, because a genus is not something apart from its differences, as was stated above (n. 1549). And even though many differences are given in a definition, still the entire definition depends on and is constituted by the ultimate difference, when the division is made "correctly," i.e., by descending from more common to less common essential differences, and not by bringing in accidental differences from the side, so to speak.

1562. **Moreover, this will be evident** [10].

Second, he clarifies by means of an example the conclusion which was drawn, saying "moreover this will be evident," namely, that the entire definition consists in the ultimate difference, on the grounds that if anyone changes the parts of such definitions an absurdity results. Thus someone might say that the definition of man is a two-footed animal having feet. But as soon as two-footed has been expressed, it is superfluous to add having feet. But if one were to say first "having feet," it would still be necessary to ask whether it was two-footed, by dividing the difference having feet.

1563. From this it is evident that insofar as those differences are many they have a definite order among themselves. But this cannot mean that there is any order in the substance of a thing; for it cannot be said that this part of a substance is prior and another subsequent, because substance is complete all at once and not successively, except in the case of those things which are deficient in being, such as motion and time.

1564. Hence it is evident that a multiplicity of parts in a definition does not signify a multiplicity of essential parts of which the essence is constituted as if they were distinct things; but all signify one thing which is made determinate by an ultimate difference. It is also evident from this that there is one substantial form for every species. Thus there is one form of lion by which it is a substance, a body, a living body, an animal, and a lion; for if there were many forms corresponding to all the differences mentioned above, all could not be included under one difference, nor could one thing be composed of them.

1565. Lastly he brings his discussion to a close with a summary. He says that with regard to definitions which are based on the divisions of genera into differences and of difference into differences, these points should constitute a preliminary statement "of the kinds of things they are": they are composed of essential predicates, they contain in themselves the parts of the specific form, and each is also a unity. He says "preliminary" because in the following discussions certain points are established about definitions and quiddities.

LESSON 13
Rejection of Universals as Substances

ARISTOTLE'S TEXT Chapter 13: 1038b1–1039a23

1. *But since our investigation has to do with substance, let us return to it. And just as the subject and the essence and the composite of these are called substance, so also is the universal. Two of these, then, have been discussed already, namely, the essence and the subject; and it has been stated that a thing is a subject in two ways: either as this particular thing (as an animal is the subject of its attributes), or as matter is the subject of actuality. But according to some thinkers the universal also seems to be in the fullest sense a cause and principle. Therefore let us treat of this.* **1038b1–8**

2. *For it seems impossible that any of those things which are predicated universally should be substance. For, first, the substance of each thing is the substance which is proper to it and belongs to nothing else, whereas the universal is common; for that is said to be universal which is suited by its nature to be found in many things. Of what particular thing, then, will it be the substance? For it is either the substance of all or of one. But it cannot be the substance of all. And if it is the substance of one, all things will also be that one; for those things whose substance is one have one essence and are themselves one.* **1038b8–15**

3. *Furthermore, substance means what is not predicated of a subject, whereas a universal is always predicated of some subject.* **1038b15–16**

4. *But while a universal cannot be a substance in the way in which the essence of a thing is, it is found in this in the way in which animal is found in man and in horse. Therefore it is evident that it has some kind of intelligible expression. However, it makes no difference if there is no definitive expression of all those things which are present in substance; for none the less this will be the substance of something, as man is the substance of the particular man in whom it is present. Hence the same thing will happen again, for substance will be the substance of that thing, as animal will be the substance of that in which it is present as its proper form.* **1038b16–23**

5. *Furthermore, it is both impossible and absurd that this particular thing, or substance, if it is composed of certain parts, should not be composed of substances or of a particular thing but of quality; for that which is not substance, i.e., quality, will then be prior both to substance and to the particular thing itself. But this is impossible; for accidental attributes cannot be prior to substance either in intelligibility or in time or in the process of generation; for they would then be separable from it.* **1038b23–29**

6. *Furthermore, Socrates will have a substance in his substance, and therefore it will be the substance of two things. And in general it follows, if man and all terms used in this way are substance, that no one of the parts in the intelligible expression is the substance of anything, nor does it exist apart from the species or in anything else. And I mean that there is no animal existing apart from particular ones, and the same is true of everything contained in the intelligible expressions of things. From these considerations it is evident to those who study the matter that no universal is a substance, and that none of the categories signify particular things but things of such and such a kind.* **1038b29–1039a2**

7. *And if this is not the case, many absurdities will follow, among them the third man.* **1039a2–3**

8. *Furthermore, it is also evident in this way that a substance cannot be composed of substances which are actually present in it, for what is actually two can never be actually one; but if something is potentially two, it will be actually one; for example, the whole line consists of two halves existing potentially. For actuality separates. Hence, if substance is one it will not consist*

of substances present in it. And in this sense Democritus is right; for he says that it is impossible for one thing to be produced from two, or two from one; because he makes indivisible continuous quantities substances. It is evident, then, that the same thing will also be true of numbers if a number is a composite of units as some say, because either the number two is not one or the unit is actually present in it. **1039a3–14**

9. But the result involves a difficulty; for if no single substance can consist of universals (because a universal signifies such and such a thing but not a particular thing), and if no single substance can be composed of actual substances, then every substance will lack composition. Hence no substance will have an intelligible expression. But it appears to all, and this has already been stated, that it is either substance alone or chiefly substance that is defined. But now it seems that not even this kind of substance is defined. Hence there will be no definition of anything, or in one sense there will be and in another there will not. The meaning of this will become clearer from what follows. **1039a14–23**

COMMENTARY

1566. Having settled the issue about substance in the sense of quiddity, the Philosopher now comes to certain conclusions about substance insofar as the universal is considered by some thinkers to be a substance; and in regard to this he does two things. First [1], he links up this discussion with the preceding one. Second [2], he carries out his plan ("For it seems").

He therefore says, first [1], that since this science is chiefly concerned with the study of substance, we must return again to the division of substance in order to see what has been said and what remains to be said. Now it is clear from the preceding discussion that substance has the following meanings. First, it means what has the nature "of a subject," namely, matter, which is related to substantial form in the same way as a subject, which is a complete substance, is related to accidental form; second, it means the essence of a thing, which refers to its form; third, it means "the composite of these," i.e., the composite of matter and form; and fourth, it means the universal, according to some thinkers.

1567. Now the division of substance given here is the same as that given at the beginning of Book VII (n. 1270), although it seems to differ; for there he gave four senses of substance: the subject, the essence, the universal and the genus. And he divided subject into three meanings: matter, form, and the composite. And since it has already been made clear that essence derives from form, he puts essence in place of form; and again since a common genus is said to be substance on the same grounds as a universal is, as will be shown, he concludes that both belong in the same class; and thus there remain only the four senses in which substance is spoken of here.

1568. Two of these, then, have been discussed already; for essence has been treated (n. 1299) and also the subject (n. 1270), which is taken in two senses. For, first, it means a particular thing and an actual being, as animal is the subject of its predicates, and as any particular substance is the subject of its accidents. Second, it means primary matter, which is "the subject of actuality," i.e., of substantial form. These things were discussed where it was shown (n. 1501) how the parts of matter pertain to the form and to the individual. But since not only the matter and the quiddity seem to be causes, but also the universal, because "according to some thinkers," i.e., the Platonists, this seems to be in the fullest sense a cause and principle, we will therefore treat "of this," i.e., the universal, in this same seventh book. And in Book VIII we will treat of composite and sensible substances, to which the things treated in this seventh book are related as principles.

1569. For it seems [2].

Here he begins to investigate whether universals are substances, and this is divided into two parts. In the first [2] he shows that universals are not substances, as some thinkers claimed. In the second (Lesson 16, [5]) he shows to what extent the statements of those making this claim are true and to what extent they are false ("But those who").

In regard to the first he does two things. First, he shows in a general way that universals are not substances. Second (Lesson 16, [2]), he shows this in a special way with regard to being and unity, which were assumed to be the substances of things in the highest degree ("And since").

The first is divided into two parts. In the first he shows that universals are not substances; and in the second (Lesson 14), he shows that they are not separate entities ("And from these").

In regard to the first he does two things. First, he shows that universals cannot be substances on the grounds that they are predicated of many things; and second [5], on the grounds that species are composed of universals as parts of their definition ("Furthermore, it is"). For he had said above, in Book V (n. 1119), that in one sense a genus is a whole inasmuch as it is predicated of several things, and in another sense it is a part inasmuch as a species is composed of a genus and a difference.

In regard to the first he does two things. First, he shows that a universal is not a substance on the grounds that it is predicated of many things. Second [4], he rejects a captious answer ("But while a universal").

1570. For the clarification of this chapter it must be noted that the term universal can be taken in two senses. First, it can be taken to mean the nature of the thing to which the intellect attributes the aspect of universality, and in this sense universals such as genera and species signify the substances of things inasmuch as they are predicated quidditatively; for animal signifies the substance of the thing of which it is predicated, and so also does man. Second, a universal can be taken insofar as it is universal, and insofar as the nature predicated of a thing falls under the aspect of universality, i.e., insofar as animal or man is considered as a one-in-many. And in this sense the Platonists claimed that animal and man in their universal aspect constitute substances.

1571. This is what Aristotle aims to disprove in this chapter by showing that animal in general or man in general is not a substance in reality, but that the form animal or man takes on this generality insofar as it exists in the mind, which understands one form as common to many inasmuch as it abstracts it from all individuating principles. Hence in support of his thesis he gives two arguments.

1572. Concerning the first of these [2] he says that in the light of the succeeding arguments it seems impossible that any one of those attributes which are predicated universally should be a substance, i.e., insofar as it is taken in its universality. This is proved, first, by the fact that while the substance of each thing is proper to each and does not belong to something else, a universal is common to many; for that is said to be universal which belongs by nature to many things and is predicated of many. Hence, if a universal is substance it must be the substance of some thing. Of what thing, then, will it be the substance? For it must either be the substance of all the things to which it belongs or of one. But it is impossible for it to be the substance of all things, because one thing cannot be the substance of many, since those things are many whose substances are many and distinct.

1573. But if it is held to be the substance of one of the things in which it is found, it follows that all other things in which it is found, and of which it is held to be the substance, are that one thing; because it must also be their substance for the same reason, since it is found in all in the same way. Now those things of which the substance and essence are one must also be one themselves. Hence, since a universal cannot be the substance of all the things of which it is predicated or of any one of them, it follows that it is not the substance of anything.

1574. Now it should be noted that he describes a universal as what is naturally disposed to exist in many, and not as what exists in many; because there are some universals which contain under themselves only one singular thing, for example, sun and moon. But this is not to be understood in the sense that the very nature of the species, considered in itself, is not naturally disposed to exist in many things; but there is something else which prevents this, as the fact that all the matter of the species is included in one individual, and the fact that it is not necessary that a species which can last forever in a single individual should be numerically many.

1575. Furthermore, substance [3].

Here he gives his second reason. He says that substance refers to something which is not predicated of a subject. But a universal is something which is always predicated of some subject. Therefore a universal is not a substance. But this argument seems not to be cogent, for it is said in the ***Categories***^1 that it belongs to the notion of substance not to exist in a subject. But to be predicated of a subject is not opposed to the notion of substance. Hence in that place second substances are posited, and these are predicated of a subject.

1576. But it must be said that in the **Categories** the Philosopher is speaking from the viewpoint of logic. Now a logician considers things insofar as they exist in the mind, and therefore he considers substances insofar as they take on the character of universality from the way in which the intellect understands them. Hence in reference to predicating, which is an act of reason, he says that substance is predicated "of a subject," i.e., of a substance subsisting outside of the mind. But the first philosopher considers things insofar as they are beings, and therefore in his view of the matter there is no difference between existing in a subject and being predicated of a subject. For he takes something to be predicated of a subject which is something in itself and belongs to some actually existing subject. And it is impossible that this be a substance, for then it would have to exist in a subject. But this is contrary to the notion of substance, as is also stated in the *Categories*.^2

1577. **But while a universal** [4].

Here he rejects the captious answer by which someone might oppose his first argument, in which he had said that all things are one whose substance and quiddity are one. For someone might say that a universal is not a substance in the sense of the essence of a thing, which is proper to one thing. Therefore with a view to rejecting this the Philosopher says "But while" it might be said, in opposition to the first argument introduced, that it is impossible for a universal to be a substance in the way in which an essence is, it is substance only as something existing in these particular things, as animal exists in man and in horse. For the nature of animal is not found in man in such a way that it is proper to him, because it is also found in horse—as if to say that the argument cannot be answered in this way.

1578. For if animal in common is a substance, it follows that there is an intelligible expression of this substance. And it makes no difference to his thesis if there is no definitive expression of all those things "which are present in substance," i.e., which are given in the definition, lest there be an infinite regress in definitions, but all parts of any definition must be further defined. For this substance must be the substance of something, even though it does not have a definition, no less than if it has. Thus we might say that, although man in common does not have a definition, it must nevertheless be the substance of the man in whom it is present, namely, of man in common. Hence the same conclusion follows as before, because, even though this common substance is not held to be proper to any one of its inferiors, it must still be proper to that common substance in which it is first found. For example, if animal in common is a substance, animal will be predicated primarily of that common substance and will signify its proper substance, whether it be definable or not. Hence, since this substance is proper to one thing, it will be impossible for it to be predicated of many things.

1579. **Furthermore, it is** [5].

He now shows that the universal is not a substance by basing his arguments on the grounds that the universal is part of the definition and essence. In regard to this he does two things. First [5], he gives the arguments in support of his thesis. Second [9], he disposes of a difficulty ("But the result").

In regard to the first part he gives four arguments. First, he says that it is both impossible and untenable that a particular thing and a substance should not be composed of substances or particular things but of those things which signify quality—if it is composed of anything (which he adds to allow for simple substances). For since those parts of which a thing is composed are prior to it, it follows that what is not substance but quality is prior both to substance and to this particular thing. But this is impossible, because it is impossible for modifications and qualities and accidents to be prior to substance either in intelligibility or in time or in generation.

1580. For it has been shown above (n. 1253) that they are not prior in intelligibility, because substance is given in the definition of accidents, and not the reverse. And from this it has also been proved above (n. 1257) that they are not prior in time. From this in turn he further proves here that it would follow that attributes would be capable of existing apart from substances; and this is impossible. And priority in generation comes under priority in time, although the reverse is not true. For even though things which are not related to the generation of something are prior in time, they are still not prior in generation; for example, a horse is not prior in generation to a lion which exists at this moment, even though it is prior to it in time. However, the parts of which a thing is composed are prior in the process of generation and therefore in time, and sometimes also in intelligibility, as was shown above (n. 1278). Hence it is impossible that substances should be composed of things which are not substances. But universals do not signify particular things, but of what sort things are, as was said about second substances in the *Categories.*^3 It is evident, then, that singular things, which are particulars, cannot be composed of universals if these are some kind of things which exist apart from singulars.

1581. But it seems that this argument is not a satisfactory one; for even though second substances, which are genera and species in the genus of substance, do not signify particular things but of what sort things are, nevertheless they do not signify of what sort things are in the same way in which attributes that signify accidental quality do, but they signify substantial quality. However, he argues here as if they signified accidental quality.

1582. But it must be said that if universals are things, as the Platonists claimed, we shall have to say that they signify not only substantial quality but also accidental quality; for every quality which is distinct from the thing of which it is the quality, is accidental. For example, whiteness differs from the body of which it is a quality, and it inheres in the body of which it is the quality as its subject; and therefore it is an accident. Hence, if universals as universals are things, they must be distinct from singulars, which are not universals. Therefore, if they signify the quality of those things, they must inhere in them as in substances and thus must signify accidental quality.

1583. However, for those who claim that genera and species are not things or natures distinct from singulars but are the singular things themselves (for example, that there is no man who is not this man), it does not follow that second substance signifies an accident or modification.

1584. **Furthermore, Socrates** [6].

He gives the second argument. He says that if universals are substances, it follows that Socrates will have a substance in his substance; for if all universals are substances, then just as man is the substance of Socrates, in a similar fashion animal will be the substance of man; and thus these two substances, one of which is man and the other animal, will exist in Socrates. His conclusion is "and therefore it will be the substance of two things," i.e., it therefore follows that animal is the substance not only of man but also of Socrates. Hence one substance will belong to two things. Yet it has been shown above that one thing has only one substance.

1585. And the result mentioned applies not only in the case of Socrates but universally in all cases. For if man and the other things which are called species in this way are substances, it also follows that no one of the parts in the intelligible structure of a species is substance, and that it cannot exist without the species in whose definitions it is given or exist in anything else; just as there is no animal "apart from particular animals," i.e., apart from the species of animal. And the same thing applies to all other predicates which are given in definitions, whether they are genera or differences. And this is true because, if those parts which are given in the definitions of species are substances, then since species are substances there will be many substances in singular things, and many things will have one substance; as was said about Socrates. From what has been said, then, it is evident that no universal is a substance, and that common predicates do not signify a particular thing but of what sort a thing is.

1586. **And if this** [7].

Then he gives the third argument. He says that, if the preceding conclusion is not admitted, many absurdities will follow, and one of these will be the need to posit a third man. This can be explained in two ways. First, it can mean that besides the two singular men, Socrates and Plato, there is a third man, who is common to both. This is not absurd according to those who posit Ideas, although it seems absurd from the viewpoint of right reason.

1587. Second, it can be explained as meaning that there is posited a third man besides a singular man and man in common, since they have a common name and intelligible expression, just as do two singular men in addition to whom a third common man is posited; and the reason is that they have a common name and definition.

1588. **Furthermore, it is** [8].

He gives the fourth argument. He says that universals are not substances for this reason that it is impossible that a substance should be composed of many substances actually present in it; for two actual things are never one actual thing, but two which are in potentiality are one actually, as is clear of the parts of a continuous quantity. The two halves of one line, for instance, exist potentially in the whole line, which is one actually. And this is because actuality has the power of separating and distinguishing; for one thing is distinguished from another by its proper form. Hence in order that many things may become one actual thing, it is necessary that all should be included under one form, and that each one should not have its own form by which it would exist in act. Hence it is evident that if a particular substance is one, it will not be composed of substances actually present in it; and thus if it is composed of universals, universals will not be substances.

1589. And in this sense Democritus is right when he says that it is impossible for one thing to be produced from two, and two from one; for it must be borne in mind that two actual existents never make one. But in failing to distinguish between the potential and the actual, he claimed that indivisible continuous quantities are substances; for he thought that, just as one thing does not contain many things actually, neither does it contain them potentially; and thus any continuous quantity is indivisible. Or this might be explained differently. I mean that Democritus was right if we assume his own position to be true, in which he claimed that indivisible quantities are the substances of things and thus are always actual, and in this way no one thing is produced from them. And just as this is true in the case of continuous quantities, in a similar way it is true in the case of numbers, if number is composed of units, as some thinkers claimed. For either the number two (or any other number) is not one thing, or the unit is not actually present in it. Thus the number two will not be two units, but something composed of units; otherwise a number would not be a unity, essentially and properly, but only accidentally, like a heap.

1590. **But the result** [9].

He poses a difficulty about the above answer. He says that the result of the foregoing discussion gives rise to a difficulty; for first (as was said), a substance cannot be composed of universals, because a universal does not signify a particular thing but of what sort a thing is; and second, a substance cannot be composed of actual substances; and thus it seems to follow that substances cannot be composed or made up of substances. It follows, then, that all substances lack composition. And thus, since no definitions are given of substances which lack composition (and this is clear from the fact that the definition is an intelligible expression having parts, as was shown above [n. 1460]), it follows that no substance has a definition. But it seems to everyone, as was shown above (n. 1331), that a definition is either of substance alone or chiefly of substance, and it has now been concluded that there is no definition of substance; hence it follows that there is no definition of anything.

1591. Now the answer to the above difficulty is that in one sense substance is composed of substances and in another it is not. But this will become clearer from the following discussions in this book and in Book VIII; for substance is composed of potential substances, not of actual ones.

LESSON 14
Rejection of Universals as Separate Substances

ARISTOTLE'S TEXT Chapter 14: 1039a24–1039b19

1. And from these facts it is evident what consequences face those who say that the Ideas are substances and are separable, and who also at the same time make the form out of genus and difference. For if there are Forms, and if animal exists in man and in horse, it is either one and the same numerically or different. **1039a24–28**

2. For it is evident that they are one in their intelligible expression, for one will express the same notion in speaking of each. Therefore, if there is a man-in-himself, who is a particular thing and is separate, the things of which he is composed, such as animal and two-footed, must also signify particular things and be separable and be substances. Hence animal will also be such. **1039a28–33**

3. If, then, the animal in horse and in man^1 is one and the same, as you are in yourself, how can one thing be present in many things which exist separately? **1039a33–1039b1**

4. And why will this animal not exist apart from itself? **1039b1–2**

5. Again, if it participates in two-footed and in many-footed, an impossible conclusion follows, for contrary attributes will belong at the same time to this thing which is one and a particular being. And if it does not, what mode of being is meant when one says that an animal is two-footed or is capable of walking? But perhaps they are combined or joined together or mixed. Yet all such views are untenable. **1039b2–6**

6. But what will happen if there is a different animal in each? There will then be an infinite number of things whose substances is animal, for man does not come from animal accidentally. **1039b7–9**

7. Again, animal-in-itself will be many things; for the animal in each will be substance, since it is not predicated of anything else. But if this is not so, man will consist of that other thing, and that will be the genus of man. **1039b9–11**

8. Further, all the things of which man is composed will be Ideas. Hence no one of them will be the Idea of one thing and the substance of something else, for this is impossible. Therefore animal-in-itself will be each of these things which are contained in animals. **1039b11–14**

9. Again, from what is it derived? And how is it derived from animal-in-itself? Or how is it possible that the animal which is a substance should exist apart from animal-in-itself? **1039b14–16**

10. Again, these are the conclusions which follow in the case of sensible things, and there are others more absurd than these. If it is impossible, then, that this should be so, it is evident that there is no Idea of these sensible things, as some affirm. **1039b16–19**

COMMENTARY

1592. Having shown that universals are not substances in an unqualified sense, here the Philosopher shows that they are not substances existing apart from sensible things. This is divided into two parts. In the first [1] he shows that universals are not substances existing apart from sensible things. In the second (Lesson 16) he clears up a point which had remained a problem in the above discussion ("It is also").

In regard to the first he does two things. First, he shows that universals are not separate substances. Second (Lesson 15), he shows that if they are separate they are not definable ("But since there are").

In regard to the first he does two

things. First, he shows the absurd consequences facing those who claim that universals are separate substances, by comparing genus with species; and second [10], by comparing genus with individuals ("Again, these are").

In regard to the first he does three things. First, he presents a division. Second [2], he proceeds to treat the first member of this division ("For it is evident"). Third [6], he proceeds to treat the second member ("But what will happen").

He therefore says, first [1], that from what has been said above it is also possible to indicate the absurd conclusions facing those who say that the Ideas, which are said to be universal forms, are substances and are separable, and at the same time claim that a specific form is composed of genus and difference; for these two positions, when taken together, i.e., that forms are composed of genus and difference, and that universal forms are separate substances, called Ideas, lead to absurd consequences. For if forms are assumed to be separate, it follows that one genus exists in many species at the same time, as animal in man and in horse. Therefore, either this animal present in man and in horse is one and the same thing numerically, or there is one animal present in man and a different one present in horse. And he introduces this division because Plato claimed that there are Ideas of species but not of genera, even though he made the general claim that universals are substances.

1593. **For it is evident** [2].

He proceeds to treat the first member of this division. First, he shows that the animal present in man and that present in horse are one and the same. Second [3], he explains the absurdities which follow from this position ("If, then").

He accordingly says, first [2], that it is evident that the animal present in man and that present in horse are one and the same in their intelligible expression; for if one states the intelligible expression of animal insofar as it is predicated of each, namely, of man and of horse, the same intelligible expression—living sensible substance—will be assigned to each of them; for a genus is predicated univocally of a species just as a species is also predicated univocally of individuals. Hence, if, because of the fact that species are predicated of all individuals according to one intelligible expression, there is a common man, who is man-in-himself, existing by himself, "and who is a particular thing," i.e., something subsistent which can be pointed to and is separable from sensible things, as the Platonists maintained, then for a similar reason the things of which a species consists, namely, genus and difference, such as animal and two-footed, must also signify particular things and be separable from their own inferiors, and be substances existing by themselves. Hence it follows that animal will be one individual and subsistent thing, which is predicated of man and of horse.

1594. **If, then, the animal** [3].

Then he points out the absurdities which follow from this position; and there are three of them.

The first is that since a genus is present in a species as something signifying the substance of a thing, then animal will be present in horse as you are in yourself, who are your own substance. Now in this way it is not possible for some one thing to be present in many things which exist separately.

For you are present only in yourself, since you are not in many things which exist separately, as in flesh and bones, which are your parts. Therefore, if animal is one and the same, it will be incapable of existing in many species, as in man and in horse, since the separate Forms, according to the Platonists, are substances which are distinct from each other.

1595. **And why will** [4].

Then he gives the second absurdity. For since man is one thing predicated of many, according to the Platonists, man is assumed not to be present in particular things but to exist outside of them. Hence, if there is one animal which is predicated of all species of animals, why will this universal animal-in-itself not exist apart from itself, namely, apart from horse or any other species of animal, as something existing separately by itself? No suitable explanation of this can be given by them.

1596. **Again, if it participates** [5].

He gives the third absurdity. He says that it is evident that a species is constituted of a genus and a difference. Therefore this is explained by the fact that a genus participates in a difference just as a subject participates in an accident. Thus we understand that man is made up of animal and two-footed in the same way that white man is made up of white and man. Or it is explained in some other way.

1597. And if a species comes to be because a genus participates in a difference, so that animal by participating in two-footed becomes a man, and by participating in many-footed becomes a horse or an octopus, an impossible conclusion follows. For when a genus which is predicated of different species is held to be one substance, it follows that contrary attributes will be present at the same time in the same animal, which is one thing in itself and a particular being, namely, something capable of being pointed to; for the differences by which a genus is divided are contraries.

1598. However, if man is not composed of animal and two-footed by way of participation, then when someone says that animal is two-footed or capable of walking, what will be the way in which one thing is constituted from these two? The implication is that the reason cannot be easily given. Therefore he adds "But perhaps they are combined," which is equivalent to saying: will it be possible to affirm that one thing arises from these two as a result of their combination, as a house arises from stones; or by being joined together, as a chest comes from pieces of wood being fitted together; or by being mixed, as a lozenge comes from the alteration of different kinds of medications? For these are the three ways in which one thing is found to come from two or more things which exist as independent substances.

1599. But all of these ways are unacceptable. For genus and difference could not be predicated of species, as parts which are combined, joined together and mixed are not predicated of their wholes. Furthermore, one thing does not enter as a whole into the composition of different things, but its parts exist separately, so that one part of it enters into the composition of this thing and another into the composition of something else, as one part of wood enters into the composition of a house and another into the composition of a chest. Hence if man and bird were to come from animal and from two-footed in the foregoing ways, it would follow that the whole nature of animal would not be present in man and in bird, but different parts would be present in each. And so, again, animal would not be the same in each.

1600. **But what will happen** [6].

He now treats the second member of the division. He says that an absurdity follows if animal is not assumed to be one in all species of animals; and this leads to four impossible consequences. He gives the first by speaking as follows: the consequences facing those who claim that universals are substances when animal is assumed to be one in all species of animals, has been made clear. But because of this someone can say that there is a different animal in each species of animal; hence there will be an infinite number of things whose substance is animal, inasmuch as this follows from the statement of the foregoing position; for animal is the substance of any species contained under animal, since it cannot be said that man comes from animal accidentally but essentially. And thus animal pertains to the substance of horse and of ox and to that of the other species, which are almost infinite in number. But that some one thing should be present in the substance of an infinite number of things seems absurd.

1601. **Again, animal-in-itself** [7].

Then he gives the second absurdity. He says that it also follows that "animal-in-itself," i.e., the universal substance animal, will be many, because animal, which is present in each species of animal, is the substance of the species of which it is predicated; for it is not predicated of the species as of something else substantially different from itself. And if the term animal is not predicated of man as something different, it will be proper to say that man will be made up of it, i.e., have animal within himself as his own substance, and that the thing being predicated, i.e., animal, is also his genus, which is predicated of him quidditatively. Hence it follows that, just as those things of which animal is predicated are many, in a similar way the universal animal is itself many.

1602. **Further, all the things** [8].

He gives the third absurdity. He says that it also follows, from the things said above, that all the things of which man consists, namely, the higher genera and species, are Ideas; and this is opposed to the position of the Platonists, who claimed that only species are Ideas of particular things, and that genera and differences are not Ideas of species. They did this because an Idea is the proper exemplar of the thing produced from the Idea so far as the form of the thing is concerned. Now the form of a genus is not proper to that of its species as the form of a species is proper to its individuals, which are formally the same and materially different.

1603. But if there are different animals for the different species of animals, then something in the substance of the genus of each species will correspond to each as its proper Idea; and thus genera also will be Ideas, and so will differences. Therefore it will not be characteristic of one of the universals to be an Idea and of another to be a substance, as the Platonists claimed when they said that genera are the substances of species and species the Ideas of individuals; for it is impossible that this should be so, as has been shown. From what has been said above, then, it follows "that animal-in-itself," i.e., the universal substance animal, is each of these things "which are contained in animals," i.e., which are contained among the species of animal.

1604. **Again from what** [9].

Here he gives the fourth absurdity. He says that there also seems to be a difficulty about the parts of which this thing, man, is composed; and how it is derived from "animal-in-itself," namely, the universal animal; or "how is it possible that the animal which is a substance should exist apart from animal-in-itself," i.e., how is it possible for man to be something apart from animal as a substance existing by itself and for it still to be true that animal is this very thing which is man? For these two views seem to be opposed, namely, that man exists apart from animal, and that animal is this very thing which is man.

1605. **Again, these are** [10].

Then he rejects the foregoing position by comparing genera to singular things. He says that the same absurd conclusions which face those who claim that genera and universals are the substances of species, also face those who hold genera to be the substances of singular sensible things (and there are even more absurd conclusions than these). And their claim is absurd inasmuch as the nature of a genus is more removed from sensible, material singulars than from intelligible and immaterial species. Hence, if it is impossible that this should be the case, it is clear that there is no Idea of these sensible things, as the Platonists said.

LESSON 15
Three Arguments Why Ideas Cannot be Defined

ARISTOTLE'S TEXT Chapter 15: 1039b20–1040b4

1. *But since there are two kinds of substance, the concrete whole and the intelligible structure of a thing (and I say that the former is substance taken as the intelligible structure conceived with matter, and the latter is the intelligible structure in general), then all things which are called substance in the former way are subject to corruption; for these are also subject to generation. But the intelligible structure is not subject to corruption in such a way that it perishes, since it is not subject to generation; for it is not the being of house that is produced, but the being of this house. But they both are and are not without generation and corruption; for it has been shown (611) that no one generates or produces these. And for this reason, too, there is neither definition nor demonstration of singular sensible substances, because they have matter whose nature is such that it is possible for them both to be and not to be; and for this reason all singular instances of these are corruptible. Now demonstration is of necessary things, and definition is scientific. And just as scientific knowledge cannot sometimes be scientific knowledge and sometimes ignorance, but what is such is opinion, so too neither can it be admitted that demonstration or definition is such (but it is opinion then which is concerned with something that can be otherwise than it is). But if this is true, it is evident that there will not be demonstration or definition of these things. For corruptible things are not evident to those having scientific knowledge; and when they have been removed from the sphere of sensory perception, even though their intelligible expressions remain the same in the mind, there will be neither demonstration nor definition of them. And for this reason when anyone, eager for setting the limits of things, defines one of these singulars, he must not ignore the fact that it is always possible to overthrow his definition; for it is not possible to define such a thing. Nor is it possible, then, to define any of the Ideas; for an Idea is of singular things (as they say), and is separable.* **1039b20–1040a9**

2. *And it is necessary that the intelligible expression of a thing should be composed of words; and one who forms a definition will not coin a word (for it would be unknown), but the attributes which are posited are common to all things. It is necessary, then, that these also apply to other things; for example, if anyone were to define you, he would say that you are an animal capable of walking or white or having some other attribute which is found in something else.* **1040a9–14**

3. *But if anyone were to say that nothing prevents all things considered separately from being present in many things, but that taken together they are present together only in this one thing, it is first necessary to say that they belong to both; e.g., two-footed animal belongs both to animal and to two-footed. And this must be the case with eternal things.* **1040a14–17**

4. *It is also necessary that they be prior existents and parts of the composite. And even more, they must be separable if man is separable; for either neither or both will be such. If, then, neither is separable, a genus will not exist apart from species; but if both are, so also will a difference be.* **1040a17–21**

5. *Again, because they are prior to being itself, they will therefore not be destroyed.* **1040a21–22**

6. *And, again, if the Ideas are composed of Ideas, less composite things are the elements of others.* **1040a22–23**

7. *It will, moreover, be necessary that those things of which an Idea is composed should be predicated of many things, as animal and two-footed. But if this is not true, how will they be*

known? For there will be an Idea which cannot be predicated of more things than one. However, this does not seem to be the case, but every Idea is capable of being participated. **1040a23–27**

8. Therefore, as was stated (671), the fact that it is impossible to give definitions of eternal things, and especially of any singular instances of these, as the sun and the moon, is hidden from these people. For people err by adding such attributes as can be removed and let the sun remain, for example, going around the earth or being hidden at night; (for according to them) if it stands still or is visible at night, it will no longer be the sun; but it is absurd if it is not so (for the sun means a certain substance); and they also err by adding attributes which are capable of belonging to something else; for example, supposing that another such thing should come into being, it would evidently be a sun. Therefore the definitive expression is common. But the sun was taken to be a singular thing, like Cleon and Socrates. For why do none of these thinkers offer any fixed limits of an Idea? For to those attempting this it would become evident that what has been said just now is true. **1040a27–1040b4**

COMMENTARY

1606. In this place the Philosopher shows that the Ideas, which the Platonists claimed to be separate, are incapable of being defined. And he does this because the Platonists posited Ideas chiefly in order that they might apply them both to definitions and demonstrations, which have to do with what is necessary, since all these sensible substances seemed to be in motion.

In regard to this he does two things. First [1], he uses arguments to show that the Ideas cannot be defined. Second [8], he uses an example ("Therefore, as was stated").

In the first member of this division [1] he presents three arguments, and the first of these he states as follows:

one kind of substance is "the intelligible structure," i.e., the essence and form, and another is the composite of matter and form, which is the concrete whole made up of matter and form. And I say that these differ; i.e., "that the latter," which is substance in the sense of the concrete whole, is substance taken as something having its intelligible structure conceived with matter; but the former, which is the form or intelligible structure or essence of a thing, is the intelligible structure or form in general, and this does not have individual matter connected with it.

1607. Therefore all those things which are called substance in the sense of a composite are capable of being corrupted; for it was shown above (n. 1423) that only those things which are composed of matter and form are subject to generation; and generation and corruption belong to the same subject.

1608. And substance in the sense of the intelligible structure or whatness of a thing is incapable of being corrupted in such a way that it is corrupted in itself. For it was shown above (nn. 1417–23) that this kind of substance is not generated but only the composite; for it is not the essence of a house that is produced (as was shown above), but what is peculiar to this house; because it is this particular house and not the intelligible structure of a house that is produced. Yet forms and quiddities of this kind sometimes are and sometimes are not "without generation and corruption," i.e., without being generated or corrupted in themselves, for they begin to be and not to be when other things are generated and corrupted. For it was shown above (n.

1420) that in the case of natural things no one "generates these," namely, their forms and quiddities; nor does this happen even in the case of artificial things; but this singular agent generates and produces this singular thing.

1609. And because singular things are generated and corrupted there can be neither definition nor demonstration of singular sensible substances; for they contain individual matter whose nature is such that anything constituted of it is capable both of being and of not being. For matter itself, considered in itself, is in potentiality to form, by means of which the material thing exists, and to privation, by reason of which the material thing does not exist. Hence all singular things included among these sensible substances whose matter is in potentiality to being and non-being are corruptible. However, the celestial bodies do not have that kind of matter which is in potentiality to being and non-being, but that which is in potentiality to place; therefore they are not corruptible.

1610. Hence, if demonstration is of necessary things, as was proved in the ***Posterior Analytics***,^1 and definition is also "scientific," i.e., productive of science, because it serves as the middle term in a demonstration, which is a syllogism producing science, then just as it is impossible for scientific knowledge sometimes to be scientific knowledge and sometimes ignorance, because what is known scientifically must always be true, "but what is such," i.e., what can sometimes be true and sometimes false, is opinion, in the same way it is impossible that there should be demonstration or definition of those things which can be otherwise than they are; but about contingent things of this kind there is only opinion.

1611. If this is so, I say, it is evident that there will be neither definition nor demonstration of these singular, sensible, corruptible things. For corruptible things of this kind cannot be clearly known by those who have scientific knowledge of them when they have passed outside the scope of the senses, through which they are known. Hence, "even though the intelligible expressions" or forms of these singular things, by which they can be known, "remain in the soul," there will be neither definition nor demonstration of them. And for this reason when anyone, "eager for setting the limits of things," i.e., the definition of anything, defines a singular thing, he must not ignore the fact that it is always possible to remove the singular while the intelligible expression as such which he forms in his mind remains. And this is true because it is impossible to give a genuine definition of a singular; for in the case of those things which are truly defined the knowledge of the thing defined remains as long as the knowledge of the definition remains in the mind.

1612. Therefore, if a singular thing cannot be defined, it is impossible to define an Idea; for an Idea must be a singular thing, according to those who posit Ideas, since they claim that an Idea is something which subsists of itself apart from all other things; and this is what *singular thing* means.

1613. **And it is necessary** [2].

Then he gives the second argument; and in regard to this he does two things. First, he gives the argument; and second [3], he rejects an answer which avoids the question ("But if").

Now it was necessary that he should add this argument to the foregoing one, since the argument given has already proved that the singular is not definable because it is corruptible and material, and the Platonists did not assign these two properties to the Ideas. Hence, lest his proof should be rendered ineffective, he adds another argument [2], and states it as follows.

1614. It is necessary that every definitive expression should be composed of several words; for one who defines a thing does not convey its meaning by giving only one word, because if he were to give only one the thing defined would still remain unknown to us. For when a single better known word is given it is possible to know the name of the thing defined but not the thing defined, unless its principles are given; for it is by its principles that everything becomes known.

1615. Now the resolving of the thing defined into its principles—which those forming definitions intend to do—is possible only when several words are given. Therefore he says that, if only one word is given, the thing defined will still remain unknown; but if many words are given, they must be common to all things [of their class].

1616. For if in the definition of any singular thing certain words are given which are proper only to that thing itself, they will be synonymous names of the same singular thing. Hence it is not the thing which will be made known when words of this kind are given, but perhaps a less well known word. For example, if we were to ask who Tullius is, and one were to answer, Marcus and Cicero, it would not be an apt definition.

1617. Therefore, if a singular thing is defined, certain words must be given which are applicable to many things. Hence the definition must fit not only the singular thing whose definition is under investigation but also other things; and this is opposed to the notion of a true definition; for example, if someone intended to define you, and said that you are an animal capable of walking or a white animal or anything else that applies to you, this definition would not only fit you but other things as well.

1618. It is evident, then, that a singular thing lacks a definition not only because it is corruptible and material but also because it is singular. Hence, neither is an Idea defined. The reason for this is the one which the Philosopher gives here: if the words taken to define a thing express the individual in terms of the things by which it is individuated, the words will be synonymous. But if they express the nature and common attributes without individuation, the definition will not be a proper definition of the thing defined, because all forms, accidental or substantial, which do not subsist of themselves, are, when considered in themselves, common to many. And if some are found in only one thing, as the form of the sun, this does not come from the form, inasmuch as^2 it is of itself suited to be in many things, but from the matter; for the whole matter of the species is collected in one individual. Or this comes from its final cause, because one sun is sufficient for the perfection of the universe.

1619. **But if anyone** [3].

Then he rejects an answer which is evasive. For someone could say that while any of those attributes given in the definition of a singular Idea are proper to many individually, yet taken together they are proper to only one thing, viz., to the one whose definition is under investigation.

He rejects this answer in two ways. First [3], with reference to the Ideas themselves; and second [7], with reference to those things of which they are the Ideas ("It will, moreover").

In regard to the first he does two things. First, he rejects the answer mentioned above, showing that it still does not follow that the definition belongs only to the thing defined; and second [4], that it does not belong to it primarily ("It is also necessary").

Hence he says [3] that in opposing this answer it must be said, first, that the definition assigned to any Idea also belongs to other Ideas; for example, if the definition of the Idea of man is two-footed animal, these two belong "to animal and to two-footed," i.e., to the Idea of animal and to the Idea of two-footed; for those two Ideas combined would also be two-footed animal. Hence this definition, two-footed animal, will not be proper to the Idea of man. And this absurdity also follows "in the case of eternal things," i.e., if we consider the definition of an Idea, which is an eternal singular, from the Platonists' point of view, and if we consider that the definition given to one Idea is proper to the others.

1620. **It is also** [4].

Then he exposes the second consequence, namely, that the definition assigned to the Idea of man does not belong primarily to this Idea; and this is opposed to the notion of a definition, for a definition is shown to be true primarily of the thing defined.

He proves this in three ways. First, he says that it is necessary not only that the definition given to man should belong to animal and to two-footed, but also that these—animal and two-footed—should be prior to man and be his parts inasmuch as man is composed of both.

1621. But according to the position of the Platonists it would rather follow that both of these—animal and two-footed—are separable from man and from other animals, if man is assumed to be separable from individuals; because just as man is above individuals, in a similar fashion genus and difference are above man. For it is necessary either that nothing common be separable, or that both of these—animal and two-footed—be separable from man. Now if nothing common is separable, it follows that a genus will not exist apart from its species, and thus the genus will not signify substance. But if a genus exists apart from its species, then for a like reason a difference will also exist apart, for this is more common than a species. But if both animal and two-footed are separable from man, it follows that they are prior in the way in which the separate man is prior to the individual. And thus it further follows that the definition assigned to man belongs to certain prior things—to animal and to two-footed.

1622. **Again, because** [5].

Second, he proves the same point by means of another argument. He says that it is evident from the following consideration that animal and two-footed are prior to man in being; for those things are prior in being which are not destroyed when other things are destroyed, although when they are destroyed other things are destroyed. For example, the number one is prior to the number two because, when the number one is destroyed, the number two is destroyed; but not the reverse. And when animal and two-footed are destroyed, man is destroyed, although when man is destroyed the former—animal and two-footed—are not destroyed. Hence animal and two-footed are evidently prior to man.

1623. **And again** [6].

He then proves the same point by a

third argument. He says that the same conclusion is evident if we maintain not only that animal and two-footed are separable from man, as being Ideas of man, as was proved above in the first argument, but also that man is composed of them, insomuch that in this way a separate Idea turns out to be composed of separate Ideas. For it is evident that animal and two-footed, of which man is composed, would be less composite than man, who is composed of them. But what is less composite is prior. Hence it follows again that animal and two-footed are prior to man, not only because they are separate, as the first argument advanced, but also because man is composite, as this third argument advanced.

1624. **It will, moreover** [7].

Then he gives an additional argument to reject the answer given above. He says that it not only follows that the definition assigned to the Idea of man is common to other prior Ideas, namely, to animal and to two-footed, of which the Idea of man is supposed to be composed, but also that these very things—animal and two-footed—will be predicated of many things and not just of man. And this will occur not only when they are taken in themselves, as the foregoing answer of these men stated, but also when they are taken together.

1625. For if these elements of which the Idea of man is composed, animal and two-footed, are not predicated of many things, how is it known that they belong to the Idea of man, as was concluded above (nn. 1542–50)? For it would follow that there is some Idea which cannot be predicated of more things than one, since it is evident that the Idea of animal can be predicated of many individuals. Hence, if these two together—animal and two-footed—can be predicated of only one thing, it follows that two-footed restricts animal to one thing so that some Idea, two-footed, is predicated of only one thing. But this does not seem to be true, since every Idea is capable of being participated in by many things; for from one examplar there arise many things which resemble that exemplar. Therefore the foregoing answer cannot be true.

1626. Moreover, it must be understood that by the same argument it can also be adequately shown that no singular thing among these sensible things can be defined by any properties or united forms, whatever they may be. For any Idea, and also any form, taken in itself, is naturally disposed to exist in many things; and thus no matter how they may be combined there will be an exact definition of this singular thing only accidentally, inasmuch as it is possible for all of these forms taken together to be found in only one thing. It is obvious, then, that the principle of individuation is not a collection of accidents (as some said), but designated matter, as the Philosopher has stated (n. 1496).

1627. **Therefore, as was stated** [8].

Then he gives the third and chief argument to show that Ideas cannot be defined. He says that, since it has been stated above (n. 1609) that individuals cannot be defined because of their corruptibility, as the first argument advanced, and since those attributes which are included in definitions are common ones, as the second argument advanced, the truth of the statement that it is impossible to define singulars among eternal things is not apparent, especially in the case of those which are unique in one species, as the sun and the moon. For since the things in question are eternal, the argument based on the corruptibility of singular things does not seem to be conclusive when applied to them. And because these things are unique in their species, the argument from the commonness of the parts of a definition does not seem to be conclusive in their regard; for in this case all attributes proper to one species alone are proper to one individual alone.

1628. But those who think that these things are definable are deceived to such an extent that they make many errors in defining such things. They err in one respect inasmuch as they add in the definitions of these things such attributes as can be removed and let the things themselves remain, namely, the sun and the moon; for example, in defining the sun they say that it is something "going around the earth," i.e., revolving around the earth, or "hidden at night," i.e., invisible during the night. For if the sun were to stand still and not revolve around the earth, or if it appeared without being invisible at night, it would not be the sun if it had been defined properly. However, it would be absurd if it were not the sun when these attributes were removed, for *the sun* signifies a substance; but these things by which it is defined are certain of its accidents.

1629. And they not only err in this way but also make a further mistake when they define the sun by an attribute which is suited to belong to something else; for supposing that "another such thing should come into being," i.e., some body having such a form, or the same form and species, it is evident that it would be a sun, inasmuch as *sun* signifies a species; and in this way it can be defined. Hence, "the definitive expression is common," i.e., the intelligible expression of the species *sun*. But this sun would be a singular thing like Cleon or Socrates. Thus it is certain that even though the Ideas are also claimed to be eternal and unique in their species, they still cannot be defined.

1630. Hence none of those who posit Ideas reveal "any fixed limits," i.e., definition, of an Idea. For if they were to give the definition of some Idea, as that of man or horse, it would become evident, in opposition to those attempting to define an Idea, that what has just been said is true: an Idea is indefinable.

LESSON 16

Composition in Sensible Substances. Non-Substantiality of Unity and Being. Plato's Doctrine of Ideas

ARISTOTLE'S TEXT Chapter 16: 1040b5–1041a5

1. It is also evident that many of the things which are thought to be substances are potential, as the parts of animals; for none of them are separate. But when they have been separated, all are then like matter, for example, earth, fire and air; for none of them constitute a unity but they are like a heap of things before they are arranged and some one thing is produced from them. But someone might very easily suppose that the parts of living things and the parts of the soul which are close to them exist in actuality as well as in potency, because they have principles of motion consisting in something in their joints; and for this reason some animals live when they have been divided. Yet all parts exist potentially when they are one and continuous by nature, not by compulsion or by being joined together; for such a thing is a mutilation. **1040b5–16**

2. And since the term one is used in the same senses as the term being, and the substance of unity is one, and those things whose substance is one are numerically one, it is evident that neither unity nor being can be the substance of things, as neither can the being of an element or a principle. But we look for the principle in order to reduce the thing to something better known. Therefore, among these unity and being are substance to a greater degree than principle, element or cause. **1040b16–19**

3. But neither are these substance, if nothing that is common is substance; for substance is not present in anything else but itself and in that which has it, of which it is the substance. **1040b19–24**

4. Furthermore, unity will not be present in many things at the same time; but what is common is present in many things at the same time. Hence it is evident that nothing universal exists apart from singular things. **1040b25–27**

5. But those who speak of the Forms are right in a sense when they make them separate, if^1 they are substances; but in a sense they are wrong, because they say that a Form is one in many things. And the reason for this is that they cannot explain what are the incorruptible substances of this kind which exist apart from singular, sensible substances. Therefore they make them specifically the same as corruptible things (for we know these things); i.e., they invent a man himself and a horse itself by adding the word itself to sensible things. Hence, even if we did not see the stars, none the less, as I should presume, there would be eternal substances besides those which we see. Hence, even if we do not now know what they are, perhaps it is still necessary that there should be some. It is evident, then, that no universal predicates are substance, and that one substance is not composed of substances. **1040b27–1041a5**

COMMENTARY

1631. Here the Philosopher clears up a point which remained a difficulty above, namely, how a substance is composed of parts, when he showed above (n. 1318) that a substance could be composed neither of its accidental attributes nor of actually existing substances (n. 1588). Therefore he shows here [1] that the parts of which substances are composed are not actually existing substances but potential ones. He says that, since it was stated above (n. 1263) that there are some things which are thought by all to be substances, namely, sensible substances and their parts, it is evident that most substances of this kind are potential and not actual, as is clear of the parts of animals and all other parts.

1632. He says that the parts of these substances are many, because since each whole is composed of many parts, there must be more component parts than composite wholes. And it is evident that parts exist potentially, because none of them are separate, but all parts as parts are rather united in the whole.

1633. For everything which is actual must be distinct from other things, because one thing is distinguished from another by its own actuality and form, as was stated above (n. 1588). But when those things which are assumed to be parts have been separated from each other when the whole is dissolved, they are then actual beings, not as parts but as matter existing under the privation of the form of the whole. This is evident, for example, of earth, fire and air, which, when they are parts of a compound, are not actually existing things but exist potentially in the compound; but when they are separated, they are then actually existing things and not parts. For none of the elements "before they are arranged," i.e., before they reach their proper state of mixture by way of alteration, and before one compound comes from them, together form a unity, except in the sense that a heap of stones is one in a qualified sense and not in an unqualified one. Or better "none of them," i.e., they do not constitute a unity before some one thing is produced from them by arrangement.

1634. For even though all parts exist potentially, someone might very readily suppose that the parts of living things and those of the soul which are close to them are actual as well as potential, i.e., they are in potentiality close to actuality; and the reason is that living bodies are organic bodies having parts which are formally distinct. Hence they most of all are close to being actual; and this is because they have a principle of motion in some determinate part, since one part moves another. This is clear, for instance, in the case of their joints, in which the principle of motion of one of the two connected parts seems to be found, since one can be moved and another at rest, as is stated in ***The Motion of Animals***.^1

1635. And since not only the parts of the body are in potentiality close to actuality, but also the parts of the soul, therefore some animals live after they have been divided, as segmented animals. And this is possible because in the whole animal there is one soul actually and there are many souls potentially. But when division is made the several souls become actual. This happens because of the imperfection of such animals which require very little diversity in their parts, for they have a soul with imperfect ability to function and incapable of acting in different ways, for which a number of different organs are necessary.

1636. Yet even though these parts of the soul and the parts of living things are close to actuality, nevertheless they are all potential when the whole is one and continuous by nature. But this would not be the case if one thing came into being by force, as, for example, when the parts of one living thing are tied to those of another; or by grafting, as happens in the case of plants. For before the scion which is to be inserted is united with the plant, it is actual, but afterwards it is potential. "For such a thing," namely, to be one by force or grafting, "is a mutilation," i.e., something injurious to nature and opposed to nature.

1637. **And since** [2].

Here he shows in a special way that unity and being are not substances; and in regard to this he does two things. First, he states his thesis. He says that unity is predicated of things in the same way that being is, since they are interchangeable, and unity is predicated of a thing because of its substance. For one thing has one substance, and those things are numerically one whose substance is numerically one. And it is also evident that a thing is called a being because of its own substance.

1638. Since this is true, I say, it is clear that neither unity nor being can be the substance of things, but they are predicated rather of substance as their subject. And in a similar way neither does "the being of an element or a principle," i.e., the very notion of a principle or element, express the substance of the thing called a principle or element. But we look for the principle or element in order to refer it to something better known, namely, to the substance of the subject.

1639. Yet being and unity are substance to a greater degree than a principle, element and cause, since they are closer to the substance of things; for principle, element and cause signify only the relationship of one thing to another, but being and unity signify something proper to a thing by reason of its own substance. Yet neither being nor unity is the substance itself of a thing.

1640. **But neither** [3].

Second, he proves his thesis by two arguments. He gives the first of these when he says that since these—unity and being—are common attributes, they cannot be substances if nothing common is substance, as has been proved (n. 1585). That nothing common is substance is clear from the fact that substance can only be present in the thing to which it belongs and of which it is the substance. Hence it is impossible that substance should be common to several things.

1641. **Furthermore, unity** [4].

Here he gives the second argument. He says that unity itself cannot be present in many things at the same time; for this is opposed to the notion of unity even though it is maintained that there is a unity which exists by itself as a substance. But what is common is present in many things at the same time, for common means what may be predicated of many things and be present in many things. Hence it is clear that a common unity cannot be one in the sense that it is one substance. Furthermore, it is evident from all the points already discussed above in this chapter that no universal—either being or unity or genera or species—has a separate being apart from singular things.

1642. **But those who** [5].

He shows in what sense Plato's statements are true, and in what sense they are not. He says that the Platonists, who assume that there are certain ideal forms, are right insofar as they claim that these are separate, because they hold that they are the substances of singular things; for by definition a substance is something that exists of itself. Now unity cannot be something that exists of itself if it exists in some singular thing, and the reason is that if it does exist in one singular thing it cannot exist in others; for, as has already been stated (680:C 1641), no self-subsistent unity can be present in many things. Hence considering Plato's doctrine that the separate Forms are substance, he was right insofar as he maintained that they are separate.

1643. But the Platonists were not right when they said that there is one form in many things; for these two statements seem to be opposed, namely, that something may be separate and exist of itself, and that it may still have being in many things. The reason why the Platonists were led to posit separate substances of this kind, yet have them existing in many things, is that they discovered through the use of reason that there must be some incorruptible and incorporeal substances, since the notion of substance is not bound up with corporeal dimensions. But "they cannot explain" which substances are of this kind which are incorruptible and exist apart from these singular and sensible substances, i.e., they cannot describe and make them known, because our knowledge begins from the senses and therefore we can ascend to incorporeal things, which transcend the senses, only insofar as we may be guided by sensible substances.

1644. Therefore in order that they might convey some knowledge of incorporeal, incorruptible substances, "they make," i.e., they suppose, them to be specifically the same as corruptible substances, just as they find among these corruptible substances a singular corruptible man and similarly a singular corruptible horse. Hence they claimed that among those separate substances there is a substance which is man, and another which is horse, and so on for other things, but in a different way; because according to the doctrine of the Platonists we know these separate substances on the grounds that we speak of "man himself," i.e., man-in-himself, "and horse itself," i.e., horse-in-itself. And thus in order to designate separate substances "we add this word," i.e., the term "itself," or in itself, to each sensible substance.

1645. From this it appears that the Platonists wanted those separate substances to be specifically the same as these sensible substances; and to differ only in that they gave to separate substances the name of a form in itself, but not to sensible substances. The reason for this is that singular substances contain many things which are not parts of the form, and they said that separate substances contain only those elements which pertain to the specific form and to the nature of the specific form. Hence this separate man was called man-in-himself, because he contained only those elements which pertain to the nature of the form; but this singular man contains many other things besides those which pertain to the form, and for this reason he is not called man-in-himself.

1646. Now there is a defect in this position comparable to that of maintaining that we do not see the stars and other incorruptible bodies but that it was nevertheless certain by reason that there existed incorruptible bodies, and then maintaining that incorruptible bodies were specifically the same as the bodies of corruptible things; as if we were to say that ox and man and horse and other substances of this kind were incorruptible bodies, as the poets imagined a ram (Aries) and a bull (Taurus) and the like to be present in the stars. Therefore even if we did not see the stars, none the less, "as I should presume," there would be "eternal corporeal substances," i.e., the stars, in addition to those substances which we did then see, namely, corruptible bodies of this kind, and they would be of a different species than these. And in a similar way, even if we do not now know how to express what separate substances are and of what nature they are, perhaps it is still necessary that there should be some separate substances in addition to sensible ones, and of a different species than these. And he says "perhaps" because he has not yet proved that there are any separate substances apart from matter. However, he will prove this in later books (XII & XIII).

1647. Last of all he draws the conclusion at which he aims throughout the whole chapter. He says that two things are evident from what has been said: first, that no universal predicates are substances; and second, that no substance consists of substances having actual existence, or according to another text, "one substance is not composed of substances." For he has shown above (nn. 1584–5) that substance in the sense of this particular thing does not consist of common attributes which signify of what sort a thing is.

LESSON 17

The Role of Nature and Substance in the Sense of Essence as Principle and Cause

ARISTOTLE'S TEXT Chapter 17: 1041a6–1041b33

1. *But let us state both what and what kind of thing it is necessary to say substance is, as though we were making a fresh start; for perhaps from these things we shall come to an understanding of that kind of substance which is separate from sensible substances. Hence, since substance is a principle and cause, let us proceed from this starting point.* **1041a6–10**

2. *Now the why of a thing is always investigated in the following way: why does one thing belong to something else? For to ask why a musical man is a musical man, is either to ask (as has been said) why the man is musical, or to ask about something else. Therefore to ask why a thing is itself is to make no inquiry at all; for both the fact that a thing is such and its existence must be evident from the first; and I mean, for example, that the moon undergoes an eclipse. And in the case of all things there is one reason and one cause of the fact that a thing is itself, for example, why a man is a man, or why the musical is musical—unless one were to say that each thing is indivisible in relation to itself. But this is what being one really is. However, this is common to all things and is small.^1 But someone might ask, "Why is man such and such an animal?" This, then, is evident, that he is not asking why he who is a man is a man. Therefore one is asking why something is predicated of something else; for if this were not so, the inquiry would be about nothing, for example, "Why does it thunder?" The answer is, "because sound is produced in the clouds." For what is being investigated is one thing as predicated in this way of something else. And "Why are these things," for example, bricks and stones, "a house?" It is evident, then, that he is asking about the cause. And this—to speak logically—is the quiddity. Now in the case of some things this is that for the sake of which a thing exists [its end or goal], as, say, in the case of a house or a bed. But in the case of other things it is the thing which first moves them, for this also is a cause. Such a cause is sought in the process of generation and corruption, while the other is also sought in the case of being.* **1041a10–32**

3. *Now the object of our inquiry is most obscure in cases concerned with things not predicated of others, as when we ask what man is; because a single term is used and it is not said definitely that he is this or that.* **1041a32–1041b2**

4. *But in dealing with this question corrections must be; for if this is not done, it will turn out that asking something and asking nothing will have something in common. But since it is necessary to assume that the thing exists, it is clear that the question is why the matter is such and such, for example, why are these materials a house? Because these are the ones that constitute the being of a house. And why is this individual a man? or why is a thing having such and such a body a man? Hence what is being sought is the cause of the matter, and this is the specifying principle by reason of which something exists; and this is substance.* **1041b2–9**

5. *Hence it is evident that there is no inquiry or teaching as regards simple things, but that there is a different method of investigating such things.* **1041b9–11**

6. *Now since what is composed is composed of something in such a way that the whole is one, though not as a heap of things, but as a syllable is, a syllable is not the same as its letters, i.e., ba is not the same as the letters b and a; nor is flesh the same as fire; for when these are dissociated, they no longer exist, for example, flesh and the like; but the elements exist, and fire and earth exist. Hence a syllable is a determinate thing, and not merely the elements of speech, as the vowel and the consonant, but something else as well. And flesh is not merely fire and earth, or the hot and the cold, but something else as well.* **1041b11–19**

7. *Therefore, if something must either be an element or composed of elements, then if it is an*

element the same argument will again apply; for flesh will consist of this and fire and earth and something else besides, so that there will be an infinite regress. But if it is composed of elements, it is evident that it is not composed of one (otherwise it would be that very thing itself), but of many. Hence we use the same argument in this case as we did in that of a syllable or of flesh.

1041b19–25

8. Now it would seem that this something else exists, and that it is an element and the cause of being—i.e., that it is the cause of this being flesh and of this being a syllable; and it is similar in other cases. But this element is the substance of each thing and the first cause of being.

1041b25–28

9. And since certain things are not substances, although all those which are according to nature and are constituted such by nature are substances, it is evident that in some cases this substance is a nature which is not an element but a principle. Now an element is something into which a thing is divided and which is intrinsic as matter; for example, a and b are the elements of a syllable. **1041b28–33**

COMMENTARY

1648. At the beginning of this seventh book the Philosopher had promised that he would treat of the substance of sensible things in the sense of their essence, which he has explained from the viewpoint of logic by showing that those attributes which are predicated essentially pertain to the whatness of a thing, since it was not yet evident what it is that constitutes substance in the sense of essence. Now the Platonists said that this substance is the universals, which are separate Forms. But this doctrine Aristotle rejected immediately above. Hence it remained for him to show what substance in the sense of essence really is. And in order to do this he also sets down as a premise that substance in the sense of essence has the character of a principle and cause. This is the purpose of this chapter.

Hence it is divided into two parts. In the first [1] he explains what his aim is. In the second [2] he proceeds to carry out his aim ("Now the why").

He accordingly says, first [1], that, since it has been shown that no universal predicate is a substance, as the Platonists claimed, let us state what the real truth of the matter is about substance, viz., that which is essence, "and what kind of thing" this substance is, i.e., whether it is form or matter or something of this kind. He says "Let us state this," as if we were introducing or announcing a starting point different from the dialectical one with which we began in the beginning of this seventh book to investigate the above-mentioned substance; for perhaps from the things which are to be said about the quiddities of sensible substances it will also be possible to understand that kind of substance which is separate from sensible substances. For even though separate substances are not of the same species as sensible ones, as the Platonists claimed, still a knowledge of these sensible substances is the road by which we reach a knowledge of those separate substances. And he adds what that other starting point is from which one must enter upon the proposed investigation. He says that one must proceed from this starting point in order to show what the above-mentioned kind of substance is, so that we may understand that in substance itself there is a principle and cause.

1649. **Now the why** [2].

Here he shows that substance in the

sense of essence is a principle and cause; and in regard to this he does two things. First [2], he shows that it is a principle and cause. Second [6], he shows what kind of principle it is ("Now since what").

In regard to the first he does two things. First, he explains his aim. Second [3], he rejects an interpretation which could seem opposed to the argument he has given ("Now the object").

Now the point of his argument is as follows: whatever is such that one does not ask *why* it is, but is that to which the other things under investigation are reduced, must be a principle and cause; for the question why is a question about a cause. But substance in the sense of essence is a thing of this kind; for one does not ask why man is man, but why man is something else; and it is the same in other cases. Therefore the substance of a thing in the sense of its essence is a principle and cause.

1650. Hence he says, first [2], that "the why of a thing is always investigated in the following way," i.e., we use the question why when we ask why one thing belongs to something else, and not why a thing is itself. "For to ask why a musical man is a musical man is either to ask (as has been said) why the man is musical, or to ask about something else." This is equivalent to saying that, when we ask why a musical man is a musical man, this question can be interpreted in two ways: first, that the thing which has been stated and posited is under investigation, i.e., the thing being investigated, namely, the whole, musical man, is asked about the whole, musical man. Second, that one thing is asked about another; i.e., about a man who is musical what is asked is not why he is a man, but why he is musical.

1651. And he immediately rejects the first interpretation, saying that to ask why a thing is itself, for example, why man is man, is to make no inquiry at all; for every time we ask the question why, there must be something which is evident, and something which is not evident and has to be investigated. For there are four questions which may be asked, as is stated in Book II of the ***Posterior Analytics***,^1 namely, (1) "Is it?" (2) "What is it?" (3) "Is it a fact that it is such?" and (4) "Why is it such?" Now two of these questions, namely, "What is it?" and "Why is it such?" basically coincide, as is proved in that work.^2 And just as the question "What is it?" is related to the question "Is it?" so too the question "Why is it such?" is related to the question "Is it a fact that it is such?" Hence, when one asks the question why, these two points must be evident; for inasmuch as the question "Why is it such?" bears on the same point as the question "What is it?" the fact of the thing's existence must be evident. And inasmuch as the question "Why is it such?" is distinguished from the question "What is it?" the fact that it is such must be evident. Hence he says that, when one asks why, these two things must be evident, namely, the fact that it is such, and its existence, which pertains to the question "Is it?" for example, when we ask, "Why does the moon undergo an eclipse?" it must be evident that the moon does undergo an eclipse; for if this were not evident, it would be pointless to inquire why this is so. And by the same reasoning, when one asks "What is man?" it must be evident that man exists. But this could not happen if one were to ask why a thing is itself, for example, "Why is man man?" or "Why is the musical musical?" for in knowing that a man is a man it is known why he is a man.

1652. For in the case of all things there is one reason and one cause which cannot remain unknown, just as other common notions, which are called the common conceptions of the intellect, cannot remain unknown. And the reason is that each is one with itself. Hence each is predicated of itself.

1653. Now it might be that someone should want to give another cause, saying that the reason a man is a man, and the musical is musical, and so on in other cases, is that each is indivisible in relation to itself; and thus it cannot be denied of itself so that we should say that a man is not a man. Hence it must be affirmed of itself. But this argument does not differ from the first which we gave, namely, that each thing is one with itself. For "this is what being one really is"; i.e., we maintained above that unity signifies indivisibility. Therefore it is the same thing to say that each thing is one with itself and that it is indivisible in relation to itself.

1654. But even supposing that this argument differed from the preceding one, this too is still a characteristic common to all things, namely, that each thing is indivisible in relation to itself "and is something small,"^3 i.e., it has the nature of a principle, which is small in size and great in power. Hence one cannot inquire about it as about something unknown, any more than about other common principles. Another translation reads "And it is like a tone," as if to say that it is in harmony with the truth in all things. But another text has "And it is true," and we must understand by this "self-evident." Thus it is obvious that there can be no investigation as to why a thing is itself.

1655. It follows, then, that one always asks why this thing is something else. Hence he makes this clear next. He says that, if someone might ask "Why is man such and such an animal?" it is evident that he is not asking why man is man. Thus it is clear that he is asking why one thing is predicated of something else, and not why the same thing is predicated of itself. But when someone asks why something is predicated of something else, the fact that it exists must be evident; "for if this were not so," i.e., if it were not evident that it existed, "the inquiry would be about nothing"; for one is possibly inquiring about what is not. Or it may be taken in another way as referring to the point mentioned before; "for if this were not so," i.e., if one did not inquire about one thing as predicated of something else but as predicated of itself, the inquiry would be about nothing, as has been shown.

1656. Now in asking the why of something, sometimes we are asking about the cause taken as form in matter. Hence when we ask "Why does it thunder?" the answer is, "because sound is produced in the clouds"; for here it is clear that what is being asked is one thing of another, for sound is in the clouds, or thunder in the air.

1657. But sometimes we are asking about the cause of the form in the matter, either the efficient cause or final cause; for when we ask "Why are these materials (bricks and stones) a house?" the question concerns one thing as predicated of something else, namely, bricks and stones of a house. Hence the Philosopher did not say without qualification that the question is "What is a house?" but "Why are things of this kind a house?" It is evident, then, that this question asks about a cause.

1658. Now the cause which he has been investigating is the essence, logically speaking; for the logician considers the way in which terms are predicated and not the existence of a thing. Hence he says that whatever answer is given to the question "What is this thing?" pertains to the quiddity, whether it is intrinsic, as matter and form, or extrinsic, as the agent and final cause. But the philosopher, who inquires about the existence of things and their final and efficient cause, does not include them under the quiddity since they are extrinsic. If we say, then, that a house is something which protects us from cold and heat, the quiddity is signified from the viewpoint of logic, but not from that of the philosopher. Hence he says that the thing which is being investigated as the cause of the form in the matter is the quiddity, logically speaking. Yet according to the truth of the matter and from the point of view of natural philosophy, in the case of some things (for example, a house and a bed) this cause is "that for the sake of which a thing exists," i.e., its goal [or end].

1659. He draws examples from the sphere of artificial things because it is most evident that these exist for the sake of some goal; for even though natural things also exist for some goal, this was nevertheless denied by some thinkers. Therefore, when someone asks why stones and timbers are a house, one can answer by stating the final cause: to shelter ourselves from cold and heat. But in certain cases the thing under investigation, as the cause of the form in the matter, "is that which first moves a thing," i.e., the agent; for this also is a cause, for example, if we ask "Why are stones and timbers a house?" one can answer, "because of the art of building."

1660. Yet there is this difference between the efficient and the final cause: such a cause (the efficient) is investigated as the cause of the process of generation and corruption. But the other cause (the final) is investigated not merely as the cause of the process of generation and corruption but also of being. The reason for this is that the agent causes the form in the matter by changing the matter over to that form, as takes places in the process of generation and corruption. And inasmuch as the goal moves the agent through his intending it, it is also a cause of generation and corruption. And inasmuch as the thing is directed to its goal by means of its form, it is also a cause of being. Hence, when it is said that stones and timbers are a house as a result of the art of building, it is understood that the art of building is the cause of the production of the house. But when it is said that stones and timbers are a house in order to shelter us from cold and heat, it can be understood that the house has been built for this reason, and that it is useful for this reason.

1661. Now the Philosopher is speaking here of natural substances. Hence his statement here must be understood to apply only to a natural agent, which acts by means of motion. For the Divine agent, who communicates being without motion, is the cause not only of becoming but also of being.

1662. **Now the object** [3].

Since he had said above that when one asks why, one always inquires about something as predicated of something else, and this seems in a way to give rise to a problem, therefore in this place he raises the problem about this point and solves it.

Now in regard to this he does three things. First, he raises the problem. Second [4], he solves it ("But in dealing"). Third [5], he draws a corollary from his discussion ("Hence it is evident").

He accordingly says, first (684), that "the object of our inquiry," i.e., what is investigated in any inquiry pertaining to one thing as predicated of something else, "is most obscure," or puzzling, "in cases concerned with things not predicated of others," i.e., where the inquiry is about something not predicated of something else but is about a single thing; for when one inquires "What is man?" this, I say, is obscure "because a single term is used," but it is "not said definitely that he is this or that"; i.e., the cause of the difficulty is that in such cases one single thing is expressed, as man, and in that inquiry the things to which it belongs to be a man as parts, or also the particular supposit, are not expressed.

1663. But this difficulty does not seem to have anything to do with the point at issue; for the Philosopher spoke above about the question "Why is a thing such?" and not "What is it?" and this difficulty has to do with the question "What is it?" But it must be said that the questions "What is it?" and "Why is it?" bear on the same point, as has been stated (C 1651). Hence the question "What is it?" can be changed into the question "Why is it such?" for the question "What is it?" asks about the quiddity by reason of which that thing about which one asks this question, is predicated of any of its own subjects and is proper to its own parts; for Socrates is a man because the answer to the question "What is man?" is pertinent to him. And for this reason flesh and bones are man, because the whatness of man is contained in these flesh and bones. Therefore it is the same thing to ask "What is man?" and, "Why is this (Socrates) a man?" or "Why are these things (flesh and bones) a man?" And this is the same as the question which was raised above "Why are stones and timbers a house?" Therefore he also says here that this causes a difficulty, because in this investigation *this* and *that* are not added; for if they were added it would be evident that the answer to the question which asks about the quiddity of man and to the other questions of which he spoke above would be the same.

1664. **But in dealing** [5].

He now solves the foregoing problem. He says that in order to dispose of the problem relating to the foregoing question "corrections must be made," i.e., it is necessary to correct the question given, so that in place of the question "What is man?" we will substitute the question "Why is Socrates a man?" or "Why are flesh and bones a man?" And if this question is not corrected, the absurd consequence will be that asking something and asking nothing will have something in common. For it was said above that to ask something about a thing in terms of itself is not to make any inquiry at all; but to ask something about something else is to ask about something. Therefore, since the question *why* (in which we ask something about something else) and the question *what* (in which we do not seem to ask something about something else) have something in common, unless they are corrected in the way mentioned above, it follows that a question asking nothing and a question asking something have something in common.

1665. Or to state it in another way—if this question is not corrected, it follows that those cases in which no question at all is asked and those in which a question is asked have something in common. For when a question is asked about that which is, something is asked, but when a question is asked about that which is not, nothing is asked. Hence, if in asking what a thing is we need not assume anything and ask anything else of it, this question applies both to being and to non-being. Thus the question "What is it?" would apply in common both to something and to nothing.

1666. But since in the question "What is man?" it is necessary to know the truth of the fact that man exists (otherwise there would be no question), as when we ask why there is an eclipse, we must know that an eclipse exists, it is evident that one who asks what man is, asks why he is. For in order that one may ask what a thing is, the existence of the thing has to be presupposed, because it is assumed by the question why. Thus, when we ask "What is a house?" it would be the same as asking "Why are these materials (stones and timbers) a house?" because of these, i.e., "because the parts of a house constitute the being of a house," i.e., the quiddity of a house is present in the parts of a house.

1667. For it was said above that in such cases the question why sometimes asks about the form and sometimes about the agent and sometimes about the goal of a thing. And similarly when we ask what man is, it is the same as asking "Why is this (Socrates) a man?" because the quiddity of man belongs to him. Or it would also be the same as asking "Why is a body, which is disposed in this way (organically) a man?" For this is the matter of man, as stones and bricks are the matter of a house.

1668. Hence in such questions it is evident that we are asking about "the cause of the matter," i.e., why it is made to be of this nature. Now the thing under investigation which is the cause of the matter is "the specifying principle," namely, the form by which something is. And this "is the substance," i.e., the very substance in the sense of the quiddity. Thus it follows that his thesis has been proved, i.e., that substance is a principle and cause.

1669. **Hence it is** [5].

He then draws a corollary from his discussions. He says that, since in all questions one asks about something as predicated of something else, as the cause of the matter, which is the formal cause, or the cause of the form in matter, as the final cause and the agent, it is evident that there is no inquiry about simple substances, which are not composed of matter and form. For, as has been stated, in every inquiry there must be something which is known and some investigation about something which we do not know. Now such substances are either totally known or totally unknown, as is stated in Book IX. Hence there is no inquiry about them.

1670. And for this reason there also cannot be any teaching concerning them, as there is in the speculative sciences. For teaching produces science, and science arises in us by our knowing why a thing is; for the middle term of a demonstrative syllogism, which causes science, is why a thing is so.

1671. But lest the study of such substances should seem to be foreign to the philosophy of nature, he therefore adds that the method of investigating such things is different; for we come to an understanding of these substances only from sensible substances, of which these simple substances are, in a measure, the cause. Therefore we make use of sensible substances as known, and by means of them we investigate simple substances, just as the Philosopher investigates below (Book

XII) the immaterial substances, which cause motion, by means of motion. Hence in our teaching and investigations of them we use effects as the middle term in our investigations of simple substances whose quiddities we do not know. And it is also evident that simple substances are related to sensible ones in the process of teaching as the form and other causes are related to matter; for just as we inquire about the form of sensible substances and about their goal and their efficient causes as the causes of matter, in a similar fashion we inquire about simple substances as the causes of material substances.

1672. **Now since what** [6].

Here he shows what kind of cause and principle substance is when taken as the quiddity of a thing; and in regard to this he does three things. First, he premises a certain distinction necessary for the proof of his thesis. Second [7], he raises a difficulty ("Therefore, if something"). Third [8], he solves it ("Now it would seem").

In regard to the first [6] he distinguishes one kind of composition from several others; for sometimes composition involves many things in such a way that the whole is one thing composed of many, as a house is composed of its parts and a compound is composed of elements. But sometimes a composite results from many things in such a way that the whole composite is not one thing in an unqualified sense but only in a qualified one, as is clear of a heap or pile of stones when the parts are actual, not being continuous. Hence it is many in an unqualified sense, but is one only in a qualified sense, inasmuch as many things are grouped together in place.

1673. Now it is characteristic of the notion of this kind of diversity that the composite sometimes derives its species from some one thing, which is either the form (as in a compound) or combination (as in a house) or arrangement (as in a syllable or in a number). And then the whole composite must be one without qualification. But sometimes the composite derives its species from the very multitude of collected parts, as in a heap of things and a group of people and so forth; and in such cases the whole composite is not a unity in an unqualified sense but only with qualification.

1674. Hence the Philosopher says that, since one kind of composite is constituted of something in this way "as a whole"—i.e., the whole is one—and not in the way in which a heap of stones is one but as a syllable is one (without qualification), in all such cases the composite must not be identical with its components, as a syllable is not its letters; for this syllable *ba* is not the same as these two letters *b* and *a*, nor is flesh the same as fire and earth. He proves this as follows. "When these are dissociated," i.e., when the things of which the composite is made up are separated from each other, "this"—the whole—does not remain after its dissolution. For when the elements have been actually separated, flesh does not remain; and when its letters have been separated, the syllable does not remain. "But the elements," i.e., the letters, remain after the dissolution of the syllable, and fire and earth remain after the dissolution of flesh. Therefore the syllable is something over and above its elements, and it is not only its elements, which are vowels and consonants, but there is also something else by which a syllable is a syllable. And in a similar way flesh is not merely fire and earth, or the hot and the cold, by whose power the elements are mixed, but there is also something else by which flesh is flesh.

1675. **Therefore, if something** [7].

He raises a problem relating to his principal thesis; for it was shown that there is something else in flesh and in a syllable besides their elements; for it seems that everything which is, is either an element or composed of elements. If, then, it is necessary that this additional something which is present in flesh and in a syllable over and above their elements should be either an element or composed of elements, this absurdity results.

1676. For if this is an element, the same argument will apply again both to this and to other elements, because it will have to be numbered with the others. For flesh will be composed both of this thing, which we said was something over and above the elements, and which we now claim to be an element, and of fire and earth. And since it has already been proved that in every composite which is one there must be something in addition to its elements, the same question will then apply to this something else, because, if it is an element, flesh will again be composed both of the other original element, and of the elements, and then of something else. Hence in this way there will be an infinite regress; but this is absurd.

1677. Therefore, if this something else when found is not an element but is composed of elements, it is evident that it is not composed of one element only but of many; because if it were not composed of many but of only one, it would follow that that element would be the same as the whole; for what is composed of water only is truly water. Hence, if it is composed of many elements, the same argument will again apply to this thing as applies to flesh and a syllable, because it will contain something else besides the elements of which it is composed. And the same question will again apply to this. Thus once more there will be an infinite regress.

1678. **Now it would seem** [8].

Then he solves the problem which he raised; and in regard to this he does two things. First, he solves it with reference to the way in which it first appears. Second [9], he corrects this solution and gives the true one ("And since some").

He accordingly says, first [8], that the thing which is present in composites over and above their elements would seem at first glance not to be something composed of elements, but to be an element and cause of the being of flesh and a syllable and similarly of other things. Moreover, it would seem that it is the substance of each of them in the sense of their quiddity; for substance in the sense of quiddity is the first cause of being.

1679. **And since certain things** [9].

He now corrects the above solution in two ways: first, insofar as he had said that this something else which is present in composite things over and above their elements is the substance of each; for this is true of things which are substances, but not of things which are not substances, since the form of a syllable is not a substance; second, insofar as he had said that this very thing is an element and a cause of being; for it cannot be called an element but a principle, because elements pertain to the material cause of a thing.

1680. Therefore he says that, since some things are not substances, as is clear especially of artificial things, but just those are true substances that are "according to nature," with reference to being, "and are constituted such by nature," with reference to becoming, it will be made clear that this nature which we are investigating is substance "in some cases," i.e., in that of natural beings, and not in all. And it will also be made clear that this nature is not an element but a formal principle; for that is called an element into which something is divided and which is "intrinsic" as matter; for example, the elements of the syllable *ba* are *b* and *a*. Hence, since the principle in question is not a material principle but a formal one, it will not be an element. And thus it is evident at the same time both what kind of principle substance is, and that it is neither an element nor composed of elements. The foregoing problem is solved in this way.

BOOK VIII
THE PRINCIPLES OF SENSIBLE SUBSTANCES: MATTER AND FORM

LESSON 1
Sensible Substances Have Different Kinds of Matter

ARISTOTLE'S TEXT Chapter 1: 1042a3–1042b8

1. *It is necessary, then, to argue from the points which have been made, and after making a summary, to bring our investigations to a close.* **1042a3–4**

2. *It has been stated that it is the causes, principles and elements of substances which are being sought.* **1042a4–6**

3. *Now some substances are admitted by all; but there are others about which some thinkers have expressed views peculiar to themselves. Those which are admitted by all are physical substances, such as fire, earth, water and the other simple bodies; plants and their parts; animals and the parts of animals; and finally the heaven and its parts. But certain other thinkers make the peculiar claim that the Forms and the objects of mathematics are substances.* **1042a6–12**

4. *From other arguments it also follows that there are other substances, i.e., the essence and the underlying subject. Again, from another point of view a genus is substance to a greater degree than species, and a universal to a greater degree than singular things (568). And the Ideas have a connection with the universal and the genus, for they seem to be substances on the same grounds.* **1042a12–16**

5. *Further, since the essence is substance, and the definition is the intelligible expression of the essence, for this reason we have examined both the definition and everything that is predicated essentially. And since the definition of a thing is its intelligible expression, and the intelligible expression has parts, then concerning the notion of part it was also necessary to consider what things are parts of substance and what are not, and whether these are necessary to the definition. Further, neither the universal nor the genus is substance. Related questions concerning the Ideas and the objects of mathematics must be examined later on; for some say that these are substances in addition to sensible ones. But now we must treat those things which all admit to be substances, and these are sensible substances.* **1042a17–25**

6. *All sensible substances have matter. And the underlying subject is substance; in one sense the matter (by matter I mean that which is not a particular thing actually but potentially); and in another sense the intelligible structure or form, which is a particular thing and is separable in thought; and in a third sense the thing composed of these, which alone is subject to generation and corruption, and is separable in an absolute sense. For according to the intelligible structure of substances, some are separable and others are not.* **1042a25–31**

7. *Now it is evident that matter is substance; for in every process of change between contraries there is something which underlies these changes. For example, in change of place, there is something which is now here and afterwards somewhere else; and in change of size, that which is now of such a size and afterwards smaller or greater; and in change of quality, that which is now healthy and afterwards diseased. And similarly in change of substance there is something which is now in the process of generation and afterwards in the process of corruption, and which is now a subject and this particular thing and afterwards a subject of privation.* **1042a32–1042b3**

8. *And the other changes follow upon this change, but this change does not follow upon one or two of the others. For if a thing has matter which is subject to change of place, it is not necessary*

that it also have matter which is generable and corruptible. The difference between coming-to-be in an absolute sense and coming-to-be in a qualified sense has been explained in the Physics.
1042b3–8

COMMENTARY

1681. Having dealt with substance by means of the dialectical method in Book VII, i.e., by examining the definition and its parts and other things of this kind which are considered from the viewpoint of dialectics, the Philosopher now intends in Book VIII to deal with sensible substances through their proper principles, by applying to those substances the things that were investigated above by means of the dialectical method.

This is divided into two parts. In the first [1], he links up this discussion with the preceding one; and in the second [6], he carries out his intention ("All sensible substances").

In regard to the first he does three things. First, he states in a general way what he intends to do. Second [2], he repeats some of the statements which have been made ("It has been stated"). Third [5], he links up the foregoing discussion with the one that is to come ("Further, since the essence").

He says first [1], then, that since many of the statements made about substance in Book VII belong to the consideration of dialectics, we must reason from the statements which have been made in order that the things stated from the viewpoint of dialectics may be applied to things existing in reality. And "after making a summary," i.e., after bringing these together again in a brief and summary way, we must bring our investigation to a close by completing the treatise on substance. He does this by discussing those things which were omitted from the foregoing treatise.

1682. **It has been stated** [2].

Here he repeats some of the statements which have been made, because it was stated in Book VII (n. 1260) that the principal objects of our search in this science are the causes, principles and elements of substances. For since this science investigates as its proper subject being in general, and this is divided into substance and the nine classes of accidents, and a knowledge of accidents depends upon substance, as was shown in Book VII (nn. 1342–50), it follows that this science is principally concerned with substances. And since we know each thing only when we know its principles and causes, it also follows that this science must be principally concerned with the principles, causes and elements of substances. The way in which these three differ has been shown above in Book V (nn. 751–807).

1683. **Now some substances** [3].

Then he repeats one of the points discussed above, i.e., the various senses in which substance is used. First, he gives the things which are said to be real substances. Among these there are some whose existence is admitted by all thinkers, namely, sensible substances, such as earth, water and the other elements; and above these, in the order of their nobility and perfection, plants and animals and their parts; and lastly the heaven and its parts, as the orbs and the stars, which surpass in nobility the other sensible substances. However, there are some substances whose existence is not admitted by all but only by certain particular thinkers, who claim that the Forms and the objects of mathematics have separate existence. They adopted this position because they thought that for every abstraction of the intellect there is a corresponding abstraction in reality. Thus, because the intellect considers the universal apart from particular things, as "man" apart from Socrates and Plato, they held that the Forms have separate existence of themselves. And since the intellect considers some forms apart from sensible material things, as curvature (whose concept does not contain nose as does the concept of pugnose) and a line and other things of this kind, which we call the objects of mathematics, they also held that the objects of mathematics have separate existence.

1684. **From other arguments** [4].

Here he gives the different ways in which substance is considered from the viewpoint of its intelligible structure; and there are two of these. The first is that substance means the quiddity of any natural substance, and this is merely the whatness of a natural being. In the second way substance is considered in a different sense, that is, in the sense that a genus is said to be substance to a greater degree than species, and a universal to a greater degree than singular things, as some men held according to what was treated in the questions in Book III (nn. 423–442). And with this way of considering substance, according to which both a genus and a universal are called substances, is connected the theory of Ideas, or Forms as Aristotle called them above (n. 1683); for this theory maintains that both Ideas and universals are substances on the same grounds.

1685. **Further, since the essence** [5].

He links up this discussion with the preceding one by stating what has been solved and what remains to be solved. He says that, since the essence is substance, and the intelligible expression which signifies it is the definition, for this reason it was necessary in the preceding book to deal with definition. And since a definition is composed of those attributes which are predicated of a thing essentially, for this reason it was also necessary in that book to settle the issue about essential predication (nn. 1299–1380). Further, since the definition of a thing is its intelligible expression, and this is made up of parts, then concerning the parts of a definition it was also necessary to determine what parts are parts of the thing defined and what are not; and whether the parts of the definition and those of the thing defined are the same (nn. 1482–1565). Another text has "Whether the parts of the definition must be defined," but the first version is better. In Book VII (nn. 1566–1647) it was shown also that neither the universal nor the genus is substance. Thus the entire study which may be made of definitions and substance was carried out in Book VII. But of those substances which exist in reality, it will be necessary to examine later the Ideas and the objects of mathematics, which one school of thinkers claim to subsist by themselves apart from sensible substances. This is done in the last books of this work. But now it is necessary to treat at once of those substances which all men admit to exist, namely, sensible substances, so that we may proceed from what has been made evident to what as yet remains unknown.

1686. **All sensible substances** [6].

Having linked up the foregoing discussion with the one that is to come, the Philosopher begins here to treat of sensible substances by investigating their principles. This is divided into two parts. In the first [6] he establishes what is true concerning matter and form, which are the principles of sensible substances. In the second (Lesson 5) he considers the way in which they are united to each other ("It seems that we must").

In regard to the first he does two things. First, he shows that matter and form are principles of sensible substances. Second (Lesson 3), he deals with those points which must be investigated about each of these principles ("And we must not").

In regard to the first he does two things. First, he shows that matter is a principle of sensible substances; and second (Lesson 2), that the same is true of form ("But since that which has the character of a subject").

In regard to the first he does three things. First [6], he shows what matter is by distinguishing it from the other ways in which substance is considered. Hence he says that all sensible substances have matter; and the reason is that all are in motion, and motion does not exist without matter.

1687. But it must be noted that in one sense substance means matter, and in another form, and in still another the thing composed of these. For matter is called substance, not as though it were a being considered to have actual existence in itself, but as something capable of being actual (and this is said to be a particular thing). And form, which is also termed the intelligible structure because the intelligible structure of the species is derived from it, is called substance inasmuch as it is something actual, and inasmuch as it is separable from matter in thought but not in reality. And the thing composed of these is called substance inasmuch as it is something "separable in an absolute sense," i.e., capable of existing separately by itself in reality; and it alone is subject to generation and corruption. For form and matter are generated and corrupted only by reason of something else. And although the composite is separable in an absolute sense, yet some of the other things which are called substances are separable in thought and some are not. For a form is separable in thought because it can be understood without understanding individuating sensible matter; but matter cannot be understood without understanding form, since it is apprehended only inasmuch as it is in potentiality to form. Or the statement can mean that "according to the intelligible structure of substances," i.e., of forms, some are separable in their intelligible structure, as the objects of mathematics, and some are not, as natural forms. Or again it may mean that there are certain separate forms existing without matter, about which he will establish the truth later on (nn. 2447–2454).

1688. **Now it is evident** [7].

Second, he says that in sensible substances we must posit matter as substance and subject. For in every change between contraries, there must be a subject common to the termini of the change. For example, in change of place there is a common subject which is now here and afterwards somewhere else; and in growth there is a common subject which now has so much quantity and afterwards is smaller (if the change is decrease) or greater (if it is increase). And in alteration there is a common subject which is now healthy and afterwards diseased. Hence, since there is substantial change, that is, generation and corruption, there must be a common subject which underlies the opposite changes of generation and corruption. And this is the subject for the termini that have been given, i.e., form and privation, so that sometimes this subject is actual by reason of a form, and sometimes it is the subject of the privation of that form.

1689. Now from this argument of Aristotle it is clear that substantial generation and corruption are the source from which we derive our knowledge of prime matter. For if prime matter by nature had a form of its own, it would be an actual thing by reason of that form. Hence, when an additional form would be given [to prime matter], such matter would not exist in an absolute sense by reason of that form but would become this or that being; and then there would be generation in a qualified sense but not in an absolute sense. Hence all those who held that this first subject is a body, such as air or water, claimed that generation is the same as alteration. But it is clear from this argument what we must hold prime matter to be; for it is related to all forms and privations as the subject of qualitative change is to contrary qualities.

1690. **And the other changes** [8].

Here he shows that matter is not present in the same way in all sensible substances. He says that the other changes follow upon matter which is subject to generation and corruption; for if matter is subject to generation and corruption, it follows that it is subject to alteration and change of place. But this matter, i.e., one which is subject to generation and corruption, does not follow upon all the other changes, especially change of place. For if something has "matter which is subject to change of place," i.e., by which it is potentially in a place, it does not follow that it also has "matter which is generable and corruptible," namely, one which is subject to generation and corruption. For this kind of matter is lacking in the celestial bodies, in which there is a kind of alteration inasmuch as they are illuminated and deprived of light, but neither generation nor corruption. Hence he said "one" because of change of place, or "two" because of the kind of alteration just mentioned, although this is really not alteration, because illumination is not motion but the terminus of motion. Thus we must posit matter for every change according as there is in everything that changes a coming-to-be either in an absolute sense or in a qualified one. The difference between coming-to-be in an absolute sense and in a qualified one has been explained in the ***Physics***, Book [190a32]; for coming-to-be in an absolute sense belongs to substance, and coming-to-be in a qualified sense belongs to accidents.

LESSON 2
Form Inferred from Accidental Differences in Sensible Substances. Threefold Definition of All Things

ARISTOTLE'S TEXT Chapter 2: 1042b9–1043a28

1. But since that which has the character of a subject or matter has been admitted by all to be substance, and this is what is in potentiality, it remains to explain what it is that constitutes the substance of sensible things in the sense of actuality. **1042b9–11**

2. Now Democritus is like one who thinks that there are three differences in things. For he holds that the underlying body, as matter, is the same for all things, but that it differs in contour, which is shape; or in disposition, which is position; or in distribution, which is arrangement. **1042b11–15**

3. However, there seem to be many differences inasmuch as some things are said to be by reason of the way in which their material parts are combined; for example, some things are combined by mixture, as honey-water; others by a binding, as the binding around a head; others by birdlime, as a book; others by a nail, as a chest; and others in several of these ways. Others differ by position, as a threshold and a lintel, for these differ in a sense according to their position; others differ in point of time, as dinner and breakfast; others with respect to place, as the air currents; others by reason of sensible properties, as hardness and softness, density and rarity, dryness and moistness. And some things differ by some of these differences and others by all taken together; some by excess and others by defect. **1042b15–25**

4. For this reason it is evident that being is also used in the same number of ways; for a threshold is such because it is placed in this particular position, and to be a threshold means to be placed in such and such a position; and to be ice means to be congealed in such and such a way. However, the being of some things will be defined in all of these ways: one by being mixed; others by being combined; others by being tied together; others by being condensed; and others by other differences, as a hand and a foot. **1042b25–31**

5. Further, we must consider the classes of differences, for these will be the principles of being of things, as differences in degree, or in density and rarity, and others such as these; for all are instances of excess and defect. Indeed, if [anything differs] either in figure or in smoothness and roughness [these are reducible to differences] in straightness and curvature. Further, the being of some things will consist in being mixed, and their non-being will consist in the opposite state. **1042b31–1043a1**

6. It is evident, then, from these instances that, if substance is the cause of the being of each thing which is composed of these differences, we must look for the cause of the being of each one of these among these differences. Now substances is none of these differences nor any combination of them; yet it is found analogously in each. And just as in the case of substance that which is predicated of matter is the actuality itself, in a similar way this is most true in the case of other definitions. Thus if a threshold has to be defined, we shall say that it is a piece of wood or stone placed in such and such a position; and we shall say that a house is bricks and timbers placed in such and such a position. (Or again in some cases there is also the final cause). And if ice is to be defined, we shall say that it is water frozen or condensed in such and such a way; and we shall say that a harmony is such and such a combination of high and low notes. [And we must proceed] in the same way too in other things. **1043a2–12**

7. From these instances, then, it is evident that different matters have a different actuality and intelligible structure; for of some things it is combination, of others mixing, and of others some of those differences mentioned above. **1043a12–14**

8. Therefore, among those who give definitions, those who state what a house is by saying that it is stones, bricks and timbers, are speaking of a potential house; for these are its matter. But those who say that it is a shelter for protecting goods and bodies, or by adding some other such property, speak of its actuality. And those who speak of both of these together speak of the third kind of substance, which is the thing composed of these. For the intelligible structure which is expressed by means of differences seems to be that of the form or actuality of a thing, but that which is expressed by a thing's intrinsic parts is rather that of its matter. The same thing is true of the definitions of which Archytas approved, for they are both of these together. For example, What is stillness? Rest in a large expanse of air, where air is as matter and rest as actuality or substance. What is a calm? Smoothness of the sea, where the sea is as subject or matter, and smoothness as actuality or form. **1043a14–26**

9. From what has been said, then, it is evident what sensible substance is and how it exists; for in one sense it has the character of matter, and in another the character of form (because it is actuality), and in a third sense it is the thing composed of these. **1043a26–28**

COMMENTARY

1691. Having investigated the material principle in sensible substances, the Philosopher examines their formal principle.

First [1], he links up this discussion with the foregoing one, saying that, since all recognize substance in the sense of matter and subject (for even the oldest philosophers held that matter is the substance of material things), and this kind of substance is something potential, it now remains to explain what form is, which is the actuality of sensible things.

1692. **Now Democritus is like one** [2].

Then he carries out his intention; and in regard to this he does two things. First [2], he examines the differences in sensible things which indicate a formal principle. Second [7], he draws some conclusions ("From these instances").

In regard to the first he does two things. First, he examines certain accidental differences of sensible things. Second [6], he shows how these differences are related to substantial differences ("It is evident").

In regard to the first he does two things. First, he investigates the accidental differences of sensible things. Second [4], he shows how these differences are related to those things whose differences they are ("For this reason").

In regard to the first he does two things. First [2], he gives Democritus' opinion about the differences of things. He says that Democritus is like one who thinks "that there are three differences in things," i.e., according to the principles which he gives he seems to think that all differences of things are reduced to three classes. For he held that the material principles of things are indivisible bodies, which, being of the same nature, are similar to each other; but that they constitute a diversity of things because they differ in position, shape and arrangement. Thus he seems to hold that the underlying body, as a material principle, is one and the same in nature even though it is divided into an infinite number of parts, and that it differs, i.e., is divided into different things, because of differences in shape, position and arrangement. For things differ in figure by being straight or curved; in position by being above or below, right or left; and in arrangement by being before or after.

1693. **However, there seem to be** [3].

Second, he shows that the position of Democritus is unsatisfactory, because there seem to be many other differences of things which are not reducible to the foregoing ones. For some things differ by reason of the different way in which their material parts are combined: in some things the material parts are combined by being mixed, as honey-water; in others, by being tied together by some bond, as the binding around a woman's head; in others by glue or birdlime, as occurs in books; in others by a nail, as occurs in a chest; and in others the parts are united in several of the aforesaid ways. On the other hand, some things differ from each other by their position, as a lintel and a threshold, which differ because they are placed in such and such a way—one being above and the other below. Again, some differ in point of time, as dinner, which is the late meal, from breakfast, which is the early morning meal. Others differ with respect to place, as "the air currents," i.e., the winds, of which the Aquilonian comes from the north, the Favonian from the west, the Austerian from the south, and the Subsolian from the east. Others differ "by reason of the qualities of sensible bodies," i.e., by hardness or softness and other characteristics of this kind; and some things differ in several of these ways, and others in all of them. And some differ by excess and some by defect. He adds this because the ancient philosophers held that all qualities of sensible bodies are reduced to excess or defect.

1694. **For this reason** [4].

He shows the way in which these differences are related to those things whose differences they are. In regard to this he does two things. First [4], he shows that these differences constitute the being of the things whose differences they are. Second [5], he concludes that in order to grasp the principles of being we must reduce these differences to certain primary classes of differences ("Further, we must consider").

First, then, he says that, because these differences are constitutive of the things we have mentioned above, it is evident that the being of the aforesaid realities is diversified according to these differences; for a difference completes the definition, which signifies the being of a thing. Thus a threshold is this particular thing "because it is placed in such and such a position," and its being, i.e., its proper intelligible structure, consists in being placed in such and such a position. Similarly, being ice is being condensed in such and such a way. And by each of the differences mentioned the being of things of a certain type is differentiated: some by being mixed; others by being combined; and others by other differences, as a hand and a foot and other parts of this kind which have peculiar differences of their own inasmuch as they are directed to certain definite operations.

1695. **Further, we must consider** [5].

He concludes that, since the being of things consists in their differences and has to be known in this way, it will be worth our while to grasp the classes of differences by reducing the secondary differences of a class to the primary differences; because common and proper differences of this kind will be the principles of being of a whole class. This is evident in differences of degree, of rarity and density, and in other things of this kind; for density and rarity and the like are reduced to the class of the great and small, because all these signify excess and defect. Similarly, if things differ in figure or in roughness or smoothness, these are reduced to differences of straightness and curvature, which are the primary differences of figure. Again, it is necessary that some be reduced to being mixed or not being mixed; for the being of some things consists in the fact that they are mixed, and their non-being in just the opposite state.

1696. **It is evident, then** [6].

He shows how these differences are related to the substances of things. He says that it is now evident from the foregoing that we must try to discover in these differences the formal cause of the being of each thing, if it is in this way that substance in a formal sense, or the whatness of a thing, is the cause of the being of each thing, as was clear in Book VII (nn. 1648–80). For these differences signify the form or whatness of the above-mentioned things. However, none of these differences are substance or anything akin to substance, as though belonging to the genus of substance; but the same proportion is found in them as in [the genus of] substance.

1697. For just as in the genus of substance the difference, which is predicated of the genus and qualifies it in order to constitute a species, is related to the genus as actuality or form, so also is this true in other definitions. For we must not understand that difference is form or that genus is matter, since genus and difference are predicated of the species but matter and form are not predicated of the composite. But we speak in this manner because a thing's genus is derived from its material principle, and its difference from its formal principle. The genus of man, for example, is animal, because it signifies something having a sensory nature, which is related as matter to intellectual nature from which rational, the difference of man, is taken. But rational signifies something having an intellectual nature. It is for this reason that a genus contains its differences potentially, and that genus and difference are proportionate to matter and form, as Porphyry says. And for this reason too it is said here that "actuality," i.e., difference, is predicated "of matter," i.e., of the genus; and the same thing occurs in other genera.

1698. For if one wishes to define a threshold, he shall say that it is a piece of stone or wood placed in such and such a position; and in this definition stone or wood is as matter and position as form. Similarly, in the definition of a house stones and timbers are as matter, and being combined in such and such a way as form. And again in the definitions of some things there is also added its end, on which the necessity of the form depends. And similarly in the definition of ice, water is as matter and being frozen is as form. So too in the definition of a harmony the high and low notes are as matter and the way in which they are combined is as form. The same thing applies in all other definitions.

1699. **From these instances** [7].

He draws two additional conclusions from the above. First, there are different actualities or forms for different matters. For in some things the actuality consists in being combined; in others in being mixed, or in some of the aforesaid differences.

1700. **Therefore, among those who** [8].

He states the second conclusion; since in a definition one part is related to the other as actuality to matter, some people in defining things give an inadequate definition by stating only their matter, as those who define a house by means of cement, stones and timbers, which are the material of a house; because such a definition does not signify an actual house but a potential one. Those who say that a house is a shelter for goods and living bodies state the form of a house but not its matter. However, those who state both define the composite substance, and therefore their definition is a complete definition. But the conceptual element which is derived from the differences pertains to the form, whereas that which is derived from the intrinsic parts pertains to the matter.

1701. The definitions which Archytas accepts are similar to these. E.g., stillness, which signifies the state of the atmosphere when it is windless, is rest in a large expanse of air; for if only the smallest amount of air in a vessel is at rest we do not speak of stillness. In this definition air is as matter and rest as form. Similarly, when a calm is defined as the smoothness of the sea, the sea is as matter and smoothness as form. Now in these definitions the matter is substance and the form is an accident; but in the definition of a house the matter is its parts and the actuality is the form of the whole.

1702. **From what** [9].

He summarizes the things said about form. The text is clear here.

LESSON 3

The Nature of Form as Part of a Thing's Essence. The Resemblance between Numbers and Forms

ARISTOTLE'S TEXT Chapter 3: 1043a29–1044a14

1. *And we must not disregard the fact that sometimes it is not apparent whether a name signifies the composite substance or the actuality or form; for example, whether house signifies both the form and the matter together, i.e., a shelter composed of bricks, timbers and stones arranged in such and such a way, or whether it signifies the actuality or form—a shelter; and whether line signifies twoness in length or twoness; and whether animal signifies a soul in a body or a soul, for the latter is the substance or actuality of some body.* **1043a29–36**

2. *Now animal will also apply to both, not in the sense that both are expressed by one meaning, but insofar as they are related to some one thing.* **1043a36–37**

3. *These distinctions make a difference with regard to something else, but not to the investigation of sensible substances, because the essence of this other thing consists of form or actuality. For a soul and the essence of a soul are the same, but a man and the essence of a man are not the same, unless a man is also called a soul. And in some things essence and thing are identical and in others not.* **1043a37–1043b4**

4. *Accordingly, to those who make investigations it does not seem that a syllable consists of letters and their combination, nor does a house consist of bricks and their combination. And this is true, because a combination or mixture does not consist of the things of which it is the combination or mixture. Nor likewise do any of the other differences. If a threshold, for example, is constituted by its position, the position is not constituted by the threshold, but rather the latter by the former. Nor is man animal and two-footed, but there must be something else in addition to these, if these are matter. Now this is neither an element nor a combination of the elements, but the substance; but omitting this they speak only of matter. Therefore, if this is the cause of a thing's being, and this is its substance, they will not be stating its substance.* **1043b4–14**

5. *Now this must be either eternal or corruptible without being in the process of corruption, and generated without being in the process of generation. But it has been demonstrated and made clear elsewhere that no one produces a form, nor is it generated; but it is this particular thing which is produced and comes to be from these principles.* **1043b14–18**

6. *But whether the substances of corruptible things are separable or not is not yet clear.* **1043b18–19**

7. *It is evident, however, that this may not occur in the case of some things, i.e., in the case of all those that are incapable of existing apart from particular things, for example, a house or a vessel.* **1043b19–21**

8. *Indeed, perhaps neither these particular things nor any of the others which are not produced by nature are substances. For at least one might hold that only the nature of corruptible things is substance.* **1043b21–23**

9. *For this reason the problem which confronted Antisthenes and other uninstructed people is applicable here, i.e., that one cannot define what a thing is (for according to them the definition is a lengthy statement), but one can say what it is like; for example, one cannot say what silver is, but one can say that it is like tin. Hence, of one kind of substance there can be a limit or definition, i.e., of the composite, whether it be sensible or intelligible. But this cannot be true of the primary parts of which it is composed, since the definitive concept designates something as determining something else, and one of these must have the character of matter and the other that of form.* **1043b23–32**

10. Further, it is also clear that if numbers are in any sense substances, they are such in this way and not [as groups] of units, as some claim. For a definition is like a number and is divisible into indivisible parts, because definitions are not made up of an unlimited number of parts; and this is also true of numbers. **1043b32–36**

11. And just as when any part constituting a number is subtracted or added it is no longer the same number that remains but a different one, even though the minimum is subtracted or added, so too neither the definition nor the essence will any longer be the same when anything is subtracted or added. **1043b36–1044a2**

12. And there must be something by reason of which a number is one thing, although they cannot say what makes it to be one thing; i.e., if it is one thing. For either it is not one thing but like a heap, or if it is one thing it is necessary to state what makes it to be one thing out of many. And a definition is one thing; but they are also unable to say what makes it to be one thing; and this follows as a natural consequence. For by the same argument substance is also one thing in the way we have explained, but not, as some claim, as being a kind of unit or point, but as an actuality and a kind of nature. **1044a2–9**

13. And just as number does not admit of more or less, neither does substance in the sense of form; but if this were the case [it would be that substance which is joined] to matter. **1044a9–11**

14. In regard to the generation and corruption of the foregoing substances, in what way this is possible and in what way it is impossible, and in regard to the likeness which they have to numbers, we have established these things this far. **1044a11–14**

COMMENTARY

1703. Having investigated the principles of sensible substances, and having shown that sensible substances are composed of matter and form, the Philosopher's aim here is to establish the truth about the formal and material principles of things by investigating the points which must be considered about each.

This is divided into two parts. In the first [1], he investigates the things which must be considered about the formal principle. In the second (Lesson 4), he investigates the things which must be considered about the material principle ("Concerning material substances").

1704. And since Plato was the one who devoted special treatment to the formal principle, therefore Aristotle deals with the formal principle in reference to those things which Plato posited. Now Plato claimed that species [i.e., separate Forms or Ideas] and numbers are the forms of things. Hence the first part is divided into two sections. In the first [1], he deals with the formal principle in relation to the species [or Ideas]; and in the second [10], in relation to numbers ("Further, it is also clear").

Now Plato held four things about forms in relation to the species [or Ideas]. The first of these is that specific names signify form alone and not form with matter. The second is that form is something besides the material parts. The third is that form can neither be generated nor corrupted. The fourth is that forms are separate from sensible things.

The first part is divided into four sections inasmuch as Aristotle investigates the four points just mentioned. The second [4] begins where he says "Accordingly, to those." The third [5] begins where he says "Now this must." The fourth [6] begins where he says "But whether."

1705. In regard to the first he does

three things. First [1] he raises a question. We must understand, he says, that for some men there is the problem whether a specific name signifies the composite substance or only the form or something having the status of actuality; for example, whether the word house signifies both matter and form together so that a house means a shelter made of bricks and stones properly arranged (for shelter is as form, and bricks and stones as matter), or whether this word signifies only the actuality or form, a shelter.

1706. Similarly, there is the problem whether the word line signifies twoness and length or twoness alone. He mentions this because the Platonists claimed that numbers are the forms of continuous quantities; for they said that a point is merely the number one having position, so that position is a sort of material principle, and the number one a formal principle. They likewise claimed that the number two is the form of a line, so that a line is merely twoness in length. Therefore the Philosopher asks whether the word line signifies twoness alone as form, or twoness grounded in length as form in matter. And again, there is the problem whether the word animal signifies a soul in a body as a form in matter, or only a soul, which is the form of an organic body.

1707. **Now animal will also apply** [2].

He shows what follows if one says that specific names are used in both senses, so that they sometimes signify form alone and sometimes form in matter. And the result is that animal will be taken of either in either meaning, not univocally, as though it were predicated with one meaning, but analogically, as happens in the case of those things which have one name because they are related to one thing. For the specific name will be predicated of the composite only by reason of relationship to that which is predicated according to form alone, as the Platonists held. For they maintained that man, who is a composite of matter and form, is so named because he participates in the Idea man, which is only a form.

1708. **These distinctions** [3].

Then the Philosopher shows the result to which the aforesaid search leads. He says that, while the question whether a specific name signifies the composite substance or only the form, makes a difference in regard to something else, it makes no difference to the investigation of sensible substance. For it is evident that a sensible substance is composed of matter and form.

1709. Now to what kind of thing it makes a difference, whether to those in this state or in another, he makes clear next. For it is obvious that if there is something which is only form or actuality, its essence "consists of this," i.e., the thing and its essence will be identical, as a soul is identical with its essence, or is its own quiddity. But if a thing is composed of matter and form, then in this case the thing itself and its essence will not be the same; for example, a man and the essence of a man are not the same, unless perhaps a man is said to be only a soul, as was held by those who say that specific names signify only the form. Thus it is evident that something does exist whose essence is the same as itself, namely, whatever is not composed of matter and form but is only a form.

1710. The reason for this position is that essence is what the definition signifies, and the definition signifies the nature of the species. But if there is something which is composed of matter and form, then in that thing there must be some other principle besides the nature of the species. For since matter is the principle of individuation, then in anything composed of matter and form there must be certain individuating principles distinct from the nature of the species. Hence such a thing is not just its own essence but is something in addition to this. But if such a thing exists which is only a form, it will have no individuating principles in addition to the nature of its species. For a form that exists of itself is individuated of itself. Therefore this thing is nothing else than its own essence.

1711. It is clear, then, that if the specific name signifies only the form, the essence of anything will be the same as its being, as a man will be his essence, and a horse its essence, and so also will all other things of this kind. But if specific names signify things composed of matter and form, then such things will not be the same as their essence.

1712. **Accordingly, to those who** [4].

Here he deals with the second point mentioned above, namely, that the form is something in addition to the material parts. He says that for the Platonists, in raising this question, it does not seem that a syllable consists of its elements and their combination, as if combination, which is the form of a syllable, were a material part of a syllable like its elements or letters. Nor does it seem to them that a house consists of stones and their combination, as if a house were constituted of these as material parts.

1713. And on this point their remarks are true, because, if the form were one of the material parts, it would depend on matter. But we see that this is false; for combination or mixture, which are formal principles, are not constituted of those things which are combined or mixed; nor is any other formal principle constituted of its matter, but the reverse. For a threshold is constituted by position, which is its form, and not the reverse.

1714. Therefore, if one holds that animal and two-footed are the matter of man, man will not be animal and two-footed but will be something else in addition to these. And this will not be an element or anything composed of the elements but will be only a form as the Platonists claim, who omit matter from definitions. But it seems that we must hold, in opposition to this position, that, if form alone apart from matter is the substance or principle of being of a thing, they will not be able to say that this particular thing is that separate substance; i.e., they will not be able to say that this man as a sensible entity is composed of matter and form, but that man is only a form.

1715. **Now this must** [5].

He considers the third point mentioned above, namely, the Platonists' position that forms are eternal and incorruptible. Hence he concludes, from what has been said, that either a form must be eternal, as the Platonists held when they claimed that the Ideas, which they called the forms of things, are eternal; or a form must be corruptible by reason of something else without being corrupted in itself, and similarly it must come to be by reason of something else without coming to be in itself. This is in agreement with the position of Aristotle, who does not hold that forms are separate but that they exist in matter.

1716. Further, the statement that forms can neither be corrupted nor generated in themselves (nn. 1708–15), on which each of the aforesaid points depends, Aristotle proceeds to demonstrate by reason of what was shown above, namely, that no one makes or produces a form, nor is a form generated or produced in itself; but it is this particular thing which comes to be or is generated in itself. And the reason is that everything which comes to be comes to be from matter. Hence, since this particular thing is composed of matter and form, it comes to be or is generated "from these principles," i.e., from its material and individuating principles. But it was stated above (n. 1714) that a form is not an element or anything composed of the elements. Therefore it follows that a form neither comes to be nor is generated in itself.

1717. **But whether the substances** [6].

He examines the fourth point given above, namely, Plato's position that forms are separate from matter. In regard to this he does three things. First, he exposes what the problem is in this position, saying that it is not clear whether "the substances," i.e., the forms, of corruptible things are separable as the Platonists claimed.

1718. **It is evident, however** [7].

Second, he indicates what seems to be evident on this point. He says that it is evident that the forms of some corruptible things are not separate, namely, "all those" which are incapable of existing apart from their matters, as house or vessel, because neither the form of a house nor that of a vessel can exist apart from its proper matter.

1719. **Indeed, perhaps** [8].

Third, he precludes an objection, saying that perhaps the forms of artifacts are not substances or anything in their own right, and so cannot have separate existence. Nor similarly can other artificial forms, which have no natural existence, because in artifacts the matter alone is held to be substance, whereas the forms of artifacts are accidents. Natural forms, however, belong to the class of substance; and this is why Plato did not hold that the forms of artifacts exist apart from matter but only substantial forms.

1720. **For this reason** [9].

He advances arguments that are clearly opposed to Plato's position. He says that if one holds that there are separate forms, as the Platonists maintained, the problem which the followers of Antisthenes raised, even though they seem to be uninstructed, may be used against the Platonists. For they argued that it is impossible to define a thing by means of a definition which signifies its quiddity, since a thing's quiddity is simple and is not fittingly expressed by a statement composed of many parts. For we see that "the limit," or definition, which is given to a thing, is a lengthy statement made up of many words. Therefore it does not signify what a thing is but "what it is like," i.e., something to which it is similar; as if one were to say that the definition of silver does not signify silver but signifies something like lead or tin.

1721. Hence in order to solve this problem we must say that the substance which is defined, whether it be intellectual or sensible, must be one that is composite. But since the primary parts of which a definition is composed are simple, they are incapable of definition. For it was stated above (706:C 1700) that the definitive statement joins one part to another, one of which is as form and the other as matter, because genus is derived from matter and difference from form, as was pointed out above (704:C 1696–8). Hence, if the species of things were forms only, as the Platonists held, they would be indefinable.

1722. **Further, it is also clear** [10].

Having determined what is true of forms in relation to the Ideas introduced by Plato, Aristotle now determines what is true of forms in relation to numbers. For Plato held that numbers are the forms and substances of things by establishing a kind of likeness between forms and numbers. This is divided into four parts inasmuch as there are four ways in which he likens forms to numbers.

First, he says that, if numbers are in any sense the substances or forms of things, it is evident that they are such in this way, as can be understood from the foregoing, but not as numbers of units as the Platonists said. Now a number of units is called a simple and absolute number [i.e., an abstract number], but the number applied to things is called a concrete number, as four dogs or four men; and in this way the substances of things, which are signified by a definition, can be called numbers. For a definition is divisible into two parts, one of which is as form and the other as matter, as was pointed out above (n. 1700). And it is divisible into indivisible parts; for since definitions cannot proceed to infinity, the division of a definition must terminate in certain indivisible parts. For example, if the definition of man is divided into animal and rational, and the definition of animal into animated and sensible, this will not go on to infinity. For it is impossible to have an infinite regress in material and formal causes, as was shown in Book II (n. 299). Hence he explains that the division of a definition is not like the division of a continuous quantity, which is divisible to infinity, but is like the division of a number, which is divisible into indivisible parts.

1723. **And just as when** [11].

He gives the second way in which the substance that the definition signifies is like number. He says that, if anything is added to or subtracted from any number, even if it is a bare minimum, the resulting number will not be specifically the same. For in the case of numbers the minimum is the number one, which, when added to the number three, gives rise to the number four, which is a specifically different number; but if it is subtracted from the same number, the number two remains, which is also a specifically different number. And this is true because the ultimate difference gives to a number its species.

1724. And it is similar in the case of definitions and of the essence, which the definition signifies; because, howsoever small a part has been added or subtracted, there results another definition and another specific nature. For animated sensible substance alone is the definition of animal, but if you also add rational to this, you establish the species man. And in a similar way if you subtract sensible, you establish the species plant, because the ultimate difference also determines the species.

1725. **And there must be** [12].

He gives the third way in which forms are like numbers. He says that a number is one thing. For a number is an essential unity inasmuch as the ultimate unity gives to a number its species and unity, just as in things composed of matter and form a thing is one and derives its unity and species from its form. And for this reason those who speak about the unity of a number as though a number were not essentially one cannot say what makes it to be one thing, i.e., if it is one. For since a number is composed of many units, either it is not one thing in an absolute sense but its units are joined together in the manner of a heap, which does not constitute a unity in an absolute sense, and therefore not a being in any class of things (and thus number would not be a class of being); or if it is one thing in an absolute sense and a being in itself, it is still necessary to explain what makes it one thing out of a plurality of units. But they are unable to assign a reason for this.

1726. Similarly, a definition is one thing essentially, and thus they do not have to assign anything which makes it one. This is understandable, because the substance which the definition signifies is one thing for the very same reason that a number is, i.e., essentially, because one part of it is related to the other as form [to matter]. And it is one, not as being something indivisible such as a unit and a point, as some men claimed, but because each of them is one form and a kind of nature.

1727. **And just as number** [13].

He gives the fourth way in which forms are like numbers. He says that just as a number does not admit of more or less, neither does substance in the sense of form, although perhaps substance in the sense of matter does admit of such difference. For just as the concept of number consists in some limit to which neither addition nor subtraction may be made, as has been pointed out (n. 1723), so also does the concept of form. But things admit of more or less because of the fact that matter participates in a form in a more or less perfect way. Hence too whiteness does not differ in terms of more or less, but a white thing does.

1728. **In regard to the generation** [14].

He summarizes the points discussed. He says that he has dealt with "the generation and corruption of such substances," or forms, both as to the way in which this is possible, namely, by reason of something else; and as to the way in which this is impossible, i.e., essentially; and also with the likeness which forms have to numbers, i.e., by reducing them to numbers by way of a likeness.

LESSON 4
What We Must Know about Matter. How Matter Is Found in All Things

ARISTOTLE'S TEXT Chapters 4 & 5: 1044a15–1045a6

1. Concerning material substance we must not remain ignorant of the fact that, even though all things come from the same first [principle] or from the same [principles] or first [causes], and even though the same matter is the first principle of things which come to be, still there is some proper matter of each thing; for example, the first matter of phlegm is the sweet or the fat, but of bile the bitter or something else. But perhaps these come from the same matter. **1044a15–20**

2. Further, there are several matters of the same thing when one comes from another, as phlegm comes from the fat and the sweet, if the fat comes from the sweet. And something comes from bile by dissolving bile into its first matter. For one thing comes from another in two ways: either because it is prior to the other [in the process of development] or because it comes from the dissolving of a thing into its first principle. **1044a20–25**

3. Now when there is one matter it is possible for different things to come into being by virtue of the cause of motion, as a chest and a bed come from wood. But of certain things the matter is necessarily different when the things are different; e.g., a saw cannot be made from wood, and it is not within the power of the cause of motion to do this; for he is incapable of making a saw from wool or from wood. But if the same thing can be made from different matters, it is clear that the art and the principle which acts as a mover are the same. For if both the matter and the cause of motion are different, so also will be the thing that is made. **1044a25–32**

4. Hence, when one asks what the cause of anything is, it is necessary to mention all the causes concerned, since causes are spoken of in several senses. For example, What is a man's material cause? The menstrual fluid. What is his moving cause? The seed. What is his formal cause? His essence. What is his final cause? His end. But perhaps both of these are the same. **1044a32–1044b1**

5. It is necessary also to give the proximate causes. What is the matter of man? Not earth or fire, but his proper matter. **1044b1–3**

6. Indeed, concerning natural substances which are generable it is necessary to proceed in this way, if one is to proceed correctly, granted that these are the causes, that they are of this number, and that it is necessary to know the causes. **1044b3–5**

7. In the case of natural substances which are eternal there is another procedure. Perhaps some of them do not have matter or do not have this kind of matter but only that which is subjected to change of place. **1044b6–8**

8. Thus all those things which are by nature but are not substances do not have matter, but the underlying subject is their substance. For example, What is the matter of an eclipse? There is none, but it is the moon that is the patient. What is the efficient cause destroying the light? The earth. What is the final cause? Perhaps there is none. What is the formal cause? The definition. But this will not be clear if it does not include the [efficient] cause. For example, What is an eclipse? A privation of light. And if one adds, as a result of the earth intervening, this definition is one which includes the [efficient] cause. However, in the case of sleep it is not clear what the primary subject is, although it is clear that the animal is also a primary subject. But it is such in a qualified sense. And what is the primary subject, the heart or some other part? Then, by what [is this modification produced]? And what is this modification which pertains to that [part] and not to the whole? Is this a special kind of immobility? It is, but it belongs [to the animal] by reason of some primary subject. **1044b8–20**

Chapter 5

9. But since some things are and are not, without generation and corruption, such as points, if they do in fact exist, and in general the forms and specifying principles of things, then all contraries do not come from each other. For whiteness does not come to be but white wood does; and everything which comes to be comes from something and becomes something. And white man comes from black man and white from black in different ways. Nor do all things have matter but only those which may be generated and changed into each other. There is no matter in those things which are and are not without undergoing change. **1044b21–29**

10. Again, there is the problem how the matter of each thing is related to contraries. For example, if the body is potentially healthy and the opposite of health is disease, is the body potentially both? And is water potentially wine and vinegar? Or is it related to one as matter to its form or actuality, and to the other as the privation and natural corruption [of its form or actuality]? **1044b29–34**

11. Now this raises the problem why wine is not the matter of vinegar, even though vinegar comes from it, and why the living is not the potentially dead; or whether this is not the case, but the corruptions of these occur in virtue of something else. As a matter of fact the matter of a living body is by corruption the potency and matter of a dead body, and water is the matter of vinegar; for they come from each other as night comes from day. Hence whatever things are changed into each other in this way must return to their matter. For example, if a living body is to come from a dead one [the latter must return] to its first matter, and then a living body comes into being. And vinegar [must return] to water, and then wine comes into being. **1044b34–1045a6**

COMMENTARY

1729. Having treated those points which had to be considered about the formal principle of substance, Aristotle now establishes what is true regarding the material principle. This is divided into three parts. First [1], he deals with the material principle in relation to the things which come from matter; second [3], in relation to the other causes ("Now when there is one matter"); and third [9], in relation to the change of generation and corruption, whose subject is matter ("But since some things").

In regard to the first he does two things. First [1], he shows whether there is one or several kinds of matter for all things. And in regard to the material principle he says that one must not remain ignorant of the fact that, even though all things come from the same first material principle, namely, first matter, which has no form of its own, or from the same material principles "or first [causes]," (which is added because of the four elements, the material principles common to all generable and corruptible things), and even though the same matter is "the first principle of things which come to be," (which he adds because of the fact that matter is not only a principle of being but also of coming-to-be), i.e., even though first matter and the elements are universally related to things composed of the elements, there is still some proper matter of each thing. For example, the proper matter of phlegm (not in an absolute sense but generically) is the fat and the sweet, since these have a certain relationship to phlegm by reason of their moistness. But the first matter of bile is bitter things or certain others of this kind; for in bitter things heat seems to have absolute dominion over moistness even to the extent of destroying it. Thus by reason of dryness and warmth the bitter has a relationship to bile. But perhaps these two matters, namely, the bitter and the sweet, come from some prior material principle. He adds "perhaps" because certain things have different matters, since their matters are not reducible to any prior matter, for example corruptible and incorruptible bodies.

1730. From the things which are said here then it is evident that there is one first matter for all generable and corruptible things, but different proper matters for different things.

1731. **Further, there are several matters** [2].

Second, he points out how in an opposite sense there are several matters for one and the same thing. He says that there are several matters of the same thing when one of these is the matter of another, as the matter of phlegm is the fat and the sweet, if the fat comes from the sweet. For the savor of fat is reckoned among the intermediate savors, and these are produced from extremes, which are the sweet and the bitter. But the fat is nearest to the sweet. Now in these examples we must bear in mind that he takes as the matter of each thing that from which the thing comes to be, even though it is not permanent but transitory.

1732. Therefore, lest someone should think that a thing is always said to come from a material principle, and not the reverse, he adds that something is also said to come from bile by the dissolution of bile into its first matter, and in reverse order bile is said to come from first matter. For one thing is said to come from another in two ways: either because the thing from which it comes is naturally its starting point in the process of generation (for this kind of thing is a material principle); or because the process of coming-to-be is the dissolving of a thing into its material principle, namely, in the sense that a material principle is said to come from a composite by dissolution. For a mixed body comes from the elements by the process of composition, whereas the elements come from a mixed body by the process of dissolution.

1733. **Now when there is one matter** [3].

He establishes what is true of matter in relation to the other causes. First, in relation to the agent cause alone, which produces something from matter; and this relationship pertains to matter according as it is a principle of coming-to-be. Second [4] 1737), in relation to all the causes, according as matter constitutes a principle of knowing ("Hence, when one asks").

But since he had said above [1] that there was one first matter of all things, one can inquire how a diversity of things could come from one common matter. For the ancient philosophers of nature attributed this to chance when they disregarded the agent cause and claimed that the diversity of things comes from one matter by a process of rarefaction and condensation.

1734. Therefore in rejecting this the Philosopher says, first [3], that when there is one matter it is possible for different things to come into being by reason of the cause of motion, either because there are different causes of motion, or because one and the same cause of motion is disposed in a different way for producing different effects. This is most evident in the case of things made by art. For we see that a chest and a bed are made from wood by one craftsman in virtue of the different art-forms which he himself possesses.

1735. But even though there is a first matter common to all things, nevertheless the proper matters of different things are different. Therefore, lest someone should attribute the diversity of things in their entirety to the cause of motion and in no way to the material principle, he adds that in some of the things that are different the matter is necessarily different, namely, the proper matter. For not anything at all is naturally disposed to come into being from any matter, as a saw does not come from wood. Nor is it within the power of the craftsman to bring this about; for he never assigns one matter to each work, because he is unable to make a saw either from wood or from wool, which, on account of their softness, are not suitable for the work of a saw, which is to cut.

1736. It is evident, then, that the diversity of things is a result of the efficient cause and of matter. Hence, if it is fitting that something specifically the same should be produced from a different matter, as a bowl from gold and from silver, it is obvious that the efficient principle, i.e., the art, must be the same. For if both the matter and the cause of motion were different, the thing produced would have to be different.

1737. **Hence, when one asks** [4].

He deals with matter in relation to the other causes according as matter is a principle of knowing. In regard to this he does two things. First [4], he shows that in the case of generable and corruptible things we must assign matter along with the other causes. Second [7], he shows how matter is found in natural substances which are eternal ("In the case of natural substances"). Third [8], he explains how matter is ascribed to accidents ("Thus all those things").

In regard to the first he does three things. For, first [4], since the ancient philosophers of nature assigned only the material cause, he says that when one asks what the cause of anything is, it is necessary to state all the causes "concerned," i.e., all which contribute to the being of the thing in question, since causes are spoken of in several senses. For not all things have all the causes, although natural beings, and especially generable and corruptible ones, have all the causes. For example, in the generation of man his material cause is the menstrual fluid; his active cause is the seed, in which the active power is contained; his formal cause is his essence, which is signified by the definition; and his final cause is his end [or goal]. But perhaps these two causes, namely, the end and the form, are numerically the same. He says this because in some things they are the same and in some not. For the goal of a man's generation is his soul, whereas the goal of his operations is happiness.

1738. **It is necessary also** [5].

Second, he shows that it is not only necessary to assign all the causes but also to state the proximate causes, so that by beginning with the first causes we may reach the proximate ones. For the knowledge had of a thing through first causes is only a general and incomplete knowledge, whereas that had of a thing through proximate causes is a complete knowledge. For example, if one asks about the material cause of man, one should not assign as his cause fire or earth, which are the common matter of all generable and corruptible things, but should state his proper matter, such as flesh and bones and the like.

1739. **Indeed, concerning natural substances** [6].

Third, he summarizes the foregoing. He says that it is necessary to proceed thus in regard to natural and generable substances if one is to consider the causes correctly, giving all the causes including the proximate ones. This is necessary in view of the fact that the causes are of this number, as has been explained (n. 1737). And it is necessary to grasp the causes of a thing in order that it may be known scientifically, because science is a knowledge of the cause.

1740. In **the case of natural substances** [7].

He shows how there is matter in natural substances which are eternal, namely, in the celestial bodies. He says that the matter in natural substances which are eternal, namely, in the celestial bodies, is not the same as that in bodies subject to generation and corruption. For perhaps such substances do not have matter, or if they do have matter, they do not have the sort that generable and corruptible bodies have, but only that which is subjected to local motion.

1741. For, as was said above (n. 1737), in the case of generable and corruptible things generation and corruption bring us to a knowledge of matter; because in the process of generation and corruption there must be one subject common to both privation and form. Hence, since in a celestial body there is no potentiality for privation of form but only for different places, it does not have a matter which is in potentiality to form and privation but one which is in potentiality to different places.

1742. However, a body is related to place not as matter to form but rather as subject to accident. And although in one respect a subject is related to an accident as matter is to form, still a subject is not to be identified with matter, as is stated below n. 1743). Thus a celestial body as such does not have matter in any way, if subject does not imply matter; or it has matter as regards place, if subject implies matter.

1743. **Thus all those** [8].

He shows how matter is ascribed to accidents. He says that those things which exist by nature yet are not substances but accidents, do not have a matter from which they come to be, but they have a subject, which is the substance. Now a subject bears some likeness to matter inasmuch as it is receptive of an accident. But it differs from matter in this respect, that while matter has actual being only through form, a subject is not constituted in being by an accident.

1744. Therefore, if one asks what is the cause of an eclipse, one cannot give its matter, but the moon is the subject undergoing this modification. And the efficient cause which extinguishes the light is the earth placed directly between the sun and the moon. But perhaps it is impossible to give the final cause; for those things which pertain to defect do not exist because of some end but are rather a result of natural necessity or of the necessity of the efficient cause. However, he says "perhaps" because an investigation of the causes of particular events which take place in celestial movements is especially difficult. And the formal cause of an eclipse is its definition. But this definition is not clear unless the [efficient] cause is given therein. Thus the definition of a lunar eclipse is the privation of light in the moon. But if one adds that this privation is caused by the earth being placed directly between the sun and the moon, this definition will contain the [efficient] cause.

1745. This is evident also in regard to the accident sleep. But in the case of sleep it is not clear what the primary subject is that undergoes this modification, although it is clear that the animal is the subject of sleep. However, it is not clear to what part of the animal sleep primarily belongs—whether to the heart or some other part; for some men hold that the primary organ of sensation is the brain and some the heart. However, sleep is the cessation of sensory operation. Then, having come to an agreement on the subject of sleep, it is necessary to consider from what, as its efficient cause, sleep comes—whether from the evaporation of food or physical labor or something of this kind. Next we must consider what modification sleep is, [defining] its primary subject, which will be some part of the animal and not the whole animal. For sleep is a kind of immobility. But it belongs primarily to an animal by reason of some part which is the subject of such a modification. Now in the definition of sleep we must state this primary subject, just as in the definition of every accident we must state its primary and proper subject. For color is defined by surface but not by body.

1746. **But since some things** [9].

He deals with matter in relation to the process whereby one thing is changed into something else. Therefore, first [9], he shows how change comes about in different ways in different things. Second [10], he proposes certain problems ("Again, there is the problem").

He says, first [9], that certain things sometimes are and sometimes are not but "without generation and corruption," i.e., without being generated and corrupted in themselves, for example, points and all specifying principles and forms generally, whether substantial or accidental. For properly speaking, white does not come to be, but white wood does; for everything which comes to be comes "from something," i.e., from matter, and comes to be that in which the process of coming to be is terminated, which is form. Thus everything which comes to be is composed of matter and form. Hence those things which are forms only cannot come to be in themselves. Therefore, when it is said that contraries come to be from each other, this has one meaning in the case of composite things and another in the case of simple things. For white man comes from black man in a different way than white from black, because white man signifies a composite and can therefore come to be in itself. But white signifies a form only, and therefore it comes to be from black only by reason of something else.

1747. From the above, then, it is clear that matter does not exist in everything but only in those things which are generated or transformed essentially into each other. However, those things which sometimes are and sometimes are not, without being changed essentially, are such that their matter is not that from which they come, but they have as their matter the subject in which they exist.

1748. **Again, there is the problem** [10].

He raises two questions in regard to the above. The first of these pertains to the way in which matter is related to contraries, namely, whether in all things which seem to have contrariety or opposition matter is in potentiality to each contrary equally and in the same order. For health is a certain equality of humors, whereas disease is their inequality. But both inequality and equality are related to their subject in the same order. Therefore it seems that water, which is the matter of humors, is in potentiality to wine and vinegar as contraries, and is disposed equally to both.

1749. But in solving this problem the Philosopher says that this is not true. For the form of wine is a certain positive state and nature, whereas the form of vinegar is the privation and corruption of wine. Hence matter is disposed first to wine as a positive state and form, but to vinegar as the privation and corruption of wine. And thus it is related to vinegar only through the medium of wine.

1750. **Now this raises the problem** [11].

He proposes a second problem, which is as follows. That from which a thing comes to be seems to be the matter of that thing; for example, mixed bodies come to be from the elements, which constitute their matter. Therefore, since vinegar comes from wine and a dead body from a living one, the problem arises why wine is not the matter of vinegar and a living body the matter of a dead one, since one is related to the other as potentiality is to actuality.

1751. But the answer to this is that vinegar is the corruption of wine itself, and a dead body the corruption of a living one. Hence vinegar does not come from wine as matter, or a dead body from a living one; but one is said to come from the other in virtue of something else inasmuch as it comes from its matter. Hence the matter of a bowl is not a goblet but silver. Similarly, a living body is not the matter of a dead body, but the elements are.

1752. But because a dead body is said to come from a living one or vinegar from wine, this preposition from will signify order if reference is made to the form itself of wine or living body; for in the same matter after the form of wine there is vinegar, and after the form of a living body there is a dead one. And it is in this way that we say that night comes from day. Therefore, in all things that come from each other in this way, as vinegar from wine and a dead body from a living one, the process of change is reversed only when these things are dissolved into their matter. For example, if a living body must come from a dead one, the latter must first be dissolved into its primary matter inasmuch as a dead body is dissolved into the elements; and from the elements again in due order a living body is constituted. It is the same in regard to vinegar and wine.

1753. The reason for this is that, whenever matter is disposed to different forms in a certain order, it cannot be brought back from a subsequent state to one that is prior in that order. For example, in the generation of an animal, blood comes from food; and the semen and menstrual fluid, from which the animal is generated, come from blood. But this order cannot be reversed so that blood comes from semen and food from blood, unless these are resolved into their first matter; because for each thing there is a definite mode of generation. And it is the same [in the other case], because the matter of wine is related to vinegar only through the medium of wine, namely, inasmuch as it is the corruption of wine. The same is also true of a dead body and a living one, of a blind man and one who has sight, and so on.

Therefore from such privations there can be a return to a prior form only when such things are dissolved into first matter.

1754. However, if there is some privation to which matter is immediately disposed, and this signifies nothing else than the non-existence of form in matter which lacks a disposition for form, then the process of reverting from such a privation to a [prior] form, as from darkness to illumination, will be possible because this [i.e., darkness] is nothing else than the absence of light in the transparent medium.

LESSON 5

Why Definitions and Matters Are Unities. The Union of Matter and Form

ARISTOTLE'S TEXT Chapter 6: 1045a7–1045b23

1. It seems that we must discuss next the problem which was mentioned with regard to definitions and numbers: what it is that causes them to be one. For all things which have several parts, and of which the whole is not a kind of heap but is something over and above the parts, have some cause that makes them one. For in some bodies contact is the cause of their unity, and in others stickiness or some other such quality. But a definition is one intelligible structure not by the connection of its parts, like the Iliad, but by being one thing. What is it, then, that makes man to be one; and why is he one thing and not many, for example, animal and two-footed? **1045a7–15**

2. And if, in a different way, as some claim, there is an animal-itself and a two-footed-itself, why is man not these two things? And if this were the case, men would not be such by participating in man, i.e., by participating in one thing, but in two, namely, in animal and two-footed. Hence in general man will not be one thing but many, i.e., animal and two-footed. **1045a15–20**

3. It is evident, then, that those who accept this position and discuss and define things in the way they have been accustomed to do, cannot find an answer or solution to this problem. But if (as we say) one part is as matter and the other as form, or one is in potency and the other in act, the problem with which we are dealing will no longer appear to be a difficulty. **1045a20–25**

4. For this problem is just the same as we should have if the definition of cloak were round bronze. Now let us suppose that this term is the sign of this definition. Then when one asks what causes round and bronze to be one thing, there will no longer be a problem, because one is as matter and the other as form. What is it, then, apart from the efficient cause, that causes the potential to become actual in the case of things which are generated? For there is no other cause of the potential sphere being an actual sphere; but this was the essence of each. **1045a25–33**

5. Further, some matter is intelligible and some sensible. And one part of a definition is always as matter and the other as actuality; for example, a circle is a plane figure. **1045a33–35**

6. But each of those things which do not have matter, either intelligible or sensible, is at once one thing, just as it is a being: a particular thing, a quality, or a quantity; and for this reason neither being nor unity is expressed in their definitions. And their essence is at once one thing just as it is also a being. For this reason there is not some other cause of each of these being one or of being something; for each is at once a being and a unity, not as belonging to the class of being or unity, nor because these distinctions exist separately from singular things. **1045a36–1045b7**

7. And it is because of this difficulty that some men speak of participation, and raise the question as to what causes participation and what it is to participate. For some speak of the coexistence of the soul, as Lycophron, who says that knowledge is the coexistence of the act of knowing and the soul; and others say that life is the composition or connection of soul with body. **1045b7–12**

8. The same argument applies in all cases. For being healthy will be either the coexistence or conjunction or composition of soul and health; and being a bronze triangle will be the composition of bronze and triangle; and being white will be the composition of surface and whiteness. **1045b12–16**

9. Now the reason for this position is that these thinkers are looking for some unifying principle and difference of potentiality and actuality. But, as we have pointed out, both the ultimate matter and form are the same, one potentially and the other actually. Hence to ask what the cause of their unity is, is the same as to ask what makes them one; for each particular thing is a unity, and what is potential and what is actual are in a sense one thing. Hence there is no other cause except that which causes motion from potentiality to actuality. And all those things which do not have matter are simply one. **1045b16–23**

COMMENTARY

1755. Having dealt with the material and formal principles, Aristotle now intends to settle the question about the way in which they are united to each other; and in regard to this he does three things. First [1], he raises the question. Second [3], he answers it ("It is evident"). Third [7], he rejects the false opinions about this question ("And it is because").

In regard to the first, he gives two reasons for saying that this question involves a difficulty. He says [1] that, in regard to the question which was touched on above about definitions and numbers as to what makes each of them one, it must be noted that all things which have several parts (and of which the whole is not merely a heap of parts but is something constituted of parts and is over and above the parts themselves) have something that makes them one. For in some bodies which have unity in this way, contact is the cause of their unity, and in others stickiness or something else of this kind.

1756. Now it is evident that, while a defining concept is one thing composed of many parts, it is not one thing merely by the addition of its parts, "like the *Iliad*," i.e., the poem written about the history of the Trojans, which is one thing only by way of aggregation. But a definition is one thing in an absolute sense, for it signifies one thing. It is reasonable, then, to ask what makes both the definition of man to be one thing, and man himself, whose intelligible structure is the definition. For since man is animal and two-footed, and these seem to be two things, it is reasonable to ask why man is one thing and not many.

1757. **And if, in a different way** [2].

Then he gives the reason why this question is a problem. For if what some men claim is true, i.e., if animal itself is a particular thing which exists of itself and is separate, and the same is true of two-footed, as the Platonists held, then it is reasonable to ask why man is not these two things connected together, so that particular men are such only by participating in man, and not by participating in one thing but in two, animal and two-footed. And according to this man will not be one thing but two, namely, animal and two-footed.

1758. **It is evident** [3].

He solves the above problem; and in regard to this he does two things. First, he offers an explanation that seems to provide a solution to the problem. He says that, if some men accept the things which have been said about Plato's position, and change the natures of things in this way because they hold that universals are separate as the Platonists were accustomed to define and speak of them, it will evidently be impossible to give the cause of a man's unity or solve the foregoing problem. But if, as is stated above (n. 1700), one holds that in definitions one part is as matter and the other as form, i.e., one as potentiality and the other as actuality, then it will be easy to solve the question, because there does not seem to be a problem.

1759. **For this problem** [4].

Second, he solves this problem in

the aforesaid way. First, he solves it in the case of natural substances which are generated and corrupted. He says that this problem would be the same as if we were to ask why bronze is round. For let us assume that the definition of the term cloak is round bronze, and that this term signifies this definition. Then when one asks why the definition round bronze is one, there does not seem to be any problem, because bronze is as matter and round as form. For there is no other cause of these being one except that which makes what is in potency to become actual. And in everything in which there is generation this is the agent. Hence, since this (what is in potentiality to become actual) is the essence signified by the definition, then in the case of things subject to generation and corruption it is evidently the agent which causes the definition of the essence to be one.

1760. **Further, some matter** [5].

Then he solves the above problem in regard to the objects of mathematics. He says that matter is of two kinds, sensible and intelligible. Sensible matter is what pertains to the sensible qualities, hot and cold, rare and dense and the like; and with this matter natural bodies are concreted. Now the objects of mathematics abstract from this kind of matter. But intelligible matter means what is understood without sensible qualities or differences, for example, what is continuous. And the objects of mathematics do not abstract from this kind of matter.

1761. Hence, whether in the case of sensible things or in that of the objects of mathematics, their definitions must always contain something as matter and something as form; for example, in the definition of a mathematical circle, a circle is a plane figure, plane is as matter and figure as form. For a mathematical definition and a natural definition are each one thing on the same grounds (even though there is no agent in the realm of mathematical entities as there is in the realm of natural entities), because in both cases one part of the definition is as matter and the other as form.

1762. **But each of those things** [6].

He solves the above problem in regard to the things that are wholly separate from matter. He says that in the case of all those things which do not have intelligible matter, as the objects of mathematics have, or sensible matter, as natural bodies have, that is to say, in the case of the separate substances, each one of these is at once one thing. For each of those things which have matter is not at once one thing, but they are one because unity comes to their matter. But if there is anything that is only a form, it is at once one thing, because it is impossible to posit in it anything prior in any order whatever that must await unity from a form.

1763. He gives this example: the ten categories do not derive being by adding something to being in the way that species are established by adding differences to genera, but each is itself a being. And since this is true, it is evident that being does not await something to be added to it so that it may become one of these, i.e., either a substance or quantity or quality; but each of these from the very beginning is at once either a substance or quantity or quality. This is the reason why neither unity nor being is given as a genus in definitions, because unity and being would have to be related as matter to differences, through the addition of which being would become either substance or quality.

1764. Similarly, that which is wholly separate from matter and is its own essence, as was stated above (n. 1708), is at once one thing, just as it is a being; for it contains no matter that awaits a form from which it will derive being and unity. In the case of such things, then, there is no cause that makes them one by means of motion. However, some of them have a cause which supports their substances without their substances being moved, and not as in the case of things subject to generation, which come to be through motion. For each of them is at once a particular being and a one, but not so that being and unity are certain genera or that they exist as individuals apart from singular things, as the Platonists held.

1765. **And it is because** [7].

Then he rejects the false opinion which some men held about this question; and in regard to this he does three things.

First, he states their position. He says that it is because of this problem that some, namely, the Platonists, posited participation, by which inferior beings participate in superior ones; for example, this particular man participates in man, and man in animal and two-footed. And they asked what the cause of participation is, and what it is to participate, in order that it might become clear to them why this thing which I call two-footed animal is one thing. And others held that the cause of a man's unity is a certain consubstantiality or coexistence of the soul with the body, as if soul's being with body were signified in the abstract; as if we were to speak of animation as Lycophron said that knowledge is a mean between the soul and the act of knowing; and others said that life itself is the mean whereby soul is joined to body.

1766. **The same argument** [8].

He rejects these positions. He says that if the statement made about the soul and the body is correct, i.e., that there is some mean uniting them, the same argument will apply in all things which are related as form and matter. For, according to this, being healthy will be a mean as a kind of consubstantiality or a kind of connection or bond between the soul, by which the animal subsists, and health. And being a triangle will be a mean combining figure and triangle. And being white will be a mean by which whiteness is connected with surface. This is obviously false. Hence it will be false that animation is a mean by which the soul is joined to the body, since animation means merely being ensouled.

1767. **Now the reason** [9].

He gives the reasons for the error in the above positions. He says that the reason why these thinkers held such views is that they sought for some principle which makes potentiality and actuality one thing, and looked for the differences of these as though it were necessary for them to be brought together by some one mean like things which are actual and diverse. But, as has been stated, both the ultimate matter, which is appropriated to a form, and the form itself are the same; for one of them is as potentiality and the other as actuality. Hence to ask what causes a thing is the same as to ask what causes it to be one, because each thing is one to the extent that it is a being. And potentiality and actuality are also one in a certain respect, for it is the potential that becomes actual;

and thus it is not necessary for them to be united by some bond like those things which are completely different. Hence there is no other cause that produces the unity of things which are composed of matter and form except that cause which moves things from potentiality to actuality. But those things which simply do not have matter are some one thing of themselves just as they are something existing. These explanations will suffice for Book VIII.

BOOK IX
ACTUALITY AND POTENTIALITY

LESSON 1
The Division of Potency into Active and Passive. The Nature of Incapacity and Privation

ARISTOTLE'S TEXT Chapter 1: 1045b27–1046a35

1. *We have dealt then with the primary kind of being and the one to which all the other categories of being are referred, namely, substance. For it is in reference to the concept of substance that the other categories are called beings, i.e., quantity, quality, and others which are spoken of in this way; for all involve the concept of substance, as we have stated in our first discussions. And since being is used in one sense of quiddity or quantity or quality, and in another sense of potency and actuality and activity, let us now establish the truth about potency and actuality. And first let us consider potency in the most proper sense of the term, although not the one most useful for our present purpose; for potency and actuality are found in more things than those which are referred merely to motion. But when we have spoken about this sense of potency we shall, in our discussions about actuality, also explain the other senses of potency.* **1045b27–1046a4**

2. *That the terms potency and can are used in many senses we have made evident elsewhere. And all of those senses of potency which are equivocal may be dismissed; for some senses of potency [or power] are merely figurative, as in geometry. And we say that things are possible or impossible because they either are or are not in some particular way. But all those potencies belonging to the same species are principles and are referred to one primary kind of potency, which is the principle of change in some other thing inasmuch as it is other. For one kind is a potency for being acted upon, which is in the patient and is the principle of its being passively moved by another inasmuch as it is other; and another kind of potency is the state of insusceptibility to change for the worse and to corruption by some other thing inasmuch as it is other, i.e., by a principle of change. And the intelligible character of the primary kind of potency is found in all of these terms. Again, these potencies are said to be potencies either just for acting or for being acted upon, or for acting or being acted upon well, so that in these latter kinds of potencies the notes of the prior kind are somehow present.* **1046a4–19**

3. *It is evident, then, that in one sense the potency for acting and for being acted upon are one; for a thing is potential both because it itself has the potency for being acted upon, and because something else can be acted upon by it. And in another sense these potencies are different; for the one is in the patient, since it is because it has a principle, and because matter is a principle, that the patient is acted upon and changed by something else. For what is oily is capable of being burnt, and what is yielding in some way is capable of being broken (and the supposit is capable of being expressed); and the same is true in other cases. And another kind of potency is in the agent, as the potency to heat and the potency to build—the former in the thing capable of heating, and the latter in the person capable of building. Hence, inasmuch as a thing is by nature a unity, it cannot be acted upon by itself; for it is one thing and not also something else.* **1046a19–29**

4. *And incapacity or impossibility is the privation contrary to such potency, so that every potency and incapacity belong to the same subject and refer to the same attribute. And there are various kinds of privation; for there is one kind of privation when a thing does not have some attribute which it is naturally disposed to have, either in general, or when it is naturally disposed to have it. And this is so either in a particular way, for example, completely, or even in*

any way at all. And in some cases if things are naturally disposed to have some attribute and do not have it as a result of force, we say that they are deprived of it. **1046a2935**

COMMENTARY

1768. Having established the truth about being as divided into the ten categories, the Philosopher's aim here is to establish the truth about being as divided into potency and actuality. This is divided into two parts. In the first [1] he links up this discussion with the foregoing one, and explains what he intends to do in this book. In the second [2] he carries out his announced plan ("That the terms").

He accordingly points out, first [1], that he has already discussed above the primary kind of being to which all the other categories of being are referred, namely, substance. And he explains that all the other categories are referred to substance as the primary kind of being, because all other beings—quantity, quality, and the like—involve the concept of substance. For being is said of quantity because it is the measure of substance; and of quality because it is a certain disposition of substance; and the same thing applies in the case of the other categories. This is evident from the fact that all accidents involve the concept of substance, since in the definition of any accident it is necessary to include its proper subject; for example, in the definition of *snub* it is necessary to include nose. This was made clear at the beginning of Book VII (n. 1347).

1769. But being is variously divided. One division is based on its designation as whatness (i.e., substance), quantity or quality, which is its division into the ten categories. Another is its division into potency and actuality or activity, from which the word *actuality* [or *act*] is derived, as is explained later on (n. 1805). And for this reason it is now necessary to deal with potency and actuality.

1770. It is first necessary to speak of potency in its most proper sense, although not the one which is most useful for our present purpose. For potency and actuality are referred in most cases to things in motion, because motion is the actuality of a being in potency. But the principal aim of this branch of science is to consider potency and actuality, not insofar as they are found in mobile beings, but insofar as they accompany being in general. Hence potency and actuality are also found in immobile beings, for example, in intellectual ones.

1771. And when we shall have spoken about the potency found in mobile things, and about its corresponding actuality, we will also be able to explain potency and actuality insofar as they are found in the intelligible things classed as separate substances, which are treated later on (n. 1867). This order is a fitting one, since sensible things, which are in motion, are more evident to us, and therefore by means of them we may attain a knowledge of the substances of immobile things.

1772. From this consideration the meaning of another text also becomes evident, which says, "And potency in the proper sense is not the only one which is useful for our present purpose;" because even though the potency which is present in mobile things is potency in its most proper sense, this is still not the only sense in which potency is used, as was explained (nn. 1770–71). And it is useful for our present purpose, not as though it were the principal object of our investigation, but because we may attain a knowledge of the other kinds of potency from it.

1773. **That the terms** [2].

Then he deals with potency and actuality; and this is divided into three parts. In the first [2] he discusses potency; and in the second (Lesson 5), actuality ("Since we have dealt"); and in the third (Lesson 7), the relationship of actuality to potency ("Since we have established").

The first is divided into two parts. In the first of these he discusses potency itself. In the second (Lesson 2) he discusses potency in relation to the things in which it is found ("And since some").

The first is divided into two parts. In the first he deals with potency; and in the second [4], with incapacity ("And incapacity").

In regard to the first he does two things. First, he explains the different senses of potency. Second [3], he makes evident a truth about potency from the things previously laid down ("It is evident").

He accordingly says, first [2], that it has been shown elsewhere, i.e., in Book V of this work (n. 954), that the words *potency* and *can* have a multiplicity of meanings. But in some cases this multiplicity is a multiplicity of equivocation, and in others it is a multiplicity of analogy. For some things are said to be capable or incapable because they have some principle within themselves, and this refers to those senses in which all potencies are said to be such not equivocally but analogously. But other things are not said to be capable or able because of some principle which they have within themselves; and in their case the term potency is used equivocally.

1774. Therefore, with regard to those senses in which the term potency is used equivocally, he says that these must be dismissed for the present. For the term potency is referred to some things, not because of some principle which they have, but in a figurative sense, as is done in geometry; for the square of a line is called its power *(potentia),* and a line is said to be capable of becoming its square. And similarly in the case of numbers it can be said that the number three is capable of becoming the number nine, which is its square; because when the number three is multiplied by itself the number nine results, for three times three makes nine; and when a line, which is the root of a square, is multiplied by itself, a square results. And the same thing applies in the case of numbers. Hence the root of a square bears some likeness to the matter from which a thing is made; and for this reason the root is said to be capable of becoming its square as matter is capable of becoming a thing.

1775. And similarly in the considerations of logic we say that some things are possible or impossible, not because of some potency, but because they either are or are not in some way; for those things are called possible whose opposites can be true, whereas those are called impossible whose opposites cannot be true. This difference depends on the relationship of predicate to subject, because sometimes the predicate is repugnant to the subject, as in the case of impossible things, and sometimes it is not, as in the case of possible things.

1776. Passing over these senses of potency, then, we must consider those potencies which are reduced to one species, because each of these is a principle. And all potencies spoken of in this sense are reduced to some principle from which all the others derive their meaning; and this is an active principle, which is the source of change in some other thing inasmuch as it is other. He says this because it is possible for an active principle to be at the same time in the mobile or patient, as when something moves itself; although it is not mover and moved, or agent and patient, in the same respect. Hence the principle designated as active potency is said to be a principle of change in some other thing inasmuch as it is other; because, even though an active principle can be found in the same thing as a passive principle, this still does not happen insofar as it is the same, but insofar as it is other.

1777. That the other potencies are reduced to this principle which is called active potency is evident; for in one sense passive potency means the principle by which one thing is moved by some other thing inasmuch as it is other. He says this because, even if the same thing might be acted upon by itself, this still does not happen insofar as it is the same, but insofar as it is other. Now this potency is reduced to a first active potency, because when anything undergoes change this is caused by an agent. And for this reason passive potency is also reduced to active potency.

1778. In another sense potency means a certain state of insusceptibility (or impossibility) "to change for the worse," i.e., a disposition whereby a thing is such that it cannot undergo change for the worse; i.e., that it cannot undergo corruption as a result of some other thing "inasmuch as it is other," namely, by a principle of change which is an active principle.

1779. Now it is evident that both of these senses of potency imply something within us which is referred to the undergoing of a change. For in the one sense the term designates a principle by reason of which someone cannot be acted upon; and in the other sense it designates a principle by reason of which someone can be acted upon. Hence, since the state of being acted upon depends on action, the definition "of the primary kind of potency," namely, active potency, must be given in the definition of both senses of potency. Thus these two senses of potency are reduced to the first, namely, to active potency, as to something prior.

1780. Again, in another sense potencies are spoken of not only in relation to acting and being acted upon but in relation to what is done well in each case. For example, we say that someone is capable of walking, not because he can walk in any way at all, but because he can walk well; and in an opposite sense we say of one who limps that he cannot walk. Similarly, we say that wood is capable of being burned because it can be burned easily; but we say that green wood is incapable of being burned because it cannot be burned easily. Hence it is clear that in the definitions of those potencies which are described as potencies for acting and being acted upon well, there are included the concepts of those primary potencies which were described as potencies for acting and being acted upon without qualification; for example, *to act* is included in *to act well,* and *to be acted upon* is included in *to be acted upon well.* Hence it is obvious that all of these senses of potency are reduced to one primary sense, namely, to active potency; and therefore it is also evident that this multiplicity is not the multiplicity of equivocation but of analogy.

1781. **It is evident, then** [3].

From what has been said he now indicates something that is true about the foregoing potencies. He says that in one sense the potency for acting and that for being acted upon are one, and in another sense they are not. They are one potency if the relationship of the one to the other is considered; for one is spoken of in reference to the other. For a thing can be said to have a potency for being acted upon, either because it has of itself a potency by which it may be acted upon, or because it has a potency by which something else may be acted upon by it. And in this second sense active potency is the same as passive potency; for by reason of the fact that a thing has active potency it has a power by which something else may be acted upon by it.

1782. However, if these two potencies—active and passive—are taken in reference to the subject in which they are found, then in this sense active and passive potency are different; for passive potency exists in a patient, since a patient is acted upon by reason of some principle existing within itself; and matter is of this sort. Now passive potency is nothing but the principle by which one thing is acted upon by another; for example, to be burned is to undergo a change, and the material principle by reason of which a thing is capable of being burned is the oily or the fat. Hence the potency itself is present as a passive principle in the thing capable of being burned. And similarly what yields to the thing touching it so that it receives an impression from it, as wax or something of this sort, is capable of doing so inasmuch as it is impressionable. "And the supposit," i.e., the male, is the proper subject of the modification resulting in an eunuch. The same is true of other things which are acted upon insofar as they have within themselves a principle for being acted upon, which is called passive potency. But active potency is in the agent, as heat in the thing which heats and the art of building in the builder.

1783. And since active potency and passive potency are present in different things, it is obvious that nothing is acted upon by itself inasmuch as it is naturally disposed to act or to be acted upon. However, it is possible for something to be acted upon by itself accidentally, as a physician heals himself not inasmuch as he is a physician but inasmuch as he is ill. But in this case a thing is not acted upon by itself, because, properly speaking, one of the aforesaid principles is present in one and the same thing, and not the other. For the principle of being acted upon is not present in the one having the principle of action except accidentally, as has been said (n. 1782).

1784. **And incapacity** [4].

Here he establishes the truth about incapacity, saying that incapacity (which is the contrary of the abovementioned potency or capacity) or impossibility (which is referred to incapacity of this sort) is the privation of the potency in question. However, he says this to distinguish it from the impossible which signifies some mode of falsity, which is not referred to any incapacity, just as the possible is also not referred to any potency. For since privation and possession belong to the same subject and refer to the same attribute, potency and incapacity must belong to the same subject and refer to the same attribute. Hence there are as many senses of incapacity as there are of potency, to which it is opposed.

1785. But it must be noted that the term *privation* is used in many senses. For in one sense whatever does not have some attribute can be said to be deprived of it, as when we say that a stone is deprived of sight because it does not have sight; and in another sense a thing is said to be deprived only of what it can have and does not have. And this may happen in two ways: in one way when the thing does not have it at all, as a dog is said to be deprived of sight when it does not have it; and, in another way, if it does not have it when it is naturally disposed to have it. Hence a dog is not said to be deprived of sight before the ninth day. This sense of privation is again divided. For in one sense a thing is said to be deprived of some attribute because it does not have it in a particular way, namely, completely and well; as when we say that someone who does not see well is blind. And in another sense a thing is said to be deprived of some attribute when it does not have it in any way at all; for example, we say that a person is deprived of sight who does not have sight at all. But sometimes force is included in the notion of privation, and then we say that some things are deprived of certain attributes when those which they are naturally disposed to have are removed by force.

LESSON 2
Rational and Irrational Potencies

ARISTOTLE'S TEXT Chapter 2: 1046a36–1046b28

1. *And since some such principles are present in non-living things, and others in living things and in the soul, and in the soul having reason, it is evident that some potencies will be devoid of reason and others will be rational. And for this reason all the arts and productive sciences are potencies; for they are principles of change in some other thing inasmuch as it is other.* **1046a36–1046b4**

2. *And all those potencies which are rational are open to contrary determinations, and those which are irrational are each determined to one thing; for example, what is hot is capable of heating, whereas the medical art is concerned with both sickness and health.* **1046b4–7**

3. *And the reason of this is that science is a conception [or rational plan], and the same conception explains both a thing and its privation, though not in the same way. And in one sense it is a conception of both, and in another it applies rather to the existent thing. Hence it is necessary that such sciences should deal with contraries, but with one directly and with the other indirectly; for the conception applies to one essentially, but to the other in a kind of accidental way, because it explains the contrary by negation and removal. For the contrary is the primary privation, and this is the removal of the other term.* **1046b7–15**

4. *Moreover, since contraries do not exist in the same subject, and since a science is a potency in a being which possesses a rational plan, and the soul has a principle of motion, it follows that, while what is healthful produces only health, and what is capable of heating produces only heat, and what is capable of cooling produces only cold, one who has a science may be occupied with both contraries. For reason extends to both but not in the same manner, and it exists in a soul which possesses a principle of motion. Hence the soul will initiate both by the same principle by joining both to the same rational plan. And for this reason those things whose potency is rational produce effects contrary to those whose potency is irrational; for one principle of contrary determinations is contained in the rational plan.* **1046b15–24**

5. *It is also evident that a potency for doing something well involves the potency of merely doing something or undergoing some change. But the latter does not always involve the former; for he who does a thing well must do it, but he who does something need not do it well.* **1046b24–28**

COMMENTARY

1786. Having explained the different senses in which the term potency is used, here the Philosopher establishes the truth about potency in relation to the things in which it is found. This is divided into two parts. In the first [1] he shows how these potencies differ from each other on the basis of a difference in their subjects. In the second (Lesson 3) he shows how potency and actuality are simultaneous or not in a substance ("There are some").

In regard to the first he does three things. First [1], he shows how potencies differ on the basis of a difference in their subjects. He says that, since potencies are principles both for acting and being acted upon, some of these principles are in non-living things and some in living ones. And since living things are composed of body and soul, and the principles for acting and being acted upon which are present in the body of living things do not differ from those in non-living ones, he therefore adds "and in the soul," because the principles of action which are present in the soul clearly differ from those present in non-living things.

1787. Again, there are several kinds of souls, and many of these do not differ to any great extent both in acting and in being acted upon from nonliving things which act by natural instinct; for the parts of the nutritive and sentient soul act by natural impulse. Now only the rational part of the soul has dominion over its acts, and it is in this respect that it differs from non-living things. Therefore, having pointed out the difference between souls, he adds "and in the soul having reason," because those principles of living things which are found in the rational part of the soul differ specifically from those of non-living things. Hence it is evident that some powers of the soul are irrational and others rational.

1788. He explains what he means by those which are rational, when he adds that "all the productive arts," as the building and constructive arts and the like, whose actions pass over into external matter, and all sciences which do not perform actions that pass over into external matter, as the moral and logical sciences—all arts of this kind, I say, are powers. And this is concluded from the fact that they are principles of change in some other thing inasmuch as it is other. This is the definition of active power, as is clear from what was said above.

1789. **And all those** [2].

Second, he gives the difference between the above-mentioned potencies. He says that the same rational potencies are open to contrary determinations, as the art of medicine, which is a potency, as has been explained (nn. 1404–7), can produce both health and sickness. But irrational potencies are not open to contrary determinations, but properly speaking each is determined to one thing; for example, the heat of the sun has as its proper effect to heat, although it can be the cause of coldness inasmuch as by opening the pores it causes the loss of internal heat; or by absorbing the matter of a hot humor it destroys the heat and thereby cools.

1790. **And the reason** [3].

Then the Philosopher gives the reason for the aforesaid difference, and it is as follows: a science, which is a rational potency, is a conception of the thing known existing in the mind.

Now the same conception explains both the thing and its privation, although not in the same way, because it first makes known the existing thing and subsequently its privation; for example, the power of sight itself is known properly by means of the notion of sight, and then blindness is known, which is nothing but the very lack of sight in a thing naturally disposed to have it. Hence, if science is a conception of the thing known existing in the mind, the same science must deal with contraries—with one primarily and properly, and with the other secondarily; for example, the art of medicine is cognitive and productive primarily of health and secondarily of sickness, because, as has been pointed out, this art has to do with the conception of the thing known in the mind, and this conception is of one of the contraries directly and of the other indirectly.

1791. And since the remarks which the Philosopher had made above about privation he afterwards transferred to contraries, he shows that the same conception applies to a contrary and to a privation; for just as a privation is explained by negation and removal (for example, the removal of sight explains blindness), in a similar fashion a contrary is explained by negation and removal; because privation, which is merely the removal of some attribute, is a sort of first principle among contraries. For in the case of all contraries one stands as something perfect and the other as something imperfect and the privation of the former; black, for example, is the privation of white, and cold is the privation of heat. Thus it is evident that the same science extends to contraries.

1792. **Moreover, since** [4].

He next develops this point, and he begins to give the reason for the aforesaid difference. For it is clear that natural things act by reason of the forms present in them. But contrary forms cannot exist in the same subject. Therefore it is impossible for the same natural thing to produce contrary effects. But science is a potency for acting and a principle of motion, because a person has an idea of the thing to be made and this principle of motion is in the mind. And since this is so it follows that natural things produce only one effect; for example, what is healthful produces only health, and what is capable of heating produces only heat, and what is capable of cooling produces only cold. But one who acts by science may be occupied with both contraries, because the conception of both contained in the soul is the same; for the soul possesses the principle of such motion, although not in the same way, as has been explained.

1793. Therefore, just as a natural activity proceeds to bring about its effect as though it were united to its form, which is the principle of action whose likeness remains in the effect, in a similar fashion the soul by its activity proceeds to bring about both opposites "by the same principle," i.e., by the conception which is one for the two opposites, uniting both motions to this principle and causing both to terminate in it inasmuch as the likeness of this principle is verified in both of the opposites brought into being. Therefore it is evident that rational powers produce an effect opposite to irrational powers, because a rational power produces contrary effects, whereas an irrational power produces only one effect. The reason is that a single principle of contrary effects is contained in the conception belonging to a science, as has been explained.

1794. **It is also evident** [5].

He explains the relationship of some of the senses of potency mentioned above to those which come under them. For it was stated above that a thing is said to have active or passive potency, sometimes only because it can act or be acted upon, and sometimes because it can act or be acted upon well. Therefore he says that the potency for acting or being acted upon well involves the potency for acting or being acted upon, but not the reverse. For it follows that someone acts if he acts well, but the opposite of this is not true.

LESSON 3
Rejection of the View That a Thing Has Potency Only When It Is Acting. Rejection of the View That All Things Are Possible

ARISTOTLE'S TEXT Chapters 3 & 4: 1046b29–1047b30

1. There are some, such as the members of the Megaric school, who say that a thing has a potency for acting only when it is acting, and that when it is not acting it does not have this potency; for example, one who is not building does not have the power of building, but only one who is building when he is building; and it is the same in other cases. **1046b29–32**

2. It is not difficult to see the absurd consequences of this position. For it is evident, according to this view, that a man will not be a builder if he is not building, because to be a builder is to be able to build. The same is true in the case of the other arts. Therefore, if it is impossible to have such arts unless one has at some time learnt and acquired them, and if it is impossible not to have them unless one has at some time lost them (either through forgetfulness or through some change or through the passage of time; for this cannot occur as a result of the object being destroyed, since it always exists), when one will have ceased to use an art he will not have it; and yet he will be able to build forthwith, thus somehow getting it back again. **1046b32–1047a4**

3. And the same thing will be true in the case of non-living things; for neither the cold nor the hot nor the sweet nor the bitter nor any sensible thing will exist in any way at all if they are not being sensed. Hence they will have to maintain the theory that Protagoras did. **1047a4–7**

4. In fact nothing will have senses unless it is sensing or acting. Therefore, if that is blind which does not have the power of sight, though it is designed by nature to have it, and when it is designed by nature to have it, and so long as it exists, the same persons will be blind many times during the day; and deaf as well. **1047a7–10**

5. Further, if what is deprived of a potency is incapable, it will be impossible for that to come into being which has not yet been generated; but he who says that what cannot possibly be generated either is or will be, is in error; for this is what impossible or incapable means. Hence these theories do away with both motion and generation; for what is standing will always stand, and what is sitting will always sit, because if it is sitting it will not get up, since it is impossible for anything to get up which has no possibility of doing so. **1047a10–17**

6. Therefore, if it is impossible to maintain this, it is evident that potency and actuality are distinct. But these views make potency and actuality the same, and for this reason it is no small thing which they seek to destroy. Hence it is possible for a thing to be capable of being and yet not be, and for a thing not to be and yet be capable of being. And it is similar in the case of the other categories; for example, a thing may be capable of walking and yet not walk, and be capable of not walking and yet walk. **1047a17–24**

7. Moreover, a thing has a potency if there is nothing impossible in its having the actuality of that of which it is said to have the potency. I mean, for example, that if a thing is capable of sitting, and it turns out to be sitting, there will be nothing impossible in its having a sitting position; and it is similar if it is capable of being moved or of moving something, or of standing or causing a thing to stand, or of being or coming to be, or of not being or not coming to be. **1047a24–29**

8. And the word actuality, which is combined with entelechy, is extended chiefly from motion to other things; for actuality seems to be identified mainly with motion. And for this reason they do not assign motion to non-existent things, but they do assign the other categories. For example, non-existent things are considered the objects of intellect and desire but not to be in motion. And the reason is that they would have to exist actually even though they did not exist actually; for some non-existent things are potential. Yet they do not exist, because they do not exist in complete actuality. **1047a30–1047b2**

Chapter 4

9. *Now if what has been called potential or possible is such because something follows from it, it is evident that it cannot be true to say that a thing is possible but will not be, because things which cannot possibly be would then disappear. An example would be if someone, thinking that nothing is impossible, were to affirm that it is possible for the diagonal of a square to be commensurate, even though it is not commensurate; because nothing prevents a thing that is capable of being or of coming to be from not being or not coming to be. But this conclusion necessarily follows from the things laid down above. And if we suppose that which is not but is capable of being, to be or to have come into being, nothing would be impossible. But in this case something impossible will occur; for it is impossible that a diagonal be commensurate. For to be false and to be impossible are not the same; for while it is false that you are now standing, it is not impossible.* **1047b3–12**

10. *And at the same time it is evident that, if when A exists B must exist, then if A is possible B must be possible; for if it is not necessary that B be possible, there is nothing to prevent its not being possible. Therefore, let A be possible. And if A is possible, then when A is possible, if A is assumed to exist, nothing impossible follows, but B necessarily exists. But this was supposed to be impossible. Therefore, let B be impossible. Then if B must be impossible, A must be so. But the first was supposed to be impossible; therefore so also is the second. Hence, if A is possible, B will be possible also, i.e., if they are so related that, when A exists, B must exist. Therefore, if when A and B are so related, B is not possible, then A and B will not be related in the way supposed. On the other hand, if, when A is possible, B must be possible, then if A exists, B must exist. For to say that B must be possible if A is possible, means that, if A exists both when it exists and in the way in which it is possible for it to exist, then B must also exist and exist in that way.* **1047b12–30**

COMMENTARY

1795. Having compared one kind of potency with another in the above discussion, here the Philosopher begins to explain how potency and actuality are found in the same subject. This is divided into two parts. In the first [1] he rejects the false opinions of some men. In the second (Lesson 4) he establishes the truth ("And since among").

The first is divided into two parts. In the first part he rejects the opinion of those who said that a thing is possible or potential only when it is in a state of actuality. In the second part [9] he rejects the opinion of those who maintain the reverse of this: that all things are potential or possible, even though they are not in a state of actuality ("Now if what").

In regard to the first he does two things. First, he rejects the erroneous opinion referred to. Second [7], he explains what it is to be potential or possible, and what it is to be actual ("Moreover, a thing").

In regard to the first he does three things. First, he gives this opinion. Second [2], he destroys it ("It is not difficult"). Third [6], he draws his intended conclusion ("Therefore, if it").

He accordingly says, first, that some said that a thing is in a state of potency or capability only when it is acting; for example, a man who is not actually building is incapable of building, but he is capable of building only when he is actually building; and they speak in a similar way about other things. The reason for this position seems to be that they thought that all things come about necessarily because of some connection between causes. Thus if all things come about necessarily, it follows that those things which do not, are impossible.

1796. **It is not difficult** [2].

Then he adduces arguments against the above opinion, and these reduce it to its absurd consequences. The first is as follows: to be building is to have the power or capability of building. Therefore, if no one has the power or capability of acting except when he is acting, no one is a builder except when he is building. And the same thing will be true of the other arts; for all arts are certain capabilities or potencies, as has been pointed out (n. 1786). It follows, then, that no one will have an art except when he is exercising it.

1797. But this is shown to be impossible if two assumptions are made. The first is this: if someone did not at first have an art, it would be impossible for him to have it later unless he had learned it or acquired it in some way, i.e., by discovery.

1798. The second assumption is that if someone had an art it would be impossible for him not to have the same art later unless he lost it in some way, either through forgetfulness or through some illness or through the passage of a long time during which the knowledge was not exercised; for this is the cause of forgetfulness. Now it cannot be that someone should lose an art as a result of the destruction of its object, as it sometimes happens that true knowledge is lost when a thing is changed; for example, when someone makes a true judgment that Socrates is sitting, his true judgment is destroyed when Socrates stands up. But this cannot be said about an art; for an art is not a knowledge of what exists, but of what is to be made; and so long as the matter from which an art can produce something continues to exist, the object of that art always exists. Hence an art cannot be lost when its object is destroyed, except in the ways mentioned.

1799. Now from these two assumptions the Philosopher argues as follows: if a man does not have an art except when he is exercising it, then when he begins to exercise it he has it anew. Therefore he must either have learned it or acquired it in some other way. And similarly when he ceases to exercise an art it follows that he lacks that art, and thus he loses the art which he previously had either through forgetfulness or through some change or through the passage of time. But both of these are clearly false; and therefore it is not true that someone has a potency only when he is acting.

1800. **And the same** [3].

Here he gives the second argument, which now has to do with the irrational principles present in non-living things, namely, hot and cold, sweet and bitter, and other qualities of this kind, which are active principles changing the senses and thus are potencies. Now if potency is present in a thing only when it is acting, it follows that nothing is hot or cold, sweet or bitter, and so forth, except when it is being sensed through a change in the senses. But this is clearly false; for if it were true it would follow that Protagoras' opinion would be true, since he said that all the properties and natures of things have existence only in being sensed and in being thought. And from this it would follow that contradictories would be true at the same time, since different men have contradictory opinions about the same thing. Now the Philosopher argued dialectically against this position above in Book IV (n. 636). Therefore it is false that potency exists only when there is activity.

1801. **In fact nothing** [4].

Here he gives the fourth argument, which is as follows: sense is a kind of potency. Therefore, if potency exists only when there is activity, it follows that a man has sensory power only when he is sensing, for example, the power of sight or hearing. But one who does not have the power of sight although he is naturally disposed to have it is blind; and one who does not have the power of hearing is deaf. Hence he will be blind and deaf many times on the same day. But this is clearly false, for a blind man does not afterwards regain sight nor a deaf man hearing.

1802. **Further, if what** [5].

Here he gives the fourth argument, which is as follows: it is impossible for a thing to act which does not have the power to act. Therefore, if one has a potency or power only when he is acting, it follows that when he is not acting it is impossible for him to act. But whoever says that something incapable of happening either is or will be, is mistaken. This is evident from the meaning of the word *impossible;* for the impossible is said to be false because it cannot happen. It follows, then, that something which is not is incapable of coming to be in any way. And thus potency so understood will do away with motion and generation, because one who is standing will always stand, and one who is sitting will always sit. For if anyone is sitting, he will never stand afterwards, because so long as he is not standing he does not have the power to stand. Hence it is impossible for him to stand, and consequently it is impossible for him to get up. Similarly what is not white will be incapable of being white, and thus could not be made white. The same holds true in the case of all other things.

1803. **Therefore, if** [6].

He draws his intended conclusion, saying that, if the absurdities mentioned above cannot be admitted, it is obvious that potency and actuality are distinct. But those who hold the foregoing position make potency and actuality the same insofar as they say that something has potency only when it is in a state of actuality. And from this it is evident that they wish to remove from nature something of no little importance, for they eliminate motion and generation, as has been stated (n. 1802). Hence, since this cannot be admitted, it is obvious that something is capable of being which yet is not, and that something is capable of not being which yet is. And "it is similar in the case of the other categories," or predicaments, because it is possible from someone who is not walking to walk, and conversely it is possible from someone who is walking not to walk.

1804. **Moreover, a thing** [7].

Here he explains what it is to be potential and what it is to be actual. First, he explains what it is to be potential. He says that that is said to be potential from which nothing impossible follows when it is assumed to be actual; for example, if one were to say that it is possible for someone to sit if nothing impossible follows when he is assumed to sit. And the same holds true of being moved and of moving something, and other cases of this kind.

1805. **And the word "actuality"** [8].

Second, he explains what it is to be actual. He says that the word *actuality* is used to signify entelechy and perfection, namely, the form, and other things of this kind, as any action at all, is derived properly from motion, so far as the origin of the word is concerned. For since words are signs of intellectual conceptions, we first give names to those things which we first understand, even though they may be subsequent in the order of nature. Now of all acts which are perceived by us in a sensible way, motion is the best known and most evident to us; and therefore the word actuality was first referred to motion, and from motion the word was extended to other things.

1806. And for this reason motion is not attributed to non-existent things, although certain of the other categories mentioned above are attributed to nonexistents; for we say that non-existent things are intelligible, or thinkable, or even desirable, but we do not say that they are moved. For, since to be moved means to be actual, it follows that things which do not exist actually would exist actually; but this is obviously false. For even if some nonexistent things are potential, they are still not said to be, since they are not actual.

1807. **Now if what** [9].

Having destroyed the opinion of those who claim that nothing is possible except when it is actual, the Philosopher now destroys the opposite opinion of those who claim that all things are possible; and in regard to this he does two things. First, he destroys this opinion. Second (n. 1810), he establishes a truth about the succession of possible things ("And at the same").

He accordingly says, first [9], that, if it is true that a thing is said to be possible because something follows from it, inasmuch as the possible has been defined as that from which nothing impossible follows if it is assumed to exist, it is evident that the statements of some thinkers that anything is possible even if it never will be, cannot be true, since as a result of this position impossible things will be eliminated. For example, if one were to say that the diagonal of a square can be commensurate with a side, even though it is not commensurate with it (and one might speak in the same way about other impossible things), and not think that it is impossible for the diameter of a square to be commensurate with a side, those who maintain this position, I say, speak truly in one sense and in another they do not.

1808. For there are some things which nothing will prevent us from designating as capable or possible of coming to be, even though they never will be or ever come to be; but this cannot be said of all things. Yet according to the doctrine laid down above, and which we are now to assume, only those things are capable of being or coming to be, even though they are not, from which nothing impossible follows when they are posited. However, when it is posited that the diagonal of a square is commensurate, an impossible conclusion follows. Thus it cannot be said that it is possible for the diagonal to be commensurate, for it is not only false but impossible.

1809. Now some things are false only but not impossible, as that Socrates sits or that he stands. For to be false and to be impossible are not the same; for example, it is false that you are now standing, but it is not impossible. Therefore the foregoing opinion is true of some things, because some are possible even though they are false. However, it is not true of all things, because some are both false and impossible.

1810. **And at the same** [10].

And since he had said that a thing is judged possible because nothing impossible follows from it, he indicates the way in which there are possible consequents. He says that not only is the position in question destroyed by the definition of the possible given above, but it is also evident at the same time that, if the antecedent of a conditional proposition is possible, the consequent will also be possible; for example, if this conditional proposition, "If when A is, B is," is true, then if A is possible, B must be possible.

1811. Now in order to understand this we must note that the word possible is used in two senses. It is used, first, in contradistinction to the necessary, as when we call those things possible which are capable either of being or not being. And when possible is taken in this way, the foregoing remarks do not apply. For nothing prevents the antecedent from being capable of being or not being, even though the consequent is necessary, as is clear in this conditional proposition, "If Socrates laughs, he is a man."

1812. The word possible is used in a second sense inasmuch as it is common both to those things which are necessary and to those which are capable of being or not being, according as the possible is distinguished from the impossible. And the Philosopher is speaking of the possible in this way here when he says that the consequent must be possible if the antecedent was possible.

1813. For let it be assumed that this conditional proposition is true: If A is, then B is; and let it be assumed that the antecedent, A, is possible. Then it is necessary that B either be possible or not. Now if it is necessary, then the assumption follows. But if it is not necessary, nothing prevents the opposite from being assumed, namely, that B is not possible. But this cannot stand; for A is assumed to be possible, and when it is assumed to be possible, it is at the same time assumed that nothing impossible follows from it; for the possible was defined above as that from which nothing impossible follows. But B follows from A, as was assumed, and B was assumed to be impossible; for to be impossible is the same as not to be possible. Therefore A will not be possible if B, which was held to be impossible, follows from it. Therefore let B be assumed to be impossible, and if it is impossible and, given A, B must exist, then both the first and the second, namely, A and B, will be impossible.

1814. In which place it must be noted that the following proposition is correct: if the consequent is impossible, the antecedent is impossible; but the reverse is not true. For nothing prevents something necessary from being a consequence of the impossible, as in this conditional proposition, "If man is an ass, he is an animal." Therefore what the Philosopher says here must not be understood as meaning that, if the first, i.e., the antecedent, were impossible, then the second, i.e., the consequent, would also be impossible. But it must be understood to mean that, if the consequent is impossible, both will be impossible. Therefore it is obvious that, if A and B are so related that, when A is, B must be, it necessarily follows that, if A is possible, B will be possible; and if B is not possible when A is possible, then A and B are not related in the way supposed, namely, that B follows from A. But it is necessary that when A is possible B must be possible, if when A exists it is necessary that B exist. Therefore when I say "If A is, B is," this means that B must be possible if A is possible, in the sense that it is possible for B to exist at the same time and in the way in which A is possible; for it is not possible that it should exist at any time and in any way.

LESSON 4
The Relative Priority of Actuality and Potency. The Reduction of Natural Potencies to Actuality

ARISTOTLE'S TEXT Chapter 5: 1047b31–1048a24

1. And since among all potencies some are innate, as the senses, and some are acquired by practice, as the power of playing the flute, and some by learning, as artistic powers, those which are acquired by practice and by the use of reason must be acquired by previous exercise. But this is not necessary in the case of those which are not such and which involve passivity. **1047b31–35**

2. Now that which is capable is capable of something at some time and in some way, and has all the other qualifications which must be included in the definition; and some things can cause motion according to a rational plan and their potencies are rational, whereas other things are devoid of any rational plan and their potencies are irrational. And the former potencies must exist in living things, whereas the latter exist in both kinds of things. **1047b35–1048a5**

3. And since this is so, then in the case of the latter potencies, when the thing that is capable of acting and the one that is capable of being acted upon come close to each other, the one must act and the other be acted upon; but in the case of the former potencies this is not necessary. **1048a5–8**

4. For the latter are all productive of one effect, whereas the former are productive of contrary effects. Hence they would produce contrary effects at the same time, that is, if they were to act on a proximate patient without something determining them. But this is impossible. **1048a8–10**

5. Therefore there must be some other thing which is the proper cause of this, and by this I mean appetite or choice. For whatever a thing chiefly desires this it will do, when, insofar as it is potential, it is present and comes close to the thing which is capable of being acted upon. Hence every potency endowed with reason, when it desires something of which it has the potency and insofar as it has it, must do this thing. And it has this potency when the thing capable of being acted upon is present and is disposed in a definite way; but if it is not, it will not be able to act. **1048a10–16**

6. For it is unnecessary to add this qualification: when nothing external hinders it; for the agent has the potency insofar as it is a potency for acting. But this is not true of all things but only of those which are disposed in a definite way, in the case of which external obstacles will be excluded; for they remove some of the qualifications which are given in the definition of the capable or possible. **1048a16–21**

7. And for this reason if such things wish or desire to do two things or contrary things at the same time, they will not do them; for they do not have the potency for doing both at the same time, nor is it possible to do them at the same time, since it is those things which they have the capacity of doing that they do. **1048a21–24**

COMMENTARY

1815. Having rejected the false opinions about potency and actuality the Philosopher now establishes the truth about them; and in regard to this he does two things. First [1], he shows how actuality is prior to potency in the same subject; and second [2], how potency, when it is prior to actuality, is brought to a state of actuality ("Now that which").

He accordingly says, first [1], that, since some potencies are innate in the things of which they are the potencies, as the sensory powers in animals; and some are acquired by practice, as the art of flute-playing and other operative arts of this kind; and some are acquired by teaching and learning, as medicine and other similar arts; all of the above-mentioned potencies which we have as a result of practice and the use of reason must first be exercised and their acts repeated before they are acquired. For example, one becomes a harpist by playing the harp, and one becomes a physician by studying medical matters. But other potencies which are not acquired by practice but which belong to us by nature and are passive, as is evident in the case of sensory powers, are not a result of exercise; for one does not acquire the sense of sight by seeing but actually sees because he has the power of sight.

1816. **Now that which** [2].

Here he shows how those potencies which are prior to actuality are brought to actuality; and in regard to this he does two things. First, he shows how different potencies—rational and irrational potencies—differ from each other in this respect. Second [5], he shows how rational potencies are brought to a state of actuality ("Therefore, there must").

In regard to the first he does three things. First [2], he lays down certain conditions required for the study of the aforesaid differences, and one of these is that it is necessary to consider several qualifications in the definition of the capable or potential. For the capable does not refer to just anything at all but to something definite. Hence the capable must be capable of something, such as to walk or to sit. And similarly what can act or be acted upon cannot act or be acted upon at any time whatever; for example, a tree can bear fruit only at some definite time. Therefore, when it is said that something is capable, it is necessary to determine when it is capable. And it is also necessary to determine in what way it is capable, for that which is capable can neither act nor be acted upon in every way; for example, one can walk in this way, namely, slowly, but not rapidly. And the same thing is true of the other qualifications which they are accustomed to give in the definitions of things, for example, by what instrument, in what place, and the like.

1817. Another qualification which he lays down is that some things are capable of something because of a rational plan, and the potencies for these capabilities are rational. But some capabilities are irrational, and the potencies for these are irrational. Again, rational potencies can exist only in living things, whereas irrational potencies can exist in both, i.e., in both living and nonliving things. And they exist not only in plants and in brute animals, which lack reason, but also in men themselves, in whom are found certain principles both of acting and of being acted upon which are irrational; for example, the powers of nutrition and growth, and weight, and other accidents of this kind.

1818. **And since** [3].

Second, he gives the difference between the potencies in question. He says that in the case of irrational potencies when the thing capable of being acted upon comes close to the thing which is capable of acting, then in accordance with that disposition whereby that able to be acted upon can be acted upon and that capable of acting can act, it is necessary that the one be acted upon and that the other act. This is clear, for instance, when something combustible comes in contact with fire. But in the case of rational potencies this is not necessary; for no matter how close some material may be brought to a builder, it is not necessary that he build something.

1819. **For the latter** [4].

Third, he gives the reason for the difference pointed out. He says that irrational potencies are such that each is productive of only one effect, and, therefore, when such a potency is brought close to something that is capable of being acted upon, it must produce the one effect which it is capable of producing. But one and the same rational potency is capable of producing contrary effects, as was said above (nn. 1789–93). Therefore, if, when it is brought close to something capable of being acted upon, it would be necessary for it to bring about the effect which it is capable of producing, it would follow that it would produce contrary effects at the same time; but this is impossible. For example, it would follow that a physician would induce both health and sickness.

1820. **Therefore there must** [5].

He then shows what is necessary in order for rational potencies to begin to act, seeing that closeness to the thing capable of being acted upon is not sufficient. In regard to this he does three things.

First, he reveals the principle by which a rational potency is made to act. He concludes from the above discussions that since a rational potency has a common relationship to two contrary effects, and since a definite effect proceeds from a common cause only if there is some proper principle which determines that common cause to produce one effect rather than the other, it follows that it is necessary to posit, in addition to the rational power which is common to two contrary effects, something else which particularizes it to one of them in order that it may proceed to act. And this "is appetite or choice," i.e., the choosing of one of the two, or the choice which involves reason; for it is what a man intends that he does, although this occurs only if he is in that state in which he is capable of acting and the patient is present. Hence, just as an irrational potency which is capable of acting must act when its passive object comes close to it, in a similar fashion every rational potency must act when it desires the object of which it has the potency, and in the way in which it has it. And it has the power of acting when the patient is present and is so disposed that it can be acted upon; otherwise it could not act.

1821. **For it is unnecessary** [6].

Second, he answers an implied question. For since he had said that everything capable of acting as a result of a rational plan, when it desires something of which it is the potency, acts of necessity on the patient before it, someone could ask why he did not add this qualification, namely, "when nothing external hinders it"; for it has been said that it must act if it has sufficient power to act. But this does not occur in any and every way, but only when the thing having the potency is disposed in some particular way; and in this statement external obstacles are excluded. For the things which hinder it externally remove some of the qualifications laid down in the common definition of the capable or possible, so that it is not capable at this time or in this way or the like.

1822. **And for this** [7].

Third, he instructs us to avoid the absurd conclusions which he first said would follow, namely, that a rational potency would produce contrary effects at the same time. For if it is necessary that a rational potency should do what it desires, and assuming that some should wish either by reason or by sense appetite to do two different or contrary things at the same time, it does not follow for this reason that they will do them. For they do not have power over contrary effects in such a way that they may do contrary things at the same time; but they act according to the way in which they have a potency, as has been explained (nn. 1816–20).

LESSON 5
Actuality and Its Various Meanings

ARISTOTLE'S TEXT Chapter 6: 1048a25–1048b36

1. Since we have dealt with the kind of potency which is related to motion, let us now determine about actuality both what it is and what kind of thing it is. For in making our distinctions it will become evident at the same time with regard to the potential not only that we speak of the potential as that which is disposed by nature to move something else or be moved by something else, either in an unqualified sense or in some special way, but also that we use the word in a different sense as well. And for this reason we will also come upon these points in making our investigations. **1048a25–30**

2. Now actuality is the existence of a thing not in the sense in which we say that a thing exists potentially, as when we say that Mercury is potentially in the wood, and a half in the whole, because it can be separated from it, or as we say that one who is not theorizing is a man of science if he is able to theorize; but in the sense in which each of these exists actually. **1048a30–35**

3. What we mean becomes evident in particular cases by induction, and we should not look for the boundaries of every thing, but perceive what is proportional; for it is as one who is building to one capable of building, and as one who is awake to one who is asleep, and as one who sees to one whose eyes are closed but who has the power of sight, and as that which is separated out of matter to matter, and as that which has been worked on to that which has not; and let actuality be defined by one member of this division and potency by the other. **1048a35–1048b6**

4. However, things are not all said to be actual in the same way, but proportionally, as this is in that or to that; indeed, some are as motion to potency, and others as substance to some matter. **1048b6–9**

5. But the infinite and the void and all other such things are said to exist potentially and actually in a different sense from that which applies to many beings, for example, from that which sees or walks or is visible. For these things can be verified, and verified without qualification; for what is visible is so designated sometimes because it is being seen and sometimes because it is capable of being seen. But the infinite does not exist potentially in the sense that it will ever have actual separate existence, but it exists potentially only in knowledge. For since the process of division never comes to an end, this shows that this actuality exists potentially, but not that it ever exists separately. Therefore, regarding actuality, both what it is and what kind of thing it is will be evident to us from these and similar considerations. **10489–36.**

COMMENTARY

1823. Having drawn his conclusions about potency, Aristotle now establishes the truth about actuality; and this is divided into two parts. In the first [1] he establishes what actuality is. In the second (Lesson 6) he establishes what is true when something is in potency to actuality ("However, we must").

In regard to the first he does two things. First, he links this up with the preceding discussion. He says that, since we have dealt with the kind of potency which is found in mobile things, i.e., the kind which is an active or passive principle of motion, we must now explain what actuality is and how it is related to potency; because when we will have distinguished the kinds of actuality, the truth about potency will become evident from this at the same time. For actuality is found not only in mobile things but also in immobile ones.

1824. And since potency is referred to actuality, it is evident from this that capability or potency taken in reference to action is attributed not only to something that is naturally disposed to move something else actively or be moved by something else passively, either in an unqualified sense, inasmuch as potency is referred alike to acting and being acted upon, or in some special way, inasmuch as potency is referred to what is able to act or be acted upon well; but capability or potency is also referred to that actuality which is devoid of motion. For although the word actuality is derived from motion, as was explained above (758:C 1805), it is still not motion alone that is designated as actuality. Hence, neither is potency referred only to motion. It is therefore necessary to inquire about these things in our investigations.

1825. **Now actuality** [2].

Second, he establishes the truth about actuality. First [2], he shows what actuality is; and second [4], how it is used in different senses in the case of different things ("However, things").

In regard to the first he does two things. First, he shows what actuality is. He says that a thing is actual when it exists but not in the way in which it exists when it is potential. For we say that the image of Mercury is in the wood potentially and not actually before the wood is carved; but once it has been carved the image of Mercury is then said to be in the wood actually. And in the same way we say that any part of a continuous whole is in that whole, because any part (for example, the middle one) is present potentially inasmuch as it is possible for it to be separated from the whole by dividing the whole; but after the whole has been divided, that part will now be present actually. The same thing is true of one who has a science and is not speculating, for he is capable of speculating even though he is not actually doing so; but to be speculating or contemplating is to be in a state of actuality.

1826. **What we mean** [3].

Here he answers an implied question; for someone could ask him to explain what actuality is by giving its definition. And he answers by saying that it is possible to show what we mean (i.e., by actuality) in the case of singular things by proceeding inductively from examples, "and we should not look for the boundaries of everything," i.e., the definition. For simple notions cannot be defined, since an infinite regress in definitions is impossible. But actuality is one of those first simple notions. Hence it cannot be defined.

1827. And he says that we can see what actuality is by means of the proportion existing between two things. For example, we may take the proportion of one who is building to one capable of building; and of one who is awake to one asleep; and of one who sees to one whose eyes are closed although he has the power of sight; and "of that which is separated out of matter," i.e., what is formed by means of the operation of art or of nature, and thus is separated out of unformed matter, to what is not separated out of unformed matter. And similarly we may take the proportion of what has been prepared to what has not been prepared, or of what has been worked on to what has not been worked on. But in each of these opposed pairs one member will be actual and the other potential. And thus by proceeding from particular cases we can come to an understanding in a proportional way of what actuality and potency are.

1828. **However, things** [4].

Then he shows that the term actuality is used in different senses; and he gives two different senses in which it is used. First, actuality means action, or operation. And with a view to introducing the different senses of actuality he says, first, that we do not say that all things are actual in the same way but in different ones; and this difference can be considered according to different proportions. For a proportion can be taken as meaning that, just as one thing is in another, so a third is in a fourth; for example, just as sight is in the eye, so hearing is in the ear. And the relation of substance (i.e., of form) to matter is taken according to this kind of proportion; for form is said to be in matter.

1829. There is another meaning of proportion inasmuch as we say that, just as this is related to that, so another thing is related to something else; for example, just as the power of sight is related to the act of seeing, so too the power of hearing is related to the act of hearing. And the relation of motion to motive power or of any operation to an operative potency is taken according to this kind of proportion.

1830. **But the infinite** [5].

Second, he gives the other sense in which the word actuality is used. He says that the infinite and the empty or the void, and all things of this kind, are said to exist potentially and actually in a different sense from many other beings; for example, what sees and what walks and what is visible. For it is fitting that things of this kind should sometimes exist in an unqualified sense either only potentially or only actually; for example, the visible is only actual when it is seen, and it is only potential when it is capable of being seen but is not actually being seen.

1831. But the infinite is not said to exist potentially in the sense that it may sometimes have separate actual existence alone; but in the case of the infinite, actuality and potentiality are distinguished only in thought and in knowledge. For example, in the case of the infinite in the sense of the infinitely divisible, actuality and potentiality are said to exist at the same time, because the capacity of the infinite for being divided never comes to an end; for when it is actually divided it is still potentially further divisible. However, it is never actually separated from potentiality in such a way that the whole is sometimes actually divided and is incapable of any further division. And the same thing is true of the void; for it is possible for a place to be emptied of a particular body, but not so as to be a complete void, for it continues to be filled by another body; and thus in the void potentiality always continues to be joined to actuality. The same thing is true of motion and time and other things of this kind which do not have complete being. Then at the end he makes a summary of what has been said. This is evident in the text.

LESSON 6

Matter Is Potential When Ultimately Disposed for Actuality. The Use of the Term Matter in an Extended Sense

ARISTOTLE'S TEXT Chapter 7: 1048b37–1049b3

1. *However, we must determine when each thing is in a state of potency and when it is not; for a thing is not potential at just any time at all; for example, in the process of generation is earth potentially a man? Or is it not, but rather when it has become seed? But perhaps even this is not true in an unqualified sense.* **1048b37–1049a3**

2. *Therefore, in like manner, it is not everything which will be healed by the art of medicine or by chance, but there is something which is capable of being healed, and this is what is potentially healthy. And the intelligible expression of what comes to exist actually after existing potentially as a result of intellect is that it is something which when willed comes to be if no external impediment hinders it. And in the other case, namely, in that of the thing which gets well by itself, health exists potentially when nothing within the thing hinders it. The same is true of those things which are potentially a house; for if there is nothing in these things, i.e., in the matter, which prevents them from becoming a house, and if there is nothing which must be added or taken away or changed, this is potentially a house. The same is true of all other things which have an external principle of generation. And in the case of those things which have their principle of change within themselves, a thing will also be potentially any of those things which it will be of itself if nothing external hinders this. For example, seed is not yet such, because it must be present in some other thing and be changed. But when it is already such as a result of its own principle, it is now this thing potentially; but in the other state it needs another principle; for example, earth is not yet a statue potentially, but when changed it becomes bronze.* **1049a3–18**

3. *Now it seems that the thing of which we are speaking is not a that but a thaten; for example, a chest is not wood but wooden; and wood is not earth but earthen. And the same thing would be true if earth were not something else but a "thaten." And that other thing is always potentially (in an unqualified sense) the thing which follows it, as a chest is not earth or earthen but wooden; for this is potentially a chest and the matter of a chest; and wood in an unqualified sense is the matter of a chest in an unqualified sense; but this wood is the matter of this chest. And if there is some first thing which is not said to be "thaten" as regards something else, this is prime matter; for example, if earth is of air, and air is not fire but of fire, then fire is prime matter, and is a particular thing. For a universal and a subject differ in this respect that a subject is a particular thing.* **1049a18–29**

4. *For example, the subject of modifications is man, body and animal, whereas the modification is musical or white. And when music comes to a subject, the subject is not called music but musical; and a man is not called whiteness but white; and he is not called walking or motion but what walks or is moved, like a "thaten."* **1049a29–34**

5. *Therefore all those modifying attributes which are predicated in this way have substance as their ultimate subject; whereas those which are not predicated in this way, but the predicate is a form or a particular thing, have matter and material substance as their ultimate subject. Therefore it is only fitting that the term "thaten" happens to be predicated of matter and the modifying attributes; for both are indeterminate. It has been stated, then, when a thing is said to exist potentially, and when it is not.* **1049a34–1049b3**

COMMENTARY

1832. Having shown what actuality is, here the Philosopher intends to show both when and in virtue of what sort of disposition a thing is said to be in a state of potency for actuality. In regard to this he does two things.

First [1], he states what he intends to do. He says that it is necessary to determine when a thing is in potency and when it is not. For it is not at just any time and when disposed in just any way that a thing can be said to be in potentiality even to what comes from it; for it could never be said that earth is potentially a man, since obviously it is not; but it is rather said to be potentially a man when the seed has already been generated from a preceding matter. And perhaps it never is potentially a man, as will be shown below.

1833. **Therefore, in like manner** [2].

Second, he answers the question which was raised; and in regard to this he does two things. First, he explains the sort of disposition which matter must have in order to be said to be in potency to actuality. Second [3], he shows that it is only what is in matter that gets its name from matter disposed in some particular way ("Now it seems").

In regard to the first it must be understood, as he said above in Book VII (n. 1411), that the effects of certain arts may also come about without art; for while a house is not produced without art, health may be produced without the art of medicine through the operation of nature alone. And even though what comes to be by nature may not be fortuitous or a result of chance, since nature is an efficient cause in the proper sense, whereas fortune or chance is an efficient cause in an accidental sense, nevertheless, because the one who is healed by nature is healed without the application of any art, he is said to be healed by chance. For nothing prevents an effect which is not fortuitous in itself from being said to be fortuitous in relation to someone who does not consider the proper cause of such an effect.

1834. Hence he says that it is not just anyone at all or anyone disposed in any way at all who is healed by medicine or by chance; but it is someone having the capability by reason of a definite disposition who is healed either by nature or by art; for to all active principles there correspond definite passive principles. And it is the thing having this capability, which nature or art can bring to a state of actual health by a single action, that is potentially healthy.

1835. And in order that this kind of capability or potency may be more fully known he adds its definition both with reference to the operation of art and to that of nature. Hence he says that the capable or potential is what comes to exist actually from existing potentially as a result of intellect or art. For "the intelligible expression," or definition, of the capable is this: it is something which the artist immediately brings to actuality when he wills it if no external impediment hinders it. And the patient is then said to be potentially healthy, because he becomes healthy by a single action of art. However, in the case of those who are healed by nature, each is said to be potentially healthy when there is nothing hindering health which has to be removed or changed before the healing power within the patient produces its effect in the act of healing.

1836. Now what we have said about the act of healing, which is brought about by the art of healing, can also be said about the other activities produced by the other arts. For matter is potentially a house when none of the things present in the matter prevent the house from being brought into being immediately by a single action, and when there is nothing that should be added or taken away or changed before the matter is formed into a house, as clay must be changed before bricks are made from it; and as something must be taken away from trees by hewing them and something added by joining them so that a house may be brought into being. Clay and trees, then, are not potentially houses, but bricks and wood already prepared are.

1837. And the same holds true in the case of other things whether their principle of perfection is outside of them, as in the case of artificial things, or within them, as in the case of natural things. And they are always in potency to actuality when they can be brought to actuality by their proper efficient principle without any external thing hindering them. However, seed is not such, for an animal must be produced from it through many changes; but when by its proper active principle, i.e., something in a state of actuality, it can already become such, it is then already in potency.

1838. But those things which have to be changed before they are immediately capable of being brought to actuality require a different efficient principle, namely, the one preparing the matter, which is sometimes different from the one finishing it off, which induces the final form. For example, it is obvious that earth is not yet potentially a statue, for it is not brought to actuality by a single action or by a single agent; but first it is changed by nature and becomes bronze, and afterwards it becomes a statue by art.

1839. **Now it seems** [3].

Here he shows that a compound derives its name from such matter which is in potency to actuality; and in regard to this he does three things.

First, he shows how a compound derives its name from matter, saying that what is produced from matter is not called a *that* but a *thaten (ecininum).* This expression is not used in the Latin but it is used according to the custom of the Greeks to designate what comes from something else as from matter, as if to say that matter is not predicated abstractly of what comes from it, but derivatively, as a chest is not wood but wooden; and as wood is not earth but earthen. And, again, if earth should have another matter prior to it, earth would not be that matter but "thaten," i.e., it will not be predicated of earth abstractly but derivatively.

1840. Yet such predication is made, because what is potential in a definite way is always predicated of the thing which immediately comes after it. For example, earth, which cannot be said to be potentially a chest, is not predicated of a chest either abstractly or derivately; for a chest is neither earth nor earthen but wooden, because wood is potentially a chest and the matter of a chest. Wood in general is the matter of a chest in general, and this particular wood is the matter of this particular chest.

1841. But if there is some first thing which is not referred to something else as a "thaten," i.e., something which does not have something else predicated of it derivatively in the above way, this will be first matter. For example, if air is the matter of earth, as some have said (n. 86), air will be predicated derivatively of earth, so that earth will be said to be *of* air. And similarly air will be said to be *of* fire and not fire, if fire is its matter. But if fire does not get its name from any prior matter, it will be first matter, according to the position of Heraclitus (n. 87). But here it is necessary to add "if it is something subsistent" in order to distinguish it from a universal; for a universal is predicated of other things but other things are not predicated of it—yet it is not matter, since it is not something subsistent. For a universal and a subject differ in that a subject is a particular thing whereas a universal is not.

1842. **For example** [4].

Second, he gives an example of derivative predication, saying that just as the subject of modifications, for example, man, body, or animal, has modifications predicated of it derivatively, in a similar fashion matter is predicated derivatively of that which comes from matter. Now "the modification is musical and white"; but the subject to which music accrues is not called music in the abstract, but is called musical derivatively; and man is not called whiteness but white. Nor again is man called walking or motion in the abstract, but what walks or is moved "as a thaten," i.e., what gets a name [from something else].

1843. **Therefore all** [5].

Third, he compares both methods of giving names to things. He says that all those names which are predicated derivately in this way, as the accidents mentioned, have substance as the ultimate subject which sustains them; but in all those cases in which the predicate is not derivative but is a form or a particular thing, such as wood or earth, in such predications the ultimate subject sustaining the rest is matter or material substance. And it is only fitting "that the term 'thaten' happens to be predicated" derivatively "of matter and the modifying attributes," i.e., accidents, both of which are indeterminate. For an accident is both made determinate and defined by means of its subject, and matter by means of that to which it is in potency. Lastly he summarizes his remarks, and this part is evident.

LESSON 7
The Conceptual and Temporal Priority of Actuality to Potency and Vice Versa

ARISTOTLE'S TEXT Chapter 8: 1049b4–1050a3

1. Since we have established the different senses in which the term prior is employed, it is evident that actuality is prior to potency. And by potency I mean not only that definite kind which is said to be a principle of change in another thing inasmuch as it is other, but in general every principle of motion or rest. For nature also belongs to the same thing, since it is in the same genus as potency; for it is a principle of motion, although not in another thing but in something inasmuch as it is the same. Therefore actuality is prior to all such potency both in intelligibility and in substance; and in time it is prior in one sense, and in another it is not. **1094b4–12**

2. It is evident, then, that actuality is prior to potency in intelligibility; for what is potential in a primary sense is potential because it is possible for it to become actual. I mean, for example, that it is what is capable of building that can build, and what is capable of theorizing that can theorize, and what is capable of being seen that can be seen. And the same reasoning also applies in the case of other things; and therefore it is necessary that the conception or knowledge of the one should precede that of the other. **1049b12–17**

3. And actuality is prior to potency in time in the sense that an actuality which is specifically but not numerically the same as a potency is prior to it. I mean that the matter and the seed and the thing capable of seeing, which are a man and grain and seeing potentially but not yet actually, are prior in time to this man and to grain and to the act of seeing which exist actually. But prior to these are other actually existing things from which these have been produced; for what is actual is always produced from something potential by means of something which is actual. Thus man comes from man and musician from musician; for there is always some primary mover, and a mover is already something actual. And in our previous discussions concerning substance it was stated that everything which comes to be is produced from something, and this is specifically the same as itself. **1049b17–29**

4. And for this reason it seems to be impossible that anyone should be a builder who has not built something, or that anyone should be a harpist who has not played the harp. And the same holds true of all others who are learning; for one who is learning to play the harp learns to play it by playing it. And the same holds true in other cases. **1049b29–32**

5. From this arose the sophistical argument that one who does not have a science will be doing the thing which is the object of this science; for one who is learning a science does not have it. **1049b33–34**

6. But since some part of what is coming to be has come to be, and in general some part of what is being moved has been moved (as became evident in our discussions on motion), perhaps one who is learning a science must have some part of that science. Hence it is also clear from this that actuality is prior to potency both in the process of generation and in time. **1049b35–1050a3**

COMMENTARY

1844. Having established the truth about potency and actuality, the Philosopher now compares one with the other; and this is divided into two parts. In the first part [1] he compares them from the viewpoint of priority and posteriority; in the second (Lesson 10), in terms of being better or worse ("Furthermore, that"); and in the third (Lesson 10, [5]), in reference to knowledge of the true and the false ("And it is").

In regard to the first he does two things. First, he explains his aim, saying that, since it has been established above, in Book V (n. 936), that the term *prior* is used in different senses, it is evident that actuality is prior to potency in different ways. And we are now speaking of potency not only inasmuch as it is a principle of motion in some other thing as other, as active potency was defined above (n. 1776), but universally of every principle, whether it be a principle that causes motion or a principle of immobility or rest or a principle of action devoid of motion (e.g., understanding), because nature also seems to belong to the same thing as potency.

1845. For nature is in the same genus as potency itself because each is a principle of motion, although nature is not a principle of motion in some other thing but in the thing in which it is present as such, as is made clear in Book II of the ***Physics***. [192b23] However, nature is a principle not only of motion but also of immobility. Hence actuality is prior to all such potency both in intelligibility and in substance. And in one sense it is also prior in time, and in another it is not.

1846. **It is evident** [2].

Second he proves his thesis. First [2], he shows that actuality is prior to potency in intelligibility. Second [3], he shows how it is prior in time, and how it is not ("And actuality"). Third (Lesson 10), he shows how it is prior in substance ("But actuality").

The first is proved as follows: anything that must be used in defining something else is prior to it in intelligibility, as animal is prior to man and subject to accident. But potency or capability can only be defined by means of actuality, because the first characteristic of the capable consists in the possibility of its acting or being actual. For example, a builder is defined as one who can build, and a theorist as one who can theorize, and the visible as what can be seen; and the same is true in other cases. The concept of actuality must therefore be prior to the concept of potency, and the knowledge of actuality prior to the knowledge of potency. Hence Aristotle explained above what potency is by defining it in reference to actuality, but he could not define actuality by means of something else but only made it known inductively.

1847. **And actuality** [3].

Then he shows how actuality is prior to potency in time, and how it is not. In regard to this he does two things. First [3], he makes this clear in the case of passive potencies; and second [4], in the case of certain active potencies ("And for this reason").

He accordingly says, first [3], that actuality is prior to potency in time in the sense that in the same species the agent, or what is actual, is prior to what is potential; but in numerically one and the same thing what is potential is prior in time to what is actual.

1848. This is shown as follows: if we take this man who is now actually a man, prior to him in time there was a matter which was potentially a man. And similarly seed, which is potentially grain, was prior in time to what is actually grain. And "the thing capable of seeing," i.e., having the power of sight, was prior in time to the thing actually seeing. And prior in time to the things having potential being there were certain things having actual being, namely, agents, by which the former have been brought to actuality. For what exists potentially must always be brought to actuality by an agent, which is an actual being. Hence what is potentially a man becomes actually a man as a result of the man who generates him, who is an actual being; and similarly one who is potentially musical becomes actually musical by learning from a teacher who is actually musical. And thus in the case of anything potential there is always some first thing which moves it, and this mover is actual. It follows, then, that even though the same thing numerically exists potentially prior in time to existing actually, there is still also some actual being of the same species which is prior in time to the one that exists potentially.

1849. And because someone could be perplexed about some of the statements which he had made, he therefore adds that these have been explained above; for it was pointed out in the foregoing discussions about substance—in Book VII (nn. 1383, 1417)—that everything which comes to be comes from something as matter, and by something as an agent. And it was also stated above that this agent is specifically the same as the thing which comes to be. This was made clear in the case of univocal generations, but in the case of equivocal generations there must also be some likeness between the generator and the thing generated, as was shown elsewhere (nn. 1444–47).

1850. **And for this reason** [4].

He explains the temporal sequence of actuality and potency in the case of certain active potencies; and in regard to this he does three things.

First, he explains what he intends to do. For it was said above (n. 1815) that there are certain operative potencies whose very actions must be understood to be performed or exercised beforehand, as those acquired by practice or instruction. And with regard to these he says here that in those things which are numerically the same, actuality is also prior to potency. For it seems impossible that anyone should become a builder who has not first built something; or that anyone should become a harpist who has not first played the harp.

1851. He draws this conclusion from the points laid down above; for it was said above (n. 1848) that one who is potentially musical becomes actually musical as a result of someone who is actually musical—meaning that he learns from him; and the same thing holds true of other actions. Now one could not learn an art of this kind unless he himself performed the actions associated with it; for one learns to play the harp by playing it. This is also true of the other arts. It has been shown, then, that it is impossible to have potencies of this sort unless their actions are also first present in one and the same subject numerically.

1852. **From this arose** [5].

Second, he raises a sophistical objection against the above view. He says that "a sophistical argument arose," i.e., an apparently cogent syllogism which contradicts the truth, and it runs as follows: one who is learning an art exercises the actions of that art. But one who is learning an art does not have that art. Hence one who does not have a science or an art is doing the thing which is the object of that science or art. This seems to be contrary to the truth.

1853. **But since some** [6].

Third, he answers this objection by stating a position which was discussed and proved in the ***Physics***, Book VI [236b33]; for there he proved that being moved is always prior to having been moved, because of the division of motion. For whenever any part of a motion is given, since it is divisible, we must be able to pick out some part of it which has already been completed, while the part of the motion given is going on. Therefore whatever is being moved has already been partly moved.

1854. And by the same argument, whatever is coming to be has already partly come to be; for even though the process of producing a substance, with reference to the introduction of the substantial form, is indivisible, still if we take the preceding alteration whose terminus is generation, the process is divisible, and the whole process can be called a production. Therefore, since what is coming to be has partly come to be, then what is coming to be can possess to some degree the activity of the thing in which the production is terminated. For example, what is becoming hot can heat something to some degree, but not as perfectly as something that has already become hot. Hence, since to learn is to become scientific, the one learning must already have, as it were, some part of a science or an art. It is not absurd, then, if he should exercise the action of an art to some degree; for he does not do it as perfectly as one who already has the art.

1855. But in reason itself there are also naturally inherent certain seeds or principles of the sciences and virtues, through which a man can pass to some degree into the activity of a science or a virtue before he has the habit of the science or the virtue; and when this has been acquired he acts perfectly, whereas at first he acted imperfectly. Lastly he summarizes the above discussion, as is evident in the text.

LESSON 8
Priority of Actuality to Potency in Substance

ARISTOTLE'S TEXT Chapter 8: 1050a4–1050b6

1. *But actuality is also prior in substance; (1) because those things which are subsequent in generation are prior in form and substance; for example, man is prior to boy, and human being to seed; for the one already has its form, but the other has not.* **1050a4–7**

2. *And (2) because everything which comes to be moves toward a principle, namely, its goal [or end]. For that for the sake of which a thing comes to be is a principle; and generation is for the sake of the goal. And actuality is the goal, and it is for the sake of this that potency is acquired.* **1050a7–10**

3. *For animals do not see in order that they may have the power of sight, but they have the power of sight in order that they may see.* **1050a10–11**

4. *And similarly men have the science of building in order that they may build, and they have theoretical knowledge in order that they may speculate; but they do not speculate in order that they may have theoretical knowledge, unless they are learning by practice. And these latter do not speculate [in a perfect way], but either to some degree or because they do not need to speculate.* **1050a11–14**

5. *Further, matter is in potency up to the time at which it attains its form; but when it exists actually, it then possesses its form. And the same holds true in the case of other things, even of those whose goal is motion. And for this reason, just as those who are teaching think that they have reached their goal when they exhibit their student performing, so it is with nature.* **1050a15–19**

6. *For if this were not so, Pauson's Mercury would exist again, because it would not be more evident whether scientific knowledge is internal or external, as is the case with the figure of Mercury. For the activity is the goal, and the actuality is the activity. And for this reason the term actuality is used in reference to activity and is extended to completeness.* **1050a19–23**

7. *But while in the case of some things the ultimate effect is the use (as, for example, in the case of sight the ultimate effect is the act of seeing, and no other work besides this results from the power of sight), still from some potencies something else is produced; for example, the art of building produces a house in addition to the act of building. Yet in neither case is the act any less or any more the end of the potency; for the act of building is in the thing being built, and it comes into being and exists simultaneously with the house. Therefore in those cases in which the result is something other than the use, the actuality is in the thing being produced; for example, the act of building is in the thing being built, and the act of weaving in the thing being woven. The same holds true in all other cases. And in general, motion is in the thing being moved. But in the case of those things in which nothing else is produced besides the activity, the activity is present in these, as the act of seeing is in the one seeing, and the act of speculating in the one speculating, and life in the soul. Accordingly, happiness is in the soul, for it is a kind of life.* **1050a23–1050b2**

8. *It is evident, then, that substance or form is actuality. Hence it is clear according to this argument that actuality is prior to potency in substance. And, as we have said (780), one actuality is always prior to another in time right back to that actuality which is always the first principle of motion.* **1050b2–6**

COMMENTARY

1856. Having shown that actuality is prior to potency in intelligibility and in one sense in time, the Philosopher now shows that it is prior in substance. This was the third way given above (n. 1845) in which actuality is prior to potency.

This is divided into two parts. In the first part [1] he proves his thesis by arguments taken from things which are sometimes potential and sometimes actual. In the second part (Lesson 9) he proves his thesis by comparing eternal things, which are always actual, with mobile things, which are sometimes actual and sometimes potential ("But actuality").

And since to be prior in substance is to be prior in perfection, and since perfection is attributed to two things, namely, to the form and to the goal [or end], therefore in the first part he uses two arguments to prove his thesis. The first of these pertains to the form, and the second [2] to the goal, given at the words, "And (2) because."

He accordingly says, first [1], that actuality is prior to potency not only in intelligibility and in time "but in substance," i.e., in perfection; for the form by which something is perfected is customarily signified by the term *substance.* This first part is made clear by this argument: those things which are subsequent in generation are "prior in substance and form," i.e., in perfection, because the process of generation always goes from what is imperfect to what is perfect; for example, in the process of generation man is subsequent to boy, because man comes from boy; and human being is subsequent to seed. The reason is that man and human being already have a perfect form, whereas boy and seed do not yet have such a form. Hence, since in numerically one and the same subject actuality is subsequent to potency both in generation and in time, as is evident from the above, it follows that actuality is prior to potency in substance and in intelligibility.

1857. **And (2) because** [2].

Here he proves the same point by an argument involving the goal of activity. First, he sets forth the argument. Second [3], he explains one of the principles assumed in his argument ("For animals"). Third [7], he settles an issue which could cause difficulty in the above argument ("But while").

He accordingly says, first, that everything which comes to be when it moves towards its goal moves towards a principle. For a goal, or that for the sake of which a thing comes to be, is a principle because it is the first thing intended by an agent, since it is that for the sake of which generation takes place. But actuality is the goal of potency, and therefore actuality is prior to potency and is one of its principles.

1858. **For animals** [3].

He now explains the position which he maintained above, namely, that actuality is the goal of potency. He makes this clear, first, in the case of natural active potencies. He says that animals do not see in order that they may have the power of sight, but they rather have the power of sight in order that they may see. Thus it is clear that potency exists for the sake of actuality and not vice versa.

1859. **And similarly** [4].

Second, he makes the same thing clear in the case of rational potencies. He says that men have the power of building in order that they may build; and they have "theoretical knowledge," or speculative science, in order that they may speculate. However, they do not speculate in order that they may have theoretical knowledge, unless they are learning and meditating about those matters which belong to a speculative science in order that they may acquire it. And these do not speculate perfectly but to some degree and imperfectly, as has been said above (nn. 1853–55), because speculation is not undertaken because of some need but for the sake of using science already acquired. But there is speculation on the part of those who are learning because they need to acquire science.

1860. **Further, matter** [5].

Third he makes the same point clear in the case of passive potencies. He says that matter is in potency until it receives a form or specifying principle, but then it is first in a state of actuality when it receives its form. And this is what occurs in the case of all other things which are moved for the sake of a goal. Hence, just as those who are teaching think they have attained their goal when they exhibit their pupil whom they have instructed performing those activities which belong to his art, in a similar fashion nature attains its goal when it attains actuality. Hence it is made evident in the case of natural motion that actuality is the goal of potency.

1861. **For if this were not** [6].

Fourth, he proves his thesis by an argument from the untenable consequences. He says that if a thing's perfection and goal do not consist in actuality, there would then seem to be no difference between someone wise, as Mercury was, and someone foolish, as Pauson was. For if the perfection of science were not in the one acting, Mercury would not have exhibited it in his own science, if he had "internal scientific knowledge," i.e., in reference to its internal activity, "or external," i.e., in reference to its external activity, as neither would Pauson. For it is by means of the actual use of scientific knowledge, and not by means of the potency or power, that one is shown to have a science; because activity is the goal of a science, and activity is a kind of actuality. And for this reason the term actuality is derived from activity, as has been stated above (n. 1805); and from this it was extended to form, which is called completeness or perfection.

1862. **But while** [7].

He explains a point which could cause a difficulty in the foregoing argument. For since he had said that some product is the goal of activity, one could think that this is true in all cases. But he denies this, saying that the ultimate goal or end of some active potencies consists in the mere use of those potencies, and not in something produced by their activity; for example, the ultimate goal of the power of sight is the act of seeing, and there is no product resulting from the power of sight in addition to this activity. But in the case of some active potencies something else is produced in addition to the activity; for example, the art of building also produces a house in addition to the activity of building.

1863. However, this difference does not cause actuality to be the goal of potency to a lesser degree in the case of some of these potencies and to a greater degree in the case of others; for the activity is in the thing produced, as the act of building in the thing being built; and it comes into being and exists simultaneously with the house. Hence if the house, or the thing built, is the goal, this does not exclude actuality from being the goal of potency.

1864. Now it is necessary to consider such a difference among the aforesaid potencies, because when something else is produced besides the actuality of these potencies, which is activity, the activity of such potencies is in the thing being produced and is their actuality, just as the act of building is in the thing being built, and the act of weaving in the thing being woven, and in general motion in the thing being moved. And this is true, because when some product results from the activity of a potency, the activity perfects the thing being produced and not the one performing it. Hence it is in the thing being produced as an actuality and perfection of it, but not in the one who is acting.

1865. But when nothing else is produced in addition to the activity of the potency, the actuality then exists in the agent as its perfection and does not pass over into something external in order to perfect it; for example, the act of seeing is in the one seeing as his perfection, and the act of speculating is in the one speculating, and life is in the soul (if we understand by life vital activity). Hence it has been shown that happiness also consists in an activity of the kind which exists in the one acting, and not of the kind which passes over into something external; for happiness is a good of the one who is happy, namely, his perfect life. Hence, just as life is in one who lives, in a similar fashion happiness is in one who is happy. Thus it is evident that happiness does not consist either in building or in any activity of the kind which passes over into something external, but it consists in understanding and willing.

1866. **It is evident** [8].

Lastly he retraces his steps in order to draw the main conclusion which he has in mind. He says that it has been shown from the above discussion that a thing's substance or form or specifying principle is a kind of actuality; and from this it is evident that actuality is prior to potency in substance or form. And it is prior in time, as has been stated above (n. 1848), because the actuality whereby the generator or mover or maker is actual must always exist first before the other actuality by which the thing generated or produced becomes actual after being potential. And this goes on until one comes to the first mover, which is actuality alone; for whatever passes from potency to actuality requires a prior actuality in the agent, which brings it to actuality.

LESSON 9

The Substantial Priority of Actuality in Incorruptible Things

ARISTOTLE'S TEXT Chapter 8: 1050b6–1051a3

1. *But actuality is prior to potency in a more fundamental sense; for eternal things are prior in substance to corruptible ones, and nothing eternal is potential.* **1050b6–8**

2. *The reason of this is that every potency is at the same time a potency for opposite determinations. For what is incapable of existing does not exist in any way; and it is possible for everything that is capable of existing not to exist actually. Therefore whatever is capable of existing may either be or not be, and thus the same thing is capable both of being and of not being. But what is capable of not being may possibly not be; and what may possibly not be is corruptible: either absolutely, or in the sense in which it is said to be possible for it not to be, either according to place or to quantity or to quality. And the term absolutely means in reference to substance.* **1050b8–16**

3. *Therefore nothing that is incorruptible in an absolute sense is potential in an absolute sense. But there is nothing that hinders it from being so in other respects, for example, in reference to quality or to place. Therefore all incorruptible things are actual.* **1050b16–18**

4. *And none of those things which exist necessarily are potential. In fact such things are the first; for if they did not exist, nothing would exist.* **1050b18–19**

5. *Nor is eternal motion potential, if there be such a thing; and if anything is moved eternally, it is not moved potentially except in reference to whence and whither. And nothing prevents the matter of this sort of thing from existing.* **1050b20–22**

6. *And for this reason the sun and the stars and the entire heaven are always active, and there is no need to fear, as the natural philosophers do, that they may at some time stand still. Nor do they tire in their activity; for in them there is no potency for opposite determinations, as there is in corruptible things, so that the continuity of their motion should be tiresome. For the cause of this is that their substance is matter and potency and not actuality.* **1050b22–28**

7. *Moreover, incorruptible things are imitated by those which are in a state of change, such as fire and earth; for these latter things are always active, since they have motion in themselves and of themselves.* **1050b28–30**

8. *But all other potencies which have been defined are potencies for opposite determinations; for what is capable of moving something else in this way is also capable of not moving it in this way, i.e., all those things which act by reason. And irrational potencies will also be potencies for opposite determinations by being absent or not.* **1050b30–34**

9. *If, then, there are any natures or substances such as those thinkers who in their theories proclaim the Ideas to be, there will be something much more scientific than science itself, and something much more mobile than motion itself; for the former will rather be the actualities and the latter the potencies of these. Hence it is evident that actuality is prior to potency and to every principle of change.* **1050b34–1051a3**

COMMENTARY

1867. Aristotle proved above that actuality is prior to potency in substance, definition and perfection, by arguments drawn from corruptible things themselves; but here he proves the same point by comparing eternal things with corruptible ones.

This part is divided into two members. In the first [1] he proves his thesis; and in the second [9], by the thesis thus proved, he rejects a certain statement made by Plato ("If, then").

In regard to the first he does two things. First, he proves his thesis. This he does by the following argument: eternal things are compared to corruptible ones as actuality to potency; for eternal things as such are not in potency, whereas corruptible things as such are in potency. But eternal things are prior to corruptible ones in substance and perfection; for this is evident (n. 1856). Hence actuality is prior to potency both in substance and perfection. He says that his thesis is proved in a more proper way by this argument, because actuality and potency are not considered in the same subject but in different ones, and this makes the proof more evident.

1868. **The reason** [2].

Second, he proves one assumption which he made, namely, that nothing eternal is in potency; and in regard to this he does two things. First, he gives an argument to prove this, and it runs as follows: every potency is at one and the same time a potency for opposite determinations. Now he does not say this about active potency, for it has already been shown (n. 1789) that irrational potencies are not potencies for opposite determinations; but he is speaking here of passive potency, on the basis of which a thing is said to be capable of being and not being either absolutely or in a qualified sense.

1869. Now the claim which he made he proves by an argument to the contrary; because where such potency does not exist, neither of the opposite determinations is possible; for what is incapable of being never exists in any way. For if a thing is incapable of being, it is impossible for it to be, and it is necessary for it not to be. But what is capable of being may possibly not be actual. Hence it is evident that what is capable of being may either be or not be; and thus the potency is at one and the same time a potency for opposite determinations, because the same thing is in potency both to being and non-being.

1870. But what is capable of not being may possibly not be, for these two statements are equivalent ones. Moreover, what may possibly not be is corruptible either absolutely or in a qualified sense inasmuch as it is said to be possible for it not to be. For example, if it is possible for some body not to be in place, that body is corruptible as far as place is concerned; and the same applies to quantity and quality. But that is corruptible in an absolute sense which is capable of not existing substantially. Therefore it follows that everything potential inasmuch as it is potential is corruptible.

1871. **Therefore nothing** [3].

Second, he draws from the foregoing the conclusion at which he aims; and in regard to this he does three things. First, he concludes to this thesis about eternal things, inferring from the observations made above that, if everything potential is corruptible, it follows that nothing which is incorruptible in an absolute sense is a potential being, provided that we understand incorruptible things in an absolute sense and potential being in an absolute sense in reference to substance.

1872. But nothing prevents something that is incorruptible in an absolute sense from being potential in a qualified sense, in reference either to quality or to place. For example, the moon is in a state of potency to being illuminated by the sun; and when the sun is in the east it is in a state of potency with regard to being in the west. It is evident from what has been said, then, that all eternal things as such are actual.

1873. **And none** [4].

Second, he comes to the same conclusion about necessary things as he did about eternal things, because even in corruptible things there are certain necessary aspects; for example, man is an animal, and every whole is greater than its part. Hence he says that nothing necessary is potential; for necessary things are always actual and incapable of being or not being. And those things which are necessary are the first of all things, because if they ceased to exist, none of the others would exist; for example, if essential predicates, which are referred to a subject necessarily, were taken away, accidental predicates, which can be present and not present in some subject, could not be present in any subject. It follows, then, that actuality is prior to potency.

1874. **Nor is** [5].

Third, he comes to the same conclusion about eternal motion as he did about eternal substances; and in regard to this he does three things. First, from what has been said above he concludes to his thesis. He says that, if some motion is eternal, that motion is not potential; nor is anything that is moved eternally in a state of potency to motion, but it is in a state of potency to this or to that place, i.e., inasmuch as it goes from this place to that place. For since motion is the actuality of something in potency, everything which is being moved must be in potency to the goal of that motion, not however as regards motion itself, but as regards some place to which it tends by its motion.

1875. And since what is being moved must have matter, he adds that nothing prevents a thing which is being moved by an eternal motion from having matter; because, even though it is not in potency to motion in an absolute sense, it is nevertheless in potency to this or to that place.

1876. **And for this** [6].

Second, he draws a corollary from the above discussion. For since what is being moved by an eternal motion is not in potency to motion itself (and the motion of the heavens is eternal according to the discussion in Book VIII of the **Physics** *[252b5]*), it follows that the sun and the moon and the stars and the entire heaven are always active, because they are always being moved and are acting by means of their motion.

1877. Nor is it to be feared that at some time the motion of the heavens may cease, as "some of the natural philosophers feared it would," namely, Empedocles and his followers, who held that at times the world is destroyed by discord and is restored again by friendship. Hence he says that this is not to be feared, because they are not potentially immobile.

1878. And for this reason too incorruptible things insofar as they are being moved do not tire in their activity, because "the potency for opposite determinations" is not found in them, namely, the ability to be both moved and not moved, as is found in corruptible things, which have these as a result of motion. And thus in this way continuous motion becomes laborious for them. For corruptible things labor insofar as they are moved; and the reason is that they are in a state of potency both for being moved and not being moved, and it is not proper to them by reason of their substantial nature always to be undergoing motion. Hence we see that the more laborious any motion is, the nearer also does the nature of the thing come to immobility;

for example, in the case of animals it is evident that motion in an upward direction is more laborious.

1879. Now what he says here about the continuity of celestial motion is in keeping with the nature of a celestial body, which we know by experience. But this is not prejudicial to the divine will, on which the motion and being of the heavens depend.

1880. **Moreover, incorruptible things** [7].

Third, he compares corruptible bodies with incorruptible ones from the viewpoint of activity. First, he does this insofar as they are alike. He says that the bodies of those things whose being involves change resemble incorruptible bodies insofar as they are always acting; for example, fire, which of itself always produces heat, and earth, which of itself always produces proper and natural activities. And this is true because they have motion and their own proper activity of themselves—inasmuch, namely, as their forms are principles of such motions and activities.

1881. **But all the other** [8].

Second, he compares them insofar as they are unlike. He says that in contrast with eternal things, which are always actual, the other potencies of mobile things, about which the truth has been established above, are all potencies for opposite determinations. But this is verified in a different way; for rational potencies are potencies capable of opposite determinations because they can move in this way or not, as has been said above (n. 1789); whereas irrational potencies, though acting in one way, are themselves also potencies of opposite determinations in view of the fact that they can be present in a subject or not; for example, an animal can lose its power of vision.

1882. **If, then** [9].

As a result of what has been said he rejects a doctrine of Plato. For Plato claimed that there are certain separate Forms, which he held to have being in the highest degree; say, a separate science, which he called *science-in-itself;* and he said that this is foremost in the class of knowable entities. And similarly he maintained that *motion-in-itself* is foremost in the class of mobile things. But according to the points made clear above, something else besides science-in-itself will be first in the class of knowable things; for it was shown that actuality is prior to potency in perfection, and science itself is a kind of potency. Hence speculation, which is the activity of science, will be more perfect than science is; and the same will apply in the case of other things of this kind. Lastly he summarizes his discussion, saying that actuality is prior to potency and to every principle of motion.

LESSON 10
The Relative Excellence of Actuality and Potency

ARISTOTLE'S TEXT Chapter 9: 1051a4–1051a33

1. *Furthermore, that actuality is also better and more excellent and more honorable than good potency is evident from the following: all things which are spoken of as potential are alike capable of contrary determinations; for example, what is said to be capable of being well is the same as what is capable of being ill, and simultaneously has both capabilities; for it is the same potency that is capable of being well and being ill, and of being at rest and in motion, and of building and demolishing, and of being built and being demolished. Therefore the capacity for contrary determinations belongs to the same thing at the same time; but it is impossible for contrary determinations to belong to the same thing at the same time, for example, being well and ailing. Hence one of these must be good; but the potency may be both alike or neither; and therefore the actuality is better.* **1051a4–15**

2. *And also in the case of evil things the goal or actuality must be worse than the potency; for it is the same potency that is capable of both contraries.* **1051a15–17**

3. *It is clear, then, that evil does not exist apart from things; for evil is by its very nature subsequent to potency.* **1051a17–19**

4. *Hence in those things which exist from the very beginning and are eternal, there is neither evil nor wrong nor corruption; for corruption belongs to evil things.* **1051a19–21**

5. *And it is also by activity that geometrical constructions are discovered, because they are discovered by dividing. For if they had already been divided, they would be evident; but they are now present potentially. Why, for example, are the angles of a triangle equal to two right angles? Because the angles grouped around one point are equal to two right angles. Hence, if the line next to the one side were extended, the answer would be clear to anyone seeing the construction. Again, why is an angle in a semicircle always a right angle? Because, if its three lines are equal, two of which form the base and the other rests upon the middle point of the base, the answer will be evident to anyone who sees the construction and knows the former proposition. Hence, it is evident that constructions which exist potentially are discovered when they are brought to actuality; and the reason is that the intellectual comprehension of a thing is an actuality. Hence the potency proceeds from an actuality, and it is because people make these constructions that they attain knowledge of them. For in a thing numerically one and the same, actuality is subsequent in the order of generation.* **1051a21–33**

COMMENTARY

1883. Having compared actuality and potency from the viewpoint of priority and posteriority, the Philosopher now compares them from the viewpoint of good and evil; and in regard to this he does two things.

First [1], he says that in the case of good things actuality is better than potency; and this was made clear from the fact that the potential is the same as what is capable of contrary determinations; for example, what can be well can also be ill and is in potency to both at the same time. The reason is that the potency for both is the same—for being well and ailing, and for being at rest and in motion, and for other opposites of this kind. Thus it is evident that a thing can be in potency to contrary determinations, although contrary determinations cannot be actual at the same time. Therefore, taking each contrary pair separately, one is good, as health, and the other evil, as illness. For in the case of contraries one of the two always has the character of something defective, and this pertains to evil.

1884. Therefore what is actually good is good alone. But the potency may be related "to both" alike, i.e., in a qualified sense—as being in potency. But it is neither in an absolute sense—as being actual. It follows, then, that actuality is better than potency; because what is good in an absolute sense is better than what is good in a qualified sense and is connected with evil.

1885. **And also** [2].

Second, he shows on the other hand that in the case of evil things the actuality is worse than the potency; and in regard to this he does three things.

First, he proves his thesis by the argument introduced above; for what is evil in an absolute sense and is not disposed to evil in a qualified sense is worse than what is evil in a qualified sense and is disposed both to evil and to good. Hence, since the potency for evil is not yet evil, except in a qualified sense (and the same potency is disposed to good, since it is the same potency which is related to contrary determinations), it follows that actual evil is worse than the potency for evil.

1886. **It is clear, then** [3].

Second, he concludes from what has been said that evil itself is not a nature distinct from other things which are good by nature; for evil itself is subsequent in nature to potency, because it is worse and is farther removed from perfection. Hence, since a potency cannot be something existing apart from a thing, much less can evil itself be something apart from a thing.

1887. **Hence in those** [4].

Third, he draws another conclusion. For if evil is worse than potency, and there is no potency in eternal things, as has been shown above (n. 1867), then in eternal things there will be neither evil nor wrong nor any other corruption; for corruption is a kind of evil. But this must be understood insofar as they are eternal and incorruptible; for nothing prevents them from being corrupted as regards place or some other accident of this kind.

1888. **And it is** [5].

Having compared potency and actuality from the viewpoint of priority and posteriority and from that of good and evil, he now compares them with reference to the understanding of the true and the false. In regard to this he does two things. First [5], he compares them with reference to the act of understanding; and second (Lesson 11), with reference to the true and the false ("Now the terms").

He accordingly says, first [5], that "geometrical constructions," i.e., geometrical descriptions, "are discovered," i.e., made known by discovery in the actual drawing of the figures. For geometers discover the truth which they seek by dividing lines and surfaces. And division brings into actual existence the things which exist potentially; for the parts of a continuous whole are in the whole potentially before division takes place. However, if all had been divided to the extent necessary for discovering the truth, the conclusions which are being sought would then be evident. But since divisions of this kind exist potentially in the first drawing of geometrical figures, the truth which is being sought does not therefore become evident immediately.

1889. He explains this by means of two examples, and the first of these has to do with the question, "Why are the angles of a triangle equal to two right angles?" i.e., why does a triangle have

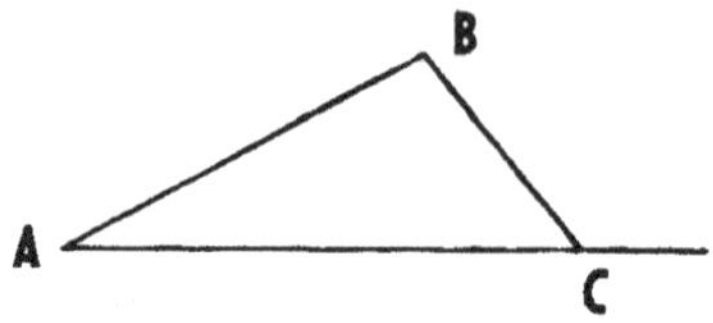

three angles equal to two right angles? This is demonstrated as follows.

Let ABC be a triangle having its base AC extended continuously and in a straight line. This extended base, then, together with the side BC of the triangle form an angle at point C, and this external angle is equal to the two interior angles opposite to it, i.e., angles ABC and BAC. Now it is evident that the two angles at point C, one exterior to the triangle and the other interior, are equal to two right angles; for it has been shown that, when one straight line falls upon another straight line, it makes two right angles or two angles equal to two right angles. Hence it follows that the interior angle at the point C together with the other two interior angles which are equal to the exterior angle, i.e., all three angles, are equal to two right angles.

1890. This, then, is what the Philosopher means when he says that it may be demonstrated that a triangle has two right angles, because the two angles which meet at the point C, one of which is interior to the triangle and the other exterior, are equal to two right angles. Hence when an angle is constructed which falls outside of the triangle and is formed by one of its sides, it immediately becomes evident to one who sees the arrangement of the figure that a triangle has three angles equal to two right angles.

1891. The second example has to do with the question, "Why is every angle

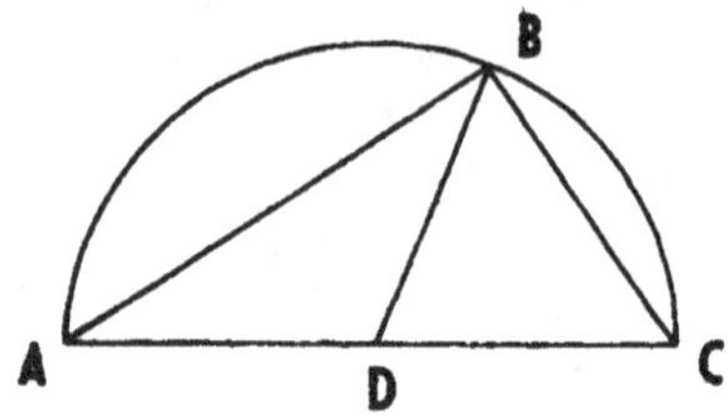

in a semicircle a right angle?" This is demonstrated as follows.

Let ABC be a semicircle, and at any point B let there be an angle subtended by the base AC, which is the diameter of the circle. I say, then, that angle B is a right angle. This is proved as follows: since the line AC is the diameter of the circle, it must pass through the center. Hence it is divided in the middle at the point D, and this is done by the line DB. Therefore the line DB is equal to the line DA, because both are drawn from the center to the circumference. In the triangle DBA, then, angle B and angle A are equal, because in every triangle having two equal sides the angles above the base are equal. Thus the two angles A and B are double the angle B alone. But the angle BDC, since it is exterior to the triangle, is equal to the two separate angles A and B. Therefore angle BDC is double the angle B alone.

1892. And it is demonstrated in the same way that angle C is equal to angle B of the triangle BDC, because the two sides DB and DC are equal since they are drawn from the center to the circumference, and the exterior angle, ADB, is equal to both. Therefore it is double the angle B alone. Hence the two angles ADB and BDC are double the whole angle ABC. But the two angles ADB and BDC are either right angles or equal to two right angles, because the line DB falls on the line AC.

Hence the angle ABC, which is in a semicircle, is a right angle.

1893. This is what the Philosopher means when he says that the angle in a semicircle may be shown to be a right angle, because the three lines are equal, namely, the two into which the base is divided, i.e., DA and DC, and the third line, BD, which is drawn from the middle of these two lines and rests upon these. And it is immediately evident to one who sees this construction, and who knows the principles of geometry, that every angle in a semicircle is a right angle.

1894. Therefore the Philosopher concludes that it has been shown that, when some things are brought from potency to actuality, their truth is then discovered. The reason for this is that understanding is an actuality, and therefore those things which are understood must be actual. And for this reason potency is known by actuality. Hence it is by making something actual that men attain knowledge, as is evident in the constructions described above. For in numerically one and the same thing actuality must be subsequent to potency in generation and in time, as has been shown above.

LESSON 11

The Reference of Truth and Falsity to Actuality. The Exclusion of Falsity from Simple and Eternal Things

ARISTOTLE'S TEXT Chapter 10: 1051a34–1052a11

1. *Now the terms being and non-being are used in one sense with reference to the categorical figures; and in another with reference to the potentiality or actuality of these or their contraries; and in still another sense they are referred most properly to truth and falsity.* **1051a34–1051b2**

2. *And in things this consists in being combined or being separated. Hence he who thinks that what is separated is separated, and that what is combined is combined, is right; but he who thinks about things otherwise than as they are, is wrong. And it is necessary to consider what we mean when we say that truth and falsity exist or do not exist. For it is not because we are right in thinking that you are white that you are white, but it is because you are white that in saying this we speak the truth.* **1051b2–9**

3. *Therefore, if some things are always combined and it is impossible for them to be separated, and others are always separated and it is impossible for them to be combined, and others admit of both contraries, then being consists in being combined and being one, and non-being consists in not being combined and being many. Therefore with regard to contingent things the same opinion or statement becomes true and false, and it is possible for it at one time to be true and at another to be false. But with regard to those things which are incapable of being otherwise than as they are, an opinion is not sometimes true and sometimes false, but one is always true and the other always false.* **1051b9–17**

4. *However, with regard to things which are not composite, what is being and non-being, and what is truth and falsity? For such things are not composite so as to exist when combined and not exist when separated; for example, the proposition "The wood is white," or the proposition "The diagonal is incommensurable." Nor will truth and falsity still be present in them in the same way as in other things. And just as truth is not the same in these things, in a similar fashion neither is being the same.* **1051b17–23**

5. *But truth or falsity is as follows: to come in contact with a thing and to express it is truth (for expression is not the same as affirmation), and not to come in contact with a thing is ignorance. For it is impossible to be deceived about a thing's quiddity, except in an accidental sense; and the same holds true in the case of incomposite things, for it is impossible to be deceived about them.* **1051b23–28**

6. *And they are all actual and not potential, for otherwise they would be generated and corrupted. But being itself is neither generated nor corrupted; otherwise it would be generated out of something. Therefore, regarding all those things which are really quiddities and actualities, it is impossible to be deceived about them, but one must either know them or not. But concerning them we may ask what they are, namely, whether they are such and such or not.* **1051b28–33**

7. *Now considering being in the sense of truth and non-being in the sense of falsity, in the case of composite beings there is truth if the thing is combined with the attribute attributed to it; in the case of simple beings the thing is just simply so. And if a thing is truly a being, it is so in some particular way; but if it is not, it does not exist at all. Again, truth means to know these beings, and there is neither falsity nor deception about them but only ignorance; but not ignorance such as blindness is, for blindness is as if one did not have intellective power at all.* **1051b33–1052a4**

8. *And concerning immobile things it is also evident that there is no deception about them as regards time, if one assumes that they are immobile. For example, if one assumes that a triangle*

does not change, he will not be of the opinion that at one time its angles are equal to two right angles and that at another time they are not; for otherwise it would change. But he might assume that one thing has such and such a property and that another has not; for example, one might assume that no even number is a prime number, or that some are and some are not. But this is impossible as regards one single number; for one will not assume that one thing is such and another is not; but whether he speaks truly or falsely, a thing is always disposed in the same way. **1052a4–11**

COMMENTARY

1895. Here the Philosopher compares actuality to potency with reference to truth and falsity; and in regard to this he does three things. First [1], he claims that truth and falsity are chiefly referred to actuality. Second [2], he explains what he aims to do ("And in things"). Third [8], he draws a corollary ("And concerning").

He accordingly says, first [1], that, since being and non-being, which is its opposite, are divided in two ways: first, into the different categories—substance, quantity, quality and so forth; and second, into the potency and actuality of one or the other of contraries (since either one of two contraries may be actual or potential), it follows that *true* and *false* are most properly predicated of what is actual.

1896. **And in things** [2].

He now proves his thesis; and in regard to this he does three things. First [2], he makes this clear in the case of continuous substances; and second [4], in that of simple substances ("However, with regard"). Third [8], he summarizes both of these ("Now considering").

In regard to the first he does two things. First, he explains his thesis, saying that in things "this," i.e., being true or false, consists merely in being combined or being separated. Hence one who thinks that to be separated which is separated in reality, has a true opinion—for example, one who thinks that man is not an ass. And the same is true of one who thinks that to be combined which is combined in reality—for example, one who thinks that man is an animal. But, on the other hand, one who relates things in thought in a different way than they are in their own proper nature has an erroneous opinion—for example, one who thinks that man is an ass, or that he is not an animal—because when a thing is or is not, it is then said to be true or false.

1897. This must be understood as follows: you are not white because we think truly that you are white; but conversely we think you are white because you are white. Hence it has been shown that the way in which a thing is disposed is the cause of truth both in thought and in speech.

1898. He adds this in order to clarify what he said above, namely, that in things truth and falsity consist in being combined and being separated. For the truth and falsity found in speech and in thought must be traced to a thing's disposition as their cause. Now when the intellect makes a combination, it receives two concepts, one of which is related to the other as a form; hence it takes one as being present in the other, because predicates are taken formally. Therefore, if such an operation of the intellect should be traced to a thing as its cause, then in composite substances the combination of matter and form, or also the combination of subject and accident, must serve as the foundation and cause of the truth in the combination which the intellect makes in itself and expresses in words. For example, when I say, "Socrates is a man," the truth of this enunciation is caused by combining the form *humanity* with *the individual matter* by means of which Socrates is *this* man; and when I say, "Man is white," the cause of the truth of this enunciation is the combining of whiteness with the subject. It is similar in other cases. And the same thing is evident in the case of separation.

1899. **Therefore, if** [3].

Second, he concludes from what has been said that, if the combining and separating of a thing is the cause of the truth and falsity in thought and in speech, the difference between truth and falsity in thought and in speech must be based on the difference between the combining and separating of what exists in reality. Now in reality such difference is found to involve combination and separation, because some things are always combined and it is impossible for them to be separated; for example, sentient nature is always united to the rational soul, and it is impossible for the latter to be separated from the former in such a way that the rational soul may exist without the power of sensation, although on the other hand a sentient soul can exist without reason. Again, some things are separated and it is impossible for them to be combined, for example, black and white, and the form of an ass and that of a man. Again, some things are open to contraries, because they can be combined and separated, as man and white and also running.

1900. However, the being in which the intellect's act of combining consists, inasmuch as there is affirmation, indicates a certain composition and union; whereas non-being, which negation signifies, does away with composition and union and indicates plurality and otherness. Hence it was shown that in the case of things which may be combined and separated one and the same statement is sometimes true and sometimes false; for example, the statement "Socrates is sitting" is true when he is sitting; but the same statement is false when he gets up. And the same holds true in the case of thought. But with regard to those things which cannot be otherwise than they are, i.e., those which are always combined or separated, it is impossible for the same thought or statement to be sometimes true and sometimes false; but what is true is always true, and what is false is always false; for example, the proposition "Man is an animal" is true, but the proposition "Man is an ass" is false.

1901. **However, with regard** [4].

He now explains how truth and falsity can be present in simple things; and in regard to this he does three things. First [4], he shows that truth is not present in the same way in simple things and in composite ones. He says that in the case of things which are not composite but simple, such as immaterial substances, truth or falsity is not present in them as a result of any combination or separation which occurs in reality, but arises because their quiddity is known or not known. For when we acquire knowledge of the quiddity of any simple being, the intellect seems to be true; and when we fail to acquire knowledge of its quiddity, but attribute something else to it, the intellect is then false.

1902. For there is no composition in simple beings as a consequence of which it could be said that, when the thing is combined, the intellect in making a combination is then true; or that, when that is separated in reality which the intellect combines, the intellect is then not true. Or to express this in a different way, there is no composition in simple things by reason of which, when we express affirmatively that it is so, its composition is signified; and when we express negatively that it is not so, its separation is signified; as, for example, in the case of composite things, when it is said that a piece of wood is white, its composition is signified, or when it is said that it is not white, or that the diagonal is not commensurable, its separation is signified.

1903. Thus it is evident that truth and falsity are not present in simple things in the same way as in composite things. Nor is this surprising, since being also is not the same in both; but the being of composite things results from their components, whereas that of simple things does not. Now truth follows being, because, as was said in Book II (n. 298) of this work, the structure of things in being and in truth is the same. Hence those things which are not similar in being are not similar in truth.

1904. **But truth** [5].

Second, he shows how truth and falsity are present in simple things. He says that in the case of simple things truth and falsity are such as will be explained; for to come in contact with a simple thing through the intellect, in such a way as to apprehend what it is "and to express it," i.e., to signify this simple thing by a word, constitutes the truth present in simple things. And since sometimes the word "to express" is taken for affirmative predication, which involves composition, he rejects this interpretation. He says that affirmation and expression are not the same, because affirmation occurs when one thing is predicated of something else, and this implies combination, whereas expression is the simple utterance of something.

1905. Therefore to come in contact with simple things through the intellect and to express them constitutes truth; but not to come in contact with them is not to know them at all. For whoever does not grasp the quiddity of a simple thing is completely ignorant of it; because one cannot both know and not know something about it, since it is not composite.

1906. Moreover, since he had said that to come in contact with simple things is to express their truth, it would seem that not to come in contact with them is to be false or in error. He did not say this, however, but said that not to come in contact with them is not to know them. Hence he gives the reason why not to come in contact with them is not to be in error about them, saying that it is possible to be in error about their quiddity only accidentally; and this must be understood as follows.

1907. It was said above in Book VII (n. 1362) and in Book VIII (n. 1710) that in the case of simple substances the thing itself and its quiddity are one and the same. Hence, since a simple substance is its own quiddity, the judgment about the knowledge of a simple substance and the judgment about the knowledge of its quiddity are one and the same. But the intellect is deceived about a quiddity only accidentally; for either a person comes in contact with a thing's quiddity through his intellect, and then he truly knows what that thing is; or he does not come in contact with it, and then he does not know what it is. Hence, with regard to such a thing the intellect is neither true nor false. This is why Aristotle says in Book III of ***The Soul,*** [427b11] that, just as a sense is always true with regard to its proper object, in a similar fashion the intellect is always true with regard to its proper object—quiddity. And the fact that the intellect is not deceived about a thing's quiddity applies not only in the case of simple substances but also in that of composite ones.

1908. Now it is necessary to consider how one may be accidentally deceived about a quiddity. For a person is deceived about a quiddity only as a result of combining or separating; and with regard to composite substances this may occur in two ways. First, it may occur by combining a definition with something defined or by separating them; for example, if someone were to say that an ass is a mortal rational animal, or that a man is not a mortal rational animal, both would be false. Second, insofar as a definition is composed of parts which are incompatible with each other; for example, if someone were to give this definition—man is a non-sensible animal. Thus a definition is said to be false in the first way because it is not the definition of this thing; and in the second way it is said to be false in itself, as the Philosopher has instructed us above in Book V (n. 1132).

1909. Now we can be deceived accidentally about the quiddity of simple substances only in the first way; for their quiddity is not composed of many parts in the combining and separating of which falsity can arise.

1910. **And they are** [6].

He adapts his remarks about simple substances to his main thesis, in which he shows that truth involves actuality rather than potency. Indeed, he had shown this to be true in the case of composite substances insofar as their truth embodies combination and separation, which designate actuality. But he shows that this is true in the case of simple substances from the fact that they do not contain falsity but only truth. And for this reason they are not potential but actual.

1911. He accordingly says that all simple substances are actual beings and are never potential ones; for if they were sometimes actual and sometimes potential, they would be generated and corrupted. But this cannot be the case, as has been shown above (n. 1715), for substances of this kind are forms alone, and for this reason they are also beings of themselves. Now what exists of itself is neither generated nor corrupted, for everything that is generated is generated from something. But being in an absolute sense cannot be generated from anything; for there is nothing apart from being but only apart from some particular being, just as there is some being apart from man. Hence this being can be generated in a qualified sense, but being in an absolute sense cannot. Hence what is a being of itself, because it is a form, from which being naturally follows, cannot be generated; and for this reason it is not sometimes potential and sometimes actual.

1912. Therefore, since truth consists chiefly in actuality, it is unfitting that there should be error or falsity in all those things which are actual only and are what something truly is, since they are quiddities or forms; but they must either be understood if they are grasped by the intellect, or not be understood at all if they are not grasped by the intellect.

1913. But even though it is impossible to be deceived about these things as regards their essence, this is nevertheless possible when "we ask what they are," i.e., whether they are of such and such a nature or not. Hence it is possible to be deceived about them accidentally, as someone might ask whether a simple substance is fire or a corporeal substance or not, because if it is held to be a corporeal substance, there will be falsity accidentally as a result of combination.

1914. **Now considering** [7].

He summarizes the statements he has made about truth and falsity both with reference to composite things and to simple ones. He says that this being which signifies truth and non-being which signifies falsity (because he who says that a man is white signifies this to be true; and he who says that a man is not white signifies this to be false), being and non-being in this sense, I say, are used in one way in the case of the composition of things. That is, there is truth if what the intellect combines is combined in reality, but there is falsity if what the intellect combines when it understands or forms a proposition is not combined in reality.

1915. And truth exists in a different way in the case of simple things, if "what is truly a being," i.e., the quiddity or substance of a simple thing, is as it is understood to be; but if it is not as it is understood to be, no truth exists in the intellect. Thus truth consists in understanding these things; but concerning them there is neither falsity nor error in the intellect, as has been explained (n. 1912), but ignorance; for if one does not grasp the quiddity of a thing, one does not know that thing in any way at all. In the case of composite things, however, one can know one of their properties and be deceived about the others.

1916. Furthermore, he shows what sort of ignorance this is when he says that this ignorance is not "a privation such as blindness," which is the privation of the power of sight. Hence that ignorance would be similar to blindness if one did not have the intellective power of acquiring knowledge of simple substances. And from this it is evident that according to the opinion of Aristotle the human intellect can acquire an understanding of simple substances. This is a point which he seems to have left unsolved in ***The Soul***, Book III. [431b18]

1917. **And concerning** [8].

Here he introduces a corollary. He says that it is evident from what has been said that there is no error about immobile things as regards time. But in the case of contingent things, which are not always so, it is possible to be in error about them as regards time; for example, if Socrates is going to sit down and someone were to judge this to be so, he could be deceived insofar as he might judge that Socrates is going to sit down when he is not. The same thing would be true if someone were to think that an eclipse will occur when it will not. But in the case of immobile things and those which always are, the above can occur only in one way, i.e., if someone were to think that these things are mobile and that they do not always exist; for he is then in error about them, but he would not be in error as regards time. Hence he says that, if someone thinks that they are immobile, he will not be deceived about them as regards time.

1918. He says this, then, because, if someone assumes that they are immobile, he will not think that they sometimes are and sometimes are not, and thus he is not deceived about them as regards time. For example, if someone thinks that a triangle is unchangeable, he will not be of the opinion that the sum of its angles will sometimes equal two right angles and sometimes will not, for it would then be both changeable and unchangeable.

1919. But in the case of immobile

things it is possible to consider under one common aspect one thing that has such and such a property and another that has not; for example, it is possible to understand that under triangle some triangles are equilateral and others are not. And it is possible to ask whether no even number is prime, or whether some are and some are not—a prime number being one which the unit alone measures. Hence among even numbers only the number two is a prime number, but none of the others. And regarding what is numerically one, in the case of immobile things it is impossible to be in error or to be deceived even in this [taking one thing that has and another that has not a certain property]. For in the case of something numerically one it is impossible for anyone to think that one individual can be so and another not be so; for what is numerically one is not divided into many. Hence he will have to say what is true or false in an unqualified sense, since what is numerically one always exists in the same way and is incapable of being diversified either in point of time or of subjects. From this it is clear that truth has to do with actuality; for immobile things as such are always actual.

BOOK X
UNITY

LESSON 1
The Kinds of Unity and the Common Meaning of Unity

ARISTOTLE'S TEXT Chapter 1: 1052a15–1052b19

1. *It was pointed out before, where we distinguished the different meanings of terms, that the term one is used in many senses. But while this is true, there are four principal senses in which things are said to be one primarily and essentially and not accidentally. For that is said to be one which is continuous, either in an unqualified sense, or in the fullest sense by nature and not by contact or by a binding. And of these, that is one to a greater degree and before all else whose motion is more indivisible and simpler.* **1052a15–21**

2. *And not only is that which is such said to be one, but so also and to a greater degree that which is a whole and has some form or specifying principle; and a thing is one to the greatest degree if it is such by nature and not by force (as those things which are united by glue or by a nail or by being tied together) and has in itself the cause of its own continuity.* **1052a21–25**

3. *And a thing is such because its motion is one and indivisible as to place and to time; so that if a thing has by nature a first principle of the primary kind of motion—I mean circular motion—it is evident that it is a primary continuous quantity. Some things are one, then, in the sense that they are continuous or whole.* **1052a25–29**

4. *And other things are one if their intelligible structure is one; and such are those whose concept is one, that is, whose concept is indivisible; and it is indivisible if the thing is specifically or numerically indivisible. Now what is numerically indivisible is the singular thing, and what is specifically indivisible is what is knowable and is the object of scientific knowledge. Hence whatever causes the unity of substances must be one in the primary sense.* **1052a29–34**

5. *The term one, then, is used of all these things, namely, of what is continuous by nature, of a whole, of the singular thing, and of the universal. And all these are one because they are indivisible. And some are indivisible in motion, and others in their concept or intelligible structure.* **1052a34–1052b1**

6. *Now it must be borne in mind that the questions as to what sort of things are one, and what the essence of oneness is, and what its intelligible structure is, should not be assumed to be the same; for the term one is used in these various senses, and each of the things to which some one of these senses applies will be one. But the essence of oneness will apply sometimes to one of these senses, and sometimes to something else (819), which is nearer to the meaning of the word; but the others are potentially one. This is like what is found in regard to element and cause by anyone who has to designate them in things and define terms. For in a sense fire is an element (and perhaps this is true of the indeterminate itself or something else of this sort), and in a sense it is not; for the essence of fire and that of an element are not the same, but fire is an element inasmuch as it is a thing and a nature. But the term signifies something which is accidental to it, namely, that something is composed of it as a primary constituent. The same is also true of cause and of one and of all such terms. Hence the essence of oneness consists in being indivisible, i.e., in being an individual thing, and in being inseparable [i.e., not separated from itself] either as to place or to form or to thought, or to being a whole and something determinate.* **1052a1–18**

COMMENTARY

1920. Above in Book IV of this work the Philosopher showed (n. 548) that this science has for its subject being and the kind of unity which is interchangeable with being. Therefore, having drawn his conclusions about accidental being (n. 1172) and about the kind of being which signifies the truth of a proposition, which he does in Book VI (n. 1223), and about essential being as divided into the ten categories, which he does in Books VII (n. 1245) and VIII (n. 1681), and as divided into potency and actuality, which he does in Book IX (n. 1768), his aim in this tenth book is to settle the issue about unity or oneness and the attributes which naturally accompany it. This is divided into two parts. In the first [1] he establishes what is true of unity in itself; and in the second (Lesson 4) he considers unity in relation to plurality ("*One* and *many*").

The first part is divided into two members. In the first he explains the different senses in which the term *one* is used. In the second (Lesson 2) he establishes a property of unity or oneness ("But the essence").

The first part is divided into three members. In the first he establishes the different senses in which the term one is used. In the second [5] he reduces all these to one common meaning ("The term *one*"). In the third [6] he explains the different ways in which the term one is used of the things of which it is predicated ("Now it must").

In regard to the first he does three things. First, he gives two senses in which the term one is used. Second [3], he exposes the notion of unity contained in these two senses ("And a thing"). Third [4], he gives two other senses of the term one ("And other things").

1921. In treating the first member of this division [1] he gives, first, the primary senses in which the term one is used. He says that he has explained in Book V (n. 749) the different meanings of the terms which pertain to the study of this science; for it was pointed out there (n. 842) that the term one is used in many senses. And while this is true, there are four principal senses in which it is employed. But let us speak of those senses in which the term one is used primarily and essentially and not accidentally; for what is accidentally one has different modes of its own.

1922. Now one of the senses in which things are said to be essentially one is that in which the continuous is said to be one; and this can be taken in two ways: either the continuous in general (i.e., anything continuous in any way at all) is called one; or only the continuous by nature is called one by continuity. And this latter is what is continuous in the fullest sense of the term, and not that which is continuous by force or by art or by any kind of contact (as is evident in the case of pieces of wood), or by any kind of continuity (as is evident in the case of things which are continuous or held together by a nail or by any other bond).

1923. And the phrase *continuous by nature* designates two things: what is a uniform whole, as a straight line or even a circular one, and what is not a uniform whole, as two lines which constitute the angle in which they are connected. And of these, lines which are said to be straight and those which are said to be circular are one to a greater degree than those which form an angle, and they are one anteriorly. For a straight line must have one motion, since one part cannot be moved and another at rest, or one be moved in this way and another in that; but the whole must be moved simultaneously and by one motion. The same holds true of a circular line.

1924. But this does not apply to two continuous quantities which form an angle; for we can imagine either that one line is at rest and the other is moved closer to it so as to form a smaller angle, or that it is moved away from it so as to form a larger angle, or even that both lines are moved in opposite directions. Hence he says that a continuous quantity whose motion is more indivisible and simpler is one to a greater degree.

1925. **And not only** [2].

Then he gives a second sense in which things are said to be essentially one; and here we must consider that what "is such," i.e., continuous, is not only said to be one but also has something more; i.e., it is a whole having some form or specifying principle, just as an animal is one, and a triangular surface is one. Hence this sense of one adds to the oneness of continuity the kind of unity which comes from the form by which a thing is a whole and has a species.

1926. And since one thing is a whole by nature and another by art, he added that "a thing is one to the greatest degree" if it is such by nature and not by force. For example, all those things which are united by glue or by some such bond so as to become a whole are joined by force. But whatever is joined by nature is one to the greatest degree, because it is clearly the cause of its own continuity; for it is such by its very nature.

1927. **And a thing is such** [3].

Then he clarifies the meaning of unity contained in these two senses of the term one. He says that a thing is such, i.e., continuous and one, because its motion is one and indivisible both as to place and to time; as to place, because whithersoever one part of a continuous thing is moved another part is also moved; and as to time, because when one part is moved another is also moved.

1928. Hence, if a thing that is continuous and whole by nature is said to be one because its motion is one, then it is evident that, if anything continuous and whole has within itself a principle of the primary kind of motion, this will be the primary kind of one in the realm of continuous quantity; for example, of all motions the primary kind is local motion, and of local motions the primary kind is circular motion, as is proved in Book VIII of the *Physics. [265a13]* And of bodies which are moved by circular motion there is one which contains the principle of such motion, i.e., the body which is moved circularly and causes the circular motion of other bodies by a daily motion. It is evident, then, that this is the one primary continuous quantity which contains the first principle of the primary kind of motion. Hence two senses of the term one are evident, namely, that in which the continuous is called one, and that in which a whole is called one.

1929. **And other things** [4].

Then he gives the other ways in which things are said to be one. He says that certain other things are said to be one, not because their motion is one, but because their intelligible structure is one. And things of this kind whose concept is one are those which are apprehended by a single intellectual act. And such things as are said to be apprehended by a single intellectual act are those of which there is a single apprehension of an undivided object.

1930. This can be so for two reasons: either because the undivided object apprehended is specifically one, or because it is numerically one. Now what is numerically undivided is the singular thing itself, which cannot be predicated of many things; and what is specifically one is undivided because it is a single object of knowledge and acquaintance. For in distinct singular things there is no nature numerically one which can be called a species, but the intellect apprehends as one that attribute in which all singulars agree. Hence the species, which is distinct in distinct individuals in reality, becomes undivided when apprehended by the intellect.

1931. And since substance is prior in intelligibility to all the other genera, and the term one is used in these senses because it has one meaning, then it follows that the primary sort of one in these senses is what is one in substance, i.e., what causes substance to be one, just as in the first two senses the primary sort of one was the continuous quantity which is moved circularly.

1932. **The term one** [5].

Here he reduces the senses of one given above to a single meaning by summarizing what he had said above. He says that the term one is used of four things: first, of what is continuous by nature; second, of a whole; third, of a singular thing; and fourth, of the universal, for example, a species. And all of these are said to be one because of one common aspect, namely, being indivisible; for properly speaking, a one is an undivided being. But the term one is used in the first two senses because a motion is undivided, and in the latter two senses because an intelligible structure or concept is undivided, inasmuch as the apprehension of a particular thing is also included under this.

1933. **Now it must** [6].

Here he shows how the term one is predicated of things which are said to be one. He says that it must be borne in mind that the term one should not be taken to mean the same thing when a thing is said to be one and when someone expresses the essence of oneness, which is its intelligible structure; just as wood too is not said to be white in the sense that whiteness is the essence of wood, but in the sense that it is an accident of it.

1934. Then he gives the following explanation of a statement which he had made, saying that, since the term one is used in many senses (as has been stated), a thing is said to be one because some one of these senses applies to it, i.e., continuous, whole, species, or singular thing. But the essence of oneness sometimes applies to something that is one in some one of the foregoing senses, as when I say that what is one in continuity is one (and the same holds true of the others); and sometimes it is attributed to something which is nearer to the nature of one, for example, what is undivided but contains within itself potentially the senses of one given above; because what is undivided as regards motion is continuous and whole, and what is undivided in meaning is singular or universal.

1935. He adds to this the example of elements and causes, viewed in the problem of identifying them in things, as when we say that such and such a thing is an element or cause by defining the term; for example, we say that that is a cause which has the essence of a cause. And in this way we say that fire is an element or "the indeterminate itself," i.e., what is unlimited in itself (which the Pythagoreans posited as a separate entity and the element of all things), or anything else of this sort for whatever reason it can be called an element. But in a sense fire is not an element, and neither is the indeterminate; for fire does not constitute the essence of an element, because the notion of fire is not the same as that of an element. It is an element, however, as existing in reality or in the natural world. But when the term element is predicated of fire, it signifies that something "has become accidental to fire," i.e., that fire is that of which something is composed as a primary constituent, and this is the formal note of an element. He says "constituent" in order to exclude privations.

1936. What has been said about an element also applies to cause and to one and to all such terms; because the things of which they are predicated are not the very things which the terms signify; for example, white man is not the very thing which the term *white* signifies, for white signifies a quality. Hence the essence of oneness consists in being undivided, i.e., in being an individual thing; and this is proper to a thing which is inseparable as to place or to form or in whatever other way it is inseparable.

LESSON 2
Unity as a Measure

ARISTOTLE'S TEXT Chapter 1: 1052b19–1053b8

1. But the essence of oneness or unity consists especially in being the first measure of each genus, and most properly of quantity; because it is from this genus that it is transferred to the others. For a measure is that by which quantity is first known; and quantity as quantity is known either by unity or by a number, and every number is known by unity. Hence all quantity as quantity is known by unity. **1052b19–22**

2. And that by which quantity is first known is unity itself; and for this reason unity is the principle of number as number. **1052b23–24**

3. And the measure of other things is also that by which each is first known. And the measure of each is a unit: in length, in breadth, in depth, and in heaviness and in rapidity. For the terms heavy and rapid are common to both contraries, since each of them has two meanings. Thus heavy is said both of what has any amount of inclination towards the center and of what has an excessive inclination; and rapid is said both of what has any amount of motion, and of what has an excessive motion. For even what is slow has a certain speed, and what is light a certain heaviness. **1052b24–31**

4. And in all these cases the measure and principle is something one and indivisible, since even in the case of lines we use the foot measure as something indivisible. For everywhere men seek as a measure something one and indivisible, and this is what is simple either in quality or in quantity. Hence wherever it seems impossible to add or to subtract anything, there the most certain measure is found. The measure of number, then, is the most certain; for men claim that the unit is indivisible in every respect. And in other cases they imitate such a measure; for any addition or subtraction might more easily escape our notice in the case of a furlong or of a talent or of anything which is always a larger measure than in that of something which is a smaller measure. Hence it is the first thing from which no perceptible subtraction can be made that all men make a measure, whether of liquids or of solids or of weight or of size; and they think they know the quantity of a thing when they know it by this measure. **1052b31–1053a8**

5. And they also measure motion by that motion which is simple and most rapid; for this takes the least time. Hence in astronomy this kind of unit is the principle and measure; for astronomers suppose the motion of the heavens to be uniform and most rapid, and they judge the other motions by this motion. And in music the diesis is the measure, because it is the smallest interval; and in speech, the letter. And all of these are one, not in the sense that there is something common to all which is one, but in the sense that we have explained. **1053a8–14**

6. However, a measure is not always numerically one, but sometimes many; for example, there are two dieses not discernible by ear but differing in their ratios. And the words by which we measure speech are many; and the diagonal of a square is measured by two quantities, and so also is a side; and so are all continuous quantities. Therefore all things have as their measure some unit, because we come to know the things of which substance is composed by dividing it either in regard to quantity or to species. Hence the unit is indivisible, because what is first in each class of things is indivisible. But not every unit is indivisible in the same way, for example, the foot and the unit; but the latter is indivisible in every respect, whereas the former belongs to that class of things which are indivisible from the viewpoint of the senses, as has already been stated (823); for perhaps every continuous thing is divisible. **1053a14–24**

7. And a measure is always of the same kind as the thing measured; for the measure of continuous quantities is a continuous quantity; and in particular the measure of length is a length; and of breath a breadth; and of width a width; and of vocal sounds a vocal sound; and of weight a weight; and of units a unit. For this is the view which must be taken, but not that the measure of numbers is a number. We should indeed have to speak in this way if we were to use parallel forms, but the meaning does not require such parallels: it would be as if the measure of units had to be designated as units and not as a unit. But number is a plurality of units.

1053a24–30

8. And for the same reason we say that knowledge and perception are the measure of things, because we know something by them; yet they are measured rather than measure. But in our own case it is as though someone else were measuring us, and we learned how big we are by means of the cubit measure being applied to so much of us. But Protagoras says that man is the measure of all things, as if he were saying the man who knows or the man who perceives; and these because the one has intellectual knowledge and the other sensory perception, which we say are the measures of the things that are placed before them. Hence, while these men say nothing extraordinary, they seem to be saying something important. **1053a31–1053b3**

9. It is evident, then, that unity in the strictest sense, according to the definition of the term, is a measure, and particularly of quantity and then of quality. And some things will be such if they are indivisible in quantity, and others if they are indivisible in quality. Therefore what is one is indivisible either in an unqualified sense or inasmuch as it is one. **1053b4–8**

COMMENTARY

1937. Having explained the various senses in which unity is predicated of things, and having stated what its essential note is, to which all its usages are reduced, i.e., being indivisible, here the Philosopher infers a property of unity from its essential note, namely, that it is a measure. This is divided into two parts. In the first [1] he shows how the notion of a measure belongs to unity and to the various classes of accidents. In the second (Lesson 3) he shows how unity in the sense of a measure is found in substances ("It is necessary").

In regard to the first part of this division he does two things. First, he indicates the class of things in which unity in the sense of a measure is primarily found, and how it is transferred from this class to the others with the proper notion of a measure. Second [8], he explains how it is transferred figuratively to the other classes ("And for the same reason").

In treating the first part he does two things. First, he indicates the class of things in which unity in the sense of a measure is first found, and how it is transferred from this class to the others. Second [6], he makes a study of measures ("However, a measure").

In regard to the first he does three things. First, he shows how unity as a measure is found in quantity, and how it is transferred from this category to the others. Second [2], he indicates the species of quantity in which it is first found ("And that by which"). Third [3], he shows how it is transferred to other species of quantity ("And the measure").

1938. He accordingly says, first [1], that, since the essential note of unity consists in being indivisible, and what is indivisible in each genus is somehow the measure of that genus, unity must be said to be in the highest degree the first measure of each genus. This is said to apply most properly to quantity, and it is from this class that the notion of a measure is transferred to other classes of things. Now a measure is nothing else than that by which a thing's quantity is known, and this is known by the unit or by a number: by a unit, as when we say one furlong or one foot; and by a number, as when we say three furlongs or three feet. Again, every number is known by the unit, because the unit taken a certain number of times gives a number. It follows, then, that every quantity is known by unity. To "quantity" he adds "as quantity," intending that this be referred to the measure of quantity; for the properties and other accidents of quantity are known in a different way.

1939. **And that by which** [2].

Then he indicates in what species of quantity unity or measure is primarily found. First, he makes it clear that the notion of a measure is primarily found in discrete quantity, which is number. He says that that by which quantity is first known is "unity itself," i.e., the unit which is the principle of number. For in other species of quantity the unit is not unity itself but something of which unity is an attribute, as when we speak of one hand or of one continuous quantity. Hence it follows that unity itself, which is the first measure, is the principle of number as number.

1940. **And the measure** [3].

Second, he shows how unity is transferred to other species of quantity; and in regard to this he does two things. First, he indicates the species of quantity to which it is transferred. He says that it is from this class, i.e., from number and from the unit, which is the principle of number, that the notion of a measure is transferred to other quantities as that by which each of them is first known. And whatever is the measure in each class of things is the unit in that class.

1941. He gives examples of this in three classes of things, i.e., in dimensions—length, breadth and width; in weight, or in what he calls heaviness; and in speed, or in what he calls rapidity, which refers to the measure of time. In the case of dimensions no one doubted that they were quantities and that they were properly susceptible to measurement, but in the case of weight and of speed there could be a difficulty because these seem to be qualities rather than quantities.

1942. He therefore explains how these pertain to the genus of quantity, and how they are susceptible to measurement. He says that heaviness and rapidity have something in common with their contraries because one contrary is found in the other; for what is heavy is in some sense light, and the reverse; and what is rapid is in some sense slow. For each of these terms is used in two senses. In one sense the term heavy is used without qualification of anything that has an inclination to be borne towards the center of the earth, without taking into consideration how great its inclination is; and in this sense heavy does not refer to the category of quantity, and it is not susceptible to measurement. In the other sense it is used of one thing in comparison with something else, namely, of what exceeds something else in terms of the above-mentioned inclination; for example, we say that earth is heavy in comparison with water, and that lead is heavy in comparison with wood. Therefore it is by reason of this excess that some notion of quantity and measure is found. The term rapid is similarly used in two senses. In one sense it is used without qualification of anything that has any motion; and in a second sense it is used of anything that has an excessive motion. And in one respect the notions of quantity and measure properly apply to it, and in another respect they do not.

1943. With a view to clarifying his statement about the condition of heaviness and rapidity in reference to contraries he adds that rapidity is found in something that is slow inasmuch as what is simply and unqualifiedly slow is more rapid in comparison with something that is slower than itself. And in a similar way heaviness is found in light things; for example, air is light in comparison with earth, and heavy in comparison with fire.

1944. **And in all cases** [4].

Then he shows how the notion of a measure is transferred from number to other kinds of quantity. He immediately makes this clear, first, in the case of dimensions and in that of weights; and second [5], in that of the rapidity of motions ("And they also measure").

He accordingly says, first [4], that the notion of a measure is transferred from number to the other kinds of quantity in this way that, just as the unit which is the measure of number is indivisible, so too all the other kinds of quantity have something that is one and indivisible as their measure and principle. For example, in measuring lines men use "the foot measure," i.e., the measure of one foot, as something indivisible; for wherever something indivisible is sought as a measure, there is something simple either in quality or in quantity; in quality, as whiteness in the case of colors, which is in a sense the measure of colors, as will be mentioned below (n. 1968); and in quantity, as the unit in the case of numbers, and the foot measure in the case of lines.

1945. Further, he points out why a measure must be something indivisible. The reason is that an exact measure must be something which can be neither added to nor subtracted from. Thus the unit is the most exact or certain measure, because the unit which is the principle of number is altogether indivisible, and whatever unity is not susceptible either to addition or to subtraction remains one. The measures of the other classes of quantity resemble this unit which is indivisible inasmuch as men take some smallest thing as a measure to the extent that this is possible. For if anything large were taken, as the furlong among distances and the talent among weights, it would escape our notice if some small portion were subtracted from or added to it. And this would always be more true of a larger measure than of a smaller one.

1946. Hence all men take this as a measure both in the case of liquids, such as oil and wine, and in that of solids, such as grain and barley; and also in that of weights and dimensions, which are designated as heaviness and continuous quantity. And this is first found to be such that nothing perceptible can be subtracted from it or added to it that might escape our notice. And men think they know the quantity of a thing exactly when they know it by the smallest measure of this kind.

1947. **And they also** [5].

Then he makes the same thing clear with regard to the rapidity of motions. He says that men also measure motion "by that motion which is simple," i.e., the motion which is uniform and quickest, because it takes the least time. Hence in astronomy they take such motion as the basis of measurement; for they take the motion of "the first heaven," i.e., the daily motion, which is regular and quickest, and they judge and measure all other motions by this.

1948. And because the low and high pitch of sounds results from the quickness and slowness of motions, as is established in the science of music, he adds as an example the measurement of sounds. He says that in music the first measure is the "diesis," i.e., the difference between two half tones; for a tone is divided into two unequal half tones, as is proved in the science of music. And similarly in speech the measure is the letter, because the shortness or length of a word is a natural consequence of the quickness or slowness of a motion.

1949. Now all these measures are something one, not in the sense that some measure is common to all, but in the sense that any measure in itself is something one, as has been pointed out.

1950. **However, a measure** [6].

After having shown in what class of things unity as a measure is primarily found, here the Philosopher clears up certain points that have to be investigated about measures.

The first of these is that, although a measure is understood to be one thing inasmuch as it comes close to being indivisible, it is not necessary that a measure be something numerically one; but sometimes many things are measures; for example, in the case of musical sounds "there are two dieses," i.e., two half tones. However, because of their smallness they are not distinguished by the sense of hearing, for the senses do not perceive the difference between two things that are very small; but their difference is perceived "in their ratios," i.e., in the different ratios which comprise their proportions, because they are caused by different numerical proportions.

1951. Similarly the things by which we measure words are also many; for the quantity of one meter or of one foot is measured by different syllables, some of which are short and some long. The same thing is true of the diameter of a circle and of the diagonal of a square, and also of the side of a square. And any continuous quantity is measured by two things, for an unknown quantity is found only by means of two known quantities.

1952. Having said this he brings this part of his discussion to a close by summarizing what has been said above, namely, that unity constitutes the measure of all things. The reason for this is that unity is the term of division. And those principles which constitute the substance of each thing are known by the division or dissolution of the whole into its component parts, whether they are quantitative parts or specific parts such as matter and form and the elements of compounds. Therefore what is one in itself must be indivisible since it is the measure by which a thing is known, because in the case of singular things whatever is first in the process of composition and last in the process of dissolution is indivisible, and it is by means of this that the thing is known, as has been explained.

1953. Yet indivisibility is not found in all things in the same way. Some things are altogether indivisible, such as the unit which is the basis of number, whereas others are not altogether indivisible but only to the senses, according as the authority of those who instituted such a measure wished to consider something as a measure; for example, the foot measure, which is indivisible in proportion [to the things measured] but not by nature. "For perhaps everything continuous is divisible"; and he says "perhaps" because of the difficulty facing those men who claimed that continuous quantity is composed of indivisible elements, or that natural continuous quantities are not infinitely divisible, but only mathematical quantities. For it is possible to find the smallest amount of flesh, as is mentioned in Book I of the *Physics*.[187b21]

1954. **And a measure** [7].

Then he gives the second point that has to be investigated about a measure. He says that "the meter," i.e., the measure, should always be of the same kind as the thing measured, i.e., of the same nature or measure as the thing measured; for example, a continuous quantity should be the measure of continuous quantities; and it is not enough that they have a common nature, as all continuous quantities do, but there must be some agreement between the measure and the thing measured in the line of their special nature. Thus a length is the measure of lengths, a width of widths, a vocal sound of vocal sounds, a weight of weights, and a unit of units.

1955. "For this is the view which must be taken" in order that we may speak without being criticized, "but not that number is the measure of numbers." Now number does not have the notion of a first measure but unity does; and if unity is a measure, then in order to signify the agreement between the measure and the thing measured it will be necessary to say that unity is the measure of units and not of numbers. Yet if the truth of the matter be taken into consideration, it will be necessary to admit also that number is the measure of numbers or even that the unit may be taken in a similar way as the measure of numbers. But it does not seem equally fitting to say that the unit is the measure of units and number of number or unity of number, because of the difference which appears to exist between the unit and number. But to observe this difference is the same as if someone were to say that it is fitting for units to be the measure of units but not the unit, because the unit differs from units as things expressed in the singular differ from those expressed in the plural. And the same argument applies to number in relation to the unit, because a number is nothing else than a plurality of units. Hence to say that the unit is the measure of number is merely to say that the unit is the measure of units.

1956. **And for the same reason** [8].

Then he shows how the term *measure* is transferred in a figurative way to another class of things. He says that, since it has been stated that a measure is that by which the quantity of a thing is known, we may say that intellectual knowledge is the measure of that which is knowable intellectually, and that sensory perception is the measure of that which is perceptible; because we know something by means of them, namely, sensible objects by means of perception and intelligible objects by means of intellectual knowledge; but we do not know them in the same way that we know something by means of a measure. For something is known by a measure as by a principle of knowledge; but things are known by sensory perception and by intellectual knowledge as by a cognitive power or cognitive habit.

1957. Therefore they are called measures figuratively, because in reality they are measured rather than measure. For it is not because we perceive or know a thing that it is so in reality; but it is because it is so in reality that we have a true knowledge or perception of it, as is said in Book IX (n. 1896). Thus it follows that in perceiving and knowing something we measure our knowledge by means of the things which exist outside the mind.

1958. However, in knowing and measuring ourselves by some other measure we know how much bodily quantity we have by applying the cubit measure to ourselves. Hence, just as the external cubit is offered as a measure of our bodily quantity, in a similar way the things known or sensuously apprehended are the measures whereby we can know whether we truly apprehend something by our senses or by our intellect.

1959. And if there is a science which is the cause of the thing known, it must be this science which measures that thing, just as the science of the master planner is the measure of things made by art, because anything made by art is complete insofar as it attains a likeness to the art. It is in this way that the science of God is related to all things. But Protagoras said that man is the measure of all things inasmuch as he knows or perceives them, because knowledge and perception are the measure of substances, i.e., of things which are intelligible and perceptible. For the followers of Protagoras, as has been stated in Book IV (344:C 637), said that things are such because we so perceive them or judge about them. Therefore, although they say nothing extraordinary or important, they nevertheless seem to be saying something of consequence, because they covertly insinuate their doctrine.

1960. **It is evident** [9].

Then he sums up the points discussed, namely, that the notion of unity involves being a measure; and this applies most properly to quantity, and then to quality and to the other genera, because anything that is a measure should be indivisible either in quantity or in quality. Thus it follows that unity is indivisible, "either in an unqualified sense" as the unit which is the basis of number, or "in a qualified sense," i.e., to the extent that it is one, as was stated with regard to the other measures.

LESSON 3
The Nature of Unity

ARISTOTLE'S TEXT Chapter 2: 1053b9–1054a19

1. It is necessary to inquire how unity is related to the substance and nature of things. In a sense this is a problem which we have examined in the questions regarding the nature of unity, and how it must be taken: whether it must be taken to be a substance, as the Pythagoreans first claimed, and later Plato, or rather whether there is some nature that underlies it, and it is necessary to describe it more meaningfully and more in the terms of those who speak of nature; for one of them said that unity is friendship, another air, and another the indeterminate. **1053b9–16**

2. If, then, it is impossible for a universal to be a substance, as has been stated in our treatment of substance and being, and being itself cannot be a substance in the sense of one thing existing apart from the many (for it is common to all of them), but it is only a predicate, it is evident that unity cannot be a substance; for being and unity are the most universal of all predicates. Hence genera are not certain natures and substances which are separable from other things; and unity cannot be a genus, for the same reasons that being and substance cannot be such. **1053b16–24**

3. Further, the same thing must be true of unity in all categories of things. Now unity and being are used in an equal number of ways. Hence, since in the category of qualities there is something which is one and a certain nature, and since the same thing is true of quantities, it is evident that we must investigate in a general way what unity is, just as we must investigate what being is, inasmuch as it is not sufficient to say that its nature is just itself. But in the sphere of colors unity is a color, for example, white; and then the other colors seem to be produced from this and from black; and black is the privation of white as darkness is of light; for it is the absence of light. If, then, all beings were colors, they would be a number. But of what? Evidently, of colors. And unity itself would be some one color, for example, white. Similarly if beings were tunes, they would be a number of minor half tones; but their substance would not be a number; and unity would be something whose substance is not unity but a minor half tone. Similarly if beings were sounds, they would be a number of elements, and unity would be a vowel. And if beings were rectilinear figures, there would be a number of figures, and unity would be a triangle. The same reasoning applies to the other genera. Therefore if in all affections, qualities, quantities and motions there are numbers and unity, and if the number is a number of particular things, and the unity is a particular unity, but unity is not its substance, then the same thing must be true of substances, because the same is true of all things. It is evident, then, that in every genus unity is a determinate nature, and that in no case is the nature of its unity merely unity. But just as in the case of colors the unity for which we must look is one color, in a similar fashion in the case of substances the unity must be one substance. **1053b24–1054a13**

4. That unity and being somehow signify the same thing is evident from the fact that they have meanings corresponding to each of the categories and are contained in none of them: neither in quiddity nor in quality, but unity is related to each in the same way that being is; and from the fact that "one man" does not express something different from "man," just as being does not exist apart from quiddity or from quality or from quantity; and because to be one is just the same as to be a particular thing. **1054a13–19**

COMMENTARY

1961. After having shown how unity in the sense of a measure is found first in quantity and then is transferred to the other categories, here the Philosopher deals with the relationship of unity to substance, i.e., whether unity constitutes the very substance of a thing. This is divided into three parts. In the first [1] he raises the question and gives the different opinions regarding it. In the second [2] he answers the question by showing that unity and being are not the substance of the things of which they are predicated ("If, then"). In the third [4] he compares unity with being ("That unity and being").

He accordingly says, first [1], that, since it has already been shown how unity in the sense of a measure belongs to quantity and to the other classes of things, it is now necessary to ask how unity relates to the substances and natures of things. This question was asked above in Book III (n. 488), in which different problems were raised.

1962. The question is whether the very thing which is called unity is a substance, i.e., something which subsists of itself, as the Pythagoreans first claimed, and as the Platonists, who followed them, later held; or rather whether there is some subsistent nature which underlies unity, in terms of which the quiddity of the thing designated as one should be more meaningfully and adequately expressed. The philosophers of nature presupposed this entity, one of them saying that unity is love, namely, Empedocles, who claimed that there are four material principles, the four elements, to which the active principles posited by him, love and hate, are said to be prior. And of these the most important is love, inasmuch as it is perfect and the principle of good things. Therefore, if the first principle is called unity, it follows according to him that unity is love. And this fits the case inasmuch as it indicates a certain union of the lover and the thing loved. Another philosopher, Diogenes, who claimed that air is the principle of all things (n. 86), said that unity is air. And still another philosopher said that unity is the indeterminate, namely, Melissus, who claimed that there was one infinite and unchangeable being, as is clear in Book I of the ***Physics***. [184b16, 185a32]

1963. **If, then** [2].

Here he answers the question which was raised. He says that unity is not a subsisting substance, of which one may predicate the term one. He proves this in two ways. First [2], by an argument; and second [3], by a comparison ("Further, the same").

He says, then, that it was proved above in Book VII (n. 1572), where he treats of being, and especially of substance, that no universal can be a substance which subsists of itself because every universal is common to many. A universal also cannot be a subsisting substance because otherwise it would have to be one thing apart from the many, and then it could not be common but would be in itself a singular thing.

1964. Unity might, it is true, be said to be common as a cause is. But the common aspect of a universal differs from that of a cause; for a cause is not predicated of its effects, since the same thing is not the cause of itself. But a universal is common in the sense of something predicated of many things; and thus it must be in some way a one-in-many, and not something subsisting apart from them.

1965. But being and unity must be predicated of all things in the most universal and common way. Hence those things which are called being and unity are not themselves subsisting substances, as Plato maintained.

1966. From this argument he concludes that no genera are natures and substances which subsist of themselves as though separable from the things of which they are predicated. This too was one of the questions debated above (n. 432). Yet this is not said in the sense that unity is a genus; for unity cannot be a genus for the very same reason that being cannot, since it is not predicated univocally. This is also true in the light of the other reasons given in Book III (nn. 493–501). And for the same reason unity and being cannot be subsisting substances.

1967. **Further, the same thing** [3].

Here he proves the same point by a comparison. He says that unity must be found in the same way in all categories of things, because being and unity are predicated in an equal number of ways of all genera. But in each genus of things we look for something that is one (implying that unity is not the very nature of what is said to be one), as is evident in the case of qualities and in that of quantities. It is clear, then, that in no genus is it sufficient to say that the nature of what is said to be one is just unity itself, but we must inquire what unity and being are.

1968. That it is necessary to investigate what unity is in the category of qualities and in that of quantities he makes clear by examples. He does this first in the case of colors; for we look for something which is one, such as whiteness, which is the primary color. Hence, if what is primary in each class of things is its unity, whiteness must constitute the unity in the class of color; and it must be in a sense the measure of the other colors, because the more perfect a thing's color the closer it comes to whiteness. He shows that whiteness is the primary color by reason of the fact that intermediate colors are produced from white and from black, and are therefore subsequent. Black is subsequent to white because it is the privation of white as darkness is of light. But this must not be understood to mean that black is pure privation in the same way that darkness is (for black is a species of color, and thus possesses the nature of color), but that blackness contains the least amount of light, which causes colors; and thus it is compared to white as the absence of light is compared to light.

1969. And since we look for something in the sphere of colors which can be said to be primary and to be one, namely, whiteness, it is evident that, if all beings were colors, they would be some number, not in the sense, however, that number would constitute subsisting things themselves, but in the sense that there would be a number of subsisting things of a particular sort, i.e., colors. And then there would be something that is the subject of unity, namely, that which is white.

1970. The same thing would be true if all things were tunes; because beings would be of a certain number, that is, a number of minor half tones or tones. Yet number is not the very substance of beings, and consequently it would be necessary to look for something which is one, namely, the minor half tone; but not in such a way that unity itself would be a substance.

1971. In a similar way too if all beings were sounds, they would be a number of beings, because there are a number of particular subjects of number, namely, "of elements," or letters. Hence the vowel, which is the primary letter (since consonants cannot be pronounced without vowels) would constitute their unity. And in a similar way if all figures were rectilinear figures, there would be a number of subjects, namely, figures; and the triangle, which is the primary rectilinear figure, would constitute their unity; for all such figures are reducible to the triangle. The same reasoning applies to every category.

1972. If it is in this way, then, that number and unity are found in all other categories: in affections, qualities, and quantities, and in motion; and if number and unity are not the substance of the things of which they are predicated, but number is predicated of certain substances, and if unity similarly requires some subject which is said to be one, the same thing must be true of substances, because being and unity are predicated in the same way of all things. It is evident, then, that in any category of things there is some nature of which the term one is predicated, not because unity itself is the nature of a thing, but because it is predicated of it.

1973. And just as when we speak of unity in the case of colors we are looking for some color which is said to be one, so too when we speak of unity in the case of substances we are looking for some substance of which unity may be predicated. And this is predicated primarily and chiefly of what is first among substances (which he investigates below [nn. 2553–66]), and subsequently of the other classes of things.

1974. **That unity and being** [4].

Since he had given the same argument for being and for unity, he now shows that unity and being somehow signify the same thing. He says "somehow" because unity and being are the same in their subject and differ only in meaning. For unity adds to being the note of undividedness, because what is one is said to be an indivisible or undivided being. He gives three reasons why unity signifies the same thing as being.

1975. The first is that unity naturally belongs to all of the different categories and not just to one of them; that is, it does not pertain just to substance or to quantity or to any other category. The same thing is also true of being.

1976. The second reason is that, when a man is said to be one, the term one does not express a different nature from man, just as being does not express a different nature from the ten categories; for, if it did express a different nature, an infinite regress would necessarily result, since that nature too would be said to be one and a being. And if being were to express a nature different from these things, an infinite regress would also follow; but if not, then the conclusion of this argument must be the same as that of the first one.

1977. The third reason is that everything is said to be one inasmuch as it is a being. Hence when a thing is dissolved it is reduced to non-being.

1978. Now in this solution of the question the Philosopher seems to contradict himself; for he first said that unity and being are not the substance of the things of which they are predicated, but here he says that unity and being do not express a nature different from the things of which they are predicated.

1979. Hence it must be noted that the term *substance* is used in two senses. In one sense it means a supposit in the genus of substance, which is called *first substance* and *hypostasis,* to which it properly belongs to subsist. In a second sense it means a thing's quiddity, which is also referred to as a thing's nature. Therefore, since universals are subsistent things according to the opinion of Plato, they signify substance not only in the second sense but also in the first. But Aristotle proves in

Book VII (n. 1572) that universals are not subsistent things, and therefore it follows that universals are not substances in the first sense but only in the second. And for this reason it is said in the ***Categories*** *[2b29]* that second substances, which are genera and species, do not signify particular things, which are subsisting substances, but "they signify the quiddity of a thing," i.e., a nature in the genus of substance.

1980. The Philosopher accordingly proved above that unity and being do not signify substance in the sense of this particular thing, but it is necessary to look for something that is one and a being, just as we look for something that is a man or an animal, as Socrates or Plato. Lastly he shows that these terms signify the natures of the things of which they are predicated and not something added, like accidents. For common attributes differ from accidents in this respect (although they agree in not being particular things), that common attributes signify the very nature of supposits, whereas accidents do not, but they signify some added nature.

1981. And Avicenna, who did not take this into account, claimed that unity and being are accidental predicates, and that they signify a nature added to the things of which they are predicated. For he was deceived by the equivocal use of the term one, because the unity which is the principle of number and has the role of a measure in the genus of quantity signifies a nature added to the things of which it is predicated, since it belongs to a class of accident. But the unity which is interchangeable with being extends to everything that is, and therefore it does not signify a nature which is limited to one category.

1982. He was also deceived by the equivocal use of the term being; for being as signifying the composition of a proposition is predicated accidentally, since composition is made by the intellect with regard to a definite time. Now to exist at this or at that particular time is to be an accidental predicate. But being as divided by the ten categories signifies the very nature of the ten categories insofar as they are actual or potential.

LESSON 4
Ways in Which One and Many Are Opposed

ARISTOTLE'S TEXT Chapter 3: 1054a20–1055a2

1. *One and many are opposed in many ways, and one of these is the opposition between one and many as between something indivisible and something divisible; for many means either what is divided or what is divisible, and one means either what is undivided or what is indivisible.* **1054a20–23**

2. *Hence, since we speak of four modes of opposition, and one of these two opposites is expressed privatively, they will be contraries and not contradictories or relative terms.* **1054a23–26**

3. *And what is one is described and made known in reference to its contrary, and what is indivisible in reference to what is divisible; for what is many and is divisible is better known to the senses than what is indivisible. Hence what is many is prior in intelligibility to what is indivisible, because of sensory perception.* **1054a26–29**

4. *And as we have already indicated in our division of contraries, same, like and equal relate to what is one; but diverse, unlike and unequal relate to what is many.* **1054a29–32**

5. *Now things are said to be the same in several ways; for in one way we say that a thing is numerically the same; and in another way we say that it is the same if it is one both in its intelligible structure and numerically; for example, you are the same as yourself in both form and matter. Again, things are the same if the intelligible structure of their primary substance is one, as equal straight lines are the same, and equal quadrangles which are equiangular, and also many other things; but in these cases equality is unity.* **1054a32–1054b3**

6. *Things are like if, while being the same in an unqualified sense or without a difference as regards their substance, they are the same in species; for example, a larger square is like a smaller one. And this likewise holds true of unequal straight lines, for these are like but not the same in an unqualified sense. And some things are said to be like if, while having the same form and admitting of difference in degree, they do not differ in degree. And other things are like if the same affection belongs to both and is one that is the same in species; for example, both what is whiter and what is less white are said to be like because they have one species. And other things are said to be such if they have more of sameness than diversity, either absolutely, or in regard to those attributes which are more important; for example, tin is like silver in being white, and gold is like fire in being red or yellowish.* **1054b3–13**

7. *It is evident, then, that the terms diverse and unlike are used in many senses; and that other or diverse is used in a way opposite to the same. Hence everything in relation to everything else is either the same or diverse. And things are diverse in another sense if their matter and intelligible structure are not one; thus you and your neighbor are diverse. A third meaning of this term is that found in mathematics. Hence for this reason everything is either diverse or the same as everything else, i.e., everything of which men predicate unity and being. For other is not the contradictory of the same, and this is why it is not predicated of non-beings (but they are said to be "not the same"), but it is predicated of all beings; for whatever is by nature a being and one is either one or not one. Hence diverse and same are opposed in this way.* **1054b13–23**

8. *But different and diverse are not the same. For that which is diverse and that from which it is diverse need not be diverse in some particular respect, because every being is either diverse or the same. But that which is different differs from something in some particular respect. Hence there must be some same thing by which they differ. Now this same thing is either a genus or a species; for everything that differs, differs either generically or specifically: generically, if they have no common matter and are not generated from each other, like those things which belong to a different figure of predication, and specifically, if they have the same genus. Genus means that*

by which both of the things that differ are said to be without difference in substance. But contraries are different, and contrariety is a kind of difference. **1054b23–32**

9. That this assumption is correct becomes clear by an induction; for all these contraries seem to be different, and they are not merely diverse, but some are generically diverse and others belong to the same category, so that they are contained in the same genus and in the same species. The kinds of things which are generically the same and those which are generically diverse have been established elsewhere. **1054b32–1055a2**

COMMENTARY

1983. After having treated of *one* considered in itself, here the Philosopher deals with *one* in comparison with *many;* and this is divided into two parts. In the first [1] he treats one and many and their concomitant attributes. In the second (Lesson 5) he establishes what is true about the contrary character of one and many; for the investigation of this involves a special difficulty ("But since it is possible").

The first member of this division is divided into two parts. In the first part he shows how one and many are opposed. In the second [4] he considers their concomitant attributes ("And as we have").

In regard to the first he does three things. First [1], he indicates how we should understand the opposition between one and many. He says that, although one and many are opposed in many ways, as will be made clear below, none the less one of these ways, and the most important one, concerns one and many insofar as they are opposed as something indivisible is opposed to something divisible, because this mode of opposition pertains to the proper notion of each.

1984. For the essential note of plurality consists in things being divided from each other or in being divisible. He says "divided" because of the things which are actually separated from each other and which are for this reason said to be many. He says "divisible" because of the things which are not actually separated from each other but come close to being separated, for example, moist things such as air and water and the like, of which we use the term *much* because they are easily divided; thus we speak of much water and much air.

1985. But the formal constituent of unity or oneness consists in being indivisible or in being undivided; for the continuous is said to be one because it is not actually divided, although it is divisible.

1986. **Hence, since** [2].

Second, he makes clear to what kind of opposition the aforesaid manner of being opposed is ultimately reduced. He says that, since there are four kinds of opposition, one of which is based on privation, it is evident that one and many are not opposed as contradictories or as relative terms, which are two kinds of opposition, but as contraries.

1987. That they are not opposed as contradictories is evident because neither of them applies to non-being, for non-being is neither one nor many. But the second member of the contradiction would have to apply to being as well as to non-being. That they are not opposed as relative terms is likewise evident, for the terms one and many are used in an absolute sense.

1988. And although he had said that one and many are opposed as what is indivisible and what is divisible, and these appear to be opposed as privation and possession, none the less he concludes that one and many are opposed as contraries; for the opposition between privation and possession is the basis of the opposition between contraries, as will be made clear below (n. 2036). For one of the two contraries is always a privation, but not a pure privation; otherwise it would not share in the nature of the genus, since contraries belong to the same genus. Each of the two contraries, then, must be a positive reality, even though one of them shares in the nature of the genus with a certain deficiency, as black in relation to white, as has been stated above (n. 1967). Therefore, since unity does not signify a pure privation, for it does not designate the mere lack of division but the very being which is undivided, it is evident that one and many are opposed not as pure privation and possession but as contraries.

1989. **And what is one** [3].

Third, he answers an implied question. Because he had said that one is related to many as what is indivisible to what is divisible, and what is indivisible seems to be the privation of what is divisible since privation is subsequent to possession or form, it seems to follow that one is subsequent to many, although he had said above (n. 1939) that one is the principle of many, from which it becomes known.

1990. In order to see the solution of this difficulty, then, it must be borne in mind that things which are prior and better known by nature are subsequent and less well known to us, because we derive our knowledge of things from the senses. Now the first things to be perceived by us are composite and confused things, as is said in Book I of the *Physics;* [184a21] and this is why the first things to be known by us are composite things. But simpler things, which are prior and more intelligible by nature, are known by us only derivatively; and this is why we define the first principles of things only by the negations of subsequent things; for example, we say that the point is what has no parts; and we know God by way of negations inasmuch as we say that God is incorporeal, unchangeable and infinite.

1991. Accordingly, even though what is one is prior by nature to what is many, yet in our knowledge it is defined and gets its name from the privation of division. This is why the Philosopher says that "what is one is described," i.e., named, "and made known," i.e., understood, "in reference to its contrary," just as the indivisible is known from the divisible. And for this reason many things are able to be perceived more easily than one thing; and what is divisible is able to be perceived more easily than what is indivisible, not in the order of nature but because of sensory perception, which is the foundation of our knowledge.

1992. But a twofold difficulty arises with regard to those things which the Philosopher is expounding. The first concerns his statement that one and many are opposed as contraries. For this appears to be impossible, because unity is the basis of plurality, whereas one of two contraries does not ground the other but rather destroys it.

1993. Hence it must be noted that, since contraries differ formally, as is said below (n. 2120), when we say that things are contraries, each of them is to be taken insofar as it has a form, but not insofar as it is a part of something having a form. For insofar as body is taken without the soul, as something having a form, it is opposed to animal as the non-living is opposed to the living. But insofar as it is not taken as something complete and informed, it is not opposed to animal but is a material part of it. We see that this is likewise true of numbers; for insofar as the number two is a kind of whole having a determinate species and form, it differs specifically from the number three; but if it is taken insofar as it is not made complete by a form, it is a part of the number three.

1994. Therefore insofar as unity itself is considered to be complete in itself and to have a certain species, it is opposed to plurality; because what is one is not many, nor is the reverse true. But insofar as it is considered to be incomplete as regards form and species, it is not opposed to plurality but is a part of it.

1995. The second difficulty has to do with the statement that plurality is prior in intelligibility to unity; for, since the concept of plurality or multitude involves unity, because a plurality is nothing else than an aggregate of units, if unity is subsequent in intelligibility to plurality, it follows that the notions of unity and plurality involve circularity, i.e., in the sense that unity is intelligible in terms of plurality and vice versa. But circularity of definition is not admissible in designating the intelligible structures of things, because the same thing would then be known both to a greater and to a lesser degree. This is impossible.

1996. The answer to this difficulty, then, must be that nothing prevents one and the same thing from being prior and subsequent in intelligibility according to different traits which are considered in it. For in multitude it is possible to consider both multitude as such and division itself. Thus from the viewpoint of division multitude is prior in intelligibility to unity; for that is one which is undivided. But multitude as multitude is subsequent in intelligibility to unity, since a multitude means an aggregate of units or ones.

1997. Now the division which is implied in the notion of that kind of unity which is interchangeable with being is not the division of continuous quantity, which is understood prior to that kind of unity which is the basis of number, but is the division which is caused by contradiction, inasmuch as two particular beings are said to be divided by reason of the fact that this being is not that being.

1998. Therefore what we first understand is *being*, and then *division*, and next *unity*, which is the privation of division, and lastly *multitude*, which is a composite of units. For even though things which are divided are many, they do not have the formal note of a many until the fact of being one is attributed to each of the particular things concerned. Yet nothing prevents us from also saying that the notion of multitude depends on that of unity insofar as multitude is measured by one; and this already involves the notion of number.

1999. **And as we have** [4].

Here he indicates the attributes which stem from unity and plurality; and in regard to this he does two things. First, he gives the attributes which naturally stem from unity and plurality. He says that sameness, likeness and equality flow from unity, as has been pointed out above in Book V (n. 911), where he divided or distinguished the various senses in which things are said to be contrary; for those things are *the same* which are one in substance; those are *like* which are one in quality; and those are *equal* which are one in quantity.

2000. And the contraries of these, *diverse, unlike* and *unequal*, pertain to plurality. For those things are diverse whose substance is not one; those are unlike whose quality is not one; and those are unequal whose quantity is not one.

2001. **Now things** [5].

He now explains the various senses in which these terms are used; and in regard to this he does two things. First, he shows how the modes of those attributes which accompany unity differ from each other. Second [7], he does the same thing for those attributes which accompany plurality ("It is evident").

In regard to the first part he does two things. First, he explains the various ways in which things are said to be *the same;* and second [6], those in which they are said to be like ("Things are *like*"). He does not make any distinctions as regards equality, however, because there are not many ways in which things are said to be equal, unless perhaps in reference to the various kinds of quantity.

2002. He accordingly gives [5] three ways in which the term *same* is used. For since same means one in substance, and substance is used of two things, namely, of the supposit itself and of the nature or species of a thing, the term same is used of three things: either of the supposit alone, as this white thing or this musical man, assuming that Socrates is white or musical; or of the nature of the supposit alone, that is, its intelligible expression or species, as Socrates and Plato are the same in terms of humanity; or of both together, as Socrates is the same as Socrates.

2003. Hence, the Philosopher, in giving these three ways in which the term is used, says that the term same is used in many senses. In one sense it means what is numerically the same, which we sometimes express by the term *itself,* as when we say that Socrates is a man and that he himself is white. For since the pronoun *itself* is reflexive, and a reflexive term brings back the same supposit, wherever the term *itself* is used it signifies that the supposit is numerically one and the same.

2004. A thing is said to be the same in another sense if it is one not only by the oneness of the supposit, as this wood and this white thing, but if it is the same both in its intelligible structure and in number, as you are the same as yourself both specifically and materially, inasmuch as matter, which is the principle of individuation is taken for the supposit, and species is taken for the nature of the supposit.

2005. Things are said to be the same in a third sense when "the intelligible structure of the primary substance," i.e., of the supposit, is one, even though there is not one supposit. And these things are the same specifically or generically but not numerically. He gives an example of this in the case of quantity, according to the opinion of those who claimed that quantities are the substances of things; and according to this opinion many straight lines are regarded as many supposits in the genus of substance, and the measure of a line is considered to be its species. This opinion maintains, then, that many straight lines are one, just as distinct supposits are one which have one specific nature in common. And since mathematicians speak of lines in the abstract, for them many equal straight lines are considered as one. And in a similar fashion many "equal quadrangles," i.e., figures which have four angles and are equal in size and "equiangular," i.e., having equal angles, are considered to be the same. And in such things as these equality provides the unity of their specific nature.

2006. **Things are "like"** [6].

Here he reveals the different ways in which things are said to be *like*, and there are four of these. The first corresponds to the third way in which things are the same; for since that is the same which is one in substance, and that is like which is one in quality, the basis of likeness must be related to the basis of sameness as quality to substance. And since he has used *equality* to designate oneness of substance, he uses *figure* and *proportion* to designate quality.

2007. It should also be noted that, since quality and quantity are rooted in substance, it follows that wherever there is oneness of substance there is oneness of quantity and quality, although this oneness or unity does not derive its name from quantity and quality but from something more basic, namely, substance. Hence, wherever there is oneness of substance we do not speak of likeness or of equality but only of identity.

2008. Diversity of substance, then, is required for likeness or equality. This is why he says that some things are said to be like even though they are not absolutely the same as to the species of their substance (provided that they are also not without difference in their underlying subject, which is called the supposit) but are specifically the same in some way. Thus a larger quadrangle is said to be like a smaller one when the angles of one are equal to those of the other and the sides containing the angles are proportional. It is evident, then, that this likeness is viewed from the standpoint of oneness of figure and proportion. And in a similar way many unequal straight lines are not the same in an absolute sense even though they are like.

2009. It can also be noted here that, when there is unity in regard to the complete concept of the species, we speak of identity. But when there is no unity in regard to the whole concept of the species, we speak of likeness; so that if someone says that things which are generically one are like, then those which are specifically one are the same, as the examples given above would seem to indicate. For he said that equal straight lines and equal quadrangles are identical with each other, whereas unequal quadrangles and unequal straight lines are said to be like.

2010. Things are said to be like in a second sense when they have in common one form which admits of difference in degree although they participate in that form without difference in degree; for example, whiteness admits of greater and lesser intensity, so that, if some things are equally white without any difference in degree, they are said to be like.

2011. Things are said to be like in a third sense when they have in common one form or affection but to a greater or lesser degree; for example, a thing which is whiter and one which is less white are said to be like because they have "one form," i.e., one quality.

2012. Things are said to be like in a fourth sense when they have in common not merely one quality but many, as those things which are said to be like because they agree in more respects than they differ, either in an absolute sense, or in regard to certain particular attributes; for example, tin is said to be like silver because it resembles it in many respects. And similarly fire is like gold, and saffron like red.

2013. **It is evident** [7].

Here he treats the attributes which naturally accompany plurality. First, he considers unlikeness and diversity;

and second [8], he treats difference ("But *different*").

He accordingly says, first [7], that, since the terms *same* and *diverse* and *like* and *unlike* are opposed to each other, and since the terms same and like are used in many senses, it is evident that the terms diverse and unlike are used in many senses; for when one of two opposites is used in many senses, the other is also used in many senses, as is said in the ***Topics***, Book I.[106b13]

2014. But omitting the many senses in which the term unlike is used, since it is quite apparent how the senses of this term are taken in contrast to those of the term like, he gives three senses in which the term *diverse*, or *other*, is employed. First, the term diverse refers to everything that is other in contrast to the same; for just as everything that is itself is said to be the same, and this is the relation of identity, in a similar fashion everything that is diverse is said to be other, and this is the relation of diversity. Hence everything is either the same as or other than everything else. Second, the term diverse, or other, is used in another sense when the matter and intelligible structure of things are not one; and in this sense you and your neighbor are diverse. The term is used in a third sense in mathematics, as when unequal straight lines are said to be diverse.

2015. And since he had said that everything is either the same as or other than everything else, lest someone think that this is true not only of beings but also of non-beings, he rejects this by saying that everything is either the same as or other than everything else in the case of those things of which the terms being and unity are predicated, but not in the case of those things which are non-beings. For same and diverse are not opposed as contradictory terms, of which one or the other must be true of any being or non-being; but they are opposed as contraries, which are only verified of beings. Hence diversity is not predicated of non-beings. But the phrase *not the same*, which is the opposite of *the same* in a contradictory sense, is also used of non-beings. However, *same* or *diverse* is used of all beings; for everything that is a being and is one in itself, when compared with something else, is either one with it, and then it is the same, or it is capable of being one with it but is not, and then it is diverse. Diverse and same, then, are opposites.

2016. But if someone were to raise the objection that diversity and sameness do not apply to all beings, since sameness is a natural consequence of oneness of substance, and diversity is a natural consequence of plurality of substance, we should have to answer that, since substance is the root of the other genera, whatever belongs to substance is transferred to all the other genera, as the Philosopher pointed out above regarding quiddity in Book VII (n. 1334).

2017. **But "different"** [8].

Then he shows how difference and diversity differ. He says that *diverse* and *different* mean different things; for any two things which are diverse need not be diverse in some particular respect, since they can be diverse in themselves. This is evident from what has been said above, because every being is either the same as or other than every other being.

2018. But that which differs from something else must differ from it in some particular respect. Hence that by which different things differ must be something that is the same in things which do not differ in this way. Now that which is the same in many things is either a genus or a species. Therefore all things that differ must differ either generically or specifically.

2019. Those things differ generically which have no common matter; for it has been said above, in Book VIII (n. 1697), that although matter is not a genus, still the essential note of a genus is taken from a thing's material constituent; for example, sensory nature is material in relation to the intellectual nature of man. Hence anything that does not possess sensory nature in common with man belongs to a different genus.

2020. And since those things which do not have a common matter are not generated from each other, it follows that those things are generically diverse which are not generated from each other. It was also necessary to add this because of the things which do not have matter, such as accidents, so that those things which belong to different categories are generically diverse, for example, a line and whiteness, neither one of which is produced from the other.

2021. Now those things are said to be specifically diverse which are the same generically and differ in form. And by genus we mean that attribute which is predicated of two things which differ specifically, as man and horse. Moreover, contraries differ, and contrariety is a type of difference.

2022. **That this assumption** [9].

Then he proves by an induction what he had said above about the formal note whereby things differ, because all things that are different seem to be such that they are not merely diverse but diverse in some particular respect. Some things, for instance, are diverse in genus; some belong to the same category and the same genus but differ in species, and some are the same in species. What things are the same or diverse in genus has been established elsewhere, namely, in Book V of this work (n. 931).

LESSON 5

Contrariety Is the Greatest and Perfect Difference

ARISTOTLE'S TEXT Chapter 4: 1055a3–1055a33

1. *But since it is possible for things which differ from each other to differ to a greater or lesser degree, there is a greatest difference.* **1055a3–4**

2. *And I call this difference contrariety. That this is the greatest difference becomes clear by induction; for things which differ generically cannot pass into each other, but they are too far apart and cannot be compared; and those things which differ specifically arise from contraries as their extremes. But the distance between extremes is the greatest; therefore the distance between contraries is the greatest.* **1055a4–10**

3. *Now what is greatest in each class is perfect (or complete); for that is greatest which nothing exceeds, and that is perfect beyond which it is impossible to find anything else; for the perfect difference is an end, just as other things are said to be perfect because they have attained their end. For there is nothing beyond the end, since in every case it is what is ultimate and contains everything else. There is nothing beyond the end, then, and what is perfect needs nothing else. It is therefore clear from these remarks that contrariety is the perfect or complete difference. And since things are said to be contrary in many ways, it follows that difference will belong to contraries perfectly in proportion to the different types of contrariety.* **1055a10–19**

4. *Since this is so, it is evident that one thing cannot have many contraries; for there can be nothing more extreme than the extreme (since, if there were, it would be the extreme); nor can there be more than two extremes for one distance.* **1055a19–21**

5. *And in general this is evident if contrariety is difference, and difference must be between two things. Hence this will also be true of the perfect difference.* **1055a22–23**

6. *And the other formulations of contraries must also be true. For the perfect difference is the greatest, since in the case of things which differ generically it is impossible to find any difference greater than in those which differ specifically; for it has been shown that there is no difference between things in a genus and those outside it, and for those specifically different the perfect difference is the greatest. And contraries are things which belong to the same genus and have the greatest difference; for the perfect difference is the greatest difference between them. And contraries are things which have the greatest difference in the same subject; for contraries have the same matter. And contraries are things which come under the same potency and have the greatest difference; for there is one science of one class of things, and in these the perfect difference is the greatest.* **1055a2333**

COMMENTARY

2023. Having settled the issue about the one and the many, and about the attributes which naturally accompany them, of which one is contrariety, which is a kind of difference, as has been pointed out (n. 2021), here the Philosopher explains contrariety, because the investigation of it involves a special difficulty. This is divided into two parts. In the first [1] he shows that contrariety is the greatest difference. In the second (Lesson 10) he inquires whether contraries differ generically or specifically ("That which is").

The first part is divided into two. In the first he settles the issue about contraries. In the second (Lesson 9) he deals with their intermediates ("And since").

The first part is divided into two. In the first he settles the issue about the nature of contraries. In the second

(Lesson 7) he raises certain difficulties about the points which have been established ("But since one thing").

The first part is divided into two. In the first he shows what contrariety is. In the second (Lesson 6) he establishes what is true of contrariety as compared with the other kinds of opposition ("The primary contrariety").

In treating the first part he does two things. First, he gives a definition of contrariety. Second [6], he reduces all the other definitions which have been assigned to contraries to the one given ("And the other").

In regard to the first he does two things. First, he gives the definition of contrariety. Second [3], he draws a corollary from this definition ("Now what is").

In regard to the first he does two things. First [1], he shows that there is a greatest difference, as follows: there is some maximum in all things which admit of difference in degree, since an infinite regress is impossible. But it is possible for one thing to differ from something else to a greater or lesser degree. Hence it is also possible for two things to differ from each other to the greatest degree; and therefore there is a greatest difference.

2024. **And I call** [2].

Second, he shows by an induction that contrariety is the greatest difference; for all things which differ must differ either generically or specifically. Now those things which differ generically cannot be compared with each other, being too far apart to admit of any difference of degree between them. This is understood to apply to those things which are changed into each other, because a certain process or way of change of one thing into another is understood from the fact that at first they differ more and afterwards less, and so on until one is changed into the other. But in the case of things which differ generically we do not find any such passage of one thing into another. Hence such things cannot be considered to differ in degree, and so cannot differ in the highest degree. Thus in things which differ generically there is no greatest difference.

2025. However, in the case of things which differ specifically there must be a greatest difference between contraries, because reciprocal processes of generation arise from contraries as their extremes. And an intermediate arises from an extreme or vice versa, or an intermediate also arises from an intermediate, as gray is produced from black or from red. Yet generations of this kind do not arise from two things as extremes; for when something passes from black to gray in the process of generation, it can still pass farther to some color which differs to a greater degree. But when it has already become white, it cannot continue farther to any color which differs to a greater degree from black, and there it must stop as in its extreme state. This is why he says that processes of generation arise from contraries as extremes. But it is evident that the distance between extremes is always the greatest. Hence it follows that contraries have the greatest difference among things which differ specifically.

2026. And since we have shown that things which differ generically are not said to have a greatest difference, although there is a greatest difference, it follows that contrariety is nothing else than the greatest difference.

2027. **Now what is greatest** [3].

He draws two corollaries from what has been said. The first is that contrariety is the perfect difference. This is proved as follows. What is greatest in any class is the same as what is perfect. This is clear from the fact that that is greatest which nothing exceeds; and that is perfect to which nothing can be added. Hence the difference of the greatest and that of the perfect [from a common referent] are seen to be the same.

2028. That that is perfect to which nothing external can be added is evident, because all things are said to be perfect when they go up to the end. Now there is nothing beyond the end, because the end is what is ultimate in every case and contains the thing. Hence nothing lies beyond the end, nor does what is perfect need anything external, but the whole is contained under its own perfection. Thus it is evident that the perfect difference is one which goes up to the end.

2029. Therefore, since contrariety is the greatest difference, as has already been proved (n. 2024), it follows that it is the perfect difference. But since things are said to be contrary in many ways, as will be stated later (n. 2039), not all contraries are said to differ perfectly; but it follows that all contraries differ perfectly in the way in which contrariety belongs to them, i.e., to some primarily and to others secondarily.

2030. **Since this is so** [4].

Here he gives the second corollary. He says that, since the foregoing remarks are true, it is evident that one thing cannot have many contraries. He proves this in two ways. He does this, first, on the grounds that contrariety is the greatest and perfect difference between extremes. But there can be no more than two extremes of one distance; for we see that one straight line has two end points. Further, there is nothing beyond the extreme. If, then, contrariety is one distance, it is impossible for two things to be equally opposed as extremes to one contrary, or for one to be more contrary and another less so, because whatever is less contrary will not be an extreme but will have something beyond it.

2031. **And in general** [5].

He now proves the same thing in another way. He says that since contrariety is a kind of difference, and every difference is a difference between two things, then the perfect difference must also be a difference between two things. Thus one thing has only one contrary.

2032. **And the other** [6].

Next he shows that all the definitions of contraries which have been given are seen to be true on the basis of the definition of contrariety posited above (n. 2023). He gives "four formulations," i.e., definitions, of contraries assigned by other thinkers. The first is that contraries are things which have the greatest difference. Now this is seen to be true on the basis of the foregoing definition, since contrariety is the perfect difference, and this causes things to differ most. For it is evident from what has been said that in the case of things which differ generically nothing can be found which differs more than things which differ specifically, because there is no difference as regards those things which lie outside the genus, as has been stated. And of things which differ specifically the greatest difference is between contraries. Hence it follows that contraries are things which differ most.

2033. The second definition is that contraries are attributes which differ to the greatest degree in the same genus. This is also seen to be true on the basis of the foregoing definition, because contrariety is the perfect difference. But the greatest difference between things which belong to the same genus is the perfect difference. Hence it follows that contraries are attributes which have the greatest difference in the same genus.

2034. The third definition is that contraries are attributes which have the greatest difference in the same subject. This is also seen to be true on the basis of the foregoing definition; for contraries have the same matter since they are generated from each other.

2035. The fourth definition is that contraries are attributes which have the greatest difference "under the same potency," i.e., the same art or science; for science is a rational potency, as has been stated in Book IX (n. 1789). This definition is also seen to be true on the basis of the foregoing definition, because there is one science of one class of things. Therefore, since contraries belong to the same genus, they must come under the same potency or science. And since contrariety is the perfect difference in the same genus, contraries must have the greatest difference among those things which come under the same science.

LESSON 6
Contrariety Based on Privation and Possession

ARISTOTLE'S TEXT Chapter 4: 1055a33–1055b29

1. *The primary contrariety is between possession and privation, not every privation (for privation has several meanings), but any which is perfect.* **1055a33–35**

2. *And the other contraries are referred to these: some because they possess them, others because they produce or can produce them, and others because they are the acquisitions or losses of them or of other contraries.* **1055a35–38**

3. *If, then, the modes of opposition are contradiction, privation, contrariety and relation, and the first of these is contradiction, and there is no intermediate between contradictories whereas there is between contraries, then it is evident that contradiction is not the same as contrariety.* **1055a38–1055b3**

4. *And privation is a kind of contradiction; for that which suffers privation, either totally or in some determinate way, is either that which is totally incapable of having some attribute, or that which does not possess it even though it is naturally fitted to do so; for we have already used this term in many senses, which have been distinguished elsewhere. Hence privation is a kind of contradiction which is found either in a determinate potency or is conceived along with something that is susceptible of it. And for this reason there is no intermediate in contradiction, although there is an intermediate in one kind of privation; for everything is either equal or not equal, but not everything is equal or unequal; but this is so only in the case of something susceptible of equality.* **1055b3–11**

5. *If, then, the processes of generation in matter start from contraries, and these are produced either from the form and the possession of the form, or from the privation of some form or specifying principle, it is evident that every contrariety will be a kind of privation.* **1055b11–14**

6. *But perhaps not every privation is contrariety. And the reason is that whatever suffers privation does so in many ways; for it is the things from which change proceeds as extremes that are contraries.* **1055b14–17**

7. *This also becomes evident by induction; for every contrariety has privation as one of its contrary terms, but not all in the same way; for inequality is the privation of equality, unlikeness the privation of likeness, and vice the privation of virtue.* **1055b17–20**

8. *And privation differs in the ways we have stated (850); for it has one meaning if a thing is merely deprived of some attribute, and another if it is deprived at a certain time or in a certain part (for example, if this happens at a certain age or in the most important part) or entirely. Hence in some cases there is an intermediate (there is a man who is neither good nor evil) and in others there is not (a number must be either even or odd). Again, some have a definite subject, and others do not. Hence it is evident that one of two contraries is always used in a privative sense.* **1055b20–27**

9. *But it is enough if this is true of the primary or generic contraries—one and many; for the others may be reduced to them.* **1055b27–29**

COMMENTARY

2036. Having defined contrariety the Philosopher now compares it with the other kinds of opposition. In regard to this he does two things. First [1], he states his thesis, namely, that the basis of contrariety is the opposition between privation and possession. Second [3], he proves it ("If, then").

In regard to the first he does two things. First, he states that the basis of contrariety is privation and possession. He says that the primary contrariety is privation and possession because privation and possession are included in every contrariety.

2037. But lest someone should think that the opposition between privation and possession and that between contraries are the same, he adds that not every privation is a contrary; for, as has been pointed out above, the term privation is used in several ways. Sometimes a thing is said to be deprived of something when it does not have in any way what it is naturally fitted to have. However, such privation is not a contrary, because it does not presuppose a positive reality which is opposed to possession, though it does presuppose a definite subject. But it is only that privation which is perfect that is said to be a contrary.

2038. And since privation by its very nature does not admit of difference in degree, a privation can be said to be perfect only by reason of some positive reality which is farther removed from possession. For example, not every privation of white is its contrary, but only that which is farthest removed from white, which must be rooted in some nature of the same genus and farthest removed from white. And according to this we say that black is the contrary of white.

2039. **And the other contraries** [2].

Second, he explains how the other contraries are derived from this first contrariety. He says that other contraries "are referred to these," namely, to privation and possession, in different ways. For some things are called contraries because they have in themselves privation and possession, for example, such things as white and black, hot and cold; others because they actually cause privation and possession, as things which cause heat and cold, or because they are virtually the active causes of privation and possession, as things capable of heating and cooling. And others are called contraries because they are acquisitions of the attributes mentioned, as the processes of becoming hot and becoming cold, or because they are the losses of these, as the destruction of heat and cold. And others again are called contraries not only because they express the aforesaid relationships to the primary contraries but also because they have the same relationships to subsequent contraries; for example, if we were to say that fire and water are contraries because they have heat and cold, which are called contraries themselves, as we have seen, because they include privation and possession.

2040. **If, then, the modes** [3].

Then he proves his thesis, namely, that the primary contrariety is privation and possession; and he does this in two ways: first, by a syllogism; second [7], by an induction ("This also").

In regard to the first he does two things. First [3], he shows that contrariety is not contradiction. He says that among the four kinds of opposition between two things—contradiction, as sitting is opposed to not-sitting; privation, as blindness is opposed to sight; contrariety, as black is opposed to white; and relation, as a son is opposed to his father—the first is contradiction.

2041. The reason is that contradiction is included in all the other kinds of opposition as something prior and simpler; for in any kind of opposition it is impossible that opposites should exist simultaneously. This follows from the fact that one of two opposites contains the negation of the other in its notion; for example, the notion of blind contains the fact of its not seeing, and the notion of black, of its not being white. And similarly the notion of son contains his not being the father of him of whom he is the son.

2042. Moreover, it is evident that there is no intermediate in contradiction; for one must either affirm or deny, as has been shown in Book IV (n. 725). However, it belongs to contraries to have an intermediate; and thus it is clear that contrariety and contradiction are not the same.

2043. **And privation** [4].

Then he shows how privation is related to contradiction by indicating the way in which they are alike and that in which they differ. He says that privation is a kind of contradiction; for the term privation is used in one sense when a thing does not have in any way some attribute which it is capable of having, for example, when an animal does not have sight. And this occurs in two ways: first, if it does not have it in any way at all; and second, if it does not have it in some definite respect, for example, at some definite time or in some definite manner, because privation is used in many senses, as has been stated in Books V (n. 1070) and IX (n. 1784).

2044. It is evident from what has been said, then, that privation is a kind of contradiction; and this is shown from the fact that a thing is said to be deprived of something because it does not have it.

2045. That it is not a simple contradiction but one of a sort is evident from the fact that according to its meaning a contradiction requires neither the aptitude nor the existence of any subject; for it may be truly affirmed of any being or non-being whatsoever. Thus we say that an animal does not see, and that wood does not see, and that a non-being does not see. A privation, however, necessarily requires some subject, and sometimes it also requires aptitude in a subject; for that which is a non-being in every respect is not said to be deprived of anything.

2046. He says, then, that privation "is found either in a determinate potency," i.e., one with a capacity for possessing something, or at least "is conceived along with something that is susceptible of it," i.e., along with a subject, even though it has no capacity for possessing something. This would be the case, for example, if we were to say that a word is invisible, or that a stone is dead.

2047. Contradiction, then, cannot have an intermediate, whereas in a sense privation has an intermediate; for everything must be either equal or not equal, whether it is a being or a non-being. However, it is not necessary to say that everything is either equal or unequal, but this is necessary only in the case of something that is susceptible of equality.

2048. Hence the opposition of contradiction has no intermediate whatsoever, whereas the opposition of privation has no intermediate in a determinate subject; but it is not without an intermediate in an absolute sense. And from this it is evident that contrariety, which is such as to have an intermediate, is closer to privation than to contradiction. Yet it still does not follow that privation is the same as contrariety.

2049. **If, then, the processes** [5].

Third, it remains to be shown that contrariety is privation, and in regard to this he does two things. First, he shows by a syllogism that contrariety is privation. He argues as follows: everything from which a process of generation arises is either a form (i.e., the possession of some form) or the privation of some specifying principle (i.e., some form). He says "everything" because generation is twofold. For things are generated absolutely in the genus of substance, but in a qualified sense in the genus of accidents; for generations arise from contraries in matter. Hence it is evident that every contrariety is a privation; for if in any process of generation one of the two extremes is a privation, and each of the contraries is an extreme in the process of generation (because contraries are generated from each other, as white from black and black from white), then one of the two contraries must be a privation.

2050. **But perhaps** [6].

Here he proves another assertion made above, that not every privation is a contrariety. He says that the reason for this is that there are many ways of being deprived; for a thing that is capable of having a form and does not have it in any way can be said to be deprived of it, and it makes no difference whether it is proximately or remotely disposed for that form. Now a contrary is always remotely disposed; for contraries are the sources, in the sense of extremes from which changes arise. Hence it was said above (n. 2038) that they are farthest removed from each other. For whether a thing is yellowish or of some other color, it is said to be deprived of whiteness if it is not white. But it is not on that account called a contrary except when it is farthest removed from whiteness, namely, when it is black. Thus it is clear that not every privation is a contrariety.

2051. And since privation requires nothing else than the absence of form (merely presupposing a disposition in a subject without conferring upon that subject any definite disposition through which the subject is close to a form or distant from it), it is evident that privation does not designate any positive reality in a subject, but presupposes a subject with an aptitude. But a contrary requires a definite disposition in a subject, by which it is farthest removed from a form. Therefore it necessarily designates in a subject some positive reality which belongs to the same class as the absent form, as black belongs to the same class as white.

2052. It should also be noted that privation is of two kinds. There is one which has an immediate relationship to the subject of the form (as darkness has an immediate relationship to the transparent medium), and between a privation of this kind and its opposite form there is reciprocal change; for the atmosphere passes from a state of illumination to one of darkness, and from a state of darkness to one of illumination. And there is another kind of privation which is related to the subject of the form only by means of the form, since it has the nature of a corruption of form; for example, blindness is the corruption of sight, and death the corruption of life. In such cases there is no reciprocal change, as has been pointed out in Book IX (n. 1785).

2053. Therefore, since it has been shown here that contrariety is the privation arising from reciprocal change which involves contraries and privation and form, it is clear that contrariety is not the type of privation which is the corruption of a form, but that which has an immediate relation to the subject of the form. Hence the objection raised in the *Categories*,[13a16] that it is impossible to revert from privation to possession, does not apply here. But contraries are changed into each other.

2054. **This also becomes** [7].

Then he shows by induction that contrariety is privation, and he does this in two ways. First, by making an induction from each type of contrary; and second [9], by reducing them to a primary kind of contrary ("But it is").

In regard to the first [7] he does two things. First, he shows by an induction that contrariety is privation. He says that the point proved above by a syllogistic argument is also made clear by an induction; for every contrariety is found to include the privation of one of the two contraries, since one of the two is always lacking in the other. Yet one contrary is not found to be the privation of the other in the same way in all types of contraries, as will be stated below (n. 2055). That one of two contraries is the privation of the other is evident from the fact that inequality is the privation of equality, and unlikeness the privation of likeness, and evil the privation of virtue.

2055. **And privation differs** [8].

Then he shows that one contrary is the privation of the other in various ways; for this is relative to different types of privation. Now this difference may be considered from two points of view. First, privation can mean either that a thing has been deprived of something in any way at all; or, that it is deprived at some definite time or in some definite way. For example, it is deprived at some definite time if this occurs at some definite age; and it is deprived in some definite part if the privation is found in some important part. Or it may also be "entirely," i.e., in the whole. For a man is said to be senseless if he lacks discretion at a mature age but not as a child. And similarly a person is said to be naked, not if any part of him is uncovered, but if many of his parts or the principal ones are left uncovered.

2056. And because of the various kinds of privation which are included under contrariety it is possible for some contraries to have an intermediate and for some not. For there is an intermediate between good and evil, since a man may be neither good nor evil. For a man is said to be good by reason of virtue, because virtue is what causes its possessor to be good. However, not everyone who lacks virtue is evil; for a boy lacks virtue, yet he is not said to be evil. But if one does not have virtue at an age when he ought to have it, he is then said to be evil. Or if someone also lacks virtue as regards certain insignificant actions and those which, so to speak, make no difference to life, he is not said to be evil, but only if he lacks virtue as to the important and necessary acts of life. But the even and the odd in numbers do not have an intermediate; for a number is said to be odd in the sense that it lacks evenness in any way at all.

2057. The second way in which privations differ is this: one kind of privation has a definite subject of its own, and another kind has not. For it was said above that everything which lacks an attribute, even though it is not naturally such as to have it, is sometimes said to be deprived of it. And according to this difference between privations it is possible for some contraries to have an intermediate or not. For example, we might say that, since man is said to be good with respect to political virtue, if evil, which includes the privation of good, requires a determinate subject, then a rustic who does not participate in civic affairs is neither good nor evil with respect to civic goodness or evil. Hence it is evident from what has been said that one of two contraries is used in a privative sense.

2058. **But it is enough** [9].

He proves the same point by reducing the other contraries to the primary ones. He says that in order to show that one of two contraries is a privation it is enough if this is found to be true in the case of the primary contraries, which are the genera of the others, for example, one and many. That these are the primary contraries is evident from the fact that all other contraries are reduced to them; for equal and unequal, like and unlike, same and other, are reduced to one and many. Moreover, difference is a kind of diversity, and contrariety is a kind of difference, as has been said above (nn. 2017 and 2023). Hence, it is evident that every contrariety is reducible to one and many. But one and many are opposed as the indivisible and the divisible, as has been pointed out above (n. 1983). Therefore it follows that all contraries include privation.

LESSON 7
Opposition of the Equal to the Large and the Small

ARISTOTLE'S TEXT Chapter 5: 1055b30–1056b2

1. *But since one thing has one contrary, someone might raise the question how the one is opposed to the many, and how the equal is opposed to the large and the small.* **1055b30–32**

2. *For we always use the term whether antithetically, for example, whether it is white or black, or whether it is white or not white. But we do not ask whether it is white or man, unless we are basing our inquiry on an assumption, asking, for example, whether it was Cleon or Socrates that came; but this is not a necessary antithesis in any one class of things. Yet even this manner of speaking came from that used in the case of opposites; for opposites alone cannot exist at the same time. And this manner of speaking is used even in asking the question which of the two came. For if it were possible that both might have come at the same time, the question would be absurd; but even if it were possible, the question would still fall in some way into an antithesis, namely, of the one or the many, for example, whether both came, or one of the two.* **1055b32–1056a3**

3. *If, then, the question whether something is such and such always has to do with opposites, and one can ask whether it is larger or smaller or equal, there is some opposition between these and the equal. For it is not contrary to one alone or to both; for why should it be contrary to the larger rather than to the smaller?* **1056a3–7**

4. *Again, the equal is contrary to the unequal. Hence it will be contrary to more things than one. But if unequal signifies the same thing as both of these together, it will be opposed to both.* **1056a7–10**

5. *And this difficulty supports those who say that the unequal is a duality.* **1056a10–11**

6. *But it follows that one thing is contrary to two; yet this is impossible.* **1056a11**

7. *Further, the equal seems to be an intermediate between the large and the small; but no contrariety seems to be intermediate, nor is this possible from its definition; for it would not be complete if it were intermediate between any two things, but rather it always has something intermediate between itself and the other term.* **1056a12–15**

8. *It follows, then, that it is opposed either as a negation or as a privation. Now it cannot be opposed as a negation or a privation of one of the two; for why should it be opposed to the large rather than to the small? Therefore it is the privative negation of both. And for this reason whether is used of both, but not of one of the two; for example, whether it is larger or equal, or whether it is equal or smaller; but there are always three things.* **1056a15–20**

9. *But it is not necessarily a privation; for not everything that is not larger or smaller is equal, but this is true of those things which are naturally capable of having these attributes. Hence the equal is what is neither large nor small but is naturally capable of being large or small; and it is opposed to both as a privative negation.* **1056a20–24**

10. *And for this reason it is also an intermediate. And what is neither good nor evil is opposed to both but is unnamed; for each of these terms is used in many senses, and their subject is not one; but more so what is neither white nor black. And neither is this said to be one thing, although the colors of which this privative negation is predicated are limited; for it must be either gray or red or some other such color.* **1056a24–30**

11. *Hence the criticism of those people is not right who think that all terms are used in a similar way, so that if there is something which is neither a shoe nor a hand, it will be intermediate between the two, since what is neither good nor evil is intermediate between what is good and what is evil, as though there were an intermediate in all cases. But this does not necessarily follow. For one term of opposition is the joint negation of things that are opposed, between*

which there is some intermediate and there is naturally some distance. But between other things there is no difference, for those things of which there are joint negations belong to a different genus. Hence their subject is not one. **1056a30–1056b2**

COMMENTARY

2059. After having shown what contrariety is, here the Philosopher settles certain difficulties concerning the points established above. In regard to this he does two things. First [1], he raises the difficulties; and second [2], he solves them ("For we always").

Now the difficulties [1] stem from the statement that one thing has one contrary; and this appears to be wrong in the case of a twofold opposition. For while the many are opposed to the one, the few are opposed to the many. And similarly the equal also seems to be opposed to two things, namely, to the large and to the small. Hence the difficulty arises as to how these things are opposed. For if they are opposed according to contrariety, then the statement which was made seems to be false, namely, that one thing has one contrary.

2060. **For we always** [2].

Then he deals with the foregoing difficulties; and, first, he examines the difficulty about the opposition between the equal and the large and the small. Second (Lesson 8), he discusses the difficulty about the opposition between the one and the many ("And one might").

In regard to the first he does two things. First, he argues the question dialectically. Second [8], he establishes the truth about this question ("It follows").

In regard to the first he does two things. First, he argues on one side of the question in order to show that the equal is contrary to the large and to the small. Second [6], he argues on the opposite side of the question ("But it follows").

In regard to the first he gives three arguments. In the first of these he does two things. First, he clarifies a presupposition of the argument by stating that we always use the term *whether* in reference to opposites; for example, when we ask whether a thing is white or black, which are opposed as contraries; and whether it is white or not white, which are opposed as contradictories. But we do not ask whether a thing is a man or white, unless we assume that something cannot be both a man and white. We then ask whether it is a man or white, just as we ask whether that is Cleon or Socrates coming, on the assumption that both are not coming at the same time. But this manner of asking about things which are not opposites does not pertain to any class of things by necessity but only by supposition. This is so because we use the term whether only of opposites by necessity, but of other things only by supposition; for only things which are opposed by nature are incapable of coexisting. And this is undoubtedly true if each part of the disjunction "whether Socrates or Cleon is coming" is not true at the same time, because, if it were possible that both of them might be coming at the same time, the above question would be absurd. And if it is true that both cannot be coming at the same time, then the above question involves the opposition between the one and the many. For it is necessary to ask whether Socrates and Cleon are both coming or only one of them. And this question involves the opposition between the one and the many. And if it is assumed that one of them is coming, then the question takes the form, whether Socrates or Cleon is coming.

2061. **If, then, the question** [3].

From the proposition which has now been made clear the argument proceeds as follows: those who ask questions concerning opposites use the term *whether*, as has been mentioned above. But we use this term in the case of the equal, the large and the small; for we ask whether one thing is more or less than or equal to another. Hence there is some kind of opposition between the equal and the large and the small. But it cannot be said that the equal is contrary to either the large or the small, because there is no reason why it should be contrary to the large rather than to the small. And again, according to what has been said before, it does not seem that it is contrary to both, because one thing has one contrary.

2062. **Again, the equal** [4].

He now gives the second argument, which runs thus: the equal is contrary to the unequal. But the unequal signifies something belonging to both the large and the small. Therefore the equal is contrary to both.

2063. **And this difficulty** [5].

Then he gives the third argument, and this is based on the opinion of Pythagoras, who attributed inequality and otherness to the number two and to any even number, and identity to an odd number. And the reason is that the equal is opposed to the unequal; but the unequal is proper to the number two; therefore the equal is contrary to the number two.

2064. **But it follows** [6].

Next, he gives two arguments for the opposite opinion. The first is as follows: the large and the small are two things. Therefore, if the equal is contrary to the large and to the small, one is contrary to two. This is impossible, as has been shown above (n. 2063).

2065. **Further, the equal** [7].

He now gives the second argument, which runs thus: there is no contrariety between an intermediate and its extremes. This is apparent to the senses, and it is also made clear from the definition of contrariety, because it is complete difference. But whatever is intermediate between any two things is not completely different from either of them, because extremes differ from each other more than from an intermediate. Thus it follows that there is no contrariety between an intermediate and its extremes. But contrariety pertains rather to things which have some intermediate between them. Now the equal seems to be the intermediate between the large and the small. Therefore the equal is not contrary to the large and to the small.

2066. **It follows, then** [8].

Here he establishes the truth about this question; and in regard to this he does three things. First, he shows that the equal is opposed to the large and to the small in a way different from that of contrariety; and he draws this conclusion from the arguments given above on each side of the question. For the first set of arguments showed that the equal is opposed to the large and to the small, whereas the second showed that it is not contrary to them. It follows, then, that it is opposed to them by some other type of opposition. And after having rejected the type of opposition according to which the equal is referred to the unequal but not to the large and the small, it follows that the equal is opposed to the large and to the small either as their negation or as their privation.

2067. He shows in two ways that in the latter type of opposition the equal is opposed to both of the others (the large and the small) and not merely to one of them. First, he says that there is no reason why the equal should be the negation or the privation of the large rather than of the small, or vice versa. Hence it must be the negation or the privation of both.

2068. He also makes this clear by an example, saying that, since the equal is opposed to both, then when we are making inquiries about the equal we use the term *whether* of both and not merely of one; for we do not ask whether one thing is more than or equal to another, or whether it is equal to or less than another. But we always give three alternatives, namely, whether it is more than or less than or equal to it.

2069. **But it is not necessarily** [9].

Second, he indicates the type of opposition by which the equal is opposed to the large and to the small. He says that the particle *not,* which is contained in the notion of the equal when we say that the equal is what is neither more nor less, does not designate a negation pure and simple but necessarily designates a privation; for a negation pure and simple refers to anything to which its own opposite affirmation does not apply; and this does not occur in the case proposed. For we do not say that everything which is not more or less is equal, but we say this only of those things which are capable of being more or less.

2070. Hence the notion of equality amounts to this, that the equal is what is neither large nor small, but is naturally capable of being either large or small, just as other privations are defined. Thus it is evident that the equal is opposed to both the large and the small as a privative negation.

2071. **And for this reason** [10].

Third, in concluding his discussion between the large and the small; and he shows that the equal is intermediate in regard to this he does two things. First, he draws his thesis as the conclusion of the foregoing argument. For since it has been said that the equal is what is neither large nor small but is naturally capable of being the one or the other, then anything that is related to contraries in this way is intermediate between them, just as what is neither good nor evil is opposed to both and is intermediate between them. Hence it follows that the equal is intermediate between the large and the small. But there is this difference between the two cases: what is neither large nor small has a name, for it is called the equal, whereas what is neither good nor evil does not have a name.

2072. The reason for this is that sometimes both of the privations of two contraries coincide in some one definite term; and then there is only one intermediate, and it can easily be given a name, as the equal. For by the fact that a thing has one and the same quantity it is neither more nor less. But sometimes the term under which both of the privations of the contraries fall is used in several senses, and there is not merely one subject of both of the privations taken together; and then it does not have one name but either remains completely unnamed, like what is neither good nor evil, and this occurs in a number of ways; or it has various names, like what is neither white nor black; for this is not some one thing. But there are certain undetermined colors of which the aforesaid privative negation is used; for what is neither white nor black must be either gray or yellow or some such color.

2073. **Hence the criticism** [11].

Then he rejects the criticism which some men offered against the view that what is neither good nor evil is an intermediate between good and evil. For they said that it would be possible on the same grounds to posit an intermediate between any two things whatsoever. Hence he says that, in view of the explanation that things having an intermediate by the negation of both extremes as indicated require a subject capable of being either extreme, it is clear that the doctrine of such an intermediate is unjustly criticized by those who think that the same could therefore be said in all cases (say, that between a shoe and a hand there is something which is neither a shoe nor a hand) because what is neither good nor evil is intermediate between good and evil, since for this reason there would be an intermediate between all things.

2074. But this is not necessarily the case, because this combination of negations which constitute an intermediate belongs to opposites having some intermediate, between which, as the extremes of one genus, there is one distance. But the other things which they adduce, such as a shoe and a hand, do not have such a difference between them that they belong to one distance; because the things of which they are the combined negations belong to a different genus. Negations of this kind, then, do not have one subject; and it is not possible to posit an intermediate between such things.

LESSON 8
Opposition between the One and the Many

ARISTOTLE'S TEXT Chapter 6: 1056b3–1057a17

1. *And one might raise similar questions about the one and the many. For if the many are opposed absolutely to the one, certain impossible conclusions will follow.* **1056b3–5**

2. *For one will then be few or a few; for the many are also opposed to the few. Further, two will be many, since the double is multiple, and the double is so designated in reference to two. Hence one will be few; for in relation to what can two be many, except to one, and therefore few? For nothing else is less than this.* **1056b5–9**

3. *Further, if much and little are in plurality what long and short are in length, and if what is much is also many, and what is many is much (unless perhaps there is some difference in the case of an easily-bounded continuum), few will be a plurality. Hence one will be a plurality, if it is few; and this will be necessary if two are many.* **1056b10–14**

4. *But perhaps, while many is said in a sense to be much, there is a difference; for example, there is much water but not many waters. But many designates those things which are divided.* **1056b14–17**

5. *In one sense much means a plurality which is excessive either absolutely or comparatively; and in a similar way few means a plurality which is deficient; and in another sense it designates number, which is opposed only to one. For it is in this sense that we say one or many, just as if we were to say "one" and in the plural "ones," as white or whites, or to compare what is measured with a measure, that is, a measure and the measurable. And it is in this sense that multiples are called such; for each number is called many because it is made up of ones and because each number is measurable by one; and number is many as the opposite of one and not of few. So therefore in this sense even two is many; but it is not such as a plurality which is excessive either absolutely or comparatively; but two is the first few absolutely, for it is the first plurality which is deficient.* **1056b17–28**

6. *For this reason Anaxagoras was wrong in speaking as he did when he said that all things were together and unlimited both in plurality and in smallness. He should have said in fewness instead of in smallness; for things could not have been unlimited in fewness, since few is not constituted by one, as some say, but by two.* **1056b28–32**

7. *The one is opposed to the many, then, as a measure is opposed to things measurable, and these are opposed as things which are not relative of themselves. But we have distinguished elsewhere the two senses in which things are said to be relative; for some are relative as contraries, and others as knowledge is relative to the knowable object, because something else is said to be relative to it.* **1056b32–1057a1**

8. *But nothing prevents one thing from being fewer than something else, for example, two; for if it is fewer, it is not few. And plurality is in a sense the genus of number, since number is many measured by one. And in a sense one and number are opposed, not as contraries but in the way in which we said that some relative terms are opposed; for they are opposed inasmuch as the one is a measure and the other something measurable. And for this reason not everything that is one is a number, for example, anything that is indivisible.* **1057a1–7**

9. *But while knowledge is similarly said to be relative to the knowable object, the relation is not similar. For knowledge might seem to be a measure, and its object to be something measured; but the truth is that while knowledge is knowable, not all that is knowable is knowledge, because in a way knowledge is measured by what is knowable.* **1057a7–12**

10. *And plurality is contrary neither to the few (though the many is contrary to this as an excessive plurality to a plurality which is exceeded), nor to the one in every sense; but they are*

contrary in the way we have described, because the one is as something indivisible and the other as something divisible. And in another sense they are relative as knowledge is relative to the knowable object, if plurality is a number and the one is a measure. **1057a12–17**

COMMENTARY

2075. Having treated the question which he had raised regarding the opposition of the equal to the large and to the small, here the Philosopher deals with the question concerning the opposition of the one to the many. In regard to this he does two things. First [1], he debates the question. Second [4], he establishes the truth ("But perhaps").

In regard to the first he does three things. First, he gives the reason for the difficulty. He says that, just as there is a difficulty about the opposition of the equal to the large and to the small, so too the difficulty can arise whether the one and the many are opposed to each other. The reason for the difficulty is that, if the many without distinction are opposed to the one, certain impossible conclusions will follow unless one distinguishes the various senses in which the term many is used, as he does later on (n. 2080).

2076. **For one will** [2].

He then proves what he had said; for he shows that, if the one is opposed to the many, the one is few or a few. He does this by two arguments, of which the first is as follows. The many are opposed to the few. Now if the many are opposed to the one in an unqualified sense and without distinction, then, since one thing has one contrary, it follows that the one is few or a few.

2077. The second argument runs thus. Two things are many. This is proved by the fact that the double is multiple. But the many are opposed to the few. Therefore two are opposed to few. But two cannot be many in relation to a few except to one; for nothing is less than two except one. It follows, then, that one is a few.

2078. **Further, if much** [3].

Then he shows that this—one is a few—is impossible; for one and a few are related to plurality as the long and the short are to length; for each one of these is a property of its respective class. But any short thing is a certain length. Hence every few is a certain plurality. Therefore if one is a few, which it seems necessary to say if two are many, it follows that one is a plurality.

2079. The one, then, will not only be much but also many; for every much is also many, unless perhaps this differs in the case of fluid things, which are easily divided, as water, oil, air and the like, which he calls here an easily-bounded continuum; for fluid things are easily limited by a foreign boundary. For in such cases the continuous is also called much, as much water or much air, since they are close to plurality by reason of the ease with which they are divided. But since any part of these is continuous, that is said to be much (in the singular) which is not said to be many (in the plural). But in other cases we use the term many only when the things are actually divided; for if wood is continuous we do not say that it is many but much; but when it becomes actually divided we not only say that it is much but also many. Therefore in other cases there is no difference between saying much and many, but only in the case of an easily-bounded continuum. Hence, if one is much, it follows that it is many. This is impossible.

2080. **But perhaps** [4].

Here he solves the difficulty which he had raised; and in regard to this he does two things. First, he shows that much is not opposed to one and to a few in the same way. Second [7], he shows how the many and the one are opposed ("The one").

In regard to the first he does two things. First, he solves the proposed difficulty; and second [6], in the light of what has been said he rejects an error ("For this reason").

And since he had touched on two points above, in the objection which he had raised, from which it would seem to follow that it is impossible for much to be many and for many to be opposed to a few, he therefore first of all makes the first point clear. He says that perhaps in some cases the term *many* is used with no difference from the term *much*. But in some cases, namely, in that of an easily-bounded continuum, much and many are taken in a different way, for example, we say of one continuous volume of water that there is much water, not many waters. And in the case of things which are actually divided, no matter what they may be, much and many are both used indifferently.

2081. **In one sense** [5].

Then he explains the second point: how the many and the few are opposed. He says that the term many is used in two senses. First, it is used in the sense of a plurality of things which is excessive, either in an absolute sense or in comparison with something. It is used in an absolute sense when we say that some things are many because they are excessive, which is the common practice with things that belong to the same class; for example, we say much rain when the rainfall is above average. It is used in comparison with something when we say that ten men are many compared with three. And in a similar way a few means "a plurality which is deficient," i.e., one which falls short of an excessive plurality.

2082. The term much is used in an absolute sense in a second way when a number is said to be a plurality; and in this way many is opposed only to one, but not to a few. For many in this sense is the plural of the word one; and so we say one and many, the equivalent of saying one and ones, as we say white and whites, and as things measured are referred to what is able to measure. For the many are measured by one, as is said below (n. 2087). And in this sense multiples are derived from many. For it is evident that a thing is said to be multiple in terms of any number; for example, in terms of the number two it is double, and in terms of the number three it is triple, and so on. For any number is many in this way, because it is referred to one, and because anything is measurable by one. This happens insofar as many is opposed to one, but not insofar as it is opposed to few.

2083. Hence two things, which are a number, are many insofar as many is opposed to one; but insofar as many signifies an excessive plurality, two things are not many but few; for nothing is fewer than two, because one is not few, as has been shown above (n. 2078). For few is a plurality which has some deficiency. But the primary plurality which is deficient is two. Hence two is the first few.

2084. **For this reason** [6].

In the light of what has been said he now rejects an error. For it should be noted that Anaxagoras claimed that the generation of things is a result of separation. Hence he posited that in the beginning all things were together in a kind of mixture, but that mind began to separate individual things from that mixture, and that this constitutes the generation of things. And since, according to him, the process of generation is infinite, he therefore claimed that there are an infinite number of things in that mixture. Hence he said that before all things were differentiated they were together, unlimited both in plurality and in smallness.

2085. And the claims which he made about the infinite in respect to its plurality and smallness are true, because the infinite is found in continuous quantities by way of division, and this infinity he signified by the phrase *in smallness*. But the infinite is found in discrete quantities by way of addition, which he signified by the phrase *in plurality*.

2086. Therefore, although Anaxagoras had been right here, he mistakenly abandoned what he had said. For it seemed to him later on that in place of the phrase *in smallness* he ought to have said *in fewness;* and this correction was not a true one, because things are not unlimited in fewness. For it is possible to find a first few, namely, two, but not one as some say. For wherever it is possible to find some first thing there is no infinite regress. However, if one were a few, there would necessarily be an infinite regress; for it would follow that one would be many, because every few is much or many, as has been stated above (n. 2078). But if one were many, something would have to be less than one, and this would be few, and that again would be much; and in this way there would be an infinite regress.

2087. **The one** [7].

Next, he shows how the one and the many are opposed; and in regard to this he does two things. First, he shows that the one is opposed to the many in a relative sense. Second [10], he shows that an absolute plurality is not opposed to few ("And plurality").

In regard to the first he does three things. First, he shows that the one is opposed to the many relatively. He says that the one is opposed to the many as a measure to what is measurable, and these are opposed relatively, but not in such a way that they are to be counted among the things which are relative of themselves. For it was said above in Book V (n. 1026) that things are said to be relative in two ways: for some things are relative to each other on an equal basis, as master and servant, father and son, great and small; and he says that these are relative as contraries; and they are relative of themselves, because each of these things taken in its quiddity is said to be relative to something else.

2088. But other things are not relative on an equal basis, but one of them is said to be relative, not because it itself is referred to something else, but because something else is referred to it, as happens, for example, in the case of knowledge and the knowable object. For what is knowable is called such relatively, not because it is referred to knowledge, but because knowledge is referred to it. Thus it is evident that things of this kind are not relative of themselves, because the knowable is not said to be relative of itself, but rather something else is said to be relative to it.

2089. **But nothing prevents** [8].

Then he shows how the one is opposed to the many as to something measurable. And because it belongs to the notion of a measure to be a minimum in some way, he therefore says, first, that one is fewer than many and also fewer than two, even though it is not a few. For if a thing is fewer, it does not follow that it is few, even though the notion of few involves being less, because every few is a certain plurality.

2090. Now it must be noted that plurality or multitude taken absolutely, which is opposed to the one which is interchangeable with being, is in a sense the genus of number; for a number is nothing else than a plurality or multitude of things measured by one. Hence one, insofar as it means an indivisible being absolutely, is interchangeable with being; but insofar as it has the character of a measure, in this respect it is limited to some particular category, that of quantity, in which the character of a measure is properly found.

2091. And in a similar way insofar as plurality or multitude signifies beings which are divided, it is not limited to any particular genus. But insofar as it signifies something measured, it is limited to the genus of quantity, of which number is a species. Hence he says that number is plurality measured by one, and that plurality is in a sense the genus of number.

2092. He does not say that it is a genus in an unqualified sense, because, just as being is not a genus properly speaking, neither is the one which is interchangeable with being nor the plurality which is opposed to it. But it is in some sense a genus, because it contains something belonging to the notion of a genus inasmuch as it is common.

2093. Therefore, when we take the one which is the principle of number and has the character of a measure, and number, which is a species of quantity and is the plurality measured by one, the one and the many are not opposed as contraries, as has already been stated above (n. 1997) of the one which is interchangeable with being and of the plurality which is opposed to it; but they are opposed in the same way as things which are relative, i.e., those of which the term one is used relatively. Hence the one and number are opposed inasmuch as the one is a measure and number is something measurable.

2094. And because the nature of these relative things is such that one of them can exist without the other, but not the other way around, this is therefore found to apply in the case of the one and number. For wherever there is a number the one must also exist; but wherever there is a one there is not necessarily a number. For if something is indivisible, as a point, we find the one there, but not number. But in the case of other relative things, each of which is said to be relative of itself, one of these does not exist without the other; for there is no master without a servant, and no servant without a master.

2095. **But while** [9].

Here he explains the similarity between the relation of the knowable object to knowledge and that of the one to the many. He says that, although knowledge is truly referred to the knowable object in the same way that number is referred to the one, or the unit, it is not considered to be similar by some thinkers; for to some, the Protagoreans, as has been said above (n. 1800), it seemed that knowledge is a measure, and that the knowable object is the thing measured. But just the opposite of this is true; for it has been pointed out that, if the one, or unit, which is a measure, exists, it is not necessary that there should be a number which is measured, although the opposite of this is true. And if there is knowledge, obviously there must be a knowable object; but if there is some knowable object it is not necessary that there should be knowledge of it. Hence it appears rather that the knowable object has the role of a measure, and knowledge the role of something measured; for in a sense knowledge is measured by the knowable object, just as a number is measured by one; for true knowledge results from the intellect apprehending a thing as it is.

2096. **And plurality** [10].

Then he shows that an absolute plurality or multitude is not opposed to a few. He says that it has been stated before that insofar as a plurality is measured it is opposed to the one as to a measure, but it is not opposed to a few. However, much, in the sense of a plurality which is excessive, is opposed to a few in the sense of a plurality which is exceeded. Similarly a plurality is not opposed to one in a single way but in two. First, it is opposed to it in the way mentioned above (n. 2081), as the divisible is opposed to the indivisible; and this is the case if the one which is interchangeable with being and the plurality which is opposed to it are understood universally. Second, plurality is opposed to the one as something relative, just as knowledge is opposed to its object. And this is the case, I say, if one understands the plurality which is number, and the one which has the character of a measure and is the basis of number.

LESSON 9
The Nature of Contraries

ARISTOTLE'S TEXT Chapter 7: 1057a18–1057b34

1. *And since there can be an intermediate between contraries, and some contraries admit of intermediates, intermediates must be composed of contraries.* **1057a18–19**

2. *For all intermediates and the things of which they are the intermediates belong to the same genus. For we call those things intermediates into which something undergoing change must first change; for example, if one should pass from the top-string note to the bottom-string note, assuming that the passage is made through the intervening register, he will first come to the intermediate sounds. And the same thing is true in the case of colors; for if one will pass from white to black, he will first come to purple and to gray before he comes to black; and it is similar in the case of other things. But it is not possible except accidentally for a change to take place from one genus to another, for example, from color to figure. Hence intermediates and the things of which they are the intermediates must belong to the same genus.* **1057a19–30**

3. *But all intermediates are intermediates between certain things that are opposed; for it is only from these that change in the strict sense can arise. And for this reason there cannot be intermediates between things that are not opposed; for otherwise there would be a change which is not from opposites.* **1057a30–33**

4. *For the opposites involved in contradiction admit of no intermediates, for this is what contradiction is: an opposition of which one or the other part applies to anything whatever and which does not have an intermediate. But of other opposites some are relative, some privative, and some contrary. And between those terms that are relative and not contrary there is no intermediate. The reason is that they do not belong to the same genus; for what is the intermediate between knowledge and the knowable object? There is an intermediate, however, between the large and the small.* **1057a33–1057b1**

5. *Now if intermediates belong to the same genus, as we have shown, and are intermediates between things that are contrary, they must be composed of these contraries.* **1057b2–4**

6. *For there will be some genus of these contraries or there will not. And if there is some genus such that it is something prior to the contraries, there will be contrary differences prior to the species, constituting them as contrary species of the genus; for species are composed of genus and differences. Thus, if white and black are contraries and the one is an expanding color and the other a contracting color, the differences "expanding" and "contracting" will be prior. Hence these things that are contrary to each other will be prior. But contrary differences are more truly contrary [than contrary species].* **1057b4–12**

7. *And the other species, the intermediate ones, will be composed of genus and differences; for example, all colors intermediate between white and black must be defined by a genus (which is color) and by differences. But these differences will not be the primary contraries; and if this were not the case, every color would be either white or black. Hence the intermediate species are different from the primary contraries.* **1057b12–18**

8. *And the primary differences will be "expanding" and "contracting," because these are primary. Moreover, it is necessary to investigate those contraries which belong to the same genus and to discover the things of which their intermediates are composed. For things belonging to the same genus must either be composed of things that are incomposite in the same genus, or must be incomposite in themselves. For contraries are not composed of each other, and thus are principles; but either all intermediates are incomposite, or none of them are. But something comes about from contraries. Hence change will affect this before reaching the contraries, for it will be less than one contrary and greater than the other, and thus this will be*

an intermediate between the contraries. All the other intermediates, then, are composites; for that intermediate which is greater than one contrary and less than the other is composed in a sense of these contraries of which it is said to be greater than one and less than the other. And since there are no other things belonging to the same genus which are prior to the contraries, all intermediates will be composed of contraries. All inferiors, then, both contraries and intermediates, must be composed of the primary contraries. **1057b18–32**

9. Hence it is evident that all intermediates belong to the same genus; that they are intermediates between contraries; and that they are composed of contraries. **1057b32–34**

COMMENTARY

2097. Having expressed his views about contraries, the Philosopher now does the same thing with regard to the intermediates between contraries; and concerning this he does two things. First [1], he indicates what his plan is. He says that, since there can be an intermediate between contraries, as has been shown above [3], and some contraries have an intermediate, it is necessary to show that intermediates are composed of contraries. He not only does this but also proves certain points needed for this proof.

2098. **For all intermediates** [2].

Then he carries out his plan; and in regard to this he does three things. First [2], he shows that intermediates belong to the same genus as contraries. Second [3], he shows that there are intermediates only between contraries ("But all intermediates"). Third [5], he establishes his main thesis, that intermediates are composed of contraries ("Now if intermediates").

He accordingly says, first [2], that all intermediates belong to the same class as the things of which they are the intermediates. He proves this by pointing out that intermediates are defined as that into which a thing undergoing change from one extreme to another first passes.

2099. He makes this clear by two examples. First, he uses the example of sounds; for some sounds are low and some are high and some are intermediate. And strings on musical instruments are distinguished by this distinction of sounds; for those strings which yield low pitched sounds are called "top-strings" because they are the basic ones, and those which yield high pitched sounds are called "bottom-strings." Hence, if a musician wishes to proceed step by step from low sounds to high ones, and so to pass through an intermediate register, he must first come to the intermediate sounds. Second, he makes this clear by using colors. For if a thing is changed from white to black, it must first pass through the intermediate colors before it reaches black. The same thing is true of other intermediates.

2100. It is evident, then, that change passes from intermediates to extremes and the reverse. But things belonging to diverse genera are changed into each other only accidentally, as is clear with regard to color and figure; for a thing is not changed from color to figure or vice versa, but from color to color, and from figure to figure. Hence intermediates and extremes must belong to the same genus.

2101. **But all intermediates** [3].

Here he shows that intermediates stand between contraries; and in regard to this he does two things. First, he shows that intermediates must stand between opposites. Second [4], he indicates the kind of opposites between which they stand, namely, contraries ("For the opposites").

He accordingly says, first [3], that all intermediates must stand between opposites. He proves this as follows: changes arise, properly speaking, only from opposites, as is proved in Book I of the ***Physics;*** [188a31] for properly speaking a thing changes from black to white; and what is sweet comes from black only accidentally inasmuch as it is possible for something sweet to become white. But intermediates stand between things which are changed into each other, as is evident from the definition of intermediates given above [2]. Therefore it is impossible that intermediates should not stand between opposites; otherwise it would follow that change would not proceed from opposites.

2102. **For the opposites** [4].

Then he indicates the kinds of opposites that can have intermediates. He says that there cannot be any intermediates whatsoever between the opposite terms of a contradiction; for contradictory opposition is such that one part of it must belong to any type of subject, whether it be a being or a non-being. For we must say that any being or non-being either is sitting or is not sitting. Thus it is evident that contradictories have no intermediate.

2103. But in the case of other opposites some involve relations, some privation and form, and some contraries. Now of opposites which are relative, some are like contraries which are related to each other on an equal basis, and these have an intermediate. But some do not have the character of contraries, for example, those which are not related to each other on an equal basis, as knowledge and a knowable object; and these do not have an intermediate. And the reason is that intermediates and extremes belong to the same genus. But these things do not belong to the same genus, since the one is related in itself, as knowledge, but the other is not, as the knowable object. How, then, can there be an intermediate between knowledge and the knowable object? But there can be "an intermediate" between the large and the small, and this is the equal, as has been stated above (n. 2102). The same thing is true of those things which are related to each other as contraries. He does not mention how things which are opposed privatively have an intermediate or how they do not, and how this opposition somehow pertains to contrariety, because he has explained these points above (nn. 2043–53).

2104. **Now if intermediates** [5].

Third, he proves the point that constitutes his main thesis. He says that, if intermediates belong to the same genus as extremes, as has been shown (n. 2098), and if again there are intermediates only between contraries, as has also been shown (n. 2104), then intermediates must be composed of the contraries between which they stand.

2105. **For there will** [6].

Then he proves his thesis; and in regard to this he does three things. First, he proves that contrary species have prior contraries of which they are composed. He proceeds as follows: there must either be a genus of contraries or not. But if there is no genus of contraries, contraries will not have an intermediate; for there is an intermediate only between those things which belong to one genus, as is evident from what has been said. But if those contraries which are assumed to have an intermediate have some genus which is prior to the contraries themselves, there must also be different contraries prior to contrary species, which make and constitute contrary species from this one genus. For species are constituted of genus and differences.

2106. He makes this clear by an example. If white and black belong to contrary species and have one genus, color, they must have certain constitutive differences, so that white is a color capable of expanding vision, and black is a contracting color. Therefore the differences "contracting" and "expanding" are prior to white and to black. Hence, since in each case there is a contrariety, it is evident that some contraries are prior to others; for contrary differences are prior to contrary species; and they are also contrary to a greater degree because they are causes of the contrariety in these species.

2107. However, it must be understood that, while "expanding" and "contracting" as referred to vision are not true differences which constitute white and black, but rather are their effects, still they are given in place of differences as signs of them, just as differences and substantial forms are sometimes designated by accidents. For the expansion of vision comes from the strength of the light, whose fullness constitutes whiteness. And the contraction of vision has as its cause the opposite of this.

2108. **And the other** [7].

He shows too that intermediate species have prior intermediates of which they are composed. He says that, since intermediates are species of the same genus, and all species are constituted of genus and differences, intermediates must be constituted of genus and differences; for example, any colors that are intermediate between white and black must be defined by their genus, color, and by certain differences; and these differences of which intermediate colors are composed cannot be the immediate "primary contraries," i.e., the differences which constitute the contrary species of white and black. Again, any color must be intermediate between white and black; for black is a contracting color and white an expanding color. Hence the differences which constitute intermediate colors must differ according to the different contraries which are constitutive of contrary species. And since differences are related to differences as species are to species, then just as intermediate colors are intermediate species between contrary species, in a similar fashion the differences which constitute them must be intermediate between the contrary differences which are called primary contraries.

2109. **And the primary** [8].

Then he shows that intermediate differences are composed of contrary differences. He says that primary contrary differences are those which can expand and contract sight, so that these differences constitute a primary type of which we compose every species of a genus. But if certain contraries did not belong to the same genus, we would still have to consider of which of these contraries the intermediates would be composed. This is not difficult to understand in the case of those things which belong to the same genus, because all things belonging to the same genus "must either be incomposite," i.e., simple things, or they must be composed "of incomposites," i.e., of simple things, which belong to the same genus. For contraries are not composed of each other, because white is not composed of black, nor black of white; nor is the contracting composed of the expanding or the reverse. Hence contraries must be principles, because the simple things in any genus are the principles of that genus.

2110. But it is necessary to say that all intermediates are composed either "of simple things," i.e., of contraries, or they are not, because the same reasoning seems to apply to all. But it cannot be said that they are not, because there is an intermediate which is composed of contraries, and according to this it is possible for change to first affect intermediates before it affects extremes. This becomes evident as follows: that in which change first occurs admits of difference in degree in relation to the two extremes; for something becomes slightly white or slightly black before it becomes completely white or completely black; and it is what is less white that becomes plain white, and what is less black that becomes plain black. And it also comes closer to white than to plain black, and closer to black than to plain white. Thus it is evident that the thing which change first affects admits of difference in degree in relation to both extremes; and for this reason contraries must have an intermediate. It follows, then, that all intermediates are composed of contraries; for the same intermediate which is more and less in relation to both extremes must be composed of both unqualified extremes, in reference to which it is said to be more and less. And since there are no extremes which are prior to contraries in the same genus, it follows that the two contrary differences which constitute intermediates are composed of contrary differences. Thus intermediates must come from contraries. This is evident because "all inferiors," i.e., all species of a genus, both contraries and intermediates, are composed of primary contraries, i.e., differences.

2111. **Hence it is evident** [9].

He brings his discussion to a close by summarizing what has been said above about intermediates. This part of the text is clear.

LESSON 10
How Contraries Differ in Species

ARISTOTLE'S TEXT Chapter 8: 1057b35–1058a28

1. That which is differentiated specifically differs from something, and it must be in both of the things which differ; for example, if animal is differentiated into species, both must be animals. Hence those things which differ specifically must belong to the same genus; for by genus I mean that by which both things are said to be one and the same, and which does not involve an accidental difference, whether it is conceived as matter or in some other way. For not only must the common attribute belong to both, for example, that both are animals, but animal itself must also be different in such things; for example, the one must be a horse and the other a man. This common attribute, then, must be specifically different in each. Therefore the one will be essentially this kind of animal and the other that kind of animal; for example, the one will be a horse and the other a man. Thus it is necessary that this difference be a difference of the genus; for by a difference of a genus I mean the difference which makes the genus itself different. **1057b35–1058a8**

2. Therefore this will be contrariety; and this also becomes clear by an induction; for all things are distinguished by opposites. **1058a8–10**

3. And it has been shown that contraries belong to the same genus; for contrariety was shown to be the perfect difference (844). And every difference in species is something of something. Hence this is the same for both and is their genus. Thus all contraries which differ specifically and not generically are contained in the same order of the categories, and they differ from each other to the greatest degree; for the difference between them is a perfect one, and they cannot be generated at the same time. The difference, then, is contrariety; for this is what it means to differ specifically, namely, to have contrariety and to belong to the same genus while being undivided. And all those things are specifically the same which do not have contrariety while being undivided; for contrarieties arise in the process of division and in the intermediate cases before one reaches the things which are undivided. **1058a10–21**

4. It is evident, then, regarding what is called the genus, that none of the things which agree in being species of the same genus are either specifically the same as the genus or specifically different from it; for matter is made known by negation, and the genus is the matter [of that of which it is considered to be the genus]; not in the sense that we speak of the genus (or race) of the Heraclidae, but in the sense that genus is found in a nature; nor is it so with reference to things that do not belong to the same genus; but they differ from them in genus, and things that differ specifically differ from those that belong to the same genus. For a contrariety must be a difference, but it need not itself differ specifically. To differ specifically, however, pertains only to things that belong to the same genus. **1058a21–28**

COMMENTARY

2112. Because the Philosopher has shown above (n. 2107) that contrariety is a kind of difference, and difference is either generic or specific, his aim here is to show how contraries differ generically and specifically. This is divided into two parts. In the first [1] he shows that difference in species is contrariety. In the second (Lesson 11) he shows how this does not apply in the case of some contraries ("But someone").

In regard to the first he does three things. First, he shows that the difference which causes difference in species belongs essentially to the same genus as the attribute which divided the nature itself of the genus into different species. Second [2], he shows that this is proper to contrariety ("Therefore this will"). Third [4], he draws a corollary from what has been said ("It is evident").

He accordingly says, first [1], that wherever there is difference in species two things must be considered, namely, that one thing differs from something else, and that there is something which is differentiated by these two. And that which is differentiated by these two must belong to both; for example, animal is something divided into various species, say, man and horse; and both of these, man and horse, must be animals. It is evident, then, that things which differ specifically from each other must belong to the same genus.

2113. For that which is one and the same for both and is not predicated of each accidentally or differentiated into each accidentally is called their genus. Hence it must have a difference which is not accidental whether the genus is assumed to have the nature of matter or is taken in some other way.

2114. Now he says this because matter is differentiated in one way by form, and genus is differentiated in another way by differences; for form is not matter itself but enters into composition with it. Hence matter is not the composite itself but is something belonging to it. But a difference is added to a genus, not as part to part, but as whole to whole; so that the genus is the very thing which is the species, and is not merely something belonging to it. But if it were a part, it would not be predicated of it.

2115. Yet since a whole can be named from one of its own parts alone, for example, if a man is said to be headed or handed, it is possible for the composite itself to be named from its matter and form. And the name which any whole gets from its material principle is that of the genus. But the name which it gets from its formal principle is the name of the difference. For example, man is called an animal because of his sensory nature, and he is called rational because of his intellective nature. Therefore, just as "handed" belongs to the whole even though the hand is a part, in a similar way genus and difference refer to the whole even though they are derived from the parts of the thing.

2116. If in the case of genus and difference, then, one considers the principle from which each is derived, the genus is related to differences as matter is to forms. But if one considers them from the viewpoint of their designating the whole, then they are related in a different way. Yet this is common to both, namely, that just as the essence of matter is divided by forms, so too the nature of a genus is divided by differences. But both differ in this respect, that, while matter is contained in both of the things divided, it is not both of them. However, the genus is both of them; because matter designates a part, but the genus designates the whole.

2117. Therefore in explaining his statement that a genus is that by which both of the things which differ specifically are said to be one and the same, he adds that, not only must the genus be common to both of the things which differ specifically (as, for instance, both are animals) as something which is undivided is common to different things, just as a house and a possession are the same, but the animal in both must differ, so that this animal is a horse and that animal is a man.

2118. He says this against the Platonists, who claimed that there are common separate natures in the sense that the common nature would not be diversified if the nature of the species were something else besides the nature of the genus. Hence from what has been said he concludes against this position that whatever is common is differentiated specifically. Hence the common nature in itself, for example, animal, must be this sort of animal with one difference, and that sort of animal with another difference, so that the one is a horse and the other is a man. Thus if animal in itself is this and that sort of animal, it follows that the difference which causes difference in species is a certain difference of the genus. And he explains the diversification of a genus which makes a difference in the generic nature itself.

2119. Now what the Philosopher says here rules out not only the opinion of Plato, who claimed that one and the same common nature exists of itself, but also the opinion of those who say that whatever pertains to the nature of the genus does not differ specifically in different species, for example, the opinion that the sensory soul of a man does not differ specifically from that in a horse.

2120. **Therefore this will** [2].

Then he shows that the difference which divides the genus essentially in the foregoing way is contrariety. He says that, since the specific difference divides the genus essentially, it is evident that this difference is contrariety.

He makes this clear, first, by an induction; for we see that all genera are divided by opposites. And this must be so; for those things which are not opposites can coexist in the same subject; and things of this kind cannot be different, since they are not necessarily in different things. Hence anything common must be divided by opposites alone.

2121. But the division of a genus into different species cannot come about by way of the other kinds of opposites. For things which are opposed as contradictories do not belong to the same genus, since negation posits nothing. The same is true of privative opposites, for privation is nothing else than negation in a subject. And relative terms, as has been explained above (n. 2103), belong to the same genus only if they are in themselves relative to each other and are in a sense contraries, as has been stated above *(ibid.)*. It is evident, then, that only contraries cause things belonging to the same genus to differ specifically.

2122. **And it has** [3].

Then he proves the same point by an argument. He says that contraries belong to the same genus, as has been shown (n. 2105). For it has been pointed out (nn. 2027–29) that contrariety is the perfect difference; and it has also been stated that difference in species is "something of something," i.e., from something. And besides this it has been noted (n. 2112) that the same genus must belong to both of the things which differ specifically. Now from these two considerations it follows that all contraries are contained in the same "order of the categories," i.e., in the same classification of predicates, yet in such a way that this is understood of all contraries which differ specifically but not generically. He says this in order to preclude the corruptible and the incorruptible, which are later said to differ generically.

2123. And contraries not only belong to one genus but they also differ from each other. This is evident, for things which differ perfectly as contraries are not generated from each other at the same time. Therefore, since difference in species requires identity of genus and the division of the genus into different species, and since both of these are found in contrariety, it follows that difference in species is contrariety. This is evident because in order for things in the same genus to differ specifically they must have contrariety of differences "while being undivided," i.e., when they are not further divided into species, as the lowest species. And these are said to be undivided inasmuch as they are not further divided formally. But particular things are said to be undivided inasmuch as they are not further divided either formally or materially. And just as those things are specifically different which have contrariety, so too those things are specifically the same which do not have contrariety, since they are not divided by any formal difference. For contrarieties arise in the process of division, not only in the highest genera but also in the intermediate ones, "before one reaches the things which are undivided," i.e., the lowest species. It is accordingly evident that, even though there is not contrariety of species in every genus, there is contrariety of differences in every genus.

2124. **It is evident** [4].

Here he draws a corollary from what has been said, namely, that none of the things which agree in being species of the same genus are said to be either specifically the same as the genus or specifically different from it; for things which are said to be specifically the same have one and the same difference, whereas things which are said to be specifically different have opposite differences. Hence, if any species is said to be specifically the same as the genus or specifically different from it, it follows that the genus will contain some difference in its definition. But this is false.

2125. This is made evident as follows: matter "is made known by negation," i.e., the nature of matter is understood by negating all forms. And in a sense genus is matter, as has been explained (nn. 2113–15); and we are now speaking of genus in the sense that it is found in the natures of things, and not in the sense that it applies to men, as the genus (or race) of the Romans or of the Heraclidae. Hence it is clear that a genus does not have a difference in its definition.

2126. Thus it is evident that no species is specifically different from its genus, nor is it specifically the same as its genus. And similarly things that do not belong to the same genus do not differ specifically from each other, properly speaking, but they do differ generically. And things that differ specifically differ from those that belong to the same genus; for a contrariety is the difference by which things differ specifically, as has been explained (n. 2120)—not that the contrariety itself of the differences need differ specifically, even though contraries differ specifically; but contrariety is found only in those things that belong to the same genus. It follows, then, that to differ specifically does not properly pertain to things that belong to different genera.

LESSON 11
The Nature of Specific Difference

ARISTOTLE'S TEXT Chapter 9: 1058a29–1058b26

1. But someone might raise the question why woman does not differ specifically from man, since male and female are opposites, and their difference is a contrariety; and why a female and a male animal do not differ specifically, although this difference belongs to animal in itself, and not as whiteness or blackness does; but it is both male and female inasmuch as it is animal. And this question is almost the same as the question why one contrariety causes things to differ specifically and another does not, for example, why "capable of walking" and "capable of flying" do this, but whiteness and blackness do not. **1058a29–36**

2. And the reason may be that the former are proper affections of the genus and the latter are less so. And since one [principle of a thing] is its intelligible structure and the other is matter, all those contrarieties in the intelligible structure of a thing cause difference in species, whereas those which are conceived with matter do not. And for this reason neither the whiteness nor blackness of man causes this. Nor do white man and black man differ specifically, even if each is designated by a single name. For inasmuch as man is considered materially, matter does not cause a difference; for individual men are not species of man for this reason, even though the flesh and bones of which this man and that man are composed are distinct. The concrete whole is other but not other in species because there is no contrariety in its intelligible structure. This is the ultimate and indivisible species. But Callias is the intelligible structure with matter; and a white man is also, because it is Callias who is white. But man is white accidentally. Hence a brazen circle and a wooden one do not differ specifically; for a brazen triangle and a wooden circle differ specifically not because of their matter but because there is contrariety in their intelligible structure. And the question arises whether matter, differing in a way itself, does not cause specific difference, or there is a sense in which it does. For why is this horse specifically different from this man, even though matter is included in their intelligible structure? Is it because contrariety is included in their intelligible structure? For white man and black horse differ specifically, but they do not do so inasmuch as the one is white and the other is black, since even if both were white they would still differ specifically. **1058a36–1058b21**

3. However, male and female are proper affections of animal, but are not such according to its substance but in the matter or body. It is for this reason that the same sperm by undergoing some modification becomes a male or a female. **1058b21–24**

4. What it is to be specifically different, then, and why some things are specifically different and others not, has been stated. **1058b24–25**

COMMENTARY

2127. Since the Philosopher has already shown that contrariety constitutes difference in species, here he indicates the kinds of things in which contrariety does not constitute difference in species; and this is divided into two parts. In the first [1], he shows that there are contraries which do not cause difference in species but belong to the same species. In the second (Lesson 12), he indicates what the contraries are which cause things to differ in genus and not merely in species ("But since contraries").

In regard to the first he does two things. First, he raises a question. Second [2], he answers it ("And the reason").

He accordingly says, first [1], that the question arises why woman does not differ specifically from man, since female and male are contraries, and difference in species is caused by contrariety, as has been established (n. 2112).

2128. Again, since it has been shown that the nature of a genus is divided into different species by those differences which are essential to the genus, the question also arises why a male and a female animal do not differ specifically, since male and female are essential differences of animal and are not accidental to animal as whiteness and blackness are; but male and female are predicated of animal as animal just as the even and the odd, whose definition contains number, are predicated of number; so that animal is given in the definition of male and female.

2129. Hence the first question presents a difficulty for two reasons: both because contrariety causes difference in species, and because the differences that divide a genus into different species are essential differences of the genus. Both of these points have been proved above (n. 2112).

2130. And since he had raised this question in certain special terms, he reduces it to a more general form. He says that this question is almost the same as asking why one kind of contrariety causes things to differ in species and another does not; for capabilities of walking and of flying, i.e., having the power to move about and to fly, cause animals to differ specifically, but whiteness and blackness do not.

2131. **And the reason** [2].

Here he answers the question that was raised, and in regard to this he does two things. First, he answers the question in a general way with reference to the issue to which he had reduced the question. Second [3], he adapts the general answer to the special terms in which he had first asked the question ("However, male and female").

He accordingly says [2] that one kind of contrariety can cause difference in species and another cannot, because some contraries are the proper affections of a genus, and others are less proper. For, since genus is taken from matter, and matter in itself has a relation to form, those differences which are taken from the different forms perfecting matter are the proper differences of a genus. But since the form of the species may be further multiplied to become distinct things by reason of designated matter, which is the subject of individual properties, the contrariety of individual accidents is related to a genus in a less proper way than the contrariety of formal differences. Hence he adds that, since the composite contains matter and form, and the one "is the intelligible structure," i.e., the form, which constitutes the species, and the other is matter, which is the principle of individuation, all those "contraries in the intelligible structure," i.e., all which have to do with the form, cause difference in species, whereas those contrarieties which have to do with matter and are proper to the individual thing, which is taken with matter, do not cause difference in species.

2132. Hence whiteness and blackness do not cause men to differ specifically; for white man and black man do not differ specifically, even if a one-word name were given to each of them, say, "white man" were called A and "black man" were called B. He adds this because "white man" does not seem to be one thing, and the same is true of "black man." Hence he says that "white man" and "black man" do not differ specifically, because man, i.e., a particular man, to whom both white and black belong, serves as matter; for man is said to be white only because this man is white. Thus since a particular man is conceived along with matter, and matter does not cause difference in species, it follows that this particular man and that particular man do not differ specifically. For many men are not many species of man on the grounds that they are many, since they are many only by reason of the diversity of their matter, i.e., because the flesh and bones of which this man and that man are composed are different. But "the concrete whole," i.e., the individual constituted of matter and form, is distinct; yet it is not specifically different because there is no contrariety as regards form. But this, namely, man, is the ultimate individual from the viewpoint of species, because the species is not further divided by a formal division. Or this, namely, the particular thing, is the ultimate individual, because it is not further divided either by a material difference or a formal one. But while there is no contrariety in distinct individuals as regard form, nevertheless there is a distinction between particular individuals; because a particular thing, such as Callias, is not a form alone but a form with individuated matter. Hence, just as difference of form causes difference of species, so too otherness in individual matter causes difference of individuals. And white is predicated of man only by way of the individual; for man is said to be white only because some particular man, such as Callias, is said to be white. Hence it is evident that man is said to be white accidentally, because a man is said to be white, not inasmuch as he is man, but inasmuch as he is this man. And this man is called "this" because of matter. Thus it is clear that white and black do not pertain to the formal difference of man but only to his material difference. Therefore "white man" and "black man" do not differ specifically, and neither do a bronze circle and a wooden circle differ specifically. And even those things which differ specifically do not do so by reason of their matter but only by reason of their form. Thus a bronze triangle and a wooden circle do not differ specifically by reason of their matter but because they have a different form.

2133. If one were to ask, then, whether matter somehow causes difference in species, the answer would seem to be that it does, because this horse is specifically different from this man, and it is no less evident that the notion of each contains individual matter. Thus it appears that matter somehow causes difference in species.—But on the other hand it is also evident that this does not come about by reason of any difference in their matter, but because there is contrariety with regard to their form. For "white man" and "black horse" differ specifically, yet they do not do so by reason of whiteness and blackness; for even if both were white they would still differ specifically. It appears, then, that the kind of contrariety which pertains to form causes difference in species, but not the kind which pertains to matter.

2134. **However, male and female** [3].

Next he adapts the general answer which he has given to the special terms in reference to which he first raised the question, namely, male and female. He says that male and female are proper affections of animal, because animal is included in the definition of each. But they do not pertain to animal by reason of its substance or form, but by reason of its matter or body. This is clear from the fact that the same sperm insofar as it undergoes a different kind of change can become a male or a female animal; because, when the heat at work is strong, a male is generated, but when it is weak, a female is generated. But this could not be the case or come about if male and female differed specifically; for specifically different things are not generated from one and the same kind of sperm, because it is the sperm that contains the active power, and every natural agent acts by way of a determinate form by which it produces its like. It follows, then, that male and female do not differ formally, and that they do not differ specifically.

2135. **What it is** [4].

Here he sums up what has been said. This is clear in the text.

LESSON 12
The Corruptible and the Incorruptible Differ Generically

ARISTOTLE'S TEXT Chapter 10: 1058b26–1059a14

1. But since contraries differ (or are other) specifically, and since corruptible and incorruptible are contraries (for privation is a definite incapacity), the corruptible and incorruptible must differ generically. **1058b26–29**

2. Now we have already spoken of these general terms. But, as will be seen, it is not necessary that every incorruptible thing should differ specifically from every corruptible thing, just as it is not necessary that a white thing should differ specifically from a black one. For the same thing can be both at the same time if it is universal; for example, man can be both white and black. But the same thing cannot be both at the same time if it is a singular; for the same man cannot be both white and black at the same time, since white is contrary to black. **1058b29–35**

3. But while some contraries belong to some things accidentally, for example, those just mentioned and many others, some cannot; and among these are the corruptible and the incorruptible. For nothing is corruptible accidentally. For what is accidental is capable of not belonging to a subject; but incorruptible is a necessary attribute of the things in which it is present; otherwise one and the same thing will be both corruptible and incorruptible, if it is possible for corruptibility not to belong to it. The corruptible, then, must either be the substance or belong to the substance of each corruptible thing. The same also holds true for the incorruptible, for both belong necessarily to things. Hence insofar as the one is corruptible and the other incorruptible, and especially on this ground, they are opposed to each other. Hence they must differ generically. **1058b35–1059a10**

4. It is clearly impossible, then, that there should be separate Forms as some claim; for in that case there would be one man who is corruptible and another who is incorruptible. Yet the separate Forms are said to be specifically the same as the individuals, and not in an equivocal sense; but things which differ generically are different to a greater degree than those which differ specifically. **1059a10–14**

COMMENTARY

2136. After having shown what contraries do not cause things to differ specifically, here the Philosopher explains what contraries cause things to differ generically. In regard to this he does three things. First [1], he establishes the truth. Second [2], he rejects the false opinion of certain men ("Now we have already"). Third [4], he draws a corollary from his discussion ("It is clearly").

He accordingly first of all [1] lays down two premises necessary for the proof of his thesis. The first of these is that contraries are formally different, as was explained above (n. 2120).

2137. The second premise is that the corruptible and the incorruptible are contraries. He proves this from the fact that the incapacity opposed to a definite capacity is a kind of privation, as has been stated in Book IX (n. 1784). Now privation is a principle of contrariety; and therefore it follows that incapacity is contrary to capacity, and that the corruptible and the incorruptible are opposed as capacity and incapacity. But they are opposed in a different way. For if capacity is taken according to its general meaning, as referring to the ability to act or to be acted upon in some way, then the term corruptible is used like the term capacity, and the term incorruptible like the term incapacity. But if the term capacity is used of something inasmuch as it is incapable of undergoing something for the worse, then contrariwise the term incorruptible is referred to capacity, and the term corruptible is referred to incapacity.

2137a. But although it seems necessary from these remarks to conclude that the corruptible and the incorruptible differ specifically, he concludes that they differ generically. And this is true because, just as form and actuality pertain to the species, so too matter and capacity pertain to the genus. Hence, just as the contrariety which pertains to form and actuality causes difference in species, so too the contrariety which pertains to capacity or potency causes difference in genus.

2138. **Now we have already** [2].

Here he rejects the false opinion of certain men; and in regard to this he does two things. First, he gives this opinion. Second [3], he shows that it is false ("But while some").

He accordingly says, first [2], that the proof which was given above regarding the corruptible and the incorruptible is based on the meaning of these universal terms, i.e., inasmuch as one signifies a capacity and the other an incapacity. But, as it seems to certain men, it is not necessary that the corruptible and the incorruptible should differ specifically, just as this is not necessary for white and black, because it is admissible for the same thing to be both white and black, although in different ways. For if what is said to be white and black is something universal, it is white and black at the same time in different subjects. Thus it is true to say that man is at the same time both white, because of Socrates, and black, because of Plato. But if it is a singular thing, it will not be both white and black at the same time (although it can now be white and afterward black) since white and black are contraries. Thus some say that some things can be corruptible and some incorruptible within the same genus, and that the same singular thing can sometimes be corruptible and sometimes incorruptible.

2139. **But while some** [3].

Here he rejects the foregoing opinion. He says that some contraries belong accidentally to the things of which they are predicated, as white and black belong to man, as has been mentioned already (n. 2131); and there are many other contraries of this kind in reference to which the view stated is verified, i.e., that contraries can exist simultaneously in the same species and successively in the same singular thing. But there are other contraries which are incapable of this, and among these are the corruptible and the incorruptible.

2140. For corruptible does not belong accidentally to any of the things of which it is predicated, because what is accidental is capable of not belonging to a thing. But corruptible belongs necessarily to the things in which it is present. If this were not so it would follow that the very same thing would sometimes be corruptible and sometimes incorruptible; but this is naturally impossible. (However, this does not prevent the divine power from being able to keep some things which are corruptible by their very nature from being corrupted.)

2141. Since the term corruptible, then, is not an accidental predicate, it must signify either the substance of the thing of which it is predicated or something belonging to the substance; for each thing is corruptible by reason of its matter, which belongs to its substance. The same argument applies to incorruptibility, because both belong to a thing necessarily. Hence it is evident that corruptible and incorruptible are opposed as essential predicates, which are predicated of a thing inasmuch as it is a thing of this kind, as such and primarily.

2142. And from this it necessarily follows that the corruptible and the incorruptible differ generically; for it is evident that contraries which belong to one genus do not belong to the substance of that genus; for "rational" and "irrational" do not belong to the substance of animal. But animal is the one or the other potentially. And whatever genus may be taken, corruptible and incorruptible must pertain to its intelligible make-up. It is impossible, then, that they should have a common genus. And this is reasonable, for there cannot be a single matter for both corruptible and incorruptible things. Now speaking from the viewpoint of the philosophy of nature, genus is taken from the matter; and thus it was said above (n. 2125) that things which do not have a common matter are other or different in genus. But speaking from the viewpoint of logic, nothing prevents them from having the same common genus inasmuch as they have one common definition, either that of substance or of quality or of quantity or something of this sort.

2143. **It is clearly impossible** [4].

Next he draws a corollary from his discussion, namely, that there cannot be separate Forms as the Platonists claimed; for they maintained that there are two men: a sensible man who is corruptible, and a separate man who is incorruptible, which they called the separate Form or Idea of man. But the separate Forms or Ideas are said to be specifically the same as individual things, according to the Platonists. And the name of the species is not predicated equivocally of the separate Form and of singular things, although the corruptible and the incorruptible differ even generically. And those things which differ generically are more widely separated than those which differ specifically.

2144. Now it must be observed that, although the Philosopher has shown that some contraries do not cause things to differ specifically, and that some cause things to differ even generically, none the less all contraries cause things to differ specifically in some way if the comparison between contraries is made with reference to some definite genus. For even though white and black do not cause difference in species within the same genus of animal, they do cause difference in species in the genus of color. And male and female cause difference in species in the genus of sex. And while living and nonliving cause difference in genus in reference to the lowest species, still in reference to the genus which is divided essentially into living and non-living they merely cause difference in species. For all differences of a genus constitute certain species, although these species can differ generically.

2145. But corruptible and incorruptible divide being essentially, because that is corruptible which is capable of not being, and that is incorruptible which is incapable of not being. Hence, since being is not a genus, it is not surprising if the corruptible and the incorruptible do not have a common genus. This brings our treatment of Book X to a close.

BOOK XI
RECAPITULATION ON THE NATURE AND SUBJECT OF META-PHYSICS.
MOTION

LESSON 1
Metaphysics Is the Science of Principles

ARISTOTLE'S TEXT Chapter 1: 1059a18–1060a2

1. That wisdom is a science of principles, then, is evident from the first chapters of this work, in which problems were raised concerning the statements of other philosophers about the principles of things. **1059a18–20**

2. But one might raise the question whether wisdom must be understood to be one science or many. For if it is one, then the objection might be raised that one science always deals with contraries; but principles are not contraries. And if it is not one but many, what kind of sciences must they be assumed to be? **1059a20–23**

3. Further, one might raise the question whether it is the office of one science or of many to study the principles of demonstration? For if it is the office of one science, why should it be the office of this science rather than of another? And if it is the office of many, what kind of sciences must these be admitted to be? **1059a23–26**

4. Further, there is the question whether it is the office of wisdom to deal with all substances or not? And if not with all, it is difficult to say with what kind it does deal. But if there is one science of all substances, the problem arises how one science can deal with many subjects. **1059a26–29**

5. Again, there is the question whether this science is a demonstration of substances alone, or also of accidents (184, 205–207); for if it is a demonstration of accidents, it is not a demonstration of substances. But if there is a different science of accidents, what is the character of each, and which of the two is wisdom? For a demonstrative science of accidents is wisdom; but that which deals with primary things is the science of substances. **1059a29–34**

6. But the science which we are seeking must not be assumed to be the one which deals with the causes mentioned in the Physics. For it does not deal with the final cause, because such is the good, and this is found in the sphere of practical affairs and in things which are in motion. And it is the first thing which causes motion (for the end is such a nature); but there is no first mover in the realm of immobile things. **1059a34–38**

7. And in general there is the question whether the science which is now being sought is concerned with sensible substances, or whether it is not concerned with these but with certain others. For, if it deals with other substances, it must be concerned with either the separate Forms or with the objects of mathematics. Now it is evident that separate Forms do not exist. **1059a38–1059b3**

8. But nevertheless even if one were to assume that these separate Forms exist, the problem would arise why the same thing should not be true of the other things of which there are Forms as is true of the objects of mathematics. I mean that they place the objects of mathematics between the Forms and sensible things as a kind of third class of entities besides the Forms and the things which exist here. But there is no third man or horse over and above man-in-himself and horse-in-itself and singular men and horses. **1059b3–9**

9. If, however, the situation is not as they say, with what kind of things must the mathematician be assumed to deal? For he is not concerned with the things which exist here, because none of these are the kind of things which the mathematical sciences study. Nor is the science which we are now seeking concerned with the objects of mathematics; for no one of these is capable of existing separately. Nor does it deal with sensible substances, for these are corruptible. **1059b9–14**

10. And in general one might raise the question to what science it belongs to consider the problem about the matter of the mathematical sciences. It is not the office of the philosophy of nature, for this science is wholly concerned with things which have in themselves a principle of rest and of motion. Nor is it the office of the science which investigates demonstration and scientific knowledge, for it is about this class of things that it makes its investigations. It follows, then, that it pertains to the philosophy which we have proposed to investigate these things. **1059b14–21**

11. And one might raise the question whether the science which is now being sought must deal with the principles which are called elements by some thinkers. But all men suppose these to be present in composite things. And it would seem rather that the science which is now being sought ought to deal with universals, for every intelligible nature and every science is of universals and not of extremes, so that in this way they would deal with the primary genera. **1059b21–27**

12. And these would become being and unity; for these most of all might be thought to contain all existing things and to be principles in the highest degree, because they are first by nature; for when they have been destroyed, everything else is destroyed, since everything is a being and one. But if one supposes them to be genera, then inasmuch as it is necessary for differences to participate in them, and no difference participates in a genus, it would seem that they must not be regarded either as genera or as principles. **1059b27–34**

13. Further, if what is more simple is more of a principle than what is less simple, and the ultimate members resulting from the subdivision of different genera are more simple than the genera themselves (for these members are indivisible, whereas genera are divided into many different species), it would seem that species are principles to a greater degree than genera. But since species are involved in the destruction of their genera, genera are like principles to a greater degree; for whatever involves something else in its destruction is a principle of that thing. These and other such points, then, are the ones which cause difficulties. **1059b34–1060a2**

COMMENTARY

2146. Because the particular sciences disregard certain things which should be investigated, there must be a universal science which examines these things. Now such things seem to be the common attributes which naturally belong to being in general (none of which are treated by the particular sciences since they do not pertain to one science rather than to another but to all in general) and to the separate substances, which lie outside the scope of every particular science. Therefore, in introducing us to such knowledge, Aristotle, after he has investigated these attributes, begins to deal particularly with the separate substances, the knowledge of which constitutes the goal to which the things studied both in this science and in the other sciences are ultimately directed.

Now in order that a clearer understanding of the separate substances may be had, Aristotle first [1] makes a summary of the points discussed both in this work and in the ***Physics*** which are useful for knowing the separate substances. Second (1055:C 2488), he investigates the separate substances in themselves (in the middle of the following book: "Since there are" [Lesson 5]).

The first part is divided into two. In the first he summarizes the points which act as a preface to the study of substances. In the second he restates the things that pertain to the study of substances (at the beginning of the following book: "The study here").

He prefaced his study of substances by doing three things. First, he raised the questions given in Book III, which he now restates under the first point of discussion. Second (Lesson 3), he expressed his views about the things that pertain to the study of this science. These are given in Book IV and are restated here under the second point of discussion ("Since the science"). Third (Lesson 8), he drew his conclusions about imperfect being, i.e., accidental being, motion, and the infinite, about which he had partly established the truth in Books II (n. 299) and VI (nn. 1171–1244) of this work, and partly in Book III of the ***Physics;*** and he gives a summary restatement of these under the third point of discussion ("Since the term *being*").

The first part is divided into two. First, he raises a question about the study of this science; and second (Lesson 2), about the things established in this science ("Further, there is").

In regard to the first he does two things. First, he asks in what way the study of this science is concerned with principles and substances. Second [6], he asks with what principles and what substances it deals ("But the science").

In regard to the first he does two things. First, he raises questions about the study of the principles of this science; and second [4], about this science's study of substances ("Further, there is the question").

In treating the first point [1] he does three things. First, he assumes that the investigations of this science are concerned with principles. He says that it is evident from Book I (nn. 93–272), in which he argued against the statements that other philosophers have made about the first principles of things, that wisdom is a science of principles. For it was shown in the Prologue to this work that wisdom considers the highest and most universal causes, and that it is the noblest of the sciences.

2147. **But one might** [2].

Second, he raises a question about the study of the principles by this science which is called wisdom. He says that one can ask whether wisdom, which considers principles, must be one science or many.

2148. However, if we say that it is one, this seems to be inconsistent, because many of the things studied in one science are contraries, since one contrary is the basis for knowing the other, and thus both contraries seem to fall under one art. But since the principles of things are many, they are not contraries, otherwise they could not be combined in one subject. Hence, wisdom, which is concerned with principles, does not seem to be one science. And if it is not one science but many, it is impossible to state what these sciences are.

2149. Now the truth of the matter is that, while wisdom is one science, it considers many principles inasmuch as they are reduced to one genus, because contraries fall under one science since they belong to one genus.

2150. **Further, one might** [3].

Third, he raises a question about the study which this science makes of the principles of demonstration. He says that it is still a problem whether the study of the principles of demonstration (for example, every whole is greater than one of its parts, and the like) belongs to the study of one science or many. If one claims that such a study belongs to one science, it seems difficult to explain why it belongs to this science rather than to another, since all sciences make common use of these principles. But if one claims that it belongs to many sciences, it seems difficult to give many such sciences.

2151. Now the truth of the matter is that there is one science which is chiefly concerned with these principles, and this is the one which investigates the common terms involved in these principles, such as being and non-being, whole and part, and the like; and the other sciences receive such principles from this science.

2152. **Further, there is** [4].

Then he raises questions about this science's study of substances; and there are two of these. First, he asks whether or not this science considers all substances. If one claims that it does not, it is difficult to indicate what substances it does consider and what not. And if one claims that it considers all substances, the question remains how one and the same science can deal with many substances, since each science treats of one thing.

2153. The truth is that, although this science deals especially with the separate substances, it does treat all substances inasmuch as all belong to one common class of essential being.

2154. **Again, there is** [5].

Second, he asks whether there is demonstration only with regard to substances or also with regard to accidents; for, if demonstration, properly speaking, were concerned with accidents, there would be no demonstration with regard to substances, since it is the function of demonstration to infer the essential accidents of substances. But if one claims that there is one demonstrative science of substances and another of essential accidents, the question remains as to which science each of these is, and whether each is worthy of the name of wisdom. For, on the one hand, it does seem that the science which deals with accidents is wisdom, because demonstration is properly concerned with accidents, and demonstrative science is the most certain. Thus it seems that wisdom, which is a demonstrative science, deals with accidents. But, on the other hand, it seems to deal with substances; for since substances are the primary kind of being, it seems that the science which treats of them is the primary science.

2155. Now the truth is that wisdom considers both substances and accidents inasmuch as they have being in common, which constitutes the subject of wisdom; but its demonstrations are concerned chiefly with substances, which are the primary kind of essential beings, and of these it demonstrates the accidents.

2156. **But the science** [6].

Then he raises more specific questions about the study of this science. First [6], he asks about the substances which this science considers; and second [11], about the principles which it considers ("And one might").

In treating the first point he raises four questions. The first [6] has to do with the causes of sensible substances. He says that it does not seem that we should hold that the science which we are seeking is concerned with the four classes of causes discussed in the ***Physics**, [194b15 ff.]* because it seems to deal especially with the final cause, which is the most important of all.—But this science does not seem to deal with "the final cause," or goal, because an end or goal has the nature of the good. Now the good relates to operations and to things which are in motion. Hence in the case of immovable things, such as the objects of mathematics, nothing is demonstrated by way of the final cause. It is also evident that the end is what first moves a thing, for it moves the efficient cause. But there does not seem to be a first cause of motion in the case of immovable things.

2157. Now the truth of the matter is that this science considers the classes of causes mentioned, especially the formal and final cause. And furthermore, the end, which is the first cause of motion, is altogether immovable, as will be shown below (n. 2526).

2158. **And in general** [7].

Second, he raises a question about the study of sensible substances. He asks whether this science is concerned with sensible substances or not. For if it is concerned with them, it does not seem to differ from the philosophy of nature. But if it is concerned with other substances, it is difficult to state what these substances are. For it must deal with either "the separate Forms," i.e., the Ideas, which the Platonists posited, or with the objects of mathematics, which some supposed to exist as an intermediate class of things between the Ideas and sensible substances, for example, surfaces, lines, figures and the like. But it is evident from the previous books that "separate Forms do not exist," i.e., separate Ideas; and so he immediately raises the question about the objects of mathematics.

2159. Now the true answer to this question is that this science deals with sensible substances inasmuch as they are substances, but not inasmuch as they are sensible and movable; for this latter belongs properly to the philosophy of nature. But the proper study of this science has to do with substances which are neither Ideas nor separate mathematical entities but primary movers, as will be seen below (n. 2488).

2160. **But nevertheless** [8].

Third, he raises a third difficulty as a secondary issue. For, since he had said that there are evidently no separate Forms, he poses the question whether the objects of mathematics are separate. First, he shows that they are not. For if one claims that there are separate Forms and separate mathematical entities over and above sensible substances, why is not the same thing true of all things which have Forms as is true of the objects of mathematics? So that just as the objects of mathematics are assumed to be intermediate between the separate Forms and sensible substances as a third class of things over and above the separate Forms and the singular things which exist here (for example, a mathematical line over and above the Form of a line and the perceptible line), in a similar fashion there should be a third man and a third "horse over and above man-in-himself and horse-in-itself" (i.e., the ideal man and the ideal horse, which the Platonists called Ideas) and individual men and horses. But the Platonists did not posit intermediates in such cases as these but only in that of the objects of mathematics.

2161. **If, however** [9].

Then he argues on the other side of the question; for, if the objects of mathematics are not separate, it is difficult to indicate the things with which the mathematical sciences deal. For they do not seem to deal with sensible things as such, because no lines and circles such as the mathematical sciences investigate are found in sensible things. It seems necessary to hold, then, that there are certain separate lines and circles.

2162. Now the truth of the matter is that the objects of mathematics are not separate from sensible things in being but only in their intelligible structure, as has been shown above in Book VI (n. 1162) and will be considered below (n. 2185).

2163. And since he had interjected as a secondary issue this difficulty about the separateness of the objects of mathematics because he had said that forms evidently are not separate, therefore when he says, "Nor is the science which we are now seeking concerned with the objects of mathematics," he returns to the main question that was raised, namely, with what kind of substances this science deals. And since he had shown that it does not deal with separate Forms (for there are no separate Forms), he now shows by the same reasoning that it does not deal with the objects of mathematics; for neither are they separate in being. And it does not seem to deal with sensible substances, because these are destructible and in motion.

2164. The true answer to this question is the one given above.

2165. **And in general one might** [10].

Then he gives a fourth difficulty by asking to what science it belongs "to consider the problems about the matter of the mathematical sciences," i.e., to investigate the things with which the mathematical sciences are concerned. This does not pertain to the philosophy of nature, because it is wholly concerned with those things which have in themselves a principle of rest and of motion and are called natural beings. Therefore he does not examine this problem. Similarly, the investigation of this problem does not seem to belong to that science which is called mathematical, which has as its aim the demonstration and knowledge of mathematical entities; for this kind of science presupposes matter of this sort or a subject of this sort, and some science does investigate this subject. It follows, then, that it is the business of this philosophical science to consider the things of which the mathematical sciences treat.

2166. **And one might** [11].

Then he asks what kind of principles this science investigates. In regard to this he raises three questions. First, he asks whether this science studies the principles which are called elements by some thinkers. This question seems to refer to the common supposition that principles of this kind are present in, i.e., intrinsic to, the composite, so that in order to know composite things these principles must be known. But from another point of view it seems that this science is concerned with more universal things, because every intelligible nature and every science seems to be "of universals and not of extremes," i.e., not about the particular things in which the division of common genera terminates. Thus it seems that this science has to do especially with the first genera.

2167. But the truth is that this science deals chiefly with common attributes, yet without making the common factors principles in a Platonic sense. However, it does consider the intrinsic principles of things—matter and form.

2168. **And these would** [12].

Second, he raises the second problem. For, on the one hand, it seems that unity and being are principles and genera, because these most of all seem to contain all things within their general ambit. And they seem to be principles because they are first by nature; for when they are destroyed, other things are too; for everything is a being and one. Hence, if being and unity are destroyed, everything else is destroyed, but not the other way around.

2169. But, on the other hand, it seems that unity and being are not genera, and therefore they are not principles if genera are principles. For no difference participates actually in a genus, because difference is derived from form and genus from matter; for example, rational is taken from intellective nature, and animal from sensory nature. Now form is not included actually in the essence of matter, but matter is in potentiality to form. And similarly difference does not belong to the nature of a genus, but a genus contains differences potentially. And for this reason a difference does not participate in a genus, because, when I say "rational," I signify something having reason. Nor does it belong to the intelligibility of rational that it should be animal. Now that is participated in which is included in the intelligibility of the thing which participates; and for this reason it is said that a difference does not participate in a genus. But there cannot be any difference whose intelligibility does not contain unity and being. Hence unity and being cannot have any differences. Thus, they cannot be genera, since every genus has differences.

2170. Now the truth of the matter is that unity and being are not genera but are common to all things analogically.

2171. **Further, if what** [13].

Then he raises the third question. The problem now is whether genera are principles to a greater degree than species. First, he shows that species are principles to a greater degree than genera; for what is more simple is a principle to a greater degree. But species seem to be more simple, for they are the indivisible things in which the formal division of a genus terminates. But genera are divided into many different species, and therefore species seem to be principles to a greater degree than genera. But in view of the fact that genera constitute species, and not vice versa, genera seem to be principles to a greater degree; for the intelligible structure of a principle is such that, when it is destroyed, other things are destroyed.

2172. Now the truth is that universals are principles, namely, of knowing; and thus genera are principles to a greater degree because they are simpler. The reason why they are divided into more members than species are is that they contain more members potentially. But species contain many members actually. Hence they are divisible to a greater degree by the method of dissolving a composite into its simple constituents.

LESSON 2
Are There Non-Sensible Substances and Principles?

ARISTOTLE'S TEXT Chapter 2: 1060a3–1060b3

1. *Further, there is the question whether or not we must posit the existence of something besides singular things; and if not, then the science which we are now seeking must deal with these things. But they are infinite in number. And what exists apart from singular things are genera and species; but the science which we are now seeking deals with neither of these. The reason why this is impossible has already been stated.* **1060a3–7**

2. *And in general the problem is whether one must suppose that there is some substance which is separable from sensible substances (i.e., the things which exist here and now), or that the latter are beings and the things with which wisdom deals. For we seem to be looking for another kind of substance, and this constitutes the object of our study: I mean, to know whether there is something which is separable in itself and belongs to no sensible thing.* **1060a7–13**

3. *Further, if there is another kind of substance apart from sensible substances, from what kind of sensible substances must it be assumed to be separate? For why should we suppose that it exists apart from men and from horses rather than from other animals or non-living things generally? Yet to devise various eternal substances equal in number to sensible and corruptible ones would seem to be unreasonable.* **1060a13–18**

4. *But if the principle we are now seeking is not separable from bodies, what could be more of a principle of things than matter? Yet matter does not exist actually but only potentially; and thus it would seem rather that the specifying principle or form is a more important principle than matter. But the form is corruptible [according to some]; and so in general there is no eternal substance which is separate and exists of itself. But this is absurd; for such a principle and substance seems to exist and is sought by almost all accomplished thinkers as something that exists. For how will there be order in the world if there is not a principle which is eternal, separable and permanent?* **1060a19–27**

5. *Again, if there is some substance and principle of such a nature as that now being sought, and this one principle belongs to everything and is one and the same for both corruptible and eternal things, the question arises why it is, if this principle is the same for all, that some of the things which come under it should be eternal and some not; for this is absurd. But if all corruptible things have one principle, and eternal things another, we shall face the same problem if the principle of corruptible things is eternal; for if it is eternal, why are not the things which fall under this principle also eternal? But if it is corruptible, it in turn must have some other principle, and this again must have another, and so on to infinity.* **1060a27–36**

6. *But on the other hand, if one were to posit those principles which are thought to be the most unchangeable, namely, being and unity, then, first, if each of these does not signify a particular thing or a substance, how will they be separable and exist of themselves? Yet the eternal and primary principles for which we are looking must be such. But if each of these does signify a particular thing or a substance, all beings will be substances; for being is predicated of all things, and unity is predicated of some. But it is false that all beings are substances.* **1060a36–1060b6**

7. *Again, how can the statement of those be true who say that unity is the first principle and a substance, and who generate number as the first thing produced from the unit and matter and say that it is substance? For how are we to understand that the number two and each of the other numbers composed of units is one? For they say nothing about this, nor is it easy to do so.* **1060b6–12**

8. *But if someone maintains that lines and what is derived from these (I mean surfaces) are the*

first principles of things, these are not separable substances but sections and divisions; the former of surfaces, and the latter of bodies (and points are the sections and divisions of lines); and further they are the limits of these same things. And all of these exist in other things, and none are separable. **1060b12–17**

9. Again, how are we to understand that the unit and the point have substance. For every substance is generated but not the point; for the point amounts to a division. **1060b17–19**

10. There is also the problem that, while every science must be about universals and about such and such a universal, a substance is not a universal but is rather a particular and separable thing. Hence, if there is a science of principles, how are we to understand substance to be a principle? **1060b19–23**

11. Again, the question arises whether or not there is any principle apart from the concrete whole? And by this I mean the matter and what is joined to it. For if not, then everything that is in matter is corruptible. But if there is some principle, it must be the specifying principle or form. Therefore it is difficult to determine in what cases this exists apart and in what not; for in some cases it is evident that the form is not separable, for example, in that of a house. **1060b23–28**

12. Again, there is the question whether principles are the same specifically or numerically? For if they are the same numerically, all things will be the same. **1060b28–30**

COMMENTARY

2173. Having raised a question about the study of this science, Aristotle now raises a question about the things which are considered in this science. He does this, first [1], with regard to substances; and second [5], with regard to principles ("Again, if").

In treating the first issue he raises two questions. First, he asks whether or not it is necessary to posit the existence of something else in reality over and above singular things. Now if one claims that it is not, then it seems to follow that the science which we are now investigating must be concerned with singular things. But this seems to be impossible, because singular things are infinite in number, and the infinite is unknowable. And if one claims that it is necessary to posit the existence of something apart from singular things, they must be genera or species; and then this science would deal with genera and species. First, he explains why this is impossible; for it seems that neither genera nor species are principles, yet this science deals with principles.

2174. The truth of the matter is that in reality there are only singular things, and that anything else exists only in the consideration of the intellect, which abstracts common attributes from particular ones.

2175. **And in general** [2].

Then he states the second question: whether there is some substance which exists apart from sensible substances existing here and now. This question must be raised here because, if there is nothing apart from sensible substances, only sensible substances are beings. And since wisdom is the science of beings, wisdom must be concerned only with sensible substances, even though we seem in this science to be looking for some other separate reality. It belongs to this science, then, to investigate whether or not there is something apart from sensible substances. And whichever alternative is taken, another question arises.

2176. **Further, if there** [3].

He therefore poses the question

which seems to arise if one claims that there is something separate from sensible substances. The question is whether this separate thing exists apart from all sensible substances or only apart from some. And if only apart from some, it is hard to explain why we should posit a separate substance apart from some sensible substances and not from others. For there does not seem to be any reason why there should be a separate man and a separate horse apart from the men and horses we perceive by the senses, and why this should not be true also of other animals and other non-living things. But if there is some separate substance apart from all sensible substances, it follows that we must posit the existence of certain separate substances which are eternal and equal in number to sensible and corruptible substances. Thus, just as there is a corruptible man, in a similar way there would be an incorruptible man, and the same with horse and ox, and also with other natural bodies. This seems to be absurd.

2177. **But if the principle** [4].

Then he raises another question which seems to follow if there is no substance separate from sensible substances. This question asks what the first principle is, whether matter or form; for sensible substances are composed of these two principles. For at first glance it seems that nothing can be more of a principle of things than matter, which is the first subject and always continues to exist, as the first philosophers of nature claimed. Yet it would seem that matter cannot be a principle, because it is not an actuality but a potentiality. Hence, since actuality is naturally prior to potentiality, as has been pointed out in Book IX (n. 1856), the specifying principle or form, which is an actuality, seems to be this principle.

2178. But it seems that form cannot be a principle because a sensible form appears to be corruptible. If a sensible form were the first principle, then, it would seem to follow that there would be no eternal substance, separable and existing of itself. But this is clearly absurd because some such principle, eternal and separate, and some such substance, is sought by [almost all] the famous philosophers. This is reasonable, for there would not be a perpetual order of things in the world if there were no separate and eternal principle which causes things to be perpetual.

2179. The true answer to this question is that there are certain substances which are separate from sensible substances; and these are not the Forms of sensible things, as the Platonists claimed, but the primary movers, as will be shown below (n. 2492).

2180. **Again, if there** [5].

Then he raises the question about principles. First, he asks what kinds of principles there are; second [6], what they are ("But on the other hand"); and third [7], how they are related to one another ("Again, how can").

He accordingly asks [5] whether or not, if there is some separate substance and principle such as we are now seeking, it is the principle of all things, corruptible and incorruptible. Now if there is such a principle of all things, the question arises why some of the things which come from the same principle are eternal and some are not. But if there is one principle for corruptible things and another for incorruptible ones, there remains the question why, if the principle is eternal, the things coming from it are not themselves eternal. But if the principle of things is corruptible, and every corruptible thing is capable of being generated, and everything capable of being generated has a principle, it follows that the corruptible principle will have a principle, and that this will have another, and so on to infinity, as has been made clear above in Book II (n. 301).

2181. The truth of the matter is that the first principle of all things is incorruptible, and that some things are corruptible because of their great distance from that principle. These are the things in which generation and corruption are caused by an intermediate cause which is incorruptible as regards its substance but changeable as regards place.

2182. **But on the other hand** [6].

Then he asks what the principles of things are. First, he examines the opinions of those men who claimed that the principles are unity and being because these are the most unchangeable. For no matter how a thing varies, it always remains one.

2183. But the opinion of these men gives rise to two questions. The first is whether unity and being signify a particular thing, i.e., a substance; for, if they do not, they cannot be separable and exist of themselves. But we are looking for such principles which are eternal and exist separately. Yet if they do signify a particular thing or substance, it follows that all things are substances, and that nothing is an accident; for being is predicated of any existing thing at all, and unity is predicated of some. Now there are some things which involve multiplicity in their being, and the different ways in which unity is predicated truly of these is clear enough. But it is false that all things are substances; and therefore it seems that unity and being do not signify substance.

2184. **Again, how can** [7].

The second question or problem which he raises runs as follows: those who maintain that unity, or the unit, is the principle and substance of things say that number is generated as a first product from the unit and matter. And this, i.e., number, they call substance. But evidently this is not true, because, if a number is composed of the unit and matter, it must be something one, just as what is composed of a living principle and matter must be something living. But in what way is the number two or any other number, which is composed of units, one, as the Platonists claimed? This is not easy to explain, inasmuch as it can be said that they neglected to account for this as though it were easy to understand.

2185. **But if someone** [8].

Second, he examines another opinion about the principles of things. For some claimed that "lines and what is derived from them," namely, surfaces, are principles, because they held that bodies are composed of surfaces, and surfaces of lines. But it is clear that such things are not separate substances which exist of themselves; for such things are sections and divisions: lines being sections and divisions of surfaces, surfaces of bodies, and points of lines. They are also the limits of these things, i.e., points are the limits of lines, and so forth; for a point, which is at the extremity of a line, is the limit of a line. Now what is signified as actually within a line is a section of the line. The same thing is true of a line in relation to a surface, and of a surface in relation to a body; for it is evident that limits and sections are entities which exist in other things as their subjects. Hence they cannot exist apart. Lines and surfaces, then, are not principles of things.

2186. **Again, how are we** [9].

Then he introduces another argument. He says that it cannot be understood that the unit and the point have a substance, because substance begins to exist only by way of generation. But when a line is actually divided, the division itself is a point.

2187. The correct answer to these questions is that neither units nor lines nor surfaces are principles.

2188. **There is also the problem** [10].

After the question about unity and being and dimensions he now raises the question about substances. First, he asks whether substances are principles. The answer seems to be that they are not; for every science is concerned with universals and with "such and such a universal," i.e., some definite universal subject. Now a substance is not included among universals, but is rather a particular thing which exists of itself. Hence it seems that there is no science of substances. But a science is concerned with principles. Therefore substances are not principles.

2189. The truth is that, although universals do not exist of themselves, it is still necessary to consider universally the natures of things which subsist of themselves. Accordingly, genera and species, which are called second substances, are put in the category of substance; and of these there is scientific knowledge. And certain things which exist of themselves are principles; and these, because they are immaterial, pertain to intelligible knowledge, even though they surpass the comprehension of our intellect.

2190. **Again, the question** [11].

Second, he asks whether or not there is any "principle apart from the concrete whole," i.e., the natural whole or composite. He explains that by *concrete whole* he means matter, or the thing composed of matter. For if there is no principle apart from the composite of matter and form, and those principles which are said to be in matter are corruptible, it follows that nothing is eternal. And if there is some principle apart from the composite, it must be the specifying principle or form. Then the question arises in which cases the form is separate and in which it is not. For it is obvious that in some cases the form is not separate; the form of a house, for example, is not separate from matter. It was for this reason that the Platonists did not posit Ideas or Forms of artificial things, because the forms of such things are actualities which cannot exist of themselves.

2191. The correct answer to this question is that there is some principle apart from matter, and this is not the form of sensible things.

2192. **Again, there is** [12].

He now asks how the principles of all things are related to one another: whether they are the same numerically or only specifically. For, if they are the same numerically, it follows that all things are the same numerically. But if they are not the same numerically, this difference will have to be accounted for.

2193. The truth is that, if one is speaking of the extrinsic principles of things, they are the same numerically, since the first principle of all things is an agent and final cause. But the intrinsic principles of things—matter and form—are not the same numerically but only analogically, as will be shown below (nn. 2474–87).

LESSON 3
All Beings Reduced to Being and Unity

ARISTOTLE'S TEXT Chapter 3: 1060b31–1061b17

1. *Since the science of the philosopher treats of being as being in general and not of some part of it, and the term being is used in many senses and not merely in one, it follows that, if being is used equivocally and not with a common meaning, being does not fall under one science (for such terms do not have a common class). But if the term is used according to one common meaning, being will fall under one science.* **1060b31–36**

2. *Therefore the term seems to be used in the way mentioned, like the terms medical and healthy; for each of these is used in many senses. Now the term is used in each of these ways because of some kind of reference. Thus the former is used in reference to the science of medicine; the latter, to health; and still another, to something else; yet in each case the term is referred to the same thing. For both a discussion and a knife are called medical: the one because it comes from the science of medicine, and the other because it is useful to it. The same is true of the term healthy; for one thing is called healthy because it is a sign of health, and another because it produces it. The same is true of other terms. Hence the same thing is true of every instance of being; for each thing is called a being because it is either a modification or a state or a disposition or a motion or something else of this kind which belongs to being as being.* **1060b36–1061a10**

3. *And since every being is referred to something one and common, each of the contrarieties may also be referred to the primary differences and contrarieties of being, whether the primary differences are plurality and unity, likeness and unlikeness, or any others; for these have been considered.* **1061a10–15**

4. *And it makes no difference whether an existing thing is referred to being or to unity. For even if they are not the same but different, they are nevertheless interchangeable; for what is one is somehow a being, and what is a being is somehow one.* **1061a15–18**

5. *Now since it is the office of one and the same science to study all contraries, and one of each pair involves privation (though one might be puzzled how some contraries are predicated privatively, i.e., those which have an intermediate, as just and unjust), in all such cases it is necessary to hold that the privation of the one is not the privation of the whole notion of the other, but only of the last species. For example, if a man is just because of some habitual tendency to obey the laws, the unjust man will not always be deprived of the perfection completely but will fail to obey the laws in some respect; and in this respect privation will belong to him. The same holds true in other cases.* **1061a18–28**

6. *Now the mathematician in a sense studies things which are gotten by taking something away; for he speculates by removing from things all sensible qualities, such as heaviness and lightness, hardness and its contrary, and also heat and cold and other sensible contrarieties, and leaves only the quantified and the continuous (some things being such in one, some in two, and some in three dimensions). And he studies the properties of the quantified and the continuous as such and not in any other respect. And of some he considers the relative positions and attributes, and of others the commensurability and incommensurability, and of others the ratios; yet we claim that there is only one science of all these things, namely, geometry. The same holds true of being.* **1061a28–1061b4**

7. *For an investigation of the attributes of being as being, and of the contrarieties of being as being, belong to no other science than [first] philosophy; for one would not assign to the philosophy of nature the study of things insofar as they are beings but rather insofar as they participate in motion. For dialectics and sophistry are concerned with the accidents of existing things, but not as beings, nor do they deal with being as being. It follows, then, that it is the*

philosopher who speculates about the things which we have mentioned, insofar as they are beings. **1061b4–11**

8. And since every being is referred to some one common meaning, which is used in many senses, and the same applies to contraries (for they are referred to the primary differences and contrarieties of being), and such things can fall under one science, the difficulty which was stated at the beginning of this work is solved in this way. I mean the question how there can be one science of things which are many and different in genus. **1061b11–17**

COMMENTARY

2194. Having raised the foregoing questions, Aristotle now begins to assemble the things that belong to the consideration of this science. This is divided into two parts. In the first [1] he indicates the things which this science considers. In the second (Lesson 7) he compares this science with the others ("Every science").

The first part is divided into two members. First, he shows that it is the office of this science to consider all beings; and second (Lesson 4), that it has to consider the principles of demonstration ("And since the mathematician").

In considering the first part he does two things. First [1], he shows that all things are somehow reduced to one. Second [6], he shows that the study of this science extends to all things insofar as they are somehow reduced to some one thing ("Now the mathematician").

In treating the first part he does two things. First, he shows that in view of the goal of our present study it is necessary to ask whether all things are somehow reduced to one. He says that, since the science of philosophy treats being as being in such a way as to consider being in terms of its universal character and not merely in terms of the intelligible character of any particular being, and since the term *being* is used in many senses and not just in one, if the many senses of being were purely equivocal without any common meaning, not all beings would fall under one science, because they would not in any way be reduced to one common class. And one science must deal with one class of things. But if the many senses of being have one common meaning, all beings can then fall under one science. Hence, in order to answer the question that was raised as to whether this science is one even though it treats many different things, we must consider whether or not all beings are reduced to some one thing.

2195. **Therefore the term** [2].

Here he shows that all things are reduced to some one thing. In treating this he does two things. First [2], he explains his thesis. Second [5], he clears up a point that might present a difficulty ("Now since").

The first is divided into two parts. In the first he shows that all things are reduced to one. In the second [4], he explains what this one thing is to which all things are reduced ("And it makes no difference").

In regard to the first part he does two things. First, he shows that all beings are reduced to one common being; and second [3], that all contrarieties are reduced to one contrariety ("And since every").

He accordingly says, first [2], that the term *being* is used in the way mentioned above; i.e., it is used of many things according to some common meaning. He makes this clear by means of two examples: the terms *medical* and *healthy*.

2196. For both of these terms are used variously, yet in such a way that they are reduced or referred to some one thing. The term medical is used in many ways inasmuch as it is referred in one sense to a medicine and in another to something else. And similarly the term healthy is used in many ways inasmuch as it is referred in one sense to health and in another to something else. Yet in both cases the various senses have reference to the same thing, though in different ways. For example, a discussion is called medical because it comes from the science of medicine, and a knife is called medical because it is an instrument that is used by the same science. Similarly one thing is called healthy because it is a sign of health, as urine, and another because it causes health, as a medication. The same applies to other terms which are used in a similar way.

2197. It is evident that terms which are used in this way are midway between univocal and equivocal terms. In the case of univocity one term is predicated of different things with absolutely one and the same meaning; for example, the term *animal*, which is predicated of a horse and of an ox, signifies a living, sensory substance. In the case of equivocity the same term is predicated of various things with an entirely different meaning. This is clear in the case of the term *dog*, inasmuch as it is predicated both of a constellation and of a certain species of animal. But in the case of those things which are spoken of in the way mentioned previously, the same term is predicated of various things with a meaning that is partly the same and partly different—different regarding the different modes of relation, and the same regarding that to which it is related; for to be a sign of something and to be a cause of something are different, but health is one. Terms of this kind, then, are predicated analogously, because they have a proportion to one thing. The same holds true also of the many ways in which the term *being* is used; for being in an unqualified sense means what exists of itself, namely, substance; but other things are called beings because they belong to what exists of itself, namely, modifications or states or anything else of this kind. For a quality is called a being, not because it has an act of existence, but because a substance is said to be disposed by it. It is the same with other accidents. This is why he says that they belong to a being (or are of a being). It is evident, then, that the many senses of the term being have a common meaning to which they are reduced.

2198. **And since** [3].

Next he shows that all contrarieties are reduced to one first contrariety. Since all beings are reduced to one common meaning, and the contrarieties of beings, which are opposite differences, are in themselves a natural consequence of beings, it follows that contrarieties must be reduced to some primary contrariety, whatever it may be, whether it is plurality and unity, likeness and unlikeness, or whatever else are primary differences of beings. And contrarieties of this kind have to be considered in the science which establishes what is true about beings.

2199. **And it makes** [4].

Then he indicates what this common thing is to which all things are reduced. He says that it makes no difference whether things are reduced to being or to unity; for if it is said that being and unity are not the same conceptually but differ inasmuch as unity adds the note of indivisibility to being, none the less it is evident that they are interchangeable; for everything that is one is somehow a being, and everything that is a being is somehow one; because, just as a substance is a being properly and of itself, so too it is one properly and of itself. The way in which unity is related to being has been explained above in Book IV (nn. 548–60) and in Book X (n. 1974).

2200. **Now since** [5].

Then he removes a difficulty. He says that, since all contraries are investigated by one science (and the most cogent reason seems to be that in each pair of contraries one contrary is used privatively, and this is known from its opposite term), the difficulty arises how contraries which have an intermediate can be predicated as privations, since in the case of opposites which are privatively opposed there is no intermediate.

2201. The answer to this must be that in the case of such contraries one opposite is not posited as a privation removing all the intelligible notes of the other but as the privation of the last species inasmuch as it detracts from the complete intelligible constitution of the whole species. For instance, if someone is said to be just because he habitually obeys the laws, he will not always be said to be unjust, as if he were deprived of the entire notion of justice, which would be the case if he obeyed the laws in no way—but rather because he fails to obey them in some respects. Hence the privation of justice will be found in him to the extent that he falls short of the perfection of justice. It is for this reason that he can be in an intermediate state, because not everyone who lacks justice is completely deprived of it but only of some part of it. And this intermediate state is one that differs in degree. The same holds true of other contraries. The privation of sight, however, is said to consist in the total lack of sight, and therefore there is no intermediate state between blindness and sight.

2202. **Now the mathematician** [6].

Here he shows that the investigations of this science extend to all beings insofar as they are reduced to one thing. In treating this he makes a tripartite division. First, he shows by an example from geometry that it is the office of one science to consider all things which are reduced to being. He says that the science of mathematics studies "those things which are gotten by taking something away," i.e., abstract things. It makes this abstraction, not because it supposes that the things which it considers are separate in reality from sensible things, but because it considers them without considering sensible qualities. For the science of mathematics carries on its investigations by removing from the scope of its study all sensible qualities, such as lightness, heaviness, hardness, softness, heat and cold, and all other sensible qualities, and retains as its object of study only the quantified and the continuous, whether it is continuous in one dimension, as a line, or in two, as a surface, or in three, as a body. And it is primarily interested in the properties of these inasmuch as they are continuous and not in any other respect; for it does not consider the properties of surface inasmuch as it is the surface of wood or of stone. Similarly it considers the relationships between its objects. And in considering figures it also studies their accidents, and how quantities are commensurable or incommensurable, as is clear in Book X of Euclid, "and their ratios," or proportions, as is clear in Book V of the same work. Yet there is one science of all these things, and this is geometry.

2203. Now what was true for the mathematician is also true for the philosopher who studies being. He passes over a study of all particular beings and considers them only inasmuch as they pertain to being in general. And though these are many, there is nevertheless a single science of all of them inasmuch as all are reduced to one thing, as has been pointed out.

2204. **For an investigation** [7].

Second, he indicates what science it is that considers the above-mentioned things. He says that the study of the attributes of being as being does not belong to any other science but only to this branch of philosophy. If it did belong to another science, it would mostly seem to belong to the philosophy of nature or to dialectics, which seemingly are the most common of the sciences. Now according to the opinion of the ancient philosophers who did not posit any substances other than sensible ones, it would seem to be the philosophy of nature that is the common science. In this way it would follow that it is the function of the philosophy of nature to consider all substances, and consequently all beings, which are reduced to substance.—But dialectics would seem to be the common science, and also sophistry, because these consider certain accidents of beings, namely, intentions and the notions of genus and species and the like. It follows, then, that it is the philosopher who has to consider the above-mentioned things, inasmuch as they are accidents of being.

2205. **And since every** [8].

Third, from what has been said, he draws his thesis as his chief conclusion. He says that, since being is used in many senses in reference to some one thing, and since all contrarieties are referred to the first contrariety of being, such things organized in this way can fall under one science, as has been pointed out. Thus he solves the question previously raised: whether there is one science of things which are many and generically different.

LESSON 4
This Science Considers the Principles of Demonstration

ARISTOTLE'S TEXT Chapter 4: 1061b17–1061b33

1. And since the mathematician uses the common axioms in a particular way, it must be the office of first philosophy to study principles of this kind. For the axiom or principle that "when equals are subtracted from equals the remainders are equal" is common to all quantities. But mathematics, assuming [principles of this kind], makes a study of some part of the quantified as its proper subject matter, for example, lines or angles or number or some of the other kinds of quantity. Yet it does not consider them inasmuch as they are beings but inasmuch as each is continuous in one, two or three dimensions. Philosophy, however, does not investigate those things which are in some part of matter insofar as each has some attribute, but it considers each of these particular things from the standpoint of being insofar as it is being. **1061b17–27**

2. Now what applies in the case of the science of mathematics is also true of the philosophy of nature; for the philosophy of nature studies the attributes and principles of beings inasmuch as they are moved, not inasmuch as they are beings. But, as we have said, the primary science considers these attributes and principles insofar as their subjects are beings, and not in any other respect. For this reason it is necessary to hold that this science and the science of mathematics are parts of wisdom. **1061b27–33**

COMMENTARY

2206. Having shown how the investigations of this science are concerned with beings and with the attributes which belong to being as being, the Philosopher now shows how the investigations of this science are concerned with the first principles of demonstration.

This is divided into two parts. In the first [1] he shows that it is the office of this science to consider these first principles of demonstration. In the second (Lesson 5) he draws his conclusions about one principle of demonstration which is prior to the others ("There is a principle").

In regard to the first he does two things. First [1], he clarifies his thesis by considering the science of mathematics; and second [2], by considering the philosophy of nature ("Now what applies").

In the first part he uses the following argument: all the common axioms which are used by the particular sciences in a way peculiar to themselves and not in their common aspect belong to the consideration of this science. But the first principles of demonstration are used by the science of mathematics and by other particular sciences in a way peculiar to themselves. Therefore an investigation of these principles insofar as they are common belongs to the science which considers being as being.

2207. He accordingly says that, since the mathematician uses "the common axioms in a particular way," i.e., insofar as they are adapted to his subject matter, it must be the function of first philosophy to consider such principles in their common aspect. For these principles are taken as principles of the sciences insofar as they are adapted to some particular subject matter. He clarifies his statement by an example.

2208. The principle that "when equals are subtracted from equals the remainders are equal" is common to all instances of quantity which admit of equality and inequality. But the science of mathematics presupposes principles of this kind in order to make a special study of that part of quantity which constitutes its proper subject matter; for there is no mathematical science which considers the attributes common to quantity as quantity, because this is the work of first philosophy. The mathematical sciences rather consider those attributes which belong to this or to that quantity; for example, arithmetic considers the attributes that belong to number, and geometry considers those that belong to continuous quantity. Thus the arithmetician uses the above-mentioned principle only inasmuch as it has to do with numbers, and the geometer uses it inasmuch as it has to do with lines and with angles. The geometer, however, does not consider this principle inasmuch as it relates to beings as beings but inasmuch as it relates to being as continuous, whether it is continuous in one dimension, as a line; or in two, as a surface; or in three, as a body. But first philosophy does not study the parts of being inasmuch as each has certain accidents; but when it studies each of these common attributes, it studies being as being.

2209. **Now what applies** [2].

Then he makes the same thing clear by considering the philosophy of nature. He says that what applies in the case of the science of mathematics is also true of the philosophy of nature; for while the philosophy of nature studies the attributes and principles of beings, it does not consider beings as beings but as mobile. The first science, on the other hand, deals with these inasmuch as they are being, and not in any other respect. Hence, the philosophy of nature and the science of mathematics must be parts of first philosophy, just as any particular science is said to be a part of a universal science.

2210. The reason why common principles of this kind belong to the consideration of first philosophy is this: since all first self-evident propositions are those of which the predicate is included in the definition of the subject, then in order that propositions may be self-evident to all, it is necessary that their subjects and predicates should be known to all. Common notions of this type are those which are conceived by all men, as being and non-being, whole and part, equal and unequal, same and different, and so on. But these belong to the consideration of first philosophy; and therefore common propositions composed of such terms must belong chiefly to the consideration of first philosophy.

LESSON 5
The Principle of Non-Contradiction

ARISTOTLE'S TEXT Chapters 5 & 6: 1061b34–1062b19

1. There is a principle in existing things about which it is impossible to make a mistake, but of which one must always do the contrary, I mean acknowledge it as true, namely, that the same thing cannot both be and not be at one and the same time; and the same is also true of other things which are opposed in this way. **1061b34–1062a2**

2. And while there is no demonstration in the strict sense of such principles, one may employ an argument ad hominem; for it is impossible to construct a syllogism from a more certain principle than this one. But this would be necessary if there were demonstration of it in the strict sense. **1062a2–5**

3. Now anyone who wants to prove to an opponent making statements opposite to one's own that he is wrong must take some such principle which is the same as this one—that the same thing cannot both be and not be at the same time—but apparently is not the same. For this will be the only method of demonstration that can be used against one who says that opposite statements can be truly made about the same subject. **1062a5–11**

4. Accordingly, those who are to join in some discussion must understand each other to some extent. And if this does not happen, how will they join in a common discussion? Therefore each of the terms used must be understood and must signify something, and not many things but only one. But if a term does signify many things, it must be made clear to which of these it refers. Hence, one who says that this is and is not, totally denies what he affirms, and thus denies that the term signifies what it signifies. But this is impossible. Hence, if to be this has some meaning, the contradictory cannot be said to be true of the same subject. **1062a11–20**

5. Again, if a term signifies something and this is affirmed truly, it must necessarily be so; and what is necessarily so cannot not be. Hence opposite affirmations and negations cannot be true of the same subject. **1062a20–23**

6. Again, if the affirmation is in no way truer than the negation, it will not be truer to say that something is a man than to say that it is not a man. And it would also seem that it is either more or not less true to say that a man is not a horse than to say that he is not a man. Hence one will also be right in saying that the same thing is a horse; for it was assumed that opposite statements are equally true. Therefore it follows that the same thing is a man and a horse, or any other animal. Hence, while there is no demonstration in the strict sense of these principles, there is still a demonstration ad hominem against one who makes these assumptions. **1062a23–31**

7. And perhaps if one had questioned Heraclitus himself in this way, he would quickly have forced him to admit that opposite statements can never be true of the same subjects. But he adopted this view without understanding his own statement. And in general if what he said is true, not even this statement will be true—I mean that the same thing can both be and not be at one and the same time. For just as when they are separated the affirmation will not be truer than the negation, in a similar way when both are combined and taken together as though they were one affirmation, the negation will not be truer than the whole statement regarded as an affirmation. **1062a31–1062b7**

8. Again, if it is possible to affirm nothing truly, even this statement—that no affirmation is true—will be false. But if there is a true affirmation, this will refute what is said by those who raise such objections and completely destroy discussion. **1062b7–11**

Chapter 6

9. The statement made by Protagoras is similar to those mentioned; for he said that man is the measure of all things,^2 meaning simply that whatever appears so to anyone is just as it appears to him. But if this is true, it follows that the same thing is and is not, and is good and evil, and that other statements involving opposites are true; because often a particular thing appears to be good to some and just the opposite to others, and that which appears to each man is the measure. **1062b12–19**

COMMENTARY

2211. Having shown that a study of the common principles of demonstration belongs chiefly to the consideration of this philosophical science, the Philosopher now deals with the first of these principles [1]. For just as all beings must be referred to one first being, in a similar fashion all principles of demonstration must be referred to some principle which pertains in a more basic way to the consideration of this philosophical science. This principle is that the same thing cannot both be and not be at the same time. It is the first principle because its terms, *being* and *non-being*, are the first to be apprehended by the intellect.

2212. This part is divided into two members. In the first [1] he establishes the truth of this principle. In the second [3] he rejects an error ("Now anyone who").

In reference to the first part he does two things regarding this principle. First, he says that in regard to beings there is a principle of demonstration "about which it is impossible to make a mistake" (i.e., so far as its meaning is concerned), but of which we "must always do the contrary," namely, acknowledge it as true. This principle is that the same thing cannot both be and not be at one and the same time, granted of course that the other conditions which it is customary to give in the case of a contradiction are fulfilled, namely, in the same respect, in an unqualified sense, and the like. For no one can think that this principle is false, because, if someone were to think that contradictories may be true at the same time, he would then have contrary opinions at the same time; for opinions about contradictories are contrary. For example, the opinion that "Socrates is sitting" is contrary to the opinion that "Socrates is not sitting."

2213. **And while** [2].

Second, he says that, while there cannot be demonstration in the strict sense of the above-mentioned principle and other similar ones, one may offer an argument *ad hominem* in support of it. That it cannot be demonstrated in the strict sense he proves thus: no one can prove this principle by constructing a syllogism from some principle which is better known. But such would be necessary if that principle were to be demonstrated in the strict sense. However, this principle can be demonstrated by using an argument *ad hominem* against one who admits some other statement, though less known, and denies this one.

2214. **Now anyone who** [3].

Then he rejects the opinion of those who deny this principle; and this is divided into two parts. First [3], he argues against those who deny this principle. Second (Lesson 6), he shows how one can meet this opinion ("Now this difficulty").

In regard to the first he does two things. First [3], he argues against those who unqualifiedly deny this principle. Second [7], he turns his attention to certain particular opinions ("And perhaps").

In regard to the first he does two things. First, he gives the method of arguing against this error. He says that in arguing against an opponent who claims that contradictory propositions may be true, anyone who wants to show that this opinion is false ought to take some such principle which is the same as this one—that the same thing cannot both be and not be at the same time—but apparently is not the same. For, if it were evidently the same, it would not be admitted by an opponent. Yet if it were not the same, he could not prove his thesis, because a principle of this kind cannot be demonstrated from some principle which is better known. Hence, it is only in this way that a demonstration can be made against those who say that contradictories may be true of the same subject, namely, by assuming as a premise what is in fact the same as the conclusion but apparently is not.

2215. **Accordingly** [4].

Second, he begins to argue dialectically against the above-mentioned error; and in regard to this he gives three arguments. First, he argues as follows: if two men are to join in a discussion in such a way that one may communicate his view to the other in a dispute, each must understand something that the other is saying. For if this were not the case, no statement would be understood by both of them; and thus an argument with an opponent would be pointless.

2216. However, if one of them is to understand what the other is saying, each of the terms used must be understood according to its proper meaning and must therefore signify some one thing and not many things. And if it should signify many, it will be necessary to make clear which of the many things it signifies; otherwise one would not know what the other person means.

2217. Now granted that a term signifies one thing, it is evident that one who says both that *this is* and that *this is not*, for example, that Socrates is a man and that he is not a man, denies the one thing which he attributed to Socrates, namely, that he is a man, when he adds that he is not a man; and thus he denies what he first signified. Hence it follows that a word does not signify what it signifies. But this is impossible. Consequently, if a term signifies some definite thing, the contradictory cannot be truly affirmed of the same subject.

2218. **Again, if a term** [5].

Then he gives the second argument, which runs as follows: if a term signifies some attribute, and the attribute signified by the term is truly affirmed of the same subject of which the term is first predicated, this attribute must belong to the subject of which the term is predicated so long as the proposition is true. For this conditional proposition, "If Socrates is a man, Socrates is a man," is clearly true. Now every true conditional proposition is a necessary one. Hence, if the consequent is true, the antecedent must be true. But what is, cannot sometimes not be, because to be necessary and to be incapable of not being are equivalent. Therefore so long as the proposition "Socrates is a man" is true, the proposition "Socrates is not a man" cannot be true. Thus it is evident that opposite affirmations and negations cannot be true of the same subject at the same time.

2219. **Again, if the affirmation** [6].

Then he gives the third argument, which is as follows: if an affirmation is not truer than the negation opposed to it, one who says that Socrates is a man does not speak with greater truth than one who says that Socrates is not a man. But it is evident that one who says that a man is not a horse speaks either with greater or with no less truth than one who says that a man is not a man. Hence, according to this argument, he who says that a man is not a horse will speak with equal or no less truth. But if contradictory opposites are true at the same time, for example, if the proposition "Man is not a horse" is true, and the proposition "Man is a horse" is also true, then it follows that a man is a horse and also any other animal.

2220. But because someone could criticize the foregoing arguments on the grounds that the things assumed in them are less known than the intended conclusion, he therefore answers this by saying that no one of the foregoing arguments is demonstrative in the strict sense, although there can be an argument *ad hominem* against an opponent who gives this argument, because the things assumed must be admitted to be true even though they are less known absolutely than what he denies.

2221. **And perhaps** [7].

Then he rejects the above error by considering certain particular thinkers. He does this, first [7], with regard to Heraclitus; and second [9], with regard to Protagoras ("The statement").

Now Heraclitus posited two things: first, that an affirmation and a negation may be true at the same time (and from this it would follow that every proposition, affirmative as well as negative, is true); and second, that there may be an intermediate between affirmation and negation (and from this it would follow that neither an affirmation nor a negation can be true). Consequently every proposition is false.

2222. First [7], he raises an argument against Heraclitus' first position; and second [8], against his second position ("Again, if it is possible").

He accordingly says, first [7], that by giving an argument *ad hominem* in this way one may easily bring even Heraclitus, who was the author of this statement, to admit that opposite propositions may not be true of the same subject. For he seems to have accepted the opinion that they may be true of the same subject because he did not understand his own statement. And he would be forced to deny his statement in the following way: if what he said is true, namely, that one and the same thing can both be and not be at one and the same time, it follows that this very statement will not be true; for if an affirmation and a negation are taken separately, an affirmation is not truer than a negation; and if an affirmation and a negation are taken together in such a way that one affirmation results from them, the negation will not be less true of the whole statement made up of the affirmation and the negation than of the opposite affirmation. For it is clearly possible for some copulative proposition to be true, just as for some simple proposition; and it is possible to take its negation. And whether the copulative proposition be composed of two affirmative propositions, as when we say "Socrates is sitting and arguing," or of two negative propositions, as when we say "It is true that Socrates is not a stone or an ass," or of an affirmative proposition and a negative proposition, as when we say "It is true that Socrates is sitting and not arguing," nevertheless a copulative proposition is always taken to be true because one affirmative proposition is true. And he who says that it is false takes the negation as applying to the whole copulative proposition. Hence he who says that it is true that man is and is not at the same time, takes this as a kind of affirmation; and that this is not true is the negation of this. Hence, if an affirmation and a negation are true at the same time, it follows that the negation which states that this is not true, i.e., that an affirmation and a negation are true at the same time, is equally true. For if any negation is true at the same time as the affirmation opposed to it, every negation must be true at the same time as the affirmation opposed to it; for the reasoning is the same in all cases.

2223. **Again, if it is possible** [8].

Then he introduces an argument against the second position of Heraclitus: that no affirmation is true. For if it is possible to affirm that nothing is true, and if one who says that no affirmation is true does affirm something, namely, that it is true that no affirmation is true, then this statement will be false. And if some affirmative statement is true, the opinion of people such as those who oppose all statements will be rejected. And those who adopt this position destroy the whole debate, because if nothing is true, nothing can be conceded on which an argument may be based. And if an affirmation and a negation are true at the same time, it will be impossible to signify anything by a word, as was said above (n. 2215), and then the argument will cease.

2224. **The statement** [9].

Here he considers the opinion of Protagoras. He says that the statement made by Protagoras is similar to the one made by Heraclitus and by others who claim that an affirmation and a negation are true at the same time. For Protagoras says that man is the measure of all things, i.e., according to the intellect and the senses, as has been explained in Book IX (n. 1800), as if the being of a thing depended upon intellectual and sensory apprehension. And one who says that man is the measure of all things merely says that whatever appears so to anyone is true. But if this is maintained, it follows that the same thing both is and is not and is both good and evil at the same time. The same thing is also true of other opposites, because often something seems to be good to some and just the opposite to others, and the way in which things seem or appear is the measure of all things according to the opinion of Protagoras; so that, inasmuch as a thing appears, to that extent it is true.

LESSON 6
Contradictories Cannot Be True at the Same Time

ARISTOTLE'S TEXT Chapter 6: 1062b20–1063b35

1. *Now this difficulty may be solved by considering the origin of this view.* **1062b20–21**

2. *For it seems to have arisen in some cases from the opinion of the philosophers of nature, and in others from the fact that not all men apprehend the same thing in the same way, but something appears pleasant to some and the opposite to others.* **1062b21–24**

3. *For the view that nothing comes from non-being but everything from being is a doctrine common to nearly all those who have dealt with nature. Thus, since the not-white comes from what is actually white, and not from the not-white, should the not-white have come to be, what becomes not-white will have come to be from what is not not-white. Hence whiteness must come from nonbeing according to them, unless the white and the not-white are the same. But it is not hard to solve this difficulty; for we have stated in our physical treatises in what sense things which come to be come from non-being, and in what sense they come from being.* **1062b24–33**

4. *But it is also foolish to occupy oneself equally with both opinions and with the fanciful statements of those who argue against themselves, because it is evident that one or the other of them must be wrong. This is clear from the facts of sensory perception; for the same thing never appears sweet to some and the opposite to others unless in some the organ of the sense which distinguishes the above-mentioned savors has been impaired or injured. And such being the case, some must be taken as the measure and the others not. And I say that the same thing applies in the case of good and evil, of beautiful and ugly, and of other attributes of this kind. For to maintain this view is not different from maintaining that what appears to those who push their finger under their eye and make one object appear to be two must therefore be two because it appears to be so many, and yet that it must be one because to those who do not move their eye the one object appears to be one.* **1062b33–1063a10**

5. *And in general seeing that things here are subject to change and never remain the same, it would be unfitting to base our judgment of the truth on this. For in pursuing the truth one must start with those things which are always the same and never undergo a single change. Such things are those which contain the world; for they do not appear at one time to be such and at another different, but they are always the same and admit of no change.* **1063a10–17**

6. *Further, if there is motion, there is also something that is moved; and everything is moved from something and to something. Therefore that which is moved must be in that from which it is moved, and yet not be in it; and it must be moved to this and come to be in it; but contradictories cannot be true at the same time, as they claim.* **1063a17–21**

7. *And if things here are in a state of continuous change and motion as regards quantity, and one were to suppose this even though it is not true, why should they not be permanent as regards quality? For the view that contradictories may be predicated of the same subject seems to be based largely on the assumption that the quantity of bodies does not remain constant; and for this reason they say that the same thing is and is not four cubits long. But a thing's substance involves quality, and this is of a determinate nature, whereas quantity is of an indeterminate nature.* **1063a22–28**

8. *Further, when a physician orders them to take some particular food, why do they take it? For why is this particular food bread rather than not bread? Hence it would make no difference whether they ate it or not. But they take the food prescribed as though they know the truth about it and that it is the food prescribed. Yet they should not do this if there is no nature which remains fixed in the sensible world, but everything is always in a state of motion and flux.* **1063a28–35**

9. Again, if we are always undergoing change and never remain the same, what wonder is it if to us, as to those who are ill, things never appear the same? For to them also, since they are not in the same condition as when they were well, sensible qualities do not appear to be the same; yet sensible things themselves need not for this reason undergo any change, but they cause different, and not the same, impressions in those who are ill. And perhaps the same thing must happen to those who are well if the above-mentioned change takes place. However, if we do not change but always remain the same, there will be something permanent. **1063a35–1063b7**

10. Hence, in the case of those who raise the foregoing difficulties as a result of reasoning, it is not easy to meet their arguments unless they assume something and do not demand a reason for it; for every argument and demonstration comes about in this way. For those who admit nothing destroy discussion and reasoning in general, and thus there is no reasoning with such men. But in the case of those who are puzzled by the usual problems, it is easy to meet them and to reject the arguments which cause their difficulty. This becomes clear from what has been said above. **1063b7–15**

11. It is evident from these considerations, then, that opposite statements cannot be verified of the same subject at one time, nor can contrary ones, because every contrariety involves privation. This becomes clear if we reduce the definitions of all contraries to their principle. Similarly no intermediate can be predicated of one and the same subject. For if the subject is white, those who say that it is neither white nor black are wrong, for it then follows that it is white and is not white; for the second of the two terms which we have combined is true of it, and this is the contradictory of white. **1063b15–24**

12. One cannot be right, then, in holding the views either of Heraclitus or of Anaxagoras; and if this were not so it would follow that contraries would be predicated of the same subject. For when Anaxagoras says that there is a part of everything in everything else, he says that nothing is sweet any more than it is bitter, and so on with any of the other pairs of contraries, since everything is present in everything else, not potentially, but actually and separately. **1063b24–30**

13. And similarly all statements cannot be true or all false, both because of many other difficulties which might be brought forward on the basis of this position, and because, if all statements are false, anyone who says this will not speak the truth; and if all are true, it will not be false to say that all are false. **1063b30–35**

COMMENTARY

2225. Having argued against those who claim that contradictories may be verified of the same subject at the same time, the Philosopher now shows how these men can be persuaded to abandon this theory. His discussion is divided into two parts. In the first [1] he explains his thesis. In the second [11] he draws a corollary from what has been said ("It is evident").

The first part is divided into two members. In the first he explains how it is possible in some cases to deal with the above-mentioned theory. In the second [10] he indicates in what cases it can be refuted and in what not ("Hence, in the case").

In treating the first [1] he does three things. First, he describes the way in which the foregoing theory can be disqualified in some cases. He says that the above-mentioned difficulty which led some people to adopt the position that contradictories may be verified of the same subject at the same time can be dispelled if one considers its source.

2226. **For it seems** [2].

Second, he gives two sources of this position. He says that this position seems to have arisen in some cases from the opinion of the philosophers of nature, who claimed that nothing comes to be from non-being, and in others from the fact that not all men make the same judgments about the same things, but something appears pleasant to some and just the opposite to others. For if one were to believe that whatever appears is true, it would follow from this that opposites are true at the same time.

2227. **For the view** [3].

Third, he shows how the above-mentioned position might follow from the two sources just given; and he points out how it may be dealt with. First, he shows how it might follow from the opinion of the philosophers of nature; and second [4], from the belief that every appearance is true ("But it is also foolish").

He accordingly says, first [3], that the doctrine common to nearly all of the thinkers who have dealt with nature is that nothing comes to be from non-being, but everything from being. It is clear that something becomes not-white from what is actually white; but what is not-white does not come from what is not-white. Further, it is also evident that what is not-white comes from what is not not-white. Consequently, it is evident that what is not not-white becomes not-white, just as what is not-black becomes black. It is clear, then, that that from which the not-white comes to be is the white, and it is not not-white. This cannot be understood in the sense that the not-white is entirely non-being, because it would then seem to follow that something comes to be from non-being absolutely. For example, if we were to say that fire comes from what is not-fire, there would be the question how they think that that from which fire comes to be is entirely not-fire. For it would then seem to follow, according to them, that something comes to be from non-being. Hence they claimed that fire lay hidden in that from which fire comes to be, as is evident from the opinion of Anaxagoras, which is given in Book I of the ***Physics***. *[187a20]* Similarly, they believed that, if something comes to be not-white from what is not not-white, the not-white must have preexisted in that from which it comes to be, as has been explained. Thus it would follow, according to them, that that from which the not-white comes to be is both white and not-white at the same time, unless it is assumed that something comes to be from non-being.

2228. But this difficulty is not hard to solve, as the Philosopher points out; for it has been explained in Book I of the ***Physics*** *[191a23-191b34]* how a thing comes to be from being and how from nonbeing; for it has been stated that something comes to be from what is a nonbeing in act, though it is incidentally a being in act. But it comes to be properly from matter, which is in potency; for it is accidental to the process of making that the matter from which a thing comes to be should be the subject of form and of privation. Thus it is not necessary that that from which a thing comes to be should be at the same time both a being and a nonbeing in act, but that it should be of itself in potency both to being and to non-being, i.e., both to form and to privation.

2229. **But it is also foolish** [4].

Then he rejects the foregoing opinion inasmuch as it might be derived from the other source, i.e., from the view that every appearance is judged to be true. First, he rejects this source; and second [5], its cause ("And in general").

He accordingly says, first [4], that, just as it is foolish to think that contradictories may be verified of the same subject at the same time, so too "it is also foolish to occupy oneself with," i.e., to accept, both of the foregoing opinions of the philosophers who argue against themselves; for it is obvious that one or the other of them must be in error.

2230. This is evident from the facts of sensory perception; for the same thing never appears sweet to some and bitter to others, unless in some the sense organ and the power which discriminates between savors has been impaired or injured. But since this does happen in some cases, "some must be taken as the measure," i.e., the judgment of those whose senses are not impaired in this way must be taken as the rule and measure of truth. But this should not be understood to apply to those whose senses are impaired.

2231. And what is evident in the case of sensory perception must also be said to apply in the case of good and evil, of beautiful and ugly, and of all attributes of this kind which are apprehended by the intellect. For if some conceive a thing to be good and others evil, the judgment of those whose intellect has not been impaired by some bad habit or by some bad influence or by some other cause of this kind must be the norm. For if someone were to hold that it is not less fitting to believe the one group rather than the other, this would not differ in any way from saying that things are as they appear "to those who push their finger under their eye," i.e., who move their eye with their finger, and thereby make one thing appear as two, and say that it must be two because it appears to be so many, and again that it must be one because it appears to be one to those who do not move their eye with their finger. For it is obvious that we must base our judgment about the oneness of things on the judgment which the eye makes when it does not receive some strange impression, and not on the judgment which it makes when it receives such an impression. Now a man judges one visible object to be two because the form of the visible object is made to appear as two to the organ of vision when it is moved; and this double impression reaches the organ of the common sense as though there were two visible objects.

2232. **And in general** [5].

Then he rejects the basis of the position that every appearance is true. For some held this because they thought that all things are in a state of continuous flux, and that there is nothing fixed and determinate in reality; and thus it would follow that a thing is such only when it is seen.

2233. He therefore presents five arguments against this position. He says, first, that it is altogether unfitting to base our judgment about the whole truth on the fact that these sensible things which are near or close to us are undergoing change and are never permanent. But the truth must be based rather on those things which are always the same and never undergo any change as regards their substance, though they do appear to be subject to local motion. For such things are those "which contain the world," i.e., the celestial bodies, to which these corruptible bodies are compared as things that have no quantity, as the mathematicians prove. Now the celestial bodies are always the same and do not at one time appear to be such and at another different, for they admit of no change which affects their substance.

2234. **Further, if there** [6].

Then he gives the second argument against this position. The argument runs thus: if there is motion in these lower bodies, there must be something that is moved, and it must also be moved from something and to something. Hence that which is moved must already be in that from which it is moved and yet not be in it, and this must be moved to something else and be continuously coming to be in it. Thus some definite affirmation, as well as some negation, must be true. And it will not be necessary that a contradiction be true of the same subject, because according to this nothing would be moved. For if the same thing might be at the extreme to which it is moved and not be at it, there would be no reason why a thing which has not yet reached an extreme should be moved thereto, because it would already be there.

2235. **And if things** [7].

He gives the third argument; and with a view to making this clear it should be borne in mind that, when Heraclitus saw that a thing increased in size according to some definite and very small quantity over a long period of time (for example, a year), he thought that some addition would be made in any part of that time, and that it would be imperceptible because of the very small quantity involved. And because of this he was led to believe that all things, even those which seem to be static, are also being moved continuously by an imperceptible motion, and that after a long time their motion would become apparent to the senses. But his opinion about increase is false; for increase does not take place continuously in such a way that something grows in any part of time, but a body is disposed to increase during some time and then grows, as Aristotle makes quite clear in Book VIII of the ***Physics***. [261a35]

2236. Hence he says that, if the bodies around us here are in a continuous state of flux and motion as regards quantity, and one wishes to admit this even though it is not true, there is no reason why a thing cannot be unchanging as to its quality. For the opinion that contradictories are true of the same subject at the same time seems to be based largely on the assumption that the quantitative aspect of bodies does not remain constant; and thus some thought that the same thing is and is not four cubits long. But a thing's substance is defined in terms of some quality, i.e., some form; and quality is of a determinate nature in things, although quantity is of an indeterminate nature because of change, as has been pointed out.

2237. **Further, when a physician** [8].

Then he gives the fourth argument, which runs thus: if there is nothing fixed in the world as regards being or non-being, why do they take this kind of bread which the physician prescribes and not that? For according to the position given above, why is this bread rather than not-bread? He implies that the answer cannot be in the affirmative any more than in the negative. And thus it would make no difference whether one ate the bread or did not. But we see that they take the bread which the physician prescribes, implying that they form a true judgment about bread itself, and that this kind of bread is really the one which the physician prescribes. Yet this would not be the case if no nature remained fixed in the sensible world but all things are always in a state of motion and flux.

2238. **Again, if we** [9].

Then he presents the fifth argument: since the above-mentioned position assumes that there is no fixed truth in things because of the continuous change which they undergo, if the truth is identical with appearance it is necessary to say that we men, who make judgments about other things, are either in motion or are not.

2239. For if we are always undergoing change and never remain the same, it is not surprising that things never appear the same to us; and this is the case with those who are ill. For since they have been changed and are not in the same state as when they were well, the sensible qualities which they perceive by way of the senses will not seem the same to them as they did before they became ill. For to those whose sense of taste has been impaired sweet things seem bitter or tasteless; and the same is true of other sensible qualities. Yet sensible qualities themselves are not changed for this reason, but they cause different impressions in those who are ill because their senses are differently disposed. Therefore, if we men, who are continuously undergoing change, make different judgments about other things, this should not be attributed to things but to us.

2240. However, if we are not changing but always remain the same, there will therefore be something permanent in the world and consequently some fixed truth about which we can make positive judgments. For we make judgments not only about other things but also about human nature.

2241. **Hence, in the case** [10].

Then he indicates who can be disabused of the above opinion and who can not. He says that, if those who adopt the foregoing opinions do so not because of any reasoning, in the sense that they do not assume anything because they are obstinate, and do not inquire into the reasons for the things that they say but stubbornly adhere to the opinions which they hold, it is not easy for them to give up an opinion of this kind. For every argument and every demonstration comes about in this way, namely, by admitting the truth of some statement and investigating the reason for it. But those who admit nothing destroy discussion and every rational argument; and thus no appeal of reason can be addressed to them whereby they can be dislodged from their error.

2242. But if there are any who are perplexed because of certain deficiencies (for example, because they do not understand some things well), it is easy to dispel such an error by removing the difficulties which puzzle them. This is evident from the previous discussion in which he deals with the difficulties that could lead to the above-mentioned opinion.

2243. **It is evident** [11].

Then he draws three corollaries from what has been said. First, it is evident from the foregoing discussion that opposite statements cannot be verified of the same subject at one and the same time. Consequently it is clear from this that contraries cannot be verified of the same subject at the same time. And this is true because every contrariety involves privation; for one of two contraries is always a privation. This becomes evident if one wishes to reduce the definitions of contraries to their first principle; for contained in the notion of black is the privation of white. Since a privation, then, is a kind of negation having a determinate subject, it is evident that, if contraries were true of the same subject, both an affirmation and a negation would have to be true of the same subject at the same time.

2244. Now it is not only impossible for two contraries to be true of the same subject at the same time, but it is also impossible for an intermediate to be predicated of one and the same subject of which one of two extremes is predicated; for from what has been said in Book X (nn. 2101–11) it is evident that an intermediate between contraries involves the privation of both extremes, whether it is designated by one word or by many or is nameless. Hence an intermediate between white and black, such as red or yellow, contains in its definition the fact that it is neither white nor black. Therefore, if one says that some subject is red when it is really white, he is saying at the same time that it is neither white nor black. Hence he is in error; for it would follow that that subject is both white and not white at the same time; because if it is true that that subject is neither white nor black, the other part of the copulative proposition may be verified of the same subject, and this is the contradictory of being white. Thus it follows that, if an intermediate and an extreme are true of the same subject, contradictories must be true of the same subject.

2245. **One cannot** [12].

He gives the second corollary. He concludes that, if an affirmation and a negation are not true at the same time, neither the opinion of Heraclitus nor that of Anaxagoras is true. That this is so regarding the opinion of Heraclitus is evident from what has been said. Hence he shows that the same thing applies with respect to the opinion of Anaxagoras. He says that, if Anaxagoras' opinion is not false, it follows that contraries may be predicated of the same subject, and therefore that contradictories may also be predicated of the same subject. This is shown as follows. Anaxagoras claimed that anything at all comes to be from anything at all, and everything which comes to be comes from something. Hence he was not compelled to maintain that something comes to be from nothing, and thus he claimed that everything is present in everything else. Therefore, since he posited that there is a part of everything in everything else (for example, a part of flesh in bone, and a part of whiteness in blackness, and vice versa), it follows that the whole is no more sweet than bitter. The same holds true of other contrarieties. And this is so if a part of anything is present in any whole not only potentially but actually and separately. And he added this because whatever comes to be from something else must pre-exist in it potentially and not actually. Hence contraries must preexist in the same subject potentially and not actually. This does not mean that contraries exist separately in something, because the potency for contraries is the same. But Anaxagoras did not know how to distinguish between potency and actuality.

2246. **And similarly** [13].

He gives the third corollary. He concludes from what has been said that both opinions are false, i.e., the opinion of those who said that all statements are true, and the opinion of those who said that all are false. This is evident because of the many difficult and serious conclusions which result from these opinions which have been brought together here and above in Book IV (nn. 611–748); and especially "because if all statements are false," he who says that every statement is false makes a statement and thus does not speak the truth. And similarly if all statements are true, he who says that all are false will not say what is false but will speak the truth. And for this reason the position of one who claims that all statements are true is destroyed.

LESSON 7
Metaphysics Differs from All the Other Sciences

ARISTOTLE'S TEXT Chapter 7: 1063b36–1064b14

1. *Every science seeks certain principles and causes of each of the knowable objects which comes within its scope; for example, medicine and gymnastics do this, and so does each of the other sciences, productive as well as doctrinal. For each of these marks off for itself some class of things and occupies itself with this as with something that is real and a being, though not as being; but there is a certain other science distinct from these which does this.* **1063b36–1064a4**

2. *And each of the sciences mentioned somehow assumes the quiddity in some class of things and tries to prove the rest with greater or lesser certainty. Some derive the quiddity from sensory perception, and some by assuming it from some other science. Hence from such a process of induction it becomes evident that there is no demonstration of the substance and of its quiddity.* **1064a4–10**

3. *Now since there is a science of nature, it is evident that it must differ from both the practical and the productive sciences. For in the case of a productive science the source of motion is in the maker and not in the thing made, and it is either the art or some kind of potency. And similarly in the case of a practical science the motion is not in the thing done but rather in the agents. But the science of the philosopher of nature is concerned with things which have a source of motion in themselves. It is evident from these considerations, then, that the philosophy of nature must be neither practical nor productive but speculative; for it must fall in one of these classes.* **1064a10–19**

4. *And since it is necessary that each one of the sciences have some knowledge of the quiddity and must use it as a starting point, we must not fail to consider how the philosophy of nature should define things, and how it should consider the intelligible structure of the substance: whether in the same way as the term snub or rather as the term concave. For of these the notion of snub includes the matter of the object, but that of concave is expressed without matter. For snubness comes into being in a nose, and for this reason its intelligible structure includes matter; for snub is a concave nose. It is evident, then, that the intelligible structure of flesh and of eye and of the other parts of the body must always be given along with matter.* **1064a19–28**

5. *And since there is a science of being as being and as separable, one must consider whether this science should be held to be the same as the philosophy of nature or rather a science distinct from it. The philosophy of nature deals with things which have a principle of motion in themselves, and mathematics is speculative and is concerned with things which are permanent but are not separable. Therefore there is a science distinct from both of these, which treats of what is separable and immovable; that is to say, if there is some such substance, and I mean one which is separable and immovable, as we shall attempt to prove. And if there is some such nature among existing things, this will exist somewhere and will be divine, and it will be the primary and highest principle. It is evident, then, that there are three classes of speculative science: the philosophy of nature, mathematics and theology.* **1064a28–1064b3**

6. *The class of speculative sciences, then, is the highest, and of these the last mentioned is highest of all. For it is concerned with the noblest of beings, and each science is said to be higher or lower by reason of its proper object.* **1064b3–6**

7. *However, one might raise the question whether the science of being as being is universal or not. For each of the mathematical sciences deals with some one determinate class of things, but a universal science is common to all. If, then, natural substances are the primary beings, the philosophy of nature must be the primary science. But if there is another nature and substance*

which is separable and immovable, the science which treats of this must be different from and prior to the philosophy of nature, and must be universal because it is prior. **1064b6–14**

COMMENTARY

2247. Having shown with what things this science is concerned, here the Philosopher compares this science with the others. In regard to this he does three things. First [1], he indicates what is proper to the particular sciences. Second [3], he shows how the particular sciences differ from one another ("Now since"). Third [5], he compares this science with the others ("And since there is").

In treating the first member of this division he does two things, insofar as there are two characteristics which he says pertain to the particular sciences. He accordingly says, first [1], that every particular science seeks certain principles and causes of the proper object of knowledge which comes within its scope. He says *certain* principles and causes because not every science considers every class of cause.

2248. He gives as an example the science of medicine, whose object is health, and the art of gymnastics, whose object is physical exercise directed to the well-being of the body. The same thing holds true of any of the other sciences, whether they are "productive," i.e., practical, or "doctrinal," i.e., theoretical; because each of these particular sciences marks off and takes as its own some determinate class of being inasmuch as it confines itself to that class and deals with it alone. For it is concerned with that class of being as a certain kind of being, though not as being. But to consider this, namely, being as being, belongs to a science which differs from all of the particular sciences.

2249. **And each** [2].

Second, he gives another characteristic of the particular sciences. He says that each of the above-mentioned particular sciences somehow assumes the quiddity in whatever class of things is considered. Hence it has been stated at the beginning of the ***Posterior Analytics*** [71a11] that it is necessary to assume both the existence and quiddity of the subject. And having assumed this, i.e., the quiddity, which every science uses as a middle term to demonstrate certain things, such as properties and the like, it tries to demonstrate these with greater or lesser certainty; because some sciences have a more certain method of demonstrating, as the mathematical sciences, and others a less certain one, as the natural sciences.

2250. And since he had said that other sciences somehow assume the quiddity, he therefore adds that some sciences derive the quiddity from sensory perception inasmuch as they acquire a knowledge of a thing's essence from sensible accidents, and that others derive the quiddity by assuming it from other sciences, as particular sciences from universal ones.

2251. Thus it is evident that in the particular sciences there is no demonstration of the substance or the quiddity of a thing. Hence both of the things with which the particular sciences do not concern themselves, i.e., a consideration of the substance or being and its quiddity, pertain to a universal science.

2252. **Now since** [3].

Then he shows how the particular sciences differ from one another. First [3], he shows how the philosophy of nature differs from the productive sciences; and second [4], how the mathematical sciences differ from the philosophy of nature ("And since it is necessary").

He accordingly says, first [3], that, since there is a particular science of nature, it must be different "from the practical," i.e., from the sciences which govern activity and from those which govern production; for every practical science is either a science of action or a science of production.

2253. In order to understand this difference we must consider a distinction which was made above in Book IX (n. 1864), namely, that to act and to make differ; for to act is said properly of an operation which remains in the agent and does not pass over into some external matter, for instance, to understand and to perceive and so on. But to make or produce is said of an operation which passes over into some external matter which is changed, for example, to heat and to cut and the like. Hence there is a science of activity by which we are instructed how to perform correctly those operations which are called actions; and moral science is such. But that science by which we make something correctly is a productive science. The art of carpentry and the like belong to this class.

2254. Now the philosophy of nature differs from each of these sciences which govern operations; for the productive sciences do not have a principle of motion in the thing made but in the maker, and this principle is either the art, which is a directive principle, or some potency which is the principle executing the work. Similarly "the practical sciences," i.e., those governing activity, do not have a principle of motion in that upon which the activity is exercised but rather in the agents.

2255. But those things which belong to the consideration of the philosophy of nature have their principles of motion in themselves, since nature is a principle of motion in the thing in which it exists. It is evident, then, that the philosophy of nature is a science neither of action nor of production but is speculative. For the philosophy of nature must fall into one of these classes, i.e., active, productive or speculative science. Hence, if it is a science neither of action nor of production, it follows that it must be speculative.

2256. **And since** [4].

Then he shows how the mathematical sciences differ from the philosophy of nature. He says that, since each of the sciences must somehow come to know the quiddity and must use this as a starting point with a view to demonstrating, the sciences must be distinguished on the basis of a different method of defining. Hence in order to understand how the philosophy of nature differs from the other sciences we must not neglect to consider the method which the philosophy of nature uses in defining things, and how the definition should be considered in the philosophy of nature; that is, whether a thing should be defined in the way that snub is or in the way that concave is.

2257. Now the definition of snub includes sensible matter, but that of concave does not; for since snubness is found only in a definite sensible matter, because it is found only in a nose, the intelligible structure of snub must therefore include sensible matter; for snub is defined thus: snub is a concave nose. Sensible matter, however, is not included in the definition of concave or curved. Hence, just as sensible matter is included in the definition of snub, so too it must be included in the definition of flesh and of eye and of the other parts of the body. The same holds true of other natural beings.

2258. The difference between the philosophy of nature and mathematics is taken from this, because the philosophy of nature deals with those things whose definitions include sensible matter, whereas mathematics deals with those things whose definitions do not include sensible matter, although they have being in sensible matter.

2259. **And since there is** [5].

Then he compares this science with the other particular sciences; and in regard to this he does three things. First [5], he compares this science with the different particular sciences in reference to the way in which their objects are separate from matter. Second [6], he compares them from the viewpoint of nobility ("The class of speculative sciences"). Third [7], he compares them from the viewpoint of universality ("However, one").

He accordingly says, first [5], that there is a science of being insofar as it is separable; for it is the office of this science not only to establish the truth about being in common (and this is to establish the truth about being as being) but also to establish the truth about things which are separate from matter in being. Hence it is necessary to consider whether this science whose function is to consider these two things is the same as the philosophy of nature or differs from it.

2260. That it differs from the philosophy of nature he makes clear as follows: the philosophy of nature is concerned with things which have a principle of motion in themselves; therefore natural things must have a definite matter, because only that which has matter is moved. But mathematics studies immovable things; for those things whose intelligible structure does not include sensible matter must likewise not have motion in their intelligible structure, since motion is found only in sensible things.

2261. But those things which mathematics considers are not separable from matter and motion in being but only in their intelligible structure. Hence the science which treats that kind of being which is separable from matter and from motion and is immovable in every respect must be one which differs both from mathematics and from the philosophy of nature.

2262. He says here, "if there is some such substance" apart from sensible substances which is immovable in every respect. He says this because the existence of some such substance has not yet been proved, although he intends to prove this.

2263. And if there is some such nature among existing things, i.e., one which is separable and immovable, it is necessary that "such a nature exist somewhere," i.e., that it be attributed to some substance. And whatever has this nature must be something that is divine and the highest of all; because the simpler and more actual a being is, the nobler it is and the more it is prior and a cause of other things. Thus it is evident that the science which considers separate beings of this kind should be called the divine science and the science of first principles.

2264. From this he again concludes that there are three classes of speculative science: the philosophy of nature, which considers things that are movable and have sensible matter in their definition; mathematics, which considers immovable things that do not have sensible matter in their definition yet exist in sensible matter; and theology, which considers beings that are entirely separate from matter.

2265. **The class** [6].

Next he compares this science with the others from the viewpoint of nobility. He says that the speculative sciences are the noblest, because of all the sciences the speculative seek knowledge for its own sake, whereas the practical seek knowledge for the sake of some work. And among the speculative sciences there is one that is highest, namely, theology, since a science which deals with more noble beings is itself more noble; for a science is more noble in proportion to the greater nobility of its object.

2266. **However, one might** [7].

Then he compares this science with the others from the viewpoint of universality. He says that one might raise the question whether or not the science which deals with separate beings must be held to be a universal science of being as being; and that it must be such he shows by a process of elimination.

2267. For it is evident that the foregoing sciences which deal with operations are not universal sciences, and he therefore omits them. In the case of the speculative sciences it is evident that every mathematical science is concerned with some one determinate class of things. But a universal science deals with all things in common. No mathematical science, then, can be the one which treats all beings in common. Regarding the philosophy of nature it is evident that, if natural substances, which are perceptible and movable, are the primary beings, the philosophy of nature must be the primary science; because the order of the sciences corresponds with that of their subjects, as has been stated already (n. 2265). But if there is a different nature and substance over and above natural substances, which is separable and immovable, there must be a science which differs from the philosophy of nature and is prior to it. And because it is first, it must be universal; for it is the same science which treats of primary beings and of what is universal, since the primary beings are the principles of the others.

LESSON 8
No Science of Accidental Being

ARISTOTLE'S TEXT Chapter 8: 1064b15–1065b4

1. *Since the term being in its unqualified sense has many meanings, and one of these is the accidental, it is first necessary to consider this sense of being.* **1064b15–17**

2. *Now it is evident that none of the traditional sciences are concerned with the accidental. The science of building does not consider what will happen to the occupants of a house, for example, whether they will dwell there unhappily or in the opposite way; nor is the art of weaving or of shoemaking or of cooking concerned with it. But each of these sciences considers only what is proper to itself, and this is its particular end.* **1064b17–23**

3. *Further, no science considers a man insofar as he is a musician or also a grammarian; nor does any science consider the quibble that "when one who is a musician has become a grammarian he will be both at the same time, although he was not so before; but that which is and has not always been, must have come to be; and therefore he must have at the same time become both a musician and a grammarian." None of the known sciences are concerned with this except sophistry, and thus Plato was not wrong in saying that sophistry is concerned with non-being.* **1064b23–30**

4. *That it is impossible to have a science of the accidental will be evident to those who are trying to learn what the accidental is. Accordingly, we say of all things that some are always and of necessity (not necessity in the sense of what is done by force but with the meaning used in matters of demonstration); others are for the most part; and others are neither for the most part nor always and of necessity, but are such as occur by chance. For example, there might be cold weather during the dog days, but this occurs neither always and of necessity nor for the most part, though it might happen sometimes. Hence the accidental is what occurs, but neither always and of necessity nor for the most part. What the accidental is, then, has been stated; and it is evident that there is no science of it. For every science deals with what is always or for the most part, but the accidental belongs to neither of these.* **1064b30–1065a6**

5. *It is also evident that there are no causes and principles of accidental being such as there are of essential being; for if there were, everything would be of necessity. For if one thing exists when another does, and this again when something else does, and if this last thing is not a matter of chance but exists of necessity, then that of which it was the cause will also exist of necessity, and so on right down to the last thing said to be caused. But this was assumed to be accidental. Hence everything will be of necessity, and the possibility of anything happening by chance or being contingent and of coming to be or not coming to be will be entirely removed from the sphere of things which are generated. And if the cause is assumed not to exist but to be something which is coming to be, the same results will follow; for everything will come to be of necessity. For tomorrow's eclipse will occur if something else does, and this again if some other thing occurs, and the latter if still another thing occurs. And if time is subtracted in this way from the limited time between the present and tomorrow, we shall at some point reach something which exists now. Therefore, since this exists, everything which comes after it will occur of necessity, so that everything will occur of necessity.* **1065a6–21**

6. *Regarding being in the sense of what is true and accidental being, the former depends upon the combination which the mind makes and is a modification of it. It is for this reason that it is not the principles of this kind of being that are sought but of that which exists outside the mind and is separable; and the latter kind of being is not necessary but indeterminate (and by this I mean the accidental); and the causes of this kind of being are indeterminate and unordered.* **1065a21–26**

7. And that for the sake of which something exists is found both in things which come to be by nature and in those which are a result of mind. It is luck when one of these comes about accidentally; for just as a being is either essential or accidental, so also is a cause. And luck is an accidental cause of those things which come to be for some end as a result of choice. **1065a26–31**

8. And for this reason both luck and mind are concerned with the same thing; for there is no choice without mind. **1065a31–32**

9. However, the causes from which some lucky result comes to be are indeterminate; and for this reason luck is uncertain for human knowledge and is an accidental cause, although in an absolute sense it is a cause of nothing. **1065a32–35**

10. There is good or bad luck when the result is good or bad, and prosperity or misfortune when this occurs on a large scale. **1064b35–1065b1**

11. And since nothing accidental is prior to things which are essential, neither are accidental causes prior. Therefore, if luck or chance is the cause of the heavens, mind and nature are prior causes. **1065b2–4**

COMMENTARY

2268. After having restated in a summary way the points that were discussed before with regard to this science's field of study, here the Philosopher begins to summarize the things that were said about imperfect being both in Book VI (nn. 1171–1244) of this work and in the **Physics**. [III, 1-3] He does this, first [1], with regard to accidental being; and second (Lesson 9), with regard to motion ("One thing").

In treating the first member of this division he does two things. First, he states the things that have been said about accidental being. Second [7], he states those that pertain to an accidental cause ("And that for the sake").

In regard to the first he does two things. First [1], he points out what he intends to do. He says that, since, "being in its unqualified sense," i.e., taken in general, has many meanings, of which one is the accidental (as when we say, for example, that the musician is white), and these have been explained above in Book V (nn. 885–97), we ought to consider accidental being before we deal with essential being, so that when this kind of being has been disposed of we may speak in a more positive way of essential being.

2269. **Now it is evident** [2].

Second, he proceeds to carry out his plan; and in regard to this he does two things. First [2], he shows that the consideration of accidental being belongs to no science. Second [6], he excludes both this kind of being and the being which signifies the truth of a proposition from this science's field of study ("Regarding being").

In treating the first he does two things. First, he shows that no science considers accidental being; and second [4], that none can do so ("That it is impossible").

In regard to the first he does two things. First [2], he shows by a process of elimination that no science considers accidental being. He says that no one of the sciences treated by us is concerned with the accidental.

2270. Now accidental here does not mean something in one of the categories of accidents, in the sense that whiteness is an accident; for there are many sciences which deal with accidents of this kind, because such accidents have a certain species of themselves and certain determinate causes in their subject. And they are called accidents because they do not have being of themselves but exist in something else.—But here accidental means what happens accidentally; for example, it is accidental that a musician is white. For accidents of this kind do not have any species or any determinate cause. And no science is concerned with this kind of being. He proves this by induction.

2271. For the art of building does not consider what happens accidentally to the occupants of the house which it builds, whether they happen to experience some unhappiness there or live there "in the opposite way," i.e., happily; for this is accidental to a house. Similarly, the art of weaving does not consider what happens to those who use the cloth which has been woven; nor does the art of shoemaking consider what happens to those who use shoes; nor does the art of cooking consider what happens to the food, for example, whether someone uses too much of it or just what is necessary. But each of these sciences considers only what is proper to itself, i.e., its subject and the properties of its subject. This is the goal of any science.

2272. **Further, no science** [3].

Second, he gives the reason why no science considers things which are accidental. It is because the accidental is not a being in the proper sense but is rather a non-being inasmuch as it is not essentially and properly one; for one and being are convertible. Now every science deals with being, and therefore it follows that no science is concerned with the accidental.

2273. Hence he says that a musician is also a grammarian, but not inasmuch as he is a musician. And if it happens that one who is a musician becomes a grammarian, he has become both at the same time, i.e., both a grammarian and a musician, although he was not so before. But if some being exists now and was not always a being, it must have come to be. Therefore, if "a musician grammarian" is a kind of being, since it did not always exist it must have become both at the same time, i.e., both a musician and a grammarian, because any being admits of some generation. Hence, since these have not come to be at the same time, it is evident that this whole—a musician-grammarian—is not one being.

2274. Nor should it be urged that matter, which is ungenerated, has existence prior to the generation of substances; for it is not the form that properly comes to be but the composite, as has been proved in Book VII (n. 1423). Now matter does not have prior existence as an actual being but only as a potential one. But here the musician has actual prior existence. Therefore, since he who was a musician has become a grammarian, only a grammarian has come to be, and not the whole—a grammarian musician. Hence this whole is not one being.

2275. For this reason no science that is truly a science and attains certainty is concerned with accidental being. Only sophistry deals with it; and it uses the accidental as though it were something of itself in order to deceive. From this there arises the fallacy of accident, which is most effective in deceiving even those who are wise, as is stated in Book I of the ***Sophistical Refutations***. [168b6-10] Hence Plato was not wrong in saying that sophistry is concerned with non-being, because it deals with the accidental.

2276. **That it is impossible** [4].

He shows that it is impossible for any science to consider accidental being, and he does this in two ways. First, he proceeds from the definition of accidental being. He says that, if we consider what accidental being is, it will be evident that there can be no science of it. With a view to proving his point he makes a tripartite division. He says that of things which are said to be there are some which are always and of necessity (not necessity in the sense of force, but in the sense used in demonstrations, as when we say that a triangle necessarily has three angles equal to two right angles; for we use the term necessary in this way to mean what cannot be otherwise). There are others which are for the most part; for example, a man is born with five fingers on each hand. This does not happen always, since it does happen that some are born with six fingers, but it does happen for the most part. And there are others which are neither always and of necessity nor for the most part but are such as occur by chance; for example, "there might be cold weather during the dog days," i.e., during the days of the dog-star. This occurs neither always and of necessity nor for the most part, though even this kind of being sometimes occurs. But since it happens rarely, and not always and of necessity or for the most part, it is called accidental being.

2277. For things which occur either always or for the most part are such that one is the cause of the other or both are referred to one cause which is the proper cause of each. And they occur in both ways. If a cause produces its effect without fail, the effect will be one that is said to be of necessity. But if a cause can fail because of some obstacle, the effect will be one that occurs for the most part.

2278. But if it so happens in the case of two things that one is not the cause of the other and there is no single common proper cause which links them together, they will seldom be combined. Such is the case, for example, when we say "the musician builds"; for the cause of building is not the art of music but that of building, which differs completely from the art of music. The same thing is true of the previous example; for excessive heat during the dog days is a result of the sun moving closer to the earth; but that there should be cold weather at this time is a result of some other cause, such as Saturn's being somehow connected with the sun. Hence, if there is cold weather during the dog days, which are caused by the sun, this is accidental.

2279. It is evident, then, that the accidental is what occurs neither always nor for the most part. But every science is concerned with what occurs either always or for the most part, as has been proved in Book I of the *Posterior Analytics.[71b9]* Thus it is clear that there can be no science of the accidental.

2280. **It is also evident** [5].

Second, with a view to making the same point he says that accidental being has no causes and principles such as essential being has; and thus there can be no science of it, since every science is concerned with principles and causes. He proves this as follows: if accidental being should have proper causes, everything would happen of necessity; for essential beings have a cause such that when it is placed the effect necessarily follows. And if there were some cause from which an effect did not follow of necessity but only for the most part, this would be a result of some obstacle, which can be accidental. If, then, accidental being had a necessary proper cause, so that when this cause is placed its effect necessarily follows (although perhaps it is not necessary to place it), the result would be that everything happens of necessity. He proves this as follows.

2281. Let us suppose that something past or present is the cause of a future effect, and that this cause has already been placed. But when the cause has been placed, as you say, the effect necessarily follows. Therefore, if this past or present thing which has already been placed is the cause of this future effect, and this in turn is the cause of another, the effect will follow not in just any way at all but necessarily. For once the cause has been placed, that whose cause has been placed will necessarily follow, and so on right down to the last thing caused. But this was assumed to be accidental. Therefore that which was assumed to be accidental will happen of necessity. Consequently, everything will happen of necessity; and "the possibility of anything happening by chance," i.e., any fortuitous event, "or being contingent," i.e., being accidental, and "of coming to be or not coming to be," i.e., the possibility of anything being or not being, or being generated or not being generated, will be completely removed from the world.

2282. But because one can meet this argument by saying that the cause of future contingent events has not yet been placed as either present or past but is still contingent and future, and that for this reason its effects are still contingent, he therefore throws out this objection ("And if the cause"). He points out that the same unreasonable conclusion follows if it is held that the cause of future contingent events is not something that already exists in the present or in the past but is something that is coming to be and is future, because it will follow that everything happens of necessity, as has been stated before. For if that cause is future, it must be going to be at some definite time, tomorrow say, and must be quite distinct from the present. Therefore, if an eclipse, which is the proper cause of certain future events, will occur tomorrow, and everything that occurs is a result of some cause, tomorrow's eclipse must occur "if something else does," i.e., because of something that existed before, and this in turn because of something else. Thus by always anticipating or subtracting causes some part of the time between the present moment and the future eclipse will be removed. And since that time is limited, and every limited thing is used up when some part of it is removed, we shall therefore reach at some point some cause which exists now. Hence, if that cause is already posited, all future effects will follow of necessity; and thus everything will occur of necessity. But since this is impossible, it is therefore evident that things which are accidental have no determinate cause from which they necessarily follow once it has been placed. Everything that can be said about this has been given in Book VI (nn. 1171–90).

2283. **Regarding being** [6].

Then he shows that accidental being and the being which signifies the truth of a proposition must be omitted from this science. He says that there is one kind of being, "being in the sense of what is true," or being as signifying the truth of a proposition, and it consists in combination; and there is accidental being. The first consists in the combination which the intellect makes and is a modification in the operation of the intellect. Hence the principles of this kind of being are not investigated in the science which considers the kind of being that exists outside of the mind and is separable, as has been stated.

The second, i.e., accidental being, is not necessary but indeterminate. Hence it does not have a related cause but an infinite number of causes that are not related to one another. Therefore this science does not consider such being.

2284. **And that for the sake** [7].

Here he summarizes the things that have been said about an accidental cause, or luck, in Book II of the ***Physics***.*[196b2-25]* There are four points. First, he states what it is; and with a view to investigating this he prefaces his remarks with the statement, "And that for the sake of which," i.e., what exists for the sake of some end, is found both in those things which exist by nature and in those which are a result of mind. This is evident in Book II of the ***Physics***. *[197a5-15]* He adds that luck is found in those things which occur for the sake of some end, but that it is accidental. For just as we find both essential being and accidental being, so too we find essential causes and accidental causes. Luck, then, is an accidental cause "of those things which come to be for the sake of some end," i.e., some goal, not by nature but by choice. For example, when someone chooses to dig in a field in order to plant a tree and thereupon discovers a treasure, we say that this is accidental because it is unintended. And this happens by luck.

2285. **And for this reason** [8].

Second, he shows in what instances luck exists. He says that, since there is choice only where there is mind or thought, luck and thought must be concerned with the same thing. Hence luck is not found in those things which lack reason, such as plants, stones and brute animals, or in children who lack the use of reason.

2286. **However, the causes** [9].

Third, he shows that luck is uncertain. He says that there are an infinite number of causes by which something can happen by luck, as is evident in the examples given; for one can find a treasure by digging in the earth either to plant something or to make a grave or for an infinite number of other reasons. And since everything infinite is unknown, luck is therefore uncertain for human knowledge. And it is called an accidental cause, although absolutely and of itself it is the cause of nothing.

2287. **There is good** [10].

Fourth, he explains why luck is said to be good or bad. He points out that luck is said to be good or bad because the accidental result is good or bad. And if the accidental result is a great good, it is then called prosperity; and if a great evil, it is then called misfortune.

2288. **And since nothing** [11].

Fifth, he shows that luck is not the primary cause of things; for nothing that is accidental is prior to things that are essential. Hence an accidental cause is not prior to a proper cause. Thus, if luck and chance, which are accidental causes, are the causes of the heavens, mind and nature, which are proper causes, must be prior causes.

LESSON 9
The Definition of Motion

ARISTOTLE'S TEXT Chapter 9: 1065b5–1066a34

1. One thing is actual only, another potential, and others both actual and potential; and of these one is a being, another a quantity, and another one of the other categories. Motion is not something apart from things themselves; for a thing is always changed according to the categories of being, and there is nothing that is common to these and in no one category. And each belongs to all its members in a twofold way, for example, this particular thing; for sometimes this is the form of a thing and sometimes its privation. And with regard to quality, one thing is white and another black; and with regard to quantity, one is perfect and another imperfect; and with regard to motion in space, one thing tends upwards and another downwards, or one is light and another heavy. Hence there are as many kinds of motion and change as there are of being. **1065b5–14**

2. Now since each class of things is divided by potentiality and actuality, I call motion the actualization of what is potential as such. **1065b14–16**

3. That our account is true becomes evident as follows: when the buildable in the sense in which we call it such actually exists, it is being built; and this is the process of building. The same is true of learning, walking, healing, dancing and bereaving. And motion occurs when something is in this very act, and neither before nor after. Motion, then, belongs to what is potential when it is actual and is engaged in activity, not inasmuch as it is itself, but inasmuch as it is movable. **1065b16–23**

4. And by the phrase inasmuch as I mean this: bronze is potentially a statue, but the actuality of bronze inasmuch as it is bronze is not motion; for to be bronze and to be some potentiality are not the same. If they were absolutely the same in meaning, the actuality of bronze would be a kind of motion; but they are not the same. This is evident in the case of contraries; for the potentiality of being healed and that of being ill are not the same, because being healed would then be the same as being ill. But it is the subject which is both healed and ill, whether it be moisture or blood, that is one and the same. And since they are not the same, just as color and the visible object are not the same, it is the actualization of what is potential insofar as it is potential that is motion. **1065b23–33**

5. That motion is this, and that a thing is being moved when it is actual in this way, and neither before nor after, is evident. For each thing is capable of being at one time actual and at another not, for example, the buildable as buildable; and the actualization of the buildable as buildable is the process of building. For the actuality is either the process of building or this particular house. But when the house exists, it will no longer be buildable; but what is being built is what is buildable. Therefore the process of building must be its actualization; and the process of building is a kind of motion. The same reasoning also applies to other motions. **1065b34–1066a7**

6. That this account is true is evident from what others say about motion, and because it is not easy to define it otherwise. For one cannot place it in another class. **1066a7–10**

7. This is evident from what some say; for they call it otherness and inequality and non-being. **1066a10–11**

8. However, no one of these is necessarily moved, and change is not to these or from these anymore than to or from their opposites. **1066a11–13**

9. The reason for putting motion in this class is that it seems to be something indefinite; and the principles in one of the columns of opposites (60) are indefinite because they are privative, for no one of them is either a this or such or any of the other categories. **1066a13–17**

10. The reason why motion seems to be indefinite is that it cannot be identified either with the potentiality or with the actuality of existing things; for neither what is capable of having a certain quantity nor what actually has it is necessarily being moved. And motion seems to be an actuality, but an incomplete one; and the reason for this is that the potentiality of which it is the actuality is incomplete. Hence it is difficult to grasp what motion is; for it must be put under privation or under potentiality or under simple actuality; but none of these appear to be possible. It remains, then, that it must be as we have said, i.e., both an actuality and a non-actuality as explained, which is difficult to see but capable of existing. **1066a17–26**

11. That motion belongs to the thing moved is evident; for it is the actualization of the thing moved by what is capable of causing motion. **1066a26–28**

12. And the actuality of what is capable of causing motion is no other than this; for it must be the actuality of both. **1066a28–29**

13. And a thing is capable of causing motion because of its power, but it is a mover because of its activity. **1066a29–30**

14. But it is on the thing moved that it is capable of acting. Thus the actuality of both alike is one. **1066a30–31**

15. And it is one just as the distance from one to two and that from two to one are the same, and just as what goes up and what comes down are the same, although their being is not one. The same applies in the case of the mover and the thing moved. **1066a31–34**

COMMENTARY

2289. Having settled the issue about accidental being, the Philosopher now states his views about motion; and this is divided into three parts. First [1], he deals with motion in itself; second (Lesson 10), with infinity, which a property of motion and of other continuous things ("The infinite"); and third (Lesson 11), with the division of motion into its species ("Everything which is changed").

The first is divided into two parts. First [1], he explains what motion is; and second [11], he points out what the subject of motion is ("That motion").

In regard to the first he does three things. First, he prefaces his discussion with some points which are necessary for defining motion. Second [2], he defines motion ("Now since each"). Third [6], he proves that the definition of motion is a good one ("That this account").

In treating the first member of this division he gives four points from which he infers a fifth. The first is that being is divided by actuality and by potentiality. He says that one kind of being is actual only, such as the prime mover, which is God; another is potential only, such as prime matter; and others are both potential and actual, as all intermediate things. Or by the phrase *actual only* he means what already has a form completely, as what is now completely white; and by *potential only*, what does not have a form, as what is not white in any way; and by *potential and actual*, what does not yet have a form completely but is being moved to a form.

2290. The second point is that being is divided by the ten categories, as is implied when he says that there is one kind of being which exists of itself, i.e., substance, and another is quantity, and another is quality, and so on for the other categories.

2291. The third point is that motion does not have a distinct nature separate from other things; but every form insofar as it is in a state of becoming is an imperfect actuality which is called motion. For to be moved to whiteness is the same as for whiteness to begin to become actual in a subject; but it need not be in complete actuality. This is his meaning in saying that motion is not something apart from things themselves; for everything which is being changed is being changed according to the categories of being. And just as the ten categories have nothing in common as their genus, in a similar way there is no genus common to all the kinds of motion. Hence motion is not a category distinct from the others but is a natural concomitant of the other categories.

2292. The fourth point is that a thing is found in any genus in two ways, namely, perfectly and imperfectly; for example, in the genus of substance one thing has the character of a form, and another the character of a privation; and in the genus of quality there is one thing which is perfect, as a white thing, which has a perfect color, and another which is imperfect, as a black thing, which is imperfect in the genus of color. And in the genus of quantity one thing is perfect, and this is called "great," and another is imperfect, and this is called "small"; and in the genus of place, in which "motion in space" is found, i.e., local motion, one thing tends upwards and another downwards, or one is light and another heavy inasmuch as that is called light which actually rises upwards, and that heavy which actually sinks downwards; and one of these has the character of something perfect and the other the character of something imperfect. The reason is that all the categories are divided by contrary differences; and one contrary always has the character of something perfect, and the other the character of something imperfect.

2293. From these four points he infers a fifth, namely, that there are as many kinds of motion and change as there are of being. He does not say this because there is motion in every genus of being, but because, just as being is divided by actuality and potentiality and by substance and accident and the like, and in terms of perfect and imperfect, so also is motion. This follows from his assertion that motion is not something apart from things. The way in which change and motion differ will be explained below.

2294. **Now since each** [2].

Next, he defines motion. First, he gives its definition, saying that, since in each genus of being, being is divided by potentiality and actuality, motion is said to be the actualization of what is potential insofar as it is such.

2295. **That our account** [3].

Second, he explains the definition which has been given; and in regard to this he does two things. First [3], he explains what was given in the definition with regard to the subject of motion; and second [5], what was given as the genus of motion ("That motion is this").

In regard to the first member of this division he does two things. First, he explains the part of the definition, *what is potential;* and second [4], the part, *insofar as it is such* ("And by the phrase").

He accordingly says, first [3], that it is evidently true from this that motion is as we have described it to be. For it is clear that the term *buildable* signifies something in potentiality, and that the potentiality in question is presented as being brought to actuality by what is designated as being built; and this actuality is called *the process of building.* The same thing is also true of other motions, such as walking, altering, and the like. And a thing is said to be being moved when it is coming to be such and such actually and has been such and such potentially, and neither before nor after. If this is so, then, it follows that motion belongs to a thing in potentiality when it is being brought to actuality; and by this I mean that it is being brought to actuality insofar as it is movable; for a thing is said to be movable because it is in potentiality to motion. Hence a potentiality of this kind is being brought to actuality when it is actually being moved; but what is potential "inasmuch as it is itself," i.e., in reference to what it actually is and in itself, does not have to be brought to actuality by motion. For it actually is this before it begins to be moved. And neither is it being brought to actuality by motion insofar as it is in potentiality to the terminus of motion, because so long as it is being moved it still remains in potentiality to the terminus of motion. But a thing is being brought from potentiality to actuality by motion only in the case of that potentiality which is signified when a thing is said to be movable, i.e., capable of being moved.

2296. **And by the phrase** [4].

Then he explains a phrase which was given in the definition of motion, namely, *insofar as it is such*, or *inasmuch as it is of this kind*. With a view to making this clear he says that bronze is in potentiality to being a statue, and thus the subject bronze and bronze in potentiality to being a statue are the same, although they are not the same in their meaning; for the concept of bronze as bronze and that of bronze insofar as it has some potentiality are different; and this is what he means when he says that to be bronze and to be some potentiality are not the same. For if they were the same in their meaning, then just as motion is an actuality of bronze insofar as it is bronze in potentiality, in a similar way motion would be the actuality of bronze insofar as it is bronze. But bronze and the potentiality of bronze do not have the same meaning. This is evident in the case of the potentiality for contraries, because the potentiality "of being healed and that of being ill" do not have the same meaning; for the concept of a potentiality is derived from that of the actuality. Hence, if the potentiality of being healed and that of being ill were the same in meaning, it would follow that being healed and being ill are the same. But this is impossible. Therefore the potentiality for each of two contraries is not the same in meaning, although it is the same in subject. For it is the same subject which can be healed or be ill; and whether that subject is any one at all of the humors in the animal's body, or the blood, which is more natural and proper to the life and nourishment of the animal, it can be a cause of its being healed or being ill. Since, then, the potentiality of being healed and that of being ill are not the same in meaning, it is evident that neither of these is the same as its subject in meaning, because any two things which are essentially the same as some third thing are themselves essentially the same. Hence, since bronze and bronze in potentiality to being a statue are not the same in meaning, just as color and the visible object are not the same, the phrase *insofar as it is such* must be added to the statement that motion is the actualization of what is potential.

2297. **That motion is this** [5].

Then he explains the term which was given as the genus in the definition of motion. That motion is this is evident, he says, because the said motion then exists "when it" (the actuality of what is potential) "is actual in this way," and neither before nor after. For obviously every movable thing can be at one time in a state of actualization and at another not; for the buildable as buildable at one time is in a state of potentiality and at another time is in a state of actualization. He says "the buildable as buildable" because the matter of a house is in potentiality to two things, namely, to the form of a house, and to the process of being built. And it is possible for it at one time to be in a state of potentiality to both and at another to be in a state of actuality. But the potentiality which the matter of a house has for being built is signified by the term *buildable*. Therefore the buildable as buildable becomes actual when it is being built; and thus the process of building is the actuality of the buildable as buildable.

2298. He proves this as follows: the matter of a house is in potentiality to only two actualities, namely, the act of building the house and the form of the house. But the term *buildable* signifies a potentiality belonging to the matter of the house. Therefore, since there is some actuality corresponding to every potentiality, the potentiality signified by the term buildable must correspond to one of these two actualities, namely, either to the form of the house or to the act of building. But the form of the house is not the actuality of the buildable as buildable, because when the form of the house develops, the house is no longer buildable but is already built. But the buildable is in a state of actuality when the house is actually being built. Therefore the act of building must be the actuality of the buildable. Now the act of building is a kind of motion; and thus motion is the actuality of the buildable. The same explanation holds for all other motions. It is evident, then, that motion is the actuality of what is potential.

2299. **That this account** [6].

Then he proves that the definition given is a good one. First, he gives a general proof. He says that it is evident that this definition of motion is a good one if we consider what others have said about motion when they defined it; and also because it cannot easily be defined in a different way. For it cannot be put in any other class than in that of actuality.

2300. **This is evident** [7].

Second, he states what others have said about motion. He says that some have said that motion is otherness, others inequality, and others non-being. And perhaps they spoke of it thus because the thing being moved gradually loses its initial state, and so long as it is being moved it is always in different states and comes closer to its goal.

2301. **However, no one** [8].

Third, he shows that the definitions given above are not suitable ones; for they do not fit motion so far as its subject is concerned, i.e., the thing moved. For if motion were non-being or inequality or otherness, it would follow that every non-being or whatever is other or unequal is moved, but it is not necessary that any of these should be moved. Hence motion is not as they have described it to be. The same thing is also apparent with regard to the termini of motion, which are the limits from which and to which there is motion. For motion is not to non-being or inequality or otherness rather than to their opposites, nor is motion from these rather than from their opposites. For there can be motion from nonbeing to being and vice versa, and from otherness to likeness, and from inequality to equality and vice versa.

2302. **The reason** [9].

Fourth, he shows why some defined motion in the foregoing way. He says that the reason why they put motion in the above-mentioned class is that motion seems to be something indefinite, and things which are privative are indefinite. Hence they assumed that motion is a kind of privation.

2303. It should also be noted, as has been pointed out in Book I (n. 127) of this work, that the Pythagoreans posited two orders of things, and in one of these, which they called the order of good things, they placed things which seem to be perfect, for example, light, right, male, rest, and the like; and in the other order, which they listed under evil, they placed darkness, left, female, motion and the like. And they said that all such things are indefinite and privative because no one of them seems to signify "either a this," i.e., substance, "or such," i.e., quality, or any of the other categories.

2304. **The reason why** [10].

Fifth, he points out why motion is placed in the class of the indefinite. The reason for this, he says, is that motion can be placed neither in the class of the potential nor in that of the actual; for if it were placed in the class of the potential, it would follow that whatever is in potentiality to something, for example, to have some quantity, would be moved to that quantity. But this is not necessary, because, before a thing begins to be moved to some quantity, it is in potentiality to that quantity. Moreover, it is not being moved when it already actually has that quantity to which it was in potentiality, but the motion has then already been terminated.

2305. But motion must be a kind of actuality, as has been proved above (n. 2294), although it is an imperfect one. The reason for this is that the thing of which it is the actuality is imperfect, and this is a possible or potential being; for if it were a perfect actuality, the whole potentiality for some definite actuality which is in the matter would be eliminated. Hence perfect actualities are not actualities of something in potentiality but of something in actuality. But motion belongs to something that is in potentiality, because it does not eliminate the potentiality of that thing. For so long as there is motion, the potentiality for that to which it tends by its motion remains in the thing moved. But only the previous potentiality for being moved is eliminated, though not completely; for what is being moved is still in potentiality to motion, because everything which is being moved will be moved, because of the division of continuous motion, as is proved in Book VI of the ***Physics***.*[234b10]* It follows, then, that motion is the actuality of what is potential; and thus it is an imperfect actuality and the actuality of something imperfect.

2306. It is because of this that it is difficult to grasp what motion is; for it seems necessary to place motion either in the class of privation, as is evident from the definitions given above, or in the class of potentiality, or in that of simple and complete actuality—none of which may be moved. It follows, then, that motion is as we have described it to be, namely, an actuality, and that it is not called a perfect actuality. This is difficult to grasp, although it can nevertheless be true, because when this is admitted nothing untenable follows.

2307. Some have defined motion by saying that it is the gradual passage from potentiality to actuality. But they erred, because motion must be given in the definition of a passage, since it is a kind of motion. Similarly, time is placed in the definition of the gradual, and motion in the definition of time.

2308. **That motion belongs** [11].

Then he explains what the subject of motion is. First, he shows that it is the thing moved; because every actuality is found in the thing whose actuality it is. But motion is the actuality of the movable by what is capable of causing motion. Hence it follows that motion is found in the movable or thing moved; and that it is the actualization of this is clear from the above discussion.

2309. **And the actuality** [12].

Second, he shows how motion is related to a mover; and he gives two points, namely, that motion is the actuality of what is capable of causing motion, and that the actuality of the thing capable of causing motion and that of the thing moved do not differ; for motion must be the actuality of both.

2310. **And a thing is capable** [13].

Third, he proves the first of these two points, namely, that motion is the actuality of what is capable of causing motion. For the actuality of a thing is that by which it becomes actual. But a thing is said to be capable of causing motion because of its power of moving, and it is said to be a mover because of its activity, i.e., because it is actual. Hence, since a thing is said to be a mover because of motion, motion will be the actuality of what is capable of causing motion.

2311. **But it is** [14].

Fourth, he proves the second of these points, namely, that the actuality of what is capable of causing motion and the actuality of what is capable of being moved are one and the same motion. He does this as follows: it has been stated that motion is the actuality of what is capable of causing motion inasmuch as it causes motion; and a thing is said to be movable inasmuch as motion is caused in it; but the thing capable of causing motion causes that motion which is found in the thing moved and not a different one. This is what he means when he says that it is on what is movable that the mover is capable of acting. It follows, then, that the actuality of the mover and that of the thing moved are one and the same motion.

2312. **And it is one** [15].

Fifth, he clarifies this by an example. He says that the distance from one to two and from two to one are the same, although they differ conceptually; and for this reason the distance is signified differently, namely, by the terms *double* and *half*. Similarly, the path of an ascent and that of a descent are one, but they differ conceptually; and for this reason some are called ascenders and others descenders. The same applies to a mover and to the thing moved; for the actuality of both is essentially one motion, although they differ conceptually. For the actuality of a mover functions as that from which motion comes, whereas the actuality of the thing moved functions as that in which motion occurs. And the actuality of the thing moved is not that from which motion comes, nor is the actuality of the mover that in which motion occurs. Hence the actuality of the thing causing motion is called action, and that of the thing moved is called undergoing or suffering.

2313. But if action and undergoing are essentially the same thing, it seems that they should not be different categories. However, it should be borne in mind that the categories are distinguished on the basis of a different way of predicating; and thus inasmuch as the same term is differently predicated of different things, it belongs to different categories; for inasmuch as place is predicated of a thing that locates, it belongs to the genus of quantity, but inasmuch as it is predicated denominatively of the located thing it constitutes the category *where*. Similarly, inasmuch as motion is predicated of the subject in which it is found, it constitutes the category of undergoing; but inasmuch as it is predicated of that from which it comes, it constitutes the category of action.

LESSON 10
The Infinite

ARISTOTLE'S TEXT Chapter 10: 1066a35–1067a37

1. *The infinite is either what cannot be spanned because it is not naturally fitted to be spanned (just as the spoken word is invisible); or what is imperfectly spanned; or what is spanned with difficulty; or what is not actually spanned, although it admits of being spanned or of having a terminus.* **1066a35–1066b1**

2. *Further, a thing may be infinite either by addition or by subtraction or by both.* **1066b1**

3. *That the infinite should be a separate entity and be perceptible is impossible. For if it is neither a continuous quantity nor a plurality, and is a substance and not an accident, it will be indivisible; for what is divisible is either a continuous quantity or a plurality. But if it is indivisible, it is not infinite, except in the sense in which the spoken word is invisible. But people do not use the term in this sense, nor is this the sense of the infinite which we are investigating, but the infinite in the sense of what cannot be spanned.* **1066b1–7**

4. *Further, how can the infinite exist of itself if number and continuous quantity, of which the infinite is an attribute, do not exist of themselves?* **1066b7–8**

5. *Again, if the infinite is an accident, it cannot, inasmuch as it is infinite, be an element of existing things, just as the invisible is not an element of speech although the spoken word is invisible. It is also evident that the infinite cannot be actual; for any part of it which might be taken would be infinite, since infinity and the infinite are the same if the infinite is a substance and is not predicated of a subject. Hence it is either indivisible, or if it is divisible, the parts into which it is divided are infinite in number. But it is impossible that the same thing should be many infinites; for, just as a part of air is air, so too a part of the infinite must be infinite if the infinite is a substance and principle. Therefore it cannot be divided into parts, and so is indivisible. But this cannot apply to the actually infinite, for it must be a quantity. Hence it is an accidental attribute. But if this is so, then, as we have said, it cannot be it that is a principle, but that of which it is an accident, for example, air or the even. This investigation, then, is universal.* **1066b8–22**

6. *That the infinite does not exist in sensible things is made clear as follows: if it is the nature of a body to be bounded by surfaces, then no body, whether it is perceptible or intelligible, can be infinite.* **1066b22–24**

7. *Nor can there be any separate and infinite number; for a number or that which has a number is numerable.* **1066b24–26**

8. *This is evident from the following argument drawn from nature: the infinite can be neither composite nor simple. It cannot be a composite body if the elements are limited in number; for the contraries must be equal, and no one of them must be infinite; for if the active power of one of two elemental bodies is inferior to that of the other, the finite body will be destroyed by the infinite body. And that each should be infinite is impossible, because a body is what is extended in all directions, and the infinite is what is extended without limit; so if the infinite is a body, it must be infinite in all directions.* **1066b26–34**

9. *Nor can the infinite be a single simple body: neither, as some say, something apart from the elements, from which they generate these (for there is no such body apart from the elements, because everything can be dissolved into that of which it is composed; but there does not appear to be anything apart from the simple bodies), nor fire, nor any of the other elements. For unless some of them are infinite, the whole, even though it is finite, could not be or become any one of them, as Heraclitus says that all things at one time become fire. The same reasoning also applies*

to "the one," which the philosophers of nature posited as an entity over and above the elements (997). For everything is changed from a contrary, for example, from hot to cold. **1066b34–1067a7**

10. Again, a sensible body is somewhere, and the place of the whole and that of a part (of the earth, for example) is the same. **1067a7–8**

11. Hence, if the infinite is composed of like parts, it will be immovable or will always be undergoing motion. But this is impossible. For why should it be moved upwards rather than downwards or in some other direction? For example, if it were a clod of earth, where would it move to or where remain at rest? For the place of the body naturally fitted to this will be infinite. Will it then occupy the whole place? And how will it do this? And what then will be its place of rest and of motion? For if it rests everywhere, it will not be in motion. And if it is moved everywhere, it will not be at rest. **1067a8–15**

12. And if the whole is composed throughout of unlike parts, their places will also be unlike. And, first, the body of the whole will be one only by contact and, second, the parts will be either finite or infinite in species. But they cannot be finite, for some would then be infinite and some not (if the whole is infinite), for example, fire or water. But such an infinite element would necessitate the destruction of contrary elements. But if the parts are infinite and simple, their places will be infinite, and the elements will be infinite in number. And since this is impossible, their places will be finite and the whole finite. **1067a15–23**

13. And in general there cannot be an infinite body and a place for bodies if every sensible body has either heaviness or lightness; for it will tend either to the center or upwards. But the infinite—either the whole or a half of it—is incapable of any of these motions. For how can you divide it? Or how can one part tend upwards and another downwards, or one part tend to the extreme and another to the center? **1067a23–28**

14. Further, every sensible body is in a place, and there are six kinds of place, but these cannot pertain to an infinite body. **1067a28–30**

15. And in general if a place cannot be infinite, neither can a body be infinite; for to be in a place is to be somewhere, and this means to be either down or up or in some one of the other places, and each of these is a limit. **1067a30–33**

16. And the infinite is not the same in the case of continuous quantity, of motion, and of time, as though it were a single reality; but the secondary member is said to be infinite inasmuch as the primary one is; for example, motion is said to be infinite in reference to the continuous quantity in which it is moved or altered or increased, and time is said to be such in reference to motion. **1067a33–37**

COMMENTARY

2314. Having given his views about motion, here the Philosopher deals with the infinite, which is an attribute of motion and of any quantity in general. In regard to this he does three things. First [1], he distinguishes the various senses in which the term *infinite* is used. Second [3], he shows that the actually infinite does not exist ("That the infinite"). Third [16], he explains how the infinite is found in different things ("And the infinite").

In regard to the first he does two things. First, he explains the different senses in which the term infinite is used; and second [2], the various senses in which things are said to be potentially infinite ("Further, a thing").

In regard to the first [1] part it should be borne in mind that every finite thing may be spanned by division. Hence the infinite, properly speaking, is what cannot be spanned by measurement; and therefore the term *infinite* is used in the same number of senses as the term *untraversable.*

2315. Now each of these is used in four ways. First, the infinite or untraversable means what cannot be spanned by measurement because it does not belong to the class of things which are naturally fitted to be spanned; for example, we say that the point or the unit or something which is not a quantity and is not measurable is infinite or untraversable; and in this sense the spoken word is said to be invisible because it does not belong to the class of things which are visible.

2316. Second, the infinite or untraversable means what has not yet been spanned although it has begun to be spanned. This is his meaning in saying "what is imperfectly spanned."

2317. Third, the infinite or untraversable means what is spanned with difficulty. Thus we may say that the depth of the sea or the height of the sky is infinite, or that any long distance is immeasurable or untraversable or infinite, because it surpasses our powers of measurement although in itself it is capable of being spanned.

2318. Fourth, the infinite or untraversable means what belongs to the class of things which are naturally fitted to be spanned, or to have some limit set to them, but are not actually spanned; for example, if a line is limitless. This sense of the infinite is the true and proper one.

2319. **Further, a thing** [2].

Second, he explains the various senses in which things are said to be *potentially infinite.* He says that in one sense a thing is said to be infinite by addition, as a number; for it is always possible to add a unit to any number, and in this respect number is capable of infinite increase.

2320. In another sense a thing is said to be infinite by subtraction or division inasmuch as a continuous quantity is said to be infinitely divisible.

2321. In a third sense it is possible for a thing to be infinite from both points of view; for example, time is said to be infinite both as regards division, because it is continuous, and as regards addition, because it is a number. It is in a similar way that the infinite is found in motion.

2322. **That the infinite** [3].

Then he shows that the actually infinite does not exist; and in regard to this it should be noted that the Platonists held that the infinite is separate from sensible things and is a principle of them, whereas the philosophers of nature held that the infinite exists in sensible things, not in the sense that it is a substance, but rather in the sense that it is an accident of some sensible body. He therefore shows, first [3], that the infinite is not a separate entity; and second [6], that the actually infinite does not exist in sensible things ("That the infinite does not").

In treating the first member of this division he gives three arguments. The first is as follows: if the infinite is a substance which exists of itself and is not an accident of some subject, the infinite must lack continuous quantity and plurality, because continuous quantity and number constitute the subject of the infinite. But if it lacks continuous quantity and plurality, it must be indivisible, because everything divisible is either a continuous quantity or a plurality. But if it is indivisible, it is infinite only in the first sense of the term, as a spoken word is said to be invisible. However, we are not investigating this sense of the term here, nor did they use the term in this sense; but we are considering the fourth sense, i.e., what is untraversable. Therefore, all things considered, if the infinite were an independently existing substance, it would not be truly infinite. This position destroys itself in this way.

2323. **Further, how can** [4].

Then he gives the second argument, which runs thus: infinity is an attribute of number and of continuous quantity. But number and continuous quantity are not things which have separate existence, as has been shown in Book I (n. 239) and will be shown below (n. 2324). Therefore much less is the infinite a separate substance.

2324. **Again, if the infinite** [5].

Here he gives the third argument, which runs as follows. Let us suppose that the infinite is either a substance which is separate from sensible things or an accident belonging to some separate subject, for example, to continuous quantity or to number—which are separate according to the Platonists. Now if the infinite is assumed to be an accident, it cannot be the infinite as infinite that is a principle of existing things, but rather the subject of the infinite; just as what is invisible is not said to be a principle of speech, but the spoken word, although the spoken word is invisible in this sense.

2325. And if the infinite is assumed to be a substance and is not predicated of a subject, it is also evident that it cannot be actually infinite; for it is either divisible or indivisible. But if the infinite itself as infinite is a substance and is divisible, any part of it which might be taken would necessarily be infinite; because infinity and the infinite are the same "if the infinite is a substance," i.e., if infinity expresses the proper intelligible structure of the infinite. Hence, just as a part of water is water and a part of air is air, so too any part of the infinite is infinite if the infinite is a divisible substance. We must say, then, that the infinite is either indivisible or divisible into many infinites. But many infinite things cannot possibly constitute one finite thing; for the infinite is not greater than the infinite, but every whole is greater than any of its parts.

2326. It follows, then, that the infinite is indivisible. But that any indivisible thing should be actually infinite is impossible, because the infinite must be a quantity. Therefore it remains that it is not a substance but an accident. But if the infinite is an accident, it is not the infinite that is a principle, but the subject of which it is an accident (as was said above), whether it be air, as some of the natural philosophers claimed, or the even, as the Pythagoreans claimed. Thus it follows that the infinite cannot be both a substance and a principle of beings at the same time. Last, he concludes that this investigation is a general one which goes beyond the study of natural things.

2327. **That the infinite does not exist** [6].

Then he proves that the actually infinite does not exist in sensible things. First [6], he proves this by probable arguments; and second [8], by arguments drawn from nature ("This is evident").

He accordingly says, first [6], that it is obvious that the actually infinite is not found in sensible things; and he proves two points. First, he says that there is no infinite body in the sensible world, for it is the nature of a body to be bounded by surfaces. But no body with a definite surface is infinite. Therefore no body is infinite, "whether it be perceptible," i.e., a natural body, "or intelligible," i.e., a mathematical one.

2328. **Nor can there be** [7].

Second, he shows in the following way that there is no infinite number in sensible things. Every number and everything which has a number is numerable. But nothing numerable is infinite, because what is numerable can be spanned by numeration. Therefore no number is infinite.

2329. Now these arguments do not pertain to natural philosophy, because they are not based on the principles of a natural body but on certain principles which are common and probable and not necessary. For anyone who would claim that a body is infinite would not maintain that its surface has limits, for this characteristic belongs to the nature of a finite body. And anyone who would claim that there is an infinite multitude would not hold that it is a number, because number is multitude measured by one, as has been explained in Book X (n. 2090). But nothing measured is infinite.

2330. **This is evident** [8].

Next, he proves that the actually infinite does not exist within sensible things, by using arguments drawn from nature. He does this, first [8], with reference to the active and passive powers of bodies; and second [10], with reference to place and the thing in place ("Again, a sensible body").

Now active and passive powers, place and thing in place are proper to natural bodies as such; and therefore he says that these arguments are drawn from nature. He accordingly says, first [8], that, if a body is perceptible and infinite, it will be either a simple body or a composite body or compound.

2331. First, he shows that a composite body cannot be infinite, if we assume that simple bodies, which are the elements of composite bodies, are finite in number. He proves this as follows: either all the elements must be infinite in quantity, or one must be infinite and the others finite, otherwise an infinite body could not be composed of elements which are finite in number.

2332. But that one of the elements should be infinite and the rest finite is impossible; because in the case of a compound contraries must somehow be equalized in order that the compound may be preserved in being, for otherwise that contrary which exceeds the others will destroy them. But if one contrary is infinite and the rest finite, no equality will be established, since there is no proportion between the infinite and the finite. A compound, then, could not exist, for the infinite element would destroy the others.

2333. And since someone might say that a body which is finite in quantity has greater power, and that equality is achieved in this way (for example, if someone were to say that in a compound air is infinite and fire finite), he therefore adds that, even if we suppose that the active power of one body which is assumed to be infinite falls short of the active power of any one of the others, because these are assumed to be finite, the finite element will be destroyed by the infinite one; for a finite body must have a finite power, and then finite fire will have a finite power. Hence, if from infinite air a portion of air equal to the fire is taken out, its power will be less than that of the whole infinite air, but proportioned to the power of fire. Let us suppose, then, that the power of fire is a hundred times greater than that of air. Hence, if we take away a hundredfold of air from infinite air it will be equal to fire in power; and thus the whole infinite air will have a greater infinite power than fire and will destroy it. It is impossible, then, that one element of a compound should be infinite and the rest finite.

2334. Similarly, it is impossible that all should be infinite, because a body is what is extended in every dimension. But the infinite is what is infinite in dimension. Hence an infinite body must have an infinite dimension in every direction. But two bodies cannot be in the same place. Therefore two infinite bodies cannot be combined into one.

2335. **Nor can the infinite** [9].

Second, he proves that the infinite cannot be a simple body. There cannot be a simple body apart from the elements, from which all of them are generated, as some claimed air to be, because each thing is dissolved into the elements of which it is composed. But we see that compounds are dissolved only into the four elements; and therefore there cannot be a simple body apart from the four elements.

2336. Nor can fire or any of the other elements be infinite, because no element could possibly exist except the one which is infinite, since it would fill every place. Again, if there were some finite element it would have to be changed into that infinite element because of the very great power of the latter; just as Heraclitus claimed that at some time all things must be changed into the element fire because of its very great power.

2337. And the same argument therefore applies to the one simple body which the natural philosophers posited as an entity over and above the elements themselves; for it would have to be opposed to the other elements as a kind of contrary, since according to them there is change from that one body alone into the others. But every change in things is from one contrary to another. Therefore, since one of two contraries destroys the other, it follows that, if that body which is supposed to exist apart from the elements is infinite, it will destroy the others.

2338. The philosopher omits the celestial body here, because, while it is something apart from the four elements, it is not contrary or repugnant to them in any way, nor are these bodies naturally derived from it. For the philosophers of nature who posited an actually infinite body did not attain any knowledge of this fifth essence or nature. Yet in *The Heavens [271b1]* Aristotle proves that even a celestial body, which moves circularly, is not actually infinite.

2339. **Again, a sensible body** [10].

Then he proves that a sensible body is not infinite; and he does this by means of arguments based upon place and a thing in place. He gives three arguments. As a sort of preamble to the first he considers two points necessary for its development. The first is that every sensible body is in a place. He emphasizes *sensible* in order to distinguish this kind of body from a mathematical one, to which place and contact are attributed only figuratively.

2340. The second point is that the natural place of a whole and that of a part are the same, i.e., the place in which it naturally rests and to which it is naturally moved. This is clear, for instance, in the case of earth and of any part of it, for the natural place of each is down.

2341. **Hence, if the infinite** [11].

After giving these two points he states his argument, which runs as follows. If a sensible body is assumed to be infinite, either its parts will all be specifically the same, as is the case with bodies having like parts, such as air, earth, blood, and so on, or they will be specifically different.

2342. But if all of its parts are specifically the same, it will follow that the whole will always be at rest or always in motion. Each one of these is impossible and incompatible with the facts of sensory perception.

2343. **For why should it** (*ibid.*).

Then he shows that the other alternative has to be accepted; for it has already been assumed that the natural place of a whole and that of a part are the same. And it is evident that every body is at rest when it is in its natural place, and that it naturally moves to its natural place when it is outside of it. If, then, the whole place occupied by a body having an infinite number of like parts is natural to it, this place must be natural to each part, and thus the whole and each of its parts will be at rest. But if it is not natural to it, the whole and each of its parts will then be outside their proper place; and thus the whole and any part of it will always be in motion.

2344. For it cannot be said that some part of a place is natural to the whole and to its parts, and that some part of a place is not; because, if a body were infinite and every body were in a place, its place would also have to be infinite. But in infinite place there is no dividedness by reason of which one part of it is the natural place of the body and another is not, because there must be some fixed proportion and distance between a place which is natural and one which is not, and this cannot apply to an infinite place. This is what he means when he says that an infinite body or one of its parts will not be moved downwards rather than upwards or in some other direction, because in an infinite place it is impossible to find any fixed proportion between these parts.

2345. He gives an example of this. If we assume that the earth is infinite, it will be impossible to give any reason why it should be in motion or at rest in one place rather than in another, because the whole infinite place will be equally fitted by nature to the infinite body which occupies this place. Hence, if some part of a place is naturally fitted to a clod of earth, the same will apply to another part; and if one part is not naturally fitted to a place, neither will another be. If, then, an infinite body is in a place, it will fill the whole of that infinite place. Yet how can it be at rest and in motion at the same time? For if it rests everywhere, it will not be in motion; or if it is in motion everywhere, it follows that no part of it will be at rest.

2346. **And if the whole** [12].

Then the Philosopher examines the other alternative, namely, the supposition that the whole is not composed of like parts. He says that it follows, first, that, if "the body of the whole," i.e., of the universe, is composed of specifically unlike parts, it will be one only by contact, as a pile of stones is one. But things specifically different, such as fire, air and water, cannot be continuous; and this is not to be one in an absolute sense.

2347. Again, if this whole is composed of parts which are specifically unlike, they will be either infinite in species, i.e., so that the different parts of the whole are infinite in species; or they will be finite in species, i.e., so that the diversity of species found among the parts amount to some fixed number.

2348. But that the elements cannot be finite in species is clear from what was proposed in the preceding argument; for it would be impossible for an infinite whole to be composed of parts which are finite in number, unless either all parts were infinite in quantity, which is impossible, since an infinite body must be infinite in any of its parts, or at least unless some part or parts were infinite. Therefore, if a whole were infinite and its parts were different species infinite in number, it would follow that some of them would be infinite and some finite in quantity—for example, if one were to assume that water is infinite and fire finite. But this position introduces corruption among contraries, because an infinite contrary would destroy other contraries, as has been shown above (n. 2332). Therefore they cannot be finite in number.

2349. But if the parts of the universe were infinite in species, and these must be assumed to be simple, it would follow that places would be infinite and that the elements would be infinite. But both of these are impossible; for since each simple body has a place naturally fitted to it which is specifically different from the place of another body, if there were an infinite number of simple bodies which are different in species, it would also follow that there are an infinite number of places which are different in species. This is obviously false; for the species of places are limited in number, and these are up and down, and so on. It is also impossible that the elements should be infinite in number, because it would then follow that they would remain unknown; and if they were unknown, all things would be unknown. Therefore, if the elements cannot be infinite, places must be finite, and consequently the whole must be finite.

2350. **And in general** [13].

Here he gives the second argument. He says that, since every sensible body has a place, it is impossible for any sensible body to be infinite, granted the assumption that every sensible body has heaviness and lightness—which would be true according to the opinion of the ancient natural philosophers, who claimed that bodies are actually infinite. Aristotle, however, is of the opinion that there is a sensible body which does not have heaviness or lightness, namely, a celestial body, as he proved in ***The Heavens***.[269b30] He introduces this circumstantially, as admitted by his opponents, but not in the sense that it is unqualifiedly true. If every sensible body, then, is either heavy or light and some sensible body is infinite, it must be heavy or light; and therefore it must be moved upwards or towards the center; for a light thing is defined as one that rises upwards, and a heavy thing as one that tends towards the center. But this cannot apply to the infinite, either to the whole of it or to a part; for the center of a body is found only when a proportion is established between the boundaries by dividing the whole. But the infinite cannot be divided according to any proportion; and therefore neither up and down nor boundary and center can be found there.

2351. This argument must be understood to apply even if one assumes that there is a third kind of body which is neither heavy nor light; for such a body is naturally moved around the center, and this could not be the case with an infinite body.

2352. **Further, every sensible body** [14].

The Philosopher now gives the

third argument, which runs thus: every sensible body is in a place. But there are six kinds of place: up and down, right and left, before and behind; and it is impossible to attribute these to an infinite body, since they are the limits of distances. Thus it is impossible that a place should be attributed to an infinite body; and therefore no sensible body is infinite. However, in saying that there are six kinds of place he does not mean that these places are distinguished because of the elements (for their motions are distinguished merely in terms of up and down) but only because, just as up and down are out of the question so far as an infinite body is concerned, so are all the other differences of place.

2353. **And in general if** [15].

He gives the fourth argument, which is as follows. Every sensible body is in a place; but it is impossible for a place to be infinite; and therefore it is impossible for a body to be infinite. The way in which it is impossible for a place to be infinite he proves thus: whatever has a common term predicated of it must also have predicated of it any of the things which fall under that common term; for example, whatever is an animal must belong to some particular species of animal, and whatever is man must be some particular man. Similarly, whatever occupies an infinite place must be "somewhere," i.e., it must occupy some place. But to occupy some place is to be up or down or to be in some one of the other kinds of place. However, none of these can be infinite because each is the limit of some distance. It is impossible, then, that a place should be infinite, and the same applies to a body.

2354. **And the infinite** [16].

Then he shows how the potentially infinite is found in different things. He says that it is found in continuous quantity, in motion, and in time, and it is not predicated of them univocally but in a primary and a secondary way. And the secondary member among them is always said to be infinite inasmuch as the primary member is; for example, motion is said to be infinite in reference to the continuous quantity in which something is moved locally or increased or altered; and time is said to be infinite in reference to motion. This must be understood as follows: infinite divisibility is attributed to what is continuous, and this is done first with reference to continuous quantity, from which motion derives its continuity. This is evident in the case of local motion because the parts of local motion are considered in relation to the parts of continuous quantity. The same thing is evident in the case of the motion of increase, because increase is noted in terms of the addition of continuous quantity. However, this is not as evident in the case of alteration, although in a sense it also applies there; because quality, which is the realm of alteration, is divided accidentally upon the division of continuous quantity. Again, the intensification and abatement of a quality is also noted inasmuch as its subject, which has continuous quantity, participates in some quality to a greater or lesser degree. And motion is referred to continuity, and so is a continuous time; for since time in itself is a number, it is continuous only in a subject, just as ten measures of cloth are continuous because the cloth is continuous. The term infinite, then, must be used of these three things in the same order of priority as the term continuous is.

LESSON 11
Motion and Change

ARISTOTLE'S TEXT Chapter 11: 1067b1–1068a7

1. Everything which is changed is changed either accidentally, as when we say that a musician walks; or it is changed without qualification because something belonging to it is changed, as what is changed in some of its parts; for example, the body is said to be healed because the eye is. And there is some primary thing which is moved of itself, and this is what is essentially movable. **1067b1–5**

2. The same division applies to a mover, for it causes motion either accidentally or in some part of itself or essentially. **1067b6–7**

3. And there is a primary mover and something which is moved. And there is also a time in which it is moved, and something from which it is moved, and something to which it is moved. But the forms and modifications and place to which things in motion are moved are immovable, as science and heat. Heat is not motion, but heating is. **1067b7–12**

4. Now change which is not accidental is not found in all things, but between contraries and between their intermediates and between contradictories. We may be convinced of this by induction. Whatever is changed is changed either from a subject to a subject, or from a non-subject to a non-subject, or from a subject to a non-subject, or from a non-subject to a subject. And by subject I mean what is expressed by an affirmative term. Hence there must be three changes; for to go from a non-subject to a non-subject is not change, because, since the limits are neither contraries nor contradictories, there is no opposition. **1067b12–21**

5. The change from a non-subject to a subject which is its contradictory is generation; and if it is unqualified, it is generation in an unqualified sense, and if in a part, partial generation; and the change from a subject to a non-subject is destruction. **1067b21–25**

6. If non-being has several different meanings, then neither that which involves a combination or separation of terms, nor that which refers to potentiality and is opposed to being in an unqualified sense, is capable of being moved (for what is not-white or not-good can be moved only accidentally, since what is not-white may be a man). But non-being in an unqualified sense cannot be moved in any way, because it is impossible for non-being to be moved. And if this is so, generation cannot be motion, because non-being is generated. For even if it is most certainly generated accidentally, it will still be true to say that what is generated in an unqualified sense is non-being. The same argument applies to rest. These are the difficulties, then, which result from this view. And if everything moved is in a place, though non-being is not in a place, it would have to be somewhere. Nor is destruction motion; for the contrary of motion is motion or rest, but the contrary of destruction is generation. **1067b25–1068a1**

7. And since every motion is a kind of change, and the three changes are those described, and of these those which refer to generation and destruction are not motions, and these are changes between contradictories, only change from a subject to a subject must be motion. And the subjects are either contraries or their intermediates—for privation is given as a contrary—and they are expressed by an affirmative term, for example, naked or toothless or black. **1068a1–7**

COMMENTARY

2355. Having explained what motion is, and having dealt with the infinite, which is a certain attribute of motion, here the Philosopher establishes the truth about the parts of motion. This is divided into two parts. In the first [1] he distinguishes the parts of motion; and in the second (Lesson

13) he explains the connection between motion and its parts ("Things which are").

The first is divided into three members, corresponding to the three divisions which he makes in motion, although one of these is included under the other as a subdivision of the preceding division.

In regard to the first he does two things. First [1], he divides motion with regard to the thing moved; and second [2], with regard to a mover ("The same division").

He accordingly says, first [1], that a thing may be changed in three ways. In one way a thing may be changed only accidentally, as when something is said to be changed because the thing to which it belongs is changed, whether it belongs to it as an accident to a subject, as when we say that a musician walks, or as a substantial form to matter, as the soul belongs to the body which is moved; or as a part is said to be moved when the whole is moved, or also as something contained is moved when its container is moved, as a sailor is said to be in motion when his ship is in motion.

2356. In a second way a thing is said to be changed without qualification because some part of it is changed, as those things which are moved in some part; for example, the body of a man is said to be healed because the eye is; and this is to be moved essentially but not in the first instance.

2357. In a third way a thing is said to be moved primarily and of itself; as when some whole is moved in its totality, for example, when a stone is moved downwards.

2358. **The same division** [2].

He then gives the same division with regard to a mover; for a thing is said to be a mover in three ways. First, a thing is said to cause motion accidentally; as when a musician builds.

2359. Second, a thing is said to be a mover in regard to some one of its parts; as when a man strikes and injures someone with his hand.

2360. Third, a thing is said to be a mover essentially; as when fire heats and a physician heals.

2361. **And there is** [3].

Then he gives a second division of motion or change, and in regard to this he does three things. First [3], he prefaces his discussion with certain points which are necessary for an understanding of the division of motion. Second [4], he divides motion ("Now change"). Third [5], he explains the division of change ("The change").

He says, first, that there are five things found in every change. First, there is a primary mover; second, something which is moved; third, a time during which the motion takes place, because every motion occurs in time; fourth, a starting point from which motion begins; and fifth, a terminus to which the motion proceeds. However, motion or change is not divided into species either on the basis of the mover or of the thing moved or of time, because these are common to every change; but it is divided on the basis of the starting point from which it begins and the terminus to which it proceeds.

2362. He therefore explains the last two, saying that "the forms," i.e., specifying principles, "modifications," i.e., qualities, and "place," are limits of motion, because those things which are movable are moved with respect to these. He uses the term *forms*, because of generation; *modifications*, because of alterations; and *place*, because of local motion. He gives examples of modifications by using science and heat. And because it might seem to some that heat is the same as alteration, and then it would follow that heat is motion and not a limit or terminus of motion, he therefore says that heat is not motion but heating is.

2363. **Now change** [4].

Then, passing over two parts of the first division, he takes the third, namely, change which is neither accidental nor in a part, and subdivides it according to its limits. He says that change which is not accidental is not found between just any limits whatever; but its limits must either be contraries, as change from white to black, or intermediates, as change from black to red and from red to gray; or there is change between contradictories, as from white to not-white, and vice versa. He says nothing of privative opposites because they are found between contradictories and contraries and are understood to come under these.

2364. He shows by induction that change takes place only between the above-mentioned limits; for the limits of change admit of four possible combinations: first, when both limits are affirmative or positive terms, as when something is said to be changed from white to black, and this change he describes as one from subject to subject; second, when both limits are negative terms, as when something is said to be changed from not-white to not-black, or in his words, from non-subject to non-subject; third, when the starting point from which change begins is a positive term and the terminus to which it proceeds is a negative one, as when a thing is said to be changed from white to not-white, or as he says, from subject to non-subject; fourth, when the starting point of change is a negative term and the terminus to which it proceeds is a positive one, as when a thing is said to be changed from not-white to white, or as he says, from a non-subject to a subject. He explains the meaning of the term *subject* which he had used, as what is signified by an affirmative or positive term.

2365. Now one of these four combinations is useless; for there is no change from a non-subject to a non-subject, because two negative terms, such as not-white and not-black, are neither contraries nor contradictories since they are not opposites; for they can be affirmed truly of the same subject because there are many things which are neither white nor black. Hence, since change is between opposites, as is proved in Book I of the ***Physics***, *[188b21]* it follows that there is no change from a non-subject to a non-subject. Therefore there must be three kinds of change, two of which relate to contradiction and the other to contrariety.

2366. **The change** [5].

Then he shows what these three changes are; and in regard to this he does three things. First, he shows that generation and destruction are two of these. Second [6], he shows that neither of these is motion ("If non-being"). Third [7], he draws his conclusion as to which change is called motion ("And since every").

He accordingly says, first [5], that of the three changes mentioned above, that which is from a non-subject to a subject, or between contradictory terms, is called generation. And this is twofold; for there is change either from non-being in an unqualified sense to being in an unqualified sense (generation in an unqualified sense), and this occurs when a movable subject is changed substantially; or there is change from non-being to being, not in an unqualified sense but in a qualified one, for example, change from not-white to white (generation in a qualified sense).

2367. But that change which proceeds from a subject to a non-subject is called destruction; and in this change we also distinguish between destruction in an unqualified sense and in a qualified one, just as we did in the case of generation.

2368. **If non-being** [6].

Then the Philosopher shows that neither of these changes is motion. First [6], he shows that this is true of generation; and second *(ibid.)*, that it is true of destruction ("Nor is destruction").

He accordingly says, first [6], that the term *non-being* is used in the same number of senses as *being* is. One meaning is the combination and separation found in a proposition; and since this does not exist in reality but only in the mind, it cannot be moved.

2369. Being and non-being are used in another sense with reference to actuality and potentiality. That which is actual is a being in an unqualified sense, but that which is potential only is a non-being. He therefore says that even that sort of non-being which is a being potentially but not actually cannot be moved.

2370. He explains why he had said that actual non-being is opposed to being in an unqualified sense, when he adds "for what is not-white." For potentiai being, which is opposed to actual being and is not being in an unqualified sense, can be moved, because what is not not-white actually or not-good actually can be moved, but only accidentally. For what is moved is not the not-white itself, but the subject in which this privation is found, and this is an actual being. For that which is not white may be a man, but that which is an actual non-being in an unqualified sense, i.e., in substance, cannot be moved at all. Now if all of these statements are true, I say, it is impossible for non-being to be moved. And if this is the case, generation cannot be motion, because non-being is generated. For generation, as has been pointed out (n. 2366), proceeds from non-being to being. Hence, if generation in an unqualified sense were motion, it would follow that non-being in an unqualified sense would be moved.

2371. But one can raise an objection to this process of reasoning by saying that non-being is generated only accidentally; for "the subject of generation," i.e., a being in potentiality, is generated essentially. But non-being signifies privation in a matter. Hence it is generated only accidentally.

2372. **For even if** (*ibid.*).

Then he refutes this objection. He says that, even if a being is generated only accidentally, nevertheless it is true to say that what is generated in an unqualified sense is non-being. And of each of these it is true to say that it cannot be moved. Similarly it cannot be at rest, because non-being in an unqualified sense is neither in motion nor at rest. These are the untenable results if one maintains that generation is motion.

2373. In order to show that nonbeing is not moved, he adds that everything which is moved is in a place because local motion is the first of all motions, whereas non-being in an unqualified sense is not in a place; for [were it moved] it would then be somewhere. Hence it cannot be moved; and therefore generation is not motion.

2374. **Nor is destruction** (*ibid.*).

From these considerations he further shows that destruction is not motion; for the only thing that is opposed to motion is motion or rest. But destruction is opposed to generation. Therefore, if destruction were motion, generation would have to be either motion or rest. But this cannot be true, as has been shown.

2375. **And since every motion** [7].

Next he shows which change is said to be motion. He says that every motion is a kind of change. But there are only three changes, and two of these, which involve contradictories, i.e., generation and destruction, are not motion. It follows, then, that only change from a subject to a subject is motion. And since the subjects between which motion takes place must be opposed to each other, they must be contraries or intermediates; for even though a privation is expressed by an affirmative term, such as naked, toothless, and black, it is regarded as a contrary, because privation is the primary contrariety, as has been pointed out in Book X (852:C 2049). And he says that black is a privation not in an unqualified sense but inasmuch as it participates deficiently in the nature of its genus.

LESSON 12

Motion Pertains to Quantity, Quality and Place

ARISTOTLE'S TEXT Chapter 12: 1068a8–1068b25

1. *If the categories are divided into substance, quality, place, action, passion, relation and quantity, there must be three kinds of motion, namely, of quality, of quantity and of place.* **1068a8–10**

2. *There is no motion of substance, because substance has no contrary.* **1068a10–11**

3. *Nor is there motion of relation; for it is possible that, when one of two relative things has undergone a change, the other may be truly referred to under a new term even though it has not been changed in any way. Hence the motion of these relative things will be accidental.* **1068a11–13**

4. *Nor is there motion of agent or of patient as of mover and thing moved, because there is no motion of motion or generation of generation. There are two ways in which there might be motion of motion. First, motion might be of the subject moved, as a man is moved because he is changed from white to black. Thus motion might be heated or cooled or might change its place or might increase. But this is impossible, for change is not a subject. Or, second, some other subject might be changed from change to some other form of being, as a man might be changed from sickness to health. But this is possible only accidentally; for every motion is a change from one thing to something else. The same applies to generation and destruction; although the opposites involved in these changes are different from those of motion. Therefore a man changes at the same time from health to sickness, and from this change itself to another. And it is evident that, if a man has become ill, he will be changed into something else whatever it may be (for he can come to rest); and further this will always be to some opposite which is not contingent; and that change will be from something to something else. Hence, its opposite will be becoming healthy; but this will happen accidentally; for example, there is a change from recollection to forgetting, because the subject to which forgetting belongs is changed, sometimes to a state of knowledge and sometimes to one of ignorance.* **1068a13–33**

5. *Further, the process will go on to infinity if there is change of change and generation of generation. Therefore, if the latter comes to be, the former must also; for example, if generation in an unqualified sense at one time was coming to be, that which is coming to be something was also coming to be. Hence that which was coming to be in an unqualified sense did not yet exist, but there was something which was coming to be, or which has already come to be. Therefore, if this also at one time was coming to be, then at that time it was not coming to be something. However, since there is no first term in infinite things, neither will there be a subsequent one. Hence it is impossible for anything to come to be or be moved or be changed in any way.* **1068a33–1068b6**

6. *Further, of the same thing of which there is contrary motion and rest there is also generation and destruction. Hence when that which is coming to be becomes that which is coming to be, it is then being destroyed; for it is not destroyed as soon as it is generated or afterwards; for that which is being destroyed must be.* **1068b6–10**

7. *Further, there must be some matter underlying the thing which is coming to be or being changed. What then will it be that becomes motion or generation in the same way that a body or a soul or something else of this kind is alterable? Further, what is the thing to which motion proceeds; for motion must be of this particular thing from this to that, and yet the latter should not be a motion at all. In what way then is this to take place? For there can be no learning of learning, and therefore no generation of generation.* **1068b10–15**

8. *And since there is no motion of substance or of relation or of action or of passion, it follows*

that there is motion of quality, of quantity and of location; for each of these admits of contrariety. By quality I mean, not that which comes under the category of substance (for even difference is quality), but the passive power in virtue of which a thing is said to be acted upon or to be incapable of being acted upon. **1068b15–20**

9. The immovable is what is totally incapable of being moved, or what is moved with difficulty over a long period of time or begins to be moved slowly, or what is naturally fit to be moved but is not capable of being moved when it is so fit, and where, and in the way in which it would naturally be moved. And this is the only kind of immobility which I call rest; for rest is contrary to motion. Hence it will be the privation of what is receptive of motion. **1068b20–25**

COMMENTARY

2376. Having divided change into generation, destruction and motion, here he subdivides the other member of this division, i.e., motion, on the basis of the categories in which it takes place. In regard to this he does two things. First [1], he indicates the categories in which motion can be found. Second [9], he explains the different senses in which the term *immovable* is used ("The immovable").

In regard to the first he does three things. First, he sets forth his thesis. Second [2], he proves this ("There is no motion"). Third [8], he draws his main conclusion ("And since").

He accordingly says, first [1], that, since the categories are divided into substance, quality and so on, and since there cannot be motion in the other categories, there are therefore three categories of being in which motion can be found; that is, quality, quantity and location, for which he substitutes the term *place*, because location merely signifies being in a place; and to be moved with respect to place is merely to be moved with respect to one's location. For motion with respect to place is not attributed to a subject in which place inheres but to the thing in place.

2377. Now it should be noted that he seems to omit three categories, namely, temporal situation (*quando*), posture and accoutrement; for since temporal situation signifies being in time, and time is the measure of motion, the reason why there is no motion in the category of temporal situation or in that of action and of passion, which signify motion itself under special aspects, is the same. And posture adds nothing to location except a definite arrangement of parts, which is nothing else than a definite relationship of parts to each other. And accoutrement implies the relation of one clothed to his clothing. Hence the reason why there does not seem to be motion with respect to posture and to accoutrement and to relation seems to be the same.

2378. **There is no motion** [2].

Next, he proves his thesis; and in regard to this he does three things. First [2] he shows that there is no motion with respect to substance; second [3], that there is no motion with respect to relation ("Nor is there motion"); and third [4], that there is no motion with respect to action and passion ("Nor is there motion of agent").

He accordingly proves, first [2], that there cannot be motion with respect to substance because motion is a change from subject to subject. Therefore the two subjects between which there is motion are either contraries or intermediates. Hence, since nothing is contrary to substance, it follows that there cannot be motion with respect to substance, but only generation and destruction, whose limits are opposed to each other as contradictories and not as contraries, as has been stated above (n. 2366).

2379. Now it seems that his statement that "substance has no contrary" is false, because fire clearly appears to be contrary to water, and because Aristotle had proved in Book I of *The Heavens* [270a12] that the heavens are not destructible since they do not have a contrary, whereas other bodies, which are corruptible, have a contrary.

2380. Hence some said that there is nothing contrary to the whole composite substance because the subject of contraries must be one; but nothing prevents a substantial form from having a contrary. For they said that heat is the substantial form of fire. But this cannot be true, because substantial forms are not perceptible of themselves. And again it is evident that in other bodies heat and cold are accidents. But what belongs to the category of substance cannot be an accident in anything.

2381. Others have said that heat and cold are not the substantial forms of fire and water, but that their substantial forms are contraries differing in degree, and are, so to speak, intermediate between substance and accidents. But this is wholly unreasonable; for, since form is the principle of a species, if the forms of fire and of water are not truly substantial, neither are fire and water true species in the category of substance. It is impossible, then, that there should be an intermediate between substance and accidents, because they belong to different categories, and between such things an intermediate does not fall, as has been shown above in Book X (n. 2102); and also because the definitions of substance and accident have no intermediate. For a substance is a being of itself, whereas an accident is not a being of itself but has being in something else.

2382. It is necessary then to say that substantial forms cannot be contraries, because contraries are extremes of a certain definite distance, and in a sense they are continuous, since motion is from one contrary to another. In those categories, then, in which no such continuous and definite distance is found, it is impossible to find a contrary, as is clear in the case of numbers. For the distance between one number and another does not mean continuity but the addition of units. Hence number is not contrary to number, nor similarly is figure contrary to figure.

2383. The same thing applies to substances because the intelligible structure of each species consists in a definite unity. But since form is the basis of difference, if substantial forms are not contrary to each other, it follows that contrariety cannot be found between differences.

2384. It is necessary to say, then, that a substantial form, considered in itself, constitutes a species in the category of substance; but according as one form implies the privation of another, different forms are the principles of contrary differences. For in one respect a privation is a contrary, and living and nonliving, rational and irrational, and the like are opposed in this way.

2385. **Nor is there motion of relation** [3].

Next, he shows that there is no motion in the proper sense in the category of relation except accidentally. For just as a thing is moved accidentally when motion takes place in it only as a result of something else being moved, in a similar way motion is said to be accidental to a thing when it takes place in it only because something else is moved. Now we find this in the category of relation; for unless something else is changed, it is not true to say that change occurs in relation; for example, the unequal comes from the equal only when there has been change in quantity. Similarly the like comes from the unlike only when there has been a change in quality. Thus we see that one of two relative things is said to be changed when change affects the other one of them; for example, a thing which is unmoved of itself changes from left to right when some other thing changes its place. Hence it follows that there is motion in the category of relation only accidentally.

2386. **Nor is there motion of agent** [4].

Here he shows that motion does not occur with respect to either action or passion. He proves this by four arguments, of which the first is as follows: action and passion constitute motion and designate it. If, then, motion were to occur in action and in passion, it would follow that there would be motion of motion and generation of generation and change of change. But this is impossible. Therefore it is also impossible that there should be motion in action and in passion. That it is impossible for motion to be moved he proves thus: there are two ways in which there might be motion of motion: first, there might be motion of motion as of a subject which is moved, or, second, as of the limit of motion. And motion might be the subject of motion, as we say that there is motion of a man because a man is moved since he is changed from white to black. In a similar way motion would be moved, and would either be heated or cooled, or changed with respect to place, or increase. But this is impossible; because motion cannot be the subject of heat or of cold or of similar attributes. It follows, then, that there cannot be motion of motion if motion is regarded as a subject.

2387. But neither can there be motion of motion as of a limit, some other subject being changed from one species of change to another, as a man might be changed from sickness to health; for this is possible only accidentally.

2388. Hence he shows next that it is impossible for motion to be moved essentially because every motion is a change from one thing to something else. Similarly generation and destruction are a change from one thing to something else, even though in their case the limits of change are not opposed to each other as they are in that of motion, as has been said above (n. 2363). If, then, there is change from one change to another, as from becoming sick to some other process of change, it will follow that, while a thing is being changed from health to sickness, it is being changed at the same time from that change to another; because, while one of the limits of a change is arising, a change from one limit to another occurs. Thus if two processes of change are the limits of one change, it follows that while the original change is occurring, a change into another takes place. And so at the same time that a thing is being moved from health to sickness it will be being changed from becoming healthy to some other change.

2389. But this seems to be true only inasmuch as one change succeeds another. And it is possible that any other change may succeed this one by which something is being moved from health to sickness, for example, becoming white or becoming black or change of place or any other change. Hence it is evident that, if someone is becoming ill because he is being moved from health to sickness, he can be changed from this change to any other. Nor is this surprising, because he can even be changed from this change to a state of repose; for it is possible that someone might come to rest after this change.

2390. But since every change is "always to an opposite which is not contingent," i.e., an opposite which cannot be true at the same time as the opposed term, it follows that, if there is a change from change to change, it will always be to an opposite change, which he calls not contingent. And that change in which the transition takes place will have to be from one thing to something else. Hence the transition from a change of becoming ill will only be to the opposite change, which is called becoming healthy.

2391. And so two contrary positions seem to follow, namely, that an opposite change passes from one change to any other, and only to its opposite. And from this it further follows that, at the same time that something is being changed to one of its opposites, it is also being changed to a change as if it were another opposite. This seems to be impossible, for it would follow that nature inclines to opposite effects at the same time. Hence it cannot be that anything is changed essentially from one change to another.

2392. But this can happen accidentally; for example, a person may change from recollection to forgetfulness because the subject is changed, sometimes in relation to one extreme and sometimes to the other—not that it may be the mover's intention that at the same time that he is being changed to one extreme he is at the same time intending to move to the other.

2393. **Further, the process** [4].

Then he gives the second argument, which runs thus: if there is change of change, as limit of limit, or generation of generation, one change must be reached only by another change, as one quality is reached only by a preceding alteration; and thus it will be possible to reach that preceding change only by a prior change, and so on to infinity.

2394. But this cannot be the case, because, if it is assumed that there are an infinite number of changes related in such a way that one leads to the other, the preceding must exist if the following does. Let us suppose that there is a particular instance of the generation of a generation in an unqualified sense, which is the generation of substance. Then, if the generation in an unqualified sense sometimes comes to be, and again if the coming to be of generation in an unqualified sense itself at one time came to be, it will follow that that which is coming to be in an unqualified sense did not yet exist, but there was generation in one respect, namely, the very generation of the process of generation. And if this generation also came to be at some time, since it is not possible to have either an infinite regress or any first term among infinite things, it is impossible ever to come to any first process of generation. But if the preceding member in a series does not exist, there will be no succeeding member, as has been pointed out above, and the consequence will be that "there will not be a subsequent one," i.e., one which follows it. It follows, then, that nothing can come to be or be moved or be changed. But this is impossible. Hence change of change is impossible.

2395. **Further, of the same thing** [6].

Then he gives the third argument, which is as follows. Contrary motions, and rest and motion, and generation and destruction, belong to the same subject, because opposites are suited by nature to come to be in the same subject. Therefore, if some subject is being changed from generation to destruction, at the same time that it is being generated it will be undergoing change leading to destruction, which is to be changed into non-being; for the terminus of destruction is non-being. Now what is being changed into non-being is being destroyed. Hence it follows that a thing is being destroyed at the same time that it is being generated.

2396. But this cannot be true; for while a thing is coming to be it is not being destroyed, nor is it corrupted immediately afterwards. For since destruction is a process from being to nonbeing, that which is being destroyed must be. And thus there will have to be an intermediate state of rest between generation, which is a change to being, and destruction, which is a change to non-being. Hence there is no change from generation to destruction.

2397. **Further, there must be** [7].

Then he gives the fourth argument, which runs as follows. In everything that is being generated two things must be present: first, the matter of the thing which is generated, and, second, that in which the generation is terminated. If, then, there is generation of generation, both generation and motion will have to have some matter, such as an alterable body or a soul or something of this kind. But it is impossible to assign matter of this kind to generation and to motion.

2398. Similarly, there must also be something in which the process of change is terminated, because some part, namely, the matter of the thing generated, must be moved from one attribute to another, and that in which motion is terminated cannot be motion but is the terminus of motion. For of the kind of change which we call learning there is not some other learning which is terminated in it, which is a learning of learning. Hence there is nothing to conclude but that there is no generation of generation.

2399. **And since** [8].

Here he draws as his conclusion his main thesis. He says that, since there cannot be motion either in the category of substance or in that of relation or in that of action and passion, it follows that motion belongs to quality, quantity and location; for in these categories there can be contrariety, which stands between the termini of motion, as has been pointed out.

2400. But since quality is sometimes used to mean substantial form, he adds that, when there is said to be motion in quality, it is not understood to signify substance, in view of the fact that substantial difference is predicated as something qualitative; but it refers to the kind of quality by which something is said to be acted upon or to be incapable of this. For there is alteration, properly speaking, only in terms of susceptible qualities, as is proved in Book VII of the *Physics*.[244b4]

2401. **The immovable** [9].

Then he explains the different senses in which the term *immovable* is used; and he gives three of these. First, the immovable means what is completely incapable of being moved; for example, God is immovable.

2402. Second, it means what can be moved with difficulty, as a huge boulder.

2403. Third, it means what is naturally fit to be moved but cannot be moved when it is fit, and where, and in the way in which it is fit to be moved. And only this kind of immobility is properly called *rest*, because rest is contrary to motion. Hence rest must be the privation of motion in what is susceptible of motion.

LESSON 13
Concepts Related to Motion

ARISTOTLE'S TEXT Chapter 12: 1068b26–1069a14

1. Things which are in one primary place are together in place, and those which are in different places are separate, and those whose extremities are together are in contact. And an intermediate is that at which something continuously changing according to its nature naturally arrives before it reaches the limit to which it is changing. That is contrary in place which is most distant in a straight line. That is subsequent which comes after a starting point (the order being determined by position or form or in some other way) and has nothing in the same genus between itself and that which it follows; for example, lines in the case of a line, and units in the case of a unit, or a house in the case of a house. But there is nothing to prevent something else from coming between. For that which follows something is subsequent and comes after something else; for one does not follow two, nor does [the first day of] the new moon follow the second. Again, what is subsequent and in contact is contiguous. And since every change is between opposites, and these are contraries and contradictories, and since there is no intermediate between contradictories, it is evident that an intermediate is between contraries. The continuous has something of the nature of the contiguous; and I call two things continuous when both have the same extremity in which they are in contact and are uninterrupted.

1068b26–1069a7

2. It is evident, then, that the continuous belongs to those things from which one thing results in virtue of their contact. And it is evident that the subsequent is the first of these; for things which are subsequent are not necessarily in contact, but what is in contact is subsequent. But if it is in contact it is not necessarily continuous. And in things in which there is no contact there is no natural coherence. The point, then, is not the same as the unit; for contact belongs to the former but not to the latter, but only successiveness, and there is an intermediate between the former but not between the latter. **1069a7–14**

COMMENTARY

2404. He explains the terms which apply to motion, especially local motion. First [1], he explains them. Second [2], he draws a corollary from his remarks ("It is evident").

He accordingly says, first [1], that things which are "in one primary place," i.e., a proper place, are said to be *together in place;* for if some things are in one common place, they are not for this reason said to be together, for then all things which are contained in the circumference of the heavens would be said to be together.

2405. Things which are in different places are said to be *separate.*

2406. And those whose extremities are said to touch one another are said to be *in contact;* for example, two bodies whose surfaces are joined.

2407. And an *intermediate* between two things is that at which it is natural for something that continuously changes to arrive before it reaches its limit; for example, if there is continuous motion from *a* to *c*, the thing being changed first arrives at *b* before it reaches *c*.

2408. Again, that which is most distant in a straight line is *contrary in place;* for that which is most distant cannot be measured by a curved line, because an infinite number of unlike sections of circles can be drawn between two points, but there can be only one straight line between two points. Now a measure must be definite and fixed. And that which is most distant as to place admits of being above and below, which are the extremity and the center of the universe.

2409. That is said to be *subsequent* which comes after some starting point, whether the order is determined by position or by form or in some other way; for example, two comes after one. And there must also be nothing of the same genus between that which is subsequent and that which it follows, as lines are subsequent to a line and units to a unit and a house to a house. But nothing prevents something of another genus from being an intermediate between two things one of which follows the other; for example, there may be one intermediate horse between two houses. In order to make the above distinction clear he adds that what is said to follow something must be subsequent and come after something. For one does not come after two, since it is first; nor does the first day of the new moon follow the second, but the other way around.

2410. Then he says that the *contiguous* means what is subsequent and in contact with something else—for example, if two bodies are so related that one touches the other.

2411. Then he says that, since every change is between opposites, and the opposites between which there is change are either contraries or contradictories, as has been shown (1008:C 2363), and since there is no intermediate between contradictories, it is evident that there is an intermediate only between contraries; for that which is intermediate is between the limits of a motion, as is clear from the definition given above. His introduction of this is timely; for since he said that those things are subsequent between which there is no intermediate, it was fitting that he should indicate between what things it is possible to have an intermediate.

2412. Then he shows what the *continuous* is. He says that the continuous adds something to the contiguous; for there is continuity when both of those things which are in contact and together have one and the same extremity, as the parts of a line are continuous in relation to a point.

2413. **It is evident** [2].

Then he draws three corollaries from what has been said. The first is that continuity belongs to those things from which one thing naturally results in virtue of their contact; and this is because the continuous requires identical extremities.

2414. The second corollary is that, of these three things—the subsequent, the contiguous and the continuous—the first and most common is the subsequent; for not everything that is subsequent is in contact, but everything which is in contact is subsequent or consecutive. For things which are in contact are arranged according to their position, and no one of them is an intermediate. Similarly, the contiguous is prior to and more common than the continuous, because, if a thing is continuous, there must be contact. For what is one must be together, unless perhaps plurality is understood in the phrase *being together*. For in that case the continuous would not involve being in contact. But the continuous must involve contact in the way in which something one is together. Yet if there is contact it does not follow that there is continuity; for example, if certain things are together it does not follow that they are one. But in things in which there is no contact "there is no natural coherence," i.e., natural union, which is a property of the continuous.

2415. The third corollary is that the point and the unit are not the same, as the Platonists claimed when they said that the point is the unit having position. That they are not the same is evident for two reasons: first, because there is contact between points but not between units, which only follow each other; second, because there is always some intermediate between two points, as is proved in Book V of the ***Physics***.*[227a30]* But it is not necessary that there should be an intermediate between two units.

BOOK XII
MOBILE AND IMMOBILE SUBSTANCE.
THE PRIME MOVER

LESSON 1
Metaphysics Studies Substance

ARISTOTLE'S TEXT Chapter 1: 1069a18–1069a30

1. *The study here is concerned with substance; for it is the principles and causes of substances which are being investigated.* **1069a18–19**

2. *For if the totality of things is a kind of whole, substance is its first part; and if things constitute a whole by reason of succession, substance is also first, and then quality or quantity.* **1069a19–22**

3. *And in like manner the latter are not to be regarded as beings in an unqualified sense, but as qualities and motions of being. Otherwise the not-straight and not-white would be beings; for we say that they are—for example, "the not-white is."* **1069a22–24**

4. *Again, none of the other genera can exist separately.* **1069a24**

5. *The ancient philosophers testify to this in practice, for it was of substance that they sought the principles, elements and causes. Present-day thinkers, however, maintain that universals are substances; for genera are universals, and they say that these are principles and substances to a greater degree because they investigate the matter dialectically. But the ancient philosophers regarded particular things as substances, for example, fire and earth, and not a common body.* **1069a25–30**

COMMENTARY

2416. Having summarized in the preceding book the points that were previously made regarding imperfect being both in this work and in the ***Physics***, *[III, 1-3]* in this book the Philosopher aims to summarize the things that have been said about being in its unqualified sense, i.e., substance, both in Books VII and VIII of this work and in Book I of the ***Physics***, *[1-6]* and to add anything that is missing in order to make his study of substances complete. This is divided into two parts. First [1], he shows that this science is chiefly concerned with substances. Second (Lesson 2), he gives his views about the classes of substances ("Now there are three").

In regard to the first he does two things. First, he states his thesis. He says that in this science "the study," i.e., the principal inquiry, has to do with substances. For since this science, being the first and the one called wisdom, investigates the first principles of beings, the principles and causes of substances must constitute its main object of study; for these are the first principles of beings. The way in which principle and cause differ has been pointed out in Book V (n. 760).

2417. **For if the totality** [2].

He proves his thesis in four ways. The first proof runs thus. Since substance is prior to the other kinds of beings, the first science should be one that is chiefly concerned with the primary kind of being. He shows that substance is the primary kind of being by using an analogous case in the realm of sensible things, among which order is found in two ways. One kind of order is found among sensible things inasmuch as the parts of any whole have a certain natural arrangement; for example, the first part of an animal is the heart, and the first part of a house the foundation. Another kind of order is found among sensible things inasmuch as some follow others and one thing is not constituted from them either by continuity or by contact. It is in this sense that one speaks of the first and second lines of an army. Hence, just as there is some first part in any whole, and also some first entity among things that follow one another, so too substance is the first of all other beings. This is what he means when he says "For if the totality," i.e., the universe of beings, is a kind of whole, substance is its first part, just as the foundation is the first part of a house. And if beings are like things that follow one another, substance again will be first, and then quantity, and then the other categories.

2418. But Averroes, failing to consider that this statement is analogical because he considered it impossible for anyone to think that all the other genera of beings should be parts of one continuous whole, departs from the obvious sense of the text and explains it in a different way. He says that by these two orders Aristotle meant the twofold relationship which can be conceived between things. The first is that beings are related as things having one nature and one genus, which would be true if being were their common genus, or in whatever way it might be common to them. He says that this is Aristotle's meaning when he says "If the totality of things is a kind of whole." The second is that beings are related as things having nothing in common. He says that this is Aristotle's meaning when he says "And if things constitute a whole by reason of succession"; for in either case it follows that substance is prior to the other kinds of being.

2419. **But in like manner** [3].

Then he gives a second proof of his thesis. He says that quantity and quality and the like are not beings in an unqualified sense, as will be said below. For being means something having existence, but it is substance alone that subsists. And accidents are called beings, not because they are but rather because by them something is; for example, whiteness is said to be because by it the subject is white. Hence Aristotle says that accidents, as quality and motion, are not called beings in an unqualified sense, but beings of a being.

2420. Nor is it surprising if accidents are called beings even though they are not beings in an unqualified sense, because even privations and negations are called beings in a sense, for example, the not-white and the not-straight. For we say that the not-white is, not because the not-white has being, but because some subject is deprived of whiteness. Accidents and privations have this in common, then, that being is predicated of both by reason of their subject. Yet they differ in this respect that, while a subject has being of some kind by reason of its accidents, it does not have being of any kind by reason of privations, but is deficient in being.

2421. Therefore, since accidents are not beings in an unqualified sense, but only substances are, this science, which considers being as being, is not chiefly concerned with accidents but with substances.

2422. **Again, none** [4].

Then he gives a third proof of his thesis that the other kinds of beings cannot exist apart from substance. For accidents can exist only in a subject, and therefore the study of accidents is included in that of substance.

2423. **The ancient philosophers** [5].

He gives a fourth proof of his thesis. He says that the ancient philosophers also testify to the fact that the philosopher is concerned with substances, because in seeking the causes of being they looked for the causes only of substance. And some of the moderns also did this, but in a different way; for they did not seek principles, causes and elements in the same way, but differently. For the moderns—the Platonists—claimed that universals are substances to a greater degree than particular things; for they said that genera, which are universals, are principles and causes of substances to a greater degree than particular things. They did this because they investigated things from the viewpoint of dialectics; for they thought that universals, which are separate according to their mode of definition from sensible things, are also separate in reality, and that they are the principles of particular things. But the ancient philosophers, such as Democritus and Empedocles, claimed that the substances and principles of things are particular entities, such as fire and earth, but not this common principle, body.

LESSON 2
Three Classes of Substances

ARISTOTLE'S TEXT Chapters 1 & 2: 1069a30–1069b32

1. Now there are three classes of substances. One is sensible, and of this class one kind is eternal and another perishable. The latter, such as plants and animals, all men recognize. But it is the eternal whose elements we must grasp, whether they are one or many. Another class is the immovable, which certain thinkers claim to have separate existence, some dividing it into two kinds, others maintaining that the separate Forms and the objects of mathematics are of one nature, and still others holding that only the objects of mathematics belong to this class. The first two classes of substance belong to the philosophy of nature since they involve motion; but the last belongs to a different science if there is no principle common to these three.

1069a30–1069b2

Chapter 2

2. Sensible substance is capable of being changed. And if change proceeds from opposites or from intermediates, yet not from all opposites (for the spoken word is not white) but only from a contrary, then there must be some underlying subject which can be changed from one contrary to another; for contraries themselves are not changed. Further, this subject remains, whereas a contrary does not remain. Therefore there is some third thing besides the contraries, and this is matter. **1069b3–9**

3. If, then, there are four kinds of change: either in substance or in quality or in quantity or in place, and if change in substance is generation and destruction without qualification, and change in quantity is increase and decrease, and change in attribute is alteration, and change in place is local motion, then the changes occurring in each case must be changes to contrary states. Therefore it must be the matter which is capable of being changed to both states.

1069b9–15

4. And since being is twofold, every change is from potential being to actual being, for example, from potentially white to actually white. The same is true of increase and decrease. Hence not only can a thing come to be accidentally from nonbeing, but all things come to be from being, i.e., from potential being, not from actual being. **1069b15–20**

5. And this is the "One" of Anaxagoras; for it is better to maintain this view than to claim that "all things were together." And this is the "mixture" of Empedocles and Anaximander, and it recalls the statement of Democritus that all things were together potentially but not at all actually. Hence all these thinkers were touching upon matter. **1069b20–24**

6. Now all things which undergo change have matter, but different things have different matters; and of eternal things, those which are incapable of being generated but can be moved by local motion have matter. Yet they do not have that kind of matter which is subject to generation, but only such as is subject to motion from one place to another. **1069b24–26**

7. And one might raise the question from what kind of non-being generation could come about; for non-being is spoken of in three senses. If, then, one kind of non-being is potentiality, still it is not from anything at all that a thing comes to be, but different things come from different things. Nor is it enough to say that "all things were together," since they differ in their matter, for otherwise why would an infinite number of things be generated and not just one thing? For mind is one, so that if matter were also one, only that could come to be actually whose matter was in potentiality. **1069b26–32**

COMMENTARY

2424. Having explained that philosophy is concerned chiefly with substances, here the Philosopher begins to deal with substances. This is divided into two parts. In the first [1] he makes a division of substance; and in the second [2] he treats the parts of this division ("Sensible substance").

He accordingly says, first [1], that there are three classes of substances. One is sensible, and this is divided into two kinds; for some sensible substances are eternal (the celestial bodies) and others perishable. Sensible and perishable substances, such as animals and plants, are recognized by all.

2425. But it is "the other class of sensible substance," i.e., the eternal, whose principles we aim to discover in this book, whether their principles are one or many. He will investigate this by considering the separate substances, which are both the sources of motion and the ends of the celestial bodies, as will be made clear below (nn. 2590–92). He uses elements in the broad sense here in place of principles; for strictly an element is only an intrinsic cause.

2426. The third class of substance is the immovable and imperceptible. This class is not evident to all, but some men claim that it is separate from sensible things. The opinions of these men differ; for some divide separate substances into two kinds—the separate Forms, which they call Ideas, and the objects of mathematics. For just as a twofold method of separating is found in reason, one by which the objects of mathematics are separated from sensible matter, and another by which universals are separated from particular things, in a similar way they maintained that both universals, which they called separate Forms, and also the objects of mathematics, are separate in reality. But others reduced these two classes—the separate Forms and the objects of mathematics—to one nature. Both of these groups were Platonists. But another group, the Pythagoreans, did not posit separate Forms, but only the objects of mathematics.

2427. Among these three classes of substances there is this difference, namely, that sensible substances, whether they are perishable or eternal, belong to the consideration of the philosophy of nature, which establishes the nature of movable being; for sensible substances of this kind are in motion. But separable and immovable substances belong to the study of a different science and not to the same science if there is no principle common to both kinds of substance; for if there were a common principle, the study of both kinds of substance would belong to the science which considers that common principle. The philosophy of nature, then, considers sensible substances only inasmuch as they are actual and in motion. Hence this science (first philosophy) considers both sensible substances and immovable substances inasmuch as both are beings and substances.

2428. **Sensible substance** [2].

Then he establishes the truth about the above-mentioned substances. He does this, first [2], with regard to sensible substances; and second (Lesson 5), with regard to immovable substances ("And since there are three").

The first is divided into two parts. First, he investigates the principles of sensible substances; and second (Lesson 4), he inquires whether the principles of substances and those of the other categories are the same ("In one sense").

In regard to the first he does two things. First, he investigates the nature of matter; and second (Lesson 3), the nature of form ("The causes or principles").

In regard to the first he does two things. First, he states his views about matter. Second [7], he meets a difficulty ("And one might raise the question").

In regard to the first he does two things. First, he shows that there is matter in sensible substances; and he also shows what kind of being matter is. Second [6], he shows how matter differs in different kinds of sensible substances ("Now all things").

In regard to the first he does two things. First, he proceeds as described. Second [4], he meets an argument by which some of the ancient philosophers denied generation ("And since being is twofold").

In regard to the first he does two things. First, he shows that there is matter in sensible substances. Second [3], he shows what kind of being matter is ("If, then, there are").

He accordingly says, first [2], that sensible substance is changeable, as has been pointed out, and every change is either from opposites or from intermediates, as has been shown above (nn. 723–24). Yet change does not proceed from any opposites whatever; for the white comes from the not-white, but not from just any not-white; for a word is not-white, yet a body does not become white from a word, but from a not-white which is black or some intermediate color. Hence he says that change proceeds from an opposite which is a contrary. And there can be no rejoinder based on change in substance on the ground that there is nothing contrary to substance. For in substance there is privation which is included in a sense among contraries, as has been shown in Book X (nn. 2050–53).

2429. Hence, since every change is from one contrary to another, there must be some underlying subject which can be changed from one contrary to another. The Philosopher proves this in two ways. First, he argues on the ground that one contrary is not changed into another; for blackness itself does not become whiteness, so that, if there is a change from black to white, there must be something besides blackness which becomes white.

2430. He proves the same point in another way, namely, from the fact that throughout every change something is found to remain. For example, in a change from black to white a body remains, whereas the other thing—the contrary black—does not remain. Therefore it is evident that matter is some third entity besides the contraries.

2431. **If, then, there are** [3].

He now shows what kind of being matter is. He says that there are four kinds of change: simple generation and destruction, which is change in substance; increase and decrease, which is change in quantity; alteration, which is change in affections (and constitutes the third species of quality); and "local motion," or change of place, which pertains to the *where* of a thing. Now it has been shown that all of these changes involve the contrarieties that belong to each of these classes; for example, alteration involves contrariety of quality, increase involves contrariety of quantity, and so on for the others. And since in every change there is besides the contraries some third entity which is called matter, the thing undergoing the change, i.e., the subject of the change, considered just in itself, must be in potentiality to both contraries, otherwise it would not be susceptible of both or admit of change from one to the other. Thus, just as a body which is changed from white to black, *qua* body, is in potentiality to each of the two contraries, in a similar way in the generation of substance the matter, as the subject of generation and destruction, is of itself in potentiality both to form and to privation, and has actually of itself neither form nor privation.

2432. **And since being** [4].

Here the Philosopher establishes the truth about matter itself, and in regard to this he does two things. First, he meets a difficulty. Second [5], he shows how some of the ancient philosophers offered a solution similar to the one mentioned above ("And this is the 'One'").

He meets the difficulty of the ancient philosophers who did away with generation because they did not think that anything could come from non-being, since nothing comes from nothing, or that anything could come from being, since a thing would then be before it came to be.

2433. The Philosopher meets this difficulty by showing how a thing comes to be both from being and from non-being. He says that being is twofold—actual and potential. Hence everything which is changed is changed from a state of potential being to one of actual being; for example, a thing is changed from being potentially white to being actually white. The same thing holds true of the motion of increase and decrease, since something is changed from being potentially large or small to being actually large or small. In the category of substance, then, all things come to be both from being and from non-being. A thing comes to be accidentally from non-being inasmuch as it comes to be from a matter subject to privation, in reference to which it is called non-being. And a thing comes to be essentially from being—not actual being but potential being—i.e., from matter, which is potential being, as has been shown above (n. 2431).

2434. Now it should be borne in mind that certain later thinkers wanted to oppose the above-mentioned principle of the ancient philosophers of nature (who denied generation and destruction and claimed that generation is merely alteration) when they said that generation comes about through detachment from some mixture or confused mass.

2435. Hence, when the Philosopher in the third part of his division says "And this is the one [5]," he shows that all who expressed this view wanted to adopt a position similar to the one mentioned above, but did not succeed in doing so. Therefore he says that this, namely, matter, which is in potentiality to all forms, is the "One" of which Anaxagoras spoke; for Anaxagoras said that everything which is generated from something else is present in that thing from which it comes to be. And so, not knowing how to distinguish between potentiality and actuality, he said that in the beginning all things were mixed together in one whole. But it is more fitting to posit a matter in which all things are present potentially than to posit one in which all things are present actually and simultaneously, as seems to be the case from what Anaxagoras said. This is what Empedocles also claimed, namely, that in the beginning all things were mixed or mingled together by friendship and later were separated out by strife. Anaximander similarly held that all contraries originally existed in one confused mass. And Democritus said that everything which comes to be first exists potentially and then actually. Hence it is evident that all these philosophers touched upon matter to some extent but did not fully comprehend it.

2436. **Now all things** [6].

He shows that matter is not present in all sensible substances in the same way. He says that all things which undergo change must have matter, but of a different kind. For things which "are changed substantially," i.e., generated and destroyed, have a matter which is subject to generation and destruction, i.e., one which is in itself in potentiality both to forms and to privations. But the celestial bodies, which are eternal and not subject to generation, yet admit of change of place, have matter—not one which admits of generation and destruction or one which is in potentiality to form and to privation, but one which is in potentiality to the termini of local motion, i.e., the point from which motion begins and the point to which it tends.

2437. **And one might raise** [7].

Then he meets a difficulty that pertains to the points established above. He says that, since generation is a change from non-being to being, one can ask from what sort of non-being generation proceeds; for non-being is said of three things. First, it is said of what does not exist in any way; and from this kind of non-being nothing is generated, because in reality nothing comes from nothing. Second, it is said of privation, which is considered in a subject; and while something is generated from this kind of non-being, the generation is accidental, i.e., inasmuch as something is generated from a subject to which some privation occurs. Third, it is said of matter itself, which, taken in itself, is not an actual being but a potential one. And from this kind of non-being something is generated essentially; or in his words, if one kind of non-being is potentiality, then from such a principle, i.e., non-being, something is generated essentially.

2438. Yet even though something is generated from that kind of non-being which is being in potentiality, still a thing is not generated from every kind of non-being, but different things come from different matters. For everything capable of being generated has a definite matter from which it comes to be, because there must be a proportion between form and matter. For even though first matter is in potentiality to all forms, it nevertheless receives them in a certain order. For first of all it is in potency to the forms of the elements, and through the intermediary of these, insofar as they are mixed in different proportions, it is in potency to different forms. Hence not everything can come to be directly from everything else unless perhaps by being resolved into first matter.

2439. This view is opposed to that of Anaxagoras, who claimed that anything at all comes to be from anything else. Nor is his assumption that all things were together in the beginning sufficient to support this view. For things differ by reason of matter inasmuch as there are different matters for different things. For if the matter of all things were one, as it is according to the opinion of Anaxagoras, why would an infinite number of things be generated and not just one thing? For Anaxagoras claimed that there is one agent, mind; and therefore, if matter too were one, only one thing would necessarily come to be, namely, that to which matter is in potentiality. For where there is one agent and one matter there must be one effect, as has been stated in Book X.

2440. This argument holds good

against Anaxagoras inasmuch as he claimed that mind needs matter in order to produce some effect. And if he claims that the first principle of things is mind, which produces matter itself, the first principle of the diversity of things will proceed from the order apprehended by the above-mentioned mind, which, inasmuch as it aims to produce different things, establishes different matters having an aptitude for a diversity of things.

LESSON 3
Characteristics of Forms

ARISTOTLE'S TEXT Chapters 2 & 3: 1069b32–1070a30

1. The causes or principles of things, then, are three. Two of these are the pair of contraries, of which one is the formal determinant or specifying principle, and the other the privation, and the third, matter. **1069b32–34**

Chapter 3

2. It should be noted next that neither matter nor form comes to be, and I mean the last matter and form. For everything which changes something else changes it from something to something. That by which it is changed is the first [i.e., immediate] mover; that which is changed is the matter; and that to which it is changed is the form. Hence there will be an infinite regress if not only the bronze becomes round but also roundness itself or bronze comes to be. Therefore there must be some stopping point. **1069b35–1070a4**

3. Again, it should be noted that every substance comes to be from something having the same name; for both things which are by nature as well as other things are substances. For things come to be either by art or by nature or by luck or spontaneously. Art is a principle in another, but nature is a principle in the subject itself; for man begets man. The remaining causes are the privations of these. **1070a4–9**

4. There are three kinds of substance. First, there is matter, which is a particular thing in appearance; for whatever things are one by contact and not by natural union are matter and subject. Second, there is the nature [i.e., the form], which is a determinate thing inasmuch as it is a kind of positive state; and third, there is the singular thing which is composed of these, such as Socrates or Callias. **1070a9–13**

5. Now in some cases the "this" [i.e., the form] does not exist apart from the composite substance; for example, the form of a house, unless it is the art. Nor is there generation and destruction of these forms, but it is in a different sense that house apart from matter, and health, and everything which comes to be by art, do and do not exist. But if the "this" does exist apart from matter, it is only in the case of those things which are by nature. Hence Plato was not wrong in saying that the Forms are things which exist by nature, i.e., if there are separate Forms different from these other things, such as fire, flesh and head. For all of these are matter, and they are the ultimate matter of substance in the fullest sense. **1070a13–20**

6. Hence efficient causes are causes as things which are prior to their effects; but those things which are causes in the sense of the formal determinant are simultaneous with their effects. For it is when a man becomes healthy that health also exists; and the shape of the bronze sphere comes to be at the same time as the bronze sphere. But whether any form continues to exist afterwards is a question that requires investigation. For nothing prevents this from being so in certain cases, for example, if the soul is of this sort, not every soul but the intellectual; for perhaps it is impossible that every soul should continue to exist. **1070a21–26**

7. It is evident, then, that it is not necessary on these grounds that the Ideas should exist; for man begets man, and the singular man begets a singular man. The same thing also holds true in the case of the arts; for the art of medicine is the formal determinant of health. **1070a26–30**

COMMENTARY

2441. Having stated his views about matter, the Philosopher now considers form, and in regard to this he does two things. First [1], he deals with form in itself; and second [4], with form in relation to the composite ("There are three kinds").

In regard to the first part he does

three things. First, he points out that form is a principle. He says that there are three causes, or three principles, of changeable substances. Two of these are contraries: one being "the specifying principle," i.e., the form, the other privation, which is in a sense a contrary, and the third, matter. For it has been shown already (nn. 2428–29) that in every change there must be a subject and two contraries, and therefore these are required in the generation of substance.

2442. **It should be noted** [2].

Second, he shows that neither matter nor form is generated. He says that neither matter nor "form comes to be," or is generated.—But this must be understood of the last matter and the last form; for some matter is generated, namely, the subject of alteration, since it is a composite substance.

2443. That neither the last matter nor the last form is generated he proves thus. In every change there must be some subject of the change, which is matter; and something by which it is changed, which is the principle imparting motion; and something to which it is changed, which is the specifying principle or form. Hence if both the form and the matter are generated, for example, if not only this whole—bronze sphere—is generated, but also the sphericity and the bronze, it follows that both form and matter have matter and form; and thus there will be an infinite regress in matters and forms. This is impossible. Hence, in the process of generation there must be some stopping point, so that the last matter and last form are not generated.

2444. **Again, it should be** [3].

Third, he points out that things acquire their form from agents like themselves. He says that every substance comes to be "from an agent having the same name," i.e., an agent similar in form. For all substances which are generated come to be either by nature or by art or by luck or "spontaneously," namely, by chance; i.e., they are not directly an object of design. Art differs from nature, because art is a principle of action in something other than the thing moved, whereas nature is a principle of action and motion in the thing in which it is present. Now things produced by art obviously come to be from something similar to themselves in form; for it is by means of the form of the house in his mind that the builder causes the house which exists in matter. The same thing is also apparent in the case of natural things, for man begets man. However, this does not seem to be true in some cases, for some things are not generated by agents similar to themselves in species; for example, the heat found in lower bodies is generated by the sun, not by heat. Yet while there is no likeness in species, there must still be some kind of likeness, even though it is an imperfect one, because the matter of lower bodies cannot acquire perfect likeness to a higher agent. And since this is true in the case of things which come to be both by art and by nature, it is evident that each thing is generated by its like.

2445. For "the remaining causes," luck and chance, are defects and privations as it were of nature and of art; for luck is intellect producing an effect over and above the one at which it aims; and chance is nature producing an effect over and above the one at which it aims. Hence those things which come to be by luck and by chance are not similar to their agents in form, since luck and chance are not causes in the strict sense but only accidentally. Therefore in a sense animals which are generated from decomposed matter seem to come into being by chance inasmuch as they are not generated by agents similar to themselves in species. Nor do they have a definite efficient cause in the realm of lower bodies, but only a higher efficient cause.

2446. **There are three kinds** [4].

Then he establishes what is true of form in relation to the composite substance, and in regard to this he does three things. First, he divides substance into matter, form and composite. He says that there are three kinds of substance. First, according to appearances, matter seems to be substance and a determinate thing; and it was for this reason that the first natural philosophers claimed that matter alone is substance. They did this because they saw that in the case of artifacts, which come to be by contact and not by natural union, only the matter or underlying subject seems to be substance; for artificial forms are accidents. Second, the nature of a thing also seems to be substance and a determinate thing—the nature of a thing being that in which the process of natural generation is terminated, i.e., the form, which is as it were a kind of permanent state. The third kind of substance is the composite of matter and form, for example, singular things such as Callias and Socrates.

2447. **Now in some cases** [5].

Second, he says that some forms evidently do not exist apart from the composite substance, for example, the form of a house does not exist apart from matter; for the form of a house is an accident, and the matter of a house is a substance, and an accident exists only in a substance.

2448. I say that this is true unless the form of the house should be taken "as the art," i.e., as existing in the mind of the artisan, for in this way it does exist apart from matter. But there is neither generation nor destruction of these artificial forms as existing in the mind of the artisan; for the house which exists in the mind without matter, and health, and all things of this kind, begin to be and cease to be in a different way from those things which come to be by generation and destruction, i.e., by teaching or by discovery.

2449. But if any forms do exist apart from composite substances, this will be true of those natural forms which are substances. Hence Plato was not wrong in saying "that the Forms," i.e., the separate Forms, are things which exist by nature. But I say that he was not wrong, not in an unqualified sense, but only if there are other forms which differ from sensible ones, such as flesh, head and the like, which are the last matter of a particular composite substance, which is substance in the fullest sense.

2450. **Hence efficient causes** [6].

Third, he shows that there are no universal forms apart from composite substances. In regard to this he does two things. First, he makes his purpose clear by differentiating between formal and efficient causes. He says that efficient causes are prior to their effects; and this must be so because efficient causes are the source of the motion which terminates in the thing made. But the formal cause, which is a cause in the sense of the intelligible structure of a thing, begins to be when the thing of which it is the form begins to be. For health begins to be when a man is healed, and the shape of a bronze sphere begins to be when the bronze sphere comes into being. It is evident, then, that forms are not separate from composite substances; for if they were separate, they would have to be eternal, since of such things there is directly neither generation nor destruction, as has been shown (n. 1420; n. 1687); and thus they would be prior to the substances of which they are the forms.

2451. But even though forms are not prior to composite substances, it is still necessary to investigate whether any form remains after the composite substance has been destroyed. For nothing prevents some forms from continuing to exist after the composite ceases to exist; for example, we might say that the soul is of this sort—not every soul but only the intellective. For perhaps it is impossible that every soul should be such that it continues to exist after the body has been destroyed, because the other parts of the soul do not operate without bodily organs, whereas the intellect does not operate by way of a bodily organ. He says "perhaps" because it is not his present intention to demonstrate this point; but this belongs to the science which treats of the soul. And just as the parts of the soul other than the intellect do not continue to exist after the composite substance has been destroyed, in a similar fashion neither do other forms of perishable things.

2452. Now we should observe that it is Aristotle's view regarding the intellective soul that it did not exist before the body as Plato claimed, and also that it is not destroyed when the body is, as the ancient philosophers held inasmuch as they failed to distinguish between intellect and sense. For he did not exclude the intellective soul from the generality of other forms as regards their not existing prior to composite substances, but only as regards their not continuing to exist after the composite substances have been destroyed.

2453. From this consideration it is also evident that one cannot degrade the intellective soul as some men attempt to do, saying that the possible intellect alone or the agent intellect alone is imperishable. For these men claim not only that the intellect which they say is imperishable (whether it be the possible or the agent intellect) is a separate substance and thus not a form, but also that, if it is a form of the kind which remains after the body has perished, it must exist prior to the body. And in this respect there would be no difference between those who hold that a separate intellect is the form of man and those who hold that separate Forms are the forms of sensible things. This is the view which Aristotle aims to reject here.

2454. **It is evident** [7].

Second, he rejects the argument by which they maintained that there are separate Ideas. For the Platonists said that it was necessary to posit Ideas in order that particular things might be formed in likeness to them. But this is not necessary, because in the realm of lower bodies one finds an adequate cause of the formation of everything that comes to be. For a natural agent produces something like itself. For man begets man; but it is not the universal man who begets a singular man, but the singular man begets a singular man. Hence it is not necessary to hold that there is a separate universal man by reason of which the singular man here receives, or shares in, the form of the species. The same thing is evident of those things which come to be by art, because the medical art is the formal determinant and likeness of health in the mind, as has also been shown above (1040:C 2450).

LESSON 4
The Principles of Movable Substances

ARISTOTLE'S TEXT Chapters 4 & 5: 1070a31–1071b2

1. In one sense the causes and principles of different things are different; but in another sense they are not, for, if one speaks universally and proportionally, they are the same for all. **1070a31–33**

2. And one might raise the question whether the principles and elements of substances and of relations are the same or different; and the same question may be asked of each of the other categories. **1070a33–35**

3. But it would be absurd if the principles and elements of all things were the same; for then substance and relations would be derived from the same principles. How then will this be [common]? For there is nothing common existing apart from substance and the other categories; and an element is prior to the things of which it is the element. But substance is not an element of relations, nor is any of these an element of substance. **1070a35–1070b4**

4. Further, how is it possible for the elements of all things to be the same? For none of the elements can be the same as a composite of elements; for example, neither b nor a is the same as ba; nor can any of the intelligibles, such as being and unity, be an element; for these belong to each composite thing. Hence none of them can be either a substance or a relation. But it must be one or the other. Therefore the elements of all things are not the same. **1070b4–10**

5. Or, as we say, there is a sense in which they are the same and a sense in which they are not; for example, perhaps the elements of sensible bodies are the hot as form, the cold as privation, and that which primarily and of its own nature is potentially both of these as matter. And not only these are substances, but so also are the things of which they are the principles. And so also is any unity which comes to be from the hot and the cold, as flesh and bone; for the thing produced from these must differ from them. The elements and principles of these things, then, are the same, although the elements of different things are different. However, it cannot be said that the elements of all things are the same in this sense, but only proportionally, just as if one were to say that there are three principles, form, privation and matter. But each of these is different in each class of things; for example, in the case of colors there is white, black and surface; and there is darkness, light and air, from which day and night are derived. **1070b10–21**

6. And since not only the things which are intrinsic to a being are its causes, but also certain external things, as the moving cause, it is evident that principle and element differ, although both are causes. And principle is divided into these two kinds; and whatever causes motion or makes it cease is a kind of principle. Hence analogically there are three elements and four causes or principles; but they differ in different things, and the first cause of motion is different in different things: for example, health, sickness and body, and the moving cause is the art of medicine; form, a certain kind of disorder, and bricks, and the moving cause is the art of building. Principle is also divided into these. **1070b22–30**

7. And since in the case of physical things the moving cause of man is man, while in the case of objects of thought the moving cause is the form or its contrary, in one sense there will be three causes and in another sense four. For in a sense the art of medicine is health, and the art of building is the form of a house, and man begets man. **1070b30–34**

8. And besides these there is that which as the first of all things imparts motion to all things. **1070b34–35**

Chapter 5

9. Since some things are separable and some are not, it is the former which are substances. And for this reason these (substances) are the causes of all things, because without substances there can be no affections and motions. **1070b36–1071a2**

10. Next, all of these causes are perhaps soul and body, or intellect, appetite and body. **1071a2–3**

11. Again, there is another sense in which the principles of things are proportionally the same, i.e., as actuality and potentiality; but these are different for different things and apply to them in different ways. For in some cases the same thing is at one time actual and at another time potential, as wine, flesh or man. Now these principles fall into the classes of causes mentioned; for a form is an actuality if it can exist apart, and so also is the thing composed of matter and form, and so also is a privation, such as darkness and suffering; but matter is in potentiality, for it is what is capable of becoming both. But it is in another way that the distinction of actuality and potentiality applies to those things of which the matter is not the same, and the form is not the same, but different. For example, the cause of man is his elements—fire and earth as matter, and his proper form—and if there is anything external, such as his father; and besides these there is the sun and the oblique circle, which are neither matter nor species nor privation nor form, but are moving causes. **1071a3–17**

12. Further, we must note that some of these causes can be expressed universally and some not. The first principles of all things are those first "this," one actually, one potentially. Therefore these principles are not universals, for the principle of a singular thing is a singular thing. For while man taken universally is a principle of man, there is no universal man, but Peleus is the cause of Achilles, and your father is the cause of you; and b and a taken either absolutely or particularly are the causes of the syllable ba. Further, there are different causes and elements of different things, as has been stated, and the causes of things which do not belong to the same genus, as colors, sounds, substances and quantity, are different, except in a proportional way. And the causes of things which belong to the same species are different, not specifically, but in the sense that the causes of singular things are different; that is, your matter and form and moving cause are different from mine, although they are the same in their universal intelligibility. **1071a17–29**

13. And to ask whether the principles and elements of substances and of relations and of qualities are the same or different, is clearly to raise questions about terms that are used in many senses. But the principles of different things are not the same but different, except that in a sense they are the same for all. They are the same for all proportionally because each thing has matter, form, privation and a moving cause. And the causes of substances may be regarded as the causes of all things because when they are destroyed all things are destroyed. And again that which is first in complete reality is the cause of all things. However, in a sense the primary [i.e., proximate] causes of things are different, i.e., all the contraries which are not predicated either as genera or as terms having many meanings. And again the matter of different things is different. We have stated what the principles of sensible things are, then, and how many there are, and how they are the same and how different. **1071a29–1071b2**

COMMENTARY

2455. Having stated his position regarding the principles of sensible substances, the Philosopher's aim here is to investigate whether the principles of substances and those of the other classes of things are the same or different. For if they are the same, it is evident that, when the principles of substances are given, the principles of all the other classes of things are also given. In regard to this he does three things. First [1], he states what is true. Second [2], he introduces a question relating to the answer proposed ("And one might"). Third [13], he gives a summary of what is true ("And to ask").

He says, first, that in one sense the principles and causes of different things are different, and in another sense they are the same for all things, i.e., universally and proportionally.

2456. **And one might** [2].

Then he examines the true answer given above, by raising a question; and in regard to this he does three things. First [2], he raises the question. Second [3], he argues on one side of the question ("But it would be"). Third [5], he settles the issue ("Or, as we say").

He accordingly says, first [2], that one might raise the question whether the principles of substances and those of relations, and also those of the other categories, are the same or different.

2457. He makes special reference to relations because they seem to be farther removed from substance than the rest of the categories are inasmuch as they have a more imperfect mode of being. And for this reason they inhere in substance by means of the other categories; for example, equal and unequal, double and half, inhere in substance by way of quantity; and mover and thing moved, father and son, master and slave, inhere in substance by way of action and passion. The reason is that, while substance is something which exists of itself, and quantity and quality are things which exist in something else, relations are things which not only exist in something else but also have being in reference to something else.

2458. **But it would be** [3].

Then he argues on one side of the question mentioned above. He gives two arguments to show that the principles of substance and those of the other classes of things are not the same. The first argument is as follows. If the principles of substance and those of the other classes of things are the same, the same principles must either exist apart from substance and from the other categories, or they must belong to the category of substance or to some other category.

2459. But it cannot be said that they exist apart from substance and from the other categories, because then they would have to be prior both to substance and to the other categories; for a principle is prior to the things which come from it. Therefore, since what is prior is found to be more common, as animal is prior to man, it follows that, if some principle is prior both to substance and to the other categories, there must be some principle which is common both to substance and to the other categories. This applies especially to the opinion of the Platonists, who claimed that universals are principles—particularly being and unity as the most common principles of all things.

2460. Neither can it be said that the most common principles of all categories belong either to the category of substance or to that of relation or to any other category. For since principles are of the same kind as the things which come from them, it seems impossible that substance should be a principle of relations, or vice versa. Therefore the principles of substance and those of the other categories are not the same.

2461. **Further, how is it** [4].

He gives a second argument, which runs thus: no element is the same as a composite of elements, for nothing is the cause or element of itself; for example, an element of this syllable *ba* is the letter *b* or the letter *a*.

2462. And since there would seem to be a rejoinder to this based on the principles laid down by Plato, namely, being and unity, since each thing composed of principles is one and a being, he therefore next rejects this argument. He says that it is also impossible that any of the intelligible elements—unity and being—should be the same as the things which are derived from them. He calls them intelligible, both because universals are grasped by the intellect, and because Plato claimed that they are separate from sensible things.

2463. He proves that elements of this kind differ from the things of which they are the elements, because "elements of this kind," i.e., unity and being, are found in each of the things composed of them, whereas no one of the things composed of them is found in other things. Hence it is evident that these elements also differ from the things composed of them. If it is true, then, that elements are not the same as the things composed of them; and if the elements of substances and those of the other classes of things are the same, it follows that none of them belong either to the category of substance or to any other category. But this is impossible, because everything which exists must belong to some category. Hence it is impossible that all the categories should have the same principles.

2464. **Or, as we say** [5].

Then he solves the question which was raised, and in regard to this he does two things. First [5], shows that the principles of all categories are proportionally the same; and second [12], that they are universally the same ("Further, we must note"). For he laid down these two qualifications above (n. 2455) when he said that there are the same first principles for all things universally and proportionally.

The first part is divided into two members inasmuch as he gives two ways in which the principles of all things are proportionally the same. He begins to treat the second [11] where he says, "Again, there is."

In regard to the first he does two things. First, he shows how the principles of all things are proportionally the same. Second [8], he shows how they are the same without qualification ("And besides").

In regard to the first he does two things. First, he shows that the principles of all things are proportionally the same as regards their intrinsic causes; and second [6], as regards both their intrinsic and their extrinsic causes ("And since not only").

He accordingly says, first [5], that in one respect it is true to say that the principles of all things are the same, and in another respect it is not.

2465. He explains this by saying that it would be the same as if we were to hold that the principle of sensible bodies in the line of specifying principle or form is the hot and in the line of privation is the cold, and that the matter of sensible bodies is what is of itself in potentiality to these two; for matter taken in itself is a principle that is susceptible both of form and of privation. He says "perhaps" because, while heat is not a substantial form of sensible bodies and cold is not a privation but both are qualities, still he uses them as form and privation in the category of substance in order to make the case more evident. Hence he adds that principles of this kind are substances, not as species in a genus, but as principles.

2466. Again, we say that things which are composed of these, i.e., the things of which these are the principles, namely, fire and water, are substances, granted that we understand fire to be composed of hot as a form and of its own matter, and water of cold as a privation and of matter; or again, granted that some one thing comes to be from the mixture of hot and cold, the above-mentioned contraries, hot and cold, and matter are the principles of these things; because that which comes to be from hot and cold must be something different from hot and cold, i.e., from the first bodies of which we imagine these to be the forms.

2467. Therefore the principles and elements of these things, i.e., of the simple bodies and the things composed of them, are the same. But other things have different proximate principles. However, the principles and elements of all these things are the same only proportionally. We might, for example, say that, just as the three things mentioned above—hot, cold, and their subject—have the character of form, privation and matter respectively in the generation of simple bodies, so too in every other genus there are three things which are proportioned to each other as form, privation and matter. But these three differ for different classes of things. For example, in the genus of color, white has the character of form, black the character of privation, and surface the character of matter or subject; and in the genus of distinctions of time, light has the character of form, darkness the character of privation, and air the character of matter or subject; and from these three principles day and night come to be.

2468. **And since not only** [6].

Then he shows that the same thing is true of intrinsic and extrinsic causes, and in regard to this he does two things. First [6], he shows that, when we enumerate the intrinsic and extrinsic causes together, there are four causes proportionally of all things. Second [7], he shows how they are reduced to three ("And since in the case").

He accordingly says, first [6], that, since not only what is intrinsic is a cause, but also what is extrinsic, i.e., a mover, it is evident that principle and element differ. For principle in the strict sense means an extrinsic cause, as a mover, since it is from this that motion proceeds; whereas element in the strict sense means an intrinsic cause, of which a thing is composed.

2469. Yet both are called causes, i.e., both extrinsic principles and intrinsic ones. And in a sense principle is divided into these, i.e., into intrinsic causes and extrinsic causes. For there are certain intrinsic principles, as has been shown in Book V (nn. 755–56); for example, the foundation of a house is a principle of it in the sense of matter, and a soul is a principle of a man in the sense of form. But that which causes motion or makes it cease, i.e., which brings it to rest, is a principle but not an element; because an element is an intrinsic principle from which a thing comes to be, as has been stated in Book V (nn. 795–98).

2470. It is clear, then, that analogously, or proportionally, the elements of all things are three in number—matter, form and privation. For privations are called elements not essentially but accidentally, i.e., because the matter to which a privation is accidentally related is an element. For matter existing under one form contains within itself the privation of another form.—But the causes and principles of things are four in number inasmuch as we may add the moving cause to the three elements. Aristotle does not mention the final cause, however, because a goal is a principle only inasmuch as it is present in the intention of the moving cause.

2471. Therefore the causes and principles of all things analogously are four in number—matter, form, privation, and the source of motion. Yet they are not the same in all cases but differ in different things. For just as it has been said above (n. 2467) that matter, form and privation differ in different things, so too the first of the causes, which has the character of a mover, differs in different cases.

2472. He clarifies this by giving examples. In the case of things healed, health has the character of form, sickness the character of privation, the body the character of matter, and the art of medicine the character of a mover; and in the case of things built, the shape of a house is the form, "a certain kind of disorder," i.e., the opposite of the order which the house requires, is the privation, bricks are the matter, and the art of building is the mover. Principles, then, are divided into these four kinds.

2473. **And since in the case** [7].

He now reduces these four kinds of causes to three on the ground that in the case of artifacts and in that of natural things the mover and the form are specifically the same. He accordingly says that this is clear because (*a*) in the case of natural things man is a mover inasmuch as he has a form; and (*b*) in the case of things which are made by mind or intellect the cause of motion is the form conceived by the mind, or even the contrary of the form through whose removal the form is induced. Therefore it is evident that in one sense there are three causes, inasmuch as the mover and the form are specifically the same, and in another sense there are four, inasmuch as these two causes differ numerically. For in a sense the art of medicine is health, and the art of building is the form of the house, i.e., inasmuch as the art itself is a kind of likeness and intelligible representation of the form which is in the matter. And similarly in the case of things which come to be through generation the generator is similar in form to the thing generated; for man begets man.

2474. **And besides these** [8].

Then he shows that, although first principles are not identically the same beings in all things but only proportionally the same, none the less the first principles of all things are the same in an unqualified sense. He proves this by three arguments. First, he shows that the moving cause is the first of the causes which have been given because it is the one which makes the form or the privation exist in matter. Now in the class of movers it is possible to reach a single cause, as has been proved in Book VIII of the ***Physics***.*[256a4-256b3]* Therefore this first mover, which is one and the same for all, is the first principle of all things.

2475. **Since some things** [9].

Second, he proves the same point in a different way. For some beings (substances) are capable of separate existence, and others (accidents) are not, because modifications and motions and accidents of this kind cannot exist apart from substances. It is evident, then, that the first principles in the category of substance are also the causes of all the other categories. This applies not only to the first moving cause but also to intrinsic causes; for the matter and form of a substance are the causes of its accidents.

2476. **Next, all of these** [10].

Third, he shows that we must also reach certain first principles in the category of substance; for first principles in the category of substance are living animated substances according to the thought of Aristotle, who claimed that the celestial bodies are animated. Hence in the category of substance the first principles which have the character of form and matter will be soul and body, or also body and intellect or appetite; for assuming that a celestial body is animated, its soul has none of the different parts of the soul except intellect and appetite; for the other parts of the soul are directed to the preservation of bodies which are capable of being generated and destroyed. Intellect and appetite also have the character of a mover.

2477. **Again, there is another sense** [11].

Then he gives a second way in which the principles of all things are proportionally the same. He says that the principles of all things are proportionally the same in another sense inasmuch as we say that actuality and potentiality are the principles of all things.

2478. But in this case two differences are to be observed. The first is that a different potentiality and a different actuality are principles in different things. The second is that potentiality and actuality are found in different things in different ways.

2479. Then the second difference is first clarified. He says that in some cases the same thing is at one time actual and at another time potential, as is evident of all things which admit of generation and destruction and are movable and contingent; for example, wine, flesh and man are at one time actual and at another potential. But some things are always actual, as the eternal substances.

2480. And since he had said that the way in which the principles of all things are proportionally the same differs from the one previously given, he next shows how these principles (actuality and potentiality) are reduced to the same class. He says that these principles (actuality and potentiality) fall under the classes of causes mentioned above, which are form, privation, matter and mover; because form is an actuality, whether it is separable from the composite, as the Platonists claimed, or whether there is something composed of both, i.e., of form and matter. And similarly privation is in a sense an actuality, for example, darkness or "suffering," i.e., sickness. But matter is in potentiality, because of itself it is capable of receiving both form and privation. It is evident, then, that actuality and potentiality amount to the same thing as matter, form and privation; and that in a sense actuality and potentiality differ in different things, because they are not present in all things in the same way but in different ways.

2481. And since he had said that actuality and potentiality not only apply to different things in different ways but also differ for different things, he next explains this by saying that it is in a different way that the distinction of actuality and potentiality applies to different things of which the matter, which is in potentiality, is not the same, and the form, which is actuality, is not the same but different. For example, the material cause of a man is his elements, namely, fire and the like, and his formal cause is "his proper form," i.e., his soul, and his moving cause is something extrinsic—his father being a proximate efficient cause, and the sun and "the oblique circle," or zodiac, through which the sun moves together with the other planets which cause generation in lower bodies by their motion, being remote efficient causes. But extrinsic causes of this sort are neither matter nor form nor privation nor anything conforming to or specifically the same as these so that it could be said that they are reduced to these causes as actuality and potentiality. They are reduced to a different class of cause because they are movers, and these are also reduced to actuality. But things which differ from man have a different proper matter and a different proper form and some proper agent.

2482. **Further, we must note** [12].

Since it has been shown already (n. 2467) how the principles of all things are proportionally the same, Aristotle now wishes to show how the principles of all things are universally the same; for both of these points were mentioned above (n. 2464). He accordingly says that we must see how some principles are predicated universally and how some are not. The first principles which are understood to be most universal are actuality and potentiality, for these divide being as being. They are called universal principles because they are signified and understood in a universal way, but not so that universals themselves are subsisting principles, as the Platonists claimed, because the principle of each singular thing can only be a singular thing; for the principle of an effect taken universally is a universal, as man of man. But since there is no subsisting universal man, there will be no universal principle of universal man, but only this particular man will be the principle of this particular man; for example, Peleus is the father of Achilles, and your father is the father of you. And this particular letter *b* is a principle of this particular syllable *ba,* but *b* taken universally is a principle of *ba* taken universally. Therefore principles signified universally are the same for all things.

2483. Then he introduces a third way in which the principles of substances are universally the principles of all things, i.e., inasmuch as accidents are caused by substances. Now just as actuality and potentiality are the universal principles of all things because they flow from being as being, so also, to the extent that the community of things caused is lessened, the community of the principles must also be lessened. For things which do not belong to the same genus, as colors, sounds, substance and quantity, have different causes and elements, as has been pointed out (n. 2467), even though these are proportionally the same for all things. And things which belong to the same genus but are numerically different have different principles, not formally, but numerically. For example, your matter and form and moving cause are one thing and mine are another, but in their universal intelligibility they are the same; for soul and body are the form and matter of man, but this soul and this body are the form and the matter of this man.

2484. **And to ask** [13].

Here he summarizes what has been said in this chapter. He says that to ask whether the principles and elements of substances and of relations and of qualities and of the other categories are the same or different is to raise questions about terms which are used in various senses, because the principles of different things are not the same except in a certain respect but different.

2485. For the principles of all things are the same in a certain respect, either proportionally, as when we say that in each class of things we find certain principles which have the character of matter, form, privation and moving cause; or in the sense that the causes of substances are the causes of all things, because when they are destroyed other things are destroyed; or because the principles are "complete reality," i.e., actuality, and potentiality. The principles of all things, then, are the same in these three ways.

2486. But in another respect the principles are different, because contraries, which are principles of things, and matter itself are not predicated in the same way; for they are not genera, nor are they even predicated of things in many ways as though they were equivocal. Hence we cannot say that they are the same without qualification but only analogously.

2487. Last, he concludes by saying that he has shown the number of principles which sensible substances have and how they are the same or different.

LESSON 5
An Eternal Immovable Substance Must Exist

ARISTOTLE'S TEXT Chapter 6: 1071b3–1071b22

1. Since there are three classes of substance (1028), two of which are physical and one immovable, concerning the latter it is necessary to affirm that an eternal immovable substance must exist. For substances are the primary kind of beings, and if all of them are perishable, all things are perishable. But it is impossible either that motion should have come to be or that it should perish, for it always existed; and the same is true of time, for there cannot be a before and an after if there is no time. Motion is continuous, then, in the sense that time is; for time is either the same as motion or a property of it. Now the only continuous motion is that which pertains to place, and of this only that which is circular. **1071b3–11**

2. But even if there is something which is capable of imparting or producing motion, but is not actually doing so, motion will still not exist; for that which has a potentiality may possibly not exercise it. Hence nothing is to be gained if we invent certain eternal substances, as do those who posit the separate Forms, unless there is some principle among them which is capable of causing change (83). This is not sufficient, then, nor is another substance besides the separate Forms sufficient; for if it does not act, there will be no eternal motion. **1071b12–17**

3. And even if it does act this will still not be sufficient, if its essence is a potentiality; for there will be no eternal motion, since what is potential may possibly not be. Hence there must be a principle of the kind whose substance is an actuality. **1071b17–20**

4. Further, such substances must also be immaterial; for they must be eternal if anything else is. Hence they are actualities. **1071b20–22**

COMMENTARY

2488. After having shown what the principles of sensible substances are, here the Philosopher begins to establish the truth about the immovable substances, which are separate from matter. This topic is divided into two parts. First [1], he treats substances of this sort by giving his own opinion. Second, he treats them by giving the opinions of other thinkers. He does this in the following book ("Concerning the substance of sensible things").

The first part is divided into two members. First, he proves that there is a substance which is eternal, immovable and separate from matter. Second (Lesson 7) he investigates the attributes of this substance ("Now the first mover").

In regard to the first he does three things. First, he proves that an eternal substance must exist. Second (Lesson 6), he deals with a question arising from the foregoing discussion ("There is a difficulty, however"); and third (Lesson 6, [6]), from the answer given to the question which was raised he proceeds to clarify a truth previously established ("Hence, Chaos or Night").

In regard to the first he does two things. First, he shows that it is necessary to posit an eternal substance. Second (1056:C 2492), he shows what kind of substance it must be ("But even if there is").

He accordingly says, first [1], that it has been pointed out above (n. 2424) that there are three classes of substances. Two of these are natural substances, because they undergo motion—one being eternal, as the heavens, and the other perishable, as plants and animals. And besides these there is a third class, which is immovable and not natural; and of this kind of substance it is now necessary to speak. With a view to investigating this kind of substance it is first necessary to prove that an eternal immovable substance must exist. He proceeds as follows.

2489. Substances are the primary kind of beings, as has been shown above (nn. 2417–23), and when primary things are destroyed none of the others remain. Therefore, if no substance is eternal but all are perishable, it follows that nothing is eternal but that "all things are perishable," i.e., they do not always exist. But this is impossible. Hence there must be an eternal substance.

2490. That it is impossible for nothing to be eternal he proves from the fact that motion cannot have come to be or "perish," i.e., it cannot have come to be anew or at some time totally cease to be. For it has been shown in Book VIII of the ***Physics****[251b10-252b5]* that motion is eternal without qualification. It also seems impossible that time should not be eternal; for if time began to be at some time or will cease to be at some time it would follow that prior to time there was the non-being of time, and also that there will be time after the non-being of time. But this seems to be impossible, because there could be no before or after if time did not exist, since time is nothing else than the measure of before and after in motion. Thus it would follow that time existed before it began to be, and that it will exist after it ceases to be. Hence it seems that time must be eternal.

2491. And if time is continuous and eternal, motion must be continuous and eternal, because motion and time are either the same thing, as some claimed, or time is a property of motion, as is really the case. For time is the measure of motion, as is evident in Book IV of the ***Physics***. [221a1] However, it must not be thought that every motion can be eternal and continuous, since this can be true only of local motion; and among local motions this is true only of circular motion, as is proved in Book VIII of the ***Physics***.[264b9-265b16]

2492. **But even if** [2].

Then he shows what kind of substance this eternal substance must be, and in regard to this he does three things. First, he shows that in order to account for the eternity of motion it is necessary to posit an eternal substance which is always moving or acting. He says that, since it is necessary, on the assumption that motion is eternal, that there be an eternal substance which is capable of imparting or producing motion, it is also necessary that this be a mover or agent which is always acting, because if it were "capable of imparting or producing motion," i.e., if it had the power to produce or cause motion, and was not actually doing so, it would follow that there would be no actual motion. For that which has the power of causing motion may possibly not be causing it, since that which has the power of acting may possibly not act; and thus motion would not be eternal. Assuming, then, that motion is eternal, it is necessary to posit an eternal substance which is actually moving or acting.

2493. Next, he concludes from this that nothing is to be gained by accepting the opinion of Plato, who posited eternal substances, since this is not sufficient to account for the eternity of motion. For the assumption that there are certain separate and eternal substances is not sufficient to account for this unless there is some principle among them which can cause change;

but this does not seem to fit the separate Forms. For Plato claimed that the separate Forms are nothing else than universals existing apart from matter. But universals as such do not cause motion; for every active or motive principle is a singular thing, as has been pointed out above (n. 2482). Neither the separate Forms, then, nor any other separate substances besides the Forms, such as the separate mathematical entities posited by some, are sufficient to account for the eternity of motion, because even the objects of mathematics as such are not principles of motion. And if there is no eternal active substance, there will be no eternal motion, because the principle of motion is an eternal substance which is a mover or agent.

2494. **And even if** [3].

Second, he shows that, in order for motion to be eternal it is necessary not only that an eternal substance exist, which is a mover or agent, but also that its essence be an actuality. Hence he says that the eternity of motion is not adequately accounted for even if it is supposed that an eternal substance does act yet is potential in essence. For example, it would not be sufficient to hold that the first principles are fire or water, as the ancient natural philosophers did, because then motion could not be eternal. For if a mover is such that its essence contains potentiality, it can possibly not be, because whatever is in potentiality may possibly not be. Hence it would be possible for motion not to be, and so it would not be necessary and eternal. Therefore it follows that there must be a first principle of motion of the sort whose essence is not in potentiality but is only an actuality.

2495. **Further, such substances** [4].

Third, he further concludes that this kind of substance must be immaterial. He says that it also follows from the foregoing (nn. 2488–94) that substances of this kind, which are the principles of eternal motion, must be free from matter; for matter is in potentiality. Therefore they must be eternal if something else is eternal, as motion and time. Thus it follows that they are actualities.

2496. He concludes in this way last because of the question which he will next raise. From this reasoning, then, it is evident that here Aristotle firmly thought and believed that motion must be eternal and also time; otherwise he would not have based his plan of investigating immaterial substances on this conviction.

2497. Yet it should be noted that the arguments which he introduces in Book VIII of the ***Physics***, [250b10-253a21] which he assumes as the basis of his procedure here, are not demonstrations in the strict sense but only dialectical arguments; unless perhaps they are arguments against the positions of the ancient natural philosophers regarding the beginning of motion, inasmuch as he aims to destroy these positions.

2498. And aside from the other arguments which he does not touch upon here, it is evident that the argument which he does give here to prove that time is eternal is not demonstrative. For if we suppose that at some moment time began to be, it is not necessary to assume a prior moment except in imaginary time; just as when we say that there is no body outside of the heavens, what we mean by "outside" is merely an imaginary something. Hence, just as it is not necessary to posit some place outside of the heavens, even though "outside" seems to signify place, so too neither is it necessary that there be a time before time began to be or a time after time will cease to be, even though before and after signify time.

2499. But even if the arguments which prove that motion and time are eternal are not demonstrative and necessarily conclusive, still the things which are proved about the eternity and immateriality of the first substance necessarily follow; for, even if the world were not eternal, it would still have to be brought into being by something that has prior existence. And if this cause were not eternal, it too would have to be produced by something else. But since there cannot be an infinite series, as has been proved in Book II (nn. 301–4), it is necessary to posit an eternal substance whose essence contains no potentiality and is therefore immaterial.

LESSON 6
Eternal Motion Requires An Eternal Mover

ARISTOTLE'S TEXT Chapters 6 & 7: 1071b22–1072a26

1. *There is a difficulty, however; for it seems that, while everything which is acting is able to act, not everything which is able to act is acting; so potentiality is prior.* **1071b22–24**

2. *But if this is so, no beings will exist; for everything may be capable of being, but still not be. And if we take what the theologians say, who generate everything from Night, or what the philosophers of nature say, who affirm that "all things were together," they express the same impossible view. For how will things be moved, if there is no actual cause? Matter will not move itself, but technical knowledge will move it; nor will menstrual blood or earth move themselves, but semen or seed will move them.* **1071b25–31**

3. *This is the reason why some men, such as Leucippus and Plato, posit something which is always actual; for they say that motion always exists. But they do not say why it exists, or what it is, or how this is so, or what its cause is. For nothing is moved by chance, but there must always be something existing which moves it. Now things are moved in one way by nature, and in another by force or by mind or by some other agent. What kind of motion, then, is prior? For this makes the greatest difference. Plato cannot explain what it is that he sometimes thinks is the source of motion, i.e., what moves itself; for according to him the soul is later than motion and simultaneous with the heavens.* **1071b31–1072a3**

4. *Now to think that potentiality is prior to actuality is in one sense right and in another not; and we have explained how this is so.* **1072a3–4**

5. *That actuality is prior is affirmed by Anaxagoras (for mind is an actuality), and by Empedocles in his theory of love and strife, and by those who say that motion always existed, as Plato and Leucippus.* **1072a4–7**

6. *Hence Chaos or Night did not exist for an infinite time, but the same things have always existed, either in a cycle or in some other way, granted that actuality is prior to potentiality.* **1072a7–9**

7. *Therefore, if something is always moved in the same cycle, there must be something which always continues to act in the same way. But if there is to be generation and destruction, there must be something else which acts in different ways. Hence this must act in one way of itself, and in another way in virtue of something else, i.e., either in virtue of some third agent or of the first. Now it must be in virtue of the first; for this is the cause both of the second and of the third. The first is preferable, then; for it was the cause of that whose being is always to be the same, and something else was the cause of that whose being is to be different; and obviously both of these account for eternal diversity. Therefore, if motion always exhibits these characteristics, why is it necessary to look for other principles?*

Chapter 7

And since this is a possible account of the matter, and if this is not so all things will come from Night (1060) or "all things were together" (1060) or something comes from non-being (1034), these difficulties are solved. And there is something which is always being moved with an unceasing motion, and this is circular motion. This is evident not only in theory but in fact; and for this reason the first heaven will be eternal. **1072a9–23**

8. *Therefore there is also something which causes it to move. And since that which is moved and causes motion is intermediate, there must be something which causes motion and is unmoved, which is eternal and both a substance and an actuality.* **1072a23–26**

COMMENTARY

2500. He raises a question about a point already dealt with. The question is whether actuality is prior absolutely to potentiality so that the first principle of things can be held to be one whose substance is actuality. In regard to this he does three things. First [1], he gives an argument to show what is false, namely, that potentiality is prior absolutely to actuality. Second [2], he argues on the other side of the question ("But if this is so"). Third [4], he answers the question ("Now to think").

He accordingly says, first [1], that it has been pointed out that an eternal substance is an actuality, although there is a difficulty regarding this. For potentiality seems to be prior to actuality, since one thing is prior to another when the sequence of their being cannot be reversed (see n. 950). Now potentiality seems to be related to actuality in this way, because everything which is acting seems to be able to act, but not everything which is able to act is acting; and so it seems that potentiality is prior to actuality.

2501. **But if this is so** [2].

Then he argues on the opposite side of the question, and in regard to this he does two things. First, he gives an argument reducing the counter-position to absurdity. He says that, if potentiality is prior absolutely to actuality, it follows that at some time nothing may exist; for the contingent is what can come to be but has not yet done so. Hence, if the first beings are potential, it follows that they do not exist actually; and so no other being will exist.

2502. This can be taken in two ways. First, according to the opinion of certain of the ancients, who were called the theological poets, such as Orpheus and certain others, who claimed that the world "is generated from Night," i.e., from a simple pre-existent privation. Second, according to the later physicists, i.e., philosophers of nature and their followers, who, when they saw that nothing comes from nothing in the natural world, claimed that all things were together in a kind of mixture, which they called Chaos. (Anaxagoras, for example, held this view.) Thus they held that all things exist potentially and not actually.

2503. But whether this position is stated in the former or in the latter way the same impossible conclusion follows, provided that potentiality is prior absolutely to actuality. For those things which are in potentiality only, or which come entirely under privation, or belong to some confused mass, cannot be moved so as to be brought to actuality unless there is some moving cause which is existing actually. For in things made by art the matter does not move itself, but an agent moves it, i.e., "technical knowledge," or art. Neither does the menstrual blood, which is the matter from which an animal is generated, move itself, but "semen," i.e., the sperm of the animal, moves it. Nor does earth, which is the material from which plants are generated, move itself, but "the seed," i.e., the seeds of plants, move it.

2504. **This is the reason** [3].

Second, he shows how some of the philosophers of nature agreed with this argument. He says that this is the reason why some philosophers—Leucippus, the companion of Democritus, and Plato—claimed that something actual always exists. For they said that motion had always existed even before the world; Leucippus attributed motion to the atoms, which are mobile of themselves, from which he supposed the world to be composed; and Plato attributed it to the elements, which he said were moved by disorderly motions before the formation of the world, and afterwards were brought into order by God.

2505. Now they seem to be right in claiming that motion has always existed. But they were wrong in failing to point out which kind of motion has always existed; nor did they give the cause of motion, either by stating this in an absolute sense or by giving the reason for their own position. Yet "nothing is moved by chance," i.e., without some fixed cause, but there must always be something existing which is the cause of motion. For example, we now see that some things are moved in this way by nature or by force or by mind or by some other agent. Hence they should also have stated what the first cause of motion is, whether nature or force or mind; for it makes a great deal of difference which of these is held to be the cause of motion.—Plato cannot be excused on the ground that he held the principle of motion to be something that moves itself, which he asserted to be a soul, since the soul did not exist of itself before the formation of the world, but only existed after the disorderly state of motion. For according to him the soul was created at the same time as the heavens, which he claimed to be animated; and thus it could not be the principle of that disorderly motion.

2506. **Now to think** [4].

Then he answers the question which was raised, and concerning this he does two things. First, he returns to the points established in Book IX regarding the relationship of potentiality to actuality. He says that the opinion that potentiality is prior to actuality is in one sense right and in another not. The sense in which it is right has been explained in Book IX (nn. 1844–49); for it was stated there that actuality is prior absolutely to potentiality. But in one and the same subject which is being moved from potentiality to actuality, potentiality is prior to actuality in time, although actuality is prior both in nature and in perfection.

2507. **That actuality is prior** [5].

Second, he strengthens his answer by giving the opinions of some of the philosophers. He says that the absolute priority of actuality is asserted by Anaxagoras, because he claimed that the first principle of motion is an intellect; for intellect is a kind of actuality. The same thing is also asserted by Empedocles, who claimed that love and strife are the causes of motion; and also by Leucippus and Plato, who claimed that motion has always existed.

2508. **Hence Chaos or Night** [6].

Then he uses the answer to the question given above to clarify a point previously established, and in regard to this he does three things. First [6], in the light of the things established above he concludes that generation must be eternal. Second [7], on the ground that generation is eternal he concludes that the motion of the heavens must be eternal ("Therefore, if something"). Third [8], on the ground that the motion of the heavens is eternal he concludes that the first unmoved mover must be eternal ("Therefore there is").

He accordingly says, first [6], that, if actuality is prior absolutely to potentiality, it follows that it is false to hold, with the ancient philosophers of nature, who thought potentiality to be prior absolutely to actuality, that all things pre-existed potentially for an infinite time in a kind of confused mass, which they called Chaos. And false also is the opinion of the theological poets, who claimed for the same reason that the simple privation of things had existed for an infinite time before things began to be actually. Some called this privation of things "Night," and perhaps the reason for their doing so is that among qualities and simple forms light is found to be more common and prior (since they thought that nothing exists except sensible things), and night is the privation of light. Both opinions are false, then, if actuality is prior to potentiality.

2509. But since we see that things which are generated and destroyed pass from potentiality to actuality, it will be necessary to say that the same things which begin to be actually after being potentially have always existed in some way. Either the very things which begin to be actually after being potentially have always existed according to circular generation, inasmuch as they claimed that things which are generated were formerly the same specifically but not numerically, and this is what occurs in circular generation. For from the moist earth vapors are derived, and these turn into rain, by which the earth is again made moist. Similarly sperm comes from a man, and from sperm a man again comes to be. Thus things which come to be are brought back the same in species by reason of circular generation. Or again those things which come to be actually after being potentially have always been the same things in a different way, as Anaxagoras claimed that they had actual prior existence in the things from which they are generated.

2510. **Therefore, if something** [7].

Then he concludes that the motion of the celestial bodies must be eternal on the ground that generation is eternal. Therefore, granted that there is no other motion by which things that pass from potentiality to actuality have always been the same except that which proceeds according to the cycle of generation, he concludes from what has been shown in the philosophy of nature (especially in Book II of ***Generation*** [336a23 ff.]) that, if something remains the same throughout the cycle of generation, something must also remain numerically the same, which will act in the same way so as to cause the eternal motion of things. For none of the things which are generated and destroyed can be the cause of the eternality which is found in generation and destruction, because no one of them always exists, nor even all of them, since they do not exist at the same time, as has been shown in Book VIII of the **Physics**.[258b26] It follows, then, that there must be some eternal agent which always acts in a uniform way so as to cause the eternal motion of things. This is the first heaven, which is moved and causes all things to be changed by its daily motion.

2511. But that which always acts in the same way only causes something that is always in the same state; and obviously those things which are generated and destroyed do not remain in the same state, for at one time they are generated and at another destroyed. This being so, if generation and destruction are to occur in the realm of lower bodies, it is necessary to posit some agent which is always in different states when it acts. He says that this agent is the body [the sun] which is moved in the oblique circle called the zodiac. For since this circle falls away on either side of the equinoctial circle, the body which is moved circularly through the zodiac must be at one time nearer and at another farther away; and by reason of its being near or far away it causes contraries. For we see that those things which are generated when the sun comes closer to the earth are destroyed when the sun recedes (for example, plants are born in the spring and wither away in the autumn); for both the sun and the other planets are moved in the circle of the zodiac. But the fixed stars are also said to be moved over the poles of the zodiac and not over the equinoctial poles, as Ptolemy proved. *[Almagest, VIII, 3]* And the coming to be and ceasing to be of everything which is generated and destroyed is caused by the motion of these stars, but more evidently by the motion of the sun.

2512. Therefore this mover which acts in different ways must be one that "acts in one way of itself," i.e., by its own power, inasmuch as it causes the diversity found in generation and destruction. And it must act "in another way in virtue of something else," i.e., by the power of some other agent, inasmuch as it causes eternal generation and destruction. Hence this second agent must act either "in virtue of some third agent," i.e., by the power of some other agent, "or of the first," i.e., by the power of the first agent, which always acts in the same way. And since it is not possible to assign some other agent by whose power this first agent brings about the eternal motion of things, it is therefore necessary according to this "that it act in the same way"; that is, that by its power it causes the eternal generation and destruction of things. For it—the first agent—which always acts in the same way, is the cause of that which acts in different ways. For that which acts in different ways acts eternally, and that which acts in the same way is the cause of the eternality of any motion. Hence it is the cause of the eternality of that which acts in different ways inasmuch as the latter acts eternally in this way; and it is also the cause of that which is produced by it, namely, eternal generation and destruction. From this it is also evident that the second agent, which acts in different ways, acts by the power "of the first agent," i.e., the first heaven or first orb, which always acts in the same way.

2513. Hence it is clear that the first agent, which always acts in the same way, is more powerful and nobler, because it is the cause of that "whose being is always to be the same," i.e., of eternality. But the cause of that whose being is to be different is another agent, which acts in different ways. And it is evident that both of these combined, i.e., both the first agent, which always acts in the same way, and the second agent, which acts in different ways, are the cause of that which both always is and is in different states, namely, the fact that generation and destruction are eternal.

2514. Again, he concludes from this that, if the motions of the heavens are such that eternal generation and destruction in the realm of lower bodies can be caused by them, it is not necessary to look for any other principles (such as the Ideas, which the Platonists posited, or love and hate, which Empedocles posited), because it is possible to account for the eternal generation and destruction of things in the above way.

2515. And if this way is not accepted, the untenable conclusions to which the first philosophers were led will follow, namely, that all things "will come from Night," i.e., from a simple privation, or "all things were together," or something comes from non-being.

2516. Therefore it is evident that, if the above-mentioned position is accepted, i.e., that eternal generation and destruction are caused by the eternal motion of the heavens, the foregoing untenable conclusions are eliminated. And it will follow that something is always being moved in an unceasing motion, which is circular motion. This becomes apparent not only by reasoning but from the effect itself and by perception. Hence, since the first heaven always causes motion by means of this motion, it must be eternal.

2517. **Therefore, there is** [8].

From what has been said above he next infers that there is an eternal unmoved mover. For since everything which is being moved is being moved by something else, as has been proved in the ***Physics***, *[254b6-256a4]* if both the heavens and their motion are eternal, there must be an eternal mover. But since three classes are found among movers and things moved: the lowest of which is something that is merely moved, the highest something that moves but is unmoved, and the intermediate something that both moves and is moved, we must assume that there is an eternal mover which is unmoved. For it has been proved in Book VIII of the ***Physics*** [256a4-256a20] that, since there cannot be an infinite number of movers and things moved, we must come to some first unmoved mover. For even if one might come to something that moves itself, it would again be necessary for the above reason to come to some unmoved mover, as has been proved in that work.

2518. Again, if the first mover is eternal and unmoved, it must not be a potential being (because any potential being is naturally fitted to be moved) but an independent substance whose essence is actuality.—This is the conclusion which he drew above (n. 2499). But it was necessary to raise this question, which was discussed among the ancients, in order that when it has been solved the course to be followed in reaching a first being whose substance is actuality will be made more evident.

LESSON 7
How the First Mover Causes Motion

ARISTOTLE'S TEXT Chapter 7: 1072a26–1072b14

1. Now the first mover causes motion as something intelligible and something appetible; for these alone cause motion without being moved. And what is first in the class of the appetible and in that of the intelligible is the same; for it is the apparent good which is the object of concupiscible appetite, and the real good which is the primary object of will. For we desire a thing because it seems good rather than consider it good because we desire it; for understanding is the principle of desire. And the intellect is moved by an intelligible object. **1072a26–30**

2. And one of the two columns of opposites is the intelligible in itself; and in this class primary substance is first, and in substance that which is simple and exists actually. However, one and simple are not the same; for one signifies a measure, and simple signifies a state. **1072a30–34**

3. But that which is good and that which is desirable in itself are in the same column of opposites; and that which is first in each class is always best, or analogous to the best. That the final cause belongs to the class of immovable things is shown by a process of division; for the final cause of a thing is either that which exists or that which does not. **1072a34–1072b3**

4. And it causes motion as something loved, whereas by that which is [first] moved other things are moved. Therefore, if a thing is moved, it is possible for it to be other than it is. Hence, local motion, which is the primary kind of motion, is also the actuality of that which is [first] moved; and in this respect the thing first moved can differ in place though not in substance. But since there is something which moves yet is itself immovable and exists actually, this can in no way be other than it is. For the primary kind of change is local motion, and of local motion the first is circular motion; and this is the motion which the first mover causes. Hence the first mover necessarily exists; and insofar as it is necessary it is good, and thus is a principle. For necessary has all of these meanings: that which seems to be done by force; that without which something does not fare well; and that which cannot be other than it is, but is absolutely necessary (416–22). It is on such a principle, then, that the heavens and the natural world depend. **1072b3–14**

COMMENTARY

2519. After having shown that there is an eternal, immaterial, immovable substance whose essence is actuality, the Philosopher now proceeds to investigate the attributes of this substance. In treating this he does three things. First [1], he considers the perfection of this substance. Second (Lesson 9), he asks whether it is one or many ("We must not"). Third (Lesson 11), he considers its operation ("The things which pertain").

In regard to the first he does two things. First, he shows the perfection of this substance. Second (Lesson 8, [6]), he proves that it is incorporeal ("And it has been shown").

In regard to the first he does two things. First, he shows its perfection. Second (Lesson 8, [5]), he rejects a contrary opinion ("And all those").

In regard to the first he does two things. First, he explains how the unmoved mover causes motion; and second [2], he infers from this what is comprised in its perfection ("And one of the two").

He accordingly says, first [1], that, since it has been shown that the first mover is unmoved, it must cause motion in the way in which the desirable and the intelligible do; for only these, the desirable and the intelligible, are found to cause motion without being moved.

2520. He proves this as follows. Motion is twofold: natural and voluntary, or according to appetite. Now that which causes motion by means of natural motion necessarily undergoes motion, since a natural mover is one that begets and alters things. For both heavy and light bodies are moved locally directly by their begetter. But that which begets and alters things directly must exist in different states. Hence it has also been pointed out above (n. 2510) that the cause of generation and destruction acts in different ways. Now in the case of voluntary and appetitive motion, will and appetite have the character of moved movers, as is evident in Book III of ***The Soul****. [433b15 ff.]* Hence it remains that only that which causes motion as something appetible is an unmoved mover.

2521. Now it is said that the first mover causes motion as something appetible because the motion of the heavens has this mover as its end or goal, for this motion is caused by some proximate mover which moves on account of the first unmoved mover in order that it may be assimilated in its causality to the first mover and bring to actuality whatever is virtually contained in it. For the motion of the heavens does not have the generation and destruction of lower bodies as its end, since an end or goal is nobler than the things ordained to it. Therefore the first mover causes motion as something appetible.

2522. But in our own case that which causes motion as a desirable good differs from that which causes motion as an intelligible good, though each causes motion as an unmoved mover. This is particularly evident in the case of an incontinent person; for according to his reason he is moved by an intelligible good, but according to his concupiscible power he is moved by something pleasant to the senses, which, while it seems to be good, is not good absolutely but only with some qualification.—However, this kind of difference cannot be found in the first intelligible and the first desirable good. But the first intelligible and the first desirable good must be the same. The reason is that a concupiscible good, which is not an intelligible good, is merely an apparent good; but the first good "must be an object of will," i.e., an object desired by intellectual appetite. For will belongs to the intellectual order and not merely to that of concupiscible appetite. And this is so because what is desired by the concupiscible power seems to be good because it is desired; for concupiscence perverts the judgment of reason insofar as something pleasant to sense seems to be good to reason. But what is desired by intellectual appetite is desired because it seems to be good in itself. For "understanding" as such, i.e., the act of intellection, which is moved in a way by an intelligible object, "is the principle of desire." Therefore it is evident that the object of concupiscible appetite is good only when it is desired through a dictate of reason. Hence it cannot be the first good, but only that which, because it is good, moves desire and is at once both appetible and intelligible.

2523. **And one of the two** [2].

Since he has proved that the first mover is both intelligible and appetible, it now remains to show from this how perfection is found in the first mover. In regard to this he does three things. First [2], he shows the perfection of the first mover in itself by considering the formal character of the intelligible and the appetible; second [4], in relation to the first sphere ("And it causes motion"); and third (Lesson 8), in relation to the thing that desires and understands it ("And its course of life").

In treating the first part he does two things. First, he proves that the first mover is perfect on the ground that it is intelligible; and second [3], on the ground that it is appetible ("But that which is good").

He says, first [2], that, just as movers and things moved are related to one another, so also are intelligible things. He calls this latter relationship an intelligible column of opposites because one intelligible is the first principle for understanding another, just as one mover is also the cause of the motion of another.

2524. Therefore, just as it has been shown (n. 2518) from the series of movers and things moved that the first mover is a simple substance and an actuality, in a similar fashion the same thing is found to be true from the series of intelligible things. For it is evident that substance is the first of intelligible things, because we understand accidents only by means of substance, through which they are defined; and among substances a simple intelligible substance is prior to a composite one; for simple things are included in the concept of composite things. And of the simple entities contained in the class of substance the actually intelligible are prior to the potentially intelligible; for potentiality is defined by means of actuality. It follows, then, that the first intelligible entity is a simple substance which is an actuality.

2525. And lest he should seem to be adopting the opinion of Plato, who claimed that the first principle of things is the intelligible one-in-itself, he therefore explains the difference between being one and being simple. He says that *one* and *simple* do not signify the same thing, but one signifies a measure, as has been pointed out in Book X (nn. 1950–52), and simple signifies that state whereby something is such as not to be composed of many things.

2526. **But that which is good** [3].

Then he proves the same point from the formal character of the appetible. He says that that which is good and that which is desirable in itself belong to the same class. For that which is prior in the class of intelligible things is also a greater good in the class of appetible things, or is something analogous to it. He says this because intelligible things are actual insofar as they exist in the intellect, whereas appetible things are actual insofar as they exist in reality; for good and evil are in things, as has been pointed out in Book VI (n. 1240).

2527. Hence, just as the concept of intelligible substance is prior to that of intelligible accidents, the same relationship holds for the goods which correspond proportionally to these concepts. Therefore the greatest good will be a simple substance, which is an actuality, because it is the first of intelligible things. It is evident, then, that the first mover is identical with the first intelligible and the first appetible good, which is the greatest good.

2528. But since what is appetible and what is good have the character of an end or goal, and there does not seem to be an end in the realm of immovable things, as has been explained in the dialectical discussions in Book III (nn. 374–75), he therefore removes this difficulty. He says that the division in which the various senses of end or goal are distinguished shows that a final cause can be found in a way in the realm of immovable things. Now one thing can be the goal of another in two ways: first, as something having prior existence, as the center of the world is said to be a goal which is prior to the motion of heavy bodies; and nothing prevents a goal of this kind from existing in the realm of immovable things. For a thing can tend by its motion to participate in some degree in something immovable; and the first mover can be a goal in this way. Second, one thing is said to be the goal of another, not as something that exists actually, but only as existing in the intention of the agent by whose activity it is produced, as health is the goal of the activity of the medical art. An end or goal of this kind does not exist in the realm of immovable things.

2529. **And it causes motion** [4].

He now relates the first unmoved mover to the first sphere. He says that, since the first unmoved mover causes motion as something loved, there must be something which is first moved by it, through which it moves other things. This is the first heaven. Therefore, since we suppose motion to be eternal, the first sphere must be moved eternally, and it in turn must move other things. And it is better to speak of it as something loved rather than as something desired, since there is desire only of something that is not yet possessed, but there is love even of something that is possessed.

2530. And if it must be moved eternally, it must be incapable of being other than it is but must always remain substantially the same. Hence the primary kind of motion, by which "the first sphere" is moved, necessarily "is local motion," i.e., motion as regards place; because that which is moved "according to the other kinds of motion," i.e., generation and destruction, increase and decrease, and alteration, must differ as regards something intrinsic, namely, substance, quantity or quality. But that which is moved with local motion differs as regards place, which is extrinsic to the thing in place, but not as regards substance or any intrinsic disposition of substance.

2531. Therefore, since the first sphere differs as regards place but not as regards substance, the first mover, which is immovable and always actual, can in no way be other than it is, because it cannot be moved. For if it were moved, it would be moved especially with the primary kind of motion, which is local motion, of which the first type is circular. But it is not moved with this motion, since it moves other things with this motion. For the first mover is not moved with that kind of motion by which it imparts motion, just as the first cause of alteration is not itself altered. Hence it is not moved circularly, and so cannot be moved in any way. Therefore it cannot be other than it is; and thus it follows that the primary kind of motion exists in that which is moved of necessity; for that is necessary which cannot not be. But it is not necessary in the sense in which things forced are necessary, but its necessity consists in its good state. And the thing which moves it is a principle of motion as an object of desire, or a goal.

2532. That its necessity is such becomes evident from the different meanings of the term *necessary*, for it is used in three senses. First it means that which happens by force, i.e., what cannot fail to happen because of the power exerted by the thing applying force.

Second, it means that without which a thing does not fare well—either that without which a goal cannot be attained at all (as food is necessary for the life of an animal), or that without which something is not in a perfect state (as a horse is necessary for a journey in the sense that it is not easy to make a journey without one). Third, it means that which cannot be other than it is, but is necessary absolutely and essentially.

2533. Therefore, when it is said that an orb is moved of necessity, such necessity cannot be called necessity of force; for in imperishable things there is not found anything that is outside their nature, but in the case of things which are forced what occurs is not natural. Similarly such necessity cannot be absolute necessity, because the first thing which is moved moves itself, as is proved in Book VIII of the ***Physics***,*[256b14 ff.]* and what moves itself has within itself the power to move or not move. It follows, then, that the necessity of the first motion is necessity from the end, inasmuch as there cannot be a fitting order to the end unless such motion is eternal.

2534. Hence it is on this principle, i.e., the first mover viewed as an end, that the heavens depend both for the eternality of their substance and the eternality of their motion. Consequently the whole of nature depends on such a principle, because all natural things depend on the heavens and on such motion as they possess.

2535. It should also be noted that Aristotle says here that the necessity of the first motion is not absolute necessity but necessity from the end, and the end is the principle which he later calls God inasmuch as things are assimilated to God through motion. Now assimilation to a being that wills and understands (as he shows God to be) is in the line of will and understanding, just as things made by art are assimilated to the artist inasmuch as his will is fulfilled in them. This being so, it follows that the necessity of the first motion is totally subject to the will of God.

LESSON 8
The Perfection of the First Substance

ARISTOTLE'S TEXT Chapter 7: 1072b14–1073a13

1. *And its course of life is like the best which we enjoy for a short time; for it is always in that state, though this is impossible for us.* **1072b14–16**

2. *For its operation is also pleasure. This is why being awake, sensing and understanding are most pleasant, and hopes and memories are pleasant because of them. Now understanding in itself has to do with what is best in itself, and the highest type of understanding has to do with what is best in the highest degree.* **1072b16–19**

3. *And an intellect understands itself insofar as it takes on its intelligible object; for it becomes intelligible by attaining and understanding its object, so that an intellect and its intelligible object are the same. For that which is receptive of something intelligible and of substance is an intellect; and it is actual when it possesses this. Hence it is the latter rather than the former state which seems to constitute the divine state of intellect; and its act of understanding is the most pleasant and best. Therefore, if God is in that pleasurable state in which we sometimes are, this is wondrous; and if He is in that state in a higher degree, this is even more wondrous; and He is in that state.* **1072b19–26**

4. *Life, then, also belongs to Him; for intellectual activity is life, and God is that activity; and the essential activity of God is the life which is best and eternal. And we say that God is an animal, eternal and most excellent. Hence life and continuous and eternal duration belong to God; for this is what God is.* **1072b26–30**

5. *And all those, such as the Pythagoreans and Speusippus, who think that the greatest good and excellence are not found in the [first] principle (because they are of the opinion that, while the principles of plants and animals are causes, it is in the things that come from these that goodness and perfection are found) are in error. For seed comes from other things which are prior and perfect, and it is not seed that is first but the perfect being. For example, one might say that the man is prior to the seed, not the man who comes from the seed, but another man from whom the seed comes. Therefore it is evident from what has been said that there is a substance which is eternal and immovable and separate from sensible things.* **1072b30–1073a5**

6. *And it has been shown that this substance can have no magnitude, but is without parts and indivisible; for it causes motion for an infinite time, and nothing finite has an infinite power. And since every magnitude is either finite or infinite, this substance cannot have finite magnitude; and it cannot have infinite magnitude, because there is no infinite magnitude at all.* **1073a5–11**

7. *It has also been shown (1066) that it lacks potentiality and is unalterable; for all the other kinds of motion are subsequent to local motion. It is clear, then, that these things are of this sort.* **1073a11–13**

COMMENTARY

2536. Here the Philosopher relates the first being, which causes motion as something intelligible and something desirable, to that which understands and desires it. For if the first mover causes motion inasmuch as it is the first thing understood and desired, the first thing moved by it must understand and desire it. This is true according to the opinion of Aristotle inasmuch as he considered a heaven to be animated by a soul which understands and desires.

In regard to this he does three things. First [1], he shows that pleasure naturally belongs to the soul of a heaven, which desires and understands, as a result of its understanding and desiring the first mover. He says that "its course of life," i.e., the pleasurable state of the thing understanding and desiring the first intelligible being, is like the best which we can enjoy for a short time. For that which understands and desires this being is always in such a pleasurable state, though this is impossible for us, i.e., that we should always be in that state which is pleasant and best.

2537. **For its operation** [2].

Then he proves his statement. Pleasure attends the activity of the thing that understands and desires the first principle, for pleasure follows upon the operation connatural to anything that understands and desires, as is evident in Book X of the *Ethics*. [1174b15 ff.] A sign of this is that pleasure is greatest when a person is awake and actually sensing and understanding. For intellect and sense in actual use are to intellect and sense in potential use as being awake is to being asleep.—That these states are the most pleasant is clear from the fact that other states are pleasant only because of these; for hope and memory are pleasant inasmuch as they bring past or future pleasant activities into consciousness as present.

2538. Hence, since pleasure consists in the actual use of intellect and sense, it is evident "that understanding," i.e., the activity of the intellect as such, is concerned with what is best in itself; for an intelligible good surpasses a sensible good just as an unchangeable and universal good surpasses a changeable and particular good. It also follows that the pleasure experienced in intellectual activity is of a higher kind than that experienced in sensory activity. Hence the best and most perfect intellectual activity is concerned with what is best in the highest degree, so that the greatest pleasure follows. Therefore it is evident that the greatest pleasure is experienced in those intellectual activities by which the first mover is understood, who is also the first intelligible object.

2539. **And an intellect** [3].

Then he shows that the act of understanding and the pleasure found in the first intelligible object are even more perfect than those found in the thing that understands and desires it. He says that it is characteristic of an intellect to understand itself inasmuch as it takes on or conceives within itself some intelligible object; for an intellect becomes intelligible by reason of the fact that it apprehends something intelligible. Hence, since the intellect becomes intelligible by conceiving some intelligible object, it follows that the intellect and its intelligible object are the same.

2540. He explains how an intellect attains its intelligible object. For an intellect is related to an intelligible object as potentiality is to actuality, and as something perfectible to its perfection. And just as something perfectible is receptive of a perfection, so too an intellect is receptive of its intelligible object. Now its proper intelligible object is substance, since the object of the intellect is a quiddity. Hence he says that the intellect is receptive of something intelligible and of substance. And since each thing becomes actual inasmuch as it attains its own perfection, it follows that the intellect becomes actual inasmuch as it receives its intelligible object. Now to be intelligible is to be actual in the class of intelligible things. And since each thing is active to the extent that it is actual, it follows that the intellect becomes active or operative, i.e., understanding, to the extent that it attains its intelligible object.

2541. But it should be borne in mind that material substances are not actually intelligible but only potentially; and they become actually intelligible by reason of the fact that the likenesses of them which are gotten by way of the sensory powers are made immaterial by the agent intellect. And these likenesses are not substances but certain intelligible forms received into the possible intellect. But according to Plato the intelligible forms of material things are self-subsistent entities. Hence he claimed that our intellect becomes actually understanding by coming in contact with separate self-subsistent forms of this kind. But in Aristotle's opinion the intelligible forms of material things are not substances which subsist of themselves.

2542. Yet there is an intelligible substance which subsists of itself, and it is of this that he is now speaking. For the first mover must be a substance which is both understanding and intelligible. Hence it follows that the relationship between the intellect of the first sphere and the first intelligible substance, which causes motion, is similar to the relationship which the Platonists posited between our intellect and the separate intelligible Forms, inasmuch as our intellect becomes actual by coming in contact with and participating in these Forms, as Plato himself says. Hence the intellect of the first sphere becomes actually understanding through some kind of contact with the first intelligible substance.

2543. Further, since the cause of some attribute of a thing has that attribute in a higher degree, it follows that anything that is divine and noble, such as understanding and taking pleasure, which is found in the intellect having the contact, is found in a much higher degree in the first intelligible object with which it is in contact. Hence its intellectual activity is most pleasant and best. But the first intelligible object of this kind is God. Therefore, since the pleasure which we experience in understanding is the highest, although we can enjoy it only for a short time, if God is always in that state in which we sometimes are, His happiness is wondrous. But if He is always in that state (which we enjoy for only a short time) in a higher degree, this is even more wondrous.

2544. **Life, then, also belongs** [4].

Third, since he has said that intellectual activity is proper to God, he shows how this applies to Him. He says that God is life itself, and he proves this as follows. "Intellectual activity," i.e., understanding, is a kind of life; and it is the most perfect kind of life that there is. For according to what has been shown, actuality is more perfect than potentiality; and therefore an intellect which is actually understanding leads a more perfect life than one which is potentially understanding, just as being awake is more perfect than being asleep. But the first being, God, is actuality itself; for His intellect is His intellectual activity; otherwise He would be related to His intellectual activity as potentiality to actuality. Moreover, it has been shown (n. 2517) that His substance is actuality. Thus it follows that the very substance of God is life, and that His actuality is His life, and that it is the life which is best and eternal and subsists of itself. This is why common opinion holds that God is an animal which is eternal and best; for around us life is clearly apparent only in animals, and therefore God is called an animal because life belongs to Him. Hence, from what has been said it is evident that life and continuous and eternal duration belong to God, because God is identical with His own eternal life; for He and His life are not different.

2545. **And all those** [5].

Then he rejects the opinion of those who attributed imperfection to the first principle. He says that the opinion of all those who claim that goodness and excellence are not found in the first principle are false. He cites as examples the Pythagoreans and Speusippus (n. 2644), who acted on the supposition that, while the principles of plants and animals are causes of goodness and perfection, goodness and perfection are not found in these principles but in the things produced from them. Thus seeds, which are imperfect principles of plants and animals, come from other individual things which are prior and perfect.

2546. He rejects this opinion by disposing of the view which influenced these thinkers. For it is not seed that is first absolutely, but the perfect being. Hence, if someone says that the man is prior to the seed, it is not the man who is said to be born from the seed in question, but a different man from whom the seed comes. For it has been proved above (nn. 2500–03) that actuality is prior absolutely to potentiality, though in one and the same subject potentiality is prior to actuality in the order of generation and of time.

2547. In view of the points established he terminates his discussion by concluding that it is evident that there is a substance which is eternal and unchangeable and separate from sensible things.

2548. **And it has been shown** [6].

Then he proceeds to examine certain points which still remain to be considered about the above-mentioned substance. First, he shows that it is incorporeal. He says that it has been proved in Book VIII of the ***Physics*** [266a26-266b6] that this kind of substance can have no magnitude but is without parts and indivisible.

2549. He briefly restates the proof, saying that a substance of this kind moves in infinite time, since the first mover is eternal, as he said above (n. 2547). And from this it follows that its power is infinite. For we see that the more powerful any inferior mover is, the more capable it is of acting for a longer time. But nothing finite can have an infinite power. Hence it follows that the above-mentioned substance is not finite in magnitude. Moreover, it cannot be infinite in magnitude because an infinite magnitude is impossible, as has been proved above (n. 2548). Therefore, since every magnitude is either finite or infinite, it follows that the above-mentioned substance lacks magnitude in every way.

2550. Moreover, the power of this substance is not said to be infinite in a privative sense, in the way that infinity pertains to quantity; but the term is used in a negative sense, i.e., inasmuch as it is not limited to some definite effect. It cannot be said of a heavenly body, however, that its power is infinite even though it may move inferior bodies in an infinite time, because it causes motion only by being moved, and thus its influence is from the first mover. Nor can it be said that the power of a heavenly body is infinite even though it has being in infinite time, because it has no active power of being but only the ability to receive. Hence its infinite duration points to the infinite power of an external principle. But in order to receive indestructible existence from an infinite power a heavenly body must not have any principle of destruction or any potentiality to non-existence.

2551. **It has also been shown** [7].

Second, since he has shown above (n. 2517) that the first mover is not moved with local motion, he next shows that it is not moved with the other kinds of motion. He says that it is also impossible for the first mover to be alterable, for it has been shown above (n. 2517) that it is not moved with local motion. But all other motions are subsequent to such motion, which pertains to place. Therefore, when the former is removed, so also must the latter be. Hence whatever is found to be moved with the other kinds of motion is moved with local motion.

2552. Last, he concludes that the things discussed above are evidently such as he has established them to be.

LESSON 9
The Number of Primary Movers

ARISTOTLE'S TEXT Chapter 8: 1073a14–1073b17

1. We must not neglect the question whether it is necessary to posit one such substance or more than one, and if the latter, how many; and we must also recall the lack of statements on this point by other philosophers, because they have said nothing about the number of these substances which can be clearly stated. The theory of Ideas makes no proper study of this problem; for the proponents of the Ideas say that the Ideas are numbers, and they speak of numbers sometimes as unlimited and sometimes as limited to the number ten. But as to the reason why there should be so many numbers, nothing is said apodictically. **1073a14–22**

2. However, we must discuss this question by beginning with what has already been laid down and established. For the first principle and primary being is both essentially and accidentally immovable, but it causes the primary motion, which is eternal and unique. And since that which is moved must be moved by something else, the first mover must be essentially immovable, and eternal motion must be caused by an eternal mover, and a single motion by a single thing. **1073a22–28**

3. Now we see that, besides the simple local motion which we say the first immovable substance causes, there are other local motions—those of the planets—which are eternal (for a body which is moved in a circle is eternal and never stands still, as has been proved in our treatises on nature). Each of these motions, then, must also be caused by a substance which is essentially immovable and eternal. For the nature of the stars is eternal, being a kind of substance; and that which causes motion is eternal and prior to that which is moved; and that which is prior to a substance must be a substance. Hence it is evident that there must be as many substances as there are motions of the stars, and that these substances are eternal in nature, essentially immovable, and without magnitude, for the reason given above. It is evident, then, that these movers are substances, and that one of these is first and another second according to the same order as the motions of the stars. **1073a28–1073b3**

4. But it is now necessary to discover the number of these motions from that branch of the mathematical sciences which is most akin to philosophy, namely, astronomy. For this science studies the kind of substance which is sensible but eternal, whereas the other mathematical sciences, such as the science of numbers and geometry, are not concerned with any kind of substance. That there are many motions belonging to the bodies which are moved is evident even to those who have given little consideration to the matter; for each of the wandering stars has more than one motion. As to the number of these motions, in order that we may have some definite number in mind for the purpose of understanding this point, let us now state what some of the mathematicians say; but for the rest, this we must investigate partly for ourselves and partly accept the opinion of other investigators. And if anyone in treating this subject should be found to form a different opinion from the one stated here, we must respect both views but accept the more certain. **1073b3–17**

COMMENTARY

2553. Having shown what it is that constitutes the perfection of an immaterial substance, here the Philosopher asks whether this substance is one or many; and in regard to this he does three things. First [1], he indicates that it is necessary to treat this question because nothing definite has been said about it by other thinkers. Second [2], he shows that there are many such substances ("However, we must discuss"). Third [4], he shows how many there are ("But it is now necessary").

He accordingly says, first [1], that we must not neglect the question whether it is necessary to posit only one such substance which is eternal and immaterial or many; and if the latter, how many. But we must also "recall the lack of statements on this point by other philosophers," i.e., the fact that others have said nothing that is clear and evident about the number of these substances.

2554. This is made clear as follows. Those who made a special claim for immaterial substances were the proponents of the Ideas. Now the opinion about the nature of the Ideas contains no theory about any definite number, because there are assumed to be Ideas of all things which share in a common name. But since those who posited Ideas said that they are numbers, it would seem that we could get some notion about how many numbers there are. However, they did not always say the same thing on this point. Sometimes they said that the species of numbers are unlimited. This is true of numbers by reason of their proper nature, because whenever a unit is added it always produces a different species of number. Hence, since in the case of numbers infinite additions can be made, the species of numbers may increase to infinity. At other times they said that the species of numbers are limited to the number ten. This refers to the naming of numbers, for the names of all numbers after ten seem to repeat in some way the name of a primary number. But they cannot show by any definite argument why there should be just so many numbers, i.e., ten, and not more or fewer. Nor is this to be wondered at, since this limitation of the species of numbers is not a real limitation but a nominal one. Other thinkers offer the argument that the number ten is generated from the progression of numbers up to the number four, which is the first square number. For one plus two equals three; and when three is added to this, the number six results; and when four is added to this, the number ten results.

2555. **However, we must discuss** [2].

He now shows that there must be many substances of this kind; and in regard to this he does two things. First, he returns to the points established about the first principle. He says that, since other thinkers have said nothing demonstrative about the number of separate substances, we must discuss this question by beginning with what has already been laid down and established. For it has been said above that, while the first principle of beings is one which is neither essentially nor accidentally moved, it still causes a single motion, which is the first and eternal motion. For since everything which is moved must be moved by something else, as has been shown in Book VIII of the ***Physics***, *[254b6 ff.]* the first mover must be altogether immovable, and eternal motion must be caused by an eternal mover, and a single motion by a single mover.

2556. **Now we see** [3].

Second, he shows that after the first principle it is necessary to posit a number of eternal substances. He says that besides the simple local motion of the universe (one that lasts a day—during which the entire heavens revolve—and is uniform and the most simple), which the first immovable substance causes, we observe the local motions of the planets, which are also eternal; because the circular body, i.e., a heaven, is also eternal. Therefore the eternity of motion is not destroyed as a result of the destruction of a movable being. And "it never stands still," i.e., it is incapable of coming to rest. Hence this motion is not broken by rest. These points have been proved in the philosophy of nature, both in the ***Physics*** [VIII, 8 & 9] as well as in ***The Heavens***.[I, 2; II, 3-8] Each of these motions, then, must be caused by a mover which is essentially unmoved and an eternal substance.

2557. Now this must be so because the stars are eternal and are substances. Hence their mover must also be eternal and a substance; for a mover is prior to the thing moved, and that which is prior to a substance must be a substance. It is clear, then, that there must be as many substances as there are motions of the stars, and that these substances must be by nature eternal and essentially immovable and without magnitude, for the reason given above (nn. 2548–50), i.e., because they move in infinite time and therefore have infinite power. Hence it is evident that there are immaterial substances which are as numerous as the motions of the stars, and that they also have the same order as the motions of the stars.

2558. Now it must be borne in mind that after the first motion Aristotle computes only the motions of the planets, because at his time the motion of the fixed stars had not been detected. Hence he thought that the eighth sphere, in which the fixed stars are located, was the first one to be moved, and that its mover was the first principle. But later on astronomers perceived that the motion of the fixed stars was in an opposite direction to the first motion, so that above the sphere of the fixed stars it was necessary to posit another sphere, which surrounds the entire heavens and turns the whole in its daily motion. This is the first sphere, which is moved by the first mover of which Aristotle spoke.

2559. But Avicenna claimed that the first sphere is moved directly, not by the first principle, but by an intelligence which is caused by the first principle. For since the first mover is absolutely one, Avicenna thought that only one thing could be caused by it; and this is the first intelligence, in which a plurality of potentiality and actuality is found inasmuch as it derives being from the first principle. For it is related to that on which it depends for its existence as something potential to something actual. Hence the first intelligence can immediately cause many things; for inasmuch as it understands itself as having some potentiality, it causes the substance of the orb which it moves, but insofar as it understands itself as possessing actual existence from some other cause, it causes the soul of its orb. Again, inasmuch as it understands its own principle, it causes the next intelligence, which moves a lower orb, and so on down to the sphere of the moon.

2560. But this is not necessary. For an efficient cause in the realm of superior substances does not act like an efficient cause in the realm of material things, in the sense that a single effect is produced by a single cause, because among higher substances cause and thing caused have intelligible existence. Hence insofar as many things can be understood by a single superior substance, many effects can be produced by a single superior substance. And it seems quite fitting that the first motion of corporeal things, on which all other motions depend, should have as its cause the principle of immaterial substances, so that there should be some connection and order between sensible and intelligible things. A problem can arise, however, regarding the Philosopher's statement that the order of separate substances corresponds to the order of motions and bodies moved. For of all the planets the sun is the largest in size, and its effect is more evident in lower bodies; and even the motions of the other planets are arranged in accordance with the motion of the sun, and in a sense are subsequent to it. Hence it seems that the substance which moves the sun is nobler than the substances which move the other planets, even though the sun is not located above the other planets. But since among bodies one which contains is more formal, and is thereby nobler and more perfect, and is related to a contained body as a whole to a part, as is said in Book IV of the ***Physics;*** [211a30] and since the sphere of a superior planet contains that of an inferior planet, therefore a superior planet, to which its whole sphere is subordinated, must have a higher and more universal power than an inferior planet, and must produce more lasting effects because it is nearer to the first sphere, which by its motion causes the eternality of things, as has been pointed out above (1065:C 2510). And this is the reason, as Ptolemy says in the ***Quadripartitum***, why the effects of Saturn correspond to universal places and times, and those of Jupiter to years, and those of Mars, the sun, Venus and Mercury to months, and those of the moon to days.

2561. This is also the reason why the effects of the planets appear in lower bodies in accordance with the order among the planets. For the first three highest planets seem to be directed to effects which pertain to the existence of a thing taken in itself; for the very stability of a thing's act of being is attributed to Saturn, and its perfection and state of well-being to Jupiter, and the power by which it protects itself from what is harmful and drives it away, to Mars. The other three planets seem to have as their proper effects the motion of a being. The sun is a universal principle of motion, and for this reason its operation is most evident in the case of lower motions. For Venus seems to have as its proper effect a more limited one, namely, the process of generation, by which a thing attains its form, and one to which all the other motions among lower bodies are directed. Mercury seems to have as its proper effect the multiplication of things, i.e., the distinction of individuals in the same species; and for this reason it has various motions. It is also mixed with the natures of all the planets, as the astronomers say. The changing of matter and the disposing of it to receive all celestial impressions belongs properly to the moon; and for this reason it seems that it is the planet which transmits celestial impressions and applies them to inferior matter.

2562. Hence the higher a celestial body, the more universal, lasting, and powerful its effect. And since the celestial bodies are the instruments, so to speak, of the separate substances which cause motion, it follows that a substance which moves a higher orb has a more universal knowledge and power, and must therefore be nobler.

2563. **But it is now necessary** [4].

Then he investigates the number of these substances; and this is divided into two parts. In the first part [4] he first investigates the number of celestial motions; and in the second (Lesson 10, [3]), he infers from this the number of substances which cause motion ("Hence it is reasonable").

In regard to the first he does two things. First, he indicates the source from which we must derive the number of celestial motions. Second (Lesson 10, [1]), he gives the different opinions about this ("Now Eudoxus").

He says, first (1081), that we must use the science of astronomy in studying the number of revolutions or celestial motions, which is a subject that belongs particularly to this branch of the mathematical sciences. For of these sciences only astronomy speculates about sensible and eternal substances, i.e., celestial bodies. But the other mathematical sciences do not consider any substance, as is clear in the case of arithmetic, which treats of numbers, and in the case of geometry, which treats of continuous quantity. Number and continuous quantity are accidents.

2564. That there are many motions belonging to the bodies which move about in the heavens, i.e., the planets, is evident even to those who have little acquaintance with the science of astronomy; for "each of the wandering stars," i.e., the planets, is moved by several motions and not just by one. Now the planets are called "wandering stars," not because their motions are irregular, but because they do not always maintain the same pattern and position in relation to the other stars, as these do among themselves and for this reason are called "fixed."

2565. That there are many motions of stars of this kind is detected in three ways. There is one motion which is perceived by plain sight. There is another which is perceived only by instruments and calculation; and of these motions, some are grasped after a very long period of time, and others after a short one. There is also a third motion, which is demonstrated by reason; for the motion of the wandering stars is found at one time to be more rapid and at another slower; and sometimes a planet seems to be moving forward, and sometimes backward. And because this cannot be in keeping with the nature of a celestial body, whose motion ought to be regular in all respects, it has been necessary to posit different motions by which this irregularity might be reduced to a fitting order.

2566. As to the number of planetary motions, let us now state what the mathematicians say about this, so that with this in mind we may conceive some definite number. But as to the other things which have not been stated, we must either investigate these for ourselves or in this matter accept the opinion of those who do investigate the problem. The same thing applies if some view should appear later on in addition to those which are now stated by men who treat this kind of problem. And since in choosing or rejecting opinions of this kind a person should not be influenced either by a liking or dislike for the one introducing the opinion, but rather by the certainty of truth, he therefore says that we must respect both parties, namely, those whose opinion we follow, and those whose opinion we reject. For both have diligently sought the truth and have aided us in this matter. Yet we must "be persuaded by the more certain," i.e., we must follow the opinion of those who have attained the truth with greater certitude.

LESSON 10
The Number of Unmoved Movers

ARISTOTLE'S TEXT Chapter 8: 1073b17–1074b14

1. *Now Eudoxus claimed that the motion both of the sun and of the moon involves for each three spheres. The first of these is the sphere of the stars whose positions remain unchanged; the second, the one which passes through the middle of the zodiac; and the third, the one which moves obliquely in the latitude of the animals in the zodiac. But the circle in which the moon is moved is inclined at a greater angle than that in which the sun is moved. He also claimed that the motion of the wandering stars involves four spheres for each. The first and second of these are the same as those mentioned above. The sphere of the fixed stars is the one which imparts motion to all of the spheres, and the sphere which is situated below this and moves through the middle of the zodiac is common to all of the planets. The third sphere for each of the planets has its poles in the circle which passes through the middle signs of the zodiac; and the motion of the fourth sphere is in a circle which is inclined at a greater angle to the middle of this sphere; and while the poles of the third sphere are peculiar to each of the other planets, those of Venus and of Mercury are the same.* **1073b17–32**

2. *And Callippus assumed the position of the spheres to be the same as Eudoxus did, i.e., as regards the arrangement of their distances, and he gave the same number of spheres to Jupiter and to Saturn as Eudoxus did. But he thought that two spheres should be added both to the sun and to the moon if appearances are to be saved. And to each of the other planets he added one sphere. However, if all spheres taken together are to account for appearances, there must be additional spheres for each of the other planets, one less in number than those mentioned above, which revolve the planets and always restore to the same place the first sphere of the star which is next in order below. For only in this way can all the spheres account for the motion of the planets. Therefore, since, as regards the spheres in which the planets themselves are carried along, some are eight in number and others twenty-five in number, and of these only those in which the lowest planet is carried along do not need to be revolved, then the spheres which revolve the first two planets will be six in number, and those which revolve the last four will be sixteen in number. The total number of spheres, then, both those which carry the planets along and those which revolve them, will be fifty-five. And if one has not added to the moon and to the sun the motions which we have mentioned, the total number of spheres will be forty-seven. Let the number of the spheres, then, be so many.* **1073b32–1074a15**

3. *Hence it is reasonable to suppose that there are as many substances and immovable principles and perceptible principles. Therefore the statement of necessity is to be left to more powerful thinkers.* **1074a15–17**

4. *However, if there can be no celestial motion which is not related to the motion of a star, and further if every nature and substance which is unchangeable and has in itself reached the highest good must be thought to be an end, there will be no other nature besides these; but this must be the number of substances. For if there were others, they would cause motion as being ends of local motion.* **1074a17–23**

5. *But there cannot be other motions besides those mentioned. And it is reasonable to suppose this from the bodies that are moved. For if everything which moves exists by nature for the sake of that which is moved, and all motion is the motion of something moved, no motion will exist for itself or for the sake of another motion, but all motions will exist for the sake of the stars. For if one motion should exist for the sake of another, the latter must also exist for the sake of another. Hence, since an infinite regress is impossible, the end of every motion must be one of the divine bodies which move about in the heavens.* **1074a23–31**

6. And it is evident that there is only one heaven. For if there were many heavens, as there are many men, the principle of each would be one in species but many in number. But all things which are many in number have matter; for many individuals have one and the same intelligible structure, for example, man, whereas Socrates is one; but the primary quiddity has no matter, for it is complete reality. Therefore the first mover, which is immovable, is one both in its intelligible structure and in number; and therefore what is moved eternally and continuously is only one. Hence there is only one heaven. **1074a31–38**

7. Now traditions have been handed down from our predecessors and the ancient thinkers, and left to posterity in the form of a myth, that these heavenly bodies are gods, and that the divine encompasses the whole of nature. But the rest of the traditions have been added later in the form of a myth for the persuasion of the multitude, the general welfare, and the passing of laws. For they say that the gods have human form and are similar to some of the other animals; and they add other statements which follow upon these and are similar to the ones mentioned. Now if anyone will separate these statements and accept only the first, that they thought the first substances to be gods, this will be considered to be a divine statement. And though every art and every philosophy has often been discovered and again lost, the opinions of these early thinkers have been preserved as relics to the present day. Therefore the opinions of our forefathers and those which have come down to us from the first thinkers are evident only to this extent. **10734a38–1074b14**

COMMENTARY

2567. Aristotle states the opinions which the astronomers of his time held about the number of planetary motions. First [1], he gives the opinion of Eudoxus; and second [2], that of Callippus ("And Callippus").

Now in regard to the first opinion it must be understood that Plato, in attributing unfailing circularity and order to the celestial motions, made mathematical hypotheses by which the apparent irregular motions of the planets can be explained; for he claimed that the motions of the planets are circular and arranged in an orderly way. And the Pythagoreans, with a view to putting into due order the irregularity which appears in the planetary motions on account of their standing still and moving backwards, and their rapidity and slowness, and their apparent differences in size, claimed that the motions of the planets involve eccentric spheres and small circles which they called epicycles; and Ptolemy also subscribes to this view.

2568. However, something contrary to the points demonstrated in the philosophy of nature seems to follow from this hypothesis; for not every motion will be either towards or away from or around the center of the world. Furthermore it follows that a sphere containing an eccentric sphere either is not of equal density, or there is a vacuum between one sphere and another, or there is some body besides the substance of the spheres that lies between them which will not be a circular body and will have no motion of its own.

2569. Further, from the hypothesis of epicycles it follows either that the sphere by which the epicycle is moved is not whole and continuous, or that it is divisible, expansible and compressible in the way in which air is divided, expanded and compressed when a body is moved. It also follows that the body itself of a star is moved by itself and not merely by the motion of an orb; and that from the motion of the celestial bodies there will arise the sound about which the Pythagoreans agreed.

2570. Yet all conclusions of this kind are contrary to the truths established in the philosophy of nature. Therefore Eudoxus, seeing this and seeking to avoid it, claimed that for each planet in the world there are many concentric spheres, each of which has its proper motion, and that as a result of all of these motions the observable motion of the planets is accounted for. Hence Eudoxus held that the motion of the sun as well as that of the moon involves three spheres.

2571. For the first motion of the sun as well as that of the moon, which is the daily motion, is that by which they are moved from east to west; and he calls this motion "that of the stars whose positions remain unchanged," i.e., of the stars which do not wander, namely, the fixed stars; for, as was said above (n. 2558), since the motion of the fixed stars, which is from west to east, was not yet discovered to be contrary to the first motion, it was thought that the daily motion was proper to the eighth sphere, which is the sphere of the fixed stars. It was not thought, however, that the first sphere alone might be sufficient to move all the spheres of the planets by a daily motion, as Ptolemy assumed; but he thought that each planet had its own sphere which would move it by a daily motion. Therefore with a view to explaining this motion he posited a first sphere for both the sun and the moon.

2572. He also posited a second sphere to account for the motion of the sun and the moon. This passes through the middle of the zodiac with what is called "longitudinal motion," according to which both the sun and the moon are moved from west to east in an opposite direction to the motion of the firmament.

2573. He posited a third sphere to account for the oblique motion across the latitude of the animals symbolized in the zodiac, inasmuch as a planet sometimes seems to be farther south and sometimes farther north of the middle line of the zodiac. But this motion is more apparent and has a broader spread in the case of the moon than in that of the sun. Hence he adds that the motion by which the moon is carried along is inclined at a greater angle than the sun's motion. And Ptolemy attributed latitudinal motion to the moon but not to the sun. Hence Eudoxus posited a third motion, as Simplicius says, because he thought that the sun also deviated from the middle line of the zodiac towards the two poles; and he made this assumption because the sun does not always rise in the same place during the summer solstice and during the winter solstice. But if it returned in latitude and in longitude at the same time by means of the declination of the great circle [i.e., the ecliptic] along which the sun travels, one sphere would suffice for this. Since this is not the case, however, but it passes through its course in longitude at one time and returns in latitude at another time, for this reason it was necessary to posit a third sphere. And he claimed that this third sphere of the sun is moved in the same direction as the second sphere, but about a different axis and on different poles. He also claimed that this third sphere of the moon is moved in the same direction as the first sphere. But in each case he claimed that the motion of this third sphere was slower than that of the second.

2574. And he claimed that the motion of each of the other five planets involves four spheres, with the first and second sphere of each planet having the same function as the first and second sphere of the sun and of the moon; because the first motion, which he assumed to be that of the fixed stars, and the second motion, which passes in longitude through the middle line of the zodiac, appear to be common to all the planets.

2575. Next, he posited a third sphere for each of the planets in order to account for their latitudinal motion, and he assumed that the poles about which it is revolved were located in the middle line of the zodiac. But since he claimed that all spheres are concentric, it would follow from this that the zodiac would pass through the poles of the great circle of the third sphere, and it would follow in the opposite way that the great circle of the third sphere would pass through the poles of the zodiac. Hence it would follow that the motion of the third sphere would carry a planet right up to the poles of the zodiac, which is never seen to occur.

2576. Therefore he had to posit a fourth sphere, which is the one that would carry the planet, and it would revolve in an opposite direction to the third sphere, namely, from east to west, in equal time, so as to prevent the planet from being diverted farther in latitude from the zodiac. This is what Aristotle means when he says that Eudoxus claimed that the fourth motion of the star is in a circle inclined at an angle to the middle of the third sphere, i.e., to its great circle.

2577. Therefore, if he posited four spheres for each of the five planets, it follows that there would be twenty spheres for these five planets. And if the three spheres of the sun and the three spheres of the moon are added to this number, there will be twenty-six spheres in all, granted that the body of each planet is understood to be fastened to the last of its own spheres.

2578. **And Callippus assumed** [2].

Then he gives the opinion of Callippus about the number of spheres. Now Callippus, as Simplicius tells us, was associated with Aristotle at Athens when the discoveries of Eudoxus were corrected and supplemented by him. Hence Callippus maintained the same theory of the spheres as Eudoxus did; and he explained the positions of the spheres by the arrangement of their distances, because he gave to the planets and to their motions and spheres the same order as Eudoxus did.

2579. And he agreed with Eudoxus as to the number of spheres of Jupiter and Saturn, because he assigned four spheres to each of these; but Callippus thought that two spheres must be added both to the sun and to the moon, if one wants to adopt a theory about them which accords with their motions. He seems to have added these two spheres in order to account for the rapidity and slowness which appears in their motions. The sun would then have five spheres, and the moon likewise would have five. He also added one sphere to each of the remaining planets—Mars, Venus and Mercury—thus giving each of them also five spheres. Perhaps they added this fifth sphere to account for the backward motion and the standing still which appear in these stars. These spheres are called deferent spheres, then, because the body of a planet is carried along by them.

2580. But in addition to these spheres they posited others, which they called revolving spheres. It would appear that they were led to posit these because the last sphere of a higher planet, for example, of Saturn, must share in the motion of all the higher planets, so that its motion gets away somewhat from that of the first sphere. Hence the first sphere of Jupiter, whose poles are fastened in some way to the highest sphere of Saturn, shared to some extent in the motion of the spheres of Saturn, and thus it was not moved uniformly by the daily motion like the first sphere of Saturn. Therefore it seemed necessary to posit another sphere which revolves this first sphere in order to restore the speed which it loses because of the higher planets. And by the same reasoning it was necessary to posit another sphere which revolves the second sphere of Jupiter, and a third sphere which revolves the third sphere of Jupiter. But it was unnecessary to posit another sphere which revolves the fourth sphere, because the motion of the first sphere, to which the star is fixed, must be composed of all the higher motions. Hence Jupiter has four deferent spheres and three revolving spheres. And in a similar way the other planets have as many revolving spheres, minus one, as deferent spheres.

2581. Therefore he says that, if all spheres taken together must account for and explain the apparent motion of the planets, it is necessary to posit, in addition to the deferent spheres mentioned above, other spheres, one less in number, which revolve and restore to the same place the first sphere of the star next in order below; for only in this way can the motions of the planets accord with all appearances.

2582. Therefore, since the deferent spheres which belong to Saturn and to Jupiter are eight in number, because each is assumed to have four spheres; and since those which belong to the other five planets are twenty-five in number, because each of these has five spheres, and of these only those at the end which carry and regulate the star are not revolved, it follows that the revolving spheres of the first two planets, i.e., of Saturn and Jupiter, are six in number, and that those of the last four planets are sixteen in number. But since after Saturn and Jupiter there are five other planets, he evidently omits one of them, i.e., either Mars or Mercury, so that his statement regarding the last four refers to the four lowest; or he omits the moon, so that he refers to the four planets immediately following. Now he omits this either by error, which sometimes happens in the case of numbers, or for some reason which is unknown to us; because the writings of Callippus are not extant, as Simplicius tells us. Hence the total number of deferent spheres and of revolving spheres together is fifty-five.

2583. But because the difficulty could arise whether it is necessary to add two spheres to the sun and two to the moon, as Callippus did, or whether only two spheres must be given to each, as Eudoxus claimed, he therefore says that, if one does not add two motions to the sun and two to the moon, as Callippus did, it follows that the total number of spheres will be forty-seven; for four deferent spheres would then be subtracted from the above number—two for the sun and two for the moon—and also the same number of revolving spheres; and when eight is subtracted from fifty-five, forty-seven remains.

2584. But it must be noted that, if above (n. 2582), when he said that the revolving spheres of the last four planets are sixteen in number, he omitted the moon, then if two deferent spheres are subtracted from the moon and two from the sun, four revolving spheres are not subtracted but only two, granted that the spheres of the moon do not have revolving spheres; and thus six spheres are subtracted from the first number of spheres, i.e., four deferent and two revolving spheres; and then it follows that the total number of spheres is forty-nine. Hence it seems that Aristotle did not wish to omit the moon but rather Mars, unless one says that Aristotle had forgotten that he had assigned revolving spheres to the moon, and that this is the reason the mistake was made, which does not seem likely.

2585. Last, he draws his conclusion that the number of spheres is that mentioned.

2586. **Hence it is reasonable** [3].

Then he infers the number of immaterial substances from the number of celestial motions; and in regard to this he does three things. First [3], he draws the conclusion at which he aims. Second [4], he rejects certain suppositions which could weaken the foregoing inference ("However, if there can be"). Third [7], he compares the points demonstrated about separate substance with the opinions of the ancients and with the common opinions held about these things during his own time ("Now traditions have").

He says, first [3], that, since the number of celestial spheres and the number of celestial motions is as has been stated, it is reasonable to suppose that there are the same number of immaterial substances and immobile principles, and even the same number of "perceptible principles," i.e., celestial bodies. He uses the term *reasonable* in order to imply that this conclusion is a probable one and not one that is necessary. Hence he adds that he is leaving the necessity of this to those who are stronger and more capable of discovering it than he is.

2587. **However, if there can be** [4].

Here the Philosopher rejects those suppositions by which the conclusion given above could be weakened; and there are three of these. The first is that one could say that there are certain separate substances to which no celestial motion corresponds.

2588. In order to reject this he says that, if there can be no celestial motions which are not connected with the motion of some star, and again if every immutable substance which has reached "in itself the highest good," i.e., which has reached its own perfection without motion, must be considered an end of some motion, there will be no immutable and immaterial nature besides those substances which are the ends of celestial motions; but the number of separate substances will correspond necessarily to the number of celestial motions.

2589. Yet the first assumption is not necessary, namely, that every immaterial and immutable substance is the end of some celestial motion. For it can be said that there are separate substances too high to be proportioned to the celestial motions as their ends. And this is not an absurd supposition. For immaterial substances do not exist for the sake of corporeal things, but rather the other way around.

2590. **But there cannot be** [5].

Then he rejects the second supposition which could weaken the inference mentioned above. For one could say that there are many more motions in the heavens than have been counted, but that these cannot be perceived because they produce no diversity in the motion of one of the celestial bodies which are perceived by the sense of sight and are called stars.

2591. And in order to reject this he had already equivalently said that there can be no celestial motion which is not connected with the motion of some star. His words here are that there cannot be other motions in the heavens besides those which produce the diversity in the motions of the stars, whether they be the motions mentioned or others, either the same in number or more or fewer.

2592. This can be taken as a probable conclusion from the bodies which are moved; for if every mover exists for the sake of something moved, and every motion belongs to something which is moved, there can be no motion which exists for itself or merely for the sake of another motion, but all motions must exist for the sake of the stars. For otherwise, if one motion exists for the sake of another, then for the same reason this motion also must exist for the sake of another. Now since an infinite regress is impossible, it follows that the end of every motion is one of the celestial bodies which are moved, as the stars. Hence there cannot be any celestial motion as a result of which some diversity in a star cannot be perceived.

2593. **And it is evident** [6].

Then he rejects a third supposition by which the above inference could be weakened. For someone might say that there are many worlds, and that in each of these there are as many spheres and motions as there are in this world, or even more, and thus it is necessary to posit many immaterial substances.

2594. He rejects this position by saying that there is evidently only one heaven. If there were many numerically and the same specifically, as there are many men, a similar judgment would also have to be made about the first principle of each heaven, which is an immovable mover, as has been stated (n. 2555). For there would have to be many first principles which are specifically one and numerically many.

2595. But this view is impossible, because all things which are specifically one and numerically many contain matter. For they are not differentiated from the viewpoint of their intelligible structure or form, because all the individuals have a common intelligible structure, for example, man. It follows, then, that they are distinguished by their matter. Thus Socrates is one not only in his intelligible structure, as man, but also in number.

2596. However, the first principle, "since it is a quiddity," i.e., since it is its own essence and intelligible structure, does not contain matter, because its substance is "complete reality," i.e., actuality, whereas matter is in potentiality. It remains, then, that the first unmoved mover is one not only in its intelligible structure but also in number. Hence the first eternal motion, which is caused by it, must be unique. It therefore follows that there is only one heaven.

2597. **Now traditions** [7].

He shows how the points discovered about an immaterial substance compare with both the ancient and common opinions. He says that certain traditions about the separate substances have been handed down from the ancient philosophers, and these have been bequeathed to posterity in the form of a myth, to the effect that these substances are gods, and that the divine encompasses the whole of nature. This follows from the above points, granted that all immaterial substances are called gods. But if only the first principle is called God, there is only one God, as is clear from what has been said. The rest of the tradition has been introduced in the form of a myth in order to persuade the multitude, who cannot grasp intelligible things, and inasmuch as it was expedient for the passing of laws and for the benefit of society, that by inventions of this kind the multitude might be persuaded to aim at virtuous acts and avoid evil ones. He explains the mythological part of this tradition by adding that they said that the gods have the form of men and of certain other animals. For they concocted the fables that certain men as well as other animals have been turned into gods; and they added certain statements consequent upon these and similar to the ones which have just been mentioned. Now if among these traditions someone wishes to accept only the one which was first noted above, namely, that the gods are immaterial substances, this will be considered a divine statement, and one that is probably true. And it is so because every art and every philosophy has often been discovered by human power and again lost, either because of wars, which prevent study, or because of floods or other catastrophes of this kind.

2598. It was also necessary for Aristotle to maintain this view in order to save the eternity of the world. For it was evident that at one time men began to philosophize and to discover the arts; and it would seem absurd that the human race should be without these for an infinite period of time. Hence he says that philosophy and the various arts were often discovered and lost, and that the opinions of those ancient thinkers are preserved as relics up to the present day.

2599. Last, he concludes that "the opinion of our forefathers," i.e., the one received from those who philosophized and after whom philosophy was lost, is evident to us only in this way, i.e., in the form of a myth, as has been stated above (1088:C 2597).

LESSON 11
The Dignity of the First Intelligence

ARISTOTLE'S TEXT Chapter 9: 1074b15–1075a10

1. The things which pertain to intellect (or mind) involve certain difficulties; for of the things apparent to us it seems to be the most divine; but how it is so gives rise to certain difficulties. **1074b15–17**

2. For if it is not actually understanding, but is in a sense like one asleep, what dignity will it have? Or if it is understanding, but its chief good is different from itself, then, since its essence is not an act of understanding but a potentiality, it will not be the best substance; for it is by reason of its act of understanding that dignity belongs to it. **1074b17–21**

3. Furthermore, whether its substance is its power to understand or its act of understanding, what does it understand? For it understands either itself or something else; and if something else, either the same thing always or something different. **1074b21–23**

4. Does it make any difference or not, then, whether it understands what is good or what is contingent? Or is it absurd that it should ponder about certain things? **1074b23–25**

5. Hence it is evident that it understands what is most divine and honorable, and that it does not change; for a change would be for the worse, and this would already be motion. **1074b25–27**

6. Therefore, if the first mover is not its act of understanding but a potency, it is reasonable to assume, first, that the continuity of its act of understanding is laborious to it. **1074b28–29**

7. Second, that there is evidently something else more honorable than intellect, namely, what it understands. For both the power to understand and understanding itself belong even to one who understands the basest thing. This must accordingly be avoided; for there are some things which it is better not to see than to see. But this will not be so if the act of understanding is the best of things. Therefore, if there is a most powerful intellect, it must understand itself. **1074b29–34**

8. And its act of understanding is an understanding of understanding. But science, perception, opinion and thought always seem to be about something else and only indirectly about themselves. **1074b34–36**

9. Again, if understanding is something different from being understood, from which of these does the intellect derive its goodness? For the essence of understanding and that of being understood are not the same. **1074b36–38**

10. But in certain cases is not understanding identical with the thing understood? For in the productive sciences the object is the substance or quiddity without matter; and in the theoretical sciences the intelligible structure is both the object and the understanding of it. Therefore, since the object of understanding does not differ from the act of understanding in the case of things which have no matter, they will be the same; and the act of understanding will be identical with the thing understood. **1074b38–1075a5**

11. Yet the difficulty still remains whether the thing that it understands is composite; for if it is, the intellect will be changed in passing from one part of the whole to another. **1075a5–6**

12. Now whatever does not have matter is indivisible, for example, the human mind. **1075a6–7**

13. And the act of understanding composite things involves time. For it does not possess its goodness at this or at that moment but attains the greatest good over a whole period of time, and this is something different from itself. And an intellect which understands itself is in this state through all eternity. **1075a8–10**

COMMENTARY

2600. Having settled the issue about the perfection and oneness of this immaterial substance, the Philosopher now meets certain difficulties concerning its activity; for it has been shown above (nn. 2519–35) that the first immaterial substance causes motion as an intelligible object and a desirable good. This is divided into two parts. In the first [1] he settles certain difficulties about the first immaterial substance insofar as it is an intelligible good and an intellect; and in the second (Lesson 12), insofar as it is a desirable good ("We must also inquire").

In regard to the first he does two things. First, he gives the reason for the difficulty concerning the intellect of the first substance. Second [2], he raises and meets this difficulty ("For if it is not").

He accordingly says, first [1], that, the things which pertain to the intellect of the first immaterial substance involve certain difficulties, and these seem to arise as follows. The Philosopher has shown that the intellect which understands and desires the first mover, which causes motion as an object of understanding and of desire, has something nobler than itself, namely, what is understood and desired by it. He has also shown that the first intelligible object itself is also an intellect. Hence for a like reason it could appear that the first intellect also has something nobler and higher than itself, and that it therefore is not the highest and best thing. But this is contrary to the truths which are apparent about the first principle; and so he says here that it seems evident to all that this principle is the noblest. Yet certain difficulties emerge if one wishes to explain how it is "noblest," i.e., best and most perfect.

2601. **For if it is not** [2].

Then he clears up these difficulties; and in regard to this he does three things. First, he raises the difficulties. Second [5], he prefaces his discussion with certain prerequisites for meeting all the questions raised ("Hence it is evident"). Third [6], he solves these difficulties ("Therefore, if the first mover").

In regard to the first he does two things. First [2], he raises the questions in which he is chiefly interested. Second [4], he introduces an additional question whose solution is necessary for solving the questions raised ("Does it make").

First of all he raises two questions. He asks, first, how the intellect of the first mover is related to its own act of understanding; and second [3], how it is related to its own intelligible object ("Furthermore, whether").

Now it should be noted that an intellect can be related to its own act of understanding in three ways: first, actual understanding does not belong to it but only potential or habitual understanding; second, actual understanding does belong to it; and third, it is identical with its own act of understanding or its own knowledge, which are the same thing.

2602. He accordingly says, first [2], that, if the intellect of the first mover is not actually understanding but only potentially or habitually understanding, it will have no dignity; for the goodness and nobility of an intellect consists in its actually understanding, and an intellect that is only potentially or habitually understanding is like one asleep. For one asleep has certain powers which enable him to perform vital operations even though he is not using them, and thus he is said to be half alive; and during sleep there is no difference between happiness and unhappiness or between virtue and vice. But if the intellect of the first intelligence is actually understanding, yet its chief good, which is its activity, is something different from itself because its "act of understanding," i.e., its intellectual activity, is not identical with its own essence, then its essence is related to its act of understanding as potentiality to actuality, and as something perfectible to its perfection. It accordingly follows that the first intellect is not the best substance; for it is by reason of its act of understanding that honor and nobility belong to it, and nothing that is noble in comparison with something else is noblest in itself. It seems to follow, then, that the essence of the first intellect is not the best, whether it understands only potentially or actually, unless one assumes along with this that its very essence is identical with its act of understanding, as he will establish later on (n. 2608).

2603. **Furthermore, whether its substance** [3].

Before he answers the questions raised he asks another about the intelligible object of the first mover. He says that, whether the essence of the first mover is its power to understand or its "act of understanding," i.e., its intellectual activity or thought (this was the first question raised), we must still ask what it understands? For it understands either itself or something else. And if it understands something else, it must understand either the same thing always or something different, i.e., sometimes one thing and sometimes another.

2604. **Does it make any difference** [4].

So before he answers the foregoing questions, he introduces another question whose solution is useful in giving the answer; that is, whether it makes any difference or none at all to the nobility or perfection of the intellect that it should understand what is good and noble or what is contingent.

2605. By using an instance he shows that it does make a difference, because it seems incongruous and unreasonable that anyone should ponder or employ the operation of his intellect on things that are base. That this should not be the case would demand that the nobility of the intellect be independent of the nobility of its object, and that the understanding of base things be no different from the understanding of good things. But this is quite impossible, since activities are evidently specified by their proper objects. Hence the nobler an object, the nobler must be the operation.

2606. **Hence it is evident** [5].

He prefaces his discussion with certain points necessary for answering the main questions. First, he gives two points. He infers the first of these from the solution of the question which he interjected. For, if it does make a difference to the nobility of the intellect whether it understands what is good or what is contingent, as has been stated (n. 2605), then, since the first intellect is the noblest, it obviously knows what is most divine and most honorable.

2607. The second point is the solution given to the last part of the second main question. The question was whether the intellect of the first mover changes from one intelligible object to another. Now it is evident that it does not change from one object to another.

For, since it understands what is most divine, if it were to change from one object to another, it would change to a less noble one; but this is fitting only to something tending to defect and destruction. Moreover, this change from one intelligible object to another would be a kind of motion; and therefore it could not be fitting to the first mover, since he is immovable in every respect.

2608. **Therefore, if the first mover** [6].

He now answers the questions first raised. First, he gives the correct solution to the first question; and second [7], the solution to the second question ("Second, that").

He answers the first question as follows. If the substance of the first mover "is not its act of understanding," i.e., its own intellectual activity, but an intellective potency, "it is reasonable," i.e., it seems to follow as a probable conclusion, that "the continuity of its act of understanding," i.e., of its intellectual operation, is laborious to it. For whatever is in potentiality to something else is related both to this something else and to its opposite, because what can be can also not be. Hence, if the substance of the first mover is related to its act of understanding as potentiality to actuality, then according to the nature of its own substance it will be able both to understand and not to understand. Therefore continuous understanding will not be proper to it by reason of its own substance.

2609. In order not to be sometimes like one asleep it must derive the continuity of its intellectual activity from something else. Now whatever a thing acquires from something else and does not have by its own nature is probably laborious to it, because this is true in our case; for when we act continuously we labor. But this conclusion is not necessary, because that which one thing acquires from something else is laborious to it only if the thing acquired or something connected with it is contrary to its nature. Therefore, even though the continuity of the motion of the heavens depends on some external principle, such motion is not laborious.

2610. Hence Aristotle was content here to reduce to absurdity the probable conclusion which follows, because the untenable conclusion which necessarily follows is evident, namely, that the goodness and perfection of the first mover will depend on some higher entity; for then it would not be the first and best.

2611. **Second, that there is** [7].

He now answers the second question; and in regard to this he does three things. First, he establishes the correct answer to the second question. Second [8], he argues on the opposite side of the question ("And its act of understanding"). Third [10], he answers the arguments given ("But in certain cases").

He accordingly says, first [7], that, since it has been shown (n. 2608) that the substance of the first mover is not an intellective potency but is itself an act of understanding, it is evident from this that, if the first mover does not understand itself but something else, it follows that this other thing, i.e., what is understood by it, is nobler than the first mover.

2612. He proves this as follows. Actual understanding itself, i.e., thinking, also belongs to one who understands the basest thing. Hence it is evident that some actual understanding must be avoided, because there are some things which it is better not to see than to see. But this would not be the case if the act of understanding were the best of things, because then no act of understanding would have to be avoided. Therefore, since some act of understanding must be avoided because of the baseness of the thing understood, it follows that the nobility of the intellect, which is found in its understanding, will depend on the nobility of its object. Hence the intelligible object is nobler than the act of understanding.

2613. Since it has been shown that the first mover is its own act of understanding, it follows that if it understands something different from itself, this other thing will be nobler than it is. Therefore, since the first mover is the noblest and most powerful, it must understand itself; and in its case intellect and thing understood must be the same.

2614. Now we must bear in mind that the Philosopher's aim is to show that God does not understand something else but only himself, inasmuch as the thing understood is the perfection of the one understanding and of his activity, which is understanding. It is also evident that nothing else can be understood by God in such a way that it would be the perfection of His intellect. It does not follow, however, that all things different from Himself are not known by Him; for by understanding Himself He knows all other things.

2615. This is made clear as follows. Since God is His own act of understanding and is the noblest and most powerful being, His act of understanding must be most perfect. Therefore He understands Himself most perfectly. Now the more perfectly a principle is known, the more perfectly is its effect known in it; for things derived from principles are contained in the power of their principle. Therefore, since the heavens and the whole of nature depend on the first principle, which is God, God obviously knows all things by understanding Himself.

2616. And the baseness of any object of knowledge does not lessen His dignity; for the actual understanding of anything more base is to be avoided only insofar as the intellect becomes absorbed in it, and when in actually understanding that thing the intellect is drawn away from the understanding of nobler things. For if in understanding some noblest object base things are also understood, the baseness of the things understood does not lessen the nobility of the act of understanding.

2617. **And its act of understanding** [8].

Then he raises two objections against the correct solution. The first is as follows. The first mover understands himself, as has been shown above (n. 2615); and he is his own act of understanding, as has also been shown (n. 2608). Hence his act of understanding does not differ from his act of understanding his own thought. But this is contrary to what seems to be true, because perception, science, opinion and thought always seem to be about something else. And if they are sometimes about themselves, as when someone perceives that he perceives, or knows that he knows, or is of the opinion that he has an opinion, or thinks that he is thinking, this seems to be something in addition to the principal act or operation; for the principal act here seems to be that whereby someone understands an intelligible object. But that someone should understand that he is understanding something intelligible seems to be accessory to the principal act. Thus if the first mover's act of understanding consists solely in his understanding his own thought, it seems to follow that his act of understanding is not the most important thing.

2618. **Again, if understanding** [9].

Then he raises a second objection against the correct solution. He says that the act of understanding and the thing understood are obviously different; and even if it were possible for an intellect and its object to be the same in reality, they would not be the same in their formal structure. Hence, if the first mover is himself both his act of understanding and the object that is being understood, which is the best of things, there still seems to be the problem as to which of these confers goodness on him, namely, his act of understanding or the thing understood.

2619. **But in certain cases** [10].

He now answers the objections raised. He says that in certain cases the thing understood is the same as the knowledge of it. This becomes clear when we draw a distinction between the sciences; for one kind of science is productive and another is speculative. In the case of a productive science the thing understood, taken without matter, is the science of that thing; for example, it is clear that a house without matter, insofar as it exists in the mind of the builder, is the very art of building; and similarly health in the mind of the physician is the medical art itself. Thus a productive art is evidently nothing else than the substance or quiddity of the thing made; for every artist proceeds to his work from a knowledge of the quiddity which he intends to produce.

2620. In the case of the speculative sciences it is evident that the concept, which defines the thing itself, is the thing understood and the science or knowledge of that thing. For an intellect has knowledge by reason of the fact that it possesses the concept of a thing. Therefore, since in the case of all those things which do not have matter the intellect when actually understanding does not differ from the thing understood, then in the case of the first substance, which is separate from matter in the highest degree, the act of understanding and the thing understood are evidently the same in the highest degree. Hence there is just one act of understanding pertaining to the thing understood; that is, the act of understanding the thing understood is not distinct from that of understanding the act of understanding.

2621. **Yet the difficulty** [11].

Here he raises a third question in addition to the two dealt with above. For since it has been shown (n. 2544) that the first mover understands himself, and a thing is understood in two ways: first, by way of a simple understanding, as we understand a quiddity, and second, by way of a composite understanding, as we know a proposition, the question therefore arises whether the first mover understands himself by way of a simple understanding, or by way of a composite one. This is what he refers to when he says that the difficulty still remains whether the object of God's understanding is composite.

2622. Now he shows that it is not composite when he says (1099) "for if it is"; and he gives three arguments in support of this. The first goes as follows. In every composite object of understanding there are several parts, which can be understood separately. For even though this composite object of understanding *Man runs*, insofar as it is one composite object, is understood all at once, none the less its parts can be understood separately. For the term *man* can be understood by itself, and so also can the term *runs*. Hence, whoever understands some composite object can be changed when his act of understanding passes from one part to another. Therefore, if the first intelligible object is composite, it follows that the intellect can change when its act of understanding passes from one part of this object to another. But the contrary of this has been proved above (n. 2619).

2623. **Now whatever** [12].

Then he gives the second argument. Whatever does not have matter is simple and indivisible. But the first intellect does not have matter. Therefore it is simple and indivisible.

2624. He gives as an example the human intellect, and this example can be taken in two ways. First, it can be taken as a comparison, meaning that the human intellect is indivisible in its own essence, because it is an immaterial form in every respect.

2625. It can also be taken in a second and better way as a contrast, meaning that the human intellect knows composite things because it derives its intelligible objects from material things. And this is not true of the first intellect.

2626. **And the act** [13].

He gives the third argument. An act of understanding which is concerned with composite things does not possess its perfection always but attains it over a period of time. This is clear from the fact that it does not attain its good in knowing one part or another, but its greatest good is something else, which is a kind of whole. Hence the truth (which is the good of the intellect), is not found in simple things but in a composite one. Further, simple things are prior to composite things as regards both generation and time, so that whatever does not possess its own good in knowing parts which can be understood separately but in knowing the whole which is constituted of them, attains its good at some particular moment and does not always possess it.—However, the first mover's act of understanding, which is of himself, is eternal and always in the same state. Therefore the thing understood by the intellect of the first mover is not composite.

LESSON 12
God Is the Final Cause of All Things. The Order of the Universe

ARISTOTLE'S TEXT Chapter 10: 1075a11–1076a4

1. *We must also inquire how the nature of the whole [universe] contains the good and the highest good, whether as something separate and self-subsisting or as the order of its parts.* **1075a11–13**

2. *Or is it in both ways, as an army does? For the good of an army consists both in its order and in its commander, but mainly in the latter; for he does not exist for the sake of the order, but the order exists for him.* **1075a13–15**

3. *And all things, both plants and animals (those that swim and those that fly), are ordered together in some way, but not alike; and things are not such that there is no relation between one thing and another, but there is a connection. For all things are ordered together to one end, but in the same way as in a household, where the children are not permitted to do just as they please, but all or most of the things done are arranged in an orderly way, while the slaves and livestock do little for the common good but act for the most part at random. For the nature of each of these constitutes such a principle. I mean that by it all must be able to be distinguished. And there are other activities which all have in common for the sake of the whole.* **1075a16–25**

4. *And we must not fail to consider all the impossible and incongruous conclusions that confront those who explain things differently, and what sort of views are expressed by the more popular thinkers, among whom the fewest difficulties appear.* **1075a25–27**

5. *For all these thinkers derive all things from contraries. But neither "all things" nor "from contraries" is correct; nor do they explain how the things in which contraries are present come from contraries.* **1075a28–30**

6. *For contraries cannot be acted upon by one another. But this difficulty is solved by us in a reasonable way on the ground that there is a third element. Some thinkers make one of the contraries matter, as those who make the unequal the matter of the equal, or the many the matter of the one. But this is also met in the same way; for matter, as one, is contrary to nothing.* **1075a30–34**

7. *Further, [according to them] all things except the one will exist by participating in evil; for evil itself is one of the two elements.* **1075a34–36**

8. *For other thinkers consider neither good nor evil as principles, even though the good is in the fullest sense a principle of things.* **1075a36–37**

9. *The former are right in holding that the good is a principle, but they do not say how it is a principle: whether as an end or as a mover or as a form.* **1075a38–1075b1**

10. *And Empedocles' doctrine is also unreasonable; for he identifies the good with friendship, although the latter is a principle both as a mover (for it combines things), and as matter (for it is a part of the mixture). Therefore, even if it happens that the same thing is a principle both as matter and as a mover, still their being is not the same. In what respect, then, is friendship a principle? And it is also unreasonable that strife should be indestructible; for the essence of evil, for him, is precisely this strife.* **1075b1–7**

11. *Again, Anaxagoras makes the good a principle as a mover; for his "Intellect" causes motion. But it causes motion for the sake of some goal, and therefore there must be something other than intellect, unless it is as we say; for the art of medicine is in a sense health. It is also unreasonable not to provide something that is contrary to the good or to intellect.* **1075b8–11**

12. *But all who speak of contraries fail to make use of them as such, except that some make use of imagery. And none of them explain why some things are destructible and others are not; for*

they derive all things from the same principles. Again, some derive beings from non-being, while others, lest they be driven to this, make all things one. **1075b11–16**

13. *Further, no one explains why there is always generation, and what its cause is.* **1075b16–17**

14. *And those who posit two principles of things must assume a first principle which is superior. This also holds for those who posit separate Forms, because there is another principle which is more important; for why has matter participated in the Forms or why does it participate in them?* **1075b17–20**

15. *And for other thinkers there must be something contrary to wisdom or the noblest science; but this is not so in our case. For there is nothing contrary to what is primary, since all contraries involve matter, and things having matter are in potentiality; and ignorance is contrary to the particular knowledge which is the contrary into which it can pass. But there is nothing contrary to what is primary.* **1075b20–24**

16. *Further, if nothing exists except sensible things, there will be no principle, no order, no generation, no heavenly bodies; but every principle will have a principle, as is maintained by all the theologians and natural philosophers.* **1075b24–27**

17. *Now if there are separate Forms and numbers, they will not be causes of anything; but if they are, they will certainly not be causes of motion.* **1075b27–28**

18. *Again, how will extension or continuous quantity be composed of parts which are unextended? For number cannot either as a mover or as a form produce a continuum.* **1075b28–30**

19. *Further, no one of the contraries will be a productive principle and a mover, because it would be possible for it not to be. And in any case its activity would be subsequent to its potentiality. No beings, then, would be eternal. But some are. Therefore one of these premises must be rejected. How this may be done has been explained.* **1075b30–34**

20. *Again, as to the way in which numbers, or soul and body, or forms and things in general are one, no one states anything; nor is it possible to do so unless he says, as we do, that a mover makes them one.* **1075b34–37**

21. *And those who say that mathematical number is the primary reality and that there is always one substance after another and give different principles for each, make the substance of the universe itself a group of substances unrelated to each other (for one substance confers nothing upon another, either by being or not being), and give us many principles. But beings do not want to be badly disposed.—"Many rulers are not good; therefore let there be one ruler."* **1075b37–1076a4**

COMMENTARY

2627. Having shown how the first mover is both an intelligence and an intelligible object, here the Philosopher aims to investigate how the first mover is a good and an object of desire; and in regard to this he does two things. First [1], he shows how the good is present in the universe, according to his opinion; and second [4], according to the opinions of other philosophers ("And we must not fail").

In regard to the first he does two things. First, he raises a question. Second [2], he answers it ("Or is it").

Now this question arises because of a statement which was made above to the effect that the first mover causes motion as something good and desirable; for good, inasmuch as it is the end or goal of a thing, is twofold. For an end is extrinsic to the thing ordained to it, as when we say that a place is the end of something that is moved locally. Or it is intrinsic, as a form is the end of the process of generation or alteration; and a form already acquired is a kind of intrinsic good of the thing whose form it is. Now the form of any whole which is one through the arrangement of its parts is the order of that whole. Hence it follows that it is a good of that whole.

2628. Therefore the Philosopher asks [1] whether the nature of the whole universe has its good and highest good, i.e., its proper end, as something separate from itself, or whether this consists in the ordering of its parts in the way in which the good of any natural being is its own form.

2629. **Or is it** [2].

Then he answers the question raised; and in regard to this he does two things. First, he shows that the universe has both a separate good and a good of order. Second [3], he shows the ways in which the parts of the universe contribute to its order ("And all things").

He accordingly says, first [2], that the universe has its good and end in both ways. For there is a separate good, which is the first mover, on which the heavens and the whole of nature depend as their end or desirable good, as has been shown (n. 2521). And since all things having one end must agree in their ordination to that end, some order must be found in the parts of the universe; and so the universe has both a separate good and a good of order.

2630. We see this, for example, in the case of an army; for the good of the army is found both in the order itself of the army and in the commander who has charge of the army. But the good of the army is found in a higher degree in its commander than in its order, because the goodness of an end takes precedence over that of the things which exist for the sake of the end. Now the order of an army exists for the purpose of achieving the good of its commander, namely, his will to attain victory. But the opposite of this is not true, i.e., that the good of the commander exists for the sake of the good of order.

2631. And since the formal character of things which exist for the sake of an end is derived from the end, it is therefore necessary not only that the good of the army exist for the sake of the commander, but also that the order of the army depend on the commander, since its order exists for the sake of the commander. In this way too the separate good of the universe, which is the first mover, is a greater good than the good of order which is found in the universe. For the whole order of the universe exists for the sake of the first mover inasmuch as the things contained in the mind and will of the first mover are realized in the ordered universe. Hence the whole order of the universe must depend on the first mover.

2632. **And all things** [3].

Here he shows the ways in which the parts of the universe contribute to its order. He says that all things in the universe are ordered together in some way, but not all are ordered alike, for example, sea animals, birds, and plants. Yet even though they are not ordered in the same way, they are still not disposed in such a way that one of them has no connection with another; but there is some affinity and relationship of one with another. For plants exist for the sake of animals, and animals for the sake of men. That all things are related to each other is evident from the fact that all are connected together to one end.

2633. That all are not ordered in the same way is made clear by an example; for in an ordered household or family different ranks of members are found. For example, under the head of the family there is a first rank, namely, that of the sons, and a second rank, which is that of the slaves, and a third rank, which is that of the domestic animals, as dogs and the like. For ranks of this kind have a different relation to the order of the household, which is imposed by the head of the family, who governs the household. For it is not proper for the sons to act in a haphazard and disorderly way, but all or most of the things that they do are ordered. This is not the case with the slaves or domestic animals, however, because they share to a very small degree in the order which exists for the common good. But in their case we find many things which are contingent and haphazard; and this is because they have little connection with the ruler of the household, who aims at the common good of the household.

2634. And just as the order of the family is imposed by the law and precept of the head of the family, who is the principle of each of the things which are ordered in the household, with a view to carrying out the activities which pertain to the order of the household, in a similar fashion the nature of physical things is the principle by which each of them carries out the activity proper to it in the order of the universe. For just as any member of the household is disposed to act through the precept of the head of the family, in a similar fashion any natural being is disposed by its own nature. Now the nature of each thing is a kind of inclination implanted in it by the first mover, who directs it to its proper end; and from this it is clear that natural beings act for the sake of an end even though they do not know that end, because they acquire their inclination to their end from the first intelligence.

2635. However, not all things are disposed to this end in the same way. For there is something common to all things, since all things must succeed in being distinguished; that is, they must have discrete and proper operations, and must also be differentiated essentially from each other; and in this respect order is lacking in none of them. But there are some things which not only have this but are also such that all their activities "participate in the whole," i.e., are directed to the common good of the whole. This is found to be true of those things which contain nothing contrary to their nature, nor any element of chance, but everything proceeds according to the right order.

2636. For it is evident, as has been pointed out (1104:C 2632–34), that each natural being is directed to the common good by reason of its proper natural activity. Hence those things which never fail in their proper natural activity have all their activities contributing to the whole. But those which sometimes fail in their proper natural activity do not have all their activities contributing to the whole; and lower bodies are of this kind.

2637. The answer briefly stated, then, is that order requires two things: a distinction between the things ordered, and the contribution of the distinct things to the whole. As regard the first of these, order is found in all things without fail; but as regards the second, order is found in some things, and these are the things which are highest and closest to the first principle, as the separate substances and the heavenly bodies, in which there is no element of chance or anything contrary to their nature. But order is lacking in some things, namely, in [lower] bodies, which are sometimes subject to chance and to things which are contrary to their nature. This is so because of their distance from the first principle, which is always the same.

2638. **And we must not** [4].

Then he deals with the end and order of the universe according to the opinion of other philosophers. In regard to this he does two things. First, he explains what he aims to do. He says that we must state all the impossible or incongruous conclusions facing those who express views different from our own about the good and order of the universe; and we must also state the kind of views held by those men who give a better explanation of things and in whose statements fewer difficulties appear.

2639. **For all these** [5].

He then carries out his plan. In regard to this he does two things. First [5], he gives the opinion of those who held that the principles of things are contraries; and second [16], the opinion of those who held that the principles of things are separate natures ("Further, if nothing").

In treating the first point he does two things. First [5], he explains in what way those men are wrong who say that the principles of things are contraries. He says that all the ancient philosophers held that all things come from contraries as their principles; and they were wrong on three counts. First, they were wrong in holding that things come from contraries; and second, in saying that *all* things come from contraries; and third, in failing to explain how things are produced from contraries.

2640. **For contraries** [6].

Second, he indicates how they were wrong in the three ways mentioned above. He explains how they erred, first, in holding that things come from contraries; and second [7], in claiming that *all* things come from contraries ("Further, [according to them]"); and third [12], in failing to show how things come from contraries ("But all who speak").

He accordingly says, first [6], that they were wrong in saying that things comes from contraries, because contraries taken in themselves cannot be acted upon by one another; for whiteness is not acted upon by blackness or vice versa, and one thing could come from them only if they were influenced by one another and so were reduced to an intermediate state.

2641. But in Aristotle's opinion this difficulty is easily solved, because besides the two contraries he also posited a third principle, matter. Hence one of the two contraries can be acted upon by the other in the sense that matter, which is the subject of one contrary, can be acted upon by the other contrary.

2642. But others claimed that matter is one of the two contraries and not something distinct from them, as is evident in the case of those who held that the contraries, the unequal and the equal, and the one and the many, are principles. For they attribute inequality and plurality to matter, and equality and unity to form, as is found in Plato's opinion, although the natural philosophers held the opposite. But this statement of theirs is met in the same way, because matter, which is one thing as the common subject of contraries, is contrary to nothing.

2643. **Further, [according to them]** [7].

Then the Philosopher explains how

these thinkers were wrong in saying that *all* things come from contraries; and in regard to this he does two things. First, he shows the unreasonable conclusion which follows from this view. For it is evident that the primary contraries are good and evil, because one of two contraries is always the privation of the other and so has the character of evil. Therefore, if all things come from contraries, it follows that all things participate in evil as well as in unity, i.e., good, which is a principle; for good is posited as one of the two elements, and everything else is supposed to come from these two principles. But this is not true, because destruction and evil are not found in the heavenly bodies or in the nature of the separate substances.

2644. **For other thinkers** [8].

Second, he shows that the position of all those who held that all things come from contraries is not in agreement with the position of certain of the philosophers. For if all things come from contraries, it follows, as has been pointed out, that good and evil are the first principles of things. But some did not claim that good and evil are principles but said that the good is the principle of all things.

2645. **The former** [9].

Third, he indicates the error made even by those who claimed that the good is a principle of things. He makes this clear, first, in a general way. He says that, even though some philosophers are right in holding that the good is a principle of all things, they are still wrong in failing to show how it is a principle, i.e., whether as an end or as a form or as a mover. For these things are characterized by perfection and goodness, whereas matter, which is perfected only by form, does not have the character of something good and perfect; and therefore he makes no mention of it.

2646. **And Empedocles' doctrine** [10].

Next, he turns to certain particular opinions. First, he considers the opinion of Empedocles. He says that Empedocles made the unreasonable assumption that the good is a principle of things; for he claimed that love is a principle, identifying it with the good. However, he said that love is a principle in two ways. For he claimed that it is a moving principle inasmuch as its function is to unite things and bring them together; and he also claimed that it is a material principle inasmuch as he asserts that love is a part of compounds, since he assumed that bodies are compounds of the four elements and of friendship and strife. And even though the same principle can be both matter and a mover, it is not such under the same formal aspect. For fire can be a mover according to its form, and a material principle according to its matter; but it cannot be both in the same respect, because a mover as such is actual, whereas matter as such is potential. Hence it must still be explained in what respect love has the character of a material principle, and in what respect it has the character of a mover—and this he fails to do.

2647. Another incongruity which follows from Empedocles' opinion is his positing strife as a first indestructible principle; for strife in itself seems to be essentially evil, and evil, in the opinions of those who are right, is not set down as a principle, but only the good, as has been stated (n. 2644).

2648. **Again, Anaxagoras** [11].

Third, he turns to the opinion of Anaxagoras. He says that Anaxagoras makes the good to be a first principle of things as a mover; for he said that an intellect moves all things. But it is evident that "an intellect always causes motion for the sake of some goal," i.e., an end. Hence Anaxagoras must posit some other principle by reason of which this intellect causes motion, unless perhaps he should say, as we have, that an intellect and its intelligible object can be the same; and that an intellect moves for its own sake; which is true in a sense of those things which act by intellect, according to our view. For the art of medicine acts for the sake of health, and health is in a sense the art of medicine itself, as has been pointed out above (n. 2619 and n. 1407).

2649. Another unreasonable consequence which is contrary to the opinion of Anaxagoras also seems to follow if the common view is maintained, namely, that contraries are the principles of all things. For according to this view it would be absurd for him not to make some principle contrary to the good and to intellect.

2650. **But all who speak** [12].

He explains the third error which he noted above (nn. 2639–40), namely, that those who held the principles to be contraries did not explain how things come from contraries as their principles. He says that all those who speak of contraries as principles fail to make use of them in accounting for what appears in the world, unless "some make use of imagery," i.e., unless someone wishes to indulge his fancy or to speak figuratively.

2651. **And none of them** (*ibid.*).

First, he shows that they cannot account for the differences between destructible and indestructible things. He accordingly says that none of the ancient philosophers give any reason why some beings are destructible and some are not. Some of them claimed that all things are derived from the same principles, namely, contraries; and this is the opinion of the ancient natural philosophers. Others, the theological poets, held that all things come from non-being. Hence he said above (n. 2515) that they generate the world from non-being. And so although both groups assign the origin of all things, they cannot explain why things are distinguished into destructible and indestructible. Hence others, in order not to be driven to this, i.e., to posit that all things come from non-being or to account for the difference between things, held that all things are one, thereby entirely doing away with the distinction between things. This is the view of Parmenides and Melissus.

2652. **Further, no one** [13].

Second, he shows that they were also wrong in another respect, namely, in being unable to explain why generation is eternal or to state what the universal cause of generation is; for neither of the contraries is a universal cause of generation.

2653. **And those who** [14].

Third, he states how those men were wrong who claimed that the principles of things are contraries; for they must maintain that one of two contraries is a superior principle, since one contrary has the character of a privation. Or he means that it is necessary to posit some principle, which is more important than both contraries, by which it is possible to explain why certain things are attributed to one of the contraries as their principle and why certain others are attributed to the other contrary; for example, why at one time strife will cause the elements to separate and why at another time friendship will cause them to combine.

2654. This difficulty also faces those who posit separate Forms; for they must assign some principle which is superior to the Forms, since it is evident that things which are generated and destroyed do not always participate in a form in the same way. Hence it is necessary to posit some principle by which it is possible to explain why this individual formerly participated or now participates in a form.

2655. **And for other thinkers** [15].

Here he gives a fourth incongruity which faces these thinkers. He says that the philosophers who claim that the principles of things are contraries must admit that there is something contrary to the primary kind of wisdom or noblest science, because wisdom is concerned with the first principle, as has been shown in Book I (n. 35). Therefore, if there is nothing contrary to the first principle (for all pairs of contraries have a nature which is in potentiality to each pair), and according to us the first principle is immaterial, as is clear from what has been said (n. 2495), then it follows that there is nothing contrary to the first principle, and that there is no science which is contrary to the primary science, but merely ignorance.

2656. **Further, if nothing** [16].

Next, he turns to the opinion of those who posited separate substances. First, he points out that an incongruity faces those who fail to posit such substances. He says that, if nothing exists except sensible things, there will be no first principle, as has been noted (n. 2489), no order of things such as has been described, no eternal generation, and no principles of the kind which we have posited above (n. 2503); but every principle will always have a principle, and so on to infinity. Thus Socrates will be begotten by Plato and the latter by someone else and so on to infinity, as was seen to be the view of all of the ancient philosophers of nature. For they did not posit a first universal principle over and above these particular and sensible principles.

2657. **Now if there** [17].

Then he shows that an unreasonable consequence faces those who posit certain separate natures. He does this, first, with regard to those who posited a certain connection in origin among natures of this kind; and second [21], with regard to those who did not hold this position ("And those who say").

Concerning the first he draws out four untenable consequences. The first [17] of these is that the separate Forms and numbers, which some posited over and above sensible things, seem not to be causes of anything. But if they are causes of something, it seems that nothing will be a cause of motion, because things of this kind do not seem to have the character of a moving cause.

2658. **Again, how will** [18].

Second, he brings forward another incongruity. For number is not continuous quantity, but continuous quantity is constituted only of continuous quantities. Hence it seems impossible to explain how continuous quantity or extension comes from numbers, which are not continuous. For it cannot be said that number is the cause of continuous quantity either as a moving cause or as a formal cause.

2659. **Further, no one** [19].

Then he gives the third untenable consequence. He says that, if the separate Forms and numbers are first principles, it follows, since contrariety is not found in forms and numbers, that first principles will not be contraries, because they are not held to be productive principles or movers. Hence it will follow that there is no generation or motion; for if the first principles are not efficient causes of motion but are subsequently caused from first principles, it will follow that they are contained in the potency of prior principles; and what can be can also not be. The conclusion, then, is that generation and motion are not eternal. But they are eternal, as has been proved above (nn. 2490–91). Therefore one of the premises must be rejected, namely, the one holding that first principles are not movers. The way in which the first principles are movers has been stated in Book I (nn. 50–51).

2660. **Again, as to the way** [20].

He gives the fourth incongruity. He says that none of these philosophers can state what it is that makes number, or soul and body, or in general form and the thing to which form belongs, a unity, unless he says that a mover does this, as we explained above in Book VIII (n. 1759). Forms and numbers, however, do not have the character of a mover.

2661. **And those who say** [21].

Here he indicates the unreasonable consequence facing those who claim that natures of this kind are unrelated things. He says that those who claim that mathematical number is the primary reality, as the Pythagoreans did, and "that there is always one substance after another" in this way, i.e., consecutively (so that after number comes continuous quantity, and after continuous quantity come sensible things), and who say that there is a different principle for each nature, so that there are certain principles for numbers, others for continuous quantity, and others for sensible things—those who speak in this way, I say, make the substances of the universe a group of substances unrelated to each other, i.e., without order, inasmuch as one part confers nothing on any other part whether it exists or does not. And they likewise make their many principles to be unrelated.

2662. Now this cannot be the case, because beings do not want to be badly disposed; for the disposition of natural things is the best possible. We observe this in the case of particular things, because each is best disposed in its own nature. Hence we must understand this to be the case to a much greater degree in the whole universe.

2663. But many rulers are not good. For example, it would not be good for different families which shared nothing in common to live in a single home. Hence it follows that the whole universe is like one principality and one kingdom, and must therefore be governed by one ruler. Aristotle's conclusion is that there is one ruler of the whole universe, the first mover, and one first intelligible object, and one first good, whom above he called God (n. 2544), who is blessed for ever and ever. Amen.